CUMULATIVE PROBABILITIES FOR THE STANDARD NORMAL DISTRIBUTION

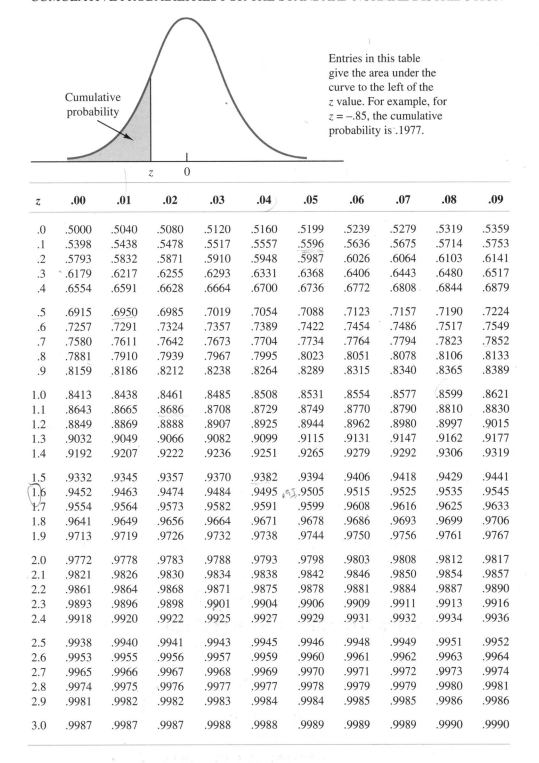

Cumulative probability

Entries in this table give the area under the curve to the left of the z value. For example, for z = −.85, the cumulative probability is .1977.

z	.00	.01	.02	.03	.04	.05	.06	.07	.08	.09
.0	.5000	.5040	.5080	.5120	.5160	.5199	.5239	.5279	.5319	.5359
.1	.5398	.5438	.5478	.5517	.5557	.5596	.5636	.5675	.5714	.5753
.2	.5793	.5832	.5871	.5910	.5948	.5987	.6026	.6064	.6103	.6141
.3	.6179	.6217	.6255	.6293	.6331	.6368	.6406	.6443	.6480	.6517
.4	.6554	.6591	.6628	.6664	.6700	.6736	.6772	.6808	.6844	.6879
.5	.6915	.6950	.6985	.7019	.7054	.7088	.7123	.7157	.7190	.7224
.6	.7257	.7291	.7324	.7357	.7389	.7422	.7454	.7486	.7517	.7549
.7	.7580	.7611	.7642	.7673	.7704	.7734	.7764	.7794	.7823	.7852
.8	.7881	.7910	.7939	.7967	.7995	.8023	.8051	.8078	.8106	.8133
.9	.8159	.8186	.8212	.8238	.8264	.8289	.8315	.8340	.8365	.8389
1.0	.8413	.8438	.8461	.8485	.8508	.8531	.8554	.8577	.8599	.8621
1.1	.8643	.8665	.8686	.8708	.8729	.8749	.8770	.8790	.8810	.8830
1.2	.8849	.8869	.8888	.8907	.8925	.8944	.8962	.8980	.8997	.9015
1.3	.9032	.9049	.9066	.9082	.9099	.9115	.9131	.9147	.9162	.9177
1.4	.9192	.9207	.9222	.9236	.9251	.9265	.9279	.9292	.9306	.9319
1.5	.9332	.9345	.9357	.9370	.9382	.9394	.9406	.9418	.9429	.9441
1.6	.9452	.9463	.9474	.9484	.9495	.9505	.9515	.9525	.9535	.9545
1.7	.9554	.9564	.9573	.9582	.9591	.9599	.9608	.9616	.9625	.9633
1.8	.9641	.9649	.9656	.9664	.9671	.9678	.9686	.9693	.9699	.9706
1.9	.9713	.9719	.9726	.9732	.9738	.9744	.9750	.9756	.9761	.9767
2.0	.9772	.9778	.9783	.9788	.9793	.9798	.9803	.9808	.9812	.9817
2.1	.9821	.9826	.9830	.9834	.9838	.9842	.9846	.9850	.9854	.9857
2.2	.9861	.9864	.9868	.9871	.9875	.9878	.9881	.9884	.9887	.9890
2.3	.9893	.9896	.9898	.9901	.9904	.9906	.9909	.9911	.9913	.9916
2.4	.9918	.9920	.9922	.9925	.9927	.9929	.9931	.9932	.9934	.9936
2.5	.9938	.9940	.9941	.9943	.9945	.9946	.9948	.9949	.9951	.9952
2.6	.9953	.9955	.9956	.9957	.9959	.9960	.9961	.9962	.9963	.9964
2.7	.9965	.9966	.9967	.9968	.9969	.9970	.9971	.9972	.9973	.9974
2.8	.9974	.9975	.9976	.9977	.9977	.9978	.9979	.9979	.9980	.9981
2.9	.9981	.9982	.9982	.9983	.9984	.9984	.9985	.9985	.9986	.9986
3.0	.9987	.9987	.9987	.9988	.9988	.9989	.9989	.9989	.9990	.9990

ESSENTIALS OF
STATISTICS FOR BUSINESS AND ECONOMICS 7e

ESSENTIALS OF STATISTICS FOR BUSINESS AND ECONOMICS 7e

David R. Anderson
University of Cincinnati

Dennis J. Sweeney
University of Cincinnati

Thomas A. Williams
Rochester Institute of Technology

Jeffrey D. Camm
University of Cincinnati

James J. Cochran
Louisiana Tech University

CENGAGE
Learning®

Australia • Brazil • Japan • Korea • Mexico • Singapore • Spain • United Kingdom • United States

Essentials of Statistics for Business and Economics, Seventh Edition
David R. Anderson, Dennis J. Sweeney, Thomas A. Williams, Jeffrey D. Camm, James J. Cochran

Senior Vice President, Global Product Manager, Higher Education: Jack W. Calhoun

Vice President, General Manager, Social Science & Qualitative Business: Erin Joyner

Product Director: Joe Sabatino

Product Manager: Aaron Arnsparger

Content Developer: Maggie Kubale

Product Assistant: Anne Merrill

Sr. Content Project Manager: Tamborah Moore

Media Developer: Chris Valentine

Manufacturing Planner: Ron Montgomery

Marketing Director: Natalie Livingston

Associate Marketing Manager: Roy Rosa

Marketing Manager: Heather Mooney

Marketing Communications Manager: Sarah Greber

Production Service: MPS

Sr. Art Director: Stacy Jenkins Shirley

Internal Designer: Michael Stratton/cmiller design

Cover Designer: Craig Ramsdell

Cover Image: © Mark Edward Atkinson

Rights Acquisitions Specialist Text and Images: John Hill

Text Permissions Researcher: Pinky Subi/PMG

Image Permissions: Dharanivel Baskar/PMG

For product information and technology assistance, contact us at **Cengage Learning Customer & Sales Support, 1-800-354-9706**

For permission to use material from this text or product, submit all requests online at **www.cengage.com/permissions**
Further permissions questions can be emailed to **permissionrequest@cengage.com**

Microsoft Excel® is a registered trademark of Microsoft Corporation. © 2013 Microsoft.

Library of Congress Control Number: 2013932884

Pkg ISBN-13: 978-1-133-62965-8

Pkg ISBN-10: 1-133-62965-2

Student Edition ISBN 13: 978-1-133-58779-8

Student Edition ISBN 10: 1-133-58779-8

Cengage Learning
200 First Stamford Place, 4th Floor
Stamford, CT 06902
USA

Cengage Learning is a leading provider of customized learning solutions with office locations around the globe, including Singapore, the United Kingdom, Australia, Mexico, Brazil, and Japan. Locate your local office at: **www.cengage.com/global**

Cengage Learning products are represented in Canada by Nelson Education, Ltd.

To learn more about Cengage Learning Solutions, visit **www.cengage.com**

Purchase any of our products at your local college store or at our preferred online store **www.cengagebrain.com**

Printed in Canada
1 2 3 4 5 6 7 17 16 15 14 13

Dedicated to
Marcia, Cherri, Robbie, Karen, and Teresa

Brief Contents

Contents

Chapter 4   Introduction to Probability   176

Preface

This text is the 7th edition of *ESSENTIALS OF STATISTICS FOR BUSINESS AND ECONOMICS*. With this edition we welcome two eminent scholars to our author team: Jeffrey D. Camm of the University of Cincinnati and James J. Cochran of Louisiana Tech University. Both Jeff and Jim are accomplished teachers, researchers, and practitioners in the fields of statistics and business analytics. Jim is a fellow of the American Statistical Association. You can read more about their accomplishments in the About the Authors section that follows this preface. We believe that the addition of Jeff and Jim as our coauthors will both maintain and improve the effectiveness of *Essentials of Statistics for Business and Economics*.

The purpose of *Essentials of Statistics for Business and Economics* is to give students, primarily those in the fields of business administration and economics, a conceptual introduction to the field of statistics and its many applications. The text is applications oriented and written with the needs of the nonmathematician in mind; the mathematical prerequisite is knowledge of algebra.

Applications of data analysis and statistical methodology are an integral part of the organization and presentation of the text material. The discussion and development of each technique is presented in an application setting, with the statistical results providing insights to decisions and solutions to problems.

Although the book is applications oriented, we have taken care to provide sound methodological development and to use notation that is generally accepted for the topic being covered. Hence, students will find that this text provides good preparation for the study of more advanced statistical material. A bibliography to guide further study is included as an appendix.

The text introduces the student to the software packages of Minitab 16 and Microsoft® Office Excel 2013 and emphasizes the role of computer software in the application of statistical analysis. Minitab is illustrated as it is one of the leading statistical software packages for both education and statistical practice. Excel is not a statistical software package, but the wide availability and use of Excel make it important for students to understand the statistical capabilities of this package. Minitab and Excel procedures are provided in appendixes so that instructors have the flexibility of using as much computer emphasis as desired for the course. StatTools, a commercial Excel add-in developed by Palisade Corporation, extends the range of statistical options for Excel users. We show how to download and install StatTools in an appendix to Chapter 1, and most chapters include a chapter appendix that shows the steps required to accomplish a statistical procedure using StatTools. We have made the use of StatTools optional so that instructors who want to teach using only the standard tools available in Excel can do so.

Changes in the Seventh Edition

We appreciate the acceptance and positive response to the previous editions of *Essentials of Statistics for Business and Economics*. Accordingly, in making modifications for this new edition, we have maintained the presentation style and readability of those editions. There have been many changes made throughout the text to enhance its educational effectiveness. The most significant changes in the new edition are summarized here.

Content Revisions

- **Descriptive Statistics—Chapters 2 and 3.** We have substantially revised these chapters to incorporate new material on data visualization, best practices, and much more. Chapter 2 has been reorganized to include new material on side-by-side and stacked bar charts and a new section has been added on data visualization and best practices in creating effective displays. Chapter 3 now includes coverage of the geometric mean in the section on measures of location. The geometric mean has many applications in the computation of growth rates for financial assets, annual percentage rates, and so on. Chapter 3 also includes a new section on data dashboards and how summary statistics can be incorporated to enhance their effectiveness.

- **Comparisons Involving Proportions and a Test of Independence—Chapter 11.** This chapter has undergone a major revision. We have replaced the section on goodness of fit tests with a new section on testing the equality of three or more population proportions. This section includes a procedure for making multiple comparison tests between all pairs of population proportions. The section on the test of independence has been rewritten to clarify that the test concerns the independence of two categorical variables. Revised appendices with step-by-step instructions for Minitab, Excel, and StatTools are included.

- **New Case Problems.** We have added 7 new case problems to this edition; the total number of cases is 25. Three new descriptive statistics cases have been added to Chapters 2 and 3. Four new case problems involving regression appear in Chapters 12 and 13. These case problems provide students with the opportunity to analyze larger data sets and prepare managerial reports based on the results of their analysis.

- **New Statistics in Practice Applications.** Each chapter begins with a Statistics in Practice vignette that describes an application of the statistical methodology to be covered in the chapter. New to this edition is a Statistics in Practice for Chapter 2 describing the use of data dashboards and data visualization at the Cincinnati Zoo. We have also added a new Statistics in Practice to Chapter 4 describing how a NASA team used probability to assist the rescue of 33 Chilean miners trapped by a cave-in.

- **New Examples and Exercises Based on Real Data.** We continue to make a significant effort to update our text examples and exercises with the most current real data and referenced sources of statistical information. In this edition, we have added approximately 200 new examples and exercises based on real data and referenced sources. Using data from sources also used by *The Wall Street Journal, USA Today, Barron's,* and others, we have drawn from actual studies to develop explanations and to create exercises that demonstrate the many uses of statistics in business and economics. We believe that the use of real data helps generate more student interest in the material and enables the student to learn about both the statistical methodology and its application. The seventh edition contains over 300 examples and exercises based on real data.

Features and Pedagogy

Authors Anderson, Sweeney, Williams, Camm, and Cochran have continued many of the features that appeared in previous editions. Important ones for students are noted here.

Methods Exercises and Applications Exercises

The end-of-section exercises are split into two parts, Methods and Applications. The Methods exercises require students to use the formulas and make the necessary computations. The Applications exercises require students to use the chapter material in real-world situations. Thus, students first focus on the computational "nuts and bolts" and then move on to the subtleties of statistical application and interpretation.

Self Test Exercises

Certain exercises are identified as "Self Test Exercises." Completely worked-out solutions for these exercises are provided in Appendix D. Students can attempt the Self Test Exercises and immediately check the solution to evaluate their understanding of the concepts presented in the chapter.

Margin Annotations and Notes and Comments

Margin annotations that highlight key points and provide additional insights for the student are a key feature of this text. These annotations, which appear in the margins, are designed to provide emphasis and enhance understanding of the terms and concepts being presented in the text.

At the end of many sections, we provide Notes and Comments designed to give the student additional insights about the statistical methodology and its application. Notes and Comments include warnings about or limitations of the methodology, recommendations for application, brief descriptions of additional technical considerations, and other matters.

Data Files Accompany the Text

Over 200 data files are available on the website that accompanies the text. The data sets are available in both Minitab and Excel formats. Webfile logos are used in the text to identify the data sets that are available on the website. Data sets for all case problems as well as data sets for larger exercises are included.

Acknowledgments

We would like to acknowledge the work of our reviewers, who provided comments and suggestions of ways to continue to improve our text. Thanks to

David H. Carhart
Bentley University

Joan M. Donohue
University of South
Carolina

Patrick Jaska
University of Mary
Hardin-Baylor

Andres Jauregui
Columbus State University

C. P. Kartha
University of Michigan—
Flint

Joseph A. Scazzero
Eastern Michigan
University

Timothy Scheppa
Concordia University
Wisconsin

Matthew J. Stollak
St. Norbert College

Daniel R. Strang
SUNY Geneseo

Daniel A. Talley
Dakota State University

David M. Taurisano
Utica College

Rahmat O. Tavallali
Walsh University

Jennifer VanGilder
Ursinus College

Ahmad Vessal
California State University
Northridge

Tatsuma Wada
Wayne State University

Bruce Watson
Boston University

Carol A. Keeth Williams
Central Virginia
Community College

Mark Wilson
St. Bonaventure University

Zachary Wong
Sonoma State University

Steven T. Yen
University of Tennessee

Jiang Zhang
Robert B. Willumstad
School of Business
Adelphi University

We continue to owe a debt to our many colleagues and friends for their helpful comments and suggestions in the development of this and earlier editions of our text. Among them are:

Alan Smith
Robert Morris College

Ali Arshad
College of Santa Fe

Bennie Waller
Francis Marion University

Carlton Scott
University of California—Irvine

Charles Reichert
University of Wisconsin—Superior

Charles Zimmerman
Robert Morris College

Dale DeBoer
University of Colorado—Colorado Springs

Elaine Parks
Laramie County Community College

Gary Nelson
Central Community College—Columbus Campus

Gipsie Ranney
Belmont University

Habtu Braha
Coppin State College

Karen Gutermuth
Virginia Military Institute

Larry Scheuermann
University of Louisiana, Lafayette

Md. Mahbubul Kabir
Lyon College

Nader Ebrahimi
University of New Mexico

Raj Devasagayam
St. Norbert College

Robert Cochran
University of Wyoming

H. Robert Gadd
Southern Adventist University

Stephen Smith
Gordon College

Timothy Bergquist
Northwest Christian College

Wibawa Sutanto
Prairie View A&M University

Yan Yu
University of Cincinnati

Zhiwei Zhu
University of Louisiana at Lafayette

We thank our associates from business and industry who supplied the Statistics in Practice features. We recognize them individually by a credit line in each of the articles. We are also indebted to our Product Director, Joe Sabatino; our Product Manager Aaron Arnsparger; our Content Developer Maggie Kubale; our Content Project Manager, Tamborah Moore; our Project Manager at MPS, Lynn Lustberg; our Media Developer Chris Valentine; and others at Cengage Learning for their editorial counsel and support during the preparation of this text.

David R. Anderson
Dennis J. Sweeney
Thomas A. Williams
Jeffrey D. Camm
James J. Cochran

About the Authors

David R. Anderson. David R. Anderson is Professor Emeritus of Quantitative Analysis in the Lindner College of Business at the University of Cincinnati. Born in Grand Forks, North Dakota, he earned his B.S., M.S., and Ph.D. degrees from Purdue University. Professor Anderson has served as Head of the Department of Quantitative Analysis and Operations Management and as Associate Dean of the College of Business at the University of Cincinnati. In addition, he was the coordinator of the College's first Executive Program.

At the University of Cincinnati, Professor Anderson has taught introductory statistics for business students as well as graduate-level courses in regression analysis, multivariate analysis, and management science. He has also taught statistical courses at the Department of Labor in Washington, D.C. He has been honored with nominations and awards for excellence in teaching and excellence in service to student organizations.

Professor Anderson has coauthored 10 textbooks in the areas of statistics, management science, linear programming, and production and operations management. He is an active consultant in the field of sampling and statistical methods.

Dennis J. Sweeney. Dennis J. Sweeney is Professor Emeritus of Quantitative Analysis and Founder of the Center for Productivity Improvement at the University of Cincinnati. Born in Des Moines, Iowa, he earned a B.S.B.A. degree from Drake University and his M.B.A. and D.B.A. degrees from Indiana University, where he was an NDEA Fellow. Professor Sweeney has worked in the management science group at Procter & Gamble and spent a year as a visiting professor at Duke University. Professor Sweeney served as Head of the Department of Quantitative Analysis and as Associate Dean of the College of Business at the University of Cincinnati.

Professor Sweeney has published more than 30 articles and monographs in the area of management science and statistics. The National Science Foundation, IBM, Procter & Gamble, Federated Department Stores, Kroger, and Cincinnati Gas & Electric have funded his research, which has been published in *Management Science, Operations Research, Mathematical Programming, Decision Sciences,* and other journals.

Professor Sweeney has coauthored 10 textbooks in the areas of statistics, management science, linear programming, and production and operations management.

Thomas A. Williams. Thomas A. Williams is Professor Emeritus of Management Science in the College of Business at Rochester Institute of Technology. Born in Elmira, New York, he earned his B.S. degree at Clarkson University. He did his graduate work at Rensselaer Polytechnic Institute, where he received his M.S. and Ph.D. degrees.

Before joining the College of Business at RIT, Professor Williams served for seven years as a faculty member in the College of Business at the University of Cincinnati, where he developed the undergraduate program in Information Systems and then served as its coordinator. At RIT he was the first chairman of the Decision Sciences Department. He teaches courses in management science and statistics, as well as graduate courses in regression and decision analysis.

Professor Williams is the coauthor of 11 textbooks in the areas of management science, statistics, production and operations management, and mathematics. He has been a consultant for numerous Fortune 500 companies and has worked on projects ranging from the use of data analysis to the development of large-scale regression models.

Jeffrey D. Camm.   Jeffrey D. Camm is Professor of Quantitative Analysis, Head of the Department of Operations, Business Analytics, and Information Systems and College of Business Research Fellow in the Lindner College of Business at the University of Cincinnati. Born in Cincinnati, Ohio, he holds a B.S. from Xavier University and a Ph.D. from Clemson University. He has been at the University of Cincinnati since 1984 and has been a visiting scholar at Stanford University and a visiting professor of business administration at the Tuck School of Business at Dartmouth College.

Dr. Camm has published over 30 papers in the general area of optimization applied to problems in operations management. He has published his research in *Science, Management Science, Operations Research, Interfaces,* and other professional journals. At the University of Cincinnati, he was named the Dornoff Fellow of Teaching Excellence and he was the 2006 recipient of the INFORMS Prize for the Teaching of Operations Research Practice. A firm believer in practicing what he preaches, he has served as an operations research consultant to numerous companies and government agencies. From 2005 to 2010 he served as editor-in-chief of *Interfaces* and is currently on the editorial board of *INFORMS Transactions on Education.*

James J. Cochran.   James J. Cochran is the Bank of Ruston Barnes, Thompson, & Thurman Endowed Research Professor of Quantitative Analysis at Louisiana Tech University. Born in Dayton, Ohio, he earned his B.S., M.S., and M.B.A. degrees from Wright State University and a Ph.D. from the University of Cincinnati. He has been at Louisiana Tech University since 2000 and has been a visiting scholar at Stanford University, Universidad de Talca, the University of South Africa, and Pôle Universitaire Léonard De Vinci.

Professor Cochran has published over two dozen papers in the development and application of operations research and statistical methods. He has published his research in *Management Science, The American Statistician, Communications in Statistics—Theory and Methods, European Journal of Operational Research, Journal of Combinatorial Optimization,* and other professional journals. He was the 2008 recipient of the INFORMS Prize for the Teaching of Operations Research Practice and the 2010 recipient of the Mu Sigma Rho Statistical Education Award. Professor Cochran was elected to the International Statistics Institute in 2005 and named a Fellow of the American Statistical Association in 2011. A strong advocate for effective operations research and statistics education as a means of improving the quality of applications to real problems, Professor Cochran has organized and chaired teaching effectiveness workshops in Montevideo, Uruguay; Cape Town, South Africa; Cartagena, Colombia; Jaipur, India; Buenos Aires, Argentina; Nairobi, Kenya; and Buea, Cameroon. He has served as an operations research consultant to numerous companies and not-for-profit organizations. From 2007 through 2012 he served as editor-in-chief of *INFORMS Transactions on Education* and is on the editorial board of *Interfaces,* the *Journal of the Chilean Institute of Operations Research,* the *Journal of Quantitative Analysis in Sports,* and *ORiON.*

CHAPTER 1

Data and Statistics

CONTENTS

STATISTICS IN PRACTICE:
BLOOMBERG BUSINESSWEEK

1.1 APPLICATIONS IN BUSINESS
AND ECONOMICS
Accounting
Finance
Marketing
Production
Economics
Information Systems

1.2 DATA
Elements, Variables, and
Observations
Scales of Measurement
Categorical and Quantitative Data
Cross-Sectional and Time
Series Data

1.3 DATA SOURCES
Existing Sources
Statistical Studies
Data Acquisition Errors

1.4 DESCRIPTIVE STATISTICS

1.5 STATISTICAL INFERENCE

1.6 COMPUTERS AND
STATISTICAL ANALYSIS

1.7 DATA MINING

1.8 ETHICAL GUIDELINES FOR
STATISTICAL PRACTICE

STATISTICS *in* PRACTICE

BLOOMBERG BUSINESSWEEK*
NEW YORK, NEW YORK

With a global circulation of more than 1 million, *Bloomberg Businessweek* is one of the most widely read business magazines in the world. Bloomberg's 1700 reporters in 145 service bureaus around the world enable *Bloomberg Businessweek* to deliver a variety of articles of interest to the global business and economic community. Along with feature articles on current topics, the magazine contains articles on international business, economic analysis, information processing, and science and technology. Information in the feature articles and the regular sections helps readers stay abreast of current developments and assess the impact of those developments on business and economic conditions.

Most issues of *Bloomberg Businessweek,* formerly *BusinessWeek,* provide an in-depth report on a topic of current interest. Often, the in-depth reports contain statistical facts and summaries that help the reader understand the business and economic information. Examples of articles and reports include the impact of businesses moving important work to cloud computing, the crisis facing the U.S. Postal Service, and why the debt crisis is even worse than we think. In addition, *Bloomberg Businessweek* provides a variety of statistics about the state of the economy, including production indexes, stock prices, mutual funds, and interest rates.

Bloomberg Businessweek also uses statistics and statistical information in managing its own business. For example, an annual survey of subscribers helps the company learn about subscriber demographics, reading habits, likely purchases, lifestyles, and so on. *Bloomberg Businessweek* managers use statistical summaries from the survey to provide better services to subscribers and advertisers. One recent North American subscriber survey indicated that 90% of *Bloomberg Businessweek*

Bloomberg Businessweek uses statistical facts and summaries in many of its articles. © Kyodo/Photoshot.

subscribers use a personal computer at home and that 64% of *Bloomberg Businessweek* subscribers are involved with computer purchases at work. Such statistics alert *Bloomberg Businessweek* managers to subscriber interest in articles about new developments in computers. The results of the subscriber survey are also made available to potential advertisers. The high percentage of subscribers using personal computers at home and the high percentage of subscribers involved with computer purchases at work would be an incentive for a computer manufacturer to consider advertising in *Bloomberg Businessweek.*

In this chapter, we discuss the types of data available for statistical analysis and describe how the data are obtained. We introduce descriptive statistics and statistical inference as ways of converting data into meaningful and easily interpreted statistical information.

*The authors are indebted to Charlene Trentham, Research Manager, for providing this Statistics in Practice.

Frequently, we see the following types of statements in newspapers and magazines:

- The median price for an existing single-family home is $186,000, up 7.6% from a year earlier (*The Wall Street Journal,* November 8, 2012).
- Women account for 14.1% of the executive officers in Fortune 500 companies (*The Wall Street Journal,* April 30, 2012).

- The average annual cost for a college education is $17,100 for public, in-state universities and $38,600 for private universities (*Money Magazine,* March 2012).
- A Yahoo Finance survey reported 51% of workers say the key to getting ahead is internal politics, while 27% say the key to getting ahead is hard work (*USA Today,* September 29, 2012).
- The median age of a first marriage is 29 for men and 26 for women (Associated Press, December 25, 2011).
- The percentage of U.S. workers getting less than six hours of sleep per night is 30% (*The Wall Street Journal,* August 4, 2012).
- The average credit card debt is $5,204 per person (PRWeb website, April 5, 2012).

The numerical facts in the preceding statements ($186,000, 7.6%, 14.1%, $17,100, $38,600, 51%, 27%, 29, 26, 30%, and $5,204) are called **statistics**. In this usage, the term statistics refers to numerical facts such as averages, medians, percentages, and maximums that help us understand a variety of business and economic situations. However, as you will see, the field, or subject, of statistics involves much more than numerical facts. In a broader sense, statistics is the art and science of collecting, analyzing, presenting, and interpreting data. Particularly in business and economics, the information provided by collecting, analyzing, presenting, and interpreting data gives managers and decision makers a better understanding of the business and economic environment and thus enables them to make more informed and better decisions. In this text, we emphasize the use of statistics for business and economic decision making.

Chapter 1 begins with some illustrations of the applications of statistics in business and economics. In Section 1.2 we define the term *data* and introduce the concept of a data set. This section also introduces key terms such as *variables* and *observations,* discusses the difference between quantitative and categorical data, and illustrates the uses of cross-sectional and time series data. Section 1.3 discusses how data can be obtained from existing sources or through survey and experimental studies designed to obtain new data. The important role that the Internet now plays in obtaining data is also highlighted. The uses of data in developing descriptive statistics and in making statistical inferences are described in Sections 1.4 and 1.5. The last three sections of Chapter 1 provide the role of the computer in statistical analysis, an introduction to data mining, and a discussion of ethical guidelines for statistical practice. A chapter-ending appendix includes an introduction to the add-in StatTools which can be used to extend the statistical options for users of Microsoft Excel.

Applications in Business and Economics

In today's global business and economic environment, anyone can access vast amounts of statistical information. The most successful managers and decision makers understand the information and know how to use it effectively. In this section, we provide examples that illustrate some of the uses of statistics in business and economics.

Accounting

Public accounting firms use statistical sampling procedures when conducting audits for their clients. For instance, suppose an accounting firm wants to determine whether the amount of accounts receivable shown on a client's balance sheet fairly represents the actual amount of accounts receivable. Usually the large number of individual accounts receivable makes reviewing and validating every account too time-consuming and expensive. As common practice in such situations, the audit staff selects a subset of the accounts called a sample.

After reviewing the accuracy of the sampled accounts, the auditors draw a conclusion as to whether the accounts receivable amount shown on the client's balance sheet is acceptable.

Finance

Financial analysts use a variety of statistical information to guide their investment recommendations. In the case of stocks, analysts review financial data such as price/earnings ratios and dividend yields. By comparing the information for an individual stock with information about the stock market averages, an analyst can begin to draw a conclusion as to whether the stock is a good investment. For example, *The Wall Street Journal* (March 19, 2012) reported that the average dividend yield for the S&P 500 companies was 2.2%. Microsoft showed a dividend yield of 2.42%. In this case, the statistical information on dividend yield indicates a higher dividend yield for Microsoft than the average dividend yield for the S&P 500 companies. This and other information about Microsoft would help the analyst make an informed buy, sell, or hold recommendation for Microsoft stock.

Marketing

Electronic scanners at retail checkout counters collect data for a variety of marketing research applications. For example, data suppliers such as ACNielsen and Information Resources, Inc., purchase point-of-sale scanner data from grocery stores, process the data, and then sell statistical summaries of the data to manufacturers. Manufacturers spend hundreds of thousands of dollars per product category to obtain this type of scanner data. Manufacturers also purchase data and statistical summaries on promotional activities such as special pricing and the use of in-store displays. Brand managers can review the scanner statistics and the promotional activity statistics to gain a better understanding of the relationship between promotional activities and sales. Such analyses often prove helpful in establishing future marketing strategies for the various products.

Production

Today's emphasis on quality makes quality control an important application of statistics in production. A variety of statistical quality control charts are used to monitor the output of a production process. In particular, an x-bar chart can be used to monitor the average output. Suppose, for example, that a machine fills containers with 12 ounces of a soft drink. Periodically, a production worker selects a sample of containers and computes the average number of ounces in the sample. This average, or x-bar value, is plotted on an x-bar chart. A plotted value above the chart's upper control limit indicates overfilling, and a plotted value below the chart's lower control limit indicates underfilling. The process is termed "in control" and allowed to continue as long as the plotted x-bar values fall between the chart's upper and lower control limits. Properly interpreted, an x-bar chart can help determine when adjustments are necessary to correct a production process.

Economics

Economists frequently provide forecasts about the future of the economy or some aspect of it. They use a variety of statistical information in making such forecasts. For instance, in forecasting inflation rates, economists use statistical information on such indicators as the Producer Price Index, the unemployment rate, and manufacturing capacity utilization. Often these statistical indicators are entered into computerized forecasting models that predict inflation rates.

Information Systems

Information systems administrators are responsible for the day-to-day operation of an organization's computer networks. A variety of statistical information helps administrators assess the performance of computer networks, including local area networks (LANs), wide area networks (WANs), network segments, intranets, and other data communication systems. Statistics such as the mean number of users on the system, the proportion of time any component of the system is down, and the proportion of bandwidth utilized at various times of the day are examples of statistical information that help the system administrator better understand and manage the computer network.

Applications of statistics such as those described in this section are an integral part of this text. Such examples provide an overview of the breadth of statistical applications. To supplement these examples, practitioners in the fields of business and economics provided chapter-opening Statistics in Practice articles that introduce the material covered in each chapter. The Statistics in Practice applications show the importance of statistics in a wide variety of business and economic situations.

Data

Data are the facts and figures collected, analyzed, and summarized for presentation and interpretation. All the data collected in a particular study are referred to as the **data set** for the study. Table 1.1 shows a data set containing information for 60 nations that participate in the World Trade Organization. The World Trade Organization encourages the free flow of international trade and provides a forum for resolving trade dispute.

Elements, Variables, and Observations

Elements are the entities on which data are collected. Each nation listed in Table 1.1 is an element with the nation or element name shown in the first column. With 60 nations, the data set contains 60 elements.

A **variable** is a characteristic of interest for the elements. The data set in Table 1.1 includes the following five variables:

- WTO Status: The nation's membership status in the World Trade Organization; this can be either as a member or an observer.
- Per Capita GDP ($): The total output of the nation divided by the number of people in the nation; this is commonly used to compare economic productivity of the nations.
- Trade Deficit ($1000s): The difference between total dollar value of the nation's imports and total dollar value of the nation's exports.
- Fitch Rating: The nation's sovereign credit rating as appraised by the Fitch Group[1]; the credit ratings range from a high of AAA to a low of F and can be modified by + or −.
- Fitch Outlook: An indication of the direction the credit rating is likely to move over the upcoming two years; the outlook can be negative, stable, or positive.

Measurements collected on each variable for every element in a study provide the data. The set of measurements obtained for a particular element is called an **observation**. Referring to Table 1.1, we see that the first observation contains the following measurements:

---

[1]The Fitch Group is one of three nationally recognized statistical rating organizations designated by the U.S. Securities and Exchange Commission. The other two are Standard and Poor's and Moody's investor service.

TABLE 1.1   DATA SET FOR 60 NATIONS IN THE WORLD TRADE ORGANIZATION

Nation	WTO Status	Per Capita GDP ($)	Trade Deficit ($1000s)	Fitch Rating	Fitch Outlook
Armenia	Member	5,400	2,673,359	BB−	Stable
Australia	Member	40,800	−33,304,157	AAA	Stable
Austria	Member	41,700	12,796,558	AAA	Stable
Azerbaijan	Observer	5,400	−16,747,320	BBB−	Positive
Bahrain	Member	27,300	3,102,665	BBB	Stable
Belgium	Member	37,600	−14,930,833	AA+	Negative
Brazil	Member	11,600	−29,796,166	BBB	Stable
Bulgaria	Member	13,500	4,049,237	BBB−	Positive
Canada	Member	40,300	−1,611,380	AAA	Stable
Cape Verde	Member	4,000	874,459	B+	Stable
Chile	Member	16,100	−14,558,218	A+	Stable
China	Member	8,400	−156,705,311	A+	Stable
Colombia	Member	10,100	−1,561,199	BBB−	Stable
Costa Rica	Member	11,500	5,807,509	BB+	Stable
Croatia	Member	18,300	8,108,103	BBB−	Negative
Cyprus	Member	29,100	6,623,337	BBB	Negative
Czech Republic	Member	25,900	−10,749,467	A+	Positive
Denmark	Member	40,200	−15,057,343	AAA	Stable
Ecuador	Member	8,300	1,993,819	B−	Stable
Egypt	Member	6,500	28,486,933	BB	Negative
El Salvador	Member	7,600	5,019,363	BB	Stable
Estonia	Member	20,200	802,234	A+	Stable
France	Member	35,000	118,841,542	AAA	Stable
Georgia	Member	5,400	4,398,153	B+	Positive
Germany	Member	37,900	−213,367,685	AAA	Stable
Hungary	Member	19,600	−9,421,301	BBB−	Negative
Iceland	Member	38,000	−504,939	BB+	Stable
Ireland	Member	39,500	−59,093,323	BBB+	Negative
Israel	Member	31,000	6,722,291	A	Stable
Italy	Member	30,100	33,568,668	A+	Negative
Japan	Member	34,300	31,675,424	AA	Negative
Kazakhstan	Observer	13,000	−33,220,437	BBB	Positive
Kenya	Member	1,700	9,174,198	B+	Stable
Latvia	Member	15,400	2,448,053	BBB−	Positive
Lebanon	Observer	15,600	13,715,550	B	Stable
Lithuania	Member	18,700	3,359,641	BBB	Positive
Malaysia	Member	15,600	−39,420,064	A−	Stable
Mexico	Member	15,100	1,288,112	BBB	Stable
Peru	Member	10,000	−7,888,993	BBB	Stable
Philippines	Member	4,100	15,667,209	BB+	Stable
Poland	Member	20,100	19,552,976	A−	Stable
Portugal	Member	23,200	21,060,508	BBB−	Negative
South Korea	Member	31,700	−37,509,141	A+	Stable
Romania	Member	12,300	13,323,709	BBB−	Stable
Russia	Observer	16,700	−151,400,000	BBB	Positive
Rwanda	Member	1,300	939,222	B	Stable
Serbia	Observer	10,700	8,275,693	BB−	Stable
Seychelles	Observer	24,700	666,026	B	Stable
Singapore	Member	59,900	−27,110,421	AAA	Stable
Slovakia	Member	23,400	−2,110,626	A+	Stable
Slovenia	Member	29,100	2,310,617	AA−	Negative
South Africa	Member	11,000	3,321,801	BBB+	Stable

Sweden	Member	40,600	−10,903,251	AAA	Stable
Switzerland	Member	43,400	−27,197,873	AAA	Stable
Thailand	Member	9,700	2,049,669	BBB	Stable
Turkey	Member	14,600	71,612,947	BB+	Positive
UK	Member	35,900	162,316,831	AAA	Negative
Uruguay	Member	15,400	2,662,628	BB	Positive
USA	Member	48,100	784,438,559	AAA	Stable
Zambia	Member	1,600	−1,805,198	B+	Stable

Member, 5,400, 2,673,359, BB−, and Stable. The second observation contains the following measurements: Member, 40,800, −33,304,157, AAA, and Stable, and so on. A data set with 60 elements contains 60 observations.

Scales of Measurement

Data collection requires one of the following scales of measurement: nominal, ordinal, interval, or ratio. The scale of measurement determines the amount of information contained in the data and indicates the most appropriate data summarization and statistical analyses.

When the data for a variable consist of labels or names used to identify an attribute of the element, the scale of measurement is considered a **nominal scale**. For example, referring to the data in Table 1.1, the scale of measurement for the WTO Status variable is nominal because the data "member" and "observer" are labels used to identify the status category for the nation. In cases where the scale of measurement is nominal, a numerical code as well as a nonnumerical label may be used. For example, to facilitate data collection and to prepare the data for entry into a computer database, we might use a numerical code for WTO Status variable by letting 1 denote a member nation in the World Trade Organization and 2 denote an observer nation. The scale of measurement is nominal even though the data appear as numerical values.

The scale of measurement for a variable is considered an **ordinal scale** if the data exhibit the properties of nominal data and in addition, the order or rank of the data is meaningful. For example, referring to the data in Table 1.1, the scale of measurement for the Fitch Rating is ordinal because the rating labels which range from AAA to F can be rank ordered from best credit rating AAA to poorest credit rating F. The rating letters provide the labels similar to nominal data, but in addition, the data can also be ranked or ordered based on the credit rating, which makes the measurement scale ordinal. Ordinal data can also be recorded by a numerical code, for example, your class rank in school.

The scale of measurement for a variable is an **interval scale** if the data have all the properties of ordinal data and the interval between values is expressed in terms of a fixed unit of measure. Interval data are always numeric. College admission SAT scores are an example of interval-scaled data. For example, three students with SAT math scores of 620, 550, and 470 can be ranked or ordered in terms of best performance to poorest performance in math. In addition, the differences between the scores are meaningful. For instance, student 1 scored $620 - 550 = 70$ points more than student 2, while student 2 scored $550 - 470 = 80$ points more than student 3.

The scale of measurement for a variable is a **ratio scale** if the data have all the properties of interval data and the ratio of two values is meaningful. Variables such as distance, height, weight, and time use the ratio scale of measurement. This scale requires that a zero value be included to indicate that nothing exists for the variable at the zero point.

For example, consider the cost of an automobile. A zero value for the cost would indicate that the automobile has no cost and is free. In addition, if we compare the cost of $30,000 for one automobile to the cost of $15,000 for a second automobile, the ratio property shows that the first automobile is $30,000/$15,000 = 2 times, or twice, the cost of the second automobile.

Categorical and Quantitative Data

Data can be classified as either categorical or quantitative. Data that can be grouped by specific categories are referred to as **categorical data**. Categorical data use either the nominal or ordinal scale of measurement. Data that use numeric values to indicate how much or how many are referred to as **quantitative data**. Quantitative data are obtained using either the interval or ratio scale of measurement.

The statistical method appropriate for summarizing data depends upon whether the data are categorical or quantitative.

A **categorical variable** is a variable with categorical data, and a **quantitative variable** is a variable with quantitative data. The statistical analysis appropriate for a particular variable depends upon whether the variable is categorical or quantitative. If the variable is categorical, the statistical analysis is limited. We can summarize categorical data by counting the number of observations in each category or by computing the proportion of the observations in each category. However, even when the categorical data are identified by a numerical code, arithmetic operations such as addition, subtraction, multiplication, and division do not provide meaningful results. Section 2.1 discusses ways for summarizing categorical data.

Arithmetic operations provide meaningful results for quantitative variables. For example, quantitative data may be added and then divided by the number of observations to compute the average value. This average is usually meaningful and easily interpreted. In general, more alternatives for statistical analysis are possible when data are quantitative. Section 2.2 and Chapter 3 provide ways of summarizing quantitative data.

Cross-Sectional and Time Series Data

For purposes of statistical analysis, distinguishing between cross-sectional data and time series data is important. **Cross-sectional data** are data collected at the same or approximately the same point in time. The data in Table 1.1 are cross-sectional because they describe the five variables for the 60 World Trade Organization nations at the same point in time. **Time series data** are data collected over several time periods. For example, the time series in Figure 1.1 shows the U.S. average price per gallon of conventional regular gasoline between 2007 and 2012. Note that gasoline prices peaked in the summer of 2008 and then dropped sharply in the fall of 2008. Since 2008, the average price per gallon has continued to climb steadily, approaching an all-time high again in 2012.

Graphs of time series data are frequently found in business and economic publications. Such graphs help analysts understand what happened in the past, identify any trends over time, and project future values for the time series. The graphs of time series data can take on a variety of forms, as shown in Figure 1.2. With a little study, these graphs are usually easy to understand and interpret. For example, Panel (A) in Figure 1.2 is a graph that shows the Dow Jones Industrial Average Index from 2002 to 2012. In April 2002, the popular stock market index was near 10,000. Over the next five years the index rose to its all-time high of slightly over 14,000 in October 2007. However, notice the sharp decline in the time series after the high in 2007. By March 2009, poor economic conditions had caused the Dow Jones Industrial Average Index to return to the 7000 level. This was a scary and discouraging period for investors. However, by late 2009, the index was showing a recovery by reaching 10,000. The index has climbed steadily and was above 13,000 in early 2012.

FIGURE 1.1   U.S. AVERAGE PRICE PER GALLON FOR CONVENTIONAL
REGULAR GASOLINE

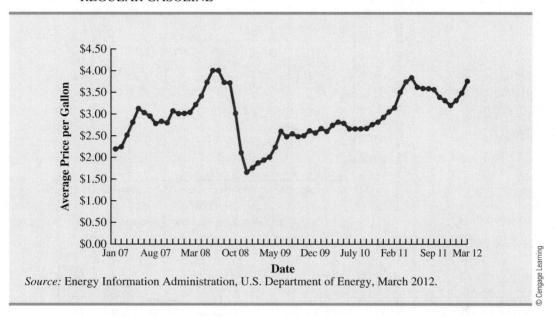

Source: Energy Information Administration, U.S. Department of Energy, March 2012.

The graph in Panel (B) shows the net income of McDonald's Inc. from 2005 to 2011. The declining economic conditions in 2008 and 2009 were actually beneficial to McDonald's as the company's net income rose to all-time highs. The growth in McDonald's net income showed that the company was thriving during the economic downturn as people were cutting back on the more expensive sit-down restaurants and seeking less-expensive alternatives offered by McDonald's. McDonald's net income continued to new all-time highs in 2010 and 2011.

Panel (C) shows the time series for the occupancy rate of hotels in South Florida over a one-year period. The highest occupancy rates, 95% and 98%, occur during the months of February and March when the climate of South Florida is attractive to tourists. In fact, January to April of each year is typically the high-occupancy season for South Florida hotels. On the other hand, note the low occupancy rates during the months of August to October, with the lowest occupancy rate of 50% occurring in September. High temperatures and the hurricane season are the primary reasons for the drop in hotel occupancy during this period.

NOTES AND COMMENTS

1. An observation is the set of measurements obtained for each element in a data set. Hence, the number of observations is always the same as the number of elements. The number of measurements obtained for each element equals the number of variables. Hence, the total number of data items can be determined by multiplying the number of observations by the number of variables.

2. Quantitative data may be discrete or continuous. Quantitative data that measure how many (e.g., number of calls received in 5 minutes) are discrete. Quantitative data that measure how much (e.g., weight or time) are continuous because no separation occurs between the possible data values.

FIGURE 1.2   A VARIETY OF GRAPHS OF TIME SERIES DATA

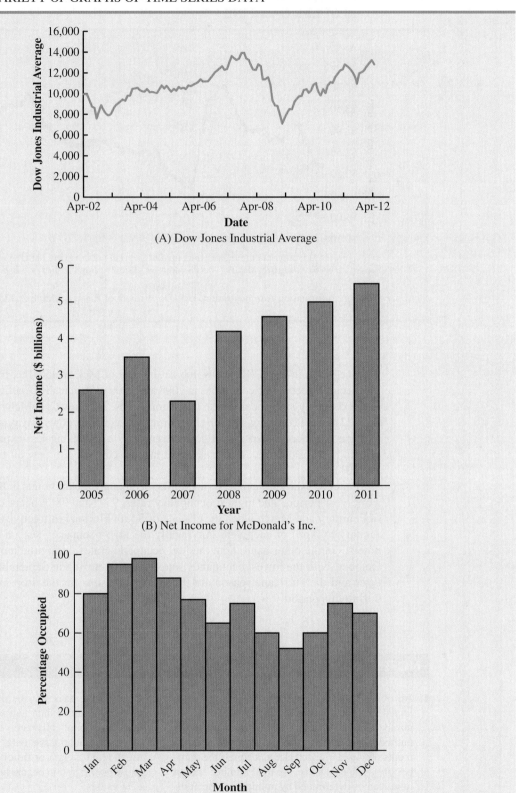

(A) Dow Jones Industrial Average

(B) Net Income for McDonald's Inc.

(C) Occupancy Rate of South Florida Hotels

1.3 # Data Sources

Data can be obtained from existing sources or from surveys and experimental studies designed to collect new data.

Existing Sources

In some cases, data needed for a particular application already exist. Companies maintain a variety of databases about their employees, customers, and business operations. Data on employee salaries, ages, and years of experience can usually be obtained from internal personnel records. Other internal records contain data on sales, advertising expenditures, distribution costs, inventory levels, and production quantities. Most companies also maintain detailed data about their customers. Table 1.2 shows some of the data commonly available from internal company records.

Organizations that specialize in collecting and maintaining data make available substantial amounts of business and economic data. Companies access these external data sources through leasing arrangements or by purchase. Dun & Bradstreet, Bloomberg, and Dow Jones & Company are three firms that provide extensive business database services to clients. ACNielsen and Information Resources, Inc., built successful businesses collecting and processing data that they sell to advertisers and product manufacturers.

Data are also available from a variety of industry associations and special interest organizations. The Travel Industry Association of America maintains travel-related information such as the number of tourists and travel expenditures by states. Such data would be of interest to firms and individuals in the travel industry. The Graduate Management Admission Council maintains data on test scores, student characteristics, and graduate management education programs. Most of the data from these types of sources are available to qualified users at a modest cost.

The Internet is an important source of data and statistical information. Almost all companies maintain websites that provide general information about the company as well as data on sales, number of employees, number of products, product prices, and product specifications. In addition, a number of companies now specialize in making information available over the Internet. As a result, one can obtain access to stock quotes, meal prices at restaurants, salary data, and an almost infinite variety of information.

Government agencies are another important source of existing data. For instance, the U.S. Department of Labor maintains considerable data on employment rates, wage rates, size of the labor force, and union membership. Table 1.3 lists selected governmental agencies

TABLE 1.2 EXAMPLES OF DATA AVAILABLE FROM INTERNAL COMPANY RECORDS

Source	Some of the Data Typically Available
Employee records	Name, address, social security number, salary, number of vacation days, number of sick days, and bonus
Production records	Part or product number, quantity produced, direct labor cost, and materials cost
Inventory records	Part or product number, number of units on hand, reorder level, economic order quantity, and discount schedule
Sales records	Product number, sales volume, sales volume by region, and sales volume by customer type
Credit records	Customer name, address, phone number, credit limit, and accounts receivable balance
Customer profile	Age, gender, income level, household size, address, and preferences

TABLE 1.3   EXAMPLES OF DATA AVAILABLE FROM SELECTED GOVERNMENT AGENCIES

Government Agency	Some of the Data Available
Census Bureau	Population data, number of households, and household income
Federal Reserve Board	Data on the money supply, installment credit, exchange rates, and discount rates
Office of Management and Budget	Data on revenue, expenditures, and debt of the federal government
Department of Commerce	Data on business activity, value of shipments by industry, level of profits by industry, and growing and declining industries
Bureau of Labor Statistics	Consumer spending, hourly earnings, unemployment rate, safety records, and international statistics

© Cengage Learning

and some of the data they provide. Most government agencies that collect and process data also make the results available through a website. Figure 1.3 shows the homepage for the U.S. Bureau of Labor Statistics website.

Statistical Studies

The largest experimental statistical study ever conducted is believed to be the 1954 Public Health Service experiment for the Salk polio vaccine. Nearly 2 million children in grades 1, 2, and 3 were selected from throughout the United States.

Sometimes the data needed for a particular application are not available through existing sources. In such cases, the data can often be obtained by conducting a statistical study. Statistical studies can be classified as either *experimental* or *observational*.

In an experimental study, a variable of interest is first identified. Then one or more other variables are identified and controlled so that data can be obtained about how they influence the variable of interest. For example, a pharmaceutical firm might be interested in conducting an experiment to learn how a new drug affects blood pressure. Blood pressure is the variable of interest in the study. The dosage level of the new drug is another variable

FIGURE 1.3   U.S. BUREAU OF LABOR STATISTICS HOMEPAGE

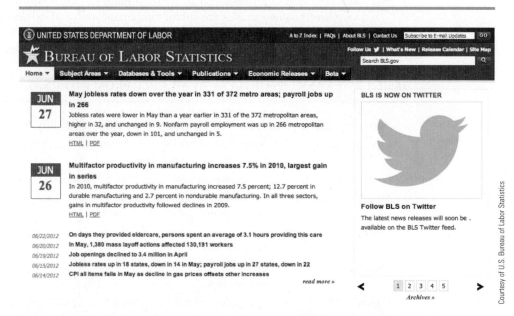

Courtesy of U.S. Bureau of Labor Statistics

that is hoped to have a causal effect on blood pressure. To obtain data about the effect of the new drug, researchers select a sample of individuals. The dosage level of the new drug is controlled, as different groups of individuals are given different dosage levels. Before and after data on blood pressure are collected for each group. Statistical analysis of the experimental data can help determine how the new drug affects blood pressure.

Nonexperimental, or observational, statistical studies make no attempt to control the variables of interest. A survey is perhaps the most common type of observational study. For instance, in a personal interview survey, research questions are first identified. Then a questionnaire is designed and administered to a sample of individuals. Some restaurants use observational studies to obtain data about customer opinions on the quality of food, quality of service, atmosphere, and so on. A customer opinion questionnaire used by Chops City Grill in Naples, Florida, is shown in Figure 1.4. Note that the customers who fill out the questionnaire are asked to provide ratings for 12 variables, including overall experience, greeting by hostess, manager (table visit), overall service, and so on. The response categories of excellent, good, average, fair, and poor provide categorical data that enable Chops City Grill management to maintain high standards for the restaurant's food and service.

Anyone wanting to use data and statistical analysis as aids to decision making must be aware of the time and cost required to obtain the data. The use of existing data sources is desirable when data must be obtained in a relatively short period of time. If important data are not readily available from an existing source, the additional time and cost involved in obtaining the data must be taken into account. In all cases, the decision maker should

Studies of smokers and nonsmokers are observational studies because researchers do not determine or control who will smoke and who will not smoke.

FIGURE 1.4   CUSTOMER OPINION QUESTIONNAIRE USED BY CHOPS CITY GRILL RESTAURANT IN NAPLES, FLORIDA consider the contribution of the statistical analysis to the decision-making process. The cost of data acquisition and the subsequent statistical analysis should not exceed the savings generated by using the information to make a better decision.

Data Acquisition Errors

Managers should always be aware of the possibility of data errors in statistical studies. Using erroneous data can be worse than not using any data at all. An error in data acquisition occurs whenever the data value obtained is not equal to the true or actual value that would be obtained with a correct procedure. Such errors can occur in a number of ways. For example, an interviewer might make a recording error, such as a transposition in writing the age of a 24-year-old person as 42, or the person answering an interview question might misinterpret the question and provide an incorrect response.

Experienced data analysts take great care in collecting and recording data to ensure that errors are not made. Special procedures can be used to check for internal consistency of the data. For instance, such procedures would indicate that the analyst should review the accuracy of data for a respondent shown to be 22 years of age but reporting 20 years of work experience. Data analysts also review data with unusually large and small values, called outliers, which are candidates for possible data errors. In Chapter 3 we present some of the methods statisticians use to identify outliers.

Errors often occur during data acquisition. Blindly using any data that happen to be available or using data that were acquired with little care can result in misleading information and bad decisions. Thus, taking steps to acquire accurate data can help ensure reliable and valuable decision-making information.

Descriptive Statistics

Most of the statistical information in newspapers, magazines, company reports, and other publications consists of data that are summarized and presented in a form that is easy for the reader to understand. Such summaries of data, which may be tabular, graphical, or numerical, are referred to as **descriptive statistics**.

Refer to the data set in Table 1.1 showing data for 60 nations that participate in the World Trade Organization. Methods of descriptive statistics can be used to summarize these data. For example, consider the variable Fitch Outlook that indicates the direction the nation's credit rating is likely to move over the next two years. The Fitch Outlook is recorded as being negative, stable, or positive. A tabular summary of the data showing the number of nations with each of the Fitch Outlook ratings is shown in Table 1.4. A graphical summary of the same data, called a bar chart, is shown in Figure 1.5. These types of summaries make the data easier to interpret. Referring to Table 1.4 and Figure 1.5, we can see that the majority of Fitch Outlook credit ratings are stable, with 65% of the nations

TABLE 1.4   FREQUENCIES AND PERCENT FREQUENCIES FOR THE FITCH CREDIT RATING OUTLOOK OF 60 NATIONS

Fitch Outlook	Frequency	Percent Frequency (%)
Positive	10	16.7
Stable	39	65.0
Negative	11	18.3

FIGURE 1.5   BAR CHART FOR THE FITCH CREDIT RATING OUTLOOK FOR 60 NATIONS

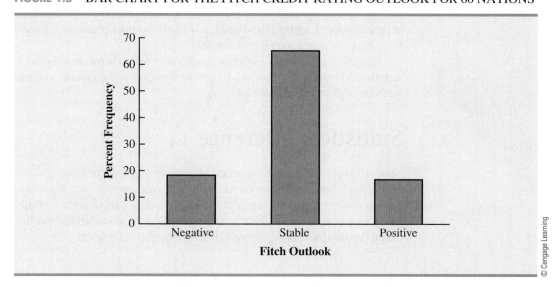

having this rating. Negative and positive outlook credit ratings are similar, with slightly more nations having a negative outlook (18.3%) than a positive outlook (16.7%).

A graphical summary of the data for quantitative variable Per Capita GDP in Table 1.1, called a histogram, is provided in Figure 1.6. Using the histogram, it is easy to see that Per Capita GDP for the 60 nations ranges from $0 to $60,000, with the highest concentration between $10,000 and $20,000. Only one nation had a Per Capita GDP exceeding $50,000.

In addition to tabular and graphical displays, numerical descriptive statistics are used to summarize data. The most common numerical measure is the average, or mean. Using

FIGURE 1.6   HISTOGRAM OF PER CAPITA GDP FOR 60 NATIONS

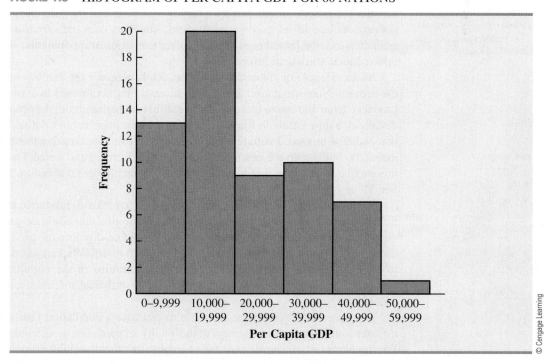

the data on Per Capita GDP for the 60 nations in Table 1.1, we can compute the average by adding Per Capita GDP for all 60 nations and dividing the total by 60. Doing so provides an average Per Capita GDP of $21,387. This average provides a measure of the central tendency, or central location of the data.

There is a great deal of interest in effective methods for developing and presenting descriptive statistics. Chapters 2 and 3 devote attention to the tabular, graphical, and numerical methods of descriptive statistics.

 1.5 Statistical Inference

Many situations require information about a large group of elements (individuals, companies, voters, households, products, customers, and so on). But, because of time, cost, and other considerations, data can be collected from only a small portion of the group. The larger group of elements in a particular study is called the **population**, and the smaller group is called the **sample**. Formally, we use the following definitions.

POPULATION

A population is the set of all elements of interest in a particular study.

SAMPLE

A sample is a subset of the population.

The U.S. government conducts a census every 10 years. Market research firms conduct sample surveys every day.

The process of conducting a survey to collect data for the entire population is called a **census**. The process of conducting a survey to collect data for a sample is called a **sample survey**. As one of its major contributions, statistics uses data from a sample to make estimates and test hypotheses about the characteristics of a population through a process referred to as **statistical inference**.

As an example of statistical inference, let us consider the study conducted by Norris Electronics. Norris manufactures a high-intensity lightbulb used in a variety of electrical products. In an attempt to increase the useful life of the lightbulb, the product design group developed a new lightbulb filament. In this case, the population is defined as all lightbulbs that could be produced with the new filament. To evaluate the advantages of the new filament, 200 bulbs with the new filament were manufactured and tested. Data collected from this sample showed the number of hours each lightbulb operated before filament burnout. See Table 1.5.

Suppose Norris wants to use the sample data to make an inference about the average hours of useful life for the population of all lightbulbs that could be produced with the new filament. Adding the 200 values in Table 1.5 and dividing the total by 200 provides the sample average lifetime for the lightbulbs: 76 hours. We can use this sample result to estimate that the average lifetime for the lightbulbs in the population is 76 hours. Figure 1.7 provides a graphical summary of the statistical inference process for Norris Electronics.

Whenever statisticians use a sample to estimate a population characteristic of interest, they usually provide a statement of the quality, or precision, associated with the estimate. For the Norris example, the statistician might state that the point estimate of the average

TABLE 1.5   HOURS UNTIL BURNOUT FOR A SAMPLE OF 200 LIGHTBULBS FOR THE NORRIS ELECTRONICS EXAMPLE

Norris

107	73	68	97	76	79	94	59	98	57
54	65	71	70	84	88	62	61	79	98
66	62	79	86	68	74	61	82	65	98
62	116	65	88	64	79	78	79	77	86
74	85	73	80	68	78	89	72	58	69
92	78	88	77	103	88	63	68	88	81
75	90	62	89	71	71	74	70	74	70
65	81	75	62	94	71	85	84	83	63
81	62	79	83	93	61	65	62	92	65
83	70	70	81	77	72	84	67	59	58
78	66	66	94	77	63	66	75	68	76
90	78	71	101	78	43	59	67	61	71
96	75	64	76	72	77	74	65	82	86
66	86	96	89	81	71	85	99	59	92
68	72	77	60	87	84	75	77	51	45
85	67	87	80	84	93	69	76	89	75
83	68	72	67	92	89	82	96	77	102
74	91	76	83	66	68	61	73	72	76
73	77	79	94	63	59	62	71	81	65
73	63	63	89	82	64	85	92	64	73

© Cengage Learning

FIGURE 1.7   THE PROCESS OF STATISTICAL INFERENCE FOR THE NORRIS ELECTRONICS EXAMPLE

© Cengage Learning

lifetime for the population of new lightbulbs is 76 hours with a margin of error of ±4 hours. Thus, an interval estimate of the average lifetime for all lightbulbs produced with the new filament is 72 hours to 80 hours. The statistician can also state how confident he or she is that the interval from 72 hours to 80 hours contains the population average.

1.6   Computers and Statistical Analysis

Statisticians frequently use computer software to perform the statistical computations required with large amounts of data. For example, computing the average lifetime for the 200 lightbulbs in the Norris Electronics example (see Table 1.5) would be quite tedious without a computer. To facilitate computer usage, many of the data sets in this book are available on the website that accompanies the text. The data files may be downloaded in either Minitab or Excel formats. In addition, the Excel add-in StatTools can be downloaded from the website. End-of-chapter appendixes cover the step-by-step procedures for using Minitab, Excel, and the Excel add-in StatTools to implement the statistical techniques presented in the chapter.

Minitab and Excel data sets and the Excel add-in StatTools are available on the website for this text.

1.7   Data Mining

With the aid of magnetic card readers, bar code scanners, and point-of-sale terminals, most organizations obtain large amounts of data on a daily basis. And, even for a small local restaurant that uses touch screen monitors to enter orders and handle billing, the amount of data collected can be substantial. For large retail companies, the sheer volume of data collected is hard to conceptualize, and figuring out how to effectively use these data to improve profitability is a challenge. Mass retailers such as Walmart capture data on 20 to 30 million transactions every day, telecommunication companies such as France Telecom and AT&T generate over 300 million call records per day, and Visa processes 6800 payment transactions per second or approximately 600 million transactions per day. Storing and managing the transaction data is a substantial undertaking.

The term *data warehousing* is used to refer to the process of capturing, storing, and maintaining the data. Computing power and data collection tools have reached the point where it is now feasible to store and retrieve extremely large quantities of data in seconds. Analysis of the data in the warehouse may result in decisions that will lead to new strategies and higher profits for the organization.

The subject of **data mining** deals with methods for developing useful decision-making information from large databases. Using a combination of procedures from statistics, mathematics, and computer science, analysts "mine the data" in the warehouse to convert it into useful information, hence the name *data mining*. Dr. Kurt Thearling, a leading practitioner in the field, defines data mining as "the automated extraction of predictive information from (large) databases." The two key words in Dr. Thearling's definition are "automated" and "predictive." Data mining systems that are the most effective use automated procedures to extract information from the data using only the most general or even vague queries by the user. And data mining software automates the process of uncovering hidden predictive information that in the past required hands-on analysis.

The major applications of data mining have been made by companies with a strong consumer focus, such as retail businesses, financial organizations, and communication companies. Data mining has been successfully used to help retailers such as Amazon and Barnes & Noble determine one or more related products that customers who have already purchased a specific product are also likely to purchase. Then, when a customer logs on to the company's website and purchases a product, the website uses pop-ups to alert the customer about additional products that the customer is likely to purchase. In another application, data mining may be used to identify customers who are likely to spend more than $20 on a particular shopping trip. These customers may then be identified as the ones to receive special e-mail or regular mail discount offers to encourage them to make their next shopping trip before the discount termination date.

Data mining is a technology that relies heavily on statistical methodology such as multiple regression, logistic regression, and correlation. But it takes a creative integration of all these methods and computer science technologies involving artificial intelligence and machine learning to make data mining effective. A substantial investment in time and money is required to implement commercial data mining software packages developed by firms such as Oracle, Teradata, and SAS. The statistical concepts introduced in this text will be helpful in understanding the statistical methodology used by data mining software packages and enable you to better understand the statistical information that is developed.

Because statistical models play an important role in developing predictive models in data mining, many of the concerns that statisticians deal with in developing statistical models are also applicable. For instance, a concern in any statistical study involves the issue of model reliability. Finding a statistical model that works well for a particular sample of data does not necessarily mean that it can be reliably applied to other data. One of the common statistical approaches to evaluating model reliability is to divide the sample data set into two parts: a training data set and a test data set. If the model developed using the training data is able to accurately predict values in the test data, we say that the model is reliable. One advantage that data mining has over classical statistics is that the enormous amount of data available allows the data mining software to partition the data set so that a model developed for the training data set may be tested for reliability on other data. In this sense, the partitioning of the data set allows data mining to develop models and relationships and then quickly observe if they are repeatable and valid with new and different data. On the other hand, a warning for data mining applications is that with so much data available, there is a danger of overfitting the model to the point that misleading associations and cause/effect conclusions appear to exist. Careful interpretation of data mining results and additional testing will help avoid this pitfall.

1.8   Ethical Guidelines for Statistical Practice

Ethical behavior is something we should strive for in all that we do. Ethical issues arise in statistics because of the important role statistics plays in the collection, analysis, presentation, and interpretation of data. In a statistical study, unethical behavior can take a variety of forms including improper sampling, inappropriate analysis of the data, development of misleading graphs, use of inappropriate summary statistics, and/or a biased interpretation of the statistical results.

As you begin to do your own statistical work, we encourage you to be fair, thorough, objective, and neutral as you collect data, conduct analyses, make oral presentations, and present written reports containing information developed. As a consumer of statistics, you should also be aware of the possibility of unethical statistical behavior by others. When you see statistics in newspapers, on television, on the Internet, and so on, it is a good idea to view the information with some skepticism, always being aware of the source as well as the purpose and objectivity of the statistics provided.

The American Statistical Association, the nation's leading professional organization for statistics and statisticians, developed the report "Ethical Guidelines for Statistical Practice"[2] to help statistical practitioners make and communicate ethical decisions and assist students in learning how to perform statistical work responsibly. The report contains 67 guidelines organized into eight topic areas: Professionalism; Responsibilities to Funders, Clients, and Employers; Responsibilities in Publications and Testimony; Responsibilities to Research Subjects; Responsibilities to Research Team Colleagues; Responsibilities to Other Statisticians or Statistical Practitioners; Responsibilities Regarding Allegations of Misconduct; and Responsibilities of Employers Including Organizations, Individuals, Attorneys, or Other Clients Employing Statistical Practitioners.

---

[2]American Statistical Association, "Ethical Guidelines for Statistical Practice," 1999.

One of the ethical guidelines in the professionalism area addresses the issue of running multiple tests until a desired result is obtained. Let us consider an example. In Section 1.5 we discussed a statistical study conducted by Norris Electronics involving a sample of 200 high-intensity lightbulbs manufactured with a new filament. The average lifetime for the sample, 76 hours, provided an estimate of the average lifetime for all lightbulbs produced with the new filament. However, consider this. Because Norris selected a sample of bulbs, it is reasonable to assume that another sample would have provided a different average lifetime.

Suppose Norris's management had hoped the sample results would enable them to claim that the average lifetime for the new lightbulbs was 80 hours or more. Suppose further that Norris's management decides to continue the study by manufacturing and testing repeated samples of 200 lightbulbs with the new filament until a sample mean of 80 hours or more is obtained. If the study is repeated enough times, a sample may eventually be obtained—by chance alone—that would provide the desired result and enable Norris to make such a claim. In this case, consumers would be misled into thinking the new product is better than it actually is. Clearly, this type of behavior is unethical and represents a gross misuse of statistics in practice.

Several ethical guidelines in the responsibilities and publications and testimony area deal with issues involving the handling of data. For instance, a statistician must account for all data considered in a study and explain the sample(s) actually used. In the Norris Electronics study the average lifetime for the 200 bulbs in the original sample is 76 hours; this is considerably less than the 80 hours or more that management hoped to obtain. Suppose now that after reviewing the results showing a 76 hour average lifetime, Norris discards all the observations with 70 or fewer hours until burnout, allegedly because these bulbs contain imperfections caused by startup problems in the manufacturing process. After discarding these lightbulbs, the average lifetime for the remaining lightbulbs in the sample turns out to be 82 hours. Would you be suspicious of Norris's claim that the lifetime for their lightbulbs is 82 hours?

If the Norris lightbulbs showing 70 or fewer hours until burnout were discarded to simply provide an average lifetime of 82 hours, there is no question that discarding the lightbulbs with 70 or fewer hours until burnout is unethical. But, even if the discarded lightbulbs contain imperfections due to startup problems in the manufacturing process—and, as a result, should not have been included in the analysis—the statistician who conducted the study must account for all the data that were considered and explain how the sample actually used was obtained. To do otherwise is potentially misleading and would constitute unethical behavior on the part of both the company and the statistician.

A guideline in the shared values section of the American Statistical Association report states that statistical practitioners should avoid any tendency to slant statistical work toward predetermined outcomes. This type of unethical practice is often observed when unrepresentative samples are used to make claims. For instance, in many areas of the country smoking is not permitted in restaurants. Suppose, however, a lobbyist for the tobacco industry interviews people in restaurants where smoking is permitted in order to estimate the percentage of people who are in favor of allowing smoking in restaurants. The sample results show that 90% of the people interviewed are in favor of allowing smoking in restaurants. Based upon these sample results, the lobbyist claims that 90% of all people who eat in restaurants are in favor of permitting smoking in restaurants. In this case we would argue that only sampling persons eating in restaurants that allow smoking has biased the results. If only the final results of such a study are reported, readers unfamiliar with the details of the study (i.e., that the sample was collected only in restaurants allowing smoking) can be misled.

The scope of the American Statistical Association's report is broad and includes ethical guidelines that are appropriate not only for a statistician, but also for consumers of statistical information. We encourage you to read the report to obtain a better perspective of ethical issues as you continue your study of statistics and to gain the background for determining how to ensure that ethical standards are met when you start to use statistics in practice.

Summary

Statistics is the art and science of collecting, analyzing, presenting, and interpreting data. Nearly every college student majoring in business or economics is required to take a course in statistics. We began the chapter by describing typical statistical applications for business and economics.

Data consist of the facts and figures that are collected and analyzed. Four scales of measurement used to obtain data on a particular variable include nominal, ordinal, interval, and ratio. The scale of measurement for a variable is nominal when the data are labels or names used to identify an attribute of an element. The scale is ordinal if the data demonstrate the properties of nominal data and the order or rank of the data is meaningful. The scale is interval if the data demonstrate the properties of ordinal data and the interval between values is expressed in terms of a fixed unit of measure. Finally, the scale of measurement is ratio if the data show all the properties of interval data and the ratio of two values is meaningful.

For purposes of statistical analysis, data can be classified as categorical or quantitative. Categorical data use labels or names to identify an attribute of each element. Categorical data use either the nominal or ordinal scale of measurement and may be nonnumeric or numeric. Quantitative data are numeric values that indicate how much or how many. Quantitative data use either the interval or ratio scale of measurement. Ordinary arithmetic operations are meaningful only if the data are quantitative. Therefore, statistical computations used for quantitative data are not always appropriate for categorical data.

In Sections 1.4 and 1.5 we introduced the topics of descriptive statistics and statistical inference. Descriptive statistics are the tabular, graphical, and numerical methods used to summarize data. The process of statistical inference uses data obtained from a sample to make estimates or test hypotheses about the characteristics of a population. The last three sections of the chapter provide information on the role of computers in statistical analysis, an introduction to the relative new field of data mining, and a summary of ethical guidelines for statistical practice.

Glossary

Statistics The art and science of collecting, analyzing, presenting, and interpreting data.
Data The facts and figures collected, analyzed, and summarized for presentation and interpretation.
Data set All the data collected in a particular study.
Elements The entities on which data are collected.
Variable A characteristic of interest for the elements.
Observation The set of measurements obtained for a particular element.
Nominal scale The scale of measurement for a variable when the data are labels or names used to identify an attribute of an element. Nominal data may be nonnumeric or numeric.
Ordinal scale The scale of measurement for a variable if the data exhibit the properties of nominal data and the order or rank of the data is meaningful. Ordinal data may be nonnumeric or numeric.
Interval scale The scale of measurement for a variable if the data demonstrate the properties of ordinal data and the interval between values is expressed in terms of a fixed unit of measure. Interval data are always numeric.
Ratio scale The scale of measurement for a variable if the data demonstrate all the properties of interval data and the ratio of two values is meaningful. Ratio data are always numeric.

Categorical data Labels or names used to identify an attribute of each element. Categorical data use either the nominal or ordinal scale of measurement and may be nonnumeric or numeric.
Quantitative data Numeric values that indicate how much or how many of something. Quantitative data are obtained using either the interval or ratio scale of measurement.
Categorical variable A variable with categorical data.
Quantitative variable A variable with quantitative data.
Cross-sectional data Data collected at the same or approximately the same point in time.
Time series data Data collected over several time periods.
Descriptive statistics Tabular, graphical, and numerical summaries of data.
Population The set of all elements of interest in a particular study.
Sample A subset of the population.
Census A survey to collect data on the entire population.
Sample survey A survey to collect data on a sample.
Statistical inference The process of using data obtained from a sample to make estimates or test hypotheses about the characteristics of a population.
Data mining The process of using procedures from statistics and computer science to extract useful information from extremely large databases.

Supplementary Exercises

1. Discuss the differences between statistics as numerical facts and statistics as a discipline or field of study.

2. The U.S. Department of Energy provides fuel economy information for a variety of motor vehicles. A sample of 10 automobiles is shown in Table 1.6 (Fuel Economy website, February 22, 2008). Data show the size of the automobile (compact, midsize, or large), the number of cylinders in the engine, the city driving miles per gallon, the highway driving miles per gallon, and the recommended fuel (diesel, premium, or regular).
   a. How many elements are in this data set?
   b. How many variables are in this data set?
   c. Which variables are categorical and which variables are quantitative?
   d. What type of measurement scale is used for each of the variables?

3. Refer to Table 1.6.
   a. What is the average miles per gallon for city driving?
   b. On average, how much higher is the miles per gallon for highway driving as compared to city driving?

TABLE 1.6   FUEL ECONOMY INFORMATION FOR 10 AUTOMOBILES

Car	Size	Cylinders	City MPG	Highway MPG	Fuel
Audi A8	Large	12	13	19	Premium
BMW 328Xi	Compact	6	17	25	Premium
Cadillac CTS	Midsize	6	16	25	Regular
Chrysler 300	Large	8	13	18	Premium
Ford Focus	Compact	4	24	33	Regular
Hyundai Elantra	Midsize	4	25	33	Regular
Jeep Grand Cherokee	Midsize	6	17	26	Diesel
Pontiac G6	Compact	6	15	22	Regular
Toyota Camry	Midsize	4	21	31	Regular
Volkswagen Jetta	Compact	5	21	29	Regular

TABLE 1.7   DATA FOR EIGHT CORDLESS TELEPHONES

Brand	Model	Price ($)	Overall Score	Voice Quality	Handset on Base	Talk Time (Hours)
AT&T	CL84100	60	73	Excellent	Yes	7
AT&T	TL92271	80	70	Very Good	No	7
Panasonic	4773B	100	78	Very Good	Yes	13
Panasonic	6592T	70	72	Very Good	No	13
Uniden	D2997	45	70	Very Good	No	10
Uniden	D1788	80	73	Very Good	Yes	7
Vtech	DS6521	60	72	Excellent	No	7
Vtech	CS6649	50	72	Very Good	Yes	7

© Cengage Learning

[Handwritten annotations below columns: ord, I, I, N, N, R]

c.   What percentage of the cars have four-cylinder engines?

d.   What percentage of the cars use regular fuel?

4.   Table 1.7 shows data for eight cordless telephones (*Consumer Reports,* November 2012). The Overall Score, a measure of the overall quality for the cordless telephone, ranges from 0 to 100. Voice Quality has possible ratings of poor, fair, good, very good, and excellent. Talk Time is the manufacturer's claim of how long the handset can be used when it is fully charged.

   a.   How many elements are in this data set?

   b.   For the variables Price, Overall Score, Voice Quality, Handset on Base, and Talk Time, which variables are categorical and which variables are quantitative?

   c.   What scale of measurement is used for each variable?

5.   Refer to the data set in Table 1.7.

   a.   What is the average price for the cordless telephones?

   b.   What is the average talk time for the cordless telephones?

   c.   What percentage of the cordless telephones has a voice quality of excellent?

   d.   What percentage of the cordless telephones has a handset on the base?

6.   J.D. Power and Associates surveys new automobile owners to learn about the quality of recently purchased vehicles. The following questions were asked in the *J.D. Power Initial Quality Survey,* May 2012.

   a.   Did you purchase or lease the vehicle?

   b.   What price did you pay?

   c.   What is the overall attractiveness of your vehicle's exterior? (Unacceptable, Average, Outstanding, or Truly Exceptional)

   d.   What is your average miles-per-gallon?

   e.   What is your overall rating of your new vehicle? (1- to 10-point scale with 1 unacceptable and 10 truly exceptional)

   Comment on whether each question provides categorical or quantitative data.

7.   The Kroger Company is one of the largest grocery retailers in the United States, with over 2000 grocery stores across the country. Kroger uses an online customer opinion questionnaire to obtain performance data about its products and services and learn about what motivates its customers (Kroger website, April 2012). In the survey, Kroger customers were asked if they would be willing to pay more for products that had each of the following four characteristics. The four questions were: Would you pay more for

   products that have a brand name?

   products that are environmentally friendly?

   products that are organic?

   products that have been recommended by others?

   For each question, the customers had the option of responding Yes if they would pay more or No if they would not pay more.

      a.   Are the data collected by Kroger in this example categorical or quantitative?

      b.   What measurement scale is used?

8. The *FinancialTimes*/Harris Poll is a monthly online poll of adults from six countries in Europe and the United States. A January poll included 1015 adults in the United States. One of the questions asked was, "How would you rate the Federal Bank in handling the credit problems in the financial markets?" Possible responses were Excellent, Good, Fair, Bad, and Terrible (Harris Interactive website, January 2008).

      a.   What was the sample size for this survey?

      b.   Are the data categorical or quantitative?

      c.   Would it make more sense to use averages or percentages as a summary of the data for this question?

      d.   Of the respondents in the United States, 10% said the Federal Bank is doing a good job. How many individuals provided this response?

9. The Commerce Department reported receiving the following applications for the Malcolm Baldrige National Quality Award: 23 from large manufacturing firms, 18 from large service firms, and 30 from small businesses.

      a.   Is type of business a categorical or quantitative variable?

      b.   What percentage of the applications came from small businesses?

10. The Bureau of Transportation Statistics Omnibus Household Survey is conducted annually and serves as an information source for the U.S. Department of Transportation. In one part of the survey the person being interviewed was asked to respond to the following statement: "Drivers of motor vehicles should be allowed to talk on a hand-held cell phone while driving." Possible responses were strongly agree, somewhat agree, somewhat disagree, and strongly disagree. Forty-four respondents said that they strongly agree with this statement, 130 said that they somewhat agree, 165 said they somewhat disagree, and 741 said they strongly disagree with this statement (Bureau of Transportation website, August 2010).

      a.   Do the responses for this statement provide categorical or quantitative data?

      b.   Would it make more sense to use averages or percentages as a summary of the responses for this statement?

      c.   What percentage of respondents strongly agree with allowing drivers of motor vehicles to talk on a hand-held cell phone while driving?

      d.   Do the results indicate general support for or against allowing drivers of motor vehicles to talk on a hand-held cell phone while driving?

11. J.D. Power and Associates conducts vehicle quality surveys to provide automobile manufacturers with consumer satisfaction information about their products (Vehicle Quality Survey, January 2010). Using a sample of vehicle owners from recent vehicle purchase records, the survey asks the owners a variety of questions about their new vehicles, such as those shown below. For each question, state whether the data collected are categorical or quantitative and indicate the measurement scale being used.

      a.   What price did you pay for the vehicle?

      b.   How did you pay for the vehicle? (Cash, Lease, or Finance)

      c.   How likely would you be to recommend this vehicle to a friend? (Definitely Not, Probably Not, Probably Will, and Definitely Will)

      d.   What is the current mileage?

      e.   What is your overall rating of your new vehicle? A 10-point scale, ranging from 1 for unacceptable to 10 for truly exceptional, was used.

12. The Hawaii Visitors Bureau collects data on visitors to Hawaii. The following questions were among 16 asked in a questionnaire handed out to passengers during incoming airline flights.

      •   This trip to Hawaii is my: 1st, 2nd, 3rd, 4th, etc.

      •   The primary reason for this trip is: (10 categories, including vacation, convention, honeymoon)

- Where I plan to stay: (11 categories, including hotel, apartment, relatives, camping)
- Total days in Hawaii

a. What is the population being studied?

b. Is the use of a questionnaire a good way to reach the population of passengers on incoming airline flights?

c. Comment on each of the four questions in terms of whether it will provide categorical or quantitative data.

13. Figure 1.8 provides a bar chart showing the amount of federal spending for the years 2004 to 2010 (Congressional Budget Office website, May 15, 2011).

a. What is the variable of interest?

b. Are the data categorical or quantitative?

c. Are the data time series or cross-sectional?

d. Comment on the trend in federal spending over time.

14. The following data show the number of rental cars in service for three rental car companies: Hertz, Avis, and Dollar. The data are for the years 2007–2010 and are in thousands of vehicles (Auto Rental News website, May 15, 2011).

		Cars in Service (1000s)		
Company	2007	2008	2009	2010
Hertz	327	311	286	290
Dollar	167	140	106	108
Avis	204	220	300	270

a. Construct a time series graph for the years 2007 to 2010 showing the number of rental cars in service for each company. Show the time series for all three companies on the same graph.

b. Comment on who appears to be the market share leader and how the market shares are changing over time.

c. Construct a bar chart showing rental cars in service for 2010. Is this chart based on cross-sectional or time series data?

FIGURE 1.8 FEDERAL SPENDING

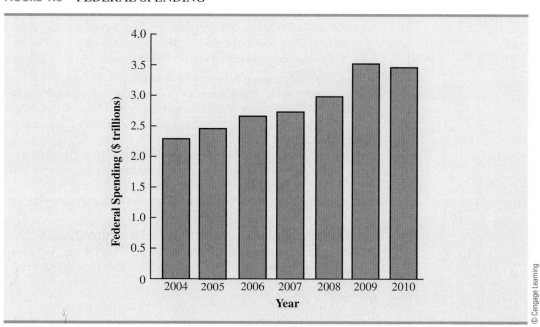

FIGURE 1.9   NUMBER OF RECREATIONAL BOATING ACCIDENTS

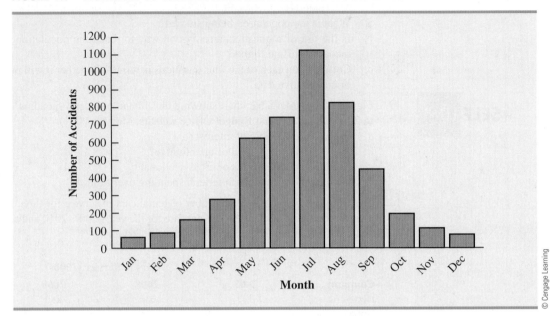

15. Every year, the U.S. Coast Guard collects data and compiles statistics on reported recreational boating accidents. These statistics are derived from accident reports that are filed by the owners/operators of recreational vessels involved in accidents. In 2009, 4730 recreational boating accident reports were filed. Figure 1.9 provides a bar chart summarizing the number of accident reports that were filed each month (U.S. Coast Guard's Boating Safety Division website, August 2010).
    a. Are the data categorical or quantitative?
    b. Are the data time series or cross-sectional?
    c. In what month were the most accident reports filed? Approximately how many?
    d. There were 61 accident reports filed in January and 76 accident reports filed in December. What percentage of the total number of accident reports for the year was filed in these two months? Does this seem reasonable?
    e. Comment on the overall shape of the bar graph.

16. The Energy Information Administration of the U.S. Department of Energy provided time series data for the U.S. average price per gallon of conventional regular gasoline between January 2007 and March 2012 (Energy Information Administration website, April 2012). Use the Internet to obtain the average price per gallon of conventional regular gasoline since March 2012.
    a. Extend the graph of the time series shown in Figure 1.1.
    b. What interpretations can you make about the average price per gallon of conventional regular gasoline since March 2012?
    c. Does the time series continue to show a summer increase in the average price per gallon? Explain.

17. A manager of a large corporation recommends a $10,000 raise be given to keep a valued subordinate from moving to another company. What internal and external sources of data might be used to decide whether such a salary increase is appropriate?

18. A random telephone survey of 1021 adults (aged 18 and older) was conducted by Opinion Research Corporation on behalf of CompleteTax, an online tax preparation and e-filing service. The survey results showed that 684 of those surveyed planned to file their taxes electronically (CompleteTax Tax Prep Survey 2010).

    a. Develop a descriptive statistic that can be used to estimate the percentage of all taxpayers who file electronically.

    b. The survey reported that the most frequently used method for preparing the tax return is to hire an accountant or professional tax preparer. If 60% of the people surveyed had their tax return prepared this way, how many people used an accountant or professional tax preparer?

    c. Other methods that the person filing the return often used include manual preparation, use of an online tax service, and use of a software tax program. Would the data for the method for preparing the tax return be considered categorical or quantitative?

19. A *Bloomberg Businessweek* North American subscriber study collected data from a sample of 2861 subscribers. Fifty-nine percent of the respondents indicated an annual income of $75,000 or more, and 50% reported having an American Express credit card.

    a. What is the population of interest in this study?

    b. Is annual income a categorical or quantitative variable?

    c. Is ownership of an American Express card a categorical or quantitative variable?

    d. Does this study involve cross-sectional or time series data?

    e. Describe any statistical inferences *Bloomberg Businessweek* might make on the basis of the survey.

20. A survey of 131 investment managers in *Barron's* Big Money poll revealed the following:

    - 43% of managers classified themselves as bullish or very bullish on the stock market.
    - The average expected return over the next 12 months for equities was 11.2%.
    - 21% selected health care as the sector most likely to lead the market in the next 12 months.
    - When asked to estimate how long it would take for technology and telecom stocks to resume sustainable growth, the managers' average response was 2.5 years.

    a. Cite two descriptive statistics.

    b. Make an inference about the population of all investment managers concerning the average return expected on equities over the next 12 months.

    c. Make an inference about the length of time it will take for technology and telecom stocks to resume sustainable growth.

21. A seven-year medical research study reported that women whose mothers took the drug DES during pregnancy were twice as likely to develop tissue abnormalities that might lead to cancer as were women whose mothers did not take the drug.

    a. This study compared two populations. What were the populations?

    b. Do you suppose the data were obtained in a survey or an experiment?

    c. For the population of women whose mothers took the drug DES during pregnancy, a sample of 3980 women showed that 63 developed tissue abnormalities that might lead to cancer. Provide a descriptive statistic that could be used to estimate the number of women out of 1000 in this population who have tissue abnormalities.

    d. For the population of women whose mothers did not take the drug DES during pregnancy, what is the estimate of the number of women out of 1000 who would be expected to have tissue abnormalities?

    e. Medical studies often use a relatively large sample (in this case, 3980). Why?

22. The Nielsen Company surveyed consumers in 47 markets from Europe, Asia-Pacific, the Americas, and the Middle East to determine which factors are most important in determining where they buy groceries. Using a scale of 1 (low) to 5 (high), the highest rated factor was *good value for money,* with an average point score of 4.32. The second highest rated factor was *better selection of high-quality brands and products,* with an average point score of 3.78, and the lowest rated factor was *uses recyclable bags and packaging,* with an average point score of 2.71 (Nielsen website, February 24, 2008). Suppose that you have been hired by a grocery store chain to conduct a similar study to determine what factors customers at the chain's stores in Charlotte, North Carolina, think are most important in determining where they buy groceries.
   a. What is the population for the survey that you will be conducting?
   b. How would you collect the data for this study?

23. Pew Research Center is a nonpartisan polling organization that provides information about issues, attitudes, and trends shaping America. In a recent poll, Pew researchers found that 47% of American adult respondents reported getting at least some local news on their cell phone or tablet computer (Pew Research website, May 14, 2011). Further findings showed that 42% of respondents who own cell phones or tablet computers use those devices to check local weather reports and 37% use the devices to find local restaurants or other businesses.
   a. One statistic concerned using cell phones or tablet computers for local news. What population is that finding applicable to?
   b. Another statistic concerned using cell phones or tablet computers to check local weather reports and to find local restaurants. What population is this finding applicable to?
   c. Do you think the Pew researchers conducted a census or a sample survey to obtain their results? Why?
   d. If you were a restaurant owner, would you find these results interesting? Why? How could you take advantage of this information?

24. A sample of midterm grades for five students showed the following results: 72, 65, 82, 90, 76. Which of the following statements are correct, and which should be challenged as being too generalized?
   a. The average midterm grade for the sample of five students is 77.
   b. The average midterm grade for all students who took the exam is 77.
   c. An estimate of the average midterm grade for all students who took the exam is 77.
   d. More than half of the students who take this exam will score between 70 and 85.
   e. If five other students are included in the sample, their grades will be between 65 and 90.

25. Table 1.8 shows a data set containing information for 25 of the shadow stocks tracked by the American Association of Individual Investors. Shadow stocks are common stocks of smaller companies that are not closely followed by Wall Street analysts. The data set is also on the website that accompanies the text in the file named Shadow02.
   a. How many variables are in the data set?
   b. Which of the variables are categorical and which are quantitative?
   c. For the Exchange variable, show the frequency and the percent frequency for AMEX, NYSE, and OTC. Construct a bar graph similar to Figure 1.5 for the Exchange variable.
   d. Show the frequency distribution for the Gross Profit Margin using the five intervals: 0–14.9, 15–29.9, 30–44.9, 45–59.9, and 60–74.9. Construct a histogram similar to Figure 1.6.
   e. What is the average price/earnings ratio?

TABLE 1.8   DATA SET FOR 25 SHADOW STOCKS

Company	Exchange	Ticker Symbol	Market Cap ($ millions)	Price/ Earnings Ratio	Gross Profit Margin (%)
DeWolfe Companies	AMEX	DWL	36.4	8.4	36.7
North Coast Energy	OTC	NCEB	52.5	6.2	59.3
Hansen Natural Corp.	OTC	HANS	41.1	14.6	44.8
MarineMax, Inc.	NYSE	HZO	111.5	7.2	23.8
Nanometrics Incorporated	OTC	NANO	228.6	38.0	53.3
TeamStaff, Inc.	OTC	TSTF	92.1	33.5	4.1
Environmental Tectonics	AMEX	ETC	51.1	35.8	35.9
Measurement Specialties	AMEX	MSS	101.8	26.8	37.6
SEMCO Energy, Inc.	NYSE	SEN	193.4	18.7	23.6
Party City Corporation	OTC	PCTY	97.2	15.9	36.4
Embrex, Inc.	OTC	EMBX	136.5	18.9	59.5
Tech/Ops Sevcon, Inc.	AMEX	TO	23.2	20.7	35.7
ARCADIS NV	OTC	ARCAF	173.4	8.8	9.6
Qiao Xing Universal Tele.	OTC	XING	64.3	22.1	30.8
Energy West Incorporated	OTC	EWST	29.1	9.7	16.3
Barnwell Industries, Inc.	AMEX	BRN	27.3	7.4	73.4
Innodata Corporation	OTC	INOD	66.1	11.0	29.6
Medical Action Industries	OTC	MDCI	137.1	26.9	30.6
Instrumentarium Corp.	OTC	INMRY	240.9	3.6	52.1
Petroleum Development	OTC	PETD	95.9	6.1	19.4
Drexler Technology Corp.	OTC	DRXR	233.6	45.6	53.6
Gerber Childrenswear Inc.	NYSE	GCW	126.9	7.9	25.8
Gaiam, Inc.	OTC	GAIA	295.5	68.2	60.7
Artesian Resources Corp.	OTC	ARTNA	62.8	20.5	45.5
York Water Company	OTC	YORW	92.2	22.9	74.2

WEB file

Shadow02

© Cengage Learning

Appendix   An Introduction to StatTools

StatTools is a professional add-in that expands the statistical capabilities available with Microsoft Excel. StatTools software can be downloaded from the website that accompanies this text.

Excel does not contain statistical functions or data analysis tools to perform all the statistical procedures discussed in the text. StatTools is a Microsoft Excel statistics add-in that extends the range of statistical and graphical options for Excel users. Most chapters include a chapter appendix that shows the steps required to accomplish a statistical procedure using StatTools. For those students who want to make more extensive use of the software, StatTools offers an excellent Help facility. The StatTools Help system includes detailed explanations of the statistical and data analysis options available, as well as descriptions and definitions of the types of output provided.

Getting Started with StatTools

StatTools software may be downloaded and installed on your computer by accessing the website that accompanies this text. After downloading and installing the software, perform the following steps to use StatTools as an Excel add-in.

Step 1. Click the **Start** button on the taskbar and then point to **All Programs**
Step 2. Point to the folder entitled **Palisade Decision Tools**
Step 3. Click **StatTools for Excel**

FIGURE 1.10   THE STATTOOLS - DATA SET MANAGER DIALOG BOX

These steps will open Excel and add the StatTools tab next to the Add-Ins tab on the Excel Ribbon. Alternately, if you are already working in Excel, these steps will make StatTools available.

Using StatTools

Nations

Before conducting any statistical analysis, we must create a StatTools data set using the StatTools Data Set Manager. Let us use the Excel worksheet for the 60 nations in the World Trade Organization data set in Table 1.1 to show how this is done. The following steps show how to create a StatTools data set for this application.

Step 1. Open the Excel file named Nations
Step 2. Select any cell in the data set (for example, cell A1)
Step 3. Click the **StatTools** tab on the Ribbon
Step 4. In the **Data** group, click **Data Set Manager**
Step 5. When StatTools asks if you want to add the range $A$1:$F$61 as a new StatTools data set, click **Yes**
Step 6. When the StatTools - Data Set Manager dialog box appears, click **OK**

Figure 1.10 shows the StatTools - Data Set Manager dialog box that appears in step 6. By default, the name of the new StatTools data set is Data Set #1. You can replace the name

FIGURE 1.11   THE STATTOOLS - APPLICATION SETTINGS DIALOG BOX

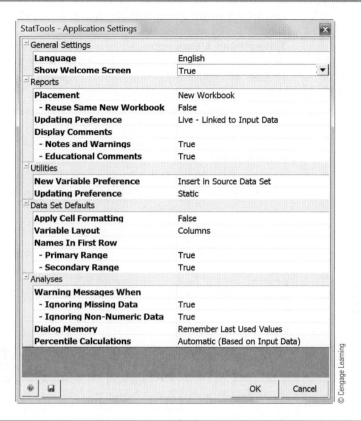

Data Set #1 in step 6 with a more descriptive name. And, if you select the Apply Cell Format option, the column labels will be highlighted in blue and the entire data set will have outside and inside borders. You can select the Data Set Manager at any time in your analysis to make these types of changes.

Recommended Application Settings

StatTools allows the user to specify some of the application settings that control such things as where statistical output is displayed and how calculations are performed. The following steps show how to access the StatTools - Application Settings dialog box.

Step 1. Click the **StatTools** tab on the Ribbon
Step 2. In the **Tools Group**, click **Utilities**
Step 3. Choose **Application Settings** from the list of options

Figure 1.11 shows that the StatTools - Application Settings dialog box has five sections: General Settings; Reports; Utilities; Data Set Defaults; and Analyses. Let us show how to make changes in the Reports section of the dialog box.

Figure 1.11 shows that the Placement option currently selected is **New Workbook**. Using this option, the StatTools output will be placed in a new workbook. But suppose you would like to place the StatTools output in the current (active) workbook. If you click the words **New Workbook**, a downward-pointing arrow will appear to the right. Clicking this arrow will display a list of all the placement options, including **Active Workbook**; we recommend using this option. Figure 1.11 also shows that the Updating

Preferences option in the Reports section is currently **Live - Linked to Input Data**. With live updating, anytime one or more data values are changed StatTools will automatically change the output previously produced; we also recommend using this option. Note that there are two options available under Display Comments: **Notes and Warnings** and **Educational Comments**. Because these options provide useful notes and information regarding the output, we recommend using both options. Thus, to include educational comments as part of the StatTools output you will have to change the value of False for Educational Comments to True.

The StatTools - Settings dialog box contains numerous other features that enable you to customize the way that you want StatTools to operate. You can learn more about these features by selecting the Help option located in the Tools group, or by clicking the Help icon located in the lower left-hand corner of the dialog box. When you have finished making changes in the application settings, click OK at the bottom of the dialog box and then click Yes when StatTools asks you if you want to save the new application settings.

CHAPTER 2

Descriptive Statistics: Tabular and Graphical Displays

CONTENTS

STATISTICS *in* PRACTICE

COLGATE-PALMOLIVE COMPANY*
NEW YORK, NEW YORK

The Colgate-Palmolive Company started as a small soap and candle shop in New York City in 1806. Today, Colgate-Palmolive employs more than 40,000 people working in more than 200 countries and territories around the world. Although best known for its brand names of Colgate, Palmolive, and Fab, the company also markets Mennen, Hill's Science Diet, and Hill's Prescription Diet products.

The Colgate-Palmolive Company uses statistics in its quality assurance program for home laundry detergent products. One concern is customer satisfaction with the quantity of detergent in a carton. Every carton in each size category is filled with the same amount of detergent by weight, but the volume of detergent is affected by the density of the detergent powder. For instance, if the powder density is on the heavy side, a smaller volume of detergent is needed to reach the carton's specified weight. As a result, the carton may appear to be underfilled when opened by the consumer.

To control the problem of heavy detergent powder, limits are placed on the acceptable range of powder density. Statistical samples are taken periodically, and the density of each powder sample is measured. Data summaries are then provided for operating personnel so that corrective action can be taken if necessary to keep the density within the desired quality specifications.

A frequency distribution for the densities of 150 samples taken over a one-week period and a histogram are shown in the accompanying table and figure. Density levels above .40 are unacceptably high. The frequency distribution and histogram show that the operation is meeting its quality guidelines with all of the densities less than or equal to .40. Managers viewing these statistical summaries would be pleased with the quality of the detergent production process.

In this chapter, you will learn about tabular and graphical methods of descriptive statistics such as frequency distributions, bar charts, histograms, stem-and-leaf displays, crosstabulations, and others. The goal of

The Colgate-Palmolive Company uses statistical summaries to help maintain the quality of its products. © Kurt Brady/Alamy.

these methods is to summarize data so that the data can be easily understood and interpreted.

Frequency Distribution of Density Data

Density	Frequency
.29–.30	30
.31–.32	75
.33–.34	32
.35–.36	9
.37–.38	3
.39–.40	1
Total	150

Histogram of Density Data

*The authors are indebted to William R. Fowle, Manager of Quality Assurance, Colgate-Palmolive Company, for providing this Statistics in Practice.

As indicated in Chapter 1, data can be classified as either categorical or quantitative. **Categorical data** use labels or names to identify categories of like items, and **quantitative data** are numerical values that indicate how much or how many. This chapter introduces the use of tabular and graphical displays for summarizing both categorical and quantitative data. Tabular and graphical displays can be found in annual reports, newspaper articles, and research studies. Everyone is exposed to these types of presentations. Hence, it is important to understand how they are constructed and how they should be interpreted.

We begin with a discussion of the use of tablular and graphical displays to summarize the data for a single variable. This is followed by a discussion of the use of tabular and graphical displays to summarize the data for two variables in a way that reveals the relationship between the two variables. **Data visualization** is a term often used to describe the use of graphical displays to summarize and present information about a data set. The last section of this chapter provides an introduction to data visualization and provides guidelines for creating effective graphical displays.

Modern statistical software packages provide extensive capabilities for summarizing data and preparing visual presentations. Minitab and Excel are two packages that are widely available. In the chapter appendixes, we show some of their capabilities.

2.1 Summarizing Data for a Categorical Variable

Frequency Distribution

We begin the discussion of how tabular and graphical displays can be used to summarize categorical data with the definition of a **frequency distribution**.

> **FREQUENCY DISTRIBUTION**
>
> A frequency distribution is a tabular summary of data showing the number (frequency) of observations in each of several nonoverlapping categories or classes.

Let us use the following example to demonstrate the construction and interpretation of a frequency distribution for categorical data. Coca-Cola, Diet Coke, Dr. Pepper, Pepsi, and Sprite are five popular soft drinks. Assume that the data in Table 2.1 show the soft drink selected in a sample of 50 soft drink purchases.

TABLE 2.1 DATA FROM A SAMPLE OF 50 SOFT DRINK PURCHASES

Coca-Cola	Coca-Cola	Coca-Cola	Sprite	Coca-Cola
Diet Coke	Dr. Pepper	Diet Coke	Dr. Pepper	Diet Coke
Pepsi	Sprite	Coca-Cola	Pepsi	Pepsi
Diet Coke	Coca-Cola	Sprite	Diet Coke	Pepsi
Coca-Cola	Diet Coke	Pepsi	Pepsi	Pepsi
Coca-Cola	Coca-Cola	Coca-Cola	Coca-Cola	Pepsi
Dr. Pepper	Coca-Cola	Coca-Cola	Coca-Cola	Coca-Cola
Diet Coke	Sprite	Coca-Cola	Coca-Cola	Dr. Pepper
Pepsi	Coca-Cola	Pepsi	Pepsi	Pepsi
Pepsi	Diet Coke	Coca-Cola	Dr. Pepper	Sprite

TABLE 2.2

FREQUENCY
DISTRIBUTION OF
SOFT DRINK
PURCHASES

Soft Drink	Frequency
Coca-Cola	19
Diet Coke	8
Dr. Pepper	5
Pepsi	13
Sprite	5
Total	50

To develop a frequency distribution for these data, we count the number of times each soft drink appears in Table 2.1. Coca-Cola appears 19 times, Diet Coke appears 8 times, Dr. Pepper appears 5 times, Pepsi appears 13 times, and Sprite appears 5 times. These counts are summarized in the frequency distribution in Table 2.2.

This frequency distribution provides a summary of how the 50 soft drink purchases are distributed across the five soft drinks. This summary offers more insight than the original data shown in Table 2.1. Viewing the frequency distribution, we see that Coca-Cola is the leader, Pepsi is second, Diet Coke is third, and Sprite and Dr. Pepper are tied for fourth. The frequency distribution summarizes information about the popularity of the five soft drinks.

Relative Frequency and Percent Frequency Distributions

A frequency distribution shows the number (frequency) of observations in each of several nonoverlapping classes. However, we are often interested in the proportion, or percentage, of observations in each class. The *relative frequency* of a class equals the fraction or proportion of observations belonging to a class. For a data set with n observations, the relative frequency of each class can be determined as follows:

RELATIVE FREQUENCY

$$\text{Relative frequency of a class} = \frac{\text{Frequency of the class}}{n} \qquad (2.1)$$

The *percent frequency* of a class is the relative frequency multiplied by 100.

A **relative frequency distribution** gives a tabular summary of data showing the relative frequency for each class. A **percent frequency distribution** summarizes the percent frequency of the data for each class. Table 2.3 shows a relative frequency distribution and a percent frequency distribution for the soft drink data. In Table 2.3 we see that the relative frequency for Coca-Cola is 19/50 = .38, the relative frequency for Diet Coke is 8/50 = .16, and so on. From the percent frequency distribution, we see that 38% of the purchases were Coca-Cola, 16% of the purchases were Diet Coke, and so on. We can also note that 38% + 26% + 16% = 80% of the purchases were for the top three soft drinks.

Bar Charts and Pie Charts

A **bar chart** is a graphical display for depicting categorical data summarized in a frequency, relative frequency, or percent frequency distribution. On one axis of the chart (usually the horizontal axis), we specify the labels that are used for the classes (categories). A frequency, relative frequency, or percent frequency scale can be used for the other axis of the chart

TABLE 2.3   RELATIVE FREQUENCY AND PERCENT FREQUENCY DISTRIBUTIONS OF SOFT DRINK PURCHASES

Soft Drink	Relative Frequency	Percent Frequency
Coca-Cola	.38	38
Diet Coke	.16	16
Dr. Pepper	.10	10
Pepsi	.26	26
Sprite	.10	10
Total	1.00	100

FIGURE 2.1   BAR CHART OF SOFT DRINK PURCHASES

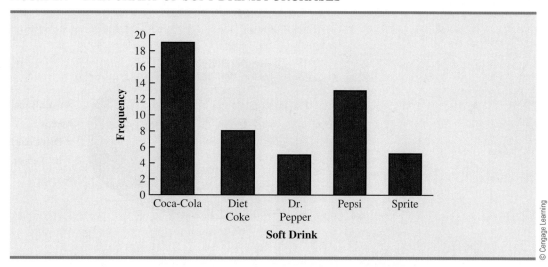

In quality control applications, bar charts are used to identify the most important causes of problems. When the bars are arranged in descending order of height from left to right with the most frequently occurring cause appearing first, the bar chart is called a Pareto diagram. *This diagram is named for its founder, Vilfredo Pareto, an Italian economist.*

(usually the vertical axis). Then, using a bar of fixed width drawn above each class label, we extend the length of the bar until we reach the frequency, relative frequency, or percent frequency of the class. For categorical data, the bars should be separated to emphasize the fact that each category is separate. Figure 2.1 shows a bar chart of the frequency distribution for the 50 soft drink purchases. Note how the graphical display shows Coca-Cola, Pepsi, and Diet Coke to be the most preferred brands.

The **pie chart** provides another graphical display for presenting relative frequency and percent frequency distributions for categorical data. To construct a pie chart, we first draw a circle to represent all the data. Then we use the relative frequencies to subdivide the circle into sectors, or parts, that correspond to the relative frequency for each class. For example, because a circle contains 360 degrees and Coca-Cola shows a relative frequency of .38, the sector of the pie chart labeled Coca-Cola consists of .38(360) = 136.8 degrees. The sector of the pie chart labeled Diet Coke consists of .16(360) = 57.6 degrees. Similar calculations for the other classes yield the pie chart in Figure 2.2.

FIGURE 2.2   PIE CHART OF SOFT DRINK PURCHASES

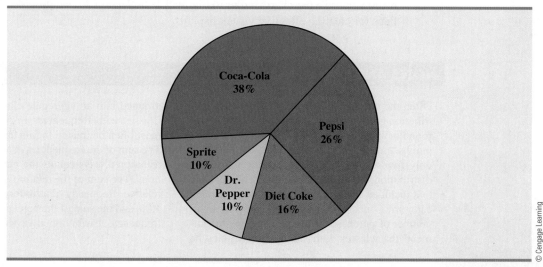

FIGURE 2.3   THREE-DIMENSIONAL PIE CHART OF SOFT DRINK PURCHASES

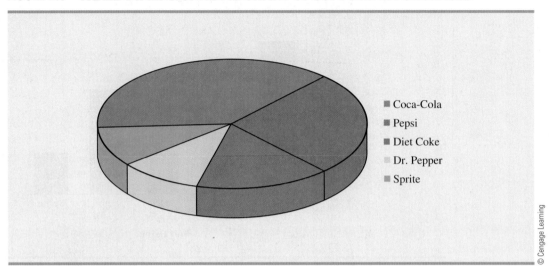

The numerical values shown for each sector can be frequencies, relative frequencies, or percent frequencies.

Numerous options involving the use of colors, shading, legends, text font, and three-dimensional perspectives are available to enhance the visual appearance of bar and pie charts. When used carefully, such options can provide a more effective display. But this is not always the case. For instance, consider the three-dimensional pie chart for the soft drink data shown in Figure 2.3. Compare it to the simpler presentation shown in Figure 2.2. The three-dimensional perspective adds no new understanding. In fact, because you have to view the three-dimensional pie chart in Figure 2.3 at an angle rather than straight overhead, it can be more difficult to visualize. The use of a legend in Figure 2.3 also forces your eyes to shift back and forth between the key and the chart. The simpler chart shown in Figure 2.2, which shows the percentages and classes directly on the pie, is more effective.

In general, pie charts are not the best way to present percentages for comparison. Research has shown that people are much better at accurately judging differences in length rather than differences in angles (or slices). When making such comparisons, we recommend you use a bar chart similar to Figure 2.1. In Section 2.5 we provide additional guidelines for creating effective visual displays.

NOTES AND COMMENTS

1. Often the number of classes in a frequency distribution is the same as the number of categories found in the data, as is the case for the soft drink purchase data in this section. The data involve only five soft drinks, and a separate frequency distribution class was defined for each one. Data that included all soft drinks would require many categories, most of which would have a small number of purchases. Most statisticians recommend that classes with smaller frequencies be grouped into an aggregate class called "other." Classes with frequencies of 5% or less would most often be treated in this fashion.

2. The sum of the frequencies in any frequency distribution always equals the number of observations. The sum of the relative frequencies in any relative frequency distribution always equals 1.00, and the sum of the percentages in a percent frequency distribution always equals 100.

Exercises

Methods

1. The response to a question has three alternatives: A, B, and C. A sample of 120 responses provides 60 A, 24 B, and 36 C. Show the frequency and relative frequency distributions.

2. A partial relative frequency distribution is given.

Class	Relative Frequency
A	.22
B	.18
C	.40
D	

    a. What is the relative frequency of class D?
    b. The total sample size is 200. What is the frequency of class D?
    c. Show the frequency distribution.
    d. Show the percent frequency distribution.

3. A questionnaire provides 58 Yes, 42 No, and 20 no-opinion answers.
    a. In the construction of a pie chart, how many degrees would be in the section of the pie showing the Yes answers?
    b. How many degrees would be in the section of the pie showing the No answers?
    c. Construct a pie chart.
    d. Construct a bar chart.

Applications

WEB file

Syndicated

4. For the 2010–2011 viewing season, the top five syndicated programs were *Wheel of Fortune* (WoF), *Two and Half Men* (THM), *Jeopardy* (Jep), *Judge Judy* (JJ), and the *Oprah Winfrey Show* (OWS) (Nielsen Media Research website, April 16, 2012). Data indicating the preferred shows for a sample of 50 viewers follow.

WoF	Jep	JJ	Jep	THM
THM	WoF	OWS	Jep	THM
Jep	OWS	WoF	WoF	WoF
WoF	THM	OWS	THM	WoF
THM	JJ	JJ	Jep	THM
OWS	OWS	JJ	JJ	Jep
JJ	WoF	THM	WoF	WoF
THM	THM	WoF	JJ	JJ
Jep	THM	WoF	Jep	Jep
WoF	THM	OWS	OWS	Jep

    a. Are these data categorical or quantitative?
    b. Provide frequency and percent frequency distributions.
    c. Construct a bar chart and a pie chart.
    d. On the basis of the sample, which television show has the largest viewing audience? Which one is second?

5. In alphabetical order, the six most common last names in the United States are Brown, Johnson, Jones, Miller, Smith, and Williams (*The World Almanac,* 2012). Assume that a sample of 50 individuals with one of these last names provided the following data.

2012Names

Brown	Williams	Williams	Williams	Brown
Smith	Jones	Smith	Johnson	Smith
Miller	Smith	Brown	Williams	Johnson
Johnson	Smith	Smith	Johnson	Brown
Williams	Miller	Johnson	Williams	Johnson
Williams	Johnson	Jones	Smith	Brown
Johnson	Smith	Smith	Brown	Jones
Jones	Jones	Smith	Smith	Miller
Miller	Jones	Williams	Miller	Smith
Jones	Johnson	Brown	Johnson	Miller

Summarize the data by constructing the following:

a.   Relative and percent frequency distributions
b.   A bar chart
c.   A pie chart
d.   Based on these data, what are the three most common last names?

6.   Nielsen Media Research provided the list of the 25 top-rated single shows in television history (*The World Almanac*, 2012). The following data show the television network that produced each of these 25 top-rated shows.

2012Networks

CBS	CBS	NBC	FOX	CBS
CBS	NBC	NBC	NBC	ABC
ABC	NBC	ABC	ABC	NBC
CBS	NBC	CBS	ABC	NBC
NBC	CBS	CBS	ABC	CBS

a.   Construct a frequency distribution, percent frequency distribution, and bar chart for the data.
b.   Which network or networks have done the best in terms of presenting top-rated television shows? Compare the performance of ABC, CBS, and NBC.

7.   The Canmark Research Center Airport Customer Satisfaction Survey uses an online questionnaire to provide airlines and airports with customer satisfaction ratings for all aspects of the customers' flight experience (airportsurvey website, July, 2012). After completing a flight, customers receive an e-mail asking them to go to the website and rate a variety of factors, including the reservation process, the check-in process, luggage policy, cleanliness of gate area, service by flight attendants, food/beverage selection, on-time arrival, and so on. A five-point scale, with Excellent (E), Very Good (V), Good (G), Fair (F), and Poor (P), is used to record customer ratings. Assume that passengers on a Delta Airlines flight from Myrtle Beach, South Carolina, to Atlanta, Georgia, provided the following ratings for the question, "Please rate the airline based on your overall experience with this flight." The sample ratings are shown below.

AirSurvey

E	E	G	V	V	E	V	V	V	E
E	G	V	E	E	V	E	E	E	V
V	V	V	F	V	E	V	E	G	E
G	E	V	E	V	E	V	V	V	V
E	E	V	V	E	P	E	V	P	V

a.   Use a percent frequency distribution and a bar chart to summarize these data. What do these summaries indicate about the overall customer satisfaction with the Delta flight?
b.   The online survey questionnaire enabled respondents to explain any aspect of the flight that failed to meet expectations. Would this be helpful information to a manager looking for ways to improve the overall customer satisfaction on Delta flights? Explain.

8. Data for a sample of 55 members of the Baseball Hall of Fame in Cooperstown, New York, are shown here. Each observation indicates the primary position played by the Hall of Famers: pitcher (P), catcher (H), 1st base (1), 2nd base (2), 3rd base (3), shortstop (S), left field (L), center field (C), and right field (R).

BaseballHall

L	P	C	H	2	P	R	1	S	S	1	L	P	R	P
P	P	P	R	C	S	L	R	P	C	C	P	P	R	P
2	3	P	H	L	P	1	C	P	P	P	S	1	L	R
R	1	2	H	S	3	H	2	L	P				

a. Construct frequency and relative frequency distributions to summarize the data.
b. What position provides the most Hall of Famers?
c. What position provides the fewest Hall of Famers?
d. What outfield position (L, C, or R) provides the most Hall of Famers?
e. Compare infielders (1, 2, 3, and S) to outfielders (L, C, and R).

9. The Pew Research Center's Social & Demographic Trends project found that 46% of U.S. adults would rather live in a different type of community than the one where they are living now (Pew Research Center, January 29, 2009). The national survey of 2260 adults asked: "Where do you live now?" and "What do you consider to be the ideal community?" Response options were City (C), Suburb (S), Small Town (T), or Rural (R). A representative portion of this survey for a sample of 100 respondents is as follows.

Where do you live now?

LivingArea

S	T	R	C	R	R	T	C	S	T	C	S	C	S	T
S	S	C	S	S	T	T	C	C	S	T	C	S	T	C
T	R	S	S	T	C	S	C	T	C	T	C	T	C	R
C	C	R	T	C	S	S	T	S	C	C	C	R	S	C
S	S	C	C	S	C	R	T	T	T	C	R	T	C	R
C	T	R	R	C	T	C	C	R	T	T	R	S	R	T
T	S	S	S	S	S	C	C	R	T					

What do you consider to be the ideal community?

S	C	R	R	R	S	T	S	S	T	T	S	C	S	T
C	C	R	T	R	S	T	T	S	S	C	C	T	T	S
S	R	C	S	C	C	S	C	R	C	T	S	R	R	R
C	T	S	T	T	T	R	R	S	C	C	R	R	S	S
S	T	C	T	T	C	R	T	T	T	C	T	T	R	R
C	S	R	T	C	T	C	C	T	T	T	R	C	R	T
T	C	S	S	C	S	T	S	S	R					

a. Provide a percent frequency distribution for each question.
b. Construct a bar chart for each question.
c. Where are most adults living now?
d. Where do most adults consider the ideal community?
e. What changes in living areas would you expect to see if people moved from where they currently live to their ideal community?

10. Virtual Tourist provides ratings for hotels throughout the world. Ratings provided by 649 guests at the Sheraton Anaheim Hotel, located near the Disneyland Resort in Anaheim, California, can be found in the file HotelRatings (Virtual Tourist website, February 25, 2013). Possible responses were Excellent, Very Good, Average, Poor, and Terrible.

HotelRatings

a. Construct a frequency distribution.
b. Construct a percent frequency distribution.
c. Construct a bar chart for the percent frequency distribution.
d. Comment on how guests rate their stay at the Sheraton Anaheim Hotel.
e. Results for 1679 guests who stayed at Disney's Grand Californian provided the following frequency distribution.

Rating	Frequency
Excellent	807
Very Good	521
Average	200
Poor	107
Terrible	44

Compare the ratings for Disney's Grand Californian with the results obtained for the Sheraton Anaheim Hotel.

2.2   Summarizing Data for a Quantitative Variable

Frequency Distribution

As defined in Section 2.1, a frequency distribution is a tabular summary of data showing the number (frequency) of observations in each of several nonoverlapping categories or classes. This definition holds for quantitative as well as categorical data. However, with quantitative data we must be more careful in defining the nonoverlapping classes to be used in the frequency distribution.

For example, consider the quantitative data in Table 2.4. These data show the time in days required to complete year-end audits for a sample of 20 clients of Sanderson and Clifford, a small public accounting firm. The three steps necessary to define the classes for a frequency distribution with quantitative data are

1. Determine the number of nonoverlapping classes.
2. Determine the width of each class.
3. Determine the class limits.

Let us demonstrate these steps by developing a frequency distribution for the audit time data in Table 2.4.

Number of classes Classes are formed by specifying ranges that will be used to group the data. As a general guideline, we recommend using between 5 and 20 classes. For a small number of data items, as few as five or six classes may be used to summarize the data. For a larger number of data items, a larger number of classes is usually required. The goal is to use enough classes to show the variation in the data, but not so many classes that some contain only a few data items. Because the number of data items in Table 2.4 is relatively small ($n = 20$), we chose to develop a frequency distribution with five classes.

Width of the classes The second step in constructing a frequency distribution for quantitative data is to choose a width for the classes. As a general guideline, we recommend that the width be the same for each class. Thus the choices of the number of classes and the width of classes are not independent decisions. A larger number of classes means a smaller class width, and vice versa. To determine an approximate class width, we begin by identifying the largest and smallest data values. Then, with the desired number of classes specified, we can use the following expression to determine the approximate class width.

$$\text{Approximate class width} = \frac{\text{Largest data value} - \text{Smallest data value}}{\text{Number of classes}} \tag{2.2}$$

TABLE 2.4

YEAR-END AUDIT TIMES (IN DAYS)

12	14	19	18
15	15	18	17
20	27	22	23
22	21	33	28
14	18	16	13

© Cengage Learning

WEB file

Audit

Making the classes the same width reduces the chance of inappropriate interpretations by the user.

The approximate class width given by equation (2.2) can be rounded to a more convenient value based on the preference of the person developing the frequency distribution. For example, an approximate class width of 9.28 might be rounded to 10 simply because 10 is a more convenient class width to use in presenting a frequency distribution.

For the data involving the year-end audit times, the largest data value is 33 and the smallest data value is 12. Because we decided to summarize the data with five classes, using equation (2.2) provides an approximate class width of $(33 - 12)/5 = 4.2$. We therefore decided to round up and use a class width of five days in the frequency distribution.

No single frequency distribution is best for a data set. Different people may construct different, but equally acceptable, frequency distributions. The goal is to reveal the natural grouping and variation in the data.

In practice, the number of classes and the appropriate class width are determined by trial and error. Once a possible number of classes is chosen, equation (2.2) is used to find the approximate class width. The process can be repeated for a different number of classes. Ultimately, the analyst uses judgment to determine the combination of the number of classes and class width that provides the best frequency distribution for summarizing the data.

For the audit time data in Table 2.4, after deciding to use five classes, each with a width of five days, the next task is to specify the class limits for each of the classes.

Class limits   Class limits must be chosen so that each data item belongs to one and only one class. The *lower class limit* identifies the smallest possible data value assigned to the class. The *upper class limit* identifies the largest possible data value assigned to the class. In developing frequency distributions for categorical data, we did not need to specify class limits because each data item naturally fell into a separate class. But with quantitative data, such as the audit times in Table 2.4, class limits are necessary to determine where each data value belongs.

Using the audit time data in Table 2.4, we selected 10 days as the lower class limit and 14 days as the upper class limit for the first class. This class is denoted 10–14 in Table 2.5. The smallest data value, 12, is included in the 10–14 class. We then selected 15 days as the lower class limit and 19 days as the upper class limit of the next class. We continued defining the lower and upper class limits to obtain a total of five classes: 10–14, 15–19, 20–24, 25–29, and 30–34. The largest data value, 33, is included in the 30–34 class. The difference between the lower class limits of adjacent classes is the class width. Using the first two lower class limits of 10 and 15, we see that the class width is $15 - 10 = 5$.

With the number of classes, class width, and class limits determined, a frequency distribution can be obtained by counting the number of data values belonging to each class. For example, the data in Table 2.4 show that four values—12, 14, 14, and 13— belong to the 10–14 class. Thus, the frequency for the 10–14 class is 4. Continuing this counting process for the 15–19, 20–24, 25–29, and 30–34 classes provides the frequency distribution in Table 2.5. Using this frequency distribution, we can observe the following:

1. The most frequently occurring audit times are in the class of 15–19 days. Eight of the 20 audit times belong to this class.
2. Only one audit required 30 or more days.

TABLE 2.5

FREQUENCY DISTRIBUTION FOR THE AUDIT TIME DATA

Audit Time (days)	Frequency
10–14	4
15–19	8
20–24	5
25–29	2
30–34	1
Total	20

© Cengage Learning

Other conclusions are possible, depending on the interests of the person viewing the frequency distribution. The value of a frequency distribution is that it provides insights about the data that are not easily obtained by viewing the data in their original unorganized form.

Class midpoint   In some applications, we want to know the midpoints of the classes in a frequency distribution for quantitative data. The **class midpoint** is the value halfway between the lower and upper class limits. For the audit time data, the five class midpoints are 12, 17, 22, 27, and 32.

Relative Frequency and Percent Frequency Distributions

We define the relative frequency and percent frequency distributions for quantitative data in the same manner as for categorical data. First, recall that the relative frequency is the proportion

TABLE 2.6   RELATIVE FREQUENCY AND PERCENT FREQUENCY DISTRIBUTIONS FOR
THE AUDIT TIME DATA

Audit Time (days)	Relative Frequency	Percent Frequency
10–14	.20	20
15–19	.40	40
20–24	.25	25
25–29	.10	10
30–34	.05	5
Total	1.00	100

© Cengage Learning

of the observations belonging to a class. With n observations,

$$\text{Relative frequency of class} = \frac{\text{Frequency of the class}}{n}$$

The percent frequency of a class is the relative frequency multiplied by 100.

Based on the class frequencies in Table 2.5 and with $n = 20$, Table 2.6 shows the relative frequency distribution and percent frequency distribution for the audit time data. Note that .40 of the audits, or 40%, required from 15 to 19 days. Only .05 of the audits, or 5%, required 30 or more days. Again, additional interpretations and insights can be obtained by using Table 2.6.

Dot Plot

One of the simplest graphical summaries of data is a **dot plot**. A horizontal axis shows the range for the data. Each data value is represented by a dot placed above the axis. Figure 2.4 is the dot plot for the audit time data in Table 2.4. The three dots located above 18 on the horizontal axis indicate that an audit time of 18 days occurred three times. Dot plots show the details of the data and are useful for comparing the distribution of the data for two or more variables.

Histogram

A common graphical display of quantitative data is a **histogram**. This graphical display can be prepared for data previously summarized in either a frequency, relative frequency, or percent frequency distribution. A histogram is constructed by placing the variable of interest on the horizontal axis and the frequency, relative frequency, or percent frequency on the vertical axis. The frequency, relative frequency, or percent frequency of each class is shown by drawing a rectangle whose base is determined by the class limits on the horizontal axis and whose height is the corresponding frequency, relative frequency, or percent frequency.

FIGURE 2.4   DOT PLOT FOR THE AUDIT TIME DATA

© Cengage Learning

FIGURE 2.5   HISTOGRAM FOR THE AUDIT TIME DATA

Figure 2.5 is a histogram for the audit time data. Note that the class with the greatest frequency is shown by the rectangle appearing above the class of 15–19 days. The height of the rectangle shows that the frequency of this class is 8. A histogram for the relative or percent frequency distribution of these data would look the same as the histogram in Figure 2.5 with the exception that the vertical axis would be labeled with relative or percent frequency values.

As Figure 2.5 shows, the adjacent rectangles of a histogram touch one another. Unlike a bar graph, a histogram contains no natural separation between the rectangles of adjacent classes. This format is the usual convention for histograms. Because the classes for the audit time data are stated as 10–14, 15–19, 20–24, 25–29, and 30–34, one-unit spaces of 14 to 15, 19 to 20, 24 to 25, and 29 to 30 would seem to be needed between the classes. These spaces are eliminated when constructing a histogram. Eliminating the spaces between classes in a histogram for the audit time data helps show that all values between the lower limit of the first class and the upper limit of the last class are possible.

One of the most important uses of a histogram is to provide information about the shape, or form, of a distribution. Figure 2.6 contains four histograms constructed from relative frequency distributions. Panel A shows the histogram for a set of data moderately skewed to the left. A histogram is said to be skewed to the left if its tail extends farther to the left. This histogram is typical for exam scores, with no scores above 100%, most of the scores above 70%, and only a few really low scores. Panel B shows the histogram for a set of data moderately skewed to the right. A histogram is said to be skewed to the right if its tail extends farther to the right. An example of this type of histogram would be for data such as housing prices; a few expensive houses create the skewness in the right tail.

Panel C shows a symmetric histogram. In a symmetric histogram, the left tail mirrors the shape of the right tail. Histograms for data found in applications are never perfectly symmetric, but the histogram for many applications may be roughly symmetric. Data for SAT scores, heights and weights of people, and so on lead to histograms that are roughly symmetric. Panel D shows a histogram highly skewed to the right. This histogram was constructed from data on the amount of customer purchases over one day at a women's apparel store. Data from applications in business and economics often lead to histograms that are skewed to the right. For instance, data on housing prices, salaries, purchase amounts, and so on often result in histograms skewed to the right.

FIGURE 2.6   HISTOGRAMS SHOWING DIFFERING LEVELS OF SKEWNESS

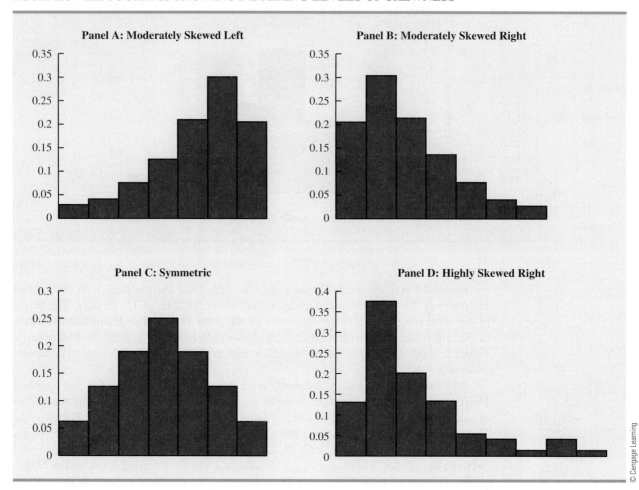

Cumulative Distributions

A variation of the frequency distribution that provides another tabular summary of quantitative data is the **cumulative frequency distribution**. The cumulative frequency distribution uses the number of classes, class widths, and class limits developed for the frequency distribution. However, rather than showing the frequency of each class, the cumulative frequency distribution shows the number of data items with values *less than or equal to the upper class limit* of each class. The first two columns of Table 2.7 provide the cumulative frequency distribution for the audit time data.

To understand how the cumulative frequencies are determined, consider the class with the description "less than or equal to 24." The cumulative frequency for this class is simply the sum of the frequencies for all classes with data values less than or equal to 24. For the frequency distribution in Table 2.5, the sum of the frequencies for classes 10–14, 15–19, and 20–24 indicates that $4 + 8 + 5 = 17$ data values are less than or equal to 24. Hence, the cumulative frequency for this class is 17. In addition, the cumulative frequency distribution in Table 2.7 shows that four audits were completed in 14 days or less and 19 audits were completed in 29 days or less.

TABLE 2.7 CUMULATIVE FREQUENCY, CUMULATIVE RELATIVE FREQUENCY, AND CUMULATIVE PERCENT FREQUENCY DISTRIBUTIONS FOR THE AUDIT TIME DATA

Audit Time (days)	Cumulative Frequency	Cumulative Relative Frequency	Cumulative Percent Frequency
Less than or equal to 14	4	.20	20
Less than or equal to 19	12	.60	60
Less than or equal to 24	17	.85	85
Less than or equal to 29	19	.95	95
Less than or equal to 34	20	1.00	100

© Cengage Learning

As a final point, we note that a **cumulative relative frequency distribution** shows the proportion of data items, and a **cumulative percent frequency distribution** shows the percentage of data items with values less than or equal to the upper limit of each class. The cumulative relative frequency distribution can be computed either by summing the relative frequencies in the relative frequency distribution or by dividing the cumulative frequencies by the total number of items. Using the latter approach, we found the cumulative relative frequencies in column 3 of Table 2.7 by dividing the cumulative frequencies in column 2 by the total number of items ($n = 20$). The cumulative percent frequencies were again computed by multiplying the relative frequencies by 100. The cumulative relative and percent frequency distributions show that .85 of the audits, or 85%, were completed in 24 days or less, .95 of the audits, or 95%, were completed in 29 days or less, and so on.

Stem-and-Leaf Display

A **stem-and-leaf display** is a graphical display used to show simultaneously the rank order and shape of a distribution of data. To illustrate the use of a stem-and-leaf display, consider the data in Table 2.8. These data result from a 150-question aptitude test given to 50 individuals recently interviewed for a position at Haskens Manufacturing. The data indicate the number of questions answered correctly.

To develop a stem-and-leaf display, we first arrange the leading digits of each data value to the left of a vertical line. To the right of the vertical line, we record the last digit for each data value. Based on the top row of data in Table 2.8 (112, 72, 69, 97, and 107),

TABLE 2.8 NUMBER OF QUESTIONS ANSWERED CORRECTLY ON AN APTITUDE TEST

WEB file

ApTest

112	72	69	97	107
73	92	76	86	73
126	128	118	127	124
82	104	132	134	83
92	108	96	100	92
115	76	91	102	81
95	141	81	80	106
84	119	113	98	75
68	98	115	106	95
100	85	94	106	119

© Cengage Learning

the first five entries in constructing a stem-and-leaf display would be as follows:

```
 6 | 9
 7 | 2
 8 |
 9 | 7
10 | 7
11 | 2
12 |
13 |
14 |
```

For example, the data value 112 shows the leading digits 11 to the left of the line and the last digit 2 to the right of the line. Similarly, the data value 72 shows the leading digit 7 to the left of the line and last digit 2 to the right of the line. Continuing to place the last digit of each data value on the line corresponding to its leading digit(s) provides the following:

```
 6 | 9  8
 7 | 2  3  6  3  6  5
 8 | 6  2  3  1  1  0  4  5
 9 | 7  2  2  6  2  1  5  8  8  5  4
10 | 7  4  8  0  2  6  6  0  6
11 | 2  8  5  9  3  5  9
12 | 6  8  7  4
13 | 2  4
14 | 1
```

With this organization of the data, sorting the digits on each line into rank order is simple. Doing so provides the stem-and-leaf display shown here.

```
 6 | 8  9
 7 | 2  3  3  5  6  6
 8 | 0  1  1  2  3  4  5  6
 9 | 1  2  2  2  4  5  5  6  7  8  8
10 | 0  0  2  4  6  6  6  7  8
11 | 2  3  5  5  8  9  9
12 | 4  6  7  8
13 | 2  4
14 | 1
```

The numbers to the left of the vertical line (6, 7, 8, 9, 10, 11, 12, 13, and 14) form the *stem,* and each digit to the right of the vertical line is a *leaf.* For example, consider the first row with a stem value of 6 and leaves of 8 and 9.

```
6 | 8   9
```

This row indicates that two data values have a first digit of six. The leaves show that the data values are 68 and 69. Similarly, the second row

```
7 | 2   3   3   5   6   6
```

indicates that six data values have a first digit of seven. The leaves show that the data values are 72, 73, 73, 75, 76, and 76.

To focus on the shape indicated by the stem-and-leaf display, let us use a rectangle to contain the leaves of each stem. Doing so, we obtain the following:

```
 6 | 8  9
 7 | 2  3  3  5  6  6
 8 | 0  1  1  2  3  4  5  6
 9 | 1  2  2  2  4  5  5  6  7  8  8
10 | 0  0  2  4  6  6  6  7  8
11 | 2  3  5  5  8  9  9
12 | 4  6  7  8
13 | 2  4
14 | 1
```

Rotating this page counterclockwise onto its side provides a picture of the data that is similar to a histogram with classes of 60–69, 70–79, 80–89, and so on.

Although the stem-and-leaf display may appear to offer the same information as a histogram, it has two primary advantages.

1. The stem-and-leaf display is easier to construct by hand.
2. Within a class interval, the stem-and-leaf display provides more information than the histogram because the stem-and-leaf shows the actual data.

Just as a frequency distribution or histogram has no absolute number of classes, neither does a stem-and-leaf display have an absolute number of rows or stems. If we believe that our original stem-and-leaf display condensed the data too much, we can easily stretch the display by using two or more stems for each leading digit. For example, to use two stems for each leading digit, we would place all data values ending in 0, 1, 2, 3, and 4 in one row and all values ending in 5, 6, 7, 8, and 9 in a second row. The following stretched stem-and-leaf display illustrates this approach.

In a stretched stem-and-leaf display, whenever a stem value is stated twice, the first value corresponds to leaf values of 0–4, and the second value corresponds to leaf values of 5–9.

```
 6 | 8  9
 7 | 2  3  3
 7 | 5  6  6
 8 | 0  1  1  2  3  4
 8 | 5  6
 9 | 1  2  2  2  4
 9 | 5  5  6  7  8  8
10 | 0  0  2  4
10 | 6  6  6  7  8
11 | 2  3
11 | 5  5  8  9  9
12 | 4
12 | 6  7  8
13 | 2  4
13 |
14 | 1
```

Note that values 72, 73, and 73 have leaves in the 0–4 range and are shown with the first stem value of 7. The values 75, 76, and 76 have leaves in the 5–9 range and are shown with the second stem value of 7. This stretched stem-and-leaf display is similar to a frequency distribution with intervals of 65–69, 70–74, 75–79, and so on.

The preceding example showed a stem-and-leaf display for data with as many as three digits. Stem-and-leaf displays for data with more than three digits are possible. For example, consider the following data on the number of hamburgers sold by a fast-food restaurant for each of 15 weeks.

1565	1852	1644	1766	1888	1912	2044	1812
1790	1679	2008	1852	1967	1954	1733	

A stem-and-leaf display of these data follows.

Leaf unit = 10

```
15 | 6
16 | 4  7
17 | 3  6  9
18 | 1  5  5  8
19 | 1  5  6
20 | 0  4
```

A single digit is used to define each leaf in a stem-and-leaf display. The leaf unit indicates how to multiply the stem-and-leaf numbers in order to approximate the original data. Leaf units may be 100, 10, 1, 0.1, and so on.

Note that a single digit is used to define each leaf and that only the first three digits of each data value have been used to construct the display. At the top of the display we have specified Leaf unit = 10. To illustrate how to interpret the values in the display, consider the first stem, 15, and its associated leaf, 6. Combining these numbers, we obtain 156. To reconstruct an approximation of the original data value, we must multiply this number by 10, the value of the *leaf unit*. Thus, $156 \times 10 = 1560$ is an approximation of the original data value used to construct the stem-and-leaf display. Although it is not possible to reconstruct the exact data value from this stem-and-leaf display, the convention of using a single digit for each leaf enables stem-and-leaf displays to be constructed for data having a large number of digits. For stem-and-leaf displays where the leaf unit is not shown, the leaf unit is assumed to equal 1.

NOTES AND COMMENTS

1. A bar chart and a histogram are essentially the same thing; both are graphical presentations of the data in a frequency distribution. A histogram is just a bar chart with no separation between bars. For some discrete quantitative data, a separation between bars is also appropriate. Consider, for example, the number of classes in which a college student is enrolled. The data may assume only integer values. Intermediate values such as 1.5, 2.73, and so on are not possible. With continuous quantitative data, however, such as the audit times in Table 2.4, a separation between bars is not appropriate.

2. The appropriate values for the class limits with quantitative data depend on the level of accuracy of the data. For instance, with the audit time data of Table 2.4 the limits used were integer values. If the data were rounded to the nearest tenth of a day (e.g., 12.3, 14.4, and so on), then the limits would be stated in tenths of days. For instance, the first class would be 10.0–14.9. If the data were recorded to the nearest hundredth of a day (e.g., 12.34, 14.45, and so on), the limits would be stated in hundredths of days. For instance, the first class would be 10.00–14.99.

3. An *open-end* class requires only a lower class limit or an upper class limit. For example, in the audit time data of Table 2.4, suppose two of the audits had taken 58 and 65 days. Rather than continue with the classes of width 5 with classes 35–39, 40–44, 45–49, and so on, we could simplify the frequency distribution to show an open-end class of "35 or more." This class would have a frequency of 2. Most often the open-end class appears at the upper end of the distribution. Sometimes an open-end class appears at the lower end of the distribution, and occasionally such classes appear at both ends.

4. The last entry in a cumulative frequency distribution always equals the total number of observations. The last entry in a cumulative relative frequency distribution always equals 1.00 and the last entry in a cumulative percent frequency distribution always equals 100.

Exercises

Methods

11. Consider the following data.

Frequency

14	21	23	21	16
19	22	25	16	16
24	24	25	19	16
19	18	19	21	12
16	17	18	23	25
20	23	16	20	19
24	26	15	22	24
20	22	24	22	20

a. Develop a frequency distribution using classes of 12–14, 15–17, 18–20, 21–23, and 24–26.
b. Develop a relative frequency distribution and a percent frequency distribution using the classes in part (a).

12. Consider the following frequency distribution.

Class	Frequency
10–19	10
20–29	14
30–39	17
40–49	7
50–59	2

Construct a cumulative frequency distribution and a cumulative relative frequency distribution.

13. Construct a histogram for the data in exercise 12.

14. Consider the following data.

8.9   10.2   11.5   7.8   10.0   12.2   13.5   14.1   10.0   12.2
6.8   9.5   11.5   11.2   14.9   7.5   10.0   6.0   15.8   11.5

a. Construct a dot plot.
b. Construct a frequency distribution.
c. Construct a percent frequency distribution.

15. Construct a stem-and-leaf display for the following data.

11.3	9.6	10.4	7.5	8.3	10.5	10.0
9.3	8.1	7.7	7.5	8.4	6.3	8.8

16. Construct a stem-and-leaf display for the following data. Use a leaf unit of 10.

1161	1206	1478	1300	1604	1725	1361	1422
1221	1378	1623	1426	1557	1730	1706	1689

Applications

17. A doctor's office staff studied the waiting times for patients who arrive at the office with a request for emergency service. The following data with waiting times in minutes were collected over a one-month period.

2   5   10   12   4   4   5   17   11   8   9   8   12   21   6   8   7   13   18   3

Use classes of 0–4, 5–9, and so on in the following:
a. Show the frequency distribution.
b. Show the relative frequency distribution.

c.   Show the cumulative frequency distribution.
d.   Show the cumulative relative frequency distribution.
e.   What proportion of patients needing emergency service wait 9 minutes or less?

18. CBSSports.com developed the Total Player Ratings system to rate players in the National Basketball Association (NBA) based upon various offensive and defensive statistics. The following data show the average number of points scored per game (PPG) for 50 players with the highest ratings for a portion of the 2012–2013 NBA season. (CBSSports.com website, February 25, 2013).

NBAPlayerPts

27.0	28.8	26.4	27.1	22.9	28.4	19.2	21.0	20.8	17.6
21.1	19.2	21.2	15.5	17.2	16.7	17.6	18.5	18.3	18.3
23.3	16.4	18.9	16.5	17.0	11.7	15.7	18.0	17.7	14.6
15.7	17.2	18.2	17.5	13.6	16.3	16.2	13.6	17.1	16.7
17.0	17.3	17.5	14.0	16.9	16.3	15.1	12.3	18.7	14.6

Use classes with number of points per game of 10–11.9, 12–13.9, 14–15.9, and so on.
a.   Show the frequency distribution.
b.   Show the relative frequency distribution.
c.   Show the cumulative percent frequency distribution.
d.   Develop a histogram for the average number of points scored per game.
e.   Do the data appear to be skewed? Explain.
f.   What percentage of the players averaged at least 20 points per game?

19. Based on the tons handled in a year, the ports listed below are the 25 busiest ports in the United States (*The 2013 World Almanac*).

Ports

Port	Tons Handled (Millions)	Port	Tons Handled (Millions)
Baltimore	39.6	Norfolk Harbor	41.6
Baton Rouge	55.5	Pascagoula	37.3
Beaumont	77.0	Philadelphia	34.0
Corpus Christi	73.7	Pittsburgh	33.8
Duluth-Superior	36.6	Plaquemines	55.8
Houston	227.1	Port Arthur	30.2
Hunnington	61.5	Savannah	34.7
Lake Charles	54.6	South Louisiana	236.3
Long Beach	75.4	St. Louis	30.8
Los Angeles	62.4	Tampa	34.2
Mobile	55.7	Texas City	56.6
New Orleans	72.4	Valdez	31.9
New York	139.2		

a.   What is the largest number of tons handled? What is the smallest number of tons handled?
b.   Using a class width of 25, develop a frequency distribution of the data starting with 25–49.9, 50–74.9, 75–99.9 and so on.
c.   Prepare a histogram. Interpret the histogram.

20. The London School of Economics and the Harvard Business School conducted a study of how chief executive officers (CEOs) spend their day. The study found that CEOs spend on average about 18 hours per week in meetings, not including conference calls, business

meals, and public events (*The Wall Street Journal,* February 14, 2012). Shown below is the time spent per week in meetings (hours) for a sample of 25 CEOs.

CEOTime

14	15	18	23	15
19	20	13	15	23
23	21	15	20	21
16	15	18	18	19
19	22	23	21	12

a.   What is the least amount of time spent per week on meetings? The highest?
b.   Use a class width of two hours to prepare a frequency distribution and a percent frequency distribution for the data.
c.   Prepare a histogram and comment on the shape of the distribution.

21.   *Fortune* provides a list of America's largest corporations based on annual revenue. Shown below are the 50 largest corporations, with annual revenue expressed in billions of dollars (*CNN Money* website, January 15, 2010).

LargeCorp

Corporation	Revenue	Corporation	Revenue
Amerisource Bergen	71	Lowe's	48
Archer Daniels Midland	70	Marathon Oil	74
AT&T	124	McKesson	102
Bank of America	113	Medco Health	51
Berkshire Hathaway	108	MetLife	55
Boeing	61	Microsoft	60
Cardinal Health	91	Morgan Stanley	62
Caterpillar	51	Pepsico	43
Chevron	263	Pfizer	48
Citigroup	112	Procter & Gamble	84
ConocoPhillips	231	Safeway	44
Costco Wholesale	72	Sears Holdings	47
CVS Caremark	87	State Farm Insurance	61
Dell	61	Sunoco	52
Dow Chemical	58	Target	65
ExxonMobil	443	Time Warner	47
Ford Motors	146	United Parcel Service	51
General Electric	149	United Technologies	59
Goldman Sachs	54	UnitedHealth Group	81
Hewlett-Packard	118	Valero Energy	118
Home Depot	71	Verizon	97
IBM	104	Walgreen	59
JPMorgan Chase	101	Walmart	406
Johnson & Johnson	64	WellPoint	61
Kroger	76	Wells Fargo	52

Summarize the data by constructing the following:
a.   A frequency distribution (classes 0–49, 50–99, 100–149, and so on).
b.   A relative frequency distribution.
c.   A cumulative frequency distribution.
d.   A cumulative relative frequency distribution.
e.   What do these distributions tell you about the annual revenue of the largest corporations in America?
f.   Show a histogram. Comment on the shape of the distribution.
g.   What is the largest corporation in America and what is its annual revenue?

22.   *Entrepreneur* magazine ranks franchises using performance measures such as growth rate, number of locations, startup costs, and financial stability. The number of locations for the top 20 U.S. franchises follow (*The World Almanac,* 2012).

Franchise

Franchise	No. U.S. Locations	Franchise	No. U.S. Locations
Hampton Inns	1864	Jan-Pro Franchising Intl. Inc.	12,394
ampm	3183	Hardee's	1901
McDonald's	32,805	Pizza Hut Inc.	13,281
7-Eleven Inc.	37,496	Kumon Math & Reading Centers	25,199
Supercuts	2130	Dunkin' Donuts	9947
Days Inn	1877	KFC Corp.	16,224
Vanguard Cleaning Systems	2155	Jazzercise Inc.	7683
		Anytime Fitness	1618
Servpro	1572	Matco Tools	1431
Subway	34,871	Stratus Building Solutions	5018
Denny's Inc.	1668		

Use classes 0–4999, 5000–9999, 10,000–14,999, and so forth to answer the following questions.

a.   Construct a frequency distribution and a percent frequency distribution of the number of U.S. locations for these top-ranked franchises.

b.   Construct a histogram of these data.

c.   Comment on the shape of the distribution.

23.   The *Nielsen Home Technology Report* provided information about home technology and its usage. The following data are the hours of personal computer usage during one week for a sample of 50 persons.

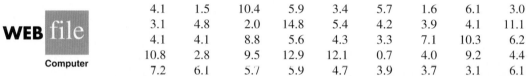

Computer

4.1	1.5	10.4	5.9	3.4	5.7	1.6	6.1	3.0	3.7
3.1	4.8	2.0	14.8	5.4	4.2	3.9	4.1	11.1	3.5
4.1	4.1	8.8	5.6	4.3	3.3	7.1	10.3	6.2	7.6
10.8	2.8	9.5	12.9	12.1	0.7	4.0	9.2	4.4	5.7
7.2	6.1	5.7	5.9	4.7	3.9	3.7	3.1	6.1	3.1

Summarize the data by constructing the following:

a.   A frequency distribution (use a class width of three hours)

b.   A relative frequency distribution

c.   A histogram

d.   Comment on what the data indicate about personal computer usage at home.

24.   *Money* magazine listed top career opportunities for work that is enjoyable, pays well, and will still be around 10 years from now (*Money,* November 2009). Shown below are 20 top career opportunities, with the median pay and top pay for workers with two to seven years of experience in the field. Data are shown in thousands of dollars.

Careers

Career	Median Pay	Top Pay
Account Executive	81	157
Certified Public Accountant	74	138
Computer Security Consultant	100	138
Director of Communications	78	135
Financial Analyst	80	109
Finance Director	121	214
Financial Research Analyst	66	155
Hotel General Manager	77	146
Human Resources Manager	72	111
Investment Banking	106	221
IT Business Analyst	83	119
IT Project Manager	99	140

Career	Median Pay	Top Pay
Marketing Manager	77	126
Quality-Assurance Manager	80	122
Sales Representative	67	125
Senior Internal Auditor	76	106
Software Developer	79	116
Software Program Manager	110	152
Systems Engineer	87	130
Technical Writer	67	100

Develop a stem-and-leaf display for both the median pay and the top pay. Comment on what you learn about the pay for these careers.

25.   A psychologist developed a new test of adult intelligence. The test was administered to 20 individuals, and the following data were obtained.

114	99	131	124	117	102	106	127	119	115
98	104	144	151	132	106	125	122	118	118

Construct a stem-and-leaf display for the data.

26.   The 2011 Cincinnati Flying Pig Half-Marathon (13.1 miles) had 10,897 finishers (Cincinnati Flying Pig Marathon website). The following data show the ages for a sample of 40 half-marathoners.

Marathon

49	33	40	37	56
44	46	57	55	32
50	52	43	64	40
46	24	30	37	43
31	43	50	36	61
27	44	35	31	43
52	43	66	31	50
72	26	59	21	47

a.   Construct a stretched stem-and-leaf display.
b.   What age group had the largest number of runners?
c.   What age occurred most frequently?

2.3   Summarizing Data for Two Variables Using Tables

Thus far in this chapter, we have focused on using tabular and graphical displays to summarize the data for a single categorical or quantitative variable. Often a manager or decision maker needs to summarize the data for two variables in order to reveal the relationship—if any—between the variables. In this section, we show how to construct a tabular summary of the data for two variables.

Crosstabulation

A **crosstabulation** is a tabular summary of data for two variables. Although both variables can be either categorical or quantitative, crosstabulations in which one variable is categorical and the other variable is quantitative are just as common. We will illustrate this latter case by considering the following application based on data from Zagat's Restaurant Review. Data showing the quality rating and the typical meal price were collected for a sample of

TABLE 2.9   QUALITY RATING AND MEAL PRICE DATA FOR 300 LOS ANGELES
RESTAURANTS

Restaurant

Restaurant	Quality Rating	Meal Price ($)
1	Good	18
2	Very Good	22
3	Good	28
4	Excellent	38
5	Very Good	33
6	Good	28
7	Very Good	19
8	Very Good	11
9	Very Good	23
10	Good	13
.	.	.
.	.	.
.	.	.

© Cengage Learning

300 restaurants in the Los Angeles area. Table 2.9 shows the data for the first 10 restaurants.
Quality rating is a categorical variable with rating categories of good, very good, and excellent. Meal price is a quantitative variable that ranges from $10 to $49.

A crosstabulation of the data for this application is shown in Table 2.10. The labels shown in the margins of the table define the categories (classes) for the two variables. In the left margin, the row labels (good, very good, and excellent) correspond to the three rating categories for the quality rating variable. In the top margin, the column labels ($10–19, $20–29, $30–39, and $40–49) show that the meal price data have been grouped into four classes. Because each restaurant in the sample provides a quality rating and a meal price, each restaurant is associated with a cell appearing in one of the rows and one of the columns of the crosstabulation. For example, Table 2.9 shows restaurant 5 as having a very good quality rating and a meal price of $33. This restaurant belongs to the cell in row 2 and column 3 of the crosstabulation shown in Table 2.10. In constructing a crosstabulation, we simply count the number of restaurants that belong to each of the cells.

Grouping the data for a quantitative variable enables us to treat the quantitative variable as if it were a categorical variable when creating a crosstabulation.

Although four classes of the meal price variable were used to construct the crosstabulation shown in Table 2.10, the crosstabulation of quality rating and meal price could have been developed using fewer or more classes for the meal price variable. The issues involved in deciding how to group the data for a quantitative variable in a crosstabulation are similar to the issues involved in deciding the number of classes to use when constructing a frequency distribution for a quantitative variable. For this application, four classes of meal price were considered a reasonable number of classes to reveal any relationship between quality rating and meal price.

TABLE 2.10   CROSSTABULATION OF QUALITY RATING AND MEAL PRICE DATA
FOR 300 LOS ANGELES RESTAURANTS

Quality Rating	Meal Price				Total
	$10–19	**$20–29**	**$30–39**	**$40–49**	
Good	42	40	2	0	84
Very Good	34	64	46	6	150
Excellent	2	14	28	22	66
Total	78	118	76	28	300

© Cengage Learning

In reviewing Table 2.10, we see that the greatest number of restaurants in the sample (64) have a very good rating and a meal price in the $20–29 range. Only two restaurants have an excellent rating and a meal price in the $10–19 range. Similar interpretations of the other frequencies can be made. In addition, note that the right and bottom margins of the crosstabulation provide the frequency distributions for quality rating and meal price separately. From the frequency distribution in the right margin, we see that data on quality ratings show 84 restaurants with a good quality rating, 150 restaurants with a very good quality rating, and 66 restaurants with an excellent quality rating. Similarly, the bottom margin shows the frequency distribution for the meal price variable.

Dividing the totals in the right margin of the crosstabulation by the total for that column provides a relative and percent frequency distribution for the quality rating variable.

Quality Rating	Relative Frequency	Percent Frequency
Good	.28	28
Very Good	.50	50
Excellent	.22	22
Total	1.00	100

From the percent frequency distribution we see that 28% of the restaurants were rated good, 50% were rated very good, and 22% were rated excellent.

Dividing the totals in the bottom row of the crosstabulation by the total for that row provides a relative and percent frequency distribution for the meal price variable.

Meal Price	Relative Frequency	Percent Frequency
$10–19	.26	26
$20–29	.39	39
$30–39	.25	25
$40–49	.09	9
Total	1.00	100

Note that the sum of the values in the relative frequency column do not add exactly to 1.00 and the sum of the values in the percent frequency distribution do not add exactly to 100; the reason is that the values being summed are rounded. From the percent frequency distribution we see that 26% of the meal prices are in the lowest price class ($10–19), 39% are in the next higher class, and so on.

The frequency and relative frequency distributions constructed from the margins of a crosstabulation provide information about each of the variables individually, but they do not shed any light on the relationship between the variables. The primary value of a crosstabulation lies in the insight it offers about the relationship between the variables. A review of the crosstabulation in Table 2.10 reveals that restaurants with higher meal prices received higher quality ratings than restaurants with lower meal prices.

Converting the entries in a crosstabulation into row percentages or column percentages can provide more insight into the relationship between the two variables. For row percentages, the results of dividing each frequency in Table 2.10 by its corresponding row total are shown in Table 2.11. Each row of Table 2.11 is a percent frequency distribution of meal price for one of the quality rating categories. Of the restaurants with the lowest quality rating (good), we see that the greatest percentages are for the less expensive restaurants (50% have $10–19 meal prices and 47.6% have $20–29 meal prices). Of the restaurants with the highest quality rating (excellent), we see that the greatest

TABLE 2.11   ROW PERCENTAGES FOR EACH QUALITY RATING CATEGORY

	Meal Price				
Quality Rating	$10–19	$20–29	$30–39	$40–49	Total
Good	50.0	47.6	2.4	0.0	100
Very Good	22.7	42.7	30.6	4.0	100
Excellent	3.0	21.2	42.4	33.4	100

© Cengage Learning

percentages are for the more expensive restaurants (42.4% have $30–39 meal prices and 33.4% have $40–49 meal prices). Thus, we continue to see that restaurants with higher meal prices received higher quality ratings.

Crosstabulations are widely used to investigate the relationship between two variables. In practice, the final reports for many statistical studies include a large number of crosstabulations. In the Los Angeles restaurant survey, the crosstabulation is based on one categorical variable (quality rating) and one quantitative variable (meal price). Crosstabulations can also be developed when both variables are categorical and when both variables are quantitative. When quantitative variables are used, however, we must first create classes for the values of the variable. For instance, in the restaurant example we grouped the meal prices into four classes ($10–19, $20–29, $30–39, and $40–49).

Simpson's Paradox

The data in two or more crosstabulations are often combined or aggregated to produce a summary crosstabulation showing how two variables are related. In such cases, conclusions drawn from two or more separate crosstabulations can be reversed when the data are aggregated into a single crosstabulation. The reversal of conclusions based on aggregate and unaggregated data is called **Simpson's paradox**. To provide an illustration of Simpson's paradox we consider an example involving the analysis of verdicts for two judges in two different courts.

Judges Ron Luckett and Dennis Kendall presided over cases in Common Pleas Court and Municipal Court during the past three years. Some of the verdicts they rendered were appealed. In most of these cases the appeals court upheld the original verdicts, but in some cases those verdicts were reversed. For each judge a crosstabulation was developed based upon two variables: Verdict (upheld or reversed) and Type of Court (Common Pleas and Municipal). Suppose that the two crosstabulations were then combined by aggregating the type of court data. The resulting aggregated crosstabulation contains two variables: Verdict (upheld or reversed) and Judge (Luckett or Kendall). This crosstabulation shows the number of appeals in which the verdict was upheld and the number in which the verdict was reversed for both judges. The following crosstabulation shows these results along with the column percentages in parentheses next to each value.

	Judge		
Verdict	Luckett	Kendall	Total
Upheld	129 (86%)	110 (88%)	239
Reversed	21 (14%)	15 (12%)	36
Total (%)	150 (100%)	125 (100%)	275

A review of the column percentages shows that 86% of the verdicts were upheld for Judge Luckett, while 88% of the verdicts were upheld for Judge Kendall. From this aggregated crosstabulation, we conclude that Judge Kendall is doing the better job because a greater percentage of Judge Kendall's verdicts are being upheld.

The following unaggregated crosstabulations show the cases tried by Judge Luckett and Judge Kendall in each court; column percentages are shown in parentheses next to each value.

Judge Luckett

Verdict	Common Pleas	Municipal Court	Total
Upheld	29 (91%)	100 (85%)	129
Reversed	3 (9%)	18 (15%)	21
Total (%)	32 (100%)	118 (100%)	150

Judge Kendall

Verdict	Common Pleas	Municipal Court	Total
Upheld	90 (90%)	20 (80%)	110
Reversed	10 (10%)	5 (20%)	15
Total (%)	100 (100%)	25 (100%)	125

From the crosstabulation and column percentages for Judge Luckett, we see that the verdicts were upheld in 91% of the Common Pleas Court cases and in 85% of the Municipal Court cases. From the crosstabulation and column percentages for Judge Kendall, we see that the verdicts were upheld in 90% of the Common Pleas Court cases and in 80% of the Municipal Court cases. Thus, when we unaggregate the data, we see that Judge Luckett has a better record because a greater percentage of Judge Luckett's verdicts are being upheld in both courts. This result contradicts the conclusion we reached with the aggregated data crosstabulation that showed Judge Kendall had the better record. This reversal of conclusions based on aggregated and unaggregated data illustrates Simpson's paradox.

The original crosstabulation was obtained by aggregating the data in the separate crosstabulations for the two courts. Note that for both judges the percentage of appeals that resulted in reversals was much higher in Municipal Court than in Common Pleas Court. Because Judge Luckett tried a much higher percentage of his cases in Municipal Court, the aggregated data favored Judge Kendall. When we look at the crosstabulations for the two courts separately, however, Judge Luckett shows the better record. Thus, for the original crosstabulation, we see that the *type of court* is a hidden variable that cannot be ignored when evaluating the records of the two judges.

Because of the possibility of Simpson's paradox, realize that the conclusion or interpretation may be reversed depending upon whether you are viewing unaggregated or aggregate crosstabulation data. Before drawing a conclusion, you may want to investigate whether the aggregate or unaggregate form of the crosstabulation provides the better insight and conclusion. Especially when the crosstabulation involves aggregated data, you should investigate whether a hidden variable could affect the results such that separate or unaggregated crosstabulations provide a different and possibly better insight and conclusion.

Exercises

Methods

27. The following data are for 30 observations involving two categorical variables, x and y. The categories for x are A, B, and C; the categories for y are 1 and 2.

Observation	x	y	Observation	x	y
1	A	1	16	B	2
2	B	1	17	C	1
3	B	1	18	B	1
4	C	2	19	C	1
5	B	1	20	B	1
6	C	2	21	C	2
7	B	1	22	B	1
8	C	2	23	C	2
9	A	1	24	A	1
10	B	1	25	B	1
11	A	1	26	C	2
12	B	1	27	C	2
13	C	2	28	A	1
14	C	2	29	B	1
15	C	2	30	B	2

Crosstab

a. Develop a crosstabulation for the data, with x as the row variable and y as the column variable.
b. Compute the row percentages.
c. Compute the column percentages.
d. What is the relationship, if any, between x and y?

28. The following observations are for two quantitative variables, x and y.

Observation	x	y	Observation	x	y
1	28	72	11	13	98
2	17	99	12	84	21
3	52	58	13	59	32
4	79	34	14	17	81
5	37	60	15	70	34
6	71	22	16	47	64
7	37	77	17	35	68
8	27	85	18	62	67
9	64	45	19	30	39
10	53	47	20	43	28

Crosstab2

a. Develop a crosstabulation for the data, with x as the row variable and y as the column variable. For x use classes of 10–29, 30–49, and so on; for y use classes of 40–59, 60–79, and so on.
b. Compute the row percentages.
c. Compute the column percentages.
d. What is the relationship, if any, between x and y?

Applications

29. The Daytona 500 is a 500-mile automobile race held annually at the Daytona International Speedway in Daytona Beach, Florida. The following crosstabulation shows the automobile make by average speed of the 25 winners from 1988 to 2012 (*The 2013 World Almanac*).
    a. Compute the row percentages.
    b. What percentage of winners driving a Chevrolet won with an average speed of at least 150 miles per hour?

	Average Speed in Miles per Hour					
Make	130–139.9	140–149.9	150–159.9	160–169.9	170–179.9	Total
Buick	1					1
Chevrolet	3	5	4	3	1	16
Dodge		2				2
Ford	2	1	2	1		6
Total	6	8	6	4	1	25

    c.   Compute the column percentages.

    d.   What percentage of winning average speeds 160–169.9 miles per hour were Chevrolets?

30.   The following crosstabulation shows the average speed of the 25 winners by year of the Daytona 500 automobile race (*The 2013 World Almanac*).

	Year					
Average Speed	1988–1992	1993–1997	1998–2002	2003–2007	2008–2012	Total
130–139.9	1			2	3	6
140–149.9	2	2	1	2	1	8
150–159.9		3	1	1	1	6
160–169.9	2		2			4
170–179.9			1			1
Total	5	5	5	5	5	25

    a.   Calculate the row percentages.

    b.   What is the apparent relationship between average winning speed and year? What might be the cause of this apparent relationship?

31.   Recently, management at Oak Tree Golf Course received a few complaints about the condition of the greens. Several players complained that the greens are too fast. Rather than react to the comments of just a few, the Golf Association conducted a survey of 100 male and 100 female golfers. The survey results are summarized here.

Male Golfers

	Greens Condition	
Handicap	Too Fast	Fine
Under 15	10	40
15 or more	25	25

Female Golfers

	Greens Condition	
Handicap	Too Fast	Fine
Under 15	1	9
15 or more	39	51

    a.   Combine these two crosstabulations into one with Male and Female as the row labels and Too Fast and Fine as the column labels. Which group shows the highest percentage saying that the greens are too fast?

    b.   Refer to the initial crosstabulations. For those players with low handicaps (better players), which group (male or female) shows the highest percentage saying the greens are too fast?

    c.   Refer to the initial crosstabulations. For those players with higher handicaps, which group (male or female) shows the highest percentage saying the greens are too fast?

    d.   What conclusions can you draw about the preferences of men and women concerning the speed of the greens? Are the conclusions you draw from part (a) as compared with parts (b) and (c) consistent? Explain any apparent inconsistencies.

32. Table 2.12 shows a data set containing information for 45 mutual funds that are part of the *Morningstar Funds 500* for 2008. The data set includes the following five variables:

TABLE 2.12   FINANCIAL DATA FOR A SAMPLE OF 45 MUTUAL FUNDS

Fund Name	Fund Type	Net Asset Value ($)	5-Year Average Return (%)	Expense Ratio (%)	Morningstar Rank
Amer Cent Inc & Growth Inv	DE	28.88	12.39	0.67	2-Star
American Century Intl Disc	IE	14.37	30.53	1.41	3-Star
American Century Tax-Free Bond	FI	10.73	3.34	0.49	4-Star
American Century Ultra	DE	24.94	10.88	0.99	3-Star
Ariel	DE	46.39	11.32	1.03	2-Star
Artisan Intl Val	IE	25.52	24.95	1.23	3-Star
Artisan Small Cap	DE	16.92	15.67	1.18	3-Star
Baron Asset	DE	50.67	16.77	1.31	5-Star
Brandywine	DE	36.58	18.14	1.08	4-Star
Brown Cap Small	DE	35.73	15.85	1.20	4-Star
Buffalo Mid Cap	DE	15.29	17.25	1.02	3-Star
Delafield	DE	24.32	17.77	1.32	4-Star
DFA U.S. Micro Cap	DE	13.47	17.23	0.53	3-Star
Dodge & Cox Income	FI	12.51	4.31	0.44	4-Star
Fairholme	DE	31.86	18.23	1.00	5-Star
Fidelity Contrafund	DE	73.11	17.99	0.89	5-Star
Fidelity Municipal Income	FI	12.58	4.41	0.45	5-Star
Fidelity Overseas	IE	48.39	23.46	0.90	4-Star
Fidelity Sel Electronics	DE	45.60	13.50	0.89	3-Star
Fidelity Sh-Term Bond	FI	8.60	2.76	0.45	3-Star
Fidelity	DE	39.85	14.40	0.56	4-Star
FPA New Income	FI	10.95	4.63	0.62	3-Star
Gabelli Asset AAA	DE	49.81	16.70	1.36	4-Star
Greenspring	DE	23.59	12.46	1.07	3-Star
Janus	DE	32.26	12.81	0.90	3-Star
Janus Worldwide	IE	54.83	12.31	0.86	2-Star
Kalmar Gr Val Sm Cp	DE	15.30	15.31	1.32	3-Star
Managers Freemont Bond	FI	10.56	5.14	0.60	5-Star
Marsico 21st Century	DE	17.44	15.16	1.31	5-Star
Mathews Pacific Tiger	IE	27.86	32.70	1.16	3-Star
Meridan Value	DE	31.92	15.33	1.08	4-Star
Oakmark I	DE	40.37	9.51	1.05	2-Star
PIMCO Emerg Mkts Bd D	FI	10.68	13.57	1.25	3-Star
RS Value A	DE	26.27	23.68	1.36	4-Star
T. Rowe Price Latin Am	IE	53.89	51.10	1.24	4-Star
T. Rowe Price Mid Val	DE	22.46	16.91	0.80	4-Star
Templeton Growth A	IE	24.07	15.91	1.01	3-Star
Thornburg Value A	DE	37.53	15.46	1.27	4-Star
USAA Income	FI	12.10	4.31	0.62	3-Star
Vanguard Equity-Inc	DE	24.42	13.41	0.29	4-Star
Vanguard Global Equity	IE	23.71	21.77	0.64	5-Star
Vanguard GNMA	FI	10.37	4.25	0.21	5-Star
Vanguard Sht-Tm TE	FI	15.68	2.37	0.16	3-Star
Vanguard Sm Cp Idx	DE	32.58	17.01	0.23	3-Star
Wasatch Sm Cp Growth	DE	35.41	13.98	1.19	4-Star

MutualFunds

© Cengage Learning

Fund Type: The type of fund, labeled DE (Domestic Equity), IE (International Equity), and FI (Fixed Income)

Net Asset Value ($): The closing price per share

5-Year Average Return (%): The average annual return for the fund over the past 5 years

Expense Ratio (%): The percentage of assets deducted each fiscal year for fund expenses

Morningstar Rank: The risk adjusted star rating for each fund; Morningstar ranks go from a low of 1-Star to a high of 5-Stars

a. Prepare a crosstabulation of the data on Fund Type (rows) and the average annual return over the past 5 years (columns). Use classes of 0–9.99, 10–19.99, 20–29.99, 30–39.99, 40–49.99, and 50–59.99 for the 5-Year Average Return (%).

b. Prepare a frequency distribution for the data on Fund Type.

c. Prepare a frequency distribution for the data on 5-Year Average Return (%).

d. How has the crosstabulation helped in preparing the frequency distributions in parts (b) and (c)?

e. What conclusions can you draw about the fund type and the average return over the past 5 years?

33. Refer to the data in Table 2.12.

a. Prepare a crosstabulation of the data on Fund Type (rows) and the Expense Ratio (%) (columns). Use classes of .25–.49, .50–.74, .75–.99, 1.00–1.24, and 1.25–1.49 for Expense Ratio (%).

b. Prepare a percent frequency distribution for Expense Ratio (%).

c. What conclusions can you draw about fund type and the expense ratio?

34. The file named BankFail contains a list of 492 banks that failed from 2000–2012 (Federal Deposit Insurance Corporation website, March 9, 2013). The file contains the name of the bank, city, state, and year of failure.

WEB file

BankFail

a. Construct a crosstabulation with state as the rows and year as the columns.

b. Which three states have had the most failed banks?

c. Give the frequency distribution of bank failures by year. Comment on what appears to be happening with bank failures over time.

35. The U.S. Department of Energy's Fuel Economy Guide provides fuel efficiency data for cars and trucks (Fuel Economy website, September 8, 2012). A portion of the data for 149 compact, midsize, and large cars is shown in Table 2.13. The data set contains the following variables:

Size: Compact, Midsize, and Large

Displacement: Engine size in liters

Cylinders: Number of cylinders in the engine

WEB file

FuelData2012

TABLE 2.13   FUEL EFFICIENCY DATA FOR 311 CARS

Car	Size	Displacement	Cylinders	Drive	Fuel Type	City MPG	Hwy MPG
1	Compact	2.0	4	F	P	22	30
2	Compact	2.0	4	A	P	21	29
3	Compact	2.0	4	A	P	21	31
•	•	•	•	•	•	•	•
•	•	•	•	•	•	•	•
•	•	•	•	•	•	•	•
94	Midsize	3.5	6	A	R	17	25
95	Midsize	2.5	4	F	R	23	33
•	•	•	•	•	•	•	•
•	•	•	•	•	•	•	•
•	•	•	•	•	•	•	•
148	Large	6.7	12	R	P	11	18
149	Large	6.7	12	R	P	11	18

Drive: All wheel (A), front wheel (F), and rear wheel (R)

Fuel Type: Premium (P) or regular (R) fuel

City MPG: Fuel efficiency rating for city driving in terms of miles per gallon

Hwy MPG: Fuel efficiency rating for highway driving in terms of miles per gallon

The complete data set is contained in the file named FuelData2012.

a.   Prepare a crosstabulation of the data on Size (rows) and Hwy MPG (columns). Use classes of 15–19, 20–24, 25–29, 30–34, 35–39, and 40–44 for Hwy MPG.
b.   Comment on the relationship beween Size and Hwy MPG.
c.   Prepare a crosstabulation of the data on Drive (rows) and City MPG (columns). Use classes of 10–14, 15–19, 20–24, 25–29, 30–34, 35–39, and 40–44 for City MPG.
d.   Comment on the relationship between Drive and City MPG.
e.   Prepare a crosstabulation of the data on Fuel Type (rows) and City MPG (columns). Use classes of 10–14, 15–19, 20–24, 25–29, 30–34, 35–39, and 40–44 for City MPG.
f.   Comment on the relationship between Fuel Type and City MPG.

2.4 Summarizing Data for Two Variables Using Graphical Displays

In the previous section we showed how a crosstabulation can be used to summarize the data for two variables and help reveal the relationship between the variables. In most cases, a graphical display is more useful for recognizing patterns and trends in the data.

In this section, we introduce a variety of graphical displays for exploring the relationships between two variables. Displaying data in creative ways can lead to powerful insights and allow us to make "common-sense inferences" based on our ability to visually compare, contrast, and recognize patterns. We begin with a discussion of scatter diagrams and trendlines.

Scatter Diagram and Trendline

A **scatter diagram** is a graphical display of the relationship between two quantitative variables, and a **trendline** is a line that provides an approximation of the relationship. As an illustration, consider the advertising/sales relationship for a stereo and sound equipment store in San Francisco. On 10 occasions during the past three months, the store used weekend television commercials to promote sales at its stores. The managers want to investigate whether a relationship exists between the number of commercials shown and sales at the store during the following week. Sample data for the 10 weeks with sales in hundreds of dollars are shown in Table 2.14.

TABLE 2.14   SAMPLE DATA FOR THE STEREO AND SOUND EQUIPMENT STORE

Stereo

Week	Number of Commercials x	Sales ($100s) y
1	2	50
2	5	57
3	1	41
4	3	54
5	4	54
6	1	38
7	5	63
8	3	48
9	4	59
10	2	46

FIGURE 2.7   SCATTER DIAGRAM AND TRENDLINE FOR THE STEREO AND SOUND EQUIPMENT STORE

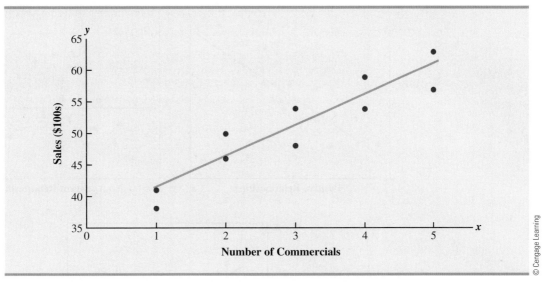

Figure 2.7 shows the scatter diagram and the trendline[1] for the data in Table 2.14. The number of commercials (x) is shown on the horizontal axis and the sales (y) are shown on the vertical axis. For week 1, $x = 2$ and $y = 50$. A point with those coordinates is plotted on the scatter diagram. Similar points are plotted for the other nine weeks. Note that during two of the weeks one commercial was shown, during two of the weeks two commercials were shown, and so on.

The scatter diagram in Figure 2.7 indicates a positive relationship between the number of commercials and sales. Higher sales are associated with a higher number of commercials. The relationship is not perfect in that all points are not on a straight line. However, the general pattern of the points and the trendline suggest that the overall relationship is positive.

Some general scatter diagram patterns and the types of relationships they suggest are shown in Figure 2.8. The top left panel depicts a positive relationship similar to the one for the number of commercials and sales example. In the top right panel, the scatter diagram shows no apparent relationship between the variables. The bottom panel depicts a negative relationship where y tends to decrease as x increases.

Side-by-Side and Stacked Bar Charts

In Section 2.1 we said that a bar chart is a graphical display for depicting categorical data summarized in a frequency, relative frequency, or percent frequency distribution. Side-by-side bar charts and stacked bar charts are extensions of basic bar charts that are used to display and compare two variables. By displaying two variables on the same chart, we may better understand the relationship between the variables.

A **side-by-side bar chart** is a graphical display for depicting multiple bar charts on the same display. To illustrate the construction of a side-by-side chart, recall the application involving the quality rating and meal price data for a sample of 300 restaurants located in the Los Angeles area. Quality rating is a categorical variable with rating categories of good, very good, and excellent. Meal price is a quantitative variable that ranges from $10 to $49. The crosstabulation displayed in Table 2.10 shows that the data for meal price were

---

[1]The equation of the trendline is $y = 36.15 + 4.95x$. The slope of the trendline is 4.95 and the y-intercept (the point where the trendline intersects the y-axis) is 36.15. We will discuss in detail the interpretation of the slope and y-intercept for a linear trendline in Chapter 12 when we study simple linear regression.

FIGURE 2.8   TYPES OF RELATIONSHIPS DEPICTED BY SCATTER DIAGRAMS

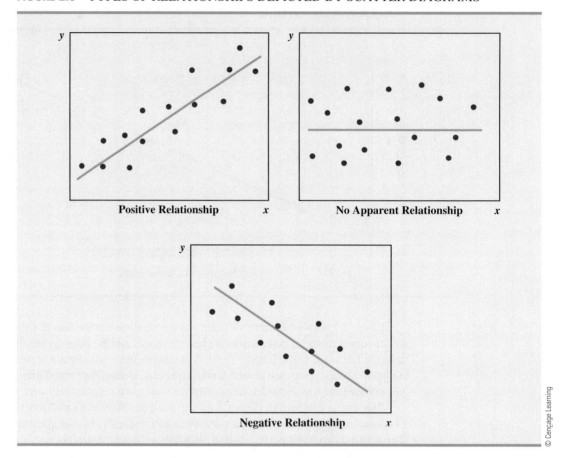

grouped into four classes: $10–19, $20–29, $30–39, and $40–49. We will use these classes to construct a side-by-side bar chart.

Figure 2.9 shows a side-by-side chart for the restaurant data. The color of each bar indicates the quality rating (blue = good, red = very good, and green = excellent). Each bar is constructed by extending the bar to the point on the vertical axis that represents the frequency

FIGURE 2.9   SIDE-BY-SIDE BAR CHART FOR THE QUALITY AND MEAL PRICE DATA

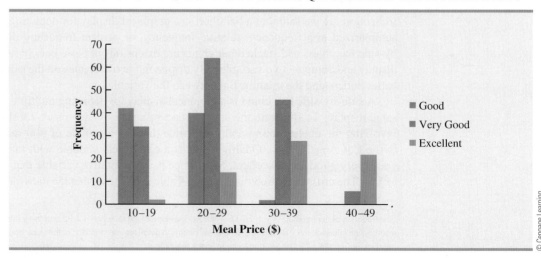

with which that quality rating occurred for each of the meal price categories. Placing each meal price category's quality rating frequency adjacent to one another allows us to quickly determine how a particular meal price category is rated. We see that the lowest meal price category ($10–$19) received mostly good and very good ratings, but very few excellent ratings. The highest price category ($40–49), however, shows a much different result. This meal price category received mostly excellent ratings, some very good ratings, but no good ratings.

Figure 2.9 also provides a good sense of the relationship between meal price and quality rating. Notice that as the price increases (left to right), the height of the blue bars decreases and the height of the green bars generally increases. This indicates that as price increases, the quality rating tends to be better. The very good rating, as expected, tends to be more prominent in the middle price categories as indicated by the dominance of the red bars in the middle of the chart.

Stacked bar charts are another way to display and compare two variables on the same display. A **stacked bar chart** is a bar chart in which each bar is broken into rectangular segments of a different color showing the relative frequency of each class in a manner similar to a pie chart. To illustrate a stacked bar chart we will use the quality rating and meal price data summarized in the crosstabulation shown in Table 2.10.

We can convert the frequency data in Table 2.10 into column percentages by dividing each element in a particular column by the total for that column. For instance, 42 of the 78 restaurants with a meal price in the $10–19 range had a good quality rating. In other words, (42/78)100 or 53.8% of the 78 restaurants had a good rating. Table 2.15 shows the column percentages for each meal price category. Using the data in Table 2.15 we constructed the stacked bar chart shown in Figure 2.10. Because the stacked bar chart is based on

TABLE 2.15   COLUMN PERCENTAGES FOR EACH MEAL PRICE CATEGORY

Quality Rating	Meal Price			
	$10–19	$20–29	$30–39	$40–49
Good	53.8%	33.9%	2.6%	0.0%
Very Good	43.6	54.2	60.5	21.4
Excellent	2.6	11.9	36.8	78.6
Total	100.0%	100.0%	100.0%	100.0%

FIGURE 2.10   STACKED BAR CHART FOR QUALITY RATING AND MEAL PRICE DATA

percentages, Figure 2.10 shows even more clearly than Figure 2.9 the relationship between the variables. As we move from the low price category ($10–19) to the high price category ($40–49), the length of the blue bars decreases and the length of the green bars increases.

NOTE AND COMMENT

A stacked bar chart can also be used to display frequencies rather than percentage frequencies. In this case, the different color segments of each bar represent the contribution to the total for that bar, rather than the percentage contribution.

Exercises

Methods

Scatter

36. The following 20 observations are for two quantitative variables, x and y.

Observation	x	y	Observation	x	y
1	−22	22	11	−37	48
2	−33	49	12	34	−29
3	2	8	13	9	−18
4	29	−16	14	−33	31
5	−13	10	15	20	−16
6	21	−28	16	−3	14
7	−13	27	17	−15	18
8	−23	35	18	12	17
9	14	−5	19	−20	−11
10	3	−3	20	−7	−22

a. Develop a scatter diagram for the relationship between x and y.
b. What is the relationship, if any, between x and y?

37. Consider the following data on two categorical variables. The first variable, x, can take on values A, B, C, or D. The second variable, y, can take on values I or II. The following table gives the frequency with which each combination occurs.

x	I	II
A	143	857
B	200	800
C	321	679
D	420	580

a. Construct a side-by-side bar chart with x on the horizontal axis.
b. Comment on the relationship between x and y.

38. The following crosstabulation summarizes the data for two categorical variables, x and y. The variable x can take on values low, medium, or high and the variable y can take on values yes or no.

x	Yes	No	Total
Low	20	10	30
Medium	15	35	50
High	20	5	25
Total	55	50	105

a. Compute the row percentages.
b. Construct a stacked percent frequency bar chart with x on the horizontal axis.

Applications

39. A study on driving speed (miles per hour) and fuel efficiency (miles per gallon) for midsize automobiles resulted in the following data:

MPG

Driving Speed	30 50 40 55 30 25 60 25 50 55
Fuel Efficiency	28 25 25 23 30 32 21 35 26 25

a. Construct a scatter diagram with driving speed on the horizontal axis and fuel efficiency on the vertical axis.
b. Comment on any apparent relationship between these two variables.

40. The Current Results website lists the average annual high and low temperatures (degrees Fahrenheit) and average annual snowfall (inches) for 51 major U.S. cities, based on data from 1981 to 2010. The data are contained in the file *Snow*. For example, the average low temperature for Columbus, Ohio, is 44 degrees and the average annual snowfall is 27.5 inches.

Snow

a. Construct a scatter diagram with the average annual low temperature on the horizontal axis and the average annual snowfall on the vertical axis.
b. Does there appear to be any relationship between these two variables?
c. Based on the scatter diagram, comment on any data points that seem to be unusual.

41. People often wait until middle age to worry about having a healthy heart. However, recent studies have shown that earlier monitoring of risk factors such as blood pressure can be very beneficial (*The Wall Street Journal*, January 10, 2012). Having higher than normal blood pressure, a condition known as hypertension, is a major risk factor for heart disease. Suppose a large sample of individuals of various ages and gender was selected and that each individual's blood pressure was measured to determine if they have hypertension. For the sample data, the following table shows the percentage of individuals with hypertension.

Hypertension

Age	Male	Female
20–34	11.0%	9.0%
35–44	24.0%	19.0%
45–54	39.0%	37.0%
55–64	57.0%	56.0%
65–74	62.0%	64.0%
75+	73.30%	79.0%

a. Develop a side-by-side bar chart with age on the horizontal axis, the percentage of individuals with hypertension on the vertical axis, and side-by-side bars based on gender.
b. What does the display you developed in part (a), indicate about hypertension and age?
c. Comment on differences by gender.

42. Smartphones are advanced mobile phones with Internet, photo, and music and video capability (The Pew Research Center, Internet & American Life Project, 2011). The following survey results show smartphone ownership by age.

WEB file

Smartphones

Age Category	Smartphone (%)	Other Cell Phone (%)	No Cell Phone (%)
18–24	49	46	5
25–34	58	35	7
35–44	44	45	11
45–54	28	58	14
55–64	22	59	19
65+	11	45	44

a. Construct a stacked bar chart to display the above survey data on type of mobile phone ownership. Use age category as the variable on the horizontal axis.
b. Comment on the relationship between age and smartphone ownership.
c. How would you expect the results of this survey to be different if conducted in 2021?

43. The Northwest regional manager of an outdoor equipment retailer conducted a study to determine how managers at three store locations are using their time. A summary of the results is shown in the following table.

WEB file

ManagerTime

Store Location	Percentage of Manager's Work Week Spent on			
	Meetings	Reports	Customers	Idle
Bend	18	11	52	19
Portland	52	11	24	13
Seattle	32	17	37	14

a. Create a stacked bar chart with store location on the horizontal axis and percentage of time spent on each task on the vertical axis.
b. Create a side-by-side bar chart with store location on the horizontal axis and side-by-side bars of the percentage of time spent on each task.
c. Which type of bar chart (stacked or side-by-side) do you prefer for these data? Why?

2.5 Data Visualization: Best Practices in Creating Effective Graphical Displays

Data visualization is a term used to describe the use of graphical displays to summarize and present information about a data set. The goal of data visualization is to communicate as effectively and clearly as possible, the key information about the data. In this section, we provide guidelines for creating an effective graphical display, discuss how to select an appropriate type of display given the purpose of the study, illustrate the use of data dashboards, and show how the Cincinnati Zoo and Botanical Garden uses data visualization techniques to improve decision making.

TABLE 2.16 PLANNED AND ACTUAL SALES BY SALES REGION ($1000s)

WEB file

PlannedActual

Sales Region	Planned Sales ($1000s)	Actual Sales ($1000s)
Northeast	540	447
Northwest	420	447
Southeast	575	556
Southwest	360	341

© Cengage Learning

Creating Effective Graphical Displays

The data presented in Table 2.16 show the forecasted or planned value of sales ($1000s) and the actual value of sales ($1000s) by sales region in the United States for Gustin Chemical for the past year. Note that there are two quantitative variables (planned sales and actual sales) and one categorical variable (sales region). Suppose we would like to develop a graphical display that would enable management of Gustin Chemical to visualize how each sales region did relative to planned sales and simultaneously enable management to visualize sales performance across regions.

Figure 2.11 shows a side-by-side bar chart of the planned versus actual sales data. Note how this bar chart makes it very easy to compare the planned versus actual sales in a region, as well as across regions. This graphical display is simple, contains a title, is well labeled, and uses distinct colors to represent the two types of sales. Note also that the scale of the vertical axis begins at zero. The four sales regions are separated by space so that it is clear that they are distinct, whereas the planned versus actual sales values are side-by-side for easy comparison within each region. The side-by-side bar chart in Figure 2.11 makes it easy to see that the Southwest region is the lowest in both planned and actual sales and that the Northwest region slightly exceeded its planned sales.

Creating an effective graphical display is as much art as it is science. By following the general guidelines listed below you can increase the likelihood that your display will effectively convey the key information in the data.

- Give the display a clear and concise title.
- Keep the display simple. Do not use three dimensions when two dimensions are sufficient.

FIGURE 2.11 SIDE-BY-SIDE BAR CHART FOR PLANNED VERSUS ACTUAL SALES

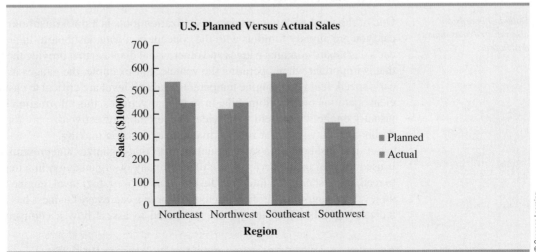

© Cengage Learning

- Clearly label each axis and provide the units of measure.
- If color is used to distinguish categories, make sure the colors are distinct.
- If multiple colors or line types are used, use a legend to define how they are used and place the legend close to the representation of the data.

Choosing the Type of Graphical Display

In this chapter we discussed a variety of graphical displays, including bar charts, pie charts, dot plots, histograms, stem-and-leaf plots, scatter diagrams, side-by-side bar charts, and stacked bar charts. Each of these types of displays was developed for a specific purpose. In order to provide guidelines for choosing the appropriate type of graphical display, we now provide a summary of the types of graphical displays categorized by their purpose. We note that some types of graphical displays may be used effectively for multiple purposes.

Displays Used to Show the Distribution of Data

- Bar Chart—Used to show the frequency distribution and relative frequency distribution for categorical data
- Pie Chart—Used to show the relative frequency and percent frequency for categorical data
- Dot Plot—Used to show the distribution for quantitative data over the entire range of the data
- Histogram—Used to show the frequency distribution for quantitative data over a set of class intervals
- Stem-and-Leaf Display—Used to show both the rank order and shape of the distribution for quantitative data

Displays Used to Make Comparisons

- Side-by-Side Bar Chart—Used to compare two variables
- Stacked Bar Charts—Used to compare the relative frequency or percent frequency of two categorical variables

Displays Used to Show Relationships

- Scatter diagram—Used to show the relationship between two quantitative variables
- Trendline—Used to approximate the relationship of data in a scatter diagram

Data Dashboards

Data dashboards are also referred to as digital dashboards.

One of the most widely used data visualization tools is a **data dashboard**. If you drive a car, you are already familiar with the concept of a data dashboard. In an automobile, the car's dashboard contains gauges and other visual displays that provide the key information that is important when operating the vehicle. For example, the gauges used to display the car's speed, fuel level, engine temperature, and oil level are critical to ensure safe and efficient operation of the automobile. In some new vehicles, this information is even displayed visually on the windshield to provide an even more effective display for the driver. Data dashboards play a similar role for managerial decision making.

A data dashboard is a set of visual displays that organizes and presents information that is used to monitor the performance of a company or organization in a manner that is easy to read, understand, and interpret. Just as a car's speed, fuel level, engine temperature, and oil level are important information to monitor in a car, every business has key performance indicators (KPIs)[2] that need to be monitored to assess how a company is performing.

---

[2] Key performance indicators are sometimes referred to as Key Performance Metrics (KPMs).

Examples of KPIs are inventory on hand, daily sales, percentage of on-time deliveries, and sales revenue per quarter. A data dashboard should provide timely summary information (potentially from various sources) on KPIs that is important to the user, and it should do so in a manner that informs rather than overwhelms its user.

To illustrate the use of a data dashboard in decision making, we will discuss an application involving the Grogan Oil Company. Grogan has offices located in three cities in Texas: Austin (its headquarters), Houston, and Dallas. Grogan's Information Technology (IT) call center, located in the Austin office, handles calls from employees regarding computer-related problems involving software, Internet, and e-mail issues. For example, if a Grogan employee in Dallas has a computer software problem, the employee can call the IT call center for assistance.

The data dashboard shown in Figure 2.12 was developed to monitor the performance of the call center. This data dashboard combines several displays to monitor the call center's KPIs. The data presented are for the current shift, which started at 8:00 A.M. The stacked bar chart in the upper left-hand corner shows the call volume for each type of problem (software, Internet, or e-mail) over time. This chart shows that call volume is heavier during the first few hours of the shift, calls concerning e-mail issues appear to decrease over time, and volume of calls regarding software issues is highest at midmorning. The pie chart in the upper

FIGURE 2.12   GROGAN OIL INFORMATION TECHNOLOGY CALL CENTER DATA DASHBOARD

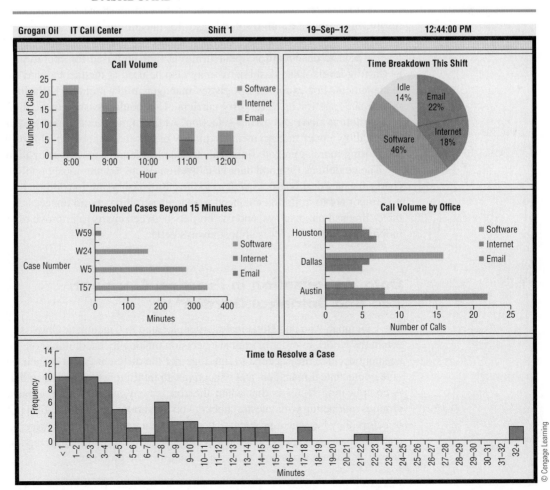

© Cengage Learning

right-hand corner of the dashboard shows the percentage of time that call-center employees spent on each type of problem or not working on a call (idle). Both of these charts are important displays in determining optimal staffing levels. For instance, knowing the call mix and how stressed the system is—as measured by percentage of idle time—can help the IT manager make sure there are enough call center employees available with the right level of expertise.

The side-by-side bar chart below the pie chart shows the call volume by type of problem for each of Grogan's offices. This allows the IT manager to quickly identify if there is a particular type of problem by location. For example, it appears that the office in Austin is reporting a relatively high number of issues with e-mail. If the source of the problem can be identified quickly, then the problem for many might be resolved quickly. Also, note that a relatively high number of software problems are coming from the Dallas office. The higher call volume in this case was simply due to the fact that the Dallas office is currently installing new software, and this has resulted in more calls to the IT call center. Because the IT manager was alerted to this by the Dallas office last week, the IT manager knew there would be an increase in calls coming from the Dallas office and was able to increase staffing levels to handle the expected increase in calls.

For each unresolved case that was received more than 15 minutes ago, the bar chart shown in the middle left-hand side of the data dashboard displays the length of time that each of these cases has been unresolved. This chart enables Grogan to quickly monitor the key problem cases and decide whether additional resources may be needed to resolve them. The worst case, T57, has been unresolved for over 300 minutes and is actually left over from the previous shift. Finally, the histogram at the bottom shows the distribution of the time to resolve the problem for all resolved cases for the current shift.

The Grogan Oil data dashboard illustrates the use of a dashboard at the operational level. The data dashboard is updated in real time and used for operational decisions such as staffing levels. Data dashboards may also be used at the tactical and strategic levels of management. For example, a logistics manager might monitor KPIs for on-time performance and cost for its third-party carriers. This could assist in tactical decisions such as transportation mode and carrier selection. At the highest level, a more strategic dashboard would allow upper management to quickly assess the financial health of the company by monitoring more aggregate financial, service level, and capacity utilization information.

The guidelines for good data visualization discussed previously apply to the individual charts in a data dashboard, as well as to the entire dashboard. In addition to those guidelines, it is important to minimize the need for screen scrolling, avoid unnecessary use of color or three-dimensional displays, and use borders between charts to improve readability. As with individual charts, simpler is almost always better.

Data Visualization in Practice: Cincinnati Zoo and Botanical Garden[3]

The Cincinnati Zoo and Botanical Garden, located in Cincinnati, Ohio, is the second oldest zoo in the world. In order to improve decision making by becoming more data-driven, management decided they needed to link together the different facets of their business and provide nontechnical managers and executives an intuitive way to better understand their data. A complicating factor is that when the zoo is busy, managers are expected to be on the grounds interacting with guests, checking on operations, and anticipating issues as they arise or before they become a problem. Therefore, being able to monitor what is happening on a real-time basis was a key factor in deciding what to do. Zoo management concluded that a data visualization strategy was needed to address the problem.

[3] The authors are indebted to John Lucas of the Cincinnati Zoo and Botanical Garden for providing this application.

FIGURE 2.13   DATA DASHBOARD FOR THE CINCINNATI ZOO

Because of its ease of use, real-time updating capability, and iPad compatibility, the Cincinnati Zoo decided to implement its data visualization strategy using IBM's Cognos advanced data visualization software. Using this software, the Cincinnati Zoo developed the data dashboard shown in Figure 2.13 to enable zoo management to track the following key performance indicators:

- Item Analysis (sales volumes and sales dollars by location within the zoo)
- Geo Analytics (using maps and displays of where the day's visitors are spending their time at the zoo)
- Customer Spending
- Cashier Sales Performance
- Sales and Attendance Data versus Weather Patterns
- Performance of the zoo's Loyalty Rewards Program

An iPad mobile application was also developed to enable the zoo's managers to be out on the grounds and still see and anticipate what is occurring on a real-time basis. The Cincinnati Zoo's iPad data dashboard, shown in Figure 2.14, provides managers with access to the following information:

- Real-time attendance data, including what "types" of guests are coming to the zoo
- Real-time analysis showing which items are selling the fastest inside the zoo
- Real-time geographical representation of where the zoo's visitors live

FIGURE 2.14   THE CINCINNATI ZOO iPAD DATA DASHBOARD

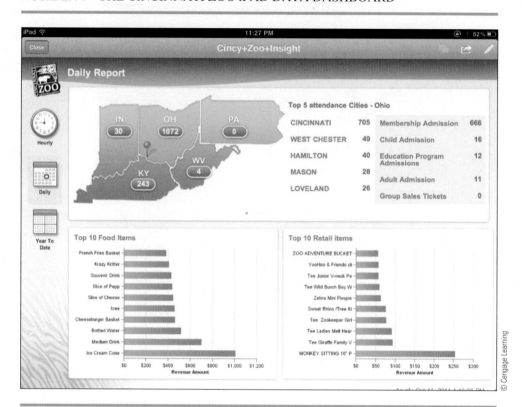

Having access to the data shown in Figures 2.13 and 2.14 allows the zoo managers to make better decisions on staffing levels within the zoo, which items to stock based upon weather and other conditions, and how to better target its advertising based on geodemographics.

The impact that data visualization has had on the zoo has been significant. Within the first year of use, the system has been directly responsible for revenue growth of over $500,000, increased visitation to the zoo, enhanced customer service, and reduced marketing costs.

NOTES AND COMMENTS

1. A variety of software is available for data visualization. Among the more popular packages are Cognos, JMP, Spotfire, and Tableau.
2. Radar charts and bubble charts are two other commonly used charts for displaying relationships between multiple variables. However, many experts in data visualization recommend against using these charts because they can be overcomplicated. Instead, the use of simpler displays such as bar charts and scatter diagrams is recommended.
3. A very powerful tool for visualizing geographic data is a Geographic Information System (GIS).

A GIS uses color, symbols, and text on a map to help you understand how variables are distributed geographically. For example, a company interested in trying to locate a new distribution center might wish to better understand how the demand for its product varies throughout the United States. A GIS can be used to map the demand where red regions indicate high demand, blue lower demand, and no color for regions where the product is not sold. Locations closer to red high-demand regions might be good candidate sites for further consideration.

Summary

A set of data, even if modest in size, is often difficult to interpret directly in the form in which it is gathered. Tabular and graphical displays can be used to summarize and present data so that patterns are revealed and the data are more easily interpreted. Frequency distributions, relative frequency distributions, percent frequency distributions, bar charts, and pie charts were presented as tabular and graphical displays for summarizing the data for a single categorical variable. Frequency distributions, relative frequency distributions, percent frequency distributions, histograms, cumulative frequency distributions, cumulative relative frequency distributions, cumulative percent frequency distributions, and stem-and-leaf displays were presented as ways of summarizing the data for a single quantitative variable.

A crosstabulation was presented as a tabular display for summarizing the data for two variables and a scatter diagram was introduced as a graphical display for summarizing the data for two quantitative variables. We also showed that side-by-side bar charts and stacked bar charts are just extensions of basic bar charts that can be used to display and compare two categorical variables. Guidelines for creating effective graphical displays and how to choose the most appropriate type of display were discussed. Data dashboards were introduced to illustrate how a set of visual displays can be developed that organizes and presents information that is used to monitor a company's performance in a manner that is easy to read, understand, and interpret. Figure 2.15 provides a summary of the tabular and graphical methods presented in this chapter.

FIGURE 2.15 TABULAR AND GRAPHICAL DISPLAYS FOR SUMMARIZING DATA

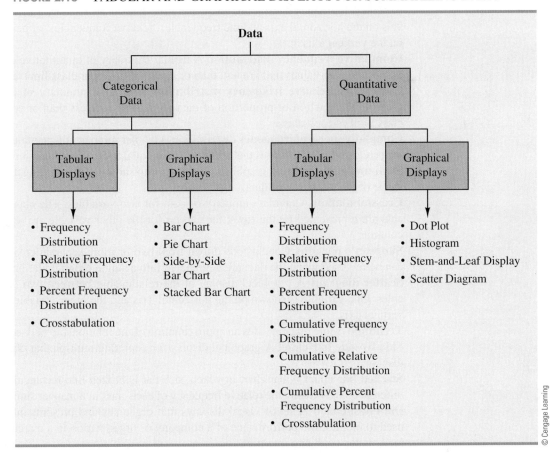

With large data sets, computer software packages are essential in constructing tabular and graphical summaries of data. In the chapter appendixes, we show how Minitab, Excel, and StatTools can be used for this purpose.

Glossary

Categorical data Labels or names used to identify categories of like items.

Quantitative data Numerical values that indicate how much or how many.

Data visualization A term used to describe the use of graphical displays to summarize and present information about a data set.

Frequency distribution A tabular summary of data showing the number (frequency) of observations in each of several nonoverlapping categories or classes.

Relative frequency distribution A tabular summary of data showing the fraction or proportion of observations in each of several nonoverlapping categories or classes.

Percent frequency distribution A tabular summary of data showing the percentage of observations in each of several nonoverlapping classes.

Bar chart A graphical device for depicting categorical data that have been summarized in a frequency, relative frequency, or percent frequency distribution.

Pie chart A graphical device for presenting data summaries based on subdivision of a circle into sectors that correspond to the relative frequency for each class.

Class midpoint The value halfway between the lower and upper class limits.

Dot plot A graphical device that summarizes data by the number of dots above each data value on the horizontal axis.

Histogram A graphical display of a frequency distribution, relative frequency distribution, or percent frequency distribution of quantitative data constructed by placing the class intervals on the horizontal axis and the frequencies, relative frequencies, or percent frequencies on the vertical axis.

Cumulative frequency distribution A tabular summary of quantitative data showing the number of data values that are less than or equal to the upper class limit of each class.

Cumulative relative frequency distribution A tabular summary of quantitative data showing the fraction or proportion of data values that are less than or equal to the upper class limit of each class.

Cumulative percent frequency distribution A tabular summary of quantitative data showing the percentage of data values that are less than or equal to the upper class limit of each class.

Stem-and-leaf display A graphical display used to show simultaneously the rank order and shape of a distribution of data.

Crosstabulation A tabular summary of data for two variables. The classes for one variable are represented by the rows; the classes for the other variable are represented by the columns.

Simpson's paradox Conclusions drawn from two or more separate crosstabulations that can be reversed when the data are aggregated into a single crosstabulation.

Scatter diagram A graphical display of the relationship between two quantitative variables. One variable is shown on the horizontal axis and the other variable is shown on the vertical axis.

Trendline A line that provides an approximation of the relationship between two variables.

Side-by-side bar chart A graphical display for depicting multiple bar charts on the same display.

Stacked bar chart A bar chart in which each bar is broken into rectangular segments of a different color showing the relative frequency of each class in a manner similar to a pie chart.

Data dashboard A set of visual displays that organizes and presents information that is used to monitor the performance of a company or organization in a manner that is easy to read, understand, and interpret.

Key Formulas

Relative Frequency

$$\frac{\text{Frequency of the class}}{n} \qquad \textbf{(2.1)}$$

Approximate Class Width

$$\frac{\text{Largest data value } - \text{ Smallest data value}}{\text{Number of classes}} \qquad \textbf{(2.2)}$$

Supplementary Exercises

44. Approximately 1.5 million high school students take the SAT each year and nearly 80% of the college and universities without open admissions policies use SAT scores in making admission decisions (College Board, March 2009). The current version of the SAT includes three parts: reading comprehension, mathematics, and writing. A perfect combined score for all three parts is 2400. A sample of SAT scores for the combined three-part SAT are as follows:

NewSAT

1665	1525	1355	1645	1780
1275	2135	1280	1060	1585
1650	1560	1150	1485	1990
1590	1880	1420	1755	1375
1475	1680	1440	1260	1730
1490	1560	940	1390	1175

   a. Show a frequency distribution and histogram. Begin with the first class starting at 800 and use a class width of 200.
   b. Comment on the shape of the distribution.
   c. What other observations can be made about the SAT scores based on the tabular and graphical summaries?

45. The Pittsburgh Steelers defeated the Arizona Cardinals 27 to 23 in professional football's 43rd Super Bowl. With this win, its sixth championship, the Pittsburgh Steelers became the team with the most wins in the 43-year history of the event (*Tampa Tribune*, February 2,

SuperBowl

Super Bowl	State	Won By Points	Super Bowl	State	Won By Points	Super Bowl	State	Won By Points
1	CA	25	16	MI	5	31	LA	14
2	FL	19	17	CA	10	32	CA	7
3	FL	9	18	FL	19	33	FL	15
4	LA	16	19	CA	22	34	GA	7
5	FL	3	20	LA	36	35	FL	27
6	FL	21	21	CA	19	36	LA	3
7	CA	7	22	CA	32	37	CA	27
8	TX	17	23	FL	4	38	TX	3
9	LA	10	24	LA	45	39	FL	3
10	FL	4	25	FL	1	40	MI	11
11	CA	18	26	MN	13	41	FL	12
12	LA	17	27	CA	35	42	AZ	3
13	FL	4	28	GA	17	43	FL	4
14	CA	12	29	FL	23			
15	LA	17	30	AZ	10			

2009). The Super Bowl has been played in eight different states: Arizona (AZ), California
(CA), Florida (FL), Georgia (GA), Louisiana (LA), Michigan (MI), Minnesota (MN), and
Texas (TX). Data in the table show the state where the Super Bowls were played and the
point margin of victory for the winning team.

a. Show a frequency distribution and bar chart for the state where the Super Bowl was
    played.
b. What conclusions can you draw from your summary in part (a)? What percentage of
    Super Bowls were played in the states of Florida or California? What percentage of
    Super Bowls were played in northern or cold-weather states?
c. Show a stretched stem-and-leaf display for the point margin of victory for the winning
    team. Show a histogram.
d. What conclusions can you draw from your summary in part (c)? What percentage of
    Super Bowls have been close games with the margin of victory less than 5 points?
    What percentage of Super Bowls have been won by 20 or more points?
e. The closest Super Bowl occurred when the New York Giants beat the Buffalo Bills.
    Where was this game played and what was the winning margin of victory? The biggest
    point margin in Super Bowl history occurred when the San Francisco 49ers beat the
    Denver Broncos. Where was this game played and what was the winning margin of
    victory?

46. Data showing the population by state in millions of people follow (*The World Almanac,*
    2012).

2012Population

State	Population	State	Population	State	Population
Alabama	4.8	Louisiana	4.5	Ohio	11.5
Alaska	0.7	Maine	1.3	Oklahoma	3.8
Arizona	6.4	Maryland	5.8	Oregon	4.3
Arkansas	2.9	Massachusetts	6.5	Pennsylvania	12.7
California	37.3	Michigan	9.9	Rhode Island	1.0
Colorado	5.0	Minnesota	5.3	South Carolina	4.6
Connecticut	3.6	Mississippi	3.0	South Dakota	0.8
Delaware	0.9	Missouri	6.0	Tennessee	6.3
Florida	18.8	Montana	0.9	Texas	25.1
Georgia	9.7	Nebraska	1.8	Utah	2.8
Hawaii	1.4	Nevada	2.7	Vermont	0.6
Idaho	1.6	New Hampshire	1.3	Virginia	8.0
Illinois	12.8	New Jersey	8.8	Washington	6.7
Indiana	6.5	New Mexico	2.0	West Virginia	1.9
Iowa	3.0	New York	19.4	Wisconsin	5.7
Kansas	2.9	North Carolina	9.5	Wyoming	0.6
Kentucky	4.3	North Dakota	0.7		

a. Develop a frequency distribution, a percent frequency distribution, and a histogram.
    Use a class width of 2.5 million.
b. Does there appear to be any skewness in the distribution? Explain.
c. What observations can you make about the population of the 50 states?

47. A startup company's ability to gain funding is a key to success. The funds raised (in
    millions of dollars) by 50 startup companies appear below (*The Wall Street Journal,*
    March 10, 2011).

StartUps

81	61	103	166	168
80	51	130	77	78
69	119	81	60	20
73	50	110	21	60
192	18	54	49	63

91	272	58	54	40
47	24	57	78	78
154	72	38	131	52
48	118	40	49	55
54	112	129	156	31

    a. Construct a stem-and-leaf display.

    b. Comment on the display.

48. Consumer complaints are frequently reported to the Better Business Bureau. In 2011, the industries with the most complaints to the Better Business Bureau were banks, cable and satellite television companies, collection agencies, cellular phone providers, and new car dealerships (*USA Today,* April 16, 2012). The results for a sample of 200 complaints are contained in the file BBB.

    a. Show the frequency and percent frequency of complaints by industry.

    b. Construct a bar chart of the percent frequency distribution.

    c. Which industry had the highest number of complaints?

    d. Comment on the percentage frequency distribution for complaints.

49. Dividend yield is the annual dividend paid by a company expressed as a percentage of the price of the stock (Dividend/Stock Price × 100). The dividend yield for the Dow Jones Industrial Average companies is shown in Table 2.17 (*The Wall Street Journal,* June 8, 2009).

    a. Construct a frequency distribution and percent frequency distribution.

    b. Construct a histogram.

    c. Comment on the shape of the distribution.

    d. What do the tabular and graphical summaries indicate about the dividend yields among the Dow Jones Industrial Average companies?

    e. What company has the highest dividend yield? If the stock for this company currently sells for $14 per share and you purchase 500 shares, how much dividend income will this investment generate in one year?

50. The U.S Census Bureau estimates the characteristics of the U.S. population through a survey the bureau administers every 10 years. Below is a crosstabulation of age versus education level of achievement (U.S. Census Bureau website, March 9, 2013).

TABLE 2.17   DIVIDEND YIELD FOR DOW JONES INDUSTRIAL AVERAGE COMPANIES

Company	Dividend Yield %	Company	Dividend Yield %
3M	3.6	IBM	2.1
Alcoa	1.3	Intel	3.4
American Express	2.9	JPMorgan Chase	0.5
AT&T	6.6	Johnson & Johnson	3.6
Bank of America	0.4	Kraft Foods	4.4
Boeing	3.8	McDonald's	3.4
Caterpillar	4.7	Merck	5.5
Chevron	3.9	Microsoft	2.5
Cisco Systems	0.0	Pfizer	4.2
Coca-Cola	3.3	Procter & Gamble	3.4
DuPont	5.8	Travelers	3.0
ExxonMobil	2.4	United Technologies	2.9
General Electric	9.2	Verizon	6.3
Hewlett-Packard	0.9	Wal-Mart Stores	2.2
Home Depot	3.9	Walt Disney	1.5

Age	Below High School	High School Graduate	Some College No Degree	Associate's Degree	Bachelor's Degree	Advanced Degree	Total
25–34	4766	11,175	7765	3903	9860	3657	41,126
35–44	4732	11,568	6593	4166	8858	4530	40,447
45–54	4616	14,559	7413	4705	8434	4616	44,343
55–64	3681	11,079	6123	3256	6583	4637	35,359
65–74	3563	7418	3290	1383	2955	2326	20,935
75 & older	4344	6639	2472	812	2101	1289	17,657
Total	25,702	62,438	33,656	18,225	38,791	21,055	199,867

    a.   Calculate the row percentages.

    b.   Calculate the column percentages. Compare the percent frequency distributions for a Bachelor's Degree versus an Advanced Degree.

51. Western University has only one women's softball scholarship remaining for the coming year. The final two players that Western is considering are Allison Fealey and Emily Janson. The coaching staff has concluded that the speed and defensive skills are virtually identical for the two players, and that the final decision will be based on which player has the best batting average. Crosstabulations of each player's batting performance in their junior and senior years of high school are as follows:

	Allison Fealey				Emily Janson	
Outcome	Junior	Senior		Outcome	Junior	Senior
Hit	15	75		**Hit**	70	35
No Hit	25	175		**No Hit**	130	85
Total At-Bats	40	250		**Total At Bats**	200	120

A player's batting average is computed by dividing the number of hits a player has by the total number of at-bats. Batting averages are represented as a decimal number with three places after the decimal.

    a.   Calculate the batting average for each player in her junior year. Then calculate the batting average of each player in her senior year. Using this analysis, which player should be awarded the scholarship? Explain.

    b.   Combine or aggregate the data for the junior and senior years into one crosstabulation as follows:

	Player	
Outcome	Fealey	Janson
Hit		
No Hit		
Total At-Bats		

Calculate each player's batting average for the combined two years. Using this analysis, which player should be awarded the scholarship? Explain.

    c.   Are the recommendations you made in parts (a) and (b) consistent? Explain any apparent inconsistencies.

FortuneBest

52. *Fortune* magazine publishes an annual survey of the best companies to work for. The data in the file named FortuneBest shows the rank, company name, the size of the company, and the percentage job growth for full-time employees for the coming year for 98 companies (*Fortune* magazine website, February 25, 2013).

a. Construct a crosstabulation with Job Growth (%) as the row variable and Size as the column variable. Use classes of −10 to −1, 0–9, 10–19 and so on for Growth Rate (%).

b. Show the frequency distribution for Job Growth (%) and the frequency distribution for Size.

c. Using the crosstabulation constructed in part (a), develop a crosstabulation showing column percentages.

d. Using the crosstabulation constructed in part (a), develop a crosstabulation showing row percentages.

e. Comment on the relationship between the percentage job growth for full-time employees and the size of the company.

53. Table 2.18 shows a portion of the data for a sample of 103 private colleges and universities. The complete data set is contained in the file named Colleges. The data include the name of the college or university, the year the institution was founded, the tuition and fees (not including room and board) for the most recent academic year, and the percentage of full-time, first-time bachelor's degree-seeking undergraduate students who obtain their degree in six years or less (*The World Almanac*, 2012)

a. Construct a crosstabulation with Year Founded as the row variable and Tuition & Fees as the column variable. Use classes starting with 1600 and ending with 2000 in increments of 50 for Year Founded. For Tuition & Fees, use classes starting with 1 and ending with 45,000 in increments of 5000.

b. Compute the row percentages for the crosstabulation in part (a).

c. What relationship, if any, do you notice between Year Founded and Tuition & Fees?

54. Refer to the data set in Table 2.18.

a. Construct a crosstabulation with Year Founded as the row variable and % Graduate as the column variable. Use classes starting with 1600 and ending with 2000 in increments of 50 for Year Founded. For % Graduate, use classes starting with 35% and ending with 100% in increments of 5%.

b. Compute the row percentages for your crosstabulation in part (a).

c. Comment on any relationship between the variables.

55. Refer to the data set in Table 2.18.

a. Construct a scatter diagram to show the relationship between Year Founded and Tuition & Fees.

b. Comment on any relationship between the variables.

TABLE 2.18   DATA FOR A SAMPLE OF PRIVATE COLLEGES AND UNIVERSITIES

Colleges

School	Year Founded	Tuition & Fees	% Graduate
American University	1893	$36,697	79.00
Baylor University	1845	$29,754	70.00
Belmont University	1951	$23,680	68.00
.	.	.	.
.	.	.	.
.	.	.	.
Wofford College	1854	$31,710	82.00
Xavier University	1831	$29,970	79.00
Yale University	1701	$38,300	98.00

© Cengage Learning

56. Refer to the data set in Table 2.18.
   a.   Prepare a scatter diagram to show the relationship between Tuition & Fees and % Graduate.
   b.   Comment on any relationship between the variables.

57. Google has changed its strategy with regard to how much and over which media it invests in advertising. The following table shows Google's marketing budget in millions of dollars for 2008 and 2011 (*The Wall Street Journal,* March 27, 2012).

	2008	**2011**
Internet	26.0	123.3
Newspaper, etc.	4.0	20.7
Television	0.0	69.3

   a.   Construct a side-by-side bar chart with year as the variable on the horizontal axis. Comment on any trend in the display.
   b.   Convert the above table to percentage allocation for each year. Construct a stacked bar chart with year as the variable on the horizontal axis.
   c.   Is the display in part (a) or part (b) more insightful? Explain.

58. A zoo has categorized its visitors into three categories: member, school, and general. The member category refers to visitors who pay an annual fee to support the zoo. Members receive certain benefits such as discounts on merchandise and trips planned by the zoo. The school category includes faculty and students from day care and elementary and secondary schools; these visitors generally receive a discounted rate. The general category includes all other visitors. The zoo has been concerned about a recent drop in attendance. To help better understand attendance and membership, a zoo staff member has collected the following data:

	Attendance			
Visitor Category	**2008**	**2009**	**2010**	**2011**
General	153,713	158,704	163,433	169,106
Member	115,523	104,795	98,437	81,217
School	82,885	79,876	81,970	81,290
Total	352,121	343,375	343,840	331,613

Zoo

   a.   Construct a bar chart of total attendance over time. Comment on any trend in the data.
   b.   Construct a side-by-side bar chart showing attendance by visitor category with year as the variable on the horizontal axis.
   c.   Comment on what is happening to zoo attendance based on the charts from parts (a) and (b).

Case Problem 1 Pelican Stores

Pelican Stores, a division of National Clothing, is a chain of women's apparel stores operating throughout the country. The chain recently ran a promotion in which discount coupons were sent to customers of other National Clothing stores. Data collected for a sample of 100 in-store credit card transactions at Pelican Stores during one day while the promotion was running are contained in the file named PelicanStores. Table 2.19 shows a portion of the data set. The Proprietary Card method of payment refers to charges made using a National Clothing charge card. Customers who made a purchase using a discount coupon are referred to as promotional customers and customers who made a purchase but did not use a discount coupon are referred to as regular customers. Because the promotional coupons were not

TABLE 2.19   DATA FOR A SAMPLE OF 100 CREDIT CARD PURCHASES AT PELICAN STORES

PelicanStores

Customer	Type of Customer	Items	Net Sales	Method of Payment	Gender	Marital Status	Age
1	Regular	1	39.50	Discover	Male	Married	32
2	Promotional	1	102.40	Proprietary Card	Female	Married	36
3	Regular	1	22.50	Proprietary Card	Female	Married	32
4	Promotional	5	100.40	Proprietary Card	Female	Married	28
5	Regular	2	54.00	MasterCard	Female	Married	34
.	.	.	.	.	.	.	.
.	.	.	.	.	.	.	.
.	.	.	.	.	.	.	.
96	Regular	1	39.50	MasterCard	Female	Married	44
97	Promotional	9	253.00	Proprietary Card	Female	Married	30
98	Promotional	10	287.59	Proprietary Card	Female	Married	52
99	Promotional	2	47.60	Proprietary Card	Female	Married	30
100	Promotional	1	28.44	Proprietary Card	Female	Married	44

sent to regular Pelican Stores customers, management considers the sales made to people presenting the promotional coupons as sales it would not otherwise make. Of course, Pelican also hopes that the promotional customers will continue to shop at its stores.

Most of the variables shown in Table 2.19 are self-explanatory, but two of the variables require some clarification.

Items   The total number of items purchased
Net Sales   The total amount ($) charged to the credit card

Pelican's management would like to use this sample data to learn about its customer base and to evaluate the promotion involving discount coupons.

Managerial Report

Use the tabular and graphical methods of descriptive statistics to help management develop a customer profile and to evaluate the promotional campaign. At a minimum, your report should include the following:

1. Percent frequency distribution for key variables.
2. A bar chart or pie chart showing the number of customer purchases attributable to the method of payment.
3. A crosstabulation of type of customer (regular or promotional) versus net sales. Comment on any similarities or differences present.
4. A scatter diagram to explore the relationship between net sales and customer age.

Case Problem 2   Motion Picture Industry

The motion picture industry is a competitive business. More than 50 studios produce a total of 300 to 400 new motion pictures each year, and the financial success of each motion picture varies considerably. The opening weekend gross sales ($millions), the total gross sales ($millions), the number of theaters the movie was shown in, and the number of weeks the motion picture was in release are common variables used to measure the success of a motion picture. Data collected for the top 100 motion pictures produced in 2011 are

TABLE 2.20   PERFORMANCE DATA FOR 10 MOTION PICTURES

Motion Picture	Opening Gross Sales ($millions)	Total Gross Sales ($millions)	Number of Theaters	Weeks in Release
Harry Potter and the Deathly Hallows Part 2	169.19	381.01	4375	19
Transformers: Dark of the Moon	97.85	352.39	4088	15
The Twilight Saga: Breaking Dawn Part 1	138.12	281.29	4066	14
The Hangover Part II	85.95	254.46	3675	16
Pirates of the Caribbean: On Stranger Tides	90.15	241.07	4164	19
Fast Five	86.20	209.84	3793	15
Mission: Impossible— Ghost Protocol	12.79	208.55	3555	13
Cars 2	66.14	191.45	4115	25
Sherlock Holmes: A Game of Shadows	39.64	186.59	3703	13
Thor	65.72	181.03	3963	16

WEB file

2011Movies

© Cengage Learning

contained in the file named 2011Movies (Box Office Mojo, March 17, 2012). Table 2.20 shows the data for the first 10 motion pictures in this file.

Managerial Report

Use the tabular and graphical methods of descriptive statistics to learn how these variables contribute to the success of a motion picture. Include the following in your report.

1. Tabular and graphical summaries for each of the four variables along with a discussion of what each summary tells us about the motion picture industry.
2. A scatter diagram to explore the relationship between Total Gross Sales and Opening Weekend Gross Sales. Discuss.
3. A scatter diagram to explore the relationship between Total Gross Sales and Number of Theaters. Discuss.
4. A scatter diagram to explore the relationship between Total Gross Sales and Number of Weeks in Release. Discuss.

Appendix 2.1   Using Minitab for Tabular and Graphical Presentations

Minitab offers extensive capabilities for constructing tabular and graphical summaries of data. In this appendix we show how Minitab can be used to construct several graphical summaries and the tabular summary of a crosstabulation. The graphical methods presented include the dot plot, the histogram, the stem-and-leaf display, and the scatter diagram.

Dot Plot

Audit

We use the audit time data in Table 2.4 to demonstrate. The data are in column C1 of a Minitab worksheet. The following steps will generate a dot plot.

Step 1. Select the **Graph** menu and choose **Dotplot**
Step 2. Select **One Y, Simple** and click **OK**
Step 3. When the Dotplot-One Y, Simple dialog box appears:
  Enter C1 in the **Graph Variables** box
  Click **OK**

Histogram

Audit

We show how to construct a histogram with frequencies on the vertical axis using the audit time data in Table 2.4. The data are in column C1 of a Minitab worksheet. The following steps will generate a histogram for audit times.

Step 1. Select the **Graph** menu
Step 2. Choose **Histogram**
Step 3. When the Histograms dialog box appears:
  Choose **Simple** and click **OK**
Step 4. When the Histogram-Simple dialog box appears:
  Enter C1 in the **Graph Variables** box
  Click **OK**
Step 5. When the Histogram appears:*
  Position the mouse pointer over any one of the bars
  Double-click
Step 6. When the Edit Bars dialog box appears:
  Click the **Binning** tab
  Select **Cutpoint** for Interval Type
  Select **Midpoint/Cutpoint positions** for Interval Definition
  Enter 10:35/5 in the **Midpoint/Cutpoint positions** box
  Click **OK**

Note that Minitab also provides the option of scaling the x-axis so that the numerical values appear at the midpoints of the histogram rectangles. If this option is desired, modify step 6 to include Select **Midpoint** for Interval Type and Enter 12:32/5 in the **Midpoint/ Cutpoint positions** box. These steps provide the same histogram with the midpoints of the histogram rectangles labeled 12, 17, 22, 27, and 32.

Stem-and-Leaf Display

ApTest

We use the aptitude test data in Table 2.8 to demonstrate the construction of a stem-and-leaf display. The data are in column C1 of a Minitab worksheet. The following steps will generate the stretched stem-and-leaf display shown in Section 2.3.

Step 1. Select the **Graph** menu
Step 2. Choose **Stem-and-Leaf**
Step 3. When the Stem-and-Leaf dialog box appears:
  Enter C1 in the **Graph Variables** box
  Click **OK**

---

*Steps 5 and 6 are optional but are shown here to demonstrate user flexibility in displaying the histogram. The entry 10:35/5 in step 6 indicates that 10 is the starting value for the histogram, 35 is the ending value for the histogram, and 5 is the class width.

Scatter Diagram

Stereo

We use the stereo and sound equipment store data in Table 2.14 to demonstrate the construction of a scatter diagram. The weeks are numbered from 1 to 10 in column C1, the data for number of commercials are in column C2, and the data for sales are in column C3 of a Minitab worksheet. The following steps will generate the scatter diagram shown in Figure 2.7.

Step 1. Select the **Graph** menu
Step 2. Choose **Scatterplot**
Step 3. Select **Simple** and click **OK**
Step 4. When the Scatterplot-Simple dialog box appears:
Enter C3 under **Y variables** and C2 under **X variables**
Click **OK**

Crosstabulation

Restaurant

We use the data from Zagat's restaurant review, part of which is shown in Table 2.9, to demonstrate. The restaurants are numbered from 1 to 300 in column C1 of the Minitab worksheet. The quality ratings are in column C2, and the meal prices are in column C3.

Minitab can only create a crosstabulation for qualitative variables and meal price is a quantitative variable. So we need to first code the meal price data by specifying the class to which each meal price belongs. The following steps will code the meal price data to create four classes of meal price in column C4: $10–19, $20–29, $30–39, and $40–49.

Step 1. Select the **Data** menu
Step 2. Choose **Code**
Step 3. Choose **Numeric to Text**
Step 4. When the Code-Numeric to Text dialog box appears:
Enter C3 in the **Code data from columns** box
Enter C4 in the **Store coded data in columns** box
Enter 10:19 in the first **Original values** box and $10–19 in the adjacent **New** box
Enter 20:29 in the second **Original values** box and $20–29 in the adjacent **New** box
Enter 30:39 in the third **Original values** box and $30–39 in the adjacent **New** box
Enter 40:49 in the fourth **Original values** box and $40–49 in the adjacent **New** box
Click **OK**

For each meal price in column C3 the associated meal price category will now appear in column C4. We can now develop a crosstabulation for quality rating and the meal price categories by using the data in columns C2 and C4. The following steps will create a cross-tabulation containing the same information as shown in Table 2.10.

Step 1. Select the **Stat** menu
Step 2. Choose **Tables**
Step 3. Choose **Cross Tabulation and Chi-Square**
Step 4. When the Cross Tabulation and Chi-Square dialog box appears:
Enter C2 in the **For rows** box and C4 in the **For columns** box
Select **Counts** under Display
Click **OK**

Appendix 2.2 Using Excel for Tabular and Graphical Presentations

Excel offers extensive capabilities for constructing tabular and graphical summaries of data. In this appendix, we show how Excel can be used to construct a frequency distribution, relative frequency distribution, percent frequency distribution, bar chart, pie chart, histogram, scatter diagram, crosstabulation, side-by-side bar chart, and stacked bar chart.

Using Excel to Construct a Frequency Distribution, a Relative Frequency Distribution, and a Percent Frequency Distribution

SoftDrink

We can use Excel's Recommended PivotTables tool to construct a frequency distribution for the sample of 50 soft drink purchases. Open the file named SoftDrink. The data are in cell A2:A51 and a label is in cell A1.

The following steps describe how to use Excel's Recommended PivotTables tool to construct a frequency distribution for the sample of 50 soft drink purchases.

Step 1. Select any cell in the data set (cells A1:A51)
Step 2. Click **Insert** on the Ribbon
Step 3. In the **Tables Group** choose **Recommended PivotTables**; a preview showing the frequency distribution appears
Step 4. Click **OK**; the frequency distribution will appear in a new worksheet

The worksheet in Figure 2.16 shows the frequency distribution for the 50 soft drink purchases created using these steps. Also shown is the PivotTable Fields dialog box, a key component of every PivotTable report. We will discuss the use of the PivotTable Fields dialog box later in this appendix.

Editing options You can easily change the column headings in the frequency distribution output. For instance, to change the current heading in cell A3 (Row Labels) to "Soft Drink" click in cell A3 and type "Soft Drink"; to change the current heading in cell B3 (Count of Brand Purchases) to "Frequency," click in cell B3 and type "Frequency"; and to change the current heading in A9 (Grand Total) to "Total," click in cell A9 and type "Total." The foreground and background worksheets shown in Figure 2.17 contain the revised headings; in addition, the label "Relative Frequency" was entered into cell C3 and the label "Percent Frequency" was added into cell D3 to illustrate how to compute relative and percent frequency distributions.

Enter functions and formulas Refer to Figure 2.17 as we describe how to create the relative and percent frequency distributions for the soft drink purchases. The formula worksheet is in the background and the value worksheet is in the foreground. To compute the relative frequency for Coca-Cola using equation (2.1), we entered the formula =B4/$B$9 into cell C4; the result, 0.38, is the relative frequency for Coca-Cola. Copying cell C4 to cells C5:C8 computes the relative frequencies for each of the other soft drinks. To compute the percent frequency for Coca-Cola, we entered the formula =C4*100 into cell D4. The result, 38, indicates that 38% of the soft drink purchases were Coca-Cola. Copying cell D4 to cells D5:D8 computes the percent frequencies for each of the other soft drinks. To compute the total of the relative frequencies, we entered the formula =SUM(C4:C8) into cell C9. And to compute the total of the percent frequencies we copied cell C9 to cell C10.

FIGURE 2.16   FREQUENCY DISTRIBUTION OF SOFT DRINK PURCHASES
CONSTRUCTED USING EXCEL'S RECOMMENDED PIVOTTABLES TOOL

	A	B	C	D
1				
2				
3	**Row Labels** ▾	**Count of Brand Purchased**		
4	Coca-Cola	19		
5	Diet Coke	8		
6	Dr. Pepper	5		
7	Pepsi	13		
8	Sprite	5		
9	**Grand Total**	**50**		
10				

PivotTable Fields   ▾ ✕

Choose fields to add to report: ⚙ ▾

☑ **Brand Purchased**

MORE TABLES...

Drag fields between areas below:

▼ FILTERS   ▥ COLUMNS

≡ ROWS   Σ VALUES

Brand Purchased   ▾   Count of Brand Purc... ▾

☐ Defer Layout Update   UPDATE

© Cengage Learning

Using Excel to Construct a Bar Chart and a Pie Chart

SoftDrink

We can use Excel's Recommended Charts tool to construct a bar chart and a pie chart for the sample of 50 soft drink purchases. Open the file named SoftDrink. The data are in cell A2:A51 and a label is in cell A1.

The following steps describe how to use Excel's Recommended Charts tool to construct a bar chart for the sample of 50 soft drink purchases.

FIGURE 2.17   RELATIVE FREQUENCY AND PERCENT FREQUENCY DISTRIBUTIONS OF SOFT DRINK PURCHASES CONSTRUCTED USING EXCEL FUNCTIONS

	A	B	C	D	E
1					
2					
3	Soft Drink	Frequency	Relative Frequency	Percent Frequency	
4	Coca-Cola	19	=B4/$B$9	=C4*100	
5	Diet Coke	8	=B5/$B$9	=C5*100	
6	Dr. Pepper	5	=B6/$B$9	=C6*100	
7	Pepsi	13	=B7/$B$9	=C7*100	
8	Sprite	5	=B8/$B$9	=C8*100	
9	Total	50	=SUM(C4:C8)	=SUM(D4:D8)	
10					

	A	B	C	D	E
1					
2					
3	Soft Drink	Frequency	Relative Frequency	Percent Frequency	
4	Coca-Cola	19	0.38	38	
5	Diet Coke	8	0.16	16	
6	Dr. Pepper	5	0.1	10	
7	Pepsi	13	0.26	26	
8	Sprite	5	0.1	10	
9	Total	50	1	100	
10					

PivotTable Fields   ▾ ✕

Choose fields to add to report: ⚙ ▾

☑ **Brand Purchased**

MORE TABLES...

Drag fields between areas below:

▼ FILTERS   ▮ COLUMNS

≡ ROWS   Σ VALUES

Brand Purchased   ▾   Frequency   ▾

☐ Defer Layout Update   UPDATE

© Cengage Learning

Step 1. Select any cell in the data set (cells A1:A51)
Step 2. Click **Insert** on the Ribbon
Step 3. In the **Charts Group** choose **Recommended Charts**; a preview showing the chart appears
Step 4. Click **OK**; the bar chart will appear in a new worksheet

Excel refers to the bar chart in Figure 2.18 as a Clustered Column chart.

The worksheet in Figure 2.18 shows the bar chart for the 50 soft drink purchases created using these steps. Also shown are the frequency distribution and PivotTable Fields dialog box that were created by Excel in order to construct the bar chart. Thus, using Excel's

FIGURE 2.18 BAR CHART OF SOFT DRINK PURCHASES CONSTRUCTED USING EXCEL'S RECOMMENDED CHARTS TOOL

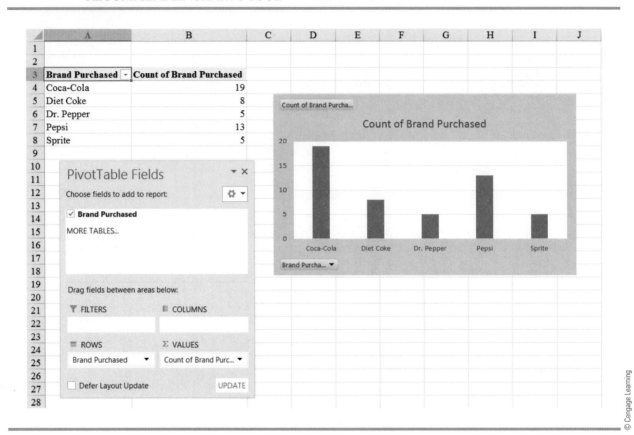

Recommended Charts tool you can construct a bar chart and a frequency distribution at the same time.

Editing options You can easily edit the bar chart to display a different chart title and add axis titles. For instance, suppose you would like to use "Bar Chart of Soft Drink Purchases" as the chart title and insert "Soft Drink" for the horizontal axis title and "Frequency" for the vertical axis title.

Step 1. Click the **Chart Title** and replace it with **Bar Chart of Soft Drink Purchases**
Step 2. Click the **Chart Elements** button + (located next to the top right corner of the chart)
Step 3. When the list of chart elements appears:
 Click **Axis Titles** (creates placeholders for the axis titles)
Step 4. Click the **Horizontal (Category) Axis Title** and replace it with **Soft Drink**
Step 5. Click the **Vertical (Value) Axis Title** and replace it with **Frequency**

The edited bar chart is shown in Figure 2.19.

Creating a pie chart To display a pie chart, select the bar chart (by clicking anywhere in the chart) to display three tabs (**Analyze, Design**, and **Format**) located on the Ribbon under the heading **PivotChart Tools**. Click the **Design Tab** and choose the **Change Chart Type** option to display the Change Chart Type dialog box. Click the **Pie** option and then **OK** to display a pie chart of the soft drink purchases.

FIGURE 2.19   EDITED BAR CHART OF SOFT DRINK PURCHASES CONSTRUCTED USING EXCEL'S RECOMMENDED CHARTS TOOL

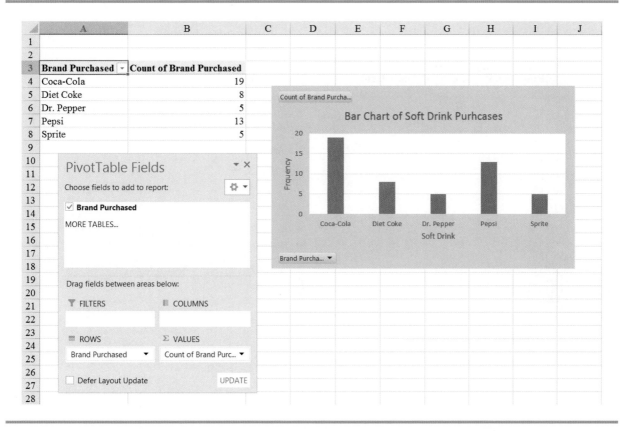

Using Excel to Construct a Frequency Distribution

Audit

Previously we illustrated how to use Excel's Recommended PivotTables tool to construct a frequency distribution. We can also use Excel's PivotTable tool directly to construct a frequency distribution. We illustrate this here for the audit time data. Open the file named Audit. The data are in cells A2:A21 and a label is in cell A1.

The following steps describe how to use Excel's PivotTable tool to construct a frequency distribution for the audit time data. When using Excel's PivotTable tool, each column of data is referred to as a field. Thus, for the audit time example, the data appearing in cells A2:A21 and the label in cell A1 are referred to as the Audit Time field.

Step 1. Select any cell in the data set (cells A1:A21)

Step 2. Click **Insert** on the Ribbon

Step 3. In the **Tables Group** choose **PivotTable**

Step 4. When the **Create PivotTable** dialog box appears:

Click **OK**; a PivotTable and PivotTable Fields dialog box will appear in a new worksheet

Step 5. In the **PivotTable Fields** dialog box:

Drag the **Audit Time** field to the **Rows** area

Drag the **Audit Time** field to the **Values** area

Step 6. Click on **Sum of Audit Time** in the **Values** area

FIGURE 2.20   PIVOTTABLE FIELD LIST AND INITIAL PIVOTTABLE USED TO CONSTRUCT A FREQUENCY DISTRIBUTION FOR THE AUDIT TIME DATA

	A	B	C	D	E	F	G	H
1								
2								
3	**Row Labels** ▾	**Count of Audit Time**						
4	12	1						
5	13	1						
6	14	2						
7	15	2						
8	16	1						
9	17	1						
10	18	3						
11	19	1						
12	20	1						
13	21	1						
14	22	2						
15	23	1						
16	27	1						
17	28	1						
18	33	1						
19	**Grand Total**	**20**						
20								
21								
22								
23								

PivotTable Fields   ▾ ✕

Choose fields to add to report: ⚙ ▾

☑ **Audit Time**

MORE TABLES...

Drag fields between areas below:

▼ FILTERS   ▥ COLUMNS

≡ ROWS   Σ VALUES
Audit Time   ▾   Count of Audit Time   ▾

☐ Defer Layout Update   UPDATE

Step 7. Click **Value Field Settings** from the list of options that appears

Step 8. When the Value Field Settings dialog box appears:
Under **Summarize value field by**, choose **Count**
Click **OK**

Figure 2.20 shows the resulting PivotTable Fields list and the corresponding PivotTable. To construct the frequency distribution shown in Table 2.5, we must group the rows containing the audit times. The resulting steps accomplish this.

Step 1. Right-click cell A4 in the PivotTable or any other cell containing an audit time

Step 2. Choose **Group** from the list of options that appears

Step 3. When the Grouping dialog box appears:
Enter 10 in the **Starting at** box
Enter 34 in the **Ending at** box
Enter 5 in the **By** box
Click **OK**

Figure 2.21 shows the completed PivotTable Fields list and the corresponding PivotTable. We see that with the exception of the column headings, the PivotTable provides the same information as the frequency distribution shown in Table 2.5.

Editing options   You can easily change the labels in the PivotTable to match the labels in Table 2.5. For instance, to change the current heading in cell A3 (Row Labels) to "Audit

FIGURE 2.21   FREQUENCY DISTRIBUTION FOR THE AUDIT TIME DATA CONSTRUCTED USING EXCEL'S PIVOTTABLE TOOL

The same Excel procedures we followed in the first section of this appendix can now be used to develop relative and percent frequency distributions, if desired.

Time (days)," click in cell A3 and type "Audit Time (days)"; to change the current heading in cell B3 (Count of Audit Time) to "Frequency," click in cell B3 and type "Frequency"; and to change the current heading in A9 (Grand Total) to "Total," click in cell A9 and type "Total."

Using Excel's Recommended Charts Tool to Construct a Histogram

In Figure 2.21 we showed the results of using Excel's PivotTable tool to construct a frequency distribution for the audit time data. We will use these results to illustrate how Excel's Recommended Charts tool can be used to construct a histogram for depicting quantitative data summarized in a frequency distribution. Refer to Figure 2.21 as we describe the steps involved.

The following steps describe how to use Excel's Recommended Charts tool to construct a histogram for the audit time data.

Step 1. Select any cell in the PivotTable report (cells A3:B9 in Figure 2.21)
Step 2. Click **Insert** on the Ribbon

Step 3. In the **Charts Group** choose **Recommended Charts**; a preview showing the chart appears

Step 4. Click **OK**

Excel refers to the bar chart in Figure 2.22 as a Clustered Column chart.

The worksheet in Figure 2.22 shows the chart for the audit time data created using these steps. With the exception of the gaps separating the bars, this resembles the histogram for the audit time data shown in Figure 2.5. We can easily edit this chart to remove the gaps between the bars and enter more descriptive axis labels and chart heading.

Editing options In addition to removing the gaps between the bars, suppose you would like to use "Histogram for Audit Time Data" as the chart title and insert "Audit Time (days)" for the horizontal axis title and "Frequency" for the vertical axis title.

Step 1. Right-click any bar in the chart and choose **Format Data Series** from the list of options that appear

Step 2. When the Format Data Series dialog box appears:

     Go to the **Series Options** section

     Set the **Gap Width** to 0

     Click the **Close** button ✕ at the top right of the dialog box

Step 3. Click the **Chart Title** and replace it with **Histogram for Audit Time Data**

Step 4. Click the **Chart Elements** button ➕ (located next to the top right corner of the chart)

FIGURE 2.22   INITIAL CHART USED TO CONSTRUCT A HISTOGRAM FOR THE AUDIT TIME DATA

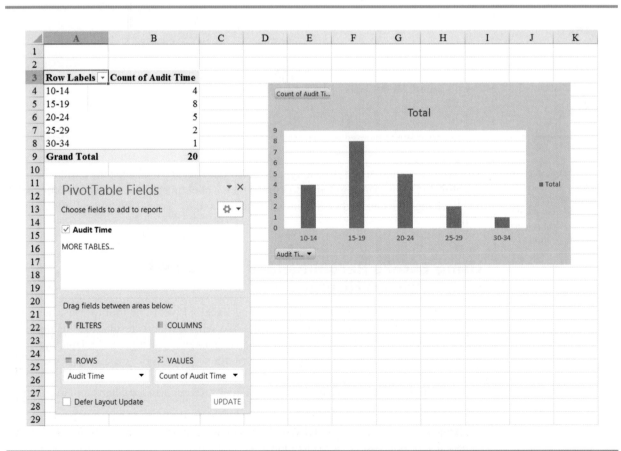

FIGURE 2.23   HISTOGRAM FOR THE AUDIT TIME DATA CREATED USING EXCEL'S RECOMMENDED CHARTS TOOL

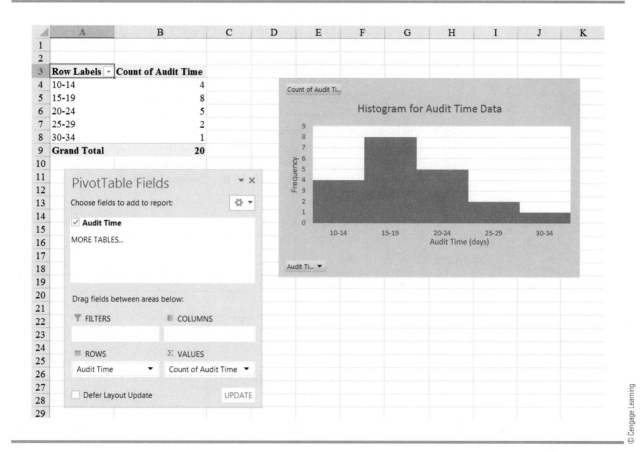

Step 5. When the list of chart elements appears:
Click **Axis Titles** (creates placeholders for the axis titles)
Click **Legends** to remove the check in the Legends box
Step 6. Click the **Horizontal (Category) Axis Title** and replace it with **Audit Time (days)**
Step 7. Click the **Vertical (Value) Axis Title** and replace it with **Frequency**

The edited histogram for the audit time is shown in Figure 2.23.

Using Excel's PivotTable Tool to Construct a Crosstabulation

Excel's PivotTable tool can be used to summarize the data for two or more variables simultaneously. We will illustrate the use of Excel's PivotTable tool by showing how to develop a crosstabulation of quality ratings and meal prices for the sample of 300 restaurants located in the Los Angeles area. Open the webfile Restaurant. The data are in cells B2:C301 and labels are in column A and cells B1:C1.

Each of the three columns in the Restaurant data set labeled, Restaurant, Quality Rating, and Meal Price ($), is considered a field by Excel. Fields may be chosen to represent rows, columns, or values in the PivotTable. The following steps describe how to use Excel's PivotTable tool to construct a crosstabulation of quality ratings and meal prices.

Step 1. Select cell A1 or any cell in the data set
Step 2. Click **Insert** on the Ribbon
Step 3. In the **Tables Group** choose **PivotTable**
Step 4. When the Create PivotTable dialog box appears:
　　　　Click **OK** and a PivotTable and PivotTable Fields dialog box
　　　　　　will appear in a new worksheet
Step 5. In the **PivotTable Fields** dialog box:
　　　　Drag the **Quality Rating** field to the **Rows** area
　　　　Drag the **Meal Price** field to the **Columns** area
　　　　Drag the **Restaurant** field to the **Values** area
Step 6. Click on **Sum of Restaurant** in the **Values** area
Step 7. Click **Value Field Settings** from the list of options that appears
Step 8. When the Value Field Settings dialog box appears:
　　　　Under **Summarize value field by**, choose **Count**
　　　　Click **OK**

Figure 2.24 shows the PivotTable Fields list and the corresponding PivotTable created following the above steps. For readability, columns H:AC have been hidden.

Editing options   To complete the PivotTable we need to group the rows containing the meal prices and place the rows for quality rating in the proper order. The following steps accomplish this.

Step 1. Right-click cell B4 in the PivotTable or any other cell containing meal prices
Step 2. Choose **Group** from the list of options that appears

FIGURE 2.24   INITIAL PIVOTTABLE FIELDS DIALOG BOX AND PIVOTTABLE FOR
　　　　　　　THE RESTAURANT DATA

FIGURE 2.25   FINAL PIVOTTABLE FOR THE RESTAURANT DATA

	A	B	C	D	E	F	G
1							
2							
3	**Count of Restaurant**	**Column Labels** ▾					
4	**Row Labels** ▾	**10-19**	**20-29**	**30-39**	**40-49**	**Grand Total**	
5	Good		42	40	2		84
6	Very Good		34	64	46	6	150
7	Excellent		2	14	28	22	66
8	**Grand Total**		78	118	76	28	300
9							

PivotTable Fields   ▾ ✕

Choose fields to add to report: ⚙ ▾

☑ **Restaurant**
☑ **Quality Rating**
☑ **Meal Price ($)**

MORE TABLES...

Drag fields between areas below:

▼ FILTERS   ▥ COLUMNS

                             Meal Price ($)   ▾

≡ ROWS   Σ VALUES

Quality Rating   ▾   Count of Restaurant ▾

☐ Defer Layout Update   UPDATE

© Cengage Learning

Step 3. When the Grouping dialog box appears:
Enter 10 in the **Starting at** box
Enter 49 in the **Ending at** box
Enter 10 in the **By** box
Click **OK**
Step 4. Right click on **Excellent** in cell A5
Step 5. Choose **Move** and click **Move "Excellent" to End**

The final PivotTable is shown in Figure 2.25. Note that it provides the same information as the crosstabulation shown in Table 2.10.

Using Excel's Charts Tool to Construct a Scatter Diagram and a Trendline

WEB file

Stereo

We can use Excel's Charts tool to construct a scatter diagram and a trendline for the stereo and sound equipment store data. Open the file named Stereo. The data are in cells B2:C11 and the labels are in column A and cells B1:C1.

The following steps describe how to use Excel's Charts tool to construct a scatter diagram from the data in the worksheet.

Step 1. Select cells B1:C11
Step 2. Click the **Insert** tab on the Ribbon
Step 3. In the **Charts Group**, click **Insert Scatter (X,Y)** or **Bubble Chart** ⣿ ▾

FIGURE 2.26   INITIAL SCATTER DIAGRAM FOR THE STEREO AND SOUND EQUIPMENT STORE USING EXCEL'S RECOMMENDED CHARTS TOOL

Step 4. When the list of scatter diagram subtypes appears:
   Click **Scatter** (the chart in the upper left corner)

The worksheet in Figure 2.26 shows the scatter diagram produced using these steps.

Editing options You can easily edit the scatter diagram to display a different chart title, add axis titles, and display the trendline. For instance, suppose you would like to use "Scatter Diagram for the Stereo and Sound Equipment Store" as the chart title and insert "Number of Commercials" for the horizontal axis title and "Sales ($1000s)" for the vertical axis title.

Step 1. Click the **Chart Title** and replace it with **Scatter Diagram for the Stereo and Sound Equipment Store**

Step 2. Click the **Chart Elements** button ⊞ (located next to the top right corner of the chart)

Step 3. When the list of chart elements appears:
   Click **Axis Titles** (creates placeholders for the axis titles)
   Click **Gridlines** (to deselect the Gridlines option)
   Click **Trendline**

Step 4. Click the **Horizontal (Value) Axis Title** and replace it with **Number of Commercials**

Step 5. Click the **Vertical (Value) Axis Title** and replace it with **Sales ($1000s)**

Step 6. To change the trendline from a dashed line to a solid line, right-click on the trendline and select the **Format Trendline** option

Step 7. When the Format Trendline dialog box appears:
   Select the **Fill & Line** option ⬧
   In the **Dash type** box, select **Solid**
   Close the Format Trendline dialog box

The edited scatter diagram and trendline are shown in Figure 2.27.

FIGURE 2.27   EDITED SCATTER DIAGRAM AND TRENDLINE FOR THE STEREO AND SOUND
EQUIPMENT STORE USING EXCEL'S RECOMMENDED CHARTS TOOL

Using Excel's Recommended Charts Tool to Construct Side-by-Side and Stacked Bar Charts

In Figure 2.25 we showed the results of using Excel's PivotTable tool to construct a frequency distribution for the sample of 300 restaurants in the Los Angeles area. We will use these results to illustrate how Excel's Recommended Charts tool can be used to construct side-by-side and stacked bar charts for the restaurant data using the Pivot-Table output.

The following steps describe how to use Excel's Recommended Charts tool to construct a side-by-side bar chart for the restaurant data using the PivotTable tool output shown in Figure 2.25.

Step 1. Select any cell in the PivotTable report (cells A3:F8 in Figure 2.25)
Step 2. Click **Insert** on the Ribbon
Step 3. In the **Charts Group** choose **Recommended Charts**; a preview showing a bar chart with quality rating on the horizontal axis appears
Step 4. Click **OK**
Step 5. Click **Design** on the Ribbon (located below the PivotCharts Tools heading)
Step 6. In the **Data Group** choose **Switch Row/Column**; a bar chart with meal price on the horizontal axis appears

Excel refers to the bar chart in Figure 2.28 as a Clustered Column chart.

The worksheet in Figure 2.28 shows the side-by-side chart for the restaurant data created using these steps.

Editing options   We can easily edit the side-by-side bar chart to enter a chart heading and axis labels. Suppose you would like to use "Side-by-Side Bar Chart" as the chart title, insert "Meal Price ($)" for the horizontal axis title, and insert "Frequency" for the vertical axis title.

FIGURE 2.28   SIDE-BY-SIDE CHART FOR THE RESTAURANT DATA CONSTRUCTED USING EXCEL'S RECOMMENDED CHARTS TOOL

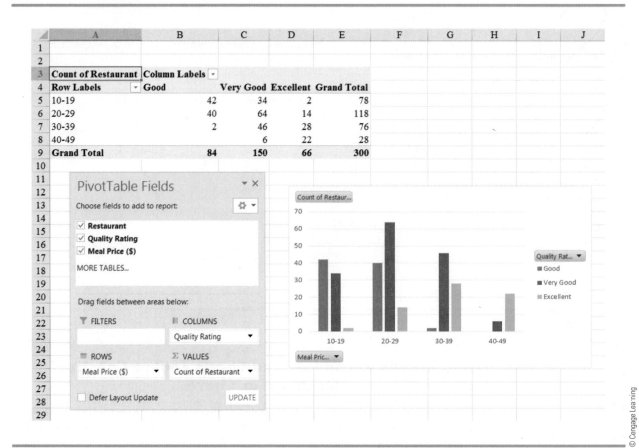

© Cengage Learning

Step 1. Click the **Chart Elements** button ⊞ (located next to the top right corner of the chart)

Step 2. When the list of chart elements appears:
       Click **Chart Title** (creates placeholder for the chart title)
       Click **Axis Titles** (creates placeholders for the axis titles)

Step 3. Click the **Chart Title** and replace it with **Side-by-Side Bar Chart**

Step 4. Click the **Horizontal (Category) Axis Title** and replace it with **Meal Price ($)**

Step 5. Click the **Vertical (Value) Axis Title** and replace it with **Frequency**

The edited side-by-side chart is shown in Figure 2.29.

You can easily change the side-by-side bar chart to a stacked bar chart using the following steps.

Step 1. Click **Design** on the Ribbon

Step 2. In the **Type Group** click **Change Chart Type**

Step 3. When the Change Chart Type dialog box appears:
       Select the **Stacked Columns** option
       Click **OK**

Once you have created a side-by-side bar chart or a stacked bar chart, you can easily switch back and forth between the two chart types by reapplying steps 7 and 8.

FIGURE 2.29   EDITED SIDE-BY-SIDE CHART FOR THE RESTAURANT DATA CONSTRUCTED USING EXCEL'S RECOMMENDED CHARTS TOOL

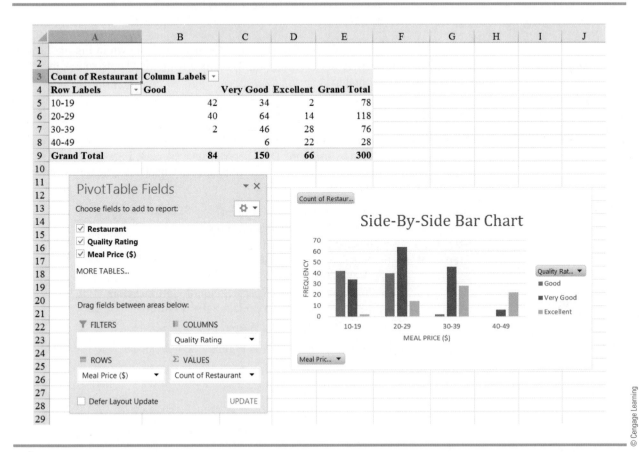

Appendix 2.3   Using StatTools for Tabular and Graphical Presentations

In this appendix we show how StatTools can be used to construct a histogram and a scatter diagram.

Histogram

We use the audit time data in Table 2.4 to illustrate. Begin by using the Data Set Manager to create a StatTools data set for these data using the procedure described in the appendix in Chapter 1. The following steps will generate a histogram.

WEB file

Audit

Step 1. Click the **StatTools** tab on the Ribbon
Step 2. In the **Analyses Group,** click **Summary Graphs**
Step 3. Choose the **Histogram** option
Step 4. When the StatTools - Histogram dialog box appears:
　　　　In the **Variables** section, select **Audit Time**
　　　　In the **Options** section,
　　　　　　Enter 5 in the **Number of Bins** box
　　　　　　Enter 9.5 in the **Histogram Minimum** box

Enter 34.5 in the **Histogram Maximum** box
Choose **Categorical** in the **X-Axis** box
Choose **Frequency** in the **Y-Axis** box
Click **OK**

A histogram for the audit time data similar to the histogram shown in Figure 2.5 will appear. The only difference is the histogram developed using StatTools shows the class midpoints on the horizontal axis.

Scatter Diagram

Stereo

We use the stereo and sound equipment data in Table 2.14 to demonstrate the construction of a scatter diagram. Begin by using the Data Set Manager to create a StatTools data set for these data using the procedure described in the appendix in Chapter 1. The following steps will generate a scatter diagram.

Step 1. Click the **StatTools** tab on the Ribbon
Step 2. In the **Analyses Group,** click **Summary Graphs**
Step 3. Choose the **Scatterplot** option
Step 4. When the StatTools - Scatterplot dialog box appears:
In the **Variables** section,
In the column labeled **X**, select **No. of Commercials**
In the column labeled **Y**, select **Sales Volume**
Click **OK**

A scatter diagram similar to the one shown in Figure 2.26 will appear.

CHAPTER 3

Descriptive Statistics: Numerical Measures

SMALL FRY DESIGN*
SANTA ANA, CALIFORNIA

Founded in 1997, Small Fry Design is a toy and accessory company that designs and imports products for infants. The company's product line includes teddy bears, mobiles, musical toys, rattles, and security blankets and features high-quality soft toy designs with an emphasis on color, texture, and sound. The products are designed in the United States and manufactured in China.

Small Fry Design uses independent representatives to sell the products to infant furnishing retailers, children's accessory and apparel stores, gift shops, upscale department stores, and major catalog companies. Currently, Small Fry Design products are distributed in more than 1000 retail outlets throughout the United States.

Cash flow management is one of the most critical activities in the day-to-day operation of this company. Ensuring sufficient incoming cash to meet both current and ongoing debt obligations can mean the difference between business success and failure. A critical factor in cash flow management is the analysis and control of accounts receivable. By measuring the average age and dollar value of outstanding invoices, management can predict cash availability and monitor changes in the status of accounts receivable. The company set the following goals: The average age for outstanding invoices should not exceed 45 days, and the dollar value of invoices more than 60 days old should not exceed 5% of the dollar value of all accounts receivable.

In a recent summary of accounts receivable status, the following descriptive statistics were provided for the age of outstanding invoices:

Mean	40 days
Median	35 days
Mode	31 days

*The authors are indebted to John A. McCarthy, President of Small Fry Design, for providing this Statistics in Practice.

Small Fry Design uses descriptive statistics to monitor its accounts receivable and incoming cash flow. © Robert Dant/Alamy

Interpretation of these statistics shows that the mean or average age of an invoice is 40 days. The median shows that half of the invoices remain outstanding 35 days or more. The mode of 31 days, the most frequent invoice age, indicates that the most common length of time an invoice is outstanding is 31 days. The statistical summary also showed that only 3% of the dollar value of all accounts receivable was more than 60 days old. Based on the statistical information, management was satisfied that accounts receivable and incoming cash flow were under control.

In this chapter, you will learn how to compute and interpret some of the statistical measures used by Small Fry Design. In addition to the mean, median, and mode, you will learn about other descriptive statistics such as the range, variance, standard deviation, percentiles, and correlation. These numerical measures will assist in the understanding and interpretation of data.

In Chapter 2 we discussed tabular and graphical presentations used to summarize data. In this chapter, we present several numerical measures that provide additional alternatives for summarizing data.

We start by developing numerical summary measures for data sets consisting of a single variable. When a data set contains more than one variable, the same numerical measures can be computed separately for each variable. However, in the two-variable case, we will also develop measures of the relationship between the variables.

Numerical measures of location, dispersion, shape, and association are introduced. If the measures are computed for data from a sample, they are called **sample statistics**. If the measures are computed for data from a population, they are called **population parameters**. In statistical inference, a sample statistic is referred to as the **point estimator** of the corresponding population parameter. In Chapter 7 we will discuss in more detail the process of point estimation.

In the three chapter appendixes, we show how Minitab, Excel, and StatTools can be used to compute the numerical measures described in the chapter.

3.1   Measures of Location

Mean

The mean is sometimes referred to as the arithmetic mean.

Perhaps the most important measure of location is the **mean**, or average value, for a variable. The mean provides a measure of central location for the data. If the data are for a sample, the mean is denoted by $\bar{x}$; if the data are for a population, the mean is denoted by the Greek letter μ.

In statistical formulas, it is customary to denote the value of variable x for the first observation by x_1, the value of variable x for the second observation by x_2, and so on. In general, the value of variable x for the ith observation is denoted by x_i. For a sample with n observations, the formula for the sample mean is as follows.

The sample mean $\bar{x}$ is a sample statistic.

SAMPLE MEAN

$$\bar{x} = \frac{\sum x_i}{n} \tag{3.1}$$

In the preceding formula, the numerator is the sum of the values of the n observations. That is,

$$\sum x_i = x_1 + x_2 + \cdots + x_n$$

The Greek letter $\sum$ is the summation sign.

To illustrate the computation of a sample mean, let us consider the following class size data for a sample of five college classes.

$$46 \quad 54 \quad 42 \quad 46 \quad 32$$

We use the notation x_1, x_2, x_3, x_4, x_5 to represent the number of students in each of the five classes.

$$x_1 = 46 \qquad x_2 = 54 \qquad x_3 = 42 \qquad x_4 = 46 \qquad x_5 = 32$$

Hence, to compute the sample mean, we can write

$$\bar{x} = \frac{\sum x_i}{n} = \frac{x_1 + x_2 + x_3 + x_4 + x_5}{5} = \frac{46 + 54 + 42 + 46 + 32}{5} = 44$$

The sample mean class size is 44 students.

To provide a visual perspective of the mean and to show how it can be influenced by extreme values, consider the dot plot for the class size data shown in Figure 3.1. Treating the horizontal axis used to create the dot plot as a long narrow board in which each of the

FIGURE 3.1   THE MEAN AS THE CENTER OF BALANCE FOR THE DOT PLOT OF THE
CLASSROOM SIZE DATA

dots has the same fixed weight, the mean is the point at which we would place a fulcrum or
pivot point under the board in order to balance the dot plot. This is the same principle by
which a see-saw on a playground works, the only difference being that the see-saw is
pivoted in the middle so that as one end goes up, the other end goes down. In the dot plot
we are locating the pivot point based upon the location of the dots. Now consider what happens to the balance if we increase the largest value from 54 to 114. We will have to move
the fulcrum under the new dot plot in a positive direction in order to reestablish balance.
To determine how far we would have to shift the fulcrum, we simply compute the sample
mean for the revised class size data.

$$\bar{x} = \frac{\Sigma x_i}{n} = \frac{x_1 + x_2 + x_3 + x_4 + x_5}{5} = \frac{46 + 114 + 42 + 46 + 32}{5} = \frac{280}{5} = 56$$

Thus, the mean for the revised class size data is 56, an increase of 12 students. In other
words, we have to shift the balance point 12 units to the right to establish balance under the
new dot plot.

    Another illustration of the computation of a sample mean is given in the following situ-
ation. Suppose that a college placement office sent a questionnaire to a sample of business
school graduates requesting information on monthly starting salaries. Table 3.1 shows the
collected data. The mean monthly starting salary for the sample of 12 business college
graduates is computed as

$$\bar{x} = \frac{\Sigma x_i}{n} = \frac{x_1 + x_2 + \cdots + x_{12}}{12}$$

$$= \frac{3850 + 3950 + \cdots + 3880}{12}$$

$$= \frac{47,280}{12} = 3940$$

TABLE 3.1   MONTHLY STARTING SALARIES FOR A SAMPLE OF 12 BUSINESS SCHOOL
GRADUATES

Graduate	Monthly Starting Salary ($)	Graduate	Monthly Starting Salary ($)
1	3850	7	3890
2	3950	8	4130
3	4050	9	3940
4	3880	10	4325
5	3755	11	3920
6	3710	12	3880

WEB file

2012StartSalary

Equation (3.1) shows how the mean is computed for a sample with n observations. The formula for computing the mean of a population remains the same, but we use different notation to indicate that we are working with the entire population. The number of observations in a population is denoted by N and the symbol for a population mean is μ.

The sample mean $\bar{x}$ is a point estimator of the population mean μ.

POPULATION MEAN

$$\mu = \frac{\sum x_i}{N}$$

(3.2)

Weighted Mean

In the formulas for the sample mean and population mean, each x_i is given equal importance or weight. For instance, the formula for the sample mean can be written as follows:

$$\bar{x} = \frac{\sum x_i}{n} = \frac{1}{n}\left(\sum x_i\right) = \frac{1}{n}(x_1 + x_2 + \cdots + x_n) = \frac{1}{n}(x_1) + \frac{1}{n}(x_2) + \cdots + \frac{1}{n}(x_n)$$

This shows that each observation in the sample is given a weight of $1/n$. Although this practice is most common, in some instances the mean is computed by giving each observation a weight that reflects its relative importance. A mean computed in this manner is referred to as a **weighted mean**. The weighted mean is computed as follows.

WEIGHTED MEAN

$$\bar{x} = \frac{\sum w_i x_i}{\sum w_i}$$

(3.3)

where

$$w_i = \text{weight for observation } i$$

When the data are from a sample, equation (3.3) provides the weighted sample mean. If the data are from a population, μ replaces $\bar{x}$ and equation (3.3) provides the weighted population mean.

As an example of the need for a weighted mean, consider the following sample of five purchases of a raw material over the past three months.

Purchase	Cost per Pound ($)	Number of Pounds
1	3.00	1200
2	3.40	500
3	2.80	2750
4	2.90	1000
5	3.25	800

Note that the cost per pound varies from $2.80 to $3.40, and the quantity purchased varies from 500 to 2750 pounds. Suppose that a manager wanted to know the mean cost per pound of the raw material. Because the quantities ordered vary, we must use the formula for a weighted mean. The five cost-per-pound data values are $x_1 = 3.00$, $x_2 = 3.40$, $x_3 = 2.80$, $x_4 = 2.90$, and $x_5 = 3.25$. The weighted mean cost per pound is found by weighting each cost by its corresponding quantity. For this example, the weights are $w_1 = 1200$, $w_2 = 500$, $w_3 = 2750$, $w_4 = 1000$, and $w_5 = 800$. Based on equation (3.3), the weighted mean is calculated as follows:

$$\bar{x} = \frac{1200(3.00) + 500(3.40) + 2750(2.80) + 1000(2.90) + 800(3.25)}{1200 + 500 + 2750 + 1000 + 800}$$

$$= \frac{18,500}{6250} = 2.96$$

Thus, the weighted mean computation shows that the mean cost per pound for the raw material is $2.96. Note that using equation (3.1) rather than the weighted mean formula in equation (3.3) would provide misleading results. In this case, the sample mean of the five cost-per-pound values is $(3.00 + 3.40 + 2.80 + 2.90 + 3.25)/5 = 15.35/5 = \$3.07$, which overstates the actual mean cost per pound purchased.

The choice of weights for a particular weighted mean computation depends upon the application. An example that is well known to college students is the computation of a grade point average (GPA). In this computation, the data values generally used are 4 for an A grade, 3 for a B grade, 2 for a C grade, 1 for a D grade, and 0 for an F grade. The weights are the number of credit hours earned for each grade. Exercise 16 at the end of this section provides an example of this weighted mean computation. In other weighted mean computations, quantities such as pounds, dollars, or volume are frequently used as weights. In any case, when observations vary in importance, the analyst must choose the weight that best reflects the importance of each observation in the determination of the mean.

Median

The **median** is another measure of central location. The median is the value in the middle when the data are arranged in ascending order (smallest value to largest value). With an odd number of observations, the median is the middle value. An even number of observations has no single middle value. In this case, we follow convention and define the median as the average of the values for the middle two observations. For convenience the definition of the median is restated as follows.

MEDIAN

Arrange the data in ascending order (smallest value to largest value).

(a) For an odd number of observations, the median is the middle value.
(b) For an even number of observations, the median is the average of the two middle values.

Let us apply this definition to compute the median class size for the sample of five college classes. Arranging the data in ascending order provides the following list.

32   42   46   46   54

Because $n = 5$ is odd, the median is the middle value. Thus the median class size is 46 students. Even though this data set contains two observations with values of 46, each observation is treated separately when we arrange the data in ascending order.

Suppose we also compute the median starting salary for the 12 business college graduates in Table 3.1. We first arrange the data in ascending order.

3710   3755   3850   3880   3880   3890   3920   3940   3950   4050   4130   4325

Middle Two Values

Because $n = 12$ is even, we identify the middle two values: 3890 and 3920. The median is the average of these values.

$$\text{Median} = \frac{3890 + 3920}{2} = 3905$$

The procedure we used to compute the median depends upon whether there is an odd number of observations or an even number of observations. Let us now describe a more conceptual and visual approach using the monthly starting salary for the 12 business college graduates. As before, we begin by arranging the data in ascending order.

3710   3755   3850   3880   3880   3890   3920   3940   3950   4050   4130   4325

Once the data are in ascending order, we trim pairs of extreme high and low values until no further pairs of values can be trimmed without completely eliminating all the data. For instance, after trimming the lowest observation (3710) and the highest observation (4325) we obtain a new data set with 10 observations.

3710   3755   3850   3880   3880   3890   3920   3940   3950   4050   4130   4325

We then trim the next lowest remaining value (3755) and the next highest remaining value (4130) to produce a new data set with eight observations.

3710   3755   3850   3880   3880   3890   3920   3940   3950   4050   4130   4325

Continuing this process we obtain the following results.

3710   3755   3850   3880   3880   3890   3920   3940   3950   4050   4130   4325
3710   3755   3850   3880   3880   3890   3920   3940   3950   4050   4130   4325
3710   3755   3850   3880   3880   3890   3920   3940   3950   4050   4130   4325

At this point no further trimming is possible without eliminating all the data. So, the median is just the average of the remaining two values. When there is an even number of observations, the trimming process will always result in two remaining values, and the average of these values will be the median. When there is an odd number of observations, the trimming process will always result in one final value, and this value will be the median. Thus, this method works whether the number of observations is odd or even.

The median is the measure of location most often reported for annual income and property value data because a few extremely large incomes or property values can inflate the mean. In such cases, the median is the preferred measure of central location.

Although the mean is the more commonly used measure of central location, in some situations the median is preferred. The mean is influenced by extremely small and large data values. For instance, suppose that the highest paid graduate (see Table 3.1) had a starting salary of $10,000 per month (maybe the individual's family owns the company). If we change the highest monthly starting salary in Table 3.1 from $4325 to $10,000 and recompute the mean, the sample mean changes from $3940 to $4413. The median of $3905, however, is unchanged, because $3890 and $3920 are still the middle two values. With the extremely high starting salary included, the median provides a better measure of central location than the mean. We can generalize to say that whenever a data set contains extreme values, the median is often the preferred measure of central location.

Geometric Mean

The **geometric mean** is a measure of location that is calculated by finding the nth root of the product of n values. The general formula for the geometric mean, denoted $\bar{x}_g$, follows.

GEOMETRIC MEAN

$$\bar{x}_g = \sqrt[n]{(x_1)(x_2)\cdots(x_n)} = [(x_1)(x_2)\cdots(x_n)]^{1/n} \qquad (3.4)$$

The geometric mean is often used in analyzing growth rates in financial data. In these types of situations the arithmetic mean or average value will provide misleading results.

To illustrate the use of the geometric mean, consider Table 3.2, which shows the percentage annual returns, or growth rates, for a mutual fund over the past 10 years. Suppose we want to compute how much $100 invested in the fund at the beginning of year 1 would be worth at the end of year 10. Let's start by computing the balance in the fund at the end of year 1. Because the percentage annual return for year 1 was -22.1%, the balance in the fund at the end of year 1 would be

$$\$100 - .221(\$100) = \$100(1 - .221) = \$100(.779) = \$77.90$$

The growth factor for each year is 1 plus .01 times the percentage return. A growth factor less than 1 indicates negative growth, while a growth factor greater than 1 indicates positive growth. The growth factor cannot be less than zero.

Note that .779 is identified as the growth factor for year 1 in Table 3.2. This result shows that we can compute the balance at the end of year 1 by multiplying the value invested in the fund at the beginning of year 1 times the growth factor for year 1.

The balance in the fund at the end of year 1, $77.90, now becomes the beginning balance in year 2. So, with a percentage annual return for year 2 of 28.7%, the balance at the end of year 2 would be

$$\$77.90 + .287(\$77.90) = \$77.90(1 + .287) = \$77.90(1.287) = \$100.2573$$

Note that 1.287 is the growth factor for year 2. And, by substituting $100(.779) for $77.90 we see that the balance in the fund at the end of year 2 is

$$\$100(.779)(1.287) = \$100.2573$$

In other words, the balance at the end of year 2 is just the initial investment at the beginning of year 1 times the product of the first two growth factors. This result can be generalized to

---

TABLE 3.2   PERCENTAGE ANNUAL RETURNS AND GROWTH FACTORS FOR THE MUTUAL FUND DATA

Year	Return (%)	Growth Factor
1	−22.1	0.779
2	28.7	1.287
3	10.9	1.109
4	4.9	1.049
5	15.8	1.158
6	5.5	1.055
7	−37.0	0.630
8	26.5	1.265
9	15.1	1.151
10	2.1	1.021

show that the balance at the end of year 10 is the initial investment times the product of all 10 growth factors.

$$\$100[(.779)(1.287)(1.109)(1.049)(1.158)(1.055)(.630)(1.265)(1.151)(1.021)] =$$

$$\$100(1.334493) = \$133.4493$$

The nth root can be computed using most calculators or by using the POWER function in Excel. For instance, using Excel, the 10th root of 1.334493 = POWER (1.334493,1/10) or 1.029275.

So, a $100 investment in the fund at the beginning of year 1 would be worth $133.4493 at the end of year 10. Note that the product of the 10 growth factors is 1.334493. Thus, we can compute the balance at the end of year 10 for any amount of money invested at the beginning of year 1 by multiplying the value of the initial investment times 1.334493. For instance, an initial investment of $2500 at the beginning of year 1 would be worth $2500(1.334493) or approximately $3336 at the end of year 10.

But what was the mean percentage annual return or mean rate of growth for this investment over the 10-year period? Let us see how the geometric mean of the 10 growth factors can be used to answer to this question. Because the product of the 10 growth factors is 1.334493, the geometric mean is the 10th root of 1.334493 or

$$\bar{x}_g = \sqrt[10]{1.334493} = 1.029275$$

The geometric mean tells us that annual returns grew at an average annual rate of $(1.029275 - 1)100\%$ or 2.9275%. In other words, with an average annual growth rate of 2.9275%, a $100 investment in the fund at the beginning of year 1 would grow to $100(1.029275)^{10} = \$133.4493$ at the end of 10 years.

It is important to understand that the arithmetic mean of the percentage annual returns does not provide the mean annual growth rate for this investment. The sum of the 10 annual percentage returns in Table 3.2 is 50.4. Thus, the arithmetic mean of the 10 percentage annual returns is 50.4/10 = 5.04%. A broker might try to convince you to invest in this fund by stating that the mean annual percentage return was 5.04%. Such a statement is not only misleading, it is inaccurate. A mean annual percentage return of 5.04% corresponds to an average growth factor of 1.0504. So, if the average growth factor were really 1.0504, $100 invested in the fund at the beginning of year 1 would have grown to $100(1.0504)^{10} = \$163.51$ at the end of 10 years. But, using the 10 annual percentage returns in Table 3.2, we showed that an initial $100 investment is worth $133.45 at the end of 10 years. The broker's claim that the mean annual percentage return is 5.04% grossly overstates the true growth for this mutual fund. The problem is that the sample mean is only appropriate for an additive process. For a multiplicative process, such as applications involving growth rates, the geometric mean is the appropriate measure of location.

While the applications of the geometric mean to problems in finance, investments, and banking are particularly common, the geometric mean should be applied any time you want to determine the mean rate of change over several successive periods. Other common applications include changes in populations of species, crop yields, pollution levels, and birth and death rates. Also note that the geometric mean can be applied to changes that occur over any number of successive periods of any length. In addition to annual changes, the geometric mean is often applied to find the mean rate of change over quarters, months, weeks, and even days.

Mode

Another measure of location is the **mode**. The mode is defined as follows.

> MODE
>
> The mode is the value that occurs with greatest frequency.

To illustrate the identification of the mode, consider the sample of five class sizes. The only value that occurs more than once is 46. Because this value, occurring with a frequency of 2, has the greatest frequency, it is the mode. As another illustration, consider the sample of starting salaries for the business school graduates. The only monthly starting salary that occurs more than once is $3880. Because this value has the greatest frequency, it is the mode.

Situations can arise for which the greatest frequency occurs at two or more different values. In these instances more than one mode exists. If the data contain exactly two modes, we say that the data are *bimodal*. If data contain more than two modes, we say that the data are *multimodal*. In multimodal cases the mode is almost never reported because listing three or more modes would not be particularly helpful in describing a location for the data.

Percentiles

A **percentile** provides information about how the data are spread over the interval from the smallest value to the largest value. For data that do not contain numerous repeated values, the *p*th percentile divides the data into two parts. Approximately *p* percent of the observations have values less than the *p*th percentile; approximately $(100 - p)$ percent of the observations have values greater than the *p*th percentile. The *p*th percentile is formally defined as follows.

> PERCENTILE
>
> The *p*th percentile is a value such that *at least p* percent of the observations are less than or equal to this value and *at least* $(100 - p)$ percent of the observations are greater than or equal to this value.

Colleges and universities frequently report admission test scores in terms of percentiles. For instance, suppose an applicant obtains a raw score of 54 on the verbal portion of an admission test. How this student performed in relation to other students taking the same test may not be readily apparent. However, if the raw score of 54 corresponds to the 70th percentile, we know that approximately 70% of the students scored lower than this individual and approximately 30% of the students scored higher than this individual.

The following procedure can be used to compute the *p*th percentile.

> CALCULATING THE *p*TH PERCENTILE
>
> **Step 1.** Arrange the data in ascending order (smallest value to largest value).
> **Step 2.** Compute an index *i*
>
> $$i = \left(\frac{p}{100}\right)n$$
>
> where *p* is the percentile of interest and *n* is the number of observations.
> **Step 3.** (a) If *i is not an integer, round up.* The next integer *greater* than *i* denotes the position of the *p*th percentile.
> (b) If *i is an integer*, the *p*th percentile is the average of the values in positions *i* and $i + 1$.

Following these steps makes it easy to calculate percentiles.

As an illustration of this procedure, let us determine the 85th percentile for the starting salary data in Table 3.1.

Step 1. Arrange the data in ascending order.

3710 3755 3850 3880 3880 3890 3920 3940 3950 4050 4130 4325

Step 2.

$$i = \left(\frac{p}{100}\right)n = \left(\frac{85}{100}\right)12 = 10.2$$

Step 3. Because i is not an integer, *round up*. The position of the 85th percentile is the next integer greater than 10.2, the 11th position.

Returning to the data, we see that the 85th percentile is the data value in the 11th position, or 4130.

As another illustration of this procedure, let us consider the calculation of the 50th percentile for the starting salary data. Applying step 2, we obtain

$$i = \left(\frac{50}{100}\right)12 = 6$$

Because i is an integer, step 3(b) states that the 50th percentile is the average of the sixth and seventh data values; thus the 50th percentile is $(3890 + 3920)/2 = 3905$. Note that the *50th percentile is also the median.*

Quartiles

Quartiles are just specific percentiles; thus, the steps for computing percentiles can be applied directly in the computation of quartiles.

It is often desirable to divide data into four parts, with each part containing approximately one-fourth, or 25% of the observations. The division points are referred to as the **quartiles** and are defined as

Q_1 = first quartile, or 25th percentile

Q_2 = second quartile, or 50th percentile (also the median)

Q_3 = third quartile, or 75th percentile.

To compute the quartiles for the starting salary data, we begin by arranging the data in ascending order.

3710 3755 3850 3880 3880 3890 3920 3940 3950 4050 4130 4325

We already identified Q_2, the second quartile (median), as 3905. The computations of quartiles Q_1 and Q_3 require the use of the rule for finding the 25th and 75th percentiles. These calculations follow.

For Q_1,

$$i = \left(\frac{p}{100}\right)n = \left(\frac{25}{100}\right)12 = 3$$

Because i is an integer, step 3(b) indicates that the first quartile, or 25th percentile, is the average of the third and fourth data values; thus, $Q_1 = (3850 + 3880)/2 = 3865$.

For Q_3,

$$i = \left(\frac{p}{100}\right)n = \left(\frac{75}{100}\right)12 = 9$$

Again, because i is an integer, step 3(b) indicates that the third quartile, or 75th percentile, is the average of the ninth and tenth data values; thus, $Q_3 = (3950 + 4050)/2 = 4000$.

The quartiles divide the starting salary data into four parts, with each part containing 25% of the observations.

25% of the data		25% of the data		25% of the data		25% of the data	

3710	3755	3850	3880	3880	3890	3920	3940	3950	4050	4130	4325

$$Q_1 = 3865 \qquad\qquad Q_2 = 3905 \qquad\qquad Q_3 = 4000$$
$$\text{(Median)}$$

We defined the quartiles as the 25th, 50th, and 75th percentiles. Thus, we computed the quartiles in the same way as percentiles. However, other conventions are sometimes used to compute quartiles, and the actual values reported for quartiles may vary slightly depending on the convention used. Nevertheless, the objective of all procedures for computing quartiles is to divide the data into four equal parts.

NOTES AND COMMENTS

1. It is better to use the median than the mean as a measure of central location when a data set contains extreme values. Another measure that is sometimes used when extreme values are present is the trimmed mean. The trimmed mean is obtained by deleting a percentage of the smallest and largest values from a data set and then computing the mean of the remaining values. For example, the 5% trimmed mean is obtained by removing the smallest 5% and the largest 5% of the data values and then computing the mean of the remaining values. Using the sample with $n = 12$ starting salaries, $0.05(12) = 0.6$. Rounding this value to 1 indicates that the 5% trimmed mean is obtained by removing the smallest data value and the largest data value and then computing the mean of the remaining 10 values. For the starting salary data, the 5% trimmed mean is 3924.50.

2. Other commonly used percentiles are the quintiles (the 20th, 40th, 60th, and 80th percentiles) and the deciles (the 10th, 20th, 30th, 40th, 50th, 60th, 70th, 80th, and 90th percentiles).

Exercises

Methods

1. Consider a sample with data values of 10, 20, 12, 17, and 16. Compute the mean and median.
2. Consider a sample with data values of 10, 20, 21, 17, 16, and 12. Compute the mean and median.
3. Consider the following data and corresponding weights.

x_i	Weight (w_i)
3.2	6
2.0	3
2.5	2
5.0	8

a. Compute the weighted mean.
b. Compute the sample mean of the four data values without weighting. Note the difference in the results provided by the two computations.

4.   Consider the following data.

Period	Rate of Return (%)
1	−6.0
2	−8.0
3	−4.0
4	2.0
5	5.4

What is the mean growth rate over these five periods?

5.   Consider a sample with data values of 27, 25, 20, 15, 30, 34, 28, and 25. Compute the 20th, 25th, 65th, and 75th percentiles.

6.   Consider a sample with data values of 53, 55, 70, 58, 64, 57, 53, 69, 57, 68, and 53. Compute the mean, median, and mode.

Applications

7.   The average number of minutes Americans commute to work is 27.7 minutes (*Sterling's Best Places*, April 13, 2012). The average commute time in minutes for 48 cities are as follows:

Albuquerque	23.3	Jacksonville	26.2	Phoenix	28.3
Atlanta	28.3	Kansas City	23.4	Pittsburgh	25.0
Austin	24.6	Las Vegas	28.4	Portland	26.4
Baltimore	32.1	Little Rock	20.1	Providence	23.6
Boston	31.7	Los Angeles	32.2	Richmond	23.4
Charlotte	25.8	Louisville	21.4	Sacramento	25.8
Chicago	38.1	Memphis	23.8	Salt Lake City	20.2
Cincinnati	24.9	Miami	30.7	San Antonio	26.1
Cleveland	26.8	Milwaukee	24.8	San Diego	24.8
Columbus	23.4	Minneapolis	23.6	San Francisco	32.6
Dallas	28.5	Nashville	25.3	San Jose	28.5
Denver	28.1	New Orleans	31.7	Seattle	27.3
Detroit	29.3	New York	43.8	St. Louis	26.8
El Paso	24.4	Oklahoma City	22.0	Tucson	24.0
Fresno	23.0	Orlando	27.1	Tulsa	20.1
Indianapolis	24.8	Philadelphia	34.2	Washington, D.C.	32.8

a.   What is the mean commute time for these 48 cities?
b.   Compute the median commute time.
c.   Compute the mode.
d.   Compute the third quartile.

8.   During the 2007–2008 NCAA college basketball season, men's basketball teams attempted an all-time high number of 3-point shots, averaging 19.07 shots per game (Associated Press Sports, January 24, 2009). In an attempt to discourage so many 3-point shots and encourage more inside play, the NCAA rules committee moved the 3-point line back from 19 feet, 9 inches to 20 feet, 9 inches at the beginning of the 2008–2009 basketball season. Shown in the following table are the 3-point shots taken and the 3-point shots made for a sample of 19 NCAA basketball games during the 2008–2009 season.

3Points

3-Point Shots	Shots Made	3-Point Shots	Shots Made
23	4	17	7
20	6	19	10
17	5	22	7
18	8	25	11
13	4	15	6
16	4	10	5
8	5	11	3
19	8	25	8
28	5	23	7
21	7		

a. What is the mean number of 3-point shots taken per game?
b. What is the mean number of 3-point shots made per game?
c. Using the closer 3-point line, players were making 35.2% of their shots. What percentage of shots were players making from the new 3-point line?
d. What was the impact of the NCAA rules change that moved the 3-point line back to 20 feet, 9 inches for the 2008–2009 season? Would you agree with the Associated Press Sports article that stated, "Moving back the 3-point line hasn't changed the game dramatically"? Explain.

9. Endowment income is a critical part of the annual budgets at colleges and universities. A study by the National Association of College and University Business Officers reported that the 435 colleges and universities surveyed held a total of $413 billion in endowments. The 10 wealthiest universities are shown below (*The Wall Street Journal*, January 27, 2009). Amounts are in billion of dollars.

University	Endowment ($billion)	University	Endowment ($billion)
Columbia	7.2	Princeton	16.4
Harvard	36.6	Stanford	17.2
M.I.T.	10.1	Texas	16.1
Michigan	7.6	Texas A&M	6.7
Northwestern	7.2	Yale	22.9

a. What is the mean endowment for these universities?
b. What is the median endowment?
c. What is the mode endowment?
d. Compute the first and third quartiles.
e. What is the total endowment at these 10 universities? These universities represent 2.3% of the 435 colleges and universities surveyed. What percentage of the total $413 billion in endowments is held by these 10 universities?
f. *The Wall Street Journal* reported that over a recent five-month period, a downturn in the economy has caused endowments to decline 23%. What is the estimate of the dollar amount of the decline in the total endowments held by these 10 universities? Given this situation, what are some of the steps you would expect university administrators to be considering?

10. Over a nine-month period, OutdoorGearLab tested hardshell jackets designed for ice climbing, mountaineering, and backpacking. Based on the breathability, durability, versatility,

JacketRatings

features, mobility, and weight of each jacket, an overall rating ranging from 0 (lowest) to 100 (highest) was assigned to each jacket tested. The following data show the results for 20 top-of-the line jackets (OutdoorGearLab website, February 27, 2013).

42	66	67	71	78	62	61	76	71	67
61	64	61	54	83	63	68	69	81	53

a. Compute the mean, median, and mode.
b. Compute the first and third quartiles.
c. Compute and interpret the 90th percentile.

11. According to the National Education Association (NEA), teachers generally spend more than 40 hours each week working on instructional duties (NEA website, April 2012). The following data show the number of hours worked per week for a sample of 13 high school science teachers and a sample of 11 high school English teachers.

   High School Science Teachers: 53 56 54 54 55 58 49 61 54 54 52 53 54
   High School English Teachers: 52 47 50 46 47 48 49 46 55 44 47

a. What is the median number of hours worked per week for the sample of 13 high school science teachers?
b. What is the median number of hours worked per week for the sample of 11 high school English teachers?
c. Which group has the highest median number of hours worked per week? What is the difference between the median number of hours worked per week?

BigBangTheory

12. *The Big Bang Theory*, a situation comedy featuring Johnny Galecki, Jim Parsons, and Kaley Cuoco, is one of the most watched programs on network television. The first two episodes for the 2011–2012 season premiered on September 22, 2011; the first episode attracted 14.1 million viewers and the second episode attracted 14.7 million viewers. The following table shows the number of viewers in millions for the first 21 episodes of the 2011–2012 season (*The Big Bang Theory* website, April 17, 2012).

Air Date	Viewers (millions)	Air Date	Viewers (millions)
September 22, 2011	14.1	January 12, 2012	16.1
September 22, 2011	14.7	January 19, 2012	15.8
September 29, 2011	14.6	January 26, 2012	16.1
October 6, 2011	13.6	February 2, 2012	16.5
October 13, 2011	13.6	February 9, 2012	16.2
October 20, 2011	14.9	February 16, 2012	15.7
October 27, 2011	14.5	February 23, 2012	16.2
November 3, 2011	16.0	March 8, 2012	15.0
November 10, 2011	15.9	March 29, 2012	14.0
November 17, 2011	15.1	April 5, 2012	13.3
December 8, 2011	14.0		

a. Compute the minimum and maximum number of viewers.
b. Compute the mean, median, and mode.
c. Compute the first and third quartiles.
d. Has viewership grown or declined over the 2011–2012 season? Discuss.

13. In automobile mileage and gasoline-consumption testing, 13 automobiles were road tested for 300 miles in both city and highway driving conditions. The following data were recorded for miles-per-gallon performance.

    City: 16.2 16.7 15.9 14.4 13.2 15.3 16.8 16.0 16.1 15.3 15.2 15.3 16.2
    Highway: 19.4 20.6 18.3 18.6 19.2 17.4 17.2 18.6 19.0 21.1 19.4 18.5 18.7

    Use the mean, median, and mode to make a statement about the difference in performance for city and highway driving.

WEB file

StateUnemp

14. The data contained in the file named StateUnemp show the unemployment rate in March 2011 and the unemployment rate in March 2012 for every state and the District of Columbia (Bureau of Labor Statistics website, April 20, 2012). To compare unemployment rates in March 2011 with unemployment rates in March 2012, compute the first quartile, the median, and the third quartile for the March 2011 unemployment data and the March 2012 unemployment data. What do these statistics suggest about the change in unemployment rates across the states?

15. Martinez Auto Supplies has retail stores located in eight cities in California. The price they charge for a particular product in each city varies because of differing competitive conditions. For instance, the price they charge for a case of a popular brand of motor oil in each city follows. Also shown are the number of cases that Martinez Auto sold last quarter in each city.

City	Price ($)	Sales (cases)
Bakersfield	34.99	501
Los Angeles	38.99	1425
Modesto	36.00	294
Oakland	33.59	882
Sacramento	40.99	715
San Diego	38.59	1088
San Francisco	39.59	1644
San Jose	37.99	819

Compute the average sales price per case for this product during the last quarter.

SELF test

16. The grade point average for college students is based on a weighted mean computation. For most colleges, the grades are given the following data values: A (4), B (3), C (2), D (1), and F (0). After 60 credit hours of course work, a student at State University earned 9 credit hours of A, 15 credit hours of B, 33 credit hours of C, and 3 credit hours of D.
    a. Compute the student's grade point average.
    b. Students at State University must maintain a 2.5 grade point average for their first 60 credit hours of course work in order to be admitted to the business college. Will this student be admitted?

17. Morningstar tracks the total return for a large number of mutual funds. The following table shows the total return and the number of funds for four categories of mutual funds (*Morningstar Funds 500*, 2008).

Type of Fund	Number of Funds	Total Return (%)
Domestic Equity	9191	4.65
International Equity	2621	18.15
Specialty Stock	1419	11.36
Hybrid	2900	6.75

a. Using the number of funds as weights, compute the weighted average total return for the mutual funds covered by Morningstar.
b. Is there any difficulty associated with using the "number of funds" as the weights in computing the weighted average total return for Morningstar in part (a)? Discuss. What else might be used for weights?
c. Suppose you had invested $10,000 in mutual funds at the beginning of 2007 and diversified the investment by placing $2000 in Domestic Equity funds, $4000 in International Equity funds, $3000 in Specialty Stock funds, and $1000 in Hybrid funds. What is the expected return on the portfolio?

18. Based on a survey of 425 master's programs in business administration, *U.S. News & World Report* ranked the Indiana University Kelley Business School as the 20th best business program in the country (*America's Best Graduate Schools*, 2009). The ranking was based in part on surveys of business school deans and corporate recruiters. Each survey respondent was asked to rate the overall academic quality of the master's program on a scale from 1 "marginal" to 5 "outstanding." Use the sample of responses shown below to compute the weighted mean score for the business school deans and the corporate recruiters. Discuss.

Quality Assessment	Business School Deans	Corporate Recruiters
5	44	31
4	66	34
3	60	43
2	10	12
1	0	0

19. Annual revenue for Corning Supplies grew by 5.5% in 2007; 1.1% in 2008; −3.5% in 2009; −1.1% in 2010; and 1.8% in 2011. What is the mean growth annual rate over this period?

20. Suppose that at the beginning of 2004 you invested $10,000 in the Stivers mutual fund and $5,000 in the Trippi mutual fund. The value of each investment at the end of each subsequent year is provided in the table below. Which mutual fund performed better?

Year	Stivers	Trippi
2004	11,000	5,600
2005	12,000	6,300
2006	13,000	6,900
2007	14,000	7,600
2008	15,000	8,500
2009	16,000	9,200
2010	17,000	9,900
2011	18,000	10,600

21. If an asset declines in value from $5,000 to $3,500 over nine years, what is the mean annual growth rate in the asset's value over these nine years?

22. The current value of a company is $25 million. If the value of the company six year ago was $10 million, what is the company's mean annual growth rate over the past six years?

3.2   Measures of Variability

The variability in the delivery time creates uncertainty for production scheduling. Methods in this section help measure and understand variability.

In addition to measures of location, it is often desirable to consider measures of variability, or dispersion. For example, suppose that you are a purchasing agent for a large manufacturing firm and that you regularly place orders with two different suppliers. After several months of operation, you find that the mean number of days required to fill orders is 10 days for both of the suppliers. The histograms summarizing the number of working days required to fill orders from the suppliers are shown in Figure 3.2. Although the mean number of days is 10 for both suppliers, do the two suppliers demonstrate the same degree of reliability in terms of making deliveries on schedule? Note the dispersion, or variability, in delivery times indicated by the histograms. Which supplier would you prefer?

For most firms, receiving materials and supplies on schedule is important. The 7- or 8-day deliveries shown for J.C. Clark Distributors might be viewed favorably; however, a few of the slow 13- to 15-day deliveries could be disastrous in terms of keeping a workforce busy and production on schedule. This example illustrates a situation in which the variability in the delivery times may be an overriding consideration in selecting a supplier. For most purchasing agents, the lower variability shown for Dawson Supply, Inc., would make Dawson the preferred supplier.

We turn now to a discussion of some commonly used measures of variability.

Range

The simplest measure of variability is the **range**.

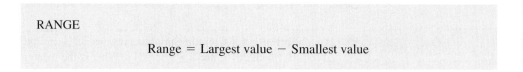

RANGE

$$\text{Range} = \text{Largest value} - \text{Smallest value}$$

Let us refer to the data on starting salaries for business school graduates in Table 3.1. The largest starting salary is 4325 and the smallest is 3710. The range is $4325 - 3710 = 615$.

FIGURE 3.2   HISTORICAL DATA SHOWING THE NUMBER OF DAYS REQUIRED TO FILL ORDERS

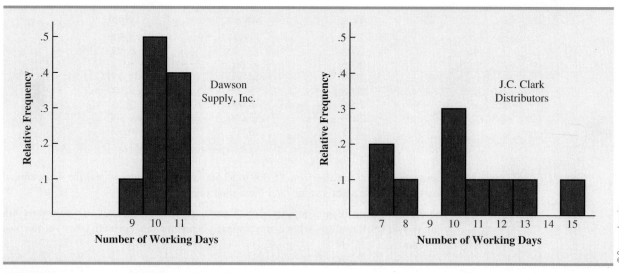

Although the range is the easiest of the measures of variability to compute, it is seldom used as the only measure. The reason is that the range is based on only two of the observations and thus is highly influenced by extreme values. Suppose the highest paid graduate received a starting salary of $10,000 per month. In this case, the range would be $10,000 - 3710 = 6290$ rather than 615. This large value for the range would not be especially descriptive of the variability in the data because 11 of the 12 starting salaries are closely grouped between 3710 and 4130.

Interquartile Range

A measure of variability that overcomes the dependency on extreme values is the **interquartile range (IQR)**. This measure of variability is the difference between the third quartile, Q_3, and the first quartile, Q_1. In other words, the interquartile range is the range for the middle 50% of the data.

INTERQUARTILE RANGE

$$IQR = Q_3 - Q_1 \tag{3.5}$$

For the data on monthly starting salaries, the quartiles are $Q_3 = 4000$ and $Q_1 = 3865$. Thus, the interquartile range is $4000 - 3865 = 135$.

Variance

The **variance** is a measure of variability that utilizes all the data. The variance is based on the difference between the value of each observation (x_i) and the mean. The difference between each x_i and the mean ($\bar{x}$ for a sample, μ for a population) is called a *deviation about the mean*. For a sample, a deviation about the mean is written ($x_i - \bar{x}$); for a population, it is written ($x_i - \mu$). In the computation of the variance, the deviations about the mean are *squared*.

If the data are for a population, the average of the squared deviations is called the *population variance*. The population variance is denoted by the Greek symbol σ^2. For a population of N observations and with μ denoting the population mean, the definition of the population variance is as follows.

POPULATION VARIANCE

$$\sigma^2 = \frac{\sum(x_i - \mu)^2}{N} \tag{3.6}$$

In most statistical applications, the data being analyzed are for a sample. When we compute a sample variance, we are often interested in using it to estimate the population variance σ^2. Although a detailed explanation is beyond the scope of this text, it can be shown that if the sum of the squared deviations about the sample mean is divided by $n - 1$, and not n, the resulting sample variance provides an unbiased estimate of the population variance. For this reason, the *sample variance,* denoted by s^2, is defined as follows.

The sample variance s^2 is a point estimator of the population variance σ^2.

SAMPLE VARIANCE

$$s^2 = \frac{\sum(x_i - \bar{x})^2}{n - 1} \tag{3.7}$$

TABLE 3.3   COMPUTATION OF DEVIATIONS AND SQUARED DEVIATIONS ABOUT
THE MEAN FOR THE CLASS SIZE DATA

Number of Students in Class (x_i)	Mean Class Size ($\bar{x}$)	Deviation About the Mean ($x_i - \bar{x}$)	Squared Deviation About the Mean ($x_i - \bar{x})^2$
46	44	2	4
54	44	10	100
42	44	−2	4
46	44	2	4
32	44	−12	144
		0	256
		$\Sigma(x_i - \bar{x})$	$\Sigma(x_i - \bar{x})^2$

To illustrate the computation of the sample variance, we will use the data on class size for the sample of five college classes as presented in Section 3.1. A summary of the data, including the computation of the deviations about the mean and the squared deviations about the mean, is shown in Table 3.3. The sum of squared deviations about the mean is $\Sigma(x_i - \bar{x})^2 = 256$. Hence, with $n - 1 = 4$, the sample variance is

$$s^2 = \frac{\Sigma(x_i - \bar{x})^2}{n - 1} = \frac{256}{4} = 64$$

The variance is useful in comparing the variability of two or more variables.

Before moving on, let us note that the units associated with the sample variance often cause confusion. Because the values being summed in the variance calculation, $(x_i - \bar{x})^2$, are squared, the units associated with the sample variance are also *squared*. For instance, the sample variance for the class size data is $s^2 = 64$ (students)^2. The squared units associated with variance make it difficult to develop an intuitive understanding and interpretation of the numerical value of the variance. We recommend that you think of the variance as a measure useful in comparing the amount of variability for two or more variables. In a comparison of the variables, the one with the largest variance shows the most variability. Further interpretation of the value of the variance may not be necessary.

As another illustration of computing a sample variance, consider the starting salaries listed in Table 3.1 for the 12 business school graduates. In Section 3.1, we showed that the sample mean starting salary was 3940. The computation of the sample variance ($s^2 = 27,440.91$) is shown in Table 3.4.

In Tables 3.3 and 3.4 we show both the sum of the deviations about the mean and the sum of the squared deviations about the mean. For any data set, the sum of the deviations about the mean will *always equal zero*. Note that in Tables 3.3 and 3.4, $\Sigma(x_i - \bar{x}) = 0$. The positive deviations and negative deviations cancel each other, causing the sum of the deviations about the mean to equal zero.

Standard Deviation

The **standard deviation** is defined to be the positive square root of the variance. Following the notation we adopted for a sample variance and a population variance, we use s to denote the sample standard deviation and σ to denote the population standard deviation. The standard deviation is derived from the variance in the following way.

TABLE 3.4   COMPUTATION OF THE SAMPLE VARIANCE FOR THE STARTING SALARY DATA

Monthly Salary (x_i)	Sample Mean ($\bar{x}$)	Deviation About the Mean ($x_i - \bar{x}$)	Squared Deviation About the Mean ($(x_i - \bar{x})^2$)
3850	3940	−90	8,100
3950	3940	10	100
4050	3940	110	12,100
3880	3940	−60	3,600
3755	3940	−185	34,225
3710	3940	−230	52,900
3890	3940	−50	2,500
4130	3940	190	36,100
3940	3940	0	0
4325	3940	385	148,225
3920	3940	−20	400
3880	3940	−60	3,600
		0	301,850
		$\sum(x_i - \bar{x})$	$\sum(x_i - \bar{x})^2$

Using equation (3.7),

$$s^2 = \frac{\sum(x_i - \bar{x})^2}{n-1} = \frac{301,850}{11} = 27,440.91$$

© Cengage Learning

STANDARD DEVIATION

The sample standard deviation s is a point estimator of the population standard deviation σ.

$$\text{Sample standard deviation} = s = \sqrt{s^2} \tag{3.8}$$

$$\text{Population standard deviation} = \sigma = \sqrt{\sigma^2} \tag{3.9}$$

Recall that the sample variance for the sample of class sizes in five college classes is $s^2 = 64$. Thus, the sample standard deviation is $s = \sqrt{64} = 8$. For the data on starting salaries, the sample standard deviation is $s = \sqrt{27,440.91} = 165.65$.

The standard deviation is easier to interpret than the variance because the standard deviation is measured in the same units as the data.

What is gained by converting the variance to its corresponding standard deviation? Recall that the units associated with the variance are squared. For example, the sample variance for the starting salary data of business school graduates is $s^2 = 27,440.91$ (dollars)^2. Because the standard deviation is the square root of the variance, the units of the variance, dollars squared, are converted to dollars in the standard deviation. Thus, the standard deviation of the starting salary data is $165.65. In other words, the standard deviation is measured in the same units as the original data. For this reason the standard deviation is more easily compared to the mean and other statistics that are measured in the same units as the original data.

Coefficient of Variation

The coefficient of variation is a relative measure of variability; it measures the standard deviation relative to the mean.

In some situations we may be interested in a descriptive statistic that indicates how large the standard deviation is relative to the mean. This measure is called the **coefficient of variation** and is usually expressed as a percentage.

COEFFICIENT OF VARIATION

$$\left(\frac{\text{Standard deviation}}{\text{Mean}} \times 100 \right)\% \qquad\qquad (3.10)$$

For the class size data, we found a sample mean of 44 and a sample standard deviation of 8. The coefficient of variation is $[(8/44) \times 100]\% = 18.2\%$. In words, the coefficient of variation tells us that the sample standard deviation is 18.2% of the value of the sample mean. For the starting salary data with a sample mean of 3940 and a sample standard deviation of 165.65, the coefficient of variation, $[(165.65/3940) \times 100]\% = 4.2\%$, tells us the sample standard deviation is only 4.2% of the value of the sample mean. In general, the coefficient of variation is a useful statistic for comparing the variability of variables that have different standard deviations and different means.

NOTES AND COMMENTS

1. Statistical software packages and spreadsheets can be used to develop the descriptive statistics presented in this chapter. After the data are entered into a worksheet, a few simple commands can be used to generate the desired output. In three chapter-ending appendixes we show how Minitab, Excel, and StatTools can be used to develop descriptive statistics.

2. The standard deviation is a commonly used measure of the risk associated with investing in stock and stock funds (*Morningstar* website, July 21, 2012). It provides a measure of how monthly returns fluctuate around the long-run average return.

3. Rounding the value of the sample mean $\bar{x}$ and the values of the squared deviations $(x_i - \bar{x})^2$ may introduce errors when a calculator is used in the computation of the variance and standard deviation. To reduce rounding errors, we recommend carrying at least six significant digits during intermediate calculations. The resulting variance or standard deviation can then be rounded to fewer digits.

4. An alternative formula for the computation of the sample variance is

$$s^2 = \frac{\sum x_i^2 - n\bar{x}^2}{n - 1}$$

where $\sum x_i^2 = x_1^2 + x_2^2 + \cdots + x_n^2$.

Exercises

Methods

23. Consider a sample with data values of 10, 20, 12, 17, and 16. Compute the range and interquartile range.

24. Consider a sample with data values of 10, 20, 12, 17, and 16. Compute the variance and standard deviation.

25. Consider a sample with data values of 27, 25, 20, 15, 30, 34, 28, and 25. Compute the range, interquartile range, variance, and standard deviation.

Applications

26. A bowler's scores for six games were 182, 168, 184, 190, 170, and 174. Using these data as a sample, compute the following descriptive statistics:
    a. Range
    b. Variance
    c. Standard deviation
    d. Coefficient of variation

27. The results of a search to find the least expensive round-trip flights to Atlanta and Salt Lake City from 14 major U.S. cities are shown in the following table. The departure date was June 20, 2012, and the return date was June 27, 2012.

WEB file

Flights

	Round-Trip Cost ($)	
Departure City	Atlanta	Salt Lake City
Cincinnati	340.10	570.10
New York	321.60	354.60
Chicago	291.60	465.60
Denver	339.60	219.60
Los Angeles	359.60	311.60
Seattle	384.60	297.60
Detroit	309.60	471.60
Philadelphia	415.60	618.40
Washington, D.C.	293.60	513.60
Miami	249.60	523.20
San Francisco	539.60	381.60
Las Vegas	455.60	159.60
Phoenix	359.60	267.60
Dallas	333.90	458.60

a. Compute the mean price for a round-trip flight into Atlanta and the mean price for a round-trip flight into Salt Lake City. Is Atlanta less expensive to fly into than Salt Lake City? If so, what could explain this difference?

b. Compute the range, variance, and standard deviation for the two samples. What does this information tell you about the prices for flights into these two cities?

28. The Australian Open is the first of the four Grand Slam professional tennis events held each year. Victoria Azarenka beat Maria Sharapova to win the 2012 Australian Open women's title (*Washington Post,* January 27, 2012). During the tournament Ms. Azarenka's serve speed reached 178 kilometers per hour. A list of the 20 Women's Singles serve speed leaders for the 2012 Australian Open is provided below.

WEB file

AustralianOpen

Player	Serve Speed (km/h)	Player	Serve Speed (km/h)
S. Williams	191	G. Arn	179
S. Lisicki	190	V. Azarenka	178
M. Keys	187	A. Ivanovic	178
L. Hradecka	187	P. Kvitova	178
J. Gajdosova	187	M. Krajicek	178
J. Hampton	181	V. Dushevina	178
B. Mattek-Sands	181	S. Stosur	178
F. Schiavone	179	S. Cirstea	177
P. Parmentier	179	M. Barthel	177
N. Petrova	179	P. Ormaechea	177

a. Compute the mean, variance, and standard deviation for the serve speeds.

b. A similar sample of the 20 Women's Singles serve speed leaders for the 2011 Wimbledon tournament showed a sample mean serve speed of 182.5 kilometers per hour. The variance and standard deviation were 33.3 and 5.77, respectively. Discuss any difference between the serve speeds in the Australian Open and the Wimbledon women's tournaments.

29. The *Los Angeles Times* regularly reports the air quality index for various areas of Southern California. A sample of air quality index values for Pomona provided the following data: 28, 42, 58, 48, 45, 55, 60, 49, and 50.

    a. Compute the range and interquartile range.

    b. Compute the sample variance and sample standard deviation.

    c. A sample of air quality index readings for Anaheim provided a sample mean of 48.5, a sample variance of 136, and a sample standard deviation of 11.66. What comparisons can you make between the air quality in Pomona and that in Anaheim on the basis of these descriptive statistics?

30. The following data were used to construct the histograms of the number of days required to fill orders for Dawson Supply, Inc., and J.C. Clark Distributors (see Figure 3.2).

Dawson Supply Days for Delivery:	11	10	9	10	11	11	10	11	10	10
Clark Distributors Days for Delivery:	8	10	13	7	10	11	10	7	15	12

    Use the range and standard deviation to support the previous observation that Dawson Supply provides the more consistent and reliable delivery times.

31. The results of Accounting Principals' latest Workonomix survey indicate the average American worker spends $1092 on coffee annually (*The Consumerist,* January 20, 2012). To determine if there are any differences in coffee expenditures by age group, samples of 10 consumers were selected for three age groups (18–34, 35–44, and 45 and Older). The dollar amount each consumer in the sample spent last year on coffee is provided below.

Coffee

18–34	35–44	45 and Older
1355	969	1135
115	434	956
1456	1792	400
2045	1500	1374
1621	1277	1244
994	1056	825
1937	1922	763
1200	1350	1192
1567	1586	1305
1390	1415	1510

    a. Compute the mean, variance, and standard deviation for the each of these three samples.

    b. What observations can be made based on these data?

Advertising

32. *Advertising Age* annually compiles a list of the 100 companies that spend the most on advertising. Consumer-goods company Procter & Gamble has often topped the list, spending billions of dollars annually (*Advertising Age* website, March 12, 2013). Consider the data found in the file Advertising. It contains annual advertising expenditures for a sample of 20 companies in the automotive sector and 20 companies in the department store sector.

    a. What is the mean advertising spend for each sector?

    b. What is the standard deviation for each sector?

    c. What is the range of advertising spend for each sector?

    d. What is the interquartile range for each sector?

    e. Based on this sample and your answers to parts (a) to (d), comment on any differences in the advertising spending in the automotive companies versus the department store companies.

33. Scores turned in by an amateur golfer at the Bonita Fairways Golf Course in Bonita Springs, Florida, during 2011 and 2012 are as follows:

2011 Season:	74	78	79	77	75	73	75	77
2012 Season:	71	70	75	77	85	80	71	79

a.   Use the mean and standard deviation to evaluate the golfer's performance over the two-year period.
b.   What is the primary difference in performance between 2011 and 2012? What improvement, if any, can be seen in the 2012 scores?

34.   The following times were recorded by the quarter-mile and mile runners of a university track team (times are in minutes).

Quarter-Mile Times:	.92	.98	1.04	.90	.99
Mile Times:	4.52	4.35	4.60	4.70	4.50

After viewing this sample of running times, one of the coaches commented that the quarter-milers turned in the more consistent times. Use the standard deviation and the coefficient of variation to summarize the variability in the data. Does the use of the coefficient of variation indicate that the coach's statement should be qualified?

Measures of Distribution Shape, Relative Location, and Detecting Outliers

We have described several measures of location and variability for data. In addition, it is often important to have a measure of the shape of a distribution. In Chapter 2 we noted that a histogram provides a graphical display showing the shape of a distribution. An important numerical measure of the shape of a distribution is called **skewness**.

Distribution Shape

Figure 3.3 shows four histograms constructed from relative frequency distributions. The histograms in Panels A and B are moderately skewed. The one in Panel A is skewed to the left; its skewness is $-.85$. The histogram in Panel B is skewed to the right; its skewness is $+.85$. The histogram in Panel C is symmetric; its skewness is zero. The histogram in Panel D is highly skewed to the right; its skewness is 1.62. The formula used to compute skewness is somewhat complex.[1] However, the skewness can easily be computed using statistical software. For data skewed to the left, the skewness is negative; for data skewed to the right, the skewness is positive. If the data are symmetric, the skewness is zero.

For a symmetric distribution, the mean and the median are equal. When the data are positively skewed, the mean will usually be greater than the median; when the data are negatively skewed, the mean will usually be less than the median. The data used to construct the histogram in Panel D are customer purchases at a women's apparel store. The mean purchase amount is $77.60 and the median purchase amount is $59.70. The relatively few large purchase amounts tend to increase the mean, while the median remains unaffected by the large purchase amounts. The median provides the preferred measure of location when the data are highly skewed.

z-Scores

In addition to measures of location, variability, and shape, we are also interested in the relative location of values within a data set. Measures of relative location help us determine how far a particular value is from the mean.

---

[1]The formula for the skewness of sample data:

$$\text{Skewness} = \frac{n}{(n-1)(n-2)} \Sigma \left(\frac{x_i - \bar{x}}{s} \right)^3$$

FIGURE 3.3   HISTOGRAMS SHOWING THE SKEWNESS FOR FOUR DISTRIBUTIONS

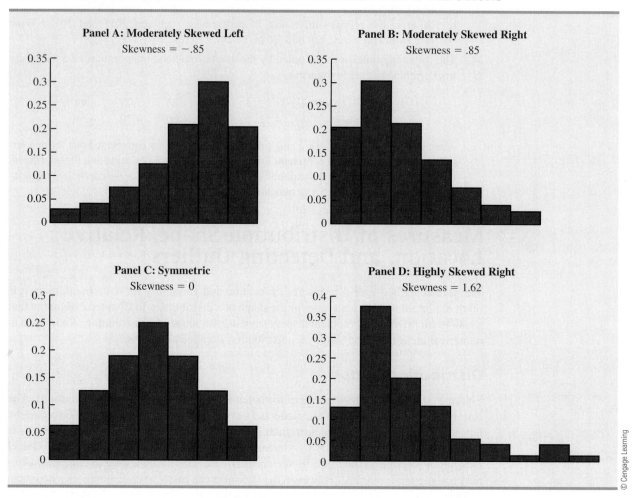

By using both the mean and standard deviation, we can determine the relative location of any observation. Suppose we have a sample of n observations, with the values denoted by $x_1, x_2, \ldots, x_n$. In addition, assume that the sample mean, $\bar{x}$, and the sample standard deviation, s, are already computed. Associated with each value, x_i, is another value called its **z-score**. Equation (3.11) shows how the z-score is computed for each x_i.

z-SCORE

$$z_i = \frac{x_i - \bar{x}}{s} \tag{3.11}$$

where

z_i = the z-score for x_i
$\bar{x}$ = the sample mean
s = the sample standard deviation

TABLE 3.5 z-SCORES FOR THE CLASS SIZE DATA

Number of Students in Class (x_i)	Deviation About the Mean $(x_i - \bar{x})$	z-Score $\left(\dfrac{x_i - \bar{x}}{s} \right)$
46	2	$2/8 = .25$
54	10	$10/8 = 1.25$
42	−2	$-2/8 = -.25$
46	2	$2/8 = .25$
32	−12	$-12/8 = -1.50$

© Cengage Learning

The z-score is often called the *standardized value*. The z-score, z_i, can be interpreted as the *number of standard deviations x_i is from the mean $\bar{x}$*. For example, $z_1 = 1.2$ would indicate that x_1 is 1.2 standard deviations greater than the sample mean. Similarly, $z_2 = -.5$ would indicate that x_2 is .5, or 1/2, standard deviation less than the sample mean. A z-score greater than zero occurs for observations with a value greater than the mean, and a z-score less than zero occurs for observations with a value less than the mean. A z-score of zero indicates that the value of the observation is equal to the mean.

The z-score for any observation can be interpreted as a measure of the relative location of the observation in a data set. Thus, observations in two different data sets with the same z-score can be said to have the same relative location in terms of being the same number of standard deviations from the mean.

The process of converting a value for a variable to a z-score is often referred to as a z transformation.

The z-scores for the class size data from Section 3.1 are computed in Table 3.5. Recall the previously computed sample mean, $\bar{x} = 44$, and sample standard deviation, $s = 8$. The z-score of -1.50 for the fifth observation shows it is farthest from the mean; it is 1.50 standard deviations below the mean. Figure 3.4 provides a dot plot of the class size data with a graphical representation of the associated z-scores on the axis below.

Chebyshev's Theorem

Chebyshev's theorem enables us to make statements about the proportion of data values that must be within a specified number of standard deviations of the mean.

FIGURE 3.4 DOT PLOT SHOWING CLASS SIZE DATA AND z-SCORES

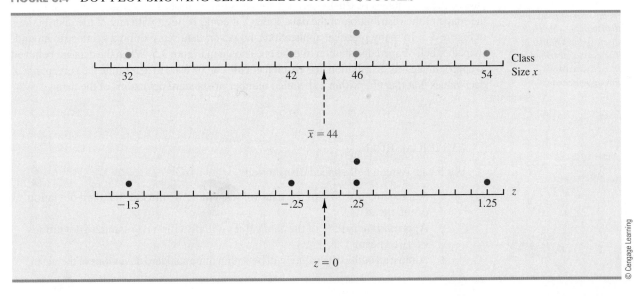

© Cengage Learning

CHEBYSHEV'S THEOREM

At least $(1 - 1/z^2)$ of the data values must be within z standard deviations of the mean, where z is any value greater than 1.

Some of the implications of this theorem, with $z = 2, 3$, and 4 standard deviations, follow.

- At least .75, or 75%, of the data values must be within $z = 2$ standard deviations of the mean.
- At least .89, or 89%, of the data values must be within $z = 3$ standard deviations of the mean.
- At least .94, or 94%, of the data values must be within $z = 4$ standard deviations of the mean.

For an example using Chebyshev's theorem, suppose that the midterm test scores for 100 students in a college business statistics course had a mean of 70 and a standard deviation of 5. How many students had test scores between 60 and 80? How many students had test scores between 58 and 82?

For the test scores between 60 and 80, we note that 60 is two standard deviations below the mean and 80 is two standard deviations above the mean. Using Chebyshev's theorem, we see that at least .75, or at least 75%, of the observations must have values within two standard deviations of the mean. Thus, at least 75% of the students must have scored between 60 and 80.

Chebyshev's theorem requires $z > 1$; but z need not be an integer.

For the test scores between 58 and 82, we see that $(58 - 70)/5 = -2.4$ indicates 58 is 2.4 standard deviations below the mean and that $(82 - 70)/5 = +2.4$ indicates 82 is 2.4 standard deviations above the mean. Applying Chebyshev's theorem with $z = 2.4$, we have

$$\left(1 - \frac{1}{z^2}\right) = \left(1 - \frac{1}{(2.4)^2}\right) = .826$$

At least 82.6% of the students must have test scores between 58 and 82.

Empirical Rule

The empirical rule is based on the normal probability distribution, which will be discussed in Chapter 6. The normal distribution is used extensively throughout the text.

One of the advantages of Chebyshev's theorem is that it applies to any data set regardless of the shape of the distribution of the data. Indeed, it could be used with any of the distributions in Figure 3.3. In many practical applications, however, data sets exhibit a symmetric mound-shaped or bell-shaped distribution like the one shown in Figure 3.5. When the data are believed to approximate this distribution, the **empirical rule** can be used to determine the percentage of data values that must be within a specified number of standard deviations of the mean.

EMPIRICAL RULE

For data having a bell-shaped distribution:

- Approximately 68% of the data values will be within one standard deviation of the mean.
- Approximately 95% of the data values will be within two standard deviations of the mean.
- Almost all of the data values will be within three standard deviations of the mean.

FIGURE 3.5   A SYMMETRIC MOUND-SHAPED OR BELL-SHAPED DISTRIBUTION

© Cengage Learning

For example, liquid detergent cartons are filled automatically on a production line. Filling weights frequently have a bell-shaped distribution. If the mean filling weight is 16 ounces and the standard deviation is .25 ounces, we can use the empirical rule to draw the following conclusions.

- Approximately 68% of the filled cartons will have weights between 15.75 and 16.25 ounces (within one standard deviation of the mean).
- Approximately 95% of the filled cartons will have weights between 15.50 and 16.50 ounces (within two standard deviations of the mean).
- Almost all filled cartons will have weights between 15.25 and 16.75 ounces (within three standard deviations of the mean).

Detecting Outliers

Sometimes a data set will have one or more observations with unusually large or unusually small values. These extreme values are called **outliers**. Experienced statisticians take steps to identify outliers and then review each one carefully. An outlier may be a data value that has been incorrectly recorded. If so, it can be corrected before further analysis. An outlier may also be from an observation that was incorrectly included in the data set; if so, it can be removed. Finally, an outlier may be an unusual data value that has been recorded correctly and belongs in the data set. In such cases it should remain.

It is a good idea to check for outliers before making decisions based on data analysis. Errors are often made in recording data and entering data into the computer. Outliers should not necessarily be deleted, but their accuracy and appropriateness should be verified.

Standardized values (z-scores) can be used to identify outliers. Recall that the empirical rule allows us to conclude that for data with a bell-shaped distribution, almost all the data values will be within three standard deviations of the mean. Hence, in using z-scores to identify outliers, we recommend treating any data value with a z-score less than -3 or greater than $+3$ as an outlier. Such data values can then be reviewed for accuracy and to determine whether they belong in the data set.

Refer to the z-scores for the class size data in Table 3.5. The z-score of -1.50 shows the fifth class size is farthest from the mean. However, this standardized value is well within the -3 to $+3$ guideline for outliers. Thus, the z-scores do not indicate that outliers are present in the class size data.

Another approach to identifying outliers is based upon the values of the first and third quartiles (Q_1 and Q_3) and the interquartile range (IQR). Using this method, we first compute the following lower and upper limits:

$$\text{Lower Limit} = Q_1 - 1.5(\text{IQR})$$
$$\text{Upper Limit} = Q_3 + 1.5(\text{IQR})$$

The approach that uses the first and third quartiles and the IQR to identify outliers does not necessarily provide the same results as the approach based upon a z-score less than −3 or greater than +3. Either or both procedures may be used.

An observation is classified as an outlier if its value is less than the lower limit or greater than the upper limit. For the monthly starting salary data shown in Table 3.1, $Q_1 = 3465$, $Q_3 = 3600$, IQR = 135, and the lower and upper limits are

$$\text{Lower Limit} = Q_1 - 1.5(\text{IQR}) = 3465 - 1.5(135) = 3262.5$$
$$\text{Upper Limit} = Q_3 + 1.5(\text{IQR}) = 3600 + 1.5(135) = 3802.5$$

Looking at the data in Table 3.1 we see that there are no observations with a starting salary less than the lower limit of 3262.5. But, there is one starting salary, 3925, that is greater than the upper limit of 3802.5. Thus, 3925 is considered to be an outlier using this alternate approach to identifying outliers.

NOTES AND COMMENTS

1. Chebyshev's theorem is applicable for any data set and can be used to state the minimum number of data values that will be within a certain number of standard deviations of the mean. If the data are known to be approximately bell-shaped, more can be said. For instance, the empirical rule allows us to say that *approximately* 95% of the data values will be within two standard deviations of the mean; Chebyshev's theorem allows us to conclude only that at least 75% of the data values will be in that interval.

2. Before analyzing a data set, statisticians usually make a variety of checks to ensure the validity of data. In a large study it is not uncommon for errors to be made in recording data values or in entering the values into a computer. Identifying outliers is one tool used to check the validity of the data.

Exercises

Methods

35. Consider a sample with data values of 10, 20, 12, 17, and 16. Compute the z-score for each of the five observations.

36. Consider a sample with a mean of 500 and a standard deviation of 100. What are the z-scores for the following data values: 520, 650, 500, 450, and 280?

37. Consider a sample with a mean of 30 and a standard deviation of 5. Use Chebyshev's theorem to determine the percentage of the data within each of the following ranges:
    a. 20 to 40
    b. 15 to 45
    c. 22 to 38
    d. 18 to 42
    e. 12 to 48

38. Suppose the data have a bell-shaped distribution with a mean of 30 and a standard deviation of 5. Use the empirical rule to determine the percentage of data within each of the following ranges:
    a. 20 to 40
    b. 15 to 45
    c. 25 to 35

Applications

39. The results of a national survey showed that on average, adults sleep 6.9 hours per night. Suppose that the standard deviation is 1.2 hours.
    a. Use Chebyshev's theorem to calculate the percentage of individuals who sleep between 4.5 and 9.3 hours.

b. Use Chebyshev's theorem to calculate the percentage of individuals who sleep between 3.9 and 9.9 hours.

c. Assume that the number of hours of sleep follows a bell-shaped distribution. Use the empirical rule to calculate the percentage of individuals who sleep between 4.5 and 9.3 hours per day. How does this result compare to the value that you obtained using Chebyshev's theorem in part (a)?

40. The Energy Information Administration reported that the mean retail price per gallon of regular grade gasoline was $3.43 (Energy Information Administration, July 2012). Suppose that the standard deviation was $.10 and that the retail price per gallon has a bell-shaped distribution.

a. What percentage of regular grade gasoline sold between $3.33 and $3.53 per gallon?

b. What percentage of regular grade gasoline sold between $3.33 and $3.63 per gallon?

c. What percentage of regular grade gasoline sold for more than $3.63 per gallon?

41. The national average for the math portion of the College Board's SAT test is 515 (*The World Almanac,* 2009). The College Board periodically rescales the test scores such that the standard deviation is approximately 100. Answer the following questions using a bell-shaped distribution and the empirical rule for the math test scores.

a. What percentage of students have an SAT math score greater than 615?

b. What percentage of students have an SAT math score greater than 715?

c. What percentage of students have an SAT math score between 415 and 515?

d. What percentage of students have an SAT math score between 315 and 615?

42. Many families in California are using backyard structures for home offices, art studios, and hobby areas as well as for additional storage. Suppose that the mean price for a customized wooden, shingled backyard structure is $3100. Assume that the standard deviation is $1200.

a. What is the z-score for a backyard structure costing $2300?

b. What is the z-score for a backyard structure costing $4900?

c. Interpret the z-scores in parts (a) and (b). Comment on whether either should be considered an outlier.

d. If the cost for a backyard shed-office combination built in Albany, California, is $13,000, should this structure be considered an outlier? Explain.

43. Florida Power & Light (FP&L) Company has enjoyed a reputation for quickly fixing its electric system after storms. However, during the hurricane seasons of 2004 and 2005, a new reality was that the company's historical approach to emergency electric system repairs was no longer good enough (*The Wall Street Journal,* January 16, 2006). Data showing the days required to restore electric service after seven hurricanes during 2004 and 2005 follow.

Hurricane	Days to Restore Service
Charley	13
Frances	12
Jeanne	8
Dennis	3
Katrina	8
Rita	2
Wilma	18

Based on this sample of seven, compute the following descriptive statistics:

a. Mean, median, and mode

b. Range and standard deviation

c. Should Wilma be considered an outlier in terms of the days required to restore electric service?

d. The seven hurricanes resulted in 10 million service interruptions to customers. Do the statistics show that FP&L should consider updating its approach to emergency electric system repairs? Discuss.

44. A sample of 10 NCAA college basketball game scores provided the following data.

NCAA

Winning Team	Points	Losing Team	Points	Winning Margin
Arizona	90	Oregon	66	24
Duke	85	Georgetown	66	19
Florida State	75	Wake Forest	70	5
Kansas	78	Colorado	57	21
Kentucky	71	Notre Dame	63	8
Louisville	65	Tennessee	62	3
Oklahoma State	72	Texas	66	6
Purdue	76	Michigan State	70	6
Stanford	77	Southern Cal	67	10
Wisconsin	76	Illinois	56	20

a. Compute the mean and standard deviation for the points scored by the winning team.
b. Assume that the points scored by the winning teams for all NCAA games follow a bell-shaped distribution. Using the mean and standard deviation found in part (a), estimate the percentage of all NCAA games in which the winning team scores 84 or more points. Estimate the percentage of NCAA games in which the winning team scores more than 90 points.
c. Compute the mean and standard deviation for the winning margin. Do the data contain outliers? Explain.

45. The Associated Press Team Marketing Report listed the Dallas Cowboys as the team with the highest ticket prices in the National Football League (*USA Today,* October 20, 2009). Data showing the average ticket price for a sample of 14 teams in the National Football League are as follows.

NFLTickets

Team	Ticket Price	Team	Ticket Price
Atlanta Falcons	72	Green Bay Packers	63
Buffalo Bills	51	Indianapolis Colts	83
Carolina Panthers	63	New Orleans Saints	62
Chicago Bears	88	New York Jets	87
Cleveland Browns	55	Pittsburgh Steelers	67
Dallas Cowboys	160	Seattle Seahawks	61
Denver Broncos	77	Tennessee Titans	61

a. What is the mean ticket price?
b. The previous year, the mean ticket price was $72.20. What was the percentage increase in the mean ticket price for the one-year period?
c. Compute the median ticket price.
d. Compute the first and third quartiles.
e. Compute the standard deviation.
f. What is the z-score for the Dallas Cowboys ticket price? Should this price be considered an outlier? Explain.

3.4 # Five-Number Summaries and Box Plots

Summary statistics and easy-to-draw graphs based on summary statistics can be used to quickly summarize large quantities of data. In this section we show how five-number summaries and box plots can be developed to identify several characteristics of a large data set.

Five-Number Summary

In a **five-number summary**, five numbers are used to summarize the data:

1. Smallest value
2. First quartile (Q_1)
3. Median (Q_2)
4. Third quartile (Q_3)
5. Largest value

To develop a five-number summary we first arrange the data in ascending order. We then identify the smallest value, the three quartiles, and the largest value. For the monthly starting salary data in Table 3.1 we obtain the following results.

$$3710 \quad 3755 \quad 3850 \mid 3880 \quad 3880 \quad 3890 \mid 3920 \quad 3940 \quad 3950 \mid 4050 \quad 4130 \quad 4325$$

$$Q_1 = 3865 \qquad \underset{\text{(Median)}}{Q_2 = 3905} \qquad Q_3 = 4000$$

We showed how to compute the median, 3905, and the quartiles, $Q_1 = 3865$ and $Q_3 = 4000$, in Section 3.1. Reviewing the data shows that the smallest value is 3710 and the largest value is 4325. Thus the five-number summary for the monthly starting salary data is 3710, 3865, 3905, 4000, 4325. Approximately one-fourth, or 25%, of the observations are between adjacent numbers in a five-number summary.

Box Plot

A **box plot** is a graphical summary of data that is based on a five-number summary. A key to the development of a box plot is the computation of the interquartile range, IQR = $Q_3 - Q_1$. Figure 3.6 shows a box plot for the monthly starting salary data. The steps used to construct the box plot follow.

1. A box is drawn with the ends of the box located at the first and third quartiles. For the monthly starting salary data, $Q_1 = 3865$ and $Q_3 = 4000$. This box contains the middle 50% of the data.

Box plots provide a convenient visual display of several characteristics of a data set.

2. A vertical line is drawn in the box at the location of the median (3905 for the monthly starting salary data).
3. By using the interquartile range, IQR = $Q_3 - Q_1$, *limits* are located at 1.5(IQR) below Q_1 and 1.5(IQR) above Q_3. For the monthly starting salary data, IQR = $Q_3 - Q_1 = 4000 - 3865 = 135$. Thus, the limits are $3865 - 1.5(135) = 3662.5$ and $4000 + 1.5(135) = 4202.5$. Data outside these limits are considered *outliers*.

FIGURE 3.6 BOX PLOT OF THE MONTHLY STARTING SALARY DATA WITH LINES SHOWING THE LOWER AND UPPER LIMITS

FIGURE 3.7   BOX PLOT OF THE MONTHLY STARTING SALARY DATA

4. The dashed lines in Figure 3.6 are called *whiskers.* The whiskers are drawn from the ends of the box to the smallest and largest values *inside the limits* computed in step 3. Thus, the whiskers end at salary values of 3710 and 4130.
5. Finally, the location of each outlier is shown with the symbol *. In Figure 3.6 we see one outlier, 4325.

In Figure 3.6 we included lines showing the location of the upper and lower limits. These lines were drawn to show how the limits are computed and where they are located. Although the limits are always computed, generally they are not drawn on the box plots. Figure 3.7 shows the usual appearance of a box plot for the monthly starting salary data.

MajorSalary

In order to compare monthly starting salaries for business school graduates by major, a sample of 111 recent graduates was selected. The major and the monthly starting salary were recorded for each graduate. Figure 3.8 shows the Minitab box plots for accounting, finance, information systems, management, and marketing majors. Note that the major is shown on the horizontal axis and each box plot is shown vertically above the corresponding major. Displaying box plots in this manner is an excellent graphical technique for making comparisons among two or more groups.

What observations can you make about monthly starting salaries by major using the box plots in Figure 3.8? Specifically, we note the following:

- The higher salaries are in accounting; the lower salaries are in management and marketing.

FIGURE 3.8   MINITAB BOX PLOTS OF MONTHLY STARTING SALARY BY MAJOR

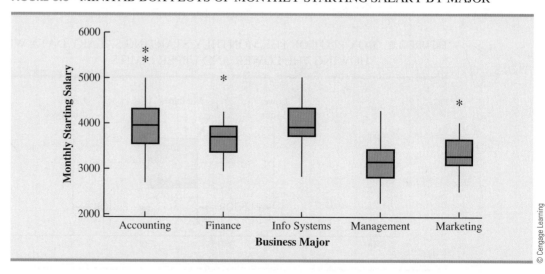

- Based on the medians, accounting and information systems have similar and higher median salaries. Finance is next with management and marketing showing lower median salaries.
- High salary outliers exist for accounting, finance, and marketing majors.
- Finance salaries appear to have the least variation, while accounting salaries appear to have the most variation.

Perhaps you can see additional interpretations based on these box plots.

NOTE AND COMMENT

In Appendix 3.1, we show how to construct a box plot for the starting salary data using Minitab. The box plot obtained looks like the one in Figure 3.7, but turned on its side.

Exercises

Methods

46. Consider a sample with data values of 27, 25, 20, 15, 30, 34, 28, and 25. Provide the five-number summary for the data.

47. Show the box plot for the data in exercise 46.

48. Show the five-number summary and the box plot for the following data: 5, 15, 18, 10, 8, 12, 16, 10, 6.

49. A data set has a first quartile of 42 and a third quartile of 50. Compute the lower and upper limits for the corresponding box plot. Should a data value of 65 be considered an outlier?

Applications

50. Naples, Florida, hosts a half-marathon (13.1-mile race) in January each year. The event attracts top runners from throughout the United States as well as from around the world. In January 2009, 22 men and 31 women entered the 19–24 age class. Finish times in minutes are as follows (*Naples Daily News,* January 19, 2009). Times are shown in order of finish.

Runners

Finish	Men	Women	Finish	Men	Women	Finish	Men	Women
1	65.30	109.03	11	109.05	123.88	21	143.83	136.75
2	66.27	111.22	12	110.23	125.78	22	148.70	138.20
3	66.52	111.65	13	112.90	129.52	23		139.00
4	66.85	111.93	14	113.52	129.87	24		147.18
5	70.87	114.38	15	120.95	130.72	25		147.35
6	87.18	118.33	16	127.98	131.67	26		147.50
7	96.45	121.25	17	128.40	132.03	27		147.75
8	98.52	122.08	18	130.90	133.20	28		153.88
9	100.52	122.48	19	131.80	133.50	29		154.83
10	108.18	122.62	20	138.63	136.57	30		189.27
						31		189.28

a. George Towett of Marietta, Georgia, finished in first place for the men and Lauren Wald of Gainesville, Florida, finished in first place for the women. Compare the first-place finish times for men and women. If the 53 men and women runners had competed as one group, in what place would Lauren have finished?

b. What is the median time for men and women runners? Compare men and women runners based on their median times.

c. Provide a five-number summary for both the men and the women.

d. Are there outliers in either group?

e. Show the box plots for the two groups. Did men or women have the most variation in finish times? Explain.

51. Annual sales, in millions of dollars, for 21 pharmaceutical companies follow.

8408	1374	1872	8879	2459	11413
608	14138	6452	1850	2818	1356
10498	7478	4019	4341	739	2127
3653	5794	8305			

a. Provide a five-number summary.

b. Compute the lower and upper limits.

c. Do the data contain any outliers?

d. Johnson & Johnson's sales are the largest on the list at $14,138 million. Suppose a data entry error (a transposition) had been made and the sales had been entered as $41,138 million. Would the method of detecting outliers in part (c) identify this problem and allow for correction of the data entry error?

e. Show a box plot.

52. *Consumer Reports* provided overall customer satisfaction scores for AT&T, Sprint, T-Mobile, and Verizon cell-phone services in major metropolitan areas throughout the United States. The rating for each service reflects the overall customer satisfaction considering a variety of factors such as cost, connectivity problems, dropped calls, static interference, and customer support. A satisfaction scale from 0 to 100 was used with 0 indicating completely dissatisfied

CellService

Metropolitan Area	AT&T	Sprint	T-Mobile	Verizon
Atlanta	70	66	71	79
Boston	69	64	74	76
Chicago	71	65	70	77
Dallas	75	65	74	78
Denver	71	67	73	77
Detroit	73	65	77	79
Jacksonville	73	64	75	81
Las Vegas	72	68	74	81
Los Angeles	66	65	68	78
Miami	68	69	73	80
Minneapolis	68	66	75	77
Philadelphia	72	66	71	78
Phoenix	68	66	76	81
San Antonio	75	65	75	80
San Diego	69	68	72	79
San Francisco	66	69	73	75
Seattle	68	67	74	77
St. Louis	74	66	74	79
Tampa	73	63	73	79
Washington	72	68	71	76

and 100 indicating completely satisfied. The ratings for the four cell-phone services in 20 metropolitan areas are as shown (*Consumer Reports,* January 2009).

a. Consider T-Mobile first. What is the median rating?

b. Develop a five-number summary for the T-Mobile service.

c. Are there outliers for T-Mobile? Explain.

d. Repeat parts (b) and (c) for the other three cell-phone services.

e. Show the box plots for the four cell-phone services on one graph. Discuss what a comparison of the box plots tells about the four services. Which service did *Consumer Reports* recommend as being best in terms of overall customer satisfaction?

53. The Philadelphia Phillies defeated the Tampa Bay Rays 4 to 3 to win the 2008 major league baseball World Series. Earlier in the major league baseball playoffs, the Philadelphia Phillies defeated the Los Angeles Dodgers to win the National League Championship, while the Tampa Bay Rays defeated the Boston Red Sox to win the American League Championship. The file MLBSalaries contains the salaries for the 28 players on each of these four teams (*USA Today* Salary Database, October 2008). The data, shown in thousands of dollars, have been ordered from the highest salary to the lowest salary for each team.

MLBSalaries

a. Analyze the salaries for the World Champion Philadelphia Phillies. What is the total payroll for the team? What is the median salary? What is the five-number summary?

b. Were there salary outliers for the Philadelphia Phillies? If so, how many and what were the salary amounts?

c. What is the total payroll for each of the other three teams? Develop the five-number summary for each team and identify any outliers.

d. Show the box plots of the salaries for all four teams. What are your interpretations? Of these four teams, does it appear that the team with the higher salaries won the league championships and the World Series?

BorderCrossings

54. The Bureau of Transportation Statistics keeps track of all border crossings through ports of entry along the U.S.-Canadian and U.S.-Mexican borders. The Web file BorderCrossings contains data on the number of personal vehicle crossings (rounded to the nearest 1000) at the 50 busiest ports of entry during the month of August (U.S. Department of Transportation website, February 28, 2013).

a. What are the mean and median number of crossings for these ports of entry?

b. What are the first and third quartiles?

c. Provide a five-number summary.

d. Do the data contain any outliers? Show a box plot.

3.5 Measures of Association Between Two Variables

Thus far we have examined numerical methods used to summarize the data for *one variable at a time.* Often a manager or decision maker is interested in the *relationship between two variables.* In this section we present covariance and correlation as descriptive measures of the relationship between two variables.

We begin by reconsidering the application concerning a stereo and sound equipment store in San Francisco as presented in Section 2.4. The store's manager wants to determine the relationship between the number of weekend television commercials shown and the sales at the store during the following week. Sample data with sales expressed in hundreds of dollars are provided in Table 3.6. It shows 10 observations ($n = 10$), one for each week. The scatter diagram in Figure 3.9 shows a positive relationship, with higher sales (y) associated with a greater number of commercials (x). In fact, the scatter diagram suggests that

TABLE 3.6   SAMPLE DATA FOR THE STEREO AND SOUND EQUIPMENT STORE

Week	Number of Commercials x	Sales Volume ($100s) y
1	2	50
2	5	57
3	1	41
4	3	54
5	4	54
6	1	38
7	5	63
8	3	48
9	4	59
10	2	46

WEB file

Stereo

a straight line could be used as an approximation of the relationship. In the following discussion, we introduce **covariance** as a descriptive measure of the linear association between two variables.

Covariance

For a sample of size n with the observations (x_1, y_1), (x_2, y_2), and so on, the sample covariance is defined as follows.

SAMPLE COVARIANCE

$$s_{xy} = \frac{\sum(x_i - \bar{x})(y_i - \bar{y})}{n - 1} \tag{3.12}$$

FIGURE 3.9   SCATTER DIAGRAM FOR THE STEREO AND SOUND EQUIPMENT STORE

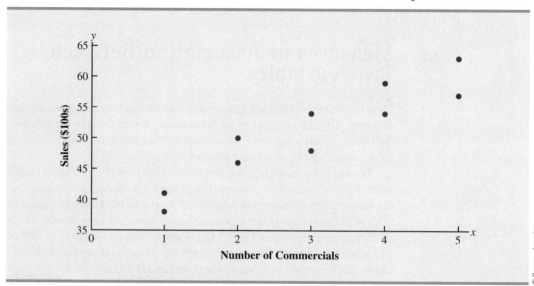

This formula pairs each x_i with a y_i. We then sum the products obtained by multiplying the deviation of each x_i from its sample mean $\bar{x}$ by the deviation of the corresponding y_i from its sample mean $\bar{y}$; this sum is then divided by $n - 1$.

To measure the strength of the linear relationship between the number of commercials x and the sales volume y in the stereo and sound equipment store problem, we use equation (3.12) to compute the sample covariance. The calculations in Table 3.7 show the computation of $\sum(x_i - \bar{x})(y_i - \bar{y})$. Note that $\bar{x} = 30/10 = 3$ and $\bar{y} = 510/10 = 51$. Using equation (3.12), we obtain a sample covariance of

$$s_{xy} = \frac{\sum(x_i - \bar{x})(y_i - \bar{y})}{n - 1} = \frac{99}{9} = 11$$

The formula for computing the covariance of a population of size N is similar to equation (3.12), but we use different notation to indicate that we are working with the entire population.

POPULATION COVARIANCE

$$\sigma_{xy} = \frac{\sum(x_i - \mu_x)(y_i - \mu_y)}{N}$$

(3.13)

In equation (3.13) we use the notation μ_x for the population mean of the variable x and μ_y for the population mean of the variable y. The population covariance σ_{xy} is defined for a population of size N.

TABLE 3.7   CALCULATIONS FOR THE SAMPLE COVARIANCE

x_i	y_i	$x_i - \bar{x}$	$y_i - \bar{y}$	$(x_i - \bar{x})(y_i - \bar{y})$
2	50	−1	−1	1
5	57	2	6	12
1	41	−2	−10	20
3	54	0	3	0
4	54	1	3	3
1	38	−2	−13	26
5	63	2	12	24
3	48	0	−3	0
4	59	1	8	8
2	46	−1	−5	5
Totals 30	510	0	0	99

$$s_{xy} = \frac{\sum(x_i - \bar{x})(y_i - \bar{y})}{n - 1} = \frac{99}{10 - 1} = 11$$

FIGURE 3.10   PARTITIONED SCATTER DIAGRAM FOR THE STEREO AND SOUND
EQUIPMENT STORE

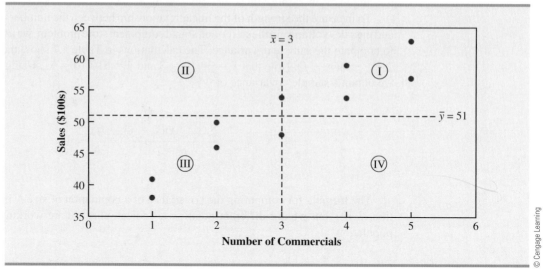

Interpretation of the Covariance

To aid in the interpretation of the sample covariance, consider Figure 3.10. It is the same as the scatter diagram of Figure 3.9 with a vertical dashed line at $\bar{x} = 3$ and a horizontal dashed line at $\bar{y} = 51$. The lines divide the graph into four quadrants. Points in quadrant I correspond to x_i greater than $\bar{x}$ and y_i greater than $\bar{y}$, points in quadrant II correspond to x_i less than $\bar{x}$ and y_i greater than $\bar{y}$, and so on. Thus, the value of $(x_i - \bar{x})(y_i - \bar{y})$ must be positive for points in quadrant I, negative for points in quadrant II, positive for points in quadrant III, and negative for points in quadrant IV.

The covariance is a measure of the linear association between two variables.

If the value of s_{xy} is positive, the points with the greatest influence on s_{xy} must be in quadrants I and III. Hence, a positive value for s_{xy} indicates a positive linear association between x and y; that is, as the value of x increases, the value of y increases. If the value of s_{xy} is negative, however, the points with the greatest influence on s_{xy} are in quadrants II and IV. Hence, a negative value for s_{xy} indicates a negative linear association between x and y; that is, as the value of x increases, the value of y decreases. Finally, if the points are evenly distributed across all four quadrants, the value of s_{xy} will be close to zero, indicating no linear association between x and y. Figure 3.11 shows the values of s_{xy} that can be expected with three different types of scatter diagrams.

Referring again to Figure 3.10, we see that the scatter diagram for the stereo and sound equipment store follows the pattern in the top panel of Figure 3.11. As we should expect, the value of the sample covariance indicates a positive linear relationship with $s_{xy} = 11$.

From the preceding discussion, it might appear that a large positive value for the covariance indicates a strong positive linear relationship and that a large negative value indicates a strong negative linear relationship. However, one problem with using covariance as a measure of the strength of the linear relationship is that the value of the covariance depends on the units of measurement for x and y. For example, suppose we are interested in the relationship between height x and weight y for individuals. Clearly the strength of the relationship should be the same whether we measure height in feet or inches. Measuring the height in inches, however, gives us much larger numerical values for $(x_i - \bar{x})$ than when we measure height in feet. Thus, with

FIGURE 3.11   INTERPRETATION OF SAMPLE COVARIANCE

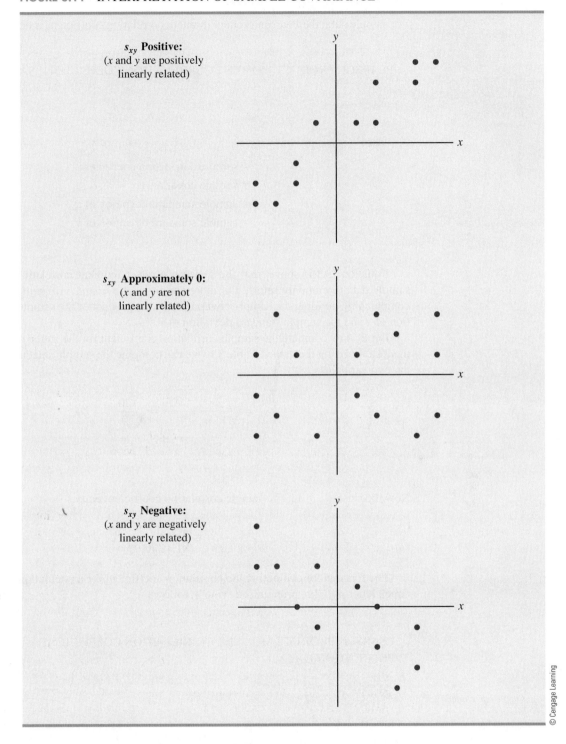

height measured in inches, we would obtain a larger value for the numerator $\sum(x_i - \bar{x})$ $(y_i - \bar{y})$ in equation (3.12)—and hence a larger covariance—when in fact the relationship does not change. A measure of the relationship between two variables that is not affected by the units of measurement for x and y is the **correlation coefficient**.

Correlation Coefficient

For sample data, the Pearson product moment correlation coefficient is defined as follows.

PEARSON PRODUCT MOMENT CORRELATION COEFFICIENT: SAMPLE DATA

$$r_{xy} = \frac{s_{xy}}{s_x s_y} \tag{3.14}$$

where

$$r_{xy} = \text{sample correlation coefficient}$$
$$s_{xy} = \text{sample covariance}$$
$$s_x = \text{sample standard deviation of } x$$
$$s_y = \text{sample standard deviation of } y$$

Equation (3.14) shows that the Pearson product moment correlation coefficient for sample data (commonly referred to more simply as the *sample correlation coefficient*) is computed by dividing the sample covariance by the product of the sample standard deviation of x and the sample standard deviation of y.

Let us now compute the sample correlation coefficient for the stereo and sound equipment store. Using the data in Table 3.6, we can compute the sample standard deviations for the two variables:

$$s_x = \sqrt{\frac{\sum(x_i - \bar{x})^2}{n-1}} = \sqrt{\frac{20}{9}} = 1.49$$

$$s_y = \sqrt{\frac{\sum(y_i - \bar{y})^2}{n-1}} = \sqrt{\frac{566}{9}} = 7.93$$

Now, because $s_{xy} = 11$, the sample correlation coefficient equals

$$r_{xy} = \frac{s_{xy}}{s_x s_y} = \frac{11}{(1.49)(7.93)} = .93$$

The formula for computing the correlation coefficient for a population, denoted by the Greek letter ρ_{xy} (rho, pronounced "row"), follows.

PEARSON PRODUCT MOMENT CORRELATION COEFFICIENT: POPULATION DATA

$$\rho_{xy} = \frac{\sigma_{xy}}{\sigma_x \sigma_y} \tag{3.15}$$

where

$$\rho_{xy} = \text{population correlation coefficient}$$
$$\sigma_{xy} = \text{population covariance}$$
$$\sigma_x = \text{population standard deviation for } x$$
$$\sigma_y = \text{population standard deviation for } y$$

The sample correlation coefficient r_{xy} is a point estimator of the population correlation coefficient ρ_{xy}.

FIGURE 3.12   SCATTER DIAGRAM DEPICTING A PERFECT POSITIVE LINEAR
RELATIONSHIP

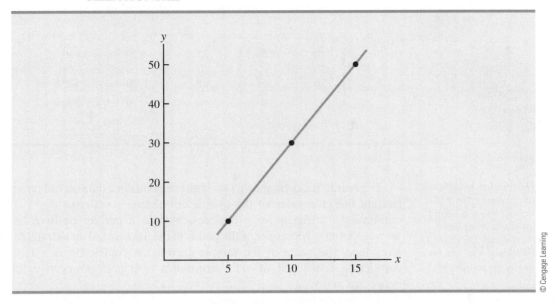

The sample correlation coefficient r_{xy} provides an estimate of the population correlation
coefficient ρ_{xy}.

Interpretation of the Correlation Coefficient

First let us consider a simple example that illustrates the concept of a perfect positive linear
relationship. The scatter diagram in Figure 3.12 depicts the relationship between x and y
based on the following sample data.

x_i	y_i
5	10
10	30
15	50

The straight line drawn through each of the three points shows a perfect linear relationship between x and y. In order to apply equation (3.14) to compute the sample correlation we must first compute s_{xy}, s_x, and s_y. Some of the computations are shown in Table 3.8.
Using the results in this table, we find

$$s_{xy} = \frac{\Sigma(x_i - \bar{x})(y_i - \bar{y})}{n-1} = \frac{200}{2} = 100$$

$$s_x = \sqrt{\frac{\Sigma(x_i - \bar{x})^2}{n-1}} = \sqrt{\frac{50}{2}} = 5$$

$$s_y = \sqrt{\frac{\Sigma(y_i - \bar{y})^2}{n-1}} = \sqrt{\frac{800}{2}} = 20$$

$$r_{xy} = \frac{s_{xy}}{s_x s_y} = \frac{100}{5(20)} = 1$$

Thus, we see that the value of the sample correlation coefficient is 1.

TABLE 3.8   COMPUTATIONS USED IN CALCULATING THE SAMPLE
CORRELATION COEFFICIENT

x_i	y_i	$x_i - \bar{x}$	$(x_i - \bar{x})^2$	$y_i - \bar{y}$	$(y_i - \bar{y})^2$	$(x_i - \bar{x})(y_i - \bar{y})$
5	10	−5	25	−20	400	100
10	30	0	0	0	0	0
15	50	5	25	20	400	100
Totals 30	90	0	50	0	800	200

$\bar{x} = 10 \quad \bar{y} = 30$

© Cengage Learning

The correlation coefficient ranges from −1 to +1. Values close to −1 or +1 indicate a strong linear relationship. The closer the correlation is to zero, the weaker the relationship.

In general, it can be shown that if all the points in a data set fall on a positively sloped straight line, the value of the sample correlation coefficient is +1; that is, a sample correlation coefficient of +1 corresponds to a perfect positive linear relationship between x and y. Moreover, if the points in the data set fall on a straight line having negative slope, the value of the sample correlation coefficient is −1; that is, a sample correlation coefficient of −1 corresponds to a perfect negative linear relationship between x and y.

Let us now suppose that a certain data set indicates a positive linear relationship between x and y but that the relationship is not perfect. The value of r_{xy} will be less than 1, indicating that the points in the scatter diagram are not all on a straight line. As the points deviate more and more from a perfect positive linear relationship, the value of r_{xy} becomes smaller and smaller. A value of r_{xy} equal to zero indicates no linear relationship between x and y, and values of r_{xy} near zero indicate a weak linear relationship.

For the data involving the stereo and sound equipment store, $r_{xy} = .93$. Therefore, we conclude that a strong positive linear relationship occurs between the number of commercials and sales. More specifically, an increase in the number of commercials is associated with an increase in sales.

In closing, we note that correlation provides a measure of linear association and not necessarily causation. A high correlation between two variables does not mean that changes in one variable will cause changes in the other variable. For example, we may find that the quality rating and the typical meal price of restaurants are positively correlated. However, simply increasing the meal price at a restaurant will not cause the quality rating to increase.

NOTE AND COMMENT

Because the correlation coefficient measures only the strength of the linear relationship between two quantitative variables, it is possible for the correlation coefficient to be near zero, suggesting no linear relationship, when the relationship between the two variables is nonlinear. For example, the following scatter diagram shows the relationship between the amount spent by a small retail store for environmental control (heating and cooling) and the daily high outside temperature over 100 days.

The sample correlation coefficient for these data is $r_{xy} = -.007$ and indicates there is no linear relationship between the two variables. However, the scatter diagram provides strong visual evidence of a nonlinear relationship. That is, we can see that as the daily high outside temperature increases, the money spent on environmental control first decreases as less heating is required and then increases as greater cooling is required.

Exercises

Methods

55. Five observations taken for two variables follow.

x_i	4	6	11	3	16
y_i	50	50	40	60	30

a. Develop a scatter diagram with x on the horizontal axis.
b. What does the scatter diagram developed in part (a) indicate about the relationship between the two variables?
c. Compute and interpret the sample covariance.
d. Compute and interpret the sample correlation coefficient.

56. Five observations taken for two variables follow.

x_i	6	11	15	21	27
y_i	6	9	6	17	12

a. Develop a scatter diagram for these data.
b. What does the scatter diagram indicate about a relationship between x and y?
c. Compute and interpret the sample covariance.
d. Compute and interpret the sample correlation coefficient.

Applications

57. Ten major college football bowl games were played in January 2010, with the University of Alabama beating the University of Texas 37 to 21 to become the national champion of college football. The results of the 10 bowl games follow (*USA Today,* January 8, 2010).

Bowl Game	Score	Predicted Point Margin	Actual Point Margin
Outback	Auburn 38 Northwestern 35	5	3
Gator	Florida State 33 West Virginia 21	1	12
Capital One	Penn State 19 LSU 17	3	2
Rose	Ohio State 26 Oregon 17	−2	9
Sugar	Florida 51 Cincinnati 24	14	27
Cotton	Mississippi State 21 Oklahoma State 7	3	14
Alamo	Texas Tech 41 Michigan State 31	9	10
Fiesta	Boise State 17 TCU 10	−4	7
Orange	Iowa 24 Georgia Tech 14	−3	10
Championship	Alabama 37 Texas 21	4	16

BowlGames

The predicted winning point margin was based on Las Vegas betting odds approximately one week before the bowl games were played. For example, Auburn was predicted to beat Northwestern in the Outback Bowl by five points. The actual winning point margin for Auburn was three points. A negative predicted winning point margin means that the team that won the bowl game was an underdog and expected to lose. For example, in the Rose Bowl, Ohio State was a two-point underdog to Oregon and ended up winning by nine points.

a. Develop a scatter diagram with predicted point margin on the horizontal axis.
b. What is the relationship between predicted and actual point margins?
c. Compute and interpret the sample covariance.
d. Compute the sample correlation coefficient. What does this value indicate about the relationship between the Las Vegas predicted point margin and the actual point margin in college football bowl games?

58. A department of transportation's study on driving speed and miles per gallon for midsize automobiles resulted in the following data:

Speed (Miles per Hour)	30	50	40	55	30	25	60	25	50	55
Miles per Gallon	28	25	25	23	30	32	21	35	26	25

Compute and interpret the sample correlation coefficient.

59. At the beginning of 2009, the economic downturn resulted in the loss of jobs and an increase in delinquent loans for housing. The national unemployment rate was 6.5% and the

Housing

Metro Area	Jobless Rate (%)	Delinquent Loan (%)	Metro Area	Jobless Rate (%)	Delinquent Loan (%)
Atlanta	7.1	7.02	New York	6.2	5.78
Boston	5.2	5.31	Orange County	6.3	6.08
Charlotte	7.8	5.38	Orlando	7.0	10.05
Chicago	7.8	5.40	Philadelphia	6.2	4.75
Dallas	5.8	5.00	Phoenix	5.5	7.22
Denver	5.8	4.07	Portland	6.5	3.79
Detroit	9.3	6.53	Raleigh	6.0	3.62
Houston	5.7	5.57	Sacramento	8.3	9.24
Jacksonville	7.3	6.99	St. Louis	7.5	4.40
Las Vegas	7.6	11.12	San Diego	7.1	6.91
Los Angeles	8.2	7.56	San Francisco	6.8	5.57
Miami	7.1	12.11	Seattle	5.5	3.87
Minneapolis	6.3	4.39	Tampa	7.5	8.42
Nashville	6.6	4.78			

percentage of delinquent loans was 6.12% (*The Wall Street Journal,* January 27, 2009). In projecting where the real estate market was headed in the coming year, economists studied the relationship between the jobless rate and the percentage of delinquent loans. The expectation was that if the jobless rate continued to increase, there would also be an increase in the percentage of delinquent loans. The data below show the jobless rate and the delinquent loan percentage for 27 major real estate markets.

   a. Compute the correlation coefficient. Is there a positive correlation between the jobless rate and the percentage of delinquent housing loans? What is your interpretation?
   b. Show a scatter diagram of the relationship between jobless rate and the percentage of delinquent housing loans.

Russell

60. The Russell 1000 is a stock market index consisting of the largest U.S. companies. The Dow Jones Industrial Average is based on 30 large companies. The file Russell gives the annual percentage returns for each of these stock indexes for the years 1988 to 2012 (1stock1 website).

   a. Plot these percentage returns using a scatter plot.
   b. Compute the sample mean and standard deviation for each index.
   c. Compute the sample correlation.
   d. Discuss similarities and differences in these two indexes.

61. The daily high and low temperatures for 14 cities around the world are shown (The Weather Channel, April 22, 2009).

WorldTemp

City	High	Low	City	High	Low
Athens	68	50	London	67	45
Beijing	70	49	Moscow	44	29
Berlin	65	44	Paris	69	44
Cairo	96	64	Rio de Janeiro	76	69
Dublin	57	46	Rome	69	51
Geneva	70	45	Tokyo	70	58
Hong Kong	80	73	Toronto	44	39

   a. What is the sample mean high temperature?
   b. What is the sample mean low temperature?
   c. What is the correlation between the high and low temperatures? Discuss.

3.6 Data Dashboards: Adding Numerical Measures to Improve Effectiveness

In Section 2.5 we provided an introduction to data visualization, a term used to describe the use of graphical displays to summarize and present information about a data set. The goal of data visualization is to communicate key information about the data as effectively and clearly as possible. One of the most widely used data visualization tools is a data dashboard, a set of visual displays that organizes and presents information that is used to monitor the performance of a company or organization in a manner that is easy to read, understand, and interpret. In this section we extend the discussion of data dashboards to show how the addition of numerical measures can improve the overall effectiveness of the display.

The addition of numerical measures, such as the mean and standard deviation of key performance indicators (KPIs), to a data dashboard is critical because numerical measures often provide benchmarks or goals by which KPIs are evaluated. In addition, graphical displays that include numerical measures as components of the display are also frequently

FIGURE 3.13   INITIAL GROGAN OIL INFORMATION TECHNOLOGY CALL CENTER DATA DASHBOARD

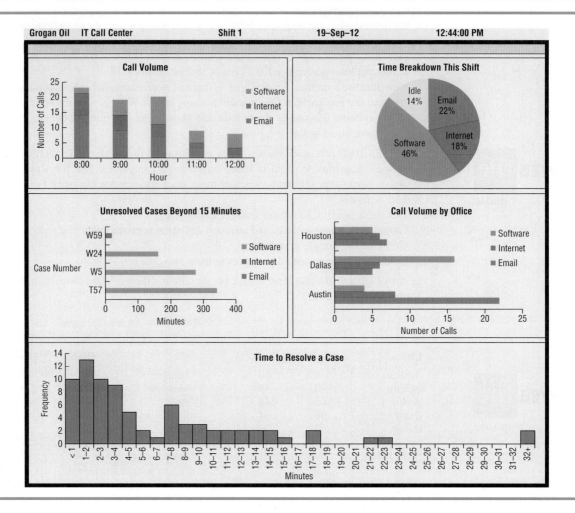

© Cengage Learning

included in data dashboards. We must keep in mind that the purpose of a data dashboard is to provide information on the KPIs in a manner that is easy to read, understand, and interpret. Adding numerical measures and graphs that utilize numerical measures can help us accomplish these objectives.

To illustrate the use of numerical measures in a data dashboard, recall the Grogan Oil Company application that we used in Section 2.5 to introduce the concept of a data dashboard. Grogan Oil has offices located in three cities in Texas: Austin (its headquarters), Houston, and Dallas. Grogan's Information Technology (IT) call center, located in the Austin office, handles calls regarding computer-related problems (software, Internet, and e-mail) from employees in the three offices. Figure 3.13 shows the data dashboard that Grogan developed to monitor the performance of the call center. The key components of this dashboard are as follows:

- The stacked bar chart in the upper left corner of the dashboard shows the call volume for each type of problem (software, Internet, or e-mail) over time.
- The pie chart in the upper right corner of the dashboard shows the percentage of time that call center employees spent on each type of problem or not working on a call (idle).
- For each unresolved case that was received more than 15 minutes ago, the bar chart shown in the middle left portion of the dashboard shows the length of time that each of these cases has been unresolved.

- The bar chart in the middle right portion of the dashboard shows the call volume by office (Houston, Dallas, Austin) for each type of problem.
- The histogram at the bottom of the dashboard shows the distribution of the time to resolve a case for all resolved cases for the current shift.

In order to gain additional insight into the performance of the call center, Grogan's IT manager has decided to expand the current dashboard by adding box plots for the time required to resolve calls received for each type of problem (e-mail, Internet, and software). In addition, a graph showing the time to resolve individual cases has been added in the lower left portion of the dashboard. Finally, the IT manager added a display of summary statistics for each type of problem and summary statistics for each of the first few hours of the shift. The updated dashboard is shown in Figure 3.14.

The IT call center has set a target performance level or benchmark of 10 minutes for the mean time to resolve a case. Furthermore, the center has decided it is undesirable for the time to resolve a case to exceed 15 minutes. To reflect these benchmarks, a black horizontal line at the mean target value of 10 minutes and a red horizontal line at the maximum acceptable level of 15 minutes have been added to both the graph showing the time to resolve cases and the box plots of the time required to resolve calls received for each type of problem.

The summary statistics in the dashboard in Figure 3.14 show that the mean time to resolve an e-mail case is 4.6 minutes, the mean time to resolve an Internet case is 5.4 minutes, and the mean time to resolve a software case is 5.2 minutes. Thus, the mean time to resolve each type of case is better than the target mean (10 minutes).

Reviewing the box plots, we see that the box associated with the e-mail cases is "larger" than the boxes associated with the other two types of cases. The summary statistics also show that the standard deviation of the time to resolve e-mail cases is larger than the standard deviations of the times to resolve the other types of cases. This leads us to take a closer look at the e-mail cases in the two new graphs. The box plot for the e-mail cases has a whisker that extends beyond 15 minutes and an outlier well beyond 15 minutes. The graph of the time to resolve individual cases (in the lower left position of the dashboard) shows that this is because of two calls on e-mail cases during the 9:00 hour that took longer than the target maximum time (15 minutes) to resolve. This analysis may lead the IT call center manager to further investigate why resolution times are more variable for e-mail cases than for Internet or software cases. Based on this analysis, the IT manager may also decide to investigate the circumstances that led to inordinately long resolution times for the two e-mail cases that took longer than 15 minutes to resolve.

The graph of the time to resolve individual cases also shows that most calls received during the first hour of the shift were resolved relatively quickly; the graph also shows that the time to resolve cases increased gradually throughout the morning. This could be due to a tendency for complex problems to arise later in the shift or possibly to the backlog of calls that accumulates over time. Although the summary statistics suggest that cases submitted during the 9:00 hour take the longest to resolve, the graph of time to resolve individual cases shows that two time-consuming e-mail cases and one time-consuming software case were reported during that hour, and this may explain why the mean time to resolve cases during the 9.00 hour is larger than during any other hour of the shift. Overall, reported cases have generally been resolved in 15 minutes or less during this shift.

Drilling down refers to functionality in interactive data dashboards that allows the user to access information and analyses at an increasingly detailed level.

Dashboards such as the Grogan Oil data dashboard are often interactive. For instance, when a manager uses a mouse or a touch screen monitor to position the cursor over the display or point to something on the display, additional information, such as the time to resolve the problem, the time the call was received, and the individual and/or the location that reported the problem, may appear. Clicking on the individual item may also take the user to a new level of analysis at the individual case level.

FIGURE 3.14 UPDATED GROGAN OIL INFORMATION TECHNOLOGY CALL CENTER DATA DASHBOARD

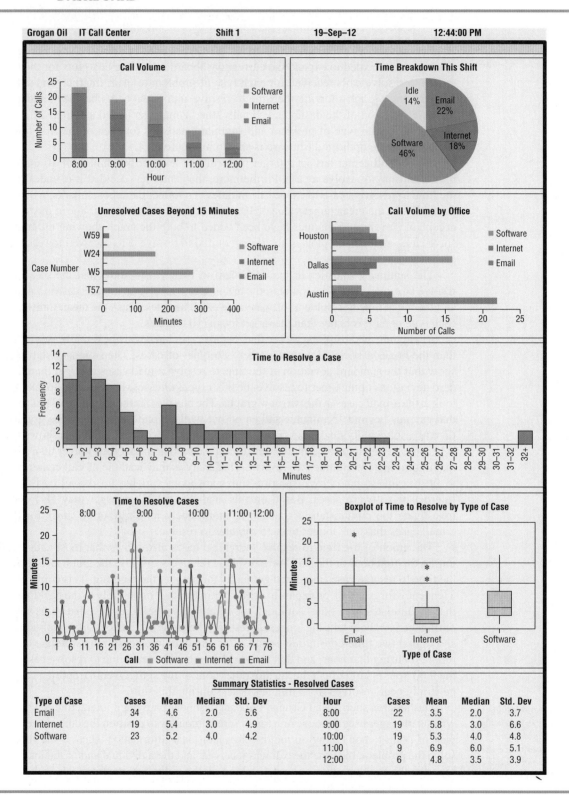

Summary

In this chapter we introduced several descriptive statistics that can be used to summarize the location, variability, and shape of a data distribution. Unlike the tabular and graphical displays introduced in Chapter 2, the measures introduced in this chapter summarize the data in terms of numerical values. When the numerical values obtained are for a sample, they are called sample statistics. When the numerical values obtained are for a population, they are called population parameters. Some of the notation used for sample statistics and population parameters follows.

	Sample Statistic	Population Parameter
Mean	$\bar{x}$	μ
Variance	s^2	σ^2
Standard deviation	s	σ
Covariance	s_{xy}	σ_{xy}
Correlation	r_{xy}	ρ_{xy}

As measures of location, we defined the mean, median, mode, weighted mean, geometric mean, percentiles, and quartiles. Next, we presented the range, interquartile range, variance, standard deviation, and coefficient of variation as measures of variability or dispersion. Our primary measure of the shape of a data distribution was the skewness. Negative values of skewness indicate a data distribution skewed to the left, and positive values of skewness indicate a data distribution skewed to the right. We then described how the mean and standard deviation could be used, applying Chebyshev's theorem and the empirical rule, to provide more information about the distribution of data and to identify outliers.

In Section 3.4 we showed how to develop a five-number summary and a box plot to provide simultaneous information about the location, variability, and shape of the distribution. In Section 3.5 we introduced covariance and the correlation coefficient as measures of association between two variables. In the final section, we showed how adding numerical measures can improve the effectiveness of data dashboards.

The descriptive statistics we discussed can be developed using statistical software packages and spreadsheets. In the chapter-ending appendixes we show how to use Minitab, Excel, and StatTools to develop the descriptive statistics introduced in this chapter.

Glossary

Sample statistic A numerical value used as a summary measure for a sample (e.g., the sample mean, $\bar{x}$, the sample variance, s^2, and the sample standard deviation, s).
Population parameter A numerical value used as a summary measure for a population (e.g., the population mean, μ, the population variance, σ^2, and the population standard deviation, σ).
Point estimator A sample statistic, such as $\bar{x}$, s^2, and s, used to estimate the corresponding population parameter.
Mean A measure of central location computed by summing the data values and dividing by the number of observations.
Weighted mean The mean obtained by assigning each observation a weight that reflects its importance.
Median A measure of central location provided by the value in the middle when the data are arranged in ascending order.
Geometric mean A measure of location that is calculated by finding the nth root of the product of n values.

Mode A measure of location, defined as the value that occurs with greatest frequency.

Percentile A value such that at least p percent of the observations are less than or equal to this value and at least $(100 - p)$ percent of the observations are greater than or equal to this value. The 50th percentile is the median.

Quartiles The 25th, 50th, and 75th percentiles, referred to as the first quartile, the second quartile (median), and third quartile, respectively. The quartiles can be used to divide a data set into four parts, with each part containing approximately 25% of the data.

Range A measure of variability, defined to be the largest value minus the smallest value.

Interquartile range (IQR) A measure of variability, defined to be the difference between the third and first quartiles.

Variance A measure of variability based on the squared deviations of the data values about the mean.

Standard deviation A measure of variability computed by taking the positive square root of the variance.

Coefficient of variation A measure of relative variability computed by dividing the standard deviation by the mean and multiplying by 100.

Skewness A measure of the shape of a data distribution. Data skewed to the left result in negative skewness; a symmetric data distribution results in zero skewness; and data skewed to the right result in positive skewness.

z-score A value computed by dividing the deviation about the mean $(x_i - \bar{x})$ by the standard deviation s. A z-score is referred to as a standardized value and denotes the number of standard deviations x_i is from the mean.

Chebyshev's theorem A theorem that can be used to make statements about the proportion of data values that must be within a specified number of standard deviations of the mean.

Empirical rule A rule that can be used to compute the percentage of data values that must be within one, two, and three standard deviations of the mean for data that exhibit a bell-shaped distribution.

Outlier An unusually small or unusually large data value.

Five-number summary A technique that uses five numbers to summarize the data: smallest value, first quartile, median, third quartile, and largest value.

Box plot A graphical summary of data based on a five-number summary.

Covariance A measure of linear association between two variables. Positive values indicate a positive relationship; negative values indicate a negative relationship.

Correlation coefficient A measure of linear association between two variables that takes on values between -1 and $+1$. Values near $+1$ indicate a strong positive linear relationship; values near -1 indicate a strong negative linear relationship; and values near zero indicate the lack of a linear relationship.

Key Formulas

Sample Mean

$$\bar{x} = \frac{\Sigma x_i}{n}$$ (3.1)

Population Mean

$$\mu = \frac{\Sigma x_i}{N}$$ (3.2)

Weighted Mean

$$\bar{x} = \frac{\Sigma w_i x_i}{w_i}$$ (3.3)

Geometric Mean

$$\bar{x}_g = \sqrt[n]{(x_1)(x_2)\cdots(x_n)} = [(x_1)(x_2)\cdots(x_n)]^{1/n} \tag{3.4}$$

Interquartile Range

$$IQR = Q_3 - Q_1 \tag{3.5}$$

Population Variance

$$\sigma^2 = \frac{\Sigma(x_i - \mu)^2}{N} \tag{3.6}$$

Sample Variance

$$s^2 = \frac{\Sigma(x_i - \bar{x})^2}{n - 1} \tag{3.7}$$

Standard Deviation

$$\text{Sample standard deviation} = s = \sqrt{s^2} \tag{3.8}$$
$$\text{Population standard deviation} = \sigma = \sqrt{\sigma^2} \tag{3.9}$$

Coefficient of Variation

$$\left(\frac{\text{Standard deviation}}{\text{Mean}} \times 100\right)\% \tag{3.10}$$

z-Score

$$z_i = \frac{x_i - \bar{x}}{s} \tag{3.11}$$

Sample Covariance

$$s_{xy} = \frac{\Sigma(x_i - \bar{x})(y_i - \bar{y})}{n - 1} \tag{3.12}$$

Population Covariance

$$\sigma_{xy} = \frac{\Sigma(x_i - \mu_x)(y_i - \mu_y)}{N} \tag{3.13}$$

Pearson Product Moment Correlation Coefficient: Sample Data

$$r_{xy} = \frac{s_{xy}}{s_x s_y} \tag{3.14}$$

Pearson Product Moment Correlation Coefficient: Population Data

$$\rho_{xy} = \frac{\sigma_{xy}}{\sigma_x \sigma_y} \tag{3.15}$$

Supplementary Exercises

62. The average number of times Americans dine out in a week fell from 4.0 in 2008 to 3.8 in 2012 (Zagat.com, April 1, 2012). The number of times a sample of 20 families dined out last week provides the following data.

6	1	5	3	7	3	0	3	1	3
4	1	2	4	1	0	5	6	3	1

   a. Compute the mean and median.
   b. Compute the first and third quartiles.
   c. Compute the range and interquartile range.
   d. Compute the variance and standard deviation.
   e. The skewness measure for these data is 0.34. Comment on the shape of this distribution. Is it the shape you would expect? Why or why not?
   f. Do the data contain outliers?

Coaches

63. *USA Today* reports that NCAA colleges and universities are paying higher salaries to a newly recruited football coach compared to what they paid their previous football coach. (*USA Today*, February 12, 2013). The annual base salaries for the previous head football coach and the new head football coach at 23 schools are given in the file Coaches.

   a. Determine the median annual salary for a previous head football coach and a new head football coach.
   b. Compute the range for salaries for both previous and new head football coaches.
   c. Compute the standard deviation for salaries for both previous and new head football coaches.
   d. Based on your answers to a-c, comment on any differences between the annual base salary a school pays a new head football coach compared to what it paid its pervious head football coach.

64. The average waiting time for a patient at an El Paso physician's office is just over 29 minutes, well above the national average of 21 minutes. In fact, El Paso has the longest physician's office waiting times in the United States (*El Paso Times,* January 8, 2012). In order to address the issue of long patient wait times, some physicians' offices are using wait tracking systems to notify patients of expected wait times. Patients can adjust their arrival times based on this information and spend less time in waiting rooms. The following data show wait times (minutes) for a sample of patients at offices that do not have an office tracking system and wait times for a sample of patients at offices with an office tracking system.

   a. What are the mean and median patient wait times for offices with a wait tracking system? What are the mean and median patient wait times for offices without a wait tracking system?

WaitTracking

Without Wait Tracking System	With Wait Tracking System
24	31
67	11
17	14
20	18
31	12
44	37
12	9
23	13
16	12
37	15

b. What are the variance and standard deviation of patient wait times for offices with a wait tracking system? What are the variance and standard deviation of patient wait times for visits to offices without a wait tracking system?

c. Do offices with a wait tracking system have shorter patient wait times than offices without a wait tracking system? Explain.

d. Considering only offices without a wait tracking system, what is the z-score for the tenth patient in the sample?

e. Considering only offices with a wait tracking system, what is the z-score for the sixth patient in the sample? How does this z-score compare with the z-score you calculated for part (d)?

f. Based on z-scores, do the data for offices without a wait tracking system contain any outliers? Based on z-scores, do the data for offices with a wait tracking system contain any outliers?

Sleep

65. U.S. companies lose $63.2 billion per year from workers with insomnia. Workers lose an average of 7.8 days of productivity per year due to lack of sleep (*Wall Street Journal*, January 23, 2013). The following data show the number of hours of sleep attained during a recent night for a sample of 20 workers.

6	5	10	5	6	9	9	5	9	5
8	7	8	6	9	8	9	6	10	8

a. What is the mean number of hours of sleep for this sample?

b. What is the variance? Standard deviation?

Smartphone

66. A study of smartphone users shows that 68% of smartphone use occurs at home and a user spends an average of 410 minutes per month using a smartphone to interact with other people (*Harvard Business Review,* January–February 2013). Consider the following data indicating the number of minutes in a month spent interacting with others via a smartphone for a sample of 50 smartphone users.

353	458	404	394	416
437	430	369	448	430
431	469	446	387	445
354	468	422	402	360
444	424	441	357	435
461	407	470	413	351
464	374	417	460	352
445	387	468	368	430
384	367	436	390	464
405	372	401	388	367

a. What is the mean number of minutes spent interacting with others for this sample? How does it compare to the mean reported in the study?

b. What is the standard deviation for this sample?

c. Are there any outliers in this sample?

67. Public transportation and the automobile are two methods an employee can use to get to work each day. Samples of times recorded for each method are shown. Times are in minutes.

Public Transportation:	28	29	32	37	33	25	29	32	41	34
Automobile:		29	31	33	32	34	30	31	32	35	33

a. Compute the sample mean time to get to work for each method.

b. Compute the sample standard deviation for each method.

c. On the basis of your results from parts (a) and (b), which method of transportation should be preferred? Explain.

d. Develop a box plot for each method. Does a comparison of the box plots support your conclusion in part (c)?

68. Consumers borrow money for many different reasons, including the purchase of a home, car, and appliances, to remodel, or to help pay for college. Approximately 75% of U.S. households carry some debt (*Wall Street Journal,* February 25, 2013). Consider the amount of household debt in the sample of 25 households shown below.

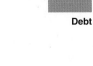

Debt

122,231	69,402	52,055	131,176	59,423
125,409	142,762	72,576	58,458	18,927
59,025	131,934	148,782	57,380	124,831
116,128	107,320	79,649	110,354	53,880
60,370	68,140	94,513	97,544	72,140

a. What is the median amount of household debt?

b. Provide a five-number summary of this sample data.

c. What is the mean household debt for this sample?

d. Does this sample contain any outliers?

e. Would you prefer to use the mean or the median when describing household debt? Why?

69. The U.S. Census Bureau's American Community Survey reported the percentage of children under 18 years of age who had lived below the poverty level during the previous 12 months (U.S. Census Bureau website, August 2008). The region of the country, Northeast (NE), Southeast (SE), Midwest (MW), Southwest (SW), and West (W), and the percentage of children under 18 who had lived below the poverty level are shown for each state.

a. What is the median poverty level percentage for the 50 states?

b. What are the first and third quartiles? What is your interpretation of the quartiles?

PovertyLevel

State	Region	Poverty %	State	Region	Poverty %
Alabama	SE	23.0	Montana	W	17.3
Alaska	W	15.1	Nebraska	MW	14.4
Arizona	SW	19.5	Nevada	W	13.9
Arkansas	SE	24.3	New Hampshire	NE	9.6
California	W	18.1	New Jersey	NE	11.8
Colorado	W	15.7	New Mexico	SW	25.6
Connecticut	NE	11.0	New York	NE	20.0
Delaware	NE	15.8	North Carolina	SE	20.2
Florida	SE	17.5	North Dakota	MW	13.0
Georgia	SE	20.2	Ohio	MW	18.7
Hawaii	W	11.4	Oklahoma	SW	24.3
Idaho	W	15.1	Oregon	W	16.8
Illinois	MW	17.1	Pennsylvania	NE	16.9
Indiana	MW	17.9	Rhode Island	NE	15.1
Iowa	MW	13.7	South Carolina	SE	22.1
Kansas	MW	15.6	South Dakota	MW	16.8
Kentucky	SE	22.8	Tennessee	SE	22.7
Louisiana	SE	27.8	Texas	SW	23.9
Maine	NE	17.6	Utah	W	11.9
Maryland	NE	9.7	Vermont	NE	13.2
Massachusetts	NE	12.4	Virginia	SE	12.2
Michigan	MW	18.3	Washington	W	15.4
Minnesota	MW	12.2	West Virginia	SE	25.2
Mississippi	SE	29.5	Wisconsin	MW	14.9
Missouri	MW	18.6	Wyoming	W	12.0

c.   Show a box plot for the data. Interpret the box plot in terms of what it tells you about the level of poverty for children in the United States. Are any states considered outliers? Discuss.

d.   Identify the states in the lower quartile. What is your interpretation of this group and what region or regions are represented most in the lower quartile?

70.   *Travel + Leisure* magazine presented its annual list of the 500 best hotels in the world (*Travel + Leisure,* January 2009). The magazine provides a rating for each hotel along with a brief description that includes the size of the hotel, amenities, and the cost per night for a double room. A sample of 12 of the top-rated hotels in the United States follows.

Travel

Hotel	Location	Rooms	Cost/Night
Boulders Resort & Spa	Phoenix, AZ	220	499
Disney's Wilderness Lodge	Orlando, FL	727	340
Four Seasons Hotel Beverly Hills	Los Angeles, CA	285	585
Four Seasons Hotel	Boston, MA	273	495
Hay-Adams	Washington, DC	145	495
Inn on Biltmore Estate	Asheville, NC	213	279
Loews Ventana Canyon Resort	Phoenix, AZ	398	279
Mauna Lani Bay Hotel	Island of Hawaii	343	455
Montage Laguna Beach	Laguna Beach, CA	250	595
Sofitel Water Tower	Chicago, IL	414	367
St. Regis Monarch Beach	Dana Point, CA	400	675
The Broadmoor	Colorado Springs, CO	700	420

a.   What is the mean number of rooms?

b.   What is the mean cost per night for a double room?

c.   Develop a scatter diagram with the number of rooms on the horizontal axis and the cost per night on the vertical axis. Does there appear to be a relationship between the number of rooms and the cost per night? Discuss.

d.   What is the sample correlation coefficient? What does it tell you about the relationship between the number of rooms and the cost per night for a double room? Does this appear reasonable? Discuss.

71.   Morningstar tracks the performance of a large number of companies and publishes an evaluation of each. Along with a variety of financial data, Morningstar includes a Fair Value estimate for the price that should be paid for a share of the company's common stock. Data for 30 companies are available in the file named FairValue. The data include the Fair Value estimate per share of common stock, the most recent price per share, and the earning per share for the company (*Morningstar Stocks 500,* 2008).

FairValue

a.   Develop a scatter diagram for the Fair Value and Share Price data with Share Price on the horizontal axis. What is the sample correlation coefficient, and what can you say about the relationship between the variables?

b.   Develop a scatter diagram for the Fair Value and Earnings per Share data with Earnings per Share on the horizontal axis. What is the sample correlation coefficient, and what can you say about the relationship between the variables?

72.   Does a major league baseball team's record during spring training indicate how the team will play during the regular season? Over the last six years, the correlation coefficient between a team's winning percentage in spring training and its winning percentage in the regular season is .18 (*The Wall Street Journal,* March 30, 2009). Shown are the winning percentages for the 14 American League teams during the 2008 season.

SpringTraining

Team	Spring Training	Regular Season	Team	Spring Training	Regular Season
Baltimore Orioles	.407	.422	Minnesota Twins	.500	.540
Boston Red Sox	.429	.586	New York Yankees	.577	.549
Chicago White Sox	.417	.546	Oakland A's	.692	.466
Cleveland Indians	.569	.500	Seattle Mariners	.500	.377
Detroit Tigers	.569	.457	Tampa Bay Rays	.731	.599
Kansas City Royals	.533	.463	Texas Rangers	.643	.488
Los Angeles Angels	.724	.617	Toronto Blue Jays	.448	.531

a. What is the correlation coefficient between the spring training and the regular season winning percentages?

b. What is your conclusion about a team's record during spring training indicating how the team will play during the regular season? What are some of the reasons why this occurs? Discuss.

73. The days to maturity for a sample of five money market funds are shown here. The dollar amounts invested in the funds are provided. Use the weighted mean to determine the mean number of days to maturity for dollars invested in these five money market funds.

Days to Maturity	Dollar Value ($millions)
20	20
12	30
7	10
5	15
6	10

74. Automobiles traveling on a road with a posted speed limit of 55 miles per hour are checked for speed by a state police radar system. Following is a frequency distribution of speeds.

Speed (miles per hour)	Frequency
45–49	10
50–54	40
55–59	150
60–64	175
65–69	75
70–74	15
75–79	10
Total	475

a. What is the mean speed of the automobiles traveling on this road?

b. Compute the variance and the standard deviation.

75. The Panama Railroad Company was established in 1850 to construct a railroad across the isthmus that would allow fast and easy access between the Atlantic and Pacific Oceans. The following table (*The Big Ditch*, Mauer and Yu, 2011) provides annual returns for Panama Railroad stock from 1853 through 1880.

Year	Return on Panama Railroad Company Stock (%)
1853	−1
1854	−9
1855	19
1856	2
1857	3
1858	36
1859	21
1860	16
1861	−5
1862	43
1863	44
1864	48
1865	7
1866	11
1867	23
1868	20
1869	−11
1870	−51
1871	−42
1872	39
1873	42
1874	12
1875	26
1876	9
1877	−6
1878	25
1879	31
1880	30

WEB file

PanamaRailroad

a. Create a graph of the annual returns on the stock. The New York Stock Exchange earned an annual average return of 8.4% from 1853 through 1880. Can you tell from the graph if the Panama Railroad Company stock outperformed the New York Stock Exchange?

b. Calculate the mean annual return on Panama Railroad Company stock from 1853 through 1880. Did the stock outperform the New York Stock Exchange over the same period?

Case Problem 1   Pelican Stores

Pelican Stores, a division of National Clothing, is a chain of women's apparel stores operating throughout the country. The chain recently ran a promotion in which discount coupons were sent to customers of other National Clothing stores. Data collected for a sample of 100 in-store credit card transactions at Pelican Stores during one day while the promotion was running are contained in the file named PelicanStores. Table 3.9 shows a portion of the data set. The proprietary card method of payment refers to charges made using a National Clothing charge card. Customers who made a purchase using a discount coupon are referred to as promotional customers and customers who made a purchase but did not use a discount coupon are referred to as regular customers. Because the promotional coupons were not sent to regular Pelican Stores customers, management considers the sales made to people presenting the promotional coupons as sales it would not otherwise make. Of course, Pelican also hopes that the promotional customers will continue to shop at its stores.

TABLE 3.9   SAMPLE OF 100 CREDIT CARD PURCHASES AT PELICAN STORES

Customer	Type of Customer	Items	Net Sales	Method of Payment	Gender	Marital Status	Age
1	Regular	1	39.50	Discover	Male	Married	32
2	Promotional	1	102.40	Proprietary Card	Female	Married	36
3	Regular	1	22.50	Proprietary Card	Female	Married	32
4	Promotional	5	100.40	Proprietary Card	Female	Married	28
5	Regular	2	54.00	MasterCard	Female	Married	34
6	Regular	1	44.50	MasterCard	Female	Married	44
7	Promotional	2	78.00	Proprietary Card	Female	Married	30
8	Regular	1	22.50	Visa	Female	Married	40
9	Promotional	2	56.52	Proprietary Card	Female	Married	46
10	Regular	1	44.50	Proprietary Card	Female	Married	36
.	.	.	.	.	.	.	.
.	.	.	.	.	.	.	.
.	.	.	.	.	.	.	.
96	Regular	1	39.50	MasterCard	Female	Married	44
97	Promotional	9	253.00	Proprietary Card	Female	Married	30
98	Promotional	10	287.59	Proprietary Card	Female	Married	52
99	Promotional	2	47.60	Proprietary Card	Female	Married	30
100	Promotional	1	28.44	Proprietary Card	Female	Married	44

PelicanStores

© Cengage Learning

Most of the variables shown in Table 3.9 are self-explanatory, but two of the variables require some clarification.

Items   The total number of items purchased
Net Sales   The total amount ($) charged to the credit card

Pelican's management would like to use this sample data to learn about its customer base and to evaluate the promotion involving discount coupons.

Managerial Report

Use the methods of descriptive statistics presented in this chapter to summarize the data and comment on your findings. At a minimum, your report should include the following:

1. Descriptive statistics on net sales and descriptive statistics on net sales by various classifications of customers.
2. Descriptive statistics concerning the relationship between age and net sales.

Case Problem 2   Motion Picture Industry

The motion picture industry is a competitive business. More than 50 studios produce several hundred new motion pictures each year, and the financial success of the motion pictures varies considerably. The opening weekend gross sales, the total gross sales, the number of theaters the movie was shown in, and the number of weeks the motion picture was in release are common variables used to measure the success of a motion picture. Data on the top 100 grossing motion pictures released in 2011 (Box Office Mojo website, March 17, 2012) are contained in a file named 2011Movies. Table 3.10 shows the data for the first 10 motion pictures in this file. Note that some movies, such as *War Horse*, were released late in 2011 and continued to run in 2012.

TABLE 3.10 PERFORMANCE DATA FOR 10 MOTION PICTURES

2011Movies

Motion Picture	Opening Gross Sales ($millions)	Total Gross Sales ($millions)	Number of Theaters	Weeks in Release
Harry Potter and the Deathly Hallows Part 2	169.19	381.01	4375	19
Transformers: Dark of the Moon	97.85	352.39	4088	15
The Twilight Saga: Breaking Dawn Part 1	138.12	281.29	4066	14
The Hangover Part II	85.95	254.46	3675	16
Pirates of the Caribbean: On Stranger Tides	90.15	241.07	4164	19
Fast Five	86.20	209.84	3793	15
Mission: Impossible—Ghost Protocol	12.79	208.55	3555	13
Cars 2	66.14	191.45	4115	25
Sherlock Holmes: A Game of Shadows	39.64	186.59	3703	13
Thor	65.72	181.03	3963	16

© Cengage Learning

Managerial Report

Use the numerical methods of descriptive statistics presented in this chapter to learn how these variables contribute to the success of a motion picture. Include the following in your report:

1. Descriptive statistics for each of the four variables along with a discussion of what the descriptive statistics tell us about the motion picture industry.
2. What motion pictures, if any, should be considered high-performance outliers? Explain.
3. Descriptive statistics showing the relationship between total gross sales and each of the other variables. Discuss.

Case Problem 3 Business Schools of Asia–Pacific

Asian

The pursuit of a higher education degree in business is now international. A survey shows that more and more Asians choose the master of business administration (MBA) degree route to corporate success. As a result, the number of applicants for MBA courses at Asia-Pacific schools continues to increase.

Across the region, thousands of Asians show an increasing willingness to temporarily shelve their careers and spend two years in pursuit of a theoretical business qualification. Courses in these schools are notoriously tough and include economics, banking, marketing, behavioral sciences, labor relations, decision making, strategic thinking, business law, and more. The data set in Table 3.11 shows some of the characteristics of the leading Asia-Pacific business schools.

Managerial Report

Use the methods of descriptive statistics to summarize the data in Table 3.11. Discuss your findings.

1. Include a summary for each variable in the data set. Make comments and interpretations based on maximums and minimums, as well as the appropriate means and

TABLE 3.11 DATA FOR 25 ASIA-PACIFIC BUSINESS SCHOOLS

Business School	Full-Time Enrollment	Students per Faculty	Local Tuition ($)	Foreign Tuition ($)	Age	%Foreign	GMAT	English Test	Work Experience	Starting Salary ($)
Melbourne Business School	200	5	24,420	29,600	28	47	Yes	No	Yes	71,400
University of New South Wales (Sydney)	228	4	19,993	32,582	29	28	Yes	No	Yes	65,200
Indian Institute of Management (Ahmedabad)	392	5	4,300	4,300	22	0	No	No	No	7,100
Chinese University of Hong Kong	90	5	11,140	11,140	29	10	Yes	No	No	31,000
International University of Japan (Niigata)	126	4	33,060	33,060	28	60	Yes	Yes	No	87,000
Asian Institute of Management (Manila)	389	5	7,562	9,000	25	50	Yes	No	Yes	22,800
Indian Institute of Management (Bangalore)	380	5	3,935	16,000	23	1	Yes	No	No	7,500
National University of Singapore	147	6	6,146	7,170	29	51	Yes	Yes	Yes	43,300
Indian Institute of Management (Calcutta)	463	8	2,880	16,000	23	0	No	No	No	7,400
Australian National University (Canberra)	42	2	20,300	20,300	30	80	Yes	Yes	Yes	46,600
Nanyang Technological University (Singapore)	50	5	8,500	8,500	32	20	Yes	No	Yes	49,300
University of Queensland (Brisbane)	138	17	16,000	22,800	32	26	No	No	Yes	49,600
Hong Kong University of Science and Technology	60	2	11,513	11,513	26	37	Yes	No	Yes	34,000
Macquarie Graduate School of Management (Sydney)	12	8	17,172	19,778	34	27	No	No	Yes	60,100
Chulalongkorn University (Bangkok)	200	7	17,355	17,355	25	6	Yes	No	Yes	17,600
Monash Mt. Eliza Business School (Melbourne)	350	13	16,200	22,500	30	30	Yes	Yes	Yes	52,500
Asian Institute of Management (Bangkok)	300	10	18,200	18,200	29	90	No	Yes	Yes	25,000
University of Adelaide	20	19	16,426	23,100	30	10	No	No	Yes	66,000
Massey University (Palmerston North, New Zealand)	30	15	13,106	21,625	37	35	No	Yes	Yes	41,400
Royal Melbourne Institute of Technology Business Graduate School	30	7	13,880	17,765	32	30	No	Yes	Yes	48,900
Jamnalal Bajaj Institute of Management Studies (Mumbai)	240	9	1,000	1,000	24	0	No	No	Yes	7,000
Curtin Institute of Technology (Perth)	98	15	9,475	19,097	29	43	Yes	No	Yes	55,000
Lahore University of Management Sciences	70	14	11,250	26,300	23	2.5	No	No	No	7,500
Universiti Sains Malaysia (Penang)	30	5	2,260	2,260	32	15	No	Yes	Yes	16,000
De La Salle University (Manila)	44	17	3,300	3,600	28	3.5	Yes	No	Yes	13,100

proportions. What new insights do these descriptive statistics provide concerning Asia-Pacific business schools?
2. Summarize the data to compare the following:
   a. Any difference between local and foreign tuition costs.
   b. Any difference between mean starting salaries for schools requiring and not requiring work experience.
   c. Any difference between starting salaries for schools requiring and not requiring English tests.
3. Do starting salaries appear to be related to tuition?
4. Present any additional graphical and numerical summaries that will be beneficial in communicating the data in Table 3.11 to others.

Case Problem 4 Heavenly Chocolates Website Transactions

Heavenly Chocolates manufactures and sells quality chocolate products at its plant and retail store located in Saratoga Springs, New York. Two years ago the company developed a website and began selling its products over the Internet. Website sales have exceeded the company's expectations, and management is now considering strategies to increase sales even further. To learn more about the website customers, a sample of 50 Heavenly Chocolate transactions was selected from the previous month's sales. Data showing the day of the week each transaction was made, the type of browser the customer used, the time spent on the website, the number of website pages viewed, and the amount spent by each of the 50 customers are contained in the file named Shoppers. A portion of the data are shown in Table 3.12.

Heavenly Chocolates would like to use the sample data to determine if online shoppers who spend more time and view more pages also spend more money during their visit to the website. The company would also like to investigate the effect that the day of the week and the type of browser have on sales.

TABLE 3.12 A SAMPLE OF 50 HEAVENLY CHOCOLATES WEBSITE TRANSACTIONS

WEB file

Shoppers

Customer	Day	Browser	Time (min)	Pages Viewed	Amount Spent ($)
1	Mon	Internet Explorer	12.0	4	54.52
2	Wed	Other	19.5	6	94.90
3	Mon	Internet Explorer	8.5	4	26.68
4	Tue	Firefox	11.4	2	44.73
5	Wed	Internet Explorer	11.3	4	66.27
6	Sat	Firefox	10.5	6	67.80
7	Sun	Internet Explorer	11.4	2	36.04
.	.	.	.	.	.
.	.	.	.	.	.
.	.	.	.	.	.
48	Fri	Internet Explorer	9.7	5	103.15
49	Mon	Other	7.3	6	52.15
50	Fri	Internet Explorer	13.4	3	98.75

© Cengage Learning

Managerial Report

Use the methods of descriptive statistics to learn about the customers who visit the Heavenly Chocolates website. Include the following in your report.

1. Graphical and numerical summaries for the length of time the shopper spends on the website, the number of pages viewed, and the mean amount spent per transaction. Discuss what you learn about Heavenly Cholcolates' online shoppers from these numerical summaries.
2. Summarize the frequency, the total dollars spent, and the mean amount spent per transaction for each day of week. What observations can you make about Hevenly Chocolates' business based on the day of the week? Discuss.
3. Summarize the frequency, the total dollars spent, and the mean amount spent per transaction for each type of browser. What observations can you make about Heavenly Chocolate's business based on the type of browser? Discuss.
4. Develop a scatter diagram and compute the sample correlation coefficient to explore the relationship between the time spent on the website and the dollar amount spent. Use the horizontal axis for the time spent on the website. Discuss.
5. Develop a scatter diagram and compute the sample correlation coefficient to explore the relationship between the the number of website pages viewed and the amount spent. Use the horizontal axis for the number of website pages viewed. Discuss.
6. Develop a scatter diagram and compute the sample correlation coefficient to explore the relationship between the time spent on the website and the number of pages viewed. Use the horizontal axis to represent the number of pages viewed. Discuss.

Case Problem 5   African Elephant Populations

Although millions of elephants once roamed across Africa, by the mid-1980s elephant populations in African nations had been devastated by poaching. Elephants are important to African ecosystems. In tropical forests, elephants create clearings in the canopy that encourage new tree growth. In savannas, elephants reduce bush cover to create an environment that is favorable to browsing and grazing animals. In addition, the seeds of many plant species depend on passing through an elephant's digestive tract before germination.

The status of the elephant now varies greatly across the continent; in some nations, strong measures have been taken to effectively protect elephant populations, while in other nations the elephant populations remain in danger due to poaching for meat and ivory, loss of habitat, and conflict with humans. Table 3.13 shows elephant populations for several African nations in 1979, 1989, and 2007 (Lemieux and Clarke, "The International Ban on Ivory Sales and Its Effects on Elephant Poaching in Africa," *British Journal of Criminology,* 49(4), 2009).

The David Sheldrick Wildlife Trust was established in 1977 to honor the memory of naturalist David Leslie William Sheldrick, who founded Warden of Tsavo East National Park in Kenya and headed the Planning Unit of the Wildlife Conservation and Management Department in that country. Management of the Sheldrick Trust would like to know what these data indicate about elephant populations in various African countries since 1979.

Managerial Report

Use methods of descriptive statistics to summarize the data and comment on changes in elephant populations in African nations since 1979. At a minimum your report should include the following.

1. The mean annual change in elephant population for each country in the 10 years from 1979 to 1989, and a discussion of which countries saw the largest changes in elephant population over this 10-year period.

TABLE 3.13   ELEPHANT POPULATIONS FOR SEVERAL AFRICAN NATIONS IN 1979, 1989, AND 2007

Country	Elephant population 1979	1989	2007
Angola	12,400	12,400	2,530
Botswana	20,000	51,000	175,487
Cameroon	16,200	21,200	15,387
Cen African Rep	63,000	19,000	3,334
Chad	15,000	3,100	6,435
Congo	10,800	70,000	22,102
Dem Rep of Congo	377,700	85,000	23,714
Gabon	13,400	76,000	70,637
Kenya	65,000	19,000	31,636
Mozambique	54,800	18,600	26,088
Somalia	24,300	6,000	70
Sudan	134,000	4,000	300
Tanzania	316,300	80,000	167,003
Zambia	150,000	41,000	29,231
Zimbabwe	30,000	43,000	99,107

AfricanElephants

© Cengage Learning

2. The mean annual change in elephant population for each country from 1989 to 2007, and a discussion of which countries saw the largest changes in elephant population over this 18-year period.
3. A comparison of your results from parts 1 and 2, and a discussion of the conclusions you can draw from this comparison.

Appendix 3.1   Descriptive Statistics Using Minitab

In this appendix, we describe how Minitab can be used to compute a variety of descriptive statistics and display box plots. We then show how Minitab can be used to obtain covariance and correlation measures for two variables.

Descriptive Statistics

2012StartSalary

Table 3.1 provided the starting salaries for 12 business school graduates. These data are in column C2 of the file 2012StartSalary. The following steps can be used to generate descriptive statistics for the starting salary data.

Step 1. Select the **Stat** menu
Step 2. Choose **Basic Statistics**
Step 3. Choose **Display Descriptive Statistics**
Step 4. When the Display Descriptive Statistics dialog box appears:
  Enter C2 in the **Variables** box
  Click **OK**

Figure 3.15 shows the descriptive statistics obtained using Minitab. Definitions of the headings follow.

N	number of data values	Minimum	minimum data value
N*	number of missing data values	Q1	first quartile
Mean	mean	Median	median
SE Mean	standard error of mean	Q3	third quartile
StDev	standard deviation	Maximum	maximum data value

FIGURE 3.15 DESCRIPTIVE STATISTICS PROVIDED BY MINITAB

N	N*	Mean	SEMean	StDev
12	0	3940.0	47.8	165.7
Minimum	Q1	Median	Q3	Maximum
3710.0	4025.0	3905.0	4025.0	4325.0

© Cengage Learning

The label SE Mean refers to the *standard error of the mean.* It is computed by dividing the standard deviation by the square root of N. The interpretation and use of this measure are discussed in Chapter 7 when we introduce the topics of sampling and sampling distributions.

The ten descriptive statistics shown in Figure 3.15 are the default descriptive statistics selected automatically by Minitab. These descriptive statistics are of interest to the majority of users. However, Minitab provides 15 additional descriptive statistics that may be selected depending upon the preferences of the user. The variance, coefficient of variation, range, interquartile range, mode, and skewness are among the additional descriptive statistics available. To select one or more of these additional descriptive statistics, modify step 4 as follows.

Step 4. When the Display Descriptive Statistics dialog box appears:
    Enter C2 in the **Variables** box
    Click **Statistics**
    Select the **descriptive statistics** you wish to obtain or
        choose **All** to obtain all 25 descriptive statistics
    Click **OK**
    Click **OK**

Finally, note that Minitab's quartiles $Q_1 = 3857.5$ and $Q_3 = 4025.0$ are slightly different from the quartiles $Q_1 = 3865$ and $Q_3 = 4000$ computed in Section 3.1. The different conventions* used to identify the quartiles explain this variation. Hence, the values of Q_1 and Q_3 provided by one convention may not be identical to the values of Q_1 and Q_3 provided by another convention. Any differences tend to be negligible, however, and the results provided should not mislead the user in making the usual interpretations associated with quartiles.

Box Plot

The following steps use the file 2012StartSalary to generate the box plot for the starting salary data.

Step 1. Select the **Graph** menu
Step 2. Choose **Boxplot**
Step 3. Under the heading **OneY** select **Simple** and click **OK**
Step 4. When the Boxplot-One Y, Simple dialog box appears:
    Enter C2 in the **Graph variables** box
    Click **OK**

Covariance and Correlation

Stereo

Table 3.6 provided the number of commercials and the sales volume for a stereo and sound equipment store. These data are available in the file Stereo, with the number of commercials in column C2 and the sales volume in column C3. The following steps show how Minitab can be used to compute the covariance for the two variables.

*With the n observations arranged in ascending order (smallest value to largest value), Minitab uses the positions given by $(n + 1)/4$ and $3(n + 1)/4$ to locate Q_1 and Q_3, respectively. When a position is fractional, Minitab interpolates between the two adjacent ordered data values to determine the corresponding quartile.

Step 1. Select the **Stat** menu
Step 2. Choose **Basic Statistics**
Step 3. Choose **Covariance**
Step 4. When the Covariance dialog box appears:
    Enter C2 C3 in the **Variables** box
    Click **OK**

To obtain the correlation coefficient for the number of commercials and the sales volume, only one change is necessary in the preceding procedure. In step 3, choose the **Correlation** option.

Appendix 3.2   Descriptive Statistics Using Excel

Excel can be used to generate the descriptive statistics discussed in this chapter. We show how Excel can be used to generate several measures of location and variability for a single variable and to generate the covariance and correlation coefficient as measures of association between two variables.

Using Excel Functions

2012StartSalary

Stereo

Excel provides functions for computing the mean, median, mode, sample variance, and sample standard deviation. We illustrate the use of these Excel functions by computing the mean, median, mode, sample variance, and sample standard deviation for the starting salary data in Table 3.1. Refer to Figure 3.16 as we describe the steps involved. The data are entered in column B.

Excel's AVERAGE function can be used to compute the mean by entering the following formula into cell E1:

$$=\text{AVERAGE}(B2{:}B13)$$

FIGURE 3.16   USING EXCEL FUNCTIONS FOR COMPUTING THE MEAN, MEDIAN, MODE, VARIANCE, AND STANDARD DEVIATION

	A	B	C	D	E
1	Graduate	Starting Salary		Mean	=AVERAGE(B2:B13)
2	1	3850		Median	=MEDIAN(B2:B13)
3	2	3950		Mode	=MODE(B2:B13)
4	3	4050		Variance	=VAR.S(B2:B13)
5	4	3880		Standard Deviation	=STDEV.S(B2:B13)
6	5	3755			
7	6	3710			
8	7	3890			
9	8	4130			
10	9	3940			
11	10	4325			
12	11	3920			
13	12	3880			

	A	B	C	D	E
1	Graduate	Starting Salary		Mean	3940
2	1	3850		Median	3905
3	2	3950		Mode	3880
4	3	4050		Variance	27440.91
5	4	3880		Standard Deviation	165.653
6	5	3755			
7	6	3710			
8	7	3890			
9	8	4130			
10	9	3940			
11	10	4325			
12	11	3920			
13	12	3880			

FIGURE 3.17   USING EXCEL FUNCTIONS FOR COMPUTING THE COVARIANCE AND CORRELATION

	A	B	C	D	E	F	G
1	Week	No. of Commercials	Sales Volume		Sample Covariance	=COVARIANCE.S(B2:B11,C2:C11)	
2	1	2	50		Sample Correlation	=CORREL(B2:B11,C2:C11)	
3	2	5	57				
4	3	1	41				
5	4	3	54				
6	5	4	54				
7	6	1	38				
8	7	5	63				
9	8	3	48				
10	9	4	59				
11	10	2	46				
12							

	A	B	C	D	E	F
1	Week	No. of Commercials	Sales Volume		Sample Covariance	11
2	1	2	50		Sample Correlation	0.930491
3	2	5	57			
4	3	1	41			
5	4	3	54			
6	5	4	54			
7	6	1	38			
8	7	5	63			
9	8	3	48			
10	9	4	59			
11	10	2	46			
12						

© Cengage Learning

To find the variance, standard deviation, and covariance for population data, follow the same steps but use the VAR.P, STDEV.P, and COV.P functions.

Similarly, the formulas =MEDIAN(B2:B13), =MODE.SNGL(B2:B13), =VAR.S(B2:B13), and =STDEV.S(B2:B13) are entered into cells E2:E5, respectively, to compute the median, mode, variance, and standard deviation for this sample. The worksheet in the foreground shows that the values computed using the Excel functions are the same as we computed earlier in the chapter.

Excel also provides functions that can be used to compute the sample covariance and the sample correlation coefficient. We show here how these functions can be used to compute the sample covariance and the sample correlation coefficient for the stereo and sound equipment store data in Table 3.6. Refer to Figure 3.17 as we present the steps involved.

Excel's sample covariance function, COVARIANCE.S, can be used to compute the sample covariance by entering the following formula into cell F1:

$$=COVARIANCE.S(B2:B11,C2:C11)$$

Similarly, the formula =CORREL(B2:B11,C2:C11) is entered into cell F2 to compute the sample correlation coefficient. The worksheet in the foreground shows the values computed using the Excel functions. Note that the value of the sample covariance (11) is the same as computed using equation (3.12). And the value of the sample correlation coefficient (.93) is the same as computed using equation (3.14).

Using Excel's Descriptive Statistics Tool

As we already demonstrated, Excel provides statistical functions to compute descriptive statistics for a data set. These functions can be used to compute one statistic at a time (e.g., mean, variance, etc.). Excel also provides a variety of Data Analysis Tools. One of these tools, called Descriptive Statistics, allows the user to compute a variety of descriptive statistics at once. We show here how it can be used to compute descriptive statistics for the starting salary data in Table 3.1.

WEB file

2012StartSalary

Step 1. Click the **Data** tab on the Ribbon
Step 2. In the **Analysis** group, click **Data Analysis**
Step 3. When the Data Analysis dialog box appears:
　　　　Choose **Descriptive Statistics**
　　　　Click **OK**

FIGURE 3.18   EXCEL'S DESCRIPTIVE STATISTICS TOOL OUTPUT

	A	B	C	D	E	F
1	Graduate	Monthly Starting Salary ($)		Monthly Starting Salary ($)		
2	1	3850				
3	2	3950		Mean	3940	
4	3	4050		Standard Error	47.82	
5	4	3880		Median	3905	
6	5	3755		Mode	3880	
7	6	3710		Standard Deviation	165.65	
8	7	3890		Sample Variance	27440.91	
9	8	4130		Kurtosis	1.72	
10	9	3940		Skewness	1.09	
11	10	4325		Range	615	
12	11	3920		Minimum	3710	
13	12	3880		Maximum	4325	
14				Sum	47280	
15				Count	12	
16						

© Cengage Learning

Step 4. When the Descriptive Statistics dialog box appears:
  Enter B1:B13 in the **Input Range** box
  Select **Grouped By Columns**
  Select **Labels in First Row**
  Select **Output Range**
  Enter D1 in the **Output Range** box (to identify the upper left-hand corner of the section of the worksheet where the descriptive statistics will appear)
  Select **Summary statistics**
  Click **OK**

Cells D1:E15 of Figure 3.18 show the descriptive statistics provided by Excel. The boldface entries are the descriptive statistics we covered in this chapter. The descriptive statistics that are not boldface are either covered subsequently in the text or discussed in more advanced texts.

NOTES AND COMMENTS

If the **Analysis** tab doesn't appear on your ribbon or if the **Data Analysis** option doesn't appear in the **Data Analysis** tab, you need to activate the **Data Analysis ToolPak** by following these three steps:

1. Click the **File** tab, then click **Options**, and then click the **Add-Ins** category.
2. In the **Manage** box, click **Excel Add-ins**, and then click **Go**. The **Add-Ins** dialog box will then appear.

3. In the **Add-Ins available** box, select the check-box next to the **Data Analysis ToolPak** add-in and click **OK**.

The **Analysis** tab will now be available with the **Data Analysis** option.

Appendix 3.3   Descriptive Statistics Using StatTools

In this appendix, we describe how StatTools can be used to compute a variety of descriptive statistics and also display box plots. We then show how StatTools can be used to obtain covariance and correlation measures for two variables.

Descriptive Statistics

2012StartSalary

We use the starting salary data in Table 3.1 to illustrate. Begin by using the Data Set Manager to create a StatTools data set for these data using the procedure described in the appendix in Chapter 1. The following steps will generate a variety of descriptive statistics.

Step 1. Click the **StatTools** tab on the Ribbon
Step 2. In the **Analyses Group,** click **Summary Statistics**
Step 3. Choose the **One-Variable Summary** option
Step 4. When the One-Variable Summary Statistics dialog box appears:
   In the **Variables** section, select **Starting Salary**
   Click **OK**

A variety of descriptive statistics as shown in Figure 3.18 will appear.

Box Plots

We use the starting salary data in Table 3.1 to illustrate. Begin by using the Data Set Manager to create a StatTools data set for these data using the procedure described in the appendix in Chapter 1. The following steps will create a box plot for these data.

2012StartSalary

Step 1. Click the **StatTools** tab on the Ribbon
Step 2. In the **Analyses Group,** click **Summary Graphs**
Step 3. Choose the **Box-Whisker Plot** option
Step 4. When the StatTools - Box-Whisker Plot dialog box appears:
   In the Variables section, select **Starting Salary**
   Click **OK**

In its box plots, StatTools defines any value that is at least 1.5 IQR, but less than 3 IQR outside the box as a mild outlier, and any value that is at least 3 IRQ outside the box as an extreme outlier. The symbol □ is used to identify a mild outlier, the symbol ■ is used to signify an extreme outlier, and x is used to identify the mean.

Covariance and Correlation

We use the stereo and sound equipment data in Table 3.6 to demonstrate the computation of the sample covariance and the sample correlation coefficient. Begin by using the Data Set Manager to create a StatTools data set for these data using the procedure described in the appendix in Chapter 1. The following steps will provide the sample covariance and sample correlation coefficient.

Stereo

Step 1. Click the **StatTools** tab on the Ribbon
Step 2. In the **Analyses Group,** click **Summary Statistics**
Step 3. Choose the **Correlation and Covariance** option
Step 4. When the StatTools - Correlation and Covariance dialog box appears:
  In the **Variables** section:
    Select **No. of Commercials**
    Select **Sales Volume**
  In the **Tables to Create** section:
    Select **Table of Correlations**
    Select **Table of Covariances**
  In the **Table Structure** section select **Symmetric**
  Click **OK**

A table showing the correlation coefficient and the covariance will appear.

CHAPTER 4

Introduction to Probability

CONTENTS

STATISTICS *in* PRACTICE

NATIONAL AERONAUTICS AND SPACE ADMINISTRATION*
WASHINGTON, D.C.

The National Aeronautics and Space Administration (NASA) is the agency of the United States government that is responsible for the U.S. civilian space program and for aeronautics and aerospace research. Best known for its manned space exploration, NASA's mission statement is to "pioneer the future in space exploration, scientific discovery and aeronautics research." NASA, with its 18,800 employees, is currently working on the design of a new Space Launch System that will take the astronauts further into space than ever before and provide the cornerstone for future human space exploration.

While NASA's primary mission is space exploration, their expertise has been called upon to assist countries and organizations throughout the world. In one such situation, the San José copper and gold mine in Copiapó, Chile, caved in, trapping 33 men more than 2000 feet underground. While it was important to bring the men safely to the surface as quickly as possible, it was imperative that the rescue effort be carefully designed and implemented to save as many miners as possible. The Chilean government asked NASA to provide assistance in developing a rescue method. In response, NASA sent a four-person team consisting of an engineer, two physicians, and a psychologist with expertise in vehicle design and issues of long-term confinement.

The probability of success and failure of various rescue methods was prominent in the thoughts of everyone involved. Since there were no historical data available that applied to this unique rescue situation, NASA scientists developed subjective probability estimates for the success and failure of various rescue

NASA scientists based probabilities on similar circumstances experienced during space flights.
© Hugo Infante/Government of Chile/Handout/Reuters.

methods based on similar circumstances experienced by astronauts returning from short- and long-term space missions. The probability estimates provided by NASA guided officials in the selection of a rescue method and provided insight as to how the miners would survive the ascent in a rescue cage.

The rescue method designed by the Chilean officials in consultation with the NASA team resulted in the construction of 13-foot-long, 924-pound steel rescue capsule that would be used to bring up the miners one at a time. All miners were rescued, with the last miner emerging 68 days after the cave-in occurred.

In this chapter you will learn about probability as well as how to compute and interpret probabilities for a variety of situations. In addition to subjective probabilities, you will learn about classical and relative frequency methods for assigning probabilities. The basic relationships of probability, conditional probability, and Bayes' theorem will be covered.

* The authors are indebted to Dr. Michael Duncan and Clinton Cragg of NASA for providing this Statistics in Practice.

Managers often base their decisions on an analysis of uncertainties such as the following:

1. What are the chances that sales will decrease if we increase prices?
2. What is the likelihood a new assembly method will increase productivity?
3. How likely is it that the project will be finished on time?
4. What is the chance that a new investment will be profitable?

Some of the earliest work on probability originated in a series of letters between Pierre de Fermat and Blaise Pascal in the 1650s.

Probability is a numerical measure of the likelihood that an event will occur. Thus, probabilities can be used as measures of the degree of uncertainty associated with the four events previously listed. If probabilities are available, we can determine the likelihood of each event occurring.

Probability values are always assigned on a scale from 0 to 1. A probability near zero indicates an event is unlikely to occur; a probability near 1 indicates an event is almost certain to occur. Other probabilities between 0 and 1 represent degrees of likelihood that an event will occur. For example, if we consider the event "rain tomorrow," we understand that when the weather report indicates "a near-zero probability of rain," it means almost no chance of rain. However, if a .90 probability of rain is reported, we know that rain is likely to occur. A .50 probability indicates that rain is just as likely to occur as not. Figure 4.1 depicts the view of probability as a numerical measure of the likelihood of an event occurring.

4.1   Experiments, Counting Rules, and Assigning Probabilities

In discussing probability, we define an **experiment** as a process that generates well-defined outcomes. On any single repetition of an experiment, one and only one of the possible experimental outcomes will occur. Several examples of experiments and their associated outcomes follow.

Experiment	Experimental Outcomes
Toss a coin	Head, tail
Select a part for inspection	Defective, nondefective
Conduct a sales call	Purchase, no purchase
Roll a die	1, 2, 3, 4, 5, 6
Play a football game	Win, lose, tie

By specifying all possible experimental outcomes, we identify the **sample space** for an experiment.

FIGURE 4.1   PROBABILITY AS A NUMERICAL MEASURE OF THE LIKELIHOOD OF AN EVENT OCCURRING

> **SAMPLE SPACE**
>
> The sample space for an experiment is the set of all experimental outcomes.

Experimental outcomes are also called sample points.

An experimental outcome is also called a **sample point** to identify it as an element of the sample space.

Consider the first experiment in the preceding table—tossing a coin. The upward face of the coin—a head or a tail—determines the experimental outcomes (sample points). If we let S denote the sample space, we can use the following notation to describe the sample space.

$$S = \{\text{Head, Tail}\}$$

The sample space for the second experiment in the table—selecting a part for inspection—can be described as follows:

$$S = \{\text{Defective, Nondefective}\}$$

Both of the experiments just described have two experimental outcomes (sample points). However, suppose we consider the fourth experiment listed in the table—rolling a die. The possible experimental outcomes, defined as the number of dots appearing on the upward face of the die, are the six points in the sample space for this experiment.

$$S = \{1, 2, 3, 4, 5, 6\}$$

Counting Rules, Combinations, and Permutations

Being able to identify and count the experimental outcomes is a necessary step in assigning probabilities. We now discuss three useful counting rules.

Multiple-step experiments The first counting rule applies to **multiple-step experiments**. Consider the experiment of tossing two coins. Let the experimental outcomes be defined in terms of the pattern of heads and tails appearing on the upward faces of the two coins. How many experimental outcomes are possible for this experiment? The experiment of tossing two coins can be thought of as a two-step experiment in which step 1 is the tossing of the first coin and step 2 is the tossing of the second coin. If we use H to denote a head and T to denote a tail, (H, H) indicates the experimental outcome with a head on the first coin and a head on the second coin. Continuing this notation, we can describe the sample space (S) for this coin-tossing experiment as follows:

$$S = \{(H, H), (H, T), (T, H), (T, T)\}$$

Thus, we see that four experimental outcomes are possible. In this case, we can easily list all the experimental outcomes.

The counting rule for multiple-step experiments makes it possible to determine the number of experimental outcomes without listing them.

> **COUNTING RULE FOR MULTIPLE-STEP EXPERIMENTS**
>
> If an experiment can be described as a sequence of k steps with n_1 possible outcomes on the first step, n_2 possible outcomes on the second step, and so on, then the total number of experimental outcomes is given by $(n_1)(n_2) \cdots (n_k)$.

Viewing the experiment of tossing two coins as a sequence of first tossing one coin ($n_1 = 2$) and then tossing the other coin ($n_2 = 2$), we can see from the counting rule that $(2)(2) = 4$ distinct experimental outcomes are possible. As shown, they are $S = \{(H, H),$

FIGURE 4.2   TREE DIAGRAM FOR THE EXPERIMENT OF TOSSING TWO COINS

(H, T), (T, H), (T, T)}. The number of experimental outcomes in an experiment involving tossing six coins is $(2)(2)(2)(2)(2)(2) = 64$.

Without the tree diagram, one might think only three experimental outcomes are possible for two tosses of a coin: 0 heads, 1 head, and 2 heads.

A **tree diagram** is a graphical representation that helps in visualizing a multiple-step experiment. Figure 4.2 shows a tree diagram for the experiment of tossing two coins. The sequence of steps moves from left to right through the tree. Step 1 corresponds to tossing the first coin, and step 2 corresponds to tossing the second coin. For each step, the two possible outcomes are head or tail. Note that for each possible outcome at step 1 two branches correspond to the two possible outcomes at step 2. Each of the points on the right end of the tree corresponds to an experimental outcome. Each path through the tree from the leftmost node to one of the nodes at the right side of the tree corresponds to a unique sequence of outcomes.

Let us now see how the counting rule for multiple-step experiments can be used in the analysis of a capacity expansion project for the Kentucky Power & Light Company (KP&L). KP&L is starting a project designed to increase the generating capacity of one of its plants in northern Kentucky. The project is divided into two sequential stages or steps: stage 1 (design) and stage 2 (construction). Even though each stage will be scheduled and controlled as closely as possible, management cannot predict beforehand the exact time required to complete each stage of the project. An analysis of similar construction projects revealed possible completion times for the design stage of 2, 3, or 4 months and possible completion times for the construction stage of 6, 7, or 8 months. In addition, because of the critical need for additional electrical power, management set a goal of 10 months for the completion of the entire project.

Because this project has three possible completion times for the design stage (step 1) and three possible completion times for the construction stage (step 2), the counting rule for multiple-step experiments can be applied here to determine a total of $(3)(3) = 9$ experimental outcomes. To describe the experimental outcomes, we use a two-number notation; for instance, $(2, 6)$ indicates that the design stage is completed in 2 months and the construction stage is completed in 6 months. This experimental outcome results in a total of $2 + 6 = 8$ months to complete the entire project. Table 4.1 summarizes the nine experimental outcomes for the KP&L problem. The tree diagram in Figure 4.3 shows how the nine outcomes (sample points) occur.

The counting rule and tree diagram help the project manager identify the experimental outcomes and determine the possible project completion times. From the information in

TABLE 4.1   EXPERIMENTAL OUTCOMES (SAMPLE POINTS) FOR THE KP&L PROJECT

Completion Time (months)

Stage 1 Design	Stage 2 Construction	Notation for Experimental Outcome	Total Project Completion Time (months)
2	6	(2, 6)	8
2	7	(2, 7)	9
2	8	(2, 8)	10
3	6	(3, 6)	9
3	7	(3, 7)	10
3	8	(3, 8)	11
4	6	(4, 6)	10
4	7	(4, 7)	11
4	8	(4, 8)	12

© Cengage Learning

FIGURE 4.3   TREE DIAGRAM FOR THE KP&L PROJECT

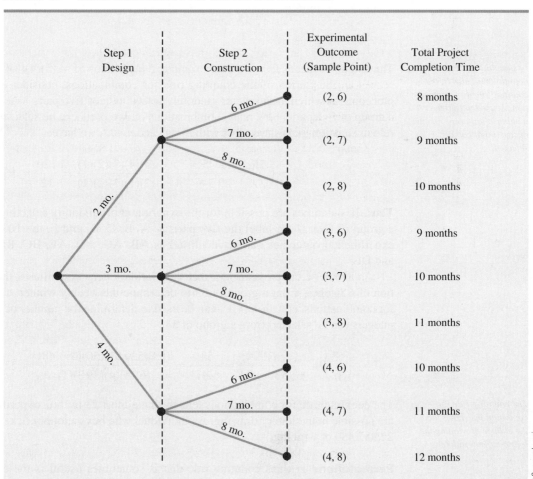

© Cengage Learning

Figure 4.3, we see that the project will be completed in 8 to 12 months, with six of the nine experimental outcomes providing the desired completion time of 10 months or less. Even though identifying the experimental outcomes may be helpful, we need to consider how probability values can be assigned to the experimental outcomes before making an assessment of the probability that the project will be completed within the desired 10 months.

Combinations A second useful counting rule allows one to count the number of experimental outcomes when the experiment involves selecting n objects from a set of N objects. It is called the counting rule for **combinations**.

COUNTING RULE FOR COMBINATIONS

The number of combinations of N objects taken n at a time is

$$C_n^N = \binom{N}{n} = \frac{N!}{n!(N-n)!} \tag{4.1}$$

where

$$N! = N(N-1)(N-2)\cdots(2)(1)$$
$$n! = n(n-1)(n-2)\cdots(2)(1)$$

and, by definition,

$$0! = 1$$

In sampling from a finite population of size N, the counting rule for combinations is used to find the number of different samples of size n that can be selected.

The notation ! means *factorial;* for example, 5 factorial is $5! = (5)(4)(3)(2)(1) = 120$.

As an illustration of the counting rule for combinations, consider a quality control procedure in which an inspector randomly selects two of five parts to test for defects. In a group of five parts, how many combinations of two parts can be selected? The counting rule in equation (4.1) shows that with $N = 5$ and $n = 2$, we have

$$C_2^5 = \binom{5}{2} = \frac{5!}{2!(5-2)!} = \frac{(5)(4)(3)(2)(1)}{(2)(1)(3)(2)(1)} = \frac{120}{12} = 10$$

Thus, 10 outcomes are possible for the experiment of randomly selecting two parts from a group of five. If we label the five parts as A, B, C, D, and E, the 10 combinations or experimental outcomes can be identified as AB, AC, AD, AE, BC, BD, BE, CD, CE, and DE.

As another example, consider that the Florida lottery system uses the random selection of 6 integers from a group of 53 to determine the weekly winner. The counting rule for combinations, equation (4.1), can be used to determine the number of ways 6 different integers can be selected from a group of 53.

$$\binom{53}{6} = \frac{53!}{6!(53-6)!} = \frac{53!}{6!47!} = \frac{(53)(52)(51)(50)(49)(48)}{(6)(5)(4)(3)(2)(1)} = 22,957,480$$

The counting rule for combinations shows that the chance of winning the lottery is very unlikely.

The counting rule for combinations tells us that almost 23 million experimental outcomes are possible in the lottery drawing. An individual who buys a lottery ticket has 1 chance in 22,957,480 of winning.

Permutations A third counting rule that is sometimes useful is the counting rule for **permutations**. It allows one to compute the number of experimental outcomes when n objects are to be selected from a set of N objects where the order of selection is important. The same n objects selected in a different order are considered a different experimental outcome.

COUNTING RULE FOR PERMUTATIONS

The number of permutations of N objects taken n at a time is given by

$$p_n^N = n! \binom{N}{n} = \frac{N!}{(N-n)!} \tag{4.2}$$

The counting rule for permutations closely relates to the one for combinations; however, an experiment results in more permutations than combinations for the same number of objects because every selection of n objects can be ordered in $n!$ different ways.

As an example, consider again the quality control process in which an inspector selects two of five parts to inspect for defects. How many permutations may be selected? The counting rule in equation (4.2) shows that with $N = 5$ and $n = 2$, we have

$$P_2^5 = \frac{5!}{(5-2)!} = \frac{5!}{3!} = \frac{(5)(4)(3)(2)(1)}{(3)(2)(1)} = \frac{120}{6} = 20$$

Thus, 20 outcomes are possible for the experiment of randomly selecting two parts from a group of five when the order of selection must be taken into account. If we label the parts A, B, C, D, and E, the 20 permutations are AB, BA, AC, CA, AD, DA, AE, EA, BC, CB, BD, DB, BE, EB, CD, DC, CE, EC, DE, and ED.

Assigning Probabilities

Now let us see how probabilities can be assigned to experimental outcomes. The three approaches most frequently used are the classical, relative frequency, and subjective methods. Regardless of the method used, two **basic requirements for assigning probabilities** must be met.

BASIC REQUIREMENTS FOR ASSIGNING PROBABILITIES

1. The probability assigned to each experimental outcome must be between 0 and 1, inclusively. If we let E_i denote the ith experimental outcome and $P(E_i)$ its probability, then this requirement can be written as

$$0 \leq P(E_i) \leq 1 \text{ for all } i \tag{4.3}$$

2. The sum of the probabilities for all the experimental outcomes must equal 1.0. For n experimental outcomes, this requirement can be written as

$$P(E_1) + P(E_2) + \cdots + P(E_n) = 1 \tag{4.4}$$

The **classical method** of assigning probabilities is appropriate when all the experimental outcomes are equally likely. If n experimental outcomes are possible, a probability of $1/n$ is assigned to each experimental outcome. When using this approach, the two basic requirements for assigning probabilities are automatically satisfied.

For an example, consider the experiment of tossing a fair coin; the two experimental outcomes—head and tail—are equally likely. Because one of the two equally likely outcomes is a head, the probability of observing a head is 1/2, or .50. Similarly, the probability of observing a tail is also 1/2, or .50.

As another example, consider the experiment of rolling a die. It would seem reasonable to conclude that the six possible outcomes are equally likely, and hence each outcome is assigned a probability of 1/6. If $P(1)$ denotes the probability that one dot appears on the upward face of the die, then $P(1) = 1/6$. Similarly, $P(2) = 1/6$, $P(3) = 1/6$, $P(4) = 1/6$, $P(5) = 1/6$, and $P(6) = 1/6$. Note that these probabilities satisfy the two basic requirements of equations (4.3) and (4.4) because each of the probabilities is greater than or equal to zero and they sum to 1.0.

The **relative frequency method** of assigning probabilities is appropriate when data are available to estimate the proportion of the time the experimental outcome will occur if the experiment is repeated a large number of times. As an example, consider a study of waiting times in the X-ray department for a local hospital. A clerk recorded the number of patients waiting for service at 9:00 A.M. on 20 successive days and obtained the following results.

Number Waiting	Number of Days Outcome Occurred
0	2
1	5
2	6
3	4
4	3
Total	20

These data show that on 2 of the 20 days, zero patients were waiting for service; on 5 of the days, one patient was waiting for service; and so on. Using the relative frequency method, we would assign a probability of $2/20 = .10$ to the experimental outcome of zero patients waiting for service, $5/20 = .25$ to the experimental outcome of one patient waiting, $6/20 = .30$ to two patients waiting, $4/20 = .20$ to three patients waiting, and $3/20 = .15$ to four patients waiting. As with the classical method, using the relative frequency method automatically satisfies the two basic requirements of equations (4.3) and (4.4).

The **subjective method** of assigning probabilities is most appropriate when one cannot realistically assume that the experimental outcomes are equally likely and when little relevant data are available. When the subjective method is used to assign probabilities to the experimental outcomes, we may use any information available, such as our experience or intuition. After considering all available information, a probability value that expresses our *degree of belief* (on a scale from 0 to 1) that the experimental outcome will occur is specified. Because subjective probability expresses a person's degree of belief, it is personal. Using the subjective method, different people can be expected to assign different probabilities to the same experimental outcome.

The subjective method requires extra care to ensure that the two basic requirements of equations (4.3) and (4.4) are satisfied. Regardless of a person's degree of belief, the probability value assigned to each experimental outcome must be between 0 and 1, inclusive, and the sum of all the probabilities for the experimental outcomes must equal 1.0.

Consider the case in which Tom and Judy Elsbernd make an offer to purchase a house. Two outcomes are possible:

$$E_1 = \text{their offer is accepted}$$
$$E_2 = \text{their offer is rejected}$$

Judy believes that the probability their offer will be accepted is .8; thus, Judy would set $P(E_1) = .8$ and $P(E_2) = .2$. Tom, however, believes that the probability that their offer will be accepted is .6; hence, Tom would set $P(E_1) = .6$ and $P(E_2) = .4$. Note that Tom's probability estimate for E_1 reflects a greater pessimism that their offer will be accepted.

Bayes' theorem (see Section 4.5) provides a means for combining subjectively determined prior probabilities with probabilities obtained by other means to obtain revised, or posterior, probabilities.

Both Judy and Tom assigned probabilities that satisfy the two basic requirements. The fact that their probability estimates are different emphasizes the personal nature of the subjective method.

Even in business situations where either the classical or the relative frequency approach can be applied, managers may want to provide subjective probability estimates. In such cases, the best probability estimates often are obtained by combining the estimates from the classical or relative frequency approach with subjective probability estimates.

Probabilities for the KP&L Project

To perform further analysis on the KP&L project, we must develop probabilities for each of the nine experimental outcomes listed in Table 4.1. On the basis of experience and judgment, management concluded that the experimental outcomes were not equally likely. Hence, the classical method of assigning probabilities could not be used. Management then decided to conduct a study of the completion times for similar projects undertaken by KP&L over the past three years. The results of a study of 40 similar projects are summarized in Table 4.2.

After reviewing the results of the study, management decided to employ the relative frequency method of assigning probabilities. Management could have provided subjective probability estimates but felt that the current project was quite similar to the 40 previous projects. Thus, the relative frequency method was judged best.

In using the data in Table 4.2 to compute probabilities, we note that outcome (2, 6)—stage 1 completed in 2 months and stage 2 completed in 6 months—occurred six times in the 40 projects. We can use the relative frequency method to assign a probability of 6/40 = .15 to this outcome. Similarly, outcome (2, 7) also occurred in six of the 40 projects, providing a 6/40 = .15 probability. Continuing in this manner, we obtain the probability assignments for the sample points of the KP&L project shown in Table 4.3. Note that $P(2, 6)$ represents the probability of the sample point (2, 6), $P(2, 7)$ represents the probability of the sample point (2, 7), and so on.

TABLE 4.2   COMPLETION RESULTS FOR 40 KP&L PROJECTS

Completion Time (months)			Number of Past Projects Having These
Stage 1 Design	**Stage 2 Construction**	**Sample Point**	**Completion Times**
2	6	(2, 6)	6
2	7	(2, 7)	6
2	8	(2, 8)	2
3	6	(3, 6)	4
3	7	(3, 7)	8
3	8	(3, 8)	2
4	6	(4, 6)	2
4	7	(4, 7)	4
4	8	(4, 8)	6
		Total	40

TABLE 4.3   PROBABILITY ASSIGNMENTS FOR THE KP&L PROJECT BASED ON THE RELATIVE FREQUENCY METHOD

Sample Point	Project Completion Time	Probability of Sample Point
(2, 6)	8 months	$P(2, 6) = 6/40 = .15$
(2, 7)	9 months	$P(2, 7) = 6/40 = .15$
(2, 8)	10 months	$P(2, 8) = 2/40 = .05$
(3, 6)	9 months	$P(3, 6) = 4/40 = .10$
(3, 7)	10 months	$P(3, 7) = 8/40 = .20$
(3, 8)	11 months	$P(3, 8) = 2/40 = .05$
(4, 6)	10 months	$P(4, 6) = 2/40 = .05$
(4, 7)	11 months	$P(4, 7) = 4/40 = .10$
(4, 8)	12 months	$P(4, 8) = 6/40 = .15$
		Total 1.00

© Cengage Learning

NOTES AND COMMENTS

1. In statistics, the notion of an experiment differs somewhat from the notion of an experiment in the physical sciences. In the physical sciences, researchers usually conduct an experiment in a laboratory or a controlled environment in order to learn about cause and effect. In statistical experiments, probability determines outcomes. Even though the experiment is repeated in exactly the same way, an entirely different outcome may occur. Because of this influence of probability on the outcome, the experiments of statistics are sometimes called *random experiments*.

2. When drawing a random sample without replacement from a population of size N, the counting rule for combinations is used to find the number of different samples of size n that can be selected.

Exercises

Methods

1. An experiment has three steps with three outcomes possible for the first step, two outcomes possible for the second step, and four outcomes possible for the third step. How many experimental outcomes exist for the entire experiment?

2. How many ways can three items be selected from a group of six items? Use the letters A, B, C, D, E, and F to identify the items, and list each of the different combinations of three items.

3. How many permutations of three items can be selected from a group of six? Use the letters A, B, C, D, E, and F to identify the items, and list each of the permutations of items B, D, and F.

4. Consider the experiment of tossing a coin three times.
   a. Develop a tree diagram for the experiment.
   b. List the experimental outcomes.
   c. What is the probability for each experimental outcome?

5. Suppose an experiment has five equally likely outcomes: E_1, E_2, E_3, E_4, E_5. Assign probabilities to each outcome and show that the requirements in equations (4.3) and (4.4) are satisfied. What method did you use?

6. An experiment with three outcomes has been repeated 50 times, and it was learned that E_1 occurred 20 times, E_2 occurred 13 times, and E_3 occurred 17 times. Assign probabilities to the outcomes. What method did you use?

7. A decision maker subjectively assigned the following probabilities to the four outcomes of an experiment: $P(E_1) = .10$, $P(E_2) = .15$, $P(E_3) = .40$, and $P(E_4) = .20$. Are these probability assignments valid? Explain.

Applications

8. In the city of Milford, applications for zoning changes go through a two-step process: a review by the planning commission and a final decision by the city council. At step 1 the planning commission reviews the zoning change request and makes a positive or negative recommendation concerning the change. At step 2 the city council reviews the planning commission's recommendation and then votes to approve or to disapprove the zoning change. Suppose the developer of an apartment complex submits an application for a zoning change. Consider the application process as an experiment.
   a. How many sample points are there for this experiment? List the sample points.
   b. Construct a tree diagram for the experiment.

9. Simple random sampling uses a sample of size n from a population of size N to obtain data that can be used to make inferences about the characteristics of a population. Suppose that, from a population of 50 bank accounts, we want to take a random sample of four accounts in order to learn about the population. How many different random samples of four accounts are possible?

10. Many students accumulate debt by the time they graduate from college. Shown in the following table is the percentage of graduates with debt and the average amount of debt for these graduates at four universities and four liberal arts colleges (*U.S. News and World Report, America's Best Colleges,* 2008).

University	% with Debt	Amount($)	College	% with Debt	Amount($)
Pace	72	32,980	Wartburg	83	28,758
Iowa State	69	32,130	Morehouse	94	27,000
Massachusetts	55	11,227	Wellesley	55	10,206
SUNY—Albany	64	11,856	Wofford	49	11,012

   a. If you randomly choose a graduate of Morehouse College, what is the probability that this individual graduated with debt?
   b. If you randomly choose one of these eight institutions for a follow-up study on student loans, what is the probability that you will choose an institution with more than 60% of its graduates having debt?
   c. If you randomly choose one of these eight institutions for a follow-up study on student loans, what is the probability that you will choose an institution whose graduates with debts have an average debt of more than $30,000?
   d. What is the probability that a graduate of Pace University does not have debt?
   e. For graduates of Pace University with debt, the average amount of debt is $32,980. Considering all graduates from Pace University, what is the average debt per graduate?

11. The National Occupant Protection Use Survey (NOPUS) was conducted to provide probability-based data on motorcycle helmet use in the United States. The survey was conducted by sending observers to randomly selected roadway sites where they collected data on motorcycle helmet use, including the number of motorcyclists wearing a Department of Transportation (DOT)-compliant helmet (National Highway Traffic Safety Administration website, January 7, 2010). Sample data consistent with the most recent NOPUS are shown below.

| | Type of Helmet | |
Region	DOT-Compliant	Noncompliant
Northeast	96	62
Midwest	86	43
South	92	49
West	76	16
Total	350	170

a. Use the data to compute the probability that a motorcyclist wears a DOT-compliant helmet.

b. The probability that a motorcyclist wore a DOT-compliant helmet five years ago was .48, and last year this probability was .63. Would the National Highway Traffic Safety Administration be pleased with the most recent survey results?

c. What is the probability of DOT-compliant helmet use by region of the country? What region has the highest probability of DOT-compliant helmet use?

12. The Powerball lottery is played twice each week in 31 states, the District of Columbia, and the Virgin Islands. To play Powerball, a participant must purchase a $2 ticket, select five numbers from the digits 1 through 59, and then select a Powerball number from the digits 1 through 35. To determine the winning numbers for each game, lottery officials draw 5 white balls out a drum of 59 white balls numbered 1 through 59 and 1 red ball out of a drum of 35 red balls numbered 1 through 35. To win the Powerball jackpot, a participant's numbers must match the numbers on the 5 white balls in any order and must also match the number on the red Powerball. The numbers 5–16–22–23–29 with a Powerball number of 6 provided the record jackpot of $580 million (Powerball website, November 29, 2012).

a. How many Powerball lottery outcomes are possible? *Hint*: Consider this a two-step experiment. Select the 5 white ball numbers and then select the 1 red Powerball number.

b. What is the probability that a $2 lottery ticket wins the Powerball lottery?

13. A company that manufactures toothpaste is studying five different package designs. Assuming that one design is just as likely to be selected by a consumer as any other design, what selection probability would you assign to each of the package designs? In an actual experiment, 100 consumers were asked to pick the design they preferred. The following data were obtained. Do the data confirm the belief that one design is just as likely to be selected as another? Explain.

Design	Number of Times Preferred
1	5
2	15
3	30
4	40
5	10

4.2   Events and Their Probabilities

In the introduction to this chapter we used the term *event* much as it would be used in everyday language. Then, in Section 4.1 we introduced the concept of an experiment and its associated experimental outcomes or sample points. Sample points and events provide the foundation for the study of probability. As a result, we must now introduce the formal definition of an **event** as it relates to sample points. Doing so will provide the basis for determining the probability of an event.

EVENT

An event is a collection of sample points.

For an example, let us return to the KP&L project and assume that the project manager is interested in the event that the entire project can be completed in 10 months or less. Referring to Table 4.3, we see that six sample points—(2, 6), (2, 7), (2, 8), (3, 6), (3, 7), and (4, 6)—provide a project completion time of 10 months or less. Let C denote the event that the project is completed in 10 months or less; we write

$$C = \{(2, 6), (2, 7), (2, 8), (3, 6), (3, 7), (4, 6)\}$$

Event C is said to occur if *any one* of these six sample points appears as the experimental outcome.

Other events that might be of interest to KP&L management include the following.

$L =$ The event that the project is completed in *less* than 10 months
$M =$ The event that the project is completed in *more* than 10 months

Using the information in Table 4.3, we see that these events consist of the following sample points.

$$L = \{(2, 6), (2, 7), (3, 6)\}$$
$$M = \{(3, 8), (4, 7), (4, 8)\}$$

A variety of additional events can be defined for the KP&L project, but in each case the event must be identified as a collection of sample points for the experiment.

Given the probabilities of the sample points shown in Table 4.3, we can use the following definition to compute the probability of any event that KP&L management might want to consider.

PROBABILITY OF AN EVENT

The probability of any event is equal to the sum of the probabilities of the sample points in the event.

Using this definition, we calculate the probability of a particular event by adding the probabilities of the sample points (experimental outcomes) that make up the event. We can now compute the probability that the project will take 10 months or less to complete. Because this event is given by $C = \{(2, 6), (2, 7), (2, 8), (3, 6), (3, 7), (4, 6)\}$, the probability of event C, denoted $P(C)$, is given by

$$P(C) = P(2, 6) + P(2, 7) + P(2, 8) + P(3, 6) + P(3, 7) + P(4, 6)$$

Refer to the sample point probabilities in Table 4.3; we have

$$P(C) = .15 + .15 + .05 + .10 + .20 + .05 = .70$$

Similarly, because the event that the project is completed in less than 10 months is given by $L = \{(2, 6), (2, 7), (3, 6)\}$, the probability of this event is given by

$$P(L) = P(2, 6) + P(2, 7) + P(3, 6)$$
$$= .15 + .15 + .10 = .40$$

Finally, for the event that the project is completed in more than 10 months, we have $M = \{(3, 8), (4, 7), (4, 8)\}$ and thus

$$P(M) = P(3, 8) + P(4, 7) + P(4, 8)$$
$$= .05 + .10 + .15 = .30$$

Using these probability results, we can now tell KP&L management that there is a .70 probability that the project will be completed in 10 months or less, a .40 probability that the project will be completed in less than 10 months, and a .30 probability that the project will be completed in more than 10 months. This procedure of computing event probabilities can be repeated for any event of interest to the KP&L management.

Any time that we can identify all the sample points of an experiment and assign probabilities to each, we can compute the probability of an event using the definition. However, in many experiments the large number of sample points makes the identification of the sample points, as well as the determination of their associated probabilities, extremely cumbersome, if not impossible. In the remaining sections of this chapter, we present some basic probability relationships that can be used to compute the probability of an event without knowledge of all the sample point probabilities.

NOTES AND COMMENTS

1. The sample space, S, is an event. Because it contains all the experimental outcomes, it has a probability of 1; that is, $P(S) = 1$.
2. When the classical method is used to assign probabilities, the assumption is that the experimental outcomes are equally likely. In such cases, the probability of an event can be computed by counting the number of experimental outcomes in the event and dividing the result by the total number of experimental outcomes.

Exercises

Methods

14. An experiment has four equally likely outcomes: E_1, E_2, E_3, and E_4.
    a. What is the probability that E_2 occurs?
    b. What is the probability that any two of the outcomes occur (e.g., E_1 or E_3)?
    c. What is the probability that any three of the outcomes occur (e.g., E_1 or E_2 or E_4)?

15. Consider the experiment of selecting a playing card from a deck of 52 playing cards. Each card corresponds to a sample point with a 1/52 probability.
    a. List the sample points in the event an ace is selected.
    b. List the sample points in the event a club is selected.
    c. List the sample points in the event a face card (jack, queen, or king) is selected.
    d. Find the probabilities associated with each of the events in parts (a), (b), and (c).

16. Consider the experiment of rolling a pair of dice. Suppose that we are interested in the sum of the face values showing on the dice.
    a. How many sample points are possible? (*Hint:* Use the counting rule for multiple-step experiments.)
    b. List the sample points.
    c. What is the probability of obtaining a value of 7?
    d. What is the probability of obtaining a value of 9 or greater?
    e. Because each roll has six possible even values (2, 4, 6, 8, 10, and 12) and only five possible odd values (3, 5, 7, 9, and 11), the dice should show even values more often than odd values. Do you agree with this statement? Explain.
    f. What method did you use to assign the probabilities requested?

Applications

17. Refer to the KP&L sample points and sample point probabilities in Tables 4.2 and 4.3.
    a. The design stage (stage 1) will run over budget if it takes 4 months to complete. List the sample points in the event the design stage is over budget.
    b. What is the probability that the design stage is over budget?
    c. The construction stage (stage 2) will run over budget if it takes 8 months to complete. List the sample points in the event the construction stage is over budget.
    d. What is the probability that the construction stage is over budget?
    e. What is the probability that both stages are over budget?

18. *Fortune* magazine publishes an annual list of the 500 largest companies in the United States. The corporate headquarters for the 500 companies are located in 38 different states. The following table shows the 8 states with the largest number of *Fortune* 500 companies (*Money*/CNN website, May 12, 2012).

State	Number of Companies	State	Number of Companies
California	53	Ohio	28
Illinois	32	Pennsylvania	23
New Jersey	21	Texas	52
New York	50	Virginia	24

   Suppose one of the 500 companies is selected at random for a follow-up questionnaire.
   a. What is the probability that the company selected has its corporate headquarters in California?
   b. What is the probability that the company selected has its corporate headquarters in California, New York, or Texas?
   c. What is the probability that the company selected has its corporate headquarters in one of the 8 states listed above?

19. Do you think the government protects investors adequately? This question was part of an online survey of investors under age 65 living in the United States and Great Britain (*Financial Times*/Harris Poll, October 1, 2009). The numbers of investors from the United States and Great Britain who answered Yes, No, or Unsure to this question are provided below.

Response	United States	Great Britain
Yes	187	197
No	334	411
Unsure	256	213

   a. Estimate the probability that an investor in the United States thinks the government is not protecting investors adequately.
   b. Estimate the probability that an investor in Great Britain thinks the government is not protecting investors adequately or is unsure the government is protecting investors adequately.
   c. For a randomly selected investor from these two countries, estimate the probability that the investor thinks the government is not protecting investors adequately.
   d. Based on the survey results, does there appear to be much difference between the perceptions of investors in the United States and investors in Great Britain regarding the issue of the government protecting investors adequately?

20. Junior Achievement USA and the Allstate Foundation surveyed teenagers aged 14 to 18 and asked at what age they think that they will become financially independent (*USA Today,* April 30, 2012). The responses of 944 teenagers who answered this survey question are as follows.

Age Financially Independent	Number of Responses
16 to 20	191
21 to 24	467
25 to 27	244
28 or older	42

Consider the experiment of randomly selecting a teenager from the population of teenagers aged 14 to 18.

a. Compute the probability of being financially independent for each of the four age categories.
b. What is the probability of being financially independent before the age of 25?
c. What is the probability of being financially independent after the age of 24?
d. Do the probabilities suggest that the teenagers may be somewhat unrealistic in their expectations about when they will become financially independent?

21. Data on U.S. work-related fatalities by cause follow (*The World Almanac,* 2012).

Cause of Fatality	Number of Fatalities
Transportation incidents	1795
Assaults and violent acts	837
Contact with objects and equipment	741
Falls	645
Exposure to harmful substances or environments	404
Fires and explosions	113

Assume that a fatality will be randomly chosen from this population.

a. What is the probability the fatality resulted from a fall?
b. What is the probability the fatality resulted from a transportation incident?
c. What cause of fatality is least likely to occur? What is the probability the fatality resulted from this cause?

4.3 Some Basic Relationships of Probability

Complement of an Event

Given an event A, the **complement of A** is defined to be the event consisting of all sample points that are *not* in A. The complement of A is denoted by A^c. Figure 4.4 is a diagram, known as a **Venn diagram**, which illustrates the concept of a complement. The rectangular area represents the sample space for the experiment and as such contains all possible sample points. The circle represents event A and contains only the sample points that belong to A. The shaded region of the rectangle contains all sample points not in event A and is by definition the complement of A.

In any probability application, either event A or its complement A^c must occur. Therefore, we have

$$P(A) + P(A^c) = 1$$

FIGURE 4.4 COMPLEMENT OF EVENT *A* IS SHADED

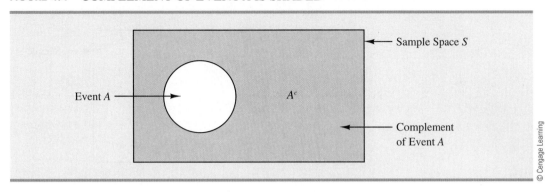

Solving for $P(A)$, we obtain the following result.

COMPUTING PROBABILITY USING THE COMPLEMENT

$$P(A) = 1 - P(A^c) \qquad (4.5)$$

Equation (4.5) shows that the probability of an event *A* can be computed easily if the probability of its complement, $P(A^c)$, is known.

As an example, consider the case of a sales manager who, after reviewing sales reports, states that 80% of new customer contacts result in no sale. By allowing *A* to denote the event of a sale and A^c to denote the event of no sale, the manager is stating that $P(A^c) = .80$. Using equation (4.5), we see that

$$P(A) = 1 - P(A^c) = 1 - .80 = .20$$

We can conclude that a new customer contact has a .20 probability of resulting in a sale.

In another example, a purchasing agent states a .90 probability that a supplier will send a shipment that is free of defective parts. Using the complement, we can conclude that there is a $1 - .90 = .10$ probability that the shipment will contain defective parts.

Addition Law

The addition law is helpful when we are interested in knowing the probability that at least one of two events occurs. That is, with events *A* and *B* we are interested in knowing the probability that event *A* or event *B* or both occur.

Before we present the addition law, we need to discuss two concepts related to the combination of events: the *union* of events and the *intersection* of events. Given two events *A* and *B*, the **union of *A* and *B*** is defined as follows.

UNION OF TWO EVENTS

The *union* of *A* and *B* is the event containing *all* sample points belonging to *A or B or both.* The union is denoted by $A \cup B$.

The Venn diagram in Figure 4.5 depicts the union of events *A* and *B*. Note that the two circles contain all the sample points in event *A* as well as all the sample points in event *B*.

FIGURE 4.5   UNION OF EVENTS *A* AND *B* IS SHADED

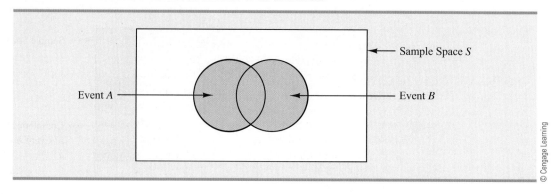

The fact that the circles overlap indicates that some sample points are contained in both *A* and *B*.

The definition of the **intersection of *A* and *B*** follows.

INTERSECTION OF TWO EVENTS

Given two events *A* and *B*, the *intersection* of *A* and *B* is the event containing the sample points belonging to *both A and B*. The intersection is denoted by $A \cap B$.

The Venn diagram depicting the intersection of events *A* and *B* is shown in Figure 4.6. The area where the two circles overlap is the intersection; it contains the sample points that are in both *A* and *B*.

Let us now continue with a discussion of the addition law. The **addition law** provides a way to compute the probability that event *A* or event *B* or both occur. In other words, the addition law is used to compute the probability of the union of two events. The addition law is written as follows.

ADDITION LAW

$$P(A \cup B) = P(A) + P(B) - P(A \cap B) \qquad \textbf{(4.6)}$$

FIGURE 4.6   INTERSECTION OF EVENTS *A* AND *B* IS SHADED

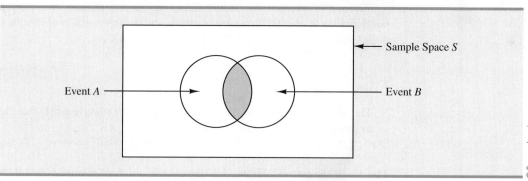

To understand the addition law intuitively, note that the first two terms in the addition law, $P(A) + P(B)$, account for all the sample points in $A \cup B$. However, because the sample points in the intersection $A \cap B$ are in both A and B, when we compute $P(A) + P(B)$, we are in effect counting each of the sample points in $A \cap B$ twice. We correct for this overcounting by subtracting $P(A \cap B)$.

As an example of an application of the addition law, let us consider the case of a small assembly plant with 50 employees. Each worker is expected to complete work assignments on time and in such a way that the assembled product will pass a final inspection. On occasion, some of the workers fail to meet the performance standards by completing work late or assembling a defective product. At the end of a performance evaluation period, the production manager found that 5 of the 50 workers completed work late, 6 of the 50 workers assembled a defective product, and 2 of the 50 workers both completed work late *and* assembled a defective product.

Let

$$L = \text{the event that the work is completed late}$$
$$D = \text{the event that the assembled product is defective}$$

The relative frequency information leads to the following probabilities.

$$P(L) = \frac{5}{50} = .10$$

$$P(D) = \frac{6}{50} = .12$$

$$P(L \cap D) = \frac{2}{50} = .04$$

After reviewing the performance data, the production manager decided to assign a poor performance rating to any employee whose work was either late or defective; thus the event of interest is $L \cup D$. What is the probability that the production manager assigned an employee a poor performance rating?

Note that the probability question is about the union of two events. Specifically, we want to know $P(L \cup D)$. Using equation (4.6), we have

$$P(L \cup D) = P(L) + P(D) - P(L \cap D)$$

Knowing values for the three probabilities on the right side of this expression, we can write

$$P(L \cup D) = .10 + .12 - .04 = .18$$

This calculation tells us that there is a .18 probability that a randomly selected employee received a poor performance rating.

As another example of the addition law, consider a recent study conducted by the personnel manager of a major computer software company. The study showed that 30% of the employees who left the firm within two years did so primarily because they were dissatisfied with their salary, 20% left because they were dissatisfied with their work assignments, and 12% of the former employees indicated dissatisfaction with *both* their salary and their work assignments. What is the probability that an employee who leaves within two years does so because of dissatisfaction with salary, dissatisfaction with the work assignment, or both?

Let

$$S = \text{the event that the employee leaves because of salary}$$
$$W = \text{the event that the employee leaves because of work assignment}$$

We have $P(S) = .30$, $P(W) = .20$, and $P(S \cap W) = .12$. Using equation (4.6), the addition law, we have

$$P(S \cup W) = P(S) + P(W) - P(S \cap W) = .30 + .20 - .12 = .38$$

We find a .38 probability that an employee leaves for salary or work assignment reasons.

Before we conclude our discussion of the addition law, let us consider a special case that arises for **mutually exclusive events**.

MUTUALLY EXCLUSIVE EVENTS

Two events are said to be mutually exclusive if the events have no sample points in common.

Events A and B are mutually exclusive if, when one event occurs, the other cannot occur. Thus, a requirement for A and B to be mutually exclusive is that their intersection must contain no sample points. The Venn diagram depicting two mutually exclusive events A and B is shown in Figure 4.7. In this case $P(A \cap B) = 0$ and the addition law can be written as follows.

ADDITION LAW FOR MUTUALLY EXCLUSIVE EVENTS
$$P(A \cup B) = P(A) + P(B)$$

FIGURE 4.7   MUTUALLY EXCLUSIVE EVENTS

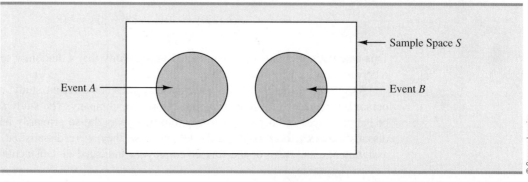

Exercises

Methods

22. Suppose that we have a sample space with five equally likely experimental outcomes: E_1, E_2, E_3, E_4, E_5. Let

$$A = \{E_1, E_2\}$$
$$B = \{E_3, E_4\}$$
$$C = \{E_2, E_3, E_5\}$$

   a. Find $P(A)$, $P(B)$, and $P(C)$.
   b. Find $P(A \cup B)$. Are A and B mutually exclusive?
   c. Find A^c, C^c, $P(A^c)$, and $P(C^c)$.
   d. Find $A \cup B^c$ and $P(A \cup B^c)$.
   e. Find $P(B \cup C)$.

23. Suppose that we have a sample space $S = \{E_1, E_2, E_3, E_4, E_5, E_6, E_7\}$, where $E_1, E_2, \ldots$, E_7 denote the sample points. The following probability assignments apply: $P(E_1) = .05$, $P(E_2) = .20$, $P(E_3) = .20$, $P(E_4) = .25$, $P(E_5) = .15$, $P(E_6) = .10$, and $P(E_7) = .05$. Let

$$A = \{E_1, E_4, E_6\}$$
$$B = \{E_2, E_4, E_7\}$$
$$C = \{E_2, E_3, E_5, E_7\}$$

   a. Find $P(A)$, $P(B)$, and $P(C)$.
   b. Find $A \cup B$ and $P(A \cup B)$.
   c. Find $A \cap B$ and $P(A \cap B)$.
   d. Are events A and C mutually exclusive?
   e. Find B^c and $P(B^c)$.

Applications

24. Clarkson University surveyed alumni to learn more about what they think of Clarkson. One part of the survey asked respondents to indicate whether their overall experience at Clarkson fell short of expectations, met expectations, or surpassed expectations. The results showed that 4% of the respondents did not provide a response, 26% said that their experience fell short of expectations, and 65% of the respondents said that their experience met expectations.
   a. If we chose an alumnus at random, what is the probability that the alumnus would say their experience *surpassed* expectations?
   b. If we chose an alumnus at random, what is the probability that the alumnus would say their experience met or surpassed expectations?

25. The Eco Pulse survey from the marketing communications firm Shelton Group asked individuals to indicate things they do that make them feel guilty (*Los Angeles Times*, August 15, 2012). Based on the survey results, there is a .39 probability that a randomly selected person will feel guilty about wasting food and a .27 probability that a randomly selected person will feel guilty about leaving lights on when not in a room. Moreover, there is a .12 probability that a randomly selected person will feel guilty for both of these reasons.
   a. What is the probability that a randomly selected person will feel guilty for either wasting food or leaving lights on when not in a room?
   b. What is the probability that a randomly selected person will not feel guilty for either of these reasons?

26. Information about mutual funds provided by Morningstar Investment Research includes the type of mutual fund (Domestic Equity, International Equity, or Fixed Income) and the Morningstar rating for the fund. The rating is expressed from 1-star (lowest rating) to 5-star (highest rating). A sample of 25 mutual funds was selected from *Morningstar Funds 500* (2008). The following counts were obtained:
    - Sixteen mutual funds were Domestic Equity funds.
    - Thirteen mutual funds were rated 3-star or less.
    - Seven of the Domestic Equity funds were rated 4-star.
    - Two of the Domestic Equity funds were rated 5-star.

    Assume that one of these 25 mutual funds will be randomly selected in order to learn more about the mutual fund and its investment strategy.
    a. What is the probability of selecting a Domestic Equity fund?
    b. What is the probability of selecting a fund with a 4-star or 5-star rating?
    c. What is the probability of selecting a fund that is both a Domestic Equity fund *and* a fund with a 4-star or 5-star rating?
    d. What is the probability of selecting a fund that is a Domestic Equity fund *or* a fund with a 4-star or 5-star rating?

27. Which NCAA college basketball conferences have the higher probability of having a team play in college basketball's national championship game? Over the last 20 years, the Atlantic Coast Conference (ACC) ranks first by having a team in the championship game 10 times. The Southeastern Conference (SEC) ranks second by having a team in the championship game 8 times. However, these two conferences have both had teams in the championship game only one time, when Arkansas (SEC) beat Duke (ACC) 76–70 in 1994 (NCAA website, April 2009). Use these data to estimate the following probabilities.
    a. What is the probability the ACC will have a team in the championship game?
    b. What is the probability the SEC will have team in the championship game?
    c. What is the probability the ACC and SEC will both have teams in the championship game?
    d. What is the probability at least one team from these two conferences will be in the championship game? That is, what is the probability a team from the ACC or SEC will play in the championship game?
    e. What is the probability that the championship game will not a have team from one of these two conferences?

28. A survey of magazine subscribers showed that 45.8% rented a car during the past 12 months for business reasons, 54% rented a car during the past 12 months for personal reasons, and 30% rented a car during the past 12 months for both business and personal reasons.
    a. What is the probability that a subscriber rented a car during the past 12 months for business or personal reasons?
    b. What is the probability that a subscriber did not rent a car during the past 12 months for either business or personal reasons?

29. High school seniors with strong academic records apply to the nation's most selective colleges in greater numbers each year. Because the number of slots remains relatively stable, some colleges reject more early applicants. Suppose that for a recent admissions class, an Ivy League college received 2851 applications for early admission. Of this group, it admitted 1033 students early, rejected 854 outright, and deferred 964 to the regular admission pool for further consideration. In the past, this school has admitted 18% of the deferred early admission applicants during the regular admission process. Counting the students admitted early and the students admitted during the regular admission process, the total class size was 2375. Let E, R, and D represent the events that a student who applies for early admission is admitted early, rejected outright, or deferred to the regular admissions pool.
    a. Use the data to estimate $P(E)$, $P(R)$, and $P(D)$.
    b. Are events E and D mutually exclusive? Find $P(E \cap D)$.

c. For the 2375 students who were admitted, what is the probability that a randomly selected student was accepted during early admission?
d. Suppose a student applies for early admission. What is the probability that the student will be admitted for early admission or be deferred and later admitted during the regular admission process?

4.4 Conditional Probability

Often, the probability of an event is influenced by whether a related event already occurred. Suppose we have an event A with probability $P(A)$. If we obtain new information and learn that a related event, denoted by B, already occurred, we will want to take advantage of this information by calculating a new probability for event A. This new probability of event A is called a **conditional probability** and is written $P(A \mid B)$. We use the notation | to indicate that we are considering the probability of event A *given* the condition that event B has occurred. Hence, the notation $P(A \mid B)$ reads "the probability of A given B."

As an illustration of the application of conditional probability, consider the situation of the promotion status of male and female officers of a major metropolitan police force in the eastern United States. The police force consists of 1200 officers, 960 men and 240 women. Over the past two years, 324 officers on the police force received promotions. The specific breakdown of promotions for male and female officers is shown in Table 4.4.

After reviewing the promotion record, a committee of female officers raised a discrimination case on the basis that 288 male officers had received promotions, but only 36 female officers had received promotions. The police administration argued that the relatively low number of promotions for female officers was due not to discrimination, but to the fact that relatively few females are members of the police force. Let us show how conditional probability could be used to analyze the discrimination charge.

Let

$$M = \text{event an officer is a man}$$
$$W = \text{event an officer is a woman}$$
$$A = \text{event an officer is promoted}$$
$$A^c = \text{event an officer is not promoted}$$

Dividing the data values in Table 4.4 by the total of 1200 officers enables us to summarize the available information with the following probability values.

$$P(M \cap A) = 288/1200 = .24 \text{ probability that a randomly selected officer is a man } and \text{ is promoted}$$

$$P(M \cap A^c) = 672/1200 = .56 \text{ probability that a randomly selected officer is a man } and \text{ is not promoted}$$

TABLE 4.4 PROMOTION STATUS OF POLICE OFFICERS OVER THE PAST TWO YEARS

	Men	Women	Total
Promoted	288	36	324
Not Promoted	672	204	876
Total	960	240	1200

TABLE 4.5   JOINT PROBABILITY TABLE FOR PROMOTIONS

Joint probabilities appear in the body of the table.	Men (M)	Women (W)	Total
Promoted (A)	.24	.03	.27
Not Promoted (A^c)	.56	.17	.73
Total	.80	.20	1.00

Marginal probabilities appear in the margins of the table.

© Cengage Learning

$$P(W \cap A) = 36/1200 \ = .03 \text{ probability that a randomly selected officer is a woman } and \text{ is promoted}$$

$$P(W \cap A^c) = 204/1200 = .17 \text{ probability that a randomly selected officer is a woman } and \text{ is not promoted}$$

Because each of these values gives the probability of the intersection of two events, the probabilities are called **joint probabilities**. Table 4.5, which provides a summary of the probability information for the police officer promotion situation, is referred to as a *joint probability table.*

The values in the margins of the joint probability table provide the probabilities of each event separately. That is, $P(M) = .80$, $P(W) = .20$, $P(A) = .27$, and $P(A^c) = .73$. These probabilities are referred to as **marginal probabilities** because of their location in the margins of the joint probability table. We note that the marginal probabilities are found by summing the joint probabilities in the corresponding row or column of the joint probability table. For instance, the marginal probability of being promoted is $P(A) = P(M \cap A) + P(W \cap A) = .24 + .03 = .27$. From the marginal probabilities, we see that 80% of the force is male, 20% of the force is female, 27% of all officers received promotions, and 73% were not promoted.

Let us begin the conditional probability analysis by computing the probability that an officer is promoted given that the officer is a man. In conditional probability notation, we are attempting to determine $P(A \mid M)$. To calculate $P(A \mid M)$, we first realize that this notation simply means that we are considering the probability of the event A (promotion) given that the condition designated as event M (the officer is a man) is known to exist. Thus $P(A \mid M)$ tells us that we are now concerned only with the promotion status of the 960 male officers. Because 288 of the 960 male officers received promotions, the probability of being promoted given that the officer is a man is $288/960 = .30$. In other words, given that an officer is a man, that officer had a 30% chance of receiving a promotion over the past two years.

This procedure was easy to apply because the values in Table 4.4 show the number of officers in each category. We now want to demonstrate how conditional probabilities such as $P(A \mid M)$ can be computed directly from related event probabilities rather than the frequency data of Table 4.4.

We have shown that $P(A \mid M) = 288/960 = .30$. Let us now divide both the numerator and denominator of this fraction by 1200, the total number of officers in the study.

$$P(A \mid M) = \frac{288}{960} = \frac{288/1200}{960/1200} = \frac{.24}{.80} = .30$$

We now see that the conditional probability $P(A \mid M)$ can be computed as .24/.80. Refer to the joint probability table (Table 4.5). Note in particular that .24 is the joint probability of

A and M; that is, $P(A \cap M) = .24$. Also note that .80 is the marginal probability that a randomly selected officer is a man; that is, $P(M) = .80$. Thus, the conditional probability $P(A \mid M)$ can be computed as the ratio of the joint probability $P(A \cap M)$ to the marginal probability $P(M)$.

$$P(A \mid M) = \frac{P(A \cap M)}{P(M)} = \frac{.24}{.80} = .30$$

The fact that conditional probabilities can be computed as the ratio of a joint probability to a marginal probability provides the following general formula for conditional probability calculations for two events A and B.

CONDITIONAL PROBABILITY

$$P(A \mid B) = \frac{P(A \cap B)}{P(B)} \qquad (4.7)$$

or

$$P(B \mid A) = \frac{P(A \cap B)}{P(A)} \qquad (4.8)$$

The Venn diagram in Figure 4.8 is helpful in obtaining an intuitive understanding of conditional probability. The circle on the right shows that event B has occurred; the portion of the circle that overlaps with event A denotes the event $(A \cap B)$. We know that once event B has occurred, the only way that we can also observe event A is for the event $(A \cap B)$ to occur. Thus, the ratio $P(A \cap B)/P(B)$ provides the conditional probability that we will observe event A given that event B has already occurred.

Let us return to the issue of discrimination against the female officers. The marginal probability in row 1 of Table 4.5 shows that the probability of promotion of an officer is $P(A) = .27$ (regardless of whether that officer is male or female). However, the critical issue in the discrimination case involves the two conditional probabilities $P(A \mid M)$ and $P(A \mid W)$. That is, what is the probability of a promotion *given* that the officer is a man, and what is the probability of a promotion *given* that the officer is a woman? If these two probabilities are equal, a discrimination argument has no basis because the chances of a promotion are the same for male and female officers. However, a difference in the two conditional probabilities will support the position that male and female officers are treated differently in promotion decisions.

FIGURE 4.8 CONDITIONAL PROBABILITY $P(A \mid B) = P(A \cap B)/P(B)$

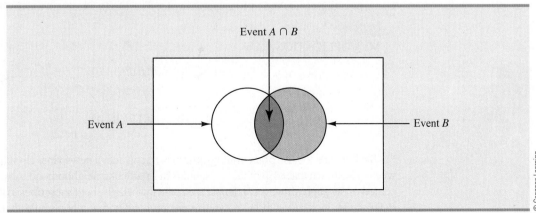

We already determined that $P(A \mid M) = .30$. Let us now use the probability values in Table 4.5 and the basic relationship of conditional probability in equation (4.7) to compute the probability that an officer is promoted given that the officer is a woman; that is, $P(A \mid W)$. Using equation (4.7), with W replacing B, we obtain

$$P(A \mid W) = \frac{P(A \cap W)}{P(W)} = \frac{.03}{.20} = .15$$

What conclusion do you draw? The probability of a promotion given that the officer is a man is .30, twice the .15 probability of a promotion given that the officer is a woman. Although the use of conditional probability does not in itself prove that discrimination exists in this case, the conditional probability values support the argument presented by the female officers.

Independent Events

In the preceding illustration, $P(A) = .27$, $P(A \mid M) = .30$, and $P(A \mid W) = .15$. We see that the probability of a promotion (event A) is affected or influenced by whether the officer is a man or a woman. Particularly, because $P(A \mid M) \neq P(A)$, we would say that events A and M are dependent events. That is, the probability of event A (promotion) is altered or affected by knowing that event M (the officer is a man) exists. Similarly, with $P(A \mid W) \neq P(A)$, we would say that events A and W are *dependent events*. However, if the probability of event A is not changed by the existence of event M—that is, $P(A \mid M) = P(A)$—we would say that events A and M are **independent events**. This situation leads to the following definition of the independence of two events.

INDEPENDENT EVENTS

Two events A and B are independent if

$$P(A \mid B) = P(A) \tag{4.9}$$

or

$$P(B \mid A) = P(B) \tag{4.10}$$

Otherwise, the events are dependent.

Multiplication Law

Whereas the addition law of probability is used to compute the probability of a union of two events, the multiplication law is used to compute the probability of the intersection of two events. The multiplication law is based on the definition of conditional probability. Using equations (4.7) and (4.8) and solving for $P(A \cap B)$, we obtain the **multiplication law**.

MULTIPLICATION LAW

$$P(A \cap B) = P(B)P(A \mid B) \tag{4.11}$$

or

$$P(A \cap B) = P(A)P(B \mid A) \tag{4.12}$$

To illustrate the use of the multiplication law, consider a newspaper circulation department where it is known that 84% of the households in a particular neighborhood subscribe to the daily edition of the paper. If we let D denote the event that a household subscribes to the daily edition, $P(D) = .84$. In addition, it is known that the probability that a household that already holds a daily subscription also subscribes to the Sunday edition (event S) is .75; that is, $P(S \mid D) = .75$. What is the probability that a household subscribes to both the Sunday and daily editions of the newspaper? Using the multiplication law, we compute the desired $P(S \cap D)$ as

$$P(S \cap D) = P(D)P(S \mid D) = .84(.75) = .63$$

We now know that 63% of the households subscribe to both the Sunday and daily editions.

Before concluding this section, let us consider the special case of the multiplication law when the events involved are independent. Recall that events A and B are independent whenever $P(A \mid B) = P(A)$ or $P(B \mid A) = P(B)$. Hence, using equations (4.11) and (4.12) for the special case of independent events, we obtain the following multiplication law.

MULTIPLICATION LAW FOR INDEPENDENT EVENTS

$$P(A \cap B) = P(A)P(B) \tag{4.13}$$

To compute the probability of the intersection of two independent events, we simply multiply the corresponding probabilities. Note that the multiplication law for independent events provides another way to determine whether A and B are independent. That is, if $P(A \cap B) = P(A)P(B)$, then A and B are independent; if $P(A \cap B) \neq P(A)P(B)$, then A and B are dependent.

As an application of the multiplication law for independent events, consider the situation of a service station manager who knows from past experience that 80% of the customers use a credit card when they purchase gasoline. What is the probability that the next two customers purchasing gasoline will each use a credit card? If we let

A = the event that the first customer uses a credit card
B = the event that the second customer uses a credit card

then the event of interest is $A \cap B$. Given no other information, we can reasonably assume that A and B are independent events. Thus,

$$P(A \cap B) = P(A)P(B) = (.80)(.80) = .64$$

To summarize this section, we note that our interest in conditional probability is motivated by the fact that events are often related. In such cases, we say the events are dependent and the conditional probability formulas in equations (4.7) and (4.8) must be used to compute the event probabilities. If two events are not related, they are independent; in this case neither event's probability is affected by whether the other event occurred.

NOTE AND COMMENT

Do not confuse the notion of mutually exclusive events with that of independent events. Two events with nonzero probabilities cannot be both mutually exclusive and independent. If one mutually exclusive event is known to occur, the other cannot occur; thus, the probability of the other event occurring is reduced to zero. They are therefore dependent.

Exercises

Methods

30. Suppose that we have two events, A and B, with $P(A) = .50$, $P(B) = .60$, and $P(A \cap B) = .40$.
    a. Find $P(A \mid B)$.
    b. Find $P(B \mid A)$.
    c. Are A and B independent? Why or why not?

31. Assume that we have two events, *A* and *B*, that are mutually exclusive. Assume further
     that we know $P(A) = .30$ and $P(B) = .40$.
     a.   What is $P(A \cap B)$?
     b.   What is $P(A \mid B)$?
     c.   A student in statistics argues that the concepts of mutually exclusive events and inde-
          pendent events are really the same, and that if events are mutually exclusive they must
          be independent. Do you agree with this statement? Use the probability information in
          this problem to justify your answer.
     d.   What general conclusion would you make about mutually exclusive and independent
          events given the results of this problem?

Applications

32. The automobile industry sold 657,000 vehicles in the United States during January 2009 (*The
     Wall Street Journal,* February 4, 2009). This volume was down 37% from January 2008 as
     economic conditions continued to decline. The Big Three U.S. automakers—General Motors,
     Ford, and Chrysler—sold 280,500 vehicles, down 48% from January 2008. A summary of
     sales by automobile manufacturer and type of vehicle sold is shown in the following table.
     Data are in thousands of vehicles. The non-U.S. manufacturers are led by Toyota, Honda, and
     Nissan. The category Light Truck includes pickup, minivan, SUV, and crossover models.

		Type of Vehicle	
		Car	Light Truck
Manufacturer	U.S.	87.4	193.1
	Non-U.S.	228.5	148.0

     a.   Develop a joint probability table for these data and use the table to answer the remain-
          ing questions.
     b.   What are the marginal probabilities? What do they tell you about the probabilities
          associated with the manufacturer and the type of vehicle sold?
     c.   If a vehicle was manufactured by one of the U.S. automakers, what is the probability
          that the vehicle was a car? What is the probability it was a light truck?
     d.   If a vehicle was not manufactured by one of the U.S. automakers, what is the prob-
          ability that the vehicle was a car? What is the probability it was a light truck?
     e.   If the vehicle was a light truck, what is the probability that it was manufactured by one
          of the U.S. automakers?
     f.   What does the probability information tell you about sales?

33. Students taking the Graduate Management Admissions Test (GMAT) were asked about
     their undergraduate major and intent to pursue their MBA as a full-time or part-time
     student. A summary of their responses follows.

		Undergraduate Major			
		Business	Engineering	Other	Totals
Intended	Full-Time	352	197	251	800
Enrollment	Part-Time	150	161	194	505
Status	Totals	502	358	445	1305

     a.   Develop a joint probability table for these data.
     b.   Use the marginal probabilities of undergraduate major (business, engineering, or other)
          to comment on which undergraduate major produces the most potential MBA students.

c. If a student intends to attend classes full-time in pursuit of an MBA degree, what is the probability that the student was an undergraduate engineering major?

d. If a student was an undergraduate business major, what is the probability that the student intends to attend classes full-time in pursuit of an MBA degree?

e. Let F denote the event that the student intends to attend classes full-time in pursuit of an MBA degree, and let B denote the event that the student was an undergraduate business major. Are events F and B independent? Justify your answer.

34. The Bureau of Transportation Statistics reports on-time performance for airlines at major U.S. airports. JetBlue, United, and US Airways share terminal C at Boston's Logan Airport. The percentage of on-time flights reported for August 2012 were 76.8% for JetBlue, 71.5% for United, and 82.2% for US Airways (Bureau of Transportation Statistics website, October 2012). Assume that 30% of the flights arriving at terminal C are JetBlue flights, 32% are United flights, and 38% US Airways flights.

a. Develop a joint probability table with three rows (the airlines) and two columns (on-time and late).

b. An announcement is made that Flight 1382 will be arriving at gate 20 of terminal C. What is the probability that Flight 1382 will arrive on time?

c. What is the most likely airline for Flight 1382? What is the probability that Flight 1382 is by this airline?

d. Suppose that an announcement is made saying that Flight 1382 will now be arriving late. What is the most likely airline for this flight? What is the probability that Flight 1382 is by this airline?

35. According to the Ameriprise Financial Money Across Generations study, 9 out of 10 parents with adult children ages 20 to 35 have helped their adult children with some type of financial assistance ranging from college, a car, rent, utilities, credit card debt, and/or down payments for houses (*Money*, January 2009). The following table with sample data consistent with the study shows the number of times parents have given their adult children financial assistance to buy a car and to pay rent.

		Pay Rent	
		Yes	No
Buy a Car	Yes	56	52
	No	14	78

a. Develop a joint probability table and use it to answer the remaining questions.

b. Using the marginal probabilities for buy a car and pay rent, are parents more likely to assist their adult children with buying a car or paying rent? What is your interpretation of the marginal probabilities?

c. If parents provided financial assistance to buy a car, what it the probability that the parents assisted with paying rent?

d. If parents did not provide financial assistance to buy a car, what is the probability the parents assisted with paying rent?

e. Is financial assistance to buy a car independent of financial assistance to pay rent? Use probabilities to justify your answer.

f. What is the probability that parents provided financial assistance for their adult children by either helping buy a car or pay rent?

36. Jamal Crawford of the National Basketball Association's Portland Trail Blazers is the best free-throw shooter on the team, making 93% of his shots (ESPN website, April 5, 2012). Assume that late in a basketball game, Jamal Crawford is fouled and is awarded two shots.

a. What is the probability that he will make both shots?

b. What is the probability that he will make at least one shot?

c. What is the probability that he will miss both shots?

d. Late in a basketball game, a team often intentionally fouls an opposing player in order to stop the game clock. The usual strategy is to intentionally foul the other team's worst free-throw shooter. Assume that the Portland Trail Blazers' center makes 58% of his free-throw shots. Calculate the probabilities for the center as shown in parts (a), (b), and (c), and show that intentionally fouling the Portland Trail Blazers' center is a better strategy than intentionally fouling Jamal Crawford. Assume as in parts (a), (b), and (c) that two shots will be awarded.

37. A joint survey by *Parade* magazine and Yahoo found that 59% of American workers say that if they could do it all over again, they would choose a different career (*USA Today,* September 24, 2012). The survey also found that 33% of American workers say they plan to retire early and 67% say they plan to wait and retire at age 65 or older. Assume that the following joint probability table applies.

		Retire Early		
		Yes	**No**	
Career	**Same**	.20	.21	.41
	Different	.13	.46	.59
		.33	.67	

a. What is the probability a worker would select the same career?

b. What is the probability a worker who would select the same career plans to retire early?

c. What is the probability a worker who would select a different career plans to retire early?

d. What do the conditional probabilities in parts (b) and (c) suggest about the reasons workers say they would select the same career?

38. The Institute for Higher Education Policy, a Washington, D.C.-based research firm, studied the payback of student loans for 1.8 million college students who had student loans that began to become due six years ago (*The Wall Street Journal,* November 27, 2012). The study found that 50% of the student loans were being paid back in a satisfactory fashion whereas 50% of the student loans were delinquent. The following joint probability table shows the probabilities of the student loan status and whether or not the student had received a college degree.

		College Degree		
		Yes	**No**	
Loan	**Satisfactory**	.26	.24	.50
Status	**Delinquent**	.16	.34	.50
		.42	.58	

a. What is the probability that a student with a student loan had received a college degree?

b. What is the probability that a student with a student loan had not received a college degree?

c. Given the student had received a college degree, what is the probability that the student has a delinquent loan?

d. Given the student had not received a college degree, what is the probability that the student has a delinquent loan?

e. What is the impact of dropping out of college without a degree for students who have a student loan?

4.5   Bayes' Theorem

In the discussion of conditional probability, we indicated that revising probabilities when new information is obtained is an important phase of probability analysis. Often, we begin the analysis with initial or **prior probability** estimates for specific events of interest. Then, from sources such as a sample, a special report, or a product test, we obtain additional information about the events. Given this new information, we update the prior probability values by calculating revised probabilities, referred to as **posterior probabilities**. **Bayes' theorem** provides a means for making these probability calculations. The steps in this probability revision process are shown in Figure 4.9.

As an application of Bayes' theorem, consider a manufacturing firm that receives shipments of parts from two different suppliers. Let A_1 denote the event that a part is from supplier 1 and A_2 denote the event that a part is from supplier 2. Currently, 65% of the parts purchased by the company are from supplier 1 and the remaining 35% are from supplier 2. Hence, if a part is selected at random, we would assign the prior probabilities $P(A_1) = .65$ and $P(A_2) = .35$.

The quality of the purchased parts varies with the source of supply. Historical data suggest that the quality ratings of the two suppliers are as shown in Table 4.6. If we let G denote the event that a part is good and B denote the event that a part is bad, the information in Table 4.6 provides the following conditional probability values.

$$P(G \mid A_1) = .98 \quad P(B \mid A_1) = .02$$
$$P(G \mid A_2) = .95 \quad P(B \mid A_2) = .05$$

The tree diagram in Figure 4.10 depicts the process of the firm receiving a part from one of the two suppliers and then discovering that the part is good or bad as a two-step experiment. We see that four experimental outcomes are possible; two correspond to the part being good and two correspond to the part being bad.

Each of the experimental outcomes is the intersection of two events, so we can use the multiplication rule to compute the probabilities. For instance,

$$P(A_1, G) = P(A_1 \cap G) = P(A_1)P(G \mid A_1)$$

FIGURE 4.9   PROBABILITY REVISION USING BAYES' THEOREM

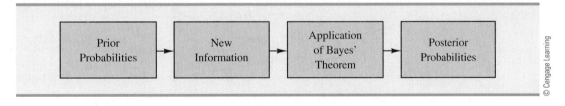

TABLE 4.6   HISTORICAL QUALITY LEVELS OF TWO SUPPLIERS

	Percentage Good Parts	Percentage Bad Parts
Supplier 1	98	2
Supplier 2	95	5

FIGURE 4.10   TREE DIAGRAM FOR TWO-SUPPLIER EXAMPLE

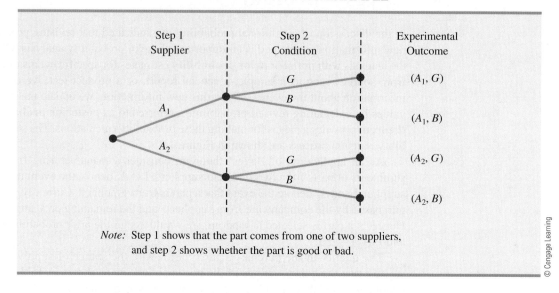

Note: Step 1 shows that the part comes from one of two suppliers,
and step 2 shows whether the part is good or bad.

The process of computing these joint probabilities can be depicted in what is called a probability tree (see Figure 4.11). From left to right through the tree, the probabilities for each branch at step 1 are prior probabilities and the probabilities for each branch at step 2 are conditional probabilities. To find the probabilities of each experimental outcome, we simply multiply the probabilities on the branches leading to the outcome. Each of these joint probabilities is shown in Figure 4.11 along with the known probabilities for each branch.

Suppose now that the parts from the two suppliers are used in the firm's manufacturing process and that a machine breaks down because it attempts to process a bad part. Given the information that the part is bad, what is the probability that it came from supplier 1 and what is the probability that it came from supplier 2? With the information in the probability tree (Figure 4.11), Bayes' theorem can be used to answer these questions.

FIGURE 4.11   PROBABILITY TREE FOR TWO-SUPPLIER EXAMPLE

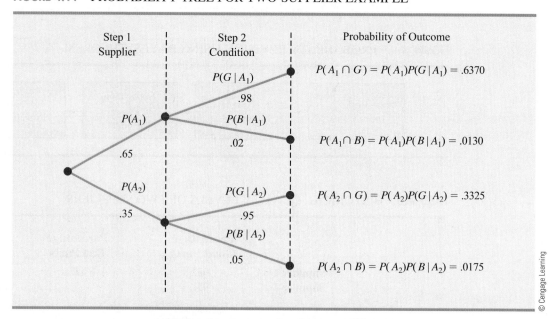

Letting B denote the event that the part is bad, we are looking for the posterior probabilities $P(A_1 \mid B)$ and $P(A_2 \mid B)$. From the law of conditional probability, we know that

$$P(A_1 \mid B) = \frac{P(A_1 \cap B)}{P(B)} \tag{4.14}$$

Referring to the probability tree, we see that

$$P(A_1 \cap B) = P(A_1)P(B \mid A_1) \tag{4.15}$$

To find $P(B)$, we note that event B can occur in only two ways: $(A_1 \cap B)$ and $(A_2 \cap B)$. Therefore, we have

$$P(B) = P(A_1 \cap B) + P(A_2 \cap B)$$
$$= P(A_1)P(B \mid A_1) + P(A_2)P(B \mid A_2) \tag{4.16}$$

Substituting from equations (4.15) and (4.16) into equation (4.14) and writing a similar result for $P(A_2 \mid B)$, we obtain Bayes' theorem for the case of two events.

The Reverend Thomas Bayes (1702–1761), a Presbyterian minister, is credited with the original work leading to the version of Bayes' theorem in use today.

BAYES' THEOREM (TWO-EVENT CASE)

$$P(A_1 \mid B) = \frac{P(A_1)P(B \mid A_1)}{P(A_1)P(B \mid A_1) + P(A_2)P(B \mid A_2)} \tag{4.17}$$

$$P(A_2 \mid B) = \frac{P(A_2)P(B \mid A_2)}{P(A_1)P(B \mid A_1) + P(A_2)P(B \mid A_2)} \tag{4.18}$$

Using equation (4.17) and the probability values provided in the example, we have

$$P(A_1 \mid B) = \frac{P(A_1)P(B \mid A_1)}{P(A_1)P(B \mid A_1) + P(A_2)P(B \mid A_2)}$$

$$= \frac{(.65)(.02)}{(.65)(.02) + (.35)(.05)} = \frac{.0130}{.0130 + .0175}$$

$$= \frac{.0130}{.0305} = .4262$$

In addition, using equation (4.18), we find $P(A_2 \mid B)$.

$$P(A_2 \mid B) = \frac{(.35)(.05)}{(.65)(.02) + (.35)(.05)}$$

$$= \frac{.0175}{.0130 + .0175} = \frac{.0175}{.0305} = .5738$$

Note that in this application we started with a probability of .65 that a part selected at random was from supplier 1. However, given information that the part is bad, the probability that the part is from supplier 1 drops to .4262. In fact, if the part is bad, it has better than a 50–50 chance that it came from supplier 2; that is, $P(A_2 \mid B) = .5738$.

Bayes' theorem is applicable when the events for which we want to compute posterior probabilities are mutually exclusive and their union is the entire sample space.[1] For the case of n mutually exclusive events $A_1, A_2, \ldots, A_n$, whose union is the entire sample space, Bayes' theorem can be used to compute any posterior probability $P(A_i \mid B)$ as shown here.

BAYES' THEOREM

$$P(A_i \mid B) = \frac{P(A_i)P(B \mid A_i)}{P(A_1)P(B \mid A_1) + P(A_2)P(B \mid A_2) + \cdots + P(A_n)P(B \mid A_n)} \qquad \textbf{(4.19)}$$

With prior probabilities $P(A_1), P(A_2), \ldots, P(A_n)$ and the appropriate conditional probabilities $P(B \mid A_1), P(B \mid A_2), \ldots, P(B \mid A_n)$, equation (4.19) can be used to compute the posterior probability of the events $A_1, A_2, \ldots, A_n$.

Tabular Approach

A tabular approach is helpful in conducting the Bayes' theorem calculations. Such an approach is shown in Table 4.7 for the parts supplier problem. The computations shown there are done in the following steps.

Step 1. Prepare the following three columns:
  Column 1—The mutually exclusive events A_i for which posterior probabilities are desired
  Column 2—The prior probabilities $P(A_i)$ for the events
  Column 3—The conditional probabilities $P(B \mid A_i)$ of the new information B given each event

Step 2. In column 4, compute the joint probabilities $P(A_i \cap B)$ for each event and the new information B by using the multiplication law. These joint probabilities are found by multiplying the prior probabilities in column 2 by the corresponding conditional probabilities in column 3; that is, $P(A_i \cap B) = P(A_i)P(B \mid A_i)$.

Step 3. Sum the joint probabilities in column 4. The sum is the probability of the new information, $P(B)$. Thus we see in Table 4.7 that there is a .0130 probability that the part came from supplier 1 and is bad and a .0175 probability that the part came from supplier 2 and is bad. Because these are the only two ways in which a bad part can be obtained, the sum .0130 + .0175 shows an overall

TABLE 4.7   TABULAR APPROACH TO BAYES' THEOREM CALCULATIONS FOR THE TWO-SUPPLIER PROBLEM

(1) Events A_i	(2) Prior Probabilities $P(A_i)$	(3) Conditional Probabilities $P(B \mid A_i)$	(4) Joint Probabilities $P(A_i \cap B)$	(5) Posterior Probabilities $P(A_i \mid B)$
A_1	.65	.02	.0130	.0130/.0305 = .4262
A_2	.35	.05	.0175	.0175/.0305 = .5738
	1.00		$P(B) = .0305$	1.0000

© Cengage Learning

---

[1] If the union of events is the entire sample space, the events are said to be collectively exhaustive.

probability of .0305 of finding a bad part from the combined shipments of the two suppliers.

Step 4. In column 5, compute the posterior probabilities using the basic relationship of conditional probability.

$$P(A_i \mid B) = \frac{P(A_i \cap B)}{P(B)}$$

Note that the joint probabilities $P(A_i \cap B)$ are in column 4 and the probability $P(B)$ is the sum of column 4.

NOTES AND COMMENTS

1. Bayes' theorem is used extensively in decision analysis. The prior probabilities are often subjective estimates provided by a decision maker. Sample information is obtained and posterior probabilities are computed for use in choosing the best decision.

2. An event and its complement are mutually exclusive, and their union is the entire sample space. Thus, Bayes' theorem is always applicable for computing posterior probabilities of an event and its complement.

Exercises

Methods

39. The prior probabilities for events A_1 and A_2 are $P(A_1) = .40$ and $P(A_2) = .60$. It is also known that $P(A_1 \cap A_2) = 0$. Suppose $P(B \mid A_1) = .20$ and $P(B \mid A_2) = .05$.
    a. Are A_1 and A_2 mutually exclusive? Explain.
    b. Compute $P(A_1 \cap B)$ and $P(A_2 \cap B)$.
    c. Compute $P(B)$.
    d. Apply Bayes' theorem to compute $P(A_1 \mid B)$ and $P(A_2 \mid B)$.

40. The prior probabilities for events A_1, A_2, and A_3 are $P(A_1) = .20$, $P(A_2) = .50$, and $P(A_3) = .30$. The conditional probabilities of event B given A_1, A_2, and A_3 are $P(B \mid A_1) = .50$, $P(B \mid A_2) = .40$, and $P(B \mid A_3) = .30$.
    a. Compute $P(B \cap A_1)$, $P(B \cap A_2)$, and $P(B \cap A_3)$.
    b. Apply Bayes' theorem, equation (4.19), to compute the posterior probability $P(A_2 \mid B)$.
    c. Use the tabular approach to applying Bayes' theorem to compute $P(A_1 \mid B)$, $P(A_2 \mid B)$, and $P(A_3 \mid B)$.

Applications

41. A consulting firm submitted a bid for a large research project. The firm's management initially felt they had a 50–50 chance of getting the project. However, the agency to which the bid was submitted subsequently requested additional information on the bid. Past experience indicates that for 75% of the successful bids and 40% of the unsuccessful bids the agency requested additional information.
    a. What is the prior probability of the bid being successful (that is, prior to the request for additional information)?
    b. What is the conditional probability of a request for additional information given that the bid will ultimately be successful?
    c. Compute the posterior probability that the bid will be successful given a request for additional information.

42. A local bank reviewed its credit card policy with the intention of recalling some of its credit cards. In the past approximately 5% of cardholders defaulted, leaving the bank unable to collect the outstanding balance. Hence, management established a prior probability of .05 that any particular cardholder will default. The bank also found that the probability of missing a monthly payment is .20 for customers who do not default. Of course, the probability of missing a monthly payment for those who default is 1.
    a. Given a customer missed a monthly payment, compute the posterior probability that the customer will default.
    b. The bank would like to recall its credit card if the probability that a customer will default is greater than .20. Should the bank recall its card if the customer misses a monthly payment? Why or why not?

43. In August 2012, tropical storm Isaac formed in the Caribbean and was headed for the Gulf of Mexico. There was an initial probability of .69 that Isaac would become a hurricane by the time it reached the Gulf of Mexico (National Hurricane Center website, August 21, 2012).
    a. What was the probability that Isaac would not become a hurricane but remain a tropical storm when it reached the Gulf of Mexico?
    b. Two days later, the National Hurricane Center projected the path of Isaac would pass directly over Cuba before reaching the Gulf of Mexico. How did passing over Cuba alter the probability that Isaac would become a hurricane by the time it reached the Gulf of Mexico? Use the following probabilities to answer this question. Hurricanes that reach the Gulf of Mexico have a .08 probability of having passed over Cuba. Tropical storms that reach the Gulf of Mexico have a .20 probability of having passed over Cuba.
    c. What happens to the probability of becoming a hurricane when a tropical storm passes over a landmass such as Cuba?

44. ParFore created a website to market golf equipment and golf apparel. Management would like a special pop-up offer to appear for female website visitors and a different special pop-up offer to appear for male website visitors. From a sample of past website visitors, ParFore's management learned that 60% of the visitors are male and 40% are female.
    a. What is the probability that a current visitor to the website is female?
    b. Suppose 30% of ParFore's female visitors previously visited the Dillard's Department Store website and 10% of ParFore's male visitors previously visited the Dillard's Department Store website. If the current visitor to ParFore's website previously visited the Dillard's website, what is the revised probability that the current visitor is female? Should the ParFore's website display the special offer that appeals to female visitors or the special offer that appeals to male visitors?

45. Professors at the University of Chicago and the University of Pennsylvania analyzed 1,613,234 putts by golfers on the Professional Golfers Association (PGA) Tour and found that 983,764 putts were made and 629,470 putts were missed (*Is Tiger Woods Loss Averse? Persistent Bias in the Face of Experience, Competition, and High Stakes*, American Economic Review, February, 2011.)
    a. What is the probability that a PGA Tour player makes a putt? What is the probability that a PGA Tour player misses a putt?
    b. Suppose that a PGA Tour player has a par putt. It is known that of putts made, 64.0% were for par while for putts missed, 20.3% were for par. What is the revised probability of making a putt given the PGA Tour player has a par putt?
    c. A birdie occurs when a player makes a putt in one stroke less than par. Suppose that a PGA Tour player has a birdie putt. It is known that of putts made, 18.8% were for birdie whereas for putts missed, 73.4% were for birdie. What is the revised probability of making a putt given the PGA Tour player has a birdie putt?
    d. Comment on the differences in the probabilities computed in parts (b) and (c).

Summary

In this chapter we introduced basic probability concepts and illustrated how probability analysis can be used to provide helpful information for decision making. We described how probability can be interpreted as a numerical measure of the likelihood that an event will occur. In addition, we saw that the probability of an event can be computed either by summing the probabilities of the experimental outcomes (sample points) comprising the event or by using the relationships established by the addition, conditional probability, and multiplication laws of probability. For cases in which additional information is available, we showed how Bayes' theorem can be used to obtain revised or posterior probabilities.

Glossary

Probability A numerical measure of the likelihood that an event will occur.

Experiment A process that generates well-defined outcomes.

Sample space The set of all experimental outcomes.

Sample point An element of the sample space. A sample point represents an experimental outcome.

Multiple-step experiment An experiment that can be described as a sequence of steps. If a multiple-step experiment has k steps with n_1 possible outcomes on the first step, n_2 possible outcomes on the second step, and so on, the total number of experimental outcomes is given by $(n_1)(n_2) \cdots (n_k)$.

Tree diagram A graphical representation that helps in visualizing a multiple-step experiment.

Combination In an experiment we may be interested in determining the number of ways n objects may be selected from among N objects without regard to the *order in which the n objects are selected*. Each selection of n objects is called a combination and the total number of combinations of N objects taken n at a time is $C_n^N = \binom{N}{n} = \dfrac{N!}{n!(N-n)!}$ for $n = 0, 1, 2, \ldots, N$.

Permutation In an experiment we may be interested in determining the number of ways n objects may be selected from among N objects when the *order in which the n objects are selected* is important. Each ordering of n objects is called a permutation and the total number of permutations of N objects taken n at a time is $P_n^N = n!\binom{N}{n} = \dfrac{N!}{(N-n)!}$ for $n = 0, 1, 2, \ldots, N$.

Basic requirements for assigning probabilities Two requirements that restrict the manner in which probability assignments can be made: (1) for each experimental outcome E_i we must have $0 \le P(E_i) \le 1$; (2) considering all experimental outcomes, we must have $P(E_1) + P(E_2) + \cdots + P(E_n) = 1.0$.

Classical method A method of assigning probabilities that is appropriate when all the experimental outcomes are equally likely.

Relative frequency method A method of assigning probabilities that is appropriate when data are available to estimate the proportion of the time the experimental outcome will occur if the experiment is repeated a large number of times.

Subjective method A method of assigning probabilities on the basis of judgment.

Event A collection of sample points.

Complement of A The event consisting of all sample points that are not in A.

Venn diagram A graphical representation for showing symbolically the sample space and operations involving events in which the sample space is represented by a rectangle and events are represented as circles within the sample space.

Union of A and B The event containing all sample points belonging to A or B or both. The union is denoted $A \cup B$.

Intersection of A and B The event containing the sample points belonging to both A and B. The intersection is denoted $A \cap B$.

Addition law A probability law used to compute the probability of the union of two events. It is $P(A \cup B) = P(A) + P(B) - P(A \cap B)$. For mutually exclusive events, $P(A \cap B) = 0$; in this case the addition law reduces to $P(A \cup B) = P(A) + P(B)$.

Mutually exclusive events Events that have no sample points in common; that is, $A \cap B$ is empty and $P(A \cap B) = 0$.

Conditional probability The probability of an event given that another event already occurred. The conditional probability of A given B is $P(A \mid B) = P(A \cap B)/P(B)$.

Joint probability The probability of two events both occurring; that is, the probability of the intersection of two events.

Marginal probability The values in the margins of a joint probability table that provide the probabilities of each event separately.

Independent events Two events A and B where $P(A \mid B) = P(A)$ or $P(B \mid A) = P(B)$; that is, the events have no influence on each other.

Multiplication law A probability law used to compute the probability of the intersection of two events. It is $P(A \cap B) = P(B)P(A \mid B)$ or $P(A \cap B) = P(A)P(B \mid A)$. For independent events it reduces to $P(A \cap B) = P(A)P(B)$.

Prior probabilities Initial estimates of the probabilities of events.

Posterior probabilities Revised probabilities of events based on additional information.

Bayes' theorem A method used to compute posterior probabilities.

Key Formulas

Counting Rule for Combinations

$$C_n^N = \binom{N}{n} = \frac{N!}{n!(N-n)!} \tag{4.1}$$

Counting Rule for Permutations

$$P_n^N = n!\binom{N}{n} = \frac{N!}{(N-n)!} \tag{4.2}$$

Computing Probability Using the Complement

$$P(A) = 1 - P(A^c) \tag{4.5}$$

Addition Law

$$P(A \cup B) = P(A) + P(B) - P(A \cap B) \tag{4.6}$$

Conditional Probability

$$P(A \mid B) = \frac{P(A \cap B)}{P(B)} \tag{4.7}$$

$$P(B \mid A) = \frac{P(A \cap B)}{P(A)} \tag{4.8}$$

Multiplication Law

$$P(A \cap B) = P(B)P(A \mid B) \tag{4.11}$$

$$P(A \cap B) = P(A)P(B \mid A) \tag{4.12}$$

Multiplication Law for Independent Events

$$P(A \cap B) = P(A)P(B) \qquad (4.13)$$

Bayes' Theorem

$$P(A_i \mid B) = \frac{P(A_i)P(B \mid A_i)}{P(A_1)P(B \mid A_1) + P(A_2)P(B \mid A_2) + \cdots + P(A_n)P(B \mid A_n)} \qquad (4.19)$$

Supplementary Exercises

46. A survey of adults aged 18 and older conducted by Princess Cruises asked how many days into your vacation does it take until you feel truly relaxed (*USA Today,* August 24, 2011). The responses were as follows: 422—a day or less; 181—2 days; 80—3 days; 121—4 or more days; and 201—never feel relaxed.
    a. How many adults participated in the Princess Cruises survey?
    b. What response has the highest probability? What is the probability of this response?
    c. What is the probability a respondent never feels truly relaxed on a vacation?
    d. What is the probability it takes a respondent 2 or more days to feel truly relaxed?

47. A financial manager made two new investments—one in the oil industry and one in municipal bonds. After a one-year period, each of the investments will be classified as either successful or unsuccessful. Consider the making of the two investments as an experiment.
    a. How many sample points exist for this experiment?
    b. Show a tree diagram and list the sample points.
    c. Let O = the event that the oil industry investment is successful and M = the event that the municipal bond investment is successful. List the sample points in O and in M.
    d. List the sample points in the union of the events $(O \cup M)$.
    e. List the sample points in the intersection of the events $(O \cap M)$.
    f. Are events O and M mutually exclusive? Explain.

48. Forty-three percent of Americans use social media and other websites to voice their opinions about television programs (*The Huffington Post,* November 23, 2011). Below are the results of a survey of 1400 individuals who were asked if they use social media and other websites to voice their opinions about television programs.

	Uses Social Media and Other Websites to Voice Opinions About Television Programs	Doesn't Use Social Media and Other Websites to Voice Opinions About Television Programs
Female	395	291
Male	323	355

    a. Show a joint probability table.
    b. What is the probability a respondent is female?
    c. What is the conditional probability a respondent uses social media and other websites to voice opinions about television programs given the respondent is female?
    d. Let F denote the event that the respondent is female and A denote the event that the respondent uses social media and other websites to voice opinions about television programs. Are F and A independent events?

49. A study of 31,000 hospital admissions in New York State found that 4% of the admissions led to treatment-caused injuries. One-seventh of these treatment-caused injuries resulted in death, and one-fourth were caused by negligence. Malpractice claims were filed in one out of 7.5 cases involving negligence, and payments were made in one out of every two claims.
    a. What is the probability a person admitted to the hospital will suffer a treatment-caused injury due to negligence?

b.   What is the probability a person admitted to the hospital will die from a treatment-caused injury?

c.   In the case of a negligent treatment-caused injury, what is the probability a malpractice claim will be paid?

50. A telephone survey to determine viewer response to a new television show obtained the following data.

Rating	Frequency
Poor	4
Below average	8
Average	11
Above average	14
Excellent	13

a.   What is the probability that a randomly selected viewer will rate the new show as average or better?

b.   What is the probability that a randomly selected viewer will rate the new show below average or worse?

51. The following crosstabulation shows household income by educational level of the head of household (*Statistical Abstract of the United States*, 2008).

	Household Income ($1000s)					
Education Level	Under 25	25.0– 49.9	50.0– 74.9	75.0– 99.9	100 or more	Total
Not H.S. Graduate	4,207	3,459	1,389	539	367	9,961
H.S. Graduate	4,917	6,850	5,027	2,637	2,668	22,099
Some College	2,807	5,258	4,678	3,250	4,074	20,067
Bachelor's Degree	885	2,094	2,848	2,581	5,379	13,787
Beyond Bach. Deg.	290	829	1,274	1,241	4,188	7,822
Total	13,106	18,490	15,216	10,248	16,676	73,736

a.   Develop a joint probability table.

b.   What is the probability of a head of household not being a high school graduate?

c.   What is the probability of a head of household having a bachelor's degree or more education?

d.   What is the probability of a household headed by someone with a bachelor's degree earning $100,000 or more?

e.   What is the probability of a household having income below $25,000?

f.   What is the probability of a household headed by someone with a bachelor's degree earning less than $25,000?

g.   Is household income independent of educational level?

52. An MBA new-matriculants survey provided the following data for 2018 students.

		Applied to More Than One School	
		Yes	No
	23 and under	207	201
	24–26	299	379
Age Group	**27–30**	185	268
	31–35	66	193
	36 and over	51	169

    a. For a randomly selected MBA student, prepare a joint probability table for the experiment consisting of observing the student's age and whether the student applied to one or more schools.

    b. What is the probability that a randomly selected applicant is 23 or under?

    c. What is the probability that a randomly selected applicant is older than 26?

    d. What is the probability that a randomly selected applicant applied to more than one school?

53. Refer again to the data from the MBA new-matriculants survey in exercise 52.

    a. Given that a person applied to more than one school, what is the probability that the person is 24–26 years old?

    b. Given that a person is in the 36-and-over age group, what is the probability that the person applied to more than one school?

    c. What is the probability that a person is 24–26 years old or applied to more than one school?

    d. Suppose a person is known to have applied to only one school. What is the probability that the person is 31 or more years old?

    e. Is the number of schools applied to independent of age? Explain.

54. In February 2012, the Pew Internet & American Life project conducted a survey that included several questions about how Internet users feel about search engines and other websites collecting information about them and using this information either to shape search results or target advertising to them (Pew Research Center, March 9, 2012). In one question, participants were asked, "If a search engine kept track of what you search for, and then used that information to personalize your future search results, how would you feel about that?" Respondents could indicate either "Would *not* be okay with it because you feel it is an invasion of your privacy" or "Would be *okay* with it, even if it means they are gathering information about you." Joint probabilities of responses and age groups are summarized in the following table.

Age	Not Okay	Okay
18–29	.1485	.0604
30–49	.2273	.0907
50+	.4008	.0723

    a. What is the probability a respondent will say *not okay* with this practice?

    b. Given a respondent is 30–49 years old, what is the probability the respondent will say *okay* with this practice?

    c. Given a respondent says *not okay* with this practice, what is the probability the respondent is 50+ years old?

    d. Is the attitude about this practice independent of the age of the respondent? Why or why not?

    e. Do attitudes toward this practice for respondents who are 18–29 years old and respondents who are 50+ years old differ?

55. A large consumer goods company ran a television advertisement for one of its soap products. On the basis of a survey that was conducted, probabilities were assigned to the following events.

$$B = \text{individual purchased the product}$$
$$S = \text{individual recalls seeing the advertisement}$$
$$B \cap S = \text{individual purchased the product and recalls seeing the advertisement}$$

The probabilities assigned were $P(B) = .20$, $P(S) = .40$, and $P(B \cap S) = .12$.

a. What is the probability of an individual's purchasing the product given that the individual recalls seeing the advertisement? Does seeing the advertisement increase the probability that the individual will purchase the product? As a decision maker, would you recommend continuing the advertisement (assuming that the cost is reasonable)?

b. Assume that individuals who do not purchase the company's soap product buy from its competitors. What would be your estimate of the company's market share? Would you expect that continuing the advertisement will increase the company's market share? Why or why not?

c. The company also tested another advertisement and assigned it values of $P(S) = .30$ and $P(B \cap S) = .10$. What is $P(B \mid S)$ for this other advertisement? Which advertisement seems to have had the bigger effect on customer purchases?

56. Cooper Realty is a small real estate company located in Albany, New York, specializing primarily in residential listings. They recently became interested in determining the likelihood of one of their listings being sold within a certain number of days. An analysis of company sales of 800 homes in previous years produced the following data.

		Days Listed Until Sold			
		Under 30	31–90	Over 90	Total
Initial Asking Price	Under $150,000	50	40	10	100
	$150,000–$199,999	20	150	80	250
	$200,000–$250,000	20	280	100	400
	Over $250,000	10	30	10	50
	Total	100	500	200	800

a. If A is defined as the event that a home is listed for more than 90 days before being sold, estimate the probability of A.

b. If B is defined as the event that the initial asking price is under $150,000, estimate the probability of B.

c. What is the probability of $A \cap B$?

d. Assuming that a contract was just signed to list a home with an initial asking price of less than $150,000, what is the probability that the home will take Cooper Realty more than 90 days to sell?

e. Are events A and B independent?

57. A company studied the number of lost-time accidents occurring at its Brownsville, Texas, plant. Historical records show that 6% of the employees suffered lost-time accidents last year. Management believes that a special safety program will reduce such accidents to 5% during the current year. In addition, it estimates that 15% of employees who had lost-time accidents last year will experience a lost-time accident during the current year.

a. What percentage of the employees will experience lost-time accidents in both years?

b. What percentage of the employees will suffer at least one lost-time accident over the two-year period?

58. According to the Open Doors Report, 9.5% of all full-time U.S. undergraduate students study abroad (Institute of International Education, November 14, 2011). Assume that 60% of the undergraduate students who study abroad are female and that 49% of the undergraduate students who do not study abroad are female.

a. Given a female undergraduate student, what is the probability that she studies abroad?

b. Given a male undergraduate student, what is the probability that he studies abroad?

c. What is the overall percentage of full-time female undergraduate students? What is the overall percentage of full-time male undergraduate students?

59. An oil company purchased an option on land in Alaska. Preliminary geologic studies assigned the following prior probabilities.

$$P(\text{high-quality oil}) = .50$$
$$P(\text{medium-quality oil}) = .20$$
$$P(\text{no oil}) = .30$$

a. What is the probability of finding oil?

b. After 200 feet of drilling on the first well, a soil test is taken. The probabilities of finding the particular type of soil identified by the test follow.

$$P(\text{soil} \mid \text{high-quality oil}) = .20$$
$$P(\text{soil} \mid \text{medium-quality oil}) = .80$$
$$P(\text{soil} \mid \text{no oil}) = .20$$

How should the firm interpret the soil test? What are the revised probabilities, and what is the new probability of finding oil?

60. The five most common words appearing in spam emails are *shipping!, today!, here!, available,* and *fingertips!* (Andy Greenberg, "The Most Common Words In Spam Email," *Forbes* website, March 17, 2010). Many spam filters separate spam from ham (e-mail not considered to be spam) through application of Bayes' theorem. Suppose that for one e-mail account, 1 in every 10 messages is spam and the proportions of spam messages that have the five most common words in spam email are given below.

shipping!	.051
today!	.045
here!	.034
available	.014
fingertips!	.014

Also suppose that the proportions of ham messages that have these words are

shipping!	.0015
today!	.0022
here!	.0022
available	.0041
fingertips!	.0011

a. If a message includes the word *shipping!,* what is the probability the message is spam? If a message includes the word *shipping!,* what is the probability the message is ham? Should messages that include the word *shipping!* be flagged as spam?

b. If a message includes the word *today!,* what is the probability the message is spam? If a message includes the word *here!,* what is the probability the message is spam? Which of these two words is a stronger indicator that a message is spam? Why?

c. If a message includes the word *available,* what is the probability the message is spam? If a message includes the word *fingertips!,* what is the probability the message is spam? Which of these two words is a stronger indicator that a message is spam? Why?

d. What insights do the results of parts (b) and (c) yield about what enables a spam filter that uses Bayes' theorem to work effectively?

Case Problem   # Hamilton County Judges

Hamilton County judges try thousands of cases per year. In an overwhelming majority of the cases disposed, the verdict stands as rendered. However, some cases are appealed, and of those appealed, some of the cases are reversed. Kristen DelGuzzi of *The Cincinnati Enquirer* conducted a study of cases handled by Hamilton County judges over a three-year period. Shown in Table 4.8 are the results for 182,908 cases handled (disposed)

TABLE 4.8   TOTAL CASES DISPOSED, APPEALED, AND REVERSED IN HAMILTON COUNTY COURTS

Common Pleas Court

Judge	Total Cases Disposed	Appealed Cases	Reversed Cases
Fred Cartolano	3037	137	12
Thomas Crush	3372	119	10
Patrick Dinkelacker	1258	44	8
Timothy Hogan	1954	60	7
Robert Kraft	3138	127	7
William Mathews	2264	91	18
William Morrissey	3032	121	22
Norbert Nadel	2959	131	20
Arthur Ney, Jr.	3219	125	14
Richard Niehaus	3353	137	16
Thomas Nurre	3000	121	6
John O'Connor	2969	129	12
Robert Ruehlman	3205	145	18
J. Howard Sundermann	955	60	10
Ann Marie Tracey	3141	127	13
Ralph Winkler	3089	88	6
Total	43,945	1762	199

Domestic Relations Court

Judge	Total Cases Disposed	Appealed Cases	Reversed Cases
Penelope Cunningham	2729	7	1
Patrick Dinkelacker	6001	19	4
Deborah Gaines	8799	48	9
Ronald Panioto	12,970	32	3
Total	30,499	106	17

Municipal Court

Judge	Total Cases Disposed	Appealed Cases	Reversed Cases
Mike Allen	6149	43	4
Nadine Allen	7812	34	6
Timothy Black	7954	41	6
David Davis	7736	43	5
Leslie Isaiah Gaines	5282	35	13
Karla Grady	5253	6	0
Deidra Hair	2532	5	0
Dennis Helmick	7900	29	5
Timothy Hogan	2308	13	2
James Patrick Kenney	2798	6	1
Joseph Luebbers	4698	25	8
William Mallory	8277	38	9
Melba Marsh	8219	34	7
Beth Mattingly	2971	13	1
Albert Mestemaker	4975	28	9
Mark Painter	2239	7	3
Jack Rosen	7790	41	13
Mark Schweikert	5403	33	6
David Stockdale	5371	22	4
John A. West	2797	4	2
Total	108,464	500	104

by 38 judges in Common Pleas Court, Domestic Relations Court, and Municipal Court. Two of the judges (Dinkelacker and Hogan) did not serve in the same court for the entire three-year period.

The purpose of the newspaper's study was to evaluate the performance of the judges. Appeals are often the result of mistakes made by judges, and the newspaper wanted to know which judges were doing a good job and which were making too many mistakes. You are called in to assist in the data analysis. Use your knowledge of probability and conditional probability to help with the ranking of the judges. You also may be able to analyze the likelihood of appeal and reversal for cases handled by different courts.

Managerial Report

Prepare a report with your rankings of the judges. Also, include an analysis of the likelihood of appeal and case reversal in the three courts. At a minimum, your report should include the following:

1. The probability of cases being appealed and reversed in the three different courts.
2. The probability of a case being appealed for each judge.
3. The probability of a case being reversed for each judge.
4. The probability of reversal given an appeal for each judge.
5. Rank the judges within each court. State the criteria you used and provide a rationale for your choice.

CHAPTER 5

Discrete Probability Distributions

CONTENTS

CITIBANK*
LONG ISLAND CITY, NEW YORK

Citibank, the retail banking division of Citigroup, offers a wide range of financial services including checking and saving accounts, loans and mortgages, insurance, and investment services. It delivers these services through a unique system referred to as Citibanking.

Citibank was one of the first banks in the United States to introduce automatic teller machines (ATMs). Citibank's ATMs, located in Citicard Banking Centers (CBCs), let customers do all of their banking in one place with the touch of a finger, 24 hours a day, 7 days a week. More than 150 different banking functions—from deposits to managing investments—can be performed with ease. Citibank customers use ATMs for 80% of their transactions.

Each Citibank CBC operates as a waiting line system with randomly arriving customers seeking service at one of the ATMs. If all ATMs are busy, the arriving customers wait in line. Periodic CBC capacity studies are used to analyze customer waiting times and to determine whether additional ATMs are needed.

Data collected by Citibank showed that the random customer arrivals followed a probability distribution known as the Poisson distribution. Using the Poisson distribution, Citibank can compute probabilities for the number of customers arriving at a CBC during any time period and make decisions concerning the number of ATMs needed. For example, let x = the number of customers arriving during a one-minute period. Assuming that

Each Citicard Banking Center operates as a waiting line system with randomly arriving customers seeking service at an ATM. © Jeff Greenberg/Alamy Limited.

a particular CBC has a mean arrival rate of two customers per minute, the following table shows the probabilities for the number of customers arriving during a one-minute period.

x	Probability
0	.1353
1	.2707
2	.2707
3	.1804
4	.0902
5 or more	.0527

Discrete probability distributions, such as the one used by Citibank, are the topic of this chapter. In addition to the Poisson distribution, you will learn about the binomial and hypergeometric distributions and how they can be used to provide helpful probability information.

*The authors are indebted to Ms. Stacey Karter, Citibank, for providing this Statistics in Practice.

In this chapter we extend the study of probability by introducing the concepts of random variables and probability distributions. Random variables and probability distributions are models for populations of data. The focus of this chapter is on probability distributions for discrete data, that is, discrete probability distributions.

We will introduce two types of discrete probability distributions. The first type is a table with one column for the values of the random variable and a second column for the associated probabilities. We will see that the rules for assigning probabilities to experimental outcomes introduced in Chapter 4 are used to assign probabilities for such a distribution. The second type of discrete probability distribution uses a special mathematical function to compute the probabilities for each value of the random variable. We present three probability distributions of this type that are widely used in practice: the binomial, Poisson, and hypergeometric distributions.

 ## 5.1 Random Variables

In Chapter 4 we defined the concept of an experiment and its associated experimental outcomes. A random variable provides a means for describing experimental outcomes using numerical values. Random variables must assume numerical values.

RANDOM VARIABLE

Random variables must assume numerical values.

A **random variable** is a numerical description of the outcome of an experiment.

In effect, a random variable associates a numerical value with each possible experimental outcome. The particular numerical value of the random variable depends on the outcome of the experiment. A random variable can be classified as being either *discrete* or *continuous* depending on the numerical values it assumes.

Discrete Random Variables

A random variable that may assume either a finite number of values or an infinite sequence of values such as $0, 1, 2, \ldots$ is referred to as a **discrete random variable**. For example, consider the experiment of an accountant taking the certified public accountant (CPA) examination. The examination has four parts. We can define a random variable as $x =$ the number of parts of the CPA examination passed. It is a discrete random variable because it may assume the finite number of values 0, 1, 2, 3, or 4.

As another example of a discrete random variable, consider the experiment of cars arriving at a tollbooth. The random variable of interest is $x =$ the number of cars arriving during a one-day period. The possible values for x come from the sequence of integers 0, 1, 2, and so on. Hence, x is a discrete random variable assuming one of the values in this infinite sequence.

Although the outcomes of many experiments can naturally be described by numerical values, others cannot. For example, a survey question might ask an individual to recall the message in a recent television commercial. This experiment would have two possible outcomes: The individual cannot recall the message and the individual can recall the message. We can still describe these experimental outcomes numerically by defining the discrete random variable x as follows: let $x = 0$ if the individual cannot recall the message and $x = 1$ if the individual can recall the message. The numerical values for this random variable are arbitrary (we could use 5 and 10), but they are acceptable in terms of the definition of a random variable—namely, x is a random variable because it provides a numerical description of the outcome of the experiment.

Table 5.1 provides some additional examples of discrete random variables. Note that in each example the discrete random variable assumes a finite number of values or an infinite sequence of values such as $0, 1, 2, \ldots$. These types of discrete random variables are discussed in detail in this chapter.

Continuous Random Variables

A random variable that may assume any numerical value in an interval or collection of intervals is called a **continuous random variable**. Experimental outcomes based on

TABLE 5.1   EXAMPLES OF DISCRETE RANDOM VARIABLES

Experiment	Random Variable (x)	Possible Values for the Random Variable
Contact five customers	Number of customers who place an order	0, 1, 2, 3, 4, 5
Inspect a shipment of 50 radios	Number of defective radios	0, 1, 2, . . . , 49, 50
Operate a restaurant for one day	Number of customers	0, 1, 2, 3, . . .
Sell an automobile	Gender of the customer	0 if male; 1 if female

© Cengage Learning

measurement scales such as time, weight, distance, and temperature can be described by continuous random variables. For example, consider an experiment of monitoring incoming telephone calls to the claims office of a major insurance company. Suppose the random variable of interest is x = the time between consecutive incoming calls in minutes. This random variable may assume any value in the interval $x \geq 0$. Actually, an infinite number of values are possible for x, including values such as 1.26 minutes, 2.751 minutes, 4.3333 minutes, and so on. As another example, consider a 90-mile section of interstate highway I-75 north of Atlanta, Georgia. For an emergency ambulance service located in Atlanta, we might define the random variable as x = number of miles to the location of the next traffic accident along this section of I-75. In this case, x would be a continuous random variable assuming any value in the interval $0 \leq x \leq 90$. Additional examples of continuous random variables are listed in Table 5.2. Note that each example describes a random variable that may assume any value in an interval of values. Continuous random variables and their probability distributions will be the topic of Chapter 6.

TABLE 5.2   EXAMPLES OF CONTINUOUS RANDOM VARIABLES

Experiment	Random Variable (x)	Possible Values for the Random Variable
Operate a bank	Time between customer arrivals in minutes	$x \geq 0$
Fill a soft drink can (max = 12.1 ounces)	Number of ounces	$0 \leq x \leq 12.1$
Construct a new library	Percentage of project complete after six months	$0 \leq x \leq 100$
Test a new chemical process	Temperature when the desired reaction takes place (min 150° F; max 212° F)	$150 \leq x \leq 212$

© Cengage Learning

NOTE AND COMMENT

One way to determine whether a random variable is discrete or continuous is to think of the values of the random variable as points on a line segment. Choose two points representing values of the random variable. If the entire line segment between the two points also represents possible values for the random variable, then the random variable is continuous.

Exercises

Methods

1. Consider the experiment of tossing a coin twice.
   a. List the experimental outcomes.
   b. Define a random variable that represents the number of heads occurring on the two tosses.
   c. Show what value the random variable would assume for each of the experimental outcomes.
   d. Is this random variable discrete or continuous?

2. Consider the experiment of a worker assembling a product.
   a. Define a random variable that represents the time in minutes required to assemble the product.
   b. What values may the random variable assume?
   c. Is the random variable discrete or continuous?

Applications

3. Three students scheduled interviews for summer employment at the Brookwood Institute. In each case the interview results in either an offer for a position or no offer. Experimental outcomes are defined in terms of the results of the three interviews.
   a. List the experimental outcomes.
   b. Define a random variable that represents the number of offers made. Is the random variable continuous?
   c. Show the value of the random variable for each of the experimental outcomes.

4. In January the U.S. unemployment rate dropped to 8.3% (U.S. Department of Labor website, February 10, 2012). The Census Bureau includes nine states in the Northeast region. Assume that the random variable of interest is the number of Northeastern states with an unemployment rate in January that was less than 8.3%. What values may this random variable assume?

5. To perform a certain type of blood analysis, lab technicians must perform two procedures. The first procedure requires either one or two separate steps, and the second procedure requires either one, two, or three steps.
   a. List the experimental outcomes associated with performing the blood analysis.
   b. If the random variable of interest is the total number of steps required to do the complete analysis (both procedures), show what value the random variable will assume for each of the experimental outcomes.

6. Listed is a series of experiments and associated random variables. In each case, identify the values that the random variable can assume and state whether the random variable is discrete or continuous.

Experiment	Random Variable (x)
a. Take a 20-question examination	Number of questions answered correctly
b. Observe cars arriving at a tollbooth for 1 hour	Number of cars arriving at tollbooth
c. Audit 50 tax returns	Number of returns containing errors
d. Observe an employee's work	Number of nonproductive hours in an eight-hour workday
e. Weigh a shipment of goods	Number of pounds

5.2 Developing Discrete Probability Distributions

The **probability distribution** for a random variable describes how probabilities are distributed over the values of the random variable. For a discrete random variable x, a **probability function**, denoted by $f(x)$, provides the probability for each value of the random variable. As such, you might suppose that the classical, subjective, and relative frequency methods of assigning probabilities introduced in Chapter 4 would be useful in developing discrete probability distributions. They are and in this section we show how. Application of this methodology leads to what we call tabular discrete probability distributions, that is, probability distributions that are presented in a table.

The classical method of assigning probabilities to values of a random variable is applicable when the experimental outcomes generate values of the random variable that are equally likely. For instance, consider the experiment of rolling a die and observing the number on the upward face. It must be one of the numbers 1, 2, 3, 4, 5, or 6 and each of these outcomes is equally likely. Thus, if we let x = number obtained on one roll of a die and $f(x)$ = the probability of x, the probability distribution of x is given in Table 5.3.

The subjective method of assigning probabilities can also lead to a table of values of the random variable together with the associated probabilities. With the subjective method the individual developing the probability distribution uses their best judgment to assign each probability. So, unlike probability distributions developed using the classical method, different people can be expected to obtain different probability distributions.

The relative frequency method of assigning probabilities to values of a random variable is applicable when reasonably large amounts of data are available. We then treat the data as if they were the population and use the relative frequency method to assign probabilities to the experimental outcomes. The use of the relative frequency method to develop discrete probability distributions leads to what is called an **empirical discrete distribution**. With the large amounts of data available today (e.g., scanner data, credit card data), this type of probability distribution is becoming more widely used in practice. Let us illustrate by considering the sale of automobiles at a dealership.

We will use the relative frequency method to develop a probability distribution for the number of cars sold per day at DiCarlo Motors in Saratoga, New York. Over the past 300 days, DiCarlo has experienced 54 days with no automobiles sold, 117 days with 1 automobile sold, 72 days with 2 automobiles sold, 42 days with 3 automobiles sold, 12 days with 4 automobiles sold, and 3 days with 5 automobiles sold. Suppose we consider the experiment of observing a day of operations at DiCarlo Motors and define the random variable of interest as x = the number of automobiles sold during a day. Using the relative frequencies

TABLE 5.3   PROBABILITY DISTRIBUTION FOR NUMBER OBTAINED ON ONE ROLL OF A DIE

Number Obtained x	Probability of x $f(x)$
1	1/6
2	1/6
3	1/6
4	1/6
5	1/6
6	1/6

TABLE 5.4 PROBABILITY DISTRIBUTION FOR THE NUMBER OF AUTOMOBILES SOLD DURING A DAY AT DICARLO MOTORS

x	$f(x)$
0	.18
1	.39
2	.24
3	.14
4	.04
5	.01
Total	1.00

© Cengage Learning

to assign probabilities to the values of the random variable x, we can develop the probability distribution for x.

In probability function notation, $f(0)$ provides the probability of 0 automobiles sold, $f(1)$ provides the probability of 1 automobile sold, and so on. Because historical data show 54 of 300 days with 0 automobiles sold, we assign the relative frequency $54/300 = .18$ to $f(0)$, indicating that the probability of 0 automobiles being sold during a day is .18. Similarly, because 117 of 300 days had 1 automobile sold, we assign the relative frequency $117/300 = .39$ to $f(1)$, indicating that the probability of exactly 1 automobile being sold during a day is .39. Continuing in this way for the other values of the random variable, we compute the values for $f(2), f(3), f(4),$ and $f(5)$ as shown in Table 5.4.

A primary advantage of defining a random variable and its probability distribution is that once the probability distribution is known, it is relatively easy to determine the probability of a variety of events that may be of interest to a decision maker. For example, using the probability distribution for DiCarlo Motors as shown in Table 5.4, we see that the most probable number of automobiles sold during a day is 1 with a probability of $f(1) = .39$. In addition, there is an $f(3) + f(4) + f(5) = .14 + .04 + .01 = .19$ probability of selling 3 or more automobiles during a day. These probabilities, plus others the decision maker may ask about, provide information that can help the decision maker understand the process of selling automobiles at DiCarlo Motors.

In the development of a probability function for any discrete random variable, the following two conditions must be satisfied.

These conditions are the analogs to the two basic requirements for assigning probabilities to experimental outcomes presented in Chapter 4.

REQUIRED CONDITIONS FOR A DISCRETE PROBABILITY FUNCTION

$$f(x) \geq 0 \tag{5.1}$$
$$\Sigma f(x) = 1 \tag{5.2}$$

Table 5.4 shows that the probabilities for the random variable x satisfy equation (5.1); $f(x)$ is greater than or equal to 0 for all values of x. In addition, because the probabilities sum to 1, equation (5.2) is satisfied. Thus, the DiCarlo Motors probability function is a valid discrete probability function.

We can also show the DiCarlo Motors probability distribution graphically. In Figure 5.1 the values of the random variable x for DiCarlo Motors are shown on the horizontal axis and the probability associated with these values is shown on the vertical axis.

FIGURE 5.1   GRAPHICAL REPRESENTATION OF THE PROBABILITY DISTRIBUTION
FOR THE NUMBER OF AUTOMOBILES SOLD DURING A DAY AT
DICARLO MOTORS

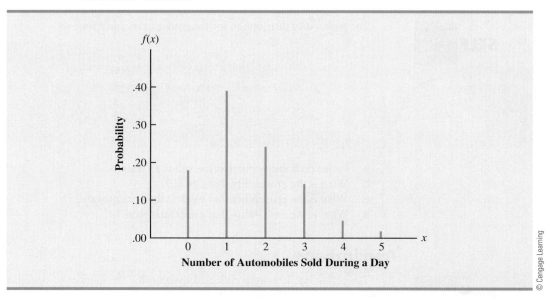

In addition to the probability distributions shown in tables, a formula that gives the
probability function, $f(x)$, for every value of x is often used to describe probability distributions. The simplest example of a discrete probability distribution given by a formula
is the **discrete uniform probability distribution**. Its probability function is defined by
equation (5.3).

DISCRETE UNIFORM PROBABILITY FUNCTION

$$f(x) = 1/n \qquad\qquad\qquad \textbf{(5.3)}$$

where

n = the number of values the random variable may assume

For example, consider again the experiment of rolling a die. We define the random
variable x to be the number of dots on the upward face. For this experiment, $n = 6$ values
are possible for the random variable; $x = 1, 2, 3, 4, 5, 6$. We showed earlier how the
probability distribution for this experiment can be expressed as a table. Since the probabilities are equally likely, the discrete uniform probability function can also be used. The
probability function for this discrete uniform random variable is

$$f(x) = 1/6 \qquad x = 1, 2, 3, 4, 5, 6$$

Several widely used discrete probability distributions are specified by formulas. Three
important cases are the binomial, Poisson, and hypergeometric distributions; these distributions are discussed later in the chapter.

Exercises

Methods

7. The probability distribution for the random variable x follows.

x	$f(x)$
20	.20
25	.15
30	.25
35	.40

    a. Is this probability distribution valid? Explain.
    b. What is the probability that $x = 30$?
    c. What is the probability that x is less than or equal to 25?
    d. What is the probability that x is greater than 30?

Applications

8. The following data were collected by counting the number of operating rooms in use at Tampa General Hospital over a 20-day period: On three of the days only one operating room was used, on five of the days two were used, on eight of the days three were used, and on four days all four of the hospital's operating rooms were used.
    a. Use the relative frequency approach to construct an empirical discrete probability distribution for the number of operating rooms in use on any given day.
    b. Draw a graph of the probability distribution.
    c. Show that your probability distribution satisfies the required conditions for a valid discrete probability distribution.

9. For unemployed persons in the United States, the average number of months of unemployment at the end of December 2009 was approximately seven months (Bureau of Labor Statistics, January 2010). Suppose the following data are for a particular region in upstate New York. The values in the first column show the number of months unemployed and the values in the second column show the corresponding number of unemployed persons.

Months Unemployed	Number Unemployed
1	1029
2	1686
3	2269
4	2675
5	3487
6	4652
7	4145
8	3587
9	2325
10	1120

    Let x be a random variable indicating the number of months a person is unemployed.
    a. Use the data to develop an empirical discrete probability distribution for x.
    b. Show that your probability distribution satisfies the conditions for a valid discrete probability distribution.

c.   What is the probability that a person is unemployed for two months or less? Unemployed for more than two months?

d.   What is the probability that a person is unemployed for more than six months?

10.   The percent frequency distributions of job satisfaction scores for a sample of information systems (IS) senior executives and middle managers are as follows. The scores range from a low of 1 (very dissatisfied) to a high of 5 (very satisfied).

Job Satisfaction Score	IS Senior Executives (%)	IS Middle Managers (%)
1	5	4
2	9	10
3	3	12
4	42	46
5	41	28

a.   Develop a probability distribution for the job satisfaction score of a senior executive.

b.   Develop a probability distribution for the job satisfaction score of a middle manager.

c.   What is the probability a senior executive will report a job satisfaction score of 4 or 5?

d.   What is the probability a middle manager is very satisfied?

e.   Compare the overall job satisfaction of senior executives and middle managers.

11.   A technician services mailing machines at companies in the Phoenix area. Depending on the type of malfunction, the service call can take 1, 2, 3, or 4 hours. The different types of malfunctions occur at about the same frequency.

a.   Develop a probability distribution for the duration of a service call.

b.   Draw a graph of the probability distribution.

c.   Show that your probability distribution satisfies the conditions required for a discrete probability function.

d.   What is the probability a service call will take three hours?

e.   A service call has just come in, but the type of malfunction is unknown. It is 3:00 P.M. and service technicians usually get off at 5:00 P.M. What is the probability the service technician will have to work overtime to fix the machine today?

12.   Time Warner Cable provides television and Internet service to over 15 million people (Time Warner Cable website, October 24, 2012). Suppose that the management of Time Warner Cable subjectively assesses a probability distribution for the number of new subscribers next year in the state of New York as follows.

x	$f(x)$
100,000	.10
200,000	.20
300,000	.25
400,000	.30
500,000	.10
600,000	.05

a.   Is this probability distribution valid? Explain.

b.   What is the probability Time Warner will obtain more than 400,000 new subscribers?

c.   What is the probability Time Warner will obtain fewer than 200,000 new subscribers?

13.   A psychologist determined that the number of sessions required to obtain the trust of a new patient is either 1, 2, or 3. Let x be a random variable indicating the number of

sessions required to gain the patient's trust. The following probability function has been proposed.

$$f(x) = \frac{x}{6} \qquad \text{for } x = 1, 2, \text{ or } 3$$

a. Is this probability function valid? Explain.
b. What is the probability that it takes exactly 2 sessions to gain the patient's trust?
c. What is the probability that it takes at least 2 sessions to gain the patient's trust?

14. The following table is a partial probability distribution for the MRA Company's projected profits (x = profit in \$1000s) for the first year of operation (the negative value denotes a loss).

x	$f(x)$
-100	.10
0	.20
50	.30
100	.25
150	.10
200	

a. What is the proper value for $f(200)$? What is your interpretation of this value?
b. What is the probability that MRA will be profitable?
c. What is the probability that MRA will make at least \$100,000?

5.3   Expected Value and Variance

Expected Value

The **expected value**, or mean, of a random variable is a measure of the central location for the random variable. The formula for the expected value of a discrete random variable x follows.

The expected value is a weighted average of the values of the random variable where the weights are the probabilities.

EXPECTED VALUE OF A DISCRETE RANDOM VARIABLE

$$E(x) = \mu = \Sigma x f(x) \tag{5.4}$$

Both the notations $E(x)$ and μ are used to denote the expected value of a random variable.

Equation (5.4) shows that to compute the expected value of a discrete random variable, we must multiply each value of the random variable by the corresponding probability $f(x)$ and then add the resulting products. Using the DiCarlo Motors automobile sales example from Section 5.2, we show the calculation of the expected value for the number of automobiles sold during a day in Table 5.5. The sum of the entries in the $xf(x)$ column shows that the expected value is 1.50 automobiles per day. We therefore know that although sales of 0, 1, 2, 3, 4, or 5 automobiles are possible on any one day, over time DiCarlo can anticipate selling an average of 1.50 automobiles per day. Assuming 30 days of operation during a month, we can use the expected value of 1.50 to forecast average monthly sales of $30(1.50) = 45$ automobiles.

The expected value does not have to be a value the random variable can assume.

Variance

The expected value provides a measure of central tendency for a random variable, but we often also want a measure of variability, or dispersion. Just as we used the variance in Chapter 3 to summarize the variability in data, we now use **variance** to summarize the variability in the values of a random variable. The formula for the variance of a discrete random variable follows.

TABLE 5.5   CALCULATION OF THE EXPECTED VALUE FOR THE NUMBER
OF AUTOMOBILES SOLD DURING A DAY AT DICARLO MOTORS

x	$f(x)$	$xf(x)$
0	.18	0(.18) = .00
1	.39	1(.39) = .39
2	.24	2(.24) = .48
3	.14	3(.14) = .42
4	.04	4(.04) = .16
5	.01	5(.01) = .05
		1.50

$$E(x) = \mu = \Sigma xf(x)$$

The variance is a weighted average of the squared deviations of a random variable from its mean. The weights are the probabilities.

VARIANCE OF A DISCRETE RANDOM VARIABLE

$$Var(x) = \sigma^2 = \Sigma(x - \mu)^2 f(x) \tag{5.5}$$

As equation (5.5) shows, an essential part of the variance formula is the deviation, $x - \mu$, which measures how far a particular value of the random variable is from the expected value, or mean, μ. In computing the variance of a random variable, the deviations are squared and then weighted by the corresponding value of the probability function. The sum of these weighted squared deviations for all values of the random variable is referred to as the *variance*. The notations $Var(x)$ and σ^2 are both used to denote the variance of a random variable.

The calculation of the variance for the probability distribution of the number of automobiles sold during a day at DiCarlo Motors is summarized in Table 5.6. We see that the variance is 1.25. The **standard deviation**, σ, is defined as the positive square root of the variance. Thus, the standard deviation for the number of automobiles sold during a day is

$$\sigma = \sqrt{1.25} = 1.118$$

The standard deviation is measured in the same units as the random variable ($\sigma = 1.118$ automobiles) and therefore is often preferred in describing the variability of a random variable. The variance σ^2 is measured in squared units and is thus more difficult to interpret.

TABLE 5.6   CALCULATION OF THE VARIANCE FOR THE NUMBER OF AUTOMOBILES
SOLD DURING A DAY AT DICARLO MOTORS

x	$x - \mu$	$(x - \mu)^2$	$f(x)$	$(x - \mu)^2 f(x)$
0	0 − 1.50 = −1.50	2.25	.18	2.25(.18) = .4050
1	1 − 1.50 = −.50	.25	.39	.25(.39) = .0975
2	2 − 1.50 = .50	.25	.24	.25(.24) = .0600
3	3 − 1.50 = 1.50	2.25	.14	2.25(.14) = .3150
4	4 − 1.50 = 2.50	6.25	.04	6.25(.04) = .2500
5	5 − 1.50 = 3.50	12.25	.01	12.25(.01) = .1225
				1.2500

$$\sigma^2 = \Sigma(x - \mu)^2 f(x)$$

Exercises

Methods

15.   The following table provides a probability distribution for the random variable x.

x	$f(x)$
3	.25
6	.50
9	.25

     a.   Compute $E(x)$, the expected value of x.
     b.   Compute σ^2, the variance of x.
     c.   Compute σ, the standard deviation of x.

16.   The following table provides a probability distribution for the random variable y.

y	$f(y)$
2	.20
4	.30
7	.40
8	.10

     a.   Compute $E(y)$.
     b.   Compute $Var(y)$ and σ.

Applications

17.   The number of students taking the SAT has risen to an all-time high of more than 1.5 million (College Board, August 26, 2008). Students are allowed to repeat the test in hopes of improving the score that is sent to college and university admission offices. The number of times the SAT was taken and the number of students are as follows.

Number of Times	Number of Students
1	721,769
2	601,325
3	166,736
4	22,299
5	6730

     a.   Let x be a random variable indicating the number of times a student takes the SAT. Show the probability distribution for this random variable.
     b.   What is the probability that a student takes the SAT more than one time?
     c.   What is the probability that a student takes the SAT three or more times?
     d.   What is the expected value of the number of times the SAT is taken? What is your interpretation of the expected value?
     e.   What is the variance and standard deviation for the number of times the SAT is taken?

18.   The American Housing Survey reported the following data on the number of times that owner-occupied and renter-occupied units had a water supply stoppage lasting 6 or more hours in the past 3 months (U.S. Census Bureau website, October 2012).

	Number of Units (1000s)	
Number of Times	Owner-Occupied	Renter-Occupied
0	439	394
1	1100	760
2	249	221
3	98	92
4 times or more	120	111

a. Define a random variable x = number of times that owner-occupied units had a water supply stoppage lasting 6 or more hours in the past 3 months and develop a probability distribution for the random variable. (Let $x = 4$ represent 4 or more times.)
b. Compute the expected value and variance for x.
c. Define a random variable y = number of times that renter-occupied units had a water supply stoppage lasting 6 or more hours in the past 3 months and develop a probability distribution for the random variable. (Let $y = 4$ represent 4 or more times.)
d. Compute the expected value and variance for y.
e. What observations can you make from a comparison of the number of water supply stoppages reported by owner-occupied units versus renter-occupied units?

19. West Virginia has one of the highest divorce rates in the nation with an annual rate of approximately 5 divorces per 1000 people (Centers for Disease Control and Prevention website, January 12, 2012). The Marital Counseling Center, Inc. (MCC) thinks that the high divorce rate in the state may require them to hire additional staff. Working with a consultant, the management of MCC has developed the following probability distribution for x = the number of new clients for marriage counseling for the next year.

x	$f(x)$
10	.05
20	.10
30	.10
40	.20
50	.35
60	.20

a. Is this probability distribution valid? Explain.
b. What is the probability MCC will obtain more than 30 new clients?
c. What is the probability MCC will obtain fewer than 20 new clients?
d. Compute the expected value and variance of x.

20. The probability distribution for damage claims paid by the Newton Automobile Insurance Company on collision insurance follows.

Payment ($)	Probability
0	.85
500	.04
1000	.04
3000	.03
5000	.02
8000	.01
10000	.01

a. Use the expected collision payment to determine the collision insurance premium that would enable the company to break even.

b. The insurance company charges an annual rate of $520 for the collision coverage. What is the expected value of the collision policy for a policyholder? (*Hint:* It is the expected payments from the company minus the cost of coverage.) Why does the policyholder purchase a collision policy with this expected value?

21. The following probability distributions of job satisfaction scores for a sample of information systems (IS) senior executives and middle managers range from a low of 1 (very dissatisfied) to a high of 5 (very satisfied).

Job Satisfaction Score	Probability IS Senior Executives	IS Middle Managers
1	.05	.04
2	.09	.10
3	.03	.12
4	.42	.46
5	.41	.28

a. What is the expected value of the job satisfaction score for senior executives?
b. What is the expected value of the job satisfaction score for middle managers?
c. Compute the variance of job satisfaction scores for executives and middle managers.
d. Compute the standard deviation of job satisfaction scores for both probability distributions.
e. Compare the overall job satisfaction of senior executives and middle managers.

22. The demand for a product of Carolina Industries varies greatly from month to month. The probability distribution in the following table, based on the past two years of data, shows the company's monthly demand.

Unit Demand	Probability
300	.20
400	.30
500	.35
600	.15

a. If the company bases monthly orders on the expected value of the monthly demand, what should Carolina's monthly order quantity be for this product?
b. Assume that each unit demanded generates $70 in revenue and that each unit ordered costs $50. How much will the company gain or lose in a month if it places an order based on your answer to part (a) and the actual demand for the item is 300 units?

23. In Gallup's Annual Consumption Habits Poll, telephone interviews were conducted for a random sample of 1014 adults aged 18 and over. One of the questions was, "How many cups of coffee, if any, do you drink on an average day?" The following table shows the results obtained (Gallup website, August 6, 2012).

Number of Cups per Day	Number of Responses
0	365
1	264
2	193
3	91
4 or more	101

Define a random variable x = number of cups of coffee consumed on an average day. Let $x = 4$ represent four or more cups.

a. Develop a probability distribution for x.
b. Compute the expected value of x.
c. Compute the variance of x.
d. Suppose we are only interested in adults who drink at least one cup of coffee on an average day. For this group, let y = the number of cups of coffee consumed on an average day. Compute the expected value of y and compare it to the expected value of x.

24. The J. R. Ryland Computer Company is considering a plant expansion to enable the company to begin production of a new computer product. The company's president must determine whether to make the expansion a medium- or large-scale project. Demand for the new product is uncertain, which for planning purposes may be low demand, medium demand, or high demand. The probability estimates for demand are .20, .50, and .30, respectively. Letting x and y indicate the annual profit in thousands of dollars, the firm's planners developed the following profit forecasts for the medium- and large-scale expansion projects.

		Medium-Scale Expansion Profit		Large-Scale Expansion Profit	
		x	$f(x)$	y	$f(y)$
	Low	50	.20	0	.20
Demand	**Medium**	150	.50	100	.50
	High	200	.30	300	.30

a. Compute the expected value for the profit associated with the two expansion alternatives. Which decision is preferred for the objective of maximizing the expected profit?
b. Compute the variance for the profit associated with the two expansion alternatives. Which decision is preferred for the objective of minimizing the risk or uncertainty?

5.4 Binomial Probability Distribution

The binomial probability distribution is a discrete probability distribution that has many applications. It is associated with a multiple-step experiment that we call the binomial experiment.

A Binomial Experiment

A **binomial experiment** exhibits the following four properties.

PROPERTIES OF A BINOMIAL EXPERIMENT

1. The experiment consists of a sequence of n identical trials.
2. Two outcomes are possible on each trial. We refer to one outcome as a *success* and the other outcome as a *failure*.
3. The probability of a success, denoted by p, does not change from trial to trial. Consequently, the probability of a failure, denoted by $1 - p$, does not change from trial to trial.
4. The trials are independent.

FIGURE 5.2   ONE POSSIBLE SEQUENCE OF SUCCESSES AND FAILURES FOR AN EIGHT-TRIAL BINOMIAL EXPERIMENT

Property 1:   The experiment consists of $n = 8$ identical trials.

Property 2:   Each trial results in either success (S) or failure (F).

Trials ⟶	1	2	3	4	5	6	7	8
Outcomes ⟶	S	F	F	S	S	F	S	S

© Cengage Learning

Jakob Bernoulli (1654–1705), the first of the Bernoulli family of Swiss mathematicians, published a treatise on probability that contained the theory of permutations and combinations, as well as the binomial theorem.

If properties 2, 3, and 4 are present, we say the trials are generated by a Bernoulli process. If, in addition, property 1 is present, we say we have a binomial experiment. Figure 5.2 depicts one possible sequence of successes and failures for a binomial experiment involving eight trials.

In a binomial experiment, our interest is in the *number of successes occurring in the n trials*. If we let x denote the number of successes occurring in the n trials, we see that x can assume the values of 0, 1, 2, 3, . . . , n. Because the number of values is finite, x is a *discrete* random variable. The probability distribution associated with this random variable is called the **binomial probability distribution**. For example, consider the experiment of tossing a coin five times and on each toss observing whether the coin lands with a head or a tail on its upward face. Suppose we want to count the number of heads appearing over the five tosses. Does this experiment show the properties of a binomial experiment? What is the random variable of interest? Note that:

1. The experiment consists of five identical trials; each trial involves the tossing of one coin.
2. Two outcomes are possible for each trial: a head or a tail. We can designate head a success and tail a failure.
3. The probability of a head and the probability of a tail are the same for each trial, with $p = .5$ and $1 - p = .5$.
4. The trials or tosses are independent because the outcome on any one trial is not affected by what happens on other trials or tosses.

Thus, the properties of a binomial experiment are satisfied. The random variable of interest is $x = $ the number of heads appearing in the five trials. In this case, x can assume the values of 0, 1, 2, 3, 4, or 5.

As another example, consider an insurance salesperson who visits 10 randomly selected families. The outcome associated with each visit is classified as a success if the family purchases an insurance policy and a failure if the family does not. From past experience, the salesperson knows the probability that a randomly selected family will purchase an insurance policy is .10. Checking the properties of a binomial experiment, we observe that:

1. The experiment consists of 10 identical trials; each trial involves contacting one family.
2. Two outcomes are possible on each trial: the family purchases a policy (success) or the family does not purchase a policy (failure).
3. The probabilities of a purchase and a nonpurchase are assumed to be the same for each sales call, with $p = .10$ and $1 - p = .90$.
4. The trials are independent because the families are randomly selected.

Because the four assumptions are satisfied, this example is a binomial experiment. The random variable of interest is the number of sales obtained in contacting the 10 families. In this case, x can assume the values of 0, 1, 2, 3, 4, 5, 6, 7, 8, 9, and 10.

Property 3 of the binomial experiment is called the *stationarity assumption* and is sometimes confused with property 4, independence of trials. To see how they differ, consider again the case of the salesperson calling on families to sell insurance policies. If, as the day wore on, the salesperson got tired and lost enthusiasm, the probability of success (selling a policy) might drop to .05, for example, by the tenth call. In such a case, property 3 (stationarity) would not be satisfied, and we would not have a binomial experiment. Even if property 4 held—that is, the purchase decisions of each family were made independently—it would not be a binomial experiment if property 3 was not satisfied.

In applications involving binomial experiments, a special mathematical formula, called the *binomial probability function,* can be used to compute the probability of x successes in the n trials. Using probability concepts introduced in Chapter 4, we will show in the context of an illustrative problem how the formula can be developed.

Martin Clothing Store Problem

Let us consider the purchase decisions of the next three customers who enter the Martin Clothing Store. On the basis of past experience, the store manager estimates the probability that any one customer will make a purchase is .30. What is the probability that two of the next three customers will make a purchase?

Using a tree diagram (Figure 5.3), we can see that the experiment of observing the three customers each making a purchase decision has eight possible outcomes. Using S

FIGURE 5.3   TREE DIAGRAM FOR THE MARTIN CLOTHING STORE PROBLEM

First Customer	Second Customer	Third Customer	Experimental Outcome	Value of x
		S	(S, S, S)	3
	S	F	(S, S, F)	2
S	F	S	(S, F, S)	2
		F	(S, F, F)	1
	S	S	(F, S, S)	2
F		F	(F, S, F)	1
	F	S	(F, F, S)	1
		F	(F, F, F)	0

S = Purchase
F = No purchase
x = Number of customers making a purchase

© Cengage Learning

to denote success (a purchase) and F to denote failure (no purchase), we are interested in experimental outcomes involving two successes in the three trials (purchase decisions). Next, let us verify that the experiment involving the sequence of three purchase decisions can be viewed as a binomial experiment. Checking the four requirements for a binomial experiment, we note that:

1. The experiment can be described as a sequence of three identical trials, one trial for each of the three customers who will enter the store.
2. Two outcomes—the customer makes a purchase (success) or the customer does not make a purchase (failure)—are possible for each trial.
3. The probability that the customer will make a purchase (.30) or will not make a purchase (.70) is assumed to be the same for all customers.
4. The purchase decision of each customer is independent of the decisions of the other customers.

Hence, the properties of a binomial experiment are present.

The number of experimental outcomes resulting in exactly x successes in n trials can be computed using the following formula.[1]

NUMBER OF EXPERIMENTAL OUTCOMES PROVIDING EXACTLY x SUCCESSES IN n TRIALS

$$\binom{n}{x} = \frac{n!}{x!(n-x)!} \tag{5.6}$$

where

$$n! = n(n-1)(n-2) \cdots (2)(1)$$

and, by definition,

$$0! = 1$$

Now let us return to the Martin Clothing Store experiment involving three customer purchase decisions. Equation (5.6) can be used to determine the number of experimental outcomes involving two purchases; that is, the number of ways of obtaining $x = 2$ successes in the $n = 3$ trials. From equation (5.6) we have

$$\binom{n}{x} = \binom{3}{2} = \frac{3!}{2!(3-2)!} = \frac{(3)(2)(1)}{(2)(1)(1)} = \frac{6}{2} = 3$$

Equation (5.6) shows that three of the experimental outcomes yield two successes. From Figure 5.3 we see these three outcomes are denoted by (S, S, F), (S, F, S), and (F, S, S).

Using equation (5.6) to determine how many experimental outcomes have three successes (purchases) in the three trials, we obtain

$$\binom{n}{x} = \binom{3}{3} = \frac{3!}{3!(3-3)!} = \frac{3!}{3!0!} = \frac{(3)(2)(1)}{3(2)(1)(1)} = \frac{6}{6} = 1$$

---

[1]This formula, introduced in Chapter 4, determines the number of combinations of n objects selected x at a time. For the binomial experiment, this combinatorial formula provides the number of experimental outcomes (sequences of n trials) resulting in x successes.

From Figure 5.3 we see that the one experimental outcome with three successes is identified by (S, S, S).

We know that equation (5.6) can be used to determine the number of experimental outcomes that result in x successes in n trials. If we are to determine the probability of x successes in n trials, however, we must also know the probability associated with each of these experimental outcomes. Because the trials of a binomial experiment are independent, we can simply multiply the probabilities associated with each trial outcome to find the probability of a particular sequence of successes and failures.

The probability of purchases by the first two customers and no purchase by the third customer, denoted (S, S, F), is given by

$$pp(1 - p)$$

With a .30 probability of a purchase on any one trial, the probability of a purchase on the first two trials and no purchase on the third is given by

$$(.30)(.30)(.70) = (.30)^2(.70) = .063$$

Two other experimental outcomes also result in two successes and one failure. The probabilities for all three experimental outcomes involving two successes follow.

Trial Outcomes				Probability of
1st Customer	**2nd Customer**	**3rd Customer**	**Experimental Outcome**	**Experimental Outcome**
Purchase	Purchase	No purchase	(S, S, F)	$pp(1 - p) = p^2(1 - p)$ $= (.30)^2(.70) = .063$
Purchase	No purchase	Purchase	(S, F, S)	$p(1 - p)p = p^2(1 - p)$ $= (.30)^2(.70) = .063$
No purchase	Purchase	Purchase	(F, S, S)	$(1 - p)pp = p^2(1 - p)$ $= (.30)^2(.70) = .063$

Observe that all three experimental outcomes with two successes have exactly the same probability. This observation holds in general. In any binomial experiment, all sequences of trial outcomes yielding x successes in n trials have the *same probability* of occurrence. The probability of each sequence of trials yielding x successes in n trials follows.

$$\text{Probability of a particular sequence of trial outcomes} = p^x(1 - p)^{(n-x)} \qquad (5.7)$$
$$\text{with } x \text{ successes in } n \text{ trials}$$

For the Martin Clothing Store, this formula shows that any experimental outcome with two successes has a probability of $p^2(1 - p)^{(3-2)} = p^2(1 - p)^1 = (.30)^2(.70)^1 = .063$.

Because equation (5.6) shows the number of outcomes in a binomial experiment with x successes and equation (5.7) gives the probability for each sequence involving x successes, we combine equations (5.6) and (5.7) to obtain the following **binomial probability function**.

BINOMIAL PROBABILITY FUNCTION

$$f(x) = \binom{n}{x} p^x (1-p)^{(n-x)} \tag{5.8}$$

where

$$x = \text{the number of successes}$$
$$p = \text{the probability of a success on one trial}$$
$$n = \text{the number of trials}$$
$$f(x) = \text{the probability of } x \text{ successes in } n \text{ trials}$$
$$\binom{n}{x} = \frac{n!}{x!(n-x)!}$$

For the binomial probability distribution, x is a discrete random variable with the probability function $f(x)$ applicable for values of $x = 0, 1, 2, \ldots, n$.

In the Martin Clothing Store example, let us use equation (5.8) to compute the probability that no customer makes a purchase, exactly one customer makes a purchase, exactly two customers make a purchase, and all three customers make a purchase. The calculations are summarized in Table 5.7, which gives the probability distribution of the number of customers making a purchase. Figure 5.4 is a graph of this probability distribution.

The binomial probability function can be applied to *any* binomial experiment. If we are satisfied that a situation demonstrates the properties of a binomial experiment and if we know the values of n and p, we can use equation (5.8) to compute the probability of x successes in the n trials.

If we consider variations of the Martin experiment, such as 10 customers rather than three entering the store, the binomial probability function given by equation (5.8) is still applicable. Suppose we have a binomial experiment with $n = 10$, $x = 4$, and $p = .30$. The probability of making exactly four sales to 10 customers entering the store is

$$f(4) = \frac{10!}{4!6!}(.30)^4(.70)^6 = .2001$$

TABLE 5.7   PROBABILITY DISTRIBUTION FOR THE NUMBER OF CUSTOMERS MAKING A PURCHASE

x	$f(x)$
0	$\frac{3!}{0!3!}(.30)^0(.70)^3 = .343$
1	$\frac{3!}{1!2!}(.30)^1(.70)^2 = .441$
2	$\frac{3!}{2!1!}(.30)^2(.70)^1 = .189$
3	$\frac{3!}{3!0!}(.30)^3(.70)^0 = \frac{.027}{1.000}$

FIGURE 5.4 GRAPHICAL REPRESENTATION OF THE PROBABILITY DISTRIBUTION FOR THE NUMBER OF CUSTOMERS MAKING A PURCHASE

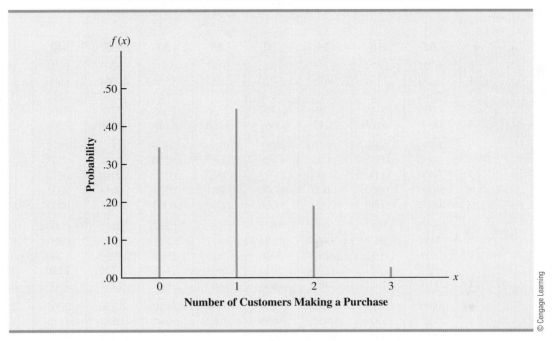

Using Tables of Binomial Probabilities

Tables have been developed that give the probability of x successes in n trials for a binomial experiment. The tables are generally easy to use and quicker than equation (5.8). Table 5 of Appendix B provides such a table of binomial probabilities. A portion of this table appears in Table 5.8. To use this table, we must specify the values of n, p, and x for the binomial experiment of interest. In the example at the top of Table 5.8, we see that the probability of $x = 3$ successes in a binomial experiment with $n = 10$ and $p = .40$ is .2150. You can use equation (5.8) to verify that you would obtain the same answer if you used the binomial probability function directly.

Now let us use Table 5.8 to verify the probability of 4 successes in 10 trials for the Martin Clothing Store problem. Note that the value of $f(4) = .2001$ can be read directly from the table of binomial probabilities, with $n = 10$, $x = 4$, and $p = .30$.

Even though the tables of binomial probabilities are relatively easy to use, it is impossible to have tables that show all possible values of n and p that might be encountered in a binomial experiment. However, with today's calculators, using equation (5.8) to calculate the desired probability is not difficult, especially if the number of trials is not large. In the exercises, you should practice using equation (5.8) to compute the binomial probabilities unless the problem specifically requests that you use the binomial probability table.

Statistical software packages such as Minitab and spreadsheet packages such as Excel also provide a capability for computing binomial probabilities. Consider the Martin Clothing Store example with $n = 10$ and $p = .30$. Figure 5.5 shows the binomial probabilities generated by Minitab for all possible values of x. Note that these values are the same as those found in the $p = .30$ column of Table 5.8. Appendix 5.1 gives the step-by-step procedure for using Minitab to generate the output in Figure 5.5. Appendix 5.2 describes how Excel can be used to compute binomial probabilities.

TABLE 5.8   SELECTED VALUES FROM THE BINOMIAL PROBABILITY TABLE
EXAMPLE: $n = 10, x = 3, p = .40; f(3) = .2150$

n	x	.05	.10	.15	.20	p .25	.30	.35	.40	.45	.50
9	0	.6302	.3874	.2316	.1342	.0751	.0404	.0207	.0101	.0046	.0020
	1	.2985	.3874	.3679	.3020	.2253	.1556	.1004	.0605	.0339	.0176
	2	.0629	.1722	.2597	.3020	.3003	.2668	.2162	.1612	.1110	.0703
	3	.0077	.0446	.1069	.1762	.2336	.2668	.2716	.2508	.2119	.1641
	4	.0006	.0074	.0283	.0661	.1168	.1715	.2194	.2508	.2600	.2461
	5	.0000	.0008	.0050	.0165	.0389	.0735	.1181	.1672	.2128	.2461
	6	.0000	.0001	.0006	.0028	.0087	.0210	.0424	.0743	.1160	.1641
	7	.0000	.0000	.0000	.0003	.0012	.0039	.0098	.0212	.0407	.0703
	8	.0000	.0000	.0000	.0000	.0001	.0004	.0013	.0035	.0083	.0176
	9	.0000	.0000	.0000	.0000	.0000	.0000	.0001	.0003	.0008	.0020
10	0	.5987	.3487	.1969	.1074	.0563	.0282	.0135	.0060	.0025	.0010
	1	.3151	.3874	.3474	.2684	.1877	.1211	.0725	.0403	.0207	.0098
	2	.0746	.1937	.2759	.3020	.2816	.2335	.1757	.1209	.0763	.0439
	3	.0105	.0574	.1298	.2013	.2503	.2668	.2522	**.2150**	.1665	.1172
	4	.0010	.0112	.0401	.0881	.1460	.2001	.2377	.2508	.2384	.2051
	5	.0001	.0015	.0085	.0264	.0584	.1029	.1536	.2007	.2340	.2461
	6	.0000	.0001	.0012	.0055	.0162	.0368	.0689	.1115	.1596	.2051
	7	.0000	.0000	.0001	.0008	.0031	.0090	.0212	.0425	.0746	.1172
	8	.0000	.0000	.0000	.0001	.0004	.0014	.0043	.0106	.0229	.0439
	9	.0000	.0000	.0000	.0000	.0000	.0001	.0005	.0016	.0042	.0098
	10	.0000	.0000	.0000	.0000	.0000	.0000	.0000	.0001	.0003	.0010

© Cengage Learning

Expected Value and Variance for the Binomial Distribution

In Section 5.3 we provided formulas for computing the expected value and variance of a discrete random variable. In the special case where the random variable has a binomial distribution with a known number of trials n and a known probability of success

FIGURE 5.5   MINITAB OUTPUT SHOWING BINOMIAL PROBABILITIES FOR THE MARTIN CLOTHING STORE PROBLEM

x	P(X = x)
0	0.0282
1	0.1211
2	0.2335
3	0.2668
4	0.2001
5	0.1029
6	0.0368
7	0.0090
8	0.0014
9	0.0001
10	0.0000

© Cengage Learning

p, the general formulas for the expected value and variance can be simplified. The results follow.

EXPECTED VALUE AND VARIANCE FOR THE BINOMIAL DISTRIBUTION

$$E(x) = \mu = np \qquad\qquad (5.9)$$
$$Var(x) = \sigma^2 = np(1 - p) \qquad\qquad (5.10)$$

For the Martin Clothing Store problem with three customers, we can use equation (5.9) to compute the expected number of customers who will make a purchase.

$$E(x) = np = 3(.30) = .9$$

Suppose that for the next month the Martin Clothing Store forecasts 1000 customers will enter the store. What is the expected number of customers who will make a purchase? The answer is $\mu = np = (1000)(.3) = 300$. Thus, to increase the expected number of purchases, Martin's must induce more customers to enter the store and/or somehow increase the probability that any individual customer will make a purchase after entering.

For the Martin Clothing Store problem with three customers, we see that the variance and standard deviation for the number of customers who will make a purchase are

$$\sigma^2 = np(1 - p) = 3(.3)(.7) = .63$$
$$\sigma = \sqrt{.63} = .79$$

For the next 1000 customers entering the store, the variance and standard deviation for the number of customers who will make a purchase are

$$\sigma^2 = np(1 - p) = 1000(.3)(.7) = 210$$
$$\sigma = \sqrt{210} = 14.49$$

NOTES AND COMMENTS

1. The binomial table in Appendix B shows values of p up to and including $p = .95$. Some sources of the binomial table only show values of p up to and including $p = .50$. It would appear that such a table cannot be used when the probability of success exceeds $p = .50$. However, the table can be used by noting that the probability of $n - x$ failures is also the probability of x successes. Thus, when the probability of success is greater than $p = .50$, we can compute the probability of $n - x$ failures instead. The probability of failure, $1 - p$, will be less than .50 when $p > .50$.

2. Some sources present the binomial table in a cumulative form. In using such a table, one must subtract entries in the table to find the probability of exactly x success in n trials. For example, $f(2) = P(x \le 2) - P(x \le 1)$. The binomial table we provide in Appendix B provides $f(2)$ directly. To compute cumulative probabilities using the binomial table in Appendix B, sum the entries in the table. For example, to determine the cumulative probability $P(x \le 2)$, compute the sum $f(0) + f(1) + f(2)$.

Exercises

Methods

25. Consider a binomial experiment with two trials and $p = .4$.
     a.   Draw a tree diagram for this experiment (see Figure 5.3).
     b.   Compute the probability of one success, $f(1)$.
     c.   Compute $f(0)$.
     d.   Compute $f(2)$.
     e.   Compute the probability of at least one success.
     f.   Compute the expected value, variance, and standard deviation.

26. Consider a binomial experiment with $n = 10$ and $p = .10$.
     a.   Compute $f(0)$.
     b.   Compute $f(2)$.
     c.   Compute $P(x \leq 2)$.
     d.   Compute $P(x \geq 1)$.
     e.   Compute $E(x)$.
     f.   Compute $Var(x)$ and σ.

27. Consider a binomial experiment with $n = 20$ and $p = .70$.
     a.   Compute $f(12)$.
     b.   Compute $f(16)$.
     c.   Compute $P(x \geq 16)$.
     d.   Compute $P(x \leq 15)$.
     e.   Compute $E(x)$.
     f.   Compute $Var(x)$ and σ.

Applications

28. For its "Music 360" survey, Nielsen Co. asked teenagers and adults how each group has listened to music in the past 12 months. Nearly two-thirds of U.S. teenagers under the age of 18 say they use Google Inc.'s video-sharing site to listen to music and 35% of the teenagers said they use Pandora Media Inc.'s custom online radio service (*The Wall Street Journal*, August 14, 2012). Suppose 10 teenagers are selected randomly to be interviewed about how they listen to music.
     a.   Is randomly selecting 10 teenagers and asking whether or not they use Pandora Media Inc.'s online service a binomial experiment?
     b.   What is the probability that none of the 10 teenagers use Pandora Media Inc.'s online radio service?
     c.   What is the probability that 4 of the 10 teenagers use Pandora Media Inc.'s online radio service?
     d.   What is the probability that at least 2 of the 10 teenagers use Pandora Media Inc.'s online radio service?

29. The Center for Medicare and Medical Services reported that there were 295,000 appeals for hospitalization and other Part A Medicare service. For this group, 40% of first-round appeals were successful (*The Wall Street Journal*, October 22, 2012). Suppose 10 first-round appeals have just been received by a Medicare appeal office.
     a.   Compute the probability that none of the appeals will be successful.
     b.   Compute the probability that exactly one of the appeals will be successful.
     c.   What is the probability that at least two of the appeals will be successful?
     d.   What is the probability that more than half of the appeals will be successful?

30. When a new machine is functioning properly, only 3% of the items produced are defective. Assume that we will randomly select two parts produced on the machine and that we are interested in the number of defective parts found.
     a.   Describe the conditions under which this situation would be a binomial experiment.
     b.   Draw a tree diagram similar to Figure 5.3 showing this problem as a two-trial experiment.

c. How many experimental outcomes result in exactly one defect being found?

d. Compute the probabilities associated with finding no defects, exactly one defect, and two defects.

31. A Randstad/Harris interactive survey reported that 25% of employees said their company is loyal to them (*USA Today,* November 11, 2009). Suppose 10 employees are selected randomly and will be interviewed about company loyalty.

a. Is the selection of 10 employees a binomial experiment? Explain.

b. What is the probability that none of the 10 employees will say their company is loyal to them?

c. What is the probability that 4 of the 10 employees will say their company is loyal to them?

d. What is the probability that at least 2 of the 10 employees will say their company is loyal to them?

32. Military radar and missile detection systems are designed to warn a country of an enemy attack. A reliability question is whether a detection system will be able to identify an attack and issue a warning. Assume that a particular detection system has a .90 probability of detecting a missile attack. Use the binomial probability distribution to answer the following questions.

a. What is the probability that a single detection system will detect an attack?

b. If two detection systems are installed in the same area and operate independently, what is the probability that at least one of the systems will detect the attack?

c. If three systems are installed, what is the probability that at least one of the systems will detect the attack?

d. Would you recommend that multiple detection systems be used? Explain.

33. Twelve of the top 20 finishers in the 2009 PGA Championship at Hazeltine National Golf Club in Chaska, Minnesota, used a Titleist brand golf ball (GolfBallTest website, November 12, 2009). Suppose these results are representative of the probability that a randomly selected PGA Tour player uses a Titleist brand golf ball. For a sample of 15 PGA Tour players, make the following calculations.

a. Compute the probability that exactly 10 of the 15 PGA Tour players use a Titleist brand golf ball.

b. Compute the probability that more than 10 of the 15 PGA Tour players use a Titleist brand golf ball.

c. For a sample of 15 PGA Tour players, compute the expected number of players who use a Titleist brand golf ball.

d. For a sample of 15 PGA Tour players, compute the variance and standard deviation of the number of players who use a Titleist brand golf ball.

34. A study conducted by the Pew Research Center showed that 75% of 18– to 34-year-olds living with their parents say they contribute to household expenses (*The Wall Street Journal*, October 22, 2012). Suppose that a random sample of fifteen 18– to 34-year-olds living with their parents is selected and asked if they contribute to household expenses.

a. Is the selection of the fifteen 18– to 34-year-olds living with their parents a binomial experiment? Explain.

b. If the sample shows that none of the fifteen 18– to 34-year-olds living with their parents contribute to household expenses, would you question the results of the Pew Research Study? Explain.

c. What is the probability that at least 10 of the fifteen 18– to 34-year-olds living with their parents contribute to household expenses?

35. A university found that 20% of its students withdraw without completing the introductory statistics course. Assume that 20 students registered for the course.

a. Compute the probability that 2 or fewer will withdraw.

b. Compute the probability that exactly 4 will withdraw.

c. Compute the probability that more than 3 will withdraw.

d. Compute the expected number of withdrawals.

36. A Gallup Poll showed that 30% of Americans are satisfied with the way things are going in the United States (Gallup website, September 12, 2012). Suppose a sample of 20 Americans is selected as part of a study of the state of the nation.
    a. Compute the probability that exactly 4 of the 20 Americans surveyed are satisfied with the way things are going in the United States.
    b. Compute the probability that at least 2 of the Americans surveyed are satisfied with the way things are going in the United States.
    c. For the sample of 20 Americans, compute the expected number of Americans who are satisfied with the way things are going in the United States.
    d. For the sample of 20 Americans, compute the variance and standard deviation of the number of Americans who are satisfied with the way things are going in the United States.

37. Twenty-three percent of automobiles are not covered by insurance (CNN, February 23, 2006). On a particular weekend, 35 automobiles are involved in traffic accidents.
    a. What is the expected number of these automobiles that are not covered by insurance?
    b. What are the variance and standard deviation?

5.5 Poisson Probability Distribution

In this section we consider a discrete random variable that is often useful in estimating the number of occurrences over a specified interval of time or space. For example, the random variable of interest might be the number of arrivals at a car wash in one hour, the number of repairs needed in 10 miles of highway, or the number of leaks in 100 miles of pipeline. If the following two properties are satisfied, the number of occurrences is a random variable described by the **Poisson probability distribution**.

The Poisson probability distribution is often used to model random arrivals in waiting line situations.

PROPERTIES OF A POISSON EXPERIMENT

1. The probability of an occurrence is the same for any two intervals of equal length.
2. The occurrence or nonoccurrence in any interval is independent of the occurrence or nonoccurrence in any other interval.

The **Poisson probability function** is defined by equation (5.11).

Siméon Poisson taught mathematics at the Ecole Polytechnique in Paris from 1802 to 1808. In 1837, he published a work entitled, "Researches on the Probability of Criminal and Civil Verdicts," which includes a discussion of what later became known as the Poisson distribution.

POISSON PROBABILITY FUNCTION

$$f(x) = \frac{\mu^x e^{-\mu}}{x!} \qquad (5.11)$$

where

$f(x)$ = the probability of x occurrences in an interval

μ = expected value or mean number of occurrences in an interval

e = 2.71828

For the Poisson probability distribution, x is a discrete random variable indicating the number of occurrences in the interval. Since there is no stated upper limit for the number of occurrences, the probability function $f(x)$ is applicable for values $x = 0, 1, 2, \ldots$ without limit. In practical applications, x will eventually become large enough so that $f(x)$ is approximately zero and the probability of any larger values of x becomes negligible.

An Example Involving Time Intervals

Bell Labs used the Poisson distribution to model the arrival of telephone calls.

Suppose that we are interested in the number of arrivals at the drive-up teller window of a bank during a 15-minute period on weekday mornings. If we can assume that the probability of a car arriving is the same for any two time periods of equal length and that the arrival or nonarrival of a car in any time period is independent of the arrival or nonarrival in any other time period, the Poisson probability function is applicable. Suppose these assumptions are satisfied and an analysis of historical data shows that the average number of cars arriving in a 15-minute period of time is 10; in this case, the following probability function applies.

$$f(x) = \frac{10^x e^{-10}}{x!}$$

The random variable here is x = number of cars arriving in any 15-minute period.

If management wanted to know the probability of exactly five arrivals in 15 minutes, we would set $x = 5$ and thus obtain

$$\text{Probability of exactly}\atop\text{5 arrivals in 15 minutes} = f(5) = \frac{10^5 e^{-10}}{5!} = .0378$$

Although this probability was determined by evaluating the probability function with $\mu = 10$ and $x = 5$, it is often easier to refer to a table for the Poisson distribution. The table provides probabilities for specific values of x and μ. We included such a table as Table 7 of Appendix B. For convenience, we reproduced a portion of this table as Table 5.9. Note that to use the table of Poisson probabilities, we need know only the values of x and μ. From Table 5.9 we see that the probability of five arrivals in a 15-minute period is found by locating the value in the row of the table corresponding to $x = 5$ and the column of the table corresponding to $\mu = 10$. Hence, we obtain $f(5) = .0378$.

A property of the Poisson distribution is that the mean and variance are equal.

In the preceding example, the mean of the Poisson distribution is $\mu = 10$ arrivals per 15-minute period. A property of the Poisson distribution is that the mean of the distribution and the variance of the distribution are *equal*. Thus, the variance for the number of arrivals during 15-minute periods is $\sigma^2 = 10$. The standard deviation is $\sigma = \sqrt{10} = 3.16$.

Our illustration involves a 15-minute period, but other time periods can be used. Suppose we want to compute the probability of one arrival in a 3-minute period. Because 10 is the expected number of arrivals in a 15-minute period, we see that $10/15 = 2/3$ is the expected number of arrivals in a 1-minute period and that $(2/3)(3 \text{ minutes}) = 2$ is the expected number of arrivals in a 3-minute period. Thus, the probability of x arrivals in a 3-minute time period with $\mu = 2$ is given by the following Poisson probability function.

$$f(x) = \frac{2^x e^{-2}}{x!}$$

The probability of one arrival in a 3-minute period is calculated as follows:

$$\text{Probability of exactly}\atop\text{1 arrival in 3 minutes} = f(1) = \frac{2^1 e^{-2}}{1!} = .2707$$

Earlier we computed the probability of five arrivals in a 15-minute period; it was .0378. Note that the probability of one arrival in a 3-minute period (.2707) is not the same. When computing a Poisson probability for a different time interval, we must first convert the mean arrival rate to the time period of interest and then compute the probability.

An Example Involving Length or Distance Intervals

Let us illustrate an application not involving time intervals in which the Poisson distribution is useful. Suppose we are concerned with the occurrence of major defects in a highway one

TABLE 5.9   SELECTED VALUES FROM THE POISSON PROBABILITY TABLES
EXAMPLE: $\mu = 10, x = 5; f(5) = .0378$

x	9.1	9.2	9.3	9.4	9.5	9.6	9.7	9.8	9.9	10
0	.0001	.0001	.0001	.0001	.0001	.0001	.0001	.0001	.0001	.0000
1	.0010	.0009	.0009	.0008	.0007	.0007	.0006	.0005	.0005	.0005
2	.0046	.0043	.0040	.0037	.0034	.0031	.0029	.0027	.0025	.0023
3	.0140	.0131	.0123	.0115	.0107	.0100	.0093	.0087	.0081	.0076
4	.0319	.0302	.0285	.0269	.0254	.0240	.0226	.0213	.0201	.0189
5	.0581	.0555	.0530	.0506	.0483	.0460	.0439	.0418	.0398	**.0378**
6	.0881	.0851	.0822	.0793	.0764	.0736	.0709	.0682	.0656	.0631
7	.1145	.1118	.1091	.1064	.1037	.1010	.0982	.0955	.0928	.0901
8	.1302	.1286	.1269	.1251	.1232	.1212	.1191	.1170	.1148	.1126
9	.1317	.1315	.1311	.1306	.1300	.1293	.1284	.1274	.1263	.1251
10	.1198	.1210	.1219	.1228	.1235	.1241	.1245	.1249	.1250	.1251
11	.0991	.1012	.1031	.1049	.1067	.1083	.1098	.1112	.1125	.1137
12	.0752	.0776	.0799	.0822	.0844	.0866	.0888	.0908	.0928	.0948
13	.0526	.0549	.0572	.0594	.0617	.0640	.0662	.0685	.0707	.0729
14	.0342	.0361	.0380	.0399	.0419	.0439	.0459	.0479	.0500	.0521
15	.0208	.0221	.0235	.0250	.0265	.0281	.0297	.0313	.0330	.0347
16	.0118	.0127	.0137	.0147	.0157	.0168	.0180	.0192	.0204	.0217
17	.0063	.0069	.0075	.0081	.0088	.0095	.0103	.0111	.0119	.0128
18	.0032	.0035	.0039	.0042	.0046	.0051	.0055	.0060	.0065	.0071
19	.0015	.0017	.0019	.0021	.0023	.0026	.0028	.0031	.0034	.0037
20	.0007	.0008	.0009	.0010	.0011	.0012	.0014	.0015	.0017	.0019
21	.0003	.0003	.0004	.0004	.0005	.0006	.0006	.0007	.0008	.0009
22	.0001	.0001	.0002	.0002	.0002	.0002	.0003	.0003	.0004	.0004
23	.0000	.0001	.0001	.0001	.0001	.0001	.0001	.0001	.0002	.0002
24	.0000	.0000	.0000	.0000	.0000	.0000	.0000	.0001	.0001	.0001

month after resurfacing. We will assume that the probability of a defect is the same for any two highway intervals of equal length and that the occurrence or nonoccurrence of a defect in any one interval is independent of the occurrence or nonoccurrence of a defect in any other interval. Hence, the Poisson distribution can be applied.

Suppose we learn that major defects one month after resurfacing occur at the average rate of two per mile. Let us find the probability of no major defects in a particular three-mile section of the highway. Because we are interested in an interval with a length of three miles, $\mu = (2 \text{ defects/mile})(3 \text{ miles}) = 6$ represents the expected number of major defects over the three-mile section of highway. Using equation (5.11), the probability of no major defects is $f(0) = 6^0 e^{-6}/0! = .0025$. Thus, it is unlikely that no major defects will occur in the three-mile section. In fact, this example indicates a $1 - .0025 = .9975$ probability of at least one major defect in the three-mile highway section.

Exercises

Methods

38. Consider a Poisson distribution with $\mu = 3$.
    a. Write the appropriate Poisson probability function.
    b. Compute $f(2)$.

c.   Compute $f(1)$.
d.   Compute $P(x \geq 2)$.

39.   Consider a Poisson distribution with a mean of two occurrences per time period.
   a.   Write the appropriate Poisson probability function.
   b.   What is the expected number of occurrences in three time periods?
   c.   Write the appropriate Poisson probability function to determine the probability of x occurrences in three time periods.
   d.   Compute the probability of two occurrences in one time period.
   e.   Compute the probability of six occurrences in three time periods.
   f.   Compute the probability of five occurrences in two time periods.

Applications

40.   Phone calls arrive at the rate of 48 per hour at the reservation desk for Regional Airways.
   a.   Compute the probability of receiving three calls in a 5-minute interval of time.
   b.   Compute the probability of receiving exactly 10 calls in 15 minutes.
   c.   Suppose no calls are currently on hold. If the agent takes 5 minutes to complete the current call, how many callers do you expect to be waiting by that time? What is the probability that none will be waiting?
   d.   If no calls are currently being processed, what is the probability that the agent can take 3 minutes for personal time without being interrupted by a call?

41.   During the period of time that a local university takes phone-in registrations, calls come in at the rate of one every two minutes.
   a.   What is the expected number of calls in one hour?
   b.   What is the probability of three calls in five minutes?
   c.   What is the probability of no calls in a five-minute period?

42.   In 2011, New York City had a total of 11,232 motor vehicle accidents that occurred on Monday through Friday between the hours of 3 P.M. and 6 P.M. (New York State Department of Motor Vehicles website, October 24, 2012). This corresponds to mean of 14.4 accidents per hour.
   a.   Compute the probability of no accidents in a 15-minute period.
   b.   Compute the probability of at least one accident in a 15-minute period.
   c.   Compute the probability of four or more accidents in a 15-minute period.

43.   Airline passengers arrive randomly and independently at the passenger-screening facility at a major international airport. The mean arrival rate is 10 passengers per minute.
   a.   Compute the probability of no arrivals in a one-minute period.
   b.   Compute the probability that three or fewer passengers arrive in a one-minute period.
   c.   Compute the probability of no arrivals in a 15-second period.
   d.   Compute the probability of at least one arrival in a 15-second period.

44.   According to the National Oceanic and Atmospheric Administration (NOAA), the state of Colorado averages 18 tornadoes every June (NOAA website, November 8, 2012). *Note*: There are 30 days in June.
   a.   Compute the mean number of tornadoes per day.
   b.   Compute the probability of no tornadoes during a day.
   c.   Compute the probability of exactly one tornado during a day.
   d.   Compute the probability of more than one tornado during a day.

45.   The National Safety Council (NSC) estimates that off-the-job accidents cost U.S. businesses almost $200 billion annually in lost productivity (National Safety Council, March 2006). Based on NSC estimates, companies with 50 employees are expected to average three employee off-the-job accidents per year. Answer the following questions for companies with 50 employees.
   a.   What is the probability of no off-the-job accidents during a one-year period?
   b.   What is the probability of at least two off-the-job accidents during a one-year period?

c.   What is the expected number of off-the-job accidents during six months?
d.   What is the probability of no off-the-job accidents during the next six months?

 5.6 # Hypergeometric Probability Distribution

The **hypergeometric probability distribution** is closely related to the binomial distribution. The two probability distributions differ in two key ways. With the hypergeometric distribution, the trials are not independent; and the probability of success changes from trial to trial.

In the usual notation for the hypergeometric distribution, r denotes the number of elements in the population of size N labeled success, and $N - r$ denotes the number of elements in the population labeled failure. The **hypergeometric probability function** is used to compute the probability that in a random selection of n elements, selected without replacement, we obtain x elements labeled success and $n - x$ elements labeled failure. For this outcome to occur, we must obtain x successes from the r successes in the population and $n - x$ failures from the $N - r$ failures. The following hypergeometric probability function provides $f(x)$, the probability of obtaining x successes in n trials.

HYPERGEOMETRIC PROBABILITY FUNCTION

$$f(x) = \frac{\dbinom{r}{x}\dbinom{N - r}{n - x}}{\dbinom{N}{n}} \qquad (5.12)$$

where

$$x = \text{the number of successes}$$
$$n = \text{the number of trials}$$
$$f(x) = \text{the probability of } x \text{ successes in } n \text{ trials}$$
$$N = \text{the number of elements in the population}$$
$$r = \text{the number of elements in the population labeled success}$$

Note that $\dbinom{N}{n}$ represents the number of ways n elements can be selected from a population of size N; $\dbinom{r}{x}$ represents the number of ways that x successes can be selected from a total of r successes in the population; and $\dbinom{N - r}{n - x}$ represents the number of ways that $n - x$ failures can be selected from a total of $N - r$ failures in the population.

For the hypergeometric probability distribution, x is a discrete random variable and the probability function $f(x)$ given by equation (5.12) is usually applicable for values of $x = 0, 1, 2, \ldots, n$. However, only values of x where the number of observed successes is *less than or equal* to the number of successes in the population ($x \leq r$) and where the number of observed failures is *less than or equal to* the number of failures in the population ($n - x \leq N - r$) are valid. If these two conditions do not hold for one or more values of x, the corresponding $f(x) = 0$ indicating that the probability of this value of x is zero.

To illustrate the computations involved in using equation (5.12), let us consider the following quality control application. Electric fuses produced by Ontario Electric are packaged in boxes of 12 units each. Suppose an inspector randomly selects 3 of the 12 fuses in a box for testing. If the box contains exactly 5 defective fuses, what is the probability that the inspector will find exactly 1 of the 3 fuses defective? In this application, $n = 3$ and $N = 12$. With $r = 5$ defective fuses in the box the probability of finding $x = 1$ defective fuse is

$$f(1) = \frac{\binom{5}{1}\binom{7}{2}}{\binom{12}{3}} = \frac{\left(\frac{5!}{1!4!}\right)\left(\frac{7!}{2!5!}\right)}{\left(\frac{12!}{3!9!}\right)} = \frac{(5)(21)}{220} = .4773$$

Now suppose that we wanted to know the probability of finding *at least* 1 defective fuse. The easiest way to answer this question is to first compute the probability that the inspector does not find any defective fuses. The probability of $x = 0$ is

$$f(0) = \frac{\binom{5}{0}\binom{7}{3}}{\binom{12}{3}} = \frac{\left(\frac{5!}{0!5!}\right)\left(\frac{7!}{3!4!}\right)}{\left(\frac{12!}{3!9!}\right)} = \frac{(1)(35)}{220} = .1591$$

With a probability of zero defective fuses $f(0) = .1591$, we conclude that the probability of finding at least 1 defective fuse must be $1 - .1591 = .8409$. Thus, there is a reasonably high probability that the inspector will find at least 1 defective fuse.

The mean and variance of a hypergeometric distribution are as follows.

$$E(x) = \mu = n\left(\frac{r}{N}\right) \tag{5.13}$$

$$Var(x) = \sigma^2 = n\left(\frac{r}{N}\right)\left(1 - \frac{r}{N}\right)\left(\frac{N-n}{N-1}\right) \tag{5.14}$$

In the preceding example $n = 3$, $r = 5$, and $N = 12$. Thus, the mean and variance for the number of defective fuses are

$$\mu = n\left(\frac{r}{N}\right) = 3\left(\frac{5}{12}\right) = 1.25$$

$$\sigma^2 = n\left(\frac{r}{N}\right)\left(1 - \frac{r}{N}\right)\left(\frac{N-n}{N-1}\right) = 3\left(\frac{5}{12}\right)\left(1 - \frac{5}{12}\right)\left(\frac{12-3}{12-1}\right) = .60$$

The standard deviation is $\sigma = \sqrt{.60} = .77$.

NOTE AND COMMENT

Consider a hypergeometric distribution with n trials. Let $p = (r/N)$ denote the probability of a success on the first trial. If the population size is large, the term $(N - n)/(N - 1)$ in equation (5.14) approaches 1. As a result, the expected value and variance can be written $E(x) = np$ and $Var(x) = np(1 - p)$. Note that these expressions are the same as the expressions used to compute the expected value and variance of a binomial distribution, as in equations (5.9) and (5.10). When the population size is large, a hypergeometric distribution can be approximated by a binomial distribution with n trials and a probability of success $p = (r/N)$.

Exercises

Methods

46. Suppose $N = 10$ and $r = 3$. Compute the hypergeometric probabilities for the following values of n and x.
   a. $n = 4, x = 1$.
   b. $n = 2, x = 2$.
   c. $n = 2, x = 0$.
   d. $n = 4, x = 2$.
   e. $n = 4, x = 4$.

47. Suppose $N = 15$ and $r = 4$. What is the probability of $x = 3$ for $n = 10$?

Applications

48. A survey showed that a majority of Americans plan on doing their holiday shopping online because they don't want to spend money on gas driving from store to store (SOASTA website, October 24, 2012). Suppose we have a group of 10 shoppers; 7 prefer to do their holiday shopping online and 3 prefer to do their holiday shopping in stores. A random sample of 3 of these 10 shoppers is selected for a more in-depth study of how the economy has impacted their shopping behavior.
   a.   What is the probability that exactly 2 prefer shopping online?
   b.   What is the probability that the majority (either 2 or 3) prefer shopping online?

49. Blackjack, or twenty-one as it is frequently called, is a popular gambling game played in Las Vegas casinos. A player is dealt two cards. Face cards (jacks, queens, and kings) and tens have a point value of 10. Aces have a point value of 1 or 11. A 52-card deck contains 16 cards with a point value of 10 (jacks, queens, kings, and tens) and four aces.
   a.   What is the probability that both cards dealt are aces or 10-point cards?
   b.   What is the probability that both of the cards are aces?
   c.   What is the probability that both of the cards have a point value of 10?
   d.   A blackjack is a 10-point card and an ace for a value of 21. Use your answers to parts (a), (b), and (c) to determine the probability that a player is dealt blackjack. (*Hint:* Part (d) is not a hypergeometric problem. Develop your own logical relationship as to how the hypergeometric probabilities from parts (a), (b), and (c) can be combined to answer this question.)

50. Axline Computers manufactures personal computers at two plants, one in Texas and the other in Hawaii. The Texas plant has 40 employees; the Hawaii plant has 20. A random sample of 10 employees is to be asked to fill out a benefits questionnaire.
   a.   What is the probability that none of the employees in the sample work at the plant in Hawaii?
   b.   What is the probability that 1 of the employees in the sample works at the plant in Hawaii?
   c.   What is the probability that 2 or more of the employees in the sample work at the plant in Hawaii?
   d.   What is the probability that 9 of the employees in the sample work at the plant in Texas?

51. The Zagat Restaurant Survey provides food, decor, and service ratings for some of the top restaurants across the United States. For 15 restaurants located in Boston, the average price of a dinner, including one drink and tip, was $48.60. You are leaving on a business trip to Boston and will eat dinner at three of these restaurants. Your company will reimburse you for a maximum of $50 per dinner. Business associates familiar with these restaurants have told you that the meal cost at one-third of these restaurants will exceed $50. Suppose that you randomly select three of these restaurants for dinner.
   a.   What is the probability that none of the meals will exceed the cost covered by your company?

b. What is the probability that one of the meals will exceed the cost covered by your company?
c. What is the probability that two of the meals will exceed the cost covered by your company?
d. What is the probability that all three of the meals will exceed the cost covered by your company?

52. The Troubled Asset Relief Program (TARP), passed by the U.S. Congress in October 2008, provided $700 billion in assistance for the struggling U.S. economy. Over $200 billion was given to troubled financial institutions with the hope that there would be an increase in lending to help jump-start the economy. But three months later, a Federal Reserve survey found that two-thirds of the banks that had received TARP funds had tightened terms for business loans (*The Wall Street Journal,* February 3, 2009). Of the 10 banks that were the biggest recipients of TARP funds, only 3 had actually increased lending during this period.

Increased Lending	Decreased Lending
BB&T	Bank of America
Sun Trust Banks	Capital One
U.S. Bancorp	Citigroup
	Fifth Third Bancorp
	J.P. Morgan Chase
	Regions Financial
	Wells Fargo

For the purposes of this exercise, assume that you will randomly select 3 of these 10 banks for a study that will continue to monitor bank lending practices. Let x be a random variable indicating the number of banks in the study that had increased lending.

a. What is $f(0)$? What is your interpretation of this value?
b. What is $f(3)$? What is your interpretation of this value?
c. Compute $f(1)$ and $f(2)$. Show the probability distribution for the number of banks in the study that had increased lending. What value of x has the highest probability?
d. What is the probability that the study will have at least one bank that had increased lending?
e. Compute the expected value, variance, and standard deviation for the random variable.

Summary

A random variable provides a numerical description of the outcome of an experiment. The probability distribution for a random variable describes how the probabilities are distributed over the values the random variable can assume. For any discrete random variable x, the probability distribution is defined by a probability function, denoted by $f(x)$, which provides the probability associated with each value of the random variable.

We introduced two types of discrete probability distributions. One type involved providing a list of the values of the random variable and the associated probabilities in a table. We showed how the relative frequency method of assigning probabilities could be used to develop empirical discrete probability distributions of this type.

The second type of discrete probability distribution we discussed involved the use of a mathematical function to provide the probabilities for the random variable. The binomial, Poisson, and hypergeometric distributions discussed were all of this type. The binomial distribution can be used to determine the probability of x successes in n trials whenever the experiment has the following properties:

1. The experiment consists of a sequence of n identical trials.
2. Two outcomes are possible on each trial, one called success and the other failure.
3. The probability of a success p does not change from trial to trial. Consequently, the probability of failure, $1 - p$, does not change from trial to trial.
4. The trials are independent.

When the four properties hold, the binomial probability function can be used to determine the probability of obtaining x successes in n trials. Formulas were also presented for the mean and variance of the binomial distribution.

The Poisson distribution is used when it is desirable to determine the probability of obtaining x occurrences over an interval of time or space. The following assumptions are necessary for the Poisson distribution to be applicable.

1. The probability of an occurrence of the event is the same for any two intervals of equal length.
2. The occurrence or nonoccurrence of the event in any interval is independent of the occurrence or nonoccurrence of the event in any other interval.

A third discrete probability distribution, the hypergeometric, was introduced in Section 5.6. Like the binomial, it is used to compute the probability of x successes in n trials. But, in contrast to the binomial, the probability of success changes from trial to trial.

Glossary

Random variable A numerical description of the outcome of an experiment.
Discrete random variable A random variable that may assume either a finite number of values or an infinite sequence of values.
Continuous random variable A random variable that may assume any numerical value in an interval or collection of intervals.
Probability distribution A description of how the probabilities are distributed over the values of the random variable.
Probability function A function, denoted by $f(x)$, that provides the probability that x assumes a particular value for a discrete random variable.
Empirical discrete distribution A discrete probability distribution for which the relative frequency method is used to assign the probabilities.
Discrete uniform probability distribution A probability distribution for which each possible value of the random variable has the same probability.
Expected value A measure of the central location of a random variable.
Variance A measure of the variability, or dispersion, of a random variable.
Standard deviation The positive square root of the variance.
Binomial experiment An experiment having the four properties stated at the beginning of Section 5.4.
Binomial probability distribution A probability distribution showing the probability of x successes in n trials of a binomial experiment.
Binomial probability function The function used to compute binomial probabilities.
Poisson probability distribution A probability distribution showing the probability of x occurrences of an event over a specified interval of time or space.
Poisson probability function The function used to compute Poisson probabilities.
Hypergeometric probability distribution A probability distribution showing the probability of x successes in n trials from a population with r successes and $N - r$ failures.
Hypergeometric probability function The function used to compute hypergeometric probabilities.

Key Formulas

Discrete Uniform Probability Function

$$f(x) = 1/n \qquad (5.3)$$

Expected Value of a Discrete Random Variable

$$E(x) = \mu = \sum x f(x) \qquad (5.4)$$

Variance of a Discrete Random Variable

$$Var(x) = \sigma^2 = \sum (x - \mu)^2 f(x) \qquad (5.5)$$

Number of Experimental Outcomes Providing Exactly x Successes in n Trials

$$\binom{n}{x} = \frac{n!}{x!(n - x)!} \qquad (5.6)$$

Binomial Probability Function

$$f(x) = \binom{n}{x} p^x (1 - p)^{(n - x)} \qquad (5.8)$$

Expected Value for the Binomial Distribution

$$E(x) = \mu = np \qquad (5.9)$$

Variance for the Binomial Distribution

$$Var(x) = \sigma^2 = np(1 - p) \qquad (5.10)$$

Poisson Probability Function

$$f(x) = \frac{\mu^x e^{-\mu}}{x!} \qquad (5.11)$$

Hypergeometric Probability Function

$$f(x) = \frac{\binom{r}{x}\binom{N - r}{n - x}}{\binom{N}{n}} \qquad (5.12)$$

Expected Value for the Hypergeometric Distribution

$$E(x) = \mu = n\left(\frac{r}{N}\right) \qquad (5.13)$$

Variance for the Hypergeometric Distribution

$$Var(x) = \sigma^2 = n\left(\frac{r}{N}\right)\left(1 - \frac{r}{N}\right)\left(\frac{N - n}{N - 1}\right) \qquad (5.14)$$

Supplementary Exercises

53. The United States Coast Guard (USCG) provides a wide variety of information on boating accidents including the wind condition at the time of the accident. The following table shows the results obtained for 4401 accidents (USCG website, November 8, 2012).

Wind Condition	Percentage of Accidents
None	9.6
Light	57.0
Moderate	23.8
Strong	7.7
Storm	1.9

Let x be a random variable reflecting the known wind condition at the time of each accident. Set $x = 0$ for none, $x = 1$ for light, $x = 2$ for moderate, $x = 3$ for strong, and $x = 4$ for storm.

a. Develop a probability distribution for x.
b. Compute the expected value of x.
c. Compute the variance and standard deviation for x.
d. Comment on what your results imply about the wind conditions during boating accidents.

54. The Car Repair Ratings website provides consumer reviews and ratings for garages in the United States and Canada. The time customers wait for service to be completed is one of the categories rated. The following table provides a summary of the wait-time ratings (1 = Slow/Delays; 10 = Quick/On Time) for 40 randomly selected garages located in the province of Ontario, Canada (Car Repair Ratings website, November 14, 2012).

Wait-Time Rating	Number of Garages
1	6
2	2
3	3
4	2
5	5
6	2
7	4
8	5
9	5
10	6

a. Develop a probability distribution for x = wait-time rating.
b. Any garage that receives a wait-time rating of at least 9 is considered to provide outstanding service. If a consumer randomly selects one of the 40 garages for their next car service, what is the probability the garage selected will provide outstanding wait-time service?
c. What is the expected value and variance for x?
d. Suppose that 7 of the 40 garages reviewed were new car dealerships. Of the 7 new car dealerships, two were rated as providing outstanding wait-time service. Compare the likelihood of a new car dealership achieving an outstanding wait-time service rating as compared to other types of service providers.

55. The budgeting process for a midwestern college resulted in expense forecasts for the coming year (in $ millions) of $9, $10, $11, $12, and $13. Because the actual expenses are unknown, the following respective probabilities are assigned: .3, .2, .25, .05, and .2.
    a. Show the probability distribution for the expense forecast.
    b. What is the expected value of the expense forecast for the coming year?
    c. What is the variance of the expense forecast for the coming year?
    d. If income projections for the year are estimated at $12 million, comment on the financial position of the college.

56. A survey showed that the average commuter spends about 26 minutes on a one-way door-to-door trip from home to work. In addition, 5% of commuters reported a one-way commute of more than one hour (Bureau of Transportation Statistics website, January 12, 2004).
    a. If 20 commuters are surveyed on a particular day, what is the probability that 3 will report a one-way commute of more than one hour?
    b. If 20 commuters are surveyed on a particular day, what is the probability that none will report a one-way commute of more than one hour?
    c. If a company has 2000 employees, what is the expected number of employees who have a one-way commute of more than one hour?
    d. If a company has 2000 employees, what is the variance and standard deviation of the number of employees who have a one-way commute of more than one hour?

57. The following table shows the percentage of individuals in each age group who use an online tax program to prepare their federal income tax return (CompleteTax website, November 9, 2012).

Age	Online Tax Program (%)
18–34	16
35–44	12
45–54	10
55–64	8
65+	2

Suppose a follow-up study consisting of personal interviews is to be conducted to determine the most important factors in selecting a method for filing taxes.
    a. How many 18–34-year-olds must be sampled to find an expected number of at least 25 who use an online tax program to prepare their federal income tax return?
    b. How many 35–44-year-olds must be sampled to find an expected number of at least 25 who use an online tax program to prepare their federal income tax return?
    c. How many 65+-year-olds must be sampled to find an expected number of at least 25 who use an online tax program to prepare their federal income tax return?
    d. If the number of 18–34-year-olds sampled is equal to the value identified in part (a), what is the standard deviation of the percentage who use an online tax program?
    e. If the number of 35–44-year-olds sampled is equal to the value identified in part (b), what is the standard deviation of the percentage who use an online tax program?

58. Many companies use a quality control technique called acceptance sampling to monitor incoming shipments of parts, raw materials, and so on. In the electronics industry, component parts are commonly shipped from suppliers in large lots. Inspection of a sample of n components can be viewed as the n trials of a binomial experiment. The outcome for each component tested (trial) will be that the component is classified as good or defective. Reynolds Electronics accepts a lot from a particular supplier if the defective components in the lot do not exceed 1%. Suppose a random sample of five items from a recent shipment is tested.
    a. Assume that 1% of the shipment is defective. Compute the probability that no items in the sample are defective.

    b.   Assume that 1% of the shipment is defective. Compute the probability that exactly one item in the sample is defective.

    c.   What is the probability of observing one or more defective items in the sample if 1% of the shipment is defective?

    d.   Would you feel comfortable accepting the shipment if one item was found to be defective? Why or why not?

59.   The unemployment rate in the state of Arizona is 4.1% (CNN Money website, May 2, 2007). Assume that 100 employable people in Arizona are selected randomly.

    a.   What is the expected number of people who are unemployed?

    b.   What are the variance and standard deviation of the number of people who are unemployed?

60.   Mahoney Custom Home Builders, Inc., of Canyon Lake, Texas, asked visitors to their website what is most important when choosing a home builder. Possible responses were quality, price, customer referral, years in business, and special features. Results showed that 23.5% of the respondents chose price as the most important factor (Mahoney Custom Homes website, November 13, 2012). Suppose a sample of 200 potential home buyers in the Canyon Lake area was selected.

    a.   How many people would you expect to choose price as the most important factor when choosing a home builder?

    b.   What is the standard deviation of the number of respondents who would choose price as the most important factor in selecting a home builder?

    c.   What is the standard deviation of the number of respondents who do not list price as the most important factor in selecting a home builder?

61.   Cars arrive at a car wash randomly and independently; the probability of an arrival is the same for any two time intervals of equal length. The mean arrival rate is 15 cars per hour. What is the probability that 20 or more cars will arrive during any given hour of operation?

62.   A new automated production process averages 1.5 breakdowns per day. Because of the cost associated with a breakdown, management is concerned about the possibility of having three or more breakdowns during a day. Assume that breakdowns occur randomly, that the probability of a breakdown is the same for any two time intervals of equal length, and that breakdowns in one period are independent of breakdowns in other periods. What is the probability of having three or more breakdowns during a day?

63.   A regional director responsible for business development in the state of Pennsylvania is concerned about the number of small business failures. If the mean number of small business failures per month is 10, what is the probability that exactly 4 small businesses will fail during a given month? Assume that the probability of a failure is the same for any two months and that the occurrence or nonoccurrence of a failure in any month is independent of failures in any other month.

64.   Customer arrivals at a bank are random and independent; the probability of an arrival in any one-minute period is the same as the probability of an arrival in any other one-minute period. Answer the following questions, assuming a mean arrival rate of three customers per minute.

    a.   What is the probability of exactly three arrivals in a one-minute period?

    b.   What is the probability of at least three arrivals in a one-minute period?

65.   A deck of playing cards contains 52 cards, four of which are aces. What is the probability that the deal of a five-card hand provides

    a.   A pair of aces?

    b.   Exactly one ace?

    c.   No aces?

    d.   At least one ace?

66.   *U.S. News & World Report*'s ranking of America's best graduate schools of business showed Harvard University and Stanford University in a tie for first place. In addition, 7 of the top 10 graduate schools of business showed students with an average undergraduate

grade point average (GPA) of 3.50 or higher (*America's Best Graduate Schools, 2009 edition, U.S. News & World Report*). Suppose that we randomly select 2 of the top 10 graduate schools of business.

a. What is the probability that exactly one school has students with an average undergraduate GPA of 3.50 or higher?
b. What is the probability that both schools have students with an average undergraduate GPA of 3.50 or higher?
c. What is the probability that neither school has students with an average undergraduate GPA of 3.50 or higher?

Appendix 5.1   Discrete Probability Distributions with Minitab

Statistical packages such as Minitab offer a relatively easy and efficient procedure for computing binomial probabilities. In this appendix, we show the step-by-step procedure for determining the binomial probabilities for the Martin Clothing Store problem in Section 5.4. Recall that the desired binomial probabilities are based on $n = 10$ and $p = .30$. Before beginning the Minitab routine, the user must enter the desired values of the random variable x into a column of the worksheet. We entered the values 0, 1, 2, . . . , 10 in column 1 (see Figure 5.5) to generate the entire binomial probability distribution. The Minitab steps to obtain the desired binomial probabilities follow.

Step 1. Select the **Calc** menu
Step 2. Choose **Probability Distributions**
Step 3. Choose **Binomial**
Step 4. When the Binomial Distribution dialog box appears:
　　　Select **Probability**
　　　Enter 10 in the **Number of trials** box
　　　Enter .3 in the **Event probability** box
　　　Enter C1 in the **Input column** box
　　　Click **OK**

The Minitab output with the binomial probabilities will appear as shown in Figure 5.5.

Minitab provides Poisson and hypergeometric probabilities in a similar manner. For instance, to compute Poisson probabilities the only differences are in step 3, where the **Poisson** option would be selected, and step 4, where the **Mean** would be entered rather than the number of trials and the probability of success.

Appendix 5.2   Discrete Probability Distributions with Excel

Excel provides functions for computing probabilities for the binomial, Poisson, and hypergeometric distributions introduced in this chapter. The Excel function for computing binomial probabilities is BINOM.DIST. It has four arguments: x (the number of successes), n (the number of trials), p (the probability of success), and cumulative. FALSE is used for the fourth argument (cumulative) if we want the probability of x successes, and TRUE is used for the fourth argument if we want the cumulative probability of x or fewer successes. Here we show how to compute the probabilities of 0 through 10 successes for the Martin Clothing Store problem in Section 5.4 (see Figure 5.5).

As we describe the worksheet development, refer to Figure 5.6; the formula worksheet is set in the background, and the value worksheet appears in the foreground. We entered the number of trials (10) into cell B1, the probability of success into cell B2, and the values for the random variable into cells B5:B15. The following steps will generate the desired probabilities:

FIGURE 5.6   EXCEL WORKSHEET FOR COMPUTING BINOMIAL PROBABILITIES

	A	B	C	D
1	Number of Trials (*n*)	10		
2	Probability of Success (*p*)	0.3		
3				
4		*x*	*f(x)*	
5		0	=BINOM.DIST(B5,$B$1,$B$2,FALSE)	
6		1	=BINOM.DIST(B6,$B$1,$B$2,FALSE)	
7		2	=BINOM.DIST(B7,$B$1,$B$2,FALSE)	
8		3	=BINOM.DIST(B8,$B$1,$B$2,FALSE)	
9		4	=BINOM.DIST(B9,$B$1,$B$2,FALSE)	
10		5	=BINOM.DIST(B10,$B$1,$B$2,FALSE)	
11		6	=BINOM.DIST(B11,$B$1,$B$2,FALSE)	
12		7	=BINOM.DIST(B12,$B$1,$B$2,FALSE)	
13		8	=BINOM.DIST(B13,$B$1,$B$2,FALSE)	
14		9	=BINOM.DIST(B14,$B$1,$B$2,FALSE)	
15		10	=BINOM.DIST(B15,$B$1,$B$2,FALSE)	
16				

	A	B	C	D
1	Number of Trials (*n*)	10		
2	Probability of Success (*p*)	0.3		
3				
4		*x*	*f(x)*	
5		0	0.0282	
6		1	0.1211	
7		2	0.2335	
8		3	0.2668	
9		4	0.2001	
10		5	0.1029	
11		6	0.0368	
12		7	0.0090	
13		8	0.0014	
14		9	0.0001	
15		10	0.0000	
16				

Step 1. Use the BINOM.DIST function to compute the probability of $x = 0$ by entering the following formula into cell C5:

=BINOM.DIST(B5,$B$1,$B$2,FALSE)

Step 2. Copy the formula in cell C5 into cells C6:C15.

The value worksheet in Figure 5.6 shows that the probabilities obtained are the same as in Figure 5.5. Poisson and hypergeometric probabilities can be computed in a similar fashion. The POISSON.DIST and HYPGEOM.DIST functions are used. Excel's Insert Function dialog box can help the user in entering the proper arguments for these functions (see Appendix E).

CHAPTER 6

Continuous Probability Distributions

CONTENTS

STATISTICS IN PRACTICE:
PROCTER & GAMBLE

PROCTER & GAMBLE*
CINCINNATI, OHIO

Procter & Gamble (P&G) produces and markets such products as detergents, disposable diapers, over-the-counter pharmaceuticals, dentifrices, bar soaps, mouthwashes, and paper towels. Worldwide, it has the leading brand in more categories than any other consumer products company. Since its merger with Gillette, P&G also produces and markets razors, blades, and many other personal care products.

As a leader in the application of statistical methods in decision making, P&G employs people with diverse academic backgrounds: engineering, statistics, operations research, and business. The major quantitative technologies for which these people provide support are probabilistic decision and risk analysis, advanced simulation, quality improvement, and quantitative methods (e.g., linear programming, regression analysis, probability analysis).

The Industrial Chemicals Division of P&G is a major supplier of fatty alcohols derived from natural substances such as coconut oil and from petroleum-based derivatives. The division wanted to know the economic risks and opportunities of expanding its fatty-alcohol production facilities, so it called in P&G's experts in probabilistic decision and risk analysis to help. After structuring and modeling the problem, they determined that the key to profitability was the cost difference between the petroleum- and coconut-based raw materials. Future costs were unknown, but the analysts were able to approximate them with the following continuous random variables.

$$x = \text{the coconut oil price per pound of fatty alcohol}$$

and

$$y = \text{the petroleum raw material price per pound of fatty alcohol}$$

Because the key to profitability was the difference between these two random variables, a third random variable, $d = x - y$, was used in the analysis. Experts were interviewed to determine the probability distributions for x and y. In turn, this information was used to develop a probability distribution for the difference in prices d. This continuous probability distribution showed

Procter & Gamble is a leader in the application of statistical methods in decision making. © John Sommers II/Reuters.

a .90 probability that the price difference would be \$.0655 or less and a .50 probability that the price difference would be \$.035 or less. In addition, there was only a .10 probability that the price difference would be \$.0045 or less.[†]

The Industrial Chemicals Division thought that being able to quantify the impact of raw material price differences was key to reaching a consensus. The probabilities obtained were used in a sensitivity analysis of the raw material price difference. The analysis yielded sufficient insight to form the basis for a recommendation to management.

The use of continuous random variables and their probability distributions was helpful to P&G in analyzing the economic risks associated with its fatty-alcohol production. In this chapter, you will gain an understanding of continuous random variables and their probability distributions, including one of the most important probability distributions in statistics, the normal distribution.

---

*The authors are indebted to Joel Kahn of Procter & Gamble for providing this Statistics in Practice.

[†]The price differences stated here have been modified to protect proprietary data.

In the preceding chapter we discussed discrete random variables and their probability distributions. In this chapter we turn to the study of continuous random variables. Specifically, we discuss three continuous probability distributions: the uniform, the normal, and the exponential.

A fundamental difference separates discrete and continuous random variables in terms of how probabilities are computed. For a discrete random variable, the probability function $f(x)$ provides the probability that the random variable assumes a particular value. With continuous random variables, the counterpart of the probability function is the **probability density function**, also denoted by $f(x)$. The difference is that the probability density function does not directly provide probabilities. However, the area under the graph of $f(x)$ corresponding to a given interval does provide the probability that the continuous random variable x assumes a value in that interval. So when we compute probabilities for continuous random variables we are computing the probability that the random variable assumes any value in an interval.

Because the area under the graph of $f(x)$ at any particular point is zero, one of the implications of the definition of probability for continuous random variables is that the probability of any particular value of the random variable is zero. In Section 6.1 we demonstrate these concepts for a continuous random variable that has a uniform distribution.

Much of the chapter is devoted to describing and showing applications of the normal distribution. The normal distribution is of major importance because of its wide applicability and its extensive use in statistical inference. The chapter closes with a discussion of the exponential distribution. The exponential distribution is useful in applications involving such factors as waiting times and service times.

6.1 Uniform Probability Distribution

Consider the random variable x representing the flight time of an airplane traveling from Chicago to New York. Suppose the flight time can be any value in the interval from 120 minutes to 140 minutes. Because the random variable x can assume any value in that interval, x is a continuous rather than a discrete random variable. Let us assume that sufficient actual flight data are available to conclude that the probability of a flight time within any 1-minute interval is the same as the probability of a flight time within any other 1-minute interval contained in the larger interval from 120 to 140 minutes. With every 1-minute interval being equally likely, the random variable x is said to have a **uniform probability distribution**. The probability density function, which defines the uniform distribution for the flight-time random variable, is

Whenever the probability is proportional to the length of the interval, the random variable is uniformly distributed.

$$f(x) = \begin{cases} 1/20 & \text{for } 120 \leq x \leq 140 \\ 0 & \text{elsewhere} \end{cases}$$

Figure 6.1 is a graph of this probability density function. In general, the uniform probability density function for a random variable x is defined by the following formula.

UNIFORM PROBABILITY DENSITY FUNCTION

$$f(x) = \begin{cases} \dfrac{1}{b - a} & \text{for } a \leq x \leq b \\ 0 & \text{elsewhere} \end{cases} \tag{6.1}$$

For the flight-time random variable, $a = 120$ and $b = 140$.

FIGURE 6.1   UNIFORM PROBABILITY DISTRIBUTION FOR FLIGHT TIME

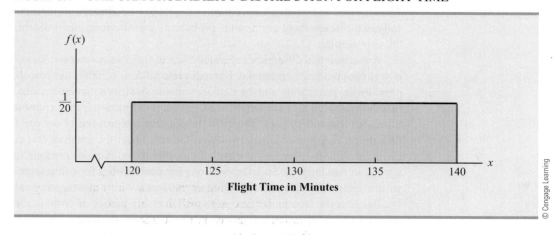

As noted in the introduction, for a continuous random variable, we consider probability only in terms of the likelihood that a random variable assumes a value within a specified interval. In the flight time example, an acceptable probability question is: What is the probability that the flight time is between 120 and 130 minutes? That is, what is $P(120 \leq x \leq 130)$? Because the flight time must be between 120 and 140 minutes and because the probability is described as being uniform over this interval, we feel comfortable saying $P(120 \leq x \leq 130) = .50$. In the following subsection we show that this probability can be computed as the area under the graph of $f(x)$ from 120 to 130 (see Figure 6.2).

Area as a Measure of Probability

Let us make an observation about the graph in Figure 6.2. Consider the area under the graph of $f(x)$ in the interval from 120 to 130. The area is rectangular, and the area of a rectangle is simply the width multiplied by the height. With the width of the interval equal to $130 - 120 = 10$ and the height equal to the value of the probability density function $f(x) = 1/20$, we have area = width × height = $10(1/20) = 10/20 = .50$.

FIGURE 6.2   AREA PROVIDES PROBABILITY OF A FLIGHT TIME BETWEEN 120 AND 130 MINUTES

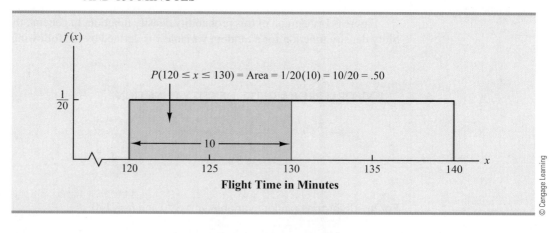

What observation can you make about the area under the graph of $f(x)$ and probability? They are identical! Indeed, this observation is valid for all continuous random variables. Once a probability density function $f(x)$ is identified, the probability that x takes a value between some lower value x_1 and some higher value x_2 can be found by computing the area under the graph of $f(x)$ over the interval from x_1 to x_2.

Given the uniform distribution for flight time and using the interpretation of area as probability, we can answer any number of probability questions about flight times. For example, what is the probability of a flight time between 128 and 136 minutes? The width of the interval is $136 - 128 = 8$. With the uniform height of $f(x) = 1/20$, we see that $P(128 \leq x \leq 136) = 8(1/20) = .40$.

Note that $P(120 \leq x \leq 140) = 20(1/20) = 1$; that is, the total area under the graph of $f(x)$ is equal to 1. This property holds for all continuous probability distributions and is the analog of the condition that the sum of the probabilities must equal 1 for a discrete probability function. For a continuous probability density function, we must also require that $f(x) \geq 0$ for all values of x. This requirement is the analog of the requirement that $f(x) \geq 0$ for discrete probability functions.

Two major differences stand out between the treatment of continuous random variables and the treatment of their discrete counterparts.

1. We no longer talk about the probability of the random variable assuming a particular value. Instead, we talk about the probability of the random variable assuming a value within some given interval.

To see that the probability of any single point is 0, refer to Figure 6.2 and compute the probability of a single point, say, $x = 125$. $P(x = 125) = P(125 \leq x \leq 125) = 0(1/20) = 0$.

2. The probability of a continuous random variable assuming a value within some given interval from x_1 to x_2 is defined to be the area under the graph of the probability density function between x_1 and x_2. Because a single point is an interval of zero width, this implies that the probability of a continuous random variable assuming any particular value exactly is zero. It also means that the probability of a continuous random variable assuming a value in any interval is the same whether or not the endpoints are included.

The calculation of the expected value and variance for a continuous random variable is analogous to that for a discrete random variable. However, because the computational procedure involves integral calculus, we leave the derivation of the appropriate formulas to more advanced texts.

For the uniform continuous probability distribution introduced in this section, the formulas for the expected value and variance are

$$E(x) = \frac{a + b}{2}$$

$$Var(x) = \frac{(b - a)^2}{12}$$

In these formulas, a is the smallest value and b is the largest value that the random variable may assume.

Applying these formulas to the uniform distribution for flight times from Chicago to New York, we obtain

$$E(x) = \frac{(120 + 140)}{2} = 130$$

$$Var(x) = \frac{(140 - 120)^2}{12} = 33.33$$

The standard deviation of flight times can be found by taking the square root of the variance. Thus, $\sigma = 5.77$ minutes.

NOTE AND COMMENT

To see more clearly why the height of a probability density function is not a probability, think about a random variable with the following uniform probability distribution.

$$f(x) = \begin{cases} 2 & \text{for } 0 \le x \le .5 \\ 0 & \text{elsewhere} \end{cases}$$

The height of the probability density function, $f(x)$, is 2 for values of x between 0 and .5. However, we know probabilities can never be greater than 1. Thus, we see that $f(x)$ cannot be interpreted as the probability of x.

Exercises

Methods

1. The random variable x is known to be uniformly distributed between 1.0 and 1.5.
   a. Show the graph of the probability density function.
   b. Compute $P(x = 1.25)$.
   c. Compute $P(1.0 \le x \le 1.25)$.
   d. Compute $P(1.20 < x < 1.5)$.

2. The random variable x is known to be uniformly distributed between 10 and 20.
   a. Show the graph of the probability density function.
   b. Compute $P(x < 15)$.
   c. Compute $P(12 \le x \le 18)$.
   d. Compute $E(x)$.
   e. Compute $Var(x)$.

Applications

3. Delta Airlines quotes a flight time of 2 hours, 5 minutes for its flights from Cincinnati to Tampa. Suppose we believe that actual flight times are uniformly distributed between 2 hours and 2 hours, 20 minutes.
   a. Show the graph of the probability density function for flight time.
   b. What is the probability that the flight will be no more than 5 minutes late?
   c. What is the probability that the flight will be more than 10 minutes late?
   d. What is the expected flight time?

4. Most computer languages include a function that can be used to generate random numbers. In Excel, the RAND function can be used to generate random numbers between 0 and 1. If we let x denote a random number generated using RAND, then x is a continuous random variable with the following probability density function.

$$f(x) = \begin{cases} 1 & \text{for } 0 \le x \le 1 \\ 0 & \text{elsewhere} \end{cases}$$

   a. Graph the probability density function.
   b. What is the probability of generating a random number between .25 and .75?
   c. What is the probability of generating a random number with a value less than or equal to .30?
   d. What is the probability of generating a random number with a value greater than .60?
   e. Generate 50 random numbers by entering =RAND() into 50 cells of an Excel worksheet.
   f. Compute the mean and standard deviation for the random numbers in part (e).

5. In October 2012, Apple introduced a much smaller variant of the Apple iPad, known as the iPad Mini. Weighing less than 11 ounces, it is about 50% lighter than the standard iPad. Battery tests for the iPad Mini showed a mean life of 10.25 hours (*The Wall Street Journal*, October 31, 2012). Assume that battery life of the iPad Mini is uniformly distributed between 8.5 and 12 hours.

    a. Give a mathematical expression for the probability density function of battery life.
    b. What is the probability that the battery life for an iPad Mini will be 10 hours or less?
    c. What is the probability that the battery life for an iPad Mini will be at least 11 hours?
    d. What is the probability that the battery life for an iPad Mini will be between 9.5 and 11.5 hours?
    e. In a shipment of 100 iPad Minis, how many should have a battery life of at least 9 hours?

6. A Gallup Daily Tracking Survey found that the mean daily discretionary spending by Americans earning over $90,000 per year was $136 per day (*USA Today*, July 30, 2012). The discretionary spending excluded home purchases, vehicle purchases, and regular monthly bills. Let $x =$ the discretionary spending per day and assume that a uniform probability density function applies with $f(x) = .00625$ for $a \leq x \leq b$.

    a. Find the values of a and b for the probability density function.
    b. What is the probability that consumers in this group have daily discretionary spending between $100 and $200?
    c. What is the probability that consumers in this group have a daily discretionary spending of $150 or more?
    d. What is the probability that consumers in this group have a daily discretionary spending of $80 or less?

7. Suppose we are interested in bidding on a piece of land and we know one other bidder is interested.[1] The seller announced that the highest bid in excess of $10,000 will be accepted. Assume that the competitor's bid x is a random variable that is uniformly distributed between $10,000 and $15,000.

    a. Suppose you bid $12,000. What is the probability that your bid will be accepted?
    b. Suppose you bid $14,000. What is the probability that your bid will be accepted?
    c. What amount should you bid to maximize the probability that you get the property?
    d. Suppose you know someone who is willing to pay you $16,000 for the property. Would you consider bidding less than the amount in part (c)? Why or why not?

6.2 Normal Probability Distribution

Abraham de Moivre, a French mathematician, published The Doctrine of Chances *in 1733. He derived the normal distribution.*

The most important probability distribution for describing a continuous random variable is the **normal probability distribution**. The normal distribution has been used in a wide variety of practical applications in which the random variables are heights and weights of people, test scores, scientific measurements, amounts of rainfall, and other similar values. It is also widely used in statistical inference, which is the major topic of the remainder of this book. In such applications, the normal distribution provides a description of the likely results obtained through sampling.

Normal Curve

The form, or shape, of the normal distribution is illustrated by the bell-shaped normal curve in Figure 6.3. The probability density function that defines the bell-shaped curve of the normal distribution follows.

---

[1]This exercise is based on a problem suggested to us by Professor Roger Myerson of Northwestern University.

FIGURE 6.3   BELL-SHAPED CURVE FOR THE NORMAL DISTRIBUTION

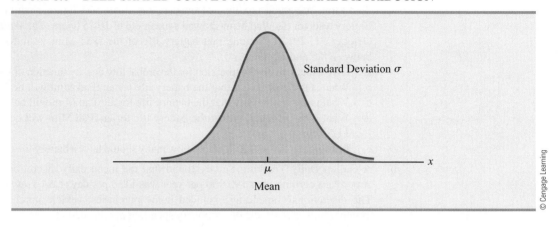

NORMAL PROBABILITY DENSITY FUNCTION

$$f(x) = \frac{1}{\sigma\sqrt{2\pi}} e^{-\frac{1}{2}\left(\frac{x-\mu}{\sigma}\right)^2} \tag{6.2}$$

where

μ = mean
σ = standard deviation
π = 3.14159
e = 2.71828

We make several observations about the characteristics of the normal distribution.

The normal curve has two parameters, μ and σ. They determine the location and shape of the normal distribution.

1. The entire family of normal distributions is differentiated by two parameters: the mean μ and the standard deviation σ.
2. The highest point on the normal curve is at the mean, which is also the median and mode of the distribution.
3. The mean of the distribution can be any numerical value: negative, zero, or positive. Three normal distributions with the same standard deviation but three different means (-10, 0, and 20) are shown here.

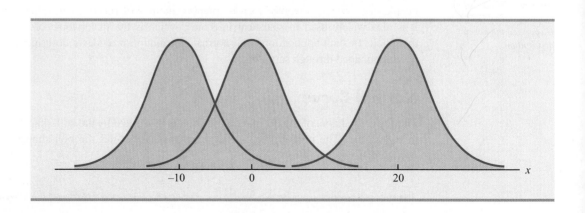

4. The normal distribution is symmetric, with the shape of the normal curve to the left of the mean a mirror image of the shape of the normal curve to the right of the mean. The tails of the normal curve extend to infinity in both directions and theoretically never touch the horizontal axis. Because it is symmetric, the normal distribution is not skewed; its skewness measure is zero.

5. The standard deviation determines how flat and wide the normal curve is. Larger values of the standard deviation result in wider, flatter curves, showing more variability in the data. Two normal distributions with the same mean but with different standard deviations are shown here.

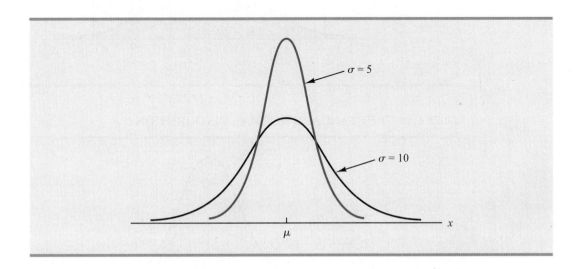

6. Probabilities for the normal random variable are given by areas under the normal curve. The total area under the curve for the normal distribution is 1. Because the distribution is symmetric, the area under the curve to the left of the mean is .50 and the area under the curve to the right of the mean is .50.

7. The percentage of values in some commonly used intervals are

These percentages are the basis for the empirical rule introduced in Section 3.3.

   a. 68.3% of the values of a normal random variable are within plus or minus one standard deviation of its mean.

   b. 95.4% of the values of a normal random variable are within plus or minus two standard deviations of its mean.

   c. 99.7% of the values of a normal random variable are within plus or minus three standard deviations of its mean.

Figure 6.4 shows properties (a), (b), and (c) graphically.

Standard Normal Probability Distribution

A random variable that has a normal distribution with a mean of zero and a standard deviation of one is said to have a **standard normal probability distribution**. The letter z is commonly used to designate this particular normal random variable. Figure 6.5 is the graph of the standard normal distribution. It has the same general appearance as other normal distributions, but with the special properties of $\mu = 0$ and $\sigma = 1$.

FIGURE 6.4   AREAS UNDER THE CURVE FOR ANY NORMAL DISTRIBUTION

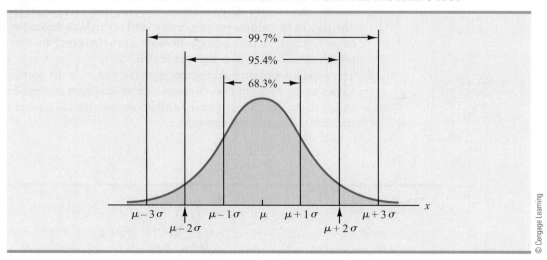

FIGURE 6.5   THE STANDARD NORMAL DISTRIBUTION

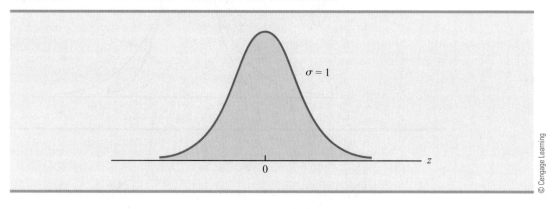

Because $\mu = 0$ and $\sigma = 1$, the formula for the standard normal probability density function is a simpler version of equation (6.2).

STANDARD NORMAL DENSITY FUNCTION

$$f(z) = \frac{1}{\sqrt{2\pi}} e^{-z^2/2}$$

As with other continuous random variables, probability calculations with any normal distribution are made by computing areas under the graph of the probability density function. Thus, to find the probability that a normal random variable is within any specific interval, we must compute the area under the normal curve over that interval.

For the normal probability density function, the height of the normal curve varies and more advanced mathematics is required to compute the areas that represent probability.

For the standard normal distribution, areas under the normal curve have been computed and are available in tables that can be used to compute probabilities. Such a table appears on the two pages inside the front cover of the text. The table on the left-hand page contains areas, or cumulative probabilities, for z values less than or equal to the mean of zero. The table on the right-hand page contains areas, or cumulative probabilities, for z values greater than or equal to the mean of zero.

The three types of probabilities we need to compute include (1) the probability that the standard normal random variable z will be less than or equal to a given value; (2) the probability that z will be between two given values; and (3) the probability that z will be greater than or equal to a given value. To see how the cumulative probability table for the standard normal distribution can be used to compute these three types of probabilities, let us consider some examples.

Because the standard normal random variable is continuous, $P(z \leq 1.00) = P(z < 1.00)$.

We start by showing how to compute the probability that z is less than or equal to 1.00; that is, $P(z \leq 1.00)$. This cumulative probability is the area under the normal curve to the left of $z = 1.00$ in the following graph.

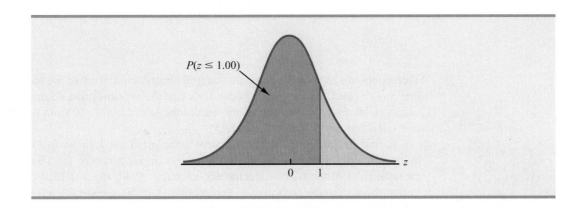

Refer to the right-hand page of the standard normal probability table inside the front cover of the text. The cumulative probability corresponding to $z = 1.00$ is the table value located at the intersection of the row labeled 1.0 and the column labeled .00. First we find 1.0 in the left column of the table and then find .00 in the top row of the table. By looking in the body of the table, we find that the 1.0 row and the .00 column intersect at the value of .8413; thus, $P(z \leq 1.00) = .8413$. The following excerpt from the probability table shows these steps.

z	.00	.01	.02
.			
.			
.			
.9	.8159	.8186	.8212
1.0	.8413	.8438	.8461
1.1	.8643	.8665	.8686
1.2	.8849	.8869	.8888
.			
.			
.			

$P(z \leq 1.00)$

To illustrate the second type of probability calculation we show how to compute the probability that z is in the interval between $-.50$ and 1.25; that is, $P(-.50 \leq z \leq 1.25)$. The following graph shows this area, or probability.

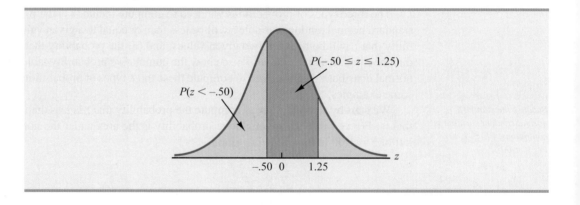

Three steps are required to compute this probability. First, we find the area under the normal curve to the left of $z = 1.25$. Second, we find the area under the normal curve to the left of $z = -.50$. Finally, we subtract the area to the left of $z = -.50$ from the area to the left of $z = 1.25$ to find $P(-.50 \le z \le 1.25)$.

To find the area under the normal curve to the left of $z = 1.25$, we first locate the 1.2 row in the standard normal probability table and then move across to the .05 column. Because the table value in the 1.2 row and the .05 column is .8944, $P(z \le 1.25) = .8944$. Similarly, to find the area under the curve to the left of $z = -.50$, we use the left-hand page of the table to locate the table value in the $-.5$ row and the .00 column; with a table value of .3085, $P(z \le -.50) = .3085$. Thus, $P(-.50 \le z \le 1.25) = P(z \le 1.25) - P(z \le -.50) = .8944 - .3085 = .5859$.

Let us consider another example of computing the probability that z is in the interval between two given values. Often it is of interest to compute the probability that a normal random variable assumes a value within a certain number of standard deviations of the mean. Suppose we want to compute the probability that the standard normal random variable is within one standard deviation of the mean; that is, $P(-1.00 \le z \le 1.00)$. To compute this probability we must find the area under the curve between -1.00 and 1.00. Earlier we found that $P(z \le 1.00) = .8413$. Referring again to the table inside the front cover of the book, we find that the area under the curve to the left of $z = -1.00$ is .1587, so $P(z \le -1.00) = .1587$. Therefore, $P(-1.00 \le z \le 1.00) = P(z \le 1.00) - P(z \le -1.00) = .8413 - .1587 = .6826$. This probability is shown graphically in the following figure.

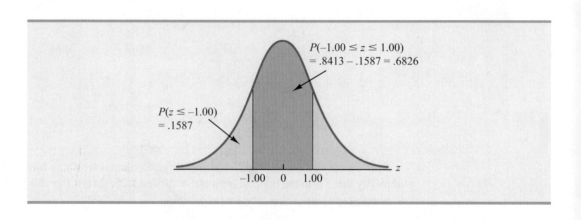

To illustrate how to make the third type of probability computation, suppose we want to compute the probability of obtaining a z value of at least 1.58; that is, $P(z \geq 1.58)$. The value in the $z = 1.5$ row and the .08 column of the cumulative normal table is .9429; thus, $P(z < 1.58) = .9429$. However, because the total area under the normal curve is 1, $P(z \geq 1.58) = 1 - .9429 = .0571$. This probability is shown in the following figure.

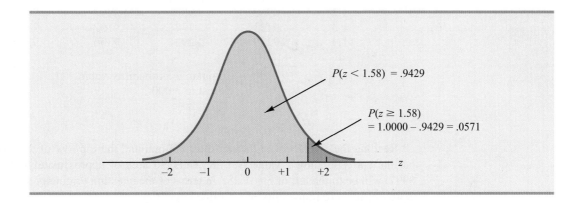

In the preceding illustrations, we showed how to compute probabilities given specified z values. In some situations, we are given a probability and are interested in working backward to find the corresponding z value. Suppose we want to find a z value such that the probability of obtaining a larger z value is .10. The following figure shows this situation graphically.

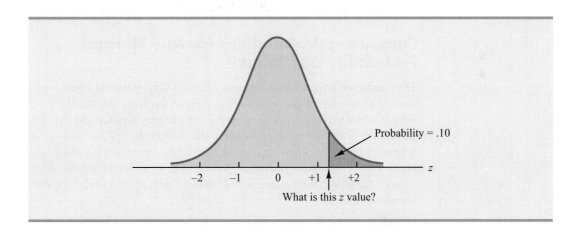

Given a probability, we can use the standard normal table in an inverse fashion to find the corresponding z value.

This problem is the inverse of those in the preceding examples. Previously, we specified the z value of interest and then found the corresponding probability, or area. In this example, we are given the probability, or area, and asked to find the corresponding z value. To do so, we use the standard normal probability table somewhat differently.

Recall that the standard normal probability table gives the area under the curve to the left of a particular z value. We have been given the information that the area in the upper tail of the curve is .10. Hence, the area under the curve to the left of the unknown z value must equal .9000. Scanning the body of the table, we find .8997 is the cumulative probability value closest to .9000. The section of the table providing this result follows.

z	.06	.07	.08	.09
.				
.				
.				
1.0	.8554	.8577	.8599	.8621
1.1	.8770	.8790	.8810	.8830
1.2	.8962	.8980	.8997	.9015
1.3	.9131	.9147	.9162	.9177
1.4	.9279	.9292	.9306	.9319
.				
.				
.				

Cumulative probability value
closest to .9000

Reading the z value from the left-most column and the top row of the table, we find that the corresponding z value is 1.28. Thus, an area of approximately .9000 (actually .8997) will be to the left of $z = 1.28$.[2] In terms of the question originally asked, there is an approximately .10 probability of a z value larger than 1.28.

The examples illustrate that the table of cumulative probabilities for the standard normal probability distribution can be used to find probabilities associated with values of the standard normal random variable z. Two types of questions can be asked. The first type of question specifies a value, or values, for z and asks us to use the table to determine the corresponding areas or probabilities. The second type of question provides an area, or probability, and asks us to use the table to determine the corresponding z value. Thus, we need to be flexible in using the standard normal probability table to answer the desired probability question. In most cases, sketching a graph of the standard normal probability distribution and shading the appropriate area will help to visualize the situation and aid in determining the correct answer.

Computing Probabilities for Any Normal Probability Distribution

The reason for discussing the standard normal distribution so extensively is that probabilities for all normal distributions are computed by using the standard normal distribution. That is, when we have a normal distribution with any mean μ and any standard deviation σ, we answer probability questions about the distribution by first converting to the standard normal distribution. Then we can use the standard normal probability table and the appropriate z values to find the desired probabilities. The formula used to convert any normal random variable x with mean μ and standard deviation σ to the standard normal random variable z follows.

The formula for the standard normal random variable is similar to the formula we introduced in Chapter 3 for computing z-scores for a data set.

CONVERTING TO THE STANDARD NORMAL RANDOM VARIABLE

$$z = \frac{x - \mu}{\sigma} \tag{6.3}$$

---

[2] We could use interpolation in the body of the table to get a better approximation of the z value that corresponds to an area of .9000. Doing so to provide one more decimal place of accuracy would yield a z value of 1.282. However, in most practical situations, sufficient accuracy is obtained by simply using the table value closest to the desired probability.

A value of x equal to its mean μ results in $z = (\mu - \mu)/\sigma = 0$. Thus, we see that a value of x equal to its mean μ corresponds to $z = 0$. Now suppose that x is one standard deviation above its mean; that is, $x = \mu + \sigma$. Applying equation (6.3), we see that the corresponding z value is $z = [(\mu + \sigma) - \mu]/\sigma = \sigma/\sigma = 1$. Thus, an x value that is one standard deviation above its mean corresponds to $z = 1$. In other words, *we can interpret z as the number of standard deviations that the normal random variable x is from its mean μ.*

To see how this conversion enables us to compute probabilities for any normal distribution, suppose we have a normal distribution with $\mu = 10$ and $\sigma = 2$. What is the probability that the random variable x is between 10 and 14? Using equation (6.3), we see that at $x = 10$, $z = (x - \mu)/\sigma = (10 - 10)/2 = 0$ and that at $x = 14$, $z = (14 - 10)/2 = 4/2 = 2$. Thus, the answer to our question about the probability of x being between 10 and 14 is given by the equivalent probability that z is between 0 and 2 for the standard normal distribution. In other words, the probability that we are seeking is the probability that the random variable x is between its mean and two standard deviations above the mean. Using $z = 2.00$ and the standard normal probability table inside the front cover of the text, we see that $P(z \leq 2) = .9772$. Because $P(z \leq 0) = .5000$, we can compute $P(.00 \leq z \leq 2.00) = P(z \leq 2) - P(z \leq 0) = .9772 - .5000 = .4772$. Hence the probability that x is between 10 and 14 is .4772.

Grear Tire Company Problem

We turn now to an application of the normal probability distribution. Suppose the Grear Tire Company developed a new steel-belted radial tire to be sold through a national chain of discount stores. Because the tire is a new product, Grear's managers believe that the mileage guarantee offered with the tire will be an important factor in the acceptance of the product. Before finalizing the tire mileage guarantee policy, Grear's managers want probability information about x = number of miles the tires will last.

From actual road tests with the tires, Grear's engineering group estimated that the mean tire mileage is $\mu = 36{,}500$ miles and that the standard deviation is $\sigma = 5000$. In addition, the data collected indicate that a normal distribution is a reasonable assumption. What percentage of the tires can be expected to last more than 40,000 miles? In other words, what is the probability that the tire mileage, x, will exceed 40,000? This question can be answered by finding the area of the darkly shaded region in Figure 6.6.

FIGURE 6.6   GREAR TIRE COMPANY MILEAGE DISTRIBUTION

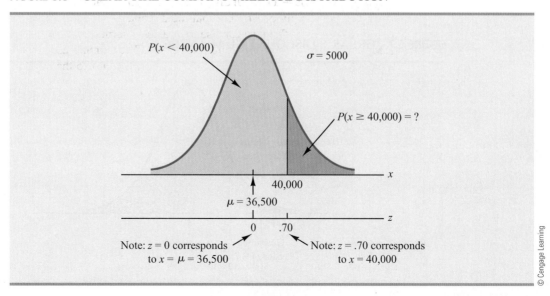

At $x = 40,000$, we have

$$z = \frac{x - \mu}{\sigma} = \frac{40,000 - 36,500}{5000} = \frac{3500}{5000} = .70$$

Refer now to the bottom of Figure 6.6. We see that a value of $x = 40,000$ on the Grear Tire normal distribution corresponds to a value of $z = .70$ on the standard normal distribution. Using the standard normal probability table, we see that the area under the standard normal curve to the left of $z = .70$ is .7580. Thus, $1.000 - .7580 = .2420$ is the probability that z will exceed .70 and hence x will exceed 40,000. We can conclude that about 24.2% of the tires will exceed 40,000 in mileage.

Let us now assume that Grear is considering a guarantee that will provide a discount on replacement tires if the original tires do not provide the guaranteed mileage. What should the guarantee mileage be if Grear wants no more than 10% of the tires to be eligible for the discount guarantee? This question is interpreted graphically in Figure 6.7.

According to Figure 6.7, the area under the curve to the left of the unknown guarantee mileage must be .10. So, we must first find the z value that cuts off an area of .10 in the left tail of a standard normal distribution. Using the standard normal probability table, we see that $z = -1.28$ cuts off an area of .10 in the lower tail. Hence, $z = -1.28$ is the value of the standard normal random variable corresponding to the desired mileage guarantee on the Grear Tire normal distribution. To find the value of x corresponding to $z = -1.28$, we have

The guaranteed mileage we need to find is 1.28 standard deviations below the mean. Thus, $x = \mu - 1.28\sigma$.

$$z = \frac{x - \mu}{\sigma} = -1.28$$
$$x - \mu = -1.28\sigma$$
$$x = \mu - 1.28\sigma$$

With $\mu = 36,500$ and $\sigma = 5000$,

$$x = 36,500 - 1.28(5000) = 30,100$$

With the guarantee set at 30,000 miles, the actual percentage eligible for the guarantee will be 9.68%.

Thus, a guarantee of 30,100 miles will meet the requirement that approximately 10% of the tires will be eligible for the guarantee. Perhaps, with this information, the firm will set its tire mileage guarantee at 30,000 miles.

FIGURE 6.7   GREAR'S DISCOUNT GUARANTEE

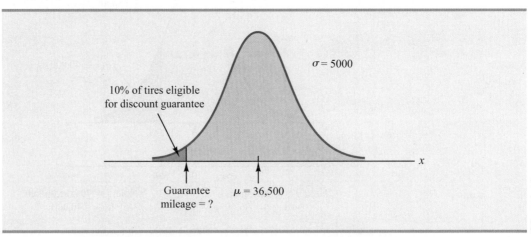

Again, we see the important role that probability distributions play in providing decision-making information. Namely, once a probability distribution is established for a particular application, it can be used to obtain probability information about the problem. Probability does not make a decision recommendation directly, but it provides information that helps the decision maker better understand the risks and uncertainties associated with the problem. Ultimately, this information may assist the decision maker in reaching a good decision.

Exercises

Methods

8. Using Figure 6.4 as a guide, sketch a normal curve for a random variable x that has a mean of $\mu = 100$ and a standard deviation of $\sigma = 10$. Label the horizontal axis with values of 70, 80, 90, 100, 110, 120, and 130.

9. A random variable is normally distributed with a mean of $\mu = 50$ and a standard deviation of $\sigma = 5$.
    a. Sketch a normal curve for the probability density function. Label the horizontal axis with values of 35, 40, 45, 50, 55, 60, and 65. Figure 6.4 shows that the normal curve almost touches the horizontal axis at three standard deviations below and at three standard deviations above the mean (in this case at 35 and 65).
    b. What is the probability the random variable will assume a value between 45 and 55?
    c. What is the probability the random variable will assume a value between 40 and 60?

10. Draw a graph for the standard normal distribution. Label the horizontal axis at values of -3, -2, -1, 0, 1, 2, and 3. Then use the table of probabilities for the standard normal distribution inside the front cover of the text to compute the following probabilities.
    a. $P(z \le 1.5)$
    b. $P(z \le 1)$
    c. $P(1 \le z \le 1.5)$
    d. $P(0 < z < 2.5)$

11. Given that z is a standard normal random variable, compute the following probabilities.
    a. $P(z \le -1.0)$
    b. $P(z \ge -1)$
    c. $P(z \ge -1.5)$
    d. $P(-2.5 \le z)$
    e. $P(-3 < z \le 0)$

12. Given that z is a standard normal random variable, compute the following probabilities.
    a. $P(0 \le z \le .83)$
    b. $P(-1.57 \le z \le 0)$
    c. $P(z > .44)$
    d. $P(z \ge -.23)$
    e. $P(z < 1.20)$
    f. $P(z \le -.71)$

13. Given that z is a standard normal random variable, compute the following probabilities.
    a. $P(-1.98 \le z \le .49)$
    b. $P(.52 \le z \le 1.22)$
    c. $P(-1.75 \le z \le -1.04)$

14. Given that z is a standard normal random variable, find z for each situation.
    a. The area to the left of z is .9750.
    b. The area between 0 and z is .4750.
    c. The area to the left of z is .7291.
    d. The area to the right of z is .1314.
    e. The area to the left of z is .6700.
    f. The area to the right of z is .3300.

15. Given that z is a standard normal random variable, find z for each situation.
    a. The area to the left of z is .2119.
    b. The area between $-z$ and z is .9030.
    c. The area between $-z$ and z is .2052.
    d. The area to the left of z is .9948.
    e. The area to the right of z is .6915.

16. Given that z is a standard normal random variable, find z for each situation.
    a. The area to the right of z is .01.
    b. The area to the right of z is .025.
    c. The area to the right of z is .05.
    d. The area to the right of z is .10.

Applications

17. The mean cost of domestic airfares in the United States rose to an all-time high of $385 per ticket (Bureau of Transportation Statistics website, November 2, 2012). Airfares were based on the total ticket value, which consisted of the price charged by the airlines plus any additional taxes and fees. Assume domestic airfares are normally distributed with a standard deviation of $110.
    a. What is the probability that a domestic airfare is $550 or more?
    b. What is the probability that a domestic airfare is $250 or less?
    c. What is the probability that a domestic airfare is between $300 and $500?
    d. What is the cost for the 3% highest domestic airfares?

18. The average return for large-cap domestic stock funds over the three years 2009–2011 was 14.4% (*AAII Journal,* February, 2012). Assume the three-year returns were normally distributed across funds with a standard deviation of 4.4%.
    a. What is the probability an individual large-cap domestic stock fund had a three-year return of at least 20%?
    b. What is the probability an individual large-cap domestic stock fund had a three-year return of 10% or less?
    c. How big does the return have to be to put a domestic stock fund in the top 10% for the three-year period?

19. In an article about the cost of health care, *Money* magazine reported that a visit to a hospital emergency room for something as simple as a sore throat has a mean cost of $328 (*Money,* January 2009). Assume that the cost for this type of hospital emergency room visit is normally distributed with a standard deviation of $92. Answer the following questions about the cost of a hospital emergency room visit for this medical service.
    a. What is the probability that the cost will be more than $500?
    b. What is the probability that the cost will be less than $250?
    c. What is the probability that the cost will be between $300 and $400?
    d. If the cost to a patient is in the lower 8% of charges for this medical service, what was the cost of this patient's emergency room visit?

20. The average price for a gallon of gasoline is $3.73 in the United States and $3.40 in Russia (*Bloomberg Businessweek,* March 5–March 11, 2012). Assume these averages are the population means in the two countries and that the probability distributions are normally distributed with a standard deviation of $.25 in the United States and a standard deviation of $.20 in Russia.
    a. What is the probability that a randomly selected gas station in the United States charges less than $3.50 per gallon?
    b. What percentage of the gas stations in Russia charge less than $3.50 per gallon?
    c. What is the probability that a randomly selected gas station in Russia charges more than the mean price in the United States?

21. A person must score in the upper 2% of the population on an IQ test to qualify for membership in Mensa, the international high-IQ society. There are 110,000 Mensa members in 100 countries throughout the world (Mensa International website, January 8, 2013). If IQ scores are normally distributed with a mean of 100 and a standard deviation of 15, what score must a person have to qualify for Mensa?

22. Television viewing reached a new high when the Nielsen Company reported a mean daily viewing time of 8.35 hours per household (*USA Today,* November 11, 2009). Use a normal probability distribution with a standard deviation of 2.5 hours to answer the following questions about daily television viewing per household.
   a. What is the probability that a household views television between 5 and 10 hours a day?
   b. How many hours of television viewing must a household have in order to be in the top 3% of all television viewing households?
   c. What is the probability that a household views television more than 3 hours a day?

23. The time needed to complete a final examination in a particular college course is normally distributed with a mean of 80 minutes and a standard deviation of 10 minutes. Answer the following questions.
   a. What is the probability of completing the exam in one hour or less?
   b. What is the probability that a student will complete the exam in more than 60 minutes but less than 75 minutes?
   c. Assume that the class has 60 students and that the examination period is 90 minutes in length. How many students do you expect will be unable to complete the exam in the allotted time?

24. The American Automobile Association (AAA) reported that families planning to travel over the Labor Day weekend would spend an average of $749 (The Associated Press, August 12, 2012). Assume that the amount spent is normally distributed with a standard deviation of $225.
   a. What is the probability that family expenses for the weekend will be less than $400?
   b. What is the probability that family expenses for the weekend will be $800 or more?
   c. What is the probability that family expenses for the weekend will be between $500 and $1000?
   d. What are the Labor Day weekend expenses for 5% of the families with the most expensive travel plans?

25. New York City is the most expensive city in the United States for lodging. The mean hotel room rate is $204 per night (*USA Today*, April 30, 2012). Assume that room rates are normally distributed with a standard deviation of $55.
   a. What is the probability that a hotel room costs $225 or more per night?
   b. What is the probability that a hotel room costs less than $140 per night?
   c. What is the probability that a hotel room costs between $200 and $300 per night?
   d. What is the cost of the 20% most expensive hotel rooms in New York City?

6.3 Normal Approximation of Binomial Probabilities

In Section 5.5 we presented the discrete binomial distribution. Recall that a binomial experiment consists of a sequence of n identical independent trials with each trial having two possible outcomes, a success or a failure. The probability of a success on a trial is the same for all trials and is denoted by p. The binomial random variable is the number of successes in the n trials, and probability questions pertain to the probability of x successes in the n trials.

   When the number of trials becomes large, evaluating the binomial probability function by hand or with a calculator is difficult. In cases where $np \geq 5$, and $n(1 - p) \geq 5$, the normal

FIGURE 6.8   NORMAL APPROXIMATION TO A BINOMIAL PROBABILITY DISTRIBUTION WITH $n = 100$ AND $p = .10$ SHOWING THE PROBABILITY OF 12 ERRORS

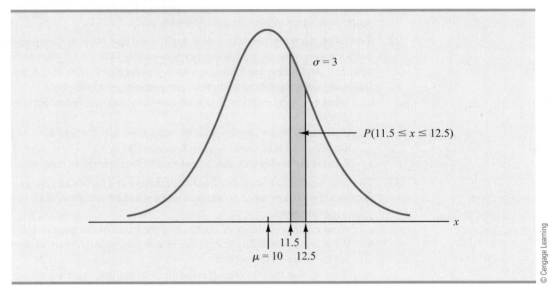

distribution provides an easy-to-use approximation of binomial probabilities. When using the normal approximation to the binomial, we set $\mu = np$ and $\sigma = \sqrt{np(1 - p)}$ in the definition of the normal curve.

Let us illustrate the normal approximation to the binomial by supposing that a particular company has a history of making errors in 10% of its invoices. A sample of 100 invoices has been taken, and we want to compute the probability that 12 invoices contain errors. That is, we want to find the binomial probability of 12 successes in 100 trials. In applying the normal approximation in this case, we set $\mu = np = (100)(.1) = 10$ and $\sigma = \sqrt{np(1 - p)} = \sqrt{(100)(.1)(.9)} = 3$. A normal distribution with $\mu = 10$ and $\sigma = 3$ is shown in Figure 6.8.

Recall that, with a continuous probability distribution, probabilities are computed as areas under the probability density function. As a result, the probability of any single value for the random variable is zero. Thus to approximate the binomial probability of 12 successes, we compute the area under the corresponding normal curve between 11.5 and 12.5. The .5 that we add and subtract from 12 is called a **continuity correction factor**. It is introduced because a continuous distribution is being used to approximate a discrete distribution. Thus, $P(x = 12)$ for the *discrete* binomial distribution is approximated by $P(11.5 \leq x \leq 12.5)$ for the *continuous* normal distribution.

Converting to the standard normal distribution to compute $P(11.5 \leq x \leq 12.5)$, we have

$$z = \frac{x - \mu}{\sigma} = \frac{12.5 - 10.0}{3} = .83 \quad \text{at } x = 12.5$$

and

$$z = \frac{x - \mu}{\sigma} = \frac{11.5 - 10.0}{3} = .50 \quad \text{at } x = 11.5$$

FIGURE 6.9   NORMAL APPROXIMATION TO A BINOMIAL PROBABILITY DISTRIBUTION WITH $n = 100$ AND $p = .10$ SHOWING THE PROBABILITY OF 13 OR FEWER ERRORS

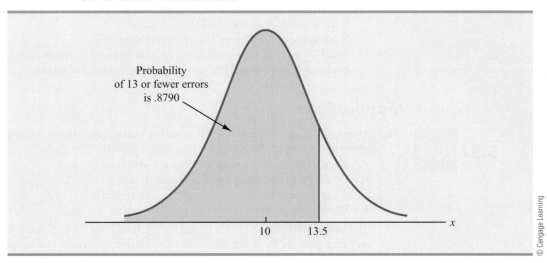

Using the standard normal probability table, we find that the area under the curve (in Figure 6.8) to the left of 12.5 is .7967. Similarly, the area under the curve to the left of 11.5 is .6915. Therefore, the area between 11.5 and 12.5 is .7967 − .6915 = .1052. The normal approximation to the probability of 12 successes in 100 trials is .1052.

For another illustration, suppose we want to compute the probability of 13 or fewer errors in the sample of 100 invoices. Figure 6.9 shows the area under the normal curve that approximates this probability. Note that the use of the continuity correction factor results in the value of 13.5 being used to compute the desired probability. The z value corresponding to $x = 13.5$ is

$$z = \frac{13.5 - 10.0}{3.0} = 1.17$$

The standard normal probability table shows that the area under the standard normal curve to the left of $z = 1.17$ is .8790. The area under the normal curve approximating the probability of 13 or fewer errors is given by the shaded portion of the graph in Figure 6.9.

Exercises

Methods

26. A binomial probability distribution has $p = .20$ and $n = 100$.
     a.   What are the mean and standard deviation?
     b.   Is this situation one in which binomial probabilities can be approximated by the normal probability distribution? Explain.
     c.   What is the probability of exactly 24 successes?
     d.   What is the probability of 18 to 22 successes?
     e.   What is the probability of 15 or fewer successes?

27. Assume a binomial probability distribution has $p = .60$ and $n = 200$.
    a. What are the mean and standard deviation?
    b. Is this situation one in which binomial probabilities can be approximated by the normal probability distribution? Explain.
    c. What is the probability of 100 to 110 successes?
    d. What is the probability of 130 or more successes?
    e. What is the advantage of using the normal probability distribution to approximate the binomial probabilities? Use part (d) to explain the advantage.

Applications

28. Although studies continue to show smoking leads to significant health problems, 20% of adults in the United States smoke. Consider a group of 250 adults.
    a. What is the expected number of adults who smoke?
    b. What is the probability that fewer than 40 smoke?
    c. What is the probability that from 55 to 60 smoke?
    d. What is the probability that 70 or more smoke?

29. An Internal Revenue Oversight Board survey found that 82% of taxpayers said that it was very important for the Internal Revenue Service (IRS) to ensure that high-income tax payers do not cheat on their tax returns (*The Wall Street Journal,* February 11, 2009).
    a. For a sample of eight taxpayers, what is the probability that at least six taxpayers say that it is very important to ensure that high-income tax payers do not cheat on their tax returns? Use the binomial distribution probability function shown in Section 5.4 to answer this question.
    b. For a sample of 80 taxpayers, what is the probability that at least 60 taxpayers say that it is very important to ensure that high-income tax payers do not cheat on their tax returns? Use the normal approximation of the binomial distribution to answer this question.
    c. As the number of trails in a binomial distribution application becomes large, what is the advantage of using the normal approximation of the binomial distribution to compute probabilities?
    d. When the number of trials for a binominal distribution application becomes large, would developers of statistical software packages prefer to use the binomial distribution probability function shown in Section 5.5 or the normal approximation of the binomial distribution shown in Section 6.3? Explain.

30. Playing video and computer games is very popular. Over 70% of households play such games. Of those individuals who play video and computer games, 18% are under 18 years old, 53% are 18–59 years old, and 29% are over 59 years old (*The Wall Street Journal,* March 6, 2012).
    a. For a sample of 800 people who play these games, how many would you expect to be under 18 years of age?
    b. For a sample of 600 people who play these games, what is the probability that fewer than 100 will be under 18 years of age?
    c. For a sample of 800 people who play these games, what is the probability that 200 or more will be over 59 years of age?

31. A Bureau of National Affairs survey found that 79% of employers provide their workers with a two-day paid Thanksgiving holiday with workers off both Thursday and Friday (*USA Today,* November 12, 2009). Nineteen percent of employers provide a one-day paid holiday with workers off Thanksgiving Day. Two percent of employers do not provide a paid Thanksgiving holiday. Consider a sample of 120 employers.
    a. What is the probability that at least 85 of the employers provide a two-day paid Thanksgiving holiday?
    b. What is the probability that between 90 and 100 employers provide a two-day paid Thanksgiving holiday? That is, what is $P(90 \leq x \leq 100)$?
    c. What is the probability that less than 20 employers provide a one-day paid Thanksgiving holiday?

6.4   Exponential Probability Distribution

The **exponential probability distribution** may be used for random variables such as the time between arrivals at a car wash, the time required to load a truck, the distance between major defects in a highway, and so on. The exponential probability density function follows.

EXPONENTIAL PROBABILITY DENSITY FUNCTION

$$f(x) = \frac{1}{\mu} e^{-x/\mu} \qquad \text{for } x \geq 0 \tag{6.4}$$

where $\mu =$ expected value or mean

As an example of the exponential distribution, suppose that x represents the loading time for a truck at the Schips loading dock and follows such a distribution. If the mean, or average, loading time is 15 minutes ($\mu = 15$), the appropriate probability density function for x is

$$f(x) = \frac{1}{15} e^{-x/15}$$

Figure 6.10 is the graph of this probability density function.

Computing Probabilities for the Exponential Distribution

In waiting line applications, the exponential distribution is often used for service time.

As with any continuous probability distribution, the area under the curve corresponding to an interval provides the probability that the random variable assumes a value in that interval. In the Schips loading dock example, the probability that loading a truck will take 6 minutes or less $P(x \leq 6)$ is defined to be the area under the curve in Figure 6.10 from $x = 0$ to $x = 6$. Similarly, the probability that the loading time will be 18 minutes or less $P(x \leq 18)$ is the area under the curve from $x = 0$ to $x = 18$. Note also that the probability that the loading time will be between 6 minutes and 18 minutes $P(6 \leq x \leq 18)$ is given by the area under the curve from $x = 6$ to $x = 18$.

FIGURE 6.10   EXPONENTIAL DISTRIBUTION FOR THE SCHIPS LOADING DOCK EXAMPLE

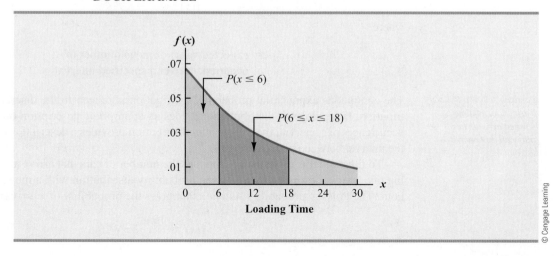

To compute exponential probabilities such as those just described, we use the following formula. It provides the cumulative probability of obtaining a value for the exponential random variable of less than or equal to some specific value denoted by x_0.

EXPONENTIAL DISTRIBUTION: CUMULATIVE PROBABILITIES

$$P(x \le x_0) = 1 - e^{-x_0/\mu} \tag{6.5}$$

For the Schips loading dock example, $x =$ loading time in minutes and $\mu = 15$ minutes. Using equation (6.5)

$$P(x \le x_0) = 1 - e^{-x_0/15}$$

Hence, the probability that loading a truck will take 6 minutes or less is

$$P(x \le 6) = 1 - e^{-6/15} = .3297$$

Using equation (6.5), we calculate the probability of loading a truck in 18 minutes or less.

$$P(x \le 18) = 1 - e^{-18/15} = .6988$$

Thus, the probability that loading a truck will take between 6 minutes and 18 minutes is equal to $.6988 - .3297 = .3691$. Probabilities for any other interval can be computed similarly.

A property of the exponential distribution is that the mean and standard deviation are equal.

In the preceding example, the mean time it takes to load a truck is $\mu = 15$ minutes. A property of the exponential distribution is that the mean of the distribution and the standard deviation of the distribution are *equal*. Thus, the standard deviation for the time it takes to load a truck is $\sigma = 15$ minutes. The variance is $\sigma^2 = (15)^2 = 225$.

Relationship Between the Poisson and Exponential Distributions

In Section 5.5 we introduced the Poisson distribution as a discrete probability distribution that is often useful in examining the number of occurrences of an event over a specified interval of time or space. Recall that the Poisson probability function is

$$f(x) = \frac{\mu^x e^{-\mu}}{x!}$$

where

$$\mu = \text{expected value or mean number of}$$
$$\text{occurrences over a specified interval}$$

If arrivals follow a Poisson distribution, the time between arrivals must follow an exponential distribution.

The continuous exponential probability distribution is related to the discrete Poisson distribution. If the Poisson distribution provides an appropriate description of the number of occurrences per interval, the exponential distribution provides a description of the length of the interval between occurrences.

To illustrate this relationship, suppose the number of cars that arrive at a car wash during one hour is described by a Poisson probability distribution with a mean of 10 cars per hour. The Poisson probability function that gives the probability of x arrivals per hour is

$$f(x) = \frac{10^x e^{-10}}{x!}$$

Because the average number of arrivals is 10 cars per hour, the average time between cars arriving is

$$\frac{1 \text{ hour}}{10 \text{ cars}} = .1 \text{ hour/car}$$

Thus, the corresponding exponential distribution that describes the time between the arrivals has a mean of $\mu = .1$ hour per car; as a result, the appropriate exponential probability density function is

$$f(x) = \frac{1}{.1} e^{-x/.1} = 10e^{-10x}$$

NOTE AND COMMENT

As we can see in Figure 6.10, the exponential distribution is skewed to the right. Indeed, the skewness measure for exponential distributions is 2. The exponential distribution gives us a good idea what a skewed distribution looks like.

Exercises

Methods

32. Consider the following exponential probability density function.

$$f(x) = \frac{1}{8} e^{-x/8} \qquad \text{for } x \geq 0$$

  a. Find $P(x \leq 6)$.
  b. Find $P(x \leq 4)$.
  c. Find $P(x \geq 6)$.
  d. Find $P(4 \leq x \leq 6)$.

33. Consider the following exponential probability density function.

$$f(x) = \frac{1}{3} e^{-x/3} \qquad \text{for } x \geq 0$$

  a. Write the formula for $P(x \leq x_0)$.
  b. Find $P(x \leq 2)$.
  c. Find $P(x \geq 3)$.
  d. Find $P(x \leq 5)$.
  e. Find $P(2 \leq x \leq 5)$.

Applications

34. Battery life between charges for the Motorola Droid Razr Maxx is 20 hours when the primary use is talk time (*The Wall Street Journal*, March 7, 2012). The battery life drops to 7 hours when the phone is primarily used for Internet applications. Assume that the battery life for both uses follows an exponential distribution.
  a. Show the probability density function for battery life for the Droid Razr Maxx phone when its primary use is talk time.
  b. What is the probability that the battery charge for a randomly selected Droid Razr Maxx phone will last no more than 15 hours when its primary use is talk time?
  c. What is the probability that the battery charge for a randomly selected Droid Razr Maxx phone will last more than 20 hours when its primary use is talk time?
  d. What is the probability that the battery charge for a randomly selected Droid Razr Maxx phone will last no more than 5 hours when its primary use is Internet applications?

35. The time between arrivals of vehicles at a particular intersection follows an exponential probability distribution with a mean of 12 seconds.
    a. Sketch this exponential probability distribution.
    b. What is the probability that the arrival time between vehicles is 12 seconds or less?
    c. What is the probability that the arrival time between vehicles is 6 seconds or less?
    d. What is the probability of 30 or more seconds between vehicle arrivals?

36. Comcast Corporation is the largest cable television company, the second largest Internet service provider, and the fourth largest telephone service provider in the United States. Generally known for quality and reliable service, the company periodically experiences unexpected service interruptions. On January 14, 2009, such an interruption occurred for the Comcast customers living in southwest Florida. When customers called the Comcast office, a recorded message told them that the company was aware of the service outage and that it was anticipated that service would be restored in two hours. Assume that two hours is the mean time to do the repair and that the repair time has an exponential probability distribution.
    a. What is the probability that the cable service will be repaired in one hour or less?
    b. What is the probability that the repair will take between one hour and two hours?
    c. For a customer who calls the Comcast office at 1:00 P.M., what is the probability that the cable service will not be repaired by 5:00 P.M.?

37. Collina's Italian Café in Houston, Texas, advertises that carryout orders take about 25 minutes (Collina's website, February 27, 2008). Assume that the time required for a carryout order to be ready for customer pickup has an exponential distribution with a mean of 25 minutes.
    a. What is the probability than a carryout order will be ready within 20 minutes?
    b. If a customer arrives 30 minutes after placing an order, what is the probability that the order will not be ready?
    c. A particular customer lives 15 minutes from Collina's Italian Café. If the customer places a telephone order at 5:20 P.M., what is the probability that the customer can drive to the café, pick up the order, and return home by 6:00 P.M.?

38. The Boston Fire Department receives 911 calls at a mean rate of 1.6 calls per hour (Mass .gov website, November 2012). Suppose the number of calls per hour follows a Poisson probability distribution.
    a. What is the mean time in minutes between 911 calls to the Boston Fire Department?
    b. Using the mean in part (a), show the probability density function for the time in minutes between 911 calls.
    c. What is the probability that there will be less than one hour between 911 calls?
    d. What is the probability that there will be 30 minutes or more between 911 calls?
    e. What is the probability that there will be more than 5 minutes, but less than 20 minutes between 911 calls?

Summary

This chapter extended the discussion of probability distributions to the case of continuous random variables. The major conceptual difference between discrete and continuous probability distributions involves the method of computing probabilities. With discrete distributions, the probability function $f(x)$ provides the probability that the random variable x assumes various values. With continuous distributions, the probability density function $f(x)$ does not provide probability values directly. Instead, probabilities are given by areas under the curve or graph of the probability density function $f(x)$. Because the area under the curve above a single point is zero, we observe that the probability of any particular value is zero for a continuous random variable.

Three continuous probability distributions—the uniform, normal, and exponential distributions—were treated in detail. The normal distribution is used widely in statistical inference and will be used extensively throughout the remainder of the text.

Glossary

Probability density function A function used to compute probabilities for a continuous random variable. The area under the graph of a probability density function over an interval represents probability.

Uniform probability distribution A continuous probability distribution for which the probability that the random variable will assume a value in any interval is the same for each interval of equal length.

Normal probability distribution A continuous probability distribution. Its probability density function is bell-shaped and determined by its mean μ and standard deviation σ.

Standard normal probability distribution A normal distribution with a mean of zero and a standard deviation of one.

Continuity correction factor A value of .5 that is added to or subtracted from a value of x when the continuous normal distribution is used to approximate the discrete binomial distribution.

Exponential probability distribution A continuous probability distribution that is useful in computing probabilities for the time it takes to complete a task.

Key Formulas

Uniform Probability Density Function

$$f(x) = \begin{cases} \dfrac{1}{b-a} & \text{for } a \leq x \leq b \\ 0 & \text{elsewhere} \end{cases} \tag{6.1}$$

Normal Probability Density Function

$$f(x) = \frac{1}{\sigma\sqrt{2\pi}} e^{-\frac{1}{2}\left(\frac{x-\mu}{\sigma}\right)^2} \tag{6.2}$$

Converting to the Standard Normal Random Variable

$$z = \frac{x-\mu}{\sigma} \tag{6.3}$$

Exponential Probability Density Function

$$f(x) = \frac{1}{\mu}e^{-x/\mu} \qquad \text{for } x \geq 0 \tag{6.4}$$

Exponential Distribution: Cumulative Probabilities

$$P(x \leq x_0) = 1 - e^{-x_0/\mu} \tag{6.5}$$

Supplementary Exercises

39. A business executive, transferred from Chicago to Atlanta, needs to sell her house in Chicago quickly. The executive's employer has offered to buy the house for $210,000, but the offer expires at the end of the week. The executive does not currently have a better offer but can afford to leave the house on the market for another month. From conversations

with her realtor, the executive believes the price she will get by leaving the house on the market for another month is uniformly distributed between $200,000 and $225,000.

a.   If she leaves the house on the market for another month, what is the mathematical expression for the probability density function of the sales price?

b.   If she leaves it on the market for another month, what is the probability she will get at least $215,000 for the house?

c.   If she leaves it on the market for another month, what is the probability she will get less than $210,000?

d.   Should the executive leave the house on the market for another month? Why or why not?

40.   The NCAA estimates that the yearly value of a full athletic scholarship at in-state public universities is $19,000 (*The Wall Street Journal,* March 12, 2012). Assume the scholarship value is normally distributed with a standard deviation of $2,100.

a.   Consider the 10% of athletic scholarships of least value. How much are they worth?

b.   What percentage of athletic scholarships are valued at $22,000 or more?

c.   Consider the 3% of athletic scholarships that are most valuable. How much are they worth?

41.   Motorola used the normal distribution to determine the probability of defects and the number of defects expected in a production process. Assume a production process produces items with a mean weight of 10 ounces. Calculate the probability of a defect and the expected number of defects for a 1000-unit production run in the following situations.

a.   The process standard deviation is .15, and the process control is set at plus or minus one standard deviation. Units with weights less than 9.85 or greater than 10.15 ounces will be classified as defects.

b.   Through process design improvements, the process standard deviation can be reduced to .05. Assume the process control remains the same, with weights less than 9.85 or greater than 10.15 ounces being classified as defects.

c.   What is the advantage of reducing process variation, thereby causing process control limits to be at a greater number of standard deviations from the mean?

42.   During early 2012, economic hardship was stretching the limits of France's welfare system. One indicator of the level of hardship was the increase in the number of people bringing items to a Paris pawnbroker; the number of people bringing items to the pawnbroker had increased to 658 per day (*Bloomberg Businessweek*, March 5–March 11, 2012). Assume the number of people bringing items to the pawnshop per day in 2012 is normally distributed with a mean of 658.

a.   Suppose you learn that on 3% of the days, 610 or fewer people brought items to the pawnshop. What is the standard deviation of the number of people bringing items to the pawnshop per day?

b.   On any given day, what is the probability that between 600 and 700 people bring items to the pawnshop?

c.   How many people bring items to the pawnshop on the busiest 3% of days?

43.   The port of South Louisiana, located 54 miles along the Mississippi River between New Orleans and Baton Rouge, is the largest bulk cargo port in the world. The U.S. Army Corps of Engineers reports that the port handles a mean of 4.5 million tons of cargo per week (*USA Today*, September 25, 2012). Assume that the number of tons of cargo handled per week is normally distributed with a standard deviation of .82 million tons.

a.   What is the probability that the port handles less than 5 million tons of cargo in a week?

b.   What is the probability that the port handles 3 or more million tons of cargo in a week?

c.   What is the probability that the port handles between 3 million and 4 million tons of cargo in a week?

d.   Assume that 85% of the time the port can handle the weekly cargo volume without extending operating hours. What is the number of tons of cargo per week that will require the port to extend its operating hours?

44.   Ward Doering Auto Sales is considering offering a special service contract that will cover the total cost of any service work required on leased vehicles. From experience,

the company manager estimates that yearly service costs are approximately normally distributed, with a mean of $150 and a standard deviation of $25.

   a. If the company offers the service contract to customers for a yearly charge of $200, what is the probability that any one customer's service costs will exceed the contract price of $200?

   b. What is Ward's expected profit per service contract?

45. A minibar in a hotel room generally provides an impression that the hotel is more upscale. PKF Hospitality research reported that minibars provide a mean annual revenue of $368 per hotel room (*USA Today*, February 9, 2012). Consider an upscale hotel in San Antonio, Texas, that has a total of 330 rooms, each with a minibar. Assume that the total monthly revenue for this hotel's minibar service is normally distributed with a standard deviation of $2,200.

   a. Using the mean annual revenue of $368 per minibar, what is the mean total monthly revenue for the minibar service at this hotel?

   b. What is the probability that the monthly minibar service provides over $12,000 in revenues for this hotel?

   c. What is the probability that the monthly minibar service provides less than $7,500 in revenues for this hotel?

   d. The hotel is considering upgrading the minibar selections to make the minibars. more interesting for its guests. New minibar offerings are expected to raise the mean annual revenue to $420 per minibar. Assume that the total monthly revenue for the hotel's new minibar service is normally distributed with a standard deviation of $2,500. Answer parts (b) and (c) for the upgraded minibar service. What is the increase in the mean annual revenue for the upgraded minibar service? Do you agree with the strategy of upgrading the hotel's minibar service? Explain.

46. Assume that the test scores from a college admissions test are normally distributed, with a mean of 450 and a standard deviation of 100.

   a. What percentage of the people taking the test score between 400 and 500?

   b. Suppose someone receives a score of 630. What percentage of the people taking the test score better? What percentage score worse?

   c. If a particular university will not admit anyone scoring below 480, what percentage of the persons taking the test would be acceptable to the university?

47. According to Salary Wizard, the average base salary for a brand manager in Houston, Texas, is $88,592 and the average base salary for a brand manager in Los Angeles, California, is $97,417 (Salary Wizard website, February 27, 2008). Assume that salaries are normally distributed, the standard deviation for brand managers in Houston is $19,900, and the standard deviation for brand managers in Los Angeles is $21,800.

   a. What is the probability that a brand manager in Houston has a base salary in excess of $100,000?

   b. What is the probability that a brand manager in Los Angeles has a base salary in excess of $100,000?

   c. What is the probability that a brand manager in Los Angeles has a base salary of less than $75,000?

   d. How much would a brand manager in Los Angeles have to make in order to have a higher salary than 99% of the brand managers in Houston?

48. A machine fills containers with a particular product. The standard deviation of filling weights is known from past data to be .6 ounce. If only 2% of the containers hold less than 18 ounces, what is the mean filling weight for the machine? That is, what must μ equal? Assume the filling weights have a normal distribution.

49. Consider a multiple-choice examination with 50 questions. Each question has four possible answers. Assume that a student who has done the homework and attended lectures has a 75% probability of answering any question correctly.

   a. A student must answer 43 or more questions correctly to obtain a grade of A. What percentage of the students who have done their homework and attended lectures will obtain a grade of A on this multiple-choice examination?

  b. A student who answers 35 to 39 questions correctly will receive a grade of C. What percentage of students who have done their homework and attended lectures will obtain a grade of C on this multiple-choice examination?

  c. A student must answer 30 or more questions correctly to pass the examination. What percentage of the students who have done their homework and attended lectures will pass the examination?

  d. Assume that a student has not attended class and has not done the homework for the course. Furthermore, assume that the student will simply guess at the answer to each question. What is the probability that this student will answer 30 or more questions correctly and pass the examination?

50. A blackjack player at a Las Vegas casino learned that the house will provide a free room if play is for four hours at an average bet of $50. The player's strategy provides a probability of .49 of winning on any one hand, and the player knows that there are 60 hands per hour. Suppose the player plays for four hours at a bet of $50 per hand.

  a. What is the player's expected payoff?
  b. What is the probability the player loses $1000 or more?
  c. What is the probability the player wins?
  d. Suppose the player starts with $1500. What is the probability of going broke?

51. The Information Systems Audit and Control Association surveyed office workers to learn about the anticipated usage of office computers for personal holiday shopping (*USA Today*, November 11, 2009). Assume that the number of hours a worker spends doing holiday shopping on an office computer follows an exponential distribution.

  a. The study reported that there is a .53 probability that a worker uses an office computer for holiday shopping 5 hours or less. Is the mean time spent using an office computer for holiday shopping closest to 5.8, 6.2, 6.6, or 7 hours?

  b. Using the mean time from part (a), what is the probability that a worker uses an office computer for holiday shopping more than 10 hours?

  c. What is the probability that a worker uses an office computer for holiday shopping between 4 and 8 hours?

52. The website for the Bed and Breakfast Inns of North America gets approximately seven visitors per minute. Suppose the number of website visitors per minute follows a Poisson probability distribution.

  a. What is the mean time between visits to the website?
  b. Show the exponential probability density function for the time between website visits.
  c. What is the probability no one will access the website in a 1-minute period?
  d. What is the probability no one will access the website in a 12-second period?

53. The American Community Survey showed that residents of New York City have the longest travel times to get to work compared to residents of other cities in the United States (U.S. Census Bureau website, August 2008). According to the latest statistics available, the average travel time to work for residents of New York City is 38.3 minutes.

  a. Assume the exponential probability distribution is applicable and show the probability density function for the travel time to work for a resident of this city.

  b. What is the probability it will take a resident of this city between 20 and 40 minutes to travel to work?

  c. What is the probability it will take a resident of this city more than one hour to travel to work?

54. The time (in minutes) between telephone calls at an insurance claims office has the following exponential probability distribution.

$$f(x) = .50e^{-.50x} \qquad \text{for } x \geq 0$$

a.   What is the mean time between telephone calls?
b.   What is the probability of having 30 seconds or less between telephone calls?
c.   What is the probability of having 1 minute or less between telephone calls?
d.   What is the probability of having 5 or more minutes without a telephone call?

Case Problem   Specialty Toys

Specialty Toys, Inc., sells a variety of new and innovative children's toys. Management learned that the preholiday season is the best time to introduce a new toy, because many families use this time to look for new ideas for December holiday gifts. When Specialty discovers a new toy with good market potential, it chooses an October market entry date.

In order to get toys in its stores by October, Specialty places one-time orders with its manufacturers in June or July of each year. Demand for children's toys can be highly volatile. If a new toy catches on, a sense of shortage in the marketplace often increases the demand to high levels and large profits can be realized. However, new toys can also flop, leaving Specialty stuck with high levels of inventory that must be sold at reduced prices. The most important question the company faces is deciding how many units of a new toy should be purchased to meet anticipated sales demand. If too few are purchased, sales will be lost; if too many are purchased, profits will be reduced because of low prices realized in clearance sales.

For the coming season, Specialty plans to introduce a new product called Weather Teddy. This variation of a talking teddy bear is made by a company in Taiwan. When a child presses Teddy's hand, the bear begins to talk. A built-in barometer selects one of five responses that predict the weather conditions. The responses range from "It looks to be a very nice day! Have fun" to "I think it may rain today. Don't forget your umbrella." Tests with the product show that, even though it is not a perfect weather predictor, its predictions are surprisingly good. Several of Specialty's managers claimed Teddy gave predictions of the weather that were as good as many local television weather forecasters.

As with other products, Specialty faces the decision of how many Weather Teddy units to order for the coming holiday season. Members of the management team suggested order quantities of 15,000, 18,000, 24,000, or 28,000 units. The wide range of order quantities suggested indicates considerable disagreement concerning the market potential. The product management team asks you for an analysis of the stock-out probabilities for various order quantities, an estimate of the profit potential, and to help make an order quantity recommendation. Specialty expects to sell Weather Teddy for $24 based on a cost of $16 per unit. If inventory remains after the holiday season, Specialty will sell all surplus inventory for $5 per unit. After reviewing the sales history of similar products, Specialty's senior sales forecaster predicted an expected demand of 20,000 units with a .95 probability that demand would be between 10,000 units and 30,000 units.

Managerial Report

Prepare a managerial report that addresses the following issues and recommends an order quantity for the Weather Teddy product.

1. Use the sales forecaster's prediction to describe a normal probability distribution that can be used to approximate the demand distribution. Sketch the distribution and show its mean and standard deviation.
2. Compute the probability of a stock-out for the order quantities suggested by members of the management team.
3. Compute the projected profit for the order quantities suggested by the management team under three scenarios: worst case in which sales = 10,000 units, most likely case in which sales = 20,000 units, and best case in which sales = 30,000 units.

4. One of Specialty's managers felt that the profit potential was so great that the order quantity should have a 70% chance of meeting demand and only a 30% chance of any stock-outs. What quantity would be ordered under this policy, and what is the projected profit under the three sales scenarios?

5. Provide your own recommendation for an order quantity and note the associated profit projections. Provide a rationale for your recommendation.

Appendix 6.1   Continuous Probability Distributions with Minitab

Let us demonstrate the Minitab procedure for computing continuous probabilities by referring to the Grear Tire Company problem where tire mileage was described by a normal distribution with $\mu = 36,500$ and $\sigma = 5000$. One question asked was: What is the probability that the tire mileage will exceed 40,000 miles?

For continuous probability distributions, Minitab provides the cumulative probability that the random variable takes on a value less than or equal to a specified constant. For the Grear tire mileage question, Minitab can be used to determine the cumulative probability that the tire mileage will be less than or equal to 40,000 miles. After obtaining the cumulative probability, we must subtract it from 1 to determine the probability that the tire mileage will exceed 40,000 miles.

Prior to using Minitab to compute a probability, we must enter the specified constant into a column of the worksheet. For the Grear tire mileage question we enter 40,000 into column C1 of the Minitab worksheet. The steps in using Minitab to compute the cumulative probability follow.

Step 1. Select the **Calc** menu
Step 2. Choose **Probability Distributions**
Step 3. Choose **Normal**
Step 4. When the Normal Distribution dialog box appears:
  Select **Cumulative probability**
  Enter 36500 in the **Mean** box
  Enter 5000 in the **Standard deviation** box
  Enter C1 in the **Input column** box (the column containing 40,000)
  Click **OK**

Minitab shows that this probability is .7580. Because we are interested in the probability that the tire mileage will be greater than 40,000, the desired probability is $1 - .7580 = .2420$.

A second question in the Grear Tire Company problem was, What mileage guarantee should Grear set to ensure that no more than 10% of the tires qualify for the guarantee? Here we are given a probability and want to find the corresponding value for the random variable. Minitab uses an inverse calculation routine to find the value of the random variable associated with a given cumulative probability. First, we must enter the cumulative probability into a column of the Minitab worksheet. In this case, the desired cumulative probability of .10 is entered into column C1. Then, the first three steps of the Minitab procedure are as already listed. In step 4, we select **Inverse cumulative probability** instead of **Cumulative probability** and complete the remaining parts of the step. Minitab then displays the mileage guarantee of 30,092 miles.

Minitab is capable of computing probabilities for other continuous probability distributions, including the exponential probability distribution. To compute exponential probabilities, follow the procedure shown previously for the normal probability distribution and choose the **Exponential** option in step 3. Step 4 is as shown, with the exception that entering the standard deviation is not required. Output for cumulative probabilities and inverse cumulative probabilities is identical to that described for the normal probability distribution.

Appendix 6.2   Continuous Probability Distributions with Excel

Excel provides the capability for computing probabilities for several continuous probability distributions, including the normal and exponential probability distributions. In this appendix, we describe how Excel can be used to compute probabilities for any normal distribution. The procedures for the exponential and other continuous distributions are similar to the one we describe for the normal distribution.

Let us return to the Grear Tire Company problem where the tire mileage was described by a normal distribution with $\mu = 36{,}500$ and $\sigma = 5000$. Assume we are interested in the probability that tire mileage will exceed 40,000 miles.

Excel's NORM.DIST function can be used to compute cumulative probabilities for a normal distribution. The general form of the function is NORM.DIST(x, μ, σ, cumulative). For the fourth argument, TRUE is specified if a cumulative probability is desired. Thus, to compute the cumulative probability that the tire mileage will be less than or equal to 40,000 miles we would enter the following formula into any cell of an Excel worksheet:

$$=\text{NORM.DIST}(40000,36500,5000,\text{TRUE})$$

At this point, .7580 will appear in the cell where the formula was entered, indicating that the probability of tire mileage being less than or equal to 40,000 miles is .7580. Therefore, the probability that tire mileage will exceed 40,000 miles is $1 - .7580 = .2420$.

Excel's NORM.INV function uses an inverse computation to find the x value corresponding to a given cumulative probability. For instance, suppose we want to find the guaranteed mileage Grear should offer so that no more than 10% of the tires will be eligible for the guarantee. We would enter the following formula into any cell of an Excel worksheet:

$$=\text{NORM.INV}(.1,36500,5000)$$

At this point, 30092 will appear in the cell where the formula was entered, indicating that the probability of a tire lasting 30,092 miles or less is .10.

The Excel function for computing exponential probabilities is EXPON.DIST. This function requires three inputs: x, the value of the variable; lambda, which is $1/\mu$, and TRUE if you would like the cumulative probability. For example, consider an exponential probability distribution with mean $\mu = 15$. The probability that the exponential variable is less than or equal to 6 can be computed by the Excel formula

$$=\text{EXPON.DIST}(6,1/15,\text{TRUE})$$

If you need help inserting functions in a worksheet, Excel's Insert Function dialog box may be used. See Appendix E.

CHAPTER 7

Sampling and Sampling Distributions

CONTENTS

MEADWESTVACO CORPORATION*
STAMFORD, CONNECTICUT

MeadWestvaco Corporation, a leading producer of packaging, coated and specialty papers, and specialty chemicals, employs more than 17,000 people. It operates worldwide in 30 countries and serves customers located in approximately 100 countries. MeadWestvaco's internal consulting group uses sampling to provide a variety of information that enables the company to obtain significant productivity benefits and remain competitive.

For example, MeadWestvaco maintains large woodland holdings, which supply the trees, or raw material, for many of the company's products. Managers need reliable and accurate information about the timberlands and forests to evaluate the company's ability to meet its future raw material needs. What is the present volume in the forests? What is the past growth of the forests? What is the projected future growth of the forests? With answers to these important questions MeadWestvaco's managers can develop plans for the future, including long-term planting and harvesting schedules for the trees.

How does MeadWestvaco obtain the information it needs about its vast forest holdings? Data collected from sample plots throughout the forests are the basis for learning about the population of trees owned by the company. To identify the sample plots, the timberland holdings are first divided into three sections based on location and types of trees. Using maps and random numbers, MeadWestvaco analysts identify random samples of 1/5- to 1/7-acre plots in each section of the forest. MeadWestvaco foresters collect data from these sample plots to learn about the forest population.

*The authors are indebted to Dr. Edward P. Winkofsky for providing this Statistics in Practice.

Random sampling of its forest holdings enables MeadWestvaco Corporation to meet future raw material needs. © Robert Crum/Shutterstock.com.

Foresters throughout the organization participate in the field data collection process. Periodically, two-person teams gather information on each tree in every sample plot. The sample data are entered into the company's continuous forest inventory (CFI) computer system. Reports from the CFI system include a number of frequency distribution summaries containing statistics on types of trees, present forest volume, past forest growth rates, and projected future forest growth and volume. Sampling and the associated statistical summaries of the sample data provide the reports essential for the effective management of MeadWestvaco's forests and timberlands.

In this chapter you will learn about simple random sampling and the sample selection process. In addition, you will learn how statistics such as the sample mean and sample proportion are used to estimate the population mean and population proportion. The important concept of a sampling distribution is also introduced.

In Chapter 1, we presented the following definitions of an element, a population, and a sample.

- An *element* is the entity on which data are collected.
- A *population* is the collection of all the elements of interest.
- A *sample* is a subset of the population.

The reason we select a sample is to collect data to make an inference and answer research questions about a population.

Let us begin by citing two examples in which sampling was used to answer a research question about a population.

1. Members of a political party in Texas were considering supporting a particular candidate for election to the U.S. Senate, and party leaders wanted to estimate the proportion of registered voters in the state favoring the candidate. A sample of 400 registered voters in Texas was selected and 160 of the 400 voters indicated a preference for the candidate. Thus, an estimate of the proportion of the population of registered voters favoring the candidate is 160/400 = .40.

2. A tire manufacturer is considering producing a new tire designed to provide an increase in mileage over the firm's current line of tires. To estimate the mean useful life of the new tires, the manufacturer produced a sample of 120 tires for testing. The test results provided a sample mean of 36,500 miles. Hence, an estimate of the mean useful life for the population of new tires was 36,500 miles.

It is important to realize that sample results provide only *estimates* of the values of the corresponding population characteristics. We do not expect exactly .40, or 40%, of the population of registered voters to favor the candidate, nor do we expect the sample mean of 36,500 miles to exactly equal the mean mileage for the population of all new tires produced. The reason is simply that the sample contains only a portion of the population. Some sampling error is to be expected. With proper sampling methods, the sample results will provide "good" estimates of the population parameters. But how good can we expect the sample results to be? Fortunately, statistical procedures are available for answering this question.

A sample mean provides an estimate of a population mean, and a sample proportion provides an estimate of a population proportion. With estimates such as these, some estimation error can be expected. This chapter provides the basis for determining how large that error might be.

Let us define some of the terms used in sampling. The **sampled population** is the population from which the sample is drawn, and a **frame** is a list of the elements that the sample will be selected from. In the first example, the sampled population is all registered voters in Texas, and the frame is a list of all the registered voters. Because the number of registered voters in Texas is a finite number, the first example is an illustration of sampling from a finite population. In Section 7.2, we discuss how a simple random sample can be selected when sampling from a finite population.

The sampled population for the tire mileage example is more difficult to define because the sample of 120 tires was obtained from a production process at a particular point in time. We can think of the sampled population as the conceptual population of all the tires that could have been made by the production process at that particular point in time. In this sense the sampled population is considered infinite, making it impossible to construct a frame to draw the sample from. In Section 7.2, we discuss how to select a random sample in such a situation.

In this chapter, we show how simple random sampling can be used to select a sample from a finite population and describe how a random sample can be taken from an infinite population that is generated by an ongoing process. We then show how data obtained from a sample can be used to compute estimates of a population mean, a population standard deviation, and a population proportion. In addition, we introduce the important concept of a sampling distribution. As we will show, knowledge of the appropriate sampling distribution enables us to make statements about how close the sample estimates are to the corresponding population parameters. The last section discusses some alternatives to simple random sampling that are often employed in practice.

7.1   The Electronics Associates Sampling Problem

The director of personnel for Electronics Associates, Inc. (EAI), has been assigned the task of developing a profile of the company's 2500 employees. The characteristics to be identified include the mean annual salary for the employees and the proportion of employees having completed the company's management training program.

Using the 2500 employees as the population for this study, we can find the annual salary and the training program status for each individual by referring to the firm's personnel records. The data set containing this information for all 2500 employees in the population is in the file named EAI.

Using the EAI data and the formulas presented in Chapter 3, we computed the population mean and the population standard deviation for the annual salary data.

$$\text{Population mean:} \quad \mu = \$51{,}800$$
$$\text{Population standard deviation:} \quad \sigma = \$4{,}000$$

The data for the training program status show that 1500 of the 2500 employees completed the training program.

Numerical characteristics of a population are called **parameters**. Letting p denote the proportion of the population that completed the training program, we see that $p = 1500/2500 = .60$. The population mean annual salary ($\mu = \$51{,}800$), the population standard deviation of annual salary ($\sigma = \$4{,}000$), and the population proportion that completed the training program ($p = .60$) are parameters of the population of EAI employees.

Often the cost of collecting information from a sample is substantially less than from a population, especially when personal interviews must be conducted to collect the information.

Now, suppose that the necessary information on all the EAI employees was not readily available in the company's database. The question we now consider is how the firm's director of personnel can obtain estimates of the population parameters by using a sample of employees rather than all 2500 employees in the population. Suppose that a sample of 30 employees will be used. Clearly, the time and the cost of developing a profile would be substantially less for 30 employees than for the entire population. If the personnel director could be assured that a sample of 30 employees would provide adequate information about the population of 2500 employees, working with a sample would be preferable to working with the entire population. Let us explore the possibility of using a sample for the EAI study by first considering how we can identify a sample of 30 employees.

7.2 Selecting a Sample

In this section we describe how to select a sample. We first describe how to sample from a finite population and then describe how to select a sample from an infinite population.

Sampling from a Finite Population

Statisticians recommend selecting a probability sample when sampling from a finite population because a probability sample allows them to make valid statistical inferences about the population. The simplest type of probability sample is one in which each sample of size n has the same probability of being selected. It is called a simple random sample. A simple random sample of size n from a finite population of size N is defined as follows.

Other methods of probability sampling are described in Section 7.7.

> **SIMPLE RANDOM SAMPLE (FINITE POPULATION)**
>
> A **simple random sample** of size n from a finite population of size N is a sample selected such that each possible sample of size n has the same probability of being selected.

One procedure for selecting a simple random sample from a finite population is to use a table of random numbers to choose the elements for the sample one at a time in such a way that, at each step, each of the elements remaining in the population has the same probability of being selected. Sampling n elements in this way will satisfy the definition of a simple random sample from a finite population.

We describe how Excel, Minitab, and StatTools can be used to generate a simple random sample in the chapter appendices.

To select a simple random sample from the finite population of EAI employees, we first construct a frame by assigning each employee a number. For example, we can assign the employees the numbers 1 to 2500 in the order that their names appear in the EAI personnel

TABLE 7.1   RANDOM NUMBERS

63271	59986	71744	51102	15141	80714	58683	93108	13554	79945
88547	09896	95436	79115	08303	01041	20030	63754	08459	28364
55957	57243	83865	09911	19761	66535	40102	26646	60147	15702
46276	87453	44790	67122	45573	84358	21625	16999	13385	22782
55363	07449	34835	15290	76616	67191	12777	21861	68689	03263
69393	92785	49902	58447	42048	30378	87618	26933	40640	16281
13186	29431	88190	04588	38733	81290	89541	70290	40113	08243
17726	28652	56836	78351	47327	18518	92222	55201	27340	10493
36520	64465	05550	30157	82242	29520	69753	72602	23756	54935
81628	36100	39254	56835	37636	02421	98063	89641	64953	99337
84649	48968	75215	75498	49539	74240	03466	49292	36401	45525
63291	11618	12613	75055	43915	26488	41116	64531	56827	30825
70502	53225	03655	05915	37140	57051	48393	91322	25653	06543
06426	24771	59935	49801	11082	66762	94477	02494	88215	27191
20711	55609	29430	70165	45406	78484	31639	52009	18873	96927
41990	70538	77191	25860	55204	73417	83920	69468	74972	38712
72452	36618	76298	26678	89334	33938	95567	29380	75906	91807
37042	40318	57099	10528	09925	89773	41335	96244	29002	46453
53766	52875	15987	46962	67342	77592	57651	95508	80033	69828
90585	58955	53122	16025	84299	53310	67380	84249	25348	04332
32001	96293	37203	64516	51530	37069	40261	61374	05815	06714
62606	64324	46354	72157	67248	20135	49804	09226	64419	29457
10078	28073	85389	50324	14500	15562	64165	06125	71353	77669
91561	46145	24177	15294	10061	98124	75732	00815	83452	97355
13091	98112	53959	79607	52244	63303	10413	63839	74762	50289

© Cengage Learning

file. Next, we refer to the table of random numbers shown in Table 7.1. Using the first row of the table, each digit, 6, 3, 2, . . . , is a random digit having an equal chance of occurring. Because the largest number in the population list of EAI employees, 2500, has four digits, we will select random numbers from the table in sets or groups of four digits. Even though we may start the selection of random numbers anywhere in the table and move systematically in a direction of our choice, we will use the first row of Table 7.1 and move from left to right. The first 7 four-digit random numbers are

The random numbers in the table are shown in groups of five for readability.

$$6327 \quad 1599 \quad 8671 \quad 7445 \quad 1102 \quad 1514 \quad 1807$$

Because the numbers in the table are random, these four-digit numbers are equally likely.

We can now use these four-digit random numbers to give each employee in the population an equal chance of being included in the random sample. The first number, 6327, is greater than 2500. It does not correspond to one of the numbered employees in the population, and hence is discarded. The second number, 1599, is between 1 and 2500. Thus the first employee selected for the random sample is number 1599 on the list of EAI employees. Continuing this process, we ignore the numbers 8671 and 7445 before identifying employees number 1102, 1514, and 1807 to be included in the random sample. This process continues until the simple random sample of 30 EAI employees has been obtained.

In implementing this simple random sample selection process, it is possible that a random number used previously may appear again in the table before the complete sample of 30 EAI employees has been selected. Because we do not want to select a employee more than one time, any previously used random numbers are ignored because the corresponding employee is already included in the sample. Selecting a sample in this manner is referred to as **sampling without replacement**. If we selected a sample such that previously used random numbers are acceptable and specific employees could be included in the sample two or more times, we would be **sampling with replacement**. Sampling with replacement is a valid way of identifying a simple random sample. However, sampling without replacement is the sampling procedure used most often in practice. When we refer to simple random sampling, we will assume the sampling is without replacement.

Sampling from an Infinite Population

Sometimes we want to select a sample from a population, but the population is infinitely large or the elements of the population are being generated by an ongoing process for which there is no limit on the number of elements that can be generated. Thus, it is not possible to develop a list of all the elements in the population. This is considered the infinite population case. With an infinite population, we cannot select a simple random sample because we cannot construct a frame consisting of all the elements. In the infinite population case, statisticians recommend selecting what is called a random sample.

RANDOM SAMPLE (INFINITE POPULATION)

A **random sample** of size n from an infinite population is a sample selected such that the following conditions are satisfied.

1. Each element selected comes from the same population.
2. Each element is selected independently.

Care and judgment must be exercised in implementing the selection process for obtaining a random sample from an infinite population. Each case may require a different selection procedure. Let us consider two examples to see what we mean by the conditions (1) each element selected comes from the same population and (2) each element is selected independently.

A common quality control application involves a production process where there is no limit on the number of elements that can be produced. The conceptual population we are sampling from is all the elements that could be produced (not just the ones that are produced) by the ongoing production process. Because we cannot develop a list of all the elements that could be produced, the population is considered infinite. To be more specific, let us consider a production line designed to fill boxes of a breakfast cereal with a mean weight of 24 ounces of breakfast cereal per box. Samples of 12 boxes filled by this process are periodically selected by a quality control inspector to determine if the process is operating properly or if, perhaps, a machine malfunction has caused the process to begin underfilling or overfilling the boxes.

With a production operation such as this, the biggest concern in selecting a random sample is to make sure that condition 1, the sampled elements are selected from the same population, is satisfied. To ensure that this condition is satisfied, the boxes must be selected at approximately the same point in time. This way the inspector avoids the possibility of selecting some boxes when the process is operating properly and other boxes when the process is not operating properly and is underfilling or overfilling the boxes. With a production process such as this, the second condition, each element is selected independently, is satisfied by designing the production process so that each box of cereal is filled independently. With this assumption, the quality control inspector only needs to worry about satisfying the same population condition.

As another example of selecting a random sample from an infinite population, consider the population of customers arriving at a fast-food restaurant. Suppose an employee is asked to select and interview a sample of customers in order to develop a profile of customers who visit the restaurant. The customer arrival process is ongoing and there is no way to obtain a list of all customers in the population. So, for practical purposes, the population for this ongoing process is considered infinite. As long as a sampling procedure is designed so that all the elements in the sample are customers of the restaurant and they are selected independently, a random sample will be obtained. In this case, the employee collecting the sample needs to select the sample from people who come into the restaurant and make a purchase to ensure that the same population condition is satisfied. If, for instance, the employee selected someone for the sample who came into the restaurant just to use the restroom, that person would not be a customer and the same population condition would be violated. So, as long as the interviewer selects the sample from people making a purchase at the restaurant, condition 1 is satisfied. Ensuring that the customers are selected independently can be more difficult.

The purpose of the second condition of the random sample selection procedure (each element is selected independently) is to prevent selection bias. In this case, selection bias would occur if the interviewer were free to select customers for the sample arbitrarily. The interviewer might feel more comfortable selecting customers in a particular age group and might avoid customers in other age groups. Selection bias would also occur if the interviewer selected a group of five customers who entered the restaurant together and asked all of them to participate in the sample. Such a group of customers would be likely to exhibit similar characteristics, which might provide misleading information about the population of customers. Selection bias such as this can be avoided by ensuring that the selection of a particular customer does not influence the selection of any other customer. In other words, the elements (customers) are selected independently.

McDonald's, the fast-food restaurant leader, implemented a random sampling procedure for this situation. The sampling procedure was based on the fact that some customers presented discount coupons. Whenever a customer presented a discount coupon, the next customer served was asked to complete a customer profile questionnaire. Because arriving customers presented discount coupons randomly and independently of other customers, this sampling procedure ensured that customers were selected independently. As a result, the sample satisfied the requirements of a random sample from an infinite population.

Situations involving sampling from an infinite population are usually associated with a process that operates over time. Examples include parts being manufactured on a production line, repeated experimental trials in a laboratory, transactions occurring at a bank, telephone calls arriving at a technical support center, and customers entering a retail store. In each case, the situation may be viewed as a process that generates elements from an infinite population. As long as the sampled elements are selected from the same population and are selected independently, the sample is considered a random sample from an infinite population.

NOTES AND COMMENTS

1. In this section we have been careful to define two types of samples: a simple random sample from a finite population and a random sample from an infinite population. In the remainder of the text, we will generally refer to both of these as either a *random sample* or simply a *sample*. We will not make a distinction of the sample being a "simple" random sample unless it is necessary for the exercise or discussion.

2. Statisticians who specialize in sample surveys from finite populations use sampling methods that provide probability samples. With a probability sample, each possible sample has a known probability of selection and a random process is used to select the elements for the sample. Simple random sampling is one of these methods. In Section 7.7, we describe some other probability sampling methods: stratified random sampling, cluster sampling, and systematic sampling. We use the term "simple" in simple random sampling to clarify that this is the probability sampling method that assures each sample of size n has the same probability of being selected.

3. The number of different simple random samples of size n that can be selected from a finite population of size N is

$$\frac{N!}{n!(N-n)!}$$

In this formula, $N!$ and $n!$ are the factorial formulas discussed in Chapter 4. For the EAI problem with $N = 2500$ and $n = 30$, this expression can be used to show that approximately 2.75×10^{69} different simple random samples of 30 EAI employees can be obtained.

Exercises

Methods

1. Consider a finite population with five elements labeled A, B, C, D, and E. Ten possible simple random samples of size 2 can be selected.
   a. List the 10 samples beginning with AB, AC, and so on.
   b. Using simple random sampling, what is the probability that each sample of size 2 is selected?
   c. Assume random number 1 corresponds to A, random number 2 corresponds to B, and so on. List the simple random sample of size 2 that will be selected by using the random digits 8 0 5 7 5 3 2.

2. Assume a finite population has 350 elements. Using the last three digits of each of the following five-digit random numbers (e.g., 601, 022, 448, . . .), determine the first four elements that will be selected for the simple random sample.

   98601   73022   83448   02147   34229   27553   84147   93289   14209

Applications

3. *Fortune* publishes data on sales, profits, assets, stockholders' equity, market value, and earnings per share for the 500 largest U.S. industrial corporations (*Fortune* 500, 2012). Assume that you want to select a simple random sample of 10 corporations from the *Fortune* 500 list. Use the last three digits in column 9 of Table 7.1, beginning with 554. Read down the column and identify the numbers of the 10 corporations that would be selected.

4. The U.S. Golf Association is considering a ban on long and belly putters. This has caused a great deal of controversy among both amateur golfers and members of the Professional Golf Association (PGA) (*Golfweek,* October 26, 2012). Shown below are the names of the top 10 finishers in the recent PGA Tour McGladrey Classic golf tournament.

1. Tommy Gainey	6. Davis Love III
2. David Toms	7. Chad Campbell
3. Jim Furyk	8. Greg Owens
4. Brendon de Jonge	9. Charles Howell III
5. D. J. Trahan	10. Arjun Atwal

   a. Select a simple random sample of three of these players to assess their opinions on the use of long and belly putters. Use random numbers from column 2 of Table 7.1 to make your selection. Start with 59986 and use the last digit, 6, as the first player selected (Davis Love III). Continue down the column to select two more players.
   b. Using the information in the third item in the Notes and Comments section, determine how many different simple random samples of size 3 can be selected from the list of 10 players.

5. A student government organization is interested in estimating the proportion of students who favor a mandatory "pass-fail" grading policy for elective courses. A list of names and addresses of the 645 students enrolled during the current quarter is available from the registrar's office. Using three-digit random numbers in row 10 of Table 7.1 and moving across the row from left to right, identify the first 10 students who would be selected using simple random sampling. The three-digit random numbers begin with 816, 283, and 610.

6. The *County and City Data Book,* published by the Census Bureau, lists information on 3139 counties throughout the United States. Assume that a national study will collect data from 30 randomly selected counties. Use four-digit random numbers from the last column of Table 7.1 to identify the numbers corresponding to the first five counties selected for the sample. Ignore the first digits and begin with the four-digit random numbers 9945, 8364, 5702, and so on.

7. Assume that we want to identify a simple random sample of 12 of the 372 doctors practicing in a particular city. The doctors' names are available from a local medical organization. Use the eighth column of five-digit random numbers in Table 7.1 to identify the 12 doctors for the sample. Ignore the first two random digits in each five-digit grouping of the random numbers. This process begins with random number 108 and proceeds down the column of random numbers.

8. The following stocks make up the Dow Jones Industrial Average (*Barron's,* July 30, 2012).

1. 3M	11. Disney	21. McDonald's
2. AT&T	12. DuPont	22. Merck
3. Alcoa	13. ExxonMobil	23. Microsoft
4. American Express	14. General Electric	24. J.P. Morgan
5. Bank of America	15. Hewlett-Packard	25. Pfizer
6. Boeing	16. Home Depot	26. Procter & Gamble
7. Caterpillar	17. IBM	27. Travelers
8. Chevron	18. Intel	28. United Technologies
9. Cisco Systems	19. Johnson & Johnson	29. Verizon
10. Coca-Cola	20. Kraft Foods	30. Wal-Mart

Suppose you would like to select a sample of six of these companies to conduct an in-depth study of management practices. Use the first two digits in each row of the ninth column of Table 7.1 to select a simple random sample of six companies.

9. The Forbes 400 is a ranked list of the 400 richest people in America (*Forbes* website, March 4, 2013). Suppose that you would like to select a simple random sample of 10 of the 400 individuals for a follow-up study about their educational background. Use the fourth column of random numbers in Table 7.1, beginning with 51102, to select the simple random sample of 10 individuals. Begin with the person ranked 102 on the list and use the last three digits in each row of the fourth column to identify the sample. What are the rankings in the list for the 10 individuals selected for the sample?

10. Indicate which of the following situations involve sampling from a finite population and which involve sampling from an infinite population. In cases where the sampled population is finite, describe how you would construct a frame.
    a. Obtain a sample of licensed drivers in the state of New York.
    b. Obtain a sample of boxes of cereal produced by the Breakfast Choice company.
    c. Obtain a sample of cars crossing the Golden Gate Bridge on a typical weekday.
    d. Obtain a sample of students in a statistics course at Indiana University.
    e. Obtain a sample of the orders that are processed by a mail-order firm.

Point Estimation

Now that we have described how to select a simple random sample, let us return to the EAI problem. A simple random sample of 30 employees and the corresponding data on annual salary and management training program participation are as shown in Table 7.2. The notation x_1, x_2, and so on is used to denote the annual salary of the first employee in the sample, the annual salary of the second employee in the sample, and so on. Participation in the management training program is indicated by Yes in the management training program column.

To estimate the value of a population parameter, we compute a corresponding characteristic of the sample, referred to as a **sample statistic**. For example, to estimate the population mean μ and the population standard deviation σ for the annual salary of EAI

TABLE 7.2   ANNUAL SALARY AND TRAINING PROGRAM STATUS FOR A SIMPLE RANDOM SAMPLE OF 30 EAI EMPLOYEES

Annual Salary ($)	Management Training Program	Annual Salary ($)	Management Training Program
$x_1 = 49,094.30$	Yes	$x_{16} = 51,766.00$	Yes
$x_2 = 53,263.90$	Yes	$x_{17} = 52,541.30$	No
$x_3 = 49,643.50$	Yes	$x_{18} = 44,980.00$	Yes
$x_4 = 49,894.90$	Yes	$x_{19} = 51,932.60$	Yes
$x_5 = 47,621.60$	No	$x_{20} = 52,973.00$	Yes
$x_6 = 55,924.00$	Yes	$x_{21} = 45,120.90$	Yes
$x_7 = 49,092.30$	Yes	$x_{22} = 51,753.00$	Yes
$x_8 = 51,404.40$	Yes	$x_{23} = 54,391.80$	No
$x_9 = 50,957.70$	Yes	$x_{24} = 50,164.20$	No
$x_{10} = 55,109.70$	Yes	$x_{25} = 52,973.60$	No
$x_{11} = 45,922.60$	Yes	$x_{26} = 50,241.30$	No
$x_{12} = 57,268.40$	No	$x_{27} = 52,793.90$	No
$x_{13} = 55,688.80$	Yes	$x_{28} = 50,979.40$	Yes
$x_{14} = 51,564.70$	No	$x_{29} = 55,860.90$	Yes
$x_{15} = 56,188.20$	No	$x_{30} = 57,309.10$	No

employees, we use the data in Table 7.2 to calculate the corresponding sample statistics: the sample mean and the sample standard deviation s. Using the formulas for a sample mean and a sample standard deviation presented in Chapter 3, the sample mean is

$$\bar{x} = \frac{\Sigma x_i}{n} = \frac{1,554,420}{30} = \$51,814$$

and the sample standard deviation is

$$s = \sqrt{\frac{\Sigma(x_i - \bar{x})^2}{n-1}} = \sqrt{\frac{325,009,260}{29}} = \$3,348$$

To estimate p, the proportion of employees in the population who completed the management training program, we use the corresponding sample proportion $\bar{p}$. Let x denote the number of employees in the sample who completed the management training program. The data in Table 7.2 show that $x = 19$. Thus, with a sample size of $n = 30$, the sample proportion is

$$\bar{p} = \frac{x}{n} = \frac{19}{30} = .63$$

By making the preceding computations, we perform the statistical procedure called *point estimation*. We refer to the sample mean $\bar{x}$ as the **point estimator** of the population mean μ, the sample standard deviation s as the point estimator of the population standard deviation σ, and the sample proportion $\bar{p}$ as the point estimator of the population proportion p. The numerical value obtained for $\bar{x}$, s, or $\bar{p}$ is called the **point estimate**. Thus, for the simple random sample of 30 EAI employees shown in Table 7.2, $51,814 is the point estimate of μ, $3,348 is the point estimate of σ, and .63 is the point estimate of p. Table 7.3 summarizes the sample results and compares the point estimates to the actual values of the population parameters.

As is evident from Table 7.3, the point estimates differ somewhat from the corresponding population parameters. This difference is to be expected because a sample, and not a census of the entire population, is being used to develop the point estimates. In the next chapter, we will show how to construct an interval estimate in order to provide information about how close the point estimate is to the population parameter.

TABLE 7.3   SUMMARY OF POINT ESTIMATES OBTAINED FROM A SIMPLE RANDOM SAMPLE OF 30 EAI EMPLOYEES

Population Parameter	Parameter Value	Point Estimator	Point Estimate
μ = Population mean annual salary	$51,800	$\bar{x}$ = Sample mean annual salary	$51,814
σ = Population standard deviation for annual salary	$4,000	s = Sample standard deviation for annual salary	$3,348
p = Population proportion having completed the management training program	.60	$\bar{p}$ = Sample proportion having completed the management training program	.63

© Cengage Learning

Practical Advice

The subject matter of most of the rest of the book is concerned with statistical inference. Point estimation is a form of statistical inference. We use a sample statistic to make an inference about a population parameter. When making inferences about a population based on a sample, it is important to have a close correspondence between the sampled population and the target population. The **target population** is the population we want to make inferences about, while the sampled population is the population from which the sample is actually taken. In this section, we have described the process of drawing a simple random sample from the population of EAI employees and making point estimates of characteristics of that same population. So the sampled population and the target population are identical, which is the desired situation. But in other cases, it is not as easy to obtain a close correspondence between the sampled and target populations.

Consider the case of an amusement park selecting a sample of its customers to learn about characteristics such as age and time spent at the park. Suppose all the sample elements were selected on a day when park attendance was restricted to employees of a single company. Then the sampled population would be composed of employees of that company and members of their families. If the target population we wanted to make inferences about were typical park customers over a typical summer, then we might encounter a significant difference between the sampled population and the target population. In such a case, we would question the validity of the point estimates being made. Park management would be in the best position to know whether a sample taken on a particular day was likely to be representative of the target population.

In summary, whenever a sample is used to make inferences about a population, we should make sure that the study is designed so that the sampled population and the target population are in close agreement. Good judgment is a necessary ingredient of sound statistical practice.

Exercises

Methods

11. The following data are from a simple random sample.

$$5 \quad 8 \quad 10 \quad 7 \quad 10 \quad 14$$

   a. What is the point estimate of the population mean?
   b. What is the point estimate of the population standard deviation?

12. A survey question for a sample of 150 individuals yielded 75 Yes responses, 55 No responses, and 20 No Opinions.
   a. What is the point estimate of the proportion in the population who respond Yes?
   b. What is the point estimate of the proportion in the population who respond No?

Applications

13. A sample of 5 months of sales data provided the following information:

Month:	1	2	3	4	5
Units Sold:	94	100	85	94	92

   a. Develop a point estimate of the population mean number of units sold per month.
   b. Develop a point estimate of the population standard deviation.

Morningstar

14. Morningstar publishes ratings data on 1208 company stocks (Morningstar website, October 24, 2012). A sample of 40 of these stocks is contained in the data set Morningstar. Use the data set to answer the following questions.
   a. Develop a point estimate of the proportion of the stocks that receive Morningstar's highest rating of 5 Stars.
   b. Develop a point estimate of the proportion of the Morningstar stocks that are rated Above Average with respect to business risk.
   c. Develop a point estimate of the proportion of the Morningstar stocks that are rated 2 Stars or less.

15. The National Football League (NFL) polls fans to develop a rating for each football game (NFL website, October 24, 2012). Each game is rated on a scale from 0 (forgettable) to 100 (memorable). The fan ratings for a random sample of 12 games are shown.

57	61	86	74	72	73
20	57	80	79	83	74

   a. Develop a point estimate of mean fan rating for the population of NFL games.
   b. Develop a point estimate of the standard deviation for the population of NFL games.

16. A sample of 426 U.S. adults age 50 and older were asked how important a variety of issues were in choosing for whom to vote in the 2012 presidential election (*AARP Bulletin*, March 2012).
   a. What is the sampled population for this study?
   b. Social Security and Medicare was cited as "very important" by 350 respondents. Estimate the proportion of the population of U.S. adults age 50 and over who believe this issue is very important.
   c. Education was cited as "very important" by 74% of the respondents. Estimate the number of respondents who believe this issue is very important.
   d. Job Growth was cited as "very important" by 354 respondents. Estimate the proportion of U.S. adults age 50 and over who believe job growth is very important.
   e. What is the target population for the inferences being made in parts (b) and (d)? Is it the same as the sampled population you identified in part (a)? Suppose you later learn that the sample was restricted to members of the American Association of Retired People (AARP). Would you still feel the inferences being made in parts (b) and (d) are valid? Why or why not?

17. One of the questions in the Pew Internet & American Life Project asked adults if they used the Internet, at least occasionally (Pew website, October 23, 2012). The results showed that 454 out of 478 adults aged 18–29 answered yes; 741 out of 833 adults aged 30–49 answered yes; and 1058 out of 1644 adults aged 50 and over answered yes.
   a. Develop a point estimate of the proportion of adults aged 18–29 who use the Internet.
   b. Develop a point estimate of the proportion of adults aged 30–49 who use the Internet.
   c. Develop a point estimate of the proportion of adults aged 50 and over who use the Internet.
   d. Comment on any relationship between age and Internet use that seems apparent.
   e. Suppose your target population of interest is that of all adults (18 years of age and over). Develop an estimate of the proportion of that population who use the Internet.

7.4 Introduction to Sampling Distributions

In the preceding section we said that the sample mean $\bar{x}$ is the point estimator of the population mean μ, and the sample proportion $\bar{p}$ is the point estimator of the population proportion p. For the simple random sample of 30 EAI employees shown in Table 7.2, the point estimate of μ is $\bar{x} = \$51,814$ and the point estimate of p is $\bar{p} = .63$. Suppose we select another simple random sample of 30 EAI employees and obtain the following point estimates:

Sample mean: $\bar{x} = \$52,670$

Sample proportion: $\bar{p} = .70$

Note that different values of $\bar{x}$ and $\bar{p}$ were obtained. Indeed, a second simple random sample of 30 EAI employees cannot be expected to provide the same point estimates as the first sample.

The ability to understand the material in subsequent chapters depends heavily on the ability to understand and use the sampling distributions presented in this chapter.

Now, suppose we repeat the process of selecting a simple random sample of 30 EAI employees over and over again, each time computing the values of $\bar{x}$ and $\bar{p}$. Table 7.4 contains a portion of the results obtained for 500 simple random samples, and Table 7.5 shows the frequency and relative frequency distributions for the 500 $\bar{x}$ values. Figure 7.1 shows the relative frequency histogram for the $\bar{x}$ values.

In Chapter 5 we defined a random variable as a numerical description of the outcome of an experiment. If we consider the process of selecting a simple random sample as an

TABLE 7.4 VALUES OF $\bar{x}$ AND $\bar{p}$ FROM 500 SIMPLE RANDOM SAMPLES OF 30 EAI EMPLOYEES

Sample Number	Sample Mean ($\bar{x}$)	Sample Proportion ($\bar{p}$)
1	51,814	.63
2	52,670	.70
3	51,780	.67
4	51,588	.53
.	.	.
.	.	.
.	.	.
500	51,752	.50

© Cengage Learning

TABLE 7.5 FREQUENCY AND RELATIVE FREQUENCY DISTRIBUTIONS OF $\bar{x}$ FROM 500 SIMPLE RANDOM SAMPLES OF 30 EAI EMPLOYEES

Mean Annual Salary ($)	Frequency	Relative Frequency
49,500.00–49,999.99	2	.004
50,000.00–50,499.99	16	.032
50,500.00–50,999.99	52	.104
51,000.00–51,499.99	101	.202
51,500.00–51,999.99	133	.266
52,000.00–52,499.99	110	.220
52,500.00–52,999.99	54	.108
53,000.00–53,499.99	26	.052
53,500.00–53,999.99	6	.012
Totals	500	1.000

© Cengage Learning

FIGURE 7.1   RELATIVE FREQUENCY HISTOGRAM OF $\bar{x}$ VALUES FROM 500 SIMPLE
RANDOM SAMPLES OF SIZE 30 EACH

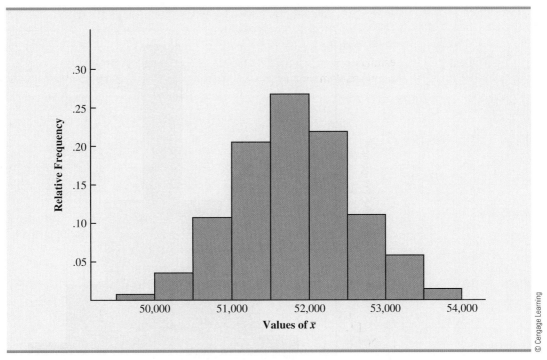

experiment, the sample mean $\bar{x}$ is the numerical description of the outcome of the experiment. Thus, the sample mean $\bar{x}$ is a random variable. As a result, just like other random variables, $\bar{x}$ has a mean or expected value, a standard deviation, and a probability distribution. Because the various possible values of $\bar{x}$ are the result of different simple random samples, the probability distribution of $\bar{x}$ is called the **sampling distribution** of $\bar{x}$. Knowledge of this sampling distribution and its properties will enable us to make probability statements about how close the sample mean $\bar{x}$ is to the population mean μ.

Let us return to Figure 7.1. We would need to enumerate every possible sample of 30 employees and compute each sample mean to completely determine the sampling distribution of $\bar{x}$. However, the histogram of 500 $\bar{x}$ values gives an approximation of this sampling distribution. From the approximation we observe the bell-shaped appearance of the distribution. We note that the largest concentration of the $\bar{x}$ values and the mean of the 500 $\bar{x}$ values is near the population mean $\mu = \$51,800$. We will describe the properties of the sampling distribution of $\bar{x}$ more fully in the next section.

The 500 values of the sample proportion $\bar{p}$ are summarized by the relative frequency histogram in Figure 7.2. As in the case of $\bar{x}$, $\bar{p}$ is a random variable. If every possible sample of size 30 were selected from the population and if a value of $\bar{p}$ were computed for each sample, the resulting probability distribution would be the sampling distribution of $\bar{p}$. The relative frequency histogram of the 500 sample values in Figure 7.2 provides a general idea of the appearance of the sampling distribution of $\bar{p}$.

In practice, we select only one simple random sample from the population. We repeated the sampling process 500 times in this section simply to illustrate that many different samples are possible and that the different samples generate a variety of values for the sample statistics $\bar{x}$ and $\bar{p}$. The probability distribution of any particular sample statistic is called the sampling distribution of the statistic. In Section 7.5 we show the characteristics of the sampling distribution of $\bar{x}$. In Section 7.6 we show the characteristics of the sampling distribution of $\bar{p}$.

FIGURE 7.2   RELATIVE FREQUENCY HISTOGRAM OF $\bar{p}$ VALUES FROM 500 SIMPLE RANDOM SAMPLES OF SIZE 30 EACH

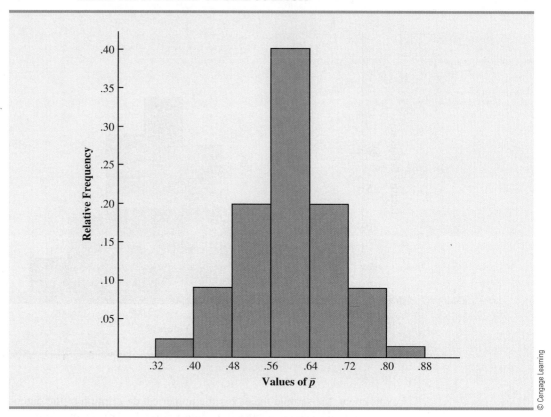

7.5 Sampling Distribution of $\bar{x}$

In the previous section we said that the sample mean $\bar{x}$ is a random variable and its probability distribution is called the sampling distribution of $\bar{x}$.

> **SAMPLING DISTRIBUTION OF $\bar{x}$**
>
> The sampling distribution of $\bar{x}$ is the probability distribution of all possible values of the sample mean $\bar{x}$.

This section describes the properties of the sampling distribution of $\bar{x}$. Just as with other probability distributions we studied, the sampling distribution of $\bar{x}$ has an expected value or mean, a standard deviation, and a characteristic shape or form. Let us begin by considering the mean of all possible $\bar{x}$ values, which is referred to as the expected value of $\bar{x}$.

Expected Value of $\bar{x}$

In the EAI sampling problem we saw that different simple random samples result in a variety of values for the sample mean $\bar{x}$. Because many different values of the random variable $\bar{x}$ are possible, we are often interested in the mean of all possible values of $\bar{x}$ that can be generated by the various simple random samples. The mean of the $\bar{x}$ random variable is the expected value of $\bar{x}$. Let $E(\bar{x})$ represent the expected value of $\bar{x}$ and μ represent the mean of the population from which we are selecting a simple random sample. It can be shown that with simple random sampling, $E(\bar{x})$ and μ are equal.

EXPECTED VALUE OF $\bar{x}$

The expected value of $\bar{x}$ equals the mean of the population from which the sample is selected.

$$E(\bar{x}) = \mu \tag{7.1}$$

where

$$E(\bar{x}) = \text{the expected value of } \bar{x}$$
$$\mu = \text{the population mean}$$

This result shows that with simple random sampling, the expected value or mean of the sampling distribution of $\bar{x}$ is equal to the mean of the population. In Section 7.1 we saw that the mean annual salary for the population of EAI employees is $\mu = \$51{,}800$. Thus, according to equation (7.1), the mean of all possible sample means for the EAI study is also $\$51{,}800$.

When the expected value of a point estimator equals the population parameter, we say the point estimator is **unbiased**. Thus, equation (7.1) shows that $\bar{x}$ is an unbiased estimator of the population mean μ.

Standard Deviation of $\bar{x}$

Let us define the standard deviation of the sampling distribution of $\bar{x}$. We will use the following notation.

$$\sigma_{\bar{x}} = \text{the standard deviation of } \bar{x}$$
$$\sigma = \text{the standard deviation of the population}$$
$$n = \text{the sample size}$$
$$N = \text{the population size}$$

It can be shown that the formula for the standard deviation of $\bar{x}$ depends on whether the population is finite or infinite. The two formulas for the standard deviation of $\bar{x}$ follow.

STANDARD DEVIATION OF $\bar{x}$

Finite Population   *Infinite Population*

$$\sigma_{\bar{x}} = \sqrt{\frac{N-n}{N-1}}\left(\frac{\sigma}{\sqrt{n}}\right) \qquad\qquad \sigma_{\bar{x}} = \frac{\sigma}{\sqrt{n}} \tag{7.2}$$

In comparing the two formulas in (7.2), we see that the factor $\sqrt{(N-n)/(N-1)}$ is required for the finite population case but not for the infinite population case. This factor is commonly referred to as the **finite population correction factor**. In many practical sampling situations, we find that the population involved, although finite, is "large," whereas the sample size is relatively "small." In such cases the finite population correction factor $\sqrt{(N-n)/(N-1)}$ is close to 1. As a result, the difference between the values of the standard deviation of $\bar{x}$ for the finite and infinite population cases becomes negligible. Then, $\sigma_{\bar{x}} = \sigma/\sqrt{n}$ becomes a good approximation to the standard deviation of $\bar{x}$ even though the population is finite. This observation leads to the following general guideline, or rule of thumb, for computing the standard deviation of $\bar{x}$.

USE THE FOLLOWING EXPRESSION TO COMPUTE THE STANDARD DEVIATION OF $\bar{x}$

$$\sigma_{\bar{x}} = \frac{\sigma}{\sqrt{n}} \tag{7.3}$$

whenever

1. The population is infinite; or
2. The population is finite *and* the sample size is less than or equal to 5% of the population size; that is, $n/N \leq .05$.

Problem 21 shows that when $n/N \leq .05$, the finite population correction factor has little effect on the value of $\sigma_{\bar{x}}$.

In cases where $n/N > .05$, the finite population version of formula (7.2) should be used in the computation of $\sigma_{\bar{x}}$. Unless otherwise noted, throughout the text we will assume that the population size is "large," $n/N \leq .05$, and expression (7.3) can be used to compute $\sigma_{\bar{x}}$.

To compute $\sigma_{\bar{x}}$, we need to know σ, the standard deviation of the population. To further emphasize the difference between $\sigma_{\bar{x}}$ and σ, we refer to the standard deviation of $\bar{x}$, $\sigma_{\bar{x}}$, as the **standard error** of the mean. In general, the term *standard error* refers to the standard deviation of a point estimator. Later we will see that the value of the standard error of the mean is helpful in determining how far the sample mean may be from the population mean. Let us now return to the EAI example and compute the standard error of the mean associated with simple random samples of 30 EAI employees.

The term standard error is used throughout statistical inference to refer to the standard deviation of a point estimator.

In Section 7.1 we saw that the standard deviation of annual salary for the population of 2500 EAI employees is $\sigma = 4000$. In this case, the population is finite, with $N = 2500$. However, with a sample size of 30, we have $n/N = 30/2500 = .012$. Because the sample size is less than 5% of the population size, we can ignore the finite population correction factor and use equation (7.3) to compute the standard error.

$$\sigma_{\bar{x}} = \frac{\sigma}{\sqrt{n}} = \frac{4000}{\sqrt{30}} = 730.3$$

Form of the Sampling Distribution of $\bar{x}$

The preceding results concerning the expected value and standard deviation for the sampling distribution of $\bar{x}$ are applicable for any population. The final step in identifying the characteristics of the sampling distribution of $\bar{x}$ is to determine the form or shape of the sampling distribution. We will consider two cases: (1) The population has a normal distribution; and (2) the population does not have a normal distribution.

Population has a normal distribution. In many situations it is reasonable to assume that the population from which we are selecting a random sample has a normal, or nearly normal, distribution. When the population has a normal distribution, the sampling distribution of $\bar{x}$ is normally distributed for any sample size.

Population does not have a normal distribution. When the population from which we are selecting a random sample does not have a normal distribution, the **central limit theorem** is helpful in identifying the shape of the sampling distribution of $\bar{x}$. A statement of the central limit theorem as it applies to the sampling distribution of $\bar{x}$ follows.

CENTRAL LIMIT THEOREM

In selecting random samples of size n from a population, the sampling distribution of the sample mean $\bar{x}$ can be approximated by a *normal distribution* as the sample size becomes large.

Figure 7.3 shows how the central limit theorem works for three different populations; each column refers to one of the populations. The top panel of the figure shows that none of the populations are normally distributed. Population I follows a uniform distribution. Population II is often called the rabbit-eared distribution. It is symmetric, but the more likely

FIGURE 7.3   ILLUSTRATION OF THE CENTRAL LIMIT THEOREM FOR THREE POPULATIONS

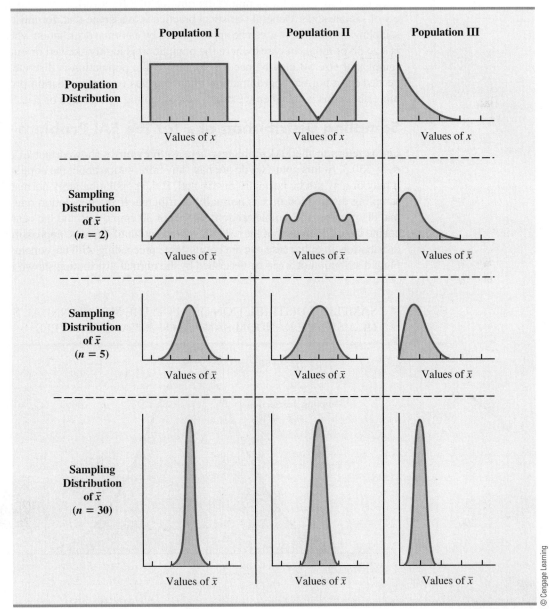

© Cengage Learning

values fall in the tails of the distribution. Population III is shaped like the exponential distribution; it is skewed to the right.

The bottom three panels of Figure 7.3 show the shape of the sampling distribution for samples of size $n = 2$, $n = 5$, and $n = 30$. When the sample size is 2, we see that the shape of each sampling distribution is different from the shape of the corresponding population distribution. For samples of size 5, we see that the shapes of the sampling distributions for populations I and II begin to look similar to the shape of a normal distribution. Even though the shape of the sampling distribution for population III begins to look similar to the shape of a normal distribution, some skewness to the right is still present. Finally, for samples of size 30, the shapes of each of the three sampling distributions are approximately normal.

From a practitioner standpoint, we often want to know how large the sample size needs to be before the central limit theorem applies and we can assume that the shape of the sampling distribution is approximately normal. Statistical researchers have investigated this question by studying the sampling distribution of $\bar{x}$ for a variety of populations and a variety of sample sizes. General statistical practice is to assume that, for most applications, the sampling distribution of $\bar{x}$ can be approximated by a normal distribution whenever the sample is size 30 or more. In cases where the population is highly skewed or outliers are present, samples of size 50 may be needed. Finally, if the population is discrete, the sample size needed for a normal approximation often depends on the population proportion. We say more about this issue when we discuss the sampling distribution of $\bar{p}$ in Section 7.6.

Sampling Distribution of $\bar{x}$ for the EAI Problem

Let us return to the EAI problem where we previously showed that $E(\bar{x}) = \$51,800$ and $\sigma_{\bar{x}} = 730.3$. At this point, we do not have any information about the population distribution; it may or may not be normally distributed. If the population has a normal distribution, the sampling distribution of $\bar{x}$ is normally distributed. If the population does not have a normal distribution, the simple random sample of 30 employees and the central limit theorem enable us to conclude that the sampling distribution of $\bar{x}$ can be approximated by a normal distribution. In either case, we are comfortable proceeding with the conclusion that the sampling distribution of $\bar{x}$ can be described by the normal distribution shown in Figure 7.4.

FIGURE 7.4   SAMPLING DISTRIBUTION OF $\bar{x}$ FOR THE MEAN ANNUAL SALARY OF A SIMPLE RANDOM SAMPLE OF 30 EAI EMPLOYEES

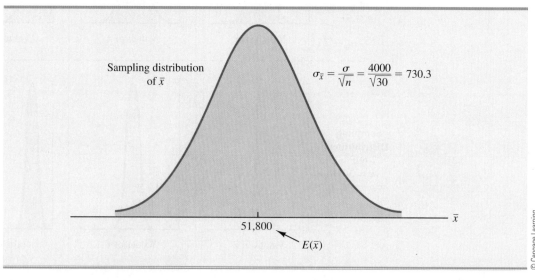

Sampling distribution of $\bar{x}$

$$\sigma_{\bar{x}} = \frac{\sigma}{\sqrt{n}} = \frac{4000}{\sqrt{30}} = 730.3$$

51,800

$E(\bar{x})$

Practical Value of the Sampling Distribution of $\bar{x}$

Whenever a simple random sample is selected and the value of the sample mean is used to estimate the value of the population mean μ, we cannot expect the sample mean to exactly equal the population mean. The practical reason we are interested in the sampling distribution of $\bar{x}$ is that it can be used to provide probability information about the difference between the sample mean and the population mean. To demonstrate this use, let us return to the EAI problem.

Suppose the personnel director believes the sample mean will be an acceptable estimate of the population mean if the sample mean is within $500 of the population mean. However, it is not possible to guarantee that the sample mean will be within $500 of the population mean. Indeed, Table 7.5 and Figure 7.1 show that some of the 500 sample means differed by more than $2,000 from the population mean. So we must think of the personnel director's request in probability terms. That is, the personnel director is concerned with the following question: What is the probability that the sample mean computed using a simple random sample of 30 EAI employees will be within $500 of the population mean?

Because we have identified the properties of the sampling distribution of $\bar{x}$ (see Figure 7.4), we will use this distribution to answer the probability question. Refer to the sampling distribution of $\bar{x}$ shown again in Figure 7.5. With a population mean of $51,800, the personnel director wants to know the probability that $\bar{x}$ is between $51,300 and $52,300. This probability is given by the darkly shaded area of the sampling distribution shown in Figure 7.5. Because the sampling distribution is normally distributed, with mean 51,800 and standard error of the mean 730.3, we can use the standard normal probability table to find the area or probability.

We first calculate the z value at the upper endpoint of the interval (52,300) and use the table to find the area under the curve to the left of that point (left tail area). Then we compute the z value at the lower endpoint of the interval (51,300) and use the table to find the area under the curve to the left of that point (another left tail area). Subtracting the second tail area from the first gives us the desired probability.

At $\bar{x} = 52,300$, we have

$$z = \frac{52,300 - 51,800}{730.30} = .68$$

FIGURE 7.5   PROBABILITY OF A SAMPLE MEAN BEING WITHIN $500 OF THE POPULATION MEAN FOR A SIMPLE RANDOM SAMPLE OF 30 EAI EMPLOYEES

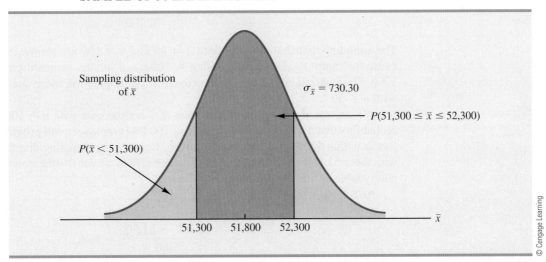

Referring to the standard normal probability table, we find a cumulative probability (area to the left of $z = .68$) of .7517.

At $\bar{x} = 51,300$, we have

$$z = \frac{51,300 - 51,800}{730.30} = -.68$$

The area under the curve to the left of $z = -.68$ is .2483. Therefore, $P(51,300 \leq \bar{x} \leq 52,300) = P(z \leq .68) - P(z < -.68) = .7517 - .2483 = .5034$.

The sampling distribution of $\bar{x}$ can be used to provide probability information about how close the sample mean $\bar{x}$ is to the population mean μ.

The preceding computations show that a simple random sample of 30 EAI employees has a .5034 probability of providing a sample mean $\bar{x}$ that is within \$500 of the population mean. Thus, there is a $1 - .5034 = .4966$ probability that the difference between $\bar{x}$ and $\mu = \$51,800$ will be more than \$500. In other words, a simple random sample of 30 EAI employees has roughly a 50–50 chance of providing a sample mean within the allowable \$500. Perhaps a larger sample size should be considered. Let us explore this possibility by considering the relationship between the sample size and the sampling distribution of $\bar{x}$.

Relationship Between the Sample Size and the Sampling Distribution of $\bar{x}$

Suppose that in the EAI sampling problem we select a simple random sample of 100 EAI employees instead of the 30 originally considered. Intuitively, it would seem that with more data provided by the larger sample size, the sample mean based on $n = 100$ should provide a better estimate of the population mean than the sample mean based on $n = 30$. To see how much better, let us consider the relationship between the sample size and the sampling distribution of $\bar{x}$.

First note that $E(\bar{x}) = \mu$ regardless of the sample size. Thus, the mean of all possible values of $\bar{x}$ is equal to the population mean μ regardless of the sample size n. However, note that the standard error of the mean, $\sigma_{\bar{x}} = \sigma/\sqrt{n}$, is related to the square root of the sample size. Whenever the sample size is increased, the standard error of the mean $\sigma_{\bar{x}}$ decreases. With $n = 30$, the standard error of the mean for the EAI problem is 730.3. However, with the increase in the sample size to $n = 100$, the standard error of the mean is decreased to

$$\sigma_{\bar{x}} = \frac{\sigma}{\sqrt{n}} = \frac{4000}{\sqrt{100}} = 400$$

The sampling distributions of $\bar{x}$ with $n = 30$ and $n = 100$ are shown in Figure 7.6. Because the sampling distribution with $n = 100$ has a smaller standard error, the values of $\bar{x}$ have less variation and tend to be closer to the population mean than the values of $\bar{x}$ with $n = 30$.

We can use the sampling distribution of $\bar{x}$ for the case with $n = 100$ to compute the probability that a simple random sample of 100 EAI employees will provide a sample mean that is within \$500 of the population mean. Because the sampling distribution is normal, with mean 51,800 and standard error of the mean 400, we can use the standard normal probability table to find the area or probability.

At $\bar{x} = 52,300$ (see Figure 7.7), we have

$$z = \frac{52,300 - 51,800}{400} = 1.25$$

FIGURE 7.6 A COMPARISON OF THE SAMPLING DISTRIBUTIONS OF $\bar{x}$ FOR SIMPLE RANDOM SAMPLES OF $n = 30$ AND $n = 100$ EAI EMPLOYEES

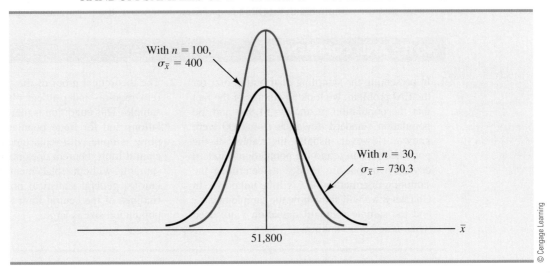

With $n = 100$,
$\sigma_{\bar{x}} = 400$

With $n = 30$,
$\sigma_{\bar{x}} = 730.3$

51,800

$\bar{x}$

© Cengage Learning

Referring to the standard normal probability table, we find a cumulative probability corresponding to $z = 1.25$ of .8944.

At $\bar{x} = 51,300$, we have

$$z = \frac{51,300 - 51,800}{400} = -1.25$$

The cumulative probability corresponding to $z = -1.25$ is .1056. Therefore, $P(51,300 \leq \bar{x} \leq 52,300) = P(z \leq 1.25) - P(z \leq -1.25) = .8944 - .1056 = .7888$. Thus, by increasing the sample size from 30 to 100 EAI employees, we increase the probability of obtaining a sample mean within \$500 of the population mean from .5034 to .7888.

FIGURE 7.7 PROBABILITY OF A SAMPLE MEAN BEING WITHIN \$500 OF THE POPULATION MEAN FOR A SIMPLE RANDOM SAMPLE OF 100 EAI EMPLOYEES

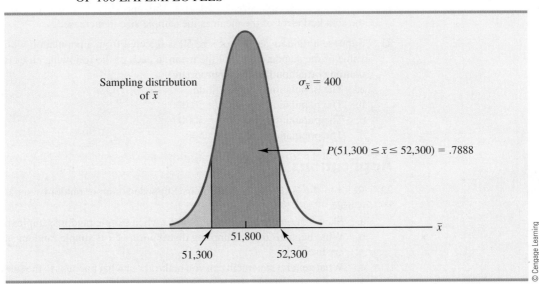

Sampling distribution of $\bar{x}$

$\sigma_{\bar{x}} = 400$

$P(51,300 \leq \bar{x} \leq 52,300) = .7888$

51,800

$\bar{x}$

51,300   52,300

© Cengage Learning

The important point in this discussion is that as the sample size is increased, the standard error of the mean decreases. As a result, the larger sample size provides a higher probability that the sample mean is within a specified distance of the population mean.

NOTES AND COMMENTS

1. In presenting the sampling distribution of $\bar{x}$ for the EAI problem, we took advantage of the fact that the population mean $\mu = 51{,}800$ and the population standard deviation $\sigma = 4000$ were known. However, usually the values of the population mean μ and the population standard deviation σ that are needed to determine the sampling distribution of $\bar{x}$ will be unknown. In Chapter 8 we will show how the sample mean $\bar{x}$ and the sample standard deviation s are used when μ and σ are unknown.

2. The theoretical proof of the central limit theorem requires independent observations in the sample. This condition is met for infinite populations and for finite populations where sampling is done with replacement. Although the central limit theorem does not directly address sampling without replacement from finite populations, general statistical practice applies the findings of the central limit theorem when the population size is large.

Exercises

Methods

18. A population has a mean of 200 and a standard deviation of 50. A sample of size 100 will be taken and the sample mean $\bar{x}$ will be used to estimate the population mean.
    a. What is the expected value of $\bar{x}$?
    b. What is the standard deviation of $\bar{x}$?
    c. Show the sampling distribution of $\bar{x}$.
    d. What does the sampling distribution of $\bar{x}$ show?

19. A population has a mean of 200 and a standard deviation of 50. Suppose a sample of size 100 is selected and $\bar{x}$ is used to estimate μ.
    a. What is the probability that the sample mean will be within ± 5 of the population mean?
    b. What is the probability that the sample mean will be within ± 10 of the population mean?

20. Assume the population standard deviation is $\sigma = 25$. Compute the standard error of the mean, $\sigma_{\bar{x}}$, for sample sizes of 50, 100, 150, and 200. What can you say about the size of the standard error of the mean as the sample size is increased?

21. Suppose a random sample of size 50 is selected from a population with $\sigma = 10$. Find the value of the standard error of the mean in each of the following cases (use the finite population correction factor if appropriate).
    a. The population size is infinite.
    b. The population size is $N = 50{,}000$.
    c. The population size is $N = 5000$.
    d. The population size is $N = 500$.

Applications

22. Refer to the EAI sampling problem. Suppose a simple random sample of 60 employees is used.
    a. Sketch the sampling distribution of $\bar{x}$ when simple random samples of size 60 are used.
    b. What happens to the sampling distribution of $\bar{x}$ if simple random samples of size 120 are used?
    c. What general statement can you make about what happens to the sampling distribution of $\bar{x}$ as the sample size is increased? Does this generalization seem logical? Explain.

23. In the EAI sampling problem (see Figure 7.5), we showed that for $n = 30$, there was .5034 probability of obtaining a sample mean within $\pm\$500$ of the population mean.
    a. What is the probability that $\bar{x}$ is within \$500 of the population mean if a sample of size 60 is used?
    b. Answer part (a) for a sample of size 120.

24. *Barron's* reported that the average number of weeks an individual is unemployed is 17.5 weeks (*Barron's*, February 18, 2008). Assume that for the population of all unemployed individuals the population mean length of unemployment is 17.5 weeks and that the population standard deviation is 4 weeks. Suppose you would like to select a sample of 50 unemployed individuals for a follow-up study.
    a. Show the sampling distribution of $\bar{x}$, the sample mean average for a sample of 50 unemployed individuals.
    b. What is the probability that a simple random sample of 50 unemployed individuals will provide a sample mean within 1 week of the population mean?
    c. What is the probability that a simple random sample of 50 unemployed individuals will provide a sample mean within 1/2 week of the population mean?

25. The College Board reported the following mean scores for the three parts of the SAT (*The World Almanac*, 2009):

Critical Reading	502
Mathematics	515
Writing	494

    Assume that the population standard deviation on each part of the test is $\sigma = 100$.
    a. What is the probability a sample of 90 test takers will provide a sample mean test score within 10 points of the population mean of 502 on the Critical Reading part of the test?
    b. What is the probability a sample of 90 test takers will provide a sample mean test score within 10 points of the population mean of 515 on the Mathematics part of the test? Compare this probability to the value computed in part (a).
    c. What is the probability a sample of 100 test takers will provide a sample mean test score within 10 of the population mean of 494 on the writing part of the test? Comment on the differences between this probability and the values computed in parts (a) and (b).

26. For the year 2010, 33% of taxpayers with adjusted gross incomes between \$30,000 and \$60,000 itemized deductions on their federal income tax return (*The Wall Street Journal*, October 25, 2012). The mean amount of deductions for this population of taxpayers was \$16,642. Assume the standard deviation is $\sigma = \$2,400$.
    a. What is the probability that a sample of taxpayers from this income group who have itemized deductions will show a sample mean within \$200 of the population mean for each of the following sample sizes: 30, 50, 100, and 400?
    b. What is the advantage of a larger sample size when attempting to estimate the population mean?

27. The Economic Policy Institute periodically issues reports on wages of entry-level workers. The institute reported that entry-level wages for male college graduates were \$21.68 per hour and for female college graduates were \$18.80 per hour in 2011 (Economic Policy Institute website, March 30, 2012). Assume the standard deviation for male graduates is \$2.30, and for female graduates it is \$2.05.
    a. What is the probability that a sample of 50 male graduates will provide a sample mean within \$.50 of the population mean, \$21.68?
    b. What is the probability that a sample of 50 female graduates will provide a sample mean within \$.50 of the population mean, \$18.80?
    c. In which of the preceding two cases, part (a) or part (b), do we have a higher probability of obtaining a sample estimate within \$.50 of the population mean? Why?
    d. What is the probability that a sample of 120 female graduates will provide a sample mean more than \$.30 below the population mean?

28. The state of California has a mean annual rainfall of 22 inches, whereas the state of New York has a mean annual rainfall of 42 inches (Current Results website, October 27, 2012). Assume that the standard deviation for both states is 4 inches. A sample of 30 years of rainfall for California and a sample of 45 years of rainfall for New York has been taken.
    a. Show the probability distribution of the sample mean annual rainfall for California.
    b. What is the probability that the sample mean is within 1 inch of the population mean for California?
    c. What is the probability that the sample mean is within 1 inch of the population mean for New York?
    d. In which case, part (b) or (c), is the probability of obtaining a sample mean within 1 inch of the population mean greater? Why?

29. The mean preparation fee H&R Block charged retail customers last year was $183 (*The Wall Street Journal,* March 7, 2012). Use this price as the population mean and assume the population standard deviation of preparation fees is $50.
    a. What is the probability that the mean price for a sample of 30 H&R Block retail customers is within $8 of the population mean?
    b. What is the probability that the mean price for a sample of 50 H&R Block retail customers is within $8 of the population mean?
    c. What is the probability that the mean price for a sample of 100 H&R Block retail customers is within $8 of the population mean?
    d. Which, if any, of the sample sizes in parts (a), (b), and (c) would you recommend to have at least a .95 probability that the sample mean is within $8 of the population mean?

30. To estimate the mean age for a population of 4000 employees, a simple random sample of 40 employees is selected.
    a. Would you use the finite population correction factor in calculating the standard error of the mean? Explain.
    b. If the population standard deviation is $\sigma = 8.2$ years, compute the standard error both with and without the finite population correction factor. What is the rationale for ignoring the finite population correction factor whenever $n/N \leq .05$?
    c. What is the probability that the sample mean age of the employees will be within ± 2 years of the population mean age?

7.6 Sampling Distribution of $\bar{p}$

The sample proportion $\bar{p}$ is the point estimator of the population proportion p. The formula for computing the sample proportion is

$$\bar{p} = \frac{x}{n}$$

where

    x = the number of elements in the sample that possess the characteristic of interest
    n = sample size

As noted in Section 7.4, the sample proportion $\bar{p}$ is a random variable and its probability distribution is called the sampling distribution of $\bar{p}$.

> **SAMPLING DISTRIBUTION OF $\bar{p}$**
>
> The sampling distribution of $\bar{p}$ is the probability distribution of all possible values of the sample proportion $\bar{p}$.

To determine how close the sample proportion $\bar{p}$ is to the population proportion p, we need to understand the properties of the sampling distribution of $\bar{p}$: the expected value of $\bar{p}$, the standard deviation of $\bar{p}$, and the shape or form of the sampling distribution of $\bar{p}$.

Expected Value of $\bar{p}$

The expected value of $\bar{p}$, the mean of all possible values of $\bar{p}$, is equal to the population proportion p.

EXPECTED VALUE OF $\bar{p}$

$$E(\bar{p}) = p \qquad (7.4)$$

where

$$E(\bar{p}) = \text{the expected value of } \bar{p}$$
$$p = \text{the population proportion}$$

Because $E(\bar{p}) = p$, $\bar{p}$ is an unbiased estimator of p. Recall from Section 7.1 we noted that $p = .60$ for the EAI population, where p is the proportion of the population of employees who participated in the company's management training program. Thus, the expected value of $\bar{p}$ for the EAI sampling problem is .60.

Standard Deviation of $\bar{p}$

Just as we found for the standard deviation of $\bar{x}$, the standard deviation of $\bar{p}$ depends on whether the population is finite or infinite. The two formulas for computing the standard deviation of $\bar{p}$ follow.

STANDARD DEVIATION OF $\bar{p}$

Finite Population	*Infinite Population*	
$\sigma_{\bar{p}} = \sqrt{\dfrac{N-n}{N-1}} \sqrt{\dfrac{p(1-p)}{n}}$	$\sigma_{\bar{p}} = \sqrt{\dfrac{p(1-p)}{n}}$	(7.5)

Comparing the two formulas in (7.5), we see that the only difference is the use of the finite population correction factor $\sqrt{(N-n)/(N-1)}$.

As was the case with the sample mean $\bar{x}$, the difference between the expressions for the finite population and the infinite population becomes negligible if the size of the finite population is large in comparison to the sample size. We follow the same rule of thumb that we recommended for the sample mean. That is, if the population is finite with $n/N \leq .05$, we will use $\sigma_{\bar{p}} = \sqrt{p(1-p)/n}$. However, if the population is finite with $n/N > .05$, the finite population correction factor should be used. Again, unless specifically noted, throughout the text we will assume that the population size is large in relation to the sample size and thus the finite population correction factor is unnecessary.

In Section 7.5 we used the term standard error of the mean to refer to the standard deviation of $\bar{x}$. We stated that in general the term standard error refers to the standard deviation of a point estimator. Thus, for proportions we use *standard error of the proportion* to refer to the standard deviation of $\bar{p}$. Let us now return to the EAI example and compute the standard error of the proportion associated with simple random samples of 30 EAI employees.

For the EAI study we know that the population proportion of employees who participated in the management training program is $p = .60$. With $n/N = 30/2500 = .012$, we can ignore the finite population correction factor when we compute the standard error of the proportion. For the simple random sample of 30 employees, $\sigma_{\bar{p}}$ is

$$\sigma_{\bar{p}} = \sqrt{\frac{p(1 - p)}{n}} = \sqrt{\frac{.60(1 - .60)}{30}} = .0894$$

Form of the Sampling Distribution of $\bar{p}$

Now that we know the mean and standard deviation of the sampling distribution of $\bar{p}$, the final step is to determine the form or shape of the sampling distribution. The sample proportion is $\bar{p} = x/n$. For a simple random sample from a large population, the value of x is a binomial random variable indicating the number of elements in the sample with the characteristic of interest. Because n is a constant, the probability of x/n is the same as the binomial probability of x, which means that the sampling distribution of $\bar{p}$ is also a discrete probability distribution and that the probability for each value of x/n is the same as the probability of x.

In Chapter 6 we also showed that a binomial distribution can be approximated by a normal distribution whenever the sample size is large enough to satisfy the following two conditions:

$$np \geq 5 \quad \text{and} \quad n(1 - p) \geq 5$$

Assuming these two conditions are satisfied, the probability distribution of x in the sample proportion, $\bar{p} = x/n$, can be approximated by a normal distribution. And because n is a constant, the sampling distribution of $\bar{p}$ can also be approximated by a normal distribution. This approximation is stated as follows:

> The sampling distribution of $\bar{p}$ can be approximated by a normal distribution whenever $np \geq 5$ and $n(1 - p) \geq 5$.

In practical applications, when an estimate of a population proportion is desired, we find that sample sizes are almost always large enough to permit the use of a normal approximation for the sampling distribution of $\bar{p}$.

Recall that for the EAI sampling problem we know that the population proportion of employees who participated in the training program is $p = .60$. With a simple random sample of size 30, we have $np = 30(.60) = 18$ and $n(1 - p) = 30(.40) = 12$. Thus, the sampling distribution of $\bar{p}$ can be approximated by a normal distribution shown in Figure 7.8.

Practical Value of the Sampling Distribution of $\bar{p}$

The practical value of the sampling distribution of $\bar{p}$ is that it can be used to provide probability information about the difference between the sample proportion and the population proportion. For instance, suppose that in the EAI problem the personnel director wants to know the probability of obtaining a value of $\bar{p}$ that is within .05 of the population proportion of EAI employees who participated in the training program. That is, what is the probability of obtaining a sample with a sample proportion $\bar{p}$ between .55 and .65? The darkly shaded area in Figure 7.9 shows this probability. Using the fact that the sampling distribution of $\bar{p}$ can be approximated by a normal distribution with a mean of .60 and a

FIGURE 7.8   SAMPLING DISTRIBUTION OF $\bar{p}$ FOR THE PROPORTION OF EAI EMPLOYEES WHO PARTICIPATED IN THE MANAGEMENT TRAINING PROGRAM

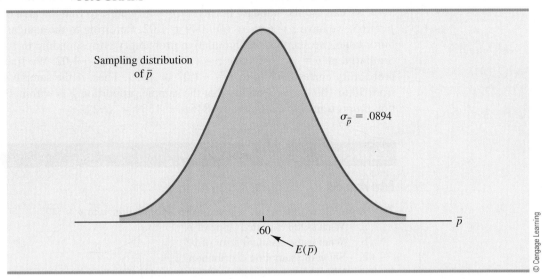

standard error of the proportion of $\sigma_{\bar{p}} = .0894$, we find that the standard normal random variable corresponding to $\bar{p} = .65$ has a value of $z = (.65 - .60)/.0894 = .56$. Referring to the standard normal probability table, we see that the cumulative probability corresponding to $z = .56$ is .7123. Similarly, at $\bar{p} = .55$, we find $z = (.55 - .60)/.0894 = -.56$. From the standard normal probability table, we find the cumulative probability corresponding to $z = -.56$ is .2877. Thus, the probability of selecting a sample that provides a sample proportion $\bar{p}$ within .05 of the population proportion p is given by $.7123 - .2877 = .4246$.

If we consider increasing the sample size to $n = 100$, the standard error of the proportion becomes

$$\sigma_{\bar{p}} = \sqrt{\frac{.60(1 - .60)}{100}} = .049$$

FIGURE 7.9   PROBABILITY OF OBTAINING $\bar{p}$ BETWEEN .55 AND .65

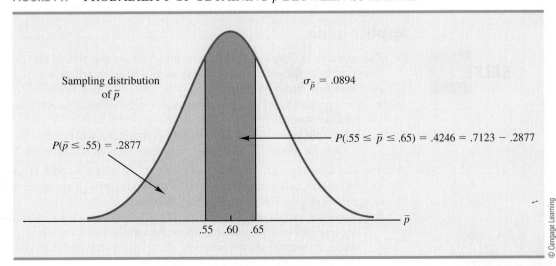

With a sample size of 100 EAI employees, the probability of the sample proportion having a value within .05 of the population proportion can now be computed. Because the sampling distribution is approximately normal, with mean .60 and standard deviation .049, we can use the standard normal probability table to find the area or probability. At $\bar{p} = .65$, we have $z = (.65 - .60)/.049 = 1.02$. Referring to the standard normal probability table, we see that the cumulative probability corresponding to $z = 1.02$ is .8461. Similarly, at $\bar{p} = .55$, we have $z = (.55 - .60)/.049 = -1.02$. We find the cumulative probability corresponding to $z = -1.02$ is .1539. Thus, if the sample size is increased from 30 to 100, the probability that the sample proportion $\bar{p}$ is within .05 of the population proportion p will increase to $.8461 - .1539 = .6922$.

Exercises

Methods

31. A sample of size 100 is selected from a population with $p = .40$.
    a. What is the expected value of $\bar{p}$?
    b. What is the standard error of $\bar{p}$?
    c. Show the sampling distribution of $\bar{p}$.
    d. What does the sampling distribution of $\bar{p}$ show?

32. A population proportion is .40. A sample of size 200 will be taken and the sample proportion $\bar{p}$ will be used to estimate the population proportion.
    a. What is the probability that the sample proportion will be within ±.03 of the population proportion?
    b. What is the probability that the sample proportion will be within ±.05 of the population proportion?

33. Assume that the population proportion is .55. Compute the standard error of the proportion, $\sigma_{\bar{p}}$, for sample sizes of 100, 200, 500, and 1000. What can you say about the size of the standard error of the proportion as the sample size is increased?

34. The population proportion is .30. What is the probability that a sample proportion will be within ±.04 of the population proportion for each of the following sample sizes?
    a. $n = 100$
    b. $n = 200$
    c. $n = 500$
    d. $n = 1000$
    e. What is the advantage of a larger sample size?

Applications

35. The president of Doerman Distributors, Inc., believes that 30% of the firm's orders come from first-time customers. A random sample of 100 orders will be used to estimate the proportion of first-time customers.
    a. Assume that the president is correct and $p = .30$. What is the sampling distribution of $\bar{p}$ for this study?
    b. What is the probability that the sample proportion $\bar{p}$ will be between .20 and .40?
    c. What is the probability that the sample proportion will be between .25 and .35?

36. *The Wall Street Journal* reported that the age at first startup for 55% of entrepreneurs was 29 years of age or less and the age at first startup for 45% of entrepreneurs was 30 years of age or more (*The Wall Street Journal*, March 19, 2012).
    a. Suppose a sample of 200 entrepreneurs will be taken to learn about the most important qualities of entrepreneurs. Show the sampling distribution of $\bar{p}$ where $\bar{p}$ is the sample proportion of entrepreneurs whose first startup was at 29 years of age or less.

b.   What is the probability that the sample proportion in part (a) will be within $\pm.05$ of its population proportion?

c.   Suppose a sample of 200 entrepreneurs will be taken to learn about the most important qualities of entrepreneurs. Show the sampling distribution of $\bar{p}$ where $\bar{p}$ is now the sample proportion of entrepreneurs whose first startup was at 30 years of age or more.

d.   What is the probability that the sample proportion in part (c) will be within $\pm.05$ of its population proportion?

e   Is the probability different in parts (b) and (d)? Why?

f.   Answer part (b) for a sample of size 400. Is the probability smaller? Why?

37.   People end up tossing 12% of what they buy at the grocery store (*Reader's Digest*, March 2009). Assume this is the true population proportion and that you plan to take a sample survey of 540 grocery shoppers to further investigate their behavior.

a.   Show the sampling distribution of $\bar{p}$, the proportion of groceries thrown out by your sample respondents.

b.   What is the probability that your survey will provide a sample proportion within $\pm.03$ of the population proportion?

c.   What is the probability that your survey will provide a sample proportion within $\pm.015$ of the population proportion?

38.   Forty-two percent of primary care doctors think their patients receive unnecessary medical care (*Reader's Digest*, December 2011/January 2012).

a.   Suppose a sample of 300 primary care doctors were taken. Show the sampling distribution of the proportion of the doctors who think their patients receive unnecessary medical care.

b.   What is the probability that the sample proportion will be within $\pm.03$ of the population proportion?

c.   What is the probability that the sample proportion will be within $\pm.05$ of the population proportion?

d.   What would be the effect of taking a larger sample on the probabilities in parts (b) and (c)? Why?

39.   In 2008 the Better Business Bureau settled 75% of complaints they received (*USA Today*, March 2, 2009). Suppose you have been hired by the Better Business Bureau to investigate the complaints they received this year involving new car dealers. You plan to select a sample of new car dealer complaints to estimate the proportion of complaints the Better Business Bureau is able to settle. Assume the population proportion of complaints settled for new car dealers is .75, the same as the overall proportion of complaints settled in 2008.

a.   Suppose you select a sample of 450 complaints involving new car dealers. Show the sampling distribution of $\bar{p}$.

b.   Based upon a sample of 450 complaints, what is the probability that the sample proportion will be within .04 of the population proportion?

c.   Suppose you select a sample of 200 complaints involving new car dealers. Show the sampling distribution of $\bar{p}$.

d.   Based upon the smaller sample of only 200 complaints, what is the probability that the sample proportion will be within .04 of the population proportion?

e.   As measured by the increase in probability, how much do you gain in precision by taking the larger sample in part (b)?

40.   The Grocery Manufacturers of America reported that 76% of consumers read the ingredients listed on a product's label. Assume the population proportion is $p = .76$ and a sample of 400 consumers is selected from the population.

a.   Show the sampling distribution of the sample proportion $\bar{p}$ where $\bar{p}$ is the proportion of the sampled consumers who read the ingredients listed on a product's label.

b.   What is the probability that the sample proportion will be within ±.03 of the population proportion?

c.   Answer part (b) for a sample of 750 consumers.

41. The Food Marketing Institute shows that 17% of households spend more than $100 per week on groceries. Assume the population proportion is $p = .17$ and a sample of 800 households will be selected from the population.

a.   Show the sampling distribution of $\bar{p}$, the sample proportion of households spending more than $100 per week on groceries.

b.   What is the probability that the sample proportion will be within ±.02 of the population proportion?

c.   Answer part (b) for a sample of 1600 households.

 7.7 ## Other Sampling Methods

This section provides a brief introduction to survey sampling methods other than simple random sampling.

We described simple random sampling as a procedure for sampling from a finite population and discussed the properties of the sampling distributions of $\bar{x}$ and $\bar{p}$ when simple random sampling is used. Other methods such as stratified random sampling, cluster sampling, and systematic sampling provide advantages over simple random sampling in some of these situations. In this section we briefly introduce these alternative sampling methods.

Stratified Random Sampling

Stratified random sampling works best when the variance among elements in each stratum is relatively small.

In **stratified random sampling**, the elements in the population are first divided into groups called *strata,* such that each element in the population belongs to one and only one stratum. The basis for forming the strata, such as department, location, age, industry type, and so on, is at the discretion of the designer of the sample. However, the best results are obtained when the elements within each stratum are as much alike as possible. Figure 7.10 is a diagram of a population divided into H strata.

After the strata are formed, a simple random sample is taken from each stratum. Formulas are available for combining the results for the individual stratum samples into one estimate of the population parameter of interest. The value of stratified random sampling depends on how homogeneous the elements are within the strata. If elements within strata are alike, the strata will have low variances. Thus relatively small sample sizes can be used to obtain good estimates of the strata characteristics. If strata are homogeneous, the stratified random sampling procedure provides results just as precise as those of simple random sampling by using a smaller total sample size.

FIGURE 7.10   DIAGRAM FOR STRATIFIED RANDOM SAMPLING

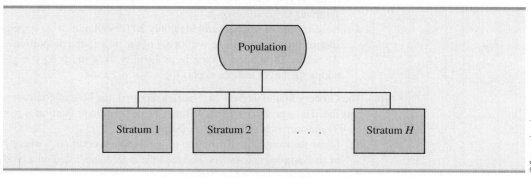

© Cengage Learning

FIGURE 7.11   DIAGRAM FOR CLUSTER SAMPLING

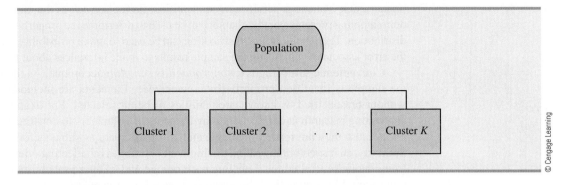

Cluster Sampling

Cluster sampling works best when each cluster provides a small-scale representation of the population.

In **cluster sampling**, the elements in the population are first divided into separate groups called *clusters*. Each element of the population belongs to one and only one cluster (see Figure 7.11). A simple random sample of the clusters is then taken. All elements within each sampled cluster form the sample. Cluster sampling tends to provide the best results when the elements within the clusters are not alike. In the ideal case, each cluster is a representative small-scale version of the entire population. The value of cluster sampling depends on how representative each cluster is of the entire population. If all clusters are alike in this regard, sampling a small number of clusters will provide good estimates of the population parameters.

One of the primary applications of cluster sampling is area sampling, where clusters are city blocks or other well-defined areas. Cluster sampling generally requires a larger total sample size than either simple random sampling or stratified random sampling. However, it can result in cost savings because of the fact that when an interviewer is sent to a sampled cluster (e.g., a city-block location), many sample observations can be obtained in a relatively short time. Hence, a larger sample size may be obtainable with a significantly lower total cost.

Systematic Sampling

In some sampling situations, especially those with large populations, it is time-consuming to select a simple random sample by first finding a random number and then counting or searching through the list of the population until the corresponding element is found. An alternative to simple random sampling is **systematic sampling**. For example, if a sample size of 50 is desired from a population containing 5000 elements, we will sample one element for every 5000/50 = 100 elements in the population. A systematic sample for this case involves selecting randomly one of the first 100 elements from the population list. Other sample elements are identified by starting with the first sampled element and then selecting every 100th element that follows in the population list. In effect, the sample of 50 is identified by moving systematically through the population and identifying every 100th element after the first randomly selected element. The sample of 50 usually will be easier to identify in this way than it would be if simple random sampling were used. Because the first element selected is a random choice, a systematic sample is usually assumed to have the properties of a simple random sample. This assumption is especially applicable when the list of elements in the population is a random ordering of the elements.

Convenience Sampling

The sampling methods discussed thus far are referred to as *probability sampling* techniques. Elements selected from the population have a known probability of being included in the sample. The advantage of probability sampling is that the sampling distribution of the appropriate sample statistic generally can be identified. Formulas such as the ones for simple random sampling presented in this chapter can be used to determine the properties of the sampling distribution. Then the sampling distribution can be used to make probability statements about the error associated with using the sample results to make inferences about the population.

Convenience sampling is a *nonprobability sampling* technique. As the name implies, the sample is identified primarily by convenience. Elements are included in the sample without prespecified or known probabilities of being selected. For example, a professor conducting research at a university may use student volunteers to constitute a sample simply because they are readily available and will participate as subjects for little or no cost. Similarly, an inspector may sample a shipment of oranges by selecting oranges haphazardly from among several crates. Labeling each orange and using a probability method of sampling would be impractical. Samples such as wildlife captures and volunteer panels for consumer research are also convenience samples.

Convenience samples have the advantage of relatively easy sample selection and data collection; however, it is impossible to evaluate the "goodness" of the sample in terms of its representativeness of the population. A convenience sample may provide good results or it may not; no statistically justified procedure allows a probability analysis and inference about the quality of the sample results. Sometimes researchers apply statistical methods designed for probability samples to a convenience sample, arguing that the convenience sample can be treated as though it were a probability sample. However, this argument cannot be supported, and we should be cautious in interpreting the results of convenience samples that are used to make inferences about populations.

Judgment Sampling

One additional nonprobability sampling technique is **judgment sampling**. In this approach, the person most knowledgeable on the subject of the study selects elements of the population that he or she feels are most representative of the population. Often this method is a relatively easy way of selecting a sample. For example, a reporter may sample two or three senators, judging that those senators reflect the general opinion of all senators. However, the quality of the sample results depends on the judgment of the person selecting the sample. Again, great caution is warranted in drawing conclusions based on judgment samples used to make inferences about populations.

NOTE AND COMMENT

We recommend using probability sampling methods when sampling from finite populations: simple random sampling, stratified random sampling, cluster sampling, or systematic sampling. For these methods, formulas are available for evaluating the "goodness" of the sample results in terms of the closeness of the results to the population parameters being estimated. An evaluation of the goodness cannot be made with convenience or judgment sampling. Thus, great care should be used in interpreting the results based on nonprobability sampling methods.

Summary

In this chapter we presented the concepts of sampling and sampling distributions. We demonstrated how a simple random sample can be selected from a finite population and how a random sample can be collected from an infinite population. The data collected from such samples can be used to develop point estimates of population parameters. Because different samples provide different values for the point estimators, point estimators such as $\bar{x}$ and $\bar{p}$ are random variables. The probability distribution of such a random variable is called a sampling distribution. In particular, we described the sampling distributions of the sample mean $\bar{x}$ and the sample proportion $\bar{p}$.

In considering the characteristics of the sampling distributions of $\bar{x}$ and $\bar{p}$, we stated that $E(\bar{x}) = \mu$ and $E(\bar{p}) = p$. Thus $\bar{x}$ and $\bar{p}$ are unbiased estimators. After developing the standard deviation or standard error formulas for these estimators, we described the conditions necessary for the sampling distributions of $\bar{x}$ and $\bar{p}$ to follow a normal distribution. Other sampling methods including stratified random sampling, cluster sampling, systematic sampling, convenience sampling, and judgment sampling were discussed.

Glossary

Sampled population The population from which the sample is taken.

Frame A listing of the elements the sample will be selected from.

Parameter A numerical characteristic of a population, such as a population mean μ, a population standard deviation σ, a population proportion p, and so on.

Simple random sample A simple random sample of size n from a finite population of size N is a sample selected such that each possible sample of size n has the same probability of being selected.

Sampling without replacement Once an element has been included in the sample, it is removed from the population and cannot be selected a second time.

Sampling with replacement Once an element has been included in the sample, it is returned to the population. A previously selected element can be selected again and therefore may appear in the sample more than once.

Random sample A random sample from an infinite population is a sample selected such that the following conditions are satisfied: (1) Each element selected comes from the same population; (2) each element is selected independently.

Sample statistic A sample characteristic, such as a sample mean $\bar{x}$, a sample standard deviation s, a sample proportion $\bar{p}$, and so on. The value of the sample statistic is used to estimate the value of the corresponding population parameter.

Point estimator The sample statistic, such as $\bar{x}$, s, or $\bar{p}$, that provides the point estimate of the population parameter.

Point estimate The value of a point estimator used in a particular instance as an estimate of a population parameter.

Target population The population for which statistical inferences such as point estimates are made. It is important for the target population to correspond as closely as possible to the sampled population.

Sampling distribution A probability distribution consisting of all possible values of a sample statistic.

Unbiased A property of a point estimator that is present when the expected value of the point estimator is equal to the population parameter it estimates.

Finite population correction factor The term $\sqrt{(N-n)/(N-1)}$ that is used in the formulas for $\sigma_{\bar{x}}$ and $\sigma_{\bar{p}}$ whenever a finite population, rather than an infinite population, is being sampled. The generally accepted rule of thumb is to ignore the finite population correction factor whenever $n/N \leq .05$.

Standard error The standard deviation of a point estimator.

Central limit theorem A theorem that enables one to use the normal probability distribution to approximate the sampling distribution of $\bar{x}$ whenever the sample size is large.

Stratified random sampling A probability sampling method in which the population is first divided into strata and a simple random sample is then taken from each stratum.

Cluster sampling A probability sampling method in which the population is first divided into clusters and then a simple random sample of the clusters is taken.

Systematic sampling A probability sampling method in which we randomly select one of the first k elements and then select every kth element thereafter.

Convenience sampling A nonprobability method of sampling whereby elements are selected for the sample on the basis of convenience.

Judgment sampling A nonprobability method of sampling whereby elements are selected for the sample based on the judgment of the person doing the study.

Key Formulas

Expected Value of $\bar{x}$

$$E(\bar{x}) = \mu \tag{7.1}$$

Standard Deviation of $\bar{x}$ (Standard Error)

Finite Population	*Infinite Population*	
$\sigma_{\bar{x}} = \sqrt{\dfrac{N-n}{N-1}}\left(\dfrac{\sigma}{\sqrt{n}}\right)$	$\sigma_{\bar{x}} = \dfrac{\sigma}{\sqrt{n}}$	(7.2)

Expected Value of $\bar{p}$

$$E(\bar{p}) = p \tag{7.4}$$

Standard Deviation of $\bar{p}$ (Standard Error)

Finite Population	*Infinite Population*	
$\sigma_{\bar{p}} = \sqrt{\dfrac{N-n}{N-1}}\sqrt{\dfrac{p(1-p)}{n}}$	$\sigma_{\bar{p}} = \sqrt{\dfrac{p(1-p)}{n}}$	(7.5)

Supplementary Exercises

42. *U.S. News & World Report* publishes comprehensive information on America's best colleges (*America's Best Colleges,* 2009 ed.). Among other things, they provide a listing of their 133 best national universities. You would like to take a sample of these universities for a follow-up study on their students. Begin at the bottom of the third column of random digits in Table 7.1. Ignoring the first two digits in each five-number group and using the three-digit random numbers beginning with 959 read *up* the column to identify the number (from 1 to 133) of the first seven universities to be included in a simple random sample. Continue by starting at the bottom of the fourth and fifth columns and reading up if necessary.

43. The latest available data showed health expenditures were $8,086 per person in the United States or 17.6% of gross domestic product (Centers for Medicare & Medicaid Services website, April 1, 2012). Use $8,086 as the population mean and suppose a survey research firm will take a sample of 100 people to investigate the nature of their health expenditures. Assume the population standard deviation is $2,500.
    a. Show the sampling distribution of the mean amount of health care expenditures for a sample of 100 people.

b. What is the probability the sample mean will be within ±$200 of the population mean?

c. What is the probability the sample mean will be greater than $9,000? If the survey research firm reports a sample mean greater than $9,000, would you question whether the firm followed correct sampling procedures? Why or why not?

44. Foot Locker uses sales per square foot as a measure of store productivity. Sales are currently running at an annual rate of $406 per square foot (*The Wall Street Journal,* March 7, 2012). You have been asked by management to conduct a study of a sample of 64 Foot Locker stores. Assume the standard deviation in annual sales per square foot for the population of all 3400 Foot Locker stores is $80.

a. Show the sampling distribution of $\bar{x}$, the sample mean annual sales per square foot for a sample of 64 Foot Locker stores.

b. What is the probability that the sample mean will be within $15 of the population mean?

c. Suppose you find a sample mean of $380. What is the probability of finding a sample mean of $380 or less? Would you consider such a sample to be an unusually low performing group of stores?

45. Allegiant Airlines charges a mean base fare of $89. In addition, the airline charges for making a reservation on its website, checking bags, and inflight beverages. These additional charges average $39 per passenger (*Bloomberg Businessweek,* October 8–14, 2012). Suppose a random sample of 60 passengers is taken to determine the total cost of their flight on Allegiant Airlines. The population standard deviation of total flight cost is known to be $40.

a. What is the population mean cost per flight?

b. What is the probability the sample mean will be within $10 of the population mean cost per flight?

c. What is the probability the sample mean will be within $5 of the population mean cost per flight?

46. After deducting grants based on need, the average cost to attend the University of Southern California (USC) is $27,175 (*U.S. News & World Report, America's Best Colleges,* 2009 ed.). Assume the population standard deviation is $7,400. Suppose that a random sample of 60 USC students will be taken from this population.

a. What is the value of the standard error of the mean?

b. What is the probability that the sample mean will be more than $27,175?

c. What is the probability that the sample mean will be within $1,000 of the population mean?

d. How would the probability in part (c) change if the sample size were increased to 100?

47. Three firms carry inventories that differ in size. Firm A's inventory contains 2000 items, firm B's inventory contains 5000 items, and firm C's inventory contains 10,000 items. The population standard deviation for the cost of the items in each firm's inventory is $\sigma = 144$. A statistical consultant recommends that each firm take a sample of 50 items from its inventory to provide statistically valid estimates of the average cost per item. Managers of the small firm state that because it has the smallest population, it should be able to make the estimate from a much smaller sample than that required by the larger firms. However, the consultant states that to obtain the same standard error and thus the same precision in the sample results, all firms should use the same sample size regardless of population size.

a. Using the finite population correction factor, compute the standard error for each of the three firms given a sample of size 50.

b. What is the probability that for each firm the sample mean $\bar{x}$ will be within ±25 of the population mean μ?

48. A researcher reports survey results by stating that the standard error of the mean is 20. The population standard deviation is 500.
    a. How large was the sample used in this survey?
    b. What is the probability that the point estimate was within ± 25 of the population mean?

49. A production process is checked periodically by a quality control inspector. The inspector selects simple random samples of 30 finished products and computes the sample mean product weights $\bar{x}$. If test results over a long period of time show that 5% of the $\bar{x}$ values are over 2.1 pounds and 5% are under 1.9 pounds, what are the mean and the standard deviation for the population of products produced with this process?

50. Fifteen percent of Australians smoke. By introducing tough laws banning brand labels on cigarette packages, Australia hopes to reduce the percentage of people smoking to 10% by 2018 (Reuters website, October 23, 2012). Answer the following questions based on a sample of 240 Australians.
    a. Show the sampling distribution of $\bar{p}$, the sample proportion of Australians who are smokers.
    b. What is the probability the sample proportion will be within $\pm .04$ of the population proportion?
    c. What is the probability the sample proportion will be within $\pm .02$ of the population proportion?

51. A market research firm conducts telephone surveys with a 40% historical response rate. What is the probability that in a new sample of 400 telephone numbers, at least 150 individuals will cooperate and respond to the questions? In other words, what is the probability that the sample proportion will be at least 150/400 = .375?

52. Advertisers contract with Internet service providers and search engines to place ads on websites. They pay a fee based on the number of potential customers who click on their ad. Unfortunately, click fraud—the practice of someone clicking on an ad solely for the purpose of driving up advertising revenue—has become a problem. Forty percent of advertisers claim they have been a victim of click fraud (*BusinessWeek,* March 13, 2006). Suppose a simple random sample of 380 advertisers will be taken to learn more about how they are affected by this practice.
    a. What is the probability that the sample proportion will be within $\pm .04$ of the population proportion experiencing click fraud?
    b. What is the probability that the sample proportion will be greater than .45?

53. The proportion of individuals insured by the All-Driver Automobile Insurance Company who received at least one traffic ticket during a five-year period is .15.
    a. Show the sampling distribution of $\bar{p}$ if a random sample of 150 insured individuals is used to estimate the proportion having received at least one ticket.
    b. What is the probability that the sample proportion will be within $\pm .03$ of the population proportion?

54. Lori Jeffrey is a successful sales representative for a major publisher of college textbooks. Historically, Lori obtains a book adoption on 25% of her sales calls. Viewing her sales calls for one month as a sample of all possible sales calls, assume that a statistical analysis of the data yields a standard error of the proportion of .0625.
    a. How large was the sample used in this analysis? That is, how many sales calls did Lori make during the month?
    b. Let $\bar{p}$ indicate the sample proportion of book adoptions obtained during the month. Show the sampling distribution of $\bar{p}$.
    c. Using the sampling distribution of $\bar{p}$, compute the probability that Lori will obtain book adoptions on 30% or more of her sales calls during a one-month period.

Appendix 7.1   Random Sampling with Minitab

If a list of the elements in a population is available in a Minitab file, Minitab can be used to select a simple random sample. For example, a list of the top 100 metropolitan areas in the United States and Canada is provided in column 1 of the data set MetAreas (*Places Rated Almanac—The Millennium Edition 2000*). Column 2 contains the overall rating of each metropolitan area. The first 10 metropolitan areas in the data set and their corresponding ratings are shown in Table 7.6.

Suppose that you would like to select a simple random sample of 30 metropolitan areas in order to do an in-depth study of the cost of living in the United States and Canada. The following steps can be used to select the sample.

MetAreas

Step 1. Select the **Calc** pull-down menu
Step 2. Choose **Random Data**
Step 3. Choose **Sample From Columns**
Step 4. When the Sample From Columns dialog box appears:
  Enter 30 in the **Number of rows to sample** box
  Enter C1 C2 in the **From columns** box below
  Enter C3 C4 in the **Store samples in** box
Step 5. Click **OK**

The random sample of 30 metropolitan areas appears in columns C3 and C4.

Appendix 7.2   Random Sampling with Excel

If a list of the elements in a population is available in an Excel file, Excel can be used to select a simple random sample. For example, a list of the top 100 metropolitan areas in the United States and Canada is provided in column A of the data set MetAreas (*Places Rated Almanac—The Millennium Edition 2000*). Column B contains the overall rating of each metropolitan area. The first 10 metropolitan areas in the data set and their corresponding ratings are shown in Table 7.6. Assume that you would like to select a simple random sample of 30 metropolitan areas in order to do an in-depth study of the cost of living in the United States and Canada.

TABLE 7.6   OVERALL RATING FOR THE FIRST 10 METROPOLITAN AREAS IN THE DATA SET METAREAS

Metropolitan Area	Rating
Albany, NY	64.18
Albuquerque, NM	66.16
Appleton, WI	60.56
Atlanta, GA	69.97
Austin, TX	71.48
Baltimore, MD	69.75
Birmingham, AL	69.59
Boise City, ID	68.36
Boston, MA	68.99
Buffalo, NY	66.10

© Cengage Learning

The rows of any Excel data set can be placed in a random order by adding an extra column to the data set and filling the column with random numbers using the =RAND() function. Then, using Excel's sort ascending capability on the random number column, the rows of the data set will be reordered randomly. The random sample of size n appears in the first n rows of the reordered data set.

In the MetAreas data set, labels are in row 1 and the 100 metropolitan areas are in rows 2 to 101. The following steps can be used to select a simple random sample of 30 metropolitan areas.

Step 1. Enter =RAND() in cell C2
Step 2. Copy cell C2 to cells C3:C101
Step 3. Select any cell in Column C
Step 4. Click the **Home** tab on the Ribbon
Step 5. In the **Editing** group, click **Sort & Filter**
Step 6. Click **Sort Smallest to Largest**

The random sample of 30 metropolitan areas appears in rows 2 to 31 of the reordered data set. The random numbers in column C are no longer necessary and can be deleted if desired.

Appendix 7.3   Random Sampling with StatTools

MetAreas

If a list of the elements in a population is available in an Excel file, StatTools Random Sample Utility can be used to select a simple random sample. For example, a list of the top 100 metropolitan areas in the United States and Canada is provided in column A of the data set MetAreas (*Places Rated Almanac—The Millennium Edition 2000*). Column B contains the overall rating of each metropolitan area. Assume that you would like to select a simple random sample of 30 metropolitan areas in order to do an in-depth study of the cost of living in the United States and Canada.

Begin by using the Data Set Manager to create a StatTools data set for these data using the procedure described in the appendix to Chapter 1. The following steps will generate a simple random sample of 30 metropolitan areas.

Step 1. Click the **StatTools** tab on the Ribbon
Step 2. In the **Data Group** click **Data Utilities**
Step 3. Choose the **Random Sample** option
Step 4. When the StatTools—Random Sample Utility dialog box appears:
    In the **Variables** section:
        Select **Metropolitan Area**
        Select **Rating**
    In the **Options** section:
        Enter 1 in the **Number of Samples** box
        Enter 30 in the **Sample Size** box
    Click **OK**

The random sample of 30 metropolitan areas will appear in columns A and B of the worksheet entitled Random Sample.

CHAPTER 8

Interval Estimation

CONTENTS

STATISTICS IN PRACTICE:
FOOD LION

FOOD LION*
SALISBURY, NORTH CAROLINA

Founded in 1957 as Food Town, Food Lion is one of the largest supermarket chains in the United States, with 1300 stores in 11 Southeastern and Mid-Atlantic states. The company sells more than 24,000 different products and offers nationally and regionally advertised brand-name merchandise, as well as a growing number of high-quality private label products manufactured especially for Food Lion. The company maintains its low price leadership and quality assurance through operating efficiencies such as standard store formats, innovative warehouse design, energy-efficient facilities, and data synchronization with suppliers. Food Lion looks to a future of continued innovation, growth, price leadership, and service to its customers.

Being in an inventory-intense business, Food Lion made the decision to adopt the LIFO (last-in, first-out) method of inventory valuation. This method matches current costs against current revenues, which minimizes the effect of radical price changes on profit and loss results. In addition, the LIFO method reduces net income thereby reducing income taxes during periods of inflation.

Food Lion establishes a LIFO index for each of seven inventory pools: Grocery, Paper/Household, Pet Supplies, Health & Beauty Aids, Dairy, Cigarette/Tobacco, and Beer/Wine. For example, a LIFO index of 1.008 for the Grocery pool would indicate that the company's grocery inventory value at current costs reflects a 0.8% increase due to inflation over the most recent one-year period.

A LIFO index for each inventory pool requires that the year-end inventory count for each product be valued at the current year-end cost and at the preceding year-end

As an inventory-intense business, Food Lion adopted the LIFO method of inventory valuation. © Davis Turner/ Bloomberg/Getty Images.

cost. To avoid excessive time and expense associated with counting the inventory in all 1200 store locations, Food Lion selects a random sample of 50 stores. Year-end physical inventories are taken in each of the sample stores. The current-year and preceding-year costs for each item are then used to construct the required LIFO indexes for each inventory pool.

For a recent year, the sample estimate of the LIFO index for the Health & Beauty Aids inventory pool was 1.015. Using a 95% confidence level, Food Lion computed a margin of error of .006 for the sample estimate. Thus, the interval from 1.009 to 1.021 provided a 95% confidence interval estimate of the population LIFO index. This level of precision was judged to be very good.

In this chapter you will learn how to compute the margin of error associated with sample estimates. You will also learn how to use this information to construct and interpret interval estimates of a population mean and a population proportion.

---

*The authors are indebted to Keith Cunningham, Tax Director, and Bobby Harkey, Staff Tax Accountant, at Food Lion for providing this Statistics in Practice.

In Chapter 7, we stated that a point estimator is a sample statistic used to estimate a population parameter. For instance, the sample mean $\bar{x}$ is a point estimator of the population mean μ and the sample proportion $\bar{p}$ is a point estimator of the population proportion p. Because a point estimator cannot be expected to provide the exact value of the population parameter, an **interval estimate** is often computed by adding and subtracting a value, called the **margin of error**, to the point estimate. The general form of an interval estimate is as follows:

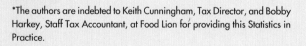

Point estimate $\pm$ Margin of error

The purpose of an interval estimate is to provide information about how close the point estimate, provided by the sample, is to the value of the population parameter.

In this chapter we show how to compute interval estimates of a population mean μ and a population proportion p. The general form of an interval estimate of a population mean is

$$\bar{x} \pm \text{Margin of error}$$

Similarly, the general form of an interval estimate of a population proportion is

$$\bar{p} \pm \text{Margin of error}$$

The sampling distributions of $\bar{x}$ and $\bar{p}$ play key roles in computing these interval estimates.

Population Mean: σ Known

In order to develop an interval estimate of a population mean, either the population standard deviation σ or the sample standard deviation s must be used to compute the margin of error. In most applications σ is not known, and s is used to compute the margin of error. In some applications, large amounts of relevant historical data are available and can be used to estimate the population standard deviation prior to sampling. Also, in quality control applications where a process is assumed to be operating correctly, or "in control," it is appropriate to treat the population standard deviation as known. We refer to such cases as the σ **known** case. In this section we introduce an example in which it is reasonable to treat σ as known and show how to construct an interval estimate for this case.

Each week Lloyd's Department Store selects a simple random sample of 100 customers in order to learn about the amount spent per shopping trip. With x representing the amount spent per shopping trip, the sample mean $\bar{x}$ provides a point estimate of μ, the mean amount spent per shopping trip for the population of all Lloyd's customers. Lloyd's has been using the weekly survey for several years. Based on the historical data, Lloyd's now assumes a known value of $\sigma = \$20$ for the population standard deviation. The historical data also indicate that the population follows a normal distribution.

Lloyd's

During the most recent week, Lloyd's surveyed 100 customers ($n = 100$) and obtained a sample mean of $\bar{x} = \$82$. The sample mean amount spent provides a point estimate of the population mean amount spent per shopping trip, μ. In the discussion that follows, we show how to compute the margin of error for this estimate and develop an interval estimate of the population mean.

Margin of Error and the Interval Estimate

In Chapter 7 we showed that the sampling distribution of $\bar{x}$ can be used to compute the probability that $\bar{x}$ will be within a given distance of μ. In the Lloyd's example, the historical data show that the population of amounts spent is normally distributed with a standard deviation of $\sigma = 20$. So, using what we learned in Chapter 7, we can conclude that the sampling distribution of $\bar{x}$ follows a normal distribution with a standard error of $\sigma_{\bar{x}} = \sigma/\sqrt{n} = 20/\sqrt{100} = 2$. This sampling distribution is shown in Figure 8.1.[1] Because

---

[1]We use the fact that the population of amounts spent has a normal distribution to conclude that the sampling distribution of $\bar{x}$ has a normal distribution. If the population did not have a normal distribution, we could rely on the central limit theorem and the sample size of $n = 100$ to conclude that the sampling distribution of $\bar{x}$ is approximately normal. In either case, the sampling distribution of $\bar{x}$ would appear as shown in Figure 8.1.

**FIGURE 8.1   SAMPLING DISTRIBUTION OF THE SAMPLE MEAN AMOUNT
SPENT FROM SIMPLE RANDOM SAMPLES OF 100 CUSTOMERS**

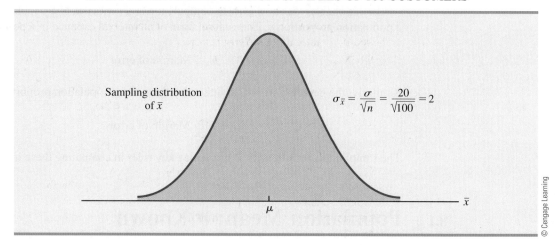

the sampling distribution shows how values of $\bar{x}$ are distributed around the population mean μ, the sampling distribution of $\bar{x}$ provides information about the possible differences between $\bar{x}$ and μ.

Using the standard normal probability table, we find that 95% of the values of any normally distributed random variable are within ± 1.96 standard deviations of the mean. Thus, when the sampling distribution of $\bar{x}$ is normally distributed, 95% of the $\bar{x}$ values must be within $\pm 1.96\ \sigma_{\bar{x}}$ of the mean μ. In the Lloyd's example we know that the sampling distribution of $\bar{x}$ is normally distributed with a standard error of $\sigma_{\bar{x}} = 2$. Because $\pm 1.96\ \sigma_{\bar{x}} = 1.96(2) = 3.92$, we can conclude that 95% of all $\bar{x}$ values obtained using a sample size of $n = 100$ will be within ± 3.92 of the population mean μ. See Figure 8.2.

**FIGURE 8.2   SAMPLING DISTRIBUTION OF $\bar{x}$ SHOWING THE LOCATION OF SAMPLE
MEANS THAT ARE WITHIN 3.92 OF μ**

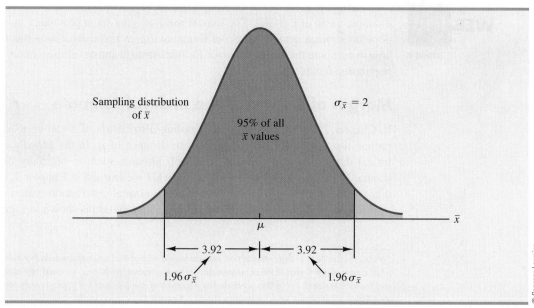

In the introduction to this chapter we said that the general form of an interval estimate of the population mean μ is $\bar{x} \pm$ margin of error. For the Lloyd's example, suppose we set the margin of error equal to 3.92 and compute the interval estimate of μ using $\bar{x} \pm 3.92$. To provide an interpretation for this interval estimate, let us consider the values of $\bar{x}$ that could be obtained if we took three *different* simple random samples, each consisting of 100 Lloyd's customers. The first sample mean might turn out to have the value shown as $\bar{x}_1$ in Figure 8.3. In this case, Figure 8.3 shows that the interval formed by subtracting 3.92 from $\bar{x}_1$ and adding 3.92 to $\bar{x}_1$ includes the population mean μ. Now consider what happens if the second sample mean turns out to have the value shown as $\bar{x}_2$ in Figure 8.3. Although this sample mean differs from the first sample mean, we see that the interval formed by subtracting 3.92 from $\bar{x}_2$ and adding 3.92 to $\bar{x}_2$ also includes the population mean μ. However, consider what happens if the third sample mean turns out to have the value shown as $\bar{x}_3$ in Figure 8.3. In this case, the interval formed by subtracting 3.92 from $\bar{x}_3$ and adding 3.92 to $\bar{x}_3$ does not include the population mean μ. Because $\bar{x}_3$ falls in the upper tail of the sampling distribution and is farther than 3.92 from μ, subtracting and adding 3.92 to $\bar{x}_3$ forms an interval that does not include μ.

Any sample mean $\bar{x}$ that is within the darkly shaded region of Figure 8.3 will provide an interval that contains the population mean μ. Because 95% of all possible sample means are in the darkly shaded region, 95% of all intervals formed by subtracting 3.92 from $\bar{x}$ and adding 3.92 to $\bar{x}$ will include the population mean μ.

Recall that during the most recent week, the quality assurance team at Lloyd's surveyed 100 customers and obtained a sample mean amount spent of $\bar{x} = 82$. Using $\bar{x} \pm 3.92$ to

FIGURE 8.3 INTERVALS FORMED FROM SELECTED SAMPLE MEANS AT LOCATIONS $\bar{x}_1, \bar{x}_2,$ AND $\bar{x}_3$

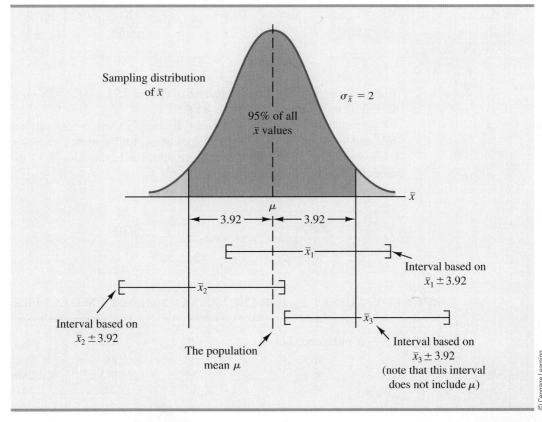

construct the interval estimate, we obtain 82 ± 3.92. Thus, the specific interval estimate of μ based on the data from the most recent week is $82 - 3.92 = 78.08$ to $82 + 3.92 = 85.92$. Because 95% of all the intervals constructed using $\bar{x} \pm 3.92$ will contain the population mean, we say that we are 95% confident that the interval 78.08 to 85.92 includes the population mean μ. We say that this interval has been established at the 95% **confidence level**. The value .95 is referred to as the **confidence coefficient**, and the interval 78.08 to 85.92 is called the 95% **confidence interval**.

This discussion provides insight as to why the interval is called a 95% confidence interval.

With the margin of error given by $z_{\alpha/2}(\sigma/\sqrt{n})$, the general form of an interval estimate of a population mean for the σ known case follows.

INTERVAL ESTIMATE OF A POPULATION MEAN: σ KNOWN

$$\bar{x} \pm z_{\alpha/2} \frac{\sigma}{\sqrt{n}} \tag{8.1}$$

where $(1 - \alpha)$ is the confidence coefficient and $z_{\alpha/2}$ is the z value providing an area of $\alpha/2$ in the upper tail of the standard normal probability distribution.

Let us use expression (8.1) to construct a 95% confidence interval for the Lloyd's example. For a 95% confidence interval, the confidence coefficient is $(1-\alpha) = .95$ and thus, $\alpha = .05$. Using the standard normal probability table, an area of $\alpha/2 = .05/2 = .025$ in the upper tail provides $z_{.025} = 1.96$. With the Lloyd's sample mean $\bar{x} = 82$, $\sigma = 20$, and a sample size $n = 100$, we obtain

$$82 \pm 1.96 \frac{20}{\sqrt{100}}$$

$$82 \pm 3.92$$

Thus, using expression (8.1), the margin of error is 3.92 and the 95% confidence interval is $82 - 3.92 = 78.08$ to $82 + 3.92 = 85.92$.

Although a 95% confidence level is frequently used, other confidence levels such as 90% and 99% may be considered. Values of $z_{\alpha/2}$ for the most commonly used confidence levels are shown in Table 8.1. Using these values and expression (8.1), the 90% confidence interval for the Lloyd's example is

$$82 \pm 1.645 \frac{20}{\sqrt{100}}$$

$$82 \pm 3.29$$

TABLE 8.1   VALUES OF $z_{\alpha/2}$ FOR THE MOST COMMONLY USED CONFIDENCE LEVELS

Confidence Level	α	$\alpha/2$	$z_{\alpha/2}$
90%	.10	.05	1.645
95%	.05	.025	1.960
99%	.01	.005	2.576

© Cengage Learning

Thus, at 90% confidence, the margin of error is 3.29 and the confidence interval is $82 - 3.29 = 78.71$ to $82 + 3.29 = 85.29$. Similarly, the 99% confidence interval is

$$82 \pm 2.576 \frac{20}{\sqrt{100}}$$

$$82 \pm 5.15$$

Thus, at 99% confidence, the margin of error is 5.15 and the confidence interval is $82 - 5.15 = 76.85$ to $82 + 5.15 = 87.15$.

Comparing the results for the 90%, 95%, and 99% confidence levels, we see that in order to have a higher degree of confidence, the margin of error and thus the width of the confidence interval must be larger.

Practical Advice

If the population follows a normal distribution, the confidence interval provided by expression (8.1) is exact. In other words, if expression (8.1) were used repeatedly to generate 95% confidence intervals, exactly 95% of the intervals generated would contain the population mean. If the population does not follow a normal distribution, the confidence interval provided by expression (8.1) will be approximate. In this case, the quality of the approximation depends on both the distribution of the population and the sample size.

In most applications, a sample size of $n \geq 30$ is adequate when using expression (8.1) to develop an interval estimate of a population mean. If the population is not normally distributed but is roughly symmetric, sample sizes as small as 15 can be expected to provide good approximate confidence intervals. With smaller sample sizes, expression (8.1) should only be used if the analyst believes, or is willing to assume, that the population distribution is at least approximately normal.

NOTES AND COMMENTS

1. The interval estimation procedure discussed in this section is based on the assumption that the population standard deviation σ is known. By σ known we mean that historical data or other information are available that permit us to obtain a good estimate of the population standard deviation prior to taking the sample that will be used to develop an estimate of the population mean. So technically we don't mean that σ is actually known with certainty. We just mean that we obtained a good estimate of the standard deviation prior to sampling and thus we won't be using the same sample to estimate both the population mean and the population standard deviation.

2. The sample size n appears in the denominator of the interval estimation expression (8.1). Thus, if a particular sample size provides too wide an interval to be of any practical use, we may want to consider increasing the sample size. With n in the denominator, a larger sample size will provide a smaller margin of error, a narrower interval, and greater precision. The procedure for determining the size of a simple random sample necessary to obtain a desired precision is discussed in Section 8.3.

Exercises

Methods

1. A simple random sample of 40 items resulted in a sample mean of 25. The population standard deviation is $\sigma = 5$.
   a. What is the standard error of the mean, $\sigma_{\bar{x}}$?
   b. At 95% confidence, what is the margin of error?

2. A simple random sample of 50 items from a population with $\sigma = 6$ resulted in a sample mean of 32.
   a. Provide a 90% confidence interval for the population mean.
   b. Provide a 95% confidence interval for the population mean.
   c. Provide a 99% confidence interval for the population mean.

3. A simple random sample of 60 items resulted in a sample mean of 80. The population standard deviation is $\sigma = 15$.
   a. Compute the 95% confidence interval for the population mean.
   b. Assume that the same sample mean was obtained from a sample of 120 items. Provide a 95% confidence interval for the population mean.
   c. What is the effect of a larger sample size on the interval estimate?

4. A 95% confidence interval for a population mean was reported to be 152 to 160. If $\sigma = 15$, what sample size was used in this study?

Applications

Houston

5. Data were collected on the amount spent by 64 customers for lunch at a major Houston restaurant. These data are contained in the file named Houston. Based on past studies the population standard deviation is known with $\sigma = \$6$.
   a. At 99% confidence, what is the margin of error?
   b. Develop a 99% confidence interval estimate of the mean amount spent for lunch.

TravelTax

6. In an attempt to assess total daily travel taxes in various cities, the Global Business Travel Association conducted a study of daily travel taxes on lodging, rental cars, and meals (GBTA Foundation website, October 30, 2012). The data in the file named TravelTax are consistent with the findings of that study for business travel to Chicago. Assume the population standard deviation is known to be $8.50 and develop a 95% confidence interval of the population mean total daily travel taxes for Chicago.

7. *The Wall Street Journal* reported that automobile crashes cost the United States $162 billion annually (*The Wall Street Journal,* March 5, 2008). The average cost per person for crashes in the Tampa, Florida, area was reported to be $1,599. Suppose this average cost was based on a sample of 50 persons who had been involved in car crashes and that the population standard deviation is $\sigma = \$600$. What is the margin of error for a 95% confidence interval? What would you recommend if the study required a margin of error of $150 or less?

8. Studies show that massage therapy has a variety of health benefits and it is not too expensive (*The Wall Street Journal,* March 13, 2012). A sample of 10 typical one-hour massage therapy sessions showed an average charge of $59. The population standard deviation for a one-hour session is $\sigma = \$5.50$.
   a. What assumptions about the population should we be willing to make if a margin of error is desired?
   b. Using 95% confidence, what is the margin of error?
   c. Using 99% confidence, what is the margin of error?

TaxReturn

9. AARP reported on a study conducted to learn how long it takes individuals to prepare their federal income tax return (*AARP Bulletin,* April 2008). The data contained in the file named TaxReturn are consistent with the study results. These data provide the time in hours required for 40 individuals to complete their federal income tax returns. Using past years' data, the population standard deviation can be assumed known with $\sigma = 9$ hours. What is the 95% confidence interval estimate of the mean time it takes an individual to complete a federal income tax return?

10. Costs are rising for all kinds of medical care. The mean monthly rent at assisted-living facilities was reported to have increased 17% over the last five years to $3,486 (*The Wall Street Journal,*

October 27, 2012). Assume this cost estimate is based on a sample of 120 facilities. From past studies, it can be assumed that the population standard deviation is $\sigma = \$650$.

a. Develop a 90% confidence interval estimate of the population mean monthly rent.

b. Develop a 95% confidence interval estimate of the population mean monthly rent.

c. Develop a 99% confidence interval estimate of the population mean monthly rent.

d. What happens to the width of the confidence interval as the confidence level is increased? Does this seem reasonable? Explain.

8.2 Population Mean: σ Unknown

William Sealy Gosset, writing under the name "Student," is the developer of the t distribution. Gosset, an Oxford graduate in mathematics, worked for the Guinness Brewery in Dublin, Ireland. He developed the t distribution while working on small-scale materials and temperature experiments.

When developing an interval estimate of a population mean we usually do not have a good estimate of the population standard deviation either. In these cases, we must use the same sample to estimate both μ and σ. This situation represents the **σ unknown** case. When s is used to estimate σ, the margin of error and the interval estimate for the population mean are based on a probability distribution known as the *t* **distribution**. Although the mathematical development of the *t* distribution is based on the assumption of a normal distribution for the population we are sampling from, research shows that the *t* distribution can be successfully applied in many situations where the population deviates significantly from normal. Later in this section we provide guidelines for using the *t* distribution if the population is not normally distributed.

The *t* distribution is a family of similar probability distributions, with a specific *t* distribution depending on a parameter known as the **degrees of freedom**. The *t* distribution with 1 degree of freedom is unique, as is the *t* distribution with 2 degrees of freedom, with 3 degrees of freedom, and so on. As the number of degrees of freedom increases, the difference between the *t* distribution and the standard normal distribution becomes smaller and smaller. Figure 8.4 shows *t* distributions with 10 and 20 degrees

FIGURE 8.4 COMPARISON OF THE STANDARD NORMAL DISTRIBUTION WITH *t* DISTRIBUTIONS HAVING 10 AND 20 DEGREES OF FREEDOM

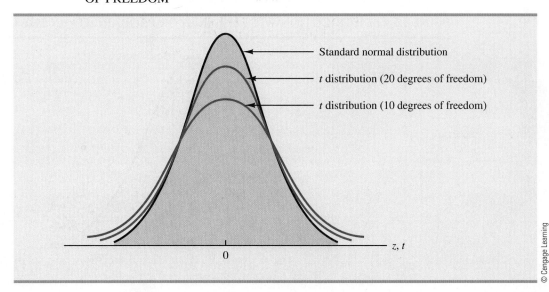

Standard normal distribution

t distribution (20 degrees of freedom)

t distribution (10 degrees of freedom)

z, t

0

© Cengage Learning

of freedom and their relationship to the standard normal probability distribution. Note that a t distribution with more degrees of freedom exhibits less variability and more closely resembles the standard normal distribution. Note also that the mean of the t distribution is zero.

We place a subscript on t to indicate the area in the upper tail of the t distribution. For example, just as we used $z_{.025}$ to indicate the z value providing a .025 area in the upper tail of a standard normal distribution, we will use $t_{.025}$ to indicate a .025 area in the upper tail of a t distribution. In general, we will use the notation $t_{\alpha/2}$ to represent a t value with an area of $\alpha/2$ in the upper tail of the t distribution. See Figure 8.5.

Table 2 in Appendix B contains a table for the t distribution. A portion of this table is shown in Table 8.2. Each row in the table corresponds to a separate t distribution with the degrees of freedom shown. For example, for a t distribution with 9 degrees of freedom, $t_{.025} = 2.262$. Similarly, for a t distribution with 60 degrees of freedom, $t_{.025} = 2.000$. As the degrees of freedom continue to increase, $t_{.025}$ approaches $z_{.025} = 1.96$. In fact, the standard normal distribution z values can be found in the infinite degrees of freedom row (labeled ∞) of the t distribution table. If the degrees of freedom exceed 100, the infinite degrees of freedom row can be used to approximate the actual t value; in other words, for more than 100 degrees of freedom, the standard normal z value provides a good approximation to the t value.

As the degrees of freedom increase, the t distribution approaches the standard normal distribution.

Margin of Error and the Interval Estimate

In Section 8.1 we showed that an interval estimate of a population mean for the σ known case is

$$\bar{x} \pm z_{\alpha/2} \frac{\sigma}{\sqrt{n}}$$

To compute an interval estimate of μ for the σ unknown case, the sample standard deviation s is used to estimate σ, and $z_{\alpha/2}$ is replaced by the t distribution value $t_{\alpha/2}$. The margin

FIGURE 8.5 t DISTRIBUTION WITH $\alpha/2$ AREA OR PROBABILITY IN THE UPPER TAIL

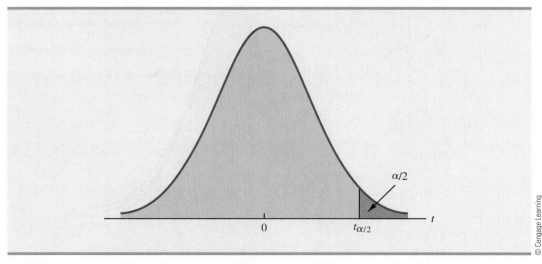

© Cengage Learning

TABLE 8.2   SELECTED VALUES FROM THE *t* DISTRIBUTION TABLE*

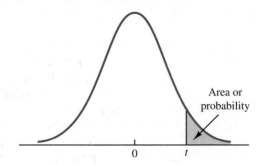

Degrees of Freedom	Area in Upper Tail					
	.20	**.10**	**.05**	**.025**	**.01**	**.005**
1	1.376	3.078	6.314	12.706	31.821	63.656
2	1.061	1.886	2.920	4.303	6.965	9.925
3	.978	1.638	2.353	3.182	4.541	5.841
4	.941	1.533	2.132	2.776	3.747	4.604
5	.920	1.476	2.015	2.571	3.365	4.032
6	.906	1.440	1.943	2.447	3.143	3.707
7	.896	1.415	1.895	2.365	2.998	3.499
8	.889	1.397	1.860	2.306	2.896	3.355
9	.883	1.383	1.833	2.262	2.821	3.250
⋮	⋮	⋮	⋮	⋮	⋮	⋮
60	.848	1.296	1.671	2.000	2.390	2.660
61	.848	1.296	1.670	2.000	2.389	2.659
62	.847	1.295	1.670	1.999	2.388	2.657
63	.847	1.295	1.669	1.998	2.387	2.656
64	.847	1.295	1.669	1.998	2.386	2.655
65	.847	1.295	1.669	1.997	2.385	2.654
66	.847	1.295	1.668	1.997	2.384	2.652
67	.847	1.294	1.668	1.996	2.383	2.651
68	.847	1.294	1.668	1.995	2.382	2.650
69	.847	1.294	1.667	1.995	2.382	2.649
⋮	⋮	⋮	⋮	⋮	⋮	⋮
90	.846	1.291	1.662	1.987	2.368	2.632
91	.846	1.291	1.662	1.986	2.368	2.631
92	.846	1.291	1.662	1.986	2.368	2.630
93	.846	1.291	1.661	1.986	2.367	2.630
94	.845	1.291	1.661	1.986	2.367	2.629
95	.845	1.291	1.661	1.985	2.366	2.629
96	.845	1.290	1.661	1.985	2.366	2.628
97	.845	1.290	1.661	1.985	2.365	2.627
98	.845	1.290	1.661	1.984	2.365	2.627
99	.845	1.290	1.660	1.984	2.364	2.626
100	.845	1.290	1.660	1.984	2.364	2.626
∞	.842	1.282	1.645	1.960	2.326	2.576

Note: A more extensive table is provided as Table 2 of Appendix B.

of error is then given by $t_{\alpha/2}\, s/\sqrt{n}$. With this margin of error, the general expression for an interval estimate of a population mean when σ is unknown follows.

INTERVAL ESTIMATE OF A POPULATION MEAN: σ UNKNOWN

$$\bar{x} \pm t_{\alpha/2}\frac{s}{\sqrt{n}} \tag{8.2}$$

where s is the sample standard deviation, $(1 - \alpha)$ is the confidence coefficient, and $t_{\alpha/2}$ is the t value providing an area of $\alpha/2$ in the upper tail of the t distribution with $n - 1$ degrees of freedom.

The reason the number of degrees of freedom associated with the t value in expression (8.2) is $n - 1$ concerns the use of s as an estimate of the population standard deviation σ. The expression for the sample standard deviation is

$$s = \sqrt{\frac{\sum(x_i - \bar{x})^2}{n - 1}}$$

Degrees of freedom refer to the number of independent pieces of information that go into the computation of $\sum(x_i - \bar{x})^2$. The n pieces of information involved in computing $\sum(x_i - \bar{x})^2$ are as follows: $x_1 - \bar{x}, x_2 - \bar{x}, \ldots, x_n - \bar{x}$. In Section 3.2 we indicated that $\sum(x_i - \bar{x}) = 0$ for any data set. Thus, only $n - 1$ of the $x_i - \bar{x}$ values are independent; that is, if we know $n - 1$ of the values, the remaining value can be determined exactly by using the condition that the sum of the $x_i - \bar{x}$ values must be 0. Thus, $n - 1$ is the number of degrees of freedom associated with $\sum(x_i - \bar{x})^2$ and hence the number of degrees of freedom for the t distribution in expression (8.2).

To illustrate the interval estimation procedure for the σ unknown case, we will consider a study designed to estimate the mean credit card debt for the population of U.S. households. A sample of $n = 70$ households provided the credit card balances shown in Table 8.3. For this situation, no previous estimate of the population standard deviation σ is available. Thus, the sample data must be used to estimate both the population mean and the population standard deviation. Using the data in Table 8.3, we compute the sample mean $\bar{x} = \$9,312$ and the sample standard deviation $s = \$4,007$. With 95% confidence and $n - 1 = 69$ degrees of

TABLE 8.3   CREDIT CARD BALANCES FOR A SAMPLE OF 70 HOUSEHOLDS

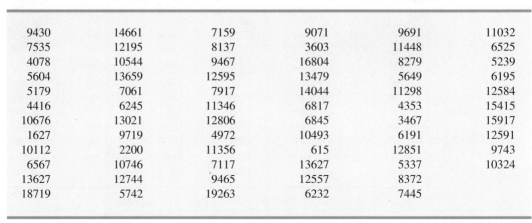

9430	14661	7159	9071	9691	11032
7535	12195	8137	3603	11448	6525
4078	10544	9467	16804	8279	5239
5604	13659	12595	13479	5649	6195
5179	7061	7917	14044	11298	12584
4416	6245	11346	6817	4353	15415
10676	13021	12806	6845	3467	15917
1627	9719	4972	10493	6191	12591
10112	2200	11356	615	12851	9743
6567	10746	7117	13627	5337	10324
13627	12744	9465	12557	8372	
18719	5742	19263	6232	7445	

freedom, Table 8.2 can be used to obtain the appropriate value for $t_{.025}$. We want the t value in the row with 69 degrees of freedom, and the column corresponding to .025 in the upper tail. The value shown is $t_{.025} = 1.995$.

We use expression (8.2) to compute an interval estimate of the population mean credit card balance.

$$9312 \pm 1.995 \frac{4007}{\sqrt{70}}$$

$$9312 \pm 955$$

The point estimate of the population mean is $9,312, the margin of error is $955, and the 95% confidence interval is $9312 - 955 = \$8,357$ to $9312 + 955 = \$10,267$. Thus, we are 95% confident that the mean credit card balance for the population of all households is between $8,357 and $10,267.

The procedures used by Minitab, Excel, and StatTools to develop confidence intervals for a population mean are described in Appendixes 8.1, 8.2, and 8.3. For the household credit card balances study, the results of the Minitab interval estimation procedure are shown in Figure 8.6. The sample of 70 households provides a sample mean credit card balance of $9,312, a sample standard deviation of $4,007, a standard error of the mean of $479, and a 95% confidence interval of $8,357 to $10,267.

Practical Advice

If the population follows a normal distribution, the confidence interval provided by expression (8.2) is exact and can be used for any sample size. If the population does not follow a normal distribution, the confidence interval provided by expression (8.2) will be approximate. In this case, the quality of the approximation depends on both the distribution of the population and the sample size.

Larger sample sizes are needed if the distribution of the population is highly skewed or includes outliers.

In most applications, a sample size of $n \geq 30$ is adequate when using expression (8.2) to develop an interval estimate of a population mean. However, if the population distribution is highly skewed or contains outliers, most statisticians would recommend increasing the sample size to 50 or more. If the population is not normally distributed but is roughly symmetric, sample sizes as small as 15 can be expected to provide good approximate confidence intervals. With smaller sample sizes, expression (8.2) should only be used if the analyst believes, or is willing to assume, that the population distribution is at least approximately normal.

Using a Small Sample

In the following example we develop an interval estimate for a population mean when the sample size is small. As we already noted, an understanding of the distribution of the population becomes a factor in deciding whether the interval estimation procedure provides acceptable results.

Scheer Industries is considering a new computer-assisted program to train maintenance employees to do machine repairs. In order to fully evaluate the program, the director of

FIGURE 8.6   MINITAB CONFIDENCE INTERVAL FOR THE CREDIT CARD BALANCE SURVEY

Variable	N	Mean	StDev	SE Mean	95% CI
NewBalance	70	9312	4007	479	(8357, 10267)

TABLE 8.4   TRAINING TIME IN DAYS FOR A SAMPLE OF 20 SCHEER
INDUSTRIES EMPLOYEES

52	59	54	42
44	50	42	48
55	54	60	55
44	62	62	57
45	46	43	56

manufacturing requested an estimate of the population mean time required for maintenance
employees to complete the computer-assisted training.

A sample of 20 employees is selected, with each employee in the sample completing
the training program. Data on the training time in days for the 20 employees are shown in
Table 8.4. A histogram of the sample data appears in Figure 8.7. What can we say about the
distribution of the population based on this histogram? First, the sample data do not support the conclusion that the distribution of the population is normal, yet we do not see any
evidence of skewness or outliers. Therefore, using the guidelines in the previous subsection,
we conclude that an interval estimate based on the t distribution appears acceptable for the
sample of 20 employees.

We continue by computing the sample mean and sample standard deviation as follows.

$$\bar{x} = \frac{\Sigma x_i}{n} = \frac{1030}{20} = 51.5 \text{ days}$$

$$s = \sqrt{\frac{\Sigma (x_i - \bar{x})^2}{n-1}} = \sqrt{\frac{889}{20-1}} = 6.84 \text{ days}$$

FIGURE 8.7   HISTOGRAM OF TRAINING TIMES FOR THE SCHEER INDUSTRIES SAMPLE

For a 95% confidence interval, we use Table 2 of Appendix B and $n - 1 = 19$ degrees of freedom to obtain $t_{.025} = 2.093$. Expression (8.2) provides the interval estimate of the population mean.

$$51.5 \pm 2.093\left(\frac{6.84}{\sqrt{20}}\right)$$

$$51.5 \pm 3.2$$

The point estimate of the population mean is 51.5 days. The margin of error is 3.2 days and the 95% confidence interval is $51.5 - 3.2 = 48.3$ days to $51.5 + 3.2 = 54.7$ days.

Using a histogram of the sample data to learn about the distribution of a population is not always conclusive, but in many cases it provides the only information available. The histogram, along with judgment on the part of the analyst, can often be used to decide whether expression (8.2) can be used to develop the interval estimate.

Summary of Interval Estimation Procedures

We provided two approaches to developing an interval estimate of a population mean. For the σ known case, σ and the standard normal distribution are used in expression (8.1) to compute the margin of error and to develop the interval estimate. For the σ unknown case, the sample standard deviation s and the t distribution are used in expression (8.2) to compute the margin of error and to develop the interval estimate.

A summary of the interval estimation procedures for the two cases is shown in Figure 8.8. In most applications, a sample size of $n \geq 30$ is adequate. If the population has a normal or approximately normal distribution, however, smaller sample sizes may be used.

FIGURE 8.8 SUMMARY OF INTERVAL ESTIMATION PROCEDURES FOR A POPULATION MEAN

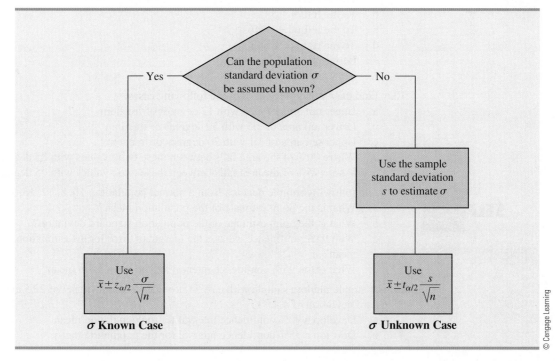

© Cengage Learning

For the σ unknown case a sample size of $n \geq 50$ is recommended if the population distribution is believed to be highly skewed or has outliers.

NOTES AND COMMENTS

1. When σ is known, the margin of error, $z_{\alpha/2}(\sigma/\sqrt{n})$, is fixed and is the same for all samples of size n. When σ is unknown, the margin of error, $t_{\alpha/2}(s/\sqrt{n})$, varies from sample to sample. This variation occurs because the sample standard deviation s varies depending upon the sample selected. A large value for s provides a larger margin of error, while a small value for s provides a smaller margin of error.

2. What happens to confidence interval estimates when the population is skewed? Consider a population that is skewed to the right with large data values stretching the distribution to the right. When such skewness exists, the sample mean $\bar{x}$ and the sample standard deviation s are positively correlated. Larger values of s tend to be associated with larger values of $\bar{x}$. Thus, when $\bar{x}$ is larger than the population mean, s tends to be larger than σ. This skewness causes the margin of error, $t_{\alpha/2}(s/\sqrt{n})$, to be larger than it would be with σ known. The confidence interval with the larger margin of error tends to include the population mean μ more often than it would if the true value of σ were used. But when $\bar{x}$ is smaller than the population mean, the correlation between $\bar{x}$ and s causes the margin of error to be small. In this case, the confidence interval with the smaller margin of error tends to miss the population mean more than it would if we knew σ and used it. For this reason, we recommend using larger sample sizes with highly skewed population distributions.

Exercises

Methods

11. For a t distribution with 16 degrees of freedom, find the area, or probability, in each region.
    a. To the right of 2.120
    b. To the left of 1.337
    c. To the left of -1.746
    d. To the right of 2.583
    e. Between -2.120 and 2.120
    f. Between -1.746 and 1.746

12. Find the t value(s) for each of the following cases.
    a. Upper tail area of .025 with 12 degrees of freedom
    b. Lower tail area of .05 with 50 degrees of freedom
    c. Upper tail area of .01 with 30 degrees of freedom
    d. Where 90% of the area falls between these two t values with 25 degrees of freedom
    e. Where 95% of the area falls between these two t values with 45 degrees of freedom

13. The following sample data are from a normal population: 10, 8, 12, 15, 13, 11, 6, 5.
    a. What is the point estimate of the population mean?
    b. What is the point estimate of the population standard deviation?
    c. With 95% confidence, what is the margin of error for the estimation of the population mean?
    d. What is the 95% confidence interval for the population mean?

14. A simple random sample with $n = 54$ provided a sample mean of 22.5 and a sample standard deviation of 4.4.
    a. Develop a 90% confidence interval for the population mean.
    b. Develop a 95% confidence interval for the population mean.

c.   Develop a 99% confidence interval for the population mean.
d.   What happens to the margin of error and the confidence interval as the confidence level is increased?

Applications

15.   Sales personnel for Skillings Distributors submit weekly reports listing the customer contacts made during the week. A sample of 65 weekly reports showed a sample mean of 19.5 customer contacts per week. The sample standard deviation was 5.2. Provide 90% and 95% confidence intervals for the population mean number of weekly customer contacts for the sales personnel.

CorporateBonds

16.   A sample containing years to maturity and yield for 40 corporate bonds is contained in the data file named CorporateBonds (*Barron's,* April 2, 2012).
a.   What is the sample mean years to maturity for corporate bonds and what is the sample standard deviation?
b.   Develop a 95% confidence interval for the population mean years to maturity.
c.   What is the sample mean yield on corporate bonds and what is the sample standard deviation?
d.   Develop a 95% confidence interval for the population mean yield on corporate bonds.

Miami

17.   The International Air Transport Association surveys business travelers to develop quality ratings for transatlantic gateway airports. The maximum possible rating is 10. Suppose a simple random sample of 50 business travelers is selected and each traveler is asked to provide a rating for the Miami International Airport. The ratings obtained from the sample of 50 business travelers follow.

6	4	6	8	7	7	6	3	3	8	10	4	8
7	8	7	5	9	5	8	4	3	8	5	5	4
4	4	8	4	5	6	2	5	9	9	8	4	8
9	9	5	9	7	8	3	10	8	9	6		

Develop a 95% confidence interval estimate of the population mean rating for Miami.

JobSearch

18.   Older people often have a hard time finding work. AARP reported on the number of weeks it takes a worker aged 55 plus to find a job. The data on number of weeks spent searching for a job contained in the file JobSearch are consistent with the AARP findings (*AARP Bulletin,* April 2008).
a.   Provide a point estimate of the population mean number of weeks it takes a worker aged 55 plus to find a job.
b.   At 95% confidence, what is the margin of error?
c.   What is the 95% confidence interval estimate of the mean?
d.   Discuss the degree of skewness found in the sample data. What suggestion would you make for a repeat of this study?

19.   The average cost per night of a hotel room in New York City is $273 (*SmartMoney,* March 2009). Assume this estimate is based on a sample of 45 hotels and that the sample standard deviation is $65.
a.   With 95% confidence, what is the margin of error?
b.   What is the 95% confidence interval estimate of the population mean?
c.   Two years ago the average cost of a hotel room in New York City was $229. Discuss the change in cost over the two-year period.

Program

20. Is your favorite TV program often interrupted by advertising? CNBC presented statistics on the average number of programming minutes in a half-hour sitcom (CNBC, February 23, 2006). The following data (in minutes) are representative of their findings.

21.06	22.24	20.62
21.66	21.23	23.86
23.82	20.30	21.52
21.52	21.91	23.14
20.02	22.20	21.20
22.37	22.19	22.34
23.36	23.44	

Assume the population is approximately normal. Provide a point estimate and a 95% confidence interval for the mean number of programming minutes during a half-hour television sitcom.

Alcohol

21. Consumption of alcoholic beverages by young women of drinking age in the United Kingdom, the United States, and Europe was reported (*The Wall Street Journal,* February 15, 2006). Data (annual consumption in liters) consistent with the findings reported in *The Wall Street Journal* article are shown for a sample of 20 European young women.

266	82	199	174	97
170	222	115	130	169
164	102	113	171	0
93	0	93	110	130

Assuming the population is roughly symmetric, construct a 95% confidence interval for the mean annual consumption of alcoholic beverages by European young women.

22. Disney's *Hannah Montana: The Movie* opened on Easter weekend in April 2009. Over the three-day weekend, the movie became the number-one box office attraction (*The Wall Street Journal,* April 13, 2009). The ticket sales revenue in dollars for a sample of 25 theaters is as follows.

TicketSales

20,200	10,150	13,000	11,320	9700
8350	7300	14,000	9940	11,200
10,750	6240	12,700	7430	13,500
13,900	4200	6750	6700	9330
13,185	9200	21,400	11,380	10,800

a. What is the 95% confidence interval estimate for the mean ticket sales revenue per theater? Interpret this result.

b. Using the movie ticket price of $7.16 per ticket, what is the estimate of the mean number of customers per theater?

c. The movie was shown in 3118 theaters. Estimate the total number of customers who saw *Hannah Montana: The Movie* and the total box office ticket sales for the three-day weekend.

(8.3) Determining the Sample Size

If a desired margin of error is selected prior to sampling, the procedures in this section can be used to determine the sample size necessary to satisfy the margin of error requirement.

In providing practical advice in the two preceding sections, we commented on the role of the sample size in providing good approximate confidence intervals when the population is not normally distributed. In this section, we focus on another aspect of the sample size issue. We describe how to choose a sample size large enough to provide a desired margin of error. To understand how this process works, we return to the σ known case presented in Section 8.1. Using expression (8.1), the interval estimate is

$$\bar{x} \pm z_{\alpha/2} \frac{\sigma}{\sqrt{n}}$$

The quantity $z_{\alpha/2}(\sigma/\sqrt{n})$ is the margin of error. Thus, we see that $z_{\alpha/2}$, the population standard deviation σ, and the sample size n combine to determine the margin of error. Once we select a confidence coefficient $1 - \alpha$, $z_{\alpha/2}$ can be determined. Then, if we have a value for σ, we can determine the sample size n needed to provide any desired margin of error. Development of the formula used to compute the required sample size n follows.

Let E = the desired margin of error:

$$E = z_{\alpha/2} \frac{\sigma}{\sqrt{n}}$$

Solving for $\sqrt{n}$, we have

$$\sqrt{n} = \frac{z_{\alpha/2}\sigma}{E}$$

Squaring both sides of this equation, we obtain the following expression for the sample size.

Equation (8.3) can be used to provide a good sample size recommendation. However, judgment on the part of the analyst should be used to determine whether the final sample size should be adjusted upward.

SAMPLE SIZE FOR AN INTERVAL ESTIMATE OF A POPULATION MEAN

$$n = \frac{(z_{\alpha/2})^2\sigma^2}{E^2} \qquad (8.3)$$

This sample size provides the desired margin of error at the chosen confidence level.

In equation (8.3), E is the margin of error that the user is willing to accept, and the value of $z_{\alpha/2}$ follows directly from the confidence level to be used in developing the interval estimate. Although user preference must be considered, 95% confidence is the most frequently chosen value ($z_{.025} = 1.96$).

Finally, use of equation (8.3) requires a value for the population standard deviation σ. However, even if σ is unknown, we can use equation (8.3) provided we have a preliminary or *planning value* for σ. In practice, one of the following procedures can be chosen.

A planning value for the population standard deviation σ must be specified before the sample size can be determined. Three methods of obtaining a planning value for σ are discussed here.

1. Use the estimate of the population standard deviation computed from data of previous studies as the planning value for σ.
2. Use a pilot study to select a preliminary sample. The sample standard deviation from the preliminary sample can be used as the planning value for σ.
3. Use judgment or a "best guess" for the value of σ. For example, we might begin by estimating the largest and smallest data values in the population. The difference between the largest and smallest values provides an estimate of the range for the data. Finally, the range divided by 4 is often suggested as a rough approximation of the standard deviation and thus an acceptable planning value for σ.

Let us demonstrate the use of equation (8.3) to determine the sample size by considering the following example. A previous study that investigated the cost of renting automobiles in the United States found a mean cost of approximately $55 per day for renting a midsize automobile. Suppose that the organization that conducted this study would like to conduct a new study in order to estimate the population mean daily rental cost for a midsize automobile in the United States. In designing the new study, the project director specifies that the population mean daily rental cost be estimated with a margin of error of $2 and a 95% level of confidence.

The project director specified a desired margin of error of $E = 2$, and the 95% level of confidence indicates $z_{.025} = 1.96$. Thus, we only need a planning value for the population standard deviation σ in order to compute the required sample size. At this point, an analyst reviewed the sample data from the previous study and found that the sample standard deviation for the daily rental cost was $9.65. Using 9.65 as the planning value for σ, we obtain

Equation (8.3) provides the minimum sample size needed to satisfy the desired margin of error requirement. If the computed sample size is not an integer, rounding up to the next integer value will provide a margin of error slightly smaller than required.

$$n = \frac{(z_{\alpha/2})^2 \sigma^2}{E^2} = \frac{(1.96)^2 (9.65)^2}{2^2} = 89.43$$

Thus, the sample size for the new study needs to be at least 89.43 midsize automobile rentals in order to satisfy the project director's $2 margin-of-error requirement. In cases where the computed n is not an integer, we round up to the next integer value; hence, the recommended sample size is 90 midsize automobile rentals.

Exercises

Methods

23. How large a sample should be selected to provide a 95% confidence interval with a margin of error of 10? Assume that the population standard deviation is 40.

24. The range for a set of data is estimated to be 36.
    a. What is the planning value for the population standard deviation?
    b. At 95% confidence, how large a sample would provide a margin of error of 3?
    c. At 95% confidence, how large a sample would provide a margin of error of 2?

Applications

25. Refer to the Scheer Industries example in Section 8.2. Use 6.84 days as a planning value for the population standard deviation.
    a. Assuming 95% confidence, what sample size would be required to obtain a margin of error of 1.5 days?
    b. If the precision statement was made with 90% confidence, what sample size would be required to obtain a margin of error of 2 days?

26. The U.S. Energy Information Administration (US EIA) reported that the average price for a gallon of regular gasoline is $3.94 (US EIA website, April 6, 2012). The US EIA updates its estimates of average gas prices on a weekly basis. Assume the standard deviation is $.25 for the price of a gallon of regular gasoline and recommend the appropriate sample size for the US EIA to use if they wish to report each of the following margins of error at 95% confidence.
    a. The desired margin of error is $.10.
    b. The desired margin of error is $.07.
    c. The desired margin of error is $.05.

27. Annual starting salaries for college graduates with degrees in business administration are generally expected to be between $30,000 and $45,000. Assume that a 95% confidence interval estimate of the population mean annual starting salary is desired. What is the planning value for the population standard deviation? How large a sample should be taken if the desired margin of error is
    a. $500?
    b. $200?
    c. $100?
    d. Would you recommend trying to obtain the $100 margin of error? Explain.

28. An online survey by ShareBuilder, a retirement plan provider, and Harris Interactive reported that 60% of female business owners are not confident they are saving enough for retirement (*SmallBiz*, Winter 2006). Suppose we would like to do a follow-up study to determine how much female business owners are saving each year toward retirement and want to use $100 as the desired margin of error for an interval estimate of the population mean. Use $1,100 as a planning value for the standard deviation and recommend a sample size for each of the following situations.
    a. A 90% confidence interval is desired for the mean amount saved.
    b. A 95% confidence interval is desired for the mean amount saved.

c.   A 99% confidence interval is desired for the mean amount saved.

d.   When the desired margin of error is set, what happens to the sample size as the confidence level is increased? Would you recommend using a 99% confidence interval in this case? Discuss.

29.   Customers arrive at a movie theater at the advertised movie time only to find that they have to sit through several previews and prepreview ads before the movie starts. Many complain that the time devoted to previews is too long (*The Wall Street Journal*, October 12, 2012). A preliminary sample conducted by *The Wall Street Journal* showed that the standard deviation of the amount of time devoted to previews was 4 minutes. Use that as a planning value for the standard deviation in answering the following questions.

a.   If we want to estimate the population mean time for previews at movie theaters with a margin of error of 75 seconds, what sample size should be used? Assume 95% confidence.

b.   If we want to estimate the population mean time for previews at movie theaters with a margin of error of 1 minute, what sample size should be used? Assume 95% confidence.

30.   There has been a trend toward less driving in the last few years, especially by young people. From 2001 to 2009 the annual vehicle miles traveled by people from 16 to 34 years of age decreased from 10,300 to 7900 miles per person (U.S. PIRG and Education Fund website, April 6, 2012). Assume the standard deviation was 2000 miles in 2009. Suppose you would like to conduct a survey to develop a 95% confidence interval estimate of the annual vehicle-miles per person for people 16 to 34 years of age at the current time. A margin of error of 100 miles is desired. How large a sample should be used for the current survey?

8.4   Population Proportion

In the introduction to this chapter we said that the general form of an interval estimate of a population proportion p is

$$\bar{p} \pm \text{Margin of error}$$

The sampling distribution of $\bar{p}$ plays a key role in computing the margin of error for this interval estimate.

In Chapter 7 we said that the sampling distribution of $\bar{p}$ can be approximated by a normal distribution whenever $np \geq 5$ and $n(1 - p) \geq 5$. Figure 8.9 shows the normal approximation

FIGURE 8.9   NORMAL APPROXIMATION OF THE SAMPLING DISTRIBUTION OF $\bar{p}$

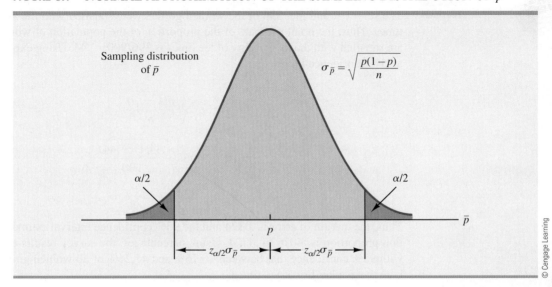

of the sampling distribution of $\bar{p}$. The mean of the sampling distribution of $\bar{p}$ is the population proportion p, and the standard error of $\bar{p}$ is

$$\sigma_{\bar{p}} = \sqrt{\frac{p(1 - p)}{n}} \qquad (8.4)$$

Because the sampling distribution of $\bar{p}$ is normally distributed, if we choose $z_{\alpha/2}\sigma_{\bar{p}}$ as the margin of error in an interval estimate of a population proportion, we know that $100(1 - \alpha)\%$ of the intervals generated will contain the true population proportion. But $\sigma_{\bar{p}}$ cannot be used directly in the computation of the margin of error because p will not be known; p is what we are trying to estimate. So $\bar{p}$ is substituted for p and the margin of error for an interval estimate of a population proportion is given by

$$\text{Margin of error} = z_{\alpha/2}\sqrt{\frac{\bar{p}(1 - \bar{p})}{n}} \qquad (8.5)$$

With this margin of error, the general expression for an interval estimate of a population proportion is as follows.

INTERVAL ESTIMATE OF A POPULATION PROPORTION

When developing confidence intervals for proportions, the quantity $z_{\alpha/2}\sqrt{\bar{p}(1 - \bar{p})/n}$ provides the margin of error.

$$\bar{p} \pm z_{\alpha/2}\sqrt{\frac{\bar{p}(1 - \bar{p})}{n}} \qquad (8.6)$$

where $1- \alpha$ is the confidence coefficient and $z_{\alpha/2}$ is the z value providing an area of $\alpha/2$ in the upper tail of the standard normal distribution.

TeeTimes

The following example illustrates the computation of the margin of error and interval estimate for a population proportion. A national survey of 900 women golfers was conducted to learn how women golfers view their treatment at golf courses in the United States. The survey found that 396 of the women golfers were satisfied with the availability of tee times. Thus, the point estimate of the proportion of the population of women golfers who are satisfied with the availability of tee times is $396/900 = .44$. Using expression (8.6) and a 95% confidence level,

$$\bar{p} \pm z_{\alpha/2}\sqrt{\frac{\bar{p}(1 - \bar{p})}{n}}$$

$$.44 \pm 1.96\sqrt{\frac{.44(1 - .44)}{900}}$$

$$.44 \pm .0324$$

Thus, the margin of error is .0324 and the 95% confidence interval estimate of the population proportion is .4076 to .4724. Using percentages, the survey results enable us to state with 95% confidence that between 40.76% and 47.24% of all women golfers are satisfied with the availability of tee times.

Determining the Sample Size

Let us consider the question of how large the sample size should be to obtain an estimate of a population proportion at a specified level of precision. The rationale for the sample size determination in developing interval estimates of p is similar to the rationale used in Section 8.3 to determine the sample size for estimating a population mean.

Previously in this section we said that the margin of error associated with an interval estimate of a population proportion is $z_{\alpha/2}\sqrt{\bar{p}(1-\bar{p})/n}$. The margin of error is based on the value of $z_{\alpha/2}$, the sample proportion $\bar{p}$, and the sample size n. Larger sample sizes provide a smaller margin of error and better precision.

Let E denote the desired margin of error.

$$E = z_{\alpha/2}\sqrt{\frac{\bar{p}(1-\bar{p})}{n}}$$

Solving this equation for n provides a formula for the sample size that will provide a margin of error of size E.

$$n = \frac{(z_{\alpha/2})^2 \bar{p}(1-\bar{p})}{E^2}$$

Note, however, that we cannot use this formula to compute the sample size that will provide the desired margin of error because $\bar{p}$ will not be known until after we select the sample. What we need, then, is a planning value for $\bar{p}$ that can be used to make the computation. Using p^* to denote the planning value for $\bar{p}$, the following formula can be used to compute the sample size that will provide a margin of error of size E.

SAMPLE SIZE FOR AN INTERVAL ESTIMATE OF A POPULATION PROPORTION

$$n = \frac{(z_{\alpha/2})^2 p^*(1-p^*)}{E^2} \tag{8.7}$$

In practice, the planning value p^* can be chosen by one of the following procedures.

1. Use the sample proportion from a previous sample of the same or similar units.
2. Use a pilot study to select a preliminary sample. The sample proportion from this sample can be used as the planning value, p^*.
3. Use judgment or a "best guess" for the value of p^*.
4. If none of the preceding alternatives apply, use a planning value of $p^* = .50$.

Let us return to the survey of women golfers and assume that the company is interested in conducting a new survey to estimate the current proportion of the population of women golfers who are satisfied with the availability of tee times. How large should the sample be if the survey director wants to estimate the population proportion with a margin of error of .025 at 95% confidence? With $E = .025$ and $z_{\alpha/2} = 1.96$, we need a planning value p^* to answer the sample size question. Using the previous survey result of $\bar{p} = .44$ as the planning value p^*, equation (8.7) shows that

$$n = \frac{(z_{\alpha/2})^2 p^*(1-p^*)}{E^2} = \frac{(1.96)^2(.44)(1-.44)}{(.025)^2} = 1514.5$$

TABLE 8.5   SOME POSSIBLE VALUES FOR $p^*(1 - p^*)$

p^*	$p^*(1 - p^*)$	
.10	(.10)(.90) = .09	
.30	(.30)(.70) = .21	
.40	(.40)(.60) = .24	
.50	(.50)(.50) = .25	← Largest value for $p^*(1 - p^*)$
.60	(.60)(.40) = .24	
.70	(.70)(.30) = .21	
.90	(.90)(.10) = .09	

© Cengage Learning

Thus, the sample size must be at least 1514.5 women golfers to satisfy the margin of error requirement. Rounding up to the next integer value indicates that a sample of 1515 women golfers is recommended to satisfy the margin of error requirement.

The fourth alternative suggested for selecting a planning value p^* is to use $p^* = .50$. This value of p^* is frequently used when no other information is available. To understand why, note that the numerator of equation (8.7) shows that the sample size is proportional to the quantity $p^*(1 - p^*)$. A larger value for the quantity $p^*(1 - p^*)$ will result in a larger sample size. Table 8.5 gives some possible values of $p^*(1 - p^*)$. Note that the largest value of $p^*(1 - p^*)$ occurs when $p^* = .50$. Thus, in case of any uncertainty about an appropriate planning value, we know that $p^* = .50$ will provide the largest sample size recommendation. In effect, we play it safe by recommending the largest necessary sample size. If the sample proportion turns out to be different from the .50 planning value, the margin of error will be smaller than anticipated. Thus, in using $p^* = .50$, we guarantee that the sample size will be sufficient to obtain the desired margin of error.

In the survey of women golfers example, a planning value of $p^* = .50$ would have provided the sample size

$$n = \frac{(z_{\alpha/2})^2 p^*(1 - p^*)}{E^2} = \frac{(1.96)^2(.50)(1 - .50)}{(.025)^2} = 1536.6$$

Thus, a slightly larger sample size of 1537 women golfers would be recommended.

NOTE AND COMMENT

The desired margin of error for estimating a population proportion is almost always .10 or less. In national public opinion polls conducted by organizations such as Gallup and Harris, a .03 or .04 margin of error is common. With such margins of error, equation (8.7) will almost always provide a sample size that is large enough to satisfy the requirements of $np \geq 5$ and $n(1 - p) \geq 5$ for using a normal distribution as an approximation for the sampling distribution of $\bar{x}$.

Exercises

Methods

31. A simple random sample of 400 individuals provides 100 Yes responses.
    a. What is the point estimate of the proportion of the population that would provide Yes responses?
    b. What is your estimate of the standard error of the proportion, $\sigma_{\bar{p}}$?
    c. Compute the 95% confidence interval for the population proportion.

32. A simple random sample of 800 elements generates a sample proportion $\bar{p} = .70$.
    a. Provide a 90% confidence interval for the population proportion.
    b. Provide a 95% confidence interval for the population proportion.

33. In a survey, the planning value for the population proportion is $p^* = .35$. How large a sample should be taken to provide a 95% confidence interval with a margin of error of .05?

34. At 95% confidence, how large a sample should be taken to obtain a margin of error of .03 for the estimation of a population proportion? Assume that past data are not available for developing a planning value for p^*.

Applications

35. The Consumer Reports National Research Center conducted a telephone survey of 2000 adults to learn about the major economic concerns for the future (*Consumer Reports,* January 2009). The survey results showed that 1760 of the respondents think the future health of Social Security is a major economic concern.
    a. What is the point estimate of the population proportion of adults who think the future health of Social Security is a major economic concern.
    b. At 90% confidence, what is the margin of error?
    c. Develop a 90% confidence interval for the population proportion of adults who think the future health of Social Security is a major economic concern.
    d. Develop a 95% confidence interval for this population proportion.

36. According to statistics reported on CNBC, a surprising number of motor vehicles are not covered by insurance (CNBC, February 23, 2006). Sample results, consistent with the CNBC report, showed 46 of 200 vehicles were not covered by insurance.
    a. What is the point estimate of the proportion of vehicles not covered by insurance?
    b. Develop a 95% confidence interval for the population proportion.

ChildOutlook

37. One of the questions on a survey of 1000 adults asked if today's children will be better off than their parents (Rasmussen Reports website October 26, 2012). Representative data are shown in the file ChildOutlook. A response of Yes indicates that the adult surveyed did think today's children will be better off than their parents. A response of No indicates that the adult surveyed did not think today's children will be better off than their parents. A response of Not Sure was given by 23% of the adults surveyed.
    a. What is the point estimate of the proportion of the population of adults who do think that today's children will be better off than their parents?
    b. At 95% confidence, what is the margin of error?
    c. What is the 95% confidence interval for the proportion of adults who do think that today's children will be better off than their parents?
    d. What is the 95% confidence interval for the proportion of adults who do not think that today's children will be better off than their parents?
    e. Which of the confidence intervals in parts (c) and (d) has the smaller margin of error? Why?

38. According to Thomson Financial, through January 25, 2006, the majority of companies reported profits had beaten estimates (*BusinessWeek,* February 6, 2006). A sample of 162 companies showed 104 beat estimates, 29 matched estimates, and 29 fell short.
    a. What is the point estimate of the proportion that fell short of estimates?
    b. Determine the margin of error and provide a 95% confidence interval for the proportion that beat estimates.
    c. How large a sample is needed if the desired margin of error is .05?

39. The percentage of people not covered by health care insurance in 2003 was 15.6% (*Statistical Abstract of the United States,* 2006). A congressional committee has been charged with conducting a sample survey to obtain more current information.
    a. What sample size would you recommend if the committee's goal is to estimate the current proportion of individuals without health care insurance with a margin of error of .03? Use a 95% confidence level.
    b. Repeat part (a) using a 99% confidence level.

40. For many years businesses have struggled with the rising cost of health care. But recently, the increases have slowed due to less inflation in health care prices and employees paying for a larger portion of health care benefits. A recent Mercer survey showed that 52% of U.S. employers were likely to require higher employee contributions for health care coverage in 2009 (*BusinessWeek,* February 16, 2009). Suppose the survey was based on a sample of 800 companies. Compute the margin of error and a 95% confidence interval for the proportion of companies likely to require higher employee contributions for health care coverage in 2009.

41. Fewer young people are driving. In 1983, 87% of 19-year-olds had a driver's license. Twenty-five years later that percentage had dropped to 75% (University of Michigan Transportation Research Institute website, April 7, 2012). Suppose these results are based on a random sample of 1200 19-year-olds in 1983 and again in 2008.
    a. At 95% confidence, what is the margin of error and the interval estimate of the number of 19-year-old drivers in 1983?
    b. At 95% confidence, what is the margin of error and the interval estimate of the number of 19-year-old drivers in 2008?
    c. Is the margin of error the same in parts (a) and (b)? Why or why not?

42. A poll for the presidential campaign sampled 491 potential voters in June. A primary purpose of the poll was to obtain an estimate of the proportion of potential voters who favored each candidate. Assume a planning value of $p^* = .50$ and a 95% confidence level.
    a. For $p^* = .50$, what was the planned margin of error for the June poll?
    b. Closer to the November election, better precision and smaller margins of error are desired. Assume the following margins of error are requested for surveys to be conducted during the presidential campaign. Compute the recommended sample size for each survey.

Survey	Margin of Error
September	.04
October	.03
Early November	.02
Pre-Election Day	.01

43. A Phoenix Wealth Management/Harris Interactive survey of 1500 individuals with net worth of $1 million or more provided a variety of statistics on wealthy people (*BusinessWeek,* September 22, 2003). The previous three-year period had been bad for the stock market, which motivated some of the questions asked.
    a. The survey reported that 53% of the respondents lost 25% or more of their portfolio value over the past three years. Develop a 95% confidence interval for the proportion of wealthy people who lost 25% or more of their portfolio value over the past three years.
    b. The survey reported that 31% of the respondents feel they have to save more for retirement to make up for what they lost. Develop a 95% confidence interval for the population proportion.
    c. Five percent of the respondents gave $25,000 or more to charity over the previous year. Develop a 95% confidence interval for the proportion who gave $25,000 or more to charity.
    d. Compare the margin of error for the interval estimates in parts (a), (b), and (c). How is the margin of error related to $\bar{p}$? When the same sample is being used to estimate a variety of proportions, which of the proportions should be used to choose the planning value p^*? Why do you think $p^* = .50$ is often used in these cases?

Summary

In this chapter we presented methods for developing interval estimates of a population mean and a population proportion. A point estimator may or may not provide a good estimate of a population parameter. The use of an interval estimate provides a measure of the precision of an estimate. Both the interval estimate of the population mean and the population proportion are of the form: point estimate $\pm$ margin of error.

We presented interval estimates for a population mean for two cases. In the σ known case, historical data or other information are used to develop an estimate of σ prior to taking a sample. Analysis of new sample data then proceeds based on the assumption that σ is known. In the σ unknown case, the sample data are used to estimate both the population mean and the population standard deviation. The final choice of which interval estimation procedure to use depends upon the analyst's understanding of which method provides the best estimate of σ.

In the σ known case, the interval estimation procedure is based on the assumed value of σ and the use of the standard normal distribution. In the σ unknown case, the interval estimation procedure uses the sample standard deviation s and the t distribution. In both cases the quality of the interval estimates obtained depends on the distribution of the population and the sample size. If the population is normally distributed the interval estimates will be exact in both cases, even for small sample sizes. If the population is not normally distributed, the interval estimates obtained will be approximate. Larger sample sizes will provide better approximations, but the more highly skewed the population is, the larger the sample size needs to be to obtain a good approximation. Practical advice about the sample size necessary to obtain good approximations was included in Sections 8.1 and 8.2. In most cases a sample of size 30 or more will provide good approximate confidence intervals.

The general form of the interval estimate for a population proportion is $\bar{p} \pm$ margin of error. In practice the sample sizes used for interval estimates of a population proportion are generally large. Thus, the interval estimation procedure is based on the standard normal distribution.

Often a desired margin of error is specified prior to developing a sampling plan. We showed how to choose a sample size large enough to provide the desired precision.

Glossary

Interval estimate An estimate of a population parameter that provides an interval believed to contain the value of the parameter. For the interval estimates in this chapter, it has the form: point estimate $\pm$ margin of error.

Margin of error The $\pm$ value added to and subtracted from a point estimate in order to develop an interval estimate of a population parameter.

σ known The case when historical data or other information provides a good value for the population standard deviation prior to taking a sample. The interval estimation procedure uses this known value of σ in computing the margin of error.

Confidence level The confidence associated with an interval estimate. For example, if an interval estimation procedure provides intervals such that 95% of the intervals formed using the procedure will include the population parameter, the interval estimate is said to be constructed at the 95% confidence level.

Confidence coefficient The confidence level expressed as a decimal value. For example, .95 is the confidence coefficient for a 95% confidence level.

Confidence interval Another name for an interval estimate.

σ unknown The more common case when no good basis exists for estimating the population standard deviation prior to taking the sample. The interval estimation procedure uses the sample standard deviation s in computing the margin of error.

t distribution A family of probability distributions that can be used to develop an interval estimate of a population mean whenever the population standard deviation σ is unknown and is estimated by the sample standard deviation s.

Degrees of freedom A parameter of the t distribution. When the t distribution is used in the computation of an interval estimate of a population mean, the appropriate t distribution has $n - 1$ degrees of freedom, where n is the size of the sample.

Key Formulas

Interval Estimate of a Population Mean: σ Known

$$\bar{x} \pm z_{\alpha/2} \frac{\sigma}{\sqrt{n}} \tag{8.1}$$

Interval Estimate of a Population Mean: σ Unknown

$$\bar{x} \pm t_{\alpha/2} \frac{s}{\sqrt{n}} \tag{8.2}$$

Sample Size for an Interval Estimate of a Population Mean

$$n = \frac{(z_{\alpha/2})^2 \sigma^2}{E^2} \tag{8.3}$$

Interval Estimate of a Population Proportion

$$\bar{p} \pm z_{\alpha/2} \sqrt{\frac{\bar{p}(1 - \bar{p})}{n}} \tag{8.6}$$

Sample Size for an Interval Estimate of a Population Proportion

$$n = \frac{(z_{\alpha/2})^2 p^*(1 - p^*)}{E^2} \tag{8.7}$$

Supplementary Exercises

44. A sample survey of 54 discount brokers showed that the mean price charged for a trade of 100 shares at $50 per share was $33.77 (*AAII Journal,* February 2006). The survey is conducted annually. With the historical data available, assume a known population standard deviation of $15.
    a. Using the sample data, what is the margin of error associated with a 95% confidence interval?
    b. Develop a 95% confidence interval for the mean price charged by discount brokers for a trade of 100 shares at $50 per share.

45. A survey conducted by the American Automobile Association showed that a family of four spends an average of $215.60 per day while on vacation. Suppose a sample of 64 families of four vacationing at Niagara Falls resulted in a sample mean of $252.45 per day and a sample standard deviation of $74.50.
    a. Develop a 95% confidence interval estimate of the mean amount spent per day by a family of four visiting Niagara Falls.
    b. Based on the confidence interval from part (a), does it appear that the population mean amount spent per day by families visiting Niagara Falls differs from the mean reported by the American Automobile Association? Explain.

46. The 92 million Americans of age 50 and over control 50 percent of all discretionary income (*AARP Bulletin,* March 2008). AARP estimated that the average annual expenditure on restaurants and carryout food was $1,873 for individuals in this age group. Suppose this estimate is based on a sample of 80 persons and that the sample standard deviation is $550.
    a. At 95% confidence, what is the margin of error?
    b. What is the 95% confidence interval for the population mean amount spent on restaurants and carryout food?
    c. What is your estimate of the total amount spent by Americans of age 50 and over on restaurants and carryout food?
    d. If the amount spent on restaurants and carryout food is skewed to the right, would you expect the median amount spent to be greater or less than $1,873?

Russia

47. Russia has recently started a push for stronger smoking regulations, much like those in Western countries, concerning cigarette advertising, smoking in public places, and so on. The webfile named Russia contains sample data that are consistent with those reported by *The Wall Street Journal* (*The Wall Street Journal*, October 16, 2012) on smoking habits of Russians. Analyze the data using Excel or Minitab and answer the following questions.
    a. Develop a point estimate and a 95% confidence interval for the proportion of Russians who smoke.
    b. Develop a point estimate and a 95% confidence interval for the mean annual per capita consumption (number of cigarettes) of a Russian.
    c. For those Russians who do smoke, estimate the number of cigarettes smoked per day.

DrugCost

48. The Health Care Cost Institute tracks health care expenditures for beneficiaries under the age of 65 who are covered by employer-sponsored private health insurance (Health Care Cost Institute website, November 4, 2012). The data contained in the file named DrugCost are consistent with the institute's findings concerning annual prescription costs per employee. Analyze the data using Excel or Minitab and answer the following questions.
    a. Develop a 90% confidence interval for the annual cost of prescription drugs.
    b. Develop a 90% confidence interval for the amount of out-of-pocket expense per employee.
    c. What is your point estimate of the proportion of employees who incurred no prescription drug costs?
    d. Which, if either, of the confidence intervals in parts (a) and (b) has a larger margin of error? Why?

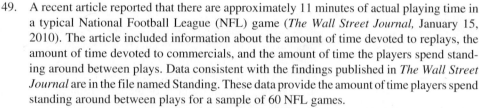

Standing

49. A recent article reported that there are approximately 11 minutes of actual playing time in a typical National Football League (NFL) game (*The Wall Street Journal,* January 15, 2010). The article included information about the amount of time devoted to replays, the amount of time devoted to commercials, and the amount of time the players spend standing around between plays. Data consistent with the findings published in *The Wall Street Journal* are in the file named Standing. These data provide the amount of time players spend standing around between plays for a sample of 60 NFL games.
    a. Use the Standing data set to develop a point estimate of the number of minutes during an NFL game that players are standing around between plays. Compare this to the actual playing time reported in the article. Are you surprised?
    b. What is the sample standard deviation?
    c. Develop a 95% confidence interval for the number of minutes players spend standing around between plays.

50. Mileage tests are conducted for a particular model of automobile. If a 98% confidence interval with a margin of error of 1 mile per gallon is desired, how many automobiles should be used in the test? Assume that preliminary mileage tests indicate the standard deviation is 2.6 miles per gallon.

51. In developing patient appointment schedules, a medical center wants to estimate the mean time that a staff member spends with each patient. How large a sample should be taken if the desired margin of error is two minutes at a 95% level of confidence? How large a sample should be taken for a 99% level of confidence? Use a planning value for the population standard deviation of eight minutes.

52. Annual salary plus bonus data for chief executive officers are presented in the *BusinessWeek* Annual Pay Survey. A preliminary sample showed that the standard deviation is $675 with data provided in thousands of dollars. How many chief executive officers should be in a sample if we want to estimate the population mean annual salary plus bonus with a margin of error of $100,000? (*Note:* The desired margin of error would be $E = 100$ if the data are in thousands of dollars.) Use 95% confidence.

53. The National Center for Education Statistics reported that 47% of college students work to pay for tuition and living expenses. Assume that a sample of 450 college students was used in the study.

    a.   Provide a 95% confidence interval for the population proportion of college students who work to pay for tuition and living expenses.

    b.   Provide a 99% confidence interval for the population proportion of college students who work to pay for tuition and living expenses.

    c.   What happens to the margin of error as the confidence is increased from 95% to 99%?

54.   A *USA Today*/CNN/Gallup survey of 369 working parents found 200 who said they spend too little time with their children because of work commitments.

    a.   What is the point estimate of the proportion of the population of working parents who feel they spend too little time with their children because of work commitments?

    b.   At 95% confidence, what is the margin of error?

    c.   What is the 95% confidence interval estimate of the population proportion of working parents who feel they spend too little time with their children because of work commitments?

55.   The Pew Research Center has conducted extensive research on the young adult population (Pew research website, November 6, 2012). One finding was that 93% of adults aged 18 to 29 use the Internet. Another finding was that 21% of those aged 18 to 28 are married. Assume the sample size associated with both findings is 500.

    a.   Develop a 95% confidence interval for the proportion of adults aged 18 to 29 who use the Internet.

    b.   Develop a 99% confidence interval for the proportion of adults aged 18 to 28 who are married.

    c.   In which case, part (a) or part (b), is the margin of error larger? Explain why.

56.   A survey of 750 likely voters in Ohio was conducted by the Rasmussen Poll just prior to the general election (Rasmussen Reports website November 4, 2012). The state of the economy was thought to be an important determinant of how people would vote. Among other things, the survey found that 165 of the respondents rated the economy as good or excellent and 315 rated the economy as poor.

    a.   Develop a point estimate of the proportion of likely voters in Ohio who rated the economy as good or excellent.

    b.   Construct a 95% confidence interval for the proportion of likely voters in Ohio who rated the economy as good or excellent.

    c.   Construct a 95% confidence interval for the proportion of likely voters in Ohio who rated the economy as poor.

    d.   Which of the confidence intervals in parts (b) and (c) is wider? Why?

57.   The *2003 Statistical Abstract of the United States* reported the percentage of people 18 years of age and older who smoke. Suppose that a study designed to collect new data on smokers and nonsmokers uses a preliminary estimate of the proportion who smoke of .30.

    a.   How large a sample should be taken to estimate the proportion of smokers in the population with a margin of error of .02? Use 95% confidence.

    b.   Assume that the study uses your sample size recommendation in part (a) and finds 520 smokers. What is the point estimate of the proportion of smokers in the population?

    c.   What is the 95% confidence interval for the proportion of smokers in the population?

58.   A well-known bank credit card firm wishes to estimate the proportion of credit card holders who carry a nonzero balance at the end of the month and incur an interest charge. Assume that the desired margin of error is .03 at 98% confidence.

    a.   How large a sample should be selected if it is anticipated that roughly 70% of the firm's card holders carry a nonzero balance at the end of the month?

    b.   How large a sample should be selected if no planning value for the proportion could be specified?

59.   Workers in several industries were surveyed to determine the proportion of workers who feel their industry is understaffed. In the government sector, 37% of the respondents said they were understaffed, in the health care sector 33% said they were understaffed, and in

the education sector 28% said they were understaffed (*USA Today,* January 11, 2010). Suppose that 200 workers were surveyed in each industry.

a. Construct a 95% confidence interval for the proportion of workers in each of these industries who feel their industry is understaffed.

b. Assuming the same sample size will be used in each industry, how large would the sample need to be to ensure that the margin of error is .05 or less for each of the three confidence intervals?

60. Although airline schedules and cost are important factors for business travelers when choosing an airline carrier, a *USA Today* survey found that business travelers list an airline's frequent flyer program as the most important factor. From a sample of $n = 1993$ business travelers who responded to the survey, 618 listed a frequent flyer program as the most important factor.

a. What is the point estimate of the proportion of the population of business travelers who believe a frequent flyer program is the most important factor when choosing an airline carrier?

b. Develop a 95% confidence interval estimate of the population proportion.

c. How large a sample would be required to report the margin of error of .01 at 95% confidence? Would you recommend that *USA Today* attempt to provide this degree of precision? Why or why not?

Case Problem 1   *Young Professional* Magazine

Young Professional magazine was developed for a target audience of recent college graduates who are in their first 10 years in a business/professional career. In its two years of publication, the magazine has been fairly successful. Now the publisher is interested in expanding the magazine's advertising base. Potential advertisers continually ask about the demographics and interests of subscribers to *Young Professional*. To collect this information, the magazine commissioned a survey to develop a profile of its subscribers. The survey results will be used to help the magazine choose articles of interest and provide advertisers with a profile of subscribers. As a new employee of the magazine, you have been asked to help analyze the survey results.

Some of the survey questions follow:

Professional

1. What is your age?
2. Are you: Male_____   Female_____
3. Do you plan to make any real estate purchases in the next two years? Yes_____ No_____
4. What is the approximate total value of financial investments, exclusive of your home, owned by you or members of your household?
5. How many stock/bond/mutual fund transactions have you made in the past year?
6. Do you have broadband access to the Internet at home? Yes_____ No_____
7. Please indicate your total household income last year. _____
8. Do you have children? Yes_____ No_____

The file entitled Professional contains the responses to these questions. Table 8.6 shows the portion of the file pertaining to the first five survey respondents.

Managerial Report

Prepare a managerial report summarizing the results of the survey. In addition to statistical summaries, discuss how the magazine might use these results to attract advertisers. You might also comment on how the survey results could be used by the magazine's editors to

TABLE 8.6   PARTIAL SURVEY RESULTS FOR *YOUNG PROFESSIONAL* MAGAZINE

Age	Gender	Real Estate Purchases	Value of Investments($)	Number of Transactions	Broadband Access	Household Income($)	Children
38	Female	No	12200	4	Yes	75200	Yes
30	Male	No	12400	4	Yes	70300	Yes
41	Female	No	26800	5	Yes	48200	No
28	Female	Yes	19600	6	No	95300	No
31	Female	Yes	15100	5	No	73300	Yes
⋮	⋮	⋮	⋮	⋮	⋮	⋮	⋮

© Cengage Learning

identify topics that would be of interest to readers. Your report should address the following issues, but do not limit your analysis to just these areas.

1. Develop appropriate descriptive statistics to summarize the data.
2. Develop 95% confidence intervals for the mean age and household income of subscribers.
3. Develop 95% confidence intervals for the proportion of subscribers who have broadband access at home and the proportion of subscribers who have children.
4. Would *Young Professional* be a good advertising outlet for online brokers? Justify your conclusion with statistical data.
5. Would this magazine be a good place to advertise for companies selling educational software and computer games for young children?
6. Comment on the types of articles you believe would be of interest to readers of *Young Professional*.

Case Problem 2   Gulf Real Estate Properties

Gulf Real Estate Properties, Inc., is a real estate firm located in southwest Florida. The company, which advertises itself as "expert in the real estate market," monitors condominium sales by collecting data on location, list price, sale price, and number of days it takes to sell each unit. Each condominium is classified as *Gulf View* if it is located directly on the Gulf of Mexico or *No Gulf View* if it is located on the bay or a golf course, near but not on the Gulf. Sample data from the Multiple Listing Service in Naples, Florida, provided recent sales data for 40 Gulf View condominiums and 18 No Gulf View condominiums. Prices are in thousands of dollars. The data are shown in Table 8.7.

Managerial Report

1. Use appropriate descriptive statistics to summarize each of the three variables for the 40 Gulf View condominiums.
2. Use appropriate descriptive statistics to summarize each of the three variables for the 18 No Gulf View condominiums.
3. Compare your summary results. Discuss any specific statistical results that would help a real estate agent understand the condominium market.
4. Develop a 95% confidence interval estimate of the population mean sales price and population mean number of days to sell for Gulf View condominiums. Interpret your results.
5. Develop a 95% confidence interval estimate of the population mean sales price and population mean number of days to sell for No Gulf View condominiums. Interpret your results.

TABLE 8.7   SALES DATA FOR GULF REAL ESTATE PROPERTIES

Gulf View Condominiums			No Gulf View Condominiums		
List Price	Sale Price	Days to Sell	List Price	Sale Price	Days to Sell
495.0	475.0	130	217.0	217.0	182
379.0	350.0	71	148.0	135.5	338
529.0	519.0	85	186.5	179.0	122
552.5	534.5	95	239.0	230.0	150
334.9	334.9	119	279.0	267.5	169
550.0	505.0	92	215.0	214.0	58
169.9	165.0	197	279.0	259.0	110
210.0	210.0	56	179.9	176.5	130
975.0	945.0	73	149.9	144.9	149
314.0	314.0	126	235.0	230.0	114
315.0	305.0	88	199.8	192.0	120
885.0	800.0	282	210.0	195.0	61
975.0	975.0	100	226.0	212.0	146
469.0	445.0	56	149.9	146.5	137
329.0	305.0	49	160.0	160.0	281
365.0	330.0	48	322.0	292.5	63
332.0	312.0	88	187.5	179.0	48
520.0	495.0	161	247.0	227.0	52
425.0	405.0	149			
675.0	669.0	142			
409.0	400.0	28			
649.0	649.0	29			
319.0	305.0	140			
425.0	410.0	85			
359.0	340.0	107			
469.0	449.0	72			
895.0	875.0	129			
439.0	430.0	160			
435.0	400.0	206			
235.0	227.0	91			
638.0	618.0	100			
629.0	600.0	97			
329.0	309.0	114			
595.0	555.0	45			
339.0	315.0	150			
215.0	200.0	48			
395.0	375.0	135			
449.0	425.0	53			
499.0	465.0	86			
439.0	428.5	158			

WEB file

GulfProp

© Cengage Learning

6. Assume the branch manager requested estimates of the mean selling price of Gulf View condominiums with a margin of error of $40,000 and the mean selling price of No Gulf View condominiums with a margin of error of $15,000. Using 95% confidence, how large should the sample sizes be?

7. Gulf Real Estate Properties just signed contracts for two new listings: a Gulf View condominium with a list price of $589,000 and a No Gulf View condominium with a list price of $285,000. What is your estimate of the final selling price and number of days required to sell each of these units?

Case Problem 3   Metropolitan Research, Inc.

Metropolitan Research, Inc., a consumer research organization, conducts surveys designed to evaluate a wide variety of products and services available to consumers. In one particular study, Metropolitan looked at consumer satisfaction with the performance of automobiles produced by a major Detroit manufacturer. A questionnaire sent to owners of one of the manufacturer's full-sized cars revealed several complaints about early transmission problems. To learn more about the transmission failures, Metropolitan used a sample of actual transmission repairs provided by a transmission repair firm in the Detroit area. Thefollowing data show the actual number of miles driven for 50 vehicles at the time of transmission failure.

Auto

85,092	32,609	59,465	77,437	32,534	64,090	32,464	59,902
39,323	89,641	94,219	116,803	92,857	63,436	65,605	85,861
64,342	61,978	67,998	59,817	101,769	95,774	121,352	69,568
74,276	66,998	40,001	72,069	25,066	77,098	69,922	35,662
74,425	67,202	118,444	53,500	79,294	64,544	86,813	116,269
37,831	89,341	73,341	85,288	138,114	53,402	85,586	82,256
77,539	88,798						

Managerial Report

1. Use appropriate descriptive statistics to summarize the transmission failure data.
2. Develop a 95% confidence interval for the mean number of miles driven until transmission failure for the population of automobiles with transmission failure. Provide a managerial interpretation of the interval estimate.
3. Discuss the implication of your statistical findings in terms of the belief that some owners of the automobiles experienced early transmission failures.
4. How many repair records should be sampled if the research firm wants the population mean number of miles driven until transmission failure to be estimated with a margin of error of 5000 miles? Use 95% confidence.
5. What other information would you like to gather to evaluate the transmission failure problem more fully?

Appendix 8.1   Interval Estimation with Minitab

We describe the use of Minitab in constructing confidence intervals for a population mean and a population proportion.

Population Mean: σ Known

Lloyd's

We illustrate interval estimation using the Lloyd's example in Section 8.1. The amounts spent per shopping trip for the sample of 100 customers are in column C1 of a Minitab worksheet. The population standard deviation $\sigma = 20$ is assumed known. The following steps can be used to compute a 95% confidence interval estimate of the population mean.

Step 1. Select the **Stat** menu
Step 2. Choose **Basic Statistics**
Step 3. Choose **1-Sample Z**
Step 4. When the 1-Sample Z dialog box appears:
          Enter C1 in the **Samples in columns** box
          Enter 20 in the **Standard deviation** box
Step 5. Click **OK**

The Minitab default is a 95% confidence level. In order to specify a different confidence level such as 90%, add the following to step 4.

> Select **Options**
> When the 1-Sample Z-Options dialog box appears:
> > Enter 90 in the **Confidence level** box
> Click **OK**

Population Mean: σ Unknown

NewBalance

We illustrate interval estimation using the data in Table 8.3 showing the credit card balances for a sample of 70 households. The data are in column C1 of a Minitab worksheet. In this case the population standard deviation σ will be estimated by the sample standard deviation s. The following steps can be used to compute a 95% confidence interval estimate of the population mean.

Step 1. Select the **Stat** menu
Step 2. Choose **Basic Statistics**
Step 3. Choose **1-Sample t**
Step 4. When the 1-Sample t dialog box appears:
> Enter C1 in the **Samples in columns** box
Step 5. Click **OK**

The Minitab default is a 95% confidence level. In order to specify a different confidence level such as 90%, add the following to step 4.

> Select **Options**
> When the 1-Sample t-Options dialog box appears:
> > Enter 90 in the **Confidence level** box
> Click **OK**

Population Proportion

TeeTimes

We illustrate interval estimation using the survey data for women golfers presented in Section 8.4. The data are in column C1 of a Minitab worksheet. Individual responses are recorded as Yes if the golfer is satisfied with the availability of tee times and No otherwise. The following steps can be used to compute a 95% confidence interval estimate of the proportion of women golfers who are satisfied with the availability of tee times.

Step 1. Select the **Stat** menu
Step 2. Choose **Basic Statistics**
Step 3. Choose **1 Proportion**
Step 4. When the 1 Proportion dialog box appears:
> Enter C1 in the **Samples in columns** box
Step 5. Select **Options**
Step 6. When the 1 Proportion-Options dialog box appears:
> Select **Use test and interval based on normal distribution**
> Click **OK**
Step 7. Click **OK**

The Minitab default is a 95% confidence level. In order to specify a different confidence level such as 90%, enter 90 in the **Confidence Level** box when the 1 Proportion-Options dialog box appears in step 6.

Note: Minitab's 1 Proportion routine uses an alphabetical ordering of the responses and selects the *second response* for the population proportion of interest. In the women golfers example, Minitab used the alphabetical ordering No–Yes and then provided the confidence interval for the proportion of Yes responses. Because Yes was the response of interest, the Minitab output was fine. However, if Minitab's alphabetical ordering does not provide the response of interest, select any cell in the column and use the sequence: Editor > Column > Value Order. It will provide you with the option of entering a user-specified order, but you must list the response of interest second in the define-an-order box.

Appendix 8.2   Interval Estimation Using Excel

We describe the use of Excel in constructing confidence intervals for a population mean and a population proportion.

Population Mean: σ Known

Lloyd's

We illustrate interval estimation using the Lloyd's example in Section 8.1. The population standard deviation $\sigma = 20$ is assumed known. The amounts spent for the sample of 100 customers are in column A of an Excel worksheet. Excel's AVERAGE and CONFIDENCE.NORM functions can be used to compute the point estimate and the margin of error for an estimate of the population mean.

> **Step 1.** Select cell C1 and enter the Excel formula =AVERAGE(A2:A101)
> **Step 2.** Select cell C2 and enter the Excel formula =CONFIDENCE.NORM(.05,20,100)

The three inputs of the CONFIDENCE.NORM function are

> Alpha = 1 − confidence coefficient = 1 − .95 = .05
> The population standard deviation = 20
> The sample size = 100

The point estimate of the population mean (82) in cell C1 and the margin of error (3.92) in cell C2 allow the confidence interval for the population mean to be easily computed.

Population Mean: σ Unknown

NewBalance

We illustrate interval estimation using the data in Table 8.3, which show the credit card balances for a sample of 70 households. The data are in column A of an Excel worksheet. The following steps can be used to compute the point estimate and the margin of error for an interval estimate of a population mean. We will use Excel's Descriptive Statistics Tool described in Chapter 3.

> **Step 1.** Click the **Data** tab on the Ribbon
> **Step 2.** In the **Analysis** group, click **Data Analysis**
> **Step 3.** Choose **Descriptive Statistics** from the list of Analysis Tools
> **Step 4.** When the Descriptive Statistics dialog box appears:
> > Enter A1:A71 in the **Input Range** box
> > Select **Grouped by Columns**
> > Select **Labels in First Row**
> > Select **Output Range**
> > Enter C1 in the Output Range box
> > Select **Summary Statistics**
> > Select **Confidence Level for Mean**
> > > Enter 95 in the Confidence Level for Mean box
> > Click **OK**

FIGURE 8.10   INTERVAL ESTIMATION OF THE POPULATION MEAN CREDIT CARD BALANCE USING EXCEL

	A	B	C	D	E	F
1	**NewBalance**		*NewBalance*			
2	9430				Point Estimate	
3	7535		Mean	9312		
4	4078		Standard Error	478.9281		
5	5604		Median	9466		
6	5179		Mode	13627		
7	4416		Standard Deviation	4007		
8	10676		Sample Variance	16056048		
9	1627		Kurtosis	-0.2960		
10	10112		Skewness	0.1879		
11	6567		Range	18648		
12	13627		Minimum	615		
13	18719		Maximum	19263		
14	14661		Sum	651840		
15	12195		Count	70	Margin of Error	
16	10544		Confidence Level(95.0%)	955		
17	13659					
70	9743					
71	10324					
72						

Note: Rows 18 to 69 are hidden.

© Cengage Learning

The summary statistics will appear in columns C and D. The point estimate of the population mean appears in cell D3. The margin of error, labeled "Confidence Level(95.0%)," appears in cell D16. The point estimate ($9,312) and the margin of error ($955) allow the confidence interval for the population mean to be easily computed. The output from this Excel procedure is shown in Figure 8.10.

Population Proportion

WEB file

Interval p

We illustrate interval estimation using the survey data for women golfers presented in Section 8.4. The data are in column A of an Excel worksheet. Individual responses are recorded as Yes if the golfer is satisfied with the availability of tee times and No otherwise. Excel does not offer a built-in routine to handle the estimation of a population proportion; however, it is relatively easy to develop an Excel template that can be used for this purpose. The template shown in Figure 8.11 provides the 95% confidence interval estimate of the proportion of women golfers who are satisfied with the availability of tee times. Note that the background worksheet in Figure 8.11 shows the cell formulas that provide the interval estimation results shown in the foreground worksheet. The following steps are necessary to use the template for this data set.

Step 1. Enter the data range A2:A901 into the =COUNTA cell formula in cell D3
Step 2. Enter Yes as the response of interest in cell D4
Step 3. Enter the data range A2:A901 into the =COUNTIF cell formula in cell D5
Step 4. Enter .95 as the confidence coefficient in cell D8

FIGURE 8.11   EXCEL TEMPLATE FOR INTERVAL ESTIMATION OF A
POPULATION PROPORTION

	A	B	C	D	E
1	**Response**		**Interval Estimate of a Population Proportion**		
2	Yes				
3	No		Sample Size	=COUNTA(A2:A901)	
4	Yes		Response of Interest	Yes	
5	Yes		Count for Response	=COUNTIF(A2:A901,D4)	
6	No		Sample Proportion	=D5/D3	
7	No				
8	No		Confidence Coefficient	0.95	
9	Yes		z Value	=NORM.S.INV(0.5+D8/2)	
10	Yes				
11	Yes		Standard Error	=SQRT(D6*(1-D6)/D3)	
12	No		Margin of Error	=D9*D11	
13	No				
14	Yes		Point Estimate	=D6	
15	No		Lower Limit	=D14-D12	
16	No		Upper Limit	=D14+D12	
17	Yes				
18	No				
901	Yes				
902					

	A	B	C	D	E	F	G
1	**Response**		**Interval Estimate of a Population Proportion**				
2	Yes						
3	No		Sample Size	900	Enter the response		
4	Yes		Response of Interest	Yes	of interest		
5	Yes		Count for Response	396			
6	No		Sample Proportion	0.4400			
7	No						
8	No		Confidence Coefficient	0.95	Enter the confidence		
9	Yes		z Value	1.960	coefficient		
10	Yes						
11	Yes		Standard Error	0.0165			
12	No		Margin of Error	0.0324			
13	No						
14	Yes		Point Estimate	0.4400			
15	No		Lower Limit	0.4076			
16	No		Upper Limit	0.4724			
17	Yes						
18	No						
901	Yes						
902							

*Note: Rows 19 to 900
are hidden.*

© Cengage Learning

The template automatically provides the confidence interval in cells D15 and D16.

This template can be used to compute the confidence interval for a population proportion for other applications. For instance, to compute the interval estimate for a new data set, enter the new sample data into column A of the worksheet and then make the changes to the four cells as shown. If the new sample data have already been summarized, the sample data do not have to be entered into the worksheet. In this case, enter the sample size into cell D3 and the sample proportion into cell D6; the worksheet template will then provide the confidence interval for the population proportion. The worksheet in Figure 8.11 is available in the file Interval p on the website that accompanies this book.

Appendix 8.3 Interval Estimation with StatTools

In this appendix we show how StatTools can be used to develop an interval estimate of a population mean for the σ unknown case and determine the sample size needed to provide a desired margin of error.

Population Mean: σ Unknown Case

In this case the population standard deviation σ will be estimated by the sample standard deviation s. We use the credit card balance data in Table 8.3 to illustrate. Begin by using the Data Set Manager to create a StatTools data set for these data using the procedure described in the appendix to Chapter 1. The following steps can be used to compute a 95% confidence interval estimate of the population mean.

NewBalance

Step 1. Click the **StatTools** tab on the Ribbon
Step 2. In the **Analyses** group, click **Statistical Inference**
Step 3. Choose the **Confidence Interval** option
Step 4. Choose Mean/Std. Deviation
Step 5. When the StatTools-Confidence Interval for Mean/Std. Deviation dialog box appears:

  For **Analysis Type** choose **One-Sample Analysis**
  In the **Variables** section, select **NewBalance**
  In the **Confidence Intervals to Calculate** section:
    Select the **For the Mean** option
    Select 95% for the **Confidence Level**
  Click **OK**

Some descriptive statistics and the confidence interval will appear.

Determining the Sample Size

In Section 8.3 we showed how to determine the sample size needed to provide a desired margin of error. The example used involved a study designed to estimate the population mean daily rental cost for a midsize automobile in the United States. The project director specified that the population mean daily rental cost be estimated with a margin of error of $2 and a 95% level of confidence. Sample data from a previous study provided a sample standard deviation of $9.65; this value was used as the planning value for the population standard deviation. The following steps can be used to compute the recommended sample size required to provide a 95% confidence interval estimate of the population mean with a margin of error of $2.

Step 1. Click the **StatTools** tab on the Ribbon
Step 2. In the **Analyses** group, click **Statistical Inference**
Step 3. Choose the **Sample Size Selection** option
Step 4. When the StatTools-Sample Size Selection dialog box appears:

  In the **Parameter to Estimate** section, select **Mean**
  In the **Confidence Interval Specification** section:
    Select **95%** for the **Confidence Level**

The half-length of interval is the margin of error.

    Enter **2** in the **Half-Length of Interval** box
    Enter **9.65** in the **Estimated Std Dev** box
  Click **OK**

The output showing a recommended sample size of 90 will appear.

Population Proportion

We illustrate using the survey data for women golfers presented in Section 8.4. Begin by using the Data Set Manager to create a StatTools data set for these data using the procedure described in the appendix to Chapter 1. The following steps can be used to compute a 95% confidence interval estimate of the population mean.

Tee Times

Step 1. Click the **StatTools** tab on the Ribbon
Step 2. In the **Analyses** group, click **Statistical Inference**
Step 3. Choose **Confidence Interval**
Step 4. Choose **Proportion**
Step 5. When the StatTools-Confidence Interval for Proportion dialog box appears:
  For **Analysis Type** choose **One-Sample Analysis**
  In the **Variables** section, select **Response**
  In the **Categories to Analyze** section, select **Yes**
  In the **Options** section, enter 95% in the **Confidence Level** box
    Click **OK**

Some descriptive statistics and the confidence interval will appear.

StatTools also provides a capability for determining the appropriate sample size to provide a desired margin of error. The steps are similar to those for determining the sample size in the previous subsection.

CHAPTER 9

Hypothesis Tests

CONTENTS

JOHN MORRELL & COMPANY*
CINCINNATI, OHIO

John Morrell & Company, which began in England in 1827, is considered the oldest continuously operating meat manufacturer in the United States. It is a wholly owned and independently managed subsidiary of Smithfield Foods, Smithfield, Virginia. John Morrell & Company offers an extensive product line of processed meats and fresh pork to consumers under 13 regional brands including John Morrell, E-Z-Cut, Tobin's First Prize, Dinner Bell, Hunter, Kretschmar, Rath, Rodeo, Shenson, Farmers Hickory Brand, Iowa Quality, and Peyton's. Each regional brand enjoys high brand recognition and loyalty among consumers.

Market research at Morrell provides management with up-to-date information on the company's various products and how the products compare with competing brands of similar products. A recent study compared a Beef Pot Roast made by Morrell to similar beef products from two major competitors. In the three-product comparison test, a sample of consumers was used to indicate how the products rated in terms of taste, appearance, aroma, and overall preference.

One research question concerned whether the Beef Pot Roast made by Morrell was the preferred choice of more than 50% of the consumer population. Letting p indicate the population proportion preferring Morrell's product, the hypothesis test for the research question is as follows:

$$H_0: p \leq .50$$
$$H_a: p > .50$$

The null hypothesis H_0 indicates the preference for Morrell's product is less than or equal to 50%. If the sample data support rejecting H_0 in favor of the

Market research at Morrell provides up-to-date information on their various products and how they compare with competing brands.
© Jeff Greenberg/Alamy

alternative hypothesis H_a, Morrell will draw the research conclusion that in a three-product comparison, their Beef Pot Roast is preferred by more than 50% of the consumer population.

In an independent taste test study using a sample of 224 consumers in Cincinnati, Milwaukee, and Los Angeles, 150 consumers selected the Beef Pot Roast made by Morrell as the preferred product. Using statistical hypothesis testing procedures, the null hypothesis H_0 was rejected. The study provided statistical evidence supporting H_a and the conclusion that the Morrell product is preferred by more than 50% of the consumer population.

The point estimate of the population proportion was $\bar{p} = 150/224 = .67$. Thus, the sample data provided support for a food magazine advertisement showing that in a three-product taste comparison, Beef Pot Roast made by Morrell was "preferred 2 to 1 over the competition."

In this chapter we will discuss how to formulate hypotheses and how to conduct tests like the one used by Morrell. Through the analysis of sample data, we will be able to determine whether a hypothesis should or should not be rejected.

---

*The authors are indebted to Marty Butler, Vice President of Marketing, John Morrell, for providing this Statistics in Practice.

In Chapters 7 and 8 we showed how a sample could be used to develop point and interval estimates of population parameters. In this chapter we continue the discussion of statistical inference by showing how hypothesis testing can be used to determine whether a statement about the value of a population parameter should or should not be rejected.

In hypothesis testing we begin by making a tentative assumption about a population parameter. This tentative assumption is called the **null hypothesis** and is denoted by H_0. We then define another hypothesis, called the **alternative hypothesis**, which is the opposite of what is stated in the null hypothesis. The alternative hypothesis is denoted by H_a. The hypothesis testing procedure uses data from a sample to test the two competing statements indicated by H_0 and H_a.

This chapter shows how hypothesis tests can be conducted about a population mean and a population proportion. We begin by providing examples that illustrate approaches to developing null and alternative hypotheses.

9.1 Developing Null and Alternative Hypotheses

It is not always obvious how the null and alternative hypotheses should be formulated. Care must be taken to structure the hypotheses appropriately so that the hypothesis testing conclusion provides the information the researcher or decision maker wants. The context of the situation is very important in determining how the hypotheses should be stated. All hypothesis testing applications involve collecting a sample and using the sample results to provide evidence for drawing a conclusion. Good questions to consider when formulating the null and alternative hypotheses are, What is the purpose of collecting the sample? What conclusions are we hoping to make?

Learning to correctly formulate hypotheses will take some practice. Expect some initial confusion over the proper choice of the null and alternative hypotheses. The examples in this section are intended to provide guidelines.

In the chapter introduction, we stated that the null hypothesis H_0 is a tentative assumption about a population parameter such as a population mean or a population proportion. The alternative hypothesis H_a is a statement that is the opposite of what is stated in the null hypothesis. In some situations it is easier to identify the alternative hypothesis first and then develop the null hypothesis. In other situations it is easier to identify the null hypothesis first and then develop the alternative hypothesis. We will illustrate these situations in the following examples.

The Alternative Hypothesis as a Research Hypothesis

Many applications of hypothesis testing involve an attempt to gather evidence in support of a research hypothesis. In these situations, it is often best to begin with the alternative hypothesis and make it the conclusion that the researcher hopes to support. Consider a particular automobile that currently attains a fuel efficiency of 24 miles per gallon in city driving. A product research group has developed a new fuel injection system designed to increase the miles-per-gallon rating. The group will run controlled tests with the new fuel injection system looking for statistical support for the conclusion that the new fuel injection system provides more miles per gallon than the current system.

Several new fuel injection units will be manufactured, installed in test automobiles, and subjected to research-controlled driving conditions. The sample mean miles per gallon for these automobiles will be computed and used in a hypothesis test to determine if it can be concluded that the new system provides more than 24 miles per gallon. In terms of the population mean miles per gallon μ, the research hypothesis $\mu > 24$ becomes the alternative hypothesis. Since the current system provides an average or mean of 24 miles per gallon, we will make the tentative assumption that the new system is not any better than the current system and choose $\mu \leq 24$ as the null hypothesis. The null and alternative hypotheses are

$$H_0: \mu \leq 24$$
$$H_a: \mu > 24$$

If the sample results lead to the conclusion to reject H_0, the inference can be made that $H_a: \mu > 24$ is true. The researchers have the statistical support to state that the new fuel injection system increases the mean number of miles per gallon. The production of automobiles with the new fuel injection system should be considered. However, if the sample results lead to the conclusion that H_0 cannot be rejected, the researchers cannot conclude

The conclusion that the research hypothesis is true is made if the sample data provide sufficient evidence to show that the null hypothesis can be rejected.

that the new fuel injection system is better than the current system. Production of automobiles with the new fuel injection system on the basis of better gas mileage cannot be justified. Perhaps more research and further testing can be conducted.

Successful companies stay competitive by developing new products, new methods, new systems, and the like, that are better than what is currently available. Before adopting something new, it is desirable to conduct research to determine if there is statistical support for the conclusion that the new approach is indeed better. In such cases, the research hypothesis is stated as the alternative hypothesis. For example, a new teaching method is developed that is believed to be better than the current method. The alternative hypothesis is that the new method is better. The null hypothesis is that the new method is no better than the old method. A new sales force bonus plan is developed in an attempt to increase sales. The alternative hypothesis is that the new bonus plan increases sales. The null hypothesis is that the new bonus plan does not increase sales. A new drug is developed with the goal of lowering blood pressure more than an existing drug. The alternative hypothesis is that the new drug lowers blood pressure more than the existing drug. The null hypothesis is that the new drug does not provide lower blood pressure than the existing drug. In each case, rejection of the null hypothesis H_0 provides statistical support for the research hypothesis. We will see many examples of hypothesis tests in research situations such as these throughout this chapter and in the remainder of the text.

The Null Hypothesis as an Assumption to Be Challenged

Of course, not all hypothesis tests involve research hypotheses. In the following discussion we consider applications of hypothesis testing where we begin with a belief or an assumption that a statement about the value of a population parameter is true. We will then use a hypothesis test to challenge the assumption and determine if there is statistical evidence to conclude that the assumption is incorrect. In these situations, it is helpful to develop the null hypothesis first. The null hypothesis H_0 expresses the belief or assumption about the value of the population parameter. The alternative hypothesis H_a is that the belief or assumption is incorrect.

As an example, consider the situation of a manufacturer of soft drink products. The label on a soft drink bottle states that it contains 67.6 fluid ounces. We consider the label correct provided the population mean filling weight for the bottles is *at least* 67.6 fluid ounces. Without any reason to believe otherwise, we would give the manufacturer the benefit of the doubt and assume that the statement provided on the label is correct. Thus, in a hypothesis test about the population mean fluid weight per bottle, we would begin with the assumption that the label is correct and state the null hypothesis as $\mu \geq 67.6$. The challenge to this assumption would imply that the label is incorrect and the bottles are being underfilled. This challenge would be stated as the alternative hypothesis $\mu < 67.6$. Thus, the null and alternative hypotheses are:

$$H_0: \mu \geq 67.6$$
$$H_a: \mu < 67.6$$

A manufacturer's product information is usually assumed to be true and stated as the null hypothesis. The conclusion that the information is incorrect can be made if the null hypothesis is rejected.

A government agency with the responsibility for validating manufacturing labels could select a sample of soft drinks bottles, compute the sample mean filling weight, and use the sample results to test the preceding hypotheses. If the sample results lead to the conclusion to reject H_0, the inference that $H_a: \mu < 67.6$ is true can be made. With this statistical support, the agency is justified in concluding that the label is incorrect and underfilling of the bottles is occurring. Appropriate action to force the manufacturer to comply with labeling standards would be considered. However, if the sample results indicate H_0 cannot be rejected, the assumption that the manufacturer's labeling is correct cannot be rejected. With this conclusion, no action would be taken.

Let us now consider a variation of the soft drink bottle filling example by viewing the same situation from the manufacturer's point of view. The bottle-filling operation has been designed to fill soft drink bottles with 67.6 fluid ounces as stated on the label. The company does not want to underfill the containers because that could result in an underfilling complaint from customers or, perhaps, a government agency. However, the company does not want to overfill containers either because putting more soft drink than necessary into the containers would be an unnecessary cost. The company's goal would be to adjust the bottle-filling operation so that the population mean filling weight per bottle is 67.6 fluid ounces as specified on the label.

Although this is the company's goal, from time to time any production process can get out of adjustment. If this occurs in our example, underfilling or overfilling of the soft drink bottles will occur. In either case, the company would like to know about it in order to correct the situation by readjusting the bottle-filling operation to the designed 67.6 fluid ounces. In a hypothesis testing application, we would again begin with the assumption that the production process is operating correctly and state the null hypothesis as $\mu = 67.6$ fluid ounces. The alternative hypothesis that challenges this assumption is that $\mu \neq 67.6$, which indicates either overfilling or underfilling is occurring. The null and alternative hypotheses for the manufacturer's hypothesis test are:

$$H_0: \mu = 67.6$$
$$H_a: \mu \neq 67.6$$

Suppose that the soft drink manufacturer uses a quality control procedure to periodically select a sample of bottles from the filling operation and computes the sample mean filling weight per bottle. If the sample results lead to the conclusion to reject H_0, the inference is made that $H_a: \mu \neq 67.6$ is true. We conclude that the bottles are not being filled properly and the production process should be adjusted to restore the population mean to 67.6 fluid ounces per bottle. However, if the sample results indicate H_0 cannot be rejected, the assumption that the manufacturer's bottle filling operation is functioning properly cannot be rejected. In this case, no further action would be taken and the production operation would continue to run.

The two preceding forms of the soft drink manufacturing hypothesis test show that the null and alternative hypotheses may vary depending upon the point of view of the researcher or decision maker. To correctly formulate hypotheses it is important to understand the context of the situation and structure the hypotheses to provide the information the researcher or decision maker wants.

Summary of Forms for Null and Alternative Hypotheses

The hypothesis tests in this chapter involve two population parameters: the population mean and the population proportion. Depending on the situation, hypothesis tests about a population parameter may take one of three forms: two use inequalities in the null hypothesis; the third uses an equality in the null hypothesis. For hypothesis tests involving a population mean, we let μ_0 denote the hypothesized value and we must choose one of the following three forms for the hypothesis test.

The three possible forms of hypotheses H_0 and H_a are shown here. Note that the equality always appears in the null hypothesis H_0.

$$H_0: \mu \geq \mu_0 \qquad H_0: \mu \leq \mu_0 \qquad H_0: \mu = \mu_0$$
$$H_a: \mu < \mu_0 \qquad H_a: \mu > \mu_0 \qquad H_a: \mu \neq \mu_0$$

For reasons that will be clear later, the first two forms are called one-tailed tests. The third form is called a two-tailed test.

In many situations, the choice of H_0 and H_a is not obvious and judgment is necessary to select the proper form. However, as the preceding forms show, the equality part of the expression (either $\geq$, $\leq$, or $=$) *always* appears in the null hypothesis. In selecting the proper form of

H_0 and H_a, keep in mind that the alternative hypothesis is often what the test is attempting to establish. Hence, asking whether the user is looking for evidence to support $\mu < \mu_0, \mu > \mu_0$, or $\mu \neq \mu_0$ will help determine H_a. The following exercises are designed to provide practice in choosing the proper form for a hypothesis test involving a population mean.

Exercises

1. The manager of the Danvers-Hilton Resort Hotel stated that the mean guest bill for a weekend is $600 or less. A member of the hotel's accounting staff noticed that the total charges for guest bills have been increasing in recent months. The accountant will use a sample of future weekend guest bills to test the manager's claim.
    a. Which form of the hypotheses should be used to test the manager's claim? Explain.

$H_0: \mu \geq 600$	$H_0: \mu \leq 600$	$H_0: \mu = 600$
$H_a: \mu < 600$	$H_a: \mu > 600$	$H_a: \mu \neq 600$

    b. What conclusion is appropriate when H_0 cannot be rejected?
    c. What conclusion is appropriate when H_0 can be rejected?

2. The manager of an automobile dealership is considering a new bonus plan designed to increase sales volume. Currently, the mean sales volume is 14 automobiles per month. The manager wants to conduct a research study to see whether the new bonus plan increases sales volume. To collect data on the plan, a sample of sales personnel will be allowed to sell under the new bonus plan for a one-month period.
    a. Develop the null and alternative hypotheses most appropriate for this situation.
    b. Comment on the conclusion when H_0 cannot be rejected.
    c. Comment on the conclusion when H_0 can be rejected.

3. A production line operation is designed to fill cartons with laundry detergent to a mean weight of 32 ounces. A sample of cartons is periodically selected and weighed to determine whether underfilling or overfilling is occurring. If the sample data lead to a conclusion of underfilling or overfilling, the production line will be shut down and adjusted to obtain proper filling.
    a. Formulate the null and alternative hypotheses that will help in deciding whether to shut down and adjust the production line.
    b. Comment on the conclusion and the decision when H_0 cannot be rejected.
    c. Comment on the conclusion and the decision when H_0 can be rejected.

4. Because of high production-changeover time and costs, a director of manufacturing must convince management that a proposed manufacturing method reduces costs before the new method can be implemented. The current production method operates with a mean cost of $220 per hour. A research study will measure the cost of the new method over a sample production period.
    a. Develop the null and alternative hypotheses most appropriate for this study.
    b. Comment on the conclusion when H_0 cannot be rejected.
    c. Comment on the conclusion when H_0 can be rejected.

(9.2) Type I and Type II Errors

The null and alternative hypotheses are competing statements about the population. Either the null hypothesis H_0 is true or the alternative hypothesis H_a is true, but not both. Ideally the hypothesis testing procedure should lead to the acceptance of H_0 when H_0 is true and the rejection of H_0 when H_a is true. Unfortunately, the correct conclusions are not always possible. Because

TABLE 9.1   ERRORS AND CORRECT CONCLUSIONS IN HYPOTHESIS TESTING

		Population Condition	
		H_0 **True**	H_a **True**
Conclusion	**Accept H_0**	Correct Conclusion	Type II Error
	Reject H_0	Type I Error	Correct Conclusion

© Cengage Learning

hypothesis tests are based on sample information, we must allow for the possibility of errors. Table 9.1 illustrates the two kinds of errors that can be made in hypothesis testing.

The first row of Table 9.1 shows what can happen if the conclusion is to accept H_0. If H_0 is true, this conclusion is correct. However, if H_a is true, we make a **Type II error**; that is, we accept H_0 when it is false. The second row of Table 9.1 shows what can happen if the conclusion is to reject H_0. If H_0 is true, we make a **Type I error**; that is, we reject H_0 when it is true. However, if H_a is true, rejecting H_0 is correct.

Recall the hypothesis testing illustration discussed in Section 9.1 in which an automobile product research group developed a new fuel injection system designed to increase the miles-per-gallon rating of a particular automobile. With the current model obtaining an average of 24 miles per gallon, the hypothesis test was formulated as follows.

$$H_0: \mu \leq 24$$
$$H_a: \mu > 24$$

The alternative hypothesis, $H_a: \mu > 24$, indicates that the researchers are looking for sample evidence to support the conclusion that the population mean miles per gallon with the new fuel injection system is greater than 24.

In this application, the Type I error of rejecting H_0 when it is true corresponds to the researchers claiming that the new system improves the miles-per-gallon rating ($\mu > 24$) when in fact the new system is not any better than the current system. In contrast, the Type II error of accepting H_0 when it is false corresponds to the researchers concluding that the new system is not any better than the current system ($\mu \leq 24$) when in fact the new system improves miles-per-gallon performance.

For the miles-per-gallon rating hypothesis test, the null hypothesis is $H_0: \mu \leq 24$. Suppose the null hypothesis is true as an equality; that is, $\mu = 24$. The probability of making a Type I error when the null hypothesis is true as an equality is called the **level of significance**. Thus, for the miles-per-gallon rating hypothesis test, the level of significance is the probability of rejecting $H_0: \mu \leq 24$ when $\mu = 24$. Because of the importance of this concept, we now restate the definition of level of significance.

LEVEL OF SIGNIFICANCE

The level of significance is the probability of making a Type I error when the null hypothesis is true as an equality.

The Greek symbol α (alpha) is used to denote the level of significance, and common choices for α are .05 and .01.

In practice, the person responsible for the hypothesis test specifies the level of significance. By selecting α, that person is controlling the probability of making a Type I error. If the cost of making a Type I error is high, small values of α are preferred. If the cost of making a Type I error is not too high, larger values of α are typically used. Applications of hypothesis testing that only control for the Type I error are called *significance tests.* Many applications of hypothesis testing are of this type.

If the sample data are consistent with the null hypothesis H_0, we will follow the practice of concluding "do not reject H_0." This conclusion is preferred over "accept H_0" because the conclusion to accept H_0 puts us at risk of making a Type II error.

Although most applications of hypothesis testing control for the probability of making a Type I error, they do not always control for the probability of making a Type II error. Hence, if we decide to accept H_0, we cannot determine how confident we can be with that decision. Because of the uncertainty associated with making a Type II error when conducting significance tests, statisticians usually recommend that we use the statement "do not reject H_0" instead of "accept H_0." Using the statement "do not reject H_0" carries the recommendation to withhold both judgment and action. In effect, by not directly accepting H_0, the statistician avoids the risk of making a Type II error. Whenever the probability of making a Type II error has not been determined and controlled, we will not make the statement "accept H_0." In such cases, only two conclusions are possible: *do not reject H_0 or reject H_0.*

Although controlling for a Type II error in hypothesis testing is not common, it can be done. More advanced texts describe procedures for determining and controlling the probability of making a Type II error.[1] If proper controls have been established for this error, action based on the "accept H_0" conclusion can be appropriate.

NOTE AND COMMENT

Walter Williams, syndicated columnist and professor of economics at George Mason University, points out that the possibility of making a Type I or a Type II error is always present in decision making (*The Cincinnati Enquirer,* August 14, 2005). He notes that the Food and Drug Administration (FDA) runs the risk of making these errors in its drug approval process. The FDA must either approve a new drug or not approve it. Thus the FDA runs the risk of making a Type I error by approving a new drug that is not safe and effective, or making a Type II error by failing to approve a new drug that is safe and effective. Regardless of the decision made, the possibility of making a costly error cannot be eliminated.

Exercises

5. Duke Energy reported that the cost of electricity for an efficient home in a particular neighborhood of Cincinnati, Ohio, was \$104 per month (*Home Energy Report,* Duke Energy, March 2012). A researcher believes that the cost of electricity for a comparable neighborhood in Chicago, Illinois, is higher. A sample of homes in this Chicago neighborhood will be taken and the sample mean monthly cost of electricity will be used to test the following null and alternative hypotheses.

$$H_0: \mu \le 104$$
$$H_a: \mu > 104$$

   a. Assume the sample data led to rejection of the null hypothesis. What would be your conclusion about the cost of electricity in the Chicago neighborhood?
   b. What is the Type I error in this situation? What are the consequences of making this error?
   c. What is the Type II error in this situation? What are the consequences of making this error?

---

[1]See, for example, D. R. Anderson, D. J. Sweeny, and T. A. Williams, *Statistics for Business and Economics,* 12th ed. (Cincinnati, OH: South-Western/Cengage Learning, 2014).

6. The label on a 3-quart container of orange juice states that the orange juice contains an average of 1 gram of fat or less. Answer the following questions for a hypothesis test that could be used to test the claim on the label.
    a. Develop the appropriate null and alternative hypotheses.
    b. What is the Type I error in this situation? What are the consequences of making this error?
    c. What is the Type II error in this situation? What are the consequences of making this error?

7. Carpetland salespersons average $8,000 per week in sales. Steve Contois, the firm's vice president, proposes a compensation plan with new selling incentives. Steve hopes that the results of a trial selling period will enable him to conclude that the compensation plan increases the average sales per salesperson.
    a. Develop the appropriate null and alternative hypotheses.
    b. What is the Type I error in this situation? What are the consequences of making this error?
    c. What is the Type II error in this situation? What are the consequences of making this error?

8. Suppose a new production method will be implemented if a hypothesis test supports the conclusion that the new method reduces the mean operating cost per hour.
    a. State the appropriate null and alternative hypotheses if the mean cost for the current production method is $220 per hour.
    b. What is the Type I error in this situation? What are the consequences of making this error?
    c. What is the Type II error in this situation? What are the consequences of making this error?

9.3 Population Mean: σ Known

In Chapter 8 we said that the σ known case corresponds to applications in which historical data and/or other information are available that enable us to obtain a good estimate of the population standard deviation prior to sampling. In such cases the population standard deviation can, for all practical purposes, be considered known. In this section we show how to conduct a hypothesis test about a population mean for the σ known case.

The methods presented in this section are exact if the sample is selected from a population that is normally distributed. In cases where it is not reasonable to assume the population is normally distributed, these methods are still applicable if the sample size is large enough. We provide some practical advice concerning the population distribution and the sample size at the end of this section.

One-Tailed Test

One-tailed tests about a population mean take one of the following two forms.

Lower Tail Test	Upper Tail Test
$H_0: \mu \geq \mu_0$	$H_0: \mu \leq \mu_0$
$H_a: \mu < \mu_0$	$H_a: \mu > \mu_0$

Let us consider an example involving a lower tail test.

The Federal Trade Commission (FTC) periodically conducts statistical studies designed to test the claims that manufacturers make about their products. For example, the label on a large can of Hilltop Coffee states that the can contains 3 pounds of coffee. The FTC knows that Hilltop's production process cannot place exactly 3 pounds of coffee in each can, even if the mean filling weight for the population of all cans filled is 3 pounds per can. However, as long as the population mean filling weight is at least 3 pounds per can, the rights of consumers will be protected. Thus, the FTC interprets the label information on a large can of coffee as a claim by Hilltop that the population mean filling weight is at least 3 pounds per can. We will show how the FTC can check Hilltop's claim by conducting a lower tail hypothesis test.

The first step is to develop the null and alternative hypotheses for the test. If the population mean filling weight is at least 3 pounds per can, Hilltop's claim is correct. This establishes the null hypothesis for the test. However, if the population mean weight is less than 3 pounds per can, Hilltop's claim is incorrect. This establishes the alternative hypothesis. With μ denoting the population mean filling weight, the null and alternative hypotheses are as follows:

$$H_0: \mu \geq 3$$
$$H_a: \mu < 3$$

Note that the hypothesized value of the population mean is $\mu_0 = 3$.

If the sample data indicate that H_0 cannot be rejected, the statistical evidence does not support the conclusion that a label violation has occurred. Hence, no action should be taken against Hilltop. However, if the sample data indicate H_0 can be rejected, we will conclude that the alternative hypothesis, $H_a: \mu < 3$, is true. In this case a conclusion of underfilling and a charge of a label violation against Hilltop would be justified.

Suppose a sample of 36 cans of coffee is selected and the sample mean $\bar{x}$ is computed as an estimate of the population mean μ. If the value of the sample mean $\bar{x}$ is less than 3 pounds, the sample results will cast doubt on the null hypothesis. What we want to know is how much less than 3 pounds must $\bar{x}$ be before we would be willing to declare the difference significant and risk making a Type I error by falsely accusing Hilltop of a label violation. A key factor in addressing this issue is the value the decision maker selects for the level of significance.

As noted in the preceding section, the level of significance, denoted by α, is the probability of making a Type I error by rejecting H_0 when the null hypothesis is true as an equality. The decision maker must specify the level of significance. If the cost of making a Type I error is high, a small value should be chosen for the level of significance. If the cost is not high, a larger value is more appropriate. In the Hilltop Coffee study, the director of the FTC's testing program made the following statement: "If the company is meeting its weight specifications at $\mu = 3$, I do not want to take action against them. But I am willing to risk a 1% chance of making such an error." From the director's statement, we set the level of significance for the hypothesis test at $\alpha = .01$. Thus, we must design the hypothesis test so that the probability of making a Type I error when $\mu = 3$ is .01.

For the Hilltop Coffee study, by developing the null and alternative hypotheses and specifying the level of significance for the test, we carry out the first two steps required in conducting every hypothesis test. We are now ready to perform the third step of hypothesis testing: collect the sample data and compute the value of what is called a test statistic.

Test statistic For the Hilltop Coffee study, previous FTC tests show that the population standard deviation can be assumed known with a value of $\sigma = .18$. In addition, these tests also show that the population of filling weights can be assumed to have a normal distribution. From the study of sampling distributions in Chapter 7 we know that if the population from which we are sampling is normally distributed, the sampling distribution of $\bar{x}$ will also be normally distributed. Thus, for the Hilltop Coffee study, the sampling distribution of $\bar{x}$ is normally distributed. With a known value of $\sigma = .18$ and a sample size of $n = 36$, Figure 9.1 shows the sampling distribution of $\bar{x}$ when the null hypothesis is true as an equality; that is, when $\mu = \mu_0 = 3$.[2] Note that the standard error of $\bar{x}$ is given by $\sigma_{\bar{x}} = \sigma/\sqrt{n} = .18/\sqrt{36} = .03$.

The standard error of $\bar{x}$ is the standard deviation of the sampling distribution of $\bar{x}$.

Because the sampling distribution of $\bar{x}$ is normally distributed, the sampling distribution of

$$z = \frac{\bar{x} - \mu_0}{\sigma_{\bar{x}}} = \frac{\bar{x} - 3}{.03}$$

---

[2]In constructing sampling distributions for hypothesis tests, it is assumed that H_0 is satisfied as an equality.

FIGURE 9.1 SAMPLING DISTRIBUTION OF $\bar{x}$ FOR THE HILLTOP COFFEE STUDY WHEN THE NULL HYPOTHESIS IS TRUE AS AN EQUALITY ($\mu = 3$)

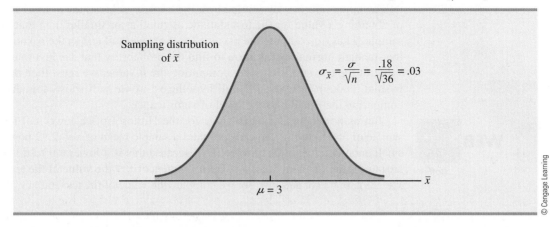

is a standard normal distribution. A value of $z = -1$ means that the value of $\bar{x}$ is one standard error below the hypothesized value of the mean, a value of $z = -2$ means that the value of $\bar{x}$ is two standard errors below the hypothesized value of the mean, and so on. We can use the standard normal probability table to find the lower tail probability corresponding to any z value. For instance, the lower tail area at $z = -3.00$ is .0013. Hence, the probability of obtaining a value of z that is three or more standard errors below the mean is .0013. As a result, the probability of obtaining a value of $\bar{x}$ that is 3 or more standard errors below the hypothesized population mean $\mu_0 = 3$ is also .0013. Such a result is unlikely if the null hypothesis is true.

For hypothesis tests about a population mean in the σ known case, we use the standard normal random variable z as a **test statistic** to determine whether $\bar{x}$ deviates from the hypothesized value of μ enough to justify rejecting the null hypothesis. With $\sigma_{\bar{x}} = \sigma/\sqrt{n}$, the test statistic is as follows.

TEST STATISTIC FOR HYPOTHESIS TESTS ABOUT A POPULATION MEAN: σ KNOWN

$$z = \frac{\bar{x} - \mu_0}{\sigma/\sqrt{n}} \tag{9.1}$$

The key question for a lower tail test is, How small must the test statistic z be before we choose to reject the null hypothesis? Two approaches can be used to answer this question: the p-value approach and the critical value approach.

p-value approach The p-value approach uses the value of the test statistic z to compute a probability called a **p-value**.

A small p-value indicates the value of the test statistic is unusual given the assumption that H_0 is true.

p-VALUE

A p-value is a probability that provides a measure of the evidence against the null hypothesis provided by the sample. Smaller p-values indicate more evidence against H_0.

The p-value is used to determine whether the null hypothesis should be rejected.

Let us see how the *p*-value is computed and used. The value of the test statistic is used to compute the *p*-value. The method used depends on whether the test is a lower tail, an upper tail, or a two-tailed test. For a lower tail test, the *p*-value is the probability of obtaining a value for the test statistic as small as or smaller than that provided by the sample. Thus, to compute the *p*-value for the lower tail test in the σ known case, we use the standard normal distribution to find the probability that *z* is less than or equal to the value of the test statistic. After computing the *p*-value, we must then decide whether it is small enough to reject the null hypothesis; as we will show, this decision involves comparing the *p*-value to the level of significance.

Coffee

Let us now compute the *p*-value for the Hilltop Coffee lower tail test. Suppose the sample of 36 Hilltop coffee cans provides a sample mean of $\bar{x} = 2.92$ pounds. Is $\bar{x} = 2.92$ small enough to cause us to reject H_0? Because this is a lower tail test, the *p*-value is the area under the standard normal curve for values of $z \leq$ the value of the test statistic. Using $\bar{x} = 2.92$, $\sigma = .18$, and $n = 36$, we compute the value of the test statistic *z*.

$$z = \frac{\bar{x} - \mu_0}{\sigma/\sqrt{n}} = \frac{2.92 - 3}{.18/\sqrt{36}} = -2.67$$

Thus, the *p*-value is the probability that *z* is less than or equal to -2.67 (the lower tail area corresponding to the value of the test statistic).

Using the standard normal probability table, we find that the lower tail area at $z = -2.67$ is .0038. Figure 9.2 shows that $\bar{x} = 2.92$ corresponds to $z = -2.67$ and a *p*-value = .0038. This *p*-value indicates a small probability of obtaining a sample mean of $\bar{x} = 2.92$ (and a test statistic of -2.67) or smaller when sampling from a population with $\mu = 3$. This

FIGURE 9.2 *p*-VALUE FOR THE HILLTOP COFFEE STUDY WHEN $\bar{x} = 2.92$ AND $z = -2.67$

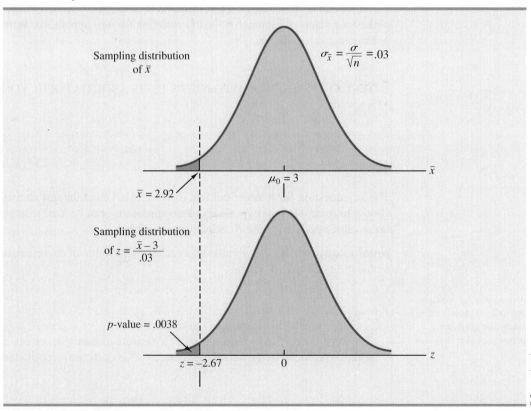

p-value does not provide much support for the null hypothesis, but is it small enough to cause us to reject H_0? The answer depends upon the level of significance for the test.

As noted previously, the director of the FTC's testing program selected a value of .01 for the level of significance. The selection of $\alpha = .01$ means that the director is willing to tolerate a probability of .01 of rejecting the null hypothesis when it is true as an equality ($\mu_0 = 3$). The sample of 36 coffee cans in the Hilltop Coffee study resulted in a p-value = .0038, which means that the probability of obtaining a value of $\bar{x} = 2.92$ or less when the null hypothesis is true as an equality is .0038. Because .0038 is less than or equal to $\alpha = .01$, we reject H_0. Therefore, we find sufficient statistical evidence to reject the null hypothesis at the .01 level of significance.

We can now state the general rule for determining whether the null hypothesis can be rejected when using the p-value approach. For a level of significance α, the rejection rule using the p-value approach is as follows:

REJECTION RULE USING p-VALUE

$$\text{Reject } H_0 \text{ if } p\text{-value} \leq \alpha$$

In the Hilltop Coffee test, the p-value of .0038 resulted in the rejection of the null hypothesis. Although the basis for making the rejection decision involves a comparison of the p-value to the level of significance specified by the FTC director, the observed p-value of .0038 means that we would reject H_0 for any value of $\alpha \geq .0038$. For this reason, the p-value is also called the *observed level of significance*.

Different decision makers may express different opinions concerning the cost of making a Type I error and may choose a different level of significance. By providing the p-value as part of the hypothesis testing results, another decision maker can compare the reported p-value to his or her own level of significance and possibly make a different decision with respect to rejecting H_0.

Critical value approach   The critical value approach requires that we first determine a value for the test statistic called the **critical value**. For a lower tail test, the critical value serves as a benchmark for determining whether the value of the test statistic is small enough to reject the null hypothesis. It is the value of the test statistic that corresponds to an area of α (the level of significance) in the lower tail of the sampling distribution of the test statistic. In other words, the critical value is the largest value of the test statistic that will result in the rejection of the null hypothesis. Let us return to the Hilltop Coffee example and see how this approach works.

In the σ known case, the sampling distribution for the test statistic z is a standard normal distribution. Therefore, the critical value is the value of the test statistic that corresponds to an area of $\alpha = .01$ in the lower tail of a standard normal distribution. Using the standard normal probability table, we find that $z = -2.33$ provides an area of .01 in the lower tail (see Figure 9.3). Thus, if the sample results in a value of the test statistic that is less than or equal to -2.33, the corresponding p-value will be less than or equal to .01; in this case, we should reject the null hypothesis. Hence, for the Hilltop Coffee study the critical value rejection rule for a level of significance of .01 is

$$\text{Reject } H_0 \text{ if } z \leq -2.33$$

In the Hilltop Coffee example, $\bar{x} = 2.92$ and the test statistic is $z = -2.67$. Because $z = -2.67 < -2.33$, we can reject H_0 and conclude that Hilltop Coffee is underfilling cans.

FIGURE 9.3   CRITICAL VALUE = −2.33 FOR THE HILLTOP COFFEE HYPOTHESIS TEST

We can generalize the rejection rule for the critical value approach to handle any level of significance. The rejection rule for a lower tail test follows.

REJECTION RULE FOR A LOWER TAIL TEST: CRITICAL VALUE APPROACH

$$\text{Reject } H_0 \text{ if } z \leq -z_\alpha$$

where $-z_\alpha$ is the critical value; that is, the z value that provides an area of α in the lower tail of the standard normal distribution.

Summary   The p-value approach to hypothesis testing and the critical value approach will always lead to the same rejection decision; that is, whenever the p-value is less than or equal to α, the value of the test statistic will be less than or equal to the critical value. The advantage of the p-value approach is that the p-value tells us *how* significant the results are (the observed level of significance). If we use the critical value approach, we only know that the results are significant at the stated level of significance.

At the beginning of this section, we said that one-tailed tests about a population mean take one of the following two forms:

Lower Tail Test	Upper Tail Test
$H_0: \mu \geq \mu_0$	$H_0: \mu \leq \mu_0$
$H_a: \mu < \mu_0$	$H_a: \mu > \mu_0$

We used the Hilltop Coffee study to illustrate how to conduct a lower tail test. We can use the same general approach to conduct an upper tail test. The test statistic z is still computed using equation (9.1). But, for an upper tail test, the p-value is the probability of obtaining a value for the test statistic as large as or larger than that provided by the sample. Thus, to compute the p-value for the upper tail test in the σ known case, we must use the standard normal distribution to find the probability that z is greater than or equal to the value of the test statistic. Using the critical value approach causes us to reject the null hypothesis if the value of the test statistic is greater than or equal to the critical value z_α; in other words, we reject H_0 if $z \geq z_\alpha$.

Let us summarize the steps involved in computing p-values for one-tailed hypothesis tests.

COMPUTATION OF p-VALUES FOR ONE-TAILED TESTS

1. Compute the value of the test statistic using equation (9.1).
2. **Lower tail test:** Using the standard normal distribution, compute the probability that z is less than or equal to the value of the test statistic (area in the lower tail).
3. **Upper tail test:** Using the standard normal distribution, compute the probability that z is greater than or equal to the value of the test statistic (area in the upper tail).

Two-Tailed Test

In hypothesis testing, the general form for a **two-tailed test** about a population mean is as follows:

$$H_0: \mu = \mu_0$$
$$H_a: \mu \neq \mu_0$$

In this subsection we show how to conduct a two-tailed test about a population mean for the σ known case. As an illustration, we consider the hypothesis testing situation facing MaxFlight, Inc.

The U.S. Golf Association (USGA) establishes rules that manufacturers of golf equipment must meet if their products are to be acceptable for use in USGA events. MaxFlight uses a high-technology manufacturing process to produce golf balls with a mean driving distance of 295 yards. Sometimes, however, the process gets out of adjustment and produces golf balls with a mean driving distance different from 295 yards. When the mean distance falls below 295 yards, the company worries about losing sales because the golf balls do not provide as much distance as advertised. When the mean distance passes 295 yards, MaxFlight's golf balls may be rejected by the USGA for exceeding the overall distance standard concerning carry and roll.

MaxFlight's quality control program involves taking periodic samples of 50 golf balls to monitor the manufacturing process. For each sample, a hypothesis test is conducted to determine whether the process has fallen out of adjustment. Let us develop the null and alternative hypotheses. We begin by assuming that the process is functioning correctly; that is, the golf balls being produced have a mean distance of 295 yards. This assumption establishes the null hypothesis. The alternative hypothesis is that the mean distance is not equal to 295 yards. With a hypothesized value of $\mu_0 = 295$, the null and alternative hypotheses for the MaxFlight hypothesis test are as follows:

$$H_0: \mu = 295$$
$$H_a: \mu \neq 295$$

If the sample mean $\bar{x}$ is significantly less than 295 yards or significantly greater than 295 yards, we will reject H_0. In this case, corrective action will be taken to adjust the manufacturing process. On the other hand, if $\bar{x}$ does not deviate from the hypothesized mean $\mu_0 = 295$ by a significant amount, H_0 will not be rejected and no action will be taken to adjust the manufacturing process.

The quality control team selected $\alpha = .05$ as the level of significance for the test. Data from previous tests conducted when the process was known to be in adjustment show that

FIGURE 9.4 SAMPLING DISTRIBUTION OF $\bar{x}$ FOR THE MAXFLIGHT HYPOTHESIS TEST

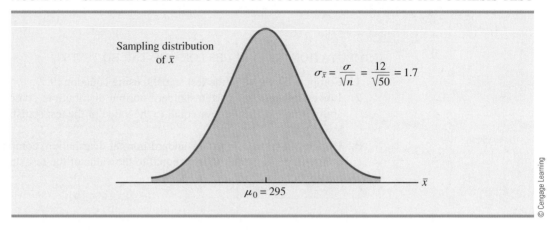

the population standard deviation can be assumed known with a value of $\sigma = 12$. Thus, with a sample size of $n = 50$, the standard error of $\bar{x}$ is

$$\sigma_{\bar{x}} = \frac{\sigma}{\sqrt{n}} = \frac{12}{\sqrt{50}} = 1.7$$

Because the sample size is large, the central limit theorem (see Chapter 7) allows us to conclude that the sampling distribution of $\bar{x}$ can be approximated by a normal distribution. Figure 9.4 shows the sampling distribution of $\bar{x}$ for the MaxFlight hypothesis test with a hypothesized population mean of $\mu_0 = 295$.

GolfTest

Suppose that a sample of 50 golf balls is selected and that the sample mean is $\bar{x} = 297.6$ yards. This sample mean provides support for the conclusion that the population mean is larger than 295 yards. Is this value of $\bar{x}$ enough larger than 295 to cause us to reject H_0 at the .05 level of significance? In the previous section we described two approaches that can be used to answer this question: the p-value approach and the critical value approach.

***p*-value approach** Recall that the p-value is a probability used to determine whether the null hypothesis should be rejected. For a two-tailed test, values of the test statistic in *either* tail provide evidence against the null hypothesis. For a two-tailed test, the p-value is the probability of obtaining a value for the test statistic *as unlikely as or more unlikely than* that provided by the sample. Let us see how the p-value is computed for the MaxFlight hypothesis test.

First we compute the value of the test statistic. For the σ known case, the test statistic z is a standard normal random variable. Using equation (9.1) with $\bar{x} = 297.6$, the value of the test statistic is

$$z = \frac{\bar{x} - \mu_0}{\sigma/\sqrt{n}} = \frac{297.6 - 295}{12/\sqrt{50}} = 1.53$$

Now to compute the p-value we must find the probability of obtaining a value for the test statistic *at least as unlikely as* $z = 1.53$. Clearly values of $z \geq 1.53$ are *at least as unlikely*. But, because this is a two-tailed test, values of $z \leq -1.53$ are also *at least as unlikely as* the value of the test statistic provided by the sample. In Figure 9.5, we see that the two-tailed p-value in this case is given by $P(z \leq -1.53) + P(z \geq 1.53)$. Because the normal curve is symmetric, we can compute this probability by finding the upper tail area at $z = 1.53$ and doubling it. The table for the standard normal distribution shows that $P(z < 1.53) = .9370$. Thus, the upper tail area is $P(z \geq 1.53) = 1.0000 - .9370 = .0630$. Doubling this, we find the p-value for the MaxFlight two-tailed hypothesis test is p-value $= 2(.0630) = .1260$.

FIGURE 9.5   *p*-VALUE FOR THE MAXFLIGHT HYPOTHESIS TEST

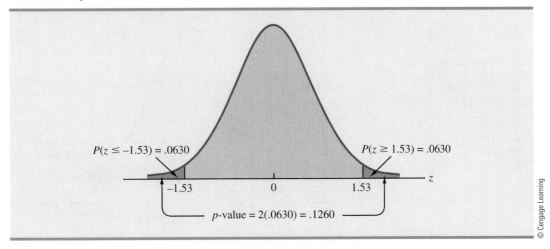

Next we compare the *p*-value to the level of significance to see whether the null hypothesis should be rejected. With a level of significance of $\alpha = .05$, we do not reject H_0 because the *p*-value $= .1260 > .05$. Because the null hypothesis is not rejected, no action will be taken to adjust the MaxFlight manufacturing process.

The computation of the *p*-value for a two-tailed test may seem a bit confusing as compared to the computation of the *p*-value for a one-tailed test. But it can be simplified by following three steps.

COMPUTATION OF *p*-VALUES FOR TWO-TAILED TESTS

1. Compute the value of the test statistic using equation (9.1).
2. If the value of the test statistic is in the upper tail, compute the probability that *z* is greater than or equal to the value of the test statistic (the upper tail area). If the value of the test statistic is in the lower tail, compute the probability that *z* is less than or equal to the value of the test statistic (the lower tail area).
3. Double the probability (or tail area) from step 2 to obtain the *p*-value.

Critical value approach   Before leaving this section, let us see how the test statistic *z* can be compared to a critical value to make the hypothesis testing decision for a two-tailed test. Figure 9.6 shows that the critical values for the test will occur in both the lower and upper tails of the standard normal distribution. With a level of significance of $\alpha = .05$, the area in each tail corresponding to the critical values is $\alpha/2 = .05/2 = .025$. Using the standard normal probability table, we find the critical values for the test statistic are $-z_{.025} = -1.96$ and $z_{.025} = 1.96$. Thus, using the critical value approach, the two-tailed rejection rule is

$$\text{Reject } H_0 \text{ if } z \leq -1.96 \text{ or if } z \geq 1.96$$

Because the value of the test statistic for the MaxFlight study is $z = 1.53$, the statistical evidence will not permit us to reject the null hypothesis at the .05 level of significance.

Summary and Practical Advice

We presented examples of a lower tail test and a two-tailed test about a population mean. Based upon these examples, we can now summarize the hypothesis testing procedures about a population mean for the σ known case as shown in Table 9.2. Note that μ_0 is the hypothesized value of the population mean.

FIGURE 9.6   CRITICAL VALUES FOR THE MAXFLIGHT HYPOTHESIS TEST

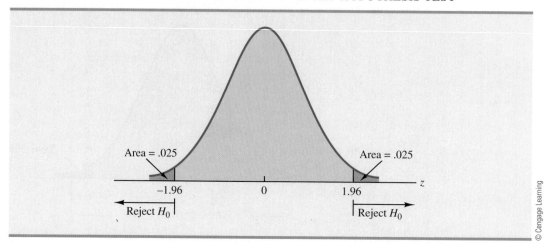

TABLE 9.2   SUMMARY OF HYPOTHESIS TESTS ABOUT A POPULATION MEAN: σ KNOWN CASE

	Lower Tail Test	**Upper Tail Test**	**Two-Tailed Test**
Hypotheses	$H_0: \mu \geq \mu_0$ $H_a: \mu < \mu_0$	$H_0: \mu \leq \mu_0$ $H_a: \mu > \mu_0$	$H_0: \mu = \mu_0$ $H_a: \mu \neq \mu_0$
Test Statistic	$z = \dfrac{\bar{x} - \mu_0}{\sigma/\sqrt{n}}$	$z = \dfrac{\bar{x} - \mu_0}{\sigma/\sqrt{n}}$	$z = \dfrac{\bar{x} - \mu_0}{\sigma/\sqrt{n}}$
Rejection Rule: *p*-**Value Approach**	Reject H_0 if p-value $\leq \alpha$	Reject H_0 if p-value $\leq \alpha$	Reject H_0 if p-value $\leq \alpha$
Rejection Rule: **Critical Value** **Approach**	Reject H_0 if $z \leq -z_\alpha$	Reject H_0 if $z \geq z_\alpha$	Reject H_0 if $z \leq -z_{\alpha/2}$ or if $z \geq z_{\alpha/2}$

The hypothesis testing steps followed in the two examples presented in this section are common to every hypothesis test.

> **STEPS OF HYPOTHESIS TESTING**
>
> **Step 1.** Develop the null and alternative hypotheses.
> **Step 2.** Specify the level of significance.
> **Step 3.** Collect the sample data and compute the value of the test statistic.
>
> *p-Value Approach*
>
> **Step 4.** Use the value of the test statistic to compute the *p*-value.
> **Step 5.** Reject H_0 if the *p*-value $\leq \alpha$.
> **Step 6.** Interpret the statistical conclusion in the context of the application.
>
> *Critical Value Approach*
>
> **Step 4.** Use the level of significance to determine the critical value and the rejection rule.
> **Step 5.** Use the value of the test statistic and the rejection rule to determine whether to reject H_0.
> **Step 6.** Interpret the statistical conclusion in the context of the application.

Practical advice about the sample size for hypothesis tests is similar to the advice we provided about the sample size for interval estimation in Chapter 8. In most applications, a sample size of $n \geq 30$ is adequate when using the hypothesis testing procedure described in this section. In cases where the sample size is less than 30, the distribution of the population from which we are sampling becomes an important consideration. If the population is normally distributed, the hypothesis testing procedure that we described is exact and can be used for any sample size. If the population is not normally distributed but is at least roughly symmetric, sample sizes as small as 15 can be expected to provide acceptable results.

Relationship Between Interval Estimation and Hypothesis Testing

In Chapter 8 we showed how to develop a confidence interval estimate of a population mean. For the σ known case, the $(1 - \alpha)\%$ confidence interval estimate of a population mean is given by

$$\bar{x} \pm z_{\alpha/2} \frac{\sigma}{\sqrt{n}}$$

In this chapter, we showed that a two-tailed hypothesis test about a population mean takes the following form:

$$H_0\colon \mu = \mu_0$$
$$H_a\colon \mu \neq \mu_0$$

where μ_0 is the hypothesized value for the population mean.

Suppose that we follow the procedure described in Chapter 8 for constructing a $100(1 - \alpha)\%$ confidence interval for the population mean. We know that $100(1 - \alpha)\%$ of the confidence intervals generated will contain the population mean and $100\alpha\%$ of the confidence intervals generated will not contain the population mean. Thus, if we reject H_0 whenever the confidence interval does not contain μ_0, we will be rejecting the null hypothesis when it is true ($\mu = \mu_0$) with probability α. Recall that the level of significance is the probability of rejecting the null hypothesis when it is true. So constructing a $100(1 - \alpha)\%$ confidence interval and rejecting H_0 whenever the interval does not contain μ_0 is equivalent to conducting a two-tailed hypothesis test with α as the level of significance. The procedure for using a confidence interval to conduct a two-tailed hypothesis test can now be summarized.

For a two-tailed hypothesis test, the null hypothesis can be rejected if the confidence interval does not include μ_0.

A CONFIDENCE INTERVAL APPROACH TO TESTING A HYPOTHESIS OF THE FORM

$$H_0\colon \mu = \mu_0$$
$$H_a\colon \mu \neq \mu_0$$

1. Select a simple random sample from the population and use the value of the sample mean $\bar{x}$ to develop the confidence interval for the population mean μ.

$$\bar{x} \pm z_{\alpha/2} \frac{\sigma}{\sqrt{n}}$$

2. If the confidence interval contains the hypothesized value μ_0, do not reject H_0. Otherwise, reject* H_0.

---

*To be consistent with the rule for rejecting H_0 when the p-value $\leq \alpha$, we would also reject H_0 using the confidence interval approach if μ_0 happens to be equal to one of the end points of the $100(1 - \alpha)\%$ confidence interval.

Let us illustrate by conducting the MaxFlight hypothesis test using the confidence interval approach. The MaxFlight hypothesis test takes the following form:

$$H_0: \mu = 295$$
$$H_a: \mu \neq 295$$

To test these hypotheses with a level of significance of $\alpha = .05$, we sampled 50 golf balls and found a sample mean distance of $\bar{x} = 297.6$ yards. Recall that the population standard deviation is $\sigma = 12$. Using these results with $z_{.025} = 1.96$, we find that the 95% confidence interval estimate of the population mean is

$$\bar{x} \pm z_{.025} \frac{\sigma}{\sqrt{n}}$$

$$297.6 \pm 1.96 \frac{12}{\sqrt{50}}$$

$$297.6 \pm 3.3$$

or

$$294.3 \text{ to } 300.9$$

This finding enables the quality control manager to conclude with 95% confidence that the mean distance for the population of golf balls is between 294.3 and 300.9 yards. Because the hypothesized value for the population mean, $\mu_0 = 295$, is in this interval, the hypothesis testing conclusion is that the null hypothesis, $H_0: \mu = 295$, cannot be rejected.

Note that this discussion and example pertain to two-tailed hypothesis tests about a population mean. However, the same confidence interval and two-tailed hypothesis testing relationship exists for other population parameters. The relationship can also be extended to one-tailed tests about population parameters. Doing so, however, requires the development of one-sided confidence intervals, which are rarely used in practice.

NOTE AND COMMENT

We have shown how to use p-values. The smaller the p-value the greater the evidence against H_0 and the more the evidence in favor of H_a. Here are some guidelines statisticians suggest for interpreting small p-values.

- Less than .01—Overwhelming evidence to conclude H_a is true.
- Between .01 and .05—Strong evidence to conclude H_a is true.
- Between .05 and .10—Weak evidence to conclude H_a is true.
- Greater than .10—Insufficient evidence to conclude H_a is true.

Exercises

Note to Student: Some of the exercises that follow ask you to use the p-value approach and others ask you to use the critical value approach. Both methods will provide the same hypothesis testing conclusion. We provide exercises with both methods to give you practice using both. In later sections and in following chapters, we will generally emphasize the p-value approach as the preferred method, but you may select either based on personal preference.

Methods

9. Consider the following hypothesis test:

$$H_0: \mu \geq 20$$
$$H_a: \mu < 20$$

A sample of 50 provided a sample mean of 19.4. The population standard deviation is 2.
   a. Compute the value of the test statistic.
   b. What is the p-value?
   c. Using $\alpha = .05$, what is your conclusion?
   d. What is the rejection rule using the critical value? What is your conclusion?

10. Consider the following hypothesis test:

$$H_0: \mu \leq 25$$
$$H_a: \mu > 25$$

A sample of 40 provided a sample mean of 26.4. The population standard deviation is 6.
   a. Compute the value of the test statistic.
   b. What is the p-value?
   c. At $\alpha = .01$, what is your conclusion?
   d. What is the rejection rule using the critical value? What is your conclusion?

11. Consider the following hypothesis test:

SELF test

$$H_0: \mu = 15$$
$$H_a: \mu \neq 15$$

A sample of 50 provided a sample mean of 14.15. The population standard deviation is 3.
   a. Compute the value of the test statistic.
   b. What is the p-value?
   c. At $\alpha = .05$, what is your conclusion?
   d. What is the rejection rule using the critical value? What is your conclusion?

12. Consider the following hypothesis test:

$$H_0: \mu \geq 80$$
$$H_a: \mu < 80$$

A sample of 100 is used and the population standard deviation is 12. Compute the p-value and state your conclusion for each of the following sample results. Use $\alpha = .01$.
   a. $\bar{x} = 78.5$
   b. $\bar{x} = 77$
   c. $\bar{x} = 75.5$
   d. $\bar{x} = 81$

13. Consider the following hypothesis test:

$$H_0: \mu \leq 50$$
$$H_a: \mu > 50$$

A sample of 60 is used and the population standard deviation is 8. Use the critical value approach to state your conclusion for each of the following sample results. Use $\alpha = .05$.
   a. $\bar{x} = 52.5$
   b. $\bar{x} = 51$
   c. $\bar{x} = 51.8$

14. Consider the following hypothesis test:

$$H_0: \mu = 22$$
$$H_a: \mu \neq 22$$

A sample of 75 is used and the population standard deviation is 10. Compute the p-value and state your conclusion for each of the following sample results. Use $\alpha = .01$.
a. $\bar{x} = 23$
b. $\bar{x} = 25.1$
c. $\bar{x} = 20$

Applications

15. Individuals filing federal income tax returns prior to March 31 received an average refund of $1,056. Consider the population of "last-minute" filers who mail their tax return during the last five days of the income tax period (typically April 10 to April 15).
a. A researcher suggests that a reason individuals wait until the last five days is that on average these individuals receive lower refunds than do early filers. Develop appropriate hypotheses such that rejection of H_0 will support the researcher's contention.
b. For a sample of 400 individuals who filed a tax return between April 10 and 15, the sample mean refund was $910. Based on prior experience a population standard deviation of $\sigma = \$1,600$ may be assumed. What is the p-value?
c. At $\alpha = .05$, what is your conclusion?
d. Repeat the preceding hypothesis test using the critical value approach.

16. In a study entitled How Undergraduate Students Use Credit Cards, it was reported that undergraduate students have a mean credit card balance of $3,173 (*Sallie Mae*, April 2009). This figure was an all-time high and had increased 44% over the previous five years. Assume that a current study is being conducted to determine if it can be concluded that the mean credit card balance for undergraduate students has continued to increase compared to the April 2009 report. Based on previous studies, use a population standard deviation $\sigma = \$1,000$.
a. State the null and alternative hypotheses.
b. What is the p-value for a sample of 180 undergraduate students with a sample mean credit card balance of $3,325?
c. Using a .05 level of significance, what is your conclusion?

17. The mean hourly wage for employees in goods-producing industries is currently $24.57 (Bureau of Labor Statistics website, April, 12, 2012). Suppose we take a sample of employees from the manufacturing industry to see if the mean hourly wage differs from the reported mean of $24.57 for the goods-producing industries.
a. State the null and alternative hypotheses we should use to test whether the population mean hourly wage in the manufacturing industry differs from the population mean hourly wage in the goods-producing industries.
b. Suppose a sample of 30 employees from the manufacturing industry showed a sample mean of $23.89 per hour. Assume a population standard deviation of $2.40 per hour and compute the p-value.
c. With $\alpha = .05$ as the level of significance, what is your conclusion?
d. Repeat the preceding hypothesis test using the critical value approach.

18. Young millennials, adults aged 18 to 34, are viewed as the future of the restaurant industry. During 2011, this group consumed a mean of 192 restaurant meals per person (NPD Group website, November 7, 2012). Conduct a hypothesis test to determine if the poor

economy has caused a change in the frequency of consuming restaurant meals by young millennials in 2012.

a. Formulate hypotheses that can be used to determine whether the annual mean number of restaurant meals per person has changed for young millennials in 2012.

b. Based on a sample, the NPD Group stated that the mean number of restaurant meals consumed by young millennials in 2012 was 182. Assume the sample size was 150 and that, based on past studies, the population standard deviation can be assumed to be $\sigma = 55$. Use the sample results to compute the test statistic and p-value for your hypothesis test.

c. At $\alpha = .05$, what is your conclusion?

19. The Internal Revenue Service (IRS) provides a toll-free help line for taxpayers to call in and get answers to questions as they prepare their tax returns. In recent years, the IRS has been inundated with taxpayer calls and has redesigned its phone service as well as posted answers to frequently asked questions on its website (*The Cincinnati Enquirer*, January 7, 2010). According to a report by a taxpayer advocate, callers using the new system can expect to wait on hold for an unreasonably long time of 12 minutes before being able to talk to an IRS employee. Suppose you select a sample of 50 callers after the new phone service has been implemented; the sample results show a mean waiting time of 10 minutes before an IRS employee comes on the line. Based upon data from past years, you decide it is reasonable to assume that the standard deviation of waiting time is 8 minutes. Using your sample results, can you conclude that the actual mean waiting time turned out to be significantly less than the 12-minute claim made by the taxpayer advocate? Use $\alpha = .05$.

20. Annual expenditure for prescription drugs was $838 per person in the Northeast region of the country (Hospital Care Cost Institute website, November 7, 2012). A sample of 60 individuals in the Midwest region showed a per person annual expenditure for prescription drugs of $745. Use a population standard deviation of $300 to answer the following questions.

a. Formulate hypotheses for a test to determine whether the sample data support the conclusion that the population annual expenditure for prescription drugs per person is lower in the Midwest region than in the Northeast region.

b. What is the value of the test statistic?

c. What is the p-value?

d. At $\alpha = .01$, what is your conclusion?

WEB file

Fowle

21. Fowle Marketing Research, Inc., bases charges to a client on the assumption that telephone surveys can be completed in a mean time of 15 minutes or less. If a longer mean survey time is necessary, a premium rate is charged. A sample of 35 surveys provided the survey times shown in the file named Fowle. Based upon past studies, the population standard deviation is assumed known with $\sigma = 4$ minutes. Is the premium rate justified?

a. Formulate the null and alternative hypotheses for this application.

b. Compute the value of the test statistic.

c. What is the p-value?

d. At $\alpha = .01$, what is your conclusion?

22. CCN and ActMedia provided a television channel targeted to individuals waiting in supermarket checkout lines. The channel showed news, short features, and advertisements. The length of the program was based on the assumption that the population mean time a shopper stands in a supermarket checkout line is 8 minutes. A sample of actual waiting times will be used to test this assumption and determine whether actual mean waiting time differs from this standard.

a. Formulate the hypotheses for this application.

b. A sample of 120 shoppers showed a sample mean waiting time of 8.4 minutes. Assume a population standard deviation of $\sigma = 3.2$ minutes. What is the p-value?

c. At $\alpha = .05$, what is your conclusion?

d. Compute a 95% confidence interval for the population mean. Does it support your conclusion?

9.4   Population Mean: σ Unknown

In this section we describe how to conduct hypothesis tests about a population mean for the σ unknown case. Because the σ unknown case corresponds to situations in which an estimate of the population standard deviation cannot be developed prior to sampling, the sample must be used to develop an estimate of both μ and σ. Thus, to conduct a hypothesis test about a population mean for the σ unknown case, the sample mean $\bar{x}$ is used as an estimate of μ and the sample standard deviation s is used as an estimate of σ.

The steps of the hypothesis testing procedure for the σ unknown case are the same as those for the σ known case described in Section 9.3. But, with σ unknown, the computation of the test statistic and p-value is a bit different. Recall that for the σ known case, the sampling distribution of the test statistic has a standard normal distribution. For the σ unknown case, however, the sampling distribution of the test statistic follows the t distribution; it has slightly more variability because the sample is used to develop estimates of both μ and σ.

In Section 8.2 we showed that an interval estimate of a population mean for the σ unknown case is based on a probability distribution known as the t distribution. Hypothesis tests about a population mean for the σ unknown case are also based on the t distribution. For the σ unknown case, the test statistic has a t distribution with $n - 1$ degrees of freedom.

> **TEST STATISTIC FOR HYPOTHESIS TESTS ABOUT A POPULATION MEAN: σ UNKNOWN**
>
> $$t = \frac{\bar{x} - \mu_0}{s/\sqrt{n}} \tag{9.2}$$

In Chapter 8 we said that the t distribution is based on an assumption that the population from which we are sampling has a normal distribution. However, research shows that this assumption can be relaxed considerably when the sample size is large enough. We provide some practical advice concerning the population distribution and sample size at the end of the section.

One-Tailed Test

AirRating

Let us consider an example of a one-tailed test about a population mean for the σ unknown case. A business travel magazine wants to classify transatlantic gateway airports according to the mean rating for the population of business travelers. A rating scale with a low score of 0 and a high score of 10 will be used, and airports with a population mean rating greater than 7 will be designated as superior service airports. The magazine staff surveyed a sample of 60 business travelers at each airport to obtain the ratings data. The sample for London's Heathrow Airport provided a sample mean rating of $\bar{x} = 7.25$ and a sample standard deviation of $s = 1.052$. Do the data indicate that Heathrow should be designated as a superior service airport?

We want to develop a hypothesis test for which the decision to reject H_0 will lead to the conclusion that the population mean rating for the Heathrow Airport is *greater* than 7. Thus, an upper tail test with $H_a: \mu > 7$ is required. The null and alternative hypotheses for this upper tail test are as follows:

$$H_0: \mu \leq 7$$
$$H_a: \mu > 7$$

We will use $\alpha = .05$ as the level of significance for the test.

Using equation (9.2) with $\bar{x} = 7.25$, $\mu_0 = 7$, $s = 1.052$, and $n = 60$, the value of the test statistic is

$$t = \frac{\bar{x} - \mu_0}{s/\sqrt{n}} = \frac{7.25 - 7}{1.052/\sqrt{60}} = 1.84$$

The sampling distribution of t has $n - 1 = 60 - 1 = 59$ degrees of freedom. Because the test is an upper tail test, the p-value is $P(t \geq 1.84)$, that is, the upper tail area corresponding to the value of the test statistic.

The t distribution table provided in most textbooks will not contain sufficient detail to determine the exact p-value, such as the p-value corresponding to $t = 1.84$. For instance, using Table 2 in Appendix B, the t distribution with 59 degrees of freedom provides the following information.

Area in Upper Tail	.20	.10	.05	.025	.01	.005
t Value (59 df)	.848	1.296	1.671	2.001	2.391	2.662

$t = 1.84$

We see that $t = 1.84$ is between 1.671 and 2.001. Although the table does not provide the exact p-value, the values in the "Area in Upper Tail" row show that the p-value must be less than .05 and greater than .025. With a level of significance of $\alpha = .05$, this placement is all we need to know to make the decision to reject the null hypothesis and conclude that Heathrow should be classified as a superior service airport.

Appendix F shows how to compute p-values using Excel or Minitab.

Because it is cumbersome to use a t table to compute p-values, and only approximate values are obtained, we show how to compute the exact p-value using Excel or Minitab. The directions can be found in Appendix F at the end of this text. Using Excel or Minitab with $t = 1.84$ provides the upper tail p-value of .0354 for the Heathrow Airport hypothesis test. With $.0354 < .05$, we reject the null hypothesis and conclude that Heathrow should be classified as a superior service airport.

The decision whether to reject the null hypothesis in the σ unknown case can also be made using the critical value approach. The critical value corresponding to an area of $\alpha = .05$ in the upper tail of a t distribution with 59 degrees of freedom is $t_{.05} = 1.671$. Thus the rejection rule using the critical value approach is to reject H_0 if $t \geq 1.671$. Because $t = 1.84 > 1.671$, H_0 is rejected. Heathrow should be classified as a superior service airport.

Two-Tailed Test

To illustrate how to conduct a two-tailed test about a population mean for the σ unknown case, let us consider the hypothesis testing situation facing Holiday Toys. The company manufactures and distributes its products through more than 1000 retail outlets. In planning production levels for the coming winter season, Holiday must decide how many units of each product to produce prior to knowing the actual demand at the retail level. For this year's most important new toy, Holiday's marketing director is expecting demand to average 40 units per retail outlet. Prior to making the final production decision based upon this estimate, Holiday decided to survey a sample of 25 retailers in order to develop more information about the demand for the new product. Each retailer was provided with information about the features of the new toy along with the cost and the suggested selling price. Then each retailer was asked to specify an anticipated order quantity.

With μ denoting the population mean order quantity per retail outlet, the sample data will be used to conduct the following two-tailed hypothesis test:

$$H_0: \mu = 40$$
$$H_a: \mu \neq 40$$

If H_0 cannot be rejected, Holiday will continue its production planning based on the marketing director's estimate that the population mean order quantity per retail outlet will be $\mu = 40$ units. However, if H_0 is rejected, Holiday will immediately reevaluate its production plan for the product. A two-tailed hypothesis test is used because Holiday wants to reevaluate the production plan if the population mean quantity per retail outlet is less than anticipated or greater than anticipated. Because no historical data are available (it's a new product), the population mean μ and the population standard deviation must both be estimated using $\bar{x}$ and s from the sample data.

Orders

The sample of 25 retailers provided a mean of $\bar{x} = 37.4$ and a standard deviation of $s = 11.79$ units. Before going ahead with the use of the t distribution, the analyst constructed a histogram of the sample data in order to check on the form of the population distribution. The histogram of the sample data showed no evidence of skewness or any extreme outliers, so the analyst concluded that the use of the t distribution with $n - 1 = 24$ degrees of freedom was appropriate. Using equation (9.2) with $\bar{x} = 37.4$, $\mu_0 = 40$, $s = 11.79$, and $n = 25$, the value of the test statistic is

$$t = \frac{\bar{x} - \mu_0}{s/\sqrt{n}} = \frac{37.4 - 40}{11.79/\sqrt{25}} = -1.10$$

Because we have a two-tailed test, the p-value is two times the area under the curve of the t distribution for $t \leq -1.10$. Using Table 2 in Appendix B, the t distribution table for 24 degrees of freedom provides the following information.

Area in Upper Tail	.20	.10	.05	.025	.01	.005
t-Value (24 df)	.857	1.318	1.711	2.064	2.492	2.797

$t = 1.10$

The t distribution table only contains positive t values. Because the t distribution is symmetric, however, the upper tail area at $t = 1.10$ is the same as the lower tail area at $t = -1.10$. We see that $t = 1.10$ is between 0.857 and 1.318. From the "Area in Upper Tail" row, we see that the area in the upper tail at $t = 1.10$ is between .20 and .10. When we double these amounts, we see that the p-value must be between .40 and .20. With a level of significance of $\alpha = .05$, we now know that the p-value is greater than α. Therefore, H_0 cannot be rejected. Sufficient evidence is not available to conclude that Holiday should change its production plan for the coming season.

Appendix F shows how the p-value for this test can be computed using Excel or Minitab. The p-value obtained is .2822. With a level of significance of $\alpha = .05$, we cannot reject H_0 because $.2822 > .05$.

The test statistic can also be compared to the critical value to make the two-tailed hypothesis testing decision. With $\alpha = .05$ and the t distribution with 24 degrees of freedom, $-t_{.025} = -2.064$ and $t_{.025} = 2.064$ are the critical values for the two-tailed test. The rejection rule using the test statistic is

Reject H_0 if $t \leq -2.064$ or if $t \geq 2.064$

TABLE 9.3 SUMMARY OF HYPOTHESIS TESTS ABOUT A POPULATION MEAN: σ UNKNOWN CASE

	Lower Tail Test	Upper Tail Test	Two-Tailed Test
Hypotheses	$H_0: \mu \geq \mu_0$ $H_a: \mu < \mu_0$	$H_0: \mu \leq \mu_0$ $H_a: \mu > \mu_0$	$H_0: \mu = \mu_0$ $H_a: \mu \neq \mu_0$
Test Statistic	$t = \dfrac{\bar{x} - \mu_0}{s/\sqrt{n}}$	$t = \dfrac{\bar{x} - \mu_0}{s/\sqrt{n}}$	$t = \dfrac{\bar{x} - \mu_0}{s/\sqrt{n}}$
Rejection Rule: **p-Value Approach**	Reject H_0 if p-value $\leq \alpha$	Reject H_0 if p-value $\leq \alpha$	Reject H_0 if p-value $\leq \alpha$
Rejection Rule: **Critical Value** **Approach**	Reject H_0 if $t \leq -t_\alpha$	Reject H_0 if $t \geq t_\alpha$	Reject H_0 if $t \leq -t_{\alpha/2}$ or if $t \geq t_{\alpha/2}$

Based on the test statistic $t = -1.10$, H_0 cannot be rejected. This result indicates that Holiday should continue its production planning for the coming season based on the expectation that $\mu = 40$.

Summary and Practical Advice

Table 9.3 provides a summary of the hypothesis testing procedures about a population mean for the σ unknown case. The key difference between these procedures and the ones for the σ known case is that s is used, instead of σ, in the computation of the test statistic. For this reason, the test statistic follows the t distribution.

The applicability of the hypothesis testing procedures of this section is dependent on the distribution of the population being sampled from and the sample size. When the population is normally distributed, the hypothesis tests described in this section provide exact results for any sample size. When the population is not normally distributed, the procedures are approximations. Nonetheless, we find that sample sizes of 30 or greater will provide good results in most cases. If the population is approximately normal, small sample sizes (e.g., $n < 15$) can provide acceptable results. If the population is highly skewed or contains outliers, sample sizes approaching 50 are recommended.

Exercises

Methods

23. Consider the following hypothesis test:

$$H_0: \mu \leq 12$$
$$H_a: \mu > 12$$

A sample of 25 provided a sample mean $\bar{x} = 14$ and a sample standard deviation $s = 4.32$.
 a. Compute the value of the test statistic.
 b. Use the t distribution table (Table 2 in Appendix B) to compute a range for the p-value.
 c. At $\alpha = .05$, what is your conclusion?
 d. What is the rejection rule using the critical value? What is your conclusion?

24. Consider the following hypothesis test:

$$H_0: \mu = 18$$
$$H_a: \mu \neq 18$$

A sample of 48 provided a sample mean $\bar{x} = 17$ and a sample standard deviation $s = 4.5$.
   a. Compute the value of the test statistic.
   b. Use the t distribution table (Table 2 in Appendix B) to compute a range for the p-value.
   c. At $\alpha = .05$, what is your conclusion?
   d. What is the rejection rule using the critical value? What is your conclusion?

25. Consider the following hypothesis test:

$$H_0: \mu \geq 45$$
$$H_a: \mu < 45$$

A sample of 36 is used. Identify the p-value and state your conclusion for each of the following sample results. Use $\alpha = .01$.
   a. $\bar{x} = 44$ and $s = 5.2$
   b. $\bar{x} = 43$ and $s = 4.6$
   c. $\bar{x} = 46$ and $s = 5.0$

26. Consider the following hypothesis test:

$$H_0: \mu = 100$$
$$H_a: \mu \neq 100$$

A sample of 65 is used. Identify the p-value and state your conclusion for each of the following sample results. Use $\alpha = .05$.
   a. $\bar{x} = 103$ and $s = 11.5$
   b. $\bar{x} = 96.5$ and $s = 11.0$
   c. $\bar{x} = 102$ and $s = 10.5$

Applications

27. Which is cheaper: eating out or dining in? The mean cost of a flank steak, broccoli, and rice bought at the grocery store is $13.04 (Money.msn website, November 7, 2012). A sample of 100 neighborhood restaurants showed a mean price of $12.75 and a standard deviation of $2 for a comparable restaurant meal.
   a. Develop appropriate hypotheses for a test to determine whether the sample data support the conclusion that the mean cost of a restaurant meal is less than fixing a comparable meal at home.
   b. Using the sample from the 100 restaurants, what is the p-value?
   c. At $\alpha = .05$, what is your conclusion?
   d. Repeat the preceding hypothesis test using the critical value approach.

28. A shareholders' group, in lodging a protest, claimed that the mean tenure for a chief executive office (CEO) was at least nine years. A survey of companies reported in *The Wall Street Journal* found a sample mean tenure of $\bar{x} = 7.27$ years for CEOs with a standard deviation of $s = 6.38$ years (*The Wall Street Journal*, January 2, 2007).
   a. Formulate hypotheses that can be used to challenge the validity of the claim made by the shareholders' group.
   b. Assume 85 companies were included in the sample. What is the p-value for your hypothesis test?
   c. At $\alpha = .01$, what is your conclusion?

Administrator

29. The national mean annual salary for a school administrator is $90,000 a year (*The Cincinnati Enquirer,* April 7, 2012). A school official took a sample of 25 school administrators in the state of Ohio to learn about salaries in that state to see if they differed from the national average.
    a. Formulate hypotheses that can be used to determine whether the population mean annual administrator salary in Ohio differs from the national mean of $90,000.
    b. The sample data for 25 Ohio administrators is contained in the file named Administrator. What is the *p*-value for your hypothesis test in part (a)?
    c. At $\alpha = .05$, can your null hypothesis be rejected? What is your conclusion?
    d. Repeat the preceding hypothesis test using the critical value approach.

ChildCare

30. The time married men with children spend on child care averages 6.4 hours per week (*Time,* March 12, 2012). You belong to a professional group on family practices that would like to do its own study to determine if the time married men in your area spend on child care per week differs from the reported mean of 6.4 hours per week. A sample of 40 married couples will be used with the data collected showing the hours per week the husband spends on child care. The sample data are contained in the file ChildCare.
    a. What are the hypotheses if your group would like to determine if the population mean number of hours married men are spending in child care differs from the mean reported by *Time* in your area?
    b. What is the sample mean and the *p*-value?
    c. Select your own level of significance. What is your conclusion?

31. The Coca-Cola Company reported that the mean per capita annual sales of its beverages in the United States was 423 eight-ounce servings (Coca-Cola Company website, February 3, 2009). Suppose you are curious whether the consumption of Coca-Cola beverages is higher in Atlanta, Georgia, the location of Coca-Cola's corporate headquarters. A sample of 36 individuals from the Atlanta area showed a sample mean annual consumption of 460.4 eight-ounce servings with a standard deviation of $s = 101.9$ ounces. Using $\alpha = .05$, do the sample results support the conclusion that mean annual consumption of Coca-Cola beverage products is higher in Atlanta?

UsedCars

32. According to the National Automobile Dealers Association, the mean price for used cars is $10,192. A manager of a Kansas City used car dealership reviewed a sample of 50 recent used car sales at the dealership in an attempt to determine whether the population mean price for used cars at this particular dealership differed from the national mean. The prices for the sample of 50 cars are shown in the file named UsedCars.
    a. Formulate the hypotheses that can be used to determine whether a difference exists in the mean price for used cars at the dealership.
    b. What is the *p*-value?
    c. At $\alpha = .05$, what is your conclusion?

33. Annual per capita consumption of milk is 21.6 gallons (*Statistical Abstract of the United States: 2006*). Being from the Midwest, you believe milk consumption is higher there and wish to support your opinion. A sample of 16 individuals from the midwestern town of Webster City showed a sample mean annual consumption of 24.1 gallons with a standard deviation of $s = 4.8$.
    a. Develop a hypothesis test that can be used to determine whether the mean annual consumption in Webster City is higher than the national mean.
    b. What is a point estimate of the difference between mean annual consumption in Webster City and the national mean?
    c. At $\alpha = .05$, test for a significant difference. What is your conclusion?

34. Joan's Nursery specializes in custom-designed landscaping for residential areas. The estimated labor cost associated with a particular landscaping proposal is based on the number of plantings of trees, shrubs, and so on to be used for the project. For cost-estimating purposes, managers use two hours of labor time for the planting of a

medium-sized tree. Actual times from a sample of 10 plantings during the past month follow (times in hours).

| 1.7 | 1.5 | 2.6 | 2.2 | 2.4 | 2.3 | 2.6 | 3.0 | 1.4 | 2.3 |

With a .05 level of significance, test to see whether the mean tree-planting time differs from two hours.

a.   State the null and alternative hypotheses.
b.   Compute the sample mean.
c.   Compute the sample standard deviation.
d.   What is the p-value?
e.   What is your conclusion?

9.5   Population Proportion

In this section we show how to conduct a hypothesis test about a population proportion p. Using p_0 to denote the hypothesized value for the population proportion, the three forms for a hypothesis test about a population proportion are as follows.

$$H_0: p \geq p_0 \qquad H_0: p \leq p_0 \qquad H_0: p = p_0$$
$$H_a: p < p_0 \qquad H_a: p > p_0 \qquad H_a: p \neq p_0$$

The first form is called a lower tail test, the second form is called an upper tail test, and the third form is called a two-tailed test.

Hypothesis tests about a population proportion are based on the difference between the sample proportion $\bar{p}$ and the hypothesized population proportion p_0. The methods used to conduct the hypothesis test are similar to those used for hypothesis tests about a population mean. The only difference is that we use the sample proportion and its standard error to compute the test statistic. The p-value approach or the critical value approach is then used to determine whether the null hypothesis should be rejected.

Let us consider an example involving a situation faced by Pine Creek golf course. Over the past year, 20% of the players at Pine Creek were women. In an effort to increase the proportion of women players, Pine Creek implemented a special promotion designed to attract women golfers. One month after the promotion was implemented, the course manager requested a statistical study to determine whether the proportion of women players at Pine Creek had increased. Because the objective of the study is to determine whether the proportion of women golfers increased, an upper tail test with $H_a: p > .20$ is appropriate. The null and alternative hypotheses for the Pine Creek hypothesis test are as follows:

$$H_0: p \leq .20$$
$$H_a: p > .20$$

If H_0 can be rejected, the test results will give statistical support for the conclusion that the proportion of women golfers increased and the promotion was beneficial. The course manager specified that a level of significance of $\alpha = .05$ be used in carrying out this hypothesis test.

The next step of the hypothesis testing procedure is to select a sample and compute the value of an appropriate test statistic. To show how this step is done for the Pine Creek upper tail test, we begin with a general discussion of how to compute the value of the test statistic for any form of a hypothesis test about a population proportion. The sampling distribution of $\bar{p}$, the point estimator of the population parameter p, is the basis for developing the test statistic.

When the null hypothesis is true as an equality, the expected value of $\bar{p}$ equals the hypothesized value p_0; that is, $E(\bar{p}) = p_0$. The standard error of $\bar{p}$ is given by

$$\sigma_{\bar{p}} = \sqrt{\frac{p_0(1 - p_0)}{n}}$$

In Chapter 7 we said that if $np \geq 5$ and $n(1 - p) \geq 5$, the sampling distribution of $\bar{p}$ can be approximated by a normal distribution.[3] Under these conditions, which usually apply in practice, the quantity

$$z = \frac{\bar{p} - p_0}{\sigma_{\bar{p}}} \qquad\qquad \textbf{(9.3)}$$

has a standard normal probability distribution. With $\sigma_{\bar{p}} = \sqrt{p_0(1 - p_0)/n}$, the standard normal random variable z is the test statistic used to conduct hypothesis tests about a population proportion.

TEST STATISTIC FOR HYPOTHESIS TESTS ABOUT A POPULATION PROPORTION

$$z = \frac{\bar{p} - p_0}{\sqrt{\dfrac{p_0(1 - p_0)}{n}}} \qquad\qquad \textbf{(9.4)}$$

WEB file

WomenGolf

We can now compute the test statistic for the Pine Creek hypothesis test. Suppose a random sample of 400 players was selected, and that 100 of the players were women. The proportion of women golfers in the sample is

$$\bar{p} = \frac{100}{400} = .25$$

Using equation (9.4), the value of the test statistic is

$$z = \frac{\bar{p} - p_0}{\sqrt{\dfrac{p_0(1 - p_0)}{n}}} = \frac{.25 - .20}{\sqrt{\dfrac{.20(1 - .20)}{400}}} = \frac{.05}{.02} = 2.50$$

Because the Pine Creek hypothesis test is an upper tail test, the p-value is the probability that z is greater than or equal to $z = 2.50$; that is, it is the upper tail area corresponding to $z \geq 2.50$. Using the standard normal probability table, we find that the area to the left of $z = 2.50$ is .9938. Thus, the p-value for the Pine Creek test is $1.0000 - .9938 = .0062$. Figure 9.7 shows this p-value calculation.

Recall that the course manager specified a level of significance of $\alpha = .05$. A p-value $= .0062 < .05$ gives sufficient statistical evidence to reject H_0 at the .05 level of significance. Thus, the test provides statistical support for the conclusion that the special promotion increased the proportion of women players at the Pine Creek golf course.

---

[3]In most applications involving hypothesis tests of a population proportion, sample sizes are large enough to use the normal approximation. The exact sampling distribution of $\bar{p}$ is discrete with the probability for each value of $\bar{p}$ given by the binomial distribution. So hypothesis testing is a bit more complicated for small samples when the normal approximation cannot be used.

FIGURE 9.7 CALCULATION OF THE p-VALUE FOR THE PINE CREEK HYPOTHESIS TEST

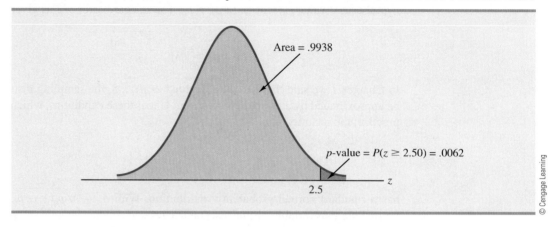

The decision whether to reject the null hypothesis can also be made using the critical value approach. The critical value corresponding to an area of .05 in the upper tail of a normal probability distribution is $z_{.05} = 1.645$. Thus, the rejection rule using the critical value approach is to reject H_0 if $z \geq 1.645$. Because $z = 2.50 > 1.645$, H_0 is rejected.

Again, we see that the p-value approach and the critical value approach lead to the same hypothesis testing conclusion, but the p-value approach provides more information. With a p-value $= .0062$, the null hypothesis would be rejected for any level of significance greater than or equal to .0062.

Summary

The procedure used to conduct a hypothesis test about a population proportion is similar to the procedure used to conduct a hypothesis test about a population mean. Although we only illustrated how to conduct a hypothesis test about a population proportion for an upper tail test, similar procedures can be used for lower tail and two-tailed tests. Table 9.4 provides a summary of the hypothesis tests about a population proportion. We assume that $np \geq 5$ and $n(1 - p) \geq 5$; thus the normal probability distribution can be used to approximate the sampling distribution of $\bar{p}$.

TABLE 9.4 SUMMARY OF HYPOTHESIS TESTS ABOUT A POPULATION PROPORTION

	Lower Tail Test	Upper Tail Test	Two-Tailed Test
Hypotheses	$H_0: p \geq p_0$ $H_a: p < p_0$	$H_0: p \leq p_0$ $H_a: p > p_0$	$H_0: p = p_0$ $H_a: p \neq p_0$
Test Statistic	$z = \dfrac{\bar{p} - p_0}{\sqrt{\dfrac{p_0(1 - p_0)}{n}}}$	$z = \dfrac{\bar{p} - p_0}{\sqrt{\dfrac{p_0(1 - p_0)}{n}}}$	$z = \dfrac{\bar{p} - p_0}{\sqrt{\dfrac{p_0(1 - p_0)}{n}}}$
Rejection Rule: **p-Value Approach**	Reject H_0 if p-value $\leq \alpha$	Reject H_0 if p-value $\leq \alpha$	Reject H_0 if p-value $\leq \alpha$
Rejection Rule: **Critical Value** **Approach**	Reject H_0 if $z \leq -z_\alpha$	Reject H_0 if $z \geq z_\alpha$	Reject H_0 if $z \leq -z_{\alpha/2}$ or if $z \geq z_{\alpha/2}$

Exercises

Methods

35. Consider the following hypothesis test:

$$H_0: p = .20$$
$$H_a: p \neq .20$$

A sample of 400 provided a sample proportion $\bar{p} = .175$.
   a. Compute the value of the test statistic.
   b. What is the p-value?
   c. At $\alpha = .05$, what is your conclusion?
   d. What is the rejection rule using the critical value? What is your conclusion?

36. Consider the following hypothesis test:

$$H_0: p \geq .75$$
$$H_a: p < .75$$

A sample of 300 items was selected. Compute the p-value and state your conclusion for each of the following sample results. Use $\alpha = .05$.
   a. $\bar{p} = .68$ c. $\bar{p} = .70$
   b. $\bar{p} = .72$ d. $\bar{p} = .77$

Applications

37. A study found that, in 2005, 12.5% of U.S. workers belonged to unions (*The Wall Street Journal*, January 21, 2006). Suppose a sample of 400 U.S. workers is collected in 2006 to determine whether union efforts to organize have increased union membership.
   a. Formulate the hypotheses that can be used to determine whether union membership increased in 2006.
   b. If the sample results show that 52 of the workers belonged to unions, what is the p-value for your hypothesis test?
   c. At $\alpha = .05$, what is your conclusion?

38. A study by *Consumer Reports* showed that 64% of supermarket shoppers believe supermarket brands to be as good as national name brands. To investigate whether this result applies to its own product, the manufacturer of a national name-brand ketchup asked a sample of shoppers whether they believed that supermarket ketchup was as good as the national brand ketchup.
   a. Formulate the hypotheses that could be used to determine whether the percentage of supermarket shoppers who believe that the supermarket ketchup was as good as the national brand ketchup differed from 64%.
   b. If a sample of 100 shoppers showed 52 stating that the supermarket brand was as good as the national brand, what is the p-value?
   c. At $\alpha = .05$, what is your conclusion?
   d. Should the national brand ketchup manufacturer be pleased with this conclusion? Explain.

39. According to the Pew Internet & American Life Project, 75% of American adults use the Internet (Pew Internet website, April 19, 2008). The Pew project authors also reported on the percentage of Americans who use the Internet by age group. The data in the file AgeGroup are consistent with their findings. These data were obtained from a sample of 100 Internet users in the 30–49 age group and 200 Internet users in the 50–64 age group. A Yes indicates the survey repondent had used the Internet; a No indicates the survey repondent had not.

a. Formulate hypotheses that could be used to determine whether the percentage of Internet users in the two age groups differs from the overall average of 75%.

b. Estimate the proportion of Internet users in the 30–49 age group. Does this proportion differ significantly from the overall proportion of .75? Use $\alpha = .05$.

c. Estimate the proportion of Internet users in the 50–64 age group. Does this proportion differ significantly from the overall proportion of .75? Use $\alpha = .05$.

d. Would you expect the proportion of users in the 18–29 age group to be larger or smaller than the proportion for the 30–49 age group? Support your conclusion with the results obtained in parts (b) and (c).

40. In 2008, 46% of business owners gave a holiday gift to their employees. A 2009 survey of business owners indicated that 35% planned to provide a holiday gift to their employees (Radio WEZV, Myrtle Beach, SC, November 11, 2009). Suppose the survey results are based on a sample of 60 business owners.

a. How many business owners in the survey planned to provide a holiday gift to their employees in 2009?

b. Suppose the business owners in the sample did as they planned. Compute the p-value for a hypothesis test that can be used to determine if the proportion of business owners providing holiday gifts had decreased from the 2008 level.

c. Using a .05 level of significance, would you conclude that the proportion of business owners providing gifts decreased? What is the smallest level of significance for which you could draw such a conclusion?

41. Ten years ago 53% of American families owned stocks or stock funds. Sample data collected by the Investment Company Institute indicate that the percentage is now 46% (*The Wall Street Journal*, October 5, 2012).

a. Develop appropriate hypotheses such that rejection of H_0 will support the conclusion that a smaller proportion of American families own stocks or stock funds in 2012 than 10 years ago.

b. Assume the Investment Company Institute sampled 300 American families to estimate that the percent owning stocks or stock funds was 46% in 2012. What is the p-value for your hypothesis test?

c. At $\alpha = .01$, what is your conclusion?

42. According to the University of Nevada Center for Logistics Management, 6% of all merchandise sold in the United States gets returned (*BusinessWeek*, January 15, 2007). A Houston department store sampled 80 items sold in January and found that 12 of the items were returned.

a. Construct a point estimate of the proportion of items returned for the population of sales transactions at the Houston store.

b. Construct a 95% confidence interval for the porportion of returns at the Houston store.

c. Is the proportion of returns at the Houston store significantly different from the returns for the nation as a whole? Provide statistical support for your answer.

Eagle

43. Eagle Outfitters is a chain of stores specializing in outdoor apparel and camping gear. They are considering a promotion that involves mailing discount coupons to all their credit card customers. This promotion will be considered a success if more than 10% of those receiving the coupons use them. Before going national with the promotion, coupons were sent to a sample of 100 credit card customers.

a. Develop hypotheses that can be used to test whether the population proportion of those who will use the coupons is sufficient to go national.

b. The file Eagle contains the sample data. Develop a point estimate of the population proportion.

c. Use $\alpha = .05$ to conduct your hypothesis test. Should Eagle go national with the promotion?

LawSuit

44. One of the reasons health care costs have been rising rapidly in recent years is the increasing cost of malpractice insurance for physicians. Also, fear of being sued causes doctors to run more precautionary tests (possibly unnecessary) just to make sure they are not guilty of missing something (*Reader's Digest*, October 2012). These precautionary tests

also add to health care costs. Data in the file LawSuit are consistent with findings in the *Reader's Digest* article and can be used to estimate the proportion of physicians over the age of 55 who have been sued at least once.

a. Formulate hypotheses that can be used to see if these data can support a finding that more than half of physicians over the age of 55 have been sued at least once.

b. Use Excel or Minitab and the file LawSuit to compute the sample proportion of physicians over the age of 55 who have been sued at least once. What is the p-value for your hypothesis test?

c. At $\alpha = .01$, what is your conclusion?

45. The American Association of Individual Investors (AAII) conducts a weekly survey of its members to measure the percent who are bullish, bearish, and neutral on the stock market for the next six months. For the week ending November 7, 2012, the survey results showed 38.5% bullish, 21.6% neutral, and 39.9% bearish (AAII website, November 12, 2012). Assume these results are based on a sample of 300 AAII members.

a. Over the long term, the proportion of bullish AAII members is .39. Conduct a hypothesis test at the 5% level of significance to see if the current sample results show that bullish sentiment differs from its long term average of .39. What are your findings?

b. Over the long term, the proportion of bearish AAII members is .30. Conduct a hypothesis test at the 1% level of significance to see if the current sample results show that bearish sentiment is above its long term average of .30. What are your findings?

c. Would you feel comfortable extending these results to all investors? Why or why not?

Summary

Hypothesis testing is a statistical procedure that uses sample data to determine whether a statement about the value of a population parameter should or should not be rejected. The hypotheses are two competing statements about a population parameter. One statement is called the null hypothesis (H_0), and the other statement is called the alternative hypothesis (H_a). In Section 9.1 we provided guidelines for developing hypotheses for situations frequently encountered in practice.

Whenever historical data or other information provides a basis for assuming that the population standard deviation is known, the hypothesis testing procedure for the population mean is based on the standard normal distribution. Whenever σ is unknown, the sample standard deviation s is used to estimate σ and the hypothesis testing procedure is based on the t distribution. In both cases, the quality of results depends on both the form of the population distribution and the sample size. If the population has a normal distribution, both hypothesis testing procedures are applicable, even with small sample sizes. If the population is not normally distributed, larger sample sizes are needed. General guidelines about the sample size were provided in Sections 9.3 and 9.4. In the case of hypothesis tests about a population proportion, the hypothesis testing procedure uses a test statistic based on the standard normal distribution.

In all cases, the value of the test statistic can be used to compute a p-value for the test. A p-value is a probability used to determine whether the null hypothesis should be rejected. If the p-value is less than or equal to the level of significance α, the null hypothesis can be rejected.

Hypothesis testing conclusions can also be made by comparing the value of the test statistic to a critical value. For lower tail tests, the null hypothesis is rejected if the value of the test statistic is less than or equal to the critical value. For upper tail tests, the null hypothesis is rejected if the value of the test statistic is greater than or equal to the critical value. Two-tailed tests consist of two critical values: one in the lower tail of the sampling distribution and one in the upper tail. In this case, the null hypothesis is rejected if the value of the test statistic is less than or equal to the critical value in the lower tail or greater than or equal to the critical value in the upper tail.

Glossary

Null hypothesis The hypothesis tentatively assumed true in the hypothesis testing procedure.

Alternative hypothesis The hypothesis concluded to be true if the null hypothesis is rejected.

Type II error The error of accepting H_0 when it is false.

Type I error The error of rejecting H_0 when it is true.

Level of significance The probability of making a Type I error when the null hypothesis is true as an equality.

One-tailed test A hypothesis test in which rejection of the null hypothesis occurs for values of the test statistic in one tail of its sampling distribution.

Test statistic A statistic whose value helps determine whether a null hypothesis should be rejected.

***p*-value** A probability that provides a measure of the evidence against the null hypothesis given by the sample. Smaller *p*-values indicate more evidence against H_0. For a lower tail test, the *p*-value is the probability of obtaining a value for the test statistic as small as or smaller than that provided by the sample. For an upper tail test, the *p*-value is the probability of obtaining a value for the test statistic as large as or larger than that provided by the sample. For a two-tailed test, the *p*-value is the probability of obtaining a value for the test statistic at least as unlikely as or more unlikely than that provided by the sample.

Critical value A value that is compared with the test statistic to determine whether H_0 should be rejected.

Two-tailed test A hypothesis test in which rejection of the null hypothesis occurs for values of the test statistic in either tail of its sampling distribution.

Key Formulas

Test Statistic for Hypothesis Tests About a Population Mean: σ Known

$$z = \frac{\bar{x} - \mu_0}{\sigma/\sqrt{n}} \tag{9.1}$$

Test Statistic for Hypothesis Tests About a Population Mean: σ Unknown

$$t = \frac{\bar{x} - \mu_0}{s/\sqrt{n}} \tag{9.2}$$

Test Statistic for Hypothesis Tests About a Population Proportion

$$z = \frac{\bar{p} - p_0}{\sqrt{\dfrac{p_0(1 - p_0)}{n}}} \tag{9.4}$$

Supplementary Exercises

46.   A production line operates with a mean filling weight of 16 ounces per container. Overfilling or underfilling presents a serious problem and when detected requires the operator to shut down the production line to readjust the filling mechanism. From past data, a population standard deviation $\sigma = .8$ ounces is assumed. A quality control inspector selects a sample

of 30 items every hour and at that time makes the decision of whether to shut down the line for readjustment. The level of significance is $\alpha = .05$.

a. State the hypothesis test for this quality control application.

b. If a sample mean of $\bar{x} = 16.32$ ounces were found, what is the p-value? What action would you recommend?

c. If a sample mean of $\bar{x} = 15.82$ ounces were found, what is the p-value? What action would you recommend?

d. Use the critical value approach. What is the rejection rule for the preceding hypothesis testing procedure? Repeat parts (b) and (c). Do you reach the same conclusion?

47. At Western University the historical mean of scholarship examination scores for freshman applications is 900. A historical population standard deviation $\sigma = 180$ is assumed known. Each year, the assistant dean uses a sample of applications to determine whether the mean examination score for the new freshman applications has changed.

a. State the hypotheses.

b. What is the 95% confidence interval estimate of the population mean examination score if a sample of 200 applications provided a sample mean $\bar{x} = 935$?

c. Use the confidence interval to conduct a hypothesis test. Using $\alpha = .05$, what is your conclusion?

d. What is the p-value?

48. Young children in the United States are exposed to an average of 4 hours of background television per day (CNN website, November 13, 2012). Having the television on in the background while children are doing other activities may have adverse consequences on a child's well-being. You have a research hypothesis that children from low-income families are exposed to more than 4 hours of daily background television. In order to test this hypothesis, you have collected information from a random sample of 60 children from low-income families and found that these children were exposed to a sample mean of 4.5 hours of daily background television.

a. Develop hypotheses that can be used to test your research hypothesis.

b. Based on a previous study, you are willing to assume that the population standard deviation is $\sigma = 0.5$ hours. What is the p-value based on your sample of 60 children from low-income families?

c. Use $\alpha = .01$ as the level of significance. What is your conclusion?

49. On Friday, Wall Street traders were anxiously awaiting the federal government's release of numbers on the January increase in nonfarm payrolls. The early consensus estimate among economists was for a growth of 250,000 new jobs (CNBC, February 3, 2006). However, a sample of 20 economists taken Thursday afternoon provided a sample mean of 266,000 with a sample standard deviation of 24,000. Financial analysts often call such a sample mean, based on late-breaking news, the *whisper number.* Treat the "consensus estimate" as the population mean. Conduct a hypothesis test to determine whether the whisper number justifies a conclusion of a statistically significant increase in the consensus estimate of economists. Use $\alpha = .01$ as the level of significance.

50. Data released by the National Center for Health Statistics showed that the mean age at which women had their first child was 25.0 in 2006 (*The Wall Street Journal,* February 4, 2009). The reporter, Sue Shellenbarger, noted that this was the first decrease in the average age at which women had their first child in several years. A recent sample of 42 women provided the data in the website file named FirstBirth concerning the age at which these women had their first child. Do the data indicate a change from 2006 in the mean age at which women had their first child? Use $\alpha = .05$.

FirstBirth

51. A recent issue of the *AARP Bulletin* reported that the average weekly pay for a woman with a high school school degree is $520 (*AARP Bulletin,* January–February, 2010). Suppose you would like to determine if the average weekly pay for all working women is significantly greater than that for women with a high school degree. Data providing the

WeeklyPay

weekly pay for a sample of 50 working women are available in the file named WeeklyPay. These data are consistent with the findings reported in the AARP article.

a. State the hypotheses that should be used to test whether the mean weekly pay for all women is significantly greater than the mean weekly pay for women with a high school degree.

b. Use the data in the file named WeeklyPay to compute the sample mean, the test statistic, and the p-value.

c. Use $\alpha = .05$. What is your conclusion?

d. Repeat the hypothesis test using the critical value approach.

52. The chamber of commerce of a Florida Gulf Coast community advertises that area residential property is available at a mean cost of $125,000 or less per lot. Suppose a sample of 32 properties provided a sample mean of $130,000 per lot and a sample standard deviation of $12,500. Use a .05 level of significance to test the validity of the advertising claim.

53. In Hamilton County, Ohio, the mean number of days needed to sell a house is 86 days (Cincinnati Multiple Listing Service, April, 2012). Data for the sale of 40 houses in a nearby county showed a sample mean of 80 days with a sample standard deviation of 20 days. Conduct a hypothesis test to determine whether the mean number of days until a house is sold in nearby counties is different than the Hamilton County mean of 86 days. Use $\alpha = .05$ for the level of significance, and state your conclusion.

54. On December 25, 2009, an airline passenger was subdued while attempting to blow up a Northwest Airlines flight headed for Detroit, Michigan. The passenger had smuggled explosives hidden in his underwear past a metal detector at an airport screening facility. As a result, the Transportation Security Administration (TSA) proposed installing full-body scanners to replace the metal detectors at the nation's largest airports. This proposal resulted in strong objections from privacy advocates who considered the scanners an invasion of privacy. On January 5–6, 2010, *USA Today* conducted a poll of 542 adults to learn what proportion of airline travelers approved of using full-body scanners (*USA Today*, January 11, 2010). The poll results showed that 455 of the respondents felt that full-body scanners would improve airline security and 423 indicated that they approved of using the devices.

a. Conduct a hypothesis test to determine if the results of the poll justify concluding that over 80% of airline travelers feel that the use of full-body scanners will improve airline security. Use $\alpha = .05$.

b. Suppose the TSA will go forward with the installation and mandatory use of full-body scanners if over 75% of airline travelers approve of using the devices. You have been told to conduct a statistical analysis using the poll results to determine if the TSA should require mandatory use of the full-body scanners. Because this is viewed as a very sensitive decision, use $\alpha = .01$. What is your recommendation?

55. An airline promotion to business travelers is based on the assumption that two-thirds of business travelers use a laptop computer on overnight business trips.

a. State the hypotheses that can be used to test the assumption.

b. What is the sample proportion from an American Express sponsored survey that found 355 of 546 business travelers use a laptop computer on overnight business trips?

c. What is the p-value?

d. Use $\alpha = .05$. What is your conclusion?

56. Virtual call centers are staffed by individuals working out of their homes. Most home agents earn $10 to $15 per hour without benefits versus $7 to $9 per hour with benefits at a traditional call center (*BusinessWeek*, January 23, 2006). Regional Airways is considering employing home agents, but only if a level of customer satisfaction greater than 80% can be maintained. A test was conducted with home service agents. In a sample of 300 customers, 252 reported that they were satisfied with service.

  a. Develop hypotheses for a test to determine whether the sample data support the conclusion that customer service with home agents meets the Regional Airways criterion.
  b. What is your point estimate of the percentage of satisfied customers?
  c. What is the p-value provided by the sample data?
  d. What is your hypothesis testing conclusion? Use $\alpha = .05$ as the level of significance.

57. The unemployment rate for 18- to 34-year-olds was reported to be 10.8% (*The Cincinnati Enquirer*, November 6, 2012). Assume that this report was based on a random sample of four hundred 18- to 34-year-olds.

  a. A political campaign manager wants to know if the sample results can be used to conclude that the unemployment rate for individuals 18 to 34 years old is significantly higher than the unemployment rate for all adults. According to the Bureau of Labor Statistics the unemployment rate for all adults was 7.9%. Develop a hypothesis test that can be used to see if the conclusion that the unemployment rate is higher for 18- to 34-year-olds can be supported
  b. Use the sample data collected for the 18- to 34-year-olds to compute the p-value for the hypothesis test in part (a). Using $\alpha = .05$, what is your conclusion?
  c. Explain to the campaign manager what can be said about the observed level of significance for the hypothesis testing results using the p-value.

58. A radio station in Myrtle Beach announced that at least 90% of the hotels and motels would be full for the Memorial Day weekend. The station advised listeners to make reservations in advance if they planned to be in the resort over the weekend. On Saturday night a sample of 58 hotels and motels showed 49 with a no-vacancy sign and 9 with vacancies. What is your reaction to the radio station's claim after seeing the sample evidence? Use $\alpha = .05$ in making the statistical test. What is the p-value?

59. In recent years more people have been working past the age of 65. In 2005, 27% of people aged 65–69 worked. A recent report from the Organization for Economic Co-operation and Development (OECD) claimed that percentage working had increased (*USA Today*, November 16, 2012). The findings reported by the OECD were consistent with taking a sample of 600 people aged 65–69 and finding that 180 of them were working.

  a. Develop a point estimate of the proportion of people aged 65–69 who are working.
  b. Set up a hypothesis test so that the rejection of H_0 will allow you to conclude that the proportion of people aged 65–69 working has increased from 2005.
  c. Conduct your hypothesis test using $\alpha = .05$. What is your conclusion?

Case Problem 1   Quality Associates, Inc.

Quality Associates, Inc., a consulting firm, advises its clients about sampling and statistical procedures that can be used to control their manufacturing processes. In one particular application, a client gave Quality Associates a sample of 800 observations taken during a time in which that client's process was operating satisfactorily. The sample standard deviation for these data was .21; hence, with so much data, the population standard deviation was assumed to be .21. Quality Associates then suggested that random samples of size 30 be taken periodically to monitor the process on an ongoing basis. By analyzing the new samples, the client could quickly learn whether the process was operating satisfactorily. When the process was not operating satisfactorily, corrective action could be taken to eliminate the problem. The design specification indicated the mean for the process should be 12. The hypothesis test suggested by Quality Associates follows.

$$H_0\colon \mu = 12$$
$$H_a\colon \mu \neq 12$$

Corrective action will be taken any time H_0 is rejected.

The following samples were collected at hourly intervals during the first day of operation of the new statistical process control procedure. These data are available in the data set Quality.

Quality

Sample 1	Sample 2	Sample 3	Sample 4
11.55	11.62	11.91	12.02
11.62	11.69	11.36	12.02
11.52	11.59	11.75	12.05
11.75	11.82	11.95	12.18
11.90	11.97	12.14	12.11
11.64	11.71	11.72	12.07
11.80	11.87	11.61	12.05
12.03	12.10	11.85	11.64
11.94	12.01	12.16	12.39
11.92	11.99	11.91	11.65
12.13	12.20	12.12	12.11
12.09	12.16	11.61	11.90
11.93	12.00	12.21	12.22
12.21	12.28	11.56	11.88
12.32	12.39	11.95	12.03
11.93	12.00	12.01	12.35
11.85	11.92	12.06	12.09
11.76	11.83	11.76	11.77
12.16	12.23	11.82	12.20
11.77	11.84	12.12	11.79
12.00	12.07	11.60	12.30
12.04	12.11	11.95	12.27
11.98	12.05	11.96	12.29
12.30	12.37	12.22	12.47
12.18	12.25	11.75	12.03
11.97	12.04	11.96	12.17
12.17	12.24	11.95	11.94
11.85	11.92	11.89	11.97
12.30	12.37	11.88	12.23
12.15	12.22	11.93	12.25

Managerial Report

1. Conduct a hypothesis test for each sample at the .01 level of significance and determine what action, if any, should be taken. Provide the test statistic and p-value for each test.
2. Compute the standard deviation for each of the four samples. Does the assumption of .21 for the population standard deviation appear reasonable?
3. Compute limits for the sample mean $\bar{x}$ around $\mu = 12$ such that, as long as a new sample mean is within those limits, the process will be considered to be operating satisfactorily. If $\bar{x}$ exceeds the upper limit or if $\bar{x}$ is below the lower limit, corrective action will be taken. These limits are referred to as upper and lower control limits for quality control purposes.
4. Discuss the implications of changing the level of significance to a larger value. What mistake or error could increase if the level of significance is increased?

Case Problem 2

Ethical Behavior of Business Students at Bayview University

During the global recession of 2008 and 2009, there were many accusations of unethical behavior by Wall Street executives, financial managers, and other corporate officers. At that time, an article appeared that suggested that part of the reason for such unethical business behavior may stem from the fact that cheating has become more prevalent among business students (*Chronicle of Higher Education,* February 10, 2009). The article reported that 56 percent of business students admitted to cheating at some time during their academic career as compared to 47 percent of nonbusiness students.

Cheating has been a concern of the dean of the College of Business at Bayview University for several years. Some faculty members in the college believe that cheating is more widespread at Bayview than at other universities, while other faculty members think that cheating is not a major problem in the college. To resolve some of these issues, the dean commissioned a study to assess the current ethical behavior of business students at Bayview. As part of this study, an anonymous exit survey was administered to a sample of 90 business students from this year's graduating class. Responses to the following questions were used to obtain data regarding three types of cheating.

> During your time at Bayview, did you ever present work copied off the Internet as your own?
>
>   Yes _____   No _____
>
> During your time at Bayview, did you ever copy answers off another student's exam?
>
>   Yes _____   No _____
>
> During your time at Bayview, did you ever collaborate with other students on projects that were supposed to be completed individually?
>
>   Yes _____   No _____

Any student who answered Yes to one or more of these questions was considered to have been involved in some type of cheating. A portion of the data collected follows. The complete data set is in the file named Bayview.

WEB file

Bayview

Student	Copied from Internet	Copied on Exam	Collaborated on Individual Project	Gender
1	No	No	No	Female
2	No	No	No	Male
3	Yes	No	Yes	Male
4	Yes	Yes	No	Male
5	No	No	Yes	Male
6	Yes	No	No	Female
.	.	.	.	.
.	.	.	.	.
.	.	.	.	.
88	No	No	No	Male
89	No	Yes	Yes	Male
90	No	No	No	Female

Managerial Report

Prepare a report for the dean of the college that summarizes your assessment of the nature of cheating by business students at Bayview University. Be sure to include the following items in your report.

1. Use descriptive statistics to summarize the data and comment on your findings.
2. Develop 95% confidence intervals for the proportion of all students, the proportion of male students, and the proportion of female students who were involved in some type of cheating.
3. Conduct a hypothesis test to determine if the proportion of business students at Bayview University who were involved in some type of cheating is less than that of business students at other institutions as reported by the *Chronicle of Higher Education*.
4. Conduct a hypothesis test to determine if the proportion of business students at Bayview University who were involved in some form of cheating is less than that of nonbusiness students at other institutions as reported by the *Chronicle of Higher Education*.
5. What advice would you give to the dean based upon your analysis of the data?

Appendix 9.1   Hypothesis Testing with Minitab

We describe the use of Minitab to conduct hypothesis tests about a population mean and a population proportion.

Population Mean: σ Known

We illustrate using the MaxFlight golf ball distance example in Section 9.3. The data are in column C1 of a Minitab worksheet. The population standard deviation $\sigma = 12$ is assumed known and the level of significance is $\alpha = .05$. The following steps can be used to test the hypothesis $H_0: \mu = 295$ versus $H_a: \mu \neq 295$.

GolfTest

Step 1. Select the **Stat** menu
Step 2. Choose **Basic Statistics**
Step 3. Choose **1-Sample Z**
Step 4. When the 1-Sample Z dialog box appears:
        Enter C1 in the **Samples in columns** box
        Enter 12 in the **Standard deviation** box
        Select **Perform Hypothesis Test**
        Enter 295 in the **Hypothesized mean** box
        Select **Options**
Step 5. When the 1-Sample Z-Options dialog box appears:
        Enter 95 in the **Confidence level** box*
        Select **not equal** in the **Alternative** box
        Click **OK**
Step 6. Click **OK**

In addition to the hypothesis testing results, Minitab provides a 95% confidence interval for the population mean.

---

*Minitab provides both hypothesis testing and interval estimation results simultaneously. The user may select any confidence level for the interval estimate of the population mean; 95% confidence is suggested here.

The procedure can be easily modified for a one-tailed hypothesis test by selecting the less than or greater than option in the **Alternative** box in step 5.

Population Mean: σ Unknown

AirRating

The ratings that 60 business travelers gave for Heathrow Airport are entered in column C1 of a Minitab worksheet. The level of significance for the test is $\alpha = .05$, and the population standard deviation σ will be estimated by the sample standard deviation s. The following steps can be used to test the hypothesis $H_0: \mu \leq 7$ against $H_a: \mu > 7$.

Step 1. Select the **Stat** menu
Step 2. Choose **Basic Statistics**
Step 3. Choose **1-Sample t**
Step 4. When the 1-Sample t dialog box appears:
      Enter C1 in the **Samples in columns** box
      Select **Perform Hypothesis Test**
      Enter 7 in the **Hypothesized mean** box
      Select **Options**
Step 5. When the 1-Sample t-Options dialog box appears:
      Enter 95 in the **Confidence level** box
      Select **greater than** in the **Alternative** box
      Click **OK**
Step 6. Click **OK**

The Heathrow Airport rating study involved a greater than alternative hypothesis. The preceding steps can be easily modified for other hypothesis tests by selecting the less than or not equal options in the **Alternative** box in step 5.

Population Proportion

WomenGolf

We illustrate using the Pine Creek golf course example in Section 9.5. The data with responses Female and Male are in column C1 of a Minitab worksheet. Minitab uses an alphabetical ordering of the responses and selects the *second response* for the population proportion of interest. In this example, Minitab uses the alphabetical ordering Female-Male to provide results for the population proportion of Male responses. Because Female is the response of interest, we change Minitab's ordering as follows: Select any cell in the column and use the sequence: Editor > Column > Value Order. Then choose the option of entering a user-specified order. Enter Male-Female in the **Define-an-order** box and click OK. Minitab's 1 Proportion routine will then provide the hypothesis test results for the population proportion of female golfers. We proceed as follows:

Step 1. Select the **Stat** menu
Step 2. Choose **Basic Statistics**
Step 3. Choose **1 Proportion**
Step 4. When the 1 Proportion dialog box appears:
      Enter C1 in the **Samples in Columns** box
      Select **Perform Hypothesis Test**
      Enter .20 in the **Hypothesized proportion** box
      Select **Options**
Step 5. When the 1 Proportion-Options dialog box appears:
      Enter 95 in the **Confidence level** box
      Select greater than in the **Alternative** box
      Select **Use test and interval based on normal distribution**
      Click **OK**
Step 6. Click **OK**

Appendix 9.2   Hypothesis Testing with Excel

Excel does not provide built-in routines for the hypothesis tests presented in this chapter. To handle these situations, we present Excel worksheets that we designed to use as templates for testing hypotheses about a population mean and a population proportion. The worksheets are easy to use and can be modified to handle any sample data. The worksheets are available on the website that accompanies this book.

Population Mean: σ Known

We illustrate using the MaxFlight golf ball distance example in Section 9.3. The data are in column A of an Excel worksheet. The population standard deviation $\sigma = 12$ is assumed known and the level of significance is $\alpha = .05$. The following steps can be used to test the hypothesis $H_0: \mu = 295$ versus $H_a: \mu \neq 295$.

Refer to Figure 9.8 as we describe the procedure. The worksheet in the background shows the cell formulas used to compute the results shown in the foreground worksheet. The data are entered into cells A2:A51. The following steps are necessary to use the template for this data set.

Hyp Sigma Known

Step 1. Enter the data range A2:A51 into the =COUNT cell formula in cell D4
Step 2. Enter the data range A2:A51 into the =AVERAGE cell formula in cell D5
Step 3. Enter the population standard deviation $\sigma = 12$ into cell D7
Step 4. Enter the hypothesized value for the population mean 295 into cell D8

The remaining cell formulas automatically provide the standard error, the value of the test statistic z, and three p-values. Because the alternative hypothesis ($\mu_0 \neq 295$) indicates a two-tailed test, the p-value (Two Tail) in cell D15 is used to make the rejection decision. With p-value $= .1255 > \alpha = .05$, the null hypothesis cannot be rejected. The p-values in cells D13 or D14 would be used if the hypotheses involved a one-tailed test.

This template can be used to make hypothesis testing computations for other applications. For instance, to conduct a hypothesis test for a new data set, enter the new sample data into column A of the worksheet. Modify the formulas in cells D4 and D5 to correspond to the new data range. Enter the population standard deviation into cell D7 and the hypothesized value for the population mean into cell D8 to obtain the results. If the new sample data have already been summarized, the new sample data do not have to be entered into the worksheet. In this case, enter the sample size into cell D4, the sample mean into cell D5, the population standard deviation into cell D7, and the hypothesized value for the population mean into cell D8 to obtain the results. The worksheet in Figure 9.8 is available in the file Hyp Sigma Known on the website that accompanies this book.

Population Mean: σ Unknown

We illustrate using the Heathrow Airport rating example in Section 9.4. The data are in column A of an Excel worksheet. The population standard deviation σ is unknown and will be estimated by the sample standard deviation s. The level of significance is $\alpha = .05$. The following steps can be used to test the hypothesis $H_0: \mu \leq 7$ versus $H_a: \mu > 7$.

Refer to Figure 9.9 as we describe the procedure. The background worksheet shows the cell formulas used to compute the results shown in the foreground version of the worksheet. The data are entered into cells A2:A61. The following steps are necessary to use the template for this data set.

Hyp Sigma Unknown

Step 1. Enter the data range A2:A61 into the =COUNT cell formula in cell D4
Step 2. Enter the data range A2:A61 into the =AVERAGE cell formula in cell D5
Step 3. Enter the data range A2:A61 into the =STDEV.S cell formula in cell D6
Step 4. Enter the hypothesized value for the population mean 7 into cell D8

FIGURE 9.8   EXCEL WORKSHEET FOR HYPOTHESIS TESTS ABOUT A POPULATION MEAN WITH σ KNOWN

	A	B	C	D	E
1	**Yards**		**Hypothesis Test about a Population Mean:**		
2	303		**σ Known Case**		
3	282				
4	289		**Sample Size**	=COUNT(A2:A51)	
5	298		**Sample Mean**	=AVERAGE(A2:A51)	
6	283				
7	317		**Population Standard Deviation**	12	
8	297		**Hypothesized Value**	295	
9	308				
10	317		**Standard Error**	=D7/SQRT(D4)	
11	293		**Test Statistic z**	=(D5-D8)/D10	
12	284				
13	290		**p-value (Lower Tail)**	=NORM.S.DIST(D11,TRUE)	
14	304		**p-value (Upper Tail)**	=1-D13	
15	290		**p-value (Two Tail)**	=2*(MIN(D13,D14))	
16	311				
50	301				
51	292				
52					

	A	B	C	D	E
1	**Yards**		**Hypothesis Test about a Population Mean:**		
2	303		**σ Known Case**		
3	282				
4	289		**Sample Size**	50	
5	298		**Sample Mean**	297.6	
6	283				
7	317		**Population Standard Deviation**	12	
8	297		**Hypothesized Value**	295	
9	308				
10	317		**Standard Error**	1.70	
11	293		**Test Statistic z**	1.53	
12	284				
13	290		**p-value (Lower Tail)**	0.9372	
14	304		**p-value (Upper Tail)**	0.0628	
15	290		**p-value (Two Tail)**	0.1255	
16	311				
50	301				
51	292				
52					

Note: Rows 17 to 49 are hidden.

The remaining cell formulas automatically provide the standard error, the value of the test statistic t, the number of degrees of freedom, and three p-values. Because the alternative hypothesis ($\mu > 7$) indicates an upper tail test, the p-value (Upper Tail) in cell D15 is used to make the decision. With p-value $= .0353 < \alpha = .05$, the null hypothesis is rejected. The p-values in cells D14 or D16 would be used if the hypotheses involved a lower tail test or a two-tailed test.

This template can be used to make hypothesis testing computations for other applications. For instance, to conduct a hypothesis test for a new data set, enter the new sample data into column A of the worksheet and modify the formulas in cells D4, D5, and D6 to correspond

FIGURE 9.9   EXCEL WORKSHEET FOR HYPOTHESIS TESTS ABOUT A POPULATION MEAN
WITH σ UNKNOWN

	A	B	C	D	E
1	**Rating**		**Hypothesis Test About a Population Mean**		
2	5		**With σ Unknown**		
3	7				
4	8		**Sample Size**	=COUNT(A2:A61)	
5	7		**Sample Mean**	=AVERAGE(A2:A61)	
6	8		**Sample Std. Deviation**	=STDEV(A2:A61)	
7	8				
8	8		**Hypothesized Value**	7	
9	7				
10	8		**Standard Error**	=D6/SQRT(D4)	
11	10		**Test Statistic _t_**	=(D5-D8)/D10	
12	6		**Degrees of Freedom**	=D4-1	
13	7				
14	8		**_p_-value (Lower Tail)**	=T.DIST(D11,D12,TRUE)	
15	8		**_p_-value (Upper Tail)**	=1-D14	
16	9		**_p_-value (Two Tail)**	=2*(MIN(D14,D15))	
17	7				
59	7				
60	7				
61	8				
62					

	A	B	C	D	E	F
1	**Rating**		**Hypothesis Test About a Population Mean**			
2	5		**With σ Unknown**			
3	7					
4	8		**Sample Size**	60		
5	7		**Sample Mean**	7.25		
6	8		**Sample Std. Deviation**	1.05		
7	8					
8	8		**Hypothesized Value**	7		
9	7					
10	8		**Standard Error**	0.136		
11	10		**Test Statistic _t_**	1.841		
12	6		**Degrees of Freedom**	59		
13	7					
14	8		**_p_-value (Lower Tail)**	0.9647		
15	8		**_p_-value (Upper Tail)**	0.0353		
16	9		**_p_-value (Two Tail)**	0.0706		
17	7					
59	7					
60	7					
61	8					
62						

Note: Rows 18 to 58 are hidden.

© Cengage Learning

to the new data range. Enter the hypothesized value for the population mean into cell D8 to obtain the results. If the new sample data have already been summarized, the new sample data do not have to be entered into the worksheet. In this case, enter the sample size into cell D4, the sample mean into cell D5, the sample standard deviation into cell D6, and the hypothesized value for the population mean into cell D8 to obtain the results. The worksheet in Figure 9.9 is available in the file Hyp Sigma Unknown on the website that accompanies this book.

Population Proportion

Hypothesis p

We illustrate using the Pine Creek golf course survey data presented in Section 9.5. The data of Male or Female golfer are in column A of an Excel worksheet. Refer to Figure 9.10 as we describe the procedure. The background worksheet shows the cell formulas used to compute the results shown in the foreground worksheet. The data are entered into cells A2:A401. The following steps can be used to test the hypothesis $H_0: p \le .20$ versus $H_a: p > .20$.

FIGURE 9.10   EXCEL WORKSHEET FOR HYPOTHESIS TESTS ABOUT A POPULATION PROPORTION

	A	B	C	D	E
1	Golfer		Hypothesis Test about a Population Proportion		
2	Female				
3	Male		Sample Size	=COUNTA(A2:A401)	
4	Female		Response of Interest	Female	
5	Male		Count for Response	=COUNTIF(A2:A903,D4)	
6	Male		Sample Proportion	=D5/D3	
7	Female				
8	Male		Hypothesized Value	0.2	
9	Male				
10	Female		Standard Error	=SQRT(D8*(1-D8)/D3)	
11	Male		Test Statistic z	=(D6-D8)/D10	
12	Male				
13	Male		p-value (Lower Tail)	=NORM.S.DIST(D11,TRUE)	
14	Male		p-value (Upper Tail)	=1-D13	
15	Male		p-value (TwoTail)	=2*MIN(D13,D14)	
16	Female				
400	Male				
401	Male				
402					

	A	B	C	D	E	F
1	Golfer		Hypothesis Test about a Population Proportion			
2	Female					
3	Male		Sample Size	400		
4	Female		Response of Interest	Female		
5	Male		Count for Response	100		
6	Male		Sample Proportion	0.25		
7	Female					
8	Male		Hypothesized Value	0.20		
9	Male					
10	Female		Standard Error	0.02		
11	Male		Test Statistic z	2.5000		
12	Male					
13	Male		p-value (Lower Tail)	0.9938		
14	Male		p-value (Upper Tail)	0.0062		
15	Male		p-value (TwoTail)	0.0124		
16	Female					
400	Male					
401	Male					
402						

Note: Rows 17 to 399 are hidden.

Step 1. Enter the data range A2:A401 into the =COUNTA cell formula in cell D3
Step 2. Enter Female as the response of interest in cell D4
Step 3. Enter the data range A2:A401 into the =COUNTIF cell formula in cell D5
Step 4. Enter the hypothesized value for the population proportion .20 into cell D8

The remaining cell formulas automatically provide the standard error, the value of the test statistic z, and three p-values. Because the alternative hypothesis ($p > .20$) indicates an upper tail test, the p-value (Upper Tail) in cell D14 is used to make the decision. With p-value $= .0062 < \alpha = .05$, the null hypothesis is rejected. The p-values in cells D13 or D15 would be used if the hypothesis involved a lower tail test or a two-tailed test.

This template can be used to make hypothesis testing computations for other applications. For instance, to conduct a hypothesis test for a new data set, enter the new sample data into column A of the worksheet. Modify the formulas in cells D3 and D5 to correspond to the new data range. Enter the response of interest into cell D4 and the hypothesized value for the population proportion into cell D8 to obtain the results. If the new sample data have already been summarized, the new sample data do not have to be entered into the worksheet. In this case, enter the sample size into cell D3, the sample proportion into cell D6, and the hypothesized value for the population proportion into cell D8 to obtain the results. The worksheet in Figure 9.10 is available in the file Hypothesis p on the website that accompanies this book.

Appendix 9.3   Hypothesis Testing with StatTools

In this appendix we show how StatTools can be used to conduct hypothesis tests about a population mean for the σ unknown case

Population Mean: σ Unknown Case

WEB file

AirRating

In this case the population standard deviation σ will be estimated by the sample standard deviation s. We use the example discussed in Section 9.4 involving ratings that 60 business travelers gave for Heathrow Airport.

Begin by using the Data Set Manager to create a StatTools data set for these data using the procedure described in the appendix in Chapter 1. The following steps can be used to test the hypothesis $H_0: \mu \le 7$ against $H_a: \mu > 7$.

Step 1. Click the **StatTools** tab on the Ribbon
Step 2. In the **Analyses** group, click **Statistical Inference**
Step 3. Choose the **Hypothesis Test** option
Step 4. Choose **Mean/Std. Deviation**
Step 5. When the StatTools - Hypothesis Test for Mean/Std. Deviation dialog box appears:

> For **Analysis Type,** choose **One-Sample Analysis**
> In the **Variables** section, select **Rating**
> In the **Hypothesis Tests to Perform** section:
> > Select the **Mean** option
> > Enter 7 in the **Null Hypothesis Value** box
> > Select **Greater Than Null Value (One-Tailed Test)** in the **Alternative Hypothesis Type** box
> If selected, remove the check in the **Standard Deviation** box
> Click **OK**

The results from the hypothesis test will appear. They include the p-value and the value of the test statistic.

Population Proportion

WomenGolf

We illustrate using the Pine Creek golf course example in Section 9.5. Begin by using the Data Set Manager to create a StatTools data set for these data using the procedure described in the appendix to Chapter 1. The following steps can be used to conduct a hypothesis test of the population proportion.

Step 1. Click the **StatTools** tab on the Ribbon
Step 2. In the **Analyses** group, click **Statistical Inference**
Step 3. Choose **Hypothesis Test**
Step 4. Choose **Proportion**
Step 5. When the StatTools - Hypothesis Test for Proportion dialog box appears:
    For **Analysis Type,** choose **One-Sample Analysis**
    In the **Variables** section, select **Golfer**
    In the **Categories to Analyze** section, select **Female**
    In the **Hypotheses About Proportion** section:
        Enter .20 in the **Null Hypothesis Value** box
        In the **Alternative Hypothesis Type** box, choose **Greater Than Null Value (One-Tailed Test)**
    Click **OK**

The results from the hypothesis test will appear. They include the *p*-value and the value of the test statistic.

CHAPTER 10

Comparisons Involving Means, Experimental Design, and Analysis of Variance

CONTENTS

U.S. FOOD AND DRUG ADMINISTRATION
WASHINGTON, D.C.

It is the responsibility of the U.S. Food and Drug Administration (FDA), through its Center for Drug Evaluation and Research (CDER), to ensure that drugs are safe and effective. But CDER does not do the actual testing of new drugs itself. It is the responsibility of the company seeking to market a new drug to test it and submit evidence that it is safe and effective. CDER statisticians and scientists then review the evidence submitted.

Companies seeking approval of a new drug conduct extensive statistical studies to support their application. The testing process in the pharmaceutical industry usually consists of three stages: (1) preclinical testing, (2) testing for long-term usage and safety, and (3) clinical efficacy testing. At each successive stage, the chance that a drug will pass the rigorous tests decreases; however, the cost of further testing increases dramatically. Industry surveys indicate that on average the research and development for one new drug costs $250 million and takes 12 years. Hence, it is important to eliminate unsuccessful new drugs in the early stages of the testing process, as well as to identify promising ones for further testing.

Statistics plays a major role in pharmaceutical research, where government regulations are stringent and rigorously enforced. In preclinical testing, a two- or three-population statistical study typically is used to determine whether a new drug should continue to be studied in the long-term usage and safety program. The populations may consist of the new drug, a control, and a standard drug. The preclinical testing process begins when a new drug is sent to the pharmacology group for evaluation of efficacy—the capacity of the drug to produce the desired effects. As part of the process, a statistician is asked to design an experiment that can be used to test the new drug. The design must specify the sample size and the statistical methods of analysis. In a two-population study, one sample is used to obtain data on the efficacy of the new drug (population 1) and a second sample is used to obtain data on the efficacy of a standard drug (population 2). Depending on the intended use, the new and standard drugs are tested in such disciplines as

Extensive statistical studies are conducted before a new drug is approved. © Lisa S./Shutterstock.com

neurology, cardiology, and immunology. In most studies, the statistical method involves hypothesis testing for the difference between the means of the new drug population and the standard drug population. If a new drug lacks efficacy or produces undesirable effects in comparison with the standard drug, the new drug is rejected and withdrawn from further testing. Only new drugs that show promising comparisons with the standard drugs are forwarded to the long-term usage and safety testing program.

Further data collection and multipopulation studies are conducted in the long-term usage and safety testing program and in the clinical testing programs. The FDA requires that statistical methods be defined prior to such testing to avoid data-related biases. In addition, to avoid human biases, some of the clinical trials are double or triple blind. That is, neither the subject nor the investigator knows what drug is administered to whom. If the new drug meets all requirements in relation to the standard drug, a new drug application (NDA) is filed with the FDA. The application is rigorously scrutinized by statisticians and scientists at the agency.

In this chapter you will learn how to construct interval estimates and make hypothesis tests about means and proportions with two populations. Techniques will be presented for analyzing independent random samples as well as matched samples.

In Chapters 8 and 9 we showed how to develop interval estimates and conduct hypothesis tests for situations involving a single population mean and a single population proportion. In Sections 10.1 to 10.3 we continue our discussion of statistical inference by showing how interval estimates and hypothesis tests can be developed for situations involving two populations when the difference between the two population means is of prime importance. For example, we may want to develop an interval estimate of the difference between the mean starting salary for a population of men and the mean starting salary for a population of women, or conduct a hypothesis test to determine whether any difference is present between the two population means.

In Section 10.4, we introduce the basic principles of an experimental study and show how they are used in a completely randomized design. We also provide a conceptual overview of the statistical procedure called analysis of variance (ANOVA). In Section 10.5 we show how ANOVA can be used to test for the equality of k population means using data obtained from a completely randomized design as well as data obtained from an observational study. So, in this sense, ANOVA extends the statistical material in Sections 10.1 to 10.3 from two population means to three or more population means.

We begin our discussion of statistical inference about two populations by showing how to develop interval estimates and conduct hypothesis tests about the difference between the means of two populations when the standard deviations of the two populations are assumed known.

10.1 Inferences About the Difference Between Two Population Means: σ_1 and σ_2 Known

Letting μ_1 denote the mean of population 1 and μ_2 denote the mean of population 2, we will focus on inferences about the difference between the means: $\mu_1 - \mu_2$. To make an inference about this difference, we select a random sample of n_1 units from population 1 and a second random sample of n_2 units from population 2. The two samples, taken separately and independently, are referred to as **independent random samples**. In this section, we assume that information is available such that the two population standard deviations, σ_1 and σ_2, can be assumed known prior to collecting the samples. We refer to this situation as the σ_1 and σ_2 known case. In the following example we show how to compute a margin of error and develop an interval estimate of the difference between the two population means when σ_1 and σ_2 are known.

Interval Estimation of $\mu_1 - \mu_2$

Greystone Department Stores, Inc., operates two stores in Buffalo, New York: One is in the inner city and the other is in a suburban shopping center. The regional manager noticed that products that sell well in one store do not always sell well in the other. The manager believes this situation may be attributable to differences in customer demographics at the two locations. Customers may differ in age, education, income, and so on. Suppose the manager asks us to investigate the difference between the mean ages of the customers who shop at the two stores.

Let us define population 1 as all customers who shop at the inner-city store and population 2 as all customers who shop at the suburban store.

μ_1 = mean of population 1 (i.e., the mean age of all customers who shop at the inner-city store)

μ_2 = mean of population 2 (i.e., the mean age of all customers who shop at the suburban store)

The difference between the two population means is $\mu_1 - \mu_2$.

To estimate $\mu_1 - \mu_2$, we will select a random sample of n_1 customers from population 1 and a random sample of n_2 customers from population 2. We then compute the two sample means.

$\bar{x}_1$ = sample mean age for the random sample of n_1 inner-city customers

$\bar{x}_2$ = sample mean age for the random sample of n_2 suburban customers

The point estimator of the difference between the two population means is the difference between the two sample means.

POINT ESTIMATOR OF THE DIFFERENCE BETWEEN TWO POPULATION MEANS

$$\bar{x}_1 - \bar{x}_2 \qquad \text{(10.1)}$$

The standard error of $\bar{x}_1 - \bar{x}_2$ is the standard deviation of the sampling distribution of $\bar{x}_1 - \bar{x}_2$.

Figure 10.1 provides an overview of the process used to estimate the difference between two population means based on two independent random samples.

As with other point estimators, the point estimator $\bar{x}_1 - \bar{x}_2$ has a standard error that describes the variation in the sampling distribution of the estimator. With two independent random samples, the standard error of $\bar{x}_1 - \bar{x}_2$ is as follows.

STANDARD ERROR OF $\bar{x}_1 - \bar{x}_2$

$$\sigma_{\bar{x}_1 - \bar{x}_2} = \sqrt{\frac{\sigma_1^2}{n_1} + \frac{\sigma_2^2}{n_2}} \qquad \text{(10.2)}$$

If both populations have a normal distribution, or if the sample sizes are large enough that the central limit theorem enables us to conclude that the sampling distributions of $\bar{x}_1$ and $\bar{x}_2$ can be approximated by a normal distribution, the sampling distribution of $\bar{x}_1 - \bar{x}_2$ will have a normal distribution with mean given by $\mu_1 - \mu_2$.

FIGURE 10.1   ESTIMATING THE DIFFERENCE BETWEEN TWO POPULATION MEANS

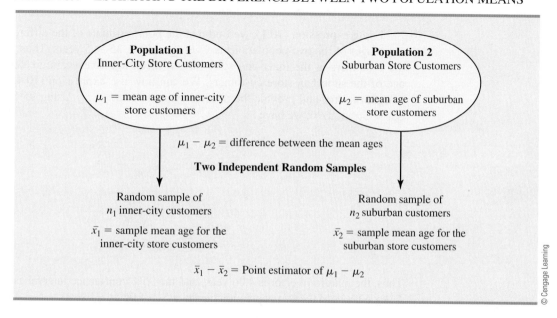

As we showed in Chapter 8, an interval estimate is given by a point estimate $\pm$ a margin of error. In the case of estimation of the difference between two population means, an interval estimate will take the following form:

$$\bar{x}_1 - \bar{x}_2 \pm \text{Margin of error}$$

With the sampling distribution of $\bar{x}_1 - \bar{x}_2$ having a normal distribution, we can write the margin of error as follows:

The margin of error is given by multiplying the standard error by $z_{\alpha/2}$.

$$\text{Margin of error} = z_{\alpha/2}\sigma_{\bar{x}_1 - \bar{x}_2} = z_{\alpha/2}\sqrt{\frac{\sigma_1^2}{n_1} + \frac{\sigma_2^2}{n_2}} \qquad (10.3)$$

Thus the interval estimate of the difference between two population means is as follows.

INTERVAL ESTIMATE OF THE DIFFERENCE BETWEEN TWO POPULATION MEANS: σ_1 AND σ_2 KNOWN

$$\bar{x}_1 - \bar{x}_2 \pm z_{\alpha/2}\sqrt{\frac{\sigma_1^2}{n_1} + \frac{\sigma_2^2}{n_2}} \qquad (10.4)$$

where $1 - \alpha$ is the confidence coefficient.

Let us return to the Greystone example. Based on data from previous customer demographic studies, the two population standard deviations are known with $\sigma_1 = 9$ years and $\sigma_2 = 10$ years. The data collected from the two independent random samples of Greystone customers provided the following results.

	Inner-City Store	**Suburban Store**
Sample Size	$n_1 = 36$	$n_2 = 49$
Sample Mean	$\bar{x}_1 = 40$ years	$\bar{x}_2 = 35$ years

Using expression (10.1), we find that the point estimate of the difference between the mean ages of the two populations is $\bar{x}_1 - \bar{x}_2 = 40 - 35 = 5$ years. Thus, we estimate that the customers at the inner-city store have a mean age five years greater than the mean age of the suburban store customers. We can now use expression (10.4) to compute the margin of error and provide the interval estimate of $\mu_1 - \mu_2$. Using 95% confidence and $z_{\alpha/2} = z_{.025} = 1.96$, we have

$$\bar{x}_1 - \bar{x}_2 \pm z_{\alpha/2}\sqrt{\frac{\sigma_1^2}{n_1} + \frac{\sigma_2^2}{n_2}}$$

$$40 - 35 \pm 1.96\sqrt{\frac{9^2}{36} + \frac{10^2}{49}}$$

$$5 \pm 4.06$$

Thus, the margin of error is 4.06 years and the 95% confidence interval estimate of the difference between the two population means is $5 - 4.06 = .94$ years to $5 + 4.06 = 9.06$ years.

Hypothesis Tests About $\mu_1 - \mu_2$

Let us consider hypothesis tests about the difference between two population means. Using D_0 to denote the hypothesized difference between μ_1 and μ_2, the three forms for a hypothesis test are as follows:

$$H_0: \mu_1 - \mu_2 \geq D_0 \qquad H_0: \mu_1 - \mu_2 \leq D_0 \qquad H_0: \mu_1 - \mu_2 = D_0$$
$$H_a: \mu_1 - \mu_2 < D_0 \qquad H_a: \mu_1 - \mu_2 > D_0 \qquad H_a: \mu_1 - \mu_2 \neq D_0$$

In many applications, $D_0 = 0$. Using the two-tailed test as an example, when $D_0 = 0$ the null hypothesis is $H_0: \mu_1 - \mu_2 = 0$. In this case, the null hypothesis is that μ_1 and μ_2 are equal. Rejection of H_0 leads to the conclusion that $H_a: \mu_1 - \mu_2 \neq 0$ is true; that is, μ_1 and μ_2 are not equal.

The steps for conducting hypothesis tests presented in Chapter 9 are applicable here. We must choose a level of significance, compute the value of the test statistic, and find the *p*-value to determine whether the null hypothesis should be rejected. With two independent random samples, we showed that the point estimator $\bar{x}_1 - \bar{x}_2$ has a standard error $\sigma_{\bar{x}_1 - \bar{x}_2}$ given by expression (10.2) and, when the sample sizes are large enough, the distribution of $\bar{x}_1 - \bar{x}_2$ can be described by a normal distribution. In this case, the test statistic for the difference between two population means when σ_1 and σ_2 are known is as follows.

TEST STATISTIC FOR HYPOTHESIS TESTS ABOUT $\mu_1 - \mu_2$: σ_1 AND σ_2 KNOWN

$$z = \frac{(\bar{x}_1 - \bar{x}_2) - D_0}{\sqrt{\dfrac{\sigma_1^2}{n_1} + \dfrac{\sigma_2^2}{n_2}}} \tag{10.5}$$

Let us demonstrate the use of this test statistic in the following hypothesis testing example.

As part of a study to evaluate differences in education quality between two training centers, a standardized examination is given to individuals who are trained at the centers. The difference between the mean examination scores is used to assess quality differences between the centers. The population means for the two centers are as follows.

$$\mu_1 = \text{the mean examination score for the population}$$
$$\text{of individuals trained at center A}$$

$$\mu_2 = \text{the mean examination score for the population}$$
$$\text{of individuals trained at center B}$$

We begin with the tentative assumption that no difference exists between the training quality provided at the two centers. Hence, in terms of the mean examination scores, the null hypothesis is that $\mu_1 - \mu_2 = 0$. If sample evidence leads to the rejection of this hypothesis, we will conclude that the mean examination scores differ for the two populations. This conclusion indicates a quality differential between the two centers and suggests that a follow-up study investigating the reason for the differential may be warranted. The null and alternative hypotheses for this two-tailed test are written as follows.

$$H_0: \mu_1 - \mu_2 = 0$$
$$H_a: \mu_1 - \mu_2 \neq 0$$

The standardized examination given previously in a variety of settings always resulted in an examination score standard deviation near 10 points. Thus, we will use this information to assume that the population standard deviations are known with $\sigma_1 = 10$ and $\sigma_2 = 10$. An $\alpha = .05$ level of significance is specified for the study.

Independent random samples of $n_1 = 30$ individuals from training center A and $n_2 = 40$ individuals from training center B are taken. The respective sample means are $\bar{x}_1 = 82$ and $\bar{x}_2 = 78$. Do these data suggest a significant difference between the population means at the two training centers? To help answer this question, we compute the test statistic using equation (10.5).

$$z = \frac{(\bar{x}_1 - \bar{x}_2) - D_0}{\sqrt{\dfrac{\sigma_1^2}{n_1} + \dfrac{\sigma_2^2}{n_2}}} = \frac{(82 - 78) - 0}{\sqrt{\dfrac{10^2}{30} + \dfrac{10^2}{40}}} = 1.66$$

Next let us compute the p-value for this two-tailed test. Because the test statistic z is in the upper tail, we first compute the area under the curve to the right of $z = 1.66$). Using the standard normal distribution table, the area to the left of $z = 1.66$ is .9515. Thus, the area in the upper tail of the distribution is $1.0000 - .9515 = .0485$. Because this test is a two-tailed test, we must double the tail area: p-value $= 2(.0485) = .0970$. Following the usual rule to reject H_0 if p-value $\leq \alpha$, we see that the p-value of .0970 does not allow us to reject H_0 at the .05 level of significance. The sample results do not provide sufficient evidence to conclude the training centers differ in quality.

In this chapter we will use the p-value approach to hypothesis testing as described in Chapter 9. However, if you prefer, the test statistic and the critical value rejection rule may be used. With $\alpha = .05$ and $z_{\alpha/2} = z_{.025} = 1.96$, the rejection rule employing the critical value approach would be reject H_0 if $z \leq -1.96$ or if $z \geq 1.96$. With $z = 1.66$, we reach the same do not reject H_0 conclusion.

In the preceding example, we demonstrated a two-tailed hypothesis test about the difference between two population means. Lower tail and upper tail tests can also be considered. These tests use the same test statistic as given in equation (10.5). The procedure for computing the p-value and the rejection rules for these one-tailed tests are the same as those presented in Chapter 9.

Practical Advice

In most applications of the interval estimation and hypothesis testing procedures presented in this section, random samples with $n_1 \geq 30$ and $n_2 \geq 30$ are adequate. In cases where either or both sample sizes are less than 30, the distributions of the populations become important considerations. In general, with smaller sample sizes, it is more important for the analyst to be satisfied that it is reasonable to assume that the distributions of the two populations are at least approximately normal.

Exercises

Methods

1. The following results come from two independent random samples taken of two populations.

Sample 1	Sample 2
$n_1 = 50$	$n_2 = 35$
$\bar{x}_1 = 13.6$	$\bar{x}_2 = 11.6$
$\sigma_1 = 2.2$	$\sigma_2 = 3.0$

a. What is the point estimate of the difference between the two population means?
b. Provide a 90% confidence interval for the difference between the two population means.
c. Provide a 95% confidence interval for the difference between the two population means.

2. Consider the following hypothesis test.

$$H_0: \mu_1 - \mu_2 \leq 0$$
$$H_a: \mu_1 - \mu_2 > 0$$

The following results are for two independent random samples taken from the two populations.

Sample 1	Sample 2
$n_1 = 40$	$n_2 = 50$
$\bar{x}_1 = 25.2$	$\bar{x}_2 = 22.8$
$\sigma_1 = 5.2$	$\sigma_2 = 6.0$

a. What is the value of the test statistic?
b. What is the p-value?
c. With $\alpha = .05$, what is your hypothesis testing conclusion?

3. Consider the following hypothesis test.

$$H_0: \mu_1 - \mu_2 = 0$$
$$H_a: \mu_1 - \mu_2 \neq 0$$

The following results are for two independent samples taken from the two populations.

Sample 1	Sample 2
$n_1 = 80$	$n_2 = 70$
$\bar{x}_1 = 104$	$\bar{x}_2 = 106$
$\sigma_1 = 8.4$	$\sigma_2 = 7.6$

a. What is the value of the test statistic?
b. What is the p-value?
c. With $\alpha = .05$, what is your hypothesis testing conclusion?

Applications

4. In a *Good Housekeeping* article, the organization reports that while washing machines have become more efficient in the last several years, washing machine manufacturers are finding it difficult to satisfy recently updated federal energy rules without sacrificing cleaning (*Good Housekeeping* website, January 20, 2013). Is there a difference in how clean front-loading washing machines and top-loading washing machines will get a load of laundry? A sample of 42 owners of top-loading washing machines and 49 front-loading washing machines purchased in 2012 were asked to rate their washing machines on how well they cleaned laundry. All washing machines are rated on a 100-point scale, with higher values indicating cleaner laundry. Ratings given by owners of top-loading machines had an average rating of 82.55, and the owners of front-loading machines provided an average rating of 77.46. Assume that the population standard deviation is 6.18 for ratings of top-loading machines and 5.97 for ratings of front-loading machines.

a. What is the point estimate of the difference between the population mean rating for top-loading washing machines and front-loading washing machines?
b. At 95% confidence, what is the margin of error?
c. What is a 95% confidence interval estimate of the difference between the population mean ratings for the two types of washing machines?

5. The average American consumed 10.6 pounds of mozzarella cheese in 2009 (U.S. Department of Agriculture, February 20, 2012). Do male and female consumers differ in the amounts of mozzarella cheese they consume? The average consumption in a survey of 35 male consumers was 12.9 pounds, and the average consumption in a survey of 50 female consumers was 8.4 pounds. Based on past surveys, the standard deviation for male consumers is assumed to be 4.4 and the standard deviation for female consumers is assumed to be 3.1.
a. What is the point estimate of the difference between the population mean consumption for males and the population mean consumption for females?
b. At 99% confidence, what is the margin of error?
c. Develop a 99% confidence interval for the difference between the two population means.

WEB file

Hotel

6. Suppose that you are responsible for making arrangements for a business convention. Because of budget cuts due to the recent recession, you have been charged with choosing a city for the convention that has the least expensive hotel rooms. You have narrowed your choices to Atlanta and Houston. The file named Hotel contains samples of prices for rooms in Atlanta and Houston that are consistent with the results reported by Smith Travel Research (*SmartMoney*, March 2009). Because considerable historical data on the prices of rooms in both cities are available, the population standard deviations for the prices can be assumed to be $20 in Atlanta and $25 in Houston. Based on the sample data, can you conclude that the mean price of a hotel room in Atlanta is lower than one in Houston?

7. *Consumer Reports* uses a survey of readers to obtain customer satisfaction ratings for the nation's largest retailers (*Consumer Reports*, March 2012). Each survey respondent is asked to rate a specified retailer in terms of six factors: quality of products, selection, value, checkout efficiency, service, and store layout. An overall satisfaction score summarizes the rating for each respondent with 100 meaning the respondent is completely satisfied in terms of all six factors. Sample data representative of independent samples of Target and Walmart customers are shown below.

Target	Walmart
$n_1 = 25$	$n_2 = 30$
$\bar{x}_1 = 79$	$\bar{x}_2 = 71$

a. Formulate the null and alternative hypotheses to test whether there is a difference between the population mean customer satisfaction scores for the two retailers.
b. Assume that experience with the *Consumer Reports* satisfaction rating scale indicates that a population standard deviation of 12 is a reasonable assumption for both retailers. Conduct the hypothesis test and report the p-value. At a .05 level of significance, what is your conclusion?
c. Which retailer, if either, appears to have the greater customer satisfaction? Provide a 95% confidence interval for the difference between the population mean customer satisfaction scores for the two retailers.

8. Will improving customer service result in higher stock prices for the companies providing the better service? "When a company's satisfaction score has improved over the prior year's

results and is above the national average (currently 75.7), studies show its shares have a good chance of outperforming the broad stock market in the long run" (*BusinessWeek,* March 2, 2009). The following satisfaction scores of three companies for the 4th quarters of 2007 and 2008 were obtained from the American Customer Satisfaction Index. Assume that the scores are based on a poll of 60 customers from each company. Because the polling has been done for several years, the standard deviation can be assumed to equal 6 points in each case.

Company	2007 Score	2008 Score
Rite Aid	73	76
Expedia	75	77
J.C. Penney	77	78

a. For Rite Aid, is the increase in the satisfaction score from 2007 to 2008 statistically significant? Use $\alpha = .05$. What can you conclude?
b. Can you conclude that the 2008 score for Rite Aid is above the national average of 75.7? Use $\alpha = .05$.
c. For Expedia, is the increase from 2007 to 2008 statistically significant? Use $\alpha = .05$.
d. When conducting a hypothesis test with the values given for the standard deviation, sample size, and α, how large must the increase from 2007 to 2008 be for it to be statistically significant?
e. Use the result of part (d) to state whether the increase for J.C. Penney from 2007 to 2008 is statistically significant.

(10.2) Inferences About the Difference Between Two Population Means: σ_1 and σ_2 Unknown

In this section we extend the discussion of inferences about the difference between two population means to the case when the two population standard deviations, σ_1 and σ_2, are unknown. In this case, we will use the sample standard deviations, s_1 and s_2, to estimate the unknown population standard deviations. When we use the sample standard deviations, the interval estimation and hypothesis testing procedures will be based on the t distribution rather than the standard normal distribution.

Interval Estimation of $\mu_1 - \mu_2$

In the following example we show how to compute a margin of error and develop an interval estimate of the difference between two population means when σ_1 and σ_2 are unknown. Clearwater National Bank is conducting a study designed to identify differences between checking account practices by customers at two of its branch banks. A random sample of 28 checking accounts is selected from the Cherry Grove Branch and an independent random sample of 22 checking accounts is selected from the Beechmont Branch. The current checking account balance is recorded for each of the checking accounts. A summary of the account balances follows:

	Cherry Grove	Beechmont
Sample Size	$n_1 = 28$	$n_2 = 22$
Sample Mean	$\bar{x}_1 = \$1,025$	$\bar{x}_2 = \$910$
Sample Standard Deviation	$s_1 = \$150$	$s_2 = \$125$

CheckAcct

Clearwater National Bank would like to estimate the difference between the mean checking account balance maintained by the population of Cherry Grove customers and the population of Beechmont customers. Let us develop the margin of error and an interval estimate of the difference between these two population means.

In Section 10.1, we provided the following interval estimate for the case when the population standard deviations, σ_1 and σ_2, are known.

$$\bar{x}_1 - \bar{x}_2 \pm z_{\alpha/2}\sqrt{\frac{\sigma_1^2}{n_1} + \frac{\sigma_2^2}{n_2}}$$

When σ_1 and σ_2 are estimated by s_1 and s_2, the t distribution is used to make inferences about the difference between two population means.

With σ_1 and σ_2 unknown, we will use the sample standard deviations s_1 and s_2 to estimate σ_1 and σ_2 and replace $z_{\alpha/2}$ with $t_{\alpha/2}$. As a result, the interval estimate of the difference between two population means is given by the following expression.

INTERVAL ESTIMATE OF THE DIFFERENCE BETWEEN TWO POPULATION MEANS: σ_1 AND σ_2 UNKNOWN

$$\bar{x}_1 - \bar{x}_2 \pm t_{\alpha/2}\sqrt{\frac{s_1^2}{n_1} + \frac{s_2^2}{n_2}} \tag{10.6}$$

where $1 - \alpha$ is the confidence coefficient.

In this expression, the use of the t distribution is an approximation, but it provides excellent results and is relatively easy to use. The only difficulty that we encounter in using expression (10.6) is determining the appropriate degrees of freedom for $t_{\alpha/2}$. Statistical software packages compute the appropriate degrees of freedom automatically. The formula used is as follows.

DEGREES OF FREEDOM: t DISTRIBUTION WITH TWO INDEPENDENT RANDOM SAMPLES

$$df = \frac{\left(\frac{s_1^2}{n_1} + \frac{s_2^2}{n_2}\right)^2}{\frac{1}{n_1-1}\left(\frac{s_1^2}{n_1}\right)^2 + \frac{1}{n_2-1}\left(\frac{s_2^2}{n_2}\right)^2} \tag{10.7}$$

Let us return to the Clearwater National Bank example and show how to use expression (10.6) to provide a 95% confidence interval estimate of the difference between the population mean checking account balances at the two branch banks. The sample data show $n_1 = 28$, $\bar{x}_1 = \$1,025$, and $s_1 = \$150$ for the Cherry Grove branch, and $n_2 = 22$, $\bar{x}_2 = \$910$, and $s_2 = \$125$ for the Beechmont branch. The calculation for degrees of freedom for $t_{\alpha/2}$ is as follows:

$$df = \frac{\left(\frac{s_1^2}{n_1} + \frac{s_2^2}{n_2}\right)^2}{\frac{1}{n_1-1}\left(\frac{s_1^2}{n_1}\right)^2 + \frac{1}{n_2-1}\left(\frac{s_2^2}{n_2}\right)^2} = \frac{\left(\frac{150^2}{28} + \frac{125^2}{22}\right)^2}{\frac{1}{28-1}\left(\frac{150^2}{28}\right)^2 + \frac{1}{22-1}\left(\frac{125^2}{22}\right)^2} = 47.8$$

We round the noninteger degrees of freedom *down* to 47 to provide a larger t-value and a more conservative interval estimate. Using the t distribution table with 47 degrees of freedom, we find $t_{.025} = 2.012$. Using expression (10.6), we develop the 95% confidence interval estimate of the difference between the two population means as follows.

$$\bar{x}_1 - \bar{x}_2 \pm t_{.025}\sqrt{\frac{s_1^2}{n_1} + \frac{s_2^2}{n_2}}$$

$$1025 - 910 \pm 2.012\sqrt{\frac{150^2}{28} + \frac{125^2}{22}}$$

$$115 \pm 78$$

The point estimate of the difference between the population mean checking account balances at the two branches is \$115. The margin of error is \$78, and the 95% confidence interval estimate of the difference between the two population means is $115 - 78 = \$37$ to $115 + 78 = \$193$.

This suggestion should help if you are using equation (10.7) to calculate the degrees of freedom by hand.

The computation of the degrees of freedom (equation (10.7)) is cumbersome if you are doing the calculation by hand, but it is easily implemented with a computer software package. However, note that the expressions s_1^2/n_1 and s_2^2/n_2 appear in both expression (10.6) and equation (10.7). These values only need to be computed once in order to evaluate both (10.6) and (10.7).

Hypothesis Tests About $\mu_1 - \mu_2$

Let us now consider hypothesis tests about the difference between the means of two populations when the population standard deviations σ_1 and σ_2 are unknown. Letting D_0 denote the hypothesized difference between μ_1 and μ_2, Section 10.1 showed that the test statistic used for the case where σ_1 and σ_2 are known is as follows.

$$z = \frac{(\bar{x}_1 - \bar{x}_2) - D_0}{\sqrt{\dfrac{\sigma_1^2}{n_1} + \dfrac{\sigma_2^2}{n_2}}}$$

The test statistic, z, follows the standard normal distribution.

When σ_1 and σ_2 are unknown, we use s_1 as an estimator of σ_1 and s_2 as an estimator of σ_2. Substituting these sample standard deviations for σ_1 and σ_2 provides the following test statistic when σ_1 and σ_2 are unknown.

> **TEST STATISTIC FOR HYPOTHESIS TESTS ABOUT $\mu_1 - \mu_2$: σ_1 AND σ_2 UNKNOWN**
>
> $$t = \frac{(\bar{x}_1 - \bar{x}_2) - D_0}{\sqrt{\dfrac{s_1^2}{n_1} + \dfrac{s_2^2}{n_2}}} \qquad \text{(10.8)}$$
>
> The degrees of freedom for t are given by equation (10.7).

Let us demonstrate the use of this test statistic in the following hypothesis testing example.

Consider a new computer software package developed to help systems analysts reduce the time required to design, develop, and implement an information system. To evaluate the benefits of the new software package, a random sample of 24 systems analysts is selected. Each analyst is given specifications for a hypothetical information system. Then 12 of the analysts are instructed to produce the information system by using current technology. The other 12 analysts are trained in the use of the new software package and then instructed to use it to produce the information system.

This study involves two populations: a population of systems analysts using the current technology and a population of systems analysts using the new software package. In terms of the time required to complete the information system design project, the population means are as follow.

$$\mu_1 = \text{the mean project completion time for systems analysts}$$
$$\text{using the current technology}$$

$$\mu_2 = \text{the mean project completion time for systems analysts}$$
$$\text{using the new software package}$$

The researcher in charge of the new software evaluation project hopes to show that the new software package will provide a shorter mean project completion time. Thus, the researcher is looking for evidence to conclude that μ_2 is less than μ_1; in this case, the difference between the two population means, $\mu_1 - \mu_2$, will be greater than zero. The research hypothesis $\mu_1 - \mu_2 > 0$ is stated as the alternative hypothesis. Thus, the hypothesis test becomes

$$H_0: \mu_1 - \mu_2 \leq 0$$
$$H_a: \mu_1 - \mu_2 > 0$$

We will use $\alpha = .05$ as the level of significance.

Suppose that the 24 analysts complete the study with the results shown in Table 10.1. Using the test statistic in equation (10.8), we have

$$t = \frac{(\bar{x}_1 - \bar{x}_2) - D_0}{\sqrt{\dfrac{s_1^2}{n_1} + \dfrac{s_2^2}{n_2}}} = \frac{(325 - 286) - 0}{\sqrt{\dfrac{40^2}{12} + \dfrac{44^2}{12}}} = 2.27$$

TABLE 10.1   COMPLETION TIME DATA AND SUMMARY STATISTICS FOR THE SOFTWARE TESTING STUDY

	Current Technology	New Software
	300	274
	280	220
	344	308
	385	336
	372	198
	360	300
	288	315
	321	258
	376	318
	290	310
	301	332
	283	263
Summary Statistics		
Sample size	$n_1 = 12$	$n_2 = 12$
Sample mean	$\bar{x}_1 = 325$ hours	$\bar{x}_2 = 286$ hours
Sample standard deviation	$s_1 = 40$	$s_2 = 44$

WEB file

SoftwareTest

© Cengage Learning

FIGURE 10.2   MINITAB OUTPUT FOR THE HYPOTHESIS TEST OF THE CURRENT AND NEW SOFTWARE TECHNOLOGY

```
Two-sample T for Current vs New

                        SE
         N   Mean  StDev  Mean
Current  12  325.0  40.0   12
New      12  286.0  44.0   13


Difference = mu (Current) - mu (New)
Estimate for difference:  39.0
95% CI for difference:  (3.3, 74.7)
T-Test of difference = 0 (vs not =): T-Value = 2.27   P-Value = 0.034   DF = 21
```

Computing the degrees of freedom using equation (10.7), we have

$$df = \frac{\left(\dfrac{s_1^2}{n_1} + \dfrac{s_2^2}{n_2}\right)^2}{\dfrac{1}{n_1 - 1}\left(\dfrac{s_1^2}{n_1}\right)^2 + \dfrac{1}{n_2 - 1}\left(\dfrac{s_2^2}{n_2}\right)^2} = \frac{\left(\dfrac{40^2}{12} + \dfrac{44^2}{12}\right)^2}{\dfrac{1}{12 - 1}\left(\dfrac{40^2}{12}\right)^2 + \dfrac{1}{12 - 1}\left(\dfrac{44^2}{12}\right)^2} = 21.8$$

Rounding down, we will use a t distribution with 21 degrees of freedom. This row of the t distribution table is as follows:

Area in Upper Tail	.20	.10	.05	.025	.01	.005
t-Value (21 df)	0.859	1.323	1.721	2.080	2.518	2.831

$t = 2.27$

Using the t distribution table, we can only determine a range for the p-value. Use of Excel or Minitab shows the exact p-value = .017.

With an upper tail test, the p-value is the area in the upper tail to the right of $t = 2.27$. From the above results, we see that the p-value is between .025 and .01. Thus, the p-value is less than $\alpha = .05$ and H_0 is rejected. The sample results enable the researcher to conclude that $\mu_1 - \mu_2 > 0$, or $\mu_1 > \mu_2$. Thus, the research study supports the conclusion that the new software package provides a smaller population mean completion time.

Minitab or Excel can be used to analyze data for testing hypotheses about the difference between two population means. The Minitab output comparing the current and new software technology is shown in Figure 10.2. The last line of the output shows $t = 2.27$ and p-value $= .017$. Note that Minitab used equation (10.7) to compute 21 degrees of freedom for this analysis.

Practical Advice

Whenever possible, equal sample sizes, $n_1 = n_2$, are recommended.

The interval estimation and hypothesis testing procedures presented in this section are robust and can be used with relatively small sample sizes. In most applications, equal or nearly equal sample sizes such that the total sample size $n_1 + n_2$ is at least 20 can be expected to provide very good results even if the populations are not normal. Larger sample sizes are recommended if the distributions of the populations are highly skewed or contain outliers. Smaller sample sizes should only be used if the analyst is satisfied that the distributions of the populations are at least approximately normal.

NOTE AND COMMENT

Another approach used to make inferences about the difference between two population means when σ_1 and σ_2 are unknown is based on the assumption that the two population standard deviations are equal ($\sigma_1 = \sigma_2 = \sigma$). Under this assumption, the two sample standard deviations are combined to provide the following *pooled sample variance:*

$$s_p^2 = \frac{(n_1 - 1)s_1^2 + (n_2 - 1)s_2^2}{n_1 + n_2 - 2}$$

The t test statistic becomes

$$t = \frac{(\bar{x}_1 - \bar{x}_2) - D_0}{s_p\sqrt{\dfrac{1}{n_1} + \dfrac{1}{n_2}}}$$

and has $n_1 + n_2 - 2$ degrees of freedom. At this point, the computation of the p-value and the interpretation of the sample results are identical to the procedures discussed earlier in this section.

A difficulty with this procedure is that the assumption that the two population standard deviations are equal is usually difficult to verify. Unequal population standard deviations are frequently encountered. Using the pooled procedure may not provide satisfactory results, especially if the sample sizes n_1 and n_2 are quite different.

The t procedure that we presented in this section does not require the assumption of equal population standard deviations and can be applied whether the population standard deviations are equal or not. It is a more general procedure and is recommended for most applications.

Exercises

Methods

9.   The following results are for independent random samples taken from two populations.

Sample 1	Sample 2
$n_1 = 20$	$n_2 = 30$
$\bar{x}_1 = 22.5$	$\bar{x}_2 = 20.1$
$s_1 = 2.5$	$s_2 = 4.8$

    a.   What is the point estimate of the difference between the two population means?
    b.   What is the degrees of freedom for the t distribution?
    c.   At 95% confidence, what is the margin of error?
    d.   What is the 95% confidence interval for the difference between the two population means?

10.   Consider the following hypothesis test.

$$H_0: \mu_1 - \mu_2 = 0$$
$$H_a: \mu_1 - \mu_2 \neq 0$$

The following results are from independent samples taken from two populations.

Sample 1	Sample 2
$n_1 = 35$	$n_2 = 40$
$\bar{x}_1 = 13.6$	$\bar{x}_1 = 10.1$
$s_1 = 5.2$	$s_2 = 8.5$

a. What is the value of the test statistic?
b. What is the degrees of freedom for the t distribution?
c. What is the p-value?
d. At $\alpha = .05$, what is your conclusion?

11. Consider the following data for two independent random samples taken from two normal populations.

Sample 1	10	7	13	7	9	8
Sample 2	8	7	8	4	6	9

a. Compute the two sample means.
b. Compute the two sample standard deviations.
c. What is the point estimate of the difference between the two population means?
d. What is the 90% confidence interval estimate of the difference between the two population means?

Applications

SELF test

12. The U.S. Department of Transportation provides the number of miles that residents of the 75 largest metropolitan areas travel per day in a car. Suppose that for a random sample of 50 Buffalo residents the mean is 22.5 miles a day and the standard deviation is 8.4 miles a day, and for an independent random sample of 40 Boston residents the mean is 18.6 miles a day and the standard deviation is 7.4 miles a day.
a. What is the point estimate of the difference between the mean number of miles that Buffalo residents travel per day and the mean number of miles that Boston residents travel per day?
b. What is the 95% confidence interval for the difference between the two population means?

WEB file

CollegeCosts

13. The average annual cost (including tuition, room, board, books, and fees) to attend a public college takes nearly a third of the annual income of a typical family with college-age children (*Money*, April 2012). At private colleges, the average annual cost is equal to about 60% of the typical family's income. The following random samples show the annual cost of attending private and public colleges. Data are in thousands of dollars.

Private Colleges

52.8	43.2	45.0	33.3	44.0
30.6	45.8	37.8	50.5	42.0

Public Colleges

20.3	22.0	28.2	15.6	24.1	28.5
22.8	25.8	18.5	25.6	14.4	21.8

a. Compute the sample mean and sample standard deviation for private and public colleges.
b. What is the point estimate of the difference between the two population means? Interpret this value in terms of the annual cost of attending private and public colleges.
c. Develop a 95% confidence interval of the difference between the mean annual cost of attending private and pubic colleges.

14. Results of the 2011 Zagat Fast-Food Survey show Americans eat an average of 6.3 meals per month at fast-food chains. Suppose that in a follow-up study of 45 consumers in

Oklahoma City and 55 consumers in Milwaukee you obtain the following results:

Oklahoma City	Milwaukee
$n_1 = 45$	$n_2 = 55$
$\bar{x}_1 = 56.1$	$\bar{x}_2 = 59.4$
$s_1 = 6.0$	$s_2 = 7.0$

   a.   Formulate a hypothesis so that, if the null hypothesis is rejected, we can conclude that the number of meals eaten at fast-food chains by consumers in Oklahoma City is significantly less than the number of meals eaten at fast-food chains by consumers in Milwaukee.

   b.   What is the value of the test statistic?

   c.   What is the p-value?

   d.   Using $\alpha = .05$, what is your conclusion?

15. Commercial real estate prices and rental rates suffered substantial declines in 2008 and 2009 (*Newsweek,* July 27, 2009). These declines were particularly severe in Asia; annual lease rates in Tokyo, Hong Kong, and Singapore declined by 40% or more. Even with such large declines, annual lease rates in Asia were still higher than those in many cities in Europe. Annual lease rates for a sample of 30 commercial properties in Hong Kong showed a mean of $1,114 per square meter with a standard deviation of $230. Annual lease rates for a sample of 40 commercial properties in Paris showed a mean lease rate of $989 per square meter with a standard deviation of $195.

   a.   On the basis of the sample results, can we conclude that the mean annual lease rate is higher in Hong Kong than in Paris? Develop appropriate null and alternative hypotheses.

   b.   Use $\alpha = .01$. What is your conclusion?

SATMath

16. The College Board provided comparisons of Scholastic Aptitude Test (SAT) scores based on the highest level of education attained by the test taker's parents. A research hypothesis was that students whose parents had attained a higher level of education would on average score higher on the SAT. The overall mean SAT math score was 514 (College Board website, January 8, 2012). SAT math scores for independent samples of students follow. The first sample shows the SAT math test scores for students whose parents are college graduates with a bachelor's degree. The second sample shows the SAT math test scores for students whose parents are high school graduates but do not have a college degree.

Student's Parents			
College Grads		High School Grads	
485	487	442	492
534	533	580	478
650	526	479	425
554	410	486	485
550	515	528	390
572	578	524	535
497	448		
592	469		

   a.   Formulate the hypotheses that can be used to determine whether the sample data support the hypothesis that students show a higher population mean math score on the SAT if their parents attained a higher level of education.

   b.   What is the point estimate of the difference between the means for the two populations?

c.   Compute the *p*-value for the hypothesis test.
d.   At $\alpha = .05$, what is your conclusion?

17. Periodically, Merrill Lynch customers are asked to evaluate Merrill Lynch financial consultants and services. Higher ratings on the client satisfaction survey indicate
better service, with 7 the maximum service rating. Independent samples of service
ratings for two financial consultants are summarized here. Consultant A has 10 years
of experience, whereas consultant B has 1 year of experience. Use $\alpha = .05$ and test
to see whether the consultant with more experience has the higher population mean
service rating.

Consultant A	Consultant B
$n_1 = 16$	$n_2 = 10$
$\bar{x}_1 = 6.82$	$\bar{x}_2 = 6.25$
$s_1 = .64$	$s_2 = .75$

a.   State the null and alternative hypotheses.
b.   Compute the value of the test statistic.
c.   What is the *p*-value?
d.   What is your conclusion?

AirDelay

18. Researchers at Purdue University and Wichita State University found that airlines are
doing a better job of getting passengers to their destinations on time (Associated Press,
April 2, 2012). AirTran Airways and Southwest Airlines were among the leaders in on-
time arrivals, with both having 88% of their flights arriving on time. But for the 12% of
flights that were delayed, how many minutes were these flights late? Sample data showing the number of minutes that delayed flights were late are provided in the file named
AirDelay. Data are shown for both airlines.
a.   Formulate the hypotheses that can be used to test for a difference between the population mean minutes late for delayed flights by these two airlines.
b.   What is the sample mean number of minutes late for delayed flights for each of these
two airlines?
c.   Using a .05 level of significance, what is the *p*-value and what is your conclusion?

(10.3) Inferences About the Difference Between Two Population Means: Matched Samples

Suppose employees at a manufacturing company can use two different methods to perform a production task. To maximize production output, the company wants to identify
the method with the smaller population mean completion time. Let μ_1 denote the population mean completion time for production method 1 and μ_2 denote the population mean
completion time for production method 2. With no preliminary indication of the preferred
production method, we begin by tentatively assuming that the two production methods have
the same population mean completion time. Thus, the null hypothesis is $H_0: \mu_1 - \mu_2 = 0$.
If this hypothesis is rejected, we can conclude that the population mean completion times
differ. In this case, the method providing the smaller mean completion time would be recommended. The null and alternative hypotheses are written as follows.

$$H_0: \mu_1 - \mu_2 = 0$$
$$H_a: \mu_1 - \mu_2 \neq 0$$

In choosing the sampling procedure that will be used to collect production time data and test the hypotheses, we consider two alternative designs. One is based on independent samples and the other is based on **matched samples**.

1. *Independent sample design:* A random sample of workers is selected and each worker in the sample uses method 1. A second independent random sample of workers is selected and each worker in this sample uses method 2. The test of the difference between population means is based on the procedures in Section 10.2.
2. *Matched sample design:* One random sample of workers is selected. Each worker first uses one method and then uses the other method. The order of the two methods is assigned randomly to the workers, with some workers performing method 1 first and others performing method 2 first. Each worker provides a pair of data values, one value for method 1 and another value for method 2.

In the matched sample design the two production methods are tested under similar conditions (i.e., with the same workers); hence this design often leads to a smaller sampling error than the independent sample design. The primary reason is that in a matched sample design, variation between workers is eliminated because the same workers are used for both production methods.

Let us demonstrate the analysis of a matched sample design by assuming it is the method used to test the difference between population means for the two production methods. A random sample of six workers is used. The data on completion times for the six workers are given in Table 10.2. Note that each worker provides a pair of data values, one for each production method. Also note that the last column contains the difference in completion times d_i for each worker in the sample.

The key to the analysis of the matched sample design is to realize that we consider only the column of differences. Therefore, we have six data values (.6, −.2, .5, .3, .0, and .6) that will be used to analyze the difference between population means of the two production methods.

Let μ_d = the mean of the *difference* in values for the population of workers. With this notation, the null and alternative hypotheses are rewritten as follows.

$$H_0: \mu_d = 0$$
$$H_a: \mu_d \neq 0$$

Other than the use of the d notation, the formulas for the sample mean and sample standard deviation are the same ones used previously in the text.

If H_0 is rejected, we can conclude that the population mean completion times differ.

The d notation is a reminder that the matched sample provides *difference* data. The sample mean and sample standard deviation for the six difference values in Table 10.2 follow.

TABLE 10.2   TASK COMPLETION TIMES FOR A MATCHED SAMPLE DESIGN

Worker	Completion Time for Method 1 (minutes)	Completion Time for Method 2 (minutes)	Difference in Completion Times (d_i)
1	6.0	5.4	.6
2	5.0	5.2	−.2
3	7.0	6.5	.5
4	6.2	5.9	.3
5	6.0	6.0	.0
6	6.4	5.8	.6

WEB file

Matched

© Cengage Learning

$$\bar{d} = \frac{\sum d_i}{n} = \frac{1.8}{6} = .30$$

$$s_d = \sqrt{\frac{\sum(d_i - \bar{d})^2}{n - 1}} = \sqrt{\frac{.56}{5}} = .335$$

It is not necessary to make the assumption that the population has a normal distribution if the sample size is large. Sample size guidelines for using the t distribution were presented in Chapters 8 and 9.

With the small sample of $n = 6$ workers, we need to make the assumption that the population of differences has a normal distribution. This assumption is necessary so that we may use the t distribution for hypothesis testing and interval estimation procedures. Based on this assumption, the following test statistic has a t distribution with $n - 1$ degrees of freedom.

TEST STATISTIC FOR HYPOTHESIS TESTS INVOLVING MATCHED SAMPLES

$$t = \frac{\bar{d} - \mu_d}{s_d/\sqrt{n}} \qquad (10.9)$$

Once the difference data are computed, the t distribution procedure for matched samples is the same as the one-population estimation and hypothesis testing procedures described in Chapters 8 and 9.

Let us use equation (10.9) to test the hypotheses H_0: $\mu_d = 0$ and H_a: $\mu_d \neq 0$, using $\alpha = .05$. Substituting the sample results $\bar{d} = .30$, $s_d = .335$, and $n = 6$ into equation (10.9), we compute the value of the test statistic.

$$t = \frac{\bar{d} - \mu_d}{s_d/\sqrt{n}} = \frac{.30 - 0}{.335/\sqrt{6}} = 2.20$$

Now let us compute the p-value for this two-tailed test. Because $t = 2.20 > 0$, the test statistic is in the upper tail of the t distribution. With $t = 2.20$, the area in the upper tail to the right of the test statistic can be found by using the t distribution table with degrees of freedom $= n - 1 = 6 - 1 = 5$. Information from the 5 degrees of freedom row of the t distribution table is as follows:

Area in Upper Tail	.20	.10	.05	.025	.01	.005
t-Value (5 df)	0.920	1.476	2.015	2.571	3.365	4.032

$t = 2.20$

Thus, we see that the area in the upper tail is between .05 and .025. Because this test is a two-tailed test, we double these values to conclude that the p-value is between .10 and .05. This p-value is greater than $\alpha = .05$. Thus, the null hypothesis H_0: $\mu_d = 0$ is not rejected. Using Excel or Minitab and the data in Table 10.2, we find the exact p-value $= .080$.

In addition we can obtain an interval estimate of the difference between the two population means by using the single population methodology of Chapter 8. At 95% confidence, the calculation follows.

$$\bar{d} \pm t_{.025} \frac{s_d}{\sqrt{n}}$$

$$.3 \pm 2.571\left(\frac{.335}{\sqrt{6}}\right)$$

$$.3 \pm .35$$

Thus, the margin of error is .35 and the 95% confidence interval for the difference between the population means of the two production methods is $-.05$ minutes to .65 minutes.

NOTES AND COMMENTS

1. In the example presented in this section, workers performed the production task with first one method and then the other method. This example illustrates a matched sample design in which each sampled element (worker) provides a pair of data values. It is also possible to use different but "similar" elements to provide the pair of data values. For example, a worker at one location could be matched with a similar worker at another location (similarity based on age, education, gender, experience, etc.). The pairs of workers would provide the difference data that could be used in the matched sample analysis.

2. A matched sample procedure for inferences about two population means generally provides better precision than the independent sample approach; therefore it is the recommended design. However, in some applications the matching cannot be achieved, or perhaps the time and cost associated with matching are excessive. In such cases, the independent sample design should be used.

Exercises

Methods

19. Consider the following hypothesis test.

$$H_0: \mu_d \leq 0$$
$$H_a: \mu_d > 0$$

The following data are from matched samples taken from two populations.

	Population	
Element	1	2
1	21	20
2	28	26
3	18	18
4	20	20
5	26	24

a. Compute the difference value for each element.
b. Compute $\bar{d}$.
c. Compute the standard deviation s_d.
d. Conduct a hypothesis test using $\alpha = .05$. What is your conclusion?

20. The following data are from matched samples taken from two populations.

	Population	
Element	1	2
1	11	8
2	7	8
3	9	6
4	12	7
5	13	10
6	15	15
7	15	14

a. Compute the difference value for each element.
b. Compute $\bar{d}$.
c. Compute the standard deviation s_d.
d. What is the point estimate of the difference between the two population means?
e. Provide a 95% confidence interval for the difference between the two population means.

Applications

21. A market research firm used a sample of individuals to rate the purchase potential of a particular product before and after the individuals saw a new television commercial about the product. The purchase potential ratings were based on a 0 to 10 scale, with higher values indicating a higher purchase potential. The null hypothesis stated that the mean rating "after" would be less than or equal to the mean rating "before." Rejection of this hypothesis would show that the commercial improved the mean purchase potential rating. Use $\alpha = .05$ and the following data to test the hypothesis and comment on the value of the commercial.

| | Purchase Rating | | | Purchase Rating | |
Individual	After	Before	Individual	After	Before
1	6	5	5	3	5
2	6	4	6	9	8
3	7	7	7	7	5
4	4	3	8	6	6

StockPrices

22. The price per share of stock for a sample of 25 companies was recorded at the beginning of 2012 and then again at the end of the 1st quarter of 2012 (*The Wall Street Journal,* April 2, 2012). How stocks perform during the 1st quarter is an indicator of what is ahead for the stock market and the economy. Use the sample data in the file entitled StockPrices to answer the following.
a. Let d_i denote the change in price per share for company i where $d_i = $ 1st quarter of 2012 price per share minus the beginning of 2012 price per share. Use the sample mean of these values to estimate the dollar amount a share of stock has changed during the 1st quarter.
b. What is the 95% confidence interval estimate of the population mean change in the price per share of stock during the first quarter? Interpret this result.

23. Bank of America's Consumer Spending Survey collected data on annual credit card charges in seven different categories of expenditures: transportation, groceries, dining out, household expenses, home furnishings, apparel, and entertainment. Using data from a sample of 42 credit card accounts, assume that each account was used to identify the annual credit card charges for groceries (population 1) and the annual credit card charges for dining out (population 2). Using the difference data, the sample mean difference was $\bar{d} = \$850$, and the sample standard deviation was $s_d = \$1,123$.
a. Formulate the null and alternative hypotheses to test for no difference between the population mean credit card charges for groceries and the population mean credit card charges for dining out.
b. Use a .05 level of significance. Can you conclude that the population means differ? What is the *p*-value?
c. Which category, groceries or dining out, has a higher population mean annual credit card charge? What is the point estimate of the difference between the population means? What is the 95% confidence interval estimate of the difference between the population means?

24. The Global Business Travel Association reported the domestic airfare for business travel for the current year and the previous year (*INC. Magazine,* February 2012). Below is a sample of 12 flights with their domestic airfares shown for both years.

Current Year	Previous Year	Current Year	Previous Year
345	315	635	585
526	463	710	650
420	462	605	545
216	206	517	547
285	275	570	508
405	432	610	580

a. Formulate the hypotheses and test for a significant increase in the mean domestic airfare for business travel for the one-year period. What is the *p*-value? Using a .05 level of significance, what is your conclusion?

b. What is the sample mean domestic airfare for business travel for each year?

c. What is the percentage change in the airfare for the one-year period?

25. The College Board SAT college entrance exam consists of three parts: math, writing, and critical reading (*The World Almanac,* 2012). Sample data showing the math and writing scores for a sample of 12 students who took the SAT follow.

Student	Math	Writing	Student	Math	Writing
1	540	474	7	480	430
2	432	380	8	499	459
3	528	463	9	610	615
4	574	612	10	572	541
5	448	420	11	390	335
6	502	526	12	593	613

a. Use a .05 level of significance and test for a difference between the population mean for the math scores and the population mean for the writing scores. What is the *p*-value and what is your conclusion?

b. What is the point estimate of the difference between the mean scores for the two tests? What are the estimates of the population mean scores for the two tests? Which test reports the higher mean score?

26. Scores in the first and fourth (final) rounds for a sample of 20 golfers who competed in PGA tournaments are shown in the following table (*Golfweek,* February 14, 2009, and February 28, 2009). Suppose you would like to determine if the mean score for the first round of a PGA Tour event is significantly different than the mean score for the fourth and final round. Does the pressure of playing in the final round cause scores to go up? Or does the increased player concentration cause scores to come down?

Player	First Round	Final Round	Player	First Round	Final Round
Michael Letzig	70	72	Aron Price	72	72
Scott Verplank	71	72	Charles Howell	72	70
D. A. Points	70	75	Jason Dufner	70	73
Jerry Kelly	72	71	Mike Weir	70	77
Soren Hansen	70	69	Carl Pettersson	68	70
D. J. Trahan	67	67	Bo Van Pelt	68	65
Bubba Watson	71	67	Ernie Els	71	70
Reteif Goosen	68	75	Cameron Beckman	70	68
Jeff Klauk	67	73	Nick Watney	69	68
Kenny Perry	70	69	Tommy Armour III	67	71

a.   Use $\alpha = .10$ to test for a statistically significantly difference between the population means for first- and fourth-round scores. What is the p-value? What is your conclusion?

b.   What is the point estimate of the difference between the two population means? For which round is the population mean score lower?

c.   What is the margin of error for a 90% confidence interval estimate for the difference between the population means? Could this confidence interval have been used to test the hypothesis in part (a)? Explain.

An Introduction to Experimental Design and Analysis of Variance

Sir Ronald Aylmer Fisher (1890–1962) invented the branch of statistics known as experimental design. In addition to being accomplished in statistics, he was a noted scientist in the field of genetics.

In Chapter 1 we stated that statistical studies can be classified as either experimental or observational. In an experimental statistical study, an experiment is conducted to generate the data. An experiment begins with identifying a variable of interest. Then one or more other variables, thought to be related, are identified and controlled, and data are collected about how those variables influence the variable of interest.

In an observational study, data are usually obtained through sample surveys and not a controlled experiment. Good design principles are employed, but the rigorous controls associated with an experimental statistical study are often not possible. For instance, in a study of the relationship between smoking and lung cancer the researcher cannot assign a smoking habit to subjects. The researcher is restricted to simply observing the effects of smoking on people who already smoke and the effects of not smoking on people who do not already smoke.

In this section we introduce the basic principles of an experimental study and show how they are used in a completely randomized design. We also provide a conceptual overview of the statistical procedure called analysis of variance (ANOVA). In the following section we show how ANOVA can be used to test for the equality of k population means using data obtained from a completely randomized design as well as data obtained from an observational study. So, in this sense, ANOVA extends the statistical material in the preceding sections from two population means to three or more population means. In later chapters, we will see that ANOVA plays a key role in analyzing the results of regression studies involving both experimental and observational data.

Cause-and-effect relationships can be difficult to establish in observational studies; such relationships are easier to establish in experimental studies.

As an example of an experimental statistical study, let us consider the problem facing Chemitech, Inc. Chemitech developed a new filtration system for municipal water supplies. The components for the new filtration system will be purchased from several suppliers, and Chemitech will assemble the components at its plant in Columbia, South Carolina. The industrial engineering group is responsible for determining the best assembly method for the new filtration system. After considering a variety of possible approaches, the group narrows the alternatives to three: method A, method B, and method C. These methods differ in the sequence of steps used to assemble the system. Managers at Chemitech want to determine which assembly method can produce the greatest number of filtration systems per week.

In the Chemitech experiment, assembly method is the independent variable or **factor**. Because three assembly methods correspond to this factor, we say that three treatments are associated with this experiment; each **treatment** corresponds to one of the three assembly methods. The Chemitech problem is an example of a **single-factor experiment**; it involves one categorical factor (method of assembly). More complex experiments may consist of multiple factors; some factors may be categorical and others may be quantitative.

The three assembly methods or treatments define the three populations of interest for the Chemitech experiment. One population is all Chemitech employees who use assembly method A, another is those who use method B, and the third is those who use method C. Note that for each population the dependent or **response variable** is the number of filtration systems assembled per week, and the primary statistical objective of the experiment is to determine whether the mean number of units produced per week is the same for all three populations (methods).

Randomization is the process of assigning the treatments to the experimental units at random. Prior to the work of Sir R. A. Fisher, treatments were assigned on a systematic or subjective basis.

Suppose a random sample of three employees is selected from all assembly workers at the Chemitech production facility. In experimental design terminology, the three randomly selected workers are the **experimental units**. The experimental design that we will use for the Chemitech problem is called a **completely randomized design**. This type of design requires that each of the three assembly methods or treatments be assigned randomly to one of the experimental units or workers. For example, method A might be randomly assigned to the second worker, method B to the first worker, and method C to the third worker. The concept of *randomization,* as illustrated in this example, is an important principle of all experimental designs.

Note that this experiment would result in only one measurement or number of units assembled for each treatment. To obtain additional data for each assembly method, we must repeat or replicate the basic experimental process. Suppose, for example, that instead of selecting just three workers at random we selected 15 workers and then randomly assigned each of the three treatments to 5 of the workers. Because each method of assembly is assigned to 5 workers, we say that five replicates have been obtained. The process of *replication* is another important principle of experimental design. Figure 10.3 shows the completely randomized design for the Chemitech experiment.

Data Collection

Once we are satisfied with the experimental design, we proceed by collecting and analyzing the data. In the Chemitech case, the employees would be instructed in how to perform the assembly method assigned to them and then would begin assembling the new filtration systems using that method. After this assignment and training, the number of units assembled by each employee during one week is as shown in Table 10.3. The sample means, sample variances, and sample standard deviations for each assembly method are also

FIGURE 10.3   COMPLETELY RANDOMIZED DESIGN FOR EVALUATING
THE CHEMITECH ASSEMBLY METHOD EXPERIMENT

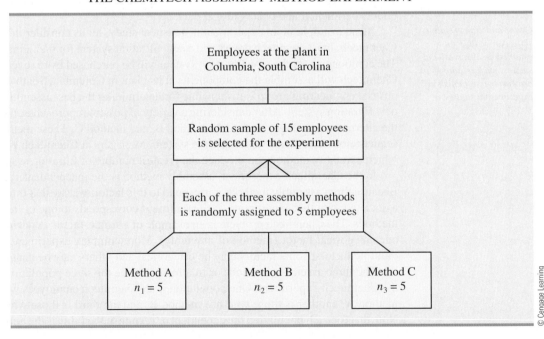

© Cengage Learning

TABLE 10.3   NUMBER OF UNITS PRODUCED BY 15 WORKERS

WEB file

Chemitech

	Method		
	A	**B**	**C**
	58	58	48
	64	69	57
	55	71	59
	66	64	47
	67	68	49
Sample mean	62	66	52
Sample variance	27.5	26.5	31.0
Sample standard deviation	5.244	5.148	5.568

© Cengage Learning

provided. Thus, the sample mean number of units produced using method A is 62; the sample mean using method B is 66; and the sample mean using method C is 52. From these data, method B appears to result in higher production rates than either of the other methods.

The real issue is whether the three sample means observed are different enough for us to conclude that the means of the populations corresponding to the three methods of assembly are different. To write this question in statistical terms, we introduce the following notation.

μ_1 = mean number of units produced per week using method A

μ_2 = mean number of units produced per week using method B

μ_3 = mean number of units produced per week using method C

Although we will never know the actual values of μ_1, μ_2, and μ_3, we want to use the sample means to test the following hypotheses.

If H_0 is rejected, we cannot conclude that all population means are different.

Rejecting H_0 means that at least two population means have different values.

$$H_0 : \mu_1 = \mu_2 = \mu_3$$
$$H_a : \text{Not all population means are equal}$$

As we will demonstrate shortly, analysis of variance (ANOVA) is the statistical procedure used to determine whether the observed differences in the three sample means are large enough to reject H_0.

Assumptions for Analysis of Variance

Three assumptions are required to use analysis of variance.

If the sample sizes are equal, analysis of variance is not sensitive to departures from the assumption of normally distributed populations.

1. **For each population, the response variable is normally distributed.** Implication: In the Chemitech experiment the number of units produced per week (response variable) must be normally distributed for each assembly method.
2. **The variance of the response variable, denoted σ^2, is the same for all of the populations.** Implication: In the Chemitech experiment, the variance of the number of units produced per week must be the same for each assembly method.
3. **The observations must be independent.** Implication: In the Chemitech experiment, the number of units produced per week for each employee must be independent of the number of units produced per week for any other employee.

Analysis of Variance: A Conceptual Overview

If the means for the three populations are equal, we would expect the three sample means to be close together. In fact, the closer the three sample means are to one another, the

FIGURE 10.4   SAMPLING DISTRIBUTION OF $\bar{x}$ GIVEN H_0 IS TRUE

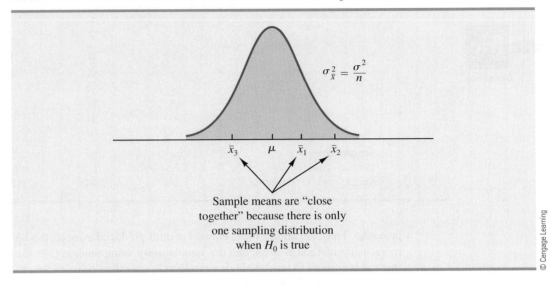

weaker the evidence we have for the conclusion that the population means differ. Alternatively, the more the sample means differ, the stronger the evidence we have for the conclusion that the population means differ. In other words, if the variability among the sample means is "small," it supports H_0; if the variability among the sample means is "large," it supports H_a.

If the null hypothesis, H_0: $\mu_1 = \mu_2 = \mu_3$, is true, we can use the variability among the sample means to develop an estimate of σ^2. First, note that if the assumptions for analysis of variance are satisfied and the null hypothesis is true, each sample will have come from the same normal distribution with mean μ and variance σ^2. Recall from Chapter 7 that the sampling distribution of the sample mean $\bar{x}$ for a simple random sample of size n from a normal population will be normally distributed with mean μ and variance σ^2/n. Figure 10.4 illustrates such a sampling distribution.

Thus, if the null hypothesis is true, we can think of each of the three sample means, $\bar{x}_1 = 62$, $\bar{x}_2 = 66$, and $\bar{x}_3 = 52$ from Table 10.3, as values drawn at random from the sampling distribution shown in Figure 10.4. In this case, the mean and variance of the three $\bar{x}$ values can be used to estimate the mean and variance of the sampling distribution. When the sample sizes are equal, as in the Chemitech experiment, the best estimate of the mean of the sampling distribution of $\bar{x}$ is the mean or average of the sample means. In the Chemitech experiment, an estimate of the mean of the sampling distribution of $\bar{x}$ is $(62 + 66 + 52)/3 = 60$. We refer to this estimate as the *overall sample mean*. An estimate of the variance of the sampling distribution of $\bar{x}$, $\sigma_{\bar{x}}^2$ is provided by the variance of the three sample means.

$$s_{\bar{x}}^2 = \frac{(62-60)^2 + (66-60)^2 + (52-60)^2}{3-1} = \frac{104}{2} = 52$$

Because $\sigma_{\bar{x}}^2 = \sigma^2/n$, solving for σ^2 gives

$$\sigma^2 = n\sigma_{\bar{x}}^2$$

Hence,

$$\text{Estimate of } \sigma^2 = n \text{ (Estimate of } \sigma_{\bar{x}}^2) = ns_{\bar{x}}^2 = 5(52) = 260$$

The result, $ns_{\bar{x}}^2 = 260$, is referred to as the *between-treatments* estimate of σ^2.

FIGURE 10.5   SAMPLING DISTRIBUTIONS OF $\bar{x}$ GIVEN H_0 IS FALSE

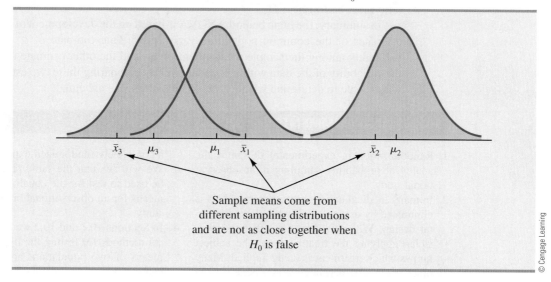

Sample means come from
different sampling distributions
and are not as close together when
H_0 is false

The between-treatments estimate of σ^2 is based on the assumption that the null hypothesis is true. In this case, each sample comes from the same population, and there is only one sampling distribution of $\bar{x}$. To illustrate what happens when H_0 is false, suppose the population means all differ. Note that because the three samples are from normal populations with different means, they will result in three different sampling distributions. Figure 10.5 shows that in this case, the sample means are not as close together as they were when H_0 was true. Thus, $s_{\bar{x}}^2$ will be larger, causing the between-treatments estimate of σ^2 to be larger. In general, when the population means are not equal, the between-treatments estimate will overestimate the population variance σ^2.

The variation within each of the samples also has an effect on the conclusion we reach in analysis of variance. When a simple random sample is selected from each population, each of the sample variances provides an unbiased estimate of σ^2. Hence, we can combine or pool the individual estimates of σ^2 into one overall estimate. The estimate of σ^2 obtained in this way is called the *pooled* or *within-treatments* estimate of σ^2. Because each sample variance provides an estimate of σ^2 based only on the variation within each sample, the within-treatments estimate of σ^2 is not affected by whether the population means are equal. When the sample sizes are equal, the within-treatments estimate of σ^2 can be obtained by computing the average of the individual sample variances. For the Chemitech experiment we obtain

$$\text{Within-treatments estimate of } \sigma^2 = \frac{27.5 + 26.5 + 31.0}{3} = \frac{85}{3} = 28.33$$

In the Chemitech experiment, the between-treatments estimate of σ^2 (260) is much larger than the within-treatments estimate of σ^2 (28.33). In fact, the ratio of these two estimates is $260/28.33 = 9.18$. Recall, however, that the between-treatments approach provides a good estimate of σ^2 only if the null hypothesis is true; if the null hypothesis is false, the between-treatments approach overestimates σ^2. The within-treatments approach provides a good estimate of σ^2 in either case. Thus, if the null hypothesis is true, the two estimates will be similar and their ratio will be close to 1. If the null hypothesis is false, the between-treatments estimate will be larger than the within-treatments estimate, and their ratio will be large. In the next section we will show how large this ratio must be to reject H_0.

In summary, the logic behind ANOVA is based on the development of two independent estimates of the common population variance σ^2. One estimate of σ^2 is based on the variability among the sample means themselves, and the other estimate of σ^2 is based on the variability of the data within each sample. By comparing these two estimates of σ^2, we will be able to determine whether the population means are equal.

NOTES AND COMMENTS

1. Randomization in experimental design is the analog of probability sampling in an observational study.
2. In many medical experiments, potential bias is eliminated by using a double-blind experimental design. With this design, neither the physician applying the treatment nor the subject knows which treatment is being applied. Many other types of experiments could benefit from this type of design.
3. In this section we provided a conceptual overview of how analysis of variance can be used to test for the equality of k population means for a completely randomized experimental design. We will see that the same procedure can also be used to test for the equality of k population means for an observational or nonexperimental study.
4. In Sections 10.1 and 10.2 we presented statistical methods for testing the hypothesis that the means of two populations are equal. ANOVA can also be used to test the hypothesis that the means of two populations are equal. In practice, however, analysis of variance is usually not used except when dealing with three or more population means.

 10.5 # Analysis of Variance and the Completely Randomized Design

In this section we show how analysis of variance can be used to test for the equality of k population means for a completely randomized design. The general form of the hypotheses tested is

$$H_0: \mu_1 = \mu_2 = \cdots = \mu_k$$
$$H_a: \text{Not all population means are equal}$$

where

$$\mu_j = \text{mean of the } j\text{th population}$$

We assume that a simple random sample of size n_j has been selected from each of the k populations or treatments. For the resulting sample data, let

$$x_{ij} = \text{value of observation } i \text{ for treatment } j$$
$$n_j = \text{number of observations for treatment } j$$
$$\bar{x}_j = \text{sample mean for treatment } j$$
$$s_j^2 = \text{sample variance for treatment } j$$
$$s_j = \text{sample standard deviation for treatment } j$$

The formulas for the sample mean and sample variance for treatment j are as follow.

$$\bar{x}_j = \frac{\sum\limits_{i=1}^{n_j} x_{ij}}{n_j} \tag{10.10}$$

$$s_j^2 = \frac{\sum\limits_{i=1}^{n_j} (x_{ij} - \bar{x}_j)^2}{n_j - 1} \tag{10.11}$$

The overall sample mean, denoted $\bar{\bar{x}}$, is the sum of all the observations divided by the total number of observations. That is,

$$\bar{\bar{x}} = \frac{\sum\limits_{j=1}^{k} \sum\limits_{i=1}^{n_j} x_{ij}}{n_T} \tag{10.12}$$

where

$$n_T = n_1 + n_2 + \cdots + n_k \tag{10.13}$$

If the size of each sample is n, $n_T = kn$; in this case equation (10.12) reduces to

$$\bar{\bar{x}} = \frac{\sum\limits_{j=1}^{k} \sum\limits_{i=1}^{n_j} x_{ij}}{kn} = \frac{\sum\limits_{j=1}^{k} \sum\limits_{i=1}^{n_j} x_{ij}/n}{k} = \frac{\sum\limits_{j=1}^{k} \bar{x}_j}{k} \tag{10.14}$$

In other words, whenever the sample sizes are the same, the overall sample mean is just the average of the k sample means.

Because each sample in the Chemitech experiment consists of $n = 5$ observations, the overall sample mean can be computed by using equation (10.14). For the data in Table 10.3 we obtained the following result.

$$\bar{\bar{x}} = \frac{62 + 66 + 52}{3} = 60$$

If the null hypothesis is true ($\mu_1 = \mu_2 = \mu_3 = \mu$), the overall sample mean of 60 is the best estimate of the population mean μ.

Between-Treatments Estimate of Population Variance

In the preceding section, we introduced the concept of a between-treatments estimate of σ^2 and showed how to compute it when the sample sizes were equal. This estimate of σ^2 is called the *mean square due to treatments* and is denoted MSTR. The general formula for computing MSTR is

$$\text{MSTR} = \frac{\sum\limits_{j=1}^{k} n_j (\bar{x}_j - \bar{\bar{x}})^2}{k - 1} \tag{10.15}$$

The numerator in equation (10.15) is called the *sum of squares due to treatments* and is denoted SSTR. The denominator, $k - 1$, represents the degrees of freedom associated with SSTR. Hence, the mean square due to treatments can be computed using the following formula.

MEAN SQUARE DUE TO TREATMENTS

$$MSTR = \frac{SSTR}{k-1} \qquad (10.16)$$

where

$$SSTR = \sum_{j=1}^{k} n_j(\bar{x}_j - \bar{\bar{x}})^2 \qquad (10.17)$$

If H_0 is true, MSTR provides an unbiased estimate of σ^2. However, if the means of the k populations are not equal, MSTR is not an unbiased estimate of σ^2; in fact, in that case, MSTR should overestimate σ^2.

For the Chemitech data in Table 10.3, we obtain the following results.

$$SSTR = \sum_{j=1}^{k} n_j(\bar{x}_j - \bar{\bar{x}})^2 = 5(62 - 60)^2 + 5(66 - 60)^2 + 5(52 - 60)^2 = 520$$

$$MSTR = \frac{SSTR}{k-1} = \frac{520}{2} = 260$$

Within-Treatments Estimate of Population Variance

Earlier, we introduced the concept of a within-treatments estimate of σ^2 and showed how to compute it when the sample sizes were equal. This estimate of σ^2 is called the *mean square due to error* and is denoted MSE. The general formula for computing MSE is

$$MSE = \frac{\sum_{j=1}^{k} (n_j - 1)s_j^2}{n_T - k} \qquad (10.18)$$

The numerator in equation (10.18) is called the *sum of squares due to error* and is denoted SSE. The denominator of MSE is referred to as the degrees of freedom associated with SSE. Hence, the formula for MSE can also be stated as follows.

MEAN SQUARE DUE TO ERROR

$$MSE = \frac{SSE}{n_T - k} \qquad (10.19)$$

where

$$SSE = \sum_{j=1}^{k} (n_j - 1)s_j^2 \qquad (10.20)$$

Note that MSE is based on the variation within each of the treatments; it is not influenced by whether the null hypothesis is true. Thus, MSE always provides an unbiased estimate of σ^2.

For the Chemitech data in Table 10.3 we obtain the following results.

$$SSE = \sum_{j=1}^{k} (n_j - 1)s_j^2 = (5 - 1)27.5 + (5 - 1)26.5 + (5 - 1)31 = 340$$

$$MSE = \frac{SSE}{n_T - k} = \frac{340}{15 - 3} = \frac{340}{12} = 28.33$$

Comparing the Variance Estimates: The *F* Test

If the null hypothesis is true, MSTR and MSE provide two independent, unbiased estimates of σ^2. If the null hypothesis is true and the ANOVA assumptions are valid, the sampling distribution of MSTR/MSE is an **F distribution** with numerator degrees of freedom equal to $k - 1$ and denominator degrees of freedom equal to $n_T - k$. In other words, if the null hypothesis is true, the value of MSTR/MSE should appear to have been selected from this F distribution.

However, if the null hypothesis is false, the value of MSTR/MSE will be inflated because MSTR overestimates σ^2. Hence, we will reject H_0 if the resulting value of MSTR/MSE appears to be too large to have been selected from an F distribution with $k - 1$ numerator degrees of freedom and $n_T - k$ denominator degrees of freedom. Because the decision to reject H_0 is based on the value of MSTR/MSE, the test statistic used to test for the equality of k population means is as follows.

TEST STATISTIC FOR THE EQUALITY OF k POPULATION MEANS

$$F = \frac{\text{MSTR}}{\text{MSE}} \qquad\qquad (10.21)$$

The test statistic follows an F distribution with $k - 1$ degrees of freedom in the numerator and $n_T - k$ degrees of freedom in the denominator.

Let us return to the Chemitech experiment and use a level of significance $\alpha = .05$ to conduct the hypothesis test. The value of the test statistic is

$$F = \frac{\text{MSTR}}{\text{MSE}} = \frac{260}{28.33} = 9.18$$

The numerator degrees of freedom is $k - 1 = 3 - 1 = 2$ and the denominator degrees of freedom is $n_T - k = 15 - 3 = 12$. Because we will only reject the null hypothesis for large values of the test statistic, the p-value is the upper tail area of the F distribution to the right of the test statistic $F = 9.18$. Figure 10.6 shows the sampling distribution of $F = \text{MSTR/MSE}$, the value of the test statistic, and the upper tail area that is the p-value for the hypothesis test.

FIGURE 10.6   COMPUTATION OF p-VALUE USING THE SAMPLING DISTRIBUTION OF MSTR/MSE

© Cengage Learning

From Table 4 of Appendix B we find the following areas in the upper tail of an F distribution with 2 numerator degrees of freedom and 12 denominator degrees of freedom.

Area in Upper Tail	.10	.05	.025	.01
F Value ($df_1 = 2$, $df_2 = 12$)	2.81	3.89	5.10	6.93

$$F = 9.18$$

Appendix F shows how to compute p-values using Minitab or Excel.

Because $F = 9.18$ is greater than 6.93, the area in the upper tail at $F = 9.18$ is less than .01. Thus, the p-value is less than .01. Minitab or Excel can be used to show that the exact p-value is .004. With p-value $\leq \alpha = .05$, H_0 is rejected. The test provides sufficient evidence to conclude that the means of the three populations are not equal. In other words, analysis of variance supports the conclusion that the population mean number of units produced per week for the three assembly methods are not equal.

As with other hypothesis testing procedures, the critical value approach may also be used. With $\alpha = .05$, the critical F value occurs with an area of .05 in the upper tail of an F distribution with 2 and 12 degrees of freedom. From the F distribution table, we find $F_{.05} = 3.89$. Hence, the appropriate upper tail rejection rule for the Chemitech experiment is

$$\text{Reject } H_0 \text{ if } F \geq 3.89$$

With $F = 9.18$, we reject H_0 and conclude that the means of the three populations are not equal. A summary of the overall procedure for testing for the equality of k population means follows.

TEST FOR THE EQUALITY OF k POPULATION MEANS

$$H_0: \mu_1 = \mu_2 = \ldots = \mu_k$$
$$H_a: \text{Not all population means are equal}$$

TEST STATISTIC

$$F = \frac{MSTR}{MSE}$$

REJECTION RULE

p-value approach: Reject H_0 if p-value $\leq \alpha$
Critical value approach: Reject H_0 if $F \geq F_\alpha$

where the value of F_α is based on an F distribution with $k - 1$ numerator degrees of freedom and $n_T - k$ denominator degrees of freedom.

ANOVA Table

The results of the preceding calculations can be displayed conveniently in a table referred to as the analysis of variance or **ANOVA table**. The general form of the ANOVA table for a completely randomized design is shown in Table 10.4; Table 10.5 is the corresponding ANOVA table for the Chemitech experiment. The sum of squares associated with the source of variation referred to as "Total" is called the total sum of squares (SST). Note that the results for the Chemitech experiment suggest that SST = SSTR + SSE, and that the degrees

TABLE 10.4 ANOVA TABLE FOR A COMPLETELY RANDOMIZED DESIGN

Source of Variation	Sum of Squares	Degrees of Freedom	Mean Square	F	p-value
Treatments	SSTR	$k - 1$	$\text{MSTR} = \dfrac{\text{SSTR}}{k - 1}$	$\dfrac{\text{MSTR}}{\text{MSE}}$	
Error	SSE	$n_T - k$	$\text{MSE} = \dfrac{\text{SSE}}{n_T - k}$		
Total	SST	$n_T - 1$			

of freedom associated with this total sum of squares is the sum of the degrees of freedom associated with the sum of squares due to treatments and the sum of squares due to error.

We point out that SST divided by its degrees of freedom $n_T - 1$ is nothing more than the overall sample variance that would be obtained if we treated the entire set of 15 observations as one data set. With the entire data set as one sample, the formula for computing the total sum of squares, SST, is

$$\text{SST} = \sum_{j=1}^{k} \sum_{i=1}^{n_j} (x_{ij} - \bar{\bar{x}})^2 \tag{10.22}$$

It can be shown that the results we observed for the analysis of variance table for the Chemitech experiment also apply to other problems. That is,

$$\text{SST} = \text{SSTR} + \text{SSE} \tag{10.23}$$

Analysis of variance can be thought of as a statistical procedure for partitioning the total sum of squares into separate components.

In other words, SST can be partitioned into two sums of squares: the sum of squares due to treatments and the sum of squares due to error. Note also that the degrees of freedom corresponding to SST, $n_T - 1$, can be partitioned into the degrees of freedom corresponding to SSTR, $k - 1$, and the degrees of freedom corresponding to SSE, $n_T - k$. The analysis of variance can be viewed as the process of **partitioning** the total sum of squares and the degrees of freedom into their corresponding sources: treatments and error. Dividing the sum of squares by the appropriate degrees of freedom provides the variance estimates, the F value, and the p-value used to test the hypothesis of equal population means.

Computer Results for Analysis of Variance

Using statistical computer packages, analysis of variance computations with large sample sizes or a large number of populations can be performed easily. Appendixes 10.2, 10.4, and 10.6 show the steps required to use Minitab, Excel, and StatTools to perform the analysis

TABLE 10.5 ANALYSIS OF VARIANCE TABLE FOR THE CHEMITECH EXPERIMENT

Source of Variation	Sum of Squares	Degrees of Freedom	Mean Square	F	p-value
Treatments	520	2	260.00	9.18	.004
Error	340	12	28.33		
Total	860	14			

FIGURE 10.7   MINITAB OUTPUT FOR THE CHEMITECH EXPERIMENT ANALYSIS OF VARIANCE

```
Source      DF        SS        MS        F        P
Factor       2     520.0     260.0     9.18    0.004
Error       12     340.0      28.3
Total       14     860.0

S = 5.323       R-Sq = 60.47%       R-Sq(adj) = 53.88%

                                    Individual 95% CIs For Mean Based on
                                    Pooled StDev
  Level   N      Mean     StDev     ---+--------+--------+--------+-------
  A       5    62.000     5.244                    (-------*-------)
  B       5    66.000     5.148                       (------*-------)
  C       5    52.000     5.568     (------*-------)
                                    ---+--------+--------+--------+-------
Pooled StDev = 5.323                49.0     56.0     63.0     70.0
```

of variance computations. In Figure 10.7 we show output for the Chemitech experiment obtained using Minitab. The first part of the computer output contains the familiar ANOVA table format. Comparing Figure 10.7 with Table 10.5, we see that the same information is available, although some of the headings are slightly different. The heading Source is used for the source of variation column, Factor identifies the treatments row, and the sum of squares and degrees of freedom columns are interchanged.

Note that following the ANOVA table the computer output contains the respective sample sizes, the sample means, and the standard deviations. In addition, Minitab provides a figure that shows individual 95% confidence interval estimates of each population mean. In developing these confidence interval estimates, Minitab uses MSE as the estimate of σ^2. Thus, the square root of MSE provides the best estimate of the population standard deviation σ. This estimate of σ on the computer output is Pooled StDev; it is equal to 5.323. To provide an illustration of how these interval estimates are developed, we will compute a 95% confidence interval estimate of the population mean for method A.

From our study of interval estimation in Chapter 8, we know that the general form of an interval estimate of a population mean is

$$\bar{x} \pm t_{\alpha/2} \frac{s}{\sqrt{n}} \tag{10.24}$$

where s is the estimate of the population standard deviation σ. Because the best estimate of σ is provided by the Pooled StDev, we use a value of 5.323 for s in expression (10.24). The degrees of freedom for the t value is 12, the degrees of freedom associated with the error sum of squares. Hence, with $t_{.025} = 2.179$ we obtain

$$62 \pm 2.179 \frac{5.323}{\sqrt{5}} = 62 \pm 5.19$$

Thus, the individual 95% confidence interval for method A goes from $62 - 5.19 = 56.81$ to $62 + 5.19 = 67.19$. Because the sample sizes are equal for the Chemitech experiment, the individual confidence intervals for methods B and C are also constructed by adding and subtracting 5.19 from each sample mean. Thus, in the figure provided by Minitab we see that the widths of the confidence intervals are the same.

Testing for the Equality of k Population Means: An Observational Study

We have shown how analysis of variance can be used to test for the equality of k population means for a completely randomized experimental design. It is important to understand that ANOVA can also be used to test for the equality of three or more population means using data obtained from an observational study. As an example, let us consider the situation at National Computer Products, Inc. (NCP).

NCP manufactures printers and fax machines at plants located in Atlanta, Dallas, and Seattle. To measure how much employees at these plants know about quality management, a random sample of 6 employees was selected from each plant and the employees selected were given a quality awareness examination. The examination scores for these 18 employees are shown in Table 10.6. The sample means, sample variances, and sample standard deviations for each group are also provided. Managers want to use these data to test the hypothesis that the mean examination score is the same for all three plants.

We define population 1 as all employees at the Atlanta plant, population 2 as all employees at the Dallas plant, and population 3 as all employees at the Seattle plant. Let

$$\mu_1 = \text{mean examination score for population 1}$$
$$\mu_2 = \text{mean examination score for population 2}$$
$$\mu_3 = \text{mean examination score for population 3}$$

Although we will never know the actual values of μ_1, μ_2, and μ_3, we want to use the sample results to test the following hypotheses.

$$H_0: \mu_1 = \mu_2 = \mu_3$$
$$H_a: \text{Not all population means are equal}$$

Exercise 34 will ask you to analyze the NCP data using the analysis of variance procedure.

Note that the hypothesis test for the NCP observational study is exactly the same as the hypothesis test for the Chemitech experiment. Indeed, the same analysis of variance methodology we used to analyze the Chemitech experiment can also be used to analyze the data from the NCP observational study.

Even though the same ANOVA methodology is used for the analysis, it is worth noting how the NCP observational statistical study differs from the Chemitech experimental statistical study. The individuals who conducted the NCP study had no control over how the plants were assigned to individual employees. That is, the plants were already in operation

TABLE 10.6 EXAMINATION SCORES FOR 18 EMPLOYEES

WEB file

NCP

	Plant 1 Atlanta	Plant 2 Dallas	Plant 3 Seattle
	85	71	59
	75	75	64
	82	73	62
	76	74	69
	71	69	75
	85	82	67
Sample mean	79	74	66
Sample variance	34	20	32
Sample standard deviation	5.83	4.47	5.66

© Cengage Learning

and a particular employee worked at one of the three plants. All that NCP could do was to select a random sample of 6 employees from each plant and administer the quality awareness examination. To be classified as an experimental study, NCP would have had to be able to randomly select 18 employees and then assign the plants to each employee in a random fashion.

NOTES AND COMMENTS

1. The overall sample mean can also be computed as a weighted average of the k sample means.

$$\bar{\bar{x}} = \frac{n_1\bar{x}_1 + n_2\bar{x}_2 + \cdots + n_k\bar{x}_k}{n_T}$$

In problems where the sample means are provided, this formula is simpler than equation (10.12) for computing the overall mean.

2. If each sample consists of n observations, equation (10.15) can be written as

$$MSTR = \frac{n\sum_{j=1}^{k}(\bar{x}_j - \bar{\bar{x}})^2}{k-1} = n\left[\frac{\sum_{j=1}^{k}(\bar{x}_j - \bar{\bar{x}})^2}{k-1}\right]$$

$$= ns_{\bar{x}}^2$$

Note that this result is the same as presented in Section 10.4 when we introduced the concept

of the between-treatments estimate of σ^2. Equation (10.15) is simply a generalization of this result to the unequal sample-size case.

3. If each sample has n observations, $n_T = kn$; thus, $n_T - k = k(n - 1)$, and equation (10.18) can be rewritten as

$$MSE = \frac{\sum_{j=1}^{k}(n-1)s_j^2}{k(n-1)} = \frac{(n-1)\sum_{j=1}^{k}s_j^2}{k(n-1)} = \frac{\sum_{j=1}^{k}s_j^2}{k}$$

In other words, if the sample sizes are the same, MSE is the average of the k sample variances. Note that it is the same result we used in Section 10.4 when we introduced the concept of the within-treatments estimate of σ^2.

Exercises

Methods

27. The following data are from a completely randomized design.

	Treatment		
	A	**B**	**C**
	162	142	126
	142	156	122
	165	124	138
	145	142	140
	148	136	150
	174	152	128
Sample mean	156	142	134
Sample variance	164.4	131.2	110.4

a. Compute the sum of squares between treatments.
b. Compute the mean square between treatments.
c. Compute the sum of squares due to error.
d. Compute the mean square due to error.
e. Set up the ANOVA table for this problem.
f. At the $\alpha = .05$ level of significance, test whether the means for the three treatments are equal.

28. In a completely randomized design, seven experimental units were used for each of the five levels of the factor. Complete the following ANOVA table.

Source of Variation	Sum of Squares	Degrees of Freedom	Mean Square	F	p-value
Treatments	300				
Error					
Total	460				

29. Refer to exercise 28.
    a. What hypotheses are implied in this problem?
    b. At the $\alpha = .05$ level of significance, can we reject the null hypothesis in part (a)? Explain.

30. In an experiment designed to test the output levels of three different treatments, the following results were obtained: SST = 400, SSTR = 150, $n_T = 19$. Set up the ANOVA table and test for any significant difference between the mean output levels of the three treatments. Use $\alpha = .05$.

31. In a completely randomized design, 12 experimental units were used for the first treatment, 15 for the second treatment, and 20 for the third treatment. Complete the following analysis of variance. At a .05 level of significance, is there a significant difference between the treatments?

Source of Variation	Sum of Squares	Degrees of Freedom	Mean Square	F	p-value
Treatments	1200				
Error					
Total	1800				

32. Develop the analysis of variance computations for the following completely randomized design. At $\alpha = .05$, is there a significant difference between the treatment means?

Exer6

	Treatment		
	A	**B**	**C**
	136	107	92
	120	114	82
	113	125	85
	107	104	101
	131	107	89
	114	109	117
	129	97	110
	102	114	120
		104	98
		89	106
$\bar{x}_j$	119	107	100
s_j^2	146.86	96.44	173.78

Applications

33. Three different methods for assembling a product were proposed by an industrial engineer. To investigate the number of units assembled correctly with each method, 30 employees were randomly selected and randomly assigned to the three proposed methods in such a way that each method was used by 10 workers. The number of units assembled correctly was recorded, and the analysis of variance procedure was applied to the resulting data set. The following results were obtained: SST = 10,800; SSTR = 4560.
    a. Set up the ANOVA table for this problem.
    b. Use $\alpha = .05$ to test for any significant difference in the means for the three assembly methods.

34. Refer to the NCP data in Table 10.6. Set up the ANOVA table and test for any significant difference in the mean examination score for the three plants. Use $\alpha = .05$.

35. To study the effect of temperature on yield in a chemical process, five batches were produced at each of three temperature levels. The results follow. Construct an analysis of variance table. Use a .05 level of significance to test whether the temperature level has an effect on the mean yield of the process.

Temperature		
50° C	60° C	70° C
34	30	23
24	31	28
36	34	28
39	23	30
32	27	31

36. Auditors must make judgments about various aspects of an audit on the basis of their own direct experience, indirect experience, or a combination of the two. In a study, auditors were asked to make judgments about the frequency of errors to be found in an audit. The judgments by the auditors were then compared to the actual results. Suppose the following data were obtained from a similar study; lower scores indicate better judgments.

WEB file

AudJudg

Direct	Indirect	Combination
17.0	16.6	25.2
18.5	22.2	24.0
15.8	20.5	21.5
18.2	18.3	26.8
20.2	24.2	27.5
16.0	19.8	25.8
13.3	21.2	24.2

Use $\alpha = .05$ to test to see whether the basis for the judgment affects the quality of the judgment. What is your conclusion?

37. Four different paints are advertised as having the same drying time. To check the manufacturer's claims, five samples were tested for each of the paints. The time in minutes until the paint was dry enough for a second coat to be applied was recorded. The following data were obtained.

Paint 1	Paint 2	Paint 3	Paint 4
128	144	133	150
137	133	143	142
135	142	137	135
124	146	136	140
141	130	131	153

At the $\alpha = .05$ level of significance, test to see whether the mean drying time is the same for each type of paint.

38. The *Consumer Reports* Restaurant Customer Satisfaction Survey is based upon 148,599 visits to full-service restaurant chains (*Consumer Reports* website). One of the variables in the study is meal price, the average amount paid per person for dinner and drinks, minus the tip. Suppose a reporter for the *Sun Coast Times* thought that it would be of interest to her readers to conduct a similar study for restaurants located on the Grand Strand section in Myrtle Beach, South Carolina. The reporter selected a sample of 8 seafood restaurants, 8 Italian restaurants, and 8 steakhouses. The following data show the meal prices ($) obtained for the 24 restaurants sampled. Use $\alpha = .05$ to test whether there is a significant difference among the mean meal price for the three types of restaurants.

Italian	Seafood	Steakhouse
$12	$16	$24
13	18	19
15	17	23
17	26	25
18	23	21
20	15	22
17	19	27
24	18	31

Summary

In this chapter we discussed procedures for developing interval estimates and conducting hypothesis tests involving two populations. First, we showed how to make inferences about the difference between two population means when independent random samples are selected. We first considered the case where the population standard deviations, σ_1 and σ_2, could be assumed known. The standard normal distribution z was used to develop the interval estimate and served as the test statistic for hypothesis tests. We then considered the case where the population standard deviations were unknown and estimated by the sample standard deviations s_1 and s_2. In this case, the t distribution was used to develop the interval estimate and served as the test statistic for hypothesis tests.

Inferences about the difference between two population means were then discussed for the matched sample design. In the matched sample design each element provides a pair of data values, one from each population. The difference between the paired data values is then used in the statistical analysis. The matched sample design is generally preferred to the independent sample design because the matched-sample procedure often improves the precision of the estimate.

In the final two sections we provided an introduction to experimental design and the analysis of variance (ANOVA). Experimental studies differ from observational studies in the sense that an experiment is conducted to generate the data. The completely randomized design was described and the analysis of variance was used to test for a treatment effect. The same analysis of variance procedure can be used to test for the difference among k population means in an observational study.

Glossary

Independent random samples Samples selected from two populations in such a way that the elements making up one sample are chosen independently of the elements making up the other sample.

Matched samples Samples in which each data value of one sample is matched with a corresponding data value of the other sample.

Factor Another word for the independent variable of interest.

Treatments Different levels of a factor.

Single-factor experiment An experiment involving only one factor with k populations or treatments.

Response variable Another word for the dependent variable of interest.

Experimental units The elements of interest in the experiment.

Completely randomized design An experimental design in which the treatments are randomly assigned to the experimental units.

F distribution A probability distribution based on the ratio of two independent estimates of the variance of a normal population. The F distribution is used in hypothesis tests about the equality of k population means.

ANOVA table A table used to summarize the analysis of variance computations and results. It contains columns showing the sources of variation, the sums of squares, the degrees of freedom, the mean squares, and the F value.

Partitioning The process of allocating the total sum of squares and degrees of freedom to the various components.

Key Formulas

Point Estimator of the Difference Between Two Population Means

$$\bar{x}_1 - \bar{x}_2 \tag{10.1}$$

Standard Error of $\bar{x}_1 - \bar{x}_2$

$$\sigma_{\bar{x}_1 - \bar{x}_2} = \sqrt{\frac{\sigma_1^2}{n_1} + \frac{\sigma_2^2}{n_2}} \tag{10.2}$$

Interval Estimate of the Difference Between Two Population Means: σ_1 and σ_2 Known

$$\bar{x}_1 - \bar{x}_2 \pm z_{\alpha/2}\sqrt{\frac{\sigma_1^2}{n_1} + \frac{\sigma_2^2}{n_2}} \tag{10.4}$$

Test Statistic for Hypothesis Tests About $\mu_1 - \mu_2$: σ_1 and σ_2 Known

$$z = \frac{(\bar{x}_1 - \bar{x}_2) - D_0}{\sqrt{\frac{\sigma_1^2}{n_1} + \frac{\sigma_2^2}{n_2}}} \tag{10.5}$$

**Interval Estimate of the Difference Between Two Population Means:
σ_1 and σ_2 Unknown**

$$\bar{x}_1 - \bar{x}_2 \pm t_{\alpha/2}\sqrt{\frac{s_1^2}{n_1} + \frac{s_2^2}{n_2}} \tag{10.6}$$

Degrees of Freedom: t Distribution with Two Independent Random Samples

$$df = \frac{\left(\dfrac{s_1^2}{n_1} + \dfrac{s_2^2}{n_2}\right)^2}{\dfrac{1}{n_1 - 1}\left(\dfrac{s_1^2}{n_1}\right)^2 + \dfrac{1}{n_2 - 1}\left(\dfrac{s_2^2}{n_2}\right)^2} \tag{10.7}$$

Test Statistic for Hypothesis Tests About $\mu_1 - \mu_2$: σ_1 and σ_2 Unknown

$$t = \frac{(\bar{x}_1 - \bar{x}_2) - D_0}{\sqrt{\dfrac{s_1^2}{n_1} + \dfrac{s_2^2}{n_2}}} \tag{10.8}$$

Test Statistic for Hypothesis Tests Involving Matched Samples

$$t = \frac{\bar{d} - \mu_d}{s_d/\sqrt{n}} \tag{10.9}$$

Sample Mean for Treatment j

$$\bar{x}_j = \frac{\sum\limits_{i=1}^{n_j} x_{ij}}{n_j} \tag{10.10}$$

Sample Variance for Treatment j

$$s_j^2 = \frac{\sum\limits_{i=1}^{n_j} (x_{ij} - \bar{x}_j)^2}{n_j - 1} \tag{10.11}$$

Overall Sample Mean

$$\bar{\bar{x}} = \frac{\sum\limits_{j=1}^{k}\sum\limits_{i=1}^{n_j} x_{ij}}{n_T} \tag{10.12}$$

where $\qquad n_T = n_1 + n_2 + \cdots + n_k \tag{10.13}$

Mean Square Due to Treatments

$$\text{MSTR} = \frac{\text{SSTR}}{k - 1} \tag{10.16}$$

Sum of Squares Due to Treatments

$$\text{SSTR} = \sum_{j=1}^{k} n_j(\bar{x}_j - \bar{\bar{x}})^2 \tag{10.17}$$

Mean Square Due to Error

$$\text{MSE} = \frac{\text{SSE}}{n_T - k} \tag{10.19}$$

Sum of Squares Due to Error

$$\text{SSE} = \sum_{j=1}^{k} (n_j - 1)s_j^2 \tag{10.20}$$

Test Statistic for the Equality of k Population Means

$$F = \frac{\text{MSTR}}{\text{MSE}} \tag{10.21}$$

Total Sum of Squares

$$\text{SST} = \sum_{j=1}^{k} \sum_{i=1}^{n_j} (x_{ij} - \bar{\bar{x}})^2 \tag{10.22}$$

Partitioning of Sum of Squares

$$\text{SST} = \text{SSTR} + \text{SSE} \tag{10.23}$$

Supplementary Exercises

CorollaNavigation

39. According to Bankrate.com, a navigation system is an expensive option that does not enhance the resale value of an automobile (Bankrate.com website, February 11, 2013). Use the data in the file CorollaNavigation, which contains recent resale prices for 40 2009 Corolla XRS sedans that have navigation systems and 50 2009 Corolla XRS sedans that do not have navigation systems, to evaluate this claim.
    a. Provide a point estimate of the difference between the population mean prices for 2009 Corolla XRS sedans that have navigation systems and 2009 Corolla XRS sedans that do not have navigation systems.
    b. Historical data indicate that a population standard deviation of $2,000 is reasonable for 2009 Corolla XRS sedans that have navigation systems and for 2009 Corolla XRS sedans that do not have navigation systems. Compute the margin of error for your estimate in part (a). Use 95% confidence.
    c. Develop a 95% confidence interval estimate of the difference between the resale prices of 2009 Corolla XRS sedans that have navigation systems and 2009 Corolla XRS sedans that do not have navigation systems.

40. Safegate Foods, Inc., is redesigning the checkout lanes in its supermarkets throughout the country and is considering two designs. Tests on customer checkout times conducted at

two stores where the two new systems have been installed result in the following summary of the data.

	System A	System B
	$n_1 = 120$	$n_2 = 100$
	$\bar{x}_1 = 4.1$ minutes	$\bar{x}_2 = 3.4$ minutes
	$\sigma_1 = 2.2$ minutes	$\sigma_2 = 1.5$ minutes

Test at the .05 level of significance to determine whether the population mean checkout times of the two systems differ. Which system is preferred?

AnesthesiologistIncome

41. In an online report, *Medscape Today News* reported that anesthesiologists earned a mean income of $309,000 in 2011 (February 22, 2013). Compensation covers salary, bonus, and profit-sharing contributions. Are there regional differences in anesthesiologist's compensation east of the Mississippi River? Suppose that in a follow-up study of 14 anesthesiologists from east of the Mississippi River and 14 anesthesiologists from west of the Mississippi River yields the following results (in $1,000's):

East of Mississippi	West of Mississippi
268	380
274	364
282	300
291	364
237	339
249	271
234	322
235	403
261	384
272	238
330	342
371	300
245	244
301	271

a. Develop a point estimate of the difference between the population incomes for anesthesiologists from east of the Mississippi River and west of the Mississippi River.

b. Develop a 99% confidence interval estimate of the difference between the population incomes for anesthesiologists from east of the Mississippi River and west of the Mississippi River.

c. Do your results suggest that annual income of anesthesiologists from east of the Mississippi River is at least as large as annual incomes of anesthesiologists from west of the Mississippi River?

42. Mutual funds are classified as *load* or *no-load* funds. Load funds require an investor to pay an initial fee based on a percentage of the amount invested in the fund. The no-load funds do not require this initial fee. Some financial advisors argue that the load mutual funds may be worth the extra fee because these funds provide a higher mean rate of return than the no-load mutual funds. A sample of 30 load mutual funds and a sample of 30 no-load mutual funds were selected. Data were collected on the annual return for the funds over a five-year period. The data are contained in the data set Mutual. The data for the first five load and first five no-load mutual funds are as follows.

Mutual

Mutual Funds—Load	Return	Mutual Funds—No-Load	Return
American National Growth	15.51	Amana Income Fund	13.24
Arch Small Cap Equity	14.57	Berger One Hundred	12.13
Bartlett Cap Basic	17.73	Columbia International Stock	12.17
Calvert World International	10.31	Dodge & Cox Balanced	16.06
Colonial Fund A	16.23	Evergreen Fund	17.61

a. Formulate H_0 and H_a such that rejection of H_0 leads to the conclusion that the load mutual funds have a higher mean annual return over the five-year period.

b. Use the 60 mutual funds in the data set Mutual to conduct the hypothesis test. What is the p-value? At $\alpha = .05$, what is your conclusion?

43. The National Association of Home Builders provided data on the cost of the most popular home remodeling projects. Sample data on cost in thousands of dollars for two types of remodeling projects are as follows.

Kitchen	Master Bedroom	Kitchen	Master Bedroom
25.2	18.0	23.0	17.8
17.4	22.9	19.7	24.6
22.8	26.4	16.9	21.0
21.9	24.8	21.8	
19.7	26.9	23.6	

a. Develop a point estimate of the difference between the population mean remodeling costs for the two types of projects.

b. Develop a 90% confidence interval for the difference between the two population means.

44. In early 2009, the economy was experiencing a recession. But how was the recession affecting the stock market? Shown are data from a sample of 15 companies. Shown for each company is the price per share of stock on January 1 and April 30 (*The Wall Street Journal*, May 1, 2009).

PriceChange

Company	January 1 ($)	April 30 ($)
Applied Materials	10.13	12.21
Bank of New York	28.33	25.48
Chevron	73.97	66.10
Cisco Systems	16.30	19.32
Coca-Cola	45.27	43.05
Comcast	16.88	15.46
Ford Motors	2.29	5.98
General Electric	16.20	12.65
Johnson & Johnson	59.83	52.36
JP Morgan Chase	31.53	33.00
Microsoft	19.44	20.26
Oracle	17.73	19.34
Pfizer	17.71	13.36
Philip Morris	43.51	36.18
Procter & Gamble	61.82	49.44

a. What is the change in the mean price per share of stock over the four-month period?
b. Provide a 90% confidence interval estimate of the change in the mean price per share of stock. Interpret the results.
c. What was the percentage change in the mean price per share of stock over the four-month period?
d. If this same percentage change were to occur for the next four months and again for the four months after that, what would be the mean price per share of stock at the end of the year 2009?

45. A study reported in the *Journal of Small Business Management* concluded that self-employed individuals do not experience higher job satisfaction than individuals who are not self-employed. In this study, job satisfaction is measured using 18 items, each of which is rated using a Likert-type scale with 1–5 response options ranging from strong agreement to strong disagreement. A higher score on this scale indicates a higher degree of job satisfaction. The sum of the ratings for the 18 items, ranging from 18–90, is used as the measure of job satisfaction. Suppose that this approach was used to measure the job satisfaction for lawyers, physical therapists, cabinetmakers, and systems analysts. The results obtained for a sample of 10 individuals from each profession follow.

SatisJob

Lawyer	Physical Therapist	Cabinetmaker	Systems Analyst
44	55	54	44
42	78	65	73
74	80	79	71
42	86	69	60
53	60	79	64
50	59	64	66
45	62	59	41
48	52	78	55
64	55	84	76
38	50	60	62

At the $\alpha = .05$ level of significance, test for any difference in the job satisfaction among the four professions.

46. The U.S. Environmental Protection Agency (EPA) monitors levels of pollutants in the air for cities across the country. Ozone pollution levels are measured using a 500-point scale; lower scores indicate little health risk, and higher scores indicate greater health risk. The following data show the peak levels of ozone pollution in four cities (Birmingham, Alabama; Memphis, Tennessee; Little Rock, Arkansas; and Jackson, Mississippi) for 10 dates in 2012 (U.S. EPA website, March 20, 2012).

OzoneLevels

| | | City | | |
Data	Birmingham AL	Memphis TN	Little Rock AR	Jackson MS
Jan 9	18	20	18	14
Jan 17	23	31	22	30
Jan 18	19	25	22	21
Jan 31	29	36	28	35
Feb 1	27	31	28	24
Feb 6	26	31	31	25
Feb 14	31	24	19	25
Feb 17	31	31	28	28
Feb 20	33	35	35	34
Feb 29	20	42	42	21

Use $\alpha = .05$ to test for any significant difference in the mean peak ozone levels among the four cities.

47. The U.S. Census Bureau computes quarterly vacancy and homeownership rates by state and metropolitan statistical area. Each metropolitan statistical area (MSA) has at least one urbanized area of 50,000 or more inhabitants. The following data are the rental vacancy rates (%) for MSAs in four geographic regions of the United States for the first quarter of 2008 (U.S. Census Bureau website, January 2009).

RentalVacancy

Midwest	Northeast	South	West
16.2	2.7	16.6	7.9
10.1	11.5	8.5	6.6
8.6	6.6	12.1	6.9
12.3	7.9	9.8	5.6
10.0	5.3	9.3	4.3
16.9	10.7	9.1	15.2
16.9	8.6	5.6	5.7
5.4	5.5	9.4	4.0
18.1	12.7	11.6	12.3
11.9	8.3	15.6	3.6
11.0	6.7	18.3	11.0
9.6	14.2	13.4	12.1
7.6	1.7	6.5	8.7
12.9	3.6	11.4	5.0
12.2	11.5	13.1	4.7
13.6	16.3	4.4	3.3
		8.2	3.4
		24.0	5.5
		12.2	
		22.6	
		12.0	
		14.5	
		12.6	
		9.5	
		10.1	

Use $\alpha = .05$ to test whether there the mean vacancy rate is the same for each geographic region.

48. Three different assembly methods have been proposed for a new product. A completely randomized experimental design was chosen to determine which assembly method results in the greatest number of parts produced per hour, and 30 workers were randomly selected and assigned to use one of the proposed methods. The number of units produced by each worker follows.

Assembly

	Method	
A	B	C
97	93	99
73	100	94
93	93	87
100	55	66
73	77	59
91	91	75
100	85	84
86	73	72
92	90	88
95	83	86

Use these data and test to see whether the mean number of parts produced is the same with each method. Use $\alpha = .05$.

49. In a study conducted to investigate browsing activity by shoppers, each shopper was initially classified as a nonbrowser, light browser, or heavy browser. For each shopper, the study obtained a measure to determine how comfortable the shopper was in a store. Higher scores indicated greater comfort. Suppose the following data were collected.

Use $\alpha = .05$ to test for differences among comfort levels for the three types of browsers.

Browsing

Nonbrowser	Light Browser	Heavy Browser
4	5	5
5	6	7
6	5	5
3	4	7
3	7	4
4	4	6
5	6	5
4	5	7

Case Problem 1   Par, Inc.

Par, Inc., is a major manufacturer of golf equipment. Management believes that Par's market share could be increased with the introduction of a cut-resistant, longer-lasting golf ball. Therefore, the research group at Par has been investigating a new golf ball coating designed to resist cuts and provide a more durable ball. The tests with the coating have been promising.

One of the researchers voiced concern about the effect of the new coating on driving distances. Par would like the new cut-resistant ball to offer driving distances comparable to those of the current-model golf ball. To compare the driving distances for the two balls, 40 balls of both the new and current models were subjected to distance tests. The testing was performed with a mechanical hitting machine so that any difference between the mean distances for the two models could be attributed to a difference in the two models. These data are available in the file named Golf.

WEB file

Golf

Model Current	New	Model Current	New	Model Current	New	Model Current	New
264	277	270	272	263	274	281	283
261	269	287	259	264	266	274	250
267	263	289	264	284	262	273	253
272	266	280	280	263	271	263	260
258	262	272	274	260	260	275	270
283	251	275	281	283	281	267	263
258	262	265	276	255	250	279	261
266	289	260	269	272	263	274	255
259	286	278	268	266	278	276	263
270	264	275	262	268	264	262	279

Managerial Report

1. Formulate and present the rationale for a hypothesis test that Par could use to compare the driving distances of the current and new golf balls.
2. Analyze the data to provide the hypothesis testing conclusion. What is the *p*-value for your test? What is your recommendation for Par, Inc.?
3. Provide descriptive statistical summaries of the data for each model.
4. What is the 95% confidence interval for the population mean driving distance of each model, and what is the 95% confidence interval for the difference between the means of the two populations?
5. Do you see a need for larger sample sizes and more testing with the golf balls? Discuss.

Case Problem 2   Wentworth Medical Center

As part of a long-term study of individuals 65 years of age or older, sociologists and physicians at the Wentworth Medical Center in upstate New York investigated the relationship between geographic location and depression. A sample of 60 individuals, all in reasonably good health, was selected; 20 individuals were residents of Florida, 20 were residents of New York, and 20 were residents of North Carolina. Each of the individuals sampled was given a standardized test to measure depression. The data collected follow; higher test scores indicate higher levels of depression. These data are contained in the file Medical1.

A second part of the study considered the relationship between geographic location and depression for individuals 65 years of age or older who had a chronic health condition such as arthritis, hypertension, and/or heart ailment. A sample of 60 individuals with such conditions was identified. Again, 20 were residents of Florida, 20 were residents of New York, and 20 were residents of North Carolina. The levels of depression recorded for this study follow. These data are contained in the file named Medical2.

WEB file

Medical1

WEB file

Medical2

	Data from Medical1			Data from Medical2	
Florida	New York	North Carolina	Florida	New York	North Carolina
3	8	10	13	14	10
7	11	7	12	9	12
7	9	3	17	15	15
3	7	5	17	12	18
8	8	11	20	16	12
8	7	8	21	24	14
8	8	4	16	18	17
5	4	3	14	14	8
5	13	7	13	15	14
2	10	8	17	17	16
6	6	8	12	20	18
2	8	7	9	11	17
6	12	3	12	23	19
6	8	9	15	19	15
9	6	8	16	17	13
7	8	12	15	14	14
5	5	6	13	9	11
4	7	3	10	14	12
7	7	8	11	13	13
3	8	11	17	11	11

Managerial Report

1. Use descriptive statistics to summarize the data from the two studies. What are your preliminary observations about the depression scores?
2. Use analysis of variance on both data sets. State the hypotheses being tested in each case. What are your conclusions?
3. Use inferences about individual treatment means where appropriate. What are your conclusions?

Case Problem 3 Compensation for Sales Professionals

Suppose that a local chapter of sales professionals in the greater San Francisco area conducted a survey of its membership to study the relationship, if any, between the years of experience and salary for individuals employed in inside and outside sales positions. On the survey, respondents were asked to specify one of three levels of years of experience: low (1–10 years), medium (11–20 years), and high (21 or more years). A portion of the data obtained follows. The complete data set, consisting of 120 observations, is contained in the file named SalesSalary.

WEB file

SalesSalary

Observation	Salary $	Position	Experience
1	53,938	Inside	Medium
2	52,694	Inside	Medium
3	70,515	Outside	Low
4	52,031	Inside	Medium
5	62,283	Outside	Low
6	57,718	Inside	Low
7	79,081	Outside	High
8	48,621	Inside	Low
9	72,835	Outside	High
10	54,768	Inside	Medium
.	.	.	.
.	.	.	.
.	.	.	.
115	58,080	Inside	High
116	78,702	Outside	Medium
117	83,131	Outside	Medium
118	57,788	Inside	High
119	53,070	Inside	Medium
120	60,259	Outside	Low

Managerial Report

1. Use descriptive statistics to summarize the data.
2. Develop a 95% confidence interval estimate of the mean annual salary for all salespersons, regardless of years of experience and type of position.
3. Develop a 95% confidence interval estimate of the mean salary for inside salespersons.
4. Develop a 95% confidence interval estimate of the mean salary for outside salespersons.
5. Use analysis of variance to test for any significant differences due to position. Use a .05 level of significance, and for now, ignore the effect of years of experience.

6. Use analysis of variance to test for any significant differences due to years of experience. Use a .05 level of significance, and for now, ignore the effect of position.

7. At the .05 level of significance test for any significant differences due to position, years of experience, and interaction.

Appendix 10.1 Inferences About Two Populations Using Minitab

We describe the use of Minitab to develop interval estimates and conduct hypothesis tests about the difference between two population means and the difference between two population proportions. Minitab provides both interval estimation and hypothesis testing results within the same module. Thus, the Minitab procedure is the same for both types of inferences. In the examples that follow, we will demonstrate interval estimation and hypothesis testing for the same two samples. We note that Minitab does not provide a routine for inferences about the difference between two population means when the population standard deviations σ_1 and σ_2 are known.

Difference Between Two Population Means: σ_1 and σ_2 Unknown

CheckAcct

We will use the data for the checking account balances example presented in Section 10.2. The checking account balances at the Cherry Grove branch are in column C1, and the checking account balances at the Beechmont branch are in column C2. In this example, we will use the Minitab 2-Sample t procedure to provide a 95% confidence interval estimate of the difference between population means for the checking account balances at the two branch banks. The output of the procedure also provides the p-value for the hypothesis test: $H_0: \mu_1 - \mu_2 = 0$ versus $H_a: \mu_1 - \mu_2 \neq 0$. The following steps are necessary to execute the procedure:

Step 1. Select the **Stat** menu
Step 2. Choose **Basic Statistics**
Step 3. Choose **2-Sample t**
Step 4. When the 2-Sample t (Test and Confidence Interval) dialog box appears:
　　　　　Select **Samples in different columns**
　　　　　Enter C1 in the **First** box
　　　　　Enter C2 in the **Second** box
　　　　　Select **Options**
Step 5. When the 2-Sample t - Options dialog box appears:
　　　　　Enter 95 in the **Confidence level** box
　　　　　Enter 0 in the **Test difference** box
　　　　　Enter not equal in the **Alternative** box
　　　　　Click **OK**
Step 6. Click **OK**

The 95% confidence interval estimate is $37 to $193, as described in Section 10.2. The p-value $= .005$ shows the null hypothesis of equal population means can be rejected at the $\alpha = .01$ level of significance. In other applications, step 5 may be modified to provide different confidence levels, different hypothesized values, and different forms of the hypotheses.

Difference Between Two Population Means with Matched Samples

Matched

We use the data on task completion times in Table 10.2 to illustrate the matched-sample procedure. The completion times for method 1 are entered into column C1 and the completion times for method 2 are entered into column C2. The Minitab steps for a matched sample are as follows:

Step 1. Select the **Stat** menu
Step 2. Choose **Basic Statistics**
Step 3. Choose **Paired t**
Step 4. When the Paired t (Test and Confidence Interval) dialog box appears:
  Select **Samples in columns**
  Enter C1 in the **First sample** box
  Enter C2 in the **Second sample** box
  Select **Options**
Step 5. When the Paired t - Options dialog box appears:
  Enter 95 in the **Confidence level**
  Enter 0 in the **Test mean** box
  Enter not equal in the **Alternative** box
  Click **OK**
Step 6. Click **OK**

The 95% confidence interval estimate is $-.05$ to $.65$, as described in Section 10.3. The p-value $= .08$ shows that the null hypothesis of no difference in completion times cannot be rejected at $\alpha = .05$. Step 5 may be modified to provide different confidence levels, different hypothesized values, and different forms of the hypothesis.

Appendix 10.2   Analysis of Variance with Minitab

Completely Randomized Design

Chemitech

In Section 10.5 we showed how analysis of variance could be used to test for the equality of k population means using data from a completely randomized design. To illustrate how Minitab can be used for this type of experimental design, we show how to test whether the mean number of units produced per week is the same for each assembly method in the Chemitech experiment introduced in Section 10.4. The sample data are entered into the first three columns of a Minitab worksheet; column 1 is labeled A, column 2 is labeled B, and column 3 is labeled C. The following steps produce the Minitab output in Figure 10.7.

Step 1. Select the **Stat** menu
Step 2. Choose **ANOVA**
Step 3. Choose **One-way (Unstacked)**
Step 4. When the One-way Analysis of Variance dialog box appears:
  Enter C1-C3 in the **Responses (in separate columns)** box
  Click **OK**

The p-value of 0.004 allows us to reject the hypothesis that the means are equal for the three assembly methods at a .01 level of significance.

Appendix 10.3   Inferences About Two Populations Using Excel

We describe the use of Excel to conduct hypothesis tests about the difference between two population means.* We begin with inferences about the difference between the means of two populations when the population standard deviations σ_1 and σ_2 are known.

---

*Excel's data analysis tools provide hypothesis testing procedures for the difference between two population means. No routines are available for interval estimation of the difference between two population means nor for inferences about the difference between two population proportions.

Difference Between Two Population Means: σ_1 and σ_2 Known

ExamScores

We will use the examination scores for the two training centers discussed in Section 10.1. The label Center A is in cell A1 and the label Center B is in cell B1. The examination scores for Center A are in cells A2:A31 and examination scores for Center B are in cells B2:B41. The population standard deviations are assumed known with $\sigma_1 = 10$ and $\sigma_2 = 10$. The Excel routine will request the input of variances which are $\sigma_1^2 = 100$ and $\sigma_2^2 = 100$. The following steps can be used to conduct a hypothesis test about the difference between the two population means.

> **Step 1.** Click the **Data** tab on the Ribbon
> **Step 2.** In the **Analysis** group, click **Data Analysis**
> **Step 3.** When the Data Analysis dialog box appears:
> > Choose **z-Test: Two Sample for Means**
> **Step 4.** When the z-Test: Two Sample for Means dialog box appears:
> > Enter A1:A31 in the **Variable 1 Range** box
> > Enter B1:B41 in the **Variable 2 Range** box
> > Enter 0 in the **Hypothesized Mean Difference** box
> > Enter 100 in the **Variable 1 Variance (known)** box
> > Enter 100 in the **Variable 2 Variance (known)** box
> > Select **Labels**
> > Enter .05 in the **Alpha** box
> > Select **Output Range** and enter C1 in the box
> > Click **OK**

The two-tailed p-value is denoted P(Z<=z) two-tail. Its value of .0977 does not allow us to reject the null hypothesis at $\alpha = .05$.

Difference Between Two Population Means: σ_1 and σ_2 Unknown

SoftwareTest

We use the data for the software testing study in Table 10.1. The data are already entered into an Excel worksheet with the label Current in cell A1 and the label New in cell B1. The completion times for the current technology are in cells A2:A13, and the completion times for the new software are in cells B2:B13. The following steps can be used to conduct a hypothesis test about the difference between two population means with σ_1 and σ_2 unknown.

> **Step 1.** Click the **Data** tab on the Ribbon
> **Step 2.** In the **Analysis** group, click **Data Analysis**
> **Step 3.** When the Data Analysis dialog box appears:
> > Choose **t-Test: Two Sample Assuming Unequal Variances**
> **Step 4.** When the t-Test: Two Sample Assuming Unequal Variances dialog box appears:
> > Enter A1:A13 in the **Variable 1 Range** box
> > Enter B1:B13 in the **Variable 2 Range** box
> > Enter 0 in the **Hypothesized Mean Difference** box
> > Select **Labels**
> > Enter .05 in the **Alpha** box
> > Select **Output Range** and enter C1 in the box
> > Click **OK**

The appropriate p-value is denoted P(T<=t) one-tail. Its value of .017 allows us to reject the null hypothesis at $\alpha = .05$.

Difference Between Two Population Means with Matched Samples

Matched

We use the matched-sample completion times in Table 10.2 to illustrate. The data are entered into a worksheet with the label Method 1 in cell A1 and the label Method 2 in cell B2. The completion times for method 1 are in cells A2:A7 and the completion times for method 2 are in cells B2:B7. The Excel procedure uses the steps previously described for the *t*-test except the user chooses the **t-Test: Paired Two Sample for Means** data analysis tool in step 3. The variable 1 range is A1:A7 and the variable 2 range is B1:B7.

The appropriate *p*-value is denoted P(T<=t) two-tail. Its value of .08 does not allow us to reject the null hypothesis at $\alpha = .05$.

Appendix 10.4   Analysis of Variance with Excel

Completely Randomized Design

In Section 10.5 we showed how analysis of variance could be used to test for the equality of *k* population means using data from a completely randomized design. To illustrate how Excel can be used to test for the equality of *k* population means for this type of experimental design, we show how to test whether the mean number of units produced per week is the same for each assembly method in the Chemitech experiment introduced in Section 10.4. The sample data are entered into worksheet rows 2 to 6 of columns A, B, and C as shown in Figure 10.8. The following steps are used to obtain the output shown in cells A8:G22; the ANOVA portion of this output corresponds to the ANOVA table shown in Table 10.5.

Chemitech

FIGURE 10.8   EXCEL SOLUTION FOR THE CHEMITECH EXPERIMENT

	A	B	C	D	E	F	G	H
1	**Method A**	**Method B**	**Method C**					
2	58	58	48					
3	64	69	57					
4	55	71	59					
5	66	64	47					
6	67	68	49					
7								
8	Anova: Single Factor							
9								
10	SUMMARY							
11	*Groups*	*Count*	*Sum*	*Average*	*Variance*			
12	Method A	5	310	62	27.5			
13	Method B	5	330	66	26.5			
14	Method C	5	260	52	31			
15								
16								
17	ANOVA							
18	*Source of Variation*	*SS*	*df*	*MS*	*F*	*P-value*	*F crit*	
19	Between Groups	520	2	260	9.1764706	0.0038184	3.8852938	
20	Within Groups	340	12	28.333333				
21								
22	Total	860	14					
23								

Step 1. Click the **Data** tab on the Ribbon

Step 2. In the **Analysis** group, click **Data Analysis**

Step 3. Choose **Anova: Single Factor** from the list of Analysis Tools

Step 4. When the Anova: Single Factor dialog box appears:

> Enter A1:C6 in **Input Range** box
>
> Select **Columns**
>
> Select **Labels in First Row**
>
> Enter .05 in the **Alpha** box
>
> Select **Output Range** and enter D1 in the box
>
> Click **OK**

The p-value of 0.004 allows us to reject the hypothesis that the means are equal for the three assembly methods at a .01 level of significance.

Appendix 10.5   Inferences About Two Populations Using StatTools

In this appendix we show how StatTools can be used to develop interval estimates and conduct hypothesis tests about the difference between two population means for the σ_1 and σ_2 unknown case.

Interval Estimation of μ_1 and μ_2

CheckAcct

We will use the data for the checking account balances example presented in Section 10.2. Begin by using the Data Set Manager to create a StatTools data set for these data using the procedure described in the appendix in Chapter 1. The following steps can be used to compute a 95% confidence interval estimate of the difference between the two population means.

Step 1. Click the **StatTools** tab on the Ribbon

Step 2. In the **Analyses** group, click **Statistical Inference**

Step 3. Select the **Confidence Interval** option

Step 4. Choose **Mean/Std. Deviation**

Step 5. When the StatTools - Confidence Interval for Mean/Std. Deviation dialog box appears:

> For **Analysis Type**, choose **Two-Sample Analysis**
>
> In the **Variables** section:
>> Select **Cherry Grove**
>>
>> Select **Beechmont**
>
> In the **Confidence Intervals to Calculate** section:
>> Select the **For the Difference of Means** option
>>
>> Select 95% for the **Confidence Level**
>
> Click **OK**

Because the sample size for Cherry Grove ($n_1 = 28$) differs from the sample size for Beechmont ($n_2 = 22$), StatTools will inform you of this difference after you click OK. A dialog box will appear saying "The variable Beechmont contains missing data. This analysis will ignore the missing data." Click OK. A Choose Variable Ordering dialog box then appears, indicating that the analysis will compare the difference between the Cherry Grove data set and the Beechmont data set. Click OK and the StatTools interval estimation output will appear.

Hypothesis Tests About μ_1 and μ_2

SoftwareTest

We will use the software evaluation example and the completion time data presented in Table 10.1. Begin by using the Data Set Manager to create a StatTools data set for these data using the procedure described in the appendix in Chapter 1. The following steps can be used to test the hypothesis: $H_0: \mu_1 - \mu_2 \leq 0$ against $H_a: \mu_1 - \mu_2 > 0$.

Step 1. Click the **StatTools** tab on the Ribbon
Step 2. In the **Analyses** group, click **Statistical Inference**
Step 3. Select the **Hypothesis Test** option
Step 4. Choose **Mean/Std. Deviation**
Step 5. When the StatTools - Hypothesis Test for Mean/Std. Deviation dialog box appears:

> For **Analysis Type**, choose **Two-Sample Analysis**
> In the **Variables** section:
>> Select **Current**
>> Select **New**
> In the **Hypothesis Test to Perform** section:
>> Select **Difference of Means**
>> Enter 0 in the **Null Hypothesis Value** box
>> Select **Greater Than Null Value (One-Tailed Test)** in the **Alternative Hypothesis Type** box
> Click **OK**

A Choose Variable Ordering dialog box then appears, indicating that the analysis will compare the difference between the Current data set and the New data set. Click OK and the StatTools interval estimation output will appear. The results of the hypothesis test will then appear.

Inferences About the Difference Between Two Population Means: Matched Samples

WEB file

Matched

StatTools can be used to develop interval estimates and conduct hypothesis tests for the difference between population means for the matched samples case. We will use the matched-sample completion times in Table 10.2 to illustrate.

Begin by using the Data Set Manager to create a StatTools data set for these data using the procedure described in the appendix in Chapter 1. The following steps can be used to compute a 95% confidence interval estimate of the difference between the population mean completion times.

Step 1. Click the **StatTools** tab on the Ribbon
Step 2. In the **Analyses** group, click **Statistical Inference**
Step 3. Select the **Confidence Interval** option
Step 4. Choose **Mean/Std. Deviation**
Step 5. When the StatTools - Confidence Interval for Mean/Std. Deviation dialog box appears:

> For **Analysis Type**, choose **Paired-Sample Analysis**
> In the **Variables** section:
>> Select **Method 1**
>> Select **Method 2**
> In the **Confidence Intervals to Calculate** section:
>> Select the **For the Difference of Means** option
>> Select 95% for the **Confidence Level**
>> If selected, remove the check in the **For the Standard Deviation box**
> Click **OK**

A Choose Variable Ordering dialog box then appears, indicating that the analysis will compare the difference between the Method 1 data set and the Method 2 data set. Click OK and the StatTools interval estimation will appear. The confidence interval will appear.

Conducting hypothesis tests for the matched samples case is very similar to conducting hypothesis tests for the difference in two means shown previously. Choose the Hypothesis Test option in step 3. Then when the Hypothesis Test for Mean/Std. Deviation dialog box appears in step 5, describe the type of hypothesis test desired.

Appendix 10.6   Analysis of a Completely Randomized Design Using StatTools

In this appendix we show how StatTools can be used to test for the equality of k population means for a completely randomized design. We use the Chemitech data in Table 10.3 to illustrate. Begin by using the Data Set Manager to create a StatTools data set for these data using the procedure described in the appendix in Chapter 1. The following steps can be used to test for the equality of the three population means.

Chemitech

Step 1. Click the **StatTools** tab on the Ribbon
Step 2. In the **Analyses** group, click **Statistical Inference**
Step 3. Choose the **One-Way ANOVA** option
Step 4. When the StatTools - One-Way ANOVA dialog box appears:
  In the **Variables** section:
    Click the **Format button** and select **Unstacked**
    Select **Method A**
    Select **Method B**
    Select **Method C**
  Select 95% in the **Confidence Level** box
  Click **OK**

Note that in step 4 we selected the Unstacked option after clicking the Format button. The Unstacked option means that the data for the three treatments appear in separate columns of the worksheet. In a stacked format, only two columns would be used. For example, the data could have been organized as follows:

	A	B	C
1	**Method**	**Units Produced**	
2	Method A	58	
3	Method A	64	
4	Method A	55	
5	Method A	66	
6	Method A	67	
7	Method B	58	
8	Method B	69	
9	Method B	71	
10	Method B	64	
11	Method B	68	
12	Method C	48	
13	Method C	57	
14	Method C	59	
15	Method C	47	
16	Method C	49	
17			

Data are frequently recorded in a stacked format. For stacked data, simply select the Stacked option after clicking the Format button.

CHAPTER 11

Comparisons Involving Proportions and a Test of Independence

CONTENTS

STATISTICS *in* PRACTICE

UNITED WAY*
ROCHESTER, NEW YORK

United Way of Greater Rochester is a nonprofit orga- nization dedicated to improving the quality of life for all people in the seven counties it serves by meeting the community's most important human care needs.

The annual United Way/Red Cross fund-raising campaign, conducted each spring, funds hundreds of programs offered by more than 200 service providers. These providers meet a wide variety of human needs— physical, mental, and social—and serve people of all ages, backgrounds, and economic means.

Because of enormous volunteer involvement, United Way of Greater Rochester is able to hold its operating costs at just eight cents of every dollar raised.

The United Way of Greater Rochester decided to conduct a survey to learn more about community per- ceptions of charities. Focus-group interviews were held with professional, service, and general worker groups to get preliminary information on perceptions. The in- formation obtained was then used to help develop the questionnaire for the survey. The questionnaire was pre- tested, modified, and distributed to 440 individuals; 323 completed questionnaires were obtained.

A variety of descriptive statistics, including fre- quency distributions and crosstabulations, were provided from the data collected. An important part of the analysis involved the use of contingency tables and chi-square tests of independence. One use of such statistical tests was to determine whether perceptions of administrative expenses were independent of occupation.

The hypotheses for the test of independence were

H_0: Perception of United Way administrative ex- penses is independent of the occupation of the respondent.

H_a: Perception of United Way administrative expenses is not independent of the occupation of the respondent.

The after-school program at Wesley House Community Center. © Jim West/Alamy

Two questions in the survey provided the data for the sta- tistical test. One question obtained data on perceptions of the percentage of funds going to administrative expenses (up to 10%, 11–20%, and 21% or more). The other ques- tion asked for the occupation of the respondent.

The chi-square test at a .05 level of significance led to rejection of the null hypothesis of independence and to the conclusion that perceptions of United Way's ad- ministrative expenses did vary by occupation. Actual ad- ministrative expenses were less than 9%, but 35% of the respondents perceived that administrative expenses were 21% or more. Hence, many had inaccurate perceptions of administrative costs. In this group, production-line, cleri- cal, sales, and professional-technical employees had more inaccurate perceptions than other groups.

The community perceptions study helped United Way of Rochester to develop adjustments to its pro- grams and fund-raising activities. In this chapter, you will learn how a statistical test of independence, such as that described here, is conducted.

*The authors are indebted to Dr. Philip R. Tyler, Marketing Consultant to the United Way, for providing this Statistics in Practice.

Many statistical applications call for a comparison of population proportions. In Sec- tion 11.1, we describe statistical inferences concerning differences in the proportions for two populations. Two samples are required, one from each population, and the statistical inference is based on the two sample proportions. Section 11.2 looks at a hypothesis test comparing the proportions of a single multinomial population with the proportions stated in a null hypothesis. One sample from the multinomial population is used, and the hypothesis test is based on comparing the sample proportions with those stated in the null hypothesis. In section 11.3, we show how contingency tables can be used to test for the independence of two variables. One sample is used for the test of independence, but measures on two variables are required for each sampled element. Both Sections 11.2 and 11.3 rely on the use of a chi-square statistical test.

Inferences About the Difference Between Two Population Proportions

Letting p_1 denote the proportion for population 1 and p_2 denote the proportion for population 2, we next consider inferences about the difference between the two population proportions: $p_1 - p_2$. To make an inference about this difference, we will select independent random samples consisting of n_1 units from population 1 and n_2 units from population 2.

Interval Estimation of $p_1 - p_2$

In the following example, we show how to compute a margin of error and develop an interval estimate of the difference between two population proportions.

A tax preparation firm is interested in comparing the quality of work at two of its regional offices. By randomly selecting samples of tax returns prepared at each office and verifying the sample returns' accuracy, the firm will be able to estimate the proportion of erroneous returns prepared at each office. Of particular interest is the difference between these proportions.

p_1 = proportion of erroneous returns for population 1 (office 1)
p_2 = proportion of erroneous returns for population 2 (office 2)
$\bar{p}_1$ = sample proportion for a simple random sample from population 1
$\bar{p}_2$ = sample proportion for a simple random sample from population 2

The difference between the two population proportions is given by $p_1 - p_2$. The point estimator of $p_1 - p_2$ is as follows.

POINT ESTIMATOR OF THE DIFFERENCE BETWEEN TWO POPULATION PROPORTIONS

$$\bar{p}_1 - \bar{p}_2 \qquad \text{(11.1)}$$

Thus, the point estimator of the difference between two population proportions is the difference between the sample proportions of two independent simple random samples.

As with other point estimators, the point estimator $\bar{p}_1 - \bar{p}_2$ has a sampling distribution that reflects the possible values of $\bar{p}_1 - \bar{p}_2$ if we repeatedly took two independent random samples. The mean of this sampling distribution is $p_1 - p_2$ and the standard error of $\bar{p}_1 - \bar{p}_2$ is as follows:

STANDARD ERROR OF $\bar{p}_1 - \bar{p}_2$

$$\sigma_{\bar{p}_1 - \bar{p}_2} = \sqrt{\frac{p_1(1 - p_1)}{n_1} + \frac{p_2(1 - p_2)}{n_2}} \qquad \text{(11.2)}$$

If the sample sizes are large enough that n_1p_1, $n_1(1 - p_1)$, n_2p_2, and $n_2(1 - p_2)$ are all greater than or equal to 5, the sampling distribution of $\bar{p}_1 - \bar{p}_2$ can be approximated by a normal distribution.

As we showed previously, an interval estimate is given by a point estimate $\pm$ a margin of error. In the estimation of the difference between two population proportions, an interval estimate will take the following form:

$$\bar{p}_1 - \bar{p}_2 \pm \text{Margin of error}$$

With the sampling distribution of $\bar{p}_1 - \bar{p}_2$ approximated by a normal distribution, we would like to use $z_{\alpha/2}\sigma_{\bar{p}_1-\bar{p}_2}$ as the margin of error. However, $\sigma_{\bar{p}_1-\bar{p}_2}$ given by equation (11.2) cannot be used directly because the two population proportions, p_1 and p_2, are unknown. Using the sample proportion $\bar{p}_1$ to estimate p_1 and the sample proportion $\bar{p}_2$ to estimate p_2, the margin of error is as follows.

$$\text{Margin of error} = z_{\alpha/2}\sqrt{\frac{\bar{p}_1(1 - \bar{p}_1)}{n_1} + \frac{\bar{p}_2(1 - \bar{p}_2)}{n_2}} \qquad (11.3)$$

The general form of an interval estimate of the difference between two population proportions is as follows.

> **INTERVAL ESTIMATE OF THE DIFFERENCE BETWEEN TWO POPULATION PROPORTIONS**
>
> $$\bar{p}_1 - \bar{p}_2 \pm z_{\alpha/2}\sqrt{\frac{\bar{p}_1(1 - \bar{p}_1)}{n_1} + \frac{\bar{p}_2(1 - \bar{p}_2)}{n_2}} \qquad (11.4)$$
>
> where $1 - \alpha$ is the confidence coefficient.

Returning to the tax preparation example, we find that independent simple random samples from the two offices provide the following information.

Office 1	Office 2
$n_1 = 250$	$n_2 = 300$
Number of returns with errors = 35	Number of returns with errors = 27

TaxPrep

The sample proportions for the two offices follow.

$$\bar{p}_1 = \frac{35}{250} = .14$$

$$\bar{p}_2 = \frac{27}{300} = .09$$

The point estimate of the difference between the proportions of erroneous tax returns for the two populations is $\bar{p}_1 - \bar{p}_2 = .14 - .09 = .05$. Thus, we estimate that office 1 has a .05, or 5%, greater error rate than office 2.

Expression (11.4) can now be used to provide a margin of error and interval estimate of the difference between the two population proportions. Using a 90% confidence interval with $z_{\alpha/2} = z_{.05} = 1.645$, we have

$$\bar{p}_1 - \bar{p}_2 \pm z_{\alpha/2} \sqrt{\frac{\bar{p}_1(1 - \bar{p}_1)}{n_1} + \frac{\bar{p}_2(1 - \bar{p}_2)}{n_2}}$$

$$.14 - .09 \pm 1.645 \sqrt{\frac{.14(1 - .14)}{250} + \frac{.09(1 - .09)}{300}}$$

$$.05 \pm .045$$

Thus, the margin of error is .045, and the 90% confidence interval is .005 to .095.

Hypothesis Tests About $p_1 - p_2$

Let us now consider hypothesis tests about the difference between the proportions of two populations. We focus on tests involving no difference between the two population proportions. In this case, the three forms for a hypothesis test are as follows:

All hypotheses considered use 0 as the difference of interest.

$$H_0: p_1 - p_2 \geq 0 \qquad H_0: p_1 - p_2 \leq 0 \qquad H_0: p_1 - p_2 = 0$$
$$H_a: p_1 - p_2 < 0 \qquad H_a: p_1 - p_2 > 0 \qquad H_a: p_1 - p_2 \neq 0$$

When we assume H_0 is true as an equality, we have $p_1 - p_2 = 0$, which is the same as saying that the population proportions are equal, $p_1 = p_2$.

We will base the test statistic on the sampling distribution of the point estimator $\bar{p}_1 - \bar{p}_2$. In equation (11.2), we showed that the standard error of $\bar{p}_1 - \bar{p}_2$ is given by

$$\sigma_{\bar{p}_1 - \bar{p}_2} = \sqrt{\frac{p_1(1 - p_1)}{n_1} + \frac{p_2(1 - p_2)}{n_2}}$$

Under the assumption H_0 is true as an equality, the population proportions are equal and $p_1 = p_2 = p$. In this case, $\sigma_{\bar{p}_1 - \bar{p}_2}$ becomes

STANDARD ERROR OF $\bar{p}_1 - \bar{p}_2$ WHEN $p_1 = p_2 = p$

$$\sigma_{\bar{p}_1 - \bar{p}_2} = \sqrt{\frac{p(1 - p)}{n_1} + \frac{p(1 - p)}{n_2}} = \sqrt{p(1 - p)\left(\frac{1}{n_1} + \frac{1}{n_2}\right)} \qquad \textbf{(11.5)}$$

With p unknown, we pool, or combine, the point estimators from the two samples ($\bar{p}_1$ and $\bar{p}_2$) to obtain a single point estimator of p as follows.

POOLED ESTIMATOR OF p WHEN $p_1 = p_2 = p$

$$\bar{p} = \frac{n_1 \bar{p}_1 + n_2 \bar{p}_2}{n_1 + n_2} \qquad \textbf{(11.6)}$$

This **pooled estimator of p** is a weighted average of $\bar{p}_1$ and $\bar{p}_2$.

Substituting $\bar{p}$ for p in equation (11.5), we obtain an estimate of the standard error of $\bar{p}_1 - \bar{p}_2$. This estimate of the standard error is used in the test statistic. The general form of the test statistic for hypothesis tests about the difference between two population proportions is the point estimator divided by the estimate of $\sigma_{\bar{p}_1 - \bar{p}_2}$.

TEST STATISTIC FOR HYPOTHESIS TESTS ABOUT $p_1 - p_2$

$$z = \frac{(\bar{p}_1 - \bar{p}_2)}{\sqrt{\bar{p}(1 - \bar{p})\left(\dfrac{1}{n_1} + \dfrac{1}{n_2}\right)}}$$ (11.7)

This test statistic applies to large sample situations where $n_1 p_1$, $n_1(1 - p_1)$, $n_2 p_2$, and $n_2(1 - p_2)$ are all greater than or equal to 5.

Let us return to the tax preparation firm example and assume that the firm wants to use a hypothesis test to determine whether the error proportions differ between the two offices. A two-tailed test is required. The null and alternative hypotheses are as follows:

$$H_0: p_1 - p_2 = 0$$
$$H_a: p_1 - p_2 \neq 0$$

If H_0 is rejected, the firm can conclude that the error rates at the two offices differ. We will use $\alpha = .10$ as the level of significance.

The sample data previously collected showed $\bar{p}_1 = .14$ for the $n_1 = 250$ returns sampled at office 1 and $\bar{p}_2 = .09$ for the $n_2 = 300$ returns sampled at office 2. We continue by computing the pooled estimate of p.

$$\bar{p} = \frac{n_1 \bar{p}_1 + n_2 \bar{p}_2}{n_1 + n_2} = \frac{250(.14) + 300(.09)}{250 + 300} = .1127$$

Using this pooled estimate and the difference between the sample proportions, the value of the test statistic is as follows.

$$z = \frac{(\bar{p}_1 - \bar{p}_2)}{\sqrt{\bar{p}(1 - \bar{p})\left(\dfrac{1}{n_1} + \dfrac{1}{n_2}\right)}} = \frac{(.14 - .09)}{\sqrt{.1127(1 - .1127)\left(\dfrac{1}{250} + \dfrac{1}{300}\right)}} = 1.85$$

In computing the p-value for this two-tailed test, we first note that $z = 1.85$ is in the upper tail of the standard normal distribution. Using $z = 1.85$ and the standard normal distribution table, we find the area in the upper tail is $1.0000 - .9678 = .0322$. Doubling this area for a two-tailed test, we find the p-value $= 2(.0322) = .0644$. With the p-value less than $\alpha = .10$, H_0 is rejected at the .10 level of significance. The firm can conclude that the error rates differ between the two offices. This hypothesis testing conclusion is consistent with the earlier interval estimation results that showed the interval estimate of the difference between the population error rates at the two offices to be .005 to .095, with Office 1 having the higher error rate.

Exercises

Methods

1. Consider the following results for independent samples taken from two populations.

Sample 1	Sample 2
$n_1 = 400$	$n_2 = 300$
$\bar{p}_1 = .48$	$\bar{p}_2 = .36$

a. What is the point estimate of the difference between the two population proportions?
b. Develop a 90% confidence interval for the difference between the two population proportions.
c. Develop a 95% confidence interval for the difference between the two population proportions.

2. Consider the following hypothesis test.

$$H_0: p_1 - p_2 = 0$$
$$H_a: p_1 - p_2 \neq 0$$

The following results are for independent samples taken from the two populations.

Sample 1	Sample 2
$n_1 = 100$	$n_2 = 140$
$\bar{p}_1 = .28$	$\bar{p}_2 = .20$

a. What is the pooled estimate of p?
b. What is the p-value?
c. What is your conclusion?

3. Consider the hypothesis test

$$H_0: p_1 - p_2 \leq 0$$
$$H_a: p_1 - p_2 > 0$$

The following results are for independent samples taken from the two populations.

Sample 1	Sample 2
$n_1 = 200$	$n_2 = 300$
$\bar{p}_1 = .22$	$\bar{p}_2 = .16$

a. What is the p-value?
b. With $\alpha = .05$, what is your hypothesis testing conclusion?

Applications

4. A *Bloomberg Businessweek*/Harris survey asked senior executives at large corporations their opinions about the economic outlook for the future. One question was, "Do you think that there will be an increase in the number of full-time employees at your company over the next 12 months?" In the current survey, 220 of 400 executives answered Yes, while in a previous year survey, 192 of 400 executives had answered Yes. Provide a 95% confidence interval estimate for the difference between the proportions at the two points in time. What is your interpretation of the interval estimate?

5. *Forbes* reports that women trust recommendations from Pinterest more than recommendations from any other social network platform (*Forbes* website, April 10, 2012). But does trust in Pinterest differ by gender? The following sample data show the number of women and men who stated in a recent sample that they trust recommendations made on Pinterest.

	Women	Men
Sample	150	170
Trust Recommendations Made on Pinterest	117	102

a. What is the point estimate of the proportion of women who trust recommendations made on Pinterest?

b. What is the point estimate of the proportion of men who trust recommendations made on Pinterest?

c. Provide a 95% confidence interval estimate of the difference between the proportion of women and men who trust recommendations made on Pinterest.

6. Researchers with Oceana, a group dedicated to preserving the ocean ecosystem, reported finding that 33% of fish sold in retail outlets, grocery stores, and sushi bars throughout the United States had been mislabeled (*San Francisco Chronicle* website, February 21, 2013). Does this mislabeling differ for different species of fish? The following data show the number labeled incorrectly for samples of tuna and mahi mahi.

	Tuna	Mahi Mahi
Sample	220	160
Mislabeled	99	56

a. What is the point estimate of the proportion of tuna that is mislabeled?

b. What is the point estimate of the proportion of mahi mahi that is mislabeled?

c. Provide a 95% confidence interval estimate of the difference between the proportion of tuna and mahi mahi that is mislabeled.

7. Minnesota had the highest turnout rate of any state for the 2012 presidential election (United States Election Project website, February 9, 2013). Political analysts wonder if turnout in rural Minnesota was higher than turnout in the urban areas of the state. A sample shows that 663 of 884 registered voters from rural Minnesota voted in the 2012 presidential election, while 414 out of 575 registered voters from urban Minnesota voted.

a. Formulate the null and alternative hypotheses that can be used to test whether registered voters in rural Minnesota were more likely than registered voters in urban Minnesota to vote in the 2012 presidential election.

b. What is the proportion of sampled registered voters in rural Minnesota that voted in the 2012 presidential election?

c. What is the proportion of sampled registered voters in urban Minnesota that voted in the 2012 presidential election?

d. At $\alpha = .05$, test the political analysts' hypothesis. What is the p-value, and what conclusion do you to draw from your results?

8. Oil wells are expensive to drill, and dry wells are a great concern to oil exploration companies. The domestic oil and natural gas producer Aegis Oil, LLC describes on its website how improvements in technologies such as three-dimensional seismic imaging have dramatically reduced the number of dry (nonproducing) wells it and other oil exploration companies drill. The following sample data for wells drilled in 2005 and 2012 show the number of dry wells that were drilled in each year.

	2005	2012
Wells Drilled	119	162
Dry Wells	24	18

a. Formulate the null and alternative hypotheses that can be used to test whether the wells drilled in 2005 were more likely to be dry than wells drilled in 2012.

b. What is the point estimate of the proportion of wells drilled in 2005 that were dry?

    c.   What is the point estimate of the proportion of wells drilled in 2012 that were dry?

    d.   What is the p-value of your hypothesis test? At $\alpha = .05$, what conclusion do you to draw from your results?

9.   The Adecco Workplace Insights Survey sampled men and women workers and asked if they expected to get a raise or promotion this year (*USA Today*, February 16, 2012). Suppose the survey sampled 200 men and 200 women. If 104 of the men replied Yes and 74 of the women replied Yes, are the results statistically significant so that you can conclude a greater proportion of men expect to get a raise or a promotion this year?

    a.   State the hypothesis test in terms of the population proportion of men and the population proportion of women.

    b.   What is the sample proportion for men? For women?

    c.   Use a .01 level of significance. What is the p-value and what is your conclusion?

10.   Winter visitors are extremely important to the economy of Southwest Florida. Hotel occupancy is an often-reported measure of visitor volume and visitor activity (*Naples Daily News*, March 22, 2012). Hotel occupancy data for February in two consecutive years are as follows.

	Current Year	Previous Year
Occupied Rooms	1470	1458
Total Rooms	1750	1800

    a.   Formulate the hypothesis test that can be used to determine if there has been an increase in the proportion of rooms occupied over the one-year period.

    b.   What is the estimated proportion of hotel rooms occupied each year?

    c.   Using a .05 level of significance, what is your hypothesis test conclusion? What is the p-value?

    d.   What is the 95% confidence interval estimate of the change in occupancy for the one-year period? Do you think area officials would be pleased with the results?

11.2 Testing the Equality of Population Proportions for Three or More Populations

In Section 11.1 we introduced methods of statistical inference for population proportions with two populations where the hypothesis test conclusion was based on the standard normal (z) test statistic. We now show how the chi-square (χ^2) test statistic can be used to make statistical inferences about the equality of population proportions for three or more populations. Using the notation

$$p_1 = \text{population proportion for population 1}$$
$$p_2 = \text{population proportion for population 2}$$

and

$$p_k = \text{population proportion for population } k$$

the hypotheses for the equality of population proportions for $k \geq 3$ populations are as follows:

$$H_0: p_1 = p_2 = \cdots = p_k$$
$$H_a: \text{Not all population proportions are equal}$$

If the sample data and the chi-square test computations indicate H_0 cannot be rejected, we cannot detect a difference among the k population proportions. However, if the sample data and the chi-square test computations indicate H_0 can be rejected, we have the statistical evidence to conclude that not all k population proportions are equal; that is, one or more population proportions differ from the other population proportions. Further analyses can be done to conclude which population proportion or proportions are significantly different from others. Let us demonstrate this chi-square test by considering an application.

Organizations such as J.D. Power and Associates use the proportion of owners likely to repurchase a particular automobile as an indication of customer loyalty for the automobile. An automobile with a greater proportion of owners likely to repurchase is concluded to have greater customer loyalty. Suppose that in a particular study we want to compare the customer loyalty for three automobiles: Chevrolet Impala, Ford Fusion, and Honda Accord. The current owners of each of the three automobiles form the three populations for the study. The three population proportions of interest are as follows:

p_1 = proportion likely to repurchase an Impala for the population of Chevrolet Impala owners

p_2 = proportion likely to repurchase a Fusion for the population of Ford Fusion owners

p_3 = proportion likely to repurchase an Accord for the population of Honda Accord owners

The hypotheses are stated as follows:

$$H_0: p_1 = p_2 = p_3$$
$$H_a: \text{Not all population proportions are equal}$$

To conduct this hypothesis test we begin by taking a sample of owners from each of the three populations. Thus we will have a sample of Chevrolet Impala owners, a sample of Ford Fusion owners, and a sample of Honda Accord owners. Each sample provides categorical data indicating whether the respondents are likely or not likely to repurchase the automobile. The data for samples of 125 Chevrolet Impala owners, 200 Ford Fusion owners, and 175 Honda Accord owners are summarized in the tabular format shown in Table 11.1. This table has two rows for the responses Yes and No and three columns, one corresponding to each of the populations. The observed frequencies are summarized in the six cells of the table corresponding to each combination of the likely to repurchase responses and the three populations.

In studies such as these, we often use the same sample size for each population. We have chosen different sample sizes in this example to show that the chi-square test is not restricted to equal sample sizes for each of the k populations.

Using Table 11.1, we see that 69 of the 125 Chevrolet Impala owners indicated that they were likely to repurchase a Chevrolet Impala. One hundred and twenty of the 200 Ford Fusion owners and 123 of the 175 Honda Accord owners indicated that they were likely to repurchase their current automobile. Also, across all three samples, 312 of the 500 owners in the study indicated that they were likely to repurchase their current automobile. The question now is how do we analyze the data in Table 11.1 to determine if the hypothesis $H_0: p_1 = p_2 = p_3$ should be rejected?

TABLE 11.1   SAMPLE RESULTS OF LIKELY TO REPURCHASE FOR THREE POPULATIONS OF AUTOMOBILE OWNERS (OBSERVED FREQUENCIES)

		Automobile Owners			
		Chevrolet Impala	Ford Fusion	Honda Accord	Total
Likely to Repurchase	Yes	69	120	123	312
	No	56	80	52	188
	Total	125	200	175	500

WEB file

AutoLoyalty

The data in Table 11.1 are the *observed frequencies* for each of the six cells that represent the six combinations of the likely to repurchase response and the owner population. If we can determine the *expected frequencies under the assumption H_0 is true*, we can use the chi-square test statistic to determine whether there is a significant difference between the observed and expected frequencies. If a significant difference exists between the observed and expected frequencies, the hypothesis H_0 can be rejected and there is evidence that not all the population proportions are equal.

Expected frequencies for the six cells of the table are based on the following rationale. First, we assume that the null hypothesis of equal population proportions is true. Then we note that in the entire sample of 500 owners, a total of 312 owners indicated that they were likely to repurchase their current automobile. Thus, 312/500 = .624 is the overall sample proportion of owners indicating they are likely to repurchase their current automobile. If H_0: $p_1 = p_2 = p_3$ is true, .624 would be the best estimate of the proportion responding likely to repurchase for each of the automobile owner populations. So if the assumption of H_0 is true, we would expect .624 of the 125 Chevrolet Impala owners, or .624(125) = 78 owners to indicate they are likely to repurchase the Impala. Using the .624 overall sample proportion, we would expect .624(200) = 124.8 of the 200 Ford Fusion owners and .624(175) = 109.2 of the Honda Accord owners to respond that they are likely to repurchase their respective model of automobile.

Let us generalize the approach to computing expected frequencies by letting e_{ij} denote the expected frequency for the cell in row i and column j of the table. With this notation, now reconsider the expected frequency calculation for the response of likely to repurchase Yes (row 1) for Chevrolet Impala owners (column 1), that is, the expected frequency e_{11}.

Note that 312 is the total number of Yes responses (row 1 total), 175 is the total sample size for Chevrolet Impala owners (column 1 total), and 500 is the total sample size. Following the logic in the preceding paragraph, we can show

$$e_{11} = \left(\frac{\text{Row 1 Total}}{\text{Total Sample Size}} \right)(\text{Column 1 Total}) = \left(\frac{312}{500} \right)125 = (.624)125 = 78$$

Starting with the first part of the above expression, we can write

$$e_{11} = \frac{(\text{Row 1 Total})(\text{Column 1 Total})}{\text{Total Sample Size}}$$

Generalizing this expression shows that the following formula can be used to provide the expected frequencies under the assumption H_0 is true.

EXPECTED FREQUENCIES UNDER THE ASSUMPTION H_0 IS TRUE

$$e_{ij} = \frac{(\text{Row } i \text{ Total})(\text{Column } j \text{ Total})}{\text{Total Sample Size}} \tag{11.8}$$

Using equation (11.8), we see that the expected frequency of Yes responses (row 1) for Honda Accord owners (column 3) would be e_{13} = (Row 1 Total)(Column 3 Total)/(Total Sample Size) = (312)(175)/500 = 109.2. Use equation (11.8) to verify the other expected frequencies are as shown in Table 11.2.

The test procedure for comparing the observed frequencies of Table 11.1 with the expected frequencies of Table 11.2 involves the computation of the following chi-square statistic:

TABLE 11.2 EXPECTED FREQUENCIES FOR LIKELY TO REPURCHASE FOR THREE POPULATIONS OF AUTOMOBILE OWNERS IF H_0 IS TRUE

		Chevrolet Impala	Ford Fusion	Honda Accord	Total
Likely to Repurchase	Yes	78	124.8	109.2	312
	No	47	75.2	65.8	188
	Total	125	200	175	500

© Cengage Learning

CHI-SQUARE TEST STATISTIC

$$\chi^2 = \sum_i \sum_j \frac{(f_{ij} - e_{ij})^2}{e_{ij}} \qquad (11.9)$$

where

f_{ij} = observed frequency for the cell in row i and column j

e_{ij} = expected frequency for the cell in row i and column j under the assumption H_0 is true

Note: In a chi-square test involving the equality of k population proportions, the above test statistic has a chi-square distribution with $k - 1$ degrees of freedom provided the expected frequency is 5 *or more* for each cell.

Reviewing the expected frequencies in Table 11.2, we see that the expected frequency is at least five for each cell in the table. We therefore proceed with the computation of the chi-square test statistic. The calculations necessary to compute the value of the test statistic are shown in Table 11.3. In this case, we see that the value of the test statistic is $\chi^2 = 7.89$.

TABLE 11.3 COMPUTATION OF THE CHI-SQUARE TEST STATISTIC FOR THE TEST OF EQUAL POPULATION PROPORTIONS

Likely to Repurchase?	Automobile Owner	Observed Frequency (f_{ij})	Expected Frequency (e_{ij})	Difference ($f_{ij} - e_{ij}$)	Squared Difference ($f_{ij} - e_{ij}$)^2	Squared Difference Divided by Expected Frequency ($f_{ij} - e_{ij}$)$^2/e_{ij}$
Yes	Impala	69	78.0	−9.0	81.00	1.04
Yes	Fusion	120	124.8	−4.8	23.04	0.18
Yes	Accord	123	109.2	13.8	190.44	1.74
No	Impala	56	47.0	9.0	81.00	1.72
No	Fusion	80	75.2	4.8	23.04	0.31
No	Accord	52	65.8	−13.8	190.44	2.89
	Total	500	500			$\chi^2 = 7.89$

© Cengage Learning

TABLE 11.4 SELECTED VALUES OF THE CHI-SQUARE DISTRIBUTION

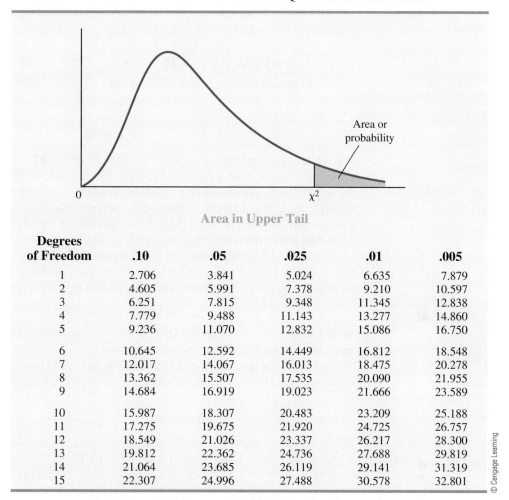

Area in Upper Tail

Degrees of Freedom	.10	.05	.025	.01	.005
1	2.706	3.841	5.024	6.635	7.879
2	4.605	5.991	7.378	9.210	10.597
3	6.251	7.815	9.348	11.345	12.838
4	7.779	9.488	11.143	13.277	14.860
5	9.236	11.070	12.832	15.086	16.750
6	10.645	12.592	14.449	16.812	18.548
7	12.017	14.067	16.013	18.475	20.278
8	13.362	15.507	17.535	20.090	21.955
9	14.684	16.919	19.023	21.666	23.589
10	15.987	18.307	20.483	23.209	25.188
11	17.275	19.675	21.920	24.725	26.757
12	18.549	21.026	23.337	26.217	28.300
13	19.812	22.362	24.736	27.688	29.819
14	21.064	23.685	26.119	29.141	31.319
15	22.307	24.996	27.488	30.578	32.801

In order to understand whether or not $\chi^2 = 7.89$ leads us to reject H_0: $p_1 = p_2 = p_3$, you will need to understand and refer to values of the chi-square distribution. Table 11.4 shows the general shape of the chi-square distribution, but note that the shape of a specific chi-square distribution depends upon the number of degrees of freedom. The table shows the upper tail areas of .10, .05, .025, .01, and .005 for chi-square distributions with up to 15 degrees of freedom. This version of the chi-square table will enable you to conduct the hypothesis tests presented in this chapter.

Since the expected frequencies shown in Table 11.2 are based on the assumption that H_0: $p_1 = p_2 = p_3$ is true, observed frequencies, f_{ij}, that are in agreement with expected frequencies, e_{ij}, provide small values of $(f_{ij} - e_{ij})^2$ in equation (11.9). If this is the case, the value of the chi-square test statistic will be relatively small and H_0 cannot be rejected. On the other hand, if the differences between the observed and expected frequencies are *large*, values of $(f_{ij} - e_{ij})^2$ and the computed value of the test statistic will be large. In this case, the null hypothesis of equal population proportions can be rejected. Thus a chi-square test for equal population proportions will always be an upper tail test with rejection of H_0 occurring when the test statistic is in the upper tail of the chi-square distribution.

The chi-square test presented in this section is always a one-tailed test with the rejection of H_0 occurring in the upper tail of the chi-square distribution.

We can use the upper tail area of the appropriate chi-square distribution and the *p*-value approach to determine whether the null hypothesis can be rejected. In the automobile brand loyalty study, the three owner populations indicate that the appropriate chi-square distribution has $k - 1 = 3 - 1 = 2$ degrees of freedom. Using row two of the chi-square distribution table, we have the following:

Area in Upper Tail	.10	.05	.025	.01	.005
χ^2 **Value (2 df)**	4.605	5.991	7.378	9.210	10.597

$$\chi^2 = 7.89$$

We see the upper tail area at $\chi^2 = 7.89$ is between .025 and .01. Thus, the corresponding upper tail area or p-value must be between .025 and .01. With p-value $\leq$ .05, we reject H_0 and conclude that the three population proportions are not all equal and thus there is a difference in brand loyalties among the Chevrolet Impala, Ford Fusion, and Honda Accord owners. Minitab or Excel procedures provided in Appendix F can be used to show $\chi^2 = 7.89$ with 2 degrees of freedom yields a p-value $= .0193$.

Instead of using the p-value, we could use the critical value approach to draw the same conclusion. With $\alpha = .05$ and 2 degrees of freedom, the critical value for the chi-square test statistic is $\chi^2 = 5.991$. The upper tail rejection region becomes

$$\text{Reject } H_0 \text{ if } \chi^2 \geq 5.991$$

With $7.89 \geq 5.991$, we reject H_0. Thus, the p-value approach and the critical value approach provide the same hypothesis-testing conclusion.

Let us summarize the general steps that can be used to conduct a chi-square test for the equality of the population proportions for three or more populations.

A CHI-SQUARE TEST FOR THE EQUALITY OF POPULATION PROPORTIONS FOR $k \geq 3$ POPULATIONS

1. State the null and alternative hypotheses.

$$H_0: p_1 = p_2 = \cdots = p_k$$
$$H_a: \text{Not all population proportions are equal}$$

2. Select a random sample from each of the populations and record the observed frequencies, f_{ij}, in a table with 2 rows and k columns.
3. Assume the null hypothesis is true and compute the expected frequencies, e_{ij}.
4. If the expected frequency, e_{ij}, is 5 or more for each cell, compute the test statistic:

$$\chi^2 = \sum_i \sum_j \frac{(f_{ij} - e_{ij})^2}{e_{ij}}$$

5. Rejection rule:

p-value approach:	Reject H_0 if p-value $\leq \alpha$
Critical value approach:	Reject H_0 if $\chi^2 \geq \chi^2_\alpha$

where the chi-square distribution has $k - 1$ degrees of freedom and α is the level of significance for the test.

A Multiple Comparison Procedure

We have used a chi-square test to conclude that the population proportions for the three populations of automobile owners are not all equal. Thus, some differences among the population proportions exist and the study indicates that customer loyalties are not all the same for the Chevrolet Impala, Ford Fusion, and Honda Accord owners. To identify where the differences between population proportions exist, we can begin by computing the three sample proportions as follows:

Brand Loyalty Sample Proportions

Chevrolet Impala	$\bar{p}_1 = 69/125\ = .5520$
Ford Fusion	$\bar{p}_2 = 120/200 = .6000$
Honda Accord	$\bar{p}_3 = 123/175 = .7029$

Since the chi-square test indicated that not all population proportions are equal, it is reasonable for us to proceed by attempting to determine where differences among the population proportions exist. For this we will rely on a multiple comparison procedure that can be used to conduct statistical tests between all pairs of population proportions. In the following, we discuss a multiple comparison procedure known as the **Marascuilo procedure**. This is a relatively straightforward procedure for making pairwise comparisons of all pairs of population proportions. We will demonstrate the computations required by this multiple comparison test procedure for the automobile customer loyalty study.

We begin by computing the absolute value of the pairwise difference between sample proportions for each pair of populations in the study. In the three-population automobile brand loyalty study we compare populations 1 and 2, populations 1 and 3, and then populations 2 and 3 using the sample proportions as follows:

Chevrolet Impala and Ford Fusion

$$|\bar{p}_1 - \bar{p}_2| = |.5520 - .6000| = .0480$$

Chevrolet Impala and Honda Accord

$$|\bar{p}_1 - \bar{p}_3| = |.5520 - .7029| = .1509$$

Ford Fusion and Honda Accord

$$|\bar{p}_2 - \bar{p}_3| = |.6000 - .7029| = .1029$$

In a second step, we select a level of significance and compute the corresponding critical value for each pairwise comparison using the following expression.

CRITICAL VALUES FOR THE MARASCUILO PAIRWISE COMPARISON PROCEDURE FOR k POPULATION PROPORTIONS

For each pairwise comparison compute a critical value as follows:

$$CV_{ij} = \sqrt{\chi_\alpha^2}\sqrt{\frac{\bar{p}_i(1 - \bar{p}_i)}{n_i} + \frac{\bar{p}_j(1 - \bar{p}_j)}{n_j}} \qquad (11.10)$$

where

χ_α^2 = chi-square with a level of significance α and $k - 1$ degrees of freedom

$\bar{p}_i$ and $\bar{p}_j$ = sample proportions for populations i and j

n_i and n_j = sample sizes for populations i and j

Using the chi-square distribution in Table 11.4, $k - 1 = 3 - 1 = 2$ degrees of freedom, and a .05 level of significance, we have $\chi^2_{.05} = 5.991$. Now using the sample proportions $\bar{p}_1 = .5520$, $\bar{p}_2 = .6000$, and $\bar{p}_3 = .7029$, the critical values for the three pairwise comparison tests are as follows:

Chevrolet Impala and Ford Fusion

$$CV_{12} = \sqrt{5.991}\sqrt{\frac{.5520(1 - .5520)}{125} + \frac{.6000(1 - .6000)}{200}} = .1380$$

Chevrolet Impala and Honda Accord

$$CV_{13} = \sqrt{5.991}\sqrt{\frac{.5520(1 - .5520)}{125} + \frac{.7029(1 - .7029)}{175}} = .1379$$

Ford Fusion and Honda Accord

$$CV_{23} = \sqrt{5.991}\sqrt{\frac{.6000(1 - .6000)}{200} + \frac{.7029(1 - .7029)}{175}} = .1198$$

If the absolute value of any pairwise sample proportion difference $|\bar{p}_i - \bar{p}_j|$ exceeds its corresponding critical value, CV_{ij}, the pairwise difference is significant at the .05 level of significance and we can conclude that the two corresponding population proportions are different. The final step of the pairwise comparison procedure is summarized in Table 11.5.

The conclusion from the pairwise comparison procedure is that the only significant difference in customer loyalty occurs between the Chevrolet Impala and the Honda Accord. Our sample results indicate that the Honda Accord had a greater population proportion of owners who say they are likely to repurchase the Honda Accord. Thus, we can conclude that the Honda Accord ($\bar{p}_3 = .7029$) has a greater customer loyalty than the Chevrolet Impala ($\bar{p}_1 = .5520$).

The results of the study are inconclusive as to the comparative loyalty of the Ford Fusion. While the Ford Fusion did not show significantly different results when compared to the Chevrolet Impala or Honda Accord, a larger sample may have revealed a significant difference between Ford Fusion and the other two automobiles in terms of customer loyalty. It is not uncommon for a multiple comparison procedure to show significance for some pairwise comparisons and yet not show significance for other pairwise comparisons in the study.

TABLE 11.5 PAIRWISE COMPARISON TESTS FOR THE AUTOMOBILE BRAND LOYALTY STUDY

Pairwise Comparison	$\|\bar{p}_i - \bar{p}_j\|$	CV_{ij}	Significant if $\|\bar{p}_i - \bar{p}_j\| > CV_{ij}$
Chevrolet Impala vs. Ford Fusion	.0480	.1380	Not significant
Chevrolet Impala vs. Honda Accord	.1509	.1379	Significant
Ford Fusion vs. Honda Accord	.1029	.1198	Not significant

NOTES AND COMMENTS

1. In Section 11.1, we used the standard normal distribution and the z test statistic to conduct hypothesis tests about the proportions of two populations. However, the chi-square test introduced in this section can also be used to conduct the hypothesis test that the proportions of two populations are equal. The results will be the same under both test procedures and the value of the test statistic χ^2 will be equal to the square of the value of the test statistic z. An advantage of the methodology in Section 11.1 is that it can be used for either a one-tailed or a two-tailed hypothesis about the proportions of two populations whereas the chi-square test in this section can be used only for two-tailed tests. Exercise 16 will give you a chance to use the chi-square test for the hypothesis that the proportions of two populations are equal.

2. Each of the k populations in this section had two response outcomes, Yes or No. In effect, each population had a binomial distribution with parameter p, the population proportion of Yes responses. An extension of the chi-square procedure in this section applies when each of the k populations has three or more possible responses. In this case, each population is said to be a **multinomial population**; that is, each of the k populations has a multinomial distribution. The chi-square calculations for the expected frequencies, e_{ij}, and the test statistic, χ^2, are the same as shown in expressions (11.8) and (11.9). The only difference is that the null hypothesis assumes that the multinomial distribution for the response variable is the same for all populations. With r responses for each of the k populations, the chi-square test statistic has $(r - 1)(k - 1)$ degrees of freedom. Exercise 18 will give you a chance to use the chi-square test to compare three populations with multinomial distributions.

Exercises

Methods

11. Use the sample data below to test the hypotheses

$$H_0: p_1 = p_2 = p_3$$
$$H_a: \text{Not all population proportions are equal}$$

where p_i is the population proportion of Yes responses for population i. Using a .05 level of significance, what is the p-value and what is your conclusion?

	Populations		
Response	1	2	3
Yes	150	150	96
No	100	150	104

12. Reconsider the observed frequencies in exercise 11.
    a. Compute the sample proportion for each population.
    b. Use the multiple comparison procedure to determine which population proportions differ significantly. Use a .05 level of significance.

Applications

13. The sample data below represent the number of late and on time flights for Delta, United, and US Airways (Bureau of Transportation Statistics, March 2012).

	Airline		
Flight	Delta	United	US Airways
Late	39	51	56
On Time	261	249	344

a. Formulate the hypotheses for a test that will determine if the population proportion of late flights is the same for all three airlines.

b. Conduct the hypothesis test with a .05 level of significance. What is the *p*-value and what is your conclusion?

c. Compute the sample proportion of late flights for each airline. What is the overall proportion of late flights for the three airlines?

14. Benson Manufacturing is considering ordering electronic components from three different suppliers. The suppliers may differ in terms of quality in that the proportion or percentage of defective components may differ among the suppliers. To evaluate the proportion of defective components for the suppliers, Benson has requested a sample shipment of 500 components from each supplier. The number of defective components and the number of good components found in each shipment are as follows.

	Supplier		
Component	A	B	C
Defective	15	20	40
Good	485	480	460

a. Formulate the hypotheses that can be used to test for equal proportions of defective components provided by the three suppliers.

b. Using a .05 level of significance, conduct the hypothesis test. What is the *p*-value and what is your conclusion?

c. Conduct a multiple comparison test to determine if there is an overall best supplier or if one supplier can be eliminated because of poor quality.

15. Kate Sanders, a researcher in the department of biology at IPFW University, studied the effect of agriculture contaminants on the stream fish population in Northeastern Indiana (April 2012). Specially designed traps collected samples of fish at each of four stream locations. A research question was, Did the differences in agricultural contaminants found at the four locations alter the proportion of the fish population by gender? Observed frequencies were as follows.

	Stream Locations			
Gender	A	B	C	D
Male	49	44	49	39
Female	41	46	36	44

a. Focusing on the proportion of male fish at each location, test the hypothesis that the population proportions are equal for all four locations. Use a .05 level of significance. What is the *p*-value and what is your conclusion?

b. Does it appear that differences in agricultural contaminants found at the four locations altered the fish population by gender?

Exercise 16 shows a chi-square test can be used when the hypothesis is about the equality of two population proportions.

16. A tax preparation firm is interested in comparing the quality of work at two of its regional offices. The observed frequencies showing the number of sampled returns with errors and the number of sampled returns that were correct are as follows.

	Regional Office	
Return	Office 1	Office 2
Error	35	27
Correct	215	273

   a. What are the sample proportions of returns with errors at the two offices?
   b. Use the chi-square test procedure to see if there is a significant difference between the population proportion of error rates for the two offices. Test the null hypothesis $H_0: p_1 = p_2$ with a .10 level of significance. What is the *p*-value and what is your conclusion? *Note*: We generally use the chi-square test of equal proportions when there are three or more populations, but this example shows that the same chi-square test can be used for testing equal proportions with two populations.
   c. In Section 11.1, a *z* test was used to conduct the above test. Either a χ^2 test statistic or a *z* test statistic may be used to test the hypothesis. However, when we want to make inferences about the proportions for two populations, we generally prefer the *z* test statistic procedure. Refer to the Notes and Comments at the end of this section and comment on why the *z* test statistic provides the user with more options for inferences about the proportions of two populations.

17. Social networking is becoming more and more popular around the world. Pew Research Center used a survey of adults in several countries to determine the percentage of adults who use social networking sites (*USA Today*, February 8, 2012). Assume that the results for surveys in Great Britain, Israel, Russia, and United States are as follows.

	Country			
Use Social Networking Sites	Great Britain	Israel	Russia	United States
Yes	344	265	301	500
No	456	235	399	500

   a. Conduct a hypothesis test to determine whether the proportion of adults using social networking sites is equal for all four countries. What is the *p*-value? Using a .05 level of significance, what is your conclusion?
   b. What are the sample proportions for each of the four countries? Which country has the largest proportion of adults using social networking sites?
   c. Using a .05 level of significance, conduct multiple pairwise comparison tests among the four countries. What is your conclusion?

Exercise 18 shows a chi-square test can also be used for multiple population tests when the categorical response variable has three or more outcomes.

18. A manufacturer is considering purchasing parts from three different suppliers. The parts received from the suppliers are classified as having a minor defect, having a major defect, or being good. Test results from samples of parts received from each of the three suppliers are shown below. Note that any test with these data is no longer a test of proportions for the three supplier populations because the categorical response variable has three outcomes: minor defect, major defect, and good.

| | Supplier | | |
Part Tested	A	B	C
Minor Defect	15	13	21
Major Defect	5	11	5
Good	130	126	124

Using the data above, conduct a hypothesis test to determine if the distribution of defects is the same for the three suppliers. Use the chi-square test calculations as presented in this section with the exception that a table with r rows and c columns results in a chi-square test statistic with $(r - 1)(c - 1)$ degrees of freedom. Using a .05 level of significance, what is the p-value and what is your conclusion.

11.3   Test of Independence

An important application of a chi-square test involves using sample data to test for the independence of two categorical variables. For this test we take one sample from a population and record the observations for two categorical variables. We will summarize the data by counting the number of responses for each combination of a category for variable 1 and a category for variable 2. The null hypothesis for this test is that the two categorical variables are independent. Thus, the test is referred to as a **test of independence**. We will illustrate this test with the following example.

A beer industry association conducts a survey to determine the preferences of beer drinkers for light, regular, and dark beers. A sample of 200 beer drinkers is taken with each person in the sample asked to indicate a preference for one of the three types of beers: light, regular, or dark. At the end of the survey questionnaire, the respondent is asked to provide information on a variety of demographics including gender: male or female. A research question of interest to the association is whether preference for the three types of beer is independent of the gender of the beer drinker. If the two categorical variables, beer preference and gender, are independent, beer preference does not depend on gender and the preference for light, regular, and dark beer can be expected to be the same for male and female beer drinkers. However, if the test conclusion is that the two categorical variables are not independent, we have evidence that beer preference is associated with or dependent upon the gender of the beer drinker. As a result, we can expect beer preferences to differ for male and female beer drinkers. In this case, a beer manufacturer could use this information to customize its promotions and advertising for the different target markets of male and female beer drinkers.

The hypotheses for this test of independence are as follows:

H_0: Beer preference is independent of gender

H_a: Beer preference is not independent of gender

The sample data will be summarized in a two-way table with beer preferences of light, regular, and dark as one of the variables and gender of male and female as the other variable. Since an objective of the study is to determine if there is difference between the beer preferences for male and female beer drinkers, we consider gender an explanatory variable and follow the usual practice of making the explanatory variable the column variable in the data tabulation table. The beer preference is the categorical response variable and is shown as the row variable. The sample results of the 200 beer drinkers in the study are summarized in Table 11.6.

TABLE 11.6 SAMPLE RESULTS FOR BEER PREFERENCES OF MALE AND FEMALE BEER DRINKERS (OBSERVED FREQUENCIES)

BeerPreference

		Gender		
		Male	Female	Total
Beer Preference	Light	51	39	90
	Regular	56	21	77
	Dark	25	8	33
	Total	132	68	200

© Cengage Learning

Because we have listed all possible combinations of beer preference and gender (that is, listed all contingencies for these two variables), tables such as Table 11.6 are called contingency tables.

The sample data are summarized based on the combination of beer preference and gender for the individual respondents. For example, 51 individuals in the study were males who preferred light beer, 56 individuals in the study were males who preferred regular beer, and so on. Let us now analyze the data in the table and test for independence of beer preference and gender.

First of all, since we selected a sample of beer drinkers, summarizing the data for each variable separately will provide some insights into the characteristics of the beer drinker population. For the categorical variable gender, we see 132 of the 200 in the sample were male. This gives us the estimate that 132/200 = .66, or 66%, of the beer drinker population is male. Similarly we estimate that 68/200 = .34, or 34%, of the beer drinker population is female. Thus male beer drinkers appear to outnumber female beer drinkers approximately 2 to 1. Sample proportions or percentages for the three types of beer are

Prefer Light Beer	90/200 = .450, or 45.0%
Prefer Regular Beer	77/200 = .385, or 38.5%
Prefer Dark Beer	33/200 = .165, or 16.5%

Across all beer drinkers in the sample, light beer is preferred most often and dark beer is preferred least often.

Let us now conduct the chi-square test to determine if beer preference and gender are independent. The computations and formulas used are the same as those used for the chi-square test in Section 11.2. Utilizing the observed frequencies in Table 11.6 for row i and column j, f_{ij}, we compute the expected frequencies, e_{ij}, under the assumption that the beer preferences and gender are independent. The computation of the expected frequencies follows the same logic and formula used in Section 11.2. Thus the expected frequency for row i and column j is given by

$$e_{ij} = \frac{(\text{Row } i \text{ Total})(\text{Column } j \text{ Total})}{\text{Sample Size}} \tag{11.11}$$

For example, $e_{11} = (90)(132)/200 = 59.40$ is the expected frequency for male beer drinkers who would prefer light beer if beer preference is independent of gender. Show that equation (11.11) can be used to find the other expected frequencies shown in Table 11.7.

Following the chi-square test procedure discussed in Section 11.2, we use the following expression to compute the value of the chi-square test statistic.

$$\chi^2 = \sum_i \sum_j \frac{(f_{ij} - e_{ij})^2}{e_{ij}} \tag{11.12}$$

TABLE 11.7   EXPECTED FREQUENCIES IF BEER PREFERENCE IS INDEPENDENT
OF THE GENDER OF THE BEER DRINKER

		Gender		
		Male	**Female**	**Total**
Beer Preference	**Light**	59.40	30.60	90
	Regular	50.82	26.18	77
	Dark	21.78	11.22	33
	Total	132	68	200

With r rows and c columns in the table, the chi-square distribution will have $(r - 1)(c - 1)$
degrees of freedom provided the expected frequency is at least 5 for each cell. Thus, in
this application we will use a chi-square distribution with $(3 - 1)(2 - 1) = 2$ degrees of
freedom. The complete steps to compute the chi-square test statistic are summarized in
Table 11.8.

We can use the upper tail area of the chi-square distribution with 2 degrees of freedom
and the p-value approach to determine whether the null hypothesis that beer preference is
independent of gender can be rejected. Using row two of the chi-square distribution table
shown in Table 11.4, we have the following:

Area in Upper Tail	**.10**	**.05**	**.025**	**.01**	**.005**
χ^2 **Value (2 df)**	4.605	5.991	7.378	9.210	10.597

$$\chi^2 = 6.45$$

Thus, we see the upper tail area at $\chi^2 = 6.45$ is between .05 and .025, and so the corresponding upper tail area or p-value must be between .05 and .025. With p-value $\leq$ .05, we reject
H_0 and conclude that beer preference is not independent of the gender of the beer drinker.
Stated another way, the study shows that beer preference can be expected to differ for male
and female beer drinkers. Minitab or Excel procedures provided in Appendix F can be used
to show $\chi^2 = 6.45$ with two degrees of freedom yields a p-value $= .0398$.

TABLE 11.8   COMPUTATION OF THE CHI-SQUARE TEST STATISTIC FOR THE TEST
OF INDEPENDENCE BETWEEN BEER PREFERENCE AND GENDER

Beer Preference	**Gender**	**Observed Frequency** f_{ij}	**Expected Frequency** e_{ij}	**Difference** $(f_{ij} - e_{ij})$	**Squared Difference** $(f_{ij} - e_{ij})^2$	**Squared Difference Divided by Expected Frequency** $(f_{ij} - e_{ij})^2/e_{ij}$
Light	Male	51	59.40	−8.40	70.56	1.19
Light	Female	39	30.60	8.40	70.56	2.31
Regular	Male	56	50.82	5.18	26.83	.53
Regular	Female	21	26.18	−5.18	26.83	1.02
Dark	Male	25	21.78	3.22	10.37	.48
Dark	Female	8	11.22	−3.22	10.37	.92
	Total	200	200			$\chi^2 = 6.45$

© Cengage Learning

Instead of using the *p*-value, we could use the critical value approach to draw the same conclusion. With $\alpha = .05$ and 2 degrees of freedom, the critical value for the chi-square test statistic is $\chi_{.05}^2 = 5.991$. The upper tail rejection region becomes

$$\text{Reject } H_0 \text{ if} \geq 5.991$$

With $6.45 \geq 5.991$, we reject H_0. Again we see that the *p*-value approach and the critical value approach provide the same conclusion.

While we now have evidence that beer preference and gender are not independent, we will need to gain additional insight from the data to assess the nature of the association between these two variables. One way to do this is to compute the probability of the beer preference responses for males and females separately. These calculations are as follows:

Beer Preference	Male	Female
Light	51/132 = .3864, or 38.64%	39/68 = .5735, or 57.35%
Regular	56/132 = .4242, or 42.42%	21/68 = .3088, or 30.88%
Dark	25/132 = .1894, or 18.94%	8/68 = .1176, or 11.76%

The bar chart for male and female beer drinkers of the three kinds of beer is shown in Figure 11.1.

What observations can you make about the association between beer preference and gender? For female beer drinkers in the sample, the highest preference is for light beer at 57.35%. For male beer drinkers in the sample, regular beer is most frequently preferred at 42.42%. While female beer drinkers have a higher preference for light beer than males, male beer drinkers have a higher preference for both regular beer and dark beer. Data visualization through bar charts such as shown in Figure 11.1 is helpful in gaining insight as to how two categorical variables are associated.

FIGURE 11.1 BAR CHART COMPARISON OF BEER PREFERENCE BY GENDER

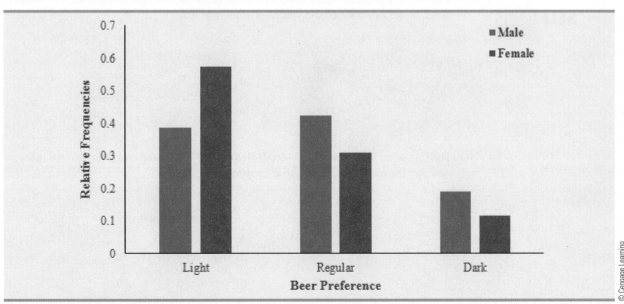

Before we leave this discussion, we summarize the steps for a test of independence.

The expected frequencies must all be 5 or more for the chi-square test to be valid.

CHI-SQUARE TEST FOR INDEPENDENCE OF TWO CATEGORICAL VARIABLES

1. State the null and alternative hypotheses.

   H_0: The two categorical variables are independent
   H_a: The two categorical variables are not independent

2. Select a random sample from the population and collect data for both variables for every element in the sample. Record the observed frequencies, f_{ij}, in a table with r rows and c columns.
3. Assume the null hypothesis is true and compute the expected frequencies, e_{ij}.
4. If the expected frequency, e_{ij}, is 5 or more for each cell, compute the test statistic:

This chi-square test is also a one-tailed test with rejection of H_0 occurring in the upper tail of a chi-square distribution with $(r-1)(c-1)$ degrees of freedom.

$$\chi^2 = \sum_i \sum_j \frac{(f_{ij} - e_{ij})^2}{e_{ij}}$$

5. Rejection rule:

p-value approach:	Reject H_0 if p-value $\leq \alpha$
Critical value approach:	Reject H_0 if $\chi^2 \geq \chi_\alpha^2$

   where the chi-square distribution has $(r-1)(c-1)$ degrees of freedom and α is the level of significance for the test.

Finally, if the null hypothesis of independence is rejected, summarizing the probabilities as shown in the above example will help the analyst determine where the association or dependence exists for the two categorical variables.

Exercises

Methods

19. The following table contains observed frequencies for a sample of 200. Test for independence of the row and column variables using $\alpha = .05$.

	Column Variable		
Row Variable	**A**	**B**	**C**
P	20	44	50
Q	30	26	30

20. The following table contains observed frequencies for a sample of 240. Test for independence of the row and column variables using $\alpha = .05$.

	Column Variable		
Row Variable	**A**	**B**	**C**
P	20	30	20
Q	30	60	25
R	10	15	30

Applications

21. A *Bloomberg Businessweek* subscriber study asked, "In the past 12 months, when traveling for business, what type of airline ticket did you purchase most often?" A second question asked if the type of airline ticket purchased most often was for domestic or international travel. Sample data obtained are shown in the following table.

	Type of Flight	
Type of Ticket	Domestic	International
First Class	29	22
Business Class	95	121
Economy Class	518	135

a. Using a .05 level of significance, is the type of ticket purchased independent of the type of flight? What is your conclusion?
b. Discuss any dependence that exists between the type of ticket and type of flight.

WorkforcePlan

22. A Deloitte employment survey asked a sample of human resource executives how their company planned to change its workforce over the next 12 months (*INC. Magazine,* February 2012). A categorical response variable showed three options: The company plans to hire and add to the number of employees, the company plans no change in the number of employees, or the company plans to lay off and reduce the number of employees. Another categorical variable indicated if the company was private or public. Sample data for 180 companies are summarized as follows.

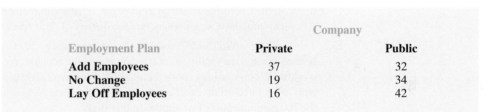

	Company	
Employment Plan	Private	Public
Add Employees	37	32
No Change	19	34
Lay Off Employees	16	42

a. Conduct a test of independence to determine if the employment plan for the next 12 months is independent of the type of company. At a .05 level of significance, what is your conclusion?
b. Discuss any differences in the employment plans for private and public companies over the next 12 months.

23. Health insurance benefits vary by the size of the company (*Atlanta Business Chronicle,* December 31, 2010). The sample data below show the number of companies providing health insurance for small, medium, and large companies. For purposes of this study, small companies are companies that have fewer than 100 employees. Medium-sized companies have 100 to 999 employees, and large companies have 1000 or more employees. The questionnaire sent to 225 employees asked whether or not the employee had health insurance and then asked the employee to indicate the size of the company.

	Size of the Company		
Health Insurance	Small	Medium	Large
Yes	36	65	88
No	14	10	12

a. Conduct a test of independence to determine whether health insurance coverage is independent of the size of the company. What is the p-value? Using a .05 level of significance, what is your conclusion?

b. A newspaper article indicated employees of small companies are more likely to lack health insurance coverage. Use percentages based on the above data to support this conclusion.

AutoQuality

24. A vehicle quality survey asked new owners a variety of questions about their recently purchased automobile (J.D. Power and Associates, March 2012). One question asked for the owner's rating of the vehicle using categorical responses of average, outstanding, and exceptional. Another question asked for the owner's education level with the categorical responses some high school, high school graduate, some college, and college graduate. Assume the sample data below are for 500 owners who had recently purchased an automobile.

Quality Rating	Education			
	Some HS	HS Grad	Some College	College Grad
Average	35	30	20	60
Outstanding	45	45	50	90
Exceptional	20	25	30	50

a. Use a .05 level of significance and a test of independence to determine if a new owner's vehicle quality rating is independent of the owner's education. What is the p-value and what is your conclusion?

b. Use the overall percentage of average, outstanding, and exceptional ratings to comment upon how new owners rate the quality of their recently purchased automobiles.

25. *The Wall Street Journal* Corporate Perceptions Study 2011 surveyed readers and asked how each rated the quality of management and the reputation of the company for over 250 worldwide corporations. Both the quality of management and the reputation of the company were rated on an excellent, good, and fair categorical scale. Assume the sample data for 200 respondents below applies to this study.

Quality of Management	Reputation of Company		
	Excellent	Good	Fair
Excellent	40	25	5
Good	35	35	10
Fair	25	10	15

a. Use a .05 level of significance and test for independence of the quality of management and the reputation of the company. What is the p-value and what is your conclusion?

b. If there is a dependence or association between the two ratings, discuss and use probabilities to justify your answer.

26. The race for the 2012 Academy Award for Actress in a Leading Role was extremely tight, featuring several worthy performances (ABC News online, February 22, 2013). The nominees were Jessica Chastain for *Zero Dark Thirty*, Jennifer Lawrence for *Silver Linings Playbook*, Emmanuelle Riva for *Amour*, Quvenzhané Wallis for *Beasts of the Southern Wild*, and Naomi Watts for *The Impossible*. In a survey, movie fans who had seen each of the movies for which these five actresses had been nominated were asked to select the

actress who was most deserving of the 2013 Academy Award for Actress in a Leading Role. The responses follow.

	18–30	31–44	45–58	Over 58
Jessica Chastain	51	50	41	42
Jennifer Lawrence	63	55	37	50
Emmanuelle Riva	15	44	56	74
Quvenzhané Wallis	48	25	22	31
Naomi Watts	36	65	62	33

a. How large was the sample in this survey?

b. Jennifer Lawrence received the 2012 Academy Award for Actress in a Leading Role for her performance in *Silver Linings Playbook*. Did the respondents favor Ms. Lawrence?

c. At $\alpha = .05$, conduct a hypothesis test to determine whether people's attitude toward the actress who was most deserving of the 2013 Academy Award for Actress in a Leading Role is independent of respondent age. What is your conclusion?

27. The National Sleep Foundation used a survey to determine whether hours of sleep per night are independent of age. A sample of individuals was asked to indicate the number of hours of sleep per night with categorical options: fewer than 6 hours, 6 to 6.9 hours, 7 to 7.9 hours, and 8 hours or more. Later in the survey, the individuals were asked to indicate their age with categorical options: age 39 or younger and age 40 or older. Sample data follow.

	Age Group	
Hours of Sleep	**39 or Younger**	**40 or Older**
Fewer Than 6	38	36
6 to 6.9	60	57
7 to 7.9	77	75
8 or More	65	92

a. Conduct a test of independence to determine whether hours of sleep are independent of age. Using a .05 level of significance, what is the *p*-value and what is your conclusion?

b. What is your estimate of the percentages of individuals who sleep fewer than 6 hours, 6 to 6.9 hours, 7 to 7.9 hours, and 8 hours or more per night?

28. On a syndicated television show the two hosts often create the impression that they strongly disagree about which movies are best. Each movie review is categorized as Pro ("thumbs up"), Con ("thumbs down"), or Mixed. The results of 160 movie ratings by the two hosts are shown here.

	Host B		
Host A	**Con**	**Mixed**	**Pro**
Con	24	8	13
Mixed	8	13	11
Pro	10	9	64

Use a test of independence with a .01 level of significance to analyze the data. What is your conclusion?

Summary

In this chapter, we described statistical procedures for comparisons involving proportions and the contingency table test for independence of two variables. In the first section, we compared a proportion for one population with the same proportion from another population. We described how to construct an interval estimate for the difference between the proportions and how to conduct a hypothesis test to learn whether the difference between the proportions was statistically significant.

In Section 11.2 we focused on testing the equality of population proportions for three or more populations. There we saw that this test is based on independent random samples selected from each of the populations. The sample data show the counts for each of two categorical responses for each population. The null hypothesis is that the population proportions are equal. Rejection of the null hypothesis supports the conclusion that the population proportions are not all equal. A chi-square test statistic is used to test this null hypothesis; this chi-square test is based on the differences between observed frequencies and expected frequencies. Expected frequencies are computed under the assumption that the null hypothesis is true. This chi-square test is an upper tailed test; large differences between observed and expected frequencies provide a large value for the chi-square test statistic and indicate that the null hypothesis should be rejected.

Section 11.3 was concerned with tests of independence for two variables. A test of independence for two variables is an extension of the methodology employed in the goodness of fit test for a multinomial population. A contingency table is used to determine the observed and expected frequencies. Then a chi-square value is computed. Large chi-square values, caused by large differences between observed and expected frequencies, lead to the rejection of the null hypothesis of independence.

Glossary

Pooled estimator of p An estimator of a population proportion obtained by computing a weighted average of the sample proportions obtained from two independent samples.

Marascuilo procedure A method for simultaneously comparing all pairs of population proportions.

Multinomial population A population in which each element is assigned to one and only one of several categories. The multinomial distribution extends the binomial distribution from two to three or more outcomes.

Test of independence A method of assessing whether two categorical variables are associated or dependent.

Contingency table A table used to summarize observed and expected frequencies for a test of independence.

Key Formulas

Point Estimator of the Difference Between Two Population Proportions

$$\bar{p}_1 - \bar{p}_2 \tag{11.1}$$

Standard Error of $\bar{p}_1 - \bar{p}_2$

$$\sigma_{\bar{p}_1 - \bar{p}_2} = \sqrt{\frac{p_1(1 - p_1)}{n_1} + \frac{p_2(1 - p_2)}{n_2}} \tag{11.2}$$

Interval Estimate of the Difference Between Two Population Proportions

$$\bar{p}_1 - \bar{p}_2 \pm z_{\alpha/2}\sqrt{\frac{\bar{p}_1(1 - \bar{p}_1)}{n_1} + \frac{\bar{p}_2(1 - \bar{p}_2)}{n_2}} \qquad (11.4)$$

Standard Error of $\bar{p}_1 - \bar{p}_2$ when $p_1 = p_2 = p$

$$\sigma_{\bar{p}_1 - \bar{p}_2} = \sqrt{p(1 - p)\left(\frac{1}{n_1} + \frac{1}{n_2}\right)} \qquad (11.5)$$

Pooled Estimator of p when $p_1 = p_2 = p$

$$\bar{p} = \frac{n_1\bar{p}_1 + n_2\bar{p}_2}{n_1 + n_2} \qquad (11.6)$$

Test Statistic for Hypothesis Tests About $p_1 - p_2$

$$z = \frac{(\bar{p}_1 - \bar{p}_2)}{\sqrt{\bar{p}(1 - \bar{p})\left(\frac{1}{n_1} + \frac{1}{n_2}\right)}} \qquad (11.7)$$

Expected Frequencies Under the Assumption H_0 Is True

$$e_{ij} = \frac{(\text{Row } i \text{ Total})(\text{Column } j \text{ Total})}{\text{Total Sample Size}} \qquad (11.8)$$

Chi-Square Test Statistic

$$\chi^2 = \sum_i \sum_j \frac{(f_{ij} - e_{ij})^2}{e_{ij}} \qquad (11.9)$$

Critical Values for the Marascuilo Pairwise Comparison Procedure for k Population Proportions

$$CV_{ij} = \sqrt{\chi_\alpha^2}\sqrt{\frac{\bar{p}_i(1 - \bar{p}_i)}{n_i} + \frac{\bar{p}_j(1 - \bar{p}_j)}{n_j}} \qquad (11.10)$$

Supplementary Exercises

29. Sudoku puzzles have become very popular in recent years; 31.1% of members of households with annual income of at least $100,000 worked Sudoku puzzles in 2012 (Statistica.com, March 10, 2013). Are there differences between the genders? The proportion of women and men from these households who worked Sudoku puzzles in 2012 can be estimated from the following sample data.

Gender	Sample size	Worked Sudoku Puzzles
Men	1200	312
Women	1600	512

a. State the hypotheses that can be used to test for a difference between the proportion for the population of men and the proportion for the population of women who worked Sudoku puzzles.

b. What is the sample proportion of men who worked Sudoku puzzles? What is the sample proportion of women?

c. Conduct the hypothesis test and compute the p-value. At a .05 level of significance, what is your conclusion?

d. What is the margin of error and 95% confidence interval estimate of the difference between the population proportions?

30. A large automobile insurance company selected samples of single and married male policyholders and recorded the number who made an insurance claim over the preceding three-year period.

Single Policyholders	Married Policyholders
$n_1 = 400$	$n_2 = 900$
Number making claims = 76	Number making claims = 90

a. Use $\alpha = .05$. Test to determine whether the claim rates differ between single and married male policyholders.

b. Provide a 95% confidence interval for the difference between the proportions for the two populations.

31. Medical tests were conducted to learn about drug-resistant tuberculosis. Of 142 cases tested in New Jersey, 9 were found to be drug-resistant. Of 268 cases tested in Texas, 5 were found to be drug-resistant. Do these data suggest a statistically significant difference between the proportions of drug-resistant cases in the two states? Use a .02 level of significance. What is the p-value, and what is your conclusion?

Occupancy

32. Vacation occupancy rates were expected to be up during March 2008 in Myrtle Beach, South Carolina (*The Sun News*, February 29, 2008). Data in the file named Occupancy will allow you to replicate the findings presented in the newspaper. The data show units rented and not rented for a random sample of vacation properties during the first week of March 2007 and March 2008.

a. Estimate the proportion of units rented during the first week of March 2007 and the first week of March 2008.

b. Provide a 95% confidence interval for the difference in proportions.

c. On the basis of your findings, does it appear March rental rates for 2008 will be up from those a year earlier?

33. The bullish sentiment of individual investors was 27.6% (*AAII Journal*, February 2009). The bullish sentiment was reported to be 48.7% one week earlier and 39.7% one month earlier. The sentiment measures were based on a poll conducted by the American Association of Individual Investors. Assume that each bullish sentiment measure was based on a sample of 240 investors.

a. Develop a 95% confidence interval for the difference between the bullish sentiment measures for the most recent two weeks.

b. Develop hypotheses so that rejection of the null hypothesis will allow us to conclude that the most recent bullish sentiment is weaker than that of one month earlier.
c. Conduct a hypothesis test of part (b) using $\alpha=.01$. What is your conclusion?

34. Phoenix Marketing International identified Bridgeport, Connecticut, Los Alamos, New Mexico, Naples, Florida, and Washington D.C. as the four U.S. cities with the highest percentage of millionaires (*USA Today*, December 7, 2011). Data consistent with that study show the following number of millionaires for samples of individuals from each of the four cities.

	City			
Milionaire	Bridgeport	Los Alamos	Naples	Washington, DC
Yes	44	35	36	34
No	456	265	364	366

a. What is the estimate of the percentage of millionaires in each of these cities?
b. Using a .05 level of significance, test for the equality of the population proportion of millionaires for these four cities. What is the *p*-value and what is your conclusion?

35. In a quality control test of parts manufactured at Dabco Corporation, an engineer sampled parts produced on the first, second, and third shifts. The research study was designed to determine if the population proportion of good parts was the same for all three shifts. Sample data follow.

	Production Shift		
Quality	First	Second	Third
Good	285	368	176
Defective	15	32	24

a. Using a .05 level of significance, conduct a hypothesis test to determine if the population proportion of good parts is the same for all three shifts. What is the *p*-value and what is your conclusion?
b. If the conclusion is that the population proportions are not all equal, use a multiple-comparison procedure to determine how the shifts differ in terms of quality. What shift or shifts need to improve the quality of parts produced?

36. Efforts by airlines to improve on-time arrival rates are showing results. Boston.com (December 22, 2012) reports that in the first 10 months of 2012 on-time arrival rates at U.S. airports were the highest they have been since 2003; during this period 82% of flights landed within 15 minutes of their scheduled time. Are there differences among the major airlines? The following data show the number of on-time arrivals for samples of flights taken from seven major U.S. airlines (American Airlines, Continental Airlines, Delta Air Lines, JetBlue Airways, Southwest Airlines, United Airlines, and US Airways) in 2012.

Arrivals	American Airlines	Continental Airlines	Delta Air Lines	JetBlue Airways	Southwest Airlines	United Airlines	US Airways
On-Time	83	54	96	60	69	66	68
Late	16	18	21	22	23	15	12

a. Use the sample data to calculate the point estimate of the population proportion of on-time arrivals for each of these seven airlines.

b. Conduct a hypothesis test to determine if the population proportion of on-time flights in 2012 is equal for these seven airlines. Using a .05 level of significance, what is the *p*-value and what is your conclusion?

37. The five most popular art museums in the world are Musée du Louvre, the Metropolitan Museum of Art, British Museum, National Gallery, and Tate Modern (*The Art Newspaper*, April 2012). Which of these five museums would visitors most frequently rate as spectacular? Samples of recent visitors of each of these museums were taken, and the results of these samples follow.

	Musée du Louvre	Metropolitan Museum of Art	British Museum	National Gallery	Tate Modern
Rated Spectacular	113	94	96	78	88
Did Not Rate Spectacular	37	46	64	42	22

a. Use the sample data to calculate the point estimate of the population proportion of visitors who rated each of these museums as spectacular.
b. Conduct a hypothesis test to determine if the population proportion of visitors who rated the museum as spectacular is equal for these five museums. Using a .05 level of significance, what is the *p*-value and what is your conclusion?

38. The Golden Snow Globe website shows that four U.S. cities with a population of at least 100,000 (Rochester, NY; Salt Lake City, UT; Madison, WI; Bridgeport, CT) had recorded between 60 and 70 inches of snow for the winter of 2012–13 as of the evening of March 9, 2013 (Golden Snow Globe website, March 13, 2013). Such large amounts of snowfall can make the local roads difficult to negotiate. Is there a difference in how well these four cities keep streets clear of snow? A sample of truck drivers who drive in each of these four cities was taken, and the drivers were asked whether the city does a satisfactory job in keeping its streets clear of snow. The results of these samples follow.

	Rochester, NY	Salt Lake City, UT	Madison, WI	Bridgeport, CT
Satisfactory	27	35	29	24
Not Satisfactory	21	21	18	21

a. Use the sample data to calculate the point estimate of the population proportion of truck drivers who rated each of these cities as satisfactory in keeping its streets clear of snow.
b. Conduct a hypothesis test to determine if the population proportion of truck drivers who rate whether the city does a satisfactory job of keeping its streets clear of snow is equal for these four cities. Using a .05 level of significance, what is the *p*-value and what is your conclusion?

39. A sample of parts provided the following contingency table data on part quality by production shift.

Shift	Number Good	Number Defective
First	368	32
Second	285	15
Third	176	24

Use $\alpha = .05$ and test the hypothesis that part quality is independent of the production shift. What is your conclusion?

40. *The Wall Street Journal* Subscriber Study showed data on the employment status of subscribers. Sample results corresponding to subscribers of the eastern and western editions are shown here.

| | Region | |
Employment Status	Eastern Edition	Western Edition
Full-Time	1105	574
Part-Time	31	15
Self-Employed/Consultant	229	186
Not Employed	485	344

Use $\alpha = .05$ and test the hypothesis that employment status is independent of the region. What is your conclusion?

41. A lending institution supplied the following data on loan approvals by four loan officers. Use $\alpha = .05$ and test to determine whether the loan approval decision is independent of the loan officer reviewing the loan application.

| | Loan Approval Decision | |
Loan Officer	Approved	Rejected
Miller	24	16
McMahon	17	13
Games	35	15
Runk	11	9

42. A Pew Research Center survey asked respondents if they would rather live in a place with a slower pace of life or a place with a faster pace of life (*USA Today*, February 13, 2009). Consider the following data showing a sample of preferences expressed by 150 men and 150 women.

| | Preferred Pace of Life | | |
Respondent	Slower	No Preference	Faster
Men	102	9	39
Women	111	12	27

a. Combine the samples of men and women. What is the overall percentage of respondents who prefer to live in a place with a slower pace of life? What is the overall percentage of respondents who prefer to live in a place with a faster pace of life? What is your conclusion?

b. Is the preferred pace of life independent of the respondent? Use $\alpha = .05$. What is your conclusion? What is your recommendation?

43. According to Ezine @rticles, the most popular flavors of ice cream in the United States are vanilla, chocolate, butter pecan, and strawberry (Ezine@rticles website, March 9, 2013), but are these preferences and age of the consumer independent? In a random survey 1000

consumers were asked their age and which of these four flavors of ice cream they preferred. The survey yielded the following results.

	Under 18	18–30	31–44	45–58	Over 58
Vanilla	155	108	99	100	129
Chocolate	39	53	47	28	30
Butter Pecan	12	15	21	20	43
Strawberry	23	14	13	17	34

Do these data suggest that consumer preference for these four flavors of ice cream and age of the consumer are independent? Use a .05 level of significance. What is your conclusion?

44. The office occupancy rates were reported for four California metropolitan areas. Do the following data suggest that the office vacancies were independent of metropolitan area? Use a .05 level of significance. What is your conclusion?

Occupancy Status	Los Angeles	San Diego	San Francisco	San Jose
Occupied	160	116	192	174
Vacant	40	34	33	26

Case Problem 1　A Bipartisan Agenda for Change

In a study conducted by Zogby International for the *Democrat and Chronicle,* more than 700 New Yorkers were polled to determine whether the New York state government works. Respondents surveyed were asked questions involving pay cuts for state legislators, restrictions on lobbyists, terms limits for legislators, and whether state citizens should be able to put matters directly on the state ballot for a vote. The results regarding several proposed reforms had broad support, crossing all demographic and political lines.

Suppose that a follow-up survey of 100 individuals who live in the western region of New York was conducted. The party affiliation (Democrat, Independent, Republican) of each individual surveyed was recorded, as well as the responses to the following three questions.

1. Should legislative pay be cut for every day the state budget is late?
   Yes _____　No _____
2. Should there be more restrictions on lobbyists?
   Yes _____　No _____
3. Should there be term limits requiring that legislators serve a fixed number of years?
   Yes _____　No _____

WEB file

NYReform

The responses were coded using 1 for a Yes response and 2 for a No response. The complete data set is available on the data disk in the file named NYReform.

Managerial Report

1. Use descriptive statistics to summarize the data from this study. What are your preliminary conclusions about the independence of the response (Yes or No) and party affiliation for each of the three questions in the survey?
2. With regard to question 1, test for the independence of the response (Yes and No) and party affiliation. Use $\alpha = .05$.

3. With regard to question 2, test for the independence of the response (Yes and No) and party affiliation. Use $\alpha = .05$.
4. With regard to question 3, test for the independence of the response (Yes and No) and party affiliation. Use $\alpha = .05$.
5. Does it appear that there is broad support for change across all political lines? Explain.

Appendix 11.1 Inferences About Two Population Proportions Using Minitab

Confidence Intervals and Hypothesis Tests

TaxPrep

We describe the use of Minitab to develop confidence intervals and conduct hypothesis tests about the difference between two population proportions. We will use the data on tax preparation errors presented in Section 11.1. The sample results for 250 tax returns prepared at office 1 are in column C1 and the sample results for 300 tax returns prepared at office 2 are in column C2. Yes denotes an error was found in the tax return and No indicates no error was found. The procedure we describe provides both a 90% confidence interval estimate of the difference between the two population proportions and hypothesis testing results for $H_0: p_1 - p_2 = 0$ vs. $H_a: p_1 - p_2 \neq 0$.

> **Step 1.** Select the **Stat** menu
> **Step 2.** Choose **Basic Statistics**
> **Step 3.** Choose **2 Proportions**
> **Step 4.** When the 2 Proportions (Test and Confidence Interval) dialog box appears:
>   Select **Samples in different columns**
>   Enter C1 in the **First** box
>   Enter C2 in the **Second** box
>   Select **Options**
> **Step 5.** When the 2 Proportions - Options dialog box appears:
>   Enter 90 in the **Confidence level** box
>   Enter 0 in the **Test difference** box
>   Enter not equal in the **Alternative** box
>   Select **Use pooled estimate of p for test**
>   Click **OK**
> **Step 6.** Click **OK**

Step 5 may be modified to provide different confidence levels, different hypothesized values, and different forms of the hypotheses.

In the tax preparation example, the data are qualitative. Yes and No are used to indicate whether an error is present. In modules involving proportions, Minitab calculates proportions for the response coming second in alphabetic order. Thus, in the tax preparation example, Minitab computes the proportion of Yes responses, which is the proportion we wanted.

If Minitab's alphabetical ordering does not compute the proportion for the response of interest, we can fix it. Select any cell in the data column, go to the Minitab menu bar, and select Editor > Column > Value Order. This sequence will provide the option of entering a user-specified order. Simply make sure that the response of interest is listed second in the define-an-order box. Minitab's 2 Proportion routine will then provide the confidence interval and hypothesis testing results for the population proportion of interest.

Finally, we note that Minitab's 2 Proportion routine uses a computational procedure different from the procedure described in the text. Thus, the Minitab output may provide slightly different interval estimates and slightly different p-values. However, results from the two methods should be close and are expected to provide the same interpretation and conclusion.

Appendix 11.2 Chi-Square Tests Using Minitab

Test the Equality of Three or More Population Proportions and Test of Independence

The Minitab procedure is identical for both of these applications. We will describe the procedure for the following situations.

1. A data set shows the responses for each element in the sample.
2. A tabular summary of the data shows the observed frequencies for the response categories.

AutoLoyalty

We begin with the automobile loyalty example presented in Section 11.2. Responses for a sample of 500 automobile owners are contained in the file named AutoLoyalty. Column C1 shows the population the owner belongs to (Chevrolet Impala, Ford Fusion, or Honda Accord) and column C2 contains the likely to purchase response (Yes or No). The Minitab steps to conduct a chi-square test using the data set follow.

Step 1. Select the **Stat** menu
Step 2. Select **Tables**
Step 3. Choose **Cross Tabulation and Chi-Square**
Step 4. When then Cross Tabulation and Chi-Square dialog box appears:
　　　　Enter C2 in the **For Rows** box
　　　　Enter C1 in the **For Columns** box
　　　　Under the **Display** options, select **Counts**
　　　　Select **Chi-Square**
Step 5. When the Cross Tabulation - Chi-Square dialog box appears:
　　　　Select **Chi-Square analysis**
　　　　Click **OK**
Step 6. Click **OK**

The output shows both a tabular summary of the data and the chi-square test results.

This procedure can also be used for a test of independence. Use the file named BeerPreference to conduct the test for the example in Section 11.3.

Next let us show how to conduct this test if a tabular summary of the data showing observed frequencies has already been obtained. We begin with a new Minitab worksheet and label the columns C1 to C3 with the titles of the three populations: Chevrolet Impala, Ford Fusion, and Honda Accord. Then we enter the observed frequencies of the Yes and No responses for each population in its corresponding column. Thus, we enter 69 and 56 in column 1, enter 120 and 80 in column 2, and enter 123 and 52 in column 3. The Minitab steps for this test are as follows.

Step 1. Select the **Stat** menu
Step 2. Select **Tables**
Step 3. Choose **Chi-Square Test (Two-Way Table in Worksheet)**
Step 4. When the Chi-Square Test dialog box appears:
　　　　Enter C1-C3 in the **Columns containing the table** box
　　　　Click **OK**

Appendix 11.3 Chi-Square Tests Using Excel

The Excel procedure for tests for the equality of population proportions and tests of independence are basically the same as both make use of the Excel chi-square function CHISQ.TEST. Regardless of the application, the user must do the following before creating an Excel worksheet that will perform the test.

1. Select a sample from the population or populations and record the data
2. Summarize the data to show observed frequencies in a tabular format

Excel's PivotTable can be used to summarize the data in step 2. Since this procedure was previously presented in Appendix 2.2, we shall not describe it in this appendix. Rather we will begin the Excel chi-square test procedure with the understanding that the user has already determined the observed frequencies for the study.

AutoLoyalty

Let us demonstrate the Excel chi-square test by considering the automobile loyalty example presented in Section 11.2. Using the data in the file named AutoLoyalty and the Excel PivotTable procedure, we obtained the observed frequencies shown in the Excel worksheet of Figure 11.2. The user must next insert Excel formulas in the worksheet to compute the expected frequencies. Using equation (11.8), the Excel formulas for expected frequencies are as shown in the background worksheet of Figure 11.2.

The last step is to insert the Excel function CHISQ.TEST. The format of this function is as follows:

$$=\text{CHISQ.TEST(Observed Frequency Cells, Expected Frequency Cells)}$$

In Figure 11.2, the observed frequency cells are B7 to D8, written B7:D8 and the expected frequency cells are B16 to D17, written B16:D17. The function =CHISQ.TEST(B7:D8,B16:D17) is shown in cell E20 of the background worksheet. This function does all the chi-square test computations and returns the *p*-value for the test.

The Excel worksheet shown in Figure 11.2 is available in the file ChiSquare.

The test of independence summarizes the observed frequencies in a tabular format very similar to the one shown in Figure 11.2. The formulas to compute expected frequencies are also very similar to the formulas shown in the background worksheet. For the goodness of fit test, the user provides the observed frequencies in a column rather than a

FIGURE 11.2 EXCEL WORKSHEET FOR THE AUTOMOBILE LOYALITY STUDY

ChiSquare

table. The user must also provide the associated expected frequencies in another column. Lastly, the CHISQ.TEST function is used to obtain the *p*-value as described above.

Appendix 11.4 Inferences About Two Population Proportions Using StatTools

Confidence Intervals

WEB file

TaxPrep

We use the data on tax preparation errors presented in Section 11.1. The sample results for 250 tax returns prepared at office 1 are in column C1 and the sample results for 300 tax returns prepared at office 2 are in column C2. Yes denotes an error was found in the tax return and No indicates no error was found. Begin by using the Data Set Manager to create a StatTools data set using the procedure described in the appendix to Chapter 1. The following steps will provide a 90% confidence interval estimate of the difference between the two population proportions.

Step 1. Click the **StatTools** tab on the Ribbon
Step 2. In the **Analyses** group, click **Statistical Inference**
Step 3. Choose **Confidence Interval**
Step 4. Choose **Proportion**
Step 5. When the StatTools - Confidence Interval for Proportion dialog box appears:
 In the **Analysis Type** box, select **Two-Sample Analysis**
 In the **Variables** section, select both **Office 1** and **Office 2**
 In the **Categories to Analyze** section, select **Yes**
 In the **Options** section, enter 90% in the **Confidence Level** box
 Click **OK**
Step 6. When the StatTools dialog box appears:
 Click **OK**
Step 7. When the Choose Variable Ordering dialog box appears:
 Click **OK**

Hypothesis Tests

WEB file

TaxPrep

We use the data on tax preparation errors presented in Section 11.1. Begin by using the Data Set Manager to create a StatTools data set using the procedure described in the appendix to Chapter 1. The follow steps will test the hypothesis that there is no difference between the two population proportions.

Step 1. Click the **StatTools** tab on the Ribbon
Step 2. In the **Analyses** group, click **Statistical Inference**
Step 3. Choose **Hypothesis Test**
Step 4. Choose **Proportion**
Step 5. When the StatTools - Hypothesis Test for Proportion dialog box appears:
 In the **Analysis Type** box, select **Two-Sample Analysis**
 In the **Variables** section, select both **Office 1** and **Office 2**
 In the **Categories to Analyze** section, select **Yes**
 In the **Hypothesis About Difference Between Proportions** section:
  Enter 0 in the **Null Hypothesis Value** box
  Select **Not Equal to Null Value (Two-Tailed Test)** in the
   Alternative Hypothesis Type box
 Click **OK**

Step 6. When the StatTools dialog box appears:
        Click **OK**
Step 7. When the Choose Variable Ordering dialog box appears:
        Click **OK**

Appendix 11.5 Chi-Square Tests Using StatTools

Test the Equality of Population Proportions and Test of Independence

The StatTools procedure is identical for both of these applications. In each case, the user must do the following before creating an Excel worksheet that can be used to perform the test.

1. Select a sample from the population or populations and record the data
2. Summarize the data to show the observed frequencies in a tabular format

We will begin the StatTools chi-square test procedure with the understanding that the user has already determined the observed frequencies for the study.

AutoLoyalty

Let us demonstrate the StatTools chi-square test by considering the automobile loyalty example presented in Section 11.2. Using the data in the file named AutoLoyalty and the Excel PivotTable procedure, we obtained the observed frequencies shown in the Excel worksheet of Figure 11.2. Note that the observed frequencies including the row and column heading are located from cell A6 to cell D8. This is all the information needed to conduct the chi-square test with StatTools. The steps are as follows.

Step 1. Select **Statistical Inference**
Step 2. Select **Chi-Square Independence Test**
Step 3. When the Chi-Square Test for Independence dialog box appears:
        Enter A6:D8 in the **Contingency Table Range** box
        Click **Table Includes Row and Column Headers**
        Click **OK**

A test of independence application would begin with a tabular summary of the observed frequencies for the two categorical variables. The three steps shown above will provide the test of independence results.

CHAPTER 12

Simple Linear Regression

CONTENTS

ALLIANCE DATA SYSTEMS*
DALLAS, TEXAS

Alliance Data Systems (ADS) provides transaction processing, credit services, and marketing services for clients in the rapidly growing customer relationship management (CRM) industry. ADS clients are concentrated in four industries: retail, petroleum/convenience stores, utilities, and transportation. In 1983, Alliance began offering end-to-end credit processing services to the retail, petroleum, and casual dining industries; today they employ more than 6500 employees who provide services to clients around the world. Operating more than 140,000 point-of-sale terminals in the United States alone, ADS processes in excess of 2.5 billion transactions annually. The company ranks second in the United States in private label credit services by representing 49 private label programs with nearly 72 million cardholders. In 2001, ADS made an initial public offering and is now listed on the New York Stock Exchange.

As one of its marketing services, ADS designs direct mail campaigns and promotions. With its database containing information on the spending habits of more than 100 million consumers, ADS can target those consumers most likely to benefit from a direct mail promotion. The Analytical Development Group uses regression analysis to build models that measure and predict the responsiveness of consumers to direct market campaigns. Some regression models predict the probability of purchase for individuals receiving a promotion, and others predict the amount spent by those consumers making a purchase.

For one particular campaign, a retail store chain wanted to attract new customers. To predict the effect of the campaign, ADS analysts selected a sample from the consumer database, sent the sampled individuals promotional materials, and then collected transaction data on the consumers' response. Sample data were collected on the amount of purchase made by the consumers responding to the campaign, as well as a variety of consumer-specific variables thought to be useful in predicting sales. The consumer-specific variable that contributed most to predicting the amount purchased was the total amount of

Alliance Data Systems analysts discuss use of a regression model to predict sales for a direct marketing campaign. © Courtesy of Alliance Data Systems.

credit purchases at related stores over the past 39 months. ADS analysts developed an estimated regression equation relating the amount of purchase to the amount spent at related stores:

$$\hat{y} = 26.7 + 0.00205x$$

where

$$\hat{y} = \text{amount of purchase}$$
$$x = \text{amount spent at related stores}$$

Using this equation, we could predict that someone spending $10,000 over the past 39 months at related stores would spend $47.20 when responding to the direct mail promotion. In this chapter, you will learn how to develop this type of estimated regression equation.

The final model developed by ADS analysts also included several other variables that increased the predictive power of the preceding equation. Some of these variables included the absence/presence of a bank credit card, estimated income, and the average amount spent per trip at a selected store. In the following chapter, we will learn how such additional variables can be incorporated into a multiple regression model.

*The authors are indebted to Philip Clemance, Director of Analytical Development at Alliance Data Systems, for providing this Statistics in Practice.

Managerial decisions often are based on the relationship between two or more variables. For example, after considering the relationship between advertising expenditures and sales, a marketing manager might attempt to predict sales for a given level of advertising expenditures. In another case, a public utility might use the relationship between the daily high temperature and the demand for electricity to predict electricity usage on the basis of next month's anticipated daily high temperatures. Sometimes a manager will rely on intuition to judge how two variables are related. However, if data can be obtained, a statistical procedure called *regression analysis* can be used to develop an equation showing how the variables are related.

The statistical methods used in studying the relationship between two variables were first employed by Sir Francis Galton (1822–1911). Galton was interested in studying the relationship between a father's height and the son's height. Galton's disciple, Karl Pearson (1857–1936), analyzed the relationship between the father's height and the son's height for 1078 pairs of subjects.

In regression terminology, the variable being predicted is called the **dependent variable**. The variable or variables being used to predict the value of the dependent variable are called the **independent variables**. For example, in analyzing the effect of advertising expenditures on sales, a marketing manager's desire to predict sales would suggest making sales the dependent variable. Advertising expenditure would be the independent variable used to help predict sales. In statistical notation, y denotes the dependent variable and x denotes the independent variable.

In this chapter we consider the simplest type of regression analysis involving one independent variable and one dependent variable in which the relationship between the variables is approximated by a straight line. It is called **simple linear regression**. Regression analysis involving two or more independent variables is called multiple regression analysis; multiple regression is covered in Chapter 13.

(12.1) Simple Linear Regression Model

Armand's Pizza Parlors is a chain of Italian-food restaurants located in a five-state area. Armand's most successful locations are near college campuses. The managers believe that quarterly sales for these restaurants (denoted by y) are related positively to the size of the student population (denoted by x); that is, restaurants near campuses with a large student population tend to generate more sales than those located near campuses with a small student population. Using regression analysis, we can develop an equation showing how the dependent variable y is related to the independent variable x.

Regression Model and Regression Equation

In the Armand's Pizza Parlors example, the population consists of all the Armand's restaurants. For every restaurant in the population, there is a value of x (student population) and a corresponding value of y (quarterly sales). The equation that describes how y is related to x and an error term is called the **regression model**. The regression model used in simple linear regression follows.

SIMPLE LINEAR REGRESSION MODEL

$$y = \beta_0 + \beta_1 x + \epsilon \tag{12.1}$$

β_0 and β_1 are referred to as the parameters of the model, and ϵ (the Greek letter epsilon) is a random variable referred to as the error term. The error term accounts for the variability in y that cannot be explained by the linear relationship between x and y.

The population of all Armand's restaurants can also be viewed as a collection of sub-populations, one for each distinct value of x. For example, one subpopulation consists of all Armand's restaurants located near college campuses with 8000 students; another subpopulation consists of all Armand's restaurants located near college campuses with 9000 students; and so on. Each subpopulation has a corresponding distribution of y values. Thus, a distribution of y values is associated with restaurants located near campuses with 8000 students; a distribution of y values is associated with restaurants located near campuses with 9000 students; and so on. Each distribution of y values has its own mean or expected value. The equation that describes how the expected value of y, denoted $E(y)$, is related to x is called the **regression equation**. The regression equation for simple linear regression follows.

SIMPLE LINEAR REGRESSION EQUATION

$$E(y) = \beta_0 + \beta_1 x \qquad\qquad (12.2)$$

The graph of the simple linear regression equation is a straight line; β_0 is the y-intercept of the regression line, β_1 is the slope, and $E(y)$ is the mean or expected value of y for a given value of x.

Examples of possible regression lines are shown in Figure 12.1. The regression line in Panel A shows that the mean value of y is related positively to x, with larger values of $E(y)$ associated with larger values of x. The regression line in Panel B shows the mean value of y is related negatively to x, with smaller values of $E(y)$ associated with larger values of x. The regression line in Panel C shows the case in which the mean value of y is not related to x; that is, the mean value of y is the same for every value of x.

Estimated Regression Equation

If the values of the population parameters β_0 and β_1 were known, we could use equation (12.2) to compute the mean value of y for a given value of x. In practice, the parameter values are not known and must be estimated using sample data. Sample statistics (denoted b_0 and b_1) are computed as estimates of the population parameters β_0 and β_1. Substituting the values of the sample statistics b_0 and b_1 for β_0 and β_1 in the regression equation, we obtain the

FIGURE 12.1   POSSIBLE REGRESSION LINES IN SIMPLE LINEAR REGRESSION

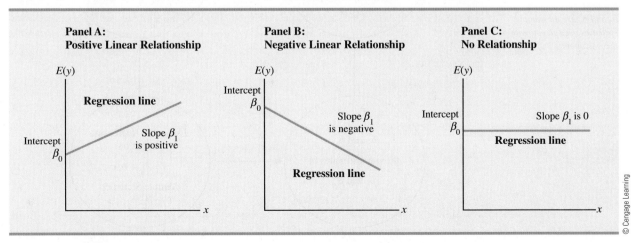

© Cengage Learning

estimated regression equation. The estimated regression equation for simple linear regression follows.

ESTIMATED SIMPLE LINEAR REGRESSION EQUATION

$$\hat{y} = b_0 + b_1 x \tag{12.3}$$

Figure 12.2 provides a summary of the estimation process for simple linear regression.

    The graph of the estimated simple linear regression equation is called the *estimated regression line*; b_0 is the y-intercept and b_1 is the slope. In the next section, we show how the least squares method can be used to compute the values of b_0 and b_1 in the estimated regression equation.

    In general, $\hat{y}$ is the point estimator of $E(y)$, the mean value of y for a given value of x. Thus, to estimate the mean or expected value of quarterly sales for all restaurants located near campuses with 10,000 students, Armand's would substitute the value of 10,000 for x in equation (12.3). In some cases, however, Armand's may be more interested in predicting sales for one particular restaurant. For example, suppose Armand's would like to predict quarterly sales for the restaurant they are considering building near Talbot College, a school with 10,000 students. As it turns out, the best predictor of y for a given value of x is also provided by $\hat{y}$. Thus, to predict quarterly sales for the restaurant located near Talbot College, Armand's would also substitute the value of 10,000 for x in equation (12.3).

The value of $\hat{y}$ provides both a point estimate of $E(y)$ for a given value of x and a prediction of an individual value of y for a given value of x.

FIGURE 12.2   THE ESTIMATION PROCESS IN SIMPLE LINEAR REGRESSION

The estimation of β_0 and β_1 is a statistical process much like the estimation of μ discussed in Chapter 7. β_0 and β_1 are the unknown parameters of interest, and b_0 and b_1 are the sample statistics used to estimate the parameters.

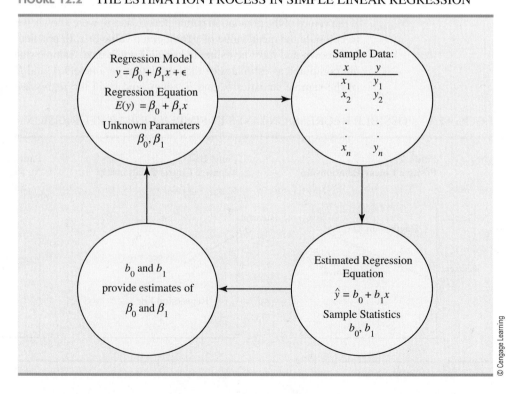

NOTES AND COMMENTS

1. Regression analysis cannot be interpreted as a procedure for establishing a cause-and-effect relationship between variables. It can only indicate how or to what extent variables are associated with each other. Any conclusions about cause and effect must be based upon the judgment of those individuals most knowledgeable about the application.

2. The regression equation in simple linear regression is $E(y) = \beta_0 + \beta_1 x$. More advanced texts in regression analysis often write the regression equation as $E(y|x) = \beta_0 + \beta_1 x$ to emphasize that the regression equation provides the mean value of y for a given value of x.

(12.2) Least Squares Method

In simple linear regression, each observation consists of two values: one for the independent variable and one for the dependent variable.

The **least squares method** is a procedure for using sample data to find the estimated regression equation. To illustrate the least squares method, suppose data were collected from a sample of 10 Armand's Pizza Parlor restaurants located near college campuses. For the ith observation or restaurant in the sample, x_i is the size of the student population (in thousands) and y_i is the quarterly sales (in thousands of dollars). The values of x_i and y_i for the 10 restaurants in the sample are summarized in Table 12.1. We see that restaurant 1, with $x_1 = 2$ and $y_1 = 58$, is near a campus with 2000 students and has quarterly sales of $58,000. Restaurant 2, with $x_2 = 6$ and $y_2 = 105$, is near a campus with 6000 students and has quarterly sales of $105,000. The largest sales value is for restaurant 10, which is near a campus with 26,000 students and has quarterly sales of $202,000.

Figure 12.3 is a scatter diagram of the data in Table 12.1. Student population is shown on the horizontal axis and quarterly sales is shown on the vertical axis. **Scatter diagrams** for regression analysis are constructed with the independent variable x on the horizontal axis and the dependent variable y on the vertical axis. The scatter diagram enables us to observe the data graphically and to draw preliminary conclusions about the possible relationship between the variables.

What preliminary conclusions can be drawn from Figure 12.3? Quarterly sales appear to be higher at campuses with larger student populations. In addition, for these data the relationship between the size of the student population and quarterly sales appears to be approximated by a straight line; indeed, a positive linear relationship is indicated between x

TABLE 12.1 STUDENT POPULATION AND QUARTERLY SALES DATA
FOR 10 ARMAND'S PIZZA PARLORS

WEB file

Armand's

Restaurant i	Student Population (1000s) x_i	Quarterly Sales ($1,000s) y_i
1	2	58
2	6	105
3	8	88
4	8	118
5	12	117
6	16	137
7	20	157
8	20	169
9	22	149
10	26	202

© Cengage Learning

FIGURE 12.3   SCATTER DIAGRAM OF STUDENT POPULATION AND QUARTERLY SALES FOR ARMAND'S PIZZA PARLORS

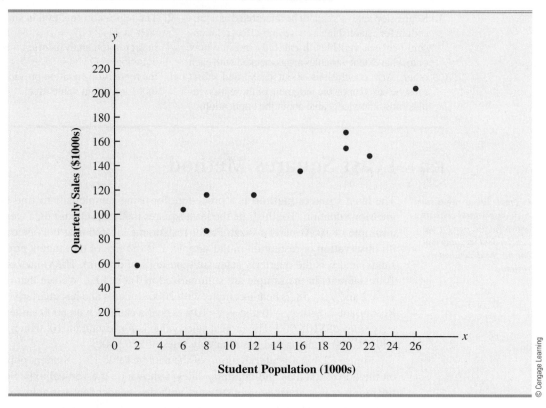

and y. We therefore choose the simple linear regression model to represent the relationship between quarterly sales and student population. Given that choice, our next task is to use the sample data in Table 12.1 to determine the values of b_0 and b_1 in the estimated simple linear regression equation. For the ith restaurant, the estimated regression equation provides

$$\hat{y}_i = b_0 + b_1 x_i \tag{12.4}$$

where

$\hat{y}_i$ = predicted value of quarterly sales ($1,000s) for the ith restaurant
b_0 = the y-intercept of the estimated regression line
b_1 = the slope of the estimated regression line
x_i = size of the student population (1000s) for the ith restaurant

With y_i denoting the observed (actual) sales for restaurant i and $\hat{y}_i$ in equation (12.4) representing the predicted value of sales for restaurant i, every restaurant in the sample will have an observed value of sales y_i and a predicted value of sales $\hat{y}_i$. For the estimated regression line to provide a good fit to the data, we want the differences between the observed sales values and the predicted sales values to be small.

The least squares method uses the sample data to provide the values of b_0 and b_1 that minimize the *sum of the squares of the deviations* between the observed values of the dependent variable y_i and the predicted values of the dependent variable $\hat{y}_i$. The criterion for the least squares method is given by expression (12.5).

Carl Friedrich Gauss (1777–1855) proposed the least squares method.

LEAST SQUARES CRITERION

$$\min \Sigma(y_i - \hat{y}_i)^2 \qquad (12.5)$$

where

y_i = observed value of the dependent variable for the ith observation

$\hat{y}_i$ = predicted value of the dependent variable for the ith observation

Differential calculus can be used to show that the values of b_0 and b_1 that minimize expression (12.5) can be found by using equations (12.6) and (12.7).

In computing b_1 with a calculator, carry as many significant digits as possible in the intermediate calculations. We recommend carrying at least four significant digits.

SLOPE AND y-INTERCEPT FOR THE ESTIMATED REGRESSION EQUATION[1]

$$b_1 = \frac{\Sigma(x_i - \bar{x})(y_i - \bar{y})}{\Sigma(x_i - \bar{x})^2} \qquad (12.6)$$

$$b_0 = \bar{y} - b_1\bar{x} \qquad (12.7)$$

where

x_i = value of the independent variable for the ith observation

y_i = value of the dependent variable for the ith observation

$\bar{x}$ = mean value for the independent variable

$\bar{y}$ = mean value for the dependent variable

n = total number of observations

Some of the calculations necessary to develop the least squares estimated regression equation for Armand's Pizza Parlors are shown in Table 12.2. With the sample of 10 restaurants, we have $n = 10$ observations. Because equations (12.6) and (12.7) require $\bar{x}$ and $\bar{y}$ we begin the calculations by computing $\bar{x}$ and $\bar{y}$.

$$\bar{x} = \frac{\Sigma x_i}{n} = \frac{140}{10} = 14$$

$$\bar{y} = \frac{\Sigma y_i}{n} = \frac{1300}{10} = 130$$

Using equations (12.6) and (12.7) and the information in Table 12.2, we can compute the slope and intercept of the estimated regression equation for Armand's Pizza Parlors. The calculation of the slope (b_1) proceeds as follows.

---

[1]An alternate formula for b_1 is

$$b_1 = \frac{\Sigma x_i y_i - (\Sigma x_i \Sigma y_i)/n}{\Sigma x_i^2 - (\Sigma x_i)^2/n}$$

This form of equation (12.6) is often recommended when using a calculator to compute b_1.

TABLE 12.2   CALCULATIONS FOR THE LEAST SQUARES ESTIMATED REGRESSION
EQUATION FOR ARMAND'S PIZZA PARLORS

Restaurant i	x_i	y_i	$x_i - \bar{x}$	$y_i - \bar{y}$	$(x_i - \bar{x})(y_i - \bar{y})$	$(x_i - \bar{x})^2$
1	2	58	−12	−72	864	144
2	6	105	−8	−25	200	64
3	8	88	−6	−42	252	36
4	8	118	−6	−12	72	36
5	12	117	−2	−13	26	4
6	16	137	2	7	14	4
7	20	157	6	27	162	36
8	20	169	6	39	234	36
9	22	149	8	19	152	64
10	26	202	12	72	864	144
Totals	140	1300			2840	568
	Σx_i	Σy_i			$\Sigma(x_i - \bar{x})(y_i - \bar{y})$	$\Sigma(x_i - \bar{x})^2$

$$b_1 = \frac{\Sigma(x_i - \bar{x})(y_i - \bar{y})}{\Sigma(x_i - \bar{x})^2}$$

$$= \frac{2840}{568}$$

$$= 5$$

The calculation of the y intercept (b_0) follows.

$$b_0 = \bar{y} - b_1\bar{x}$$

$$= 130 - 5(14)$$

$$= 60$$

Thus, the estimated regression equation is

$$\hat{y} = 60 + 5x$$

Figure 12.4 shows the graph of this equation on the scatter diagram.

The slope of the estimated regression equation ($b_1 = 5$) is positive, implying that as student population increases, sales increase. In fact, we can conclude (based on sales measured in $1,000s and student population in 1000s) that an increase in the student population of 1000 is associated with an increase of $5,000 in expected sales; that is, quarterly sales are expected to increase by $5 per student.

Using the estimated regression equation to make predictions outside the range of the values of the independent variable should be done with caution because outside that range we cannot be sure that the same relationship is valid.

If we believe the least squares estimated regression equation adequately describes the relationship between x and y, it would seem reasonable to use the estimated regression equation to predict the value of y for a given value of x. For example, if we wanted to predict quarterly sales for a restaurant to be located near a campus with 16,000 students, we would compute

$$\hat{y} = 60 + 5(16) = 140$$

Hence, we would predict quarterly sales of $140,000 for this restaurant. In the following sections we will discuss methods for assessing the appropriateness of using the estimated regression equation for estimation and prediction.

FIGURE 12.4 GRAPH OF THE ESTIMATED REGRESSION EQUATION FOR ARMAND'S PIZZA PARLORS: $\hat{y} = 60 + 5x$

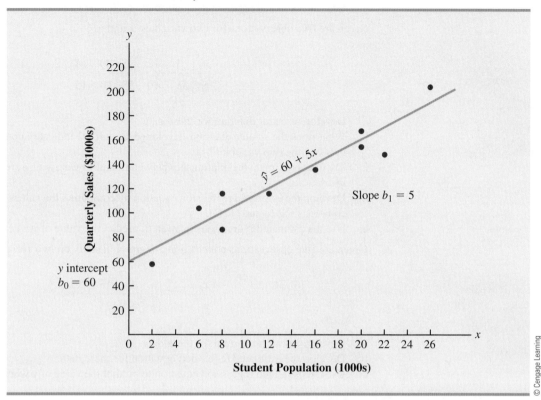

NOTE AND COMMENT

The least squares method provides an estimated regression equation that minimizes the sum of squared deviations between the observed values of the dependent variable y_i and the predicted values of the dependent variable $\hat{y}_i$. This least squares criterion is used to choose the equation that provides the best fit. If some other criterion were used, such as minimizing the sum of the absolute deviations between y_i and $\hat{y}_i$, a different equation would be obtained. In practice, the least squares method is the most widely used.

Exercises

Methods

1. Given are five observations for two variables, x and y.

x_i	1	2	3	4	5
y_i	3	7	5	11	14

a. Develop a scatter diagram for these data.
b. What does the scatter diagram developed in part (a) indicate about the relationship between the two variables?
c. Try to approximate the relationship between x and y by drawing a straight line through the data.

    d.   Develop the estimated regression equation by computing the values of b_0 and b_1 using equations (12.6) and (12.7).

    e.   Use the estimated regression equation to predict the value of y when $x = 4$.

2.   Given are five observations for two variables, x and y.

x_i	3	12	6	20	14
y_i	55	40	55	10	15

    a.   Develop a scatter diagram for these data.

    b.   What does the scatter diagram developed in part (a) indicate about the relationship between the two variables?

    c.   Try to approximate the relationship between x and y by drawing a straight line through the data.

    d.   Develop the estimated regression equation by computing the values of b_0 and b_1 using equations (12.6) and (12.7).

    e.   Use the estimated regression equation to predict the value of y when $x = 10$.

3.   Given are five observations collected in a regression study on two variables.

x_i	2	6	9	13	20
y_i	7	18	9	26	23

    a.   Develop a scatter diagram for these data.

    b.   Develop the estimated regression equation for these data.

    c.   Use the estimated regression equation to predict the value of y when $x = 6$.

Applications

4.   The following data give the percentage of women working in five companies in the retail and trade industry. The percentage of management jobs held by women in each company is also shown.

% Working	67	45	73	54	61
% Management	49	21	65	47	33

    a.   Develop a scatter diagram for these data with the percentage of women working in the company as the independent variable.

    b.   What does the scatter diagram developed in part (a) indicate about the relationship between the two variables?

    c.   Try to approximate the relationship between the percentage of women working in the company and the percentage of management jobs held by women in that company.

    d.   Develop the estimated regression equation by computing the values of b_0 and b_1.

    e.   Predict the percentage of management jobs held by women in a company that has 60% women employees.

5.   Brawdy Plastics, Inc., produces plastic seat belt retainers for General Motors at its plant in Buffalo, New York. After final assembly and painting, the parts are placed on a conveyor belt that moves the parts past a final inspection station. How fast the parts move past the final inspection station depends upon the line speed of the conveyor belt (feet per minute). Although faster line speeds are desirable, management is concerned that increasing the line speed too much may not provide enough time for inspectors to identify which parts are actually defective. To test this theory, Brawdy Plastics conducted an experiment in

which the same batch of parts, with a known number of defective parts, was inspected using a variety of line speeds. The following data were collected.

Line Speed	Number of Defective Parts found
20	23
20	21
30	19
30	16
40	15
40	17
50	14
50	11

a.   Develop a scatter diagram with the line speed as the independent variable.
b.   What does the scatter diagram developed in part (a) indicate about the relationship between the two variables?
c.   Use the least squares method to develop the estimated regression equation.
d.   Predict the number of defective parts found for a line speed of 25 feet per minute.

6.   The National Football League (NFL) records a variety of performance data for individuals and teams. To investigate the importance of passing on the percentage of games won by a team, the following data show the average number of passing yards per attempt (Yds/Att) and the percentage of games won (WinPct) for a random sample of 10 NFL teams for the 2011 season (NFL website, February 12, 2012).

WEB file

NFLPassing

Team	Yds/Att	WinPct
Arizona Cardinals	6.5	50
Atlanta Falcons	7.1	63
Carolina Panthers	7.4	38
Chicago Bears	6.4	50
Dallas Cowboys	7.4	50
New England Patriots	8.3	81
Philadelphia Eagles	7.4	50
Seattle Seahawks	6.1	44
St. Louis Rams	5.2	13
Tampa Bay Buccaneers	6.2	25

a.   Develop a scatter diagram with the number of passing yards per attempt on the horizontal axis and the percentage of games won on the vertical axis.
b.   What does the scatter diagram developed in part (a) indicate about the relationship between the two variables?
c.   Develop the estimated regression equation that could be used to predict the percentage of games won given the average number of passing yards per attempt.
d.   Provide an interpretation for the slope of the estimated regression equation.
e.   For the 2011 season, the average number of passing yards per attempt for the Kansas City Chiefs was 6.2. Use the estimated regression equation developed in part (c) to predict the percentage of games won by the Kansas City Chiefs. (*Note:* For the 2011 season the Kansas City Chiefs record was 7 wins and 9 losses.) Compare your prediction to the actual percentage of games won by the Kansas City Chiefs.

7.   A sales manager collected the following data on annual sales for new customer accounts and the number of years of experience for a sample of 10 salespersons.

Salesperson	Years of Experience	Annual Sales ($1,000s)
1	1	80
2	3	97
3	4	92
4	4	102
5	6	103
6	8	111
7	10	119
8	10	123
9	11	117
10	13	136

Sales

    a.   Develop a scatter diagram for these data with years of experience as the independent variable.

    b.   Develop an estimated regression equation that can be used to predict annual sales given the years of experience.

    c.   Use the estimated regression equation to predict annual sales for a salesperson with 9 years of experience.

8.   The American Association of Individual Investors (AAII) On-Line Discount Broker Survey polls members on their experiences with discount brokers. As part of the survey, members were asked to rate the quality of the speed of execution with their broker as well as provide an overall satisfaction rating for electronic trades. Possible responses (scores) were no opinion (0), unsatisfied (1), somewhat satisfied (2), satisfied (3), and very satisfied (4). For each broker summary scores were computed by calculating a weighted average of the scores provided by each respondent. A portion of the survey results follow (AAII website, February 7, 2012).

Brokerage	Speed	Satisfaction
Scottrade, Inc.	3.4	3.5
Charles Schwab	3.3	3.4
Fidelity Brokerage Services	3.4	3.9
TD Ameritrade	3.6	3.7
E*Trade Financial	3.2	2.9
Vanguard Brokerage Services	3.8	2.8
USAA Brokerage Services	3.8	3.6
Thinkorswim	2.6	2.6
Wells Fargo Investments	2.7	2.3
Interactive Brokers	4.0	4.0
Zecco.com	2.5	2.5

BrokerRatings

    a.   Develop a scatter diagram for these data with the speed of execution as the independent variable.

    b.   What does the scatter diagram developed in part (a) indicate about the relationship between the two variables?

    c.   Develop the least squares estimated regression equation.

    d.   Provide an interpretation for the slope of the estimated regression equation.

    e.   Suppose Zecco.com developed new software to increase its speed of execution rating. If the new software is able to increase its speed of execution rating from the current value of 2.5 to the average speed of execution rating for the other 10 brokerage firms that were surveyed, what value would you predict for the overall satisfaction rating?

9.   Companies in the U.S. car rental market vary greatly in terms of the size of the fleet, the number of locations, and annual revenue. In 2011, Hertz had 320,000 cars in service and

annual revenue of approximately $4.2 billion. The following data show the number of cars in service (1000s) and the annual revenue ($millions) for six smaller car rental companies (*Auto Rental News* website, August 7, 2012).

Company	Cars (1000s)	Revenue ($millions)
U-Save Auto Rental System, Inc.	11.5	118
Payless Car Rental System, Inc.	10.0	135
ACE Rent A Car	9.0	100
Rent-A-Wreck of America	5.5	37
Triangle Rent-A-Car	4.2	40
Affordable/Sensible	3.3	32

a. Develop a scatter diagram with the number of cars in service as the independent variable.
b. What does the scatter diagram developed in part (a) indicate about the relationship between the two variables?
c. Use the least squares method to develop the estimated regression equation.
d. For every additional car placed in service, estimate how much annual revenue will change.
e. Fox Rent-A-Car has 11,000 cars in service. Use the estimated regression equation developed in part (c) to predict annual revenue for Fox Rent-A-Car.

10. On March 31, 2009, Ford Motor Company's shares were trading at a 26-year low of $2.63. Ford's board of directors gave the CEO a grant of options and restricted shares with an estimated value of $16 million. On April 26, 2011, the price of a share of Ford had increased to $15.58, and the CEO's grant was worth $202.8 million, a gain in value of $186.8 million. The following table shows the share price in 2009 and 2011 for 10 companies, the stock-option and share grants to the CEOs in late 2008 and 2009, and the value of the options and grants in 2011. Also shown are the percentage increases in the stock price and the percentage gains in the options values (*The Wall Street Journal,* April 27, 2011).

WEB file

CEOGrants

Company	Stock Price 2009 ($)	Stock Price 2011 ($)	% Increase in Stock Price	Options and Grants Value 2009 ($ millions)	Options and Grants Value 2011 ($ millions)	% Gain in Options Value
Ford Motor	2.63	15.58	492	16.0	202.8	1168
Abercrombie & Fitch	23.80	70.47	196	46.2	196.1	324
Nabors Industries	9.99	32.06	221	37.2	132.2	255
Starbucks	9.99	32.06	221	12.4	75.9	512
Salesforce.com	32.73	137.61	320	7.8	67.0	759
Starwood Hotels	12.70	60.28	375	5.8	57.1	884
Caterpillar	27.96	111.94	300	4.0	47.5	1088
Oracle	18.07	34.97	94	61.9	97.5	58
Capital One	12.24	54.61	346	6.0	40.6	577
Dow Chemical	8.43	39.97	374	5.0	38.8	676

a. Develop a scatter diagram for these data with the percentage increase in the stock price as the independent variable.
b. What does the scatter diagram developed in part (a) indicate about the relationship between the two variables?
c. Develop the least squares estimated regression equation.
d. Provide an interpretation for the slope of the estimated regression equation.
e. Do the rewards for the CEO appear to be based on performance increases as measured by the stock price?

Computer

11. To help consumers in purchasing a laptop computer, *Consumer Reports* calculates an overall test score for each computer tested based on rating factors such as ergonomics, portability, performance, display, and battery life. Higher overall scores indicate better test results. The following data show the average retail price and the overall score for ten 13-inch models (*Consumer Reports* website, October 25, 2012).

Brand & Model	Price ($)	Overall Score
Samsung Ultrabook NP900X3C-A01US	1250	83
Apple MacBook Air MC965LL/A	1300	83
Apple MacBook Air MD231LL/A	1200	82
HP ENVY 13-2050nr Spectre XT	950	79
Sony VAIO SVS13112FXB	800	77
Acer Aspire S5-391-9880 Ultrabook	1200	74
Apple MacBook Pro MD101LL/A	1200	74
Apple MacBook Pro MD313LL/A	1000	73
Dell Inspiron I13Z-6591SLV	700	67
Samsung NP535U3C-A01US	600	63

a. Develop a scatter diagram with price as the independent variable.
b. What does the scatter diagram developed in part (a) indicate about the relationship between the two variables?
c. Use the least squares method to develop the estimated regression equation.
d. Provide an interpretation of the slope of the estimated regression equation.
e. Another laptop that *Consumer Reports* tested is the Acer Aspire S3-951-6646 Ultrabook; the price for this laptop was $700. Predict the overall score for this laptop using the estimated regression equation developed in part (c).

12. Concur Technologies, Inc., is a large expense-management company located in Redmond, Washington. *The Wall Street Journal* asked Concur to examine the data from 8.3 million expense reports to provide insights regarding business travel expenses. Their analysis of the data showed that New York was the most expensive city, with an average daily hotel room rate of $198 and an average amount spent on entertainment (including group meals and tickets for shows, sports, and other events) of $172. In comparison, the U.S. averages for these two categories were $89 for the room rate and $99 for entertainment. The following table shows the average daily hotel room rate and the amount spent on entertainment for a random sample of 9 of the 25 most visited U.S. cities (*The Wall Street Journal,* August 18, 2011).

BusinessTravel

City	Room Rate ($)	Entertainment ($)
Boston	148	161
Denver	96	105
Nashville	91	101
New Orleans	110	142
Phoenix	90	100
San Diego	102	120
San Francisco	136	167
San Jose	90	140
Tampa	82	98

a. Develop a scatter diagram for these data with the room rate as the independent variable.
b. What does the scatter diagram developed in part (a) indicate about the relationship between the two variables?
c. Develop the least squares estimated regression equation.
d. Provide an interpretation for the slope of the estimated regression equation.

e.   The average room rate in Chicago is $128, considerably higher than the U.S. average. Predict the entertainment expense per day for Chicago.

13.   A large city hospital conducted a study to investigate the relationship between the number of unauthorized days that employees are absent per year and the distance (miles) between home and work for the employees. A sample of 10 employees was selected and the following data were collected.

Distance to Work (miles)	Number of Days Absent
1	8
3	5
4	8
6	7
8	6
10	3
12	5
14	2
14	4
18	2

a.   Develop a scatter diagram for these data. Does a linear relationship appear reasonable? Explain.

b.   Develop the least squares estimated regression equation that relates the distance to work to the number of days absent.

c.   Predict the number of days absent for an employee who lives 5 miles from the hospital.

14.   Using a global-positioning-system (GPS)-based navigator for your car, you enter a destination and the system will plot a route, give spoken turn-by-turn directions, and show your progress along the route. Today, even budget units include features previously available only on more expensive models. *Consumer Reports* conducted extensive tests of GPS-based navigators and developed an overall rating based on factors such as ease of use, driver information, display, and battery life. The following data show the price and rating for a sample of 20 GPS units with 4.3-inch screens that *Consumer Reports* tested (*Consumer Reports* website, April 17, 2012).

Brand and Model	Price ($)	Rating
Garmin Nuvi 3490LMT	400	82
Garmin Nuvi 3450	330	80
Garmin Nuvi 3790T	350	77
Garmin Nuvi 3790LMT	400	77
Garmin Nuvi 3750	250	74
Garmin Nuvi 2475LT	230	74
Garmin Nuvi 2455LT	160	73
Garmin Nuvi 2370LT	270	71
Garmin Nuvi 2360LT	250	71
Garmin Nuvi 2360LMT	220	71
Garmin Nuvi 755T	260	70
Motorola Motonab TN565t	200	68
Motorola Motonab TN555	200	67
Garmin Nuvi 1350T	150	65
Garmin Nuvi 1350LMT	180	65
Garmin Nuvi 2300	160	65
Garmin Nuvi 1350	130	64
Tom Tom VIA 1435T	200	62
Garmin Nuvi 1300	140	62
Garmin Nuvi 1300LM	180	62

a. Develop a scatter diagram with price as the independent variable.
b. What does the scatter diagram developed in part (a) indicate about the relationship between the two variables?
c. Use the least squares method to develop the estimated regression equation.
d. Predict the rating for a GPS system with a 4.3-inch screen that has a price of $200.

12.3 Coefficient of Determination

For the Armand's Pizza Parlors example, we developed the estimated regression equation $\hat{y} = 60 + 5x$ to approximate the linear relationship between the size of the student population x and quarterly sales y. A question now is: How well does the estimated regression equation fit the data? In this section, we show that the **coefficient of determination** provides a measure of the goodness of fit for the estimated regression equation.

For the ith observation, the difference between the observed value of the dependent variable, y_i, and the predicted value of the dependent variable, $\hat{y}_i$, is called the i**th residual**. The ith residual represents the error in using $\hat{y}_i$ to estimate y_i. Thus, for the ith observation, the residual is $y_i - \hat{y}_i$. The sum of squares of these residuals or errors is the quantity that is minimized by the least squares method. This quantity, also known as the *sum of squares due to error,* is denoted by SSE.

SUM OF SQUARES DUE TO ERROR

$$SSE = \Sigma(y_i - \hat{y}_i)^2 \tag{12.8}$$

The value of SSE is a measure of the error in using the estimated regression equation to predict the values of the dependent variable in the sample.

In Table 12.3 we show the calculations required to compute the sum of squares due to error for the Armand's Pizza Parlors example. For instance, for restaurant 1 the values of the independent and dependent variables are $x_1 = 2$ and $y_1 = 58$. Using the estimated

TABLE 12.3   CALCULATION OF SSE FOR ARMAND'S PIZZA PARLORS

Restaurant i	x_i = Student Population (1000s)	y_i = Quarterly Sales ($1,000s)	Predicted Sales $\hat{y}_i = 60 + 5x_i$	Error $y_i - \hat{y}_i$	Squared Error $(y_i - \hat{y}_i)^2$
1	2	58	70	−12	144
2	6	105	90	15	225
3	8	88	100	−12	144
4	8	118	100	18	324
5	12	117	120	−3	9
6	16	137	140	−3	9
7	20	157	160	−3	9
8	20	169	160	9	81
9	22	149	170	−21	441
10	26	202	190	12	144
					SSE = 1530

TABLE 12.4   COMPUTATION OF THE TOTAL SUM OF SQUARES FOR ARMAND'S PIZZA PARLORS

Restaurant i	$x_i =$ Student Population (1000s)	$y_i =$ Quarterly Sales ($1,000s)	Deviation $y_i - \bar{y}$	Squared Deviation $(y_i - \bar{y})^2$
1	2	58	−72	5184
2	6	105	−25	625
3	8	88	−42	1764
4	8	118	−12	144
5	12	117	−13	169
6	16	137	7	49
7	20	157	27	729
8	20	169	39	1521
9	22	149	19	361
10	26	202	72	5184
				SST = 15,730

regression equation, we find that the predicted value of quarterly sales for restaurant 1 is $\hat{y}_1 = 60 + 5(2) = 70$. Thus, the error in using $\hat{y}_1$ to predict y_1 for restaurant 1 is $y_1 - \hat{y}_1 = 58 - 70 = -12$. The squared error, $(-12)^2 = 144$, is shown in the last column of Table 12.3. After computing and squaring the residuals for each restaurant in the sample, we sum them to obtain SSE = 1530. Thus, SSE = 1530 measures the error in using the estimated regression equation $\hat{y} = 60 + 5x$ to predict sales.

Now suppose we are asked to develop an estimate of quarterly sales without knowledge of the size of the student population. Without knowledge of any related variables, we would use the sample mean as an estimate of quarterly sales at any given restaurant. Table 12.2 showed that for the sales data, $\sum y_i = 1300$. Hence, the mean value of quarterly sales for the sample of 10 Armand's restaurants is $\bar{y} = \sum y_i/n = 1300/10 = 130$. In Table 12.4 we show the sum of squared deviations obtained by using the sample mean $\bar{y} = 130$ to predict the value of quarterly sales for each restaurant in the sample. For the ith restaurant in the sample, the difference $y_i - \bar{y}$ provides a measure of the error involved in using $\bar{y}$ to predict sales. The corresponding sum of squares, called the *total sum of squares,* is denoted SST.

TOTAL SUM OF SQUARES

$$SST = \sum(y_i - \bar{y})^2 \tag{12.9}$$

The sum at the bottom of the last column in Table 12.4 is the total sum of squares for Armand's Pizza Parlors; it is SST = 15,730.

With SST = 15,730 and SSE = 1530, the estimated regression line provides a much better fit to the data than the line y = ȳ.

In Figure 12.5 we show the estimated regression line $\hat{y} = 60 + 5x$ and the line corresponding to $\bar{y} = 130$. Note that the points cluster more closely around the estimated regression line than they do about the line $\bar{y} = 130$. For example, for the 10th restaurant in the sample we see that the error is much larger when $\bar{y} = 130$ is used to predict y_{10} than when $\hat{y}_{10} = 60 + 5(26) = 190$ is used. We can think of SST as a measure of how well the observations cluster about the $\bar{y}$ line and SSE as a measure of how well the observations cluster about the $\hat{y}$ line.

FIGURE 12.5   DEVIATIONS ABOUT THE ESTIMATED REGRESSION LINE AND THE LINE $y = \bar{y}$ FOR ARMAND'S PIZZA PARLORS

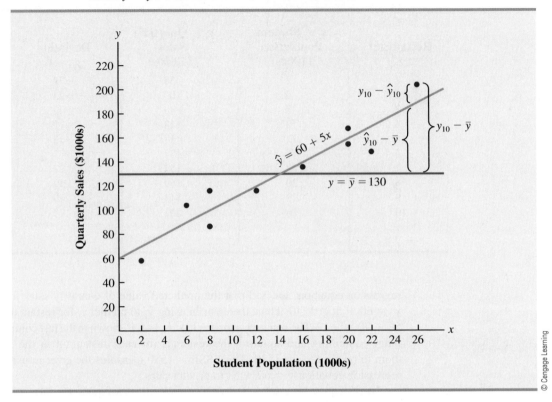

To measure how much the $\hat{y}$ values on the estimated regression line deviate from $\bar{y}$, another sum of squares is computed. This sum of squares, called the *sum of squares due to regression,* is denoted SSR.

SUM OF SQUARES DUE TO REGRESSION

$$SSR = \Sigma(\hat{y}_i - \bar{y})^2 \tag{12.10}$$

From the preceding discussion, we should expect that SST, SSR, and SSE are related. Indeed, the relationship among these three sums of squares provides one of the most important results in statistics.

RELATIONSHIP AMONG SST, SSR, AND SSE

$$SST = SSR + SSE \tag{12.11}$$

SSR can be thought of as the explained portion of SST, and SSE can be thought of as the unexplained portion of SST.

where

$\quad\quad$ SST = total sum of squares

$\quad\quad$ SSR = sum of squares due to regression

$\quad\quad$ SSE = sum of squares due to error

Equation (12.11) shows that the total sum of squares can be partitioned into two components, the sum of squares due to regression and the sum of squares due to error. Hence, if the values of any two of these sum of squares are known, the third sum of squares can be computed easily. For instance, in the Armand's Pizza Parlors example, we already know that SSE = 1530 and SST = 15,730; therefore, solving for SSR in equation (12.11), we find that the sum of squares due to regression is

$$SSR = SST - SSE = 15{,}730 - 1530 = 14{,}200$$

Now let us see how the three sums of squares, SST, SSR, and SSE, can be used to provide a measure of the goodness of fit for the estimated regression equation. The estimated regression equation would provide a perfect fit if every value of the dependent variable y_i happened to lie on the estimated regression line. In this case, $y_i - \hat{y}_i$ would be zero for each observation, resulting in SSE = 0. Because SST = SSR + SSE, we see that for a perfect fit SSR must equal SST, and the ratio (SSR/SST) must equal one. Poorer fits will result in larger values for SSE. Solving for SSE in equation (12.11), we see that SSE = SST − SSR. Hence, the largest value for SSE (and hence the poorest fit) occurs when SSR = 0 and SSE = SST.

The ratio SSR/SST, which will take values between zero and one, is used to evaluate the goodness of fit for the estimated regression equation. This ratio is called the *coefficient of determination* and is denoted by r^2.

COEFFICIENT OF DETERMINATION

$$r^2 = \frac{SSR}{SST} \tag{12.12}$$

For the Armand's Pizza Parlors example, the value of the coefficient of determination is

$$r^2 = \frac{SSR}{SST} = \frac{14{,}200}{15{,}730} = .9027$$

When we express the coefficient of determination as a percentage, r^2 can be interpreted as the percentage of the total sum of squares that can be explained by using the estimated regression equation. For Armand's Pizza Parlors, we can conclude that 90.27% of the total sum of squares can be explained by using the estimated regression equation $\hat{y} = 60 + 5x$ to predict quarterly sales. In other words, 90.27% of the variability in sales can be explained by the linear relationship between the size of the student population and sales. We should be pleased to find such a good fit for the estimated regression equation.

Correlation Coefficient

In Chapter 3 we introduced the **correlation coefficient** as a descriptive measure of the strength of linear association between two variables, x and y. Values of the correlation coefficient are always between -1 and $+1$. A value of $+1$ indicates that the two variables x and y are perfectly related in a positive linear sense. That is, all data points are on a straight line that has a positive slope. A value of -1 indicates that x and y are perfectly related in a negative linear sense, with all data points on a straight line that has a negative slope. Values of the correlation coefficient close to zero indicate that x and y are not linearly related.

In Section 3.5 we presented the equation for computing the sample correlation coefficient. If a regression analysis has already been performed and the coefficient of determination r^2 computed, the sample correlation coefficient can be computed as follows.

SAMPLE CORRELATION COEFFICIENT

$$r_{xy} = (\text{sign of } b_1)\sqrt{\text{Coefficient of determination}}$$
$$= (\text{sign of } b_1)\sqrt{r^2} \qquad (12.13)$$

where

$$b_1 = \text{the slope of the estimated regression equation } \hat{y} = b_0 + b_1 x$$

The sign for the sample correlation coefficient is positive if the estimated regression equation has a positive slope ($b_1 > 0$) and negative if the estimated regression equation has a negative slope ($b_1 < 0$).

For the Armand's Pizza Parlor example, the value of the coefficient of determination corresponding to the estimated regression equation $\hat{y} = 60 + 5x$ is .9027. Because the slope of the estimated regression equation is positive, equation (12.13) shows that the sample correlation coefficient is $+\sqrt{.9027} = +.9501$. With a sample correlation coefficient of $r_{xy} = +.9501$, we would conclude that a strong positive linear association exists between x and y.

In the case of a linear relationship between two variables, both the coefficient of determination and the sample correlation coefficient provide measures of the strength of the relationship. The coefficient of determination provides a measure between zero and one, whereas the sample correlation coefficient provides a measure between -1 and $+1$. Although the sample correlation coefficient is restricted to a linear relationship between two variables, the coefficient of determination can be used for nonlinear relationships and for relationships that have two or more independent variables. Thus, the coefficient of determination provides a wider range of applicability.

NOTES AND COMMENTS

1. In developing the least squares estimated regression equation and computing the coefficient of determination, we made no probabilistic assumptions about the error term ϵ, and no statistical tests for significance of the relationship between x and y were conducted. Larger values of r^2 imply that the least squares line provides a better fit to the data; that is, the observations are more closely grouped about the least squares line. But, using only r^2, we can draw no conclusion about whether the relationship between x and y is statistically significant. Such a conclusion must be based on considerations that involve the sample size and the properties of the appropriate sampling distributions of the least squares estimators.

2. As a practical matter, for typical data found in the social sciences, values of r^2 as low as .25 are often considered useful. For data in the physical and life sciences, r^2 values of .60 or greater are often found; in fact, in some cases, r^2 values greater than .90 can be found. In business applications, r^2 values vary greatly, depending on the unique characteristics of each application.

Exercises

Methods

15.   The data from exercise 1 follow.

x_i	1	2	3	4	5
y_i	3	7	5	11	14

The estimated regression equation for these data is $\hat{y} = .20 + 2.60x$.
   a.   Compute SSE, SST, and SSR using equations (12.8), (12.9), and (12.10).
   b.   Compute the coefficient of determination r^2. Comment on the goodness of fit.
   c.   Compute the sample correlation coefficient.

16.   The data from exercise 2 follow.

x_i	3	12	6	20	14
y_i	55	40	55	10	15

The estimated regression equation for these data is $\hat{y} = 68 - 3x$.
   a.   Compute SSE, SST, and SSR.
   b.   Compute the coefficient of determination r^2. Comment on the goodness of fit.
   c.   Compute the sample correlation coefficient.

17.   The data from exercise 3 follow.

x_i	2	6	9	13	20
y_i	7	18	9	26	23

The estimated regression equation for these data is $\hat{y} = 7.6 + .9x$. What percentage of the total sum of squares can be accounted for by the estimated regression equation? What is the value of the sample correlation coefficient?

Applications

18.   The following data show the brand, price ($), and the overall score for six stereo headphones that were tested by *Consumer Reports* (*Consumer Reports* website, March 5, 2012). The overall score is based on sound quality and effectiveness of ambient noise reduction. Scores range from 0 (lowest) to 100 (highest). The estimated regression equation for these data is $\hat{y} = 23.194 + .318x$, where x = price ($) and y = overall score.

Brand	Price ($)	Score
Bose	180	76
Skullcandy	150	71
Koss	95	61
Phillips/O'Neill	70	56
Denon	70	40
JVC	35	26

   a.   Compute SST, SSR, and SSE.
   b.   Compute the coefficient of determination r^2. Comment on the goodness of fit.
   c.   What is the value of the sample correlation coefficient?

19.   In exercise 7 a sales manager collected the following data on x = annual sales and y = years of experience. The estimated regression equation for these data is $\hat{y} = 80 + 4x$.

Sales

Salesperson	Years of Experience	Annual Sales ($1,000s)
1	1	80
2	3	97
3	4	92
4	4	102
5	6	103
6	8	111
7	10	119
8	10	123
9	11	117
10	13	136

    a. Compute SST, SSR, and SSE.
    b. Compute the coefficient of determination r^2. Comment on the goodness of fit.
    c. What is the value of the sample correlation coefficient?

20. *Bicycling,* the world's leading cycling magazine, reviews hundreds of bicycles throughout the year. The magazine's "Road-Race" category contains reviews of bikes used by riders primarily interested in racing. One of the most important factors in selecting a bike for racing is the weight of the bike. The following data show the weight (pounds) and price ($) for 10 racing bikes reviewed by the magazine (*Bicycling* website, March 8, 2012).

RacingBicycles

Brand	Weight	Price ($)
FELT F5	17.8	2100
PINARELLO Paris	16.1	6250
ORBEA Orca GDR	14.9	8370
EDDY MERCKX EMX-7	15.9	6200
BH RC1 Ultegra	17.2	4000
BH Ultralight 386	13.1	8600
CERVELO S5 Team	16.2	6000
GIANT TCR Advanced 2	17.1	2580
WILIER TRIESTINA Gran Turismo	17.6	3400
SPECIALIZED S-Works Amira SL4	14.1	8000

    a. Use the data to develop an estimated regression equation that could be used to estimate the price for a bike given the weight.
    b. Compute r^2. Did the estimated regression equation provide a good fit?
    c. Predict the price for a bike that weighs 15 pounds.

21. An important application of regression analysis in accounting is in the estimation of cost. By collecting data on volume and cost and using the least squares method to develop an estimated regression equation relating volume and cost, an accountant can estimate the cost associated with a particular manufacturing volume. Consider the following sample of production volumes and total cost data for a manufacturing operation.

Production Volume (units)	Total Cost ($)
400	4000
450	5000
550	5400
600	5900
700	6400
750	7000

a. Use these data to develop an estimated regression equation that could be used to predict the total cost for a given production volume.
b. What is the variable cost per unit produced?
c. Compute the coefficient of determination. What percentage of the variation in total cost can be explained by production volume?
d. The company's production schedule shows 500 units must be produced next month. Predict the total cost for this operation?

22. Refer to exercise 9 where the following data were used to investigate the relationship between the number of cars in service (1000s) and the annual revenue ($millions) for six smaller car rental companies (*Auto Rental News* website, August 7, 2012).

Company	Cars (1000s)	Revenue ($millions)
U-Save Auto Rental System, Inc.	11.5	118
Payless Car Rental System, Inc.	10.0	135
ACE Rent A Car	9.0	100
Rent-A-Wreck of America	5.5	37
Triangle Rent-A-Car	4.2	40
Affordable/Sensible	3.3	32

With x = cars in service (1000s) and y = annual revenue ($millions), the estimated regression equation is $\hat{y} = -17.005 + 12.966x$. For these data, SSE = 1043.03.
a. Compute the coefficient of determination r^2.
b. Did the estimated regression equation provide a good fit? Explain.
c. What is the value of the sample correlation coefficient? Does it reflect a strong or weak relationship between the number of cars in service and the annual revenue?

Model Assumptions

In conducting a regression analysis, we begin by making an assumption about the appropriate model for the relationship between the dependent and independent variable(s). For the case of simple linear regression, the assumed regression model is

$$y = \beta_0 + \beta_1 x + \epsilon$$

Then the least squares method is used to develop values for b_0 and b_1, the estimates of the model parameters β_0 and β_1, respectively. The resulting estimated regression equation is

$$\hat{y} = b_0 + b_1 x$$

We saw that the value of the coefficient of determination (r^2) is a measure of the goodness of fit of the estimated regression equation. However, even with a large value of r^2, the estimated regression equation should not be used until further analysis of the appropriateness of the assumed model has been conducted. An important step in determining whether the assumed model is appropriate involves testing for the significance of the relationship. The tests of significance in regression analysis are based on the following assumptions about the error term ϵ.

ASSUMPTIONS ABOUT THE ERROR TERM ϵ IN THE REGRESSION MODEL

$$y = \beta_0 + \beta_1 x + \epsilon$$

1. The error term ϵ is a random variable with a mean or expected value of zero; that is, $E(\epsilon) = 0$.
   Implication: β_0 and β_1 are constants, therefore $E(\beta_0) = \beta_0$ and $E(\beta_1) = \beta_1$; thus, for a given value of x, the expected value of y is

$$E(y) = \beta_0 + \beta_1 x \qquad (12.14)$$

   As we indicated previously, equation (12.14) is referred to as the regression equation.

2. The variance of ϵ, denoted by σ^2, is the same for all values of x.
   Implication: The variance of y about the regression line equals σ^2 and is the same for all values of x.

3. The values of ϵ are independent.
   Implication: The value of ϵ for a particular value of x is not related to the value of ϵ for any other value of x; thus, the value of y for a particular value of x is not related to the value of y for any other value of x.

4. The error term ϵ is a normally distributed random variable for all values of x.
   Implication: Because y is a linear function of ϵ, y is also a normally distributed random variable for all values of x.

Figure 12.6 illustrates the model assumptions and their implications; note that in this graphical interpretation, the value of $E(y)$ changes according to the specific value of x considered. However, regardless of the x value, the probability distribution of ϵ and hence the probability distributions of y are normally distributed, each with the same variance. The specific value of the error ϵ at any particular point depends on whether the actual value of y is greater than or less than $E(y)$.

At this point, we must keep in mind that we are also making an assumption or hypothesis about the form of the relationship between x and y. That is, we assume that a straight line represented by $\beta_0 + \beta_1 x$ is the basis for the relationship between the variables. We must not lose sight of the fact that some other model, for instance $y = \beta_0 + \beta_1 x^2 + \epsilon$, may turn out to be a better model for the underlying relationship.

12.5 Testing for Significance

In a simple linear regression equation, the mean or expected value of y is a linear function of x: $E(y) = \beta_0 + \beta_1 x$. If the value of β_1 is zero, $E(y) = \beta_0 + (0)x = \beta_0$. In this case, the mean value of y does not depend on the value of x and hence we would conclude that x and y are not linearly related. Alternatively, if the value of β_1 is not equal to zero, we would conclude that the two variables are related. Thus, to test for a significant regression relationship, we must conduct a hypothesis test to determine whether the value of β_1 is zero. Two tests are commonly used. Both require an estimate of σ^2, the variance of ϵ in the regression model.

Estimate of σ^2

From the regression model and its assumptions we can conclude that σ^2, the variance of ϵ, also represents the variance of the y values about the regression line. Recall that the deviations of the y values about the estimated regression line are called residuals. Thus,

FIGURE 12.6   ASSUMPTIONS FOR THE REGRESSION MODEL

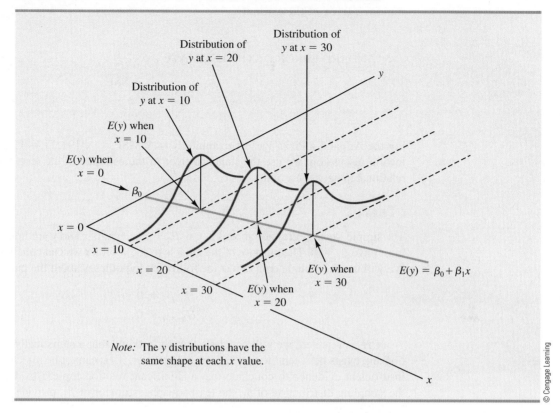

Note: The y distributions have the same shape at each x value.

SSE, the sum of squared residuals, is a measure of the variability of the actual observations about the estimated regression line. The **mean square error** (MSE) provides the estimate of σ^2; it is SSE divided by its degrees of freedom.

With $\hat{y}_i = b_0 + b_1 x_i$, SSE can be written as

$$\text{SSE} = \Sigma(y_i - \hat{y}_i)^2 = \Sigma(y_i - b_0 - b_1 x_i)^2$$

Every sum of squares has associated with it a number called its degrees of freedom. Statisticians have shown that SSE has $n - 2$ degrees of freedom because two parameters (β_0 and β_1) must be estimated to compute SSE. Thus, the mean square error is computed by dividing SSE by $n - 2$. MSE provides an unbiased estimator of σ^2. Because the value of MSE provides an estimate of σ^2, the notation s^2 is also used.

MEAN SQUARE ERROR (ESTIMATE OF σ^2)

$$s^2 = \text{MSE} = \frac{\text{SSE}}{n - 2} \tag{12.15}$$

In Section 12.3 we showed that for the Armand's Pizza Parlors example, SSE = 1530; hence,

$$s^2 = \text{MSE} = \frac{1530}{8} = 191.25$$

provides an unbiased estimate of σ^2.

To estimate σ we take the square root of s^2. The resulting value, s, is referred to as the **standard error of the estimate**.

STANDARD ERROR OF THE ESTIMATE

$$s = \sqrt{\text{MSE}} = \sqrt{\frac{\text{SSE}}{n - 2}} \qquad (12.16)$$

For the Armand's Pizza Parlors example, $s = \sqrt{\text{MSE}} = \sqrt{191.25} = 13.829$. In the following discussion, we use the standard error of the estimate in the tests for a significant relationship between x and y.

t Test

The simple linear regression model is $y = \beta_0 + \beta_1 x + \epsilon$. If x and y are linearly related, we must have $\beta_1 \neq 0$. The purpose of the t test is to see whether we can conclude that $\beta_1 \neq 0$. We will use the sample data to test the following hypotheses about the parameter β_1.

$$H_0 \colon \beta_1 = 0$$
$$H_a \colon \beta_1 \neq 0$$

If H_0 is rejected, we will conclude that $\beta_1 \neq 0$ and that a statistically significant relationship exists between the two variables. However, if H_0 cannot be rejected, we will have insufficient evidence to conclude that a significant relationship exists. The properties of the sampling distribution of b_1, the least squares estimator of β_1, provide the basis for the hypothesis test.

First, let us consider what would happen if we used a different random sample for the same regression study. For example, suppose that Armand's Pizza Parlors used the sales records of a different sample of 10 restaurants. A regression analysis of this new sample might result in an estimated regression equation similar to our previous estimated regression equation $\hat{y} = 60 + 5x$. However, it is doubtful that we would obtain exactly the same equation (with an intercept of exactly 60 and a slope of exactly 5). Indeed, b_0 and b_1, the least squares estimators, are sample statistics with their own sampling distributions. The properties of the sampling distribution of b_1 follow.

SAMPLING DISTRIBUTION OF b_1

Expected Value

$$E(b_1) = \beta_1$$

Standard Deviation

$$\sigma_{b_1} = \frac{\sigma}{\sqrt{\sum(x_i - \bar{x})^2}} \qquad (12.17)$$

Distribution Form

Normal

Note that the expected value of b_1 is equal to β_1, so b_1 is an unbiased estimator of β_1.

Because we do not know the value of σ, we develop an estimate of σ_{b_1}, denoted s_{b_1}, by estimating σ with s in equation (12.17). Thus, we obtain the following estimate of σ_{b_1}.

The standard deviation of b_1 is also referred to as the standard error of b_1. Thus, s_{b_1} provides an estimate of the standard error of b_1.

ESTIMATED STANDARD DEVIATION OF b_1

$$s_{b_1} = \frac{s}{\sqrt{\Sigma(x_i - \bar{x})^2}}$$

(12.18)

For Armand's Pizza Parlors, $s = 13.829$. Hence, using $\Sigma(x_i - \bar{x})^2 = 568$ as shown in Table 12.2, we have

$$s_{b_1} = \frac{13.829}{\sqrt{568}} = .5803$$

as the estimated standard deviation of b_1.

The t test for a significant relationship is based on the fact that the test statistic

$$\frac{b_1 - \beta_1}{s_{b_1}}$$

follows a t distribution with $n - 2$ degrees of freedom. If the null hypothesis is true, then $\beta_1 = 0$ and $t = b_1/s_{b_1}$.

Let us conduct this test of significance for Armand's Pizza Parlors at the $\alpha = .01$ level of significance. The test statistic is

$$t = \frac{b_1}{s_{b_1}} = \frac{5}{.5803} = 8.62$$

Appendixes 12.1 and 12.2 show how Minitab and Excel can be used to compute the p-value.

The t distribution table (Table 2 of Appendix D) shows that with $n - 2 = 10 - 2 = 8$ degrees of freedom, $t = 3.355$ provides an area of .005 in the upper tail. Thus, the area in the upper tail of the t distribution corresponding to the test statistic $t = 8.62$ must be less than .005. Because this test is a two-tailed test, we double this value to conclude that the p-value associated with $t = 8.62$ must be less than $2(.005) = .01$. Excel or Minitab show the p-value $= .000$. Because the p-value is less than $\alpha = .01$, we reject H_0 and conclude that β_1 is not equal to zero. This evidence is sufficient to conclude that a significant relationship exists between student population and quarterly sales. A summary of the t test for significance in simple linear regression follows.

t TEST FOR SIGNIFICANCE IN SIMPLE LINEAR REGRESSION

$$H_0: \beta_1 = 0$$
$$H_a: \beta_1 \neq 0$$

TEST STATISTIC

$$t = \frac{b_1}{s_{b_1}}$$

(12.19)

REJECTION RULE

p-value approach: Reject H_0 if p-value $\leq \alpha$

Critical value approach: Reject H_0 if $t \leq -t_{\alpha/2}$ or if $t \geq t_{\alpha/2}$

where $t_{\alpha/2}$ is based on a t distribution with $n - 2$ degrees of freedom.

Confidence Interval for β_1

The form of a confidence interval for β_1 is as follows:

$$b_1 \pm t_{\alpha/2}s_{b_1}$$

The point estimator is b_1 and the margin of error is $t_{\alpha/2}s_{b_1}$. The confidence coefficient associated with this interval is $1 - \alpha$, and $t_{\alpha/2}$ is the t value providing an area of $\alpha/2$ in the upper tail of a t distribution with $n - 2$ degrees of freedom. For example, suppose that we wanted to develop a 99% confidence interval estimate of β_1 for Armand's Pizza Parlors. From Table 2 of Appendix B we find that the t value corresponding to $\alpha = .01$ and $n - 2 = 10 - 2 = 8$ degrees of freedom is $t_{.005} = 3.355$. Thus, the 99% confidence interval estimate of β_1 is

$$b_1 \pm t_{\alpha/2}s_{b_1} = 5 \pm 3.355(.5803) = 5 \pm 1.95$$

or 3.05 to 6.95.

In using the t test for significance, the hypotheses tested were

$$H_0: \beta_1 = 0$$
$$H_a: \beta_1 \neq 0$$

At the $\alpha = .01$ level of significance, we can use the 99% confidence interval as an alternative for drawing the hypothesis testing conclusion for the Armand's data. Because 0, the hypothesized value of β_1, is not included in the confidence interval (3.05 to 6.95), we can reject H_0 and conclude that a significant statistical relationship exists between the size of the student population and quarterly sales. In general, a confidence interval can be used to test any two-sided hypothesis about β_1. If the hypothesized value of β_1 is contained in the confidence interval, do not reject H_0. Otherwise, reject H_0.

F Test

An F test, based on the F probability distribution, can also be used to test for significance in regression. With only one independent variable, the F test will provide the same conclusion as the t test; that is, if the t test indicates $\beta_1 \neq 0$ and hence a significant relationship, the F test will also indicate a significant relationship. But with more than one independent variable, only the F test can be used to test for an overall significant relationship.

The logic behind the use of the F test for determining whether the regression relationship is statistically significant is based on the development of two independent estimates of σ^2. We explained how MSE provides an estimate of σ^2. If the null hypothesis $H_0: \beta_1 = 0$ is true, the sum of squares due to regression, SSR, divided by its degrees of freedom provides another independent estimate of σ^2. This estimate is called the *mean square due to regression,* or simply the *mean square regression,* and is denoted MSR. In general,

$$MSR = \frac{SSR}{\text{Regression degrees of freedom}}$$

For the models we consider in this text, the regression degrees of freedom is always equal to the number of independent variables in the model:

$$MSR = \frac{SSR}{\text{Number of independent variables}} \tag{12.20}$$

Because we consider only regression models with one independent variable in this chapter, we have MSR = SSR/1 = SSR. Hence, for Armand's Pizza Parlors, MSR = SSR = 14,200.

If the null hypothesis (H_0: $\beta_1 = 0$) is true, MSR and MSE are two independent estimates of σ^2 and the sampling distribution of MSR/MSE follows an F distribution with numerator degrees of freedom equal to one and denominator degrees of freedom equal to $n - 2$. Therefore, when $\beta_1 = 0$, the value of MSR/MSE should be close to 1. However, if the null hypothesis is false ($\beta_1 \neq 0$), MSR will overestimate σ^2 and the value of MSR/MSE will be inflated; thus, large values of MSR/MSE lead to the rejection of H_0 and the conclusion that the relationship between x and y is statistically significant.

Let us conduct the F test for the Armand's Pizza Parlors example. The test statistic is

$$F = \frac{\text{MSR}}{\text{MSE}} = \frac{14,200}{191.25} = 74.25$$

The F test and the t test provide identical results for simple linear regression.

The F distribution table (Table 4 of Appendix B) shows that with 1 degree of freedom in the numerator and $n - 2 = 10 - 2 = 8$ degrees of freedom in the denominator, $F = 11.26$ provides an area of .01 in the upper tail. Thus, the area in the upper tail of the F distribution corresponding to the test statistic $F = 74.25$ must be less than .01. Thus, we conclude that the p-value must be less than .01. Excel or Minitab show the p-value = .000. Because the p-value is less than $\alpha = .01$, we reject H_0 and conclude that a significant relationship exists between the size of the student population and quarterly sales. A summary of the F test for significance in simple linear regression follows.

If H_0 is false, MSE still provides an unbiased estimate of σ^2 and MSR overestimates σ^2. If H_0 is true, both MSE and MSR provide unbiased estimates of σ^2; in this case the value of MSR/MSE should be close to 1.

F TEST FOR SIGNIFICANCE IN SIMPLE LINEAR REGRESSION

$$H_0: \beta_1 = 0$$
$$H_a: \beta_1 \neq 0$$

TEST STATISTIC

$$F = \frac{\text{MSR}}{\text{MSE}} \qquad (12.21)$$

REJECTION RULE

p-value approach: Reject H_0 if p-value $\leq \alpha$

Critical value approach: Reject H_0 if $F \geq F_\alpha$

where F_α is based on an F distribution with 1 degree of freedom in the numerator and $n - 2$ degrees of freedom in the denominator.

In Chapter 10 we covered analysis of variance (ANOVA) and showed how an **ANOVA table** could be used to provide a convenient summary of the computational aspects of analysis of variance. A similar ANOVA table can be used to summarize the results of the F test for significance in regression. Table 12.5 is the general form of the ANOVA table for simple linear regression. Table 12.6 is the ANOVA table with the F test computations performed for Armand's Pizza Parlors. Regression, Error, and Total are the labels for the three sources of variation, with SSR, SSE, and SST appearing as the corresponding sum of squares in column 2. The degrees of freedom, 1 for SSR, $n - 2$ for SSE, and $n - 1$ for SST, are shown in column 3. Column 4 contains the values of MSR and MSE, column 5 contains the value of $F = $ MSR/MSE, and column 6 contains the p-value corresponding to the F value in column 5.

TABLE 12.5 GENERAL FORM OF THE ANOVA TABLE FOR SIMPLE LINEAR REGRESSION

In every analysis of variance table the total sum of squares is the sum of the regression sum of squares and the error sum of squares; in addition, the total degrees of freedom is the sum of the regression degrees of freedom and the error degrees of freedom.

Source of Variation	Sum of Squares	Degrees of Freedom	Mean Square	F	p-value
Regression	SSR	1	$\text{MSR} = \dfrac{\text{SSR}}{1}$	$F = \dfrac{\text{MSR}}{\text{MSE}}$	
Error	SSE	$n - 2$	$\text{MSE} = \dfrac{\text{SSE}}{n - 2}$		
Total	SST	$n - 1$			

Almost all computer printouts of regression analysis include an ANOVA table summary of the F test for significance.

Some Cautions About the Interpretation of Significance Tests

Rejecting the null hypothesis H_0: $\beta_1 = 0$ and concluding that the relationship between x and y is significant does not enable us to conclude that a cause-and-effect relationship is present between x and y. Concluding a cause-and-effect relationship is warranted only if the analyst can provide some type of theoretical justification that the relationship is in fact causal. In the Armand's Pizza Parlors example, we can conclude that there is a significant relationship between the size of the student population x and quarterly sales y; moreover, the estimated regression equation $\hat{y} = 60 + 5x$ provides the least squares estimate of the relationship. We cannot, however, conclude that changes in student population x *cause* changes in quarterly sales y just because we identified a statistically significant relationship. The appropriateness of such a cause-and-effect conclusion is left to supporting theoretical justification and to good judgment on the part of the analyst. Armand's managers felt that increases in the student population were a likely cause of increased quarterly sales. Thus, the result of the significance test enabled them to conclude that a cause-and-effect relationship was present.

Regression analysis, which can be used to identify how variables are associated with one another, cannot be used as evidence of a cause-and-effect relationship.

In addition, just because we are able to reject H_0: $\beta_1 = 0$ and demonstrate statistical significance does not enable us to conclude that the relationship between x and y is linear. We can state only that x and y are related and that a linear relationship explains a significant portion of the variability in y over the range of values for x observed in the sample. Figure 12.7 illustrates this situation. The test for significance calls for the rejection of the null hypothesis H_0: $\beta_1 = 0$ and leads to the conclusion that x and y are significantly related,

TABLE 12.6 ANOVA TABLE FOR THE ARMAND'S PIZZA PARLORS PROBLEM

Source of Variation	Sum of Squares	Degrees of Freedom	Mean Square	F	p-value
Regression	14,200	1	$\dfrac{14{,}200}{1} = 14{,}200$	$\dfrac{14{,}200}{191.25} = 74.25$	.000
Error	1,530	8	$\dfrac{1530}{8} = 191.25$		
Total	15,730	9			

FIGURE 12.7   EXAMPLE OF A LINEAR APPROXIMATION OF A NONLINEAR RELATIONSHIP

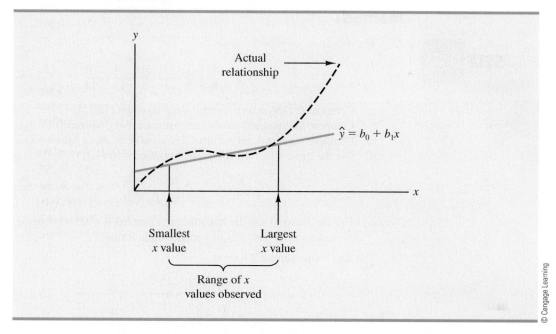

but the figure shows that the actual relationship between x and y is not linear. Although the linear approximation provided by $\hat{y} = b_0 + b_1x$ is good over the range of x values observed in the sample, it becomes poor for x values outside that range.

Given a significant relationship, we should feel confident in using the estimated regression equation for predictions corresponding to x values within the range of the x values observed in the sample. For Armand's Pizza Parlors, this range corresponds to values of x between 2 and 26. Unless other reasons indicate that the model is valid beyond this range, predictions outside the range of the independent variable should be made with caution. For Armand's Pizza Parlors, because the regression relationship has been found significant at the .01 level, we should feel confident using it to predict sales for restaurants where the associated student population is between 2000 and 26,000.

NOTES AND COMMENTS

1. The assumptions made about the error term (Section 12.4) are what allow the tests of statistical significance in this section. The properties of the sampling distribution of b_1 and the subsequent t and F tests follow directly from these assumptions.

2. Do not confuse statistical significance with practical significance. With very large sample sizes, statistically significant results can be obtained for small values of b_1; in such cases, one must exercise care in concluding that the relationship has practical significance.

3. A test of significance for a linear relationship between x and y can also be performed by using the sample correlation coefficient r_{xy}. With ρ_{xy}

denoting the population correlation coefficient, the hypotheses are as follows.

$$H_0: \rho_{xy} = 0$$
$$H_a: \rho_{xy} \neq 0$$

A significant relationship can be concluded if H_0 is rejected. The details of this test are provided in more advanced texts. However, the t and F tests presented previously in this section give the same result as the test for significance using the correlation coefficient. Conducting a test for significance using the correlation coefficient therefore is not necessary if a t or F test has already been conducted.

Exercises

Methods

23. The data from exercise 1 follow.

x_i	1	2	3	4	5
y_i	3	7	5	11	14

a. Compute the mean square error using equation (12.15).
b. Compute the standard error of the estimate using equation (12.16).
c. Compute the estimated standard deviation of b_1 using equation (12.18).
d. Use the t test to test the following hypotheses ($\alpha = .05$):

$$H_0: \beta_1 = 0$$
$$H_a: \beta_1 \neq 0$$

e. Use the F test to test the hypotheses in part (d) at a .05 level of significance. Present the results in the analysis of variance table format.

24. The data from exercise 2 follow.

x_i	3	12	6	20	14
y_i	55	40	55	10	15

a. Compute the mean square error using equation (12.15).
b. Compute the standard error of the estimate using equation (12.16).
c. Compute the estimated standard deviation of b_1 using equation (12.18).
d. Use the t test to test the following hypotheses ($\alpha = .05$):

$$H_0: \beta_1 = 0$$
$$H_a: \beta_1 \neq 0$$

e. Use the F test to test the hypotheses in part (d) at a .05 level of significance. Present the results in the analysis of variance table format.

25. The data from exercise 3 follow.

x_i	2	6	9	13	20
y_i	7	18	9	26	23

a. What is the value of the standard error of the estimate?
b. Test for a significant relationship by using the t test. Use $\alpha = .05$.
c. Use the F test to test for a significant relationship. Use $\alpha = .05$. What is your conclusion?

Applications

26. In exercise 18 the data on price ($) and the overall score for six stereo headphones tested by *Consumer Reports* were as follows (*Consumer Reports* website, March 5, 2012).

Brand	Price ($)	Score
Bose	180	76
Skullcandy	150	71
Koss	95	61
Phillips/O'Neill	70	56
Denon	70	40
JVC	35	26

    a. Does the *t* test indicate a significant relationship between price and the overall score? What is your conclusion? Use $\alpha = .05$.

    b. Test for a significant relationship using the *F* test. What is your conclusion? Use $\alpha = .05$.

    c. Show the ANOVA table for these data.

27. The number of megapixels in a digital camera is one of the most important factors in determining picture quality. But do digital cameras with more megapixels cost more? The following data show the number of megapixels and the price ($) for 10 digital cameras (*Consumer Reports,* March 2009).

DigitalCameras

Brand and Model	Megapixels	Price ($)
Canon PowerShot SD1100 IS	8	180
Casio Exilim Card EX-510	10	200
Sony Cyber-shot DSC-T70	7	230
Pentax Optio M50	8	120
Canon PowerShot G10	15	470
Canon PowerShot A590 IS	8	140
Canon PowerShot E1	10	180
Fujifilm FinePix F00FD	12	310
Sony Cyber-shot DSC-W170	10	250
Canon PowerShot A470	7	110

    a. Use these data to develop an estimated regression equation that can be used to predict the price of a digital camera given the number of megapixels.

    b. At the .05 level of significance, are the number of megapixels and the price related? Explain.

    c. Would you feel comfortable using the estimated regression equation developed in part (a) to predict the price of a digital camera given the number of megapixels? Explain.

    d. The Canon Power Shot S95 digital camera has 10 megapixels. Predict the price of this camera using the estimated regression equation developed in part (a).

28. In exercise 8 ratings data on $x =$ the quality of the speed of execution and $y =$ overall satisfaction with electronic trades provided the estimated regression equation $\hat{y} = .2046 + .9077x$ (AAII website, February 7, 2012). At the .05 level of significance, test whether speed of execution and overall satisfaction are related. Show the ANOVA table. What is your conclusion?

BrokerRatings

29. Refer to exercise 21, where data on production volume and cost were used to develop an estimated regression equation relating production volume and cost for a particular manufacturing operation. Use $\alpha = .05$ to test whether the production volume is significantly related to the total cost. Show the ANOVA table. What is your conclusion?

30. Refer to exercise 9 where the following data were used to investigate the relationship between the number of cars in service (1000s) and the annual revenue ($millions) for six smaller car rental companies (*Auto Rental News* website, August 7, 2012).

Company	Cars (1000s)	Revenue ($millions)
U-Save Auto Rental System, Inc.	11.5	118
Payless Car Rental System, Inc.	10.0	135
ACE Rent A Car	9.0	100
Rent-A-Wreck of America	5.5	37
Triangle Rent-A-Car	4.2	40
Affordable/Sensible	3.3	32

With x = cars in service (1000s) and y = annual revenue ($millions), the estimated regression equation is $\hat{y} = -17.005 + 12.966x$. For these data SSE = 1043.03 and SST = 10,568. Do these results indicate a significant relationship between the number of cars in service and the annual revenue?

RacingBicycles

31. In exercise 20, data on x = weight (pounds) and y = price ($) for 10 road-racing bikes provided the estimated regression equation $\hat{y} = 28,574 - 1439x$. (*Bicycling* website, March 8, 2012). For these data SSE = 7,102,922.54 and SST = 52,120,800. Use the F test to determine whether the weight for a bike and the price are related at the .05 level of significance.

(12.6) Using the Estimated Regression Equation for Estimation and Prediction

When using the simple linear regression model, we are making an assumption about the relationship between x and y. We then use the least squares method to obtain the estimated simple linear regression equation. If a significant relationship exists between x and y and the coefficient of determination shows that the fit is good, the estimated regression equation should be useful for estimation and prediction.

For the Armand's Pizza Parlors example, the estimated regression equation is $\hat{y} = 60 + 5x$. At the end of Section 12.1 we stated that $\hat{y}$ can be used as a *point estimator* of $E(y)$, the mean or expected value of y for a given value of x, and as a predictor of an individual value of y. For example, suppose Armand's managers want to estimate the mean quarterly sales for *all* restaurants located near college campuses with 10,000 students. Using the estimated regression equation $\hat{y} = 60 + 5x$, we see that for $x = 10$ (10,000 students), $\hat{y} = 60 + 5(10) = 110$. Thus, a *point estimate* of the mean quarterly sales for all restaurant locations near campuses with 10,000 students is $110,000. In this case we are using $\hat{y}$ as the point estimator of the mean value of y when $x = 10$.

We can also use the estimated regression equation to *predict* an individual value of y for a given value of x. For example, to predict quarterly sales for a new restaurant Armand's is considering building near Talbot College, a campus with 10,000 students, we would compute $\hat{y} = 60 + 5(10) = 110$. Hence, we would predict quarterly sales of $110,000 for such a new restaurant. In this case, we are using $\hat{y}$ as the *predictor of y* for a new observation when $x = 10$.

When we are using the estimated regression equation to estimate the mean value of y or to predict an individual value of y, it is clear that the estimate or prediction depends on the given value of x. For this reason, as we discuss in more depth the issues concerning estimation and prediction, the following notation will help clarify matters.

x^* = the given value of the independent variable x
y^* = the random variable denoting the possible values of the dependent variable y when $x = x^*$
$E(y^*)$ = the mean or expected value of the dependent variable y when $x = x^*$
$\hat{y}^* = b_0 + b_1 x^*$ = the point estimator of $E(y^*)$ and the predictor of an individual value of y^* when $x = x^*$

To illustrate the use of this notation, suppose we want to estimate the mean value of quarterly sales for *all* Armand's restaurants located near a campus with 10,000 students. For this case, $x^* = 10$ and $E(y^*)$ denotes the unknown mean value of quarterly sales for all restaurants where $x^* = 10$. Thus, the point estimate of $E(y^*)$ is provided by $\hat{y}^* = 60 + 5(10) = 110$, or $110,000. But, using this notation, $\hat{y}^* = 110$ is also the predictor of quarterly sales for the new restaurant located near Talbot College, a school with 10,000 students.

Interval Estimation

Confidence intervals and prediction intervals show the precision of the regression results. Narrower intervals provide a higher degree of precision.

Point estimators and predictors do not provide any information about the precision associated with the estimate and/or prediction. For that we must develop confidence intervals and prediction intervals. A **confidence interval** is an interval estimate of the *mean value of y* for a given value of x. A **prediction interval** is used whenever we want to *predict an individual value of y* for a new observation corresponding to a given value of x. Although the predictor of y for a given value of x is the same as the point estimator of the mean value of y for a given value of x, the interval estimates we obtain for the two cases are different. As we will show, the margin of error is larger for a prediction interval. We begin by showing how to develop an interval estimate of the mean value of y.

Confidence Interval for the Mean Value of y

In general, we cannot expect $\hat{y}^*$ to equal $E(y^*)$ exactly. If we want to make an inference about how close $\hat{y}^*$ is to the true mean value $E(y^*)$, we will have to estimate the variance of $\hat{y}^*$. The formula for estimating the variance of $\hat{y}^*$, denoted by $s_{\hat{y}^*}^2$, is

$$s_{\hat{y}^*}^2 = s^2\left[\frac{1}{n} + \frac{(x^* - \bar{x})^2}{\Sigma(x_i - \bar{x})^2}\right] \tag{12.22}$$

The estimate of the standard deviation of $\hat{y}^*$ is given by the square root of equation (12.22).

$$s_{\hat{y}^*} = s\sqrt{\frac{1}{n} + \frac{(x^* - \bar{x})^2}{\Sigma(x_i - \bar{x})^2}} \tag{12.23}$$

The computational results for Armand's Pizza Parlors in Section 12.5 provided $s = 13.829$. With $x^* = 10$, $\bar{x} = 14$, and $\Sigma(x_i - \bar{x})^2 = 568$, we can use equation (12.23) to obtain

$$s_{\hat{y}^*} = 13.829\sqrt{\frac{1}{10} + \frac{(10 - 14)^2}{568}}$$

$$= 13.829\sqrt{.1282} = 4.95$$

The general expression for a confidence interval follows.

The margin of error associated with this confidence interval is
$t_{\alpha/2}s_{\hat{y}^*}.$

CONFIDENCE INTERVAL FOR $E(y^*)$

$$\hat{y}^* \pm t_{\alpha/2}s_{\hat{y}^*} \tag{12.24}$$

where the confidence coefficient is $1 - \alpha$ and $t_{\alpha/2}$ is based on the t distribution with $n - 2$ degrees of freedom.

Using expression (12.24) to develop a 95% confidence interval of the mean quarterly sales for all Armand's restaurants located near campuses with 10,000 students, we need the value of t for $\alpha/2 = .025$ and $n - 2 = 10 - 2 = 8$ degrees of freedom. Using Table 2 of Appendix B, we have $t_{.025} = 2.306$. Thus, with $\hat{y}^* = 110$ and a margin of error of $t_{\alpha/2}s_{\hat{y}^*} = 2.306(4.95) = 11.415$, the 95% confidence interval estimate is

$$110 \pm 11.415$$

FIGURE 12.8   CONFIDENCE INTERVALS FOR THE MEAN SALES *y* AT GIVEN VALUES OF STUDENT POPULATION *x*

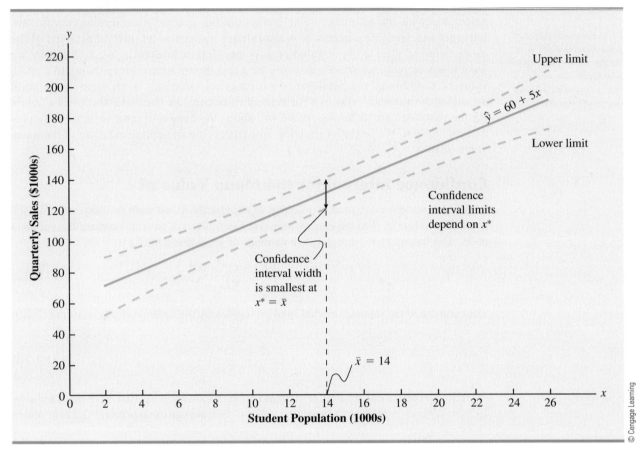

In dollars, the 95% confidence interval for the mean quarterly sales of all restaurants near campuses with 10,000 students is $110,000 ± $11,415. Therefore, the 95% confidence interval for the mean quarterly sales when the student population is 10,000 is $98,585 to $121,415.

Note that the estimated standard deviation of $\hat{y}^*$ given by equation (12.23) is smallest when $x^* - \bar{x} = 0$. In this case the estimated standard deviation of $\hat{y}^*$ becomes

$$s_{\hat{y}^*} = s\sqrt{\frac{1}{n} + \frac{(\bar{x} - \bar{x})^2}{\sum(x_i - \bar{x})^2}} = s\sqrt{\frac{1}{n}}$$

This result implies that we can make the best or most precise estimate of the mean value of *y* whenever $x^* = \bar{x}$. In fact, the further x^* is from $\bar{x}$, the larger $x^* - \bar{x}$ becomes. As a result, the confidence interval for the mean value of *y* will become wider as x^* deviates more from $\bar{x}$. This pattern is shown graphically in Figure 12.8.

Prediction Interval for an Individual Value of *y*

Instead of estimating the mean value of quarterly sales for all Armand's restaurants located near campuses with 10,000 students, suppose we want to predict quarterly sales for a new restaurant Armand's is considering building near Talbot College, a campus with 10,000 students. As noted previously, the predictor of y^*, the value of *y* corresponding to the given x^*, is

$\hat{y}^* = b_0 + b_1 x^*$. For the new restaurant located near Talbot College, $x^* = 10$ and the prediction of quarterly sales is $\hat{y}^* = 60 + 5(10) = 110$, or \$110,000. Note that the prediction of quarterly sales for the new Armand's restaurant near Talbot College is the same as the point estimate of the mean sales for all Armand's restaurants located near campuses with 10,000 students.

To develop a prediction interval, let us first determine the variance associated with using $\hat{y}^*$ as a predictor of y when $x = x^*$. This variance is made up of the sum of the following two components.

1. The variance of the y^* values about the mean $E(y^*)$, an estimate of which is given by s^2
2. The variance associated with using $\hat{y}^*$ to estimate $E(y^*)$, an estimate of which is given by $s_{\hat{y}^*}^2$

The formula for estimating the variance corresponding to the prediction of the value of y when $x = x^*$, denoted s_{pred}^2, is

$$
\begin{aligned}
s_{pred}^2 &= s^2 + s_{\hat{y}^*}^2 \\
&= s^2 + s^2 \left[\frac{1}{n} + \frac{(x^* - \bar{x})^2}{\sum (x_i - \bar{x})^2} \right] \\
&= s^2 \left[1 + \frac{1}{n} + \frac{(x^* - \bar{x})^2}{\sum (x_i - \bar{x})^2} \right]
\end{aligned}
\tag{12.25}
$$

Hence, an estimate of the standard deviation corresponding to the prediction of the value of y^* is

$$
s_{pred} = s \sqrt{1 + \frac{1}{n} + \frac{(x^* - \bar{x})^2}{\sum (x_i - \bar{x})^2}}
\tag{12.26}
$$

For Armand's Pizza Parlors, the estimated standard deviation corresponding to the prediction of quarterly sales for a new restaurant located near Talbot College, a campus with 10,000 students, is computed as follows.

$$
\begin{aligned}
s_{pred} &= 13.829 \sqrt{1 + \frac{1}{10} + \frac{(10 - 14)^2}{568}} \\
&= 13.829 \sqrt{1.282} \\
&= 14.69
\end{aligned}
$$

The general expression for a prediction interval follows.

PREDICTION INTERVAL FOR y^*

The margin of error associated with this prediction interval is $t_{\alpha/2} s_{pred}$.

$$
\hat{y}^* \pm t_{\alpha/2} s_{pred}
\tag{12.27}
$$

where the confidence coefficient is $1 - \alpha$ and $t_{\alpha/2}$ is based on a t distribution with $n - 2$ degrees of freedom.

The 95% prediction interval for quarterly sales for the new Armand's restaurant located near Talbot College can be found using $t_{\alpha/2} = t_{.025} = 2.306$ and $s_{pred} = 14.69$. Thus, with $\hat{y}^* = 110$ and a margin of error of $t_{.025} s_{pred} = 2.306(14.69) = 33.875$, the 95% prediction interval is

$$
110 \pm 33.875
$$

FIGURE 12.9 CONFIDENCE AND PREDICTION INTERVALS FOR SALES y AT GIVEN VALUES OF STUDENT POPULATION x

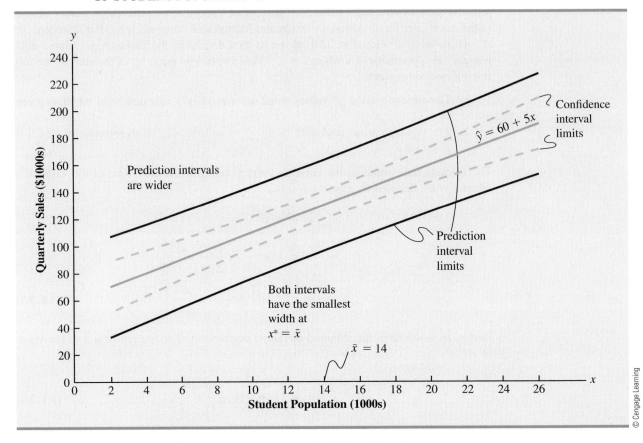

© Cengage Learning

In dollars, this prediction interval is \$110,000 ± \$33,875 or \$76,125 to \$143,875. Note that the prediction interval for the new restaurant located near Talbot College, a campus with 10,000 students, is wider than the confidence interval for the mean quarterly sales of all restaurants located near campuses with 10,000 students. The difference reflects the fact that we are able to estimate the mean value of y more precisely than we can predict an individual value of y.

In general, the lines for the confidence interval limits and the prediction interval limits both have curvature.

Confidence intervals and prediction intervals are both more precise when the value of the independent variable x^* is closer to $\bar{x}$. The general shapes of confidence intervals and the wider prediction intervals are shown together in Figure 12.9.

NOTE AND COMMENT

A prediction interval is used to predict the value of the dependent variable y for a *new observation*. As an illustration, we showed how to develop a prediction interval of quarterly sales for a new restaurant that Armand's is considering building near Talbot College, a campus with 10,000 students. The fact that the value of $x = 10$ is not one of the values of student population for the Armand's sample data in Table 12.1 is not meant to imply that prediction intervals cannot be developed for values of x in the sample data. But, for the 10 restaurants that make up the data in Table 12.1, developing a prediction interval for quarterly sales for *one of these restaurants* does not make any sense because we already know the value of quarterly sales for each of these restaurants. In other words, a prediction interval only has meaning for something new, in this case a new observation corresponding to a particular value of x that may or may not equal one of the values of x in the sample.

Exercises

Methods

32.   The data from exercise 1 follow.

x_i	1	2	3	4	5
y_i	3	7	5	11	14

  a.   Use equation (12.23) to estimate the standard deviation of $\hat{y}^*$ when $x = 4$.
  b.   Use expression (12.24) to develop a 95% confidence interval for the expected value of y when $x = 4$.
  c.   Use equation (12.26) to estimate the standard deviation of an individual value of y when $x = 4$.
  d.   Use expression (12.27) to develop a 95% prediction interval for y when $x = 4$.

33.   The data from exercise 2 follow.

x_i	3	12	6	20	14
y_i	55	40	55	10	15

  a.   Estimate the standard deviation of $\hat{y}^*$ when $x = 8$.
  b.   Develop a 95% confidence interval for the expected value of y when $x = 8$.
  c.   Estimate the standard deviation of an individual value of y when $x = 8$.
  d.   Develop a 95% prediction interval for y when $x = 8$.

34.   The data from exercise 3 follow.

x_i	2	6	9	13	20
y_i	7	18	9	26	23

  Develop the 95% confidence and prediction intervals when $x = 12$. Explain why these two intervals are different.

Applications

35.   The following data are the monthly salaries y and the grade point averages x for students who obtained a bachelor's degree in business administration.

GPA	Monthly Salary ($)
2.6	3600
3.4	3900
3.6	4300
3.2	3800
3.5	4200
2.9	3900

The estimated regression equation for these data is $\hat{y} = 2090.5 + 581.1x$ and MSE = 21,284.

a. Develop a point estimate of the starting salary for a student with a GPA of 3.0.
b. Develop a 95% confidence interval for the mean starting salary for all students with a 3.0 GPA.
c. Develop a 95% prediction interval for Ryan Dailey, a student with a GPA of 3.0.
d. Discuss the differences in your answers to parts (b) and (c).

36. In exercise 7, the data on y = annual sales ($1,000s) for new customer accounts and x = number of years of experience for a sample of 10 salespersons provided the estimated regression equation $\hat{y} = 80 + 4x$. For these data $\bar{x} = 7$, $\sum (x_i - \bar{x})^2 = 142$, and $s = 4.6098$.

Sales

a. Develop a 95% confidence interval for the mean annual sales for all salespersons with nine years of experience.
b. The company is considering hiring Tom Smart, a salesperson with nine years of experience. Develop a 95% prediction interval of annual sales for Tom Smart.
c. Discuss the differences in your answers to parts (a) and (b).

37. In exercise 5, the following data on x = the number of defective parts found and y = the line speed (feet per minute) for a production process at Brawdy Plastics provided the estimated regression equation $\hat{y} = 27.5 - .3x$.

Line Speed	Number of Defective Parts Found
20	23
20	21
30	19
30	16
40	15
40	17
50	14
50	11

For these data SSE = 16. Develop a 95% confidence interval for the mean number of defective parts for a line speed of 25 feet per minute.

38. Refer to exercise 21, where data on the production volume x and total cost y for a particular manufacturing operation were used to develop the estimated regression equation $\hat{y} = 1246.67 + 7.6x$.

a. The company's production schedule shows that 500 units must be produced next month. Predict the total cost for next month.
b. Develop a 99% prediction interval for the total cost for next month.
c. If an accounting cost report at the end of next month shows that the actual production cost during the month was $6,000, should managers be concerned about incurring such a high total cost for the month? Discuss.

39. In exercise 12, the following data on x = average daily hotel room rate and y = amount spent on entertainment (*The Wall Street Journal*, August 18, 2011) led to the estimated regression equation $\hat{y} = 17.49 + 1.0334x$. For these data SSE = 1541.4.

BusinessTravel

City	Room Rate ($)	Entertainment ($)
Boston	148	161
Denver	96	105
Nashville	91	101

(*continued*)

City	Room Rate ($)	Entertainment ($)
New Orleans	110	142
Phoenix	90	100
San Diego	102	120
San Francisco	136	167
San Jose	90	140
Tampa	82	98

a. Predict the amount spent on entertainment for a particular city that has a daily room rate of $89.

b. Develop a 95% confidence interval for the mean amount spent on entertainment for all cities that have a daily room rate of $89.

c. The average room rate in Chicago is $128. Develop a 95% prediction interval for the amount spent on entertainment in Chicago.

12.7 Computer Solution

Performing the regression analysis computations without the help of a computer can be quite time consuming. In this section we discuss how the computational burden can be minimized by using a computer software package such as Minitab.

We entered Armand's student population and sales data into a Minitab worksheet. The independent variable was named Pop and the dependent variable was named Sales to assist with interpretation of the computer output. Using Minitab, we obtained the printout for Armand's Pizza Parlors shown in Figure 12.10.[2] The interpretation of this printout follows.

FIGURE 12.10 MINITAB OUTPUT FOR THE ARMAND'S PIZZA PARLORS PROBLEM

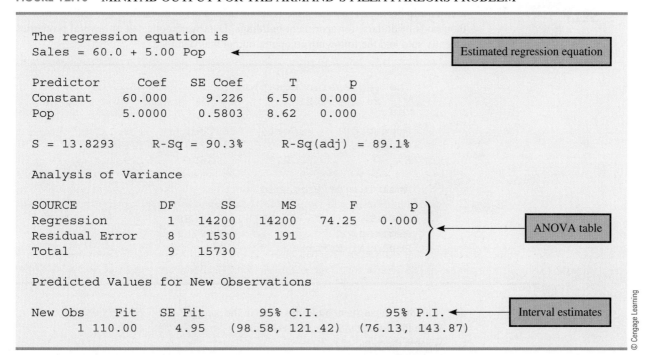

```
The regression equation is
Sales = 60.0 + 5.00 Pop          ◄——————————  Estimated regression equation


Predictor      Coef     SE Coef      T        p
Constant      60.000      9.226     6.50    0.000
Pop            5.0000     0.5803    8.62    0.000


S = 13.8293      R-Sq = 90.3%      R-Sq(adj) = 89.1%


Analysis of Variance

SOURCE            DF       SS       MS       F        p
Regression         1     14200    14200    74.25    0.000    }
Residual Error     8      1530      191                      }  ◄——  ANOVA table
Total              9     15730                               }


Predicted Values for New Observations

New Obs    Fit     SE Fit      95% C.I.            95% P.I. ◄——  Interval estimates
      1 110.00      4.95    (98.58, 121.42)    (76.13, 143.87)
```

© Cengage Learning

[2]The Minitab steps necessary to generate the output are given in Appendix 12.1.

1. Minitab prints the estimated regression equation as Sales $= 60.0 + 5.00$ Pop.
2. A table is printed that shows the values of the coefficients b_0 and b_1, the standard deviation of each coefficient, the t value obtained by dividing each coefficient value by its standard deviation, and the p-value associated with the t test. Because the p-value is zero (to three decimal places), the sample results indicate that the null hypothesis (H_0: $\beta_1 = 0$) should be rejected. Alternatively, we could compare 8.62 (located in the t-ratio column) to the appropriate critical value. This procedure for the t test was described in Section 12.5.
3. Minitab prints the standard error of the estimate, $s = 13.8293$, as well as information about the goodness of fit. Note that "R-sq $= 90.3\%$" is the coefficient of determination expressed as a percentage. The value "R-Sq(adj) $= 89.1\%$" is discussed in Chapter 13.
4. The ANOVA table is printed below the heading Analysis of Variance. Minitab uses the label Residual Error for the error source of variation. Note that DF is an abbreviation for degrees of freedom and that MSR is given as 14,200 and MSE as 191. The ratio of these two values provides the F value of 74.25 and the corresponding p-value of 0.000. Because the p-value is zero (to three decimal places), the relationship between Sales and Pop is judged statistically significant.
5. The 95% confidence interval estimate of the expected sales and the 95% prediction interval estimate of sales for an individual restaurant located near a campus with 10,000 students are printed below the ANOVA table. The confidence interval is (98.58, 121.42) and the prediction interval is (76.13, 143.87) as we showed in Section 12.6.

Exercises

Applications

40. The commercial division of a real estate firm is conducting a regression analysis of the relationship between x, annual gross rents (in thousands of dollars), and y, selling price (in thousands of dollars) for apartment buildings. Data were collected on several properties recently sold and the following computer output was obtained.

```
The regression equation is
Y = 20.0 + 7.21 X

Predictor        Coef      SE Coef          T
Constant       20.000       3.2213       6.21
X               7.210       1.3626       5.29

Analysis of Variance

SOURCE              DF           SS
Regression           1      41587.3
Residual Error       7
Total                8      51984.1
```

a. How many apartment buildings were in the sample?
b. Write the estimated regression equation.
c. What is the value of s_{b_1}?
d. Use the F statistic to test the significance of the relationship at a .05 level of significance.
e. Predict the selling price of an apartment building with gross annual rents of $50,000.

41. Following is a portion of the computer output for a regression analysis relating y = maintenance expense (dollars per month) to x = usage (hours per week) of a particular brand of computer terminal.

```
The regression equation is
Y = 6.1092 + .8951 X

Predictor           Coef        SE Coef
Constant          6.1092        0.9361
X                 0.8951        0.1490

Analysis of Variance

SOURCE             DF            SS            MS
Regression          1       1575.76       1575.76
Residual Error      8        349.14         43.64
Total               9       1924.90
```

a. Write the estimated regression equation.
b. Use a t test to determine whether monthly maintenance expense is related to usage at the .05 level of significance.
c. Use the estimated regression equation to predict monthly maintenance expense for any terminal that is used 25 hours per week.

42. A regression model relating x, number of salespersons at a branch office, to y, annual sales at the office (in thousands of dollars), provided the following computer output from a regression analysis of the data.

```
The regression equation is
Y = 80.0 + 50.00 X

Predictor           Coef        SE Coef          T
Constant           80.0         11.333        7.06
X                  50.0          5.482        9.12

Analysis of Variance

SOURCE             DF            SS            MS
Regression          1        6828.6        6828.6
Residual Error     28        2298.8          82.1
Total              29        9127.4
```

a. Write the estimated regression equation.
b. How many branch offices were involved in the study?
c. Compute the F statistic and test the significance of the relationship at a .05 level of significance.
d. Predict the annual sales at the Memphis branch office. This branch employs 12 salespersons.

43. Out-of-state tuition and fees at the top graduate schools of business can be very expensive, but the starting salary and bonus paid to graduates from many of these schools can be substantial. The following data show the out-of-state tuition and fees (rounded to the nearest $1,000) and the average starting salary and bonus paid to recent graduates (rounded to the nearest $1,000) for a sample of 20 graduate schools of business (*U.S. News & World Report 2009 Edition America's Best Graduate Schools*).

BusinessSchools

School	Tuition & Fees ($1,000s)	Salary & Bonus ($1,000s)
Arizona State University	28	98
Babson College	35	94
Cornell University	44	119
Georgetown University	40	109
Georgia Institute of Technology	30	88
Indiana University—Bloomington	35	105
Michigan State University	26	99
Northwestern University	44	123
Ohio State University	35	97
Purdue University—West Lafayette	33	96
Rice University	36	102
Stanford University	46	135
University of California—Davis	35	89
University of Florida	23	71
University of Iowa	25	78
University of Minnesota—Twin Cities	37	100
University of Notre Dame	36	95
University of Rochester	38	99
University of Washington	30	94
University of Wisconsin—Madison	27	93

a. Develop a scatter diagram with salary and bonus as the dependent variable.
b. Does there appear to be any relationship between these variables? Explain.
c. Develop an estimated regression equation that can be used to predict the starting salary and bonus paid to graduates given the cost of out-of-state tuition and fees at the school.
d. Test for a significant relationship at the .05 level of significance. What is your conclusion?
e. Did the estimated regression equation provide a good fit? Explain.
f. Suppose that we randomly select a recent graduate of the University of Virginia graduate school of business. The school has an out-of-state tuition and fees of $43,000. Predict the starting salary and bonus for this graduate.

44. Automobile racing, high-performance driving schools, and driver education programs run by automobile clubs continue to grow in popularity. All these activities require the participant to wear a helmet that is certified by the Snell Memorial Foundation, a not-for-profit organization dedicated to research, education, testing, and development of helmet safety standards. Snell "SA" (Sports Application) rated professional helmets are designed for auto racing and provide extreme impact resistance and high fire protection. One of the key factors in selecting a helmet is weight, since lower weight helmets tend to place less stress on the neck. The following data show the weight and price for 18 SA helmets (SoloRacer website, April 20, 2008).

Helmet	Weight (oz)	Price ($)
Pyrotect Pro Airflow	64	248
Pyrotect Pro Airflow Graphics	64	278
RCi Full Face	64	200
RaceQuip RidgeLine	64	200
HJC AR-10	58	300
HJC Si-12	47	700
HJC HX-10	49	900
Impact Racing Super Sport	59	340
Zamp FSA-1	66	199
Zamp RZ-2	58	299
Zamp RZ-2 Ferrari	58	299
Zamp RZ-3 Sport	52	479
Zamp RZ-3 Sport Painted	52	479
Bell M2	63	369
Bell M4	62	369
Bell M4 Pro	54	559
G Force Pro Force 1	63	250
G Force Pro Force 1 Grafx	63	280

RaceHelmets

a.   Develop a scatter diagram with weight as the independent variable.
b.   Does there appear to be any relationship between these two variables?
c.   Develop the estimated regression equation that could be used to predict the price given the weight.
d.   Test for the significance of the relationship at the .05 level of significance.
e.   Did the estimated regression equation provide a good fit? Explain.

12.8   Residual Analysis: Validating Model Assumptions

Residual analysis is the primary tool for determining whether the assumed regression model is appropriate.

As we noted previously, the *residual* for observation i is the difference between the observed value of the dependent variable (y_i) and the predicted value of the dependent variable ($\hat{y}_i$).

RESIDUAL FOR OBSERVATION i

$$y_i - \hat{y}_i \tag{12.28}$$

where

y_i is the observed value of the dependent variable
$\hat{y}_i$ is the predicted value of the dependent variable

In other words, the ith residual is the error resulting from using the estimated regression equation to predict the value of the dependent variable. The residuals for the Armand's Pizza Parlors example are computed in Table 12.7. The observed values of the dependent variable are in the second column and the predicted values of the dependent variable,

TABLE 12.7 RESIDUALS FOR ARMAND'S PIZZA PARLORS

Student Population x_i	Sales y_i	Predicted Sales $\hat{y}_i = 60 + 5x_i$	Residuals $y_i - \hat{y}_i$
2	58	70	−12
6	105	90	15
8	88	100	−12
8	118	100	18
12	117	120	−3
16	137	140	−3
20	157	160	−3
20	169	160	9
22	149	170	−21
26	202	190	12

© Cengage Learning

obtained using the estimated regression equation $\hat{y} = 60 + 5x$, are in the third column. An analysis of the corresponding residuals in the fourth column will help determine whether the assumptions made about the regression model are appropriate.

Let us now review the regression assumptions for the Armand's Pizza Parlors example. A simple linear regression model was assumed.

$$y = \beta_0 + \beta_1 x + \epsilon \qquad (12.29)$$

This model indicates that we assumed quarterly sales (y) to be a linear function of the size of the student population (x) plus an error term ϵ. In Section 12.4 we made the following assumptions about the error term ϵ.

1. $E(\epsilon) = 0$.
2. The variance of ϵ, denoted by σ^2, is the same for all values of x.
3. The values of ϵ are independent.
4. The error term ϵ has a normal distribution.

These assumptions provide the theoretical basis for the t test and the F test used to determine whether the relationship between x and y is significant, and for the confidence and prediction interval estimates presented in Section 12.6. If the assumptions about the error term ϵ appear questionable, the hypothesis tests about the significance of the regression relationship and the interval estimation results may not be valid.

The residuals provide the best information about ϵ; hence an analysis of the residuals is an important step in determining whether the assumptions for ϵ are appropriate. Much of residual analysis is based on an examination of graphical plots. In this section, we discuss the following residual plots.

1. A plot of the residuals against values of the independent variable x
2. A plot of residuals against the predicted values of the dependent variable y

Residual Plot Against x

A **residual plot** against the independent variable x is a graph in which the values of the independent variable are represented by the horizontal axis and the corresponding residual values are represented by the vertical axis. A point is plotted for each residual. The first coordinate for each point is given by the value of x_i and the second coordinate is given by the corresponding value of the residual $y_i - \hat{y}_i$. For a residual plot against x with the Armand's Pizza Parlors data from Table 12.7, the coordinates of the first point are $(2, -12)$, corresponding

FIGURE 12.11   PLOT OF THE RESIDUALS AGAINST THE INDEPENDENT VARIABLE x
FOR ARMAND'S PIZZA PARLORS

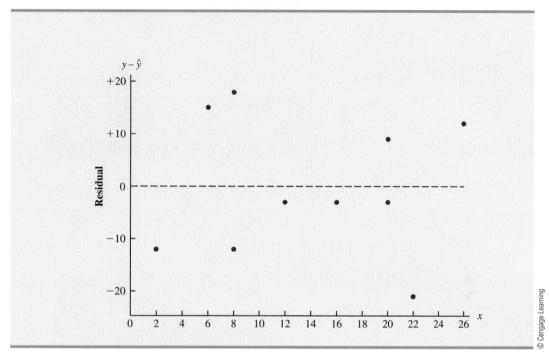

to $x_1 = 2$ and $y_1 - \hat{y}_1 = -12$; the coordinates of the second point are (6, 15), corresponding
to $x_2 = 6$ and $y_2 - \hat{y}_2 = 15$; and so on. Figure 12.11 shows the resulting residual plot.

Before interpreting the results for this residual plot, let us consider some general patterns that might be observed in any residual plot. Three examples appear in Figure 12.12.
If the assumption that the variance of ϵ is the same for all values of x and the assumed regression model is an adequate representation of the relationship between the variables, the
residual plot should give an overall impression of a horizontal band of points such as the
one in Panel A of Figure 12.12. However, if the variance of ϵ is not the same for all values
of x—for example, if variability about the regression line is greater for larger values of
x—a pattern such as the one in Panel B of Figure 12.12 could be observed. In this case, the
assumption of a constant variance of ϵ is violated. Another possible residual plot is shown
in Panel C. In this case, we would conclude that the assumed regression model is not an
adequate representation of the relationship between the variables. A curvilinear regression
model or multiple regression model should be considered.

Now let us return to the residual plot for Armand's Pizza Parlors shown in Figure 12.11.
The residuals appear to approximate the horizontal pattern in Panel A of Figure 12.12.
Hence, we conclude that the residual plot does not provide evidence that the assumptions
made for Armand's regression model should be challenged. At this point, we are confident
in the conclusion that Armand's simple linear regression model is valid.

Experience and good judgment are always factors in the effective interpretation of
residual plots. Seldom does a residual plot conform precisely to one of the patterns in
Figure 12.12. Yet analysts who frequently conduct regression studies and frequently review
residual plots become adept at understanding the differences between patterns that are
reasonable and patterns that indicate the assumptions of the model should be questioned. A
residual plot provides one technique to assess the validity of the assumptions for a regression model.

FIGURE 12.12   RESIDUAL PLOTS FROM THREE REGRESSION STUDIES

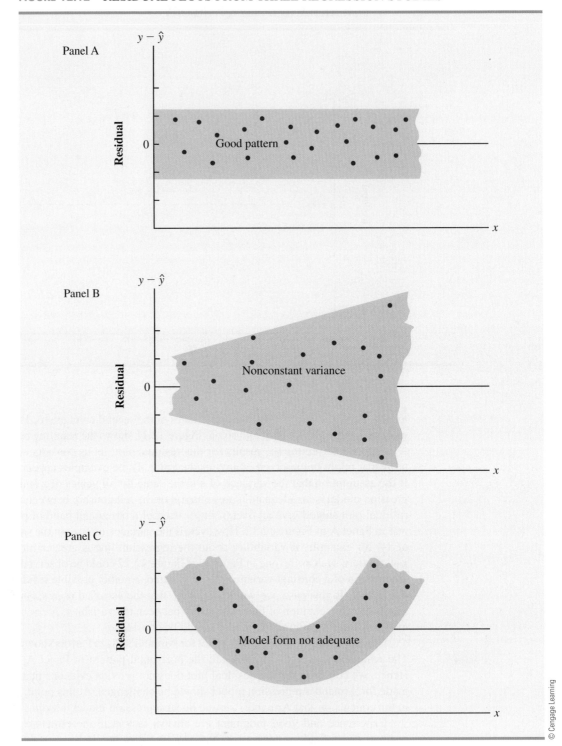

FIGURE 12.13   PLOT OF THE RESIDUALS AGAINST THE PREDICTED VALUES y FOR ARMAND'S PIZZA PARLORS

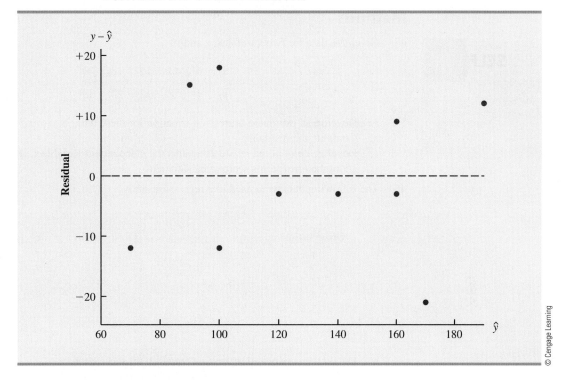

Residual Plot Against $\hat{y}$

Another residual plot represents the predicted value of the dependent variable $\hat{y}$ on the horizontal axis and the residual values on the vertical axis. A point is plotted for each residual. The first coordinate for each point is given by $\hat{y}_i$ and the second coordinate is given by the corresponding value of the ith residual $y_i - \hat{y}_i$. With the Armand's data from Table 12.7, the coordinates of the first point are $(70, -12)$, corresponding to $\hat{y}_1 = 70$ and $y_1 - \hat{y}_1 = -12$; the coordinates of the second point are $(90, 15)$; and so on. Figure 12.13 provides the residual plot. Note that the pattern of this residual plot is the same as the pattern of the residual plot against the independent variable x. It is not a pattern that would lead us to question the model assumptions. For simple linear regression, both the residual plot against x and the residual plot against $\hat{y}$ provide the same pattern. For multiple regression analysis, the residual plot against $\hat{y}$ is more widely used because of the presence of more than one independent variable.

NOTES AND COMMENTS

1. We use residual plots to validate the assumptions of a regression model. If our review indicates that one or more assumptions are questionable, a different regression model or a transformation of the data should be considered. The appropriate corrective action when the assumptions are violated must be based on good judgment; recommendations from an experienced statistician can be valuable.

2. Analysis of residuals is the primary method statisticians use to verify that the assumptions associated with a regression model are valid. Even if no violations are found, it does not necessarily follow that the model will yield good predictions. However, if additional statistical tests support the conclusion of significance and the coefficient of determination is large, we should be able to develop good estimates and predictions using the estimated regression equation.

Exercises

Methods

45. Given are data for two variables, x and y.

x_i	6	11	15	18	20
y_i	6	8	12	20	30

a. Develop an estimated regression equation for these data.
b. Compute the residuals.
c. Develop a plot of the residuals against the independent variable x. Do the assumptions about the error terms seem to be satisfied?

46. The following data were used in a regression study.

Observation	x_i	y_i	Observation	x_i	y_i
1	2	4	6	7	6
2	3	5	7	7	9
3	4	4	8	8	5
4	5	6	9	9	11
5	7	4			

a. Develop an estimated regression equation for these data.
b. Construct a plot of the residuals. Do the assumptions about the error term seem to be satisfied?

Applications

47. Data on advertising expenditures and revenue (in thousands of dollars) for the Four Seasons Restaurant follow.

Advertising Expenditures	Revenue
1	19
2	32
4	44
6	40
10	52
14	53
20	54

a. Let x equal advertising expenditures and y equal revenue. Use the method of least squares to develop a straight line approximation of the relationship between the two variables.
b. Test whether revenue and advertising expenditures are related at a .05 level of significance.
c. Prepare a residual plot of $y - \hat{y}$ versus $\hat{y}$. Use the result from part (a) to obtain the values of $\hat{y}$.
d. What conclusions can you draw from residual analysis? Should this model be used, or should we look for a better one?

48. Refer to exercise 7, where an estimated regression equation relating years of experience and annual sales was developed.
    a. Compute the residuals and construct a residual plot for this problem.
    b. Do the assumptions about the error terms seem reasonable in light of the residual plot?

RentMortgage

49. In 2011, home prices and mortgage rates dropped so low that in a number of cities the monthly cost of owning a home was less than renting. The following data show the average asking rent for 10 markets and the monthly mortgage on the median-priced home (including taxes and insurance) for 10 cities where the average monthly mortgage payment was less than the average asking rent (*The Wall Street Journal*, November 26–27, 2011).

City	Rent ($)	Mortgage ($)
Atlanta	840	539
Chicago	1062	1002
Detroit	823	626
Jacksonville, Fla.	779	711
Las Vegas	796	655
Miami	1071	977
Minneapolis	953	776
Orlando, Fla.	851	695
Phoenix	762	651
St. Louis	723	654

    a. Develop the estimated regression equation that can be used to predict the monthly mortgage given the average asking rent.
    b. Construct a residual plot against the independent variable
    c. Do the assumptions about the error term and model form seem reasonable in light of the residual plot?

Summary

In this chapter we showed how regression analysis can be used to determine how a dependent variable y is related to an independent variable x. In simple linear regression, the regression model is $y = \beta_0 + \beta_1 x + \epsilon$. The simple linear regression equation $E(y) = \beta_0 + \beta_1 x$ describes how the mean or expected value of y is related to x. We used sample data and the least squares method to develop the estimated regression equation $\hat{y} = b_0 + b_1 x$. In effect, b_0 and b_1 are the sample statistics used to estimate the unknown model parameters β_0 and β_1.

The coefficient of determination was presented as a measure of the goodness of fit for the estimated regression equation; it can be interpreted as the proportion of the variation in the dependent variable y that can be explained by the estimated regression equation. We reviewed correlation as a descriptive measure of the strength of a linear relationship between two variables.

The assumptions about the regression model and its associated error term ϵ were discussed, and t and F tests, based on those assumptions, were presented as a means for determining whether the relationship between two variables is statistically significant. We showed how to use the estimated regression equation to develop confidence interval estimates of the mean value of y and prediction interval estimates of individual values of y.

The chapter concluded with a section on the computer solution of regression problems and a section on the use of residual analysis to validate the model assumptions.

Glossary

Dependent variable The variable that is being predicted or explained. It is denoted by y.

Independent variable The variable that is doing the predicting or explaining. It is denoted by x.

Simple linear regression Regression analysis involving one independent variable and one dependent variable in which the relationship between the variables is approximated by a straight line.

Regression model The equation that describes how y is related to x and an error term; in simple linear regression, the regression model is $y = \beta_0 + \beta_1 x + \epsilon$.

Regression equation The equation that describes how the mean or expected value of the dependent variable is related to the independent variable; in simple linear regression, $E(y) = \beta_0 + \beta_1 x$.

Estimated regression equation The estimate of the regression equation developed from sample data by using the least squares method. For simple linear regression, the estimated regression equation is $\hat{y} = b_0 + b_1 x$.

Least squares method A procedure used to develop the estimated regression equation. The objective is to minimize $\sum(y_i - \hat{y}_i)^2$.

Scatter diagram A graph of bivariate data in which the independent variable is on the horizontal axis and the dependent variable is on the vertical axis.

Coefficient of determination A measure of the goodness of fit of the estimated regression equation. It can be interpreted as the proportion of the variability in the dependent variable y that is explained by the estimated regression equation.

ith residual The difference between the observed value of the dependent variable and the value predicted using the estimated regression equation; for the ith observation the ith residual is $y_i - \hat{y}_i$.

Correlation coefficient A measure of the strength of the linear relationship between two variables (previously discussed in Chapter 3).

Mean square error The unbiased estimate of the variance of the error term σ^2. It is denoted by MSE or s^2.

Standard error of the estimate The square root of the mean square error, denoted by s. It is the estimate of σ, the standard deviation of the error term ϵ.

ANOVA table The analysis of variance table used to summarize the computations associated with the F test for significance.

Confidence interval The interval estimate of the mean value of y for a given value of x.

Prediction interval The interval estimate of an individual value of y for a given value of x.

Residual analysis The analysis of the residuals used to determine whether the assumptions made about the regression model appear to be valid. Residual analysis is also used to identify outliers and influential observations.

Residual plot Graphical representation of the residuals that can be used to determine whether the assumptions made about the regression model appear to be valid.

Key Formulas

Simple Linear Regression Model

$$y = \beta_0 + \beta_1 x + \epsilon \tag{12.1}$$

Simple Linear Regression Equation

$$E(y) = \beta_0 + \beta_1 x \tag{12.2}$$

Estimated Simple Linear Regression Equation

$$\hat{y} = b_0 + b_1 x \tag{12.3}$$

Least Squares Criterion

$$\min \Sigma(y_i - \hat{y}_i)^2 \tag{12.5}$$

Slope and y-Intercept for the Estimated Regression Equation

$$b_1 = \frac{\Sigma(x_i - \bar{x})(y_i - \bar{y})}{\Sigma(x_i - \bar{x})^2} \tag{12.6}$$

$$b_0 = \bar{y} - b_1 \bar{x} \tag{12.7}$$

Sum of Squares Due to Error

$$\text{SSE} = \Sigma(y_i - \hat{y}_i)^2 \tag{12.8}$$

Total Sum of Squares

$$\text{SST} = \Sigma(y_i - \bar{y})^2 \tag{12.9}$$

Sum of Squares Due to Regression

$$\text{SSR} = \Sigma(\hat{y}_i - \bar{y})^2 \tag{12.10}$$

Relationship Among SST, SSR, and SSE

$$\text{SST} = \text{SSR} + \text{SSE} \tag{12.11}$$

Coefficient of Determination

$$r^2 = \frac{\text{SSR}}{\text{SST}} \tag{12.12}$$

Sample Correlation Coefficient

$$
\begin{aligned}
r_{xy} &= (\text{sign of } b_1)\sqrt{\text{Coefficient of determination}} \\
&= (\text{sign of } b_1)\sqrt{r^2}
\end{aligned} \tag{12.13}
$$

Mean Square Error (Estimate of σ^2)

$$s^2 = \text{MSE} = \frac{\text{SSE}}{n-2} \tag{12.15}$$

Standard Error of the Estimate

$$s = \sqrt{\text{MSE}} = \sqrt{\frac{\text{SSE}}{n-2}} \tag{12.16}$$

Standard Deviation of b_1

$$\sigma_{b_1} = \frac{\sigma}{\sqrt{\Sigma(x_i - \bar{x})^2}} \tag{12.17}$$

Estimated Standard Deviation of b_1

$$s_{b_1} = \frac{s}{\sqrt{\Sigma(x_i - \bar{x})^2}}$$

(12.18)

t Test Statistic

$$t = \frac{b_1}{s_{b_1}}$$

(12.19)

Mean Square Regression

$$\text{MSR} = \frac{\text{SSR}}{\text{Number of independent variables}}$$

(12.20)

F Test Statistic

$$F = \frac{\text{MSR}}{\text{MSE}}$$

(12.21)

Estimated Standard Deviation of $\hat{y}^*$

$$s_{\hat{y}^*} = s\sqrt{\frac{1}{n} + \frac{(x^* - \bar{x})^2}{\Sigma(x_i - \bar{x})^2}}$$

(12.23)

Confidence Interval for $E(y^*)$

$$\hat{y}^* \pm t_{\alpha/2} s_{\hat{y}^*}$$

(12.24)

Estimated Standard Deviation of an Individual Value

$$s_{\text{pred}} = s\sqrt{1 + \frac{1}{n} + \frac{(x^* - \bar{x})^2}{\Sigma(x_i - \bar{x})^2}}$$

(12.26)

Prediction Interval for y^*

$$\hat{y}^* \pm t_{\alpha/2} s_{\text{pred}}$$

(12.27)

Residual for Observation i

$$y_i - \hat{y}_i$$

(12.28)

Supplementary Exercises

50. The Dow Jones Industrial Average (DJIA) and the Standard & Poor's 500 (S&P 500) indexes are used as measures of overall movement in the stock market. The DJIA is based on the price movements of 30 large companies; the S&P 500 is an index composed of 500 stocks. Some say the S&P 500 is a better measure of stock market performance because it is broader based. The closing price for the DJIA and the S&P 500 for 15 weeks, beginning with January 6, 2012, follow (*Barron's* website, April 17, 2012).

Date	DJIA	S&P
January 6	12,360	1278
January 13	12,422	1289
January 20	12,720	1315
January 27	12,660	1316
February 3	12,862	1345
February 10	12,801	1343
February 17	12,950	1362
February 24	12,983	1366
March 2	12,978	1370
March 9	12,922	1371
March 16	13,233	1404
March 23	13,081	1397
March 30	13,212	1408
April 5	13,060	1398
April 13	12,850	1370

DJIAS&P500

a. Develop a scatter diagram with DJIA as the independent variable.
b. Develop the estimated regression equation.
c. Test for a significant relationship. Use $\alpha = .05$.
d. Did the estimated regression equation provide a good fit? Explain.
e. Suppose that the closing price for the DJIA is 13,500. Predict the closing price for the S&P 500.
f. Should we be concerned that the DJIA value of 13,500 used to predict the S&P 500 value in part (e) is beyond the range of the data used to develop the estimated regression equation?

51. The following data show Morningstar's Fair Value estimate and the Share Price for 28 companies. Fair Value is an estimate of a company's value per share that takes into account estimates of the company's growth, profitability, riskiness, and other factors over the next five years (*Morningstar Stocks 500,* 2008 edition).

Company	Fair Value ($)	Share Price ($)
Air Products and Chemicals	80	98.63
Allied Waste Industries	17	11.02
America Mobile	83	61.39
AT&T	35	41.56
Bank of America	70	41.26
Barclays PLC	68	40.37
Citigroup	53	29.44
Costco Wholesale Corp.	75	69.76
Covidien, Ltd.	58	44.29
Darden Restaurants	52	27.71
Dun & Bradstreet	87	88.63
Equifax	42	36.36
Gannett Co.	38	39.00
Genuine Parts	48	46.30
GlaxoSmithKline PLC	57	50.39
Iron Mountain	33	37.02
ITT Corporation	83	66.04
Johnson & Johnson	80	66.70
Las Vegas Sands	98	103.05
Macrovision	23	18.33
Marriott International	39	34.18
Nalco Holding Company	29	24.18

Stocks500

(*continued*)

Company	Fair Value ($)	Share Price ($)
National Interstate	25	33.10
Portugal Telecom	15	13.02
Qualcomm	48	39.35
Royal Dutch Shell Ltd.	87	84.20
SanDisk	60	33.17
Time Warner	42	27.60

a. Develop the estimated regression equation that could be used to estimate the share price given the fair value.
b. At the .05 level of significance, is there a significant relationship between the two variables?
c. Use the estimated regression equation to predict the share price for a company that has a fair value of $50.
d. Do you believe the estimated regression equation would provide a good prediction of the share price? Use r^2 to support your answer.

52. One of the biggest changes in higher education in recent years has been the growth of online universities. The Online Education Database is an independent organization whose mission is to build a comprehensive list of the top accredited online colleges. The following table shows the retention rate (%) and the graduation rate (%) for 29 online colleges (Online Education Database website, January 2009).

WEB file

OnlineEdu

College	Retention Rate (%)	Graduation Rate (%)
Western International University	7	25
South University	51	25
University of Phoenix	4	28
American InterContinental University	29	32
Franklin University	33	33
Devry University	47	33
Tiffin University	63	34
Post University	45	36
Peirce College	60	36
Everest University	62	36
Upper Iowa University	67	36
Dickinson State University	65	37
Western Governors University	78	37
Kaplan University	75	38
Salem International University	54	39
Ashford University	45	41
ITT Technical Institute	38	44
Berkeley College	51	45
Grand Canyon University	69	46
Nova Southeastern University	60	47
Westwood College	37	48
Everglades University	63	50
Liberty University	73	51
LeTourneau University	78	52
Rasmussen College	48	53
Keiser University	95	55
Herzing College	68	56
National University	100	57
Florida National College	100	61

a. Develop a scatter diagram with retention rate as the independent variable. What does the scatter diagram indicate about the relationship between the two variables?
b. Develop the estimated regression equation.
c. Test for a significant relationship. Use $\alpha = .05$.
d. Did the estimated regression equation provide a good fit?
e. Suppose you were the president of South University. After reviewing the results, would you have any concerns about the performance of your university as compared to other online universities?
f. Suppose you were the president of the University of Phoenix. After reviewing the results, would you have any concerns about the performance of your university as compared to other online universities?

53. Jensen Tire & Auto is in the process of deciding whether to purchase a maintenance contract for its new computer wheel alignment and balancing machine. Managers feel that maintenance expense should be related to usage, and they collected the following information on weekly usage (hours) and annual maintenance expense (in hundreds of dollars).

Jensen

Weekly Usage (hours)	Annual Maintenance Expense
13	17.0
10	22.0
20	30.0
28	37.0
32	47.0
17	30.5
24	32.5
31	39.0
40	51.5
38	40.0

a. Develop the estimated regression equation that relates annual maintenance expense to weekly usage.
b. Test the significance of the relationship in part (a) at a .05 level of significance.
c. Jensen expects to use the new machine 30 hours per week. Develop a 95% prediction interval for the company's annual maintenance expense.
d. If the maintenance contract costs $3,000 per year, would you recommend purchasing it? Why or why not?

54. The regional transit authority for a major metropolitan area wants to determine whether there is any relationship between the age of a bus and the annual maintenance cost. A sample of 10 buses resulted in the following data.

AgeCost

Age of Bus (years)	Maintenance Cost ($)
1	350
2	370
2	480
2	520
2	590
3	550
4	750
4	800
5	790
5	950

    a.   Develop the least squares estimated regression equation.

    b.   Test to see whether the two variables are significantly related with $\alpha = .05$.

    c.   Did the least squares line provide a good fit to the observed data? Explain.

    d.   Develop a 95% prediction interval for the maintenance cost for a specific bus that is 4 years old.

55.   Reuters reported the market beta for Xerox was 1.22 (Reuters website, January 30, 2009). Market betas for individual stocks are determined by simple linear regression. For each stock, the dependent variable is its quarterly percentage return (capital appreciation plus dividends) minus the percentage return that could be obtained from a risk-free investment (the Treasury Bill rate is used as the risk-free rate). The independent variable is the quarterly percentage return (capital appreciation plus dividends) for the stock market (S&P 500) minus the percentage return from a risk-free investment. An estimated regression equation is developed with quarterly data; the market beta for the stock is the slope of the estimated regression equation (b_1). The value of the market beta is often interpreted as a measure of the risk associated with the stock. Market betas greater than 1 indicate that the stock is more volatile than the market average; market betas less than 1 indicate that the stock is less volatile than the market average. Suppose that the following figures are the differences between the percentage return and the risk-free return for 10 quarters for the S&P 500 and Horizon Technology.

WEB file

MktBeta

S&P 500	Horizon
1.2	−.7
−2.5	−2.0
−3.0	−5.5
2.0	4.7
5.0	1.8
1.2	4.1
3.0	2.6
−1.0	2.0
.5	−1.3
2.5	5.5

    a.   Develop an estimated regression equation that can be used to predict the market beta for Horizon Technology. What is Horizon Technology's market beta?

    b.   Test for a significant relationship at the .05 level of significance.

    c.   Did the estimated regression equation provide a good fit? Explain.

    d.   Use the market betas of Xerox and Horizon Technology to compare the risk associated with the two stocks.

56.   The Toyota Camry is one of the best-selling cars in North America. The cost of a previously owned Camry depends upon many factors, including the model year, mileage, and condition. To investigate the relationship between the car's mileage and the sales price for a 2007 model year Camry, the following data show the mileage and sale price for 19 sales (PriceHub website, February 24, 2012).

WEB file

Camry

Miles (1000s)	Price ($1,000s)
22	16.2
29	16.0
36	13.8
47	11.5
63	12.5
77	12.9
73	11.2

(*continued*)

Miles (1000s)	Price ($1,000s)
87	13.0
92	11.8
101	10.8
110	8.3
28	12.5
59	11.1
68	15.0
68	12.2
91	13.0
42	15.6
65	12.7
110	8.3

a. Develop a scatter diagram with the car mileage on the horizontal axis and the price on the vertical axis.

b. What does the scatter diagram developed in part (a) indicate about the relationship between the two variables?

c. Develop the estimated regression equation that could be used to predict the price ($1,000s) given the miles (1000s).

d. Test for a significant relationship at the .05 level of significance.

e. Did the estimated regression equation provide a good fit? Explain.

f. Provide an interpretation for the slope of the estimated regression equation.

g. Suppose that you are considering purchasing a previously owned 2007 Camry that has been driven 60,000 miles. Using the estimated regression equation developed in part (c), predict the price for this car. Is this the price you would offer the seller?

AirlineSeats

57. A 2012 survey conducted by IdeaWorks provided data showing the percentage of seats available when customers try to redeem points or miles for free travel. For each airline listed, the column labeled 2011 Percentage shows the percentage of seats available in 2011 and the column labled 2012 shows the correponding percentage in 2012 (*The Wall Street Journal*, May 17, 2012).

Airline	2011 Percentage	2012 Percentage
Air Berlin	96.4	100.0
Air Canada	82.1	78.6
Air France, KLM	65.0	55.7
AirTran Airways	47.1	87.1
Alaska Airlines	64.3	59.3
American Airlines	62.9	45.7
British Airways	61.4	79.3
Cathay Pacific	66.4	70.7
Delta Air Lines	27.1	27.1
Emirates	35.7	32.9
GOL Airlines (Brazil)	100.0	97.1
Iberia	70.7	63.6
JetBlue	79.3	86.4
LAN (Chile)	75.7	78.6
Lufthansa, Swiss, Austrian	85.0	92.1
Qantas	75.0	78.6
SAS Scandinavian	52.9	57.9

(*continued*)

Airline	2011 Percentage	2012 Percentage
Singapore Airlines	90.7	90.7
Southwest	99.3	100.0
Turkish Airways	49.3	38.6
United Airlines	71.4	87.1
US Airways	25.7	33.6
Virgin Australia	91.4	90.0

a. Develop a scatter diagram with 2011 Percentage as the independent variable.
b. What does the scatter diagram developed in part (a) indicate about the relationship between the two variables?
c. Develop the estimated regression equation.
d. Test for a significant relationship. Use $\alpha = .05$.
e. Did the estimated regression equation provide a good fit?
f. Construct a residual plot. Comment on the shape of the plot as well as any unusual looking points.

Case Problem 1   Measuring Stock Market Risk

One measure of the risk or volatility of an individual stock is the standard deviation of the total return (capital appreciation plus dividends) over several periods of time. Although the standard deviation is easy to compute, it does not take into account the extent to which the price of a given stock varies as a function of a standard market index, such as the S&P 500. As a result, many financial analysts prefer to use another measure of risk referred to as *beta*.

Beta

Betas for individual stocks are determined by simple linear regression. The dependent variable is the total return for the stock and the independent variable is the total return for the stock market.* For this case problem we will use the S&P 500 index as the measure of the total return for the stock market, and an estimated regression equation will be developed using monthly data. The beta for the stock is the slope of the estimated regression equation (b_1). The data contained in the file named Beta provides the total return (capital appreciation plus dividends) over 36 months for eight widely traded common stocks and the S&P 500.

The value of beta for the stock market will always be 1; thus, stocks that tend to rise and fall with the stock market will also have a beta close to 1. Betas greater than 1 indicate that the stock is more volatile than the market, and betas less than 1 indicate that the stock is less volatile than the market. For instance, if a stock has a beta of 1.4, it is 40% *more* volatile than the market, and if a stock has a beta of .4, it is 60% *less* volatile than the market.

Managerial Report

You have been assigned to analyze the risk characteristics of these stocks. Prepare a report that includes but is not limited to the following items.
a. Compute descriptive statistics for each stock and the S&P 500. Comment on your results. Which stocks are the most volatile?
b. Compute the value of beta for each stock. Which of these stocks would you expect to perform best in an up market? Which would you expect to hold their value best in a down market?
c. Comment on how much of the return for the individual stocks is explained by the market.

---

*Various sources use different approaches for computing betas. For instance, some sources subtract the return that could be obtained from a risk-free investment (e.g., T-bills) from the dependent variable and the independent variable before computing the estimated regression equation. Some also use different indexes for the total return of the stock market; for instance, Value Line computes betas using the New York Stock Exchange composite index.

Case Problem 2   U.S. Department of Transportation

As part of a study on transportation safety, the U.S. Department of Transportation collected data on the number of fatal accidents per 1000 licenses and the percentage of licensed drivers under the age of 21 in a sample of 42 cities. Data collected over a one-year period follow. These data are contained in the file named Safety.

Safety

Percent Under 21	Fatal Accidents per 1000 Licenses	Percent Under 21	Fatal Accidents per 1000 Licenses
13	2.962	17	4.100
12	0.708	8	2.190
8	0.885	16	3.623
12	1.652	15	2.623
11	2.091	9	0.835
17	2.627	8	0.820
18	3.830	14	2.890
8	0.368	8	1.267
13	1.142	15	3.224
8	0.645	10	1.014
9	1.028	10	0.493
16	2.801	14	1.443
12	1.405	18	3.614
9	1.433	10	1.926
10	0.039	14	1.643
9	0.338	16	2.943
11	1.849	12	1.913
12	2.246	15	2.814
14	2.855	13	2.634
14	2.352	9	0.926
11	1.294	17	3.256

Managerial Report

1. Develop numerical and graphical summaries of the data.
2. Use regression analysis to investigate the relationship between the number of fatal accidents and the percentage of drivers under the age of 21. Discuss your findings.
3. What conclusion and recommendations can you derive from your analysis?

Case Problem 3   Selecting a Point-and-Shoot Digital Camera

Consumer Reports tested 166 different point-and-shoot digital cameras. Based upon factors such as the number of megapixels, weight (oz), image quality, and ease of use, they developed an overall score for each camera tested. The overall score ranges from 0 to 100, with higher scores indicating better overall test results. Selecting a camera with many options can be a difficult process, and price is certainly a key issue for most consumers. By spending more, will a consumer really get a superior camera? And do cameras that have more

TABLE 12.8   DATA FOR 28 POINT-AND-SHOOT DIGITAL CAMERAS

Observation	Brand	Price ($)	Megapixels	Weight (oz)	Score
1	Canon	330	10	7	66
2	Canon	200	12	5	66
3	Canon	300	12	7	65
4	Canon	200	10	6	62
5	Canon	180	12	5	62
6	Canon	200	12	7	61
7	Canon	200	14	5	60
8	Canon	130	10	7	60
9	Canon	130	12	5	59
10	Canon	110	16	5	55
11	Canon	90	14	5	52
12	Canon	100	10	6	51
13	Canon	90	12	7	46
14	Nikon	270	16	5	65
15	Nikon	300	16	7	63
16	Nikon	200	14	6	61
17	Nikon	400	14	7	59
18	Nikon	120	14	5	57
19	Nikon	170	16	6	56
20	Nikon	150	12	5	56
21	Nikon	230	14	6	55
22	Nikon	180	12	6	53
23	Nikon	130	12	6	53
24	Nikon	80	12	7	52
25	Nikon	80	14	7	50
26	Nikon	100	12	4	46
27	Nikon	110	12	5	45
28	Nikon	130	14	4	42

© Cengage Learning

megapixels, a factor often considered to be a good measure of photo quality, cost more than cameras with fewer megapixels? Table 12.8 shows the brand, average retail price ($), number of megapixels, weight (oz), and the overall score for 13 Canon and 15 Nikon subcompact cameras tested by *Consumer Reports* (*Consumer Reports* website, February 7, 2012).

Managerial Report

1. Develop numerical summaries of the data.
2. Using overall score as the dependent variable, develop three scatter diagrams, one using price as the independent variable, one using the number of megapixels as the independent variable, and one using weight as the independent variable. Which of the three independent variables appears to be the best predictor of overall score?
3. Using simple linear regression, develop an estimated regression equation that could be used to predict the overall score given the price of the camera. For this estimated regression equation, perform an analysis of the residuals and discuss your findings and conclusions.
4. Analyze the data using only the observations for the Canon cameras. Discuss the appropriateness of using simple linear regression and make any recommendations regarding the prediction of overall score using just the price of the camera.

Case Problem 4   Finding the Best Car Value

When trying to decide what car to buy, real value is not necessarily determined by how much you spend on the initial purchase. Instead, cars that are reliable and don't cost much to own often represent the best values. But, no matter how reliable or inexpensive a car may cost to own, it must also perform well.

To measure value, *Consumer Reports* developed a statistic referred to as a value score. The value score is based upon five-year owner costs, overall road-test scores, and predicted reliability ratings. Five-year owner costs are based on the expenses incurred in the first five years of ownership, including depreciation, fuel, maintenance and repairs, and so on. Using a national average of 12,000 miles per year, an average cost per mile driven is used as the measure of five-year owner costs. Road-test scores are the results of more than 50 tests and evaluations and are based upon a 100-point scale, with higher scores indicating better performance, comfort, convenience, and fuel economy. The highest road-test score obtained in the tests conducted by *Consumer Reports* was a 99 for a Lexus LS 460L. Predicted-reliability ratings (1 = Poor, 2 = Fair, 3 = Good, 4 = Very Good, and 5 = Excellent) are based on data from *Consumer Reports'* Annual Auto Survey.

A car with a value score of 1.0 is considered to be "average-value." A car with a value score of 2.0 is considered to be twice as good a value as a car with a value score of 1.0; a car with a value score of 0.5 is considered half as good as average; and so on. The data for 20 family sedans, including the price ($) of each car tested, follow.

WEB file

FamilySedans

Car	Price ($)	Cost/Mile	Road-Test Score	Predicted Reliability	Value Score
Nissan Altima 2.5 S (4-cyl.)	23,970	0.59	91	4	1.75
Kia Optima LX (2.4)	21,885	0.58	81	4	1.73
Subaru Legacy 2.5i Premium	23,830	0.59	83	4	1.73
Ford Fusion Hybrid	32,360	0.63	84	5	1.70
Honda Accord LX-P (4-cyl.)	23,730	0.56	80	4	1.62
Mazda6 i Sport (4-cyl.)	22,035	0.58	73	4	1.60
Hyundai Sonata GLS (2.4)	21,800	0.56	89	3	1.58
Ford Fusion SE (4-cyl.)	23,625	0.57	76	4	1.55
Chevrolet Malibu LT (4-cyl.)	24,115	0.57	74	3	1.48
Kia Optima SX (2.0T)	29,050	0.72	84	4	1.43
Ford Fusion SEL (V6)	28,400	0.67	80	4	1.42
Nissan Altima 3.5 SR (V6)	30,335	0.69	93	4	1.42
Hyundai Sonata Limited (2.0T)	28,090	0.66	89	3	1.39
Honda Accord EX-L (V6)	28,695	0.67	90	3	1.36
Mazda6 s Grand Touring (V6)	30,790	0.74	81	4	1.34
Ford Fusion SEL (V6, AWD)	30,055	0.71	75	4	1.32
Subaru Legacy 3.6R Limited	30,094	0.71	88	3	1.29
Chevrolet Malibu LTZ (V6)	28,045	0.67	83	3	1.20
Chrysler 200 Limited (V6)	27,825	0.70	52	5	1.20
Chevrolet Impala LT (3.6)	28,995	0.67	63	3	1.05

Managerial Report

1. Develop numerical summaries of the data.
2. Use regression analysis to develop an estimated regression equation that could be used to predict the value score given the price of the car.
3. Use regression analysis to develop an estimated regression equation that could be used to predict the value score given the five-year owner costs (cost/mile).

4. Use regression analysis to develop an estimated regression equation that could be used to predict the value score given the road-test score.
5. Use regression analysis to develop an estimated regression equation that could be used to predict the value score given the predicted-reliability.
6. What conclusions can you derive from your analysis?

Appendix 12.1   Regression Analysis with Minitab

WEB file

Armand's

In Section 12.7 we discussed the computer solution of regression problems by showing Minitab's output for the Armand's Pizza Parlors problem. In this appendix, we describe the steps required to generate the Minitab computer solution. First, the data must be entered in a Minitab worksheet. Student population data are entered in column C1 and quarterly sales data are entered in column C2. The variable names Pop and Sales are entered as the column headings on the worksheet. In subsequent steps, we refer to the data by using the variable names Pop and Sales or the column indicators C1 and C2. The following steps describe how to use Minitab to produce the regression results shown in Figure 12.10.

Step 1. Select the **Stat** menu
Step 2. Select the **Regression** menu
Step 3. Choose **Regression**
Step 4. When the Regression dialog box appears:
      Enter Sales in the **Response** box
      Enter Pop in the **Predictors** box
      Click the **Options** button
    When the Regression-Options dialog box appears:
      Enter 10 in the **Prediction intervals for new observations** box
      Click **OK**
    When the Regression dialog box reappears:
      Click **OK**

The Minitab regression dialog box provides additional capabilities that can be obtained by selecting the desired options. For instance, to obtain a residual plot that shows the predicted value of the dependent variable $\hat{y}$ on the horizontal axis and the standardized residual values on the vertical axis, step 4 would be as follows:

Step 4. When the Regression dialog box appears:
      Enter Sales in the **Response** box
      Enter Pop in the **Predictors** box
      Click the **Graphs** button
    When the Regression-Graphs dialog box appears:
      Select **Standardized** under Residuals for Plots
      Select **Residuals versus fits** under Residual Plots
      Click **OK**
    When the Regression dialog box reappears:
      Click **OK**

Appendix 12.2   Regression Analysis with Excel

WEB file

Armand's

In this appendix we will illustrate how Excel's Regression tool can be used to perform the regression analysis computations for the Armand's Pizza Parlors problem. Refer to Figure 12.14 as we describe the steps involved. The labels Restaurant, Population, and Sales are entered into cells A1:C1 of the worksheet. To identify each of the 10 observations, we

FIGURE 12.14   EXCEL SOLUTION TO THE ARMAND'S PIZZA PARLORS PROBLEM

	A	B	C	D	E	F	G	H	I	J
1	Restaurant	Population	Sales							
2	1	2	58							
3	2	6	105							
4	3	8	88							
5	4	8	118							
6	5	12	117							
7	6	16	137							
8	7	20	157							
9	8	20	169							
10	9	22	149							
11	10	26	202							
12										
13	SUMMARY OUTPUT									
14										
15	*Regression Statistics*									
16	Multiple R	0.9501								
17	R Square	0.9027								
18	Adjusted R Square	0.8906								
19	Standard Error	13.8293								
20	Observations	10								
21										
22	ANOVA									
23		*df*	*SS*	*MS*	*F*	*Significance F*				
24	Regression	1	14200	14200	74.2484	2.55E-05				
25	Residual	8	1530	191.25						
26	Total	9	15730							
27										
28		*Coefficients*	*Standard Error*	*t Stat*	*P-value*	*Lower 95%*	*Upper 95%*	*Lower 99.0%*	*Upper 99.0%*	
29	Intercept	60	9.2260	6.5033	0.0002	38.7247	81.2753	29.0431	90.9569	
30	Population	5	0.5803	8.6167	2.55E-05	3.6619	6.3381	3.0530	6.9470	
31										

entered the numbers 1 through 10 into cells A2:A11. The sample data are entered into cells B2:C11. The following steps describe how to use Excel to produce the regression results.

Step 1. Click the **Data** tab on the Ribbon
Step 2. In the **Analysis** group, click **Data Analysis**
Step 3. Choose **Regression** from the list of Analysis Tools
Step 4. Click **OK**
Step 5. When the Regression dialog box appears:
  Enter C1:C11 in the **Input Y Range** box
  Enter B1:B11 in the **Input X Range** box
  Select **Labels**
  Select **Confidence Level**
  Enter 99 in the **Confidence Level** box
  Select **Output Range**
  Enter A13 in the **Output Range** box
    (Any upper left-hand corner cell indicating where the output is to begin may be entered here.)
  Click **OK**

The first section of the output, entitled *Regression Statistics,* contains summary statistics such as the coefficient of determination (R Square). The second section of the output, titled ANOVA, contains the analysis of variance table. The last section of the output, which is not titled, contains the estimated regression coefficients and related information. We will begin our discussion of the interpretation of the regression output with the information contained in cells A28:I30.

Interpretation of Estimated Regression Equation Output

The y intercept of the estimated regression line, $b_0 = 60$, is shown in cell B29, and the slope of the estimated regression line, $b_1 = 5$, is shown in cell B30. The label Intercept in cell A29 and the label Population in cell A30 are used to identify these two values.

In Section 12.5 we showed that the estimated standard deviation of b_1 is $s_{b_1} = .5803$. Note that the value in cell C30 is .5803. The label Standard Error in cell C28 is Excel's way of indicating that the value in cell C30 is the standard error, or standard deviation, of b_1. Recall that the t test for a significant relationship required the computation of the t statistic, $t = b_1/s_{b_1}$. For the Armand's data, the value of t that we computed was $t = 5/.5803 = 8.62$. The label in cell D28, t Stat, reminds us that cell D30 contains the value of the t test statistic.

The value in cell E30 is the p-value associated with the t test for significance. Excel has displayed the p-value in cell E30 using scientific notation. To obtain the decimal value, we move the decimal point 5 places to the left, obtaining a value of .0000255. Because the p-value $= .0000255 < \alpha = .01$, we can reject H_0 and conclude that we have a significant relationship between student population and quarterly sales.

The information in cells F28:I30 can be used to develop confidence interval estimates of the y intercept and slope of the estimated regression equation. Excel always provides the lower and upper limits for a 95% confidence interval. Recall that in step 4 we selected Confidence Level and entered 99 in the Confidence Level box. As a result, Excel's Regression tool also provides the lower and upper limits for a 99% confidence interval. The value in cell H30 is the lower limit for the 99% confidence interval estimate of β_1 and the value in cell I30 is the upper limit. Thus, after rounding, the 99% confidence interval estimate of β_1 is 3.05 to 6.95. The values in cells F30 and G30 provide the lower and upper limits for the 95% confidence interval. Thus, the 95% confidence interval is 3.66 to 6.34.

Interpretation of ANOVA Output

The information in cells A22:F26 is a summary of the analysis of variance computations. The three sources of variation are labeled Regression, Residual, and Total. The label df in cell B23 stands for degrees of freedom, the label SS in cell C23 stands for sum of squares, and the label MS in cell D23 stands for mean square.

In Section 12.5 we stated that the mean square error, obtained by dividing the error or residual sum of squares by its degrees of freedom, provides an estimate of σ^2. The value in cell D25, 191.25, is the mean square error for the Armand's regression output. In Section 12.5 we showed that an F test could also be used to test for significance in regression. The value in cell F24, .0000255, is the p-value associated with the F test for significance. Because the p-value $= .0000255 < \alpha = .01$, we can reject H_0 and conclude that we have a significant relationship between student population and quarterly sales. The label Excel uses to identify the p-value for the F test for significance, shown in cell F23, is *Significance F*.

The label Significance F may be more meaningful if you think of the value in cell F24 as the observed level of significance for the F test.

Interpretation of Regression Statistics Output

The coefficient of determination, .9027, appears in cell B17; the corresponding label, R Square, is shown in cell A17. The square root of the coefficient of determination provides the sample correlation coefficient of .9501 shown in cell B16. Note that Excel uses the label Multiple R (cell A16) to identify this value. In cell A19, the label Standard Error is used to identify the value of the standard error of the estimate shown in cell B19. Thus, the standard error of the estimate is 13.8293. We caution the reader to keep in mind that in the Excel output, the label Standard Error appears in two different places. In the *Regression Statistics* section of the output, the label Standard Error refers to the estimate of σ. In the Estimated Regression Equation section of the output, the label *Standard Error* refers to s_{b_1}, the standard deviation of the sampling distribution of b_1.

Appendix 12.3   Regression Analysis Using StatTools

Armand's

In this appendix we show how StatTools can be used to perform the regression analysis computations for the Armand's Pizza Parlors problem. Begin by using the Data Set Manager to create a StatTools data set for these data using the procedure described in the appendix in Chapter 1. The following steps describe how StatTools can be used to provide the regression results.

Step 1. Click the **StatTools** tab on the Ribbon
Step 2. In the **Analyses** group, click **Regression and Classification**
Step 3. Choose the **Regression** option
Step 4. When the StatTools - Regression dialog box appears:
   Select **Multiple** in the **Regression Type** box
   In the **Variables** section,
      Click the **Format button** and select **Unstacked**
      In the column labeled **I** select **Population**
      In the column labeled **D** select **Sales**
   Click **OK**

The regression analysis output will appear.

Note that in step 4 we selected Multiple in the Regression Type box. In StatTools, the Multiple option is used for both simple linear regression and multiple regression. The StatTools - Regression dialog box contains a number of more advanced options for developing prediction interval estimates and producing residual plots. The StatTools Help facility provides information on using all of these options.

CHAPTER 13

Multiple Regression

CONTENTS

STATISTICS IN PRACTICE:
dunnhumby

dunnhumby*
LONDON, ENGLAND

Founded in 1989 by the husband-and-wife team of Clive Humby (a mathematician) and Edwina Dunn (a marketer), dunnhumby combines proven natural abilities with big ideas to find clues and patterns as to what customers are buying and why. The company turns these insights into actionable strategies that create dramatic growth and sustainable loyalty, ultimately improving brand value and the customer experience.

Employing more than 950 people in Europe, Asia, and the Americas, dunnhumby serves a prestigious list of companies, including Kroger, Tesco, Coca-Cola, General Mills, Kimberly-Clark, PepsiCo, Procter & Gamble, and Home Depot. dunnhumbyUSA is a joint venture between the Kroger Company and dunnhumby and has offices in New York, Chicago, Atlanta, Minneapolis, Cincinnati, and Portland.

The company's research begins with data collected about a client's customers. Data come from customer reward or discount card purchase records, electronic point-of-sale transactions, and traditional market research. Analysis of the data often translates billions of data points into detailed insights about the behavior, preferences, and lifestyles of the customers. Such insights allow for more effective merchandising programs to be activated, including strategy recommendations on pricing, promotion, advertising, and product assortment decisions.

Researchers have used a multiple regression technique referred to as logistic regression to help in their analysis of customer-based data. Using logistic regression, an estimated multiple regression equation of the following form is developed.

$$\hat{y} = b_0 + b_1 x_1 + b_2 x_2 + b_3 x_3 + \cdots + b_p x_p$$

The dependent variable $\hat{y}$ is a prediction of the probability that a customer belongs to a particular customer group. The independent variables $x_1, x_2, x_3, \ldots, x_p$ are measures of the customer's actual shopping behavior and may include the specific items purchased, number of items purchased, amount purchased, day of the week, hour of the day, and so on. The analysis helps identify the independent variables that are most relevant in

dunnhumby uses logistic regression to predict customer shopping behavior. © Micro 10x/ Shutterstock.com.

predicting the customer's group and provides a better understanding of the customer population, enabling further analysis with far greater confidence. The focus of the analysis is on understanding the customer to the point of developing merchandising, marketing, and direct marketing programs that will maximize the relevancy and service to the customer group.

In this chapter, we will introduce multiple regression and show how the concepts of simple linear regression introduced in Chapter 12 can be extended to the multiple regression case. In addition, we will show how computer software packages are used for multiple regression. In the final section of the chapter we introduce logistic regression using an example that illustrates how the technique is used in a marketing research application.

*The authors are indebted to Paul Hunter, Senior Vice President of Solutions for dunnhumby for providing this Statistics in Practice.

In Chapter 12 we presented simple linear regression and demonstrated its use in developing an estimated regression equation that describes the relationship between two variables. Recall that the variable being predicted or explained is called the dependent variable and the variable being used to predict or explain the dependent variable is called the independent variable. In this chapter we continue our study of regression analysis by considering situations involving two or more independent variables. This subject area, called **multiple regression analysis**, enables us to consider more factors and thus obtain better predictions than are possible with simple linear regression.

13.1 Multiple Regression Model

Multiple regression analysis is the study of how a dependent variable y is related to two or more independent variables. In the general case, we will use p to denote the number of independent variables.

Regression Model and Regression Equation

The concepts of a regression model and a regression equation introduced in the preceding chapter are applicable in the multiple regression case. The equation that describes how the dependent variable y is related to the independent variables $x_1, x_2, \ldots, x_p$ and an error term is called the **multiple regression model**. We begin with the assumption that the multiple regression model takes the following form.

MULTIPLE REGRESSION MODEL

$$y = \beta_0 + \beta_1 x_1 + \beta_2 x_2 + \cdots + \beta_p x_p + \epsilon \qquad (13.1)$$

In the multiple regression model, $\beta_0, \beta_1, \beta_2, \ldots, \beta_p$ are the parameters and the error term ϵ (the Greek letter epsilon) is a random variable. A close examination of this model reveals that y is a linear function of $x_1, x_2, \ldots, x_p$ (the $\beta_0 + \beta_1 x_1 + \beta_2 x_2 + \cdots + \beta_p x_p$ part) plus the error term ϵ. The error term accounts for the variability in y that cannot be explained by the linear effect of the p independent variables.

In Section 13.4 we will discuss the assumptions for the multiple regression model and ϵ. One of the assumptions is that the mean or expected value of ϵ is zero. A consequence of this assumption is that the mean or expected value of y, denoted $E(y)$, is equal to $\beta_0 + \beta_1 x_1 + \beta_2 x_2 + \cdots + \beta_p x_p$. The equation that describes how the mean value of y is related to $x_1, x_2, \ldots, x_p$ is called the **multiple regression equation**.

MULTIPLE REGRESSION EQUATION

$$E(y) = \beta_0 + \beta_1 x_1 + \beta_2 x_2 + \cdots + \beta_p x_p \qquad (13.2)$$

Estimated Multiple Regression Equation

If the values of $\beta_0, \beta_1, \beta_2, \ldots, \beta_p$ were known, equation (13.2) could be used to compute the mean value of y at given values of $x_1, x_2, \ldots, x_p$. Unfortunately, these parameter values will not, in general, be known and must be estimated from sample data. A simple random sample is used to compute sample statistics $b_0, b_1, b_2, \ldots, b_p$ that are used as the point

FIGURE 13.1 THE ESTIMATION PROCESS FOR MULTIPLE REGRESSION

In simple linear regression, b_0 and b_1 were the sample statistics used to estimate the parameters β_0 and β_1. Multiple regression parallels this statistical inference process, with b_0, $b_1, b_2, \ldots, b_p$ denoting the sample statistics used to estimate the parameters $\beta_0, \beta_1, \beta_2, \ldots, \beta_p$.

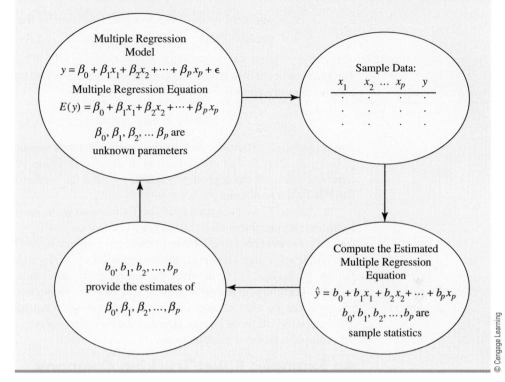

© Cengage Learning

estimators of the parameters $\beta_0, \beta_1, \beta_2, \ldots, \beta_p$. These sample statistics provide the following **estimated multiple regression equation**.

ESTIMATED MULTIPLE REGRESSION EQUATION

$$\hat{y} = b_0 + b_1 x_1 + b_2 x_2 + \cdots + b_p x_p \tag{13.3}$$

where

$b_0, b_1, b_2, \ldots, b_p$ are the estimates of $\beta_0, \beta_1, \beta_2, \ldots, \beta_p$
$\hat{y}$ = predicted value of the dependent variable

The estimation process for multiple regression is shown in Figure 13.1.

13.2 Least Squares Method

In Chapter 12, we used the **least squares method** to develop the estimated regression equation that best approximated the straight-line relationship between the dependent and independent variables. This same approach is used to develop the estimated multiple regression equation. The least squares criterion is restated as follows.

LEAST SQUARES CRITERION

$$\min \Sigma (y_i - \hat{y}_i)^2 \tag{13.4}$$

where

y_i = observed value of the dependent variable for the ith observation

$\hat{y}_i$ = predicted value of the dependent variable for the ith observation

The predicted values of the dependent variable are computed by using the estimated multiple regression equation,

$$\hat{y} = b_0 + b_1x_1 + b_2x_2 + \cdots + b_px_p$$

As expression (13.4) shows, the least squares method uses sample data to provide the values of b_0, b_1, b_2, ..., b_p that make the sum of squared residuals [the deviations between the observed values of the dependent variable (y_i) and the predicted values of the dependent variable ($\hat{y}_i$)] a minimum.

In Chapter 12 we presented formulas for computing the least squares estimators b_0 and b_1 for the estimated simple linear regression equation $\hat{y} = b_0 + b_1x$. With relatively small data sets, we were able to use those formulas to compute b_0 and b_1 by manual calculations. In multiple regression, however, the presentation of the formulas for the regression coefficients b_0, b_1, b_2, ..., b_p involves the use of matrix algebra and is beyond the scope of this text. Therefore, in presenting multiple regression, we focus on how computer software packages can be used to obtain the estimated regression equation and other information. The emphasis will be on how to interpret the computer output rather than on how to make the multiple regression computations.

An Example: Butler Trucking Company

As an illustration of multiple regression analysis, we will consider a problem faced by the Butler Trucking Company, an independent trucking company in southern California. A major portion of Butler's business involves deliveries throughout its local area. To develop better work schedules, the managers want to predict the total daily travel time for their drivers.

Initially the managers believed that the total daily travel time would be closely related to the number of miles traveled in making the daily deliveries. A simple random sample of 10 driving assignments provided the data shown in Table 13.1 and the scatter diagram shown in Figure 13.2. After reviewing this scatter diagram, the managers hypothesized that the simple linear regression model $y = \beta_0 + \beta_1x_1 + \epsilon$ could be used to describe the relationship between the total travel time (y) and the number of miles traveled (x_1). To estimate the

TABLE 13.1   PRELIMINARY DATA FOR BUTLER TRUCKING

Driving Assignment	x_1 = Miles Traveled	y = Travel Time (hours)
1	100	9.3
2	50	4.8
3	100	8.9
4	100	6.5
5	50	4.2
6	80	6.2
7	75	7.4
8	65	6.0
9	90	7.6
10	90	6.1

FIGURE 13.2   SCATTER DIAGRAM OF PRELIMINARY DATA FOR BUTLER TRUCKING

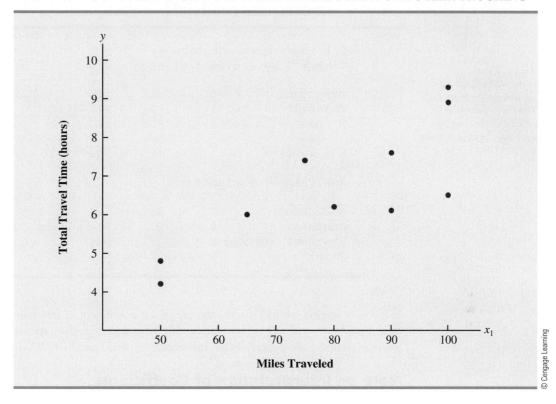

parameters β_0 and β_1, the least squares method was used to develop the estimated regression equation.

$$\hat{y} = b_0 + b_1 x_1 \qquad \text{(13.5)}$$

In Figure 13.3, we show the Minitab computer output from applying simple linear regression to the data in Table 13.1. The estimated regression equation is

$$\hat{y} = 1.27 + .0678 x_1$$

At the .05 level of significance, the F value of 15.81 and its corresponding p-value of .004 indicate that the relationship is significant; that is, we can reject H_0: $\beta_1 = 0$ because the p-value is less than $\alpha = .05$. Note that the same conclusion is obtained from the t value of 3.98 and its associated p-value of .004. Thus, we can conclude that the relationship between the total travel time and the number of miles traveled is significant; longer travel times are associated with more miles traveled. With a coefficient of determination (expressed as a percentage) of R-Sq = 66.4%, we see that 66.4% of the variability in travel time can be explained by the linear effect of the number of miles traveled. This finding is fairly good, but the managers might want to consider adding a second independent variable to explain some of the remaining variability in the dependent variable.

In attempting to identify another independent variable, the managers felt that the number of deliveries could also contribute to the total travel time. The Butler Trucking data, with the number of deliveries added, are shown in Table 13.2. The Minitab computer solution with both miles traveled (x_1) and number of deliveries (x_2) as independent variables is shown in Figure 13.4. The estimated regression equation is

The Minitab steps necessary to generate the output shown in Figure 13.4 are given in Appendix 13.1.

$$\hat{y} = -.869 + .0611 x_1 + .923 x_2 \qquad \text{(13.6)}$$

FIGURE 13.3   MINITAB OUTPUT FOR BUTLER TRUCKING WITH ONE INDEPENDENT VARIABLE

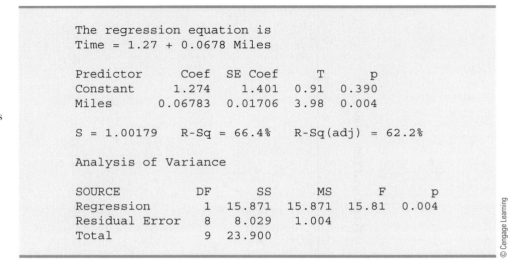

In the Minitab output the variable names Miles *and* Time *were entered as the column headings on the worksheet; thus,* x_1 = Miles *and* y = Time.

```
The regression equation is
Time = 1.27 + 0.0678 Miles

Predictor        Coef    SE Coef       T       p
Constant        1.274      1.401    0.91   0.390
Miles         0.06783    0.01706    3.98   0.004

S = 1.00179    R-Sq = 66.4%    R-Sq(adj) = 62.2%

Analysis of Variance

SOURCE           DF       SS       MS       F       p
Regression        1   15.871   15.871   15.81   0.004
Residual Error    8    8.029    1.004
Total             9   23.900
```

In the next section we will discuss the use of the coefficient of multiple determination in measuring how good a fit is provided by this estimated regression equation. Before doing so, let us examine more carefully the values of $b_1 = .0611$ and $b_2 = .923$ in equation (13.6).

Note on Interpretation of Coefficients

One observation can be made at this point about the relationship between the estimated regression equation with only the miles traveled as an independent variable and the equation that includes the number of deliveries as a second independent variable. The value of b_1 is not the same in both cases. In simple linear regression, we interpret b_1 as an estimate of the change in y for a one-unit change in the independent variable. In multiple regression analysis, this interpretation must be modified somewhat. That is, in multiple regression analysis, we interpret each regression coefficient as follows: b_i represents an estimate of the change in y corresponding to a one-unit change in x_i when all other independent variables are held constant. In the Butler Trucking example involving two independent variables, $b_1 = .0611$. Thus,

TABLE 13.2   DATA FOR BUTLER TRUCKING WITH MILES TRAVELED (x_1) AND NUMBER OF DELIVERIES (x_2) AS THE INDEPENDENT VARIABLES

WEB file

Butler

Driving Assignment	x_1 = Miles Traveled	x_2 = Number of Deliveries	y = Travel Time (hours)
1	100	4	9.3
2	50	3	4.8
3	100	4	8.9
4	100	2	6.5
5	50	2	4.2
6	80	2	6.2
7	75	3	7.4
8	65	4	6.0
9	90	3	7.6
10	90	2	6.1

FIGURE 13.4   MINITAB OUTPUT FOR BUTLER TRUCKING WITH TWO INDEPENDENT VARIABLES

In the Minitab output the variable names Miles, Deliveries, *and* Time *were entered as the column headings on the worksheet; thus,* x_1 = Miles, x_2 = Deliveries, *and* y = Time.

```
The regression equation is
Time = - 0.869 + 0.0611 Miles + 0.923 Deliveries

Predictor          Coef     SE Coef        T        p
Constant        -0.8687      0.9515    -0.91    0.392
Miles          0.061135    0.009888     6.18    0.000
Deliveries       0.9234      0.2211     4.18    0.004


S = 0.573142     R-Sq = 90.4%     R-Sq(adj) = 87.6%


Analysis of Variance

SOURCE            DF          SS        MS        F        p
Regression         2      21.601    10.800    32.88    0.000
Residual Error     7       2.299     0.328
Total              9      23.900
```

© Cengage Learning

.0611 hours is an estimate of the expected increase in travel time corresponding to an increase of 1 mile in the distance traveled when the number of deliveries is held constant. Similarly, because b_2 = .923, an estimate of the expected increase in travel time corresponding to an increase of one delivery when the number of miles traveled is held constant is .923 hours.

Exercises

Note to student: The exercises involving data in this and subsequent sections were designed to be solved using a computer software package.

Methods

1. The estimated regression equation for a model involving two independent variables and 10 observations follows.

$$\hat{y} = 29.1270 + .5906x_1 + .4980x_2$$

    a.   Interpret b_1 and b_2 in this estimated regression equation.
    b.   Predict y when x_1 = 180 and x_2 = 310.

2. Consider the following data for a dependent variable y and two independent variables, x_1 and x_2.

Exer2

x_1	x_2	y
30	12	94
47	10	108
25	17	112
51	16	178
40	5	94
51	19	175
74	7	170
36	12	117
59	13	142
76	16	211

a. Develop an estimated regression equation relating y to x_1. Predict y if $x_1 = 45$.
b. Develop an estimated regression equation relating y to x_2. Predict y if $x_2 = 15$.
c. Develop an estimated regression equation relating y to x_1 and x_2. Predict y if $x_1 = 45$ and $x_2 = 15$.

3. In a regression analysis involving 30 observations, the following estimated regression equation was obtained.

$$\hat{y} = 17.6 + 3.8x_1 - 2.3x_2 + 7.6x_3 + 2.7x_4$$

a. Interpret b_1, b_2, b_3, and b_4 in this estimated regression equation.
b. Predict y when $x_1 = 10$, $x_2 = 5$, $x_3 = 1$, and $x_4 = 2$.

Applications

4. A shoe store developed the following estimated regression equation relating sales to inventory investment and advertising expenditures.

$$\hat{y} = 25 + 10x_1 + 8x_2$$

where

$$x_1 = \text{inventory investment (\$1,000s)}$$
$$x_2 = \text{advertising expenditures (\$1,000s)}$$
$$y = \text{sales (\$1,000s)}$$

a. Predict the sales resulting from a \$15,000 investment in inventory and an advertising budget of \$10,000.
b. Interpret b_1 and b_2 in this estimated regression equation.

5. The owner of Showtime Movie Theaters, Inc., would like to predict weekly gross revenue as a function of advertising expenditures. Historical data for a sample of eight weeks follow.

Showtime

Weekly Gross Revenue ($1,000s)	Television Advertising ($1,000s)	Newspaper Advertising ($1,000s)
96	5.0	1.5
90	2.0	2.0
95	4.0	1.5
92	2.5	2.5
95	3.0	3.3
94	3.5	2.3
94	2.5	4.2
94	3.0	2.5

a. Develop an estimated regression equation with the amount of television advertising as the independent variable.
b. Develop an estimated regression equation with both television advertising and newspaper advertising as the independent variables.
c. Is the estimated regression equation coefficient for television advertising expenditures the same in part (a) and in part (b)? Interpret the coefficient in each case.
d. Predict weekly gross revenue for a week when \$3,500 is spent on television advertising and \$1,800 is spent on newspaper advertising.

6. The National Football League (NFL) records a variety of performance data for individuals and teams. To investigate the importance of passing on the percentage of games won by a

team, the following data show the conference (Conf), average number of passing yards per attempt (Yds/Att), the number of interceptions thrown per attempt (Int/Att), and the percentage of games won (Win%) for a random sample of 16 NFL teams for the 2011 season (NFL website, February 12, 2012).

NFLPassing

Team	Conf	Yds/Att	Int/Att	Win%
Arizona Cardinals	NFC	6.5	.042	50.0
Atlanta Falcons	NFC	7.1	.022	62.5
Carolina Panthers	NFC	7.4	.033	37.5
Cincinnati Bengals	AFC	6.2	.026	56.3
Detroit Lions	NFC	7.2	.024	62.5
Green Bay Packers	NFC	8.9	.014	93.8
Houstan Texans	AFC	7.5	.019	62.5
Indianapolis Colts	AFC	5.6	.026	12.5
Jacksonville Jaguars	AFC	4.6	.032	31.3
Minnesota Vikings	NFC	5.8	.033	18.8
New England Patriots	AFC	8.3	.020	81.3
New Orleans Saints	NFC	8.1	.021	81.3
Oakland Raiders	AFC	7.6	.044	50.0
San Francisco 49ers	NFC	6.5	.011	81.3
Tennessee Titans	AFC	6.7	.024	56.3
Washington Redskins	NFC	6.4	.041	31.3

a. Develop the estimated regression equation that could be used to predict the percentage of games won given the average number of passing yards per attempt.
b. Develop the estimated regression equation that could be used to predict the percentage of games won given the number of interceptions thrown per attempt.
c. Develop the estimated regression equation that could be used to predict the percentage of games won given the average number of passing yards per attempt and the number of interceptions thrown per attempt.
d. The average number of passing yards per attempt for the Kansas City Chiefs was 6.2 and the number of interceptions thrown per attempt was .036. Use the estimated regression equation developed in part (c) to predict the percentage of games won by the Kansas City Chiefs. (*Note:* For the 2011 season the Kansas City Chiefs' record was 7 wins and 9 losses.) Compare your prediction to the actual percentage of games won by the Kansas City Chiefs.

7. *PCWorld* rated four component characteristics for 10 ultraportable laptop computers: features; performance; design; and price. Each characteristic was rated using a 0–100 point scale. An overall rating, referred to as the PC World Rating, was then developed

Laptop

Model	Performance	Features	PCWorld Rating
Thinkpad X200	77	87	83
VGN-Z598U	97	85	82
U6V	83	80	81
Elitebook 2530P	77	75	78
X360	64	80	78
Thinkpad X300	56	76	78
Ideapad U110	55	81	77
Micro Express JFT2500	76	73	75
Toughbook W7	46	79	73
HP Voodoo Envy133	54	68	72

for each laptop. The data in webfile Laptop are performance rating, features rating, and the PC World Rating for the 10 laptop computers (*PCWorld* website, February 5, 2009).

    a.   Determine the estimated regression equation that can be used to predict the PC World Rating using the performance rating as the independent variable.

    b.   Determine the estimated regression equation that can be used to predict the PC World Rating using both the performance rating and the features rating.

    c.   Predict the PC World Rating for a laptop computer that has a performance rating of 80 and a features rating of 70.

8. The *Condé Nast Traveler* Gold List for 2012 provided ratings for the top 20 small cruise ships (*Condé Nast Traveler* website, March 1, 2012). The data shown below are the scores each ship received based upon the results from *Condé Nast Traveler*'s annual Readers' Choice Survey. Each score represents the percentage of respondents who rated a ship as excellent or very good on several criteria, including Shore Excursions and Food/Dining. An overall score was also reported and used to rank the ships. The highest ranked ship, the *Seabourn Odyssey,* has an overall score of 94.4, the highest component of which is 97.8 for Food/Dining.

Ships

Ship	Overall	Shore Excursions	Food/Dining
Seabourn Odyssey	94.4	90.9	97.8
Seabourn Pride	93.0	84.2	96.7
National Geographic Endeavor	92.9	100.0	88.5
Seabourn Sojourn	91.3	94.8	97.1
Paul Gauguin	90.5	87.9	91.2
Seabourn Legend	90.3	82.1	98.8
Seabourn Spirit	90.2	86.3	92.0
Silver Explorer	89.9	92.6	88.9
Silver Spirit	89.4	85.9	90.8
Seven Seas Navigator	89.2	83.3	90.5
Silver Whisperer	89.2	82.0	88.6
National Geographic Explorer	89.1	93.1	89.7
Silver Cloud	88.7	78.3	91.3
Celebrity Xpedition	87.2	91.7	73.6
Silver Shadow	87.2	75.0	89.7
Silver Wind	86.6	78.1	91.6
SeaDream II	86.2	77.4	90.9
Wind Star	86.1	76.5	91.5
Wind Surf	86.1	72.3	89.3
Wind Spirit	85.2	77.4	91.9

    a.   Determine an estimated regression equation that can be used to predict the overall score given the score for Shore Excursions.

    b.   Consider the addition of the independent variable Food/Dining. Develop the estimated regression equation that can be used to predict the overall score given the scores for Shore Excursions and Food/Dining.

    c.   Predict the overall score for a cruise ship with a Shore Excursions score of 80 and a Food/Dining Score of 90.

9. The Professional Golfers Association (PGA) maintains data on performance and earnings for members of the PGA Tour. For the 2012 season Bubba Watson led all players in total driving distance, with an average of 309.2 yards per drive. Some of the factors thought to influence driving distance are club head speed, ball speed, and launch angle. For the 2012 season Bubba Watson had an average club head speed of 124.69 miles per hour, an

PGADrivingDist

average ball speed of 184.98 miles per hour, and an average launch angle of 8.79 degrees. The file named PGADrivingDist contains data on total driving distance and the factors related to driving distance for 190 members of the PGA Tour (PGA Tour website, November 1, 2012). Descriptions for the variables in the data set follow.

Club Head Speed: Speed at which the club impacts the ball (mph).

Ball Speed: Peak speed of the golf ball at launch (mph).

Launch Angle: Vertical launch angle of the ball immediately after leaving the club (degrees).

Total Distance: The average number of yards per drive.

a. Develop an estimated regression equation that can be used to predict the average number of yards per drive given the club head speed.
b. Develop an estimated regression equation that can be used to predict the average number of yards per drive given the ball speed.
c. A recommendation has been made to develop an estimated regression equation that uses both club head speed and ball speed to predict the average number of yards per drive. Do you agree with this? Explain.
d. Develop an estimated regression equation that can be used to predict the average number of yards per drive given the ball speed and the launch angle.
e. Suppose a new member of the PGA Tour for 2013 has a ball speed of 170 miles per hour and a launch angle of 11 degrees. Use the estimated regression equation in part (d) to predict the average number of yards per drive for this player.

10. Major League Baseball (MLB) consists of teams that play in the American League and the National League. MLB collects a wide variety of team and player statistics. Some of the statistics often used to evaluate pitching performance are as follows:

ERA: The average number of earned runs given up by the pitcher per nine innings. An earned run is any run that the opponent scores off a particular pitcher except for runs scored as a result of errors.

SO/IP: The average number of strikeouts per inning pitched.

HR/IP: The average number of home runs per inning pitched.

R/IP: The number of runs given up per inning pitched.

The following data show values for these statistics for a random sample of 20 pitchers from the American League for the 2011 season (MLB website, March 1, 2012).

MLBPitching

Player	Team	W	L	ERA	SO/IP	HR/IP	R/IP
Verlander, J	DET	24	5	2.40	1.00	.10	.29
Beckett, J	BOS	13	7	2.89	.91	.11	.34
Wilson, C	TEX	16	7	2.94	.92	.07	.40
Sabathia, C	NYY	19	8	3.00	.97	.07	.37
Haren, D	LAA	16	10	3.17	.81	.08	.38
McCarthy, B	OAK	9	9	3.32	.72	.06	.43
Santana, E	LAA	11	12	3.38	.78	.11	.42
Lester, J	BOS	15	9	3.47	.95	.10	.40
Hernandez, F	SEA	14	14	3.47	.95	.08	.42
Buehrle, M	CWS	13	9	3.59	.53	.10	.45
Pineda, M	SEA	9	10	3.74	1.01	.11	.44
Colon, B	NYY	8	10	4.00	.82	.13	.52

(continued)

Player	Team	W	L	ERA	SO/IP	HR/IP	R/IP
Tomlin, J	CLE	12	7	4.25	.54	.15	.48
Pavano, C	MIN	9	13	4.30	.46	.10	.55
Danks, J	CWS	8	12	4.33	.79	.11	.52
Guthrie, J	BAL	9	17	4.33	.63	.13	.54
Lewis, C	TEX	14	10	4.40	.84	.17	.51
Scherzer, M	DET	15	9	4.43	.89	.15	.52
Davis, W	TB	11	10	4.45	.57	.13	.52
Porcello, R	DET	14	9	4.75	.57	.10	.57

a. Develop an estimated regression equation that can be used to predict the average number of runs given up per inning given the average number of strikeouts per inning pitched.

b. Develop an estimated regression equation that can be used to predict the average number of runs given up per inning given the average number of home runs per inning pitched.

c. Develop an estimated regression equation that can be used to predict the average number of runs given up per inning given the average number of strikeouts per inning pitched and the average number of home runs per inning pitched.

d. A. J. Burnett, a pitcher for the New York Yankees, had an average number of strikeouts per inning pitched of .91 and an average number of home runs per inning of .16. Use the estimated regression equation developed in part (c) to predict the average number of runs given up per inning for A. J. Burnett. (*Note:* The actual value for R/IP was .6.)

e. Suppose a suggestion was made to also use the earned run average as another independent variable in part (c). What do you think of this suggestion?

 ## 13.3   Multiple Coefficient of Determination

In simple linear regression we showed that the total sum of squares can be partitioned into two components: the sum of squares due to regression and the sum of squares due to error. The same procedure applies to the sum of squares in multiple regression.

RELATIONSHIP AMONG SST, SSR, AND SSE

$$SST = SSR + SSE \qquad (13.7)$$

where

$$SST = \text{total sum of squares} = \Sigma(y_i - \bar{y})^2$$
$$SSR = \text{sum of squares due to regression} = \Sigma(\hat{y}_i - \bar{y})^2$$
$$SSE = \text{sum of squares due to error} = \Sigma(y_i - \hat{y}_i)^2$$

Because of the computational difficulty in computing the three sums of squares, we rely on computer packages to determine those values. The analysis of variance part of the Minitab output in Figure 13.4 shows the three values for the Butler Trucking problem with two independent variables: SST = 23.900, SSR = 21.601, and SSE = 2.299. With only one independent variable (number of miles traveled), the Minitab output in Figure 13.3 shows that SST = 23.900, SSR = 15.871, and SSE = 8.029. The value of SST is the same in both cases because it does not depend on $\hat{y}$, but SSR increases and SSE decreases when a second independent variable (number of deliveries) is added. The implication is that the estimated multiple regression equation provides a better fit for the observed data.

In Chapter 12, we used the coefficient of determination, $r^2 = \text{SSR/SST}$, to measure the goodness of fit for the estimated regression equation. The same concept applies to multiple regression. The term **multiple coefficient of determination** indicates that we are measuring the goodness of fit for the estimated multiple regression equation. The multiple coefficient of determination, denoted R^2, is computed as follows.

MULTIPLE COEFFICIENT OF DETERMINATION

$$R^2 = \frac{\text{SSR}}{\text{SST}} \tag{13.8}$$

The multiple coefficient of determination can be interpreted as the proportion of the variability in the dependent variable that can be explained by the estimated multiple regression equation. Hence, when multiplied by 100, it can be interpreted as the percentage of the variability in y that can be explained by the estimated regression equation.

In the two-independent-variable Butler Trucking example, with SSR = 21.601 and SST = 23.900, we have

$$R^2 = \frac{21.601}{23.900} = .904$$

Therefore, 90.4% of the variability in travel time y is explained by the estimated multiple regression equation with miles traveled and number of deliveries as the independent variables. In Figure 13.4, we see that the multiple coefficient of determination (expressed as a percentage) is also provided by the Minitab output; it is denoted by R-Sq = 90.4%.

Adding independent variables causes the prediction errors to become smaller, thus reducing the sum of squares due to error, SSE. Because SSR = SST − SSE, when SSE becomes smaller, SSR becomes larger, causing R^2 = SSR/SST to increase.

Figure 13.3 shows that the R-Sq value for the estimated regression equation with only one independent variable, number of miles traveled (x_1), is 66.4%. Thus, the percentage of the variability in travel times that is explained by the estimated regression equation increases from 66.4% to 90.4% when number of deliveries is added as a second independent variable. In general, R^2 always increases as independent variables are added to the model.

Many analysts prefer adjusting R^2 for the number of independent variables to avoid overestimating the impact of adding an independent variable on the amount of variability explained by the estimated regression equation. With n denoting the number of observations and p denoting the number of independent variables, the **adjusted multiple coefficient of determination** is computed as follows.

ADJUSTED MULTIPLE COEFFICIENT OF DETERMINATION

$$R_a^2 = 1 - (1 - R^2)\frac{n-1}{n-p-1} \tag{13.9}$$

For the Butler Trucking example with $n = 10$ and $p = 2$, we have

$$R_a^2 = 1 - (1 - .904)\frac{10-1}{10-2-1} = .88$$

Thus, after adjusting for the two independent variables, we have an adjusted multiple coefficient of determination of .88. This value (expressed as a percentage) is provided by the Minitab output in Figure 13.4 as R-Sq(adj) = 87.6%; the value we calculated differs because we used a rounded value of R^2 in the calculation.

NOTE AND COMMENT

If the value of R^2 is small and the model contains a large number of independent variables, the adjusted coefficient of determination can take a negative value; in such cases, Minitab sets the adjusted coefficient of determination to zero.

Exercises

Methods

11. In exercise 1, the following estimated regression equation based on 10 observations was presented.

$$\hat{y} = 29.1270 + .5906x_1 + .4980x_2$$

The values of SST and SSR are 6724.125 and 6216.375, respectively.
   a. Find SSE.
   b. Compute R^2.
   c. Compute R_a^2.
   d. Comment on the goodness of fit.

12. In exercise 2, 10 observations were provided for a dependent variable y and two independent variables x_1 and x_2; for these data SST = 15,182.9, and SSR = 14,052.2.
   a. Compute R^2.
   b. Compute R_a^2.
   c. Does the estimated regression equation explain a large amount of the variability in the data? Explain.

13. In exercise 3, the following estimated regression equation based on 30 observations was presented.

$$\hat{y} = 17.6 + 3.8x_1 - 2.3x_2 + 7.6x_3 + 2.7x_4$$

The values of SST and SSR are 1805 and 1760, respectively.
   a. Compute R^2.
   b. Compute R_a^2.
   c. Comment on the goodness of fit.

Applications

14. In exercise 4, the following estimated regression equation relating sales to inventory investment and advertising expenditures was given.

$$\hat{y} = 25 + 10x_1 + 8x_2$$

The data used to develop the model came from a survey of 10 stores; for those data, SST = 16,000 and SSR = 12,000.
   a. For the estimated regression equation given, compute R^2.
   b. Compute R_a^2.
   c. Does the model appear to explain a large amount of variability in the data? Explain.

15. In exercise 5, the owner of Showtime Movie Theaters, Inc., used multiple regression analysis to predict weekly gross revenue (y) as a function of television advertising (x_1) and newspaper advertising (x_2). The estimated regression equation was

$$\hat{y} = 83.2 + 2.29x_1 + 1.30x_2$$

Showtime

The computer solution provided SST = 25.5 and SSR = 23.435.
   a. Compute and interpret R^2 and R_a^2.
   b. When television advertising was the only independent variable, $R^2 = .653$ and $R_a^2 = .595$. Do you prefer the multiple regression results? Explain.

NFLPassing

16. In exercise 6, data were given on the average number of passing yards per attempt (Yds/Att), the number of interceptions thrown per attempt (Int/Att), and the percentage of games won (Win%) for a random sample of 16 National Football League (NFL) teams for the 2011 season (NFL website, February 12, 2012).
   a. Did the estimated regression equation that uses only the average number of passing yards per attempt as the independent variable to predict the percentage of games won provide a good fit?
   b. Discuss the benefit of using both the average number of passing yards per attempt and the number of interceptions thrown per attempt to predict the percentage of games won.

PGADrivingDist

17. In exercise 9, data contained in the file named PGADrivingDist (PGA Tour website, November 1, 2012) were used to develop an estimated regression equation to predict the average number of yards per drive (y) given the ball speed (x_1) and the launch angle (x_2). The estimated regression equation was $\hat{y} = 81.6 + 1.09x_1 + 1.65x_2$.
   a. Does the estimated regression equation provide a good fit to the data? Explain.
   b. In part (b) of exercise 9, an estimated regression equation was developed using only ball speed to predict the average number of yards per drive. The estimated regression equation was $\hat{y} = 117 + 0.988x_1$. Compare the fit obtained using just ball speed to the fit obtained using ball speed and the launch angle.

MLBPitching

18. Refer to exercise 10, where Major League Baseball (MLB) pitching statistics were reported for a random sample of 20 pitchers from the American League for the 2011 season (MLB website, March 1, 2012).
   a. In part (c) of exercise 10, an estimated regression equation was developed relating the average number of runs given up per inning pitched given the average number of strikeouts per inning pitched and the average number of home runs per inning pitched. What are the values of R^2 and R_a^2?
   b. Does the estimated regression equation provide a good fit to the data? Explain.
   c. Suppose the earned run average (ERA) is used as the dependent variable in part (c) instead of the average number of runs given up per inning pitched. Does the estimated regression equation that uses the ERA provide a good fit to the data? Explain.

13.4 # Model Assumptions

In Section 13.1 we introduced the following multiple regression model.

MULTIPLE REGRESSION MODEL

$$y = \beta_0 + \beta_1 x_1 + \beta_2 x_2 + \cdots + \beta_p x_p + \epsilon \qquad (13.10)$$

The assumptions about the error term ϵ in the multiple regression model parallel those for the simple linear regression model.

ASSUMPTIONS ABOUT THE ERROR TERM ϵ IN THE MULTIPLE REGRESSION MODEL $y = \beta_0 + \beta_1 x_1 + \cdots + \beta_p x_p + \epsilon$

1. The error term ϵ is a random variable with mean or expected value of zero; that is, $E(\epsilon) = 0$.
   Implication: For given values of $x_1, x_2, \ldots, x_p$, the expected, or average, value of y is given by

   $$E(y) = \beta_0 + \beta_1 x_1 + \beta_2 x_2 + \cdots + \beta_p x_p \qquad (13.11)$$

   Equation (13.11) is the multiple regression equation we introduced in Section 13.1. In this equation, $E(y)$ represents the average of all possible values of y that might occur for the given values of $x_1, x_2, \ldots, x_p$.
2. The variance of ϵ is denoted by σ^2 and is the same for all values of the independent variables $x_1, x_2, \ldots, x_p$.
   Implication: The variance of y about the regression line equals σ^2 and is the same for all values of $x_1, x_2, \ldots, x_p$.
3. The values of ϵ are independent.
   Implication: The value of ϵ for a particular set of values for the independent variables is not related to the value of ϵ for any other set of values.
4. The error term ϵ is a normally distributed random variable reflecting the deviation between the y value and the expected value of y given by $\beta_0 + \beta_1 x_1 + \beta_2 x_2 + \cdots + \beta_p x_p$.
   Implication: Because $\beta_0, \beta_1, \ldots, \beta_p$ are constants for the given values of $x_1, x_2, \ldots, x_p$, the dependent variable y is also a normally distributed random variable.

To obtain more insight about the form of the relationship given by equation (13.11), consider the following two-independent-variable multiple regression equation.

$$E(y) = \beta_0 + \beta_1 x_1 + \beta_2 x_2$$

The graph of this equation is a plane in three-dimensional space. Figure 13.5 provides an example of such a graph. Note that the value of ϵ shown is the difference between the actual y value and the expected value of y, $E(y)$, when $x_1 = x_1^*$ and $x_2 = x_2^*$.

FIGURE 13.5   GRAPH OF THE REGRESSION EQUATION FOR MULTIPLE REGRESSION
ANALYSIS WITH TWO INDEPENDENT VARIABLES

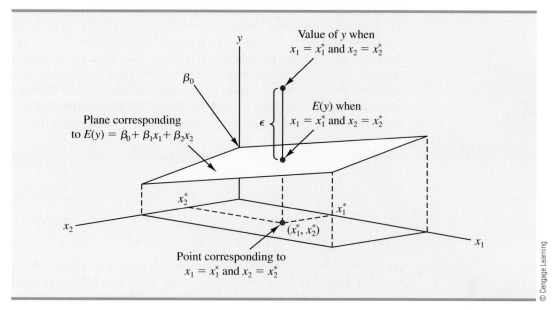

In regression analysis, the term *response variable* is often used in place of the term *dependent variable*. Furthermore, since the multiple regression equation generates a plane or surface, its graph is called a *response surface*.

 ## Testing for Significance

In this section we show how to conduct significance tests for a multiple regression relationship. The significance tests we used in simple linear regression were a *t* test and an *F* test. In simple linear regression, both tests provide the same conclusion; that is, if the null hypothesis is rejected, we conclude that $\beta_1 \neq 0$. In multiple regression, the *t* test and the *F* test have different purposes.

1. The *F* test is used to determine whether a significant relationship exists between the dependent variable and the set of all the independent variables; we will refer to the *F* test as the test for *overall significance*.
2. If the *F* test shows an overall significance, the *t* test is used to determine whether each of the individual independent variables is significant. A separate *t* test is conducted for each of the independent variables in the model; we refer to each of these *t* tests as a test for *individual significance*.

In the material that follows, we will explain the *F* test and the *t* test and apply each to the Butler Trucking Company example.

F Test

The multiple regression model as defined in Section 13.4 is

$$y = \beta_0 + \beta_1 x_1 + \beta_2 x_2 + \cdots + \beta_p x_p + \epsilon$$

The hypotheses for the *F* test involve the parameters of the multiple regression model.

$$H_0: \beta_1 = \beta_2 = \cdots = \beta_p = 0$$
$$H_a: \text{One or more of the parameters is not equal to zero}$$

If H_0 is rejected, the test gives us sufficient statistical evidence to conclude that one or more of the parameters is not equal to zero and that the overall relationship between y and the set of independent variables $x_1, x_2, \ldots, x_p$ is significant. However, if H_0 cannot be rejected, we do not have sufficient evidence to conclude that a significant relationship is present.

Before describing the steps of the F test, we need to review the concept of *mean square*. A mean square is a sum of squares divided by its corresponding degrees of freedom. In the multiple regression case, the total sum of squares has $n - 1$ degrees of freedom, the sum of squares due to regression (SSR) has p degrees of freedom, and the sum of squares due to error has $n - p - 1$ degrees of freedom. Hence, the mean square due to regression (MSR) is SSR/p and the mean square due to error (MSE) is SSE/$(n - p - 1)$.

$$\text{MSR} = \frac{\text{SSR}}{p} \tag{13.12}$$

and

$$\text{MSE} = \frac{\text{SSE}}{n - p - 1} \tag{13.13}$$

As discussed in Chapter 12, MSE provides an unbiased estimate of σ^2, the variance of the error term ϵ. If H_0: $\beta_1 = \beta_2 = \cdots = \beta_p = 0$ is true, MSR also provides an unbiased estimate of σ^2, and the value of MSR/MSE should be close to 1. However, if H_0 is false, MSR overestimates σ^2 and the value of MSR/MSE becomes larger. To determine how large the value of MSR/MSE must be to reject H_0, we make use of the fact that if H_0 is true and the assumptions about the multiple regression model are valid, the sampling distribution of MSR/MSE is an F distribution with p degrees of freedom in the numerator and $n - p - 1$ in the denominator. A summary of the F test for significance in multiple regression follows.

F TEST FOR OVERALL SIGNIFICANCE

H_0: $\beta_1 = \beta_2 = \cdots = \beta_p = 0$
H_a: One or more of the parameters is not equal to zero

TEST STATISTIC

$$F = \frac{\text{MSR}}{\text{MSE}} \tag{13.14}$$

REJECTION RULE

p-value approach: Reject H_0 if p-value $\leq \alpha$
Critical value approach: Reject H_0 if $F \geq F_\alpha$

where F_α is based on an F distribution with p degrees of freedom in the numerator and $n - p - 1$ degrees of freedom in the denominator.

Let us apply the F test to the Butler Trucking Company multiple regression problem. With two independent variables, the hypotheses are written as follows.

H_0: $\beta_1 = \beta_2 = 0$
H_a: β_1 and/or β_2 is not equal to zero

FIGURE 13.6   MINITAB OUTPUT FOR BUTLER TRUCKING WITH TWO INDEPENDENT VARIABLES, MILES TRAVELED (x_1) AND NUMBER OF DELIVERIES (x_2)

```
The regression equation is
Time = - 0.869 + 0.0611 Miles + 0.923 Deliveries

Predictor        Coef    SE Coef      T       p
Constant       -0.8687    0.9515   -0.91   0.392
Miles         0.061135  0.009888    6.18   0.000
Deliveries      0.9234    0.2211    4.18   0.004


S = 0.573142    R-Sq = 90.4%    R-Sq(adj) = 87.6%


Analysis of Variance

SOURCE           DF        SS       MS       F       p
Regression        2    21.601   10.800   32.88   0.000
Residual Error    7     2.299    0.328
Total             9    23.900
```

Figure 13.6 is the Minitab output for the multiple regression model with miles traveled (x_1) and number of deliveries (x_2) as the two independent variables. In the analysis of variance part of the output, we see that MSR = 10.8 and MSE = .328. Using equation (13.14), we obtain the test statistic.

$$F = \frac{10.8}{.328} = 32.9$$

Note that the F value on the Minitab output is $F = 32.88$; the value we calculated differs because we used rounded values for MSR and MSE in the calculation. Using $\alpha = .01$, the p-value = 0.000 in the last column of the analysis of variance table (Figure 13.6) indicates that we can reject H_0: $\beta_1 = \beta_2 = 0$ because the p-value is less than $\alpha = .01$. Alternatively, Table 4 of Appendix B shows that with two degrees of freedom in the numerator and seven degrees of freedom in the denominator, $F_{.01} = 9.55$. With $32.9 > 9.55$, we reject H_0: $\beta_1 = \beta_2 = 0$ and conclude that a significant relationship is present between travel time y and the two independent variables, miles traveled and number of deliveries.

As noted previously, the mean square error provides an unbiased estimate of σ^2, the variance of the error term ϵ. Referring to Figure 13.6, we see that the estimate of σ^2 is MSE = .328. The square root of MSE is the estimate of the standard deviation of the error term. As defined in Section 12.5, this standard deviation is called the standard error of the estimate and is denoted s. Hence, we have $s = \sqrt{\text{MSE}} = \sqrt{.328} = .573$. Note that the value of the standard error of the estimate appears in the Minitab output in Figure 13.6.

Table 13.3 is the general analysis of variance (ANOVA) table that provides the F test results for a multiple regression model. The value of the F test statistic appears in the last column and can be compared to F_{α} with p degrees of freedom in the numerator and $n - p - 1$ degrees of freedom in the denominator to make the hypothesis test conclusion. By reviewing the Minitab output for Butler Trucking Company in Figure 13.6, we see that Minitab's analysis of variance table contains this information. Moreover, Minitab also provides the p-value corresponding to the F test statistic.

TABLE 13.3   ANOVA TABLE FOR A MULTIPLE REGRESSION MODEL WITH p INDEPENDENT VARIABLES

Source	Sum of Squares	Degrees of Freedom	Mean Square	F
Regression	SSR	p	$MSR = \dfrac{SSR}{p}$	$F = \dfrac{MSR}{MSE}$
Error	SSE	$n - p - 1$	$MSE = \dfrac{SSE}{n - p - 1}$	
Total	SST	$n - 1$		

© Cengage Learning

t Test

If the F test shows that the multiple regression relationship is significant, a t test can be conducted to determine the significance of each of the individual parameters. The t test for individual significance follows.

---

t TEST FOR INDIVIDUAL SIGNIFICANCE

For any parameter β_i

$$H_0: \beta_i = 0$$
$$H_a: \beta_i \neq 0$$

TEST STATISTIC

$$t = \frac{b_i}{s_{b_i}} \tag{13.15}$$

REJECTION RULE

     p-value approach: Reject H_0 if p-value $\leq \alpha$

     Critical value approach: Reject H_0 if $t \leq -t_{\alpha/2}$ or if $t \geq t_{\alpha/2}$

where $t_{\alpha/2}$ is based on a t distribution with $n - p - 1$ degrees of freedom.

In the test statistic, s_{b_i} is the estimate of the standard deviation of b_i. The value of s_{b_i} will be provided by the computer software package.

Let us conduct the t test for the Butler Trucking regression problem. Refer to the section of Figure 13.6 that shows the Minitab output for the t-ratio calculations. Values of b_1, b_2, s_{b_1}, and s_{b_2} are as follows.

$$b_1 = .061135 \quad s_{b_1} = .009888$$
$$b_2 = .9234 \quad\quad s_{b_2} = .2211$$

Using equation (13.15), we obtain the test statistic for the hypotheses involving parameters β_1 and β_2.

$$t = .061135/.009888 = 6.18$$
$$t = .9234/.2211 = 4.18$$

Note that both of these t-ratio values and the corresponding p-values are provided by the Minitab output in Figure 13.6. Using $\alpha = .01$, the p-values of .000 and .004 on the Minitab output indicate that we can reject $H_0: \beta_1 = 0$ and $H_0: \beta_2 = 0$. Hence, both parameters are statistically significant. Alternatively, Table 2 of Appendix B shows that with $n - p - 1 = 10 - 2 - 1 = 7$ degrees of freedom, $t_{.005} = 3.499$. With $6.18 > 3.499$, we reject $H_0: \beta_1 = 0$. Similarly, with $4.18 > 3.499$, we reject $H_0: \beta_2 = 0$.

Multicollinearity

We use the term *independent variable* in regression analysis to refer to any variable being used to predict or explain the value of the dependent variable. The term does not mean, however, that the independent variables themselves are independent in any statistical sense. On the contrary, most independent variables in a multiple regression problem are correlated to some degree with one another. For example, in the Butler Trucking example involving the two independent variables x_1 (miles traveled) and x_2 (number of deliveries), we could treat the miles traveled as the dependent variable and the number of deliveries as the independent variable to determine whether those two variables are themselves related. We could then compute the sample correlation coefficient $r_{x_1 x_2}$ to determine the extent to which the variables are related. Doing so yields $r_{x_1 x_2} = .16$. Thus, we find some degree of linear association between the two independent variables. In multiple regression analysis, **multicollinearity** refers to the correlation among the independent variables.

To provide a better perspective of the potential problems of multicollinearity, let us consider a modification of the Butler Trucking example. Instead of x_2 being the number of deliveries, let x_2 denote the number of gallons of gasoline consumed. Clearly, x_1 (the miles traveled) and x_2 are related; that is, we know that the number of gallons of gasoline used depends on the number of miles traveled. Hence, we would conclude logically that x_1 and x_2 are highly correlated independent variables.

Assume that we obtain the equation $\hat{y} = b_0 + b_1 x_1 + b_2 x_2$ and find that the F test shows the relationship to be significant. Then suppose we conduct a t test on β_1 to determine whether $\beta_1 \neq 0$, and we cannot reject $H_0: \beta_1 = 0$. Does this result mean that travel time is not related to miles traveled? Not necessarily. What it probably means is that with x_2 already in the model, x_1 does not make a significant contribution to determining the value of y. This interpretation makes sense in our example; if we know the amount of gasoline consumed, we do not gain much additional information useful in predicting y by knowing the miles traveled. Similarly, a t test might lead us to conclude $\beta_2 = 0$ on the grounds that, with x_1 in the model, knowledge of the amount of gasoline consumed does not add much.

A sample correlation coefficient greater than $+.7$ or less than $-.7$ for two independent variables is a rule of thumb warning of potential problems with multicollinearity.

To summarize, in t tests for the significance of individual parameters, the difficulty caused by multicollinearity is that it is possible to conclude that none of the individual parameters are significantly different from zero when an F test on the overall multiple regression equation indicates a significant relationship. This problem is avoided when there is little correlation among the independent variables.

Statisticians have developed several tests for determining whether multicollinearity is high enough to cause problems. According to the rule of thumb test, multicollinearity is a potential problem if the absolute value of the sample correlation coefficient exceeds .7 for any two of the independent variables. The other types of tests are more advanced and beyond the scope of this text.

When the independent variables are highly correlated, it is not possible to determine the separate effect of any particular independent variable on the dependent variable.

If possible, every attempt should be made to avoid including independent variables that are highly correlated. In practice, however, strict adherence to this policy is rarely possible. When decision makers have reason to believe substantial multicollinearity is present, they must realize that separating the effects of the individual independent variables on the dependent variable is difficult.

NOTE AND COMMENT

Ordinarily, multicollinearity does not affect the way in which we perform our regression analysis or interpret the output from a study. However, when multicollinearity is severe—that is, when two or more of the independent variables are highly correlated with one another—we can have difficulty interpreting the results of t tests on the individual parameters. In addition to the type of problem illustrated in this section, severe cases of multicollinearity have been shown to result in least squares estimates that have the wrong sign. That is, in simu-

lated studies where researchers created the underlying regression model and then applied the least squares technique to develop estimates of β_0, β_1, β_2, and so on, it has been shown that under conditions of high multicollinearity the least squares estimates can have a sign opposite that of the parameter being estimated. For example, β_2 might actually be $+10$ and b_2, its estimate, might turn out to be -2. Thus, little faith can be placed in the individual coefficients if multicollinearity is present to a high degree.

Exercises

Methods

19. In exercise 1, the following estimated regression equation based on 10 observations was presented.

$$\hat{y} = 29.1270 + .5906x_1 + .4980x_2$$

Here SST = 6724.125, SSR = 6216.375, s_{b_1} = .0813, and s_{b_2} = .0567.
a. Compute MSR and MSE.
b. Compute F and perform the appropriate F test. Use $\alpha = .05$.
c. Perform a t test for the significance of β_1. Use $\alpha = .05$.
d. Perform a t test for the significance of β_2. Use $\alpha = .05$.

20. Refer to the data presented in exercise 2. The estimated regression equation for these data is

$$\hat{y} = -18.37 + 2.01x_1 + 4.74x_2$$

Here SST = 15,182.9, SSR = 14,052.2, s_{b_1} = .2471, and s_{b_2} = .9484.
a. Test for a significant relationship among x_1, x_2, and y. Use $\alpha = .05$.
b. Is β_1 significant? Use $\alpha = .05$.
c. Is β_2 significant? Use $\alpha = .05$.

21. The following estimated regression equation was developed for a model involving two independent variables.

$$\hat{y} = 40.7 + 8.63x_1 + 2.71x_2$$

After x_2 was dropped from the model, the least squares method was used to obtain an estimated regression equation involving only x_1 as an independent variable.

$$\hat{y} = 42.0 + 9.01x_1$$

a. Give an interpretation of the coefficient of x_1 in both models.
b. Could multicollinearity explain why the coefficient of x_1 differs in the two models? If so, how?

Applications

22. In exercise 4, the following estimated regression equation relating sales to inventory investment and advertising expenditures was given.

$$\hat{y} = 25 + 10x_1 + 8x_2$$

The data used to develop the model came from a survey of 10 stores; for these data SST = 16,000 and SSR = 12,000.

  a. Compute SSE, MSE, and MSR.

  b. Use an *F* test and a .05 level of significance to determine whether there is a relationship among the variables.

23. Refer to exercise 5.

  a. Use $\alpha = .01$ to test the hypotheses

$$H_0: \beta_1 = \beta_2 = 0$$
$$H_a: \beta_1 \text{ and/or } \beta_2 \text{ is not equal to zero}$$

for the model $y = \beta_0 + \beta_1 x_1 + \beta_2 x_2 + \epsilon$, where

$$x_1 = \text{television advertising (\$1,000s)}$$
$$x_2 = \text{newspaper advertising (\$1,000s)}$$

  b. Use $\alpha = .05$ to test the significance of β_1. Should x_1 be dropped from the model?

  c. Use $\alpha = .05$ to test the significance of β_2. Should x_2 be dropped from the model?

24. The National Football League (NFL) records a variety of performance data for individuals and teams. A portion of the data showing the average number of passing yards obtained per game on offense (OffPassYds/G), the average number of yards given up per game on defense (DefYds/G), and the precentage of games won (Win%), for the 2011 season follows (ESPN website, November 3, 2012).

Team	OffPassYds/G	DefYds/G	Win%
Arizona	222.9	355.1	50.0
Atlanta	262.0	333.6	62.5
Baltimore	213.9	288.9	75.0
.	.	.	.
.	.	.	.
.	.	.	.
St. Louis	179.4	358.4	12.5
Tampa Bay	228.1	394.4	25.0
Tennessee	245.2	355.1	56.3
Washington	235.8	339.8	31.3

  a. Develop an estimated regression equation that can be used to predict the percentage of games won given the average number of passing yards obtained per game on offense and the average number of yards given up per game on defense.

  b. Use the *F* test to determine the overall significance of the relationship. What is your conclusion at the .05 level of significance?

  c. Use the *t* test to determine the significance of each independent variable. What is your conclusion at the .05 level of significance?

25. The *Condé Nast Traveler* Gold List for 2012 provided ratings for the top 20 small cruise ships (*Condé Nast Traveler* website, March 1, 2012). The data shown below are the scores each ship received based upon the results from *Condé Nast Traveler*'s annual Readers' Choice Survey. Each score represents the percentage of respondents who rated a ship as excellent or very good on several criteria, including Itineraries/Schedule, Shore Excursions, and Food/Dining. An overall score was also reported and used to rank the ships. The highest ranked ship, the *Seabourn Odyssey,* has an overall score of 94.4, the highest component of which is 97.8 for Food/Dining.

Ship	Overall	Itineraries/ Schedule	Shore Excursions	Food/ Dining
Seabourn Odyssey	94.4	94.6	90.9	97.8
Seabourn Pride	93.0	96.7	84.2	96.7
National Geographic Endeavor	92.9	100.0	100.0	88.5
Seabourn Sojourn	91.3	88.6	94.8	97.1
Paul Gauguin	90.5	95.1	87.9	91.2
Seabourn Legend	90.3	92.5	82.1	98.8
Seabourn Spirit	90.2	96.0	86.3	92.0
Silver Explorer	89.9	92.6	92.6	88.9
Silver Spirit	89.4	94.7	85.9	90.8
Seven Seas Navigator	89.2	90.6	83.3	90.5
Silver Whisperer	89.2	90.9	82.0	88.6
National Geographic Explorer	89.1	93.1	93.1	89.7
Silver Cloud	88.7	92.6	78.3	91.3
Celebrity Xpedition	87.2	93.1	91.7	73.6
Silver Shadow	87.2	91.0	75.0	89.7
Silver Wind	86.6	94.4	78.1	91.6
SeaDream II	86.2	95.5	77.4	90.9
Wind Star	86.1	94.9	76.5	91.5
Wind Surf	86.1	92.1	72.3	89.3
Wind Spirit	85.2	93.5	77.4	91.9

CruiseShips

a. Determine the estimated regression equation that can be used to predict the overall score given the scores for Itineraries/Schedule, Shore Excursions, and Food/Dining.
b. Use the F test to determine the overall significance of the relationship. What is your conclusion at the .05 level of significance?
c. Use the t test to determine the significance of each independent variable. What is your conclusion at the .05 level of significance?
d. Remove any independent variable that is not significant from the estimated regression equation. What is your recommended estimated regression equation?

MLBPitching

26. In exercise 10, data showing the values of several pitching statistics for a random sample of 20 pitchers from the American League of Major League Baseball were provided (MLB website, March 1, 2012). In part (c) of this exercise an estimated regression equation was developed to predict the average number of runs given up per inning pitched (R/IP) given the average number of strikeouts per inning pitched (SO/IP) and the average number of home runs per inning pitched (HR/IP).
a. Use the F test to determine the overall significance of the relationship. What is your conclusion at the .05 level of significance?
b. Use the t test to determine the significance of each independent variable. What is your conclusion at the .05 level of significance?

Using the Estimated Regression Equation for Estimation and Prediction

The procedures for estimating the mean value of y and predicting an individual value of y in multiple regression are similar to those in regression analysis involving one independent variable. First, recall that in Chapter 12 we showed that the point estimate of the expected value of y for a given value of x was the same as the point estimate of an individual value of y. In both cases, we used $\hat{y} = b_0 + b_1 x$ as the point estimate.

In multiple regression we use the same procedure. That is, we substitute the given values of $x_1, x_2, \ldots, x_p$ into the estimated regression equation and use the corresponding value of $\hat{y}$ as the point estimate. Suppose that for the Butler Trucking example we want to use the

TABLE 13.4   THE 95% CONFIDENCE AND PREDICTION INTERVALS
FOR BUTLER TRUCKING

Value of x_1	Value of x_2	Confidence Interval		Prediction Interval	
		Lower Limit	Upper Limit	Lower Limit	Upper Limit
50	2	3.146	4.924	2.414	5.656
50	3	4.127	5.789	3.368	6.548
50	4	4.815	6.948	4.157	7.607
100	2	6.258	7.926	5.500	8.683
100	3	7.385	8.645	6.520	9.510
100	4	8.135	9.742	7.362	10.515

© Cengage Learning

estimated regression equation involving x_1 (miles traveled) and x_2 (number of deliveries)
to develop two interval estimates:

1. A *confidence interval* of the mean travel time for all trucks that travel 100 miles and
   make two deliveries
2. A *prediction interval* of the travel time for *one specific* truck that travels 100 miles
   and makes two deliveries

Using the estimated regression equation $\hat{y} = -.869 + .0611x_1 + .923x_2$ with $x_1 = 100$ and
$x_2 = 2$, we obtain the following value of $\hat{y}$.

$$\hat{y} = -.869 + .0611(100) + .923(2) = 7.09$$

Hence, the point estimate of travel time in both cases is approximately seven hours.
   To develop interval estimates for the mean value of y and for an individual value of y, we
use a procedure similar to that for regression analysis involving one independent variable.
The formulas required are beyond the scope of the text, but computer packages for multiple
regression analysis will often provide confidence intervals once the values of $x_1, x_2, \ldots, x_p$
are specified by the user. In Table 13.4 we show the 95% confidence and prediction intervals
for the Butler Trucking example for selected values of x_1 and x_2; these values were obtained
using Minitab. Note that the interval estimate for an individual value of y is wider than the
interval estimate for the expected value of y. This difference simply reflects the fact that
for given values of x_1 and x_2 we can estimate the mean travel time for all trucks with more
precision than we can predict the travel time for one specific truck.

Exercises

Methods

27. In exercise 1, the following estimated regression equation based on 10 observations was
    presented.

    $$\hat{y} = 29.1270 + .5906x_1 + .4980x_2$$

    a. Develop a point estimate of the mean value of y when $x_1 = 180$ and $x_2 = 310$.
    b. Develop a point estimate for an individual value of y when $x_1 = 180$ and $x_2 = 310$.

28. Refer to the data in exercise 2. The estimated regression equation for those data is

    $$\hat{y} = -18.4 + 2.01x_1 + 4.74x_2$$

    a. Develop a 95% confidence interval for the mean value of y when $x_1 = 45$ and $x_2 = 15$.
    b. Develop a 95% prediction interval for y when $x_1 = 45$ and $x_2 = 15$.

Applications

29. In exercise 5, the owner of Showtime Movie Theaters, Inc., used multiple regression analysis to predict weekly gross revenue (y) as a function of television advertising (x_1) and newspaper advertising (x_2). The estimated regression equation was

$$\hat{y} = 83.2 + 2.29x_1 + 1.30x_2$$

   a. What is the gross revenue expected for a week when \$3,500 is spent on television advertising ($x_1 = 3.5$) and \$1,800 is spent on newspaper advertising ($x_2 = 1.8$)?
   b. Provide a 95% confidence interval for the mean revenue of all weeks with the expenditures listed in part (a).
   c. Provide a 95% prediction interval for next week's revenue, assuming that the advertising expenditures will be allocated as in part (a).

NFL2011

30. In exercise 24, an estimated regression equation was developed relating the percentage of games won by a team in the National Football League for the 2011 season (y) given the average number of passing yards obtained per game on offense (x_1) and the average number of yards given up per game on defense (x_2) (ESPN website, November 3, 2012). The estimated regression equation was

$$\hat{y} = 60.5 + .319x_1 - .241x_2$$

   a. Predict the percentage of games won for a particular team that averages 225 passing yards per game on offense and gives up an average of 300 yards per game on defense.
   b. Develop a 95% confidence interval for the mean percentage of games won for all teams that average 225 passing yards per game on offense and gives up an average of 300 yards per game on defense.

31. The American Association of Individual Investors (AAII) On-Line Discount Broker Survey polls members on their experiences with electronic trades handled by discount brokers. As part of the survey, members were asked to rate their satisfaction with the trade price and the speed of execution, as well as provide an overall satisfaction rating. Possible responses (scores) were no opinion (0), unsatisfied (1), somewhat satisfied (2), satisfied (3), and very satisfied (4). For each broker, summary scores were computed by computing a weighted average of the scores provided by each respondent. A portion of the survey results follows (AAII website, February 7, 2012).

Broker

Brokerage	Trade Price	Speed of Execution	Satisfaction Electronic Trades
Scottrade, Inc.	3.4	3.4	3.5
Charles Schwab	3.2	3.3	3.4
Fidelity Brokerage Services	3.1	3.4	3.9
TD Ameritrade	2.9	3.6	3.7
E*Trade Financial	2.9	3.2	2.9
(Not listed)	2.5	3.2	2.7
Vanguard Brokerage Services	2.6	3.8	2.8
USAA Brokerage Services	2.4	3.8	3.6
Thinkorswim	2.6	2.6	2.6
Wells Fargo Investments	2.3	2.7	2.3
Interactive Brokers	3.7	4.0	4.0
Zecco.com	2.5	2.5	2.5
Firstrade Securities	3.0	3.0	4.0
Banc of America Investment Services	4.0	1.0	2.0

   a. Develop an estimated regression equation using trade price and speed of execution to predict overall satisfaction with the broker.

b.   Finger Lakes Investments has developed a new electronic trading system and would like to predict overall customer satisfaction assuming they can provide satisfactory levels of service levels (3) for both trade price and speed of execution. Use the estimated regression equation developed in part (a) to predict overall satisfaction level for Finger Lakes Investments if they can achieve these performance levels.

c.   Develop a 95% confidence interval estimate of the overall satisfaction of electronic trades for all brokers that provide satisfactory levels of service for both trade price and speed of execution.

d.   Develop a 95% prediction interval of overall satisfaction for Finger Lakes Investments assuming they achieve service levels of 3 for both trade price and speed of execution.

Categorical Independent Variables

The independent variables may be categorical or quantitative.

Thus far, the examples we have considered have involved quantitative independent variables such as student population, distance traveled, and number of deliveries. In many situations, however, we must work with **categorical independent variables** such as gender (male, female), method of payment (cash, credit card, check), and so on. The purpose of this section is to show how categorical variables are handled in regression analysis. To illustrate the use and interpretation of a categorical independent variable, we will consider a problem facing the managers of Johnson Filtration, Inc.

An Example: Johnson Filtration, Inc.

Johnson Filtration, Inc., provides maintenance service for water-filtration systems throughout southern Florida. Customers contact Johnson with requests for maintenance service on their water-filtration systems. To estimate the service time and the service cost, Johnson's managers want to predict the repair time necessary for each maintenance request. Hence, repair time in hours is the dependent variable. Repair time is believed to be related to two factors, the number of months since the last maintenance service and the type of repair problem (mechanical or electrical). Data for a sample of 10 service calls are reported in Table 13.5.

Let y denote the repair time in hours and x_1 denote the number of months since the last maintenance service. The regression model that uses only x_1 to predict y is

$$y = \beta_0 + \beta_1 x_1 + \epsilon$$

Using Minitab to develop the estimated regression equation, we obtained the output shown in Figure 13.7. The estimated regression equation is

$$\hat{y} = 2.15 + .304x_1 \tag{13.16}$$

TABLE 13.5   DATA FOR THE JOHNSON FILTRATION EXAMPLE

Service Call	Months Since Last Service	Type of Repair	Repair Time in Hours
1	2	Electrical	2.9
2	6	Mechanical	3.0
3	8	Electrical	4.8
4	3	Mechanical	1.8
5	2	Electrical	2.9
6	7	Electrical	4.9
7	9	Mechanical	4.2
8	8	Mechanical	4.8
9	4	Electrical	4.4
10	6	Electrical	4.5

© Cengage Learning

FIGURE 13.7   MINITAB OUTPUT FOR JOHNSON FILTRATION WITH MONTHS SINCE LAST SERVICE (x_1) AS THE INDEPENDENT VARIABLE

In the Minitab output the variable names Months *and* Time *were entered as the column headings on the worksheet; thus,* x_1 = Months *and* y = Time.

```
The regression equation is
Time = 2.15 + 0.304 Months


Predictor      Coef    SE Coef       T        p
Constant     2.1473     0.6050    3.55    0.008
Months       0.3041     0.1004    3.03    0.016


S = 0.781022    R-Sq = 53.4%    R-Sq(adj) = 47.6%


Analysis of Variance

SOURCE             DF        SS        MS       F       p
Regression          1    5.5960    5.5960    9.17   0.016
Residual Error      8    4.8800    0.6100
Total               9   10.4760
```

At the .05 level of significance, the p-value of .016 for the t (or F) test indicates that the number of months since the last service is significantly related to repair time. R-sq = 53.4% indicates that x_1 alone explains 53.4% of the variability in repair time.

To incorporate the type of repair into the regression model, we define the following variable.

$$x_2 = \begin{cases} 0 \text{ if the type of repair is mechanical} \\ 1 \text{ if the type of repair is electrical} \end{cases}$$

In regression analysis x_2 is called a **dummy** or *indicator* **variable**. Using this dummy variable, we can write the multiple regression model as

$$y = \beta_0 + \beta_1 x_1 + \beta_2 x_2 + \epsilon$$

Table 13.6 is the revised data set that includes the values of the dummy variable. Using Minitab and the data in Table 13.6, we can develop estimates of the model parameters.

TABLE 13.6   DATA FOR THE JOHNSON FILTRATION EXAMPLE WITH TYPE OF REPAIR INDICATED BY A DUMMY VARIABLE (x_2 = 0 FOR MECHANICAL; x_2 = 1 FOR ELECTRICAL)

Customer	Months Since Last Service (x_1)	Type of Repair (x_2)	Repair Time in Hours (y)
1	2	1	2.9
2	6	0	3.0
3	8	1	4.8
4	3	0	1.8
5	2	1	2.9
6	7	1	4.9
7	9	0	4.2
8	8	0	4.8
9	4	1	4.4
10	6	1	4.5

FIGURE 13.8   MINITAB OUTPUT FOR JOHNSON FILTRATION WITH MONTHS SINCE LAST SERVICE (x_1) AND TYPE OF REPAIR (x_2) AS THE INDEPENDENT VARIABLES

In the Minitab output the variable names Months, Type, *and* Time *were entered as the column headings on the worksheet; thus,* x_1 = Months, x_2 = Type, *and* y = Time.

```
The regression equation is
Time = 0.930 + 0.388 Months + 1.26 Type

Predictor      Coef    SE Coef      T       p
Constant     0.9305    0.4670    1.99   0.087
Months      0.38762   0.06257    6.20   0.000
Type         1.2627    0.3141    4.02   0.005

S = 0.459048    R-Sq = 85.9%    R-Sq(adj) = 81.9%

Analysis of Variance

SOURCE           DF       SS       MS       F       p
Regression        2   9.0009   4.5005   21.36   0.001
Residual Error    7   1.4751   0.2107
Total             9  10.4760
```

The Minitab output in Figure 13.8 shows that the estimated multiple regression equation is

$$\hat{y} = .93 + .388x_1 + 1.26x_2 \tag{13.17}$$

At the .05 level of significance, the p-value of .001 associated with the F test ($F = 21.36$) indicates that the regression relationship is significant. The t test part of the printout in Figure 13.8 shows that both months since last service (p-value $= .000$) and type of repair (p-value $= .005$) are statistically significant. In addition, R-Sq $= 85.9\%$ and R-Sq (adj) $= 81.9\%$ indicate that the estimated regression equation does a good job of explaining the variability in repair times. Thus, equation (13.17) should prove helpful in predicting the repair time necessary for the various service calls.

Interpreting the Parameters

The multiple regression equation for the Johnson Filtration example is

$$E(y) = \beta_0 + \beta_1 x_1 + \beta_2 x_2 \tag{13.18}$$

To understand how to interpret the parameters β_0, β_1, and β_2 when a categorical variable is present, consider the case when $x_2 = 0$ (mechanical repair). Using $E(y \mid \text{mechanical})$ to denote the mean or expected value of repair time *given* a mechanical repair, we have

$$E(y \mid \text{mechanical}) = \beta_0 + \beta_1 x_1 + \beta_2(0) = \beta_0 + \beta_1 x_1 \tag{13.19}$$

Similarly, for an electrical repair ($x_2 = 1$), we have

$$E(y \mid \text{electrical}) = \beta_0 + \beta_1 x_1 + \beta_2(1) = \beta_0 + \beta_1 x_1 + \beta_2 \tag{13.20}$$
$$= (\beta_0 + \beta_2) + \beta_1 x_1$$

Comparing equations (13.19) and (13.20), we see that the mean repair time is a linear function of x_1 for both mechanical and electrical repairs. The slope of both equations is β_1, but the y-intercept differs. The y-intercept is β_0 in equation (13.19) for mechanical repairs and $(\beta_0 + \beta_2)$ in equation (13.20) for electrical repairs. The interpretation of β_2 is that it indicates the difference between the mean repair time for an electrical repair and the mean repair time for a mechanical repair.

If β_2 is positive, the mean repair time for an electrical repair will be greater than that for a mechanical repair; if β_2 is negative, the mean repair time for an electrical repair will be less than that for a mechanical repair. Finally, if $\beta_2 = 0$, there is no difference in the mean repair time between electrical and mechanical repairs and the type of repair is not related to the repair time.

Using the estimated multiple regression equation $\hat{y} = .93 + .388x_1 + 1.26x_2$, we see that .93 is the estimate of β_0 and 1.26 is the estimate of β_2. Thus, when $x_2 = 0$ (mechanical repair)

$$\hat{y} = .93 + .388x_1 \tag{13.21}$$

and when $x_2 = 1$ (electrical repair)

$$\hat{y} = .93 + .388x_1 + 1.26(1) \tag{13.22}$$
$$= 2.19 + .388x_1$$

In effect, the use of a dummy variable for type of repair provides two estimated regression equations that can be used to predict the repair time, one corresponding to mechanical repairs and one corresponding to electrical repairs. In addition, with $b_2 = 1.26$, we learn that, on average, electrical repairs require 1.26 hours longer than mechanical repairs.

Figure 13.9 is the plot of the Johnson data from Table 13.6. Repair time in hours (y) is represented by the vertical axis and months since last service (x_1) is represented by the horizontal axis. A data point for a mechanical repair is indicated by an M and a data point for an electrical repair is indicated by an E. Equations (13.21) and (13.22) are plotted on the graph to show graphically the two equations that can be used to predict the repair time, one corresponding to mechanical repairs and one corresponding to electrical repairs.

FIGURE 13.9   SCATTER DIAGRAM FOR THE JOHNSON FILTRATION REPAIR DATA FROM TABLE 13.6

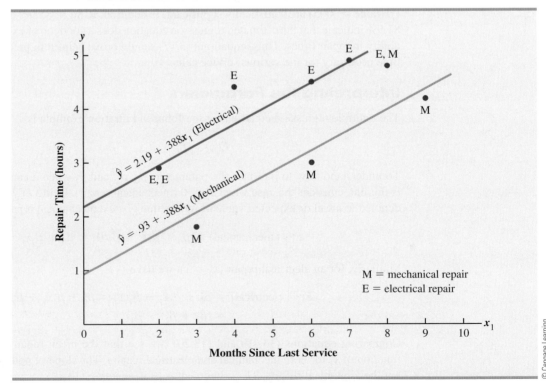

More Complex Categorical Variables

A categorical variable with k levels must be modeled using k − 1 dummy variables. Care must be taken in defining and interpreting the dummy variables.

Because the categorical variable for the Johnson Filtration example had two levels (mechanical and electrical), defining a dummy variable with zero indicating a mechanical repair and one indicating an electrical repair was easy. However, when a categorical variable has more than two levels, care must be taken in both defining and interpreting the dummy variables. As we will show, if a categorical variable has k levels, $k − 1$ dummy variables are required, with each dummy variable being coded as 0 or 1.

For example, suppose a manufacturer of copy machines organized the sales territories for a particular state into three regions: A, B, and C. The managers want to use regression analysis to help predict the number of copiers sold per week. With the number of units sold as the dependent variable, they are considering several independent variables (the number of sales personnel, advertising expenditures, and so on). Suppose the managers believe sales region is also an important factor in predicting the number of copiers sold. Because sales region is a categorical variable with three levels, A, B, and C, we will need $3 − 1 = 2$ dummy variables to represent the sales region. Each variable can be coded 0 or 1 as follows.

$$x_1 = \begin{cases} 1 \text{ if sales region B} \\ 0 \text{ otherwise} \end{cases}$$

$$x_2 = \begin{cases} 1 \text{ if sales region C} \\ 0 \text{ otherwise} \end{cases}$$

With this definition, we have the following values of x_1 and x_2.

Region	x_1	x_2
A	0	0
B	1	0
C	0	1

Observations corresponding to region A would be coded $x_1 = 0$, $x_2 = 0$; observations corresponding to region B would be coded $x_1 = 1$, $x_2 = 0$; and observations corresponding to region C would be coded $x_1 = 0$, $x_2 = 1$.

The regression equation relating the expected value of the number of units sold, $E(y)$, to the dummy variables would be written as

$$E(y) = \beta_0 + \beta_1 x_1 + \beta_2 x_2$$

To help us interpret the parameters β_0, β_1, and β_2, consider the following three variations of the regression equation.

$$E(y \mid \text{region A}) = \beta_0 + \beta_1(0) + \beta_2(0) = \beta_0$$
$$E(y \mid \text{region B}) = \beta_0 + \beta_1(1) + \beta_2(0) = \beta_0 + \beta_1$$
$$E(y \mid \text{region C}) = \beta_0 + \beta_1(0) + \beta_2(1) = \beta_0 + \beta_2$$

Thus, β_0 is the mean or expected value of sales for region A; β_1 is the difference between the mean number of units sold in region B and the mean number of units sold in region A; and β_2 is the difference between the mean number of units sold in region C and the mean number of units sold in region A.

Two dummy variables were required because sales region is a categorical variable with three levels. But the assignment of $x_1 = 0$, $x_2 = 0$ to indicate region A, $x_1 = 1$, $x_2 = 0$ to indicate region B, and $x_1 = 0, x_2 = 1$ to indicate region C was arbitrary. For example, we could have chosen $x_1 = 1, x_2 = 0$ to indicate region A, $x_1 = 0, x_2 = 0$ to indicate region B, and $x_1 = 0$, $x_2 = 1$ to indicate region C. In that case, β_1 would have been interpreted as the mean difference between regions A and B and β_2 as the mean difference between regions C and B.

The important point to remember is that when a categorical variable has k levels, $k - 1$ dummy variables are required in the multiple regression analysis. Thus, if the sales region example had a fourth region, labeled D, three dummy variables would be necessary. For example, the three dummy variables can be coded as follows.

$$x_1 = \begin{cases} 1 \text{ if sales region B} \\ 0 \text{ otherwise} \end{cases} \qquad x_2 = \begin{cases} 1 \text{ if sales region C} \\ 0 \text{ otherwise} \end{cases} \qquad x_3 = \begin{cases} 1 \text{ if sales region D} \\ 0 \text{ otherwise} \end{cases}$$

Exercises

Methods

32. Consider a regression study involving a dependent variable y, a quantitative independent variable x_1, and a categorical independent variable with two levels (level 1 and level 2).
    a. Write a multiple regression equation relating x_1 and the categorical variable to y.
    b. What is the expected value of y corresponding to level 1 of the categorical variable?
    c. What is the expected value of y corresponding to level 2 of the categorical variable?
    d. Interpret the parameters in your regression equation.

33. Consider a regression study involving a dependent variable y, a quantitative independent variable x_1, and a categorical independent variable with three possible levels (level 1, level 2, and level 3).
    a. How many dummy variables are required to represent the categorical variable?
    b. Write a multiple regression equation relating x_1 and the categorical variable to y.
    c. Interpret the parameters in your regression equation.

Applications

34. Management proposed the following regression model to predict sales at a fast-food outlet.

$$y = \beta_0 + \beta_1 x_1 + \beta_2 x_2 + \beta_3 x_3 + \epsilon$$

where

$$x_1 = \text{number of competitors within one mile}$$
$$x_2 = \text{population within one mile (1000s)}$$
$$x_3 = \begin{cases} 1 \text{ if drive-up window present} \\ 0 \text{ otherwise} \end{cases}$$
$$y = \text{sales (\$1,000s)}$$

The following estimated regression equation was developed after 20 outlets were surveyed.

$$\hat{y} = 10.1 - 4.2x_1 + 6.8x_2 + 15.3x_3$$

a. What is the expected amount of sales attributable to the drive-up window?
b. Predict sales for a store with two competitors, a population of 8000 within one mile, and no drive-up window.
c. Predict sales for a store with one competitor, a population of 3000 within one mile, and a drive-up window.

35. Refer to the Johnson Filtration problem introduced in this section. Suppose that in addition to information on the number of months since the machine was serviced and whether a mechanical or an electrical repair was necessary, the managers obtained a list showing which repairperson performed the service. The revised data follow.

Repair

Repair Time in Hours	Months Since Last Service	Type of Repair	Repairperson
2.9	2	Electrical	Dave Newton
3.0	6	Mechanical	Dave Newton
4.8	8	Electrical	Bob Jones
1.8	3	Mechanical	Dave Newton
2.9	2	Electrical	Dave Newton
4.9	7	Electrical	Bob Jones
4.2	9	Mechanical	Bob Jones
4.8	8	Mechanical	Bob Jones
4.4	4	Electrical	Bob Jones
4.5	6	Electrical	Dave Newton

a. Ignore for now the months since the last maintenance service (x_1) and the repairperson who performed the service. Develop the estimated simple linear regression equation to predict the repair time (y) given the type of repair (x_2). Recall that $x_2 = 0$ if the type of repair is mechanical and 1 if the type of repair is electrical.

b. Does the equation that you developed in part (a) provide a good fit for the observed data? Explain.

c. Ignore for now the months since the last maintenance service and the type of repair associated with the machine. Develop the estimated simple linear regression equation to predict the repair time given the repairperson who performed the service. Let $x_3 = 0$ if Bob Jones performed the service and $x_3 = 1$ if Dave Newton performed the service.

d. Does the equation that you developed in part (c) provide a good fit for the observed data? Explain.

36. This problem is an extension of the situation described in exercise 35.

a. Develop the estimated regression equation to predict the repair time given the number of months since the last maintenance service, the type of repair, and the repairperson who performed the service.

b. At the .05 level of significance, test whether the estimated regression equation developed in part (a) represents a significant relationship between the independent variables and the dependent variable.

c. Is the addition of the independent variable x_3, the repairperson who performed the service, statistically significant? Use $\alpha = .05$. What explanation can you give for the results observed?

37. The *Consumer Reports* Restaurant Customer Satisfaction Survey is based upon 148,599 visits to full-service restaurant chains (*Consumer Reports* website, February 11, 2009). Assume the following data are representative of the results reported. The variable type indicates whether the restaurant is an Italian restaurant or a seafood/steakhouse. Price indicates the average amount paid per person for dinner and drinks, minus the tip. Score reflects diners' overall satisfaction, with higher values indicating greater overall satisfaction. A score of 80 can be interpreted as very satisfied.

RestaurantRatings

Restaurant	Type	Price ($)	Score
Bertucci's	Italian	16	77
Black Angus Steakhouse	Seafood/Steakhouse	24	79
Bonefish Grill	Seafood/Steakhouse	26	85

(*continued*)

Restaurant	Type	Price ($)	Score
Bravo! Cucina Italiana	Italian	18	84
Buca di Beppo	Italian	17	81
Bugaboo Creek Steak House	Seafood/Steakhouse	18	77
Carrabba's Italian Grill	Italian	23	86
Charlie Brown's Steakhouse	Seafood/Steakhouse	17	75
Il Fornaio	Italian	28	83
Joe's Crab Shack	Seafood/Steakhouse	15	71
Johnny Carino's Italian	Italian	17	81
Lone Star Steakhouse & Saloon	Seafood/Steakhouse	17	76
LongHorn Steakhouse	Seafood/Steakhouse	19	81
Maggiano's Little Italy	Italian	22	83
McGrath's Fish House	Seafood/Steakhouse	16	81
Olive Garden	Italian	19	81
Outback Steakhouse	Seafood/Steakhouse	20	80
Red Lobster	Seafood/Steakhouse	18	78
Romano's Macaroni Grill	Italian	18	82
The Old Spaghetti Factory	Italian	12	79
Uno Chicago Grill	Italian	16	76

a. Develop the estimated regression equation to show how overall customer satisfaction is related to the independent variable average meal price.

b. At the .05 level of significance, test whether the estimated regression equation developed in part (a) indicates a significant relationship between overall customer satisfaction and average meal price.

c. Develop a dummy variable that will account for the type of restaurant (Italian or seafood/steakhouse).

d. Develop the estimated regression equation to show how overall customer satisfaction is related to the average meal price and the type of restaurant.

e. Is type of restaurant a significant factor in overall customer satisfaction?

f. Predict the *Consumer Reports* customer satisfaction score for a seafood/steakhouse that has an average meal price of $20. How much would the predicted score have changed for an Italian restaurant?

38. A 10-year study conducted by the American Heart Association provided data on how age, systolic blood pressure, and smoking relate to the risk of strokes. Assume that the following data are from a portion of this study. Risk is interpreted as the probability (times 100) that the patient will have a stroke over the next 10-year period. For the smoking variable, define a dummy variable with 1 indicating a smoker and 0 indicating a nonsmoker.

WEB file

Stroke

Risk	Age	Pressure	Smoker
12	57	152	No
24	67	163	No
13	58	155	No
56	86	177	Yes
28	59	196	No
51	76	189	Yes
18	56	155	Yes
31	78	120	No
37	80	135	Yes
15	78	98	No
22	71	152	No
36	70	173	Yes

(*continued*)

Risk	Age	Pressure	Smoker
15	67	135	Yes
48	77	209	Yes
15	60	199	No
36	82	119	Yes
8	66	166	No
34	80	125	Yes
3	62	117	No
37	59	207	Yes

a. Develop an estimated regression equation that relates risk of a stroke to the person's age, systolic blood pressure, and whether the person is a smoker.
b. Is smoking a significant factor in the risk of a stroke? Explain. Use $\alpha = .05$.
c. What is the probability of a stroke over the next 10 years for Art Speen, a 68-year-old smoker who has systolic blood pressure of 175? What action might the physician recommend for this patient?

Summary

In this chapter, we introduced multiple regression analysis as an extension of simple linear regression analysis presented in Chapter 12. Multiple regression analysis enables us to understand how a dependent variable is related to two or more independent variables. The multiple regression equation $E(y) = \beta_0 + \beta_1 x_1 + \beta_2 x_2 + \cdots + \beta_p x_p$ shows that the mean or expected value of the dependent variable y, denoted $E(y)$, is related to the values of the independent variables $x_1, x_2, \ldots, x_p$. Sample data and the least squares method are used to develop the estimated multiple regression equation $\hat{y} = b_0 + b_1 x_1 + b_2 x_2 + \cdots + b_p x_p$. In effect $b_0, b_1, b_2, \ldots, b_p$ are sample statistics used to estimate the unknown model parameters $\beta_0, \beta_1, \beta_2, \ldots, \beta_p$. Computer printouts were used throughout the chapter to emphasize the fact that statistical software packages are the only realistic means of performing the numerous computations required in multiple regression analysis.

The multiple coefficient of determination was presented as a measure of the goodness of fit of the estimated regression equation. It determines the proportion of the variation of y that can be explained by the estimated regression equation. The adjusted multiple coefficient of determination is a similar measure of goodness of fit that adjusts for the number of independent variables and thus avoids overestimating the impact of adding more independent variables.

An F test and a t test were presented as ways to determine statistically whether the relationship among the variables is significant. The F test is used to determine whether there is a significant overall relationship between the dependent variable and the set of all independent variables. The t test is used to determine whether there is a significant relationship between the dependent variable and an individual independent variable given the other independent variables in the regression model. Correlation among the independent variables, known as multicollinearity, was discussed.

The chapter concluded with a section on how dummy variables can be used to incorporate categorical data into multiple regression analysis as independent variables.

Glossary

Multiple regression analysis Regression analysis involving two or more independent variables.
Multiple regression model The mathematical equation that describes how the dependent variable y is related to the independent variables $x_1, x_2, \ldots, x_p$ and an error term ϵ.

Multiple regression equation The mathematical equation relating the expected value or mean value of the dependent variable to the values of the independent variables; that is, $E(y) = \beta_0 + \beta_1 x_1 + \beta_2 x_2 + \cdots + \beta_p x_p$.

Estimated multiple regression equation The estimate of the multiple regression equation based on sample data and the least squares method; it is $\hat{y} = b_0 + b_1 x_1 + b_2 x_2 + \cdots + b_p x_p$.

Least squares method The method used to develop the estimated regression equation. It minimizes the sum of squared residuals (the deviations between the observed values of the dependent variable, y_i, and the predicted values of the dependent variable, $\hat{y}_i$).

Multiple coefficient of determination A measure of the goodness of fit of the estimated multiple regression equation. It can be interpreted as the proportion of the variability in the dependent variable that is explained by the estimated regression equation.

Adjusted multiple coefficient of determination A measure of the goodness of fit of the estimated multiple regression equation that adjusts for the number of independent variables in the model and thus avoids overestimating the impact of adding more independent variables.

Multicollinearity The term used to describe the correlation among the independent variables.

Categorical independent variable An independent variable with categorical data.

Dummy variable A variable used to model the effect of categorical independent variables. A dummy variable may take only the value zero or one.

Key Formulas

Multiple Regression Model

$$y = \beta_0 + \beta_1 x_1 + \beta_2 x_2 + \cdots + \beta_p x_p + \epsilon \tag{13.1}$$

Multiple Regression Equation

$$E(y) = \beta_0 + \beta_1 x_1 + \beta_2 x_2 + \cdots + \beta_p x_p \tag{13.2}$$

Estimated Multiple Regression Equation

$$\hat{y} = b_0 + b_1 x_1 + b_2 x_2 + \cdots + b_p x_p \tag{13.3}$$

Least Squares Criterion

$$\min \Sigma(y_i - \hat{y}_i)^2 \tag{13.4}$$

Relationship Among SST, SSR, and SSE

$$\text{SST} = \text{SSR} + \text{SSE} \tag{13.7}$$

Multiple Coefficient of Determination

$$R^2 = \frac{\text{SSR}}{\text{SST}} \tag{13.8}$$

Adjusted Multiple Coefficient of Determination

$$R_a^2 = 1 - (1 - R^2)\frac{n-1}{n-p-1} \tag{13.9}$$

Mean Square Due to Regression

$$MSR = \frac{SSR}{p} \tag{13.12}$$

Mean Square Due to Error

$$MSE = \frac{SSE}{n - p - 1} \tag{13.13}$$

F Test Statistic

$$F = \frac{MSR}{MSE} \tag{13.14}$$

t Test Statistic

$$t = \frac{b_i}{s_{b_i}} \tag{13.15}$$

Supplementary Exercises

39. The admissions officer for Clearwater College developed the following estimated regression equation relating the final college GPA to the student's SAT mathematics score and high-school GPA.

$$\hat{y} = -1.41 + .0235x_1 + .00486x_2$$

where

$$x_1 = \text{high-school grade point average}$$
$$x_2 = \text{SAT mathematics score}$$
$$y = \text{final college grade point average}$$

   a. Interpret the coefficients in this estimated regression equation.
   b. Predict the final college GPA for a student who has a high-school average of 84 and a score of 540 on the SAT mathematics test.

40. The personnel director for Electronics Associates developed the following estimated regression equation relating an employee's score on a job satisfaction test to his or her length of service and wage rate.

$$\hat{y} = 14.4 - 8.69x_1 + 13.5x_2$$

where

$$x_1 = \text{length of service (years)}$$
$$x_2 = \text{wage rate (dollars)}$$
$$y = \text{job satisfaction test score (higher scores}$$
$$\text{indicate greater job satisfaction)}$$

   a. Interpret the coefficients in this estimated regression equation.
   b. Predict the job satisfaction test score for an employee who has four years of service and makes $6.50 per hour.

41. A partial computer output from a regression analysis follows.

```
The regression equation is
Y = 8.103 + 7.602 X1 + 3.111 X2

Predictor                 Coef          SE Coef              T
Constant               _____        2.667           _____
X1                     _____        2.105           _____
X2                     _____        0.613           _____

S = 3.335        R-Sq = 92.3%       R-Sq(adj)  =  _____ %

Analysis of Variance

SOURCE                   DF            SS            MS             F
Regression            _____        1612        _____      _____
Residual Error          12          _____      _____
Total                 _____      _____
```

a. Compute the missing entries in this output.
b. Use the F test and $\alpha = .05$ to see whether a significant relationship is present.
c. Use the t test and $\alpha = .05$ to test $H_0: \beta_1 = 0$ and $H_0: \beta_2 = 0$.
d. Compute R_a^2.

42. Recall that in exercise 39, the admissions officer for Clearwater College developed the following estimated regression equation relating final college GPA to the student's SAT mathematics score and high-school GPA.

$$\hat{y} = -1.41 + .0235x_1 + .00486x_2$$

where

$$x_1 = \text{high-school grade point average}$$
$$x_2 = \text{SAT mathematics score}$$
$$y = \text{final college grade point average}$$

A portion of the Minitab computer output follows.

```
The regression equation is
Y = -1.41 + .0235 X1 + .00486 X2

Predictor                 Coef          SE Coef              T
Constant               -1.4053         0.4848           _____
X1                     0.023467        0.008666         _____
X2                     _____       0.001077         _____

S = 0.1298       R-Sq =  _____     R-Sq(adj)  =  _____

Analysis of Variance

SOURCE                   DF            SS            MS             F
Regression            _____       1.76209       _____      _____
Residual Error        _____       _____      _____
Total                    9          1.88000
```

    a.   Complete the missing entries in this output.

    b.   Use the F test and a .05 level of significance to see whether a significant relationship is present.

    c.   Use the t test and $\alpha = .05$ to test $H_0: \beta_1 = 0$ and $H_0: \beta_2 = 0$.

    d.   Did the estimated regression equation provide a good fit to the data? Explain.

43. Recall that in exercise 40 the personnel director for Electronics Associates developed the following estimated regression equation relating an employee's score on a job satisfaction test to length of service and wage rate.

$$\hat{y} = 14.4 - 8.69x_1 + 13.5x_2$$

where

$$x_1 = \text{length of service (years)}$$
$$x_2 = \text{wage rate (dollars)}$$
$$y = \text{job satisfaction test score (higher scores indicate greater job satisfaction)}$$

A portion of the Minitab computer output follows.

```
The regression equation is
Y = 14.4 - 8.69 X1 + 13.52 X2

Predictor              Coef         SE Coef            T
Constant             14.448           8.191         1.76
X1                                    1.555        _____
X2                   13.517           2.085        _____

S = 3.773       R-Sq = _____ %   R-Sq(adj) = _____ %

Analysis of Variance

SOURCE                 DF             SS           MS          F
Regression              2         _____       _____     _____
Residual Error     _____          71.17       _____
Total                   7          720.0
```

    a.   Complete the missing entries in this output.

    b.   Compute F and test using $\alpha = .05$ to see whether a significant relationship is present.

    c.   Did the estimated regression equation provide a good fit to the data? Explain.

    d.   Use the t test and $\alpha = .05$ to test $H_0: \beta_1 = 0$ and $H_0: \beta_2 = 0$.

44. The Tire Rack, America's leading online distributor of tires and wheels, conducts extensive testing to provide customers with products that are right for their vehicle, driving style, and driving conditions. In addition, the Tire Rack maintains an independent consumer survey to help drivers help each other by sharing their long-term tire experiences. The following data show survey ratings (1 to 10 scale with 10 the highest rating) for 18 maximum performance summer tires (Tire Rack website, February 3, 2009). The variable Steering rates the tire's steering responsiveness, Tread Wear rates quickness of wear based on the driver's expectations, and Buy Again rates the driver's overall tire satisfaction and desire to purchase the same tire again.

Tire	Steering	Tread Wear	Buy Again
Goodyear Assurance TripleTred	8.9	8.5	8.1
Michelin HydroEdge	8.9	9.0	8.3
Michelin Harmony	8.3	8.8	8.2
Dunlop SP 60	8.2	8.5	7.9
Goodyear Assurance ComforTred	7.9	7.7	7.1
Yokohama Y372	8.4	8.2	8.9
Yokohama Aegis LS4	7.9	7.0	7.1
Kumho Power Star 758	7.9	7.9	8.3
Goodyear Assurance	7.6	5.8	4.5
Hankook H406	7.8	6.8	6.2
Michelin Energy LX4	7.4	5.7	4.8
Michelin MX4	7.0	6.5	5.3
Michelin Symmetry	6.9	5.7	4.2
Kumho 722	7.2	6.6	5.0
Dunlop SP 40 A/S	6.2	4.2	3.4
Bridgestone Insignia SE200	5.7	5.5	3.6
Goodyear Integrity	5.7	5.4	2.9
Dunlop SP20 FE	5.7	5.0	3.3

TireRack

a. Develop an estimated regression equation that can be used to predict the Buy Again rating given based on the Steering rating. At the .05 level of significance, test for a significant relationship.

b. Did the estimated regression equation developed in part (a) provide a good fit to the data? Explain.

c. Develop an estimated regression equation that can be used to predict the Buy Again rating given the Steering rating and the Tread Wear rating.

d. Is the addition of the Tread Wear independent variable significant? Use $\alpha = .05$.

2012FuelEcon

45. The Department of Energy and the U.S. Environmental Protection Agency's *2012 Fuel Economy Guide* provides fuel efficiency data for 2012 model year cars and trucks (Department of Energy website, April 16, 2012). The file named 2012FuelEcon provides a portion of the data for 309 cars. The column labeled Manufacturer shows the name of the company that manufactured the car; the column labeled Displacement shows the engine's displacement in liters; the column labeled Fuel shows the required or recommended type of fuel (regular or premium gasoline); the column labeled Drive identifies the type of drive (F for front wheel, R for rear wheel, and A for all wheel); and the column labeled Hwy MPG shows the fuel efficiency rating for highway driving in terms of miles per gallon.

a. Develop an estimated regression equation that can be used to predict the fuel efficiency for highway driving given the engine's displacement. Test for significance using $\alpha = .05$.

b. Consider the addition of the dummy variable FuelPremium, where the value of FuelPremium is 1 if the required or recommended type of fuel is premium gasoline and 0 if the type of fuel is regular gasoline. Develop the estimated regression equation that can be used to predict the fuel efficiency for highway driving given the engine's displacement and the dummy variable FuelPremium.

c. Use $\alpha = .05$ to determine whether the dummy variable added in part (b) is significant.

d. Consider the addition of the dummy variables FrontWheel and RearWheel. The value of FrontWheel is 1 if the car has front wheel drive and 0 otherwise; the value of RearWheel is 1 if the car has rear wheel drive and 0 otherwise. Thus, for a car that has all-wheel drive, the value of FrontWheel and the value of RearWheel is 0. Develop the estimated regression equation that can be used to predict the fuel efficiency for highway driving given the engine's displacement, the dummy variable FuelPremium, and the dummy variables FrontWheel and RearWheel.

e. For the estimated regression equation developed in part (d), test for overall significance and individual significance using $\alpha = .05$.

46. A portion of a data set containing information for 45 mutual funds that are part of the *Morningstar Funds 500* for 2008 follows. The complete data set is available in the file named MutualFunds. The data set includes the following five variables:

Fund Type: The type of fund, labeled DE (Domestic Equity), IE (International Equity), and FI (Fixed Income).

Net Asset Value ($): The closing price per share on December 31, 2007.

5-Year Average Return (%): The average annual return for the fund over the past five years.

Expense Ratio (%): The percentage of assets deducted each fiscal year for fund expenses.

Morningstar Rank: The risk adjusted star rating for each fund; Morningstar ranks go from a low of 1-Star to a high of 5-Stars.

MutualFunds

Fund Name	Fund Type	Net Asset Value ($)	5-Year Average Return (%)	Expense Ratio (%)	Morningstar Rank
Amer Cent Inc & Growth Inv	DE	28.88	12.39	.67	2-Star
American Century Intl Disc	IE	14.37	30.53	1.41	3-Star
American Century Tax-Free Bond	FI	10.73	3.34	.49	4-Star
American Century Ultra	DE	24.94	10.88	.99	3-Star
Ariel	DE	46.39	11.32	1.03	2-Star
Artisan Intl Val	IE	25.52	24.95	1.23	3-Star
Artisan Small Cap	DE	16.92	15.67	1.18	3-Star
Baron Asset	DE	50.67	16.77	1.31	5-Star
Brandywine	DE	36.58	18.14	1.08	4-Star
.	.	.	.	.	.
.	.	.	.	.	.

a. Develop an estimated regression equation that can be used to predict the 5-year average return given the type of fund. At the .05 level of significance, test for a significant relationship.

b. Did the estimated regression equation developed in part (a) provide a good fit to the data? Explain.

c. Develop the estimated regression equation that can be used to predict the 5-year average return given the type of fund, the net asset value, and the expense ratio. At the .05 level of significance, test for a significant relationship. Do you think any variables should be deleted from the estimated regression equation? Explain.

d. Morningstar Rank is a categorical variable. Because the data set contains only funds with four ranks (2-Star through 5-Star), use the following dummy variables: 3StarRank = 1 for a 3-Star fund, 0 otherwise; 4StarRank = 1 for a 4-Star fund, 0 otherwise; and 5StarRank = 1 for a 5-Star fund, 0 otherwise. Develop an estimated regression equation that can be used to predict the 5-year average return given the type of fund, the expense ratio, and the Morningstar Rank. Using $\alpha = .05$, remove any independent variables that are not significant.

e. Use the estimated regression equation developed in part (d) to predict the 5-year average return for a domestic equity fund with an expense ratio of 1.05% and a 3-Star Morningstar Rank.

47. *Fortune* magazine publishes an annual list of the 100 best companies to work for. The data in the file named FortuneBest shows a portion of the data for a random sample of 30 of the companies that made the top 100 list for 2012 (*Fortune,* February 6, 2012). The column labeled Rank shows the rank of the company in the Fortune 100 list; the column labeled Size indicates whether the company is a small, midsize, or large company; the column labeled Salaried ($1,000s) shows the average annual salary for salaried employees rounded to the nearest $1,000; and the column labeled Hourly ($1,000s) shows the average annual salary for hourly employees rounded to the nearest $1,000. *Fortune* defines large companies as having more than 10,000 employees, midsize companies as having between 2500 and 10,000 employees, and small companies as having fewer than 2500 employees.

FortuneBest

Rank	Company	Size	Salaried ($1,000s)	Hourly ($1,000s)
4	Wegmans Food Markets	Large	56	29
6	NetApp	Midsize	143	76
7	Camden Property Trust	Small	71	37
8	Recreational Equipment (REI)	Large	103	28
10	Quicken Loans	Midsize	78	54
11	Zappos.com	Midsize	48	25
12	Mercedes-Benz USA	Small	118	50
20	USAA	Large	96	47
22	The Container Store	Midsize	71	45
25	Ultimate Software	Small	166	56
37	Plante Moran	Small	73	45
42	Baptist Health South Florida	Large	126	80
50	World Wide Technology	Small	129	31
53	Methodist Hospital	Large	100	83
58	Perkins Coie	Small	189	63
60	American Express	Large	114	35
64	TDIndustries	Small	93	47
66	QuikTrip	Large	69	44
72	EOG Resources	Small	189	81
75	FactSet Research Systems	Small	103	51
80	Stryker	Large	71	43
81	SRC	Small	84	33
84	Booz Allen Hamilton	Large	105	77
91	CarMax	Large	57	34
93	GoDaddy.com	Midsize	105	71
94	KPMG	Large	79	59
95	Navy Federal Credit Union	Midsize	77	39
97	Schweitzer Engineering Labs	Small	99	28
99	Darden Restaurants	Large	57	24
100	Intercontinental Hotels Group	Large	63	26

a. Use these data to develop an estimated regression equation that could be used to predict the average annual salary for salaried employees given the average annual salary for hourly employees.

b. Use $\alpha = .05$ to test for overall significance.

c. To incorporate the effect of size, a categorical variable with three levels, we used two dummy variables: Size-Midsize and Size-Small. The value of Size-Midsize = 1 if the company is a midsize company and 0 otherwise, and the value of Size-Small = 1 if the company is a small company and 0 otherwise. Develop an estimated regression equation that could be used to predict the average annual salary for salaried employees given the average annual salary for hourly employees and the size of the company.

    d.   For the estimated regression equation developed in part (c), use the t test to determine the significance of the independent variables. Use $\alpha = .05$.

    e.   Based upon your findings in part (d), develop an estimated regression equation that can be used to predict the average annual salary for salaried employees given the average annual salary for hourly employees and the size of the company.

48.   The National Basketball Association (NBA) records a variety of statistics for each team. Five of these statistics are the percentage of games won (Win%), the percentage of field goals made (FG%), the percentage of three-point shots made (3P%), the percentage of free throws made (FT%), the average number of offensive rebounds per game (RBOff), and the average number of defensive rebounds per game (RBDef). The data contained in the file NBAStats show the values of these statistics for the 30 teams in the NBA for the 2011–2012 season (ESPN website, October 3, 2012). A portion of the data follows.

NBAStats

Team	Win%	FG%	3P%	FT%	RBOff	RBDef
Atlanta	60.6	45.4	37.0	74.0	9.9	31.3
Boston	59.1	46.0	36.7	77.8	7.7	31.1
.	.	.	.	.	.	.
.	.	.	.	.	.	.
.	.	.	.	.	.	.
Toronto	34.8	44.0	34.0	77.0	10.6	31.4
Utah	54.5	45.6	32.3	75.4	13.0	31.1
Washington	30.3	44.1	32.0	72.7	11.7	29.9

    a.   Develop an estimated regression equation that can be used to predict the percentage of games won given the percentage of field goals made. At the .05 level of significance, test for a significant relationship.

    b.   Provide an interpretation for the slope of the estimated regression equation developed in part (a).

    c.   Develop an estimated regression equation that can be used to predict the percentage of games won given the percentage of field goals made, the percentage of three-point shots made, the percentage of free throws made, the average number of offensive rebounds per game, and the average number of defensive rebounds per game (RBDef).

    d.   For the estimated regression equation developed in part (c), remove any independent variables that are not significant at the .05 level of significance and develop a new estimated regression equation using the remaining independent variables.

    e.   Assuming the estimated regression equation developed in part (d) can be used for the 2012–2013 season, predict the percentage of games won for a team with the following values for the four independent variables: FG% = 45, 3P% = 35, RBOff = 12, and RBDef = 30.

Case Problem 1   Consumer Research, Inc.

Consumer Research, Inc., is an independent agency that conducts research on consumer attitudes and behaviors for a variety of firms. In one study, a client asked for an investigation of consumer characteristics that can be used to predict the amount charged by credit card users. Data were collected on annual income, household size, and annual credit card charges for a sample of 50 consumers. The following data are contained in the file named Consumer.

Income ($1,000s)	Household Size	Amount Charged ($)	Income ($1,000s)	Household Size	Amount Charged ($)
54	3	4016	54	6	5573
30	2	3159	30	1	2583
32	4	5100	48	2	3866
50	5	4742	34	5	3586
31	2	1864	67	4	5037
55	2	4070	50	2	3605
37	1	2731	67	5	5345
40	2	3348	55	6	5370
66	4	4764	52	2	3890
51	3	4110	62	3	4705
25	3	4208	64	2	4157
48	4	4219	22	3	3579
27	1	2477	29	4	3890
33	2	2514	39	2	2972
65	3	4214	35	1	3121
63	4	4965	39	4	4183
42	6	4412	54	3	3730
21	2	2448	23	6	4127
44	1	2995	27	2	2921
37	5	4171	26	7	4603
62	6	5678	61	2	4273
21	3	3623	30	2	3067
55	7	5301	22	4	3074
42	2	3020	46	5	4820
41	7	4828	66	4	5149

Consumer

Managerial Report

1. Use methods of descriptive statistics to summarize the data. Comment on the findings.
2. Develop estimated regression equations, first using annual income as the independent variable and then using household size as the independent variable. Which variable is the better predictor of annual credit card charges? Discuss your findings.
3. Develop an estimated regression equation with annual income and household size as the independent variables. Discuss your findings.
4. What is the predicted annual credit card charge for a three-person household with an annual income of $40,000?
5. Discuss the need for other independent variables that could be added to the model. What additional variables might be helpful?

Case Problem 2   Predicting Winnings for NASCAR Drivers

Matt Kenseth won the 2012 Daytona 500, the most important race of the NASCAR season. His win was no surprise because for the 2011 season he finished fourth in the point standings with 2330 points, behind Tony Stewart (2403 points), Carl Edwards (2403 points), and Kevin Harvick (2345 points). In 2011 he earned $6,183,580 by winning three poles (fastest driver in qualifying), winning three races, finishing in the top five 12 times, and finishing in the top ten 20 times. NASCAR's point system in 2011 allocated 43 points to the driver who finished first, 42 points to the driver who finished second, and so on down to 1 point for the driver who finished in the 43rd position. In addition any driver who led a lap received

TABLE 13.7   NASCAR RESULTS FOR THE 2011 SEASON

Driver	Points	Poles	Wins	Top 5	Top 10	Winnings ($)
Tony Stewart	2403	1	5	9	19	6,529,870
Carl Edwards	2403	3	1	19	26	8,485,990
Kevin Harvick	2345	0	4	9	19	6,197,140
Matt Kenseth	2330	3	3	12	20	6,183,580
Brad Keselowski	2319	1	3	10	14	5,087,740
Jimmie Johnson	2304	0	2	14	21	6,296,360
Dale Earnhardt Jr.	2290	1	0	4	12	4,163,690
Jeff Gordon	2287	1	3	13	18	5,912,830
Denny Hamlin	2284	0	1	5	14	5,401,190
Ryan Newman	2284	3	1	9	17	5,303,020
Kurt Busch	2262	3	2	8	16	5,936,470
Kyle Busch	2246	1	4	14	18	6,161,020
Clint Bowyer	1047	0	1	4	16	5,633,950
Kasey Kahne	1041	2	1	8	15	4,775,160
A. J. Allmendinger	1013	0	0	1	10	4,825,560
Greg Biffle	997	3	0	3	10	4,318,050
Paul Menard	947	0	1	4	8	3,853,690
Martin Truex Jr.	937	1	0	3	12	3,955,560
Marcos Ambrose	936	0	1	5	12	4,750,390
Jeff Burton	935	0	0	2	5	3,807,780
Juan Montoya	932	2	0	2	8	5,020,780
Mark Martin	930	2	0	2	10	3,830,910
David Ragan	906	2	1	4	8	4,203,660
Joey Logano	902	2	0	4	6	3,856,010
Brian Vickers	846	0	0	3	7	4,301,880
Regan Smith	820	0	1	2	5	4,579,860
Jamie McMurray	795	1	0	2	4	4,794,770
David Reutimann	757	1	0	1	3	4,374,770
Bobby Labonte	670	0	0	1	2	4,505,650
David Gilliland	572	0	0	1	2	3,878,390
Casey Mears	541	0	0	0	0	2,838,320
Dave Blaney	508	0	0	1	1	3,229,210
Andy Lally	398	0	0	0	0	2,868,220
Robby Gordon	268	0	0	0	0	2,271,890
J. J. Yeley	192	0	0	0	0	2,559,500

WEB file

NASCAR

© Cengage Learning

1 bonus point, the driver who led the most laps received an additional bonus point, and the race winner was awarded 3 bonus points. But the maximum number of points a driver could earn in any race was 48. Table 13.7 shows data for the 2011 season for the top 35 drivers (NASCAR website, February 28, 2011).

Managerial Report

1. Suppose you wanted to predict Winnings ($) using only the number of poles won (Poles), the number of wins (Wins), the number of top five finishes (Top 5), or the number of top ten finishes (Top 10). Which of these four variables provides the best single predictor of winnings?

2. Develop an estimated regression equation that can be used to predict Winnings ($) given the number of poles won (Poles), the number of wins (Wins), the number of top five finishes (Top 5), and the number of top ten (Top 10) finishes. Test for individual significance and discuss your findings and conclusions.

3. Create two new independent variables: Top 2–5 and Top 6–10. Top 2–5 represents the number of times the driver finished between second and fifth place and Top 6–10 represents the number of times the driver finished between sixth and tenth place. Develop an estimated regression equation that can be used to predict Winnings ($) using Poles, Wins, Top 2–5, and Top 6–10. Test for individual significance and discuss your findings and conclusions.

4. Based upon the results of your analysis, what estimated regression equation would you recommend using to predict Winnings ($)? Provide an interpretation of the estimated regression coefficients for this equation.

Case Problem 3   # Finding the Best Car Value

When trying to decide what car to buy, real value is not necessarily determined by how much you spend on the initial purchase. Instead, cars that are reliable and don't cost much to own often represent the best values. But no matter how reliable or inexpensive a car may cost to own, it must also perform well.

To measure value, *Consumer Reports* developed a statistic referred to as a value score. The value score is based upon five-year owner costs, overall road-test scores, and predicted-reliability ratings. Five-year owner costs are based upon the expenses incurred in the first five years of ownership, including depreciation, fuel, maintenance and repairs, and so on. Using a national average of 12,000 miles per year, an average cost per mile driven is used as the measure of five-year owner costs. Road-test scores are the results of more than 50 tests and evaluations and are based on a 100-point scale, with higher scores indicating better performance, comfort, convenience, and fuel economy. The highest road-test score obtained in the tests conducted by *Consumer Reports* was a 99 for a Lexus LS 460L. Predicted-reliability ratings (1 = Poor, 2 = Fair, 3 = Good, 4 = Very Good, and 5 = Excellent) are based upon data from *Consumer Reports*' Annual Auto Survey.

CarValues

A car with a value score of 1.0 is considered to be an "average-value" car. A car with a value score of 2.0 is considered to be twice as good a value as a car with a value score of 1.0; a car with a value score of 0.5 is considered half as good as average; and so on. The data for three sizes of cars (13 small sedans, 20 family sedans, and 21 upscale sedans), including the price ($) of each car tested, are contained in the file named CarValues (*Consumer Reports* website, April 18, 2012). To incorporate the effect of size of car, a categorical variable with three values (small sedan, family sedan, and upscale sedan), use the following dummy variables:

$$\text{Family-Sedan} = \begin{cases} 1 \text{ if the car is a Family Sedan} \\ 0 \text{ otherwise} \end{cases}$$

$$\text{Upscale-Sedan} = \begin{cases} 1 \text{ if the car is an Upscale Sedan} \\ 0 \text{ otherwise} \end{cases}$$

Managerial Report

1. Treating Cost/Mile as the dependent variable, develop an estimated regression with Family-Sedan and Upscale-Sedan as the independent variables. Discuss your findings.

2. Treating Value Score as the dependent variable, develop an estimated regression equation using Cost/Mile, Road-Test Score, Predicted Reliability, Family-Sedan, and Upscale-Sedan as the independent variables.

3. Delete any independent variables that are not significant from the estimated regression equation developed in part 2 using a .05 level of significance. After deleting any independent variables that are not significant, develop a new estimated regression equation.

4. Suppose someone claims that "smaller cars provide better values than larger cars." For the data in this case, the Small Sedans represent the smallest type of car and the Upscale Sedans represent the largest type of car. Does your analysis support this claim?

Appendix 13.1   Multiple Regression with Minitab

WEB file

Butler

In Section 13.2 we discussed the computer solution of multiple regression problems by showing Minitab's output for the Butler Trucking Company problem. In this appendix we describe the steps required to generate the Minitab computer solution. First, the data must be entered in a Minitab worksheet. The miles traveled are entered in column C1, the number of deliveries are entered in column C2, and the travel times (hours) are entered in column C3. The variable names Miles, Deliveries, and Time were entered as the column headings on the worksheet. In subsequent steps, we refer to the data by using the variable names Miles, Deliveries, and Time or the column indicators C1, C2, and C3. The following steps describe how to use Minitab to produce the regression results shown in Figure 13.4.

Step 1. Select the **Stat** menu
Step 2. Select the **Regression** menu
Step 3. Choose **Regression**
Step 4. When the Regression dialog box appears:
  Enter Time in the **Response** box
  Enter Miles and Deliveries in the **Predictors** box
  Click **OK**

Appendix 13.2   Multiple Regression with Excel

In Section 13.2 we discussed the computer solution of multiple regression problems by showing Minitab's output for the Butler Trucking Company problem. In this appendix we describe how to use Excel's Regression tool to develop the estimated multiple regression equation for the Butler Trucking problem. Refer to Figure 13.10 as we describe the tasks involved. First, the labels Assignment, Miles, Deliveries, and Time are entered into cells A1:D1 of the worksheet, and the sample data into cells B2:D11. The numbers 1–10 in cells A2:A11 identify each observation.

WEB file

Butler

The following steps describe how to use the Regression tool for the multiple regression analysis.

Step 1. Click the **Data** tab on the Ribbon
Step 2. In the **Analysis** group, click **Data Analysis**
Step 3. Choose **Regression** from the list of Analysis Tools
Step 4. When the Regression dialog box appears:
  Enter D1:D11 in the **Input Y Range** box
  Enter B1:C11 in the **Input X Range** box
  Select **Labels**
  Select **Confidence Level**
  Enter 99 in the **Confidence Level** box
  Select **Output Range**

FIGURE 13.10   EXCEL OUTPUT FOR BUTLER TRUCKING WITH TWO INDEPENDENT VARIABLES

	A	B	C	D	E	F	G	H	I	J
1	**Assignment**	**Miles**	**Deliveries**	**Time**						
2	1	100	4	9.3						
3	2	50	3	4.8						
4	3	100	4	8.9						
5	4	100	2	6.5						
6	5	50	2	4.2						
7	6	80	2	6.2						
8	7	75	3	7.4						
9	8	65	4	6						
10	9	90	3	7.6						
11	10	90	2	6.1						
12										
13	SUMMARY OUTPUT									
14										
15	*Regression Statistics*									
16	Multiple R	0.9507								
17	R Square	0.9038								
18	Adjusted R Square	0.8763								
19	Standard Error	0.5731								
20	Observations	10								
21										
22	ANOVA									
23		*df*	*SS*	*MS*	*F*	*Significance F*				
24	Regression	2	21.6006	10.8003	32.8784	0.0003				
25	Residual	7	2.2994	0.3285						
26	Total	9	23.9							
27										
28		*Coefficients*	*Standard Error*	*t Stat*	*P-value*	*Lower 95%*	*Upper 95%*	*Lower 99.0%*	*Upper 99.0%*	
29	Intercept	-0.8687	0.9515	-0.9129	0.3916	-3.1188	1.3813	-4.1986	2.4612	
30	Miles	0.0611	0.0099	6.1824	0.0005	0.0378	0.0845	0.0265	0.0957	
31	Deliveries	0.9234	0.2211	4.1763	0.0042	0.4006	1.4463	0.1496	1.6972	
32										

Enter A13 in the **Output Range** box (to identify the upper left corner of
the section of the worksheet where the output will appear)
Click **OK**

In the Excel output shown in Figure 13.10 the label for the independent variable x_1 is Miles
(see cell A30), and the label for the independent variable x_2 is Deliveries (see cell A31).
The estimated regression equation is

$$\hat{y} = -.8687 + .0611x_1 + .9234x_2$$

Note that using Excel's Regression tool for multiple regression is almost the same as using
it for simple linear regression. The major difference is that in the multiple regression case a
larger range of cells is required in order to identify the independent variables.

Appendix 13.3   Multiple Regression Analysis Using StatTools

Butler

In this appendix we show how StatTools can be used to perform the regression analysis com-
putations for the Butler Trucking problem. Begin by using the Data Set Manager to create a
StatTools data set for these data using the procedure described in the appendix in Chapter 1.
The following steps describe how StatTools can be used to provide the regression results.

Step 1. Click the **StatTools** tab on the Ribbon

Step 2. In the **Analyses** group, click **Regression and Classification**

Step 3. Choose the **Regression** option

Step 4. When the StatTools - Regression dialog box appears:

     Select **Multiple** in the **Regression Type** box

     In the **Variables** section:

         Click the **Format** button and select **Unstacked**

         In the column labeled **I** select **Miles**

         In the column labeled **I** select **Deliveries**

         In the column labeled **D** select **Time**

     Click **OK**

The regression analysis output will appear.

The StatTools - Regression dialog box contains a number of more advanced options for developing prediction interval estimates and producing residual plots. The StatTools Help facility provides information on using all of these options.

APPENDIXES

Appendix A: References and Bibliography

General

Freedman, D., R. Pisani, and R. Purves. *Statistics*, 4th ed. W. W. Norton, 2007.

Hogg, R. V., and E. A. Tanis. *Probability and Statistical Inference*, 8th ed. Prentice Hall, 2009.

McKean, J. W., R. V. Hogg, and A. T. Craig. *Introduction to Mathematical Statistics*, 7th ed. Prentice Hall, 2012.

Miller, I., and M. Miller. *John E. Freund's Mathematical Statistics*, 7th ed. Pearson, 2003.

Moore, D. S., G. P. McCabe, and B. Craig. *Introduction to the Practice of Statistics*, 7th ed. Freeman, 2010.

Wackerly, D. D., W. Mendenhall, and R. L. Scheaffer. *Mathematical Statistics with Applications*, 7th ed. Cengage Learning, 2007.

Experimental Design

Cochran, W. G., and G. M. Cox. *Experimental Designs*, 2nd ed. Wiley, 1992.

Hicks, C. R., and K. V. Turner. *Fundamental Concepts in the Design of Experiments*, 5th ed. Oxford University Press, 1999.

Montgomery, D. C. *Design and Analysis of Experiments*, 8th ed. Wiley, 2012.

Winer, B. J., K. M. Michels, and D. R. Brown. *Statistical Principles in Experimental Design*, 3rd ed. McGraw-Hill, 1991.

Wu, C. F. Jeff, and M. Hamada. *Experiments: Planning, Analysis, and Optimization*, 2nd ed. Wiley, 2009.

Probability

Hogg, R. V., and E. A. Tanis. *Probability and Statistical Inference*, 8th ed. Prentice Hall, 2009.

Ross, S. M. *Introduction to Probability Models*, 10th ed. Academic Press, 2009.

Wackerly, D. D., W. Mendenhall, and R. L. Scheaffer. *Mathematical Statistics with Applications*, 7th ed. Cengage Learning, 2007.

Regression Analysis

Chatterjee, S., and A. S. Hadi. *Regression Analysis by Example*, 4th ed. Wiley, 2006.

Draper, N. R., and H. Smith. *Applied Regression Analysis*, 3rd ed. Wiley, 1998.

Graybill, F. A., and H. K. Iyer. *Regression Analysis: Concepts and Applications*. Wadsworth, 1994.

Hosmer, D. W., and S. Lemeshow. *Applied Logistic Regression*, 2nd ed. Wiley, 2000.

Kleinbaum, D. G., L. L. Kupper, and K. E. Muller. *Applied Regression Analysis and Multivariate Methods*, 4th ed. Cengage Learning, 2007.

Neter, J., W. Wasserman, M. H. Kutner, and C. Nashtsheim. *Applied Linear Statistical Models*, 5th ed. McGraw-Hill, 2004.

Mendenhall, M., T. Sincich., and T. R. Dye. *A Second Course in Statistics: Regression Analysis*, 7th ed. Prentice Hall, 2011.

Sampling

Cochran, W. G. *Sampling Techniques*, 3rd ed. Wiley, 1977.

Hansen, M. H., W. N. Hurwitz, W. G. Madow, and M. N. Hanson. *Sample Survey Methods and Theory*. Wiley, 1993.

Kish, L. *Survey Sampling*. Wiley, 2008.

Hahn, G. J., and W. Meeker. "Assumptions for Statistical Inference," *The American Statistician*, February 1993.

Levy, P. S., and S. Lemeshow. *Sampling of Populations: Methods and Applications*, 4th ed. Wiley, 2009.

Scheaffer, R. L., W. Mendenhall, and L. Ott. *Elementary Survey Sampling*, 7th ed. Duxbury Press, 2011.

Data Visualization

Cleveland, W. S. *Visualizing Data*. Hobart Press, 1993.

Cleveland, W. S. *The Elements of Graphing Data*, 2nd ed. Hobart Press, 1994.

Few, S. *Show Me the Numbers: Designing Tables and Graphs to Enlighten*. Analytics Press, 2004.

Few, S. *Information Dashboard Design: The Effective Visual Communication of Data*. O'Reilly Media, 2006.

Few, S. *Now You See It: Simple Visualization Techniques for Quantitative Analysis*. Analytics Press, 2009.

Fry, B. *Visualizing Data: Exploring and Explaining Data with the Processing Environment*. O'Reilly Media, 2008.

Robbins, N. B. *Creating More Effective Graphs*. Wiley, 2004.

Telea, A. C. *Data Visualization Principles and Practice*. A. K. Peters Ltd., 2008.

Tufte, E. R. *Envisioning Information*. Graphics Press, 1990.

Tufte, E. R. *The Visual Display of Quantitative Information*, 2nd ed. Graphics Press, 1990.

Tufte, E. R. *Visual Explanations: Images and Quantities, Evidence and Narrative*. Graphics Press, 1997.

Tufte, E. R. *Visual and Statistical Thinking: Displays of Evidence for Making Decisions*. Graphics Press, 1997.

Tufte, E. R. *Beautiful Evidence*. Graphics Press, 2006.

Wong, D. M. *The Wall Street Journal Guide to Information Graphics*. W. W. Norton & Company, 2010.

Young, F. W., P. M. Valero-Mora, and M. Friendly. *Visual Statistics: Seeing Data with Dynamic Interactive Graphics*. Wiley, 2006.

Appendix B: Tables

TABLE 1 CUMULATIVE PROBABILITIES FOR THE STANDARD NORMAL DISTRIBUTION

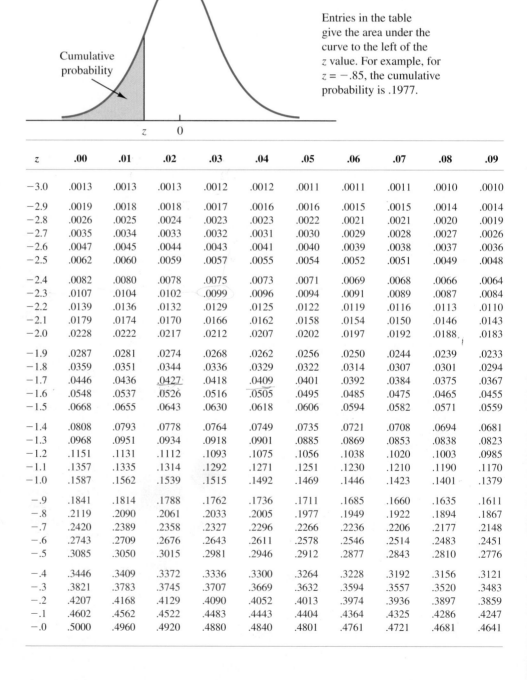

Cumulative probability

Entries in the table give the area under the curve to the left of the z value. For example, for z = −.85, the cumulative probability is .1977.

z	.00	.01	.02	.03	.04	.05	.06	.07	.08	.09
−3.0	.0013	.0013	.0013	.0012	.0012	.0011	.0011	.0011	.0010	.0010
−2.9	.0019	.0018	.0018	.0017	.0016	.0016	.0015	.0015	.0014	.0014
−2.8	.0026	.0025	.0024	.0023	.0023	.0022	.0021	.0021	.0020	.0019
−2.7	.0035	.0034	.0033	.0032	.0031	.0030	.0029	.0028	.0027	.0026
−2.6	.0047	.0045	.0044	.0043	.0041	.0040	.0039	.0038	.0037	.0036
−2.5	.0062	.0060	.0059	.0057	.0055	.0054	.0052	.0051	.0049	.0048
−2.4	.0082	.0080	.0078	.0075	.0073	.0071	.0069	.0068	.0066	.0064
−2.3	.0107	.0104	.0102	.0099	.0096	.0094	.0091	.0089	.0087	.0084
−2.2	.0139	.0136	.0132	.0129	.0125	.0122	.0119	.0116	.0113	.0110
−2.1	.0179	.0174	.0170	.0166	.0162	.0158	.0154	.0150	.0146	.0143
−2.0	.0228	.0222	.0217	.0212	.0207	.0202	.0197	.0192	.0188	.0183
−1.9	.0287	.0281	.0274	.0268	.0262	.0256	.0250	.0244	.0239	.0233
−1.8	.0359	.0351	.0344	.0336	.0329	.0322	.0314	.0307	.0301	.0294
−1.7	.0446	.0436	.0427	.0418	.0409	.0401	.0392	.0384	.0375	.0367
−1.6	.0548	.0537	.0526	.0516	.0505	.0495	.0485	.0475	.0465	.0455
−1.5	.0668	.0655	.0643	.0630	.0618	.0606	.0594	.0582	.0571	.0559
−1.4	.0808	.0793	.0778	.0764	.0749	.0735	.0721	.0708	.0694	.0681
−1.3	.0968	.0951	.0934	.0918	.0901	.0885	.0869	.0853	.0838	.0823
−1.2	.1151	.1131	.1112	.1093	.1075	.1056	.1038	.1020	.1003	.0985
−1.1	.1357	.1335	.1314	.1292	.1271	.1251	.1230	.1210	.1190	.1170
−1.0	.1587	.1562	.1539	.1515	.1492	.1469	.1446	.1423	.1401	.1379
−.9	.1841	.1814	.1788	.1762	.1736	.1711	.1685	.1660	.1635	.1611
−.8	.2119	.2090	.2061	.2033	.2005	.1977	.1949	.1922	.1894	.1867
−.7	.2420	.2389	.2358	.2327	.2296	.2266	.2236	.2206	.2177	.2148
−.6	.2743	.2709	.2676	.2643	.2611	.2578	.2546	.2514	.2483	.2451
−.5	.3085	.3050	.3015	.2981	.2946	.2912	.2877	.2843	.2810	.2776
−.4	.3446	.3409	.3372	.3336	.3300	.3264	.3228	.3192	.3156	.3121
−.3	.3821	.3783	.3745	.3707	.3669	.3632	.3594	.3557	.3520	.3483
−.2	.4207	.4168	.4129	.4090	.4052	.4013	.3974	.3936	.3897	.3859
−.1	.4602	.4562	.4522	.4483	.4443	.4404	.4364	.4325	.4286	.4247
−.0	.5000	.4960	.4920	.4880	.4840	.4801	.4761	.4721	.4681	.4641

TABLE 1   CUMULATIVE PROBABILITIES FOR THE STANDARD NORMAL DISTRIBUTION (*Continued*)

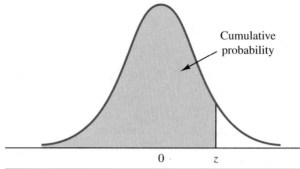

Cumulative probability

Entries in the table give the area under the curve to the left of the z value. For example, for $z = 1.25$, the cumulative probability is .8944.

z	.00	.01	.02	.03	.04	.05	.06	.07	.08	.09
.0	.5000	.5040	.5080	.5120	.5160	.5199	.5239	.5279	.5319	.5359
.1	.5398	.5438	.5478	.5517	.5557	.5596	.5636	.5675	.5714	.5753
.2	.5793	.5832	.5871	.5910	.5948	.5987	.6026	.6064	.6103	.6141
.3	.6179	.6217	.6255	.6293	.6331	.6368	.6406	.6443	.6480	.6517
.4	.6554	.6591	.6628	.6664	.6700	.6736	.6772	.6808	.6844	.6879
.5	.6915	.6950	.6985	.7019	.7054	.7088	.7123	.7157	.7190	.7224
.6	.7257	.7291	.7324	.7357	.7389	.7422	.7454	.7486	.7517	.7549
.7	.7580	.7611	.7642	.7673	.7704	.7734	.7764	.7794	.7823	.7852
.8	.7881	.7910	.7939	.7967	.7995	.8023	.8051	.8078	.8106	.8133
.9	.8159	.8186	.8212	.8238	.8264	.8289	.8315	.8340	.8365	.8389
1.0	.8413	.8438	.8461	.8485	.8508	.8531	.8554	.8577	.8599	.8621
1.1	.8643	.8665	.8686	.8708	.8729	.8749	.8770	.8790	.8810	.8830
1.2	.8849	.8869	.8888	.8907	.8925	.8944	.8962	.8980	.8997	.9015
1.3	.9032	.9049	.9066	.9082	.9099	.9115	.9131	.9147	.9162	.9177
1.4	.9192	.9207	.9222	.9236	.9251	.9265	.9279	.9292	.9306	.9319
1.5	.9332	.9345	.9357	.9370	.9382	.9394	.9406	.9418	.9429	.9441
1.6	.9452	.9463	.9474	.9484	.9495	.9505	.9515	.9525	.9535	.9545
1.7	.9554	.9564	.9573	.9582	.9591	.9599	.9608	.9616	.9625	.9633
1.8	.9641	.9649	.9656	.9664	.9671	.9678	.9686	.9693	.9699	.9706
1.9	.9713	.9719	.9726	.9732	.9738	.9744	.9750	.9756	.9761	.9767
2.0	.9772	.9778	.9783	.9788	.9793	.9798	.9803	.9808	.9812	.9817
2.1	.9821	.9826	.9830	.9834	.9838	.9842	.9846	.9850	.9854	.9857
2.2	.9861	.9864	.9868	.9871	.9875	.9878	.9881	.9884	.9887	.9890
2.3	.9893	.9896	.9898	.9901	.9904	.9906	.9909	.9911	.9913	.9916
2.4	.9918	.9920	.9922	.9925	.9927	.9929	.9931	.9932	.9934	.9936
2.5	.9938	.9940	.9941	.9943	.9945	.9946	.9948	.9949	.9951	.9952
2.6	.9953	.9955	.9956	.9957	.9959	.9960	.9961	.9962	.9963	.9964
2.7	.9965	.9966	.9967	.9968	.9969	.9970	.9971	.9972	.9973	.9974
2.8	.9974	.9975	.9976	.9977	.9977	.9978	.9979	.9979	.9980	.9981
2.9	.9981	.9982	.9982	.9983	.9984	.9984	.9985	.9985	.9986	.9986
3.0	.9987	.9987	.9987	.9988	.9988	.9989	.9989	.9989	.9990	.9990

TABLE 2   *t* DISTRIBUTION

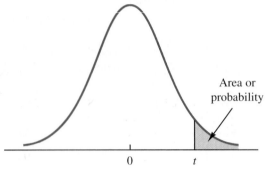

Area or probability Entries in the table give *t* values for an area or probability in the upper tail of the *t* distribution. For example, with 10 degrees of freedom and a .05 area in the upper tail, $t_{.05} = 1.812$.

Degrees of Freedom	Area in Upper Tail					
	.20	**.10**	**.05**	**.025**	**.01**	**.005**
1	1.376	3.078	6.314	12.706	31.821	63.656
2	1.061	1.886	2.920	4.303	6.965	9.925
3	.978	1.638	2.353	3.182	4.541	5.841
4	.941	1.533	2.132	2.776	3.747	4.604
5	.920	1.476	2.015	2.571	3.365	4.032
6	.906	1.440	1.943	2.447	3.143	3.707
7	.896	1.415	1.895	2.365	2.998	3.499
8	.889	1.397	1.860	2.306	2.896	3.355
9	.883	1.383	1.833	2.262	2.821	3.250
10	.879	1.372	1.812	2.228	2.764	3.169
11	.876	1.363	1.796	2.201	2.718	3.106
12	.873	1.356	1.782	2.179	2.681	3.055
13	.870	1.350	1.771	2.160	2.650	3.012
14	.868	1.345	1.761	2.145	2.624	2.977
15	.866	1.341	1.753	2.131	2.602	2.947
16	.865	1.337	1.746	2.120	2.583	2.921
17	.863	1.333	1.740	2.110	2.567	2.898
18	.862	1.330	1.734	2.101	2.552	2.878
19	.861	1.328	1.729	2.093	2.539	2.861
20	.860	1.325	1.725	2.086	2.528	2.845
21	.859	1.323	1.721	2.080	2.518	2.831
22	.858	1.321	1.717	2.074	2.508	2.819
23	.858	1.319	1.714	2.069	2.500	2.807
24	.857	1.318	1.711	2.064	2.492	2.797
25	.856	1.316	1.708	2.060	2.485	2.787
26	.856	1.315	1.706	2.056	2.479	2.779
27	.855	1.314	1.703	2.052	2.473	2.771
28	.855	1.313	1.701	2.048	2.467	2.763
29	.854	1.311	1.699	2.045	2.462	2.756
30	.854	1.310	1.697	2.042	2.457	2.750
31	.853	1.309	1.696	2.040	2.453	2.744
32	.853	1.309	1.694	2.037	2.449	2.738
33	.853	1.308	1.692	2.035	2.445	2.733
34	.852	1.307	1.691	2.032	2.441	2.728

TABLE 2 *t* DISTRIBUTION (*Continued*)

Degrees of Freedom	Area in Upper Tail					
	.20	.10	.05	.025	.01	.005
35	.852	1.306	1.690	2.030	2.438	2.724
36	.852	1.306	1.688	2.028	2.434	2.719
37	.851	1.305	1.687	2.026	2.431	2.715
38	.851	1.304	1.686	2.024	2.429	2.712
39	.851	1.304	1.685	2.023	2.426	2.708
40	.851	1.303	1.684	2.021	2.423	2.704
41	.850	1.303	1.683	2.020	2.421	2.701
42	.850	1.302	1.682	2.018	2.418	2.698
43	.850	1.302	1.681	2.017	2.416	2.695
44	.850	1.301	1.680	2.015	2.414	2.692
45	.850	1.301	1.679	2.014	2.412	2.690
46	.850	1.300	1.679	2.013	2.410	2.687
47	.849	1.300	1.678	2.012	2.408	2.685
48	.849	1.299	1.677	2.011	2.407	2.682
49	.849	1.299	1.677	2.010	2.405	2.680
50	.849	1.299	1.676	2.009	2.403	2.678
51	.849	1.298	1.675	2.008	2.402	2.676
52	.849	1.298	1.675	2.007	2.400	2.674
53	.848	1.298	1.674	2.006	2.399	2.672
54	.848	1.297	1.674	2.005	2.397	2.670
55	.848	1.297	1.673	2.004	2.396	2.668
56	.848	1.297	1.673	2.003	2.395	2.667
57	.848	1.297	1.672	2.002	2.394	2.665
58	.848	1.296	1.672	2.002	2.392	2.663
59	.848	1.296	1.671	2.001	2.391	2.662
60	.848	1.296	1.671	2.000	2.390	2.660
61	.848	1.296	1.670	2.000	2.389	2.659
62	.847	1.295	1.670	1.999	2.388	2.657
63	.847	1.295	1.669	1.998	2.387	2.656
64	.847	1.295	1.669	1.998	2.386	2.655
65	.847	1.295	1.669	1.997	2.385	2.654
66	.847	1.295	1.668	1.997	2.384	2.652
67	.847	1.294	1.668	1.996	2.383	2.651
68	.847	1.294	1.668	1.995	2.382	2.650
69	.847	1.294	1.667	1.995	2.382	2.649
70	.847	1.294	1.667	1.994	2.381	2.648
71	.847	1.294	1.667	1.994	2.380	2.647
72	.847	1.293	1.666	1.993	2.379	2.646
73	.847	1.293	1.666	1.993	2.379	2.645
74	.847	1.293	1.666	1.993	2.378	2.644
75	.846	1.293	1.665	1.992	2.377	2.643
76	.846	1.293	1.665	1.992	2.376	2.642
77	.846	1.293	1.665	1.991	2.376	2.641
78	.846	1.292	1.665	1.991	2.375	2.640
79	.846	1.292	1.664	1.990	2.374	2.639

TABLE 2   *t* DISTRIBUTION (*Continued*)

Degrees of Freedom	Area in Upper Tail					
	.20	.10	.05	.025	.01	.005
80	.846	1.292	1.664	1.990	2.374	2.639
81	.846	1.292	1.664	1.990	2.373	2.638
82	.846	1.292	1.664	1.989	2.373	2.637
83	.846	1.292	1.663	1.989	2.372	2.636
84	.846	1.292	1.663	1.989	2.372	2.636
85	.846	1.292	1.663	1.988	2.371	2.635
86	.846	1.291	1.663	1.988	2.370	2.634
87	.846	1.291	1.663	1.988	2.370	2.634
88	.846	1.291	1.662	1.987	2.369	2.633
89	.846	1.291	1.662	1.987	2.369	2.632
90	.846	1.291	1.662	1.987	2.368	2.632
91	.846	1.291	1.662	1.986	2.368	2.631
92	.846	1.291	1.662	1.986	2.368	2.630
93	.846	1.291	1.661	1.986	2.367	2.630
94	.845	1.291	1.661	1.986	2.367	2.629
95	.845	1.291	1.661	1.985	2.366	2.629
96	.845	1.290	1.661	1.985	2.366	2.628
97	.845	1.290	1.661	1.985	2.365	2.627
98	.845	1.290	1.661	1.984	2.365	2.627
99	.845	1.290	1.660	1.984	2.364	2.626
100	.845	1.290	1.660	1.984	2.364	2.626
∞	.842	1.282	1.645	1.960	2.326	2.576

TABLE 3   CHI-SQUARE DISTRIBUTION

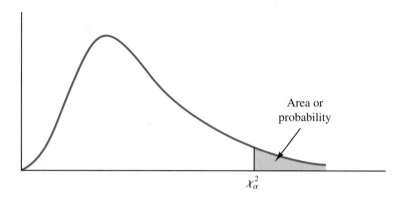

Area or probability

χ_{α}^{2}

Entries in the table give χ_{α}^{2} values, where α is the area or probability in the upper tail of the chi-square distribution. For example, with 10 degrees of freedom and a .01 area in the upper tail, $\chi_{.01}^{2} = 23.209$.

Degrees of Freedom	Area in Upper Tail									
	.995	.99	.975	.95	.90	.10	.05	.025	.01	.005
1	.000	.000	.001	.004	.016	2.706	3.841	5.024	6.635	7.879
2	.010	.020	.051	.103	.211	4.605	5.991	7.378	9.210	10.597
3	.072	.115	.216	.352	.584	6.251	7.815	9.348	11.345	12.838
4	.207	.297	.484	.711	1.064	7.779	9.488	11.143	13.277	14.860
5	.412	.554	.831	1.145	1.610	9.236	11.070	12.832	15.086	16.750
6	.676	.872	1.237	1.635	2.204	10.645	12.592	14.449	16.812	18.548
7	.989	1.239	1.690	2.167	2.833	12.017	14.067	16.013	18.475	20.278
8	1.344	1.647	2.180	2.733	3.490	13.362	15.507	17.535	20.090	21.955
9	1.735	2.088	2.700	3.325	4.168	14.684	16.919	19.023	21.666	23.589
10	2.156	2.558	3.247	3.940	4.865	15.987	18.307	20.483	23.209	25.188
11	2.603	3.053	3.816	4.575	5.578	17.275	19.675	21.920	24.725	26.757
12	3.074	3.571	4.404	5.226	6.304	18.549	21.026	23.337	26.217	28.300
13	3.565	4.107	5.009	5.892	7.041	19.812	22.362	24.736	27.688	29.819
14	4.075	4.660	5.629	6.571	7.790	21.064	23.685	26.119	29.141	31.319
15	4.601	5.229	6.262	7.261	8.547	22.307	24.996	27.488	30.578	32.801
16	5.142	5.812	6.908	7.962	9.312	23.542	26.296	28.845	32.000	34.267
17	5.697	6.408	7.564	8.672	10.085	24.769	27.587	30.191	33.409	35.718
18	6.265	7.015	8.231	9.390	10.865	25.989	28.869	31.526	34.805	37.156
19	6.844	7.633	8.907	10.117	11.651	27.204	30.144	32.852	36.191	38.582
20	7.434	8.260	9.591	10.851	12.443	28.412	31.410	34.170	37.566	39.997
21	8.034	8.897	10.283	11.591	13.240	29.615	32.671	35.479	38.932	41.401
22	8.643	9.542	10.982	12.338	14.041	30.813	33.924	36.781	40.289	42.796
23	9.260	10.196	11.689	13.091	14.848	32.007	35.172	38.076	41.638	44.181
24	9.886	10.856	12.401	13.848	15.659	33.196	36.415	39.364	42.980	45.558
25	10.520	11.524	13.120	14.611	16.473	34.382	37.652	40.646	44.314	46.928
26	11.160	12.198	13.844	15.379	17.292	35.563	38.885	41.923	45.642	48.290
27	11.808	12.878	14.573	16.151	18.114	36.741	40.113	43.195	46.963	49.645
28	12.461	13.565	15.308	16.928	18.939	37.916	41.337	44.461	48.278	50.994
29	13.121	14.256	16.047	17.708	19.768	39.087	42.557	45.722	49.588	52.335

TABLE 3   CHI-SQUARE DISTRIBUTION (*Continued*)

Degrees of Freedom	Area in Upper Tail									
	.995	.99	.975	.95	.90	.10	.05	.025	.01	.005
30	13.787	14.953	16.791	18.493	20.599	40.256	43.773	46.979	50.892	53.672
35	17.192	18.509	20.569	22.465	24.797	46.059	49.802	53.203	57.342	60.275
40	20.707	22.164	24.433	26.509	29.051	51.805	55.758	59.342	63.691	66.766
45	24.311	25.901	28.366	30.612	33.350	57.505	61.656	65.410	69.957	73.166
50	27.991	29.707	32.357	34.764	37.689	63.167	67.505	71.420	76.154	79.490
55	31.735	33.571	36.398	38.958	42.060	68.796	73.311	77.380	82.292	85.749
60	35.534	37.485	40.482	43.188	46.459	74.397	79.082	83.298	88.379	91.952
65	39.383	41.444	44.603	47.450	50.883	79.973	84.821	89.177	94.422	98.105
70	43.275	45.442	48.758	51.739	55.329	85.527	90.531	95.023	100.425	104.215
75	47.206	49.475	52.942	56.054	59.795	91.061	96.217	100.839	106.393	110.285
80	51.172	53.540	57.153	60.391	64.278	96.578	101.879	106.629	112.329	116.321
85	55.170	57.634	61.389	64.749	68.777	102.079	107.522	112.393	118.236	122.324
90	59.196	61.754	65.647	69.126	73.291	107.565	113.145	118.136	124.116	128.299
95	63.250	65.898	69.925	73.520	77.818	113.038	118.752	123.858	129.973	134.247
100	67.328	70.065	74.222	77.929	82.358	118.498	124.342	129.561	135.807	140.170

TABLE 4 *F* DISTRIBUTION

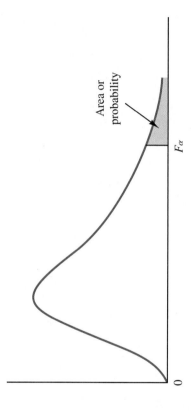

Area or probability

F_α

Entries in the table give F_α values, where α is the area or probability in the upper tail of the F distribution. For example, with 4 numerator degrees of freedom, 8 denominator degrees of freedom, and a .05 area in the upper tail, $F_{.05} = 3.84$.

Denominator Degrees of Freedom	Area in Upper Tail	Numerator Degrees of Freedom																	
		1	2	3	4	5	6	7	8	9	10	15	20	25	30	40	60	100	1000
1	.10	39.86	49.50	53.59	55.83	57.24	58.20	58.91	59.44	59.86	60.19	61.22	61.74	62.05	62.26	62.53	62.79	63.01	63.30
	.05	161.45	199.50	215.71	224.58	230.16	233.99	236.77	238.88	240.54	241.88	245.95	248.02	249.26	250.10	251.14	252.20	253.04	254.19
	.025	647.79	799.48	864.15	899.60	921.83	937.11	948.20	956.64	963.28	968.63	984.87	993.08	998.09	1001.40	1005.60	1009.79	1013.16	1017.76
	.01	4052.18	4999.34	5403.53	5624.26	5763.96	5858.95	5928.33	5980.95	6022.40	6055.93	6156.97	6208.66	6239.86	6260.35	6286.43	6312.97	6333.92	6362.80
2	.10	8.53	9.00	9.16	9.24	9.29	9.33	9.35	9.37	9.38	9.39	9.42	9.44	9.45	9.46	9.47	9.47	9.48	9.49
	.05	18.51	19.00	19.16	19.25	19.30	19.33	19.35	19.37	19.38	19.40	19.43	19.45	19.46	19.46	19.47	19.48	19.49	19.49
	.025	38.51	39.00	39.17	39.25	39.30	39.33	39.36	39.37	39.39	39.40	39.43	39.45	39.46	39.46	39.47	39.48	39.49	39.50
	.01	98.50	99.00	99.16	99.25	99.30	99.33	99.36	99.38	99.39	99.40	99.43	99.45	99.46	99.47	99.48	99.48	99.49	99.50
3	.10	5.54	5.46	5.39	5.34	5.31	5.28	5.27	5.25	5.24	5.23	5.20	5.18	5.17	5.17	5.16	5.15	5.14	5.13
	.05	10.13	9.55	9.28	9.12	9.01	8.94	8.89	8.85	8.81	8.79	8.70	8.66	8.63	8.62	8.59	8.57	8.55	8.53
	.025	17.44	16.04	15.44	15.10	14.88	14.73	14.62	14.54	14.47	14.42	14.25	14.17	14.12	14.08	14.04	13.99	13.96	13.91
	.01	34.12	30.82	29.46	28.71	28.24	27.91	27.67	27.49	27.34	27.23	26.87	26.69	26.58	26.50	26.41	26.32	26.24	26.14
4	.10	4.54	4.32	4.19	4.11	4.05	4.01	3.98	3.95	3.94	3.92	3.87	3.84	3.83	3.82	3.80	3.79	3.78	3.76
	.05	7.71	6.94	6.59	6.39	6.26	6.16	6.09	6.04	6.00	5.96	5.86	5.80	5.77	5.75	5.72	5.69	5.66	5.63
	.025	12.22	10.65	9.98	9.60	9.36	9.20	9.07	8.98	8.90	8.84	8.66	8.56	8.50	8.46	8.41	8.36	8.32	8.26
	.01	21.20	18.00	16.69	15.98	15.52	15.21	14.98	14.80	14.66	14.55	14.20	14.02	13.91	13.84	13.75	13.65	13.58	13.47
5	.10	4.06	3.78	3.62	3.52	3.45	3.40	3.37	3.34	3.32	3.30	3.324	3.21	3.19	3.17	3.16	3.14	3.13	3.11
	.05	6.61.	5.79	5.41	5.19	5.05	4.95	4.88	4.82	4.77	4.74	4.62	4.56	4.52	4.50	4.46	4.43	4.41	4.37
	.025	10.01	8.43	7.76	7.39	7.15	6.98	6.85	6.76	6.68	6.62	6.43	6.33	6.27	6.23	6.18	6.12	6.08	6.02
	.01	16.26	13.27	12.06	11.39	10.97	10.67	10.46	10.29	10.16	10.05	9.72	9.55	9.45	9.38	9.29	9.20	9.13	9.03

TABLE 4 *F* DISTRIBUTION (*Continued*)

Denominator Degrees of Freedom	Area in Upper Tail	Numerator Degrees of Freedom																	
		1	2	3	4	5	6	7	8	9	10	15	20	25	30	40	60	100	1000
6	.10	3.78	3.46	3.29	3.18	3.11	3.05	3.01	2.98	2.96	2.94	2.87	2.84	2.81	2.80	2.78	2.76	2.75	2.72
	.05	5.99	5.14	4.76	4.53	4.39	4.28	4.21	4.15	4.10	4.06	3.94	3.87	3.83	3.81	3.77	3.74	3.71	3.67
	.025	8.81	7.26	6.60	6.23	5.99	5.82	5.70	5.60	5.52	5.46	5.27	5.17	5.11	5.07	5.01	4.96	4.92	4.86
	.01	13.75	10.92	9.78	9.15	8.75	8.47	8.26	8.10	7.98	7.87	7.56	7.40	7.30	7.23	7.14	7.06	6.99	6.89
7	.10	3.59	3.26	3.07	2.96	2.88	2.83	2.78	2.75	2.72	2.70	2.63	2.59	2.57	2.56	2.54	2.51	2.50	2.47
	.05	5.59	4.74	4.35	4.12	3.97	3.87	3.79	3.73	3.68	3.64	3.51	3.44	3.40	3.38	3.34	3.30	3.27	3.23
	.025	8.07	6.54	5.89	5.52	5.29	5.12	4.99	4.90	4.82	4.76	4.57	4.47	4.40	4.36	4.31	4.25	4.21	4.15
	.01	12.25	9.55	8.45	7.85	7.46	7.19	6.99	6.84	6.72	6.62	6.31	6.16	6.06	5.99	5.91	5.82	5.75	5.66
8	.10	3.46	3.11	2.92	2.81	2.73	2.67	2.62	2.59	2.56	2.54	2.46	2.42	2.40	2.38	2.36	2.34	2.32	2.30
	.05	5.32	4.46	4.07	3.84	3.69	3.58	3.50	3.44	3.39	3.35	3.22	3.15	3.11	3.08	3.04	3.01	2.97	2.93
	.025	7.57	6.06	5.42	5.05	4.82	4.65	4.53	4.43	4.36	4.30	4.10	4.00	3.94	3.89	3.84	3.78	3.74	3.68
	.01	11.26	8.65	7.59	7.01	6.63	6.37	6.18	6.03	5.91	5.81	5.52	5.36	5.26	5.20	5.12	5.03	4.96	4.87
9	.10	3.36	3.01	2.81	2.69	2.61	2.55	2.51	2.47	2.44	2.42	2.34	2.30	2.27	2.25	2.23	2.21	2.19	2.16
	.05	5.12	4.26	3.86	3.63	3.48	3.37	3.29	3.23	3.18	3.14	3.01	2.94	2.89	2.86	2.83	2.79	2.76	2.71
	.025	7.21	5.71	5.08	4.72	4.48	4.32	4.20	4.10	4.03	3.96	3.77	3.67	3.60	3.56	3.51	3.45	3.40	3.34
	.01	10.56	8.02	6.99	6.42	6.06	5.80	5.61	5.47	5.35	5.26	4.96	4.81	4.71	4.65	4.57	4.48	4.41	4.32
10	.10	3.29	2.92	2.73	2.61	2.52	2.46	2.41	2.38	2.35	2.32	2.24	2.20	2.17	2.16	2.13	2.11	2.09	2.06
	.05	4.96	4.10	3.71	3.48	3.33	3.22	3.14	3.07	3.02	2.98	2.85	2.77	2.73	2.70	2.66	2.62	2.59	2.54
	.025	6.94	5.46	4.83	4.47	4.24	4.07	3.95	3.85	3.78	3.72	3.52	3.42	3.35	3.31	3.26	3.20	3.15	3.09
	.01	10.04	7.56	6.55	5.99	5.64	5.39	5.20	5.06	4.94	4.85	4.56	4.41	4.31	4.25	4.17	4.08	4.01	3.92
11	.10	3.23	2.86	2.66	2.54	2.45	2.39	2.34	2.30	2.27	2.25	2.17	2.12	2.10	2.08	2.05	2.03	2.01	1.98
	.05	4.84	3.98	3.59	3.36	3.20	3.09	3.01	2.95	2.90	2.85	2.72	2.65	2.60	2.57	2.53	2.49	2.46	2.41
	.025	6.72	5.26	4.63	4.28	4.04	3.88	3.76	3.66	3.59	3.53	3.33	3.23	3.16	3.12	3.06	3.00	2.96	2.89
	.01	9.65	7.21	6.22	5.67	5.32	5.07	4.89	4.74	4.63	4.54	4.25	4.10	4.01	3.94	3.86	3.78	3.71	3.61
12	.10	3.18	2.81	2.61	2.48	2.39	2.33	2.28	2.24	2.21	2.19	2.10	2.06	2.03	2.01	1.99	1.96	1.94	1.91
	.05	4.75	3.89	3.49	3.26	3.11	3.00	2.91	2.85	2.80	2.75	2.62	2.54	2.50	2.47	2.43	2.38	2.35	2.30
	.025	6.55	5.10	4.47	4.12	3.89	3.73	3.61	3.51	3.44	3.37	3.18	3.07	3.01	2.96	2.91	2.85	2.80	2.73
	.01	9.33	6.93	5.95	5.41	5.06	4.82	4.64	4.50	4.39	4.30	4.01	3.86	3.76	3.70	3.62	3.54	3.47	3.37
13	.10	3.14	2.76	2.56	2.43	2.35	2.28	2.23	2.20	2.16	2.14	2.05	2.01	1.98	1.96	1.93	1.90	1.88	1.85
	.05	4.67	3.81	3.41	3.18	3.03	2.92	2.83	2.77	2.71	2.67	2.53	2.46	2.41	2.38	2.34	2.30	2.26	2.21
	.025	6.41	4.97	4.35	4.00	3.77	3.60	3.48	3.39	3.31	3.25	3.05	2.95	2.88	2.84	2.78	2.72	2.67	2.60
	.01	9.07	6.70	5.74	5.21	4.86	4.62	4.44	4.30	4.19	4.10	3.82	3.66	3.57	3.51	3.43	3.34	3.27	3.18
14	.10	3.10	2.73	2.52	2.39	2.31	2.24	2.19	2.15	2.12	2.10	2.01	1.96	1.93	1.91	1.89	1.86	1.83	1.80
	.05	4.60	3.74	3.34	3.11	2.96	2.85	2.76	2.70	2.65	2.60	2.46	2.39	2.34	2.31	2.27	2.22	2.19	2.14
	.025	6.30	4.86	4.24	3.89	3.66	3.50	3.38	3.29	3.21	3.15	2.95	2.84	2.78	2.73	2.67	2.61	2.56	2.50
	.01	8.86	6.51	5.56	5.04	4.69	4.46	4.28	4.14	4.03	3.94	3.66	3.51	3.41	3.35	3.27	3.18	3.11	3.02
15	.10	3.07	2.70	2.49	2.36	2.27	2.21	2.16	2.12	2.09	2.06	1.97	1.92	1.89	1.87	1.85	1.82	1.79	1.76
	.05	4.54	3.68	3.29	3.06	2.90	2.79	2.71	2.64	2.59	2.54	2.40	2.33	2.28	2.25	2.20	2.16	2.12	2.07
	.025	6.20	4.77	4.15	3.80	3.58	3.41	3.29	3.20	3.12	3.06	2.86	2.76	2.69	2.64	2.59	2.52	2.47	2.40
	.01	8.68	6.36	5.42	4.89	4.56	4.32	4.14	4.00	3.89	3.80	3.52	3.37	3.28	3.21	3.13	3.05	2.98	2.88

Numerator Degrees of Freedom

Denominator Degrees of Freedom	Area in Upper Tail	1	2	3	4	5	6	7	8	9	10	15	20	25	30	40	60	100	1000
16	.10	3.05	2.67	2.46	2.33	2.24	2.18	2.13	2.09	2.06	2.03	1.94	1.89	1.86	1.84	1.81	1.78	1.76	1.72
	.05	4.49	3.63	3.24	3.01	2.85	2.74	2.66	2.59	2.54	2.49	2.35	2.28	2.23	2.19	2.15	2.11	2.07	2.02
	.025	6.12	4.69	4.08	3.73	3.50	3.34	3.22	3.12	3.05	2.99	2.79	2.68	2.61	2.57	2.51	2.45	2.40	2.32
	.01	8.53	6.23	5.29	4.77	4.44	4.20	4.03	3.89	3.78	3.69	3.41	3.26	3.16	3.10	3.02	2.93	2.86	2.76
17	.10	3.03	2.64	2.44	2.31	2.22	2.15	2.10	2.06	2.03	2.00	1.91	1.86	1.83	1.81	1.78	1.75	1.73	1.69
	.05	4.45	3.59	3.20	2.96	2.81	2.70	2.61	2.55	2.49	2.45	2.31	2.23	2.18	2.15	2.10	2.06	2.02	1.97
	.025	6.04	4.62	4.01	3.66	3.44	3.28	3.16	3.06	2.98	2.92	2.72	2.62	2.55	2.50	2.44	2.38	2.33	2.26
	.01	8.40	6.11	5.19	4.67	4.34	4.10	3.93	3.79	3.68	3.59	3.31	3.16	3.07	3.00	2.92	2.83	2.76	2.66
18	.10	3.01	2.62	2.42	2.29	2.20	2.13	2.08	2.04	2.00	1.98	1.89	1.84	1.80	1.78	1.75	1.72	1.70	1.66
	.05	4.41	3.55	3.16	2.93	2.77	2.66	2.58	2.51	2.46	2.41	2.27	2.19	2.14	2.11	2.06	2.02	1.98	1.92
	.025	5.98	4.56	3.95	3.61	3.38	3.22	3.10	3.01	2.93	2.87	2.67	2.56	2.49	2.44	2.38	2.32	2.27	2.20
	.01	8.29	6.01	5.09	4.58	4.25	4.01	3.84	3.71	3.60	3.51	3.23	3.08	2.98	2.92	2.84	2.75	2.68	2.58
19	.10	2.99	2.61	2.40	2.27	2.18	2.11	2.06	2.02	1.98	1.96	1.86	1.81	1.78	1.76	1.73	1.70	1.67	1.64
	.05	4.38	3.52	3.13	2.90	2.74	2.63	2.54	2.48	2.42	2.38	2.23	2.16	2.11	2.07	2.03	1.98	1.94	1.88
	.025	5.92	4.51	3.90	3.56	3.33	3.17	3.05	2.96	2.88	2.82	2.62	2.51	2.44	2.39	2.33	2.27	2.22	2.14
	.01	8.18	5.93	5.01	4.50	4.17	3.94	3.77	3.63	3.52	3.43	3.15	3.00	2.91	2.84	2.76	2.67	2.60	2.50
20	.10	2.97	2.59	2.38	2.25	2.16	2.09	2.04	2.00	1.96	1.94	1.84	1.79	1.76	1.74	1.71	1.68	1.65	1.61
	.05	4.35	3.49	3.10	2.87	2.71	2.60	2.51	2.45	2.39	2.35	2.20	2.12	2.07	2.04	1.99	1.95	1.91	1.85
	.025	5.87	4.46	3.86	3.51	3.29	3.13	3.01	2.91	2.84	2.77	2.57	2.46	2.40	2.35	2.29	2.22	2.17	2.09
	.01	8.10	5.85	4.94	4.43	4.10	3.87	3.70	3.56	3.46	3.37	3.09	2.94	2.84	2.78	2.69	2.61	2.54	2.43
21	.10	2.96	2.57	2.36	2.23	2.14	2.08	2.02	1.98	1.95	1.92	1.83	1.78	1.74	1.72	1.69	1.66	1.63	1.59
	.05	4.32	3.47	3.07	2.84	2.68	2.57	2.49	2.42	2.37	2.32	2.18	2.10	2.05	2.01	1.96	1.92	1.88	1.82
	.025	5.83	4.42	3.82	3.48	3.25	3.09	2.97	2.87	2.80	2.73	2.53	2.42	2.36	2.31	2.25	2.18	2.13	2.05
	.01	8.02	5.78	4.87	4.37	4.04	3.81	3.64	3.51	3.40	3.31	3.03	2.88	2.79	2.72	2.64	2.55	2.48	2.37
22	.10	2.95	2.56	2.35	2.22	2.13	2.06	2.01	1.97	1.93	1.90	1.81	1.76	1.73	1.70	1.67	1.64	1.61	1.57
	.05	4.30	3.44	3.05	2.82	2.66	2.55	2.46	2.40	2.34	2.30	2.15	2.07	2.02	1.98	1.94	1.89	1.85	1.79
	.025	5.79	4.38	3.78	3.44	3.22	3.05	2.93	2.84	2.76	2.70	2.50	2.39	2.32	2.27	2.21	2.14	2.09	2.01
	.01	7.95	5.72	4.82	4.31	3.99	3.76	3.59	3.45	3.35	3.26	2.98	2.83	2.73	2.67	2.58	2.50	2.42	2.32
23	.10	2.94	2.55	2.34	2.21	2.11	2.05	1.99	1.95	1.92	1.89	1.80	1.74	1.71	1.69	1.66	1.62	1.59	1.55
	.05	4.28	3.42	3.03	2.80	2.64	2.53	2.44	2.37	2.32	2.27	2.13	2.05	2.00	1.96	1.91	1.86	1.82	1.76
	.025	5.75	4.35	3.75	3.41	3.18	3.02	2.90	2.81	2.73	2.67	2.47	2.36	2.29	2.24	2.18	2.11	2.06	1.98
	.01	7.88	5.66	4.76	4.26	3.94	3.71	3.54	3.41	3.30	3.21	2.93	2.78	2.69	2.62	2.54	2.45	2.37	2.27
24	.10	2.93	2.54	2.33	2.19	2.10	2.04	1.98	1.94	1.91	1.88	1.78	1.73	1.70	1.67	1.64	1.61	1.58	1.54
	.05	4.26	3.40	3.01	2.78	2.62	2.51	2.42	2.36	2.30	2.25	2.11	2.03	1.97	1.94	1.89	1.84	1.80	1.74
	.025	5.72	4.32	3.72	3.38	3.15	2.99	2.87	2.78	2.70	2.64	2.44	2.33	2.26	2.21	2.15	2.08	2.02	1.94
	.01	7.82	5.61	4.72	4.22	3.90	3.67	3.50	3.36	3.26	3.17	2.89	2.74	2.64	2.58	2.49	2.40	2.33	2.22

TABLE 4 F DISTRIBUTION (*Continued*)

Numerator Degrees of Freedom

Denominator Degrees of Freedom	Area in Upper Tail	1	2	3	4	5	6	7	8	9	10	15	20	25	30	40	60	100	1000
25	.10	2.92	2.53	2.32	2.18	2.09	2.02	1.97	1.93	1.89	1.87	1.77	1.72	1.68	1.66	1.63	1.59	1.56	1.52
	.05	4.24	3.39	2.99	2.76	2.60	2.49	2.40	2.34	2.28	2.24	2.09	2.01	1.96	1.92	1.87	1.82	1.78	1.72
	.025	5.69	4.29	3.69	3.35	3.13	2.97	2.85	2.75	2.68	2.61	2.41	2.30	2.23	2.18	2.12	2.05	2.00	1.91
	.01	7.77	5.57	4.68	4.18	3.85	3.63	3.46	3.32	3.22	3.13	2.85	2.70	2.60	2.54	2.45	2.36	2.29	2.18
26	.10	2.91	2.52	2.31	2.17	2.08	2.01	1.96	1.92	1.88	1.86	1.76	1.71	1.67	1.65	1.61	1.58	1.55	1.51
	.05	4.23	3.37	2.98	2.74	2.59	2.47	2.39	2.32	2.27	2.22	2.07	1.99	1.94	1.90	1.85	1.80	1.76	1.70
	.025	5.66	4.27	3.67	3.33	3.10	2.94	2.82	2.73	2.65	2.59	2.39	2.28	2.21	2.16	2.09	2.03	1.97	1.89
	.01	7.72	5.53	4.64	4.14	3.82	3.59	3.42	3.29	3.18	3.09	2.81	2.66	2.57	2.50	2.42	2.33	2.25	2.14
27	.10	2.90	2.51	2.30	2.17	2.07	2.00	1.95	1.91	1.87	1.85	1.75	1.70	1.66	1.64	1.60	1.57	1.54	1.50
	.05	4.21	3.35	2.96	2.73	2.57	2.46	2.37	2.31	2.25	2.20	2.06	1.97	1.92	1.88	1.84	1.79	1.74	1.68
	.025	5.63	4.24	3.65	3.31	3.08	2.92	2.80	2.71	2.63	2.57	2.36	2.25	2.18	2.13	2.07	2.00	1.94	1.86
	.01	7.68	5.49	4.60	4.11	3.78	3.56	3.39	3.26	3.15	3.06	2.78	2.63	2.54	2.47	2.38	2.29	2.22	2.11
28	.10	2.89	2.50	2.29	2.16	2.06	2.00	1.94	1.90	1.87	1.84	1.74	1.69	1.65	1.63	1.59	1.56	1.53	1.48
	.05	4.20	3.34	2.95	2.71	2.56	2.45	2.36	2.29	2.24	2.19	2.04	1.96	1.91	1.87	1.82	1.77	1.73	1.66
	.025	5.61	4.22	3.63	3.29	3.06	2.90	2.78	2.69	2.61	2.55	2.34	2.23	2.16	2.11	2.05	1.98	1.92	1.84
	.01	7.64	5.45	4.57	4.07	3.75	3.53	3.36	3.23	3.12	3.03	2.75	2.60	2.51	2.44	2.35	2.26	2.19	2.08
29	.10	2.89	2.50	2.28	2.15	2.06	1.99	1.93	1.89	1.86	1.83	1.73	1.68	1.64	1.62	1.58	1.55	1.52	1.47
	.05	4.18	3.33	2.93	2.70	2.55	2.43	2.35	2.28	2.22	2.18	2.03	1.94	1.89	1.85	1.81	1.75	1.71	1.65
	.025	5.59	4.20	3.61	3.27	3.04	2.88	2.76	2.67	2.59	2.53	2.32	2.21	2.14	2.09	2.03	1.96	1.90	1.82
	.01	7.60	5.42	4.54	4.04	3.73	3.50	3.33	3.20	3.09	3.00	2.73	2.57	2.48	2.41	2.33	2.23	2.16	2.05
30	.10	2.88	2.49	2.28	2.14	2.05	1.98	1.93	1.88	1.85	1.82	1.72	1.67	1.63	1.61	1.57	1.54	1.51	1.46
	.05	4.17	3.32	2.92	2.69	2.53	2.42	2.33	2.27	2.21	2.16	2.01	1.93	1.88	1.84	1.79	1.74	1.70	1.63
	.025	5.57	4.18	3.59	3.25	3.03	2.87	2.75	2.65	2.57	2.51	2.31	2.20	2.12	2.07	2.01	1.94	1.88	1.80
	.01	7.56	5.39	4.51	4.02	3.70	3.47	3.30	3.17	3.07	2.98	2.70	2.55	2.45	2.39	2.30	2.21	2.13	2.02
40	.10	2.84	2.44	2.23	2.09	2.00	1.93	1.87	1.83	1.79	1.76	1.66	1.61	1.57	1.54	1.51	1.47	1.43	1.38
	.05	4.08	3.23	2.84	2.61	2.45	2.34	2.25	2.18	2.12	2.08	1.92	1.84	1.78	1.74	1.69	1.64	1.59	1.52
	.025	5.42	4.05	3.46	3.13	2.90	2.74	2.62	2.53	2.45	2.39	2.18	2.07	1.99	1.94	1.88	1.80	1.74	1.65
	.01	7.31	5.18	4.31	3.83	3.51	3.29	3.12	2.99	2.89	2.80	2.52	2.37	2.27	2.20	2.11	2.02	1.94	1.82
60	.10	2.79	2.39	2.18	2.04	1.95	1.87	1.82	1.77	1.74	1.71	1.60	1.54	1.50	1.48	1.44	1.40	1.36	1.30
	.05	4.00	3.15	2.76	2.53	2.37	2.25	2.17	2.10	2.04	1.99	1.84	1.75	1.69	1.65	1.59	1.53	1.48	1.40
	.025	5.29	3.93	3.34	3.01	2.79	2.63	2.51	2.41	2.33	2.27	2.06	1.94	1.87	1.82	1.74	1.67	1.60	1.49
	.01	7.08	4.98	4.13	3.65	3.34	3.12	2.95	2.82	2.72	2.63	2.35	2.20	2.10	2.03	1.94	1.84	1.75	1.62
100	.10	2.76	2.36	2.14	2.00	1.91	1.83	1.78	1.73	1.69	1.66	1.56	1.49	1.45	1.42	1.38	1.34	1.29	1.22
	.05	3.94	3.09	2.70	2.46	2.31	2.19	2.10	2.03	1.97	1.93	1.77	1.68	1.62	1.57	1.52	1.45	1.39	1.30
	.025	5.18	3.83	3.25	2.92	2.70	2.54	2.42	2.32	2.24	2.18	1.97	1.85	1.77	1.71	1.64	1.56	1.48	1.36
	.01	6.90	4.82	3.98	3.51	3.21	2.99	2.82	2.69	2.59	2.50	2.22	2.07	1.97	1.89	1.80	1.69	1.60	1.45
1000	.10	2.71	2.31	2.09	1.95	1.85	1.78	1.72	1.68	1.64	1.61	1.49	1.43	1.38	1.35	1.30	1.25	1.20	1.08
	.05	3.85	3.00	2.61	2.38	2.22	2.11	2.02	1.95	1.89	1.84	1.68	1.58	1.52	1.47	1.41	1.33	1.26	1.11
	.025	5.04	3.70	3.13	2.80	2.58	2.42	2.30	2.20	2.13	2.06	1.85	1.72	1.64	1.58	1.50	1.41	1.32	1.13
	.01	6.66	4.63	3.80	3.34	3.04	2.82	2.66	2.53	2.43	2.34	2.06	1.90	1.79	1.72	1.61	1.50	1.38	1.16

TABLE 5   BINOMIAL PROBABILITIES
Entries in the table give the probability of *x* successes in *n* trials of a binomial experiment, where *p* is the probability of a success on one trial. For example, with six trials and $p = .05$, the probability of two successes is .0305.

						p				
n	*x*	.01	.02	.03	.04	.05	.06	.07	.08	.09
2	0	.9801	.9604	.9409	.9216	.9025	.8836	.8649	.8464	.8281
	1	.0198	.0392	.0582	.0768	.0950	.1128	.1302	.1472	.1638
	2	.0001	.0004	.0009	.0016	.0025	.0036	.0049	.0064	.0081
3	0	.9703	.9412	.9127	.8847	.8574	.8306	.8044	.7787	.7536
	1	.0294	.0576	.0847	.1106	.1354	.1590	.1816	.2031	.2236
	2	.0003	.0012	.0026	.0046	.0071	.0102	.0137	.0177	.0221
	3	.0000	.0000	.0000	.0001	.0001	.0002	.0003	.0005	.0007
4	0	.9606	.9224	.8853	.8493	.8145	.7807	.7481	.7164	.6857
	1	.0388	.0753	.1095	.1416	.1715	.1993	.2252	.2492	.2713
	2	.0006	.0023	.0051	.0088	.0135	.0191	.0254	.0325	.0402
	3	.0000	.0000	.0001	.0002	.0005	.0008	.0013	.0019	.0027
	4	.0000	.0000	.0000	.0000	.0000	.0000	.0000	.0000	.0001
5	0	.9510	.9039	.8587	.8154	.7738	.7339	.6957	.6591	.6240
	1	.0480	.0922	.1328	.1699	.2036	.2342	.2618	.2866	.3086
	2	.0010	.0038	.0082	.0142	.0214	.0299	.0394	.0498	.0610
	3	.0000	.0001	.0003	.0006	.0011	.0019	.0030	.0043	.0060
	4	.0000	.0000	.0000	.0000	.0000	.0001	.0001	.0002	.0003
	5	.0000	.0000	.0000	.0000	.0000	.0000	.0000	.0000	.0000
6	0	.9415	.8858	.8330	.7828	.7351	.6899	.6470	.6064	.5679
	1	.0571	.1085	.1546	.1957	.2321	.2642	.2922	.3164	.3370
	2	.0014	.0055	.0120	.0204	.0305	.0422	.0550	.0688	.0833
	3	.0000	.0002	.0005	.0011	.0021	.0036	.0055	.0080	.0110
	4	.0000	.0000	.0000	.0000	.0001	.0002	.0003	.0005	.0008
	5	.0000	.0000	.0000	.0000	.0000	.0000	.0000	.0000	.0000
	6	.0000	.0000	.0000	.0000	.0000	.0000	.0000	.0000	.0000
7	0	.9321	.8681	.8080	.7514	.6983	.6485	.6017	.5578	.5168
	1	.0659	.1240	.1749	.2192	.2573	.2897	.3170	.3396	.3578
	2	.0020	.0076	.0162	.0274	.0406	.0555	.0716	.0886	.1061
	3	.0000	.0003	.0008	.0019	.0036	.0059	.0090	.0128	.0175
	4	.0000	.0000	.0000	.0001	.0002	.0004	.0007	.0011	.0017
	5	.0000	.0000	.0000	.0000	.0000	.0000	.0000	.0001	.0001
	6	.0000	.0000	.0000	.0000	.0000	.0000	.0000	.0000	.0000
	7	.0000	.0000	.0000	.0000	.0000	.0000	.0000	.0000	.0000
8	0	.9227	.8508	.7837	.7214	.6634	.6096	.5596	.5132	.4703
	1	.0746	.1389	.1939	.2405	.2793	.3113	.3370	.3570	.3721
	2	.0026	.0099	.0210	.0351	.0515	.0695	.0888	.1087	.1288
	3	.0001	.0004	.0013	.0029	.0054	.0089	.0134	.0189	.0255
	4	.0000	.0000	.0001	.0002	.0004	.0007	.0013	.0021	.0031
	5	.0000	.0000	.0000	.0000	.0000	.0000	.0001	.0001	.0002
	6	.0000	.0000	.0000	.0000	.0000	.0000	.0000	.0000	.0000
	7	.0000	.0000	.0000	.0000	.0000	.0000	.0000	.0000	.0000
	8	.0000	.0000	.0000	.0000	.0000	.0000	.0000	.0000	.0000

TABLE 5   BINOMIAL PROBABILITIES (*Continued*)

n	x	.01	.02	.03	.04	.05	.06	.07	.08	.09
						p				
9	0	.9135	.8337	.7602	.6925	.6302	.5730	.5204	.4722	.4279
	1	.0830	.1531	.2116	.2597	.2985	.3292	.3525	.3695	.3809
	2	.0034	.0125	.0262	.0433	.0629	.0840	.1061	.1285	.1507
	3	.0001	.0006	.0019	.0042	.0077	.0125	.0186	.0261	.0348
	4	.0000	.0000	.0001	.0003	.0006	.0012	.0021	.0034	.0052
	5	.0000	.0000	.0000	.0000	.0000	.0001	.0002	.0003	.0005
	6	.0000	.0000	.0000	.0000	.0000	.0000	.0000	.0000	.0000
	7	.0000	.0000	.0000	.0000	.0000	.0000	.0000	.0000	.0000
	8	.0000	.0000	.0000	.0000	.0000	.0000	.0000	.0000	.0000
	9	.0000	.0000	.0000	.0000	.0000	.0000	.0000	.0000	.0000
10	0	.9044	.8171	.7374	.6648	.5987	.5386	.4840	.4344	.3894
	1	.0914	.1667	.2281	.2770	.3151	.3438	.3643	.3777	.3851
	2	.0042	.0153	.0317	.0519	.0746	.0988	.1234	.1478	.1714
	3	.0001	.0008	.0026	.0058	.0105	.0168	.0248	.0343	.0452
	4	.0000	.0000	.0001	.0004	.0010	.0019	.0033	.0052	.0078
	5	.0000	.0000	.0000	.0000	.0001	.0001	.0003	.0005	.0009
	6	.0000	.0000	.0000	.0000	.0000	.0000	.0000	.0000	.0001
	7	.0000	.0000	.0000	.0000	.0000	.0000	.0000	.0000	.0000
	8	.0000	.0000	.0000	.0000	.0000	.0000	.0000	.0000	.0000
	9	.0000	.0000	.0000	.0000	.0000	.0000	.0000	.0000	.0000
	10	.0000	.0000	.0000	.0000	.0000	.0000	.0000	.0000	.0000
12	0	.8864	.7847	.6938	.6127	.5404	.4759	.4186	.3677	.3225
	1	.1074	.1922	.2575	.3064	.3413	.3645	.3781	.3837	.3827
	2	.0060	.0216	.0438	.0702	.0988	.1280	.1565	.1835	.2082
	3	.0002	.0015	.0045	.0098	.0173	.0272	.0393	.0532	.0686
	4	.0000	.0001	.0003	.0009	.0021	.0039	.0067	.0104	.0153
	5	.0000	.0000	.0000	.0001	.0002	.0004	.0008	.0014	.0024
	6	.0000	.0000	.0000	.0000	.0000	.0000	.0001	.0001	.0003
	7	.0000	.0000	.0000	.0000	.0000	.0000	.0000	.0000	.0000
	8	.0000	.0000	.0000	.0000	.0000	.0000	.0000	.0000	.0000
	9	.0000	.0000	.0000	.0000	.0000	.0000	.0000	.0000	.0000
	10	.0000	.0000	.0000	.0000	.0000	.0000	.0000	.0000	.0000
	11	.0000	.0000	.0000	.0000	.0000	.0000	.0000	.0000	.0000
	12	.0000	.0000	.0000	.0000	.0000	.0000	.0000	.0000	.0000
15	0	.8601	.7386	.6333	.5421	.4633	.3953	.3367	.2863	.2430
	1	.1303	.2261	.2938	.3388	.3658	.3785	.3801	.3734	.3605
	2	.0092	.0323	.0636	.0988	.1348	.1691	.2003	.2273	.2496
	3	.0004	.0029	.0085	.0178	.0307	.0468	.0653	.0857	.1070
	4	.0000	.0002	.0008	.0022	.0049	.0090	.0148	.0223	.0317
	5	.0000	.0000	.0001	.0002	.0006	.0013	.0024	.0043	.0069
	6	.0000	.0000	.0000	.0000	.0000	.0001	.0003	.0006	.0011
	7	.0000	.0000	.0000	.0000	.0000	.0000	.0000	.0001	.0001
	8	.0000	.0000	.0000	.0000	.0000	.0000	.0000	.0000	.0000
	9	.0000	.0000	.0000	.0000	.0000	.0000	.0000	.0000	.0000
	10	.0000	.0000	.0000	.0000	.0000	.0000	.0000	.0000	.0000
	11	.0000	.0000	.0000	.0000	.0000	.0000	.0000	.0000	.0000
	12	.0000	.0000	.0000	.0000	.0000	.0000	.0000	.0000	.0000
	13	.0000	.0000	.0000	.0000	.0000	.0000	.0000	.0000	.0000
	14	.0000	.0000	.0000	.0000	.0000	.0000	.0000	.0000	.0000
	15	.0000	.0000	.0000	.0000	.0000	.0000	.0000	.0000	.0000

TABLE 5   BINOMIAL PROBABILITIES (*Continued*)

						p				
n	*x*	.01	.02	.03	.04	.05	.06	.07	.08	.09
18	0	.8345	.6951	.5780	.4796	.3972	.3283	.2708	.2229	.1831
	1	.1517	.2554	.3217	.3597	.3763	.3772	.3669	.3489	.3260
	2	.0130	.0443	.0846	.1274	.1683	.2047	.2348	.2579	.2741
	3	.0007	.0048	.0140	.0283	.0473	.0697	.0942	.1196	.1446
	4	.0000	.0004	.0016	.0044	.0093	.0167	.0266	.0390	.0536
	5	.0000	.0000	.0001	.0005	.0014	.0030	.0056	.0095	.0148
	6	.0000	.0000	.0000	.0000	.0002	.0004	.0009	.0018	.0032
	7	.0000	.0000	.0000	.0000	.0000	.0000	.0001	.0003	.0005
	8	.0000	.0000	.0000	.0000	.0000	.0000	.0000	.0000	.0001
	9	.0000	.0000	.0000	.0000	.0000	.0000	.0000	.0000	.0000
	10	.0000	.0000	.0000	.0000	.0000	.0000	.0000	.0000	.0000
	11	.0000	.0000	.0000	.0000	.0000	.0000	.0000	.0000	.0000
	12	.0000	.0000	.0000	.0000	.0000	.0000	.0000	.0000	.0000
	13	.0000	.0000	.0000	.0000	.0000	.0000	.0000	.0000	.0000
	14	.0000	.0000	.0000	.0000	.0000	.0000	.0000	.0000	.0000
	15	.0000	.0000	.0000	.0000	.0000	.0000	.0000	.0000	.0000
	16	.0000	.0000	.0000	.0000	.0000	.0000	.0000	.0000	.0000
	17	.0000	.0000	.0000	.0000	.0000	.0000	.0000	.0000	.0000
	18	.0000	.0000	.0000	.0000	.0000	.0000	.0000	.0000	.0000
20	0	.8179	.6676	.5438	.4420	.3585	.2901	.2342	.1887	.1516
	1	.1652	.2725	.3364	.3683	.3774	.3703	.3526	.3282	.3000
	2	.0159	.0528	.0988	.1458	.1887	.2246	.2521	.2711	.2818
	3	.0010	.0065	.0183	.0364	.0596	.0860	.1139	.1414	.1672
	4	.0000	.0006	.0024	.0065	.0133	.0233	.0364	.0523	.0703
	5	.0000	.0000	.0002	.0009	.0022	.0048	.0088	.0145	.0222
	6	.0000	.0000	.0000	.0001	.0003	.0008	.0017	.0032	.0055
	7	.0000	.0000	.0000	.0000	.0000	.0001	.0002	.0005	.0011
	8	.0000	.0000	.0000	.0000	.0000	.0000	.0000	.0001	.0002
	9	.0000	.0000	.0000	.0000	.0000	.0000	.0000	.0000	.0000
	10	.0000	.0000	.0000	.0000	.0000	.0000	.0000	.0000	.0000
	11	.0000	.0000	.0000	.0000	.0000	.0000	.0000	.0000	.0000
	12	.0000	.0000	.0000	.0000	.0000	.0000	.0000	.0000	.0000
	13	.0000	.0000	.0000	.0000	.0000	.0000	.0000	.0000	.0000
	14	.0000	.0000	.0000	.0000	.0000	.0000	.0000	.0000	.0000
	15	.0000	.0000	.0000	.0000	.0000	.0000	.0000	.0000	.0000
	16	.0000	.0000	.0000	.0000	.0000	.0000	.0000	.0000	.0000
	17	.0000	.0000	.0000	.0000	.0000	.0000	.0000	.0000	.0000
	18	.0000	.0000	.0000	.0000	.0000	.0000	.0000	.0000	.0000
	19	.0000	.0000	.0000	.0000	.0000	.0000	.0000	.0000	.0000
	20	.0000	.0000	.0000	.0000	.0000	.0000	.0000	.0000	.0000

TABLE 5   BINOMIAL PROBABILITIES (*Continued*)

n	x	**.10**	**.15**	**.20**	**.25**	**.30**	**.35**	**.40**	**.45**	**.50**
						p				
2	0	.8100	.7225	.6400	.5625	.4900	.4225	.3600	.3025	.2500
	1	.1800	.2550	.3200	.3750	.4200	.4550	.4800	.4950	.5000
	2	.0100	.0225	.0400	.0625	.0900	.1225	.1600	.2025	.2500
3	0	.7290	.6141	.5120	.4219	.3430	.2746	.2160	.1664	.1250
	1	.2430	.3251	.3840	.4219	.4410	.4436	.4320	.4084	.3750
	2	.0270	.0574	.0960	.1406	.1890	.2389	.2880	.3341	.3750
	3	.0010	.0034	.0080	.0156	.0270	.0429	.0640	.0911	.1250
4	0	.6561	.5220	.4096	.3164	.2401	.1785	.1296	.0915	.0625
	1	.2916	.3685	.4096	.4219	.4116	.3845	.3456	.2995	.2500
	2	.0486	.0975	.1536	.2109	.2646	.3105	.3456	.3675	.3750
	3	.0036	.0115	.0256	.0469	.0756	.1115	.1536	.2005	.2500
	4	.0001	.0005	.0016	.0039	.0081	.0150	.0256	.0410	.0625
5	0	.5905	.4437	.3277	.2373	.1681	.1160	.0778	.0503	.0312
	1	.3280	.3915	.4096	.3955	.3602	.3124	.2592	.2059	.1562
	2	.0729	.1382	.2048	.2637	.3087	.3364	.3456	.3369	.3125
	3	.0081	.0244	.0512	.0879	.1323	.1811	.2304	.2757	.3125
	4	.0004	.0022	.0064	.0146	.0284	.0488	.0768	.1128	.1562
	5	.0000	.0001	.0003	.0010	.0024	.0053	.0102	.0185	.0312
6	0	.5314	.3771	.2621	.1780	.1176	.0754	.0467	.0277	.0156
	1	.3543	.3993	.3932	.3560	.3025	.2437	.1866	.1359	.0938
	2	.0984	.1762	.2458	.2966	.3241	.3280	.3110	.2780	.2344
	3	.0146	.0415	.0819	.1318	.1852	.2355	.2765	.3032	.3125
	4	.0012	.0055	.0154	.0330	.0595	.0951	.1382	.1861	.2344
	5	.0001	.0004	.0015	.0044	.0102	.0205	.0369	.0609	.0938
	6	.0000	.0000	.0001	.0002	.0007	.0018	.0041	.0083	.0156
7	0	.4783	.3206	.2097	.1335	.0824	.0490	.0280	.0152	.0078
	1	.3720	.3960	.3670	.3115	.2471	.1848	.1306	.0872	.0547
	2	.1240	.2097	.2753	.3115	.3177	.2985	.2613	.2140	.1641
	3	.0230	.0617	.1147	.1730	.2269	.2679	.2903	.2918	.2734
	4	.0026	.0109	.0287	.0577	.0972	.1442	.1935	.2388	.2734
	5	.0002	.0012	.0043	.0115	.0250	.0466	.0774	.1172	.1641
	6	.0000	.0001	.0004	.0013	.0036	.0084	.0172	.0320	.0547
	7	.0000	.0000	.0000	.0001	.0002	.0006	.0016	.0037	.0078
8	0	.4305	.2725	.1678	.1001	.0576	.0319	.0168	.0084	.0039
	1	.3826	.3847	.3355	.2670	.1977	.1373	.0896	.0548	.0312
	2	.1488	.2376	.2936	.3115	.2965	.2587	.2090	.1569	.1094
	3	.0331	.0839	.1468	.2076	.2541	.2786	.2787	.2568	.2188
	4	.0046	.0185	.0459	.0865	.1361	.1875	.2322	.2627	.2734
	5	.0004	.0026	.0092	.0231	.0467	.0808	.1239	.1719	.2188
	6	.0000	.0002	.0011	.0038	.0100	.0217	.0413	.0703	.1094
	7	.0000	.0000	.0001	.0004	.0012	.0033	.0079	.0164	.0313
	8	.0000	.0000	.0000	.0000	.0001	.0002	.0007	.0017	.0039

TABLE 5   BINOMIAL PROBABILITIES (*Continued*)

						p				
n	*x*	.10	.15	.20	.25	.30	.35	.40	.45	.50
9	0	.3874	.2316	.1342	.0751	.0404	.0207	.0101	.0046	.0020
	1	.3874	.3679	.3020	.2253	.1556	.1004	.0605	.0339	.0176
	2	.1722	.2597	.3020	.3003	.2668	.2162	.1612	.1110	.0703
	3	.0446	.1069	.1762	.2336	.2668	.2716	.2508	.2119	.1641
	4	.0074	.0283	.0661	.1168	.1715	.2194	.2508	.2600	.2461
	5	.0008	.0050	.0165	.0389	.0735	.1181	.1672	.2128	.2461
	6	.0001	.0006	.0028	.0087	.0210	.0424	.0743	.1160	.1641
	7	.0000	.0000	.0003	.0012	.0039	.0098	.0212	.0407	.0703
	8	.0000	.0000	.0000	.0001	.0004	.0013	.0035	.0083	.0176
	9	.0000	.0000	.0000	.0000	.0000	.0001	.0003	.0008	.0020
10	0	.3487	.1969	.1074	.0563	.0282	.0135	.0060	.0025	.0010
	1	.3874	.3474	.2684	.1877	.1211	.0725	.0403	.0207	.0098
	2	.1937	.2759	.3020	.2816	.2335	.1757	.1209	.0763	.0439
	3	.0574	.1298	.2013	.2503	.2668	.2522	.2150	.1665	.1172
	4	.0112	.0401	.0881	.1460	.2001	.2377	.2508	.2384	.2051
	5	.0015	.0085	.0264	.0584	.1029	.1536	.2007	.2340	.2461
	6	.0001	.0012	.0055	.0162	.0368	.0689	.1115	.1596	.2051
	7	.0000	.0001	.0008	.0031	.0090	.0212	.0425	.0746	.1172
	8	.0000	.0000	.0001	.0004	.0014	.0043	.0106	.0229	.0439
	9	.0000	.0000	.0000	.0000	.0001	.0005	.0016	.0042	.0098
	10	.0000	.0000	.0000	.0000	.0000	.0000	.0001	.0003	.0010
12	0	.2824	.1422	.0687	.0317	.0138	.0057	.0022	.0008	.0002
	1	.3766	.3012	.2062	.1267	.0712	.0368	.0174	.0075	.0029
	2	.2301	.2924	.2835	.2323	.1678	.1088	.0639	.0339	.0161
	3	.0853	.1720	.2362	.2581	.2397	.1954	.1419	.0923	.0537
	4	.0213	.0683	.1329	.1936	.2311	.2367	.2128	.1700	.1208
	5	.0038	.0193	.0532	.1032	.1585	.2039	.2270	.2225	.1934
	6	.0005	.0040	.0155	.0401	.0792	.1281	.1766	.2124	.2256
	7	.0000	.0006	.0033	.0115	.0291	.0591	.1009	.1489	.1934
	8	.0000	.0001	.0005	.0024	.0078	.0199	.0420	.0762	.1208
	9	.0000	.0000	.0001	.0004	.0015	.0048	.0125	.0277	.0537
	10	.0000	.0000	.0000	.0000	.0002	.0008	.0025	.0068	.0161
	11	.0000	.0000	.0000	.0000	.0000	.0001	.0003	.0010	.0029
	12	.0000	.0000	.0000	.0000	.0000	.0000	.0000	.0001	.0002
15	0	.2059	.0874	.0352	.0134	.0047	.0016	.0005	.0001	.0000
	1	.3432	.2312	.1319	.0668	.0305	.0126	.0047	.0016	.0005
	2	.2669	.2856	.2309	.1559	.0916	.0476	.0219	.0090	.0032
	3	.1285	.2184	.2501	.2252	.1700	.1110	.0634	.0318	.0139
	4	.0428	.1156	.1876	.2252	.2186	.1792	.1268	.0780	.0417
	5	.0105	.0449	.1032	.1651	.2061	.2123	.1859	.1404	.0916
	6	.0019	.0132	.0430	.0917	.1472	.1906	.2066	.1914	.1527
	7	.0003	.0030	.0138	.0393	.0811	.1319	.1771	.2013	.1964
	8	.0000	.0005	.0035	.0131	.0348	.0710	.1181	.1647	.1964
	9	.0000	.0001	.0007	.0034	.0016	.0298	.0612	.1048	.1527
	10	.0000	.0000	.0001	.0007	.0030	.0096	.0245	.0515	.0916
	11	.0000	.0000	.0000	.0001	.0006	.0024	.0074	.0191	.0417
	12	.0000	.0000	.0000	.0000	.0001	.0004	.0016	.0052	.0139
	13	.0000	.0000	.0000	.0000	.0000	.0001	.0003	.0010	.0032
	14	.0000	.0000	.0000	.0000	.0000	.0000	.0000	.0001	.0005
	15	.0000	.0000	.0000	.0000	.0000	.0000	.0000	.0000	.0000

TABLE 5   BINOMIAL PROBABILITIES (*Continued*)

n	x	.10	.15	.20	.25	.30	.35	.40	.45	.50
18	0	.1501	.0536	.0180	.0056	.0016	.0004	.0001	.0000	.0000
	1	.3002	.1704	.0811	.0338	.0126	.0042	.0012	.0003	.0001
	2	.2835	.2556	.1723	.0958	.0458	.0190	.0069	.0022	.0006
	3	.1680	.2406	.2297	.1704	.1046	.0547	.0246	.0095	.0031
	4	.0700	.1592	.2153	.2130	.1681	.1104	.0614	.0291	.0117
	5	.0218	.0787	.1507	.1988	.2017	.1664	.1146	.0666	.0327
	6	.0052	.0301	.0816	.1436	.1873	.1941	.1655	.1181	.0708
	7	.0010	.0091	.0350	.0820	.1376	.1792	.1892	.1657	.1214
	8	.0002	.0022	.0120	.0376	.0811	.1327	.1734	.1864	.1669
	9	.0000	.0004	.0033	.0139	.0386	.0794	.1284	.1694	.1855
	10	.0000	.0001	.0008	.0042	.0149	.0385	.0771	.1248	.1669
	11	.0000	.0000	.0001	.0010	.0046	.0151	.0374	.0742	.1214
	12	.0000	.0000	.0000	.0002	.0012	.0047	.0145	.0354	.0708
	13	.0000	.0000	.0000	.0000	.0002	.0012	.0045	.0134	.0327
	14	.0000	.0000	.0000	.0000	.0000	.0002	.0011	.0039	.0117
	15	.0000	.0000	.0000	.0000	.0000	.0000	.0002	.0009	.0031
	16	.0000	.0000	.0000	.0000	.0000	.0000	.0000	.0001	.0006
	17	.0000	.0000	.0000	.0000	.0000	.0000	.0000	.0000	.0001
	18	.0000	.0000	.0000	.0000	.0000	.0000	.0000	.0000	.0000
20	0	.1216	.0388	.0115	.0032	.0008	.0002	.0000	.0000	.0000
	1	.2702	.1368	.0576	.0211	.0068	.0020	.0005	.0001	.0000
	2	.2852	.2293	.1369	.0669	.0278	.0100	.0031	.0008	.0002
	3	.1901	.2428	.2054	.1339	.0716	.0323	.0123	.0040	.0011
	4	.0898	.1821	.2182	.1897	.1304	.0738	.0350	.0139	.0046
	5	.0319	.1028	.1746	.2023	.1789	.1272	.0746	.0365	.0148
	6	.0089	.0454	.1091	.1686	.1916	.1712	.1244	.0746	.0370
	7	.0020	.0160	.0545	.1124	.1643	.1844	.1659	.1221	.0739
	8	.0004	.0046	.0222	.0609	.1144	.1614	.1797	.1623	.1201
	9	.0001	.0011	.0074	.0271	.0654	.1158	.1597	.1771	.1602
	10	.0000	.0002	.0020	.0099	.0308	.0686	.1171	.1593	.1762
	11	.0000	.0000	.0005	.0030	.0120	.0336	.0710	.1185	.1602
	12	.0000	.0000	.0001	.0008	.0039	.0136	.0355	.0727	.1201
	13	.0000	.0000	.0000	.0002	.0010	.0045	.0146	.0366	.0739
	14	.0000	.0000	.0000	.0000	.0002	.0012	.0049	.0150	.0370
	15	.0000	.0000	.0000	.0000	.0000	.0003	.0013	.0049	.0148
	16	.0000	.0000	.0000	.0000	.0000	.0000	.0003	.0013	.0046
	17	.0000	.0000	.0000	.0000	.0000	.0000	.0000	.0002	.0011
	18	.0000	.0000	.0000	.0000	.0000	.0000	.0000	.0000	.0002
	19	.0000	.0000	.0000	.0000	.0000	.0000	.0000	.0000	.0000
	20	.0000	.0000	.0000	.0000	.0000	.0000	.0000	.0000	.0000

TABLE 5   BINOMIAL PROBABILITIES (*Continued*)

						p				
n	*x*	.55	.60	.65	.70	.75	.80	.85	.90	.95
2	0	.2025	.1600	.1225	.0900	.0625	.0400	.0225	.0100	.0025
	1	.4950	.4800	.4550	.4200	.3750	.3200	.2550	.1800	.0950
	2	.3025	.3600	.4225	.4900	.5625	.6400	.7225	.8100	.9025
3	0	.0911	.0640	.0429	.0270	.0156	.0080	.0034	.0010	.0001
	1	.3341	.2880	.2389	.1890	.1406	.0960	.0574	.0270	.0071
	2	.4084	.4320	.4436	.4410	.4219	.3840	.3251	.2430	.1354
	3	.1664	.2160	.2746	.3430	.4219	.5120	.6141	.7290	.8574
4	0	.0410	.0256	.0150	.0081	.0039	.0016	.0005	.0001	.0000
	1	.2005	.1536	.1115	.0756	.0469	.0256	.0115	.0036	.0005
	2	.3675	.3456	.3105	.2646	.2109	.1536	.0975	.0486	.0135
	3	.2995	.3456	.3845	.4116	.4219	.4096	.3685	.2916	.1715
	4	.0915	.1296	.1785	.2401	.3164	.4096	.5220	.6561	.8145
5	0	.0185	.0102	.0053	.0024	.0010	.0003	.0001	.0000	.0000
	1	.1128	.0768	.0488	.0284	.0146	.0064	.0022	.0005	.0000
	2	.2757	.2304	.1811	.1323	.0879	.0512	.0244	.0081	.0011
	3	.3369	.3456	.3364	.3087	.2637	.2048	.1382	.0729	.0214
	4	.2059	.2592	.3124	.3601	.3955	.4096	.3915	.3281	.2036
	5	.0503	.0778	.1160	.1681	.2373	.3277	.4437	.5905	.7738
6	0	.0083	.0041	.0018	.0007	.0002	.0001	.0000	.0000	.0000
	1	.0609	.0369	.0205	.0102	.0044	.0015	.0004	.0001	.0000
	2	.1861	.1382	.0951	.0595	.0330	.0154	.0055	.0012	.0001
	3	.3032	.2765	.2355	.1852	.1318	.0819	.0415	.0146	.0021
	4	.2780	.3110	.3280	.3241	.2966	.2458	.1762	.0984	.0305
	5	.1359	.1866	.2437	.3025	.3560	.3932	.3993	.3543	.2321
	6	.0277	.0467	.0754	.1176	.1780	.2621	.3771	.5314	.7351
7	0	.0037	.0016	.0006	.0002	.0001	.0000	.0000	.0000	.0000
	1	.0320	.0172	.0084	.0036	.0013	.0004	.0001	.0000	.0000
	2	.1172	.0774	.0466	.0250	.0115	.0043	.0012	.0002	.0000
	3	.2388	.1935	.1442	.0972	.0577	.0287	.0109	.0026	.0002
	4	.2918	.2903	.2679	.2269	.1730	.1147	.0617	.0230	.0036
	5	.2140	.2613	.2985	.3177	.3115	.2753	.2097	.1240	.0406
	6	.0872	.1306	.1848	.2471	.3115	.3670	.3960	.3720	.2573
	7	.0152	.0280	.0490	.0824	.1335	.2097	.3206	.4783	.6983
8	0	.0017	.0007	.0002	.0001	.0000	.0000	.0000	.0000	.0000
	1	.0164	.0079	.0033	.0012	.0004	.0001	.0000	.0000	.0000
	2	.0703	.0413	.0217	.0100	.0038	.0011	.0002	.0000	.0000
	3	.1719	.1239	.0808	.0467	.0231	.0092	.0026	.0004	.0000
	4	.2627	.2322	.1875	.1361	.0865	.0459	.0185	.0046	.0004
	5	.2568	.2787	.2786	.2541	.2076	.1468	.0839	.0331	.0054
	6	.1569	.2090	.2587	.2965	.3115	.2936	.2376	.1488	.0515
	7	.0548	.0896	.1373	.1977	.2670	.3355	.3847	.3826	.2793
	8	.0084	.0168	.0319	.0576	.1001	.1678	.2725	.4305	.6634

TABLE 5   BINOMIAL PROBABILITIES (*Continued*)

n	x	.55	.60	.65	.70	.75	.80	.85	.90	.95
						p				
9	0	.0008	.0003	.0001	.0000	.0000	.0000	.0000	.0000	.0000
	1	.0083	.0035	.0013	.0004	.0001	.0000	.0000	.0000	.0000
	2	.0407	.0212	.0098	.0039	.0012	.0003	.0000	.0000	.0000
	3	.1160	.0743	.0424	.0210	.0087	.0028	.0006	.0001	.0000
	4	.2128	.1672	.1181	.0735	.0389	.0165	.0050	.0008	.0000
	5	.2600	.2508	.2194	.1715	.1168	.0661	.0283	.0074	.0006
	6	.2119	.2508	.2716	.2668	.2336	.1762	.1069	.0446	.0077
	7	.1110	.1612	.2162	.2668	.3003	.3020	.2597	.1722	.0629
	8	.0339	.0605	.1004	.1556	.2253	.3020	.3679	.3874	.2985
	9	.0046	.0101	.0207	.0404	.0751	.1342	.2316	.3874	.6302
10	0	.0003	.0001	.0000	.0000	.0000	.0000	.0000	.0000	.0000
	1	.0042	.0016	.0005	.0001	.0000	.0000	.0000	.0000	.0000
	2	.0229	.0106	.0043	.0014	.0004	.0001	.0000	.0000	.0000
	3	.0746	.0425	.0212	.0090	.0031	.0008	.0001	.0000	.0000
	4	.1596	.1115	.0689	.0368	.0162	.0055	.0012	.0001	.0000
	5	.2340	.2007	.1536	.1029	.0584	.0264	.0085	.0015	.0001
	6	.2384	.2508	.2377	.2001	.1460	.0881	.0401	.0112	.0010
	7	.1665	.2150	.2522	.2668	.2503	.2013	.1298	.0574	.0105
	8	.0763	.1209	.1757	.2335	.2816	.3020	.2759	.1937	.0746
	9	.0207	.0403	.0725	.1211	.1877	.2684	.3474	.3874	.3151
	10	.0025	.0060	.0135	.0282	.0563	.1074	.1969	.3487	.5987
12	0	.0001	.0000	.0000	.0000	.0000	.0000	.0000	.0000	.0000
	1	.0010	.0003	.0001	.0000	.0000	.0000	.0000	.0000	.0000
	2	.0068	.0025	.0008	.0002	.0000	.0000	.0000	.0000	.0000
	3	.0277	.0125	.0048	.0015	.0004	.0001	.0000	.0000	.0000
	4	.0762	.0420	.0199	.0078	.0024	.0005	.0001	.0000	.0000
	5	.1489	.1009	.0591	.0291	.0115	.0033	.0006	.0000	.0000
	6	.2124	.1766	.1281	.0792	.0401	.0155	.0040	.0005	.0000
	7	.2225	.2270	.2039	.1585	.1032	.0532	.0193	.0038	.0002
	8	.1700	.2128	.2367	.2311	.1936	.1329	.0683	.0213	.0021
	9	.0923	.1419	.1954	.2397	.2581	.2362	.1720	.0852	.0173
	10	.0339	.0639	.1088	.1678	.2323	.2835	.2924	.2301	.0988
	11	.0075	.0174	.0368	.0712	.1267	.2062	.3012	.3766	.3413
	12	.0008	.0022	.0057	.0138	.0317	.0687	.1422	.2824	.5404
15	0	.0000	.0000	.0000	.0000	.0000	.0000	.0000	.0000	.0000
	1	.0001	.0000	.0000	.0000	.0000	.0000	.0000	.0000	.0000
	2	.0010	.0003	.0001	.0000	.0000	.0000	.0000	.0000	.0000
	3	.0052	.0016	.0004	.0001	.0000	.0000	.0000	.0000	.0000
	4	.0191	.0074	.0024	.0006	.0001	.0000	.0000	.0000	.0000
	5	.0515	.0245	.0096	.0030	.0007	.0001	.0000	.0000	.0000
	6	.1048	.0612	.0298	.0116	.0034	.0007	.0001	.0000	.0000
	7	.1647	.1181	.0710	.0348	.0131	.0035	.0005	.0000	.0000
	8	.2013	.1771	.1319	.0811	.0393	.0138	.0030	.0003	.0000
	9	.1914	.2066	.1906	.1472	.0917	.0430	.0132	.0019	.0000
	10	.1404	.1859	.2123	.2061	.1651	.1032	.0449	.0105	.0006
	11	.0780	.1268	.1792	.2186	.2252	.1876	.1156	.0428	.0049

TABLE 5   BINOMIAL PROBABILITIES (*Continued*)

						p				
n	*x*	.55	.60	.65	.70	.75	.80	.85	.90	.95
	12	.0318	.0634	.1110	.1700	.2252	.2501	.2184	.1285	.0307
	13	.0090	.0219	.0476	.0916	.1559	.2309	.2856	.2669	.1348
	14	.0016	.0047	.0126	.0305	.0668	.1319	.2312	.3432	.3658
	15	.0001	.0005	.0016	.0047	.0134	.0352	.0874	.2059	.4633
18	0	.0000	.0000	.0000	.0000	.0000	.0000	.0000	.0000	.0000
	1	.0000	.0000	.0000	.0000	.0000	.0000	.0000	.0000	.0000
	2	.0001	.0000	.0000	.0000	.0000	.0000	.0000	.0000	.0000
	3	.0009	.0002	.0000	.0000	.0000	.0000	.0000	.0000	.0000
	4	.0039	.0011	.0002	.0000	.0000	.0000	.0000	.0000	.0000
	5	.0134	.0045	.0012	.0002	.0000	.0000	.0000	.0000	.0000
	6	.0354	.0145	.0047	.0012	.0002	.0000	.0000	.0000	.0000
	7	.0742	.0374	.0151	.0046	.0010	.0001	.0000	.0000	.0000
	8	.1248	.0771	.0385	.0149	.0042	.0008	.0001	.0000	.0000
	9	.1694	.1284	.0794	.0386	.0139	.0033	.0004	.0000	.0000
	10	.1864	.1734	.1327	.0811	.0376	.0120	.0022	.0002	.0000
	11	.1657	.1892	.1792	.1376	.0820	.0350	.0091	.0010	.0000
	12	.1181	.1655	.1941	.1873	.1436	.0816	.0301	.0052	.0002
	13	.0666	.1146	.1664	.2017	.1988	.1507	.0787	.0218	.0014
	14	.0291	.0614	.1104	.1681	.2130	.2153	.1592	.0700	.0093
	15	.0095	.0246	.0547	.1046	.1704	.2297	.2406	.1680	.0473
	16	.0022	.0069	.0190	.0458	.0958	.1723	.2556	.2835	.1683
	17	.0003	.0012	.0042	.0126	.0338	.0811	.1704	.3002	.3763
	18	.0000	.0001	.0004	.0016	.0056	.0180	.0536	.1501	.3972
20	0	.0000	.0000	.0000	.0000	.0000	.0000	.0000	.0000	.0000
	1	.0000	.0000	.0000	.0000	.0000	.0000	.0000	.0000	.0000
	2	.0000	.0000	.0000	.0000	.0000	.0000	.0000	.0000	.0000
	3	.0002	.0000	.0000	.0000	.0000	.0000	.0000	.0000	.0000
	4	.0013	.0003	.0000	.0000	.0000	.0000	.0000	.0000	.0000
	5	.0049	.0013	.0003	.0000	.0000	.0000	.0000	.0000	.0000
	6	.0150	.0049	.0012	.0002	.0000	.0000	.0000	.0000	.0000
	7	.0366	.0146	.0045	.0010	.0002	.0000	.0000	.0000	.0000
	8	.0727	.0355	.0136	.0039	.0008	.0001	.0000	.0000	.0000
	9	.1185	.0710	.0336	.0120	.0030	.0005	.0000	.0000	.0000
	10	.1593	.1171	.0686	.0308	.0099	.0020	.0002	.0000	.0000
	11	.1771	.1597	.1158	.0654	.0271	.0074	.0011	.0001	.0000
	12	.1623	.1797	.1614	.1144	.0609	.0222	.0046	.0004	.0000
	13	.1221	.1659	.1844	.1643	.1124	.0545	.0160	.0020	.0000
	14	.0746	.1244	.1712	.1916	.1686	.1091	.0454	.0089	.0003
	15	.0365	.0746	.1272	.1789	.2023	.1746	.1028	.0319	.0022
	16	.0139	.0350	.0738	.1304	.1897	.2182	.1821	.0898	.0133
	17	.0040	.0123	.0323	.0716	.1339	.2054	.2428	.1901	.0596
	18	.0008	.0031	.0100	.0278	.0669	.1369	.2293	.2852	.1887
	19	.0001	.0005	.0020	.0068	.0211	.0576	.1368	.2702	.3774
	20	.0000	.0000	.0002	.0008	.0032	.0115	.0388	.1216	.3585

TABLE 6 VALUES OF $e^{-\mu}$

μ	$e^{-\mu}$	μ	$e^{-\mu}$	μ	$e^{-\mu}$
.00	1.0000	2.00	.1353	4.00	.0183
.05	.9512	2.05	.1287	4.05	.0174
.10	.9048	2.10	.1225	4.10	.0166
.15	.8607	2.15	.1165	4.15	.0158
.20	.8187	2.20	.1108	4.20	.0150
.25	.7788	2.25	.1054	4.25	.0143
.30	.7408	2.30	.1003	4.30	.0136
.35	.7047	2.35	.0954	4.35	.0129
.40	.6703	2.40	.0907	4.40	.0123
.45	.6376	2.45	.0863	4.45	.0117
.50	.6065	2.50	.0821	4.50	.0111
.55	.5769	2.55	.0781	4.55	.0106
.60	.5488	2.60	.0743	4.60	.0101
.65	.5220	2.65	.0707	4.65	.0096
.70	.4966	2.70	.0672	4.70	.0091
.75	.4724	2.75	.0639	4.75	.0087
.80	.4493	2.80	.0608	4.80	.0082
.85	.4274	2.85	.0578	4.85	.0078
.90	.4066	2.90	.0550	4.90	.0074
.95	.3867	2.95	.0523	4.95	.0071
1.00	.3679	3.00	.0498	5.00	.0067
1.05	.3499	3.05	.0474	6.00	.0025
1.10	.3329	3.10	.0450	7.00	.0009
1.15	.3166	3.15	.0429	8.00	.000335
1.20	.3012	3.20	.0408	9.00	.000123
				10.00	.000045
1.25	.2865	3.25	.0388		
1.30	.2725	3.30	.0369		
1.35	.2592	3.35	.0351		
1.40	.2466	3.40	.0334		
1.45	.2346	3.45	.0317		
1.50	.2231	3.50	.0302		
1.55	.2122	3.55	.0287		
1.60	.2019	3.60	.0273		
1.65	.1920	3.65	.0260		
1.70	.1827	3.70	.0247		
1.75	.1738	3.75	.0235		
1.80	.1653	3.80	.0224		
1.85	.1572	3.85	.0213		
1.90	.1496	3.90	.0202		
1.95	.1423	3.95	.0193		

TABLE 7   POISSON PROBABILITIES

Entries in the table give the probability of x occurrences for a Poisson process with a mean μ. For example, when $\mu = 2.5$, the probability of four occurrences is .1336.

					μ					
x	0.1	0.2	0.3	0.4	0.5	0.6	0.7	0.8	0.9	1.0
0	.9048	.8187	.7408	.6703	.6065	.5488	.4966	.4493	.4066	.3679
1	.0905	.1637	.2222	.2681	.3033	.3293	.3476	.3595	.3659	.3679
2	.0045	.0164	.0333	.0536	.0758	.0988	.1217	.1438	.1647	.1839
3	.0002	.0011	.0033	.0072	.0126	.0198	.0284	.0383	.0494	.0613
4	.0000	.0001	.0002	.0007	.0016	.0030	.0050	.0077	.0111	.0153
5	.0000	.0000	.0000	.0001	.0002	.0004	.0007	.0012	.0020	.0031
6	.0000	.0000	.0000	.0000	.0000	.0000	.0001	.0002	.0003	.0005
7	.0000	.0000	.0000	.0000	.0000	.0000	.0000	.0000	.0000	.0001

					μ					
x	1.1	1.2	1.3	1.4	1.5	1.6	1.7	1.8	1.9	2.0
0	.3329	.3012	.2725	.2466	.2231	.2019	.1827	.1653	.1496	.1353
1	.3662	.3614	.3543	.3452	.3347	.3230	.3106	.2975	.2842	.2707
2	.2014	.2169	.2303	.2417	.2510	.2584	.2640	.2678	.2700	.2707
3	.0738	.0867	.0998	.1128	.1255	.1378	.1496	.1607	.1710	.1804
4	.0203	.0260	.0324	.0395	.0471	.0551	.0636	.0723	.0812	.0902
5	.0045	.0062	.0084	.0111	.0141	.0176	.0216	.0260	.0309	.0361
6	.0008	.0012	.0018	.0026	.0035	.0047	.0061	.0078	.0098	.0120
7	.0001	.0002	.0003	.0005	.0008	.0011	.0015	.0020	.0027	.0034
8	.0000	.0000	.0001	.0001	.0001	.0002	.0003	.0005	.0006	.0009
9	.0000	.0000	.0000	.0000	.0000	.0000	.0001	.0001	.0001	.0002

					μ					
x	2.1	2.2	2.3	2.4	2.5	2.6	2.7	2.8	2.9	3.0
0	.1225	.1108	.1003	.0907	.0821	.0743	.0672	.0608	.0550	.0498
1	.2572	.2438	.2306	.2177	.2052	.1931	.1815	.1703	.1596	.1494
2	.2700	.2681	.2652	.2613	.2565	.2510	.2450	.2384	.2314	.2240
3	.1890	.1966	.2033	.2090	.2138	.2176	.2205	.2225	.2237	.2240
4	.0992	.1082	.1169	.1254	.1336	.1414	.1488	.1557	.1622	.1680
5	.0417	.0476	.0538	.0602	.0668	.0735	.0804	.0872	.0940	.1008
6	.0146	.0174	.0206	.0241	.0278	.0319	.0362	.0407	.0455	.0504
7	.0044	.0055	.0068	.0083	.0099	.0118	.0139	.0163	.0188	.0216
8	.0011	.0015	.0019	.0025	.0031	.0038	.0047	.0057	.0068	.0081
9	.0003	.0004	.0005	.0007	.0009	.0011	.0014	.0018	.0022	.0027
10	.0001	.0001	.0001	.0002	.0002	.0003	.0004	.0005	.0006	.0008
11	.0000	.0000	.0000	.0000	.0000	.0001	.0001	.0001	.0002	.0002
12	.0000	.0000	.0000	.0000	.0000	.0000	.0000	.0000	.0000	.0001

TABLE 7   POISSON PROBABILITIES (*Continued*)

					μ					
x	3.1	3.2	3.3	3.4	3.5	3.6	3.7	3.8	3.9	4.0
0	.0450	.0408	.0369	.0344	.0302	.0273	.0247	.0224	.0202	.0183
1	.1397	.1304	.1217	.1135	.1057	.0984	.0915	.0850	.0789	.0733
2	.2165	.2087	.2008	.1929	.1850	.1771	.1692	.1615	.1539	.1465
3	.2237	.2226	.2209	.2186	.2158	.2125	.2087	.2046	.2001	.1954
4	.1734	.1781	.1823	.1858	.1888	.1912	.1931	.1944	.1951	.1954
5	.1075	.1140	.1203	.1264	.1322	.1377	.1429	.1477	.1522	.1563
6	.0555	.0608	.0662	.0716	.0771	.0826	.0881	.0936	.0989	.1042
7	.0246	.0278	.0312	.0348	.0385	.0425	.0466	.0508	.0551	.0595
8	.0095	.0111	.0129	.0148	.0169	.0191	.0215	.0241	.0269	.0298
9	.0033	.0040	.0047	.0056	.0066	.0076	.0089	.0102	.0116	.0132
10	.0010	.0013	.0016	.0019	.0023	.0028	.0033	.0039	.0045	.0053
11	.0003	.0004	.0005	.0006	.0007	.0009	.0011	.0013	.0016	.0019
12	.0001	.0001	.0001	.0002	.0002	.0003	.0003	.0004	.0005	.0006
13	.0000	.0000	.0000	.0000	.0001	.0001	.0001	.0001	.0002	.0002
14	.0000	.0000	.0000	.0000	.0000	.0000	.0000	.0000	.0000	.0001

					μ					
x	4.1	4.2	4.3	4.4	4.5	4.6	4.7	4.8	4.9	5.0
0	.0166	.0150	.0136	.0123	.0111	.0101	.0091	.0082	.0074	.0067
1	.0679	.0630	.0583	.0540	.0500	.0462	.0427	.0395	.0365	.0337
2	.1393	.1323	.1254	.1188	.1125	.1063	.1005	.0948	.0894	.0842
3	.1904	.1852	.1798	.1743	.1687	.1631	.1574	.1517	.1460	.1404
4	.1951	.1944	.1933	.1917	.1898	.1875	.1849	.1820	.1789	.1755
5	.1600	.1633	.1662	.1687	.1708	.1725	.1738	.1747	.1753	.1755
6	.1093	.1143	.1191	.1237	.1281	.1323	.1362	.1398	.1432	.1462
7	.0640	.0686	.0732	.0778	.0824	.0869	.0914	.0959	.1002	.1044
8	.0328	.0360	.0393	.0428	.0463	.0500	.0537	.0575	.0614	.0653
9	.0150	.0168	.0188	.0209	.0232	.0255	.0280	.0307	.0334	.0363
10	.0061	.0071	.0081	.0092	.0104	.0118	.0132	.0147	.0164	.0181
11	.0023	.0027	.0032	.0037	.0043	.0049	.0056	.0064	.0073	.0082
12	.0008	.0009	.0011	.0014	.0016	.0019	.0022	.0026	.0030	.0034
13	.0002	.0003	.0004	.0005	.0006	.0007	.0008	.0009	.0011	.0013
14	.0001	.0001	.0001	.0001	.0002	.0002	.0003	.0003	.0004	.0005
15	.0000	.0000	.0000	.0000	.0001	.0001	.0001	.0001	.0001	.0002

					μ					
x	5.1	5.2	5.3	5.4	5.5	5.6	5.7	5.8	5.9	6.0
0	.0061	.0055	.0050	.0045	.0041	.0037	.0033	.0030	.0027	.0025
1	.0311	.0287	.0265	.0244	.0225	.0207	.0191	.0176	.0162	.0149
2	.0793	.0746	.0701	.0659	.0618	.0580	.0544	.0509	.0477	.0446
3	.1348	.1293	.1239	.1185	.1133	.1082	.1033	.0985	.0938	.0892
4	.1719	.1681	.1641	.1600	.1558	.1515	.1472	.1428	.1383	.1339

TABLE 7   POISSON PROBABILITIES (*Continued*)

x	5.1	5.2	5.3	5.4	5.5	5.6	5.7	5.8	5.9	6.0
5	.1753	.1748	.1740	.1728	.1714	.1697	.1678	.1656	.1632	.1606
6	.1490	.1515	.1537	.1555	.1571	.1587	.1594	.1601	.1605	.1606
7	.1086	.1125	.1163	.1200	.1234	.1267	.1298	.1326	.1353	.1377
8	.0692	.0731	.0771	.0810	.0849	.0887	.0925	.0962	.0998	.1033
9	.0392	.0423	.0454	.0486	.0519	.0552	.0586	.0620	.0654	.0688
10	.0200	.0220	.0241	.0262	.0285	.0309	.0334	.0359	.0386	.0413
11	.0093	.0104	.0116	.0129	.0143	.0157	.0173	.0190	.0207	.0225
12	.0039	.0045	.0051	.0058	.0065	.0073	.0082	.0092	.0102	.0113
13	.0015	.0018	.0021	.0024	.0028	.0032	.0036	.0041	.0046	.0052
14	.0006	.0007	.0008	.0009	.0011	.0013	.0015	.0017	.0019	.0022
15	.0002	.0002	.0003	.0003	.0004	.0005	.0006	.0007	.0008	.0009
16	.0001	.0001	.0001	.0001	.0001	.0002	.0002	.0002	.0003	.0003
17	.0000	.0000	.0000	.0000	.0000	.0001	.0001	.0001	.0001	.0001

μ

x	6.1	6.2	6.3	6.4	6.5	6.6	6.7	6.8	6.9	7.0
0	.0022	.0020	.0018	.0017	.0015	.0014	.0012	.0011	.0010	.0009
1	.0137	.0126	.0116	.0106	.0098	.0090	.0082	.0076	.0070	.0064
2	.0417	.0390	.0364	.0340	.0318	.0296	.0276	.0258	.0240	.0223
3	.0848	.0806	.0765	.0726	.0688	.0652	.0617	.0584	.0552	.0521
4	.1294	.1249	.1205	.1162	.1118	.1076	.1034	.0992	.0952	.0912
5	.1579	.1549	.1519	.1487	.1454	.1420	.1385	.1349	.1314	.1277
6	.1605	.1601	.1595	.1586	.1575	.1562	.1546	.1529	.1511	.1490
7	.1399	.1418	.1435	.1450	.1462	.1472	.1480	.1486	.1489	.1490
8	.1066	.1099	.1130	.1160	.1188	.1215	.1240	.1263	.1284	.1304
9	.0723	.0757	.0791	.0825	.0858	.0891	.0923	.0954	.0985	.1014
10	.0441	.0469	.0498	.0528	.0558	.0588	.0618	.0649	.0679	.0710
11	.0245	.0265	.0285	.0307	.0330	.0353	.0377	.0401	.0426	.0452
12	.0124	.0137	.0150	.0164	.0179	.0194	.0210	.0227	.0245	.0264
13	.0058	.0065	.0073	.0081	.0089	.0098	.0108	.0119	.0130	.0142
14	.0025	.0029	.0033	.0037	.0041	.0046	.0052	.0058	.0064	.0071
15	.0010	.0012	.0014	.0016	.0018	.0020	.0023	.0026	.0029	.0033
16	.0004	.0005	.0005	.0006	.0007	.0008	.0010	.0011	.0013	.0014
17	.0001	.0002	.0002	.0002	.0003	.0003	.0004	.0004	.0005	.0006
18	.0000	.0001	.0001	.0001	.0001	.0001	.0001	.0002	.0002	.0002
19	.0000	.0000	.0000	.0000	.0000	.0000	.0000	.0001	.0001	.0001

μ

x	7.1	7.2	7.3	7.4	7.5	7.6	7.7	7.8	7.9	8.0
0	.0008	.0007	.0007	.0006	.0006	.0005	.0005	.0004	.0004	.0003
1	.0059	.0054	.0049	.0045	.0041	.0038	.0035	.0032	.0029	.0027
2	.0208	.0194	.0180	.0167	.0156	.0145	.0134	.0125	.0116	.0107
3	.0492	.0464	.0438	.0413	.0389	.0366	.0345	.0324	.0305	.0286
4	.0874	.0836	.0799	.0764	.0729	.0696	.0663	.0632	.0602	.0573

TABLE 7   POISSON PROBABILITIES (*Continued*)

					μ					
x	7.1	7.2	7.3	7.4	7.5	7.6	7.7	7.8	7.9	8.0
5	.1241	.1204	.1167	.1130	.1094	.1057	.1021	.0986	.0951	.0916
6	.1468	.1445	.1420	.1394	.1367	.1339	.1311	.1282	.1252	.1221
7	.1489	.1486	.1481	.1474	.1465	.1454	.1442	.1428	.1413	.1396
8	.1321	.1337	.1351	.1363	.1373	.1382	.1388	.1392	.1395	.1396
9	.1042	.1070	.1096	.1121	.1144	.1167	.1187	.1207	.1224	.1241
10	.0740	.0770	.0800	.0829	.0858	.0887	.0914	.0941	.0967	.0993
11	.0478	.0504	.0531	.0558	.0585	.0613	.0640	.0667	.0695	.0722
12	.0283	.0303	.0323	.0344	.0366	.0388	.0411	.0434	.0457	.0481
13	.0154	.0168	.0181	.0196	.0211	.0227	.0243	.0260	.0278	.0296
14	.0078	.0086	.0095	.0104	.0113	.0123	.0134	.0145	.0157	.0169
15	.0037	.0041	.0046	.0051	.0057	.0062	.0069	.0075	.0083	.0090
16	.0016	.0019	.0021	.0024	.0026	.0030	.0033	.0037	.0041	.0045
17	.0007	.0008	.0009	.0010	.0012	.0013	.0015	.0017	.0019	.0021
18	.0003	.0003	.0004	.0004	.0005	.0006	.0006	.0007	.0008	.0009
19	.0001	.0001	.0001	.0002	.0002	.0002	.0003	.0003	.0003	.0004
20	.0000	.0000	.0001	.0001	.0001	.0001	.0001	.0001	.0001	.0002
21	.0000	.0000	.0000	.0000	.0000	.0000	.0000	.0000	.0001	.0001

					μ					
x	8.1	8.2	8.3	8.4	8.5	8.6	8.7	8.8	8.9	9.0
0	.0003	.0003	.0002	.0002	.0002	.0002	.0002	.0002	.0001	.0001
1	.0025	.0023	.0021	.0019	.0017	.0016	.0014	.0013	.0012	.0011
2	.0100	.0092	.0086	.0079	.0074	.0068	.0063	.0058	.0054	.0050
3	.0269	.0252	.0237	.0222	.0208	.0195	.0183	.0171	.0160	.0150
4	.0544	.0517	.0491	.0466	.0443	.0420	.0398	.0377	.0357	.0337
5	.0882	.0849	.0816	.0784	.0752	.0722	.0692	.0663	.0635	.0607
6	.1191	.1160	.1128	.1097	.1066	.1034	.1003	.0972	.0941	.0911
7	.1378	.1358	.1338	.1317	.1294	.1271	.1247	.1222	.1197	.1171
8	.1395	.1392	.1388	.1382	.1375	.1366	.1356	.1344	.1332	.1318
9	.1256	.1269	.1280	.1290	.1299	.1306	.1311	.1315	.1317	.1318
10	.1017	.1040	.1063	.1084	.1104	.1123	.1140	.1157	.1172	.1186
11	.0749	.0776	.0802	.0828	.0853	.0878	.0902	.0925	.0948	.0970
12	.0505	.0530	.0555	.0579	.0604	.0629	.0654	.0679	.0703	.0728
13	.0315	.0334	.0354	.0374	.0395	.0416	.0438	.0459	.0481	.0504
14	.0182	.0196	.0210	.0225	.0240	.0256	.0272	.0289	.0306	.0324
15	.0098	.0107	.0116	.0126	.0136	.0147	.0158	.0169	.0182	.1094
16	.0050	.0055	.0060	.0066	.0072	.0079	.0086	.0093	.0101	.0109
17	.0024	.0026	.0029	.0033	.0036	.0040	.0044	.0048	.0053	.0058
18	.0011	.0012	.0014	.0015	.0017	.0019	.0021	.0024	.0026	.0029
19	.0005	.0005	.0006	.0007	.0008	.0009	.0010	.0011	.0012	.0014
20	.0002	.0002	.0002	.0003	.0003	.0004	.0004	.0005	.0005	.0006
21	.0001	.0001	.0001	.0001	.0001	.0002	.0002	.0002	.0002	.0003
22	.0000	.0000	.0000	.0000	.0001	.0001	.0001	.0001	.0001	.0001

TABLE 7   POISSON PROBABILITIES (*Continued*)

					μ					
x	9.1	9.2	9.3	9.4	9.5	9.6	9.7	9.8	9.9	10
0	.0001	.0001	.0001	.0001	.0001	.0001	.0001	.0001	.0001	.0000
1	.0010	.0009	.0009	.0008	.0007	.0007	.0006	.0005	.0005	.0005
2	.0046	.0043	.0040	.0037	.0034	.0031	.0029	.0027	.0025	.0023
3	.0140	.0131	.0123	.0115	.0107	.0100	.0093	.0087	.0081	.0076
4	.0319	.0302	.0285	.0269	.0254	.0240	.0226	.0213	.0201	.0189
5	.0581	.0555	.0530	.0506	.0483	.0460	.0439	.0418	.0398	.0378
6	.0881	.0851	.0822	.0793	.0764	.0736	.0709	.0682	.0656	.0631
7	.1145	.1118	.1091	.1064	.1037	.1010	.0982	.0955	.0928	.0901
8	.1302	.1286	.1269	.1251	.1232	.1212	.1191	.1170	.1148	.1126
9	.1317	.1315	.1311	.1306	.1300	.1293	.1284	.1274	.1263	.1251
10	.1198	.1210	.1219	.1228	.1235	.1241	.1245	.1249	.1250	.1251
11	.0991	.1012	.1031	.1049	.1067	.1083	.1098	.1112	.1125	.1137
12	.0752	.0776	.0799	.0822	.0844	.0866	.0888	.0908	.0928	.0948
13	.0526	.0549	.0572	.0594	.0617	.0640	.0662	.0685	.0707	.0729
14	.0342	.0361	.0380	.0399	.0419	.0439	.0459	.0479	.0500	.0521
15	.0208	.0221	.0235	.0250	.0265	.0281	.0297	.0313	.0330	.0347
16	.0118	.0127	.0137	.0147	.0157	.0168	.0180	.0192	.0204	.0217
17	.0063	.0069	.0075	.0081	.0088	.0095	.0103	.0111	.0119	.0128
18	.0032	.0035	.0039	.0042	.0046	.0051	.0055	.0060	.0065	.0071
19	.0015	.0017	.0019	.0021	.0023	.0026	.0028	.0031	.0034	.0037
20	.0007	.0008	.0009	.0010	.0011	.0012	.0014	.0015	.0017	.0019
21	.0003	.0003	.0004	.0004	.0005	.0006	.0006	.0007	.0008	.0009
22	.0001	.0001	.0002	.0002	.0002	.0002	.0003	.0003	.0004	.0004
23	.0000	.0001	.0001	.0001	.0001	.0001	.0001	.0001	.0002	.0002
24	.0000	.0000	.0000	.0000	.0000	.0000	.0000	.0001	.0001	.0001

					μ					
x	11	12	13	14	15	16	17	18	19	20
0	.0000	.0000	.0000	.0000	.0000	.0000	.0000	.0000	.0000	.0000
1	.0002	.0001	.0000	.0000	.0000	.0000	.0000	.0000	.0000	.0000
2	.0010	.0004	.0002	.0001	.0000	.0000	.0000	.0000	.0000	.0000
3	.0037	.0018	.0008	.0004	.0002	.0001	.0000	.0000	.0000	.0000
4	.0102	.0053	.0027	.0013	.0006	.0003	.0001	.0001	.0000	.0000
5	.0224	.0127	.0070	.0037	.0019	.0010	.0005	.0002	.0001	.0001
6	.0411	.0255	.0152	.0087	.0048	.0026	.0014	.0007	.0004	.0002
7	.0646	.0437	.0281	.0174	.0104	.0060	.0034	.0018	.0010	.0005
8	.0888	.0655	.0457	.0304	.0194	.0120	.0072	.0042	.0024	.0013
9	.1085	.0874	.0661	.0473	.0324	.0213	.0135	.0083	.0050	.0029
10	.1194	.1048	.0859	.0663	.0486	.0341	.0230	.0150	.0095	.0058
11	.1194	.1144	.1015	.0844	.0663	.0496	.0355	.0245	.0164	.0106
12	.1094	.1144	.1099	.0984	.0829	.0661	.0504	.0368	.0259	.0176
13	.0926	.1056	.1099	.1060	.0956	.0814	.0658	.0509	.0378	.0271
14	.0728	.0905	.1021	.1060	.1024	.0930	.0800	.0655	.0514	.0387

TABLE 7   POISSON PROBABILITIES (*Continued*)

					μ					
x	11	12	13	14	15	16	17	18	19	20
15	.0534	.0724	.0885	.0989	.1024	.0992	.0906	.0786	.0650	.0516
16	.0367	.0543	.0719	.0866	.0960	.0992	.0963	.0884	.0772	.0646
17	.0237	.0383	.0550	.0713	.0847	.0934	.0963	.0936	.0863	.0760
18	.0145	.0256	.0397	.0554	.0706	.0830	.0909	.0936	.0911	.0844
19	.0084	.0161	.0272	.0409	.0557	.0699	.0814	.0887	.0911	.0888
20	.0046	.0097	.0177	.0286	.0418	.0559	.0692	.0798	.0866	.0888
21	.0024	.0055	.0109	.0191	.0299	.0426	.0560	.0684	.0783	.0846
22	.0012	.0030	.0065	.0121	.0204	.0310	.0433	.0560	.0676	.0769
23	.0006	.0016	.0037	.0074	.0133	.0216	.0320	.0438	.0559	.0669
24	.0003	.0008	.0020	.0043	.0083	.0144	.0226	.0328	.0442	.0557
25	.0001	.0004	.0010	.0024	.0050	.0092	.0154	.0237	.0336	.0446
26	.0000	.0002	.0005	.0013	.0029	.0057	.0101	.0164	.0246	.0343
27	.0000	.0001	.0002	.0007	.0016	.0034	.0063	.0109	.0173	.0254
28	.0000	.0000	.0001	.0003	.0009	.0019	.0038	.0070	.0117	.0181
29	.0000	.0000	.0001	.0002	.0004	.0011	.0023	.0044	.0077	.0125
30	.0000	.0000	.0000	.0001	.0002	.0006	.0013	.0026	.0049	.0083
31	.0000	.0000	.0000	.0000	.0001	.0003	.0007	.0015	.0030	.0054
32	.0000	.0000	.0000	.0000	.0001	.0001	.0004	.0009	.0018	.0034
33	.0000	.0000	.0000	.0000	.0000	.0001	.0002	.0005	.0010	.0020
34	.0000	.0000	.0000	.0000	.0000	.0000	.0001	.0002	.0006	.0012
35	.0000	.0000	.0000	.0000	.0000	.0000	.0000	.0001	.0003	.0007
36	.0000	.0000	.0000	.0000	.0000	.0000	.0000	.0001	.0002	.0004
37	.0000	.0000	.0000	.0000	.0000	.0000	.0000	.0000	.0001	.0002
38	.0000	.0000	.0000	.0000	.0000	.0000	.0000	.0000	.0000	.0001
39	.0000	.0000	.0000	.0000	.0000	.0000	.0000	.0000	.0000	.0001

Appendix C: Summation Notation

Appendix C is available online.

Appendix D: Self-Test Solutions and Answers to Even-Numbered Exercises

Chapter 1

2. a. 10
b. 5
c. Categorical variables: Size and Fuel Quantitiative variables: Cylinders, City MPG, and Highway MPG
d.

Variable	Measurement Scale
Size	Ordinal
Cylinders	Ratio
City MPG	Ratio
Highway MPG	Ratio
Fuel	Nominal

3. a. Average for city driving = 182/10 = 18.2 mpg
b. Average for highway driving = 261/10 = 26.1 mpg
On average, the miles per gallon for highway driving is 7.9 mpg greater than for city driving
c. 3 of 10 or 30% have four-cyclinder engines
d. 6 of 10 or 60% use regular fuel

4. a. 8
b. Categorical: Voice Quality and Handset on Base Quantitative: Price, Overall Score, and Talk Time
c. Price—ratio
Overall Score—interval
Voice Quality—ordinal
Handset on Base—nominal
Talk Time—ratio

6. a. Categorical
b. Quantitative
c. Categorical
d. Quantitative
e. Quantitative

8. a. 1015
b. Categorical
c. Percentages
d. .10(1015) = 101.5; 101 or 102 respondents

10. a. Categorical
b. Percentages
c. 15%
d. Support against

12. a. All visitors to Hawaii
b. Yes
c. First and fourth questions provide quantitative data
Second and third questions provide categorical data

13. a. Federal spending ($ trillions)
b. Quantitative
c. Time series
d. Federal spending has increased over time

14. a. Graph with time series line for each company
b. Hertz leader in 2007–2008; Avis increasing and now similar to Hertz; Dollar declining
c. A bar chart of cross-sectional data
Bar heights: Hertz 290, Dollar 108, Avis 270

18. a. 67%
b. 612
c. Categorical

20. a. 43% of managers were bullish or very bullish, and 21% of managers expected health care to be the leading industry over the next 12 months
b. The average 12-month return estimate is 11.2% for the population of investment managers
c. The sample average of 2.5 years is an estimate of how long the population of investment managers think it will take to resume sustainable growth

22. a. The population consists of all customers of the chain stores in Charlotte, North Carolina
b. Some of the ways the grocery store chain could use to collect the data are
- Customers entering or leaving the store could be surveyed
- A survey could be mailed to customers who have a shopper's club card
- Customers could be given a printed survey when they check out
- Customers could be given a coupon that asks them to complete a brief online survey; if they do, they will receive a 5% discount on their next shopping trip

24. a. Correct
b. Incorrect
c. Correct
d. Incorrect
e. Incorrect

Chapter 2

2. a. .20
b. 40
c/d.

Class	Frequency	Percent Frequency
A	44	22
B	36	18
C	80	40
D	40	20
Total	200	100

3. a. $360° \times 58/120 = 174°$
b. $360° \times 42/120 = 126°$
c.

48.3%

d.

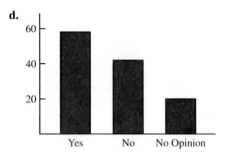

4. a. These data are categorical

b.

Show	Relative Frequency	Percent Frequency
Jep	10	20
JJ	8	16
OWS	7	14
THM	12	24
WoF	13	26
Total	50	100

c.

Syndicated Television Show

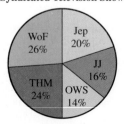

d. The largest viewing audience is for *Wheel of Fortune* and the second largest is for *Two and a Half Men*

6. a.

Network	Relative Frequency	Percent Frequency
ABC	6	24
CBS	9	36
FOX	1	4
NBC	9	36
Total	25	100

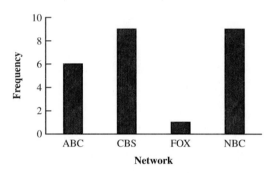

b. For these data, NBC and CBS tie for the number of top-rated shows; each has 9 (36%) of the top 25; ABC is third with 6 (24%) and the much younger FOX network has 1 (4%)

7. a.

Rating	Frequency	Percent Frequency
Excellent	20	40
Very Good	23	46
Good	4	8
Fair	1	2
Poor	2	4
Total	50	100

Management should be very pleased; 86% of the ratings are very good or excellent.

b. Review explanations from the three with Fair or Poor ratings to identify reasons for the low ratings

8. a.

Position	Frequency	Relative Frequency
P	17	.309
H	4	.073
1	5	.091
2	4	.073
3	2	.036
S	5	.091
L	6	.109
C	5	.091
R	7	.127
Totals	55	1.000

b. Pitcher
c. 3rd base
d. Right field
e. Infielders 16 to outfielders 18

10. a/b.

Rating	Frequency	Percent Frequency
Excellent	187	28.8
Very Good	252	38.8
Average	107	16.5
Poor	62	9.6
Terrible	41	6.3
Total	649	100.0

c.

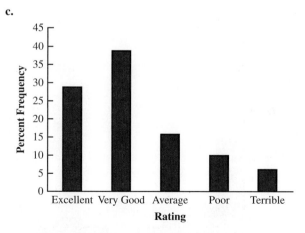

d. 67.7% rated the hotel as Excellent or Very Good; but 15.9% rated the hotel as Poor or Terrible

e. Grand California had better ratings.

12.

Class	Cumulative Frequency	Cumulative Relative Frequency
≤19	10	.20
≤29	24	.48
≤39	41	.82
≤49	48	.96
≤59	50	1.00

14. b/c.

Class	Frequency	Percent Frequency
6.0–7.9	4	20
8.0–9.9	2	10
10.0–11.9	8	40
12.0–13.9	3	15
14.0–15.9	3	15
Totals	20	100

15. Leaf unit = .1

```
 6 | 3
 7 | 5  5  7
 8 | 1  3  4  8
 9 | 3  6
10 | 0  4  5
11 | 3
```

16. Leaf unit = 10

```
11 | 6
12 | 0  2
13 | 0  6  7
14 | 2  2  7
15 | 5
16 | 0  2  8
17 | 0  2  3
```

17. a/b.

Waiting Time	Frequency	Relative Frequency
0–4	4	.20
5–9	8	.40
10–14	5	.25
15–19	2	.10
20–24	1	.05
Totals	20	1.00

c/d.

Waiting Time	Cumulative Frequency	Cumulative Relative Frequency
≤4	4	.20
≤9	12	.60
≤14	17	.85
≤19	19	.95
≤24	20	1.00

e. 12/20 = .60

18. a/b/c.

PPG	Frequency	Relative Frequency	Cumulative Percent Frequency
10–11.9	1	.02	2
12–13.9	3	.06	8
14–15.9	7	.14	22
16–17.9	19	.38	60
18–19.9	9	.18	78
20–21.9	4	.08	86
22–23.9	2	.04	90
24–25.9	0	.00	90
26–27.9	3	.06	96
28–29.9	2	.04	100
Total	50	1	

d.

e. There is skewness to the right
f. (11/50)(100) = 22%

20. a. Lowest = 12, Highest = 23
b.

Hours in Meetings per Week	Frequency	Percent Frequency
11–12	1	4
13–14	2	8
15–16	6	24
17–18	3	12
19–20	5	20
21–22	4	16
23–24	4	16
	25	100

c.

Hours per Week in Meetings

d. The distribution is slightly skewed to the left

22. a.

# U.S. Locations	Frequency	Percent Frequency
0–4999	10	50
5000–9999	3	15
10000–14999	2	10
15000–19999	1	5
20000–24999	0	0
25000–29999	1	5
30000–34999	2	10
35000–39999	1	5
Total:	20	100

b.

Number of U.S. Locations

c. The distribution is skewed to the right; the majority of the franchises in this list have fewer than 20,000 locations (50% + 15% + 15% = 80%); McDonald's, Subway, and 7-Eleven have the highest number of locations

24.

Median Pay		Top Pay	
6	6 7 7	10	0 6 9
7	2 4 6 7 7 8 9	11	1 6 9
8	0 0 1 3 7	12	2 5 6
9	9	13	0 5 8 8
10	0 6	14	0 6
11	0	15	2 5 7
12	1	16	
		17	
		18	
		19	
		20	
		21	4
		22	1

The median pay for these careers is generally in the $70 and $80 thousands. The top pay is rather evenly distributed between $100 and $160 thousand.

26. a.

2	14
2	67
3	011123
3	5677
4	003333344
4	6679
5	00022
5	5679
6	14
6	6
7	2

b. 40–44 with 9
c. 43 with 5

27. a.

		y		
		1	2	Total
	A	5	0	5
x	B	11	2	13
	C	2	10	12
	Total	18	12	30

b.

		y		
		1	2	Total
	A	100.0	0.0	100.0
x	B	84.6	15.4	100.0
	C	16.7	83.3	100.0

c.

		y	
		1	2
	A	27.8	0.0
x	B	61.1	16.7
	C	11.1	83.3
	Total	100.0	100.0

d. A values are always in y = 1
B values are most often in y = 1
C values are most often in y = 2

28. a.

		y				Grand
		20–39	40–59	60–79	80–100	Total
	10–29			1	4	5
x	30–49	2		4		6
	50–69	1	3	1		5
	70–90	4				4
	Grand Total	7	3	6	4	20

b.

		y				Grand
		20–39	40–59	60–79	80–100	Total
	10–29			20.0	80.0	100
x	30–49	33.3		66.7		100
	50–69	20.0	60.0	20.0		100
	70–90	100.0				100

c.

		20–39	40–59	60–79	80–100
	10–29	0.0	0.0	16.7	100.0
	30–49	28.6	0.0	66.7	0.0
x	50–69	14.3	100.0	16.7	0.0
	70–90	57.1	0.0	0.0	0.0
	Grand Total	100	100	100	100

d. Higher values of x are associated with lower values of y and vice versa

30. a.

	Year					
Average Speed	1988–1992	1993–1997	1998–2002	2003–2007	2008–2012	Total
130–139.9	16.7	0.0	0.0	33.3	50.0	100
140–149.9	25.0	25.0	12.5	25.0	12.5	100
150–159.9	0.0	50.0	16.7	16.7	16.7	100
160–169.9	50.0	0.0	50.0	0.0	0.0	100
170–179.9	0.0	0.0	100.0	0.0	0.0	100

b. It appears that most of the faster average winning times occur before 2003; this could be due to new regulations that take into account driver safety, fan safety, the environmental impact, and fuel consumption during races

32. a.

Fund Type	5-Year Average Return						Total
	0–9.99	10–19.99	20–29.99	30–39.99	40–49.99	50–59.99	
DE	1	25	1	0	0	0	27
FI	9	1	0	0	0	0	10
IE	0	2	3	2	0	1	8
Total	10	28	4	2	0	1	45

b.

5-Year Average Return	Frequency
0–9.99	10
10–19.99	28
20–29.99	4
30–39.99	2
40–49.99	0
50–59.99	1
Total	45

c.

Fund Type	Frequency
DE	27
FI	10
IE	8
Total	45

d. The margin of the crosstabulation shows these frequency distributions

e. Higher returns—International Equity funds
Lower returns—Fixed Income funds

34. b. Georgia (86), Florida (69) and Illinois (58)
c. Bank failures surged in 2009 and 2010 and then began a decreasing trend in 2011 and 2012

Year	Number of Bank Failures
2000	2
2001	4
2002	11
2003	3
2004	4
2005	0
2006	0
2007	3
2008	25
2009	140
2010	157
2011	92
2012	51

36. a.

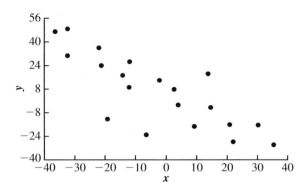

b. A negative relationship between x and y; y decreases as x increases

38. a.

		y		
		Yes	No	
x	Low	66.667	33.333	100
	Medium	30.000	70.000	100
	High	80.000	20.000	100

b.

40. a.

b. Colder average low temperature seems to lead to higher amounts of snowfall

c. Two cities have an average snowfall of nearly 100 inches of snowfall: Buffalo, New York, and Rochester, New York; both are located near large lakes in New York

42. a.

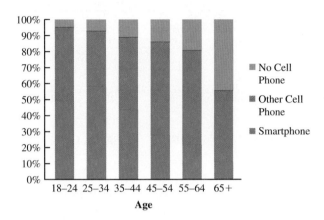

Age

b. After an increase in age 25–34, smartphone ownership decreases as age increases; the percentage of people with no cell phone increases with age; there is less variation across age groups in the percentage who own other cell phones

c. Unless a newer device replaces the smartphone, we would expect smartphone ownership would become less sensitive to age; this would be true because current users will become older and because the device will become to be seen more as a necessity than a luxury

44. a.

SAT Score	Frequency
800–999	1
1000–1199	3
1200–1399	6
1400–1599	10
1600–1799	7
1800–1999	2
2000–2199	1
Total	30

b. Nearly symmetrical

c. 33% of the scores fall between 1400 and 1599
A score below 800 or above 2200 is unusual
The average is near or slightly above 1500

46. a.

Population in Millions	Frequency	Percent Frequency
0.0–2.4	15	30.0
2.5–4.9	13	26.0
5.0–7.4	10	20.0
7.5–9.9	5	10.0
10.0–12.4	1	2.0
12.5–14.9	2	4.0
15.0–17.4	0	0.0
17.5–19.9	2	4.0
20.0–22.4	0	0.0
22.5–24.9	0	0.0
25.0–27.4	1	2.0
27.5–29.9	0	0.0
30.0–32.4	0	0.0
32.5–34.9	0	0.0
35.0–37.4	1	2.0
37.5–39.9	0	0.0
More	0	0.0

Population (millions)

b. The distribution is skewed to the right

c. Fifteen states (30%) have a population less than 2.5 million; over half the states have population less than 5 million (28 states—56%); only seven states have a population greater than 10 million (California, Florida, Illinois, New York, Ohio, Pennsylvania, and Texas); the largest state is California (37.3 million) and the smallest states are Vermont and Wyoming (600 thousand)

48. a.

Industry	Frequency	Percent Frequency
Bank	26	13
Cable	44	22
Car	42	21
Cell	60	30
Collection	28	14
Total	200	100

b.

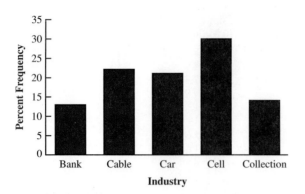

c. The cellular phone providers had the highest number of complaints

d. The percentage frequency distribution shows that the two financial industries (banks and collection agencies) had about the same number of complaints; new car dealers and cable and satellite television companies also had about the same number of complaints

50. a.

Age	Below High School	High School	Some College No Degree	Associate's Degree	Bachelor's Degree	Advanced Degree	Total
25–34	11.6	27.2	18.9	9.5	24.0	8.9	100
35–44	11.7	28.6	16.3	10.3	21.9	11.2	100
45–54	10.4	32.8	16.7	10.6	19.0	10.4	100
55–64	10.4	31.3	17.3	9.2	18.6	13.1	100
65–74	17.0	35.4	15.7	6.6	14.1	11.1	100
75 & older	24.6	37.6	14.0	4.6	11.9	7.3	100

b.

Age	Below High School	High School	Some College No Degree	Associate's Degree	Bachelor's Degree	Advanced Degree
25–34	18.5	17.9	23.1	21.4	25.4	17.4
35–44	18.4	18.5	19.6	22.9	22.8	21.5
45–54	18.0	23.3	22.0	25.8	21.7	21.9
55–64	14.3	17.7	18.2	17.9	17.0	22.0
65–74	13.9	11.9	9.8	7.6	7.6	11.0
75 & older	16.9	10.6	7.3	4.5	5.4	6.1
Total	100	100	100	100	100	100

A higher percentage of advanced degree holders are older than those holding a bachelor's degree

52. a/b. Row Totals: 12, 60, 13, 8, 4, 1; Column Totals: 32, 28, 38

c.

Job Growth (%)	Size of Company		
	Small	Midsized	Large
−10–(−1)	13	21	5
0–9	56	46	76
10–19	22	7	11
20–29	9	11	5
30–39	0	11	3
40 or more	0	4	0
Total	100	100	100

d.

Job Growth (%)	Size of Company			Total
	Small	Midsized	Large	
−10–(−1)	33	50	17	100
0–9	30	22	48	100
10–19	54	15	31	100
20–29	38	38	25	100
30–39	0	75	25	100
40 or more	0	4	0	100

e. In terms of avoiding negative job growth, large companies were better; in terms of better job growth rates, midsized companies performed better.

Chapter 3

2. 16, 16.5

4.

Period	Return (%)
1	−0.060
2	−0.080
3	−0.040
4	0.020
5	0.054

The mean growth factor over the five periods is

$$\bar{x}_g = \sqrt[n]{(x_1)(x_2)\cdots(x_5)}$$

$$= \sqrt[5]{(0.940)(0.920)(0.960)(1.020)(1.054)}$$

$$= \sqrt[5]{(0.8925)} = 0.9775$$

So the mean growth rate $(0.9775 - 1)100\% = -2.25\%$

5. Arrange data in order: 15, 20, 25, 25, 27, 28, 30, 34

$i = \dfrac{20}{100}(8) = 1.6$; round up to position 2

20th percentile = 20

$i = \dfrac{25}{100}(8) = 2$; use positions 2 and 3

25th percentile $= \dfrac{20 + 25}{2} = 22.5$

$i = \dfrac{65}{100}(8) = 5.2$; round up to position 6

65th percentile = 28

$i = \dfrac{75}{100}(8) = 6$; use positions 6 and 7

75th percentile $= \dfrac{28 + 30}{2} = 29$

6. 59, 73, 57, 53

8. a. 18.42
  b. 6.32
  c. 34.3%
  d. Reductions of only .65 shots and .9% made shots per game
   Yes, agree but not dramatically

10. a. 65.9, 66.5, 67
  b. 61, 71
  c. 79.5
   90% of the ratings are 79.5 or less; 10% of the ratings are 79.5 or greater

12. a. The minimum number of viewers who watched a new episode is 13.3 million, and the maximum number is 16.5 million
  b. The mean number of viewers who watched a new episode is 15.04 million or approximately 15.0 million; the median is also 15.0 million; the data are multimodal (13.6, 14.0, 16.1, and 16.2 million); in such cases the mode is usually not reported
  c. The data are first arranged in ascending order. The index for the first quartile is $i = \left(\dfrac{25}{100}\right)21 = 5.25$, so the first quartile is the value of the 6th observation in the sorted data, or 14.1; the index for the third quartile is $i = \left(\dfrac{75}{100}\right)21 = 15.75$, so the third quartile is the value

   of the 16th observation in the sorted data, or 16.0
  d. A graph showing the viewership data over the air dates follows: Period 1 corresponds to the first episode of the season, period 2 corresponds to the second episode, and so on

This graph shows that viewership of *The Big Bang Theory* has been relatively stable over the 2011–2012 television season

14. For March 2011

The index for the first quartile is $i = \left(\dfrac{25}{100}\right)50 = 12.50$, so the first quartile is the value of the 13th observation in the sorted data, or 6.8

The index for the median quartile is $i = \left(\dfrac{50}{100}\right)50 = 25.0$, so the median (or second quartile) is the average of the values of the 25th and 26th observations in the sorted data, or 8.0

The index for the third quartile is $i = \left(\dfrac{75}{100}\right)50 = 37.50$, so the third quartile is the value of the 38th observation in the sorted data, or 9.4

For March 2012

The minimum is 3.0

The index for the first quartile is $i = \left(\dfrac{25}{100}\right)50 = 12.50$, so the first quartile is the value of the 13th observation in the sorted data, or 6.8

The index for the median quartile is $i = \left(\dfrac{50}{100}\right)50 = 25.0$, so the median (or second quartile) is the average of the values of the 25th and 26th observations in the sorted data, or 7.35

The index for the third quartile is $i = \left(\dfrac{75}{100}\right)50 = 37.50$, so the third quartile is the value of the 38th observation in the sorted data, or 8.6

It may be easier to compare these results if we place them in a table

	March 2011	March 2012
First Quartile	6.8	6.8
Median	8.0	7.35
Third Quartile	9.4	8.6

The results show that in March 2012 approximately 25% of the states had an unemployment rate of 6.8% or less, the same as in March 2011; however, the median of 7.35% and the third quartile of 8.6% in March 2012 are both less than the corresponding values in March 2011, indicating that unemployment rates across the states are decreasing

16. a.

Grade x_i	Weight w_i
4 (A)	9
3 (B)	15
2 (C)	33
1 (D)	3
0 (F)	0
	60 credit hours

$$\bar{x} = \frac{\sum w_i x_i}{\sum_i} = \frac{9(4) + 15(3) + 33(2) + 3(1)}{9 + 15 + 33 + 3}$$

$$= \frac{150}{60} = 2.5$$

b. Yes

18. 3.8, 3.7

20.

	Stivers		Trippi	
Year	**End of Year Value ($)**	**Growth Factor**	**End of Year Value ($)**	**Growth Factor**
2004	11,000	1.100	5,600	1.120
2005	12,000	1.091	6,300	1.125
2006	13,000	1.083	6,900	1.095
2007	14,000	1.077	7,600	1.101
2008	15,000	1.071	8,500	1.118
2009	16,000	1.067	9,200	1.082
2010	17,000	1.063	9,900	1.076
2011	18,000	1.059	10,600	1.071

For the Stivers mutual fund we have
$18000 = 10000[(x_1)(x_2) \cdots (x_8)]$, so $[(x_1)(x_2) \cdots (x_8)]$
$= 1.8$ and

$$\bar{x}_g = \sqrt[n]{(x_1)(x_2) \cdots (x_8)} = \sqrt[8]{1.80} = 1.07624$$

So the mean annual return for the Stivers mutual fund is $(1.07624 - 1)100 = 7.624\%$

For the Trippi mutual fund we have
$10600 = 5000[(x_1)(x_2) \cdots (x_8)]$, so $[(x_1)(x_2) \cdots (x_8)]$
$= 2.12$ and

$$\bar{x}_g = \sqrt[n]{(x_1)(x_2) \cdots (x_8)} = \sqrt[8]{2.12} = 1.09848$$

So the mean annual return for the Trippi mutual fund is $(1.09848 - 1)100 = 9.848\%$

While the Stivers mutual fund has generated a nice annual return of 7.6%, the annual return of 9.8% earned by the Trippi mutual fund is far superior

22. $25,000,000 = 10,000,000[(x_1)(x_2) \cdots (x_6)]$,
so $[(x_1)(x_2) \cdots (x_6)] = 2.50$

so $\bar{x}_g = \sqrt[n]{(x_1)(x_2) \cdots (x_6)} = \sqrt[6]{2.50} = 1.165$
So the mean annual growth rate is $(1.165 - 1)100 = 16.5\%$

24. 16, 4

25. Range $= 34 - 15 = 19$
Arrange data in order: 15, 20, 25, 25, 27, 28, 30, 34

$$i = \frac{25}{100}(8) = 2; Q_1 = \frac{20 + 25}{2} = 22.5$$

$$i = \frac{75}{100}(8) = 6; Q_3 = \frac{28 + 30}{2} = 29$$

$$IQR = Q_3 - Q_1 = 29 - 22.5 = 6.5$$

$$\bar{x} = \frac{\sum x_i}{n} = \frac{204}{8} = 25.5$$

x_i	$(x_i - \bar{x})$	$(x_i - \bar{x})^2$
27	1.5	2.25
25	-.5	.25
20	-5.5	30.25
15	-10.5	110.25
30	4.5	20.25
34	8.5	72.25
28	2.5	6.25
25	-.5	.25
		242.00

$$s^2 = \frac{\sum(x_i - \bar{x})^2}{n - 1} = \frac{242}{8 - 1} = 34.57$$

$$s = \sqrt{34.57} = 5.88$$

26. a. Range $= 190 - 168 = 22$

b. $\bar{x} = \frac{\sum x_i}{n} = \frac{1068}{6} = 178$

$$s^2 = \frac{\sum(x_i - \bar{x})^2}{n - 1}$$

$$= \frac{4^2 + (-10)^2 + 6^2 + 12^2 + (-8)^2 + (-4)^2}{6 - 1}$$

$$= \frac{376}{5} = 75.2$$

c. $s = \sqrt{75.2} = 8.67$

d. $\frac{s}{\bar{x}}(100) = \frac{8.67}{178}(100\%) = 4.87\%$

28. a. The mean serve speed is 180.95, the variance is 21.42, and the standard deviation is 4.63

b. Although the mean serve speed for the 20 Women's Singles serve speed leaders for the 2011 Wimbledon tournament is slightly higher, the difference is very small; furthermore, given the variation in the 20 Women's Singles serve speed leaders from the 2012 Australian Open and the 20 Women's Singles serve speed leaders from the 2011 Wimbledon tournament, the difference in the mean serve speeds is most likely due to random variation in the players' performances

30. *Dawson:* range = 2, $s = .67$
   Clark: range = 8, $s = 2.58$

32. a. 1960.05, 692.85
b. 481.65, 155.06
c. 2303, 563
d. Auto: IQR = 2228 − 1717 = 511
   Dept Store: IQR = 803 − 593 = 210
e. Automotive spends more, has a larger standard deviation, larger max and min, and larger range than Department Store. Automotive spends more on advertising.

34. *Quarter-milers:* $s = .0564$, Coef. of Var. = 5.8%
   Milers: $s = .1295$, Coef. of Var. = 2.9%

36. .20, 1.50, 0, −.50, −2.20

37. a. $z = \dfrac{20 - 30}{5} = -2, z = \dfrac{40 - 30}{5} = 2 \quad 1 - \dfrac{1}{2^2} = .75$

   At least 75%

b. $z = \dfrac{15 - 30}{5} = -3, z = \dfrac{45 - 30}{5} = 3 \quad 1 - \dfrac{1}{3^2} = .89$

   At least 89%

c. $z = \dfrac{22 - 30}{5} = -1.6, z = \dfrac{38 - 30}{5} = 1.6 \quad 1 - \dfrac{1}{1.6^2} = .61$

   At least 61%

d. $z = \dfrac{18 - 30}{5} = -2.4, z = \dfrac{42 - 30}{5} = 2.4 \quad 1 - \dfrac{1}{2.4^2} = .83$

   At least 83%

e. $z = \dfrac{12 - 30}{5} = -3.6, z = \dfrac{48 - 30}{5} = 3.6 \quad 1 - \dfrac{1}{3.6^2} = .92$

   At least 92%

38. a. 95%
b. Almost all
c. 68%

39. a. $z = 2$ standard deviations

   $1 - \dfrac{1}{z^2} = 1 - \dfrac{1}{2^2} = \dfrac{3}{4}$; at least 75%

b. $z = 2.5$ standard deviations

   $1 - \dfrac{1}{z^2} = 1 - \dfrac{1}{2.5^2} = .84$; at least 84%

c. $z = 2$ standard deviations
   Empirical rule: 95%

40. a. 68%
b. 81.5%
c. 2.5%

42. a. −.67
b. 1.50
c. Neither is an outlier
d. Yes; $z = 8.25$

44. a. 76.5, 7
b. 16%, 2.5%
c. 12.2, 7.89; no outliers

46. 15, 22.5, 26, 29, 34

48. Arrange data in order: 5, 6, 8, 10, 10, 12, 15, 16, 18

   $i = \dfrac{25}{100}(9) = 2.25$; round up to position 3

   $Q_1 = 8$
   Median (5th position) = 10

   $i = \dfrac{75}{100}(9) = 6.75$; round up to position 7

   $Q_3 = 15$

   5-number summary: 5, 8, 10, 15, 18

50. a. Men's 1st place 43.73 minutes faster
b. Medians: 109.64, 131.67
   Men's median time 22.03 minutes faster
c. 65.30, 87.18, 109.64, 128.40, 148.70
   109.03, 122.08, 131.67, 147.18, 189.28
d. Men's Limits: 25.35 to 190.23; no outliers
   Women's Limits: 84.43 to 184.83; 2 outliers
e. Women runners show less variation

51. a. Arrange data in order low to high

   $i = \dfrac{25}{100}(21) = 5.25$; round up to 6th position

   $Q_1 = 1872$
   Median (11th position) = 4019

   $i = \dfrac{75}{100}(21) = 15.75$; round up to 16th position

   $Q_3 = 8305$
   5-number summary: 608, 1872, 4019, 8305, 14,138
b. IQR = $Q_3 - Q_1$ = 8305 − 1872 = 6433
   Lower limit: 1872 − 1.5(6433) = −7777.5
   Upper limit: 8305 + 1.5(6433) = 17,955
c. No; data are within limits
d. 41,138 > 27,604; 41,138 would be an outlier; data value would be reviewed and corrected

e.

52. a. 73.5
 b. 68, 71.5, 73.5, 74.5, 77
 c. Limits: 67 and 79; no outliers
 d. 66, 68, 71, 73, 75; 60.5 and 80.5
  63, 65, 66, 67.6, 69; 61.25 and 71.25
  75, 77, 78.5, 79.5, 81; 73.25 and 83.25
  No outliers for any of the services
 e. Verizon is highest rated
  Sprint is lowest rated

54. a. $\bar{x} = 177.24$, Median $= 89.5$
 b. 40, 228
 c.

Smallest	21
Q_1	40
Median	89.5
Q_3	228
Largest	995

 d. LL $= -242$
  UL $= 510$

  There are three outliers: 707, 807, and 995

 ᴇ The box plot shows the distribution is skewed to the right (positive)

55. b. There appears to be a negative linear relationship between x and y
 c.

x_i	y_i	$x_i - \bar{x}$	$y_i - \bar{y}$	$(x_i - \bar{x})(y_i - \bar{y})$
4	50	-4	4	-16
6	50	-2	4	-8
11	40	3	-6	-18
3	60	-5	14	-70
16	30	8	-16	-128
40	230	0	0	-240

$$\bar{x} = 8; \bar{y} = 46$$

$$s_{xy} = \frac{\sum(x_i - \bar{x})(y_i - \bar{y})}{n - 1} = \frac{-240}{4} = -60$$

The sample covariance indicates a negative linear association between x and y

 d. $r_{xy} = \dfrac{s_{xy}}{s_x s_y} = \dfrac{-60}{(5.43)(11.40)} = -.969$

The sample correlation coefficient of $-.969$ is indicative of a strong negative linear relationship

56. b. There appears to be a positive linear relationship between x and y
 c. $s_{xy} = 26.5$
 d. $r_{xy} = .693$

58. $-.91$; negative relationship

60. b. DJIA: $\bar{x} = 9.10$ $s = 15.37$
  Russell 1000: $\bar{x} = 9.09$ $s = 17.89$
 c. $r_{xy} = .959$
 d. The two indexes are very similar.

62. a. The mean is 2.95 and the median is 3.0
 b. The index for the first quartile is $i = \left(\dfrac{25}{100}\right)20 = 5$, so the first quartile is the mean of the values of the 5th and 6th observations in the sorted data, or $\dfrac{1 + 1}{2} = 1$

  The index for the third quartile is $i = \left(\dfrac{75}{100}\right)20 = 15$, so the third quartile is the mean of the values of the 15th and 16th observations in the sorted data, or $\dfrac{4 + 5}{2} = 4.5$

 c. The range is 7 and the interquartile range is $4.5 - 1 = 3.5$
 d. The variance is 4.37 and standard deviation is 2.09
 e. Because most people dine out relatively few times per week and a few families dine out very frequently, we would expect the data to be positively skewed; the skewness measure of 0.34 indicates the data are somewhat skewed to the right
 f. The lower limit is -4.25 and the upper limit is 9.75; no values in the data are less than the lower limit or greater than the upper limit, so the Minitab boxplot indicates there are no outliers

Boxplot of Dining Out

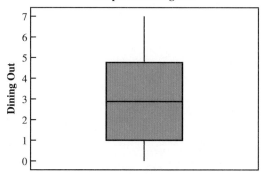

64. a. The mean and median patient wait times for offices with a wait-tracking system are 17.2 and 13.5, respectively; the mean and median patient wait times for offices without a wait-tracking system are 29.1 and 23.5, respectively
 b. The variance and standard deviation of patient wait times for offices with a wait-tracking system are 86.2 and 9.3, respectively; the variance and standard deviation of patient wait times for offices without a wait-tracking system are 275.7 and 16.6, respectively
 c. Offices with a wait-tracking system have substantially shorter patient wait times than offices without a wait-tracking system

d. $z = \dfrac{37 - 29.1}{16.6} = 0.48$

e. $z = \dfrac{37 - 17.2}{9.3} = 2.13$

As indicated by the positive z-scores, both patients had wait times that exceeded the means of their respective samples; even though the patients had the same wait time, the z-score for the sixth patient in the sample who visited an office with a wait-tracking system is much larger because that patient is part of a sample with a smaller mean and a smaller standard deviation

f. The z-scores for all patients follow

Without Wait-Tracking System	With Wait-Tracking System
−0.31	1.49
2.28	−0.67
−0.73	−0.34
−0.55	0.09
0.11	−0.56
0.90	2.13
−1.03	−0.88
−0.37	−0.45
−0.79	−0.56
0.48	−0.24

The z-scores do not indicate the existence of any outliers in either sample

66. a. $\bar{x} = 413.3$ This is slightly higher than the mean for the study

b. $s = 37.64$

c. LL = 292.5
UL = 536.5
There are no outliers

68. a. Median = 79649

b. Smallest   18927
Q_1 59423
Median   79649
Q_3 122231
Largest   148782

c. $\bar{x} = 89{,}376.36$

d. LL = −34,789
UL = 216,443
There are no outliers

e. The median is preferred as it indicates the middle of the data and is not influenced by overly large or small values.

70. a. 364 rooms

b. $457

c. −.293; slight negative correlation
Higher cost per night tends to be associated with smaller hotels

72. a. .268, low or weak positive correlation

b. Very poor predictor; spring training is practice and does not count toward standings or playoffs

74. a. 60.68

b. $s^2 = 31.23$; $s = 5.59$

Chapter 4

2. $\dbinom{6}{3} = \dfrac{6!}{3!3!} = \dfrac{6 \cdot 5 \cdot 4 \cdot 3 \cdot 2 \cdot 1}{(3 \cdot 2 \cdot 1)(3 \cdot 2 \cdot 1)} = 20$

ABC	ACE	BCD	BEF
ABD	ACF	BCE	CDE
ABE	ADE	BCF	CDF
ABF	ADF	BDE	CEF
ACD	AEF	BDF	DEF

4. b. (H,H,H), (H,H,T), (H,T,H), (H,T,T),
(T,H,H), (T,H,T), (T,T,H), (T,T,T)

c. ⅓

6. $P(E_1) = .40$, $P(E_2) = .26$, $P(E_3) = .34$
The relative frequency method was used

8. a. 4: Commission Positive—Council Approves
Commission Positive—Council Disapproves
Commission Negative—Council Approves
Commission Negative—Council Disapproves

9. $\dbinom{50}{4} = \dfrac{50!}{4!46!} = \dfrac{50 \cdot 49 \cdot 48 \cdot 47}{4 \cdot 3 \cdot 2 \cdot 1} = 230{,}300$

10. a. Using the table, $P(\text{Debt}) = .94$

b. Five of the 8 institutions, $P(\text{over } 60\%) = 5/8 = .625$

c. Two of the 8 institutions, $P(\text{more than } \$30{,}000) = 2/8 = .25$

d. $P(\text{No debt}) = 1 - P(\text{debt}) = 1 - .72 = .28$

e. A weighted average with 72% having average debt of $32,980 and 28% having no debt

Average debt per graduate $= \dfrac{.72(\$32{,}980) + .28(\$0)}{.72 + .28}$
$= \$23{,}746$

12. a. 175,223,510

b. 1 chance in 175,223,510
= .000000005707

14. a. ¼

b. ½

c. ¾

15. a. $S = \{$ace of clubs, ace of diamonds, ace of hearts, ace of spades$\}$

b. $S = \{2$ of clubs, 3 of clubs, . . . , 10 of clubs, J of clubs, Q of clubs, K of clubs, A of clubs$\}$

c. There are 12; jack, queen, or king in each of the four suits

d. For (a): 4/52 = 1/13 = .08
    For (b): 13/52 = 1/4 = .25
    For (c): 12/52 = .23

16. a. 36
  c. $\frac{1}{6}$
  d. $\frac{5}{18}$
  e. No; $P(\text{odd}) = P(\text{even}) = \frac{1}{2}$
  f. Classical

17. a. (4, 6), (4, 7), (4, 8)
  b. .05 + .10 + .15 = .30
  c. (2, 8), (3, 8), (4, 8)
  d. .05 + .05 + .15 = .25
  e. .15

18. a. .106
  b. .31
  c. .566

20. a. .2023, .4947, .2585, .0445
  b. .6970
  c. .3030
  d. Probability of being financially independent before age 25 appears unrealistically high

22. a. .40, .40, .60
  b. .80, yes
  c. $A^c = \{E_3, E_4, E_5\}$; $C^c = \{E_1, E_4\}$;
    $P(A^c) = .60$; $P(C^c) = .40$
  d. (E_1, E_2, E_5); .60
  e. .80

23. a. $P(A) = P(E_1) + P(E_4) + P(E_6)$
        $= .05 + .25 + .10 = .40$
    $P(B) = P(E_2) + P(E_4) + P(E_7)$
        $= .20 + .25 + .05 = .50$
    $P(C) = P(E_2) + P(E_3) + P(E_5) + P(E_7)$
        $= .20 + .20 + .15 + .05 = .60$
  b. $A \cup B = \{E_1, E_2, E_4, E_6, E_7\}$;
    $P(A \cup B) = P(E_1) + P(E_2) + P(E_4) + P(E_6) + P(E_7)$
        $=.05 + .20 + .25 + .10 + .05$
        $=.65$
  c. $A \cap B = \{E_4\}$; $P(A \cap B) = P(E_4) = .25$
  d. Yes, they are mutually exclusive
  e. $B^c = \{E_1, E_3, E_5, E_6\}$;
    $P(B^c) = P(E_1) + P(E_3) + P(E_5) + P(E_6)$
        $=.05 + .20 + .15 + .10$
        $=.50$

24. a. .05
  b. .70

26. a. .64
  b. .48
  c. .36
  d. .76

28. Let B = rented a car for business reasons
      P = rented a car for personal reasons
  a. $P(B \cup P) = P(B) + P(P) - P(B \cap P)$
        $=.540 + .458 - .300$
        $=.698$
  b. $P(\text{Neither}) = 1 - .698 = .302$

30. a. $P(A \mid B) = \dfrac{P(A \cap B)}{P(B)} = \dfrac{.40}{.60} = .6667$

  b. $P(B \mid A) = \dfrac{P(A \cap B)}{P(A)} = \dfrac{.40}{.50} = .80$

  c. No, because $P(A \mid B) \neq P(A)$

32. a.

	Car	Light Truck	Total
U.S.	.1330	.2939	.4269
Non-U.S.	.3478	.2253	.5731
Total	.4808	.5192	1.0000

  b. .4269, .5731 Non-U.S. higher
    .4808, .5192 Light Truck slightly higher
  c. .3115, .6885 Light Truck higher
  d. .6909, .3931 Car higher
  e. .5661, U.S. higher for Light Trucks

33. a.

	Undergraduate Major			
	Business	**Engineering**	**Other**	**Totals**
Full-Time	.2697	.1510	.1923	.6130
Part-Time	.1149	.1234	.1487	.3870
Totals	.3847	.2743	.3410	1.0000

  b. $P(B) = .3847$, $P(E) = .2743$, and $P(O) = .3410$, so business has most

  c. $P(E|F) = \dfrac{P(E \cap F)}{P(F)} = \dfrac{.1510}{.6130} = .2463$

  d. $P(F|B) = \dfrac{P(F \cap B)}{P(B)} = \dfrac{.2697}{.3847} = .7012$

  e. Independent if $P(F)P(B) = P(F \cap B)$

    $P(F)P(B) = (.6130)(.3847) = .4299$

    But $P(F \cap B) = .2697$ in the joint probability table $P(F)P(B) \neq P(F \cap B)$; events F and B are not independent

34. a.

	On Time	Late	Total
JetBlue	.2304	.0696	.30
United	.2288	.0912	.32
US Airways	.3124	.0676	.38
Total:	.7716	.2284	1.00

  b. .7716
  c. US Airways .38
  d. United .3992

36. a. .8649
  b. .9951
  c. .0049
  d. .3346, .8236, .1764
    Foul the center is best strategy

38. a. .42
  b. .58
  c. .3810
  d. .5862
  e. No degree leads to greater financial problems

39. a. Yes, because $P(A_1 \cap A_2) = 0$
  b. $P(A_1 \cap B) = P(A_1)P(B \mid A_1) = .40(.20) = .08$
    $P(A_2 \cap B) = P(A_2)P(B \mid A_2) = .60(.05) = .03$
  c. $P(B) = P(A_1 \cap B) + P(A_2 \cap B) = .08 + .03 = .11$
  d. $P(A_1 \mid B) = \dfrac{.08}{.11} = .7273$

   $P(A_2 \mid B) = \dfrac{.03}{.11} = .2727$

40. a. .10, .20, .09
  b. .51
  c. .26, .51, .23

42. M = missed payment
   D_1 = customer defaults
   D_2 = customer does not default
   $P(D_1) = .05, P(D_2) = .95, P(M \mid D_2) = .2, P(M \mid D_1) = 1$
  a. $P(D_1 \mid M) = \dfrac{P(D_1)P(M \mid D_1)}{P(D_1)P(M \mid D_1) + P(D_2)P(M \mid D_2)}$

   $= \dfrac{(.05)(1)}{(.05)(1) + (.95)(.2)}$

   $= \dfrac{.05}{.24} = .21$

  b. Yes, the probability of default is greater than .20

44. a. .40
  b. .6667; offer to female

46. a. 1005
  b. A day or less; .4199
  c. .20
  d. 382/1005 = .3801

48. a.

	A	B	Total
Female	.2896	.2133	.5029
Male	.2368	.2603	.4971
Total	.5264	.4736	1.0000

  b. .5029
  c. .5758
  d. Events are not independent

50. a. .76
  b. .24

52. b. .2022
  c. .4618
  d. .4005

54. a. .7768
  b. .2852
  c. .5161
  d. Not independent
  e. Probability of not okay higher for 50 + .8472 to .7109

56. a. .25
  b. .125
  c. .0125
  d. .10
  e. No

58. a. .1139
  b. .0761
  c. .5005, .4995

60. a. .7907, .2093, spam
  b. .6944, .6320, *today!* more likely
  c. .2750, .5858, *fingertips!* more likely
  d. These words occur more often in spam

Chapter 5

1. a. Head, Head (H, H)
   Head, Tail (H, T)
   Tail, Head (T, H)
   Tail, Tail (T, T)
  b. x = number of heads on two coin tosses
  c.

Outcome	Values of x
(H, H)	2
(H, T)	1
(T, H)	1
(T, T)	0

  d. Discrete; 0, 1, and 2

2. a. x = time in minutes to assemble product
  b. Any positive value: $x > 0$
  c. Continuous

3. Let Y = position is offered
    N = position is not offered
  a. $S = \{(Y, Y, Y), (Y, Y, N), (Y, N, Y), (Y, N, N), (N, Y, Y),$
    $(N, Y, N), (N, N, Y), (N, N, N)\}$
  b. Let N = number of offers made; N is a discrete random variable
  c.

Experimental Outcome	(Y, Y, Y)	(Y, Y, N)	(Y, N, Y)	(Y, N, N)	(N, Y, Y)	(N, Y, N)	(N, N, Y)	(N, N, N)
Value of N	3	2	2	1	2	1	1	0

4. $x = 0, 1, 2, \ldots, 9$

6. a. 0, 1, 2, . . . , 20; discrete
  b. 0, 1, 2, . . . ; discrete
  c. 0, 1, 2, . . . , 50; discrete
  d. $0 \le x \le 8$; continuous
  e. $x > 0$; continuous

7. a. $f(x) \geq 0$ for all values of x
  $\Sigma f(x) = 1$; therefore, it is a valid probability distribution
  b. Probability $x = 30$ is $f(30) = .25$
  c. Probability $x \leq 25$ is $f(20) + f(25) = .20 + .15 = .35$
  d. Probability $x > 30$ is $f(35) = .40$

8. a.

x	$f(x)$
1	3/20 = .15
2	5/20 = .25
3	8/20 = .40
4	4/20 = .20
	Total 1.00

  b. $f(x)$

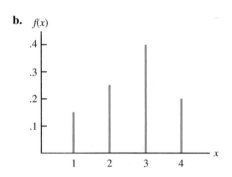

  c. $f(x) \geq 0$ for $x = 1, 2, 3, 4$
    $\Sigma f(x) = 1$

10. a.

x	1	2	3	4	5
$f(x)$	.05	.09	.03	.42	.41

  b.

x	1	2	3	4	5
$f(x)$	.04	.10	.12	.46	.28

  c. .83
  d. .28
  e. Senior executives are more satisfied

12. a. Yes
  b. .15
  c. .10

14. a. .05
  b. .70
  c. .40

16. a.

y	$f(y)$	$yf(y)$
2	.20	.4
4	.30	1.2
7	.40	2.8
8	.10	.8
Totals	1.00	5.2

$E(y) = \mu = 5.2$

b.

y	$y - \mu$	$(y - \mu)^2$	$f(y)$	$(y - \mu)^2 f(y)$
2	−3.20	10.24	.20	2.048
4	−1.20	1.44	.30	.432
7	1.80	3.24	.40	1.296
8	2.80	7.84	.10	.784
			Total	4.560

$Var(y) = 4.56$
$\sigma = \sqrt{4.56} = 2.14$

18. a/b.

x	$f(x)$	$xf(x)$	$x - \mu$	$(x - \mu)^2$	$(x - \mu)^2 f(x)$
0	.2188	.0000	−1.1825	1.3982	.3060
1	.5484	.5484	−.1825	.0333	.0183
2	.1241	.2483	.8175	.6684	.0830
3	.0489	.1466	1.8175	3.3035	.1614
4	.0598	.2393	2.8175	7.9386	.4749
Total	1.0000	1.1825			1.0435
		↑			↑
		$E(x)$			$Var(x)$

c/d.

y	$f(y)$	$yf(y)$	$y - \mu$	$(y - \mu)^2$	$(y - \mu)^2 f(y)$
0	.2497	.0000	−1.2180	1.4835	.3704
1	.4816	.4816	−.2180	.0475	.0229
2	.1401	.2801	−.7820	.6115	.0856
3	.0583	.1749	1.7820	3.1755	.1851
4	.0703	.2814	2.7820	7.7395	.5444
Total	1.0000	1.2180			1.2085
		↑			↑
		$E(y)$			$Var(y)$

  e. The expected number of times that owner-occupied units have a water supply stoppage lasting 6 or more hours in the past 3 months is 1.1825, slightly less than the expected value of 1.2180 for renter-occupied units; the variability is somewhat less for owner-occupied units (1.0435) as compared to renter-occupied units (1.2085).

20. a. 430
  b. −90; concern is to protect against the expense of a large loss

22. a. 445
  b. $1250 loss

24. a. Medium: 145; large: 140
  b. Medium: 2725; large: 12,400

25. a.

$E(x) = .2(50) + .5(30) + .3(40) = 37$
$E(y) = .2(80) + .5(50) + .3(60) = 59$
$Var(x) = .2(50 - 37)^2 + .5(30 - 37)^2 + .3(40 - 37)^2 = 61$
$Var(y) = .2(80 - 59)^2 + .5(50 - 59)^2 + .3(60 - 59)^2 = 129$

b.

x + y	f(x+y)
130	.2
80	.5
100	.3

c.

x + y	f(x + y)	(x + y)f(x + y)	x + y − E(x + y)
130	.2	26	34
80	.5	40	−16
100	.3	30	4
		E(x + y) = 96	

$[x + y − E(x + y)]^2$	$[x + y − E(x + y)]^2 f(x + y)$
1156	231.2
256	128.0
16	4.8
	Var(x + y) = 364

d.
$\sigma_{xy} = [Var(x + y) − Var(x) − Var(y)]/2 = (364−61−129)/2 = 87$ Var(x) = 61 and Var(y) = 129 were computed in part (a), so

$$\sigma_x = \sqrt{61} = 7.8102 \qquad \sigma_y = \sqrt{129} = 11.3578$$

$$\rho_{xy} = \frac{\sigma_{xy}}{\sigma_x \sigma_y} = \frac{87}{(7.8102)(11.3578)} = .98$$

The random variables x and y are positively related; both the covariance and correlation coefficient are positive; indeed, they are very highly correlated; the correlation coefficient is almost equal to 1

e. $Var(x + y) = Var(x) + Var(y) + 2\sigma_{xy}$
$= 61 + 129 + 2(87) = 364$
$Var(x) + Var(y) = 61 + 129 = 190$
The variance of the sum of x and y is greater than the sum of the variances by two times the covariance: $2(87) = 174$; the reason it is positive is that, in this case, the variables are positively related; whenever two random variables are positively related, the variance of the sum of the random variables will be greater than the sum of the variances of the individual random variables

26. a. 5%, 1%, stock 1 is riskier
b. $42.25, $25.00
c. 5.825, 2.236
d. 6.875%, 3.329%
e. −.6, strong negative relationship

27. a. Dividing each of the frequencies in the table by the total number of restaurants provides the joint probability table below; the bivariate probability for each pair of quality and meal price is shown in the body of the table; this is the bivariate probability distribution; for instance, the probability of a rating of 2 on quality and a rating of 3 on meal price is given by f(2, 3) = .18; the marginal probability distribution for quality, x, is in the rightmost column; the marginal probability for meal price, y, is in the bottom row

Quality x	Meal Price y			Total
	1	**2**	**3**	
1	0.14	0.13	0.01	0.28
2	0.11	0.21	0.18	0.50
3	0.01	0.05	0.16	0.22
Total	0.26	0.39	0.35	1.00

b. $E(x) = 1(.28) + 2(.50) + 3(.22) = 1.94$
$Var(x) = .28(1 − 1.94)^2 + .50(2 − 1.94)^2$
$\qquad + .22(3 − 1.94)^2 = .4964$

c. $E(y) = 1(.26) + 2(.39) + 3(.35) = 2.09$
$Var(y) = .26(1 − 2.09)^2 + .39(2 − 2.09)^2$
$\qquad + .35(3 − 2.09)^2 = .6019$

d. $\sigma_{xy} = [Var(x + y) − Var(x) − Var(y)]/2$
$\qquad = [1.6691 − .4964 − .6019]/2 = .2854$
Since the covariance $\sigma_{xy} = .2854$ is positive, we can conclude that as the quality rating goes up, the meal price goes up; this is as we would expect

e. $\rho_{xy} = \frac{\sigma_{xy}}{\sigma_x \sigma_y} = \frac{.2854}{\sqrt{.4964}\sqrt{.6019}} = .5221$

With a correlation coefficient of .5221, we would call this a moderately positive relationship; it is not likely to find a low-cost restaurant that is also high quality, but it is possible; there are 3 of them leading to f(3,1) = .01

28. a. Yes
b. .0135
c. .2377
d. .9140

30. a. Probability of a defective part being produced must be .03 for each part selected; parts must be selected independently
b. Let D = defective
$\qquad$ G = not defective

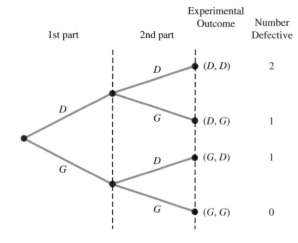

1st part	2nd part	Experimental Outcome	Number Defective
	D	(D, D)	2
D	G	(D, G)	1
	D	(G, D)	1
G	G	(G, G)	0

c. Two outcomes result in exactly one defect
d. P(no defects) = (.97)(.97) = .9409
P(1 defect) = 2(.03)(.97) = .0582
P(2 defects) = (.03)(.03) = .0009

32. a. .90
b. .99
c. .999
d. Yes

34. a. Yes
b. Yes
c. .8516

36. a. .1304
b. .9924
c. 6
d. 4.2, 2.0499

38. a. $f(x) = \dfrac{3^x e^{-3}}{x!}$
b. .2241
c. .1494
d. .8008

39. a. $f(x) = \dfrac{2^x e^{-2}}{x!}$

b. $\mu = 6$ for 3 time periods

c. $f(x) = \dfrac{6^x e^{-6}}{x!}$

d. $f(2) = \dfrac{2^2 e^{-2}}{2!} = \dfrac{4(.1353)}{2} = .2706$

e. $f(6) = \dfrac{6^6 e^{-6}}{6!} = .1606$

f. $f(5) = \dfrac{4^5 e^{-4}}{5!} = .1563$

40. a. .1952
b. .1048
c. .0183
d. .0907

42. a. For a 15-minute period the mean is 14.4/4 = 3.6

$$f(0) = \frac{3.6^0 e^{-3.6}}{0!} = e^{-3.6} = .0273$$

b. Probability = $1 - f(0) = 1 - .2073 = .9727$
c. Probability = $1 - [f(0) + f(1) + f(2) + f(3)]$
$= 1 - [.0273 + .0984 + .1771 + .2125]$
$= .4847$
Note: The value of $f(0)$ was computed in part (a) and the Poisson tables were used to compute the probabilities for $f(1)$, $f(2)$, and $f(3)$

44. a. .6
b. .5488
c. .3293
d. .1219

46. a. $f(1) = \dfrac{\dbinom{3}{1}\dbinom{10-3}{4-1}}{\dbinom{10}{4}} = \dfrac{\left(\dfrac{3!}{1!2!}\right)\left(\dfrac{7!}{3!4!}\right)}{\dfrac{10!}{4!6!}}$

$= \dfrac{(3)(35)}{210} = .50$

b. $f(2) = \dfrac{\dbinom{3}{2}\dbinom{10-3}{2-2}}{\dbinom{10}{2}} = \dfrac{(3)(1)}{45} = .067$

c. $f(0) = \dfrac{\dbinom{3}{0}\dbinom{10-3}{2-0}}{\dbinom{10}{2}} = \dfrac{(1)(21)}{45} = .4667$

d. $f(2) = \dfrac{\dbinom{3}{2}\dbinom{10-3}{4-2}}{\dbinom{10}{4}} = \dfrac{(3)(21)}{210} = .30$

e. $x = 4$ is *greater than* $r = 3$; thus, $f(4) = 0$

48. a. .5250
b. .8167

50. $N = 60$, $n = 10$
a. $r = 20$, $x = 0$

$$f(0) = \frac{\dbinom{20}{0}\dbinom{40}{10}}{\dbinom{60}{10}} = \frac{(1)\left(\dfrac{40!}{10!30!}\right)}{\dfrac{60!}{10!50!}}$$

$$= \left(\frac{40!}{10!30!}\right)\left(\frac{10!50!}{60!}\right)$$

$$= \frac{40 \cdot 39 \cdot 38 \cdot 37 \cdot 36 \cdot 35 \cdot 34 \cdot 33 \cdot 32 \cdot 31}{60 \cdot 59 \cdot 58 \cdot 57 \cdot 56 \cdot 55 \cdot 54 \cdot 53 \cdot 52 \cdot 51}$$

$= .0112$

b. $r = 20, x = 1$

$$f(1) = \frac{\binom{20}{1}\binom{40}{9}}{\binom{60}{10}} = 20\left(\frac{40!}{9!31!}\right)\left(\frac{10!50!}{60!}\right)$$

$$= .0725$$

c. $1 - f(0) - f(1) = 1 - .0112 - .0725 = .9163$

d. Same as the probability one will be from Hawaii; .0725

52. a. .2917

   b. .0083

   c. .5250, .1750; 1 bank

   d. .7083

   e. .90, .49, .70

54. a.

x	$f(x)$
1	0.150
2	0.050
3	0.075
4	0.050
5	0.125
6	0.050
7	0.100
8	0.125
9	0.125
10	0.150

b. Probability of outstanding service is $.125 + .150 = .275$

c. $E(x) = 5.925$ and $Var(x) = 9.6694$

d. New car dealership: .2857; for the remaining service providers, probability is .2727

56. a. .0596

   b. .3585

   c. 100

   d. 95, 9.75

58. a. .9510

   b. .0480

   c. .0490

60. a. 47

   b. 6

   c. 6

62. .1912

64. a. .2240

   b. .5767

66. a. .4667

   b. .4667

   c. .0667

Chapter 6

1. a.

b. $P(x = 1.25) = 0$; the probability of any single point is zero because the area under the curve above any single point is zero

c. $P(1.0 \le x \le 1.25) = 2(.25) = .50$

d. $P(1.20 < x < 1.5) = 2(.30) = .60$

2. b. .50

   c. .60

   d. 15

   e. 8.33

4. a.

b. $P(.25 < x < .75) = 1(.50) = .50$

c. $P(x \le .30) = 1(.30) = .30$

d. $P(x > .60) = 1(.40) = .40$

6. a. $a = 56, b = 216$

   b. .6250

   c. .4125

   d. .1500

10. a. .9332

   b. .8413

   c. .0919

   d. .4938

12. a. .2967

   b. .4418

   c. .3300

   d. .5910

   e. .8849

   f. .2389

13. a. $P(-1.98 \le z \le .49) = P(z \le .49) - P(z < -1.98)$
$= .6879 - .0239 = .6640$

   b. $P(.52 \le z \le 1.22) = P(z \le 1.22) - P(z < .52)$
$= .8888 - .6985 = .1903$

   c. $P(-1.75 \le z \le -1.04) = P(z \le -1.04) - P(z < -1.75) = .1492 - .0401 = .1091$

14. a. $z = 1.96$

   b. $z = 1.96$

c. $z = .61$
d. $z = 1.12$
e. $z = .44$
f. $z = .44$

15. a. The z value corresponding to a cumulative probability of .2119 is $z = -.80$
b. Compute $.9030/2 = .4515$; the cumulative probability of $.5000 + .4515 = .9515$ corresponds to $z = 1.66$
c. Compute $.2052/2 = .1026$; z corresponds to a cumulative probability of $.5000 + .1026 = .6026$, so $z = .26$
d. The z value corresponding to a cumulative probability of .9948 is $z = 2.56$
e. The area to the left of z is $1 - .6915 = .3085$, so $z = -.50$

16. a. $z = 2.33$
b. $z = 1.96$
c. $z = 1.645$
d. $z = 1.28$

18. $\mu = 14.4$ and $\sigma = 4.4$
a. At $x = 20$, $z = \dfrac{20 - 14.4}{4.4} = 1.27$

$P(z \leq 1.27) = .8980$
$P(x \geq 20) = 1 - .8980 = .1020$

b. At $x = 10$, $z = \dfrac{10 - 14.4}{4.4} = -1.00$

$P(z \leq -1.00) = .1587$
So, $P(x \leq 10) = .1587$

c. A z-value of 1.28 cuts off an area of approximately 10% in the upper tail

$x = 14.4 + 4.4(1.28) = 20.03$

A return of 20.03% or higher will put a domestic stock fund in the top 10%

20. a. .1788
b. 69.15%
c. .0495

22. a. .6553
b. 13.05 hours
c. .9838

24. a. .0606
b. .4090
c. .7351
d. $1119 or more

26. a. $\mu = np = 100(.20) = 20$
$\sigma^2 = np(1 - p) = 100(.20)(.80) = 16$
$\sigma = \sqrt{16} = 4$
b. Yes, because $np = 20$ and $n(1 - p) = 80$
c. $P(23.5 \leq x \leq 24.5)$

$z = \dfrac{24.5 - 20}{4} = 1.13 \qquad P(z \leq 1.13) = .8708$

$z = \dfrac{23.5 - 20}{4} = .88 \qquad P(z \leq .88) = .8106$

$P(23.5 \leq x \leq 24.5) = P(.88 \leq z \leq 1.13)$
$\qquad\qquad\qquad\qquad = .8708 - .8106 = .0602$

d. $P(17.5 \leq x \leq 22.5)$

$z = \dfrac{22.5 - 20}{4} = .63 \qquad P(z \leq .63) = .7357$

$z = \dfrac{17.5 - 20}{4} = -.63 \qquad P(z \leq -.63) = .2643$

$P(17.5 \leq x \leq 22.5) = P(-.63 \leq z \leq .63)$
$\qquad\qquad\qquad\qquad = .7357 - .2643 = .4714$

e. $P(x \leq 15.5)$

$z = \dfrac{15.5 - 20}{4} = -1.13 \qquad P(z \leq -1.13) = .1292$

$P(x \leq 15.5) = P(z \leq -1.13) = .1292$

28. a. $\mu = np = 250(.20) = 50$
b. $\sigma^2 = np(1 - p) = 250(.20)(1 - 20) = 40$
$\sigma = \sqrt{40} = 6.3246$
$P(x < 40) = P(x \leq 39.5)$

$z = \dfrac{x - \mu}{\sigma} = \dfrac{39.5 - 50}{6.3246} = -1.66 \qquad \text{Area} = .0485$

$P(x \leq 39.5) = .0485$
c. $P(55 \leq x \leq 60) = P(54.5 \leq x \leq 60.5)$

$z = \dfrac{x - \mu}{\sigma} = \dfrac{54.5 - 50}{6.3246} = .71 \qquad \text{Area} = .7611$

$z = \dfrac{x - \mu}{\sigma} = \dfrac{60.5 - 50}{6.3246} = 1.66 \qquad \text{Area} = .9515$

$P(54.5 \leq x \leq 60.5) = .9515 - .7611 = .1904$
d. $P(x \geq 70) = P(x \geq 69.5)$

$z = \dfrac{x - \mu}{\sigma} = \dfrac{69.5 - 50}{6.3246} - 3.08 \qquad \text{Area} = .9990$

$P(x \geq 69.5) = 1 - .9990 = .0010$

30. a. 144
b. .1841
c. .9943

32. a. .5276
b. .3935
c. .4724
d. .1341

33. a. $P(x \leq x_0) = 1 - e^{-x_0/3}$
b. $P(x \leq 2) = 1 - e^{-2/3} = 1 - .5134 = .4866$
c. $P(x \geq 3) = 1 - P(x \leq 3) = 1 - (1 - e^{-3/3})$
$\qquad\qquad = e^{-1} = .3679$
d. $P(x \leq 5) = 1 - e^{-5/3} = 1 - .1889 = .8111$
e. $P(2 \leq x \leq 5) = P(x \leq 5) - P(x \leq 2)$
$\qquad\qquad\qquad = .8111 - .4866 = .3245$

34. a. $f(x) = \dfrac{1}{20}e^{-x/20}$
b. .5276
c. .3679
d. .5105

35. a.

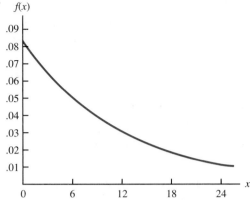

b. $P(x \le 12) = 1 - e^{-12/12} = 1 - .3679 = .6321$
c. $P(x \le 6) = 1 - e^{-6/12} = 1 - .6065 = .3935$
d. $P(x \ge 30) = 1 - P(x < 30)$
$= 1 - (1 - e^{-30/12})$
$= .0821$

36. a. .3935
   b. .2386
   c. .1353

38. a. 37.5 minutes
   b. $f(x) = \left(\dfrac{1}{37.5}\right)e^{-x/37.5}$ for $x \ge 0$
   c. .7981
   d. .4493
   e. .2886

40. a. $16,312
   b. 7.64%
   c. $22,948

42. a. $\sigma = 25.5319$
   b. .9401
   c. 706 or more

44. a. .0228
   b. $50

46. a. 38.3%
   b. 3.59% better, 96.41% worse
   c. 38.21%

48. $\mu = 19.23$ ounces

50. a. Lose $240
   b. .1788
   c. .3557
   d. .0594

52. a. $\frac{1}{7}$ minute
   b. $7e^{-7x}$
   c. .0009
   d. .2466

54. a. 2 minutes
   b. .2212
   c. .3935
   d. .0821

Chapter 7

1. a. AB, AC, AD, AE, BC, BD, BE, CD, CE, DE
   b. With 10 samples, each has a $\frac{1}{10}$ probability
   c. E and C because 8 and 0 do not apply; 5 identifies E; 7 does not apply; 5 is skipped because E is already in the sample; 3 identifies C; 2 is not needed because the sample of size 2 is complete

2. 22, 147, 229, 289

3. 459, 147, 385, 113, 340, 401, 215, 2, 33, 348

4. a. Davis Love III, Jim Fuyrk, Charles Howell III
   b. 120

6. 2782, 493, 825, 1807, 289

8. ExxonMobil, Chevron, Travelers, Microsoft, Pfizer, and Intel

10. a. finite; **b.** infinite; **c.** infinite; **d.** finite; **e.** infinite

11. a. $\bar{x} = \dfrac{\Sigma x_i}{n} = \dfrac{54}{6} = 9$
   b. $s = \sqrt{\dfrac{\Sigma(x_i - \bar{x})^2}{n - 1}}$

$\Sigma(x_i - \bar{x})^2 = (-4)^2 + (-1)^2 + 1^2 + (-2)^2 + 1^2 + 5^2$
$= 48$

$s = \sqrt{\dfrac{48}{6 - 1}} = 3.1$

12. a. .50
   b. .3667

13. a. $\bar{x} = \dfrac{\Sigma x_i}{n} = \dfrac{465}{5} = 93$
   b.

x_i	$(x_i - \bar{x})$	$(x_i - \bar{x})^2$
94	+1	1
100	+7	49
85	−8	64
94	+1	1
92	−1	1
Totals 465	0	116

$s = \sqrt{\dfrac{\Sigma(x_i - \bar{x})^2}{n - 1}} = \sqrt{\dfrac{116}{4}} = 5.39$

14. a. .05
   b. .425
   c. .20

16. a. All U.S. adults age 50 and older
   b. .8216
   c. 315
   d. .8310
   e. Target population is same as sampled population; if restricted to AARP members, inferences are questionable

18. a. 200
 b. 5
 c. Normal with $E(\bar{x}) = 200$ and $\sigma_{\bar{x}} = 5$
 d. The probability distribution of $\bar{x}$

19. a. The sampling distribution is normal with
  $E(\bar{x}) = \mu = 200$
  $\sigma_{\bar{x}} = \sigma/\sqrt{n} = 50/\sqrt{100} = 5$
  For ±5, $195 \leq \bar{x} \leq 205$
  Using the standard normal probability table:

$$\text{At } \bar{x} = 205, z = \frac{\bar{x} - \mu}{\sigma_{\bar{x}}} = \frac{5}{5} = 1$$

$$P(z \leq 1) = .8413$$

$$\text{At } \bar{x} = 195, z = \frac{\bar{x} - \mu}{\sigma_{\bar{x}}} = \frac{-5}{5} = -1$$

$$P(z < -1) = .1587$$
$$P(195 \leq \bar{x} \leq 205) = .8413 - .1587 = .6826$$

 b. For ±10, $190 \leq \bar{x} \leq 210$
  Using the standard normal probability table:

$$\text{At } \bar{x} = 210, z = \frac{\bar{x} - \mu}{\sigma_{\bar{x}}} = \frac{10}{5} = 2$$

$$P(z \leq 2) = .9772$$

$$\text{At } \bar{x} = 190, z = \frac{\bar{x} - \mu}{\sigma_{\bar{x}}} = \frac{-10}{5} = -2$$

$$P(z < -2) = .0228$$
$$P(190 \leq \bar{x} < 210) = .9772 - .0228 = .9544$$

20. 3.54, 2.50, 2.04, 1.77
 $\sigma_{\bar{x}}$ decreases as n increases

22. a. Normal with $E(\bar{x}) = 51,800$ and $\sigma_{\bar{x}} = 516.40$
 b. $\sigma_{\bar{x}}$ decreases to 365.15
 c. $\sigma_{\bar{x}}$ decreases as n increases

23. a.

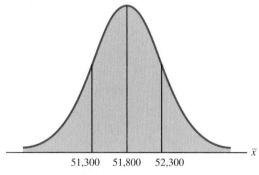

$$\sigma_{\bar{x}} = \frac{\sigma}{\sqrt{n}} = \frac{4000}{\sqrt{60}} = 516.40$$

$$\text{At } \bar{x} = 52,300, z = \frac{52,300 - 51,800}{516.40} = .97$$
$$P(\bar{x} \leq 52,300) = P(z \leq .97) = .8340$$

$$\text{At } \bar{x} = 51,300, z = \frac{51,300 - 51,800}{516.40} = -.97$$

$$P(\bar{x} < 51,300) = P(z < -.97) = .1660$$

$$P(51,300 \leq \bar{x} \leq 52,300) = .8340 - .1660 = .6680$$

 b. $\sigma_{\bar{x}} = \dfrac{\sigma}{\sqrt{n}} = \dfrac{4000}{\sqrt{120}} = 365.15$

$$\text{At } \bar{x} = 52,300, z = \frac{52,300 - 51,800}{365.15} = 1.37$$

$$P(\bar{x} \leq 52,300) = P(z \leq 1.37) = .9147$$

$$\text{At } \bar{x} = 51,300, z = \frac{51,300 - 51,800}{365.15} = -1.37$$

$$P(\bar{x} < 51,300) = P(z < -1.37) = .0853$$

$$P(51,300 \leq \bar{x} \leq 52,300) = .9147 - .0853 = .8294$$

24. a. Normal with $E(\bar{x}) = 17.5$ and $\sigma_{\bar{x}} = .57$
 b. .9198
 c. .6212

26. a. .3544, .4448, .5934, .9050
 b. Higher probability the sample mean will be close to population mean

28. a. Normal with $E(\bar{x}) = 22$ and $\sigma_{\bar{x}} = .7303$
 b. .8294
 c. .9070
 d. Part (c), larger sample size

30. a. $n/N = .01$; no
 b. 1.29, 1.30; little difference
 c. .8764

32. a. $E(\bar{p}) = .40$

$$\sigma_{\bar{p}} = \sqrt{\frac{p(1-p)}{n}} = \sqrt{\frac{(.40)(.60)}{200}} = .0346$$

  Within $\pm.03$ means $.37 \leq \bar{p} \leq .43$

$$z = \frac{\bar{p} - p}{\sigma_{\bar{p}}} = \frac{.03}{.0346} = .87$$

$$P(.37 \leq \bar{p} \leq .43) = P(-.87 \leq z \leq .87)$$
$$= .8078 - .1922$$
$$= .6156$$

 b. $z = \dfrac{\bar{p} - p}{\sigma_{\bar{p}}} = \dfrac{.05}{.0346} = 1.44$

$$P(.35 \leq \bar{p} \leq .45) = P(-1.44 \leq z \leq 1.44)$$
$$= .9251 - .0749$$
$$= .8502$$

34. a. .6156
  b. .7814
  c. .9488
  d. .9942
  e. Higher probability with larger n

35. a.

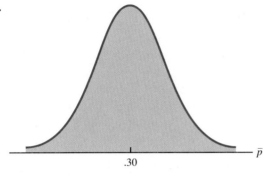

.30

$$\sigma_{\bar{p}} = \sqrt{\frac{p(1-p)}{n}} = \sqrt{\frac{.30(.70)}{100}} = .0458$$

The normal distribution is appropriate because $np =$ $100(.30) = 30$ and $n(1-p) = 100(.70) = 70$ are both greater than 5

  b. $P(.20 \le \bar{p} \le .40) = ?$

$$z = \frac{.40 - .30}{.0458} = 2.18$$

$$P(.20 \le \bar{p} \le .40) = P(-2.18 \le z \le 2.18)$$
$$= .9854 - .0146$$
$$= .9708$$

  c. $P(.25 \le \bar{p} \le .35) = ?$

$$z = \frac{.35 - .30}{.0458} = 1.09$$

$$P(.25 \le \bar{p} \le .35) = P(-1.09 \le z \le 1.09)$$
$$= .8621 - .1379$$
$$= .7242$$

36. a. Normal with $E(\bar{p}) = .55$ and $\sigma_{\bar{p}} = .0352$
  b. .8444
  c. Normal with $E(\bar{p}) = .45$ and $\sigma_{\bar{p}} = .0352$
  d. .8444
  e. No, standard error is the same in both parts
  f. .9556, the probability is larger because the increased sample size reduces the standard error
38. a. Normal with $E(\bar{p}) = .42$ and $\sigma_{\bar{p}} = .0285$
  b. .7062
  c. .9198
  d. Probabilities would increase
40. a. Normal with $E(\bar{p}) = .76$ and $\sigma_{\bar{p}} = .0214$
  b. .8384
  c. .9452
42. 122, 99, 25, 55, 115, 102, 61

44. a. Normal with $E(\bar{x}) = 406$ and $\sigma_{\bar{x}} = 10$
  b. .8664
  c. $z = -2.60$, .0047, Yes
46. a. 955
  b. .50
  c. .7062
  d. .8230
48. a. 625
  b. .7888
50. a. Normal with $E(\bar{p}) = .15$ and $\sigma_{\bar{p}} = .0230$
  b. .9182
  c. .6156
52. a. .8882
  b. .0233
54. a. 48
  b. Normal, $E(\bar{p}) = .25$, $\sigma_{\bar{p}} = .0625$
  c. .2119

Chapter 8

2. Use $\bar{x} \pm z_{\alpha/2}(\sigma/\sqrt{n})$
  a. $32 \pm 1.645(6/\sqrt{50})$
    32 ± 1.4; 30.6 to 33.4
  b. $32 \pm 1.96(6/\sqrt{50})$
    32 ± 1.66; 30.34 to 33.66
  c. $32 \pm 2.576(6/\sqrt{50})$
    32 ± 2.19; 29.81 to 34.19
4. 54
5. a. With 99% confidence $z_{\alpha/2} = z_{.005} = 2.576$
    Margin of Error $= 2.576 \sigma/\sqrt{n} = 2.576 (6/\sqrt{64}) =$ 1.93
  b. Confidence Interval: 21.52 ± 1.93 or 19.59 to 23.45
6. 39.13 to 41.49
8. a. Population is at least approximately normal
  b. 3.41
  c. 4.48
10. a. \$3388 to \$3584
  b. \$3370 to \$3602
  c. \$3333 to \$3639
  d. Width increases as confidence level increases
12. a. 2.179
  b. -1.676
  c. 2.457
  d. -1.708 and 1.708
  e. -2.014 and 2.014
13. a. $\bar{x} = \dfrac{\Sigma x_i}{n} = \dfrac{80}{8} = 10$

  b. $s = \sqrt{\dfrac{\Sigma(x_i - \bar{x})^2}{n-1}} = \sqrt{\dfrac{84}{7}} = 3.464$

  c. $t_{.025}\left(\dfrac{s}{\sqrt{n}}\right) = 2.365\left(\dfrac{3.46}{\sqrt{8}}\right) = 2.9$

d. $\bar{x} \pm t_{.025}\left(\dfrac{s}{\sqrt{n}}\right)$

     10 ± 2.9 (7.1 to 12.9)

14. a. 21.5 to 23.5

   b. 21.3 to 23.7

   c. 20.9 to 24.1

   d. A larger margin of error and a wider interval

15. $\bar{x} \pm t_{\alpha/2}(s/\sqrt{n})$

    90% confidence: $df = 64$ and $t_{.05} = 1.669$

    $19.5 \pm 1.669\left(\dfrac{5.2}{\sqrt{65}}\right)$

    19.5 ± 1.08 or (18.42 to 20.58)

    95% confidence: $df = 64$ and $t_{.025} = 1.998$

    $19.5 \pm 1.998\left(\dfrac{5.2}{\sqrt{65}}\right)$

    19.5 ± 1.29 or (18.21 to 20.79)

16. a. 9.7063, 7.9805

   b. 7.1536 to 12.2590

   c. 3.8854, 1.6194

   d. 3.3674 to 4.4034

18. a. 22 weeks

   b. 3.8020

   c. 18.20 to 25.80

   d. Larger n next time

20. $\bar{x} = 22$; 21.48 to 22.52

22. a. $9,269 to $12,541

   b. 1523

   c. 4,748,714, $34 million

24. a. Planning value of $\sigma = \dfrac{\text{Range}}{4} = \dfrac{36}{4} = 9$

   b. $n = \dfrac{z_{.025}^2 \sigma^2}{E^2} = \dfrac{(1.96)^2(9)^2}{(3)^2} = 34.57$; use $n = 35$

   c. $n = \dfrac{(1.96)^2(9)^2}{(2)^2} = 77.79$; use $n = 78$

25. a. Use $n = \dfrac{z_{\alpha/2}^2 \sigma^2}{E^2}$

      $n = \dfrac{(1.96)^2(6.84)^2}{(1.5)^2} = 79.88$; use $n = 80$

   b. $n = \dfrac{(1.645)^2(6.84)^2}{(2)^2} = 31.65$; use $n = 32$

26. a. 25

   b. 49

   c. 97

28. a. 328

   b. 465

   c. 803

   d. n gets larger; no to 99% confidence

30. 1537

31. a. $p = \dfrac{100}{400} = .25$

   b. $\sqrt{\dfrac{\bar{p}(1 - \bar{p})}{n}} = \sqrt{\dfrac{.25(.75)}{400}} = .0217$

   c. $p \pm z_{.025}\sqrt{\dfrac{\bar{p}(1 - \bar{p})}{n}}$

      $.25 \pm 1.96(.0217)$

      $.25 \pm .0424$; .2076 to .2924

32. a. .6733 to .7267

   b. .6682 to .7318

34. 1068

35. a. $\bar{p} = \dfrac{1760}{2000} = .88$

   b. Margin of error

      $z_{.05} = \sqrt{\dfrac{\bar{p}(1 - \bar{p})}{n}} = 1.645\sqrt{\dfrac{.88(1 - .88)}{2000}} = .0120$

   c. Confidence interval

      $.88 \pm .0120$ or .868 to .892

   d. Margin of error

      $z_{.05} = \sqrt{\dfrac{\bar{p}(1 - \bar{p})}{n}} = 1.96\sqrt{\dfrac{.88(1 - .88)}{2000}} = .0142$

      95% confidence interval

      $.88 \pm .0142$ or .8658 to .8942

36. a. .23

   b. .1716 to .2884

38. a. .1790

   b. .0738, .5682 to .7158

   c. 354

39. a. $n = \dfrac{z_{.025}^2 p^*(1 - p^*)}{E^2} = \dfrac{(1.96)^2(.156)(1 - .156)}{(.03)^2}$

      $= 562$

   b. $n = \dfrac{z_{.005}^2 p^*(1 - p^*)}{E^2} = \dfrac{(2.576)^2(.156)(1 - .156)}{(.03)^2}$

      $= 970.77$; use 971

40. .0346 (.4854 to .5546)

42. a. .0442

   b. 601, 1068, 2401, 9604

44. a. 4.00

   b. $29.77 to $37.77

46. a. 122

   b. $1751 to $1995

   c. $172, 316 million

   d. Less than $1873

48. a. $712.27 to $833.73

   b. $172.31 to $201.69

   c. .34

   d. part (a)

50. 37

52. 176

54. a. .5420

　b. .0508

　c. .4912 to .5928

56. a. .22

　b. .1904 to .2496

　c. .3847 to .4553

　d. Part (c) wider; sample proportion is closer to .5

58. a. 1267

　b. 1509

60. a. .3101

　b. .2898 to .3304

　c. 8219; no, this sample size is unnecessarily large

Chapter 9

2. a. $H_0: \mu \leq 14$
　　$H_a: \mu > 14$

　b. No evidence that the new plan increases sales

　c. The research hypothesis $\mu > 14$ is supported; the new plan increases sales

4. a. $H_0: \mu \geq 220$
　　$H_a: \mu < 220$

　b. Cannot conclude proposed method reduces cost

　c. Can conclude proposed method reduces cost

5. a. Conclude that the population mean monthly cost of electricity in the Chicago neighborhood is greater than \$104 and hence higher than in the comparable neighborhood in Cincinnati

　b. The Type I error is rejecting H_0 when it is true; this error occurs if the researcher concludes that the population mean monthly cost of electricity is greater than \$104 in the Chicago neighborhood when the population mean cost is actually less than or equal to \$104

　c. The Type II error is accepting H_0 when it is false; this error occurs if the researcher concludes that the population mean monthly cost for the Chicago neighborhood is less than or equal to \$104 when it is not

6. a. $H_0: \mu \leq 1$
　　$H_a: \mu > 1$

　b. Claiming $\mu > 1$ when it is not true

　c. Claiming $\mu \leq 1$ when it is not true

8. a. $H_0: \mu \geq 220$
　　$H_a: \mu < 220$

　b. Claiming $\mu < 220$ when it is not true

　c. Claiming $\mu \geq 220$ when it is not true

10. a. $z = \dfrac{\bar{x} - \mu_0}{\sigma/\sqrt{n}} = \dfrac{26.4 - 25}{6/\sqrt{40}} = 1.48$

　b. Using normal table with $z = 1.48$: p-value $=$ $1.0000 - .9306 = .0694$

　c. p-value $> .01$, do not reject H_0

　d. Reject H_0 if $z \geq 2.33$
　　$1.48 < 2.33$, do not reject H_0

11. a. $z = \dfrac{\bar{x} - \mu_0}{\sigma/\sqrt{n}} = \dfrac{14.15 - 15}{3/\sqrt{50}} = -2.00$

　b. p-value $= 2(.0228) = .0456$

　c. p-value $\leq .05$, reject H_0

　d. Reject H_0 if $z \leq -1.96$ or $z \geq 1.96$
　　$-2.00 \leq -1.96$, reject H_0

12. a. .1056; do not reject H_0

　b. .0062; reject H_0

　c. ≈ 0; reject H_0

　d. .7967; do not reject H_0

14. a. .3844; do not reject H_0

　b. .0074; reject H_0

　c. .0836; do not reject H_0

15. a. $H_0: \mu \geq 1056$
　　$H_a: \mu < 1056$

　b. $z = \dfrac{\bar{x} - \mu_0}{\sigma/\sqrt{n}} = \dfrac{910 - 1056}{1600/\sqrt{400}} = -1.83$
　　p-value $= .0336$

　c. p-value $\leq .05$, reject H_0; the mean refund of "last-minute" filers is less than \$1056

　d. Reject H_0 if $z \leq -1.645$
　　$-1.83 \leq -1.645$; reject H_0

16. a. $H_0: \mu \leq 3173$
　　$H_a: \mu > 3173$

　b. .0207

　c. Reject H_0, conclude mean credit card balance for undergraduate student has increased

18. a. $H_0: \mu = 192$
　　$H_a: \mu \neq 192$

　b. -2.23, .0258

　c. Reject H_0; mean number of restaurant meals eaten by millennials has changed

20. a. $H_0: \mu \geq 838$
　　$H_a: \mu < 838$

　b. -2.40

　c. .0082

　d. Reject H_0; conclude the annual expenditure on prescription drugs is less in the Midwest

22. a. $H_0: \mu = 8$
　　$H_a: \mu \neq 8$

　b. .1706

　c. Do not reject H_0; we cannot conclude the mean waiting time differs from 8 minutes

　d. 7.83 to 8.97; yes

24. a. $t = \dfrac{\bar{x} - \mu_0}{s/\sqrt{n}} = \dfrac{17 - 18}{4.5/\sqrt{48}} = -1.54$

　b. Degrees of freedom $= n - 1 = 47$
　　Area in lower tail is between .05 and .10
　　p-value (two-tail) is between .10 and .20
　　Exact p-value $= .1303$

　c. p-value $> .05$; do not reject H_0

　d. With $df = 47$, $t_{.025} = 2.012$
　　Reject H_0 if $t \leq -2.012$ or $t \geq 2.012$
　　$t = -1.54$; do not reject H_0

26. a. Between .02 and .05; exact p-value $= .0397$; reject H_0
   b. Between .01 and .02; exact p-value $= .0125$; reject H_0
   c. Between .10 and .20; exact p-value $= .1285$; do not reject H_0

27. a. H_0: $\mu \geq 13.04$
   H_a: $\mu < 13.04$

   b. $t = \dfrac{\bar{x} - \mu_0}{s/\sqrt{n}} = \dfrac{12.75 - 13.04}{2/\sqrt{100}} = -1.45$

   Degrees of freedom $= n - 1 = 99$
   p-value is the lower tail area at the test statistic
   Using t table: p-value is between .05 and .10
   Exact p-value corresponding to $t = -1.45$ is .0751
   c. p-value $> .05$; do not reject H_0; we cannot conclude that the cost of a restaurant meal is significantly cheaper than a comparable meal fixed at home
   d. $df = 99$; $t_{.05} = -1.66$
   Reject H_0 if $t \leq -1.66$
   $-1.45 > -1.66$; do not reject H_0

28. a. H_0: $\mu \geq 9$
   H_a: $\mu < 9$
   b. Between .005 and .01
   Exact p-value $= .0072$
   c. Reject H_0; mean tenure of a CEO is less than 9 years

30. a. H_0: $\mu = 6.4$
   H_a: $\mu \neq 6.4$
   b. Between .10 and .20
   Exact p-value $= .1268$
   c. Do not reject H_0; cannot conclude that the group consensus is wrong

32. a. H_0: $\mu = 10{,}192$
   H_a: $\mu \neq 10{,}192$
   b. Between .02 and .05
   Exact p-value $= .0304$
   c. Reject H_0; mean price at dealership differs from national mean price

34. a. H_0: $\mu = 2$
   H_a: $\mu \neq 2$
   b. 2.2
   c. .516
   d. Between .20 and .40
   Exact p-value $= .2535$
   e. Do not reject H_0; no reason to change from 2 hours for cost estimating

36. a. $z = \dfrac{\bar{p} - p_0}{\sqrt{\dfrac{p_0(1 - p_0)}{n}}} = \dfrac{.68 - .75}{\sqrt{\dfrac{.75(1 - .75)}{300}}} = -2.80$

   p-value $= .0026$
   p-value $\leq .05$; reject H_0

   b. $z = \dfrac{.72 - .75}{\sqrt{\dfrac{.75(1 - .75)}{300}}} = -1.20$

p-value $= .1151$
p-value $> .05$; do not reject H_0

   c. $z = \dfrac{.70 - .75}{\sqrt{\dfrac{.75(1 - .75)}{300}}} = -2.00$

   p-value $= .0228$
   p-value $\leq .05$; reject H_0

   d. $z = \dfrac{.77 - .75}{\sqrt{\dfrac{.75(1 - .75)}{300}}} = .80$

   p-value $= .7881$
   p-value $> .05$; do not reject H_0

38. a. H_0: $p = .64$
   H_a: $p \neq .64$

   b. $\bar{p} = 52/100 = .52$

   $z = \dfrac{\bar{p} - p_0}{\sqrt{\dfrac{p_0(1 - p_0)}{n}}} = \dfrac{.52 - .64}{\sqrt{\dfrac{.64(1 - .64)}{100}}} = -2.50$

   p-value $= 2(.0062) = .0124$
   c. p-value $\leq .05$; reject H_0
   Proportion differs from the reported .64
   d. Yes, because $\bar{p} = .52$ indicates that fewer believe the supermarket brand is as good as the name brand

40. a. 21
   b. H_0: $p \geq .46$
   H_a: $p < .46$
   p-value $\approx .0436$
   c. Yes, .0436

42. a. $\bar{p} = .15$
   b. .0718 to .2282
   c. The return rate for the Houston store is different than the national average

44. a. H_0: $p \leq .50$
   H_a: $p > .50$
   b. $\bar{p} = .6133$, p-value $= .0027$
   c. Reject H_0; proportion of physicians over the age of 55 who have been sued at least once is greater than .50

46. a. H_0: $\mu = 16$
   H_a: $\mu \neq 16$
   b. .0286; reject H_0
   Readjust line
   c. .2186; do not reject H_0
   Continue operation
   d. $z = 2.19$; reject H_0
   $z = -1.23$; do not reject H_0
   Yes, same conclusion

48. a. H_0: $\mu \leq 4$
   H_a: $\mu > 4$
   b. .0049
   c. Reject H_0; lower income children are exposed to more than 4 hours of background television

50. $t = -1.05$

p-value between .20 and .40

Exact *p*-value = .2999

Do not reject H_0; there is no evidence to conclude that the age at which women had their first child has changed

52. $t = 2.26$

p-value between .01 and .025

Exact *p*-value = .0155

Reject H_0; mean cost is greater than $125,000

54. a. $H_0: p \leq .80$

   $H_a: p > .80$

   Conclude that airline travelers feel security will be improved

b. Cannot reject H_0; mandatory use is not recommended

56. a. $H_0: p \leq .80$

   $H_a: p > .80$

b. .84

c. .0418

d. Reject H_0; more than 80% of customers are satisfied with service of home agents

58. $H_0: p \geq .90$

   $H_a: p < .90$

   p-value = .0808

   Do not reject H_0; claim of at least 90% cannot be rejected

Chapter 10

1. a. $\bar{x}_1 - \bar{x}_2 = 13.6 - 11.6 = 2$

b. $z_{\alpha/2} = z_{.05} = 1.645$

$$\bar{x}_1 - \bar{x}_2 \pm 1.645\sqrt{\frac{\sigma_1^2}{n_1} + \frac{\sigma_2^2}{n_2}}$$

$$2 \pm 1.645\sqrt{\frac{(2.2)^2}{50} + \frac{(3)^2}{35}}$$

$2 \pm .98$ (1.02 to 2.98)

c. $z_{\alpha/2} = z_{.05} = 1.96$

$$2 \pm 1.96\sqrt{\frac{(2.2)^2}{50} + \frac{(3)^2}{35}}$$

2 ± 1.17 (.83 to 3.17)

2. a. $z = \dfrac{(\bar{x}_1 - \bar{x}_2) - D_0}{\sqrt{\dfrac{\sigma_1^2}{n_1} + \dfrac{\sigma_2^2}{n_2}}} = \dfrac{(25.2 - 22.8) - 0}{\sqrt{\dfrac{(5.2)^2}{40} + \dfrac{(6)^2}{50}}} = 2.03$

b. *p*-value = $1.0000 - .9788 = .0212$

c. *p*-value $\leq .05$; reject H_0

4. a. $\bar{x}_1 - \bar{x}_2 = 82.55 - 77.46 = 5.09$

b. $z_{.025}\sqrt{\dfrac{\sigma_1^2}{n_1} + \dfrac{\sigma_2^2}{n_2}} = 1.96\sqrt{\dfrac{(6.18)^2}{42} + \dfrac{(5.97)^2}{49}} = 2.51$

c. The 95% confidence interval estimate of the difference between the population mean ratings for the two

types of washing machines is 5.09 ± 2.51 or (2.58 to 7.60); we estimate that top-loading washing machines receive a mean rating 5.09 points higher than do front-loading washing machines with a margin of error of 2.51 points

6. *p*-value = .0351

Reject H_0; mean price in Atlanta lower than mean price in Houston

8. a. Reject H_0; customer service has improved for Rite Aid

b. Do not reject H_0; the difference is not statistically significant

c. *p*-value = .0336. reject H_0; customer service has improved for Expedia

d. 1.80

e. The increase for J.C. Penney is not statistically significant

9. a. $\bar{x}_1 - \bar{x}_2 = 22.5 - 20.1 = 2.4$

b. $df = \dfrac{\left(\dfrac{s_1^2}{n_1} + \dfrac{s_2^2}{n_2}\right)^2}{\dfrac{1}{n_1 - 1}\left(\dfrac{s_1^2}{n_1}\right)^2 + \dfrac{1}{n_2 - 1}\left(\dfrac{s_2^2}{n_2}\right)^2}$

$$= \dfrac{\left(\dfrac{2.5^2}{20} + \dfrac{4.8^2}{30}\right)^2}{\dfrac{1}{19}\left(\dfrac{2.5^2}{20}\right)^2 + \dfrac{1}{29}\left(\dfrac{4.8^2}{30}\right)^2} = 45.8$$

c. $df = 45$, $t_{.025} = 2.014$

$$t_{.025}\sqrt{\dfrac{s_1^2}{n_1} + \dfrac{s_2^2}{n_2}} = 2.014\sqrt{\dfrac{2.5^2}{20} + \dfrac{4.8^2}{30}} = 2.1$$

d. 2.4 ± 2.1 (.3 to 4.5)

10. a. $t = \dfrac{(\bar{x}_1 - \bar{x}_2) - 0}{\sqrt{\dfrac{s_1^2}{n_1} + \dfrac{s_2^2}{n_2}}} = \dfrac{(13.6 - 10.1) - 0}{\sqrt{\dfrac{5.2^2}{35} + \dfrac{8.5^2}{40}}} = 2.18$

b. $df = \dfrac{\left(\dfrac{s_1^2}{n_1} + \dfrac{s_2^2}{n_2}\right)^2}{\dfrac{1}{n_1 - 1}\left(\dfrac{s_1^2}{n_1}\right)^2 + \dfrac{1}{n_2 - 1}\left(\dfrac{s_2^2}{n_2}\right)^2}$

$$= \dfrac{\left(\dfrac{5.2^2}{35} + \dfrac{8.5^2}{40}\right)^2}{\dfrac{1}{34}\left(\dfrac{5.2^2}{35}\right)^2 + \dfrac{1}{39}\left(\dfrac{8.5^2}{40}\right)^2} = 65.7$$

Use $df = 65$

c. $df = 65$, area in tail is between .01 and .025; two-tailed *p*-value is between .02 and .05

Exact *p*-value = .0329

d. *p*-value $\leq .05$; reject H_0

12. a. $\bar{x}_1 - \bar{x}_2 = 22.5 - 18.6 = 3.9$ miles

b. $df = \dfrac{\left(\dfrac{s_1^2}{n_1} + \dfrac{s_2^2}{n_2}\right)^2}{\dfrac{1}{n_1-1}\left(\dfrac{s_1^2}{n_1}\right)^2 + \dfrac{1}{n_2-1}\left(\dfrac{s_2^2}{n_2}\right)^2}$

$= \dfrac{\left(\dfrac{8.4^2}{50} + \dfrac{7.4^2}{40}\right)^2}{\dfrac{1}{49}\left(\dfrac{8.4^2}{50}\right)^2 + \dfrac{1}{39}\left(\dfrac{7.4^2}{40}\right)^2} = 87.1$

Use $df = 87$, $t_{.025} = 1.988$

$3.9 \pm 1.988\sqrt{\dfrac{8.4^2}{50} + \dfrac{7.4^2}{40}}$

3.9 ± 3.3 (.6 to 7.2)

14. a. $H_0{:}\ \mu_1 - \mu_2 \geq 0$
$H_a{:}\ \mu_1 - \mu_2 < 0$

b. $t = \dfrac{(\bar{x}_1 - \bar{x}_2) - 0}{\sqrt{\dfrac{s_1^2}{n_1} + \dfrac{s_2^2}{n_2}}} = \dfrac{(56.1 - 59.4) - 0^2}{\sqrt{\dfrac{6^2}{45} + \dfrac{7^2}{55}}} = -2.54$

c. $df = \dfrac{\left(\dfrac{s_1^2}{n_1} + \dfrac{s_2^2}{n_2}\right)^2}{\dfrac{1}{n_1-1}\left(\dfrac{s_1^2}{n_1}\right)^2 + \dfrac{1}{n_2-1}\left(\dfrac{s_2^2}{n_2}\right)^2}$

$= \dfrac{\left(\dfrac{6^2}{45} + \dfrac{7^2}{55}\right)^2}{\dfrac{1}{45-1}\left(\dfrac{6^2}{45}\right)^2 + \dfrac{1}{55-1}\left(\dfrac{7^2}{55}\right)^2} = 97.77$

Rounding down, we will use a t distribution with 97 degrees of freedom; from the t table we see that $t = -2.54$ corresponds to a p-value between .005 and .01; the exact p-value corresponding to $t = -2.54$ is .006

d. The p-value $\leq .05$, so reject H_0 and conclude that the number of meals eaten at fast-food chains is less in Oklahoma City than in Milwaukee

16. a. $H_0{:}\ \mu_1 - \mu_2 \leq 0$
$H_a{:}\ \mu_1 - \mu_2 > 0$

b. 38

c. $t = 1.80$, $df = 25$
Using t table, p-value is between .025 and .05
Exact p-value $= .0420$

d. Reject H_0; conclude higher mean score if college grad

18. a. $H_0{:}\ \mu_1 - \mu_2 = 0$
$H_a{:}\ \mu_1 - \mu_2 \neq 0$

b. 50.6 and 52.8 minutes

c. p-value greater than .40

Do not reject H_0; cannot conclude population mean delay times differ

19. a. 1, 2, 0, 0, 2

b. $\bar{d} = \Sigma d_i / n = 5/5 = 1$

c. $s_d = \sqrt{\dfrac{\Sigma(d_i - \bar{d})^2}{n-1}} = \sqrt{\dfrac{4}{5-1}} = 1$

d. $t = \dfrac{\bar{d} - \mu}{s_d/\sqrt{n}} = \dfrac{1-0}{1/\sqrt{5}} = 2.24$

$df = n - 1 = 4$
Using t table, p-value is between .025 and .05
Exact p-value $= .0443$
p-value $\leq .05$; reject H_0

20. a. 3, -1, 3, 5, 3, 0, 1

b. 2

c. 2.08

d. 2

e. .07 to 3.93

21. $H_0{:}\ \mu_d \leq 0$
$H_a{:}\ \mu_d > 0$

$\bar{d} = .625$
$s_d = 1.30$

$t = \dfrac{\bar{d} - \mu_d}{s_d/\sqrt{n}} = \dfrac{.625 - 0}{1.30/\sqrt{8}} = 1.36$

$df = n - 1 = 7$
Using t table, p-value is between .10 and .20
Exact p-value $= .1080$
p-value $> .05$; do not reject H_0; cannot conclude commercial improves mean potential to purchase

22. a. $3.41

b. $1.67 to $5.15
Very nice increase

24. a. $H_0{:}\ \mu_d \leq 0$
$H_a{:}\ \mu_d > 0$
$\bar{d} = 23$, $t = 2.05$
p-value between .05 and .025
Reject H_0; conclude airfares have increased

b. $487, $464

c. 5% increase in airfares

26. a. $t = -1.42$
Using t table, p-value is between .10 and .20
Exact p-value $= .1718$
Do not reject H_0; no difference in mean scores

b. -1.05

c. 1.28; yes

27. a. $\bar{x} = (156 + 142 + 134)/3 = 144$

$$\text{SSTR} = \sum_{j=1}^{k} n_j(\bar{x}_j - \bar{\bar{x}})^2$$

$$= 6(156 - 144)^2 + 6(142 - 144)^2 + 6(134 - 144)^2$$
$$= 1488$$

b. $MSTR = \dfrac{SSTR}{k - 1} = \dfrac{1488}{2} = 744$

c. $s_1^2 = 164.4, \quad s_2^2 = 131.2, \quad s_3^2 = 110.4$

$$SSE = \sum_{j=1}^{k} (n_j - 1)s_j^2$$

$$= 5(164.4) + 5(131.2) + 5(110.4)$$
$$= 2030$$

d. $MSE = \dfrac{SSE}{n_T - k} = \dfrac{2030}{18 - 3} = 135.3$

e.

Source of Variation	Sum of Squares	Degrees of Freedom	Mean Square	F	p-value
Treatments	1488	2	744	5.50	.0162
Error	2030	15	135.3		
Total	3518	17			

f. $F = \dfrac{MSTR}{MSE} = \dfrac{744}{135.3} = 5.50$

From the F table (2 numerator degrees of freedom and 15 denominator), p-value is between .01 and .025
Using Excel or Minitab, the p-value corresponding to $F = 5.50$ is .0162
Because p-value $\leq \alpha = .05$, we reject the hypothesis that the means for the three treatments are equal

28.

Source of Variation	Sum of Squares	Degrees of Freedom	Mean Square	F	p-value
Treatments	300	4	75	14.07	.0000
Error	160	30	5.33		
Total	460	34			

30.

Source of Variation	Sum of Squares	Degrees of Freedom	Mean Square	F	p-value
Treatments	150	2	75	4.80	.0233
Error	250	16	15.63		
Total	400	18			

Reject H_0 because p-value $\leq \alpha = .05$

32. Because p-value $= .0082$ is less than $\alpha = .05$, we reject the null hypothesis that the means of the three treatments are equal

34. $\bar{\bar{x}} = (79 + 74 + 66)/3 = 73$

$$SSTR = \sum_{j=1}^{k} n_j(\bar{x}_j - \bar{\bar{x}})^2 = 6(79 - 73)^2 + 6(74 - 73)^2$$
$$+ 6(66 - 73)^2 = 516$$

$$MSTR = \dfrac{SSTR}{k - 1} = \dfrac{516}{2} = 258$$

$$s_1^2 = 34 \qquad s_2^2 = 20 \qquad s_3^2 = 32$$

$$SSE = \sum_{j=1}^{k} (n_j - 1)s_j^2 = 5(34) + 5(20) + 5(32) = 430$$

$$MSE = \dfrac{SSE}{n_T - k} = \dfrac{430}{18 - 3} = 28.67$$

$$F = \dfrac{MSTR}{MSE} = \dfrac{258}{28.67} = 9.00$$

Source of Variation	Sum of Squares	Degrees of Freedom	Mean Square	F	p-value
Treatments	516	2	258	9.00	.003
Error	430	15	28.67		
Total	946	17			

Using F table (2 numerator degrees of freedom and 15 denominator), p-value is less than .01

Using Excel or Minitab, the p-value corresponding to $F = 9.00$ is .003

Because p-value $\leq \alpha = .05$, we reject the null hypothesis that the means for the three plants are equal; in other words, analysis of variance supports the conclusion that the population mean examination scores at the three NCP plants are not equal

36. p-value $= .0000$
Because p-value $\leq \alpha = .05$, we reject the null hypothesis that the means for the three groups are equal

38. p-value $= .0038$
Because p-value $\leq \alpha = .05$, we reject the null hypothesis that the mean meal prices are the same for the three types of restaurants

40. a. $H_0: \mu_1 - \mu_2 = 0$
$H_a: \mu_1 - \mu_2 \neq 0$
$z = 2.79$
p-value $= .0052$
Reject H_0; a significant difference between systems exists

42. a. $H_0: \mu_1 - \mu_2 \leq 0$
$H_a: \mu_1 - \mu_2 > 0$

b. $t = .60, df = 57$
Using t table, p-value is greater than .20
Exact p-value $= .2754$
Do not reject H_0; cannot conclude that funds with loads have a higher mean rate of return

44. a. A decline of $2.45

   b. 2.45 ± 2.15 (.30 to 4.60)

   c. 8% decrease

   d. $23.93

46. Not significant; p-value $= .088$

48. Not significant; p-value $= .2455$

Chapter 11

1. a. $\bar{p}_1 - \bar{p}_2 = .48 - .36 = .12$

   b. $\bar{p}_1 - \bar{p}_2 \pm z_{.05}\sqrt{\dfrac{\bar{p}_1(1 - \bar{p}_1)}{n_1} + \dfrac{\bar{p}_2(1 - \bar{p}_2)}{n_2}}$

   $.12 \pm 1.645\sqrt{\dfrac{.48(1 - .48)}{400} + \dfrac{.36(1 - .36)}{300}}$

   $.12 \pm .0614$ (.0586 to .1814)

   c. $.12 \pm 1.96\sqrt{\dfrac{.48(1 - .48)}{400} + \dfrac{.36(1 - .36)}{300}}$

   $.12 \pm .0731$ (.0469 to .1931)

2. a. .2333

   b. .1498

   c. Do not reject H_0; cannot conclude population proportions differ

3. a. $\bar{p} = \dfrac{n_1\bar{p}_1 + n_2\bar{p}_2}{n_1 + n_2} = \dfrac{200(.22) + 300(.16)}{200 + 300} = .1840$

   $z = \dfrac{\bar{p}_1 - \bar{p}_2}{\sqrt{\bar{p}(1 - \bar{p})\left(\dfrac{1}{n_1} + \dfrac{1}{n_2}\right)}}$

   $= \dfrac{.22 - .16}{\sqrt{.1840(1 - .1840)\left(\dfrac{1}{200} + \dfrac{1}{300}\right)}} = 1.70$

   p-value $= 1.0000 - .9554 = .0446$

   b. p-value $\leq .05$; reject H_0; conclude p_1 is greater than p_2

4. $\bar{p}_1 = 220/400 = .55$ $\bar{p}_2 = 192/400 = .48$

   $\bar{p}_1 - \bar{p}_2 \pm z_{.025}\sqrt{\dfrac{\bar{p}_1(1 - \bar{p}_1)}{n_1} + \dfrac{\bar{p}_2(1 - \bar{p}_2)}{n_2}}$

   $.55 - .48 \pm 1.96\sqrt{\dfrac{.55(1 - .55)}{400} + \dfrac{.48(1 - .48)}{400}}$

   $.07 \pm > .0691(.0009 \text{ to } .1391)$

6. a. .45

   b. .35

   c. $.10 \pm .0989$ or (.0011 to .1989)

8. a. $H_0: p_1 \leq p_2$
     $H_a: p_1 > p_2$

   b. .2017

   c. .1111

   d. $z = 2.10$; p-value $= .0179$
     Reject H_0; higher proportion of dry wells were drilled in 2005

10. a. $H_0: p_1 - p_2 \leq 0$
      $H_a: p_1 - p_2 > 0$

   b. .84, .81

   c. p-value $= .0094$
     Reject H_0; conclude an increase

   d. .005 to .055; yes due to increase

11. $H_0: p_1 = p_2 = p_3$

   H_a: Not all population proportions are equal
     Expected frequencies (e_{ij}):

	1	**2**	**3**	**Total**
Yes	132.0	158.4	105.6	396
No	118.0	141.6	94.4	354
Total	250	300	200	750

   Chi-square calculations $(f_{ij} - e_{ij})^2/e_{ij}$:

	1	**2**	**3**	**Total**
Yes	2.45	.45	.87	3.77
No	2.75	.50	.98	4.22
				$\chi^2 = 7.99$

   $df = k - 1 = (3 - 1) = 2$
   χ^2 table with $\chi^2 = 7.99$ shows p-value between .025 and .01
   p-value $\leq .05$, reject H_0; not all population proportions are equal

12. a. $\bar{p}_1 = 150/250 = .60$
      $\bar{p}_2 = 150/300 = .50$
      $\bar{p}_3 = 96/200 = .48$

   b. For 1 vs. 2

   $CV_{12} = \sqrt{\chi^2_{\alpha: k-1}}\sqrt{\dfrac{\bar{p}_1(1 - \bar{p}_1)}{n_1} + \dfrac{\bar{p}_2(1 - \bar{p}_2)}{n_2}}$

   $= \sqrt{5.991}\sqrt{\dfrac{.60(1 - .60)}{250} + \dfrac{.50(1 - .50)}{300}} = .1037$

p_i	p_j	Difference	n_i	n_j	Critical Value	Significant Diff > CV
.60	.50	.10	250	300	.1037	
.60	.48	.12	250	200	.1150	Yes
.50	.48	.02	300	200	.1117	

One comparison is significant, 1 vs. 3

14. a. $H_0: p_1 = p_2 = p_3$
   H_a: Not all population proportions are equal
b. Expected frequencies (e_{ij}):

Component	A	B	C	Total
Defective	25	25	25	75
Good	475	475	475	1425
Total	500	500	500	1500

Chi-square calculations $(f_{ij} - e_{ij})^2/e_{ij}$:

Component	A	B	C	Total
Defective	4.00	1.00	9.00	14.00
Good	.21	.05	.47	0.74
				$\chi^2 = 14.74$

$df = k - 1 = (3 - 1) = 2$
χ^2 table, $\chi^2 = 14.74$, p-value is less than .01
p-value $\leq .05$, reject H_0; three suppliers do not provide equal proportions of defective components
c. $\bar{p}_1 = 15/500 = .03$
   $\bar{p}_2 = 20/500 = .04$
   $\bar{p}_3 = 40/500 = .08$
For supplier A vs. supplier B

$$CV_{ij} = \sqrt{\chi^2_{\alpha: k-1}}\sqrt{\frac{\bar{p}_i(1 - \bar{p}_i)}{n_i} + \frac{\bar{p}_j(1 - \bar{p}_j)}{n_j}}$$

$$= \sqrt{5.991}\sqrt{\frac{.03(1 - .03)}{500} + \frac{.04(1 - .04)}{500}} = .0284$$

Comparison	p_i	p_j	Difference	n_i	n_j	Critical Value	Significant Diff > CV
A vs. B	.03	.04	.01	500	500	.0284	
A vs. C	.03	.08	.05	500	500	.0351	Yes
B vs. C	.04	.08	.04	500	500	.0366	Yes

Supplier A and supplier B are both significantly different from supplier C

16. a. .14, .09
   b. $\chi^2 = 3.41$, $df = 1$
   p-value between .10 and .05

Reject H_0; conclude two offices do not have equal error rates
   c. z provides options for one-tailed tests
18. $\chi^2 = 5.70$, $df = 4$
   p-value greater than .10
   Do no reject H_0; no evidence suppliers differ in quality
19. H_0: The column variable is independent of the row variable
   H_a: The column variable is not independent of the row variable
   Expected frequencies (e_{ij}):

	A	B	C	Total
P	28.5	39.9	45.6	114
Q	21.5	30.1	34.4	86
Total	50	70	80	200

Chi-square calculations $(f_{ij} - e_{ij})^2 / e_{ij}$:

	A	B	C	Total
P	2.54	.42	.42	3.38
Q	3.36	.56	.56	4.48
				$\chi^2 = 7.86$

$df = (2 - 1)(3 - 1) = 2$
Using the χ^2 table, p-value between .01 and .025
p-value $\leq .05$, reject H_0; conclude variables are not independent

20. $\chi^2 = 19.77$, $df = 4$
   p-value less than .005
   Reject H_0; conclude variables are not independent

21. a. H_0: Ticket purchased is independent of flight
   H_a: Ticket purchased is not independent of flight
   Expected frequencies:

$e_{11} = 35.59$ $e_{12} = 15.41$
$e_{21} = 150.73$ $e_{22} = 65.27$
$e_{31} = 455.68$ $e_{32} = 197.32$

Observed Frequency (f_i)	Expected Frequency (e_i)	Chi-square $(f_i - e_i)^2 / e_i$
29	35.59	1.22
22	15.41	2.82
95	150.73	20.61
121	65.27	47.59
518	455.68	8.52
135	197.32	19.68
920		$\chi^2 = 100.43$

$df = (r - 1)(c - 1) = (3 - 1)(2 - 1) = 2$
Using the χ^2 table, p-value is less than .005

p-value $\leq$ .05, reject H_0; conclude ticket purchased is not independent of the type of flight

b. Column Percentages

Type of Ticket	Type of Flight	
	Domestic	**International**
First Class	4.5%	7.9%
Business Class	14.8%	43.5%
Economy Class	80.7%	48.6%

A higher percentage of first-class and business-class tickets are purchased for international flights

22. a. $\chi^2 = 9.44$, $df = 2$
p-value is less than .01
Reject H_0; plan not independent of type of company
b.

Employment Plan	Private	Public
Add Employees	.5139	.2963
No Change	.2639	.3148
Lay Off Employees	.2222	.3889

Employment opportunities better for private companies

24. a. $\chi^2 = 6.57$, $df = 6$
p-value greater than .10
Do not reject H_0; cannot reject assumption of independence
b. 29%, 46%, and 25%
Outstanding is most frequent owner rating

26. a. 900
b. .2044, .2278, .2100, .1400, .2178

The movie fans favored Jennifer Lawrence, but three other nominees (Jessica Chastain, Emmanuelle Riva, and Naomi Watts) were each favored by almost as many of the fans

c. $\chi^2 = 77.74$; p-value is approximately 0

Reject H_0; actress and respondent age are not independent

28. $\chi^2 = 45.36$, $df = 4$
p-value less than .05
Reject H_0; conclude that the ratings of the hosts are not independent

30. a. p-value ≈ 0, reject H_0
b. .0468 to .1332

32. a. .35 and .47
b. .12 $\pm$ .1037 (.0163 to .2237)
c. Yes, we would expect occupancy rates to be higher

34. a. 8.8%, 11.7%, 9.0%, 8.5%
b. $\chi^2 = 2.48$, $df = 3$
p-value greater than .10
Do not reject H_0; cannot reject assumption that the population proportions are equal

36. Let
$p_1 =$ population proportion of on-time arrivals for American Airlines
$p_2 =$ population proportion of on-time arrivals for Continental Airlines
$p_3 =$ population proportion of on-time arrivals for Delta Air Lines
$p_4 =$ population proportion of on-time arrivals for JetBlue Airways
$p_5 =$ population proportion of on-time arrivals for Southwest Airlines
$p_6 =$ population proportion of on-time arrivals for United Airlines
$p_7 =$ population proportion of on-time arrivals for US Airways

a. .8384, .75, .8205, .7317, .75, .8148, .85
b. $\chi^2 = 7.370$
Degrees of freedom $= k - 1 = 7 - 1 = 6$
p-value $= .2880$

Do not reject H_0; no significant differences in proportion of on-time arrivals

38. Let
$p_1 =$ population proportion of truck drivers who rate Rochester, New York, as satisfactory in keeping its streets clear of snow
$p_2 =$ population proportion of truck drivers who rate Salt Lake City, Utah, as satisfactory in keeping its streets clear of snow
$p_3 =$ population proportion of truck drivers who rate Madison, Wisconsin, as satisfactory in keeping its streets clear of snow
$p_4 =$ population proportion of truck drivers who rate Bridgeport, Connecticut, as satisfactory in keeping its streets clear of snow

a. .5625, .625, .617, .5333
b. $\chi^2 = 1.16$
Degrees of freedom $= k - 1 = 4 - 1 = 3$
p-value $= .7623$
Do not reject H_0; no significant differences in the proportions who rate job as satisfactory

40. $\chi^2 = 23.37$, $df = 3$
p-value is less than .005
Reject H_0; employment status is not independent of region

42. a. 71%, 22%, slower preferred
b. $\chi^2 = 2.99$, $df = 2$
p-value greater than .10

Do not reject H_0; cannot conclude men and women differ in preference

44. $\chi^2 = 7.75$, $df = 3$

p-value is between .05 and .10

Do not reject H_0; cannot conclude office vacancies differ by metropolitan area

Chapter 12

1. a.

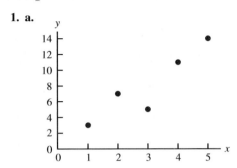

b. There appears to be a positive linear relationship between x and y

c. Many different straight lines can be drawn to provide a linear approximation of the relationship between x and y; in part (d) we will determine the equation of a straight line that "best" represents the relationship according to the least squares criterion

d. Summations needed to compute the slope and y-intercept:

$$\bar{x} = \frac{\Sigma x_i}{n} = \frac{15}{5} = 3, \quad \bar{y} = \frac{\Sigma y_i}{n} = \frac{40}{5} = 8,$$

$$\Sigma(x_i - \bar{x})(y_i - \bar{y}) = 26, \quad \Sigma(x_i - \bar{x})^2 = 10$$

$$b_1 = \frac{\Sigma(x_i - \bar{x})(y_i - \bar{y})}{\Sigma(x_i - \bar{x})^2} = \frac{26}{10} = 2.6$$

$$b_0 = \bar{y} - b_1\bar{x} = 8 - (2.6)(3) = 0.2$$

$$\hat{y} = 0.2 - 2.6x$$

e. $\hat{y} = .2 + 2.6x = .2 + 2.6(4) = 10.6$

2. b. There appears to be a negative linear relationship between x and y

d. $\hat{y} = 68 - 3x$

e. 38

4. a.

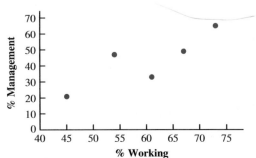

b. There appears to be a positive linear relationship between the percentage of women working in the five companies (x) and the percentage of management jobs held by women in that company (y)

c. Many different straight lines can be drawn to provide a linear approximation of the relationship between x and y; in part (d) we will determine the equation of a straight line that "best" represents the relationship according to the least squares criterion

d. $\bar{x} = \frac{\Sigma x_i}{n} = \frac{300}{5} = 60 \quad \bar{y} = \frac{\Sigma y_i}{n} = \frac{215}{5} = 43$

$$\Sigma(x_i - \bar{x})(y_i - \bar{y}) = 624 \quad \Sigma(x_i - \bar{x})^2 = 480$$

$$b_1 = \frac{\Sigma(x_i - \bar{x})(y_i - \bar{y})}{\Sigma(x_i - \bar{x})^2} = \frac{624}{480} = 1.3$$

$$b_0 = \bar{y} - b_1\bar{x} = 43 - 1.3(60) = -35$$

$$\hat{y} = -35 + 1.3x$$

e. $\hat{y} = -35 + 1.3x = -35 + 1.3(60) = 43\%$

6. c. $\hat{y} = -70.391 + 17.175x$

e. 43.8 or approximately 44%

8. c. $\hat{y} = .2046 + .9077x$

e. 3.29 or approximately 3.3

10. c. $\hat{y} = -167.81 + 2.7149x$

e. Yes

12. c. $\hat{y} = 17.49 + 1.0334x$

d. $150

14. c. $\hat{y} = 55.188 + .06357x$

d. 73

15. a. $\hat{y}_i = .2 + 2.6x_i$ and $\bar{y} = 8$

x_i	y_i	$\hat{y}_i$	$y_i - \hat{y}_i$	$(y_i - \hat{y}_i)^2$	$y_i - \bar{y}$	$(y_i - \bar{y})^2$
1	3	2.8	.2	.04	-5	25
2	7	5.4	1.6	2.56	-1	1
3	5	8.0	-3.0	9.00	-3	9
4	11	10.6	.4	.16	3	9
5	14	13.2	.8	.64	6	36
				SSE = 12.40		SST = 80

$$\text{SSR} = \text{SST} - \text{SSE} = 80 - 12.4 = 67.6$$

b. $r^2 = \dfrac{\text{SSR}}{\text{SST}} = \dfrac{67.6}{80} = .845$

The least squares line provided a good fit; 84.5% of the variability in y has been explained by the least squares line

c. $r_{xy} = \sqrt{.845} = +.9192$

16. a. SSE = 230, SST = 1850, SSR = 1620

b. $r^2 = .876$

c. $r_{xy} = -.936$

18. a.

$$x = \Sigma x_i/n = 600/6 = 100 \qquad y = \Sigma y_i/n = 330/6 = 55$$

$$SST = \Sigma(y_i - y)^2 = 1800 \quad SSE = \Sigma(y_i - \hat{y}_i)^2 = 287.624$$

$$SSR = SST - SSR = 1800 - 287.624 = 1512.376$$

b. $r^2 = \dfrac{SSR}{SST} = \dfrac{1512.376}{1800} = .84$

c. $r = \sqrt{r^2} = \sqrt{.84} = .917$

20. a. $\hat{y} = 28{,}574 - 1439x$

b. $r^2 = .864$

c. \$6989

22. a. .9013

b. Yes

c. $r_{xy} = +.95$, strong

23. a. $s^2 = MSE = \dfrac{SSE}{n-2} = \dfrac{12.4}{3} = 4.133$

b. $s = \sqrt{MSE} = \sqrt{4.133} = 2.033$

c. $\Sigma(x_i - \bar{x})^2 = 10$

$$s_{b_1} = \frac{s}{\sqrt{\Sigma(x_i - \bar{x})^2}} = \frac{2.033}{\sqrt{10}} = .643$$

d. $t = \dfrac{b_1 - \beta_1}{s_{b_1}} = \dfrac{2.6 - 0}{.643} = 4.044$

From the t table (3 degrees of freedom), area in tail is between .01 and .025

p-value is between .02 and .05

Using Excel or Minitab, the p-value corresponding to $t = 4.04$ is .0272

Because p-value $\leq \alpha$, we reject H_0: $\beta_1 = 0$

e. $MSR = \dfrac{SSR}{1} = 67.6$

$$F = \frac{MSR}{MSE} = \frac{67.6}{4.133} = 16.36$$

From the F table (1 numerator degree of freedom and 3 denominator), p-value is between .025 and .05

Using Excel or Minitab, the p-value corresponding to $F = 16.36$ is .0272

Because p-value $\leq \alpha$, we reject H_0: $\beta_1 = 0$

Source of Variation	Sum of Squares	Degrees of Freedom	Mean Square	F	p-value
Regression	67.6	1	67.6	16.36	.0272
Error	12.4	3	4.133		
Total	80	4			

24. a. 76.6667

b. 8.7560

c. .6526

d. Significant; p-value $= .0193$

e. Significant; p-value $= .0193$

26. a. In the statement of exercise 18, $\hat{y} = 23.194 + .318x$

In solving exercise 18, we found SSE $= 287.624$

$s^2 = MSE = SSE/(n-2) = 287.624/4 = 71.906$

$s = \sqrt{MSE} = \sqrt{71.906} = 8.4797$

$\Sigma(x - \bar{x})^2 = 14{,}950$

$$s_{b_1} = \frac{s}{\sqrt{\Sigma(x - \bar{x})^2}} = \frac{8.4797}{\sqrt{14{,}950}} = .0694$$

$$t = \frac{b_1}{s_{b_1}} = \frac{.318}{.0694} = 4.58$$

Using t table (4 degrees of freedom), area in tail is between .005 and .01

p-value is between .01 and .02

Using Excel, the p-value corresponding to $t = 4.58$ is .010

Because p-value $\leq \alpha$, we reject H_0: $\beta_1 = 0$; there is a significant relationship between price and overall score

b. In exercise 18 we found SSR $= 1512.376$

MSR $=$ SSR/1 $= 1512.376/1 = 1512.376$

$F =$ MSR/MSE $= 1512.376/71.906 = 21.03$

Using F table (1 degree of freedom numerator and 4 denominator), p-value is between .025 and .01

Using Excel, the p-value corresponding to $F = 11.74$ is .010

Because p-value $\leq \alpha$, we reject H_0: $\beta_1 - 0$

c.

Source of Variation	Sum of Squares	Degrees of Freedom	Mean Square	F	p-value
Regression	1512.376	1	1512.376	21.03	.010
Error	287.624	4	71.906		
Total	1800	5			

28. They are related; p-value $= .000$

30. Significant; p-value $= .004$

32. a. $s = 2.033$

$$\bar{x} = 3, \ \Sigma(x_i - \bar{x})^2 = 10$$

$$s_{\hat{y}*} = s\sqrt{\frac{1}{n} + \frac{(x* - \bar{x})^2}{\Sigma(x_i - \bar{x})^2}}$$

$$= 2.033\sqrt{\frac{1}{5} + \frac{(4-3)^2}{10}} = 1.11$$

b. $\hat{y}* = .2 + 2.6x* = .2 + 2.6(4) = 10.6$

$$\hat{y}* \pm t_{\alpha/2}s_{\hat{y}*}$$

$10.6 \pm 3.182(1.11)$

10.6 ± 3.53, or 7.07 to 14.13

c. $s_{pred} = s\sqrt{1 + \dfrac{1}{n} + \dfrac{(x^* - \bar{x})^2}{\Sigma(x_i - \bar{x})^2}}$

$= 2.033\sqrt{1 + \dfrac{1}{5} + \dfrac{(4 - 3)^2}{10}} = 2.32$

d. $\hat{y}^* \pm t_{\alpha/2}s_{pred}$

$10.6 \pm 3.182(2.32)$

10.6 ± 7.38, or 3.22 to 17.98

34. Confidence interval: 8.65 to 21.15

Prediction interval: -4.50 to 41.30

35. a. $\hat{y}^* = 2090.5 + 581.1x^* = 2090.5 + 581.1(3) = 3833.8$

b. $s = \sqrt{MSE} = \sqrt{21{,}284} = 145.89$

$\bar{x} = 3.2$, $\Sigma(x_i - \bar{x})^2 = 0.74$

$s_{\hat{y}^*} = s\sqrt{\dfrac{1}{n} + \dfrac{(x^* - \bar{x})^2}{\Sigma(x_i - \bar{x})^2}}$

$= 145.89\sqrt{\dfrac{1}{6} + \dfrac{(3 - 3.2)^2}{0.74}} = 68.54$

$\hat{y}^* \pm t_{\alpha/2}s_{\hat{y}^*}$

$3833.8 \pm 2.776(68.54) = 3833.8 \pm 190.27$

or $\$3643.53$ to $\$4024.07$

c. $s_{pred} = s\sqrt{1 + \dfrac{1}{n} + \dfrac{(x^* - \bar{x})^2}{\Sigma(x_i - \bar{x})^2}}$

$= 145.89\sqrt{1 + \dfrac{1}{6} + \dfrac{(3 - 3.2)^2}{0.74}} = 161.19$

$\hat{y}^* \pm t_{\alpha/2}s_{pred}$

$3833.8 \pm 2.776(161.19) = 3833.8 \pm 447.46$

or $\$3386.34$ to $\$4281.26$

d. As expected, the prediction interval is much wider than the confidence interval. This is due to the fact that it is more difficult to predict the starting salary for one new student with a GPA of 3.0 than it is to estimate the mean for all students with a GPA of 3.0.

36. a. $\$112{,}190$ to $\$119{,}810$

b. $\$104{,}710$ to $\$127{,}290$

38. a. $\$5046.67$

b. $\$3815.10$ to $\$6278.24$

c. Not out of line

40. a. 9

b. $\hat{y} = 20.0 + 7.21x$

c. 1.3626

d. SSE $=$ SST $-$ SSR $= 51{,}984.1 - 41{,}587.3 = 10{,}396.8$

MSE $= 10{,}396.8/7 = 1485.3$

$F = \dfrac{MSR}{MSE} = \dfrac{41{,}587.3}{1485.3} = 28.0$

From the F table (1 numerator degree of freedom and 7 denominator), p-value is less than .01

Using Excel or Minitab, the p-value corresponding to $F = 28.0$ is .0011

Because p-value $\leq \alpha = .05$, we reject H_0: $\beta_1 = 0$

e. $\hat{y} = 20.0 + 7.21(50) = 380.5$, or $\$380{,}500$

42. a. $\hat{y} = 80.0 + 50.0x$

b. 30

c. Significant; p-value $= .000$

d. $\$680{,}000$

44. b. Yes

c. $\hat{y} = 2044.38 - 28.35$ weight

d. Significant; p-value $= .000$

e. .774; a good fit

45. a. $\bar{x} = \dfrac{\Sigma x_i}{n} = \dfrac{70}{5} = 14$, $\bar{y} = \dfrac{\Sigma y_i}{n} = \dfrac{76}{5} = 15.2$,

$\Sigma(x_i - \bar{x})(y_i - \bar{y}) = 200$, $\quad \Sigma(x_i - \bar{x})^2 = 126$

$b_1 = \dfrac{\Sigma(x_i - \bar{x})(y_i - \bar{y})}{\Sigma(x_i - \bar{x})^2} = \dfrac{200}{126} = 1.5873$

$b_0 = \bar{y} - b_1\bar{x} = 15.2 - (1.5873)(14) = -7.0222$

$\hat{y} = -7.02 + 1.59x$

b.

x_i	y_i	$\hat{y}_i$	$y_i - \hat{y}_i$
6	6	2.52	3.48
11	8	10.47	-2.47
15	12	16.83	-4.83
18	20	21.60	-1.60
20	30	24.78	5.22

c.

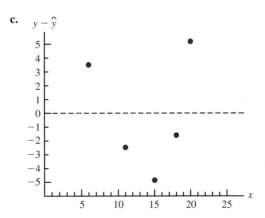

With only five observations, it is difficult to determine whether the assumptions are satisfied; however, the plot does suggest curvature in the residuals, which would indicate that the error term assumptions are not satisfied; the scatter diagram for these data also indicates that the underlying relationship between x and y may be curvilinear

46. a. $\hat{y} = 2.32 + .64x$
   b. No; the variance appears to increase for larger values of x

47. a. Let x = advertising expenditures and y = revenue
   $$\hat{y} = 29.4 + 1.55x$$

   b. SST = 1002, SSE = 310.28, SSR = 691.72

   $$MSR = \frac{SSR}{1} = 691.72$$

   $$MSE = \frac{SSE}{n-2} = \frac{310.28}{5} = 62.0554$$

   $$F = \frac{MSR}{MSE} = \frac{691.72}{62.0554} = 11.15$$

   From the F table (1 numerator degree of freedom and 5 denominator), p-value is between .01 and .025
   Using Excel or Minitab, p-value = .0206
   Because p-value $\leq \alpha$ = .05, we conclude that the two variables are related

   c.

x_i	y_i	$\hat{y}_i = 29.40 + 1.55 x_i$	$y_i - \hat{y}_i$
1	19	30.95	−11.95
2	32	32.50	−.50
4	44	35.60	8.40
6	40	38.70	1.30
10	52	44.90	7.10
14	53	51.10	1.90
20	54	60.40	−6.40

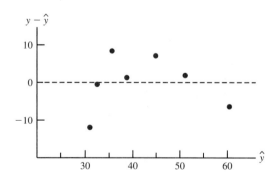

   d. The residual plot leads us to question the assumption of a linear relationship between x and y; even though the relationship is significant at the α = .05 level, it would be extremely dangerous to extrapolate beyond the range of the data

48. b. Yes

50. b. $\hat{y} = -669 + .157$ DJIA
   c. Significant; p-value = .001
   d. r^2 = .949; excellent fit

52. b. GR(%) = 25.4 + .285 RR(%)
   c. Significant; p-value = .000
   d. No; r^2 = .449
   e. Yes
   f. Yes

54. a. $\hat{y} = 220 + 132x$
   b. Significant; p-value = .000
   c. r^2 = .873; very good fit
   d. \$559.50 to \$933.90

56. b. There appears to be a negative linear relationship between the two variables
   c. $\hat{y} = 16.5 - .0588$ Miles
   d. Significant; p-value = .000
   e. r^2 = .539; reasonably good fit
   g. approximately \$13,000; no

Chapter 13

2. a. The estimated regression equation is
   $\hat{y} = 45.06 + 1.94x_1$
   An estimate of y when x_1 = 45 is
   $\hat{y} = 45.06 + 1.94(45) = 132.36$
   b. The estimated regression equation is
   $\hat{y} = 85.22 + 4.32x_2$
   An estimate of y when x_2 = 15 is
   $\hat{y} = 85.22 + 4.32(15) = 150.02$
   c. The estimated regression equation is
   $\hat{y} = -18.37 + 2.01x_1 + 4.74x_2$
   An estimate of y when x_1 = 45 and x_2 = 15 is
   $\hat{y} = -18.37 + 2.01(45) + 4.74(15) = 143.18$

4. a. \$255,000

5. a. The Minitab output is shown in Figure D13.5a
   b. The Minitab output is shown in Figure D13.5b
   c. It is 1.60 in part (a) and 2.29 in part (b); in part (a) the coefficient is an estimate of the change in revenue due to a one-unit change in television advertising expenditures; in part (b) it represents an estimate of the change in revenue due to a one-unit change in television advertising expenditures when the amount of newspaper advertising is held constant
   d. Revenue = 83.2 + 2.29(3.5) + 1.30(1.8) = 93.56 or \$93,560

6. a. Win% = −58.8 + 16.4 Yds/Att
   b. Win% = 97.5 − 1600 Int/Att
   c. Win% = −5.8 + 12.9 Yds/Att − 1084 Int/Att
   d. 35%

8. a. Overall = 69.3 + .235 Shore Excursions
   b. Overall = 45.2 + .253 Shore Excursions
             + .248 Food/Dining
   c. 87.76 or approximately 88.

FIGURE D13.5a

```
The regression equation is
Revenue = 88.6 + 1.60 TVAdv

Predictor          Coef      SE Coef          T          p
Constant         88.638        1.582      56.02      0.000
TVAdv            1.6039       0.4778       3.36      0.015


S = 1.215      R-sq = 65.3%      R-sq(adj) = 59.5%


Analysis of Variance

SOURCE             DF          SS          MS          F          p
Regression          1      16.640      16.640      11.27      0.015
Residual Error      6       8.860       1.477
Total               7      25.500
```

FIGURE D13.5b

```
The regression equation is
Revenue = 83.2 + 2.29 TVAdv + 1.30 NewsAdv

Predictor          Coef      SE Coef          T          p
Constant         83.230        1.574      52.88      0.000
TVAdv            2.2902       0.3041       7.53      0.001
NewsAdv          1.3010       0.3207       4.06      0.010


S = 0.6426      R-sq = 91.9%      R-sq(adj) = 88.7%


Analysis of Variance

SOURCE             DF          SS          MS          F          p
Regression          2      23.435      11.718      28.38      0.002
Residual Error      5       2.065       0.413
Total               7      25.500
```

10. a. R/IP = .676 − .284 SO/IP
   b. R/IP = .308 + 1.35 HR/IP
   c. R/IP = .537 − .248 SO/IP + 1.03 HR/IP
   d. .48
   e. Suggestion does not make sense

12. a. $R^2 = \dfrac{\text{SSR}}{\text{SST}} = \dfrac{14{,}052.2}{15{,}182.9} = .926$

   b. $R_a^2 = 1 - (1 - R^2)\dfrac{n-1}{n-p-1}$

   $= 1 - (1 - .926)\dfrac{10 - 1}{10 - 2 - 1} = .905$

   c. Yes; after adjusting for the number of independent variables in the model, we see that 90.5% of the variability in y has been accounted for

14. a. .75
   b. .68

15. a. $R^2 = \dfrac{\text{SSR}}{\text{SST}} = \dfrac{23.435}{25.5} = .919$

   $R_a^2 = 1 - (1 - R^2)\dfrac{n-1}{n-p-1}$

   $= 1 - (1 - .919)\dfrac{8 - 1}{8 - 2 - 1} = .887$

   b. Multiple regression analysis is preferred because both R^2 and R_a^2 show an increased percentage of the variability of y explained when both independent variables are used

16. a. No, $R^2 = .577$
   b. Better fit with multiple regression

18. a. $R^2 = .563$, $R_a^2 = .512$

   b. The fit is not very good

19. a. $MSR = \dfrac{SSR}{p} = \dfrac{6216.375}{2} = 3108.188$

$MSE = \dfrac{SSE}{n - p - 1} = \dfrac{507.75}{10 - 2 - 1} = 72.536$

   b. $F = \dfrac{MSR}{MSE} = \dfrac{3108.188}{72.536} = 42.85$

From the F table (2 numerator degrees of freedom and 7 denominator), p-value is less than .01

Using Excel or Minitab the p-value corresponding to $F = 42.85$ is .0001

Because p-value $\le \alpha$, the overall model is significant

   c. $t = \dfrac{b_1}{s_{b_1}} = \dfrac{.5906}{.0813} = 7.26$

p-value $= .0002$

Because p-value $\le \alpha$, β_1 is significant

   d. $t = \dfrac{b_2}{s_{b_2}} = \dfrac{.4980}{.0567} = 8.78$

p-value $= .0001$

Because p-value $\le \alpha$, β_2 is significant

20. a. Significant; p-value $= .000$

   b. Significant; p-value $= .000$

   c. Significant; p-value $= .002$

22. a. SSE $= 4000$, $s^2 = 571.43$,
   MSR $= 6000$

   b. Significant; p-value $= .008$

23. a. $F = 28.38$

p-value $= .002$

Because p-value $\le \alpha$, there is a significant relationship

   b. $t = 7.53$

p-value $= .001$

Because p-value $\le \alpha$, β_1 is significant and x_1 should not be dropped from the model

   c. $t = 4.06$

p-value $= .010$

Because p-value $\le \alpha$, β_2 is significant and x_2 should not be dropped from the model

24. a. $\hat{y} = 60.5 + .319\,\text{OffPassYds/G} - .241\,\text{DefYds/G}$

   b. Significant; p-value $= .000$

   c. OffPassYds/G is significant; p-value $= .000$
   DefYds/G is significant; p-value $= .011$

26. a. Significant; p-value $= .001$

   b. All significant; p-values are all $< \alpha = .05$

28. a. Using Minitab, the 95% confidence interval is 132.16 to 154.16

   b. Using Minitab, the 95% prediction interval is 111.13 at 175.18

29. a. See Minitab output in Figure D13.5b

$\hat{y} = 83.23 + 2.29(3.5) + 1.30(1.8) = 93.555$ or $\$93,555$

   b. Minitab results: 92.840 to 94.335, or $\$92,840$ to $\$94,335$

   c. Minitab results: 91.774 to 95.401, or $\$91,774$ to $\$95,401$

30. a. 59.975%

   b. 49.83 to 69.82

32. a. $E(y) = \beta_0 + \beta_1 x_1 + \beta_2 x_2$

where $x_2 = \begin{cases} 0 \text{ if level 1} \\ 1 \text{ if level 2} \end{cases}$

   b. $E(y) = \beta_0 + \beta_1 x_1 + \beta_2(0) = \beta_0 + \beta_1 x_1$

   c. $E(y) = \beta_0 + \beta_1 x_1 + \beta_2(1) = \beta_0 + \beta_1 x_1 + \beta_2$

   d. $\beta_2 = E(y \mid \text{level 2}) - E(y \mid \text{level 1})$
   β_1 is the change in $E(y)$ for a 1-unit change in x_1 holding x_2 constant

34. a. $\$15,300$

   b. $\hat{y} = 10.1 - 4.2(2) + 6.8(8) + 15.3(0) = 56.1$
   Sales prediction: $\$56,100$

   c. $\hat{y} = 10.1 - 4.2(1) + 6.8(3) + 15.3(1) = 41.6$
   Sales prediction: $\$41,600$

36. a. $\hat{y} = 1.86 + 0.291\,\text{Months} + 1.10\,\text{Type} - 0.609\,\text{Person}$

   b. Significant; p-value $= .002$

   c. Person is not significant; p-value $= .167$

38. a. $\hat{y} = -91.8 + 1.08\,\text{Age} + .252\,\text{Pressure} + 8.74\,\text{Smoker}$

   b. Significant; p-value $= .01$

   c. 95% prediction interval is 21.35 to 47.18 or a probability of .2135 to .4718; quit smoking and begin some type of treatment to reduce his blood pressure

40. b. 67.39

42. a. $\hat{y} = -1.41 + .0235 x_1 + .00486 x_2$

   b. Significant; p-value $= .0001$

   c. Both significant

   d. $R^2 = .937$; $R_a^2 = 9.19$; good fit

44. a. Buy Again $= -7.522 + 1.8151\,\text{Steering}$

   b. Yes

   c. Buy Again $= -5.388 + .6899\,\text{Steering} + .9113\,\text{Treadwear}$

   d. Significant; p-value $= .001$

46. a. $\hat{y} = 4.9090 + 10.4658\,\text{FundDE} + 21.6823\,\text{FundIE}$

   b. $R^2 = .6144$; reasonably good fit

   c. $\hat{y} = 1.1899 + 6.8969\,\text{FundDE} + 17.6800\,\text{FundIE} + 0.0265\,\text{Net Asset Value (\$)} + 6.4564\,\text{Expense Ratio (\%)}$

Net Asset Value ($) is not significant and can be deleted
  d. $\hat{y} = -4.6074 + 8.1713\,\text{FundDE} + 19.5194\,\text{FundIE}$
     $+ 5.5197\,\text{Expense Ratio (\%)} + 5.9237\,\text{3StarRank}$
     $+ 8.2367\,\text{4StarRank} + 6.6241\,\text{5StarRank}$
  e. 15.28%

48. a. $\hat{y} = -295 + 7.70\,\text{FG\%}$
  b. An increase of 1% in FG% will increase Win% by 7.7%

  c. $\hat{y} = -408 + 4.96\,\text{FG\%} + 2.37\,\text{3P\%} + .005\,\text{FT\%}$
     $+3.46\,\text{RBOff} + 3.69\,\text{RBDef}$
  d. FT% is not significant
     $\hat{y} = -408 + 4.96\,\text{FG\%} + 2.37\,\text{3P\%} + 3.46\,\text{RBOff}$
     $+ 3.69\,\text{RBDef}$
  e. 50.37

Appendix E: Microsoft Excel 2013 and Tools for Statistical Analysis

Microsoft Excel 2013, part of the Microsoft Office 2013 system, is a spreadsheet program that can be used to organize and analyze data, perform complex calculations, and create a wide variety of graphical displays. We assume that readers are familiar with basic Excel operations such as selecting cells, entering formulas, copying, and so on. But we do not assume readers are familiar with Excel 2013 or the use of Excel for statistical analysis.

The purpose of this appendix is twofold. First, we provide an overview of Excel 2013 and discuss the basic operations needed to work with Excel 2013 workbooks and worksheets. Second, we provide an overview of the tools that are available for conducting statistical analysis with Excel. These include Excel functions and formulas which allow users to conduct their own analyses and add-ins that provide more comprehensive analysis tools.

Excel's Data Analysis add-in, included with the basic Excel system, is a valuable tool for conducting statistical analysis. In the last section of this primer we provide instruction for installing the Data Analysis add-in. Other add-ins have been developed by outside suppliers to supplement the basic statistical capabilities provided by Excel. In the last section we also discuss StatTools, a commercially available add-in developed by Palisade Corporation.

Overview of Microsoft Excel 2013

When using Excel for statistical analysis, data are displayed in workbooks, each of which contains a series of worksheets that typically include the original data as well as any resulting analysis, including charts. Figure E.1 shows the layout of a blank workbook created each time Excel is opened. The workbook is named Book1 and consists of a single worksheet named Sheet1. Excel highlights the worksheet currently displayed (Sheet1) by setting the name on the worksheet tab in bold. Note that cell A1 is initially selected.

A workbook is a file containing one or more worksheets.

The wide bar located across the top of the workbook is referred to as the Ribbon. Tabs, located at the top of the Ribbon, provide quick access to groups of related commands. There are eight tabs shown on the workbook in Figure E.1: File; Home; Insert; Page Layout; Formulas; Data; Review; and View. Each tab contains a series of groups of related commands. Note that the Home tab is selected when Excel is opened. Figure E.2 displays the groups available when the Home tab is selected. Under the Home tab there are seven groups: Clipboard; Font; Alignment; Number; Styles; Cells; and Editing. Commands are arranged within each group. For example, to change selected text to boldface, click the Home tab and click the Bold button in the Font group.

Figure E.3 illustrates the location of the Quick Access Toolbar and the Formula Bar. The Quick Access Toolbar allows you to quickly access workbook options. To add or remove features on the Quick Access Toolbar click the Customize Quick Access Toolbar button ⏷ on the Quick Access Toolbar.

The Formula Bar (see Figure E.3) contains a Name box, the Insert Function Button, *fx*, and a Formula box. In Figure E.3, "A1" appears in the name box because cell A1 is selected. You can select any other cell in the worksheet by using the mouse to move the cursor to another cell and clicking or by typing the new cell location in the Name box. The Formula box is used to display the formula in the currently selected cell. For instance, if you had entered =A1+A2 into cell A3, whenever you select cell A3 the formula =A1+A2

FIGURE E.1   BLANK WORKBOOK CREATED WHEN EXCEL IS OPENED

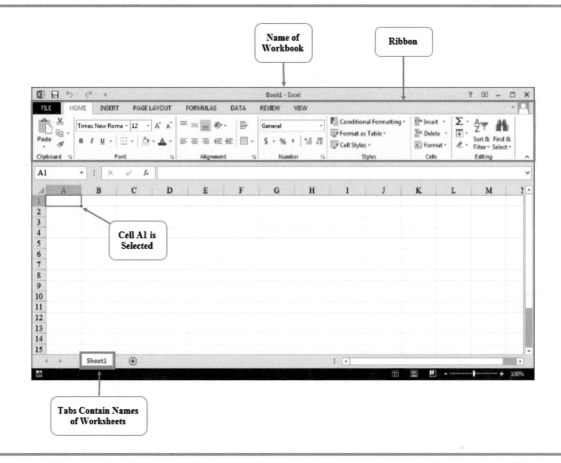

would be shown in the Formula box. This feature makes it very easy to see and edit a formula in a particular cell. The Insert Function button allows you to quickly access all of the functions available in Excel. We discuss the Insert Function button later in this appendix.

Basic Workbook Operations

Figure E.4 illustrates the worksheet options that can be performed after right-clicking on a worksheet tab. For instance, to change the name of the current worksheet from "Sheet1" to "Data," right-click the worksheet tab named "Sheet1" and select the Rename option. The current worksheet name (Sheet1) will be highlighted. Then, simply type the new name (Data) and press the Enter key to rename the worksheet.

Suppose that you wanted to create a copy of "Sheet1." After right-clicking the tab named "Sheet1," select the Move or Copy option. When the Move or Copy dialog box appears, select Create a Copy and click OK. The name of the copied worksheet will appear as "Sheet1 (2)." You can then rename it, if desired.

To add a worksheet to the workbook, right-click any worksheet tab and select the Insert option; when the Insert dialog box appears, select Worksheet and click OK. An additional blank worksheet titled "Sheet2" will appear in the workbook. You can also insert a new worksheet by clicking the New sheet tab button ⊕ that appears to the right of the last worksheet tab displayed. Worksheets can be deleted by right-clicking the worksheet tab

FIGURE E.2   PORTION OF THE HOME TAB

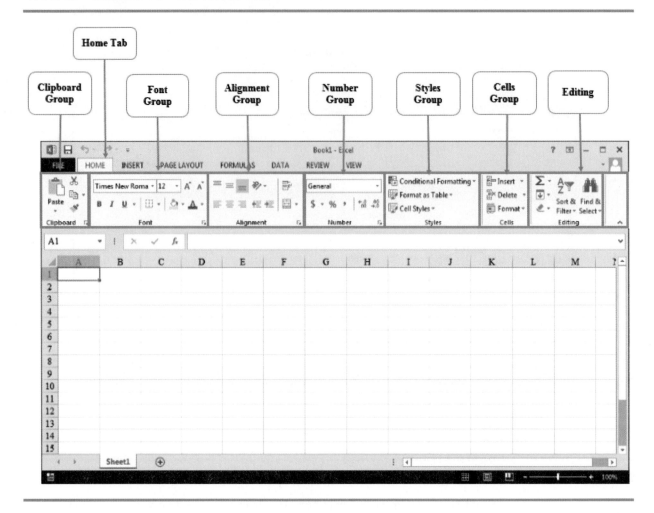

and choosing Delete. After clicking Delete, a window will appear warning you that any data appearing in the worksheet will be lost. Click Delete to confirm that you do want to delete the worksheet. Worksheets can also be moved to other workbooks or a different position in the current workbook by using the Move or Copy option.

Creating, Saving, and Opening Files

Data can be entered into an Excel worksheet by manually entering the data into the worksheet or by opening another workbook that already contains the data. As an illustration of manually entering, saving, and opening a file we will use the example from Chapter 2 involving data for a sample of 50 soft drink purchases. The original data are shown in Table E.1.

Suppose we want to enter the data for the sample of 50 soft drink purchases into Sheet1 of a new workbook. First, we enter the label "Brand Purchased" into cell A1; then we enter the data for the 50 soft drink purchases into cells A2:A51. As a reminder that this worksheet contains the data, we will change the name of the worksheet from "Sheet1" to "Data" using the procedure described previously. Figure E.5 shows the data worksheet that we just developed. Note that we have hidden rows 21–49.

FIGURE E.3   EXCEL 2013 QUICK ACCESS TOOLBAR AND FORMULA BAR

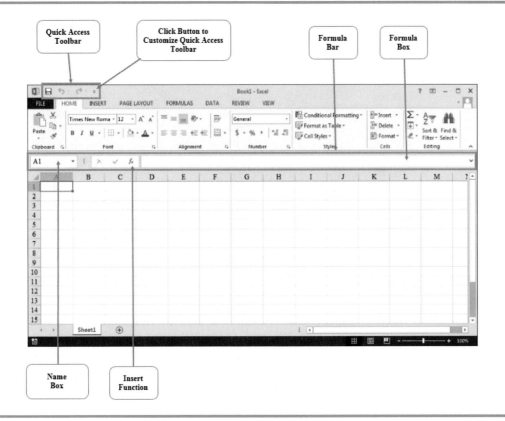

FIGURE E.4   WORKSHEET OPTIONS OBTAINED AFTER RIGHT-CLICKING
A WORKSHEET TAB

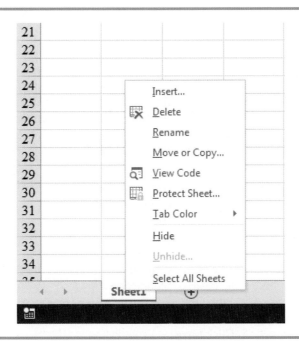

TABLE E.1   DATA FROM A SAMPLE OF 50 SOFT DRINK PURCHASES

Coca-Cola	Sprite	Pepsi
Diet Coke	Coca-Cola	Coca-Cola
Pepsi	Diet Coke	Coca-Cola
Diet Coke	Coca-Cola	Coca-Cola
Coca-Cola	Diet Coke	Pepsi
Coca-Cola	Coca-Cola	Dr. Pepper
Dr. Pepper	Sprite	Coca-Cola
Diet Coke	Pepsi	Diet Coke
Pepsi	Coca-Cola	Pepsi
Pepsi	Coca-Cola	Pepsi
Coca-Cola	Coca-Cola	Pepsi
Dr. Pepper	Pepsi	Pepsi
Sprite	Coca-Cola	Coca-Cola
Coca-Cola	Sprite	Dr. Pepper
Diet Coke	Dr. Pepper	Pepsi
Coca-Cola	Pepsi	Sprite
Coca-Cola	Diet Coke	

Before doing any analysis with these data, we recommend that you first save the file; this will prevent you from having to reenter the data in case something happens that causes Excel to close. To save the file as an Excel 2013 workbook using the filename SoftDrink we perform the following steps:

Step 1. Click the **FILE** tab
Step 2. Click **Save** in the list of options
Step 3. Select **Computer**
   Select the location where you want to save the file, either from the list of **Recent Folders** or by clicking the Browse Button and navigating to the desired folder
   When the **Save As** dialog box appears, type the filename **SoftDrink** in the **File name** box
   Click **Save**

Keyboard shortcut: To save the file, press CTRL+S.

Excel's Save command is designed to save the file as an Excel 2013 workbook. As you work with the file to do statistical analysis you should follow the practice of periodically saving the file so you will not lose any statistical analysis you may have performed. Simply click the File tab and select Save in the list of options.

Sometimes you may want to create a copy of an existing file. For instance, suppose you would like to save the soft drink data and any resulting statistical analysis in a new file named "SoftDrink Analysis." The following steps show how to create a copy of the SoftDrink workbook and analysis with the new filename, "SoftDrink Analysis."

Step 1. Click the **FILE** tab
Step 2. Click **Save As**
Step 3. Select **Computer**
   Select the location where you want to save the file, either from the list of **Recent Folders** or by clicking the Browse Button and navigating to the desired folder
   When the **Save As** dialog box appears, type the filename **SoftDrink Analysis** in the **File name** box
   Click **Save**

FIGURE E.5   WORKSHEET CONTAINING THE SOFT DRINK DATA

	A	B	C	D	E	F
1	**Brand Purchased**					
2	Coca-Cola					
3	Diet Coke					
4	Pepsi					
5	Diet Coke					
6	Coca-Cola					
7	Coca-Cola					
8	Dr. Pepper					
9	Diet Coke					
10	Pepsi					
11	Pepsi					
12	Coca-Cola					
13	Dr. Pepper					
14	Sprite					
15	Coca-Cola					
16	Diet Coke					
17	Coca-Cola					
18	Coca-Cola					
19	Sprite					
20	Coca-Cola					
50	Pepsi					
51	Sprite					
52						
53						
54						
55						

Note: Rows 21–49 are hidden.

Once the workbook has been saved, you can continue to work with the data to perform whatever type of statistical analysis is appropriate. When you are finished working with the file, click the File tab and then click Close ✗. To access the SoftDrink Analysis file at another point in time you can open the file by performing the following steps:

Step 1. Click the **FILE** tab
Step 2. Click **Open**
Step 3. Select the file name from the list of **Recent Workbooks**.

*If the file you wish to open does not appear under Recent Workbooks, select **Computer**, and click the **Browse** button. When the **Open** dialog box appears, navigate to the folder where you have saved the file, select the file, and click the **Open** button.*

The procedures we showed for saving or opening a workbook begin by clicking the File tab to access the Save and Open commands. Once you have used Excel for a while you will probably find it more convenient to add these commands to the Quick Access Toolbar.

Using Excel Functions

Excel 2013 provides a wealth of functions for data management and statistical analysis. If we know what function is needed, and how to use it, we can simply enter the function into the appropriate worksheet cell. However, if we are not sure what functions are available to accomplish a task or are not sure how to use a particular function, Excel can provide assistance. Many new functions for statistical analysis have been added with Excel 2013.

Finding the Right Excel Function

To identify the functions available in Excel, click the **FORMULA** tab on the Ribbon and then click the **Insert Function** button in the **Function Library** group. Alternatively, click the f_x button on the formula bar. Either approach provides the **Insert Function** dialog box shown in Figure E.6.

The **Search for a function** box at the top of the Insert Function dialog box enables us to type a brief description of what we want to do. After doing so and clicking **Go**, Excel will search for and display, in the **Select a function** box, the functions that may accomplish our task. In many situations, however, we may want to browse through an entire category of functions to see what is available. For this task, the **Or select a category** box is helpful. It contains a drop-down list of several categories of functions provided by Excel. Figure E.6 shows that we selected the **Statistical** category. As a result, Excel's statistical functions appear in alphabetic order in the Select a function box. We see the AVEDEV function listed first, followed by the AVERAGE function, and so on.

The AVEDEV function is highlighted in Figure E.6, indicating it is the function currently selected. The proper syntax for the function and a brief description of the function appear below the Select a function box. We can scroll through the list in the Select a function box to display the syntax and a brief description for each of the statistical functions that are available. For instance, scrolling down farther, we select the COUNTIF function

FIGURE E.6   INSERT FUNCTION DIALOG BOX

FIGURE E.7   DESCRIPTION OF THE COUNTIF FUNCTION IN THE INSERT
FUNCTION DIALOG BOX

as shown in Figure E.7. Note that COUNTIF is now highlighted, and that immediately below the Select a function box we see **COUNTIF(range,criteria)**, which indicates that the COUNTIF function contains two inputs, range and criteria. In addition, we see that the description of the COUNTIF function is "Counts the number of cells within a range that meet the given condition."

If the function selected (highlighted) is the one we want to use, we click **OK**; the **Function Arguments** dialog box then appears. The Function Arguments dialog box for the COUNTIF function is shown in Figure E.8. This dialog box assists in creating the appropriate arguments for the function selected. When finished entering the arguments, we click OK; Excel then inserts the function into a worksheet cell.

Inserting a Function into a Worksheet Cell

We will now show how to use the Insert Function and Function Arguments dialog boxes to select a function, develop its arguments, and insert the function into a worksheet cell.

Suppose we want to construct a frequency distribution for the soft drink purchase data in Table E.1. Figure E.9 displays an Excel worksheet containing the soft drink data and labels for the frequency distribution we would like to construct. We see that the frequency of Coca-Cola purchases will go into cell D2, the frequency of Diet Coke purchases will go into cell D3, and so on. Suppose we want to use the COUNTIF function to compute the frequencies and would like some assistance from Excel.

Step 1. Select cell D2
Step 2. Click f_x on the formula bar

FIGURE E.8   FUNCTION ARGUMENTS DIALOG BOX FOR THE COUNTIF FUNCTION

Function Arguments	?	⌧

COUNTIF

Range		🔢	=	reference
Criteria		🔢	=	any

=

Counts the number of cells within a range that meet the given condition.

Range   is the range of cells from which you want to count nonblank cells.

Formula result =

Help on this function   OK   Cancel

FIGURE E.9   EXCEL WORKSHEET WITH SOFT DRINK DATA AND LABELS FOR THE FREQUENCY DISTRIBUTION WE WOULD LIKE TO CONSTRUCT

	A	B	C	D	E	F
1	**Brand Purchased**		**Soft Drink**	**Frequency**		
2	Coca-Cola		Coca-Cola			
3	Diet Coke		Diet Coke			
4	Pepsi		Dr. Pepper			
5	Diet Coke		Pepsi			
6	Coca-Cola		Sprite			
7	Coca-Cola					
8	Dr. Pepper					
9	Diet Coke					
10	Pepsi					
11	Pepsi					
12	Coca-Cola					
13	Dr. Pepper					
14	Sprite					
15	Coca-Cola					
16	Diet Coke					
17	Coca-Cola					
18	Coca-Cola					
19	Sprite					
20	Coca-Cola					
50	Pepsi					
51	Sprite					
52						

FIGURE E.10   COMPLETED FUNCTION ARGUMENTS DIALOG BOX FOR THE COUNTIF FUNCTION

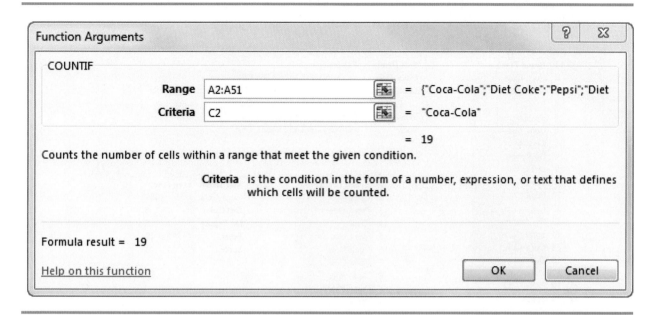

Step 3. When the Insert Function dialog box appears:
Select **Statistical** in the **Or select a category** box
Select **COUNTIF** in the **Select a function** box
Click **OK**

Step 4. When the Function Arguments dialog box appears (see Figure E.10):
Enter $A$2:$A$51 in the **Range** box
Enter C2 in the **Criteria** box (At this point, the value of the function will appear
on the next-to-last line of the dialog box. Its value is 19.)
Click **OK**

Step 5. Copy cell D2 to cells D3:D6

The worksheet then appears as in Figure E.11. The formula worksheet is in the background; the value worksheet appears in the foreground. The formula worksheet shows that the COUNTIF function was inserted into cells D2:D6. The value worksheet shows the proper class frequencies as computed.

We illustrated the use of Excel's capability to provide assistance in using the COUNTIF function. The procedure is similar for all Excel functions. This capability is especially helpful if you do not know what function to use or forget the proper name and/or inputs required for a function.

Using Excel Add-Ins

Excel's Data Analysis Add-In

Excel's Data Analysis add-in, included with the basic Excel package, is a valuable tool for conducting statistical analysis. Before you can use the Data Analysis add-in it must be installed. To see if the Data Analysis add-in has already been installed, click the DATA tab on the Ribbon. In the Analysis group you should see the Data Analysis command. If you do not have an Analysis group and/or the Data Analysis command does not appear in

FIGURE E.11   EXCEL WORKSHEET SHOWING THE USE OF EXCEL'S COUNTIF FUNCTION TO CONSTRUCT A FREQUENCY DISTRIBUTION

	A	B	C	D	E
1	**Brand Purchased**		**Soft Drink**	**Frequency**	
2	Coca-Cola		Coca-Cola	=COUNTIF($A$2:$A$51,C2)	
3	Diet Coke		Diet Coke	=COUNTIF($A$2:$A$51,C3)	
4	Pepsi		Dr. Pepper	=COUNTIF($A$2:$A$51,C4)	
5	Diet Coke		Pepsi	=COUNTIF($A$2:$A$51,C5)	
6	Coca-Cola		Sprite	=COUNTIF($A$2:$A$51,C6)	
7	Coca-Cola				
8	Dr. Pepper				
9	Diet Coke				
10	Pepsi				
11	Pepsi				
12	Coca-Cola				
13	Dr. Pepper				
14	Sprite				
15	Coca-Cola				
16	Diet Coke				
17	Coca-Cola				
18	Coca-Cola				
19	Sprite				
20	Coca-Cola				
50	Pepsi				
51	Sprite				
52					

	A	B	C	D	E
1	**Brand Purchased**		**Soft Drink**	**Frequency**	
2	Coca-Cola		Coca-Cola	19	
3	Diet Coke		Diet Coke	8	
4	Pepsi		Dr. Pepper	5	
5	Diet Coke		Pepsi	13	
6	Coca-Cola		Sprite	5	
7	Coca-Cola				
8	Dr. Pepper				
9	Diet Coke				
10	Pepsi				
11	Pepsi				
12	Coca-Cola				
13	Dr. Pepper				
14	Sprite				
15	Coca-Cola				
16	Diet Coke				
17	Coca-Cola				
18	Coca-Cola				
19	Sprite				
20	Coca-Cola				
50	Pepsi				
51	Sprite				
52					

the Analysis group, you will need to install the Data Analysis add-in. The steps needed to install the Data Analysis add-in are as follows:

Step 1. Click the **FILE** tab

Step 2. Click **Options**

Step 3. When the Excel Options dialog box appears:
Select **Add-Ins** from the list of options (on the pane on the left)
In the **Manage** box, select **Excel Add-Ins**
Click **Go**

Step 4. When the Add-Ins dialog box appears:
Select **Analysis ToolPak**
Click **OK**

Outside Vendor Add-Ins

One of the leading companies in the development of Excel add-ins for statistical analysis is Palisade Corporation. In this text we use StatTools, an Excel add-in developed by Palisade. StatTools provides a powerful statistics toolset that enables users to perform statistical analysis in the familiar Microsoft Office environment.

In the appendix to Chapter 1 we describe how to download and install the StatTools add-in and provide a brief introduction to using the software. In several appendices throughout the text we show how StatTools can be used when no corresponding basic Excel procedure is available or when additional statistical capabilities would be useful.

Typically, the add-ins offered with textbooks are designed primarily for classroom use. StatTools, however, was developed for commercial applications. As a result, students who learn how to use StatTools will be able to continue using StatTools throughout their professional career.

Here we describe how Minitab and Excel can be used to compute *p*-values for the z, t, χ^2, and F statistics that are used in hypothesis tests. As discussed in the text, only approximate *p*-values for the t, χ^2, and F statistics can be obtained by using tables. This appendix is helpful to a person who has computed the test statistic by hand, or by other means, and wishes to use computer software to compute the exact *p*-value.

Using Minitab

Minitab can be used to provide the cumulative probability associated with the z, t, χ^2, and F test statistics, so the lower tail *p*-value is obtained directly. The upper tail *p*-value is computed by subtracting the lower tail *p*-value from 1. The two-tailed *p*-value is obtained by doubling the smaller of the lower and upper tail *p*-values.

The z test statistic We use the Hilltop Coffee lower tail hypothesis test in Section 9.3 as an illustration; the value of the test statistic is $z = -2.67$. The Minitab steps used to compute the cumulative probability corresponding to $z = -2.67$ follow.

> **Step 1.** Select the **Calc** menu
> **Step 2.** Choose **Probability Distributions**
> **Step 3.** Choose **Normal**
> **Step 4.** When the Normal Distribution dialog box appears:
> > Select **Cumulative probability**
> > Enter 0 in the **Mean** box
> > Enter 1 in the **Standard deviation** box
> > Select **Input Constant**
> > Enter -2.67 in the **Input Constant** box
> > Click **OK**

Minitab provides the cumulative probability of .0038. This cumulative probability is the lower tail *p*-value used for the Hilltop Coffee hypothesis test.

For an upper tail test, the *p*-value is computed from the cumulative probability provided by Minitab as follows:

$$p\text{-value} = 1 - \text{cumulative probability}$$

For instance, the upper tail *p*-value corresponding to a test statistic of $z = -2.67$ is $1 - .0038 = .9962$. The two-tailed *p*-value corresponding to a test statistic of $z = -2.67$ is two times the minimum of the upper and lower tail *p*-values; that is, the two-tailed *p*-value corresponding to $z = -2.67$ is $2(.0038) = .0076$.

The t test statistic We use the Heathrow Airport example from Section 9.4 as an illustration; the value of the test statistic is $t = 1.84$ with 59 degrees of freedom. The Minitab steps used to compute the cumulative probability corresponding to $t = 1.84$ follow.

Step 1. Select the **Calc** menu
Step 2. Choose **Probability Distributions**
Step 3. Choose **t**
Step 4. When the t Distribution dialog box appears:
　　　　Select **Cumulative probability**
　　　　Enter 59 in the **Degrees of freedom** box
　　　　Select **Input Constant**
　　　　Enter 1.84 in the **Input Constant** box
　　　　Click **OK**

Minitab provides a cumulative probability of .9646, and hence the lower tail *p*-value = .9646. The Heathrow Airport example is an upper tail test; the upper tail *p*-value is 1 − .9646 = .0354. In the case of a two-tailed test, we would use the minimum of .9646 and .0354 to compute *p*-value = 2(.0354) = .0708.

The χ^2 test statistic Suppose we are conducting an upper tail test and the value of the test statistic is $\chi^2 = 28.18$ with 23 degrees of freedom. The Minitab steps used to compute the cumulative probability corresponding to $\chi^2 = 28.18$ follow.

Step 1. Select the **Calc** menu
Step 2. Choose **Probability Distributions**
Step 3. Choose **Chi-Square**
Step 4. When the Chi-Square Distribution dialog box appears:
　　　　Select **Cumulative probability**
　　　　Enter 23 in the **Degrees of freedom** box
　　　　Select **Input Constant**
　　　　Enter 28.18 in the **Input Constant** box
　　　　Click **OK**

Minitab provides a cumulative probability of .7909, which is the lower tail *p*-value. The upper tail *p*-value = 1 − the cumulative probability, or 1 − .7909 = .2091. The two-tailed *p*-value is two times the minimum of the lower and upper tail *p*-values. Thus, the two-tailed *p*-value is 2(.2091) = .4182. We are conducting an upper tail test, so we use *p*-value = .2091.

The F test statistic Suppose we are conducting a two-tailed test and the test statistic is $F = 2.40$ with 25 numerator degrees of freedom and 15 denominator degrees of freedom. The Minitab steps to compute the cumulative probability corresponding to $F = 2.40$ follow.

Step 1. Select the **Calc** menu
Step 2. Choose **Probability Distributions**
Step 3. Choose **F**
Step 4. When the F Distribution dialog box appears:
　　　　Select **Cumulative probability**
　　　　Enter 25 in the **Numerator degrees of freedom** box
　　　　Enter 15 in the **Denominator degrees of freedom** box
　　　　Select **Input Constant**
　　　　Enter 2.40 in the **Input Constant** box
　　　　Click **OK**

Minitab provides the cumulative probability and hence a lower tail *p*-value = .9594. The upper tail *p*-value is 1 − .9594 = .0406. Because we are conducting a two-tailed test, the minimum of .9594 and .0406 is used to compute *p*-value = 2(.0406) = .0812.

Using Excel

p-Value

Excel functions and formulas can be used to compute p-values associated with the z, t, χ^2, and F test statistics. We provide a template in the data file named p-Value for use in computing these p-values. Using the template, it is only necessary to enter the value of the test statistic and, if necessary, the appropriate degrees of freedom. Refer to Figure F.1 as we describe how the template is used. For users interested in the Excel functions and formulas being used, just click on the appropriate cell in the template.

The z test statistic We use the Hilltop Coffee lower tail hypothesis test in Section 9.3 as an illustration; the value of the test statistic is $z = -2.67$. To use the p-value template for this hypothesis test, simply enter -2.67 into cell B6 (see Figure F.1). After doing so, p-values for all three types of hypothesis tests will appear. For Hilltop Coffee, we would use the lower tail p-value = .0038 in cell B9. For an upper tail test, we would use the p-value in cell B10, and for a two-tailed test we would use the p-value in cell B11.

The t test statistic We use the Heathrow Airport example from Section 9.4 as an illustration; the value of the test statistic is $t = 1.84$ with 59 degrees of freedom. To use the p-value template for this hypothesis test, enter 1.84 into cell E6 and enter 59 into cell E7

FIGURE F.1   EXCEL WORKSHEET FOR COMPUTING p-VALUES

	A	B	C	D	E	F
1	**Computing p-Values**					
2						
3						
4	**Using the Test Statistic z**			**Using the Test Statistic t**		
5						
6	**Enter z -->**	-2.67		**Enter t -->**	1.84	
7				**df -->**	59	
8						
9	**p-value (Lower Tail)**	0.0038		**p-value (Lower Tail)**	0.9646	
10	**p-value (Upper Tail)**	0.9962		**p-value (Upper Tail)**	0.0354	
11	**p-value (Two Tail)**	0.0076		**p-value (Two Tail)**	0.0708	
12						
13						
14						
15						
16	**Using the Test Statistic Chi Square**			**Using the Test Statistic F**		
17						
18	**Enter Chi Square -->**	28.18		**Enter F -->**	2.40	
19	**df -->**	23		**Numerator df -->**	25	
20				**Denominator df -->**	15	
21						
22	**p-value (Lower Tail)**	0.7909		**p-value (Lower Tail)**	0.9594	
23	**p-value (Upper Tail)**	0.2091		**p-value (Upper Tail)**	0.0406	
24	**p-value (Two Tail)**	0.4181		**p-value (Two Tail)**	0.0812	
25						

(see Figure F.1). After doing so, p-values for all three types of hypothesis tests will appear. The Heathrow Airport example involves an upper tail test, so we would use the upper tail p-value $= .0354$ provided in cell E10 for the hypothesis test.

The χ^2 test statistic Suppose we are conducting an upper tail test and the value of the test statistic is $\chi^2 = 28.18$ with 23 degrees of freedom. To use the p-value template for this hypothesis test, enter 28.18 into cell B18 and enter 23 into cell B19 (see Figure F.1). After doing so, p-values for all three types of hypothesis tests will appear. We are conducting an upper tail test, so we would use the upper tail p-value $= .2091$ provided in cell B23 for the hypothesis test.

The F test statistic Suppose we are conducting a two-tailed test and the test statistic is $F = 2.40$ with 25 numerator degrees of freedom and 15 denominator degrees of freedom. To use the p-value template for this hypothesis test, enter 2.40 into cell E18, enter 25 into cell E19, and enter 15 into cell E20 (see Figure F.1). After doing so, p-values for all three types of hypothesis tests will appear. We are conducting a two-tailed test, so we would use the two-tailed p-value $= .0812$ provided in cell E24 for the hypothesis test.

Index

Essentials of Statistics for Business and Economics 7e WEBfiles